Mr. Harry Paul Jacofsky
2860 Oceanside Rd.
Oceanside, N. Y.
OR 8-1998

The New Medicare and Social Security Provisions

by Jerome B. Cohen

Young people are going to pay much more heavily from January 1, 1966 on for the medical care and old age security of their elders, and ultimately for their own social security, too, of course, as a result of the Social Security Amendments of 1965. While the new benefits have been widely publicized less has been said about the forthcoming higher costs.

Highlights of the new provisions are:

THE COSTS

The maximum amount of an employee's wages subject to tax will be raised from the current $4,800 to $6,600 from January 1, 1966 on.

In 1965 wages up to $4,800 were taxable at a rate of 3.625%, for a maximum of $174. In 1966, wages up to $6,600 will be taxed at a rate of 4.2% (including medicare) for a maximum of $277.20. Thus, if you earn $6,600 or more you will be paying $103.20 *more* in 1966 for medicare and increased social security benefits. Your employer, too, will have to pay the same $277.20 for you for these benefits. The $277.20 consists of $254.10 for social security and $23.10 for the new medicare.

Rates will go even higher after 1966 as the following tabulation shows:

1

SOCIAL SECURITY AND MEDICARE TAX RATES FOR EMPLOYEES

Calendar Year	Social Security Rate	Medicare (Hospital Part) Rate	Combined Rate
1963-1965	3.625%	—	—
1966	3.85	.35%	4.2%
1967-1968	3.9	.5	4.4
1969-1972	4.4	.5	4.9
1973-1975	4.85	.55	5.4
1976-1979	4.85	.6	5.45
1980-1986	4.85	.7	5.55
1987 and after	4.85	.8	5.65

Both employer and employee will each pay at these rates. This will result in the maximum amount of the tax payable by an employee moving up as follows:

MAXIMUM TAX PAYABLE BY EMPLOYEE

Calendar Year	Tax
1963-1965	$174.00
1966	277.20
1967-1968	290.40
1969-1972	323.40
1973-1975	356.40
1976-1979	359.70
1980-1986	366.30
1987 and after	372.90

For the self-employed, rates and taxes will, of course, also move up. Self-employed income must be at least $400 a year for the tax to apply. As in the case of wages, self-employed income up to $6,600 a year is taxable during 1966 and thereafter, as compared with $4,800 in 1965. Self-employed medical doctors, formerly excluded, are now covered for 1965 and thereafter.

Social security and medicare tax rates for the self-employed are as follows:

SOCIAL SECURITY AND MEDICARE TAX RATES FOR SELF-EMPLOYED

CALENDAR YEAR	SOCIAL SECURITY RATE	MEDICARE (HOSPITAL PART) RATE	COMBINED RATE
1963-1965	5.4%	—	—
1966	5.8	.35%	6.15%
1967-1968	5.9	.5	6.4
1969-1972	6.6	.5	7.1
1973-1975	7.0	.55	7.55
1976-1979	7.0	.6	7.6
1980-1986	7.0	.7	7.7
1987 and after	7.0	.8	7.8

Thus the maximum tax for social security and medicare payable by the self-employed will rise from $259.20 in 1965 to $405.90 in 1966 and to $514.80 on January 1, 1987.

If students work as waiters, waitresses, busboys, etc., they will be interested to know that after 1965 cash tips received count as wages for social security and medicare purposes if they amount to a total of $20 a month or more in connection with work for any one employer. Every employee is required to report his tips in writing to his employer and pay tax on them, although the employer is not required to pay a tax on them.

THE MEDICARE BENEFITS

None of the new medicare benefits apply to you until you become sixty-five!

The Social Security Amendments of 1965 which were signed into law by President Johnson on July 30, 1965 provide two different kinds of health insurance for people 65 or older:

> *HOSPITAL INSURANCE* which will pay most of the cost of hospital services and certain other post-hospital expenses;

> *MEDICAL INSURANCE* which will help pay for part of the cost of doctors' services and certain other medical expenses.

All social security beneficiaries 65 or over are automatically entitled to *HOSPITAL INSURANCE* and need not take any action.

They will be covered by the *MEDICAL INSURANCE* program, however, only if they apply for it which they must do not later than March 31, 1966.

There is no extra cost for *HOSPITAL INSURANCE* for those now 65 or older. For *MEDICAL INSURANCE*, however, there is a charge of $3 a month, which will be deducted from the social security benefit checks beginning with the check to be received in July 1966.

Both hospital and medical insurance under the Social Security Act do not begin, for those 65 and older, until July 1, 1966.

What Hospital Services Are Covered?

Beginning in July 1966 the hospital insurance program will pay the cost of covered services for the following hospital and post-hospital care:

Up to 60 days in a participating hospital (except for the first $40) and all but $10 per day for an additional 30 days for each spell of illness.* (There is a lifetime limit of 190 days, however, for treatment in mental hospitals.)

Up to 20 days in an extended care facility (a qualified, skilled nursing home or a convalescent section of a hospital) and all but $5 per day for an additional 80 days for each spell of illness. (This part of the program begins on January 1, 1967.)

Up to 100 home health visits by nurses or other health workers from qualified home health agencies (but not from doctors) in the 365 days following release from a hospital after a stay of 3 days or more, or from an extended care facility.

Eighty percent of the cost of outpatient diagnostic tests in a hospital (after the patient pays the first $20) for each 20-day period of diagnostic testing.

For services in a hospital or extended care facility, benefit payments will cover the cost of services in semi-private accommodations plus the cost of drugs, supplies, and most services customarily furnished by the institution.

Some services are *not* covered. No payment will be made under hospital insurance for the services of physicians, including the services

---

* A "spell of illness" begins on the first day of receipt of covered services as a patient in a hospital or extended care facility. It ends after the patient has been out of a hospital or extended care facility for 60 consecutive days.

of anesthetists, radiologists, physiatrists and pathologists. Payment will *not* be made for private nurses, custodial care, or for items furnished for the patient's convenience.

Each person covered will receive through the mail a health insurance card shortly before July 1, 1966.

What Medical Services Are Covered?

If a person 65 or over decides to take medical insurance at a cost of $3 per month additionally, beginning in July 1966, the medical insurance program will help pay for the following services:

Physicians' and surgeons' services in the hospital, doctor's office, home or elsewhere.

Up to 100 home health visits under an approved plan each year with no need for prior hospitalization. This is in addition to the 100 visits provided under the hospital insurance program.

A number of other medical and health services, such as diagnostic services, X ray or other radiation treatments, surgical dressings and splints, casts, and rental of medical equipment.

Medical insurance does *not* pay for the full cost of these services. There is a $50 deductible; that is, the insured patient pays the first $50 in each calendar year for these services and then pays 20% of the remaining costs. The medical insurance pays 80% of the reasonable charges for additional services, beyond the $50 deductible. For example, if covered medical bills were $500 in a given year, the medical insurance program would pay $360; the patient would pay $140, the first $50 plus 20% of the remaining $450.

The medical insurance program does *not* cover some services such as the cost of routine physical check-ups, drug prescriptions, eye glasses, hearing aids, and ordinary dental treatment.

The law provides that the $3 per month premium rate for medical insurance will be continued through 1967. In each odd-numbered year beginning with 1967, the cost of the medical insurance program will be studied. If the premium rate, including the government's share, is not enough to cover the cost of the program for the following two years, the rate may be changed.

Anyone who is 65 or over and who enrolls for medical insurance is not under any obligation to continue it beyond the end of the next odd-numbered year. Thus, if there is at any time an increase in the premium rate, the insured will have the opportunity to drop out of the program.

For further information see "A Brief Explanation of 'Medicare' — Health Insurance for the Aged," OASI-1965-2, U.S. Department of Health, Education and Welfare, Social Security Administration, Washington, 3rd edition, August 1965.

NEW INCOME TAX PROVISIONS ON MEDICAL EXPENSES

To dovetail with the new medicare program, there are new income tax provisions on medical expenses for those 65 and over. The Social Security Amendments of 1965 provide that, effective January 1, 1967, the following income tax changes are to take effect:

(a) There will also apply to persons 65 years of age or over, the provisions of the income tax law which now limit medical expense deductions for persons under age 65 to amounts in excess of 3% of adjusted gross income. Thus after January 1, 1967 older persons will no longer be allowed full deduction for medical expenses.

(b) All taxpayers, regardless of age, who itemize their income tax deductions, will be allowed a special deduction of $150 per year or one-half of the premiums paid for health insurance, whichever is smaller. The special deduction must be listed on the tax return separately from the medical expense computation. However, that part of the paid health insurance premium which is in excess of the special deduction can be entered as part of medical expenses, subject to the 3% rule.

(c) There will also apply to persons 65 years of age and over the rule, applicable to taxpayers under age 65, that only outlays for drugs and medicines in excess of 1% of adjusted gross income can be taken as tax deductions.

Thus, for the calendar year 1967 and thereafter, the 3% adjusted gross income limitation for medical expenses and the 1% adjusted gross income limitation for drugs and medicines will apply to those 65 and over.

(d) In 1965 and 1966 there are maximum amounts, or limits, on the amounts which may be deducted as medical expenses. Starting January 1, 1967 and thereafter, all of the presently existing maximum limitations on the medical expense deduction for *all* taxpayers are eliminated by the Social Security Amendments of 1965. Therefore, for the calendar year 1967 and subsequent years, except for the 3% and 1% limitations mentioned above, all medical expenses allowed will be deductible regardless of the age of the taxpayer.

THE REVISED SOCIAL SECURITY PROVISIONS

Increased Benefits

If you are receiving social security benefits the amount will be increased by 7%, with back payment of the increase being made for January 1965 and following months.

Those who first apply for benefits in the future will also get the 7% increase over benefits payable under the prior law.

For those who retire or become eligible for social security disability or survivor benefits in future years, benefit amounts even higher than those resulting from the 7% increase will be possible. This is because the maximum amount of earnings that can count toward social security benefits each year will be increased to $6,600 in 1966. In due course it will be possible to achieve an average monthly wage as high as $550 (1/12 of $6,600). The new benefit formula, based on average monthly wage (AMW) is 62.97% of the first $110 of AMW, plus 22.9% of the next $290 of AMW, plus 21.4% of AMW in excess of $400. The new benefit rates based on this formula are given in Table A.

Benefits for Students

Benefits may now be paid to certain students up to age 22.

If you are eligible for social security benefits as the unmarried son or daughter of a person receiving old-age or disability insurance benefits or a person who has died, you may qualify for benefits, if you continue as a full-time student, until you reach age 22.

If you were receiving social security payments which were stopped when you reached 18 and you are a full-time student under 22 years of age and still unmarried, your benefits may now be started again. Payments may be made for months back to January 1965.

If you are receiving social security benefits and are approaching your 18th birthday, your benefits may be continued if you are a full-time

TABLE A
EXAMPLES OF MONTHLY CASH BENEFIT PAYMENTS[1]

Average Yearly Earnings After 1950	$800 or less	$1800	$3000	$3600	$4200	$4800	$5400	$6600
Retirement at 65 Disability benefits	$ 44.00	$ 78.20	$101.70	$112.40	$124.20	$135.90	$146.00	$168.00
Retirement at 64	41.10	73.00	95.00	105.00	116.00	126.90	136.30	156.80
Retirement at 63	38.20	67.80	88.20	97.50	107.70	117.80	126.60	145.60
Retirement at 62	35.20	62.60	81.40	90.00	99.40	108.80	116.80	134.40
Wife's benefit at 65 or with child in her care	22.00	39.10	50.90	56.20	62.10	68.00	73.00	84.00
Wife's benefit at 64	20.20	35.90	46.70	51.60	57.00	62.40	67.00	77.00
Wife's benefit at 63	18.40	32.60	42.50	46.90	51.80	56.70	60.90	70.00
Wife's benefit at 62	16.50	29.40	38.20	42.20	46.60	51.00	54.80	63.00
One child of retired or disabled worker	22.00	39.10	50.90	56.20	62.10	68.00	73.00	84.00
Widow age 62 or over	44.00	64.60	83.90	92.80	102.50	112.20	120.50	138.60
Widow at 60, no child	38.20	56.00	72.80	80.50	88.90	97.30	104.50	120.20
Widow under 62 and 1 child	66.00	117.40	152.60	168.60	186.40	204.00	219.00	252.00
Widow under 62 and 2 children	66.00	120.00	202.40	240.00	279.60	306.00	328.00	368.00
One surviving child	44.00	58.70	76.30	84.30	93.20	102.00	109.50	126.00
Two surviving children	66.00	117.40	152.60	168.60	186.40	204.00	219.00	252.00
Maximum family payment	66.00	120.00	202.40	240.00	280.80	309.20	328.00	368.00
Lump-sum death payment	132.00	234.60	255.00	255.00	255.00	255.00	255.00	255.00

[1] Generally, in figuring average yearly earnings after 1950, 5 years of low earnings or no earnings can be excluded. The maximum earnings creditable for social security are $3600 for 1951-1954; $4200 for 1955-1958; $4800 for 1959-1965; and $6600 starting in 1966. Because of this, the benefits shown in the last two columns on the right will not generally be payable for some years to come. When a person is entitled to more than one benefit, the amount actually payable is limited to the largest of the benefits.

Source: Social Security Administration.

student. For further information about this, or to get your benefits started again if you are eligible, you or your parent should get in touch with your social security office.

If you were already 18 or over when one of your parents became entitled to old-age or disability insurance benefits or died, but you were not yet 22 in January 1965, you may now be eligible for social security benefits beginning with January 1965 if you have not married. Your social security office will need your own and your parent's social security account number and your birth certificate.

For more information about benefits for students up to age 22, ask your social security office for Leaflet No. OASI-1965-4a — "A Brief Explanation of Social Security Benefits for Students Up To Age 22," U.S. Department of Health, Education and Welfare, Social Security Administration, Washington, August 1965.

Benefits for Widows at Age 60

The widow of an insured worker, beginning with September 1965, may start receiving benefits as early as age 60 if she decides to accept a reduced monthly amount.

The amount of the reduction is five-ninths of 1% for each month a benefit is received before age 62 (6⅔% reduction for each year). The closer she is to 62 when she starts receiving benefits, the smaller the reduction will be. On the average, a widow who accepts benefits before age 62 will collect about the same value in total benefits over the years, but in smaller installments to take account of the longer period during which she will be paid.

If You Work After You Apply for Benefits

After 1965 if you earn no more than $1,500 in a year, you may receive benefits for all months of the year. Under the law in effect through 1965, the payments you receive are reduced if you work and earn more than $1,200 in a year.

If you earn more than $1,500 in a year after 1965, the general rule is that $1 in benefits will be withheld for each $2 of earnings over $1,500 and up to $2,700. In addition, $1 in benefits will be withheld for each $1 of earnings over $2,700. There are two exceptions to this rule:

If in any month you neither earn more than $125 working for someone else nor do substantial work in a business of your own, there will be no deduction from your benefit for that month no matter how much you earn in the rest of the year.

After you are 72 there will be no deduction from the benefits because of work after you reached 72.

Another change in the law is important for people 65 or over who receive royalties because of copyrights or patents they obtained before they reached 65. After 1965, this income may be excluded in figuring earnings.

If you work after applying for old-age insurance benefits, your additional earnings may increase the amount of your monthly payment.

The Social Security Administration will use its electronic computers to determine whether your recent earnings will increase your benefit amount. If so, the increase will be made automatically and you will not have to apply to have your benefit refigured.

On account of this change, you cannot lose by applying as soon as you are 65 for any benefits due you even though you continue to work.

Disability Provisions Changed

Under the old law disability benefits could be paid only to a worker whose disability was expected to continue over a long and indefinite period or to result in death. The new law provides that an insured worker whose disability is expected to last for at least 12 months may qualify for disability benefits beginning with the seventh month of his disability. The first month for which payments can be made under this change is September 1965.

Workers whose applications for disability insurance benefits have been denied because their disability was not expected to continue indefinitely, but who are severely disabled, should get in touch with their social security office.

The new law also liberalizes the requirements affecting people who are disabled by blindness.

For further information see "A Brief Explanation of Changes in Social Security Disability Benefits," OASI-1965-8, U.S. Department of Health, Education and Welfare, Social Security Administration, Washington, September 1965.

Benefits for Divorced Women

Under the new law, a divorced woman may receive benefits on her former husband's account. To do so, however, she must have been married to him at least 20 years before the divorce and he must have been contributing (or obligated by a court to contribute) to her support when he became entitled to social security benefits or died. Under the old law, a divorced woman could receive benefits on her former husband's account only if she had a child in her care receiving benefits based on his earnings.

A woman who is divorced while she is receiving benefits based on her husband's earnings may continue to receive benefits if she and her husband had been married at least 20 years. Benefits payable under this provision can begin for September 1965.

Continuing Benefits for Widows Who Remarry

If a woman could have qualified for benefits as a widow and remarried after reaching age 60, she will be eligible for whichever benefit is larger: either one-half the retirement benefit of her former husband, or a wife's benefit based on the earnings of her present husband.

FINALLY, STUDENTS PLEASE NOTE!

Tips Will Count!

Cash tips you receive in your work for one employer, provided they amount to $20 or more in a month, will now count toward social security benefits for you and your family. Beginning in 1966, you will be required to report in writing to your employer the amount of tips you receive and to pay social security contributions on the tips. Your employer will include your tips in his social security tax reports and Form W-2 along with your wages, but he will not have to match your social security contribution on the tips. The law requires that you report to your employer the amount of your tips within 10 days after the month in which you receive them. Leaflet No. 6 explains in more detail how to report your tips for social security. Ask for it at your local social security office.

FOR FURTHER INFORMATION on the 1965 changes see "Social Security Amendments-1965—A Brief Explanation," OASI-1965-1, U.S. Department of Health, Education and Welfare, Social Security Administration, Washington, 3rd edition, August 1965.

INDEX

This book has been set on the Linotype *in 12 and 10 point Garamond No. 3, leaded 1 point. Chapter numbers are in 42 point Venus Bold Extended and chapter titles in 16 point Venus Bold Extended caps. The size of the type page is 27 by 46½ picas.*

PERSONAL FINANCE

PRINCIPLES AND CASE PROBLEMS

with "The New Medicare and Social Security Provisions"

By

Jerome B. Cohen Ph.D.

Professor of Economics, and
Supervisor of Finance and Investments,
Bernard M. Baruch School of Business
and Public Administration
City University of New York

and

Arthur W. Hanson LL.B., D.C.S.

Professor of Accounting, Emeritus, Graduate School of
Business Administration, Harvard University, and
Attorney at Law

1964 · THIRD EDITION

RICHARD D. IRWIN, INC.

HOMEWOOD, ILLINOIS

THIRD EDITION

First Printing, July, 1964
Second Printing, April, 1965
Third Printing, January, 1966

Library of Congress Catalog Card No. 64–21027

PRINTED IN THE UNITED STATES OF AMERICA

To HARRY H. BINGHAM—*A Great Editor*

PREFACE

SINCE 1940, more than 650 colleges and universities have introduced courses in personal finance or some name-variant thereof. This is clear recognition of the growing complexity of the many financial decisions and judgments which the average individual and family must make during a lifetime. How can a young family with limited income possibly afford enough insurance to provide real protection? The government urges you to save by buying United States savings bonds; mutual funds urge that you place your surplus with them; the New York Stock Exchange and its member firms urge you to start a monthly investment program in common stock. Which should you do if you cannot do all three? In borrowing $50 you can pay as much as 1,040 per cent per annum or as little as 6 per cent. In buying a $10,000 house, one type of mortgage can cost over $1,000 more than another. Will you know the difference when you come to buy? If you die without leaving a will, an inflexible state law determines how your estate is to be distributed. Do you know the provisions of the law, and is this the way you would want to leave your estate? If you had invested $10,000 in 1946, one decision would have raised your fund to only a little over $14,500 a dozen years later, while another would have brought it up to $186,000.

These are merely a very few of the perplexing financial choices which you will encounter and will answer, competently or poorly, over the next forty or fifty years. If education has any purpose, it is to pass on to the next generation the cumulative wisdom of previous generations and to prepare young people to face and solve real problems of the real world. If the following pages have any value, the measure of their worth will be the degree to which they will help you to reason wisely, to understand, and to come to sensible decisions on the host of financial dilemmas which will beset you over a lifetime.

Since most of us have no funds to administer before we start earning an income, we have begun this book with income and occupation, the source of whatever financial resources the typical individual or family can acquire. Next, attention has been given to basic expenditures which usually consume the major share of total income. The remainder of the volume is devoted to that residual segment of resources, small though it may be, which can provide comforts, satisfactions, and security beyond the basic needs. At first this segment may be a mere emergency fund of dollars to fall back on in case of need. A combination of some of these surplus dollars and borrowing may bring the benefit of extra goods and services to enhance our well-being before we are able to buy them outright. Witness the young married couples in Suburbia! As the savings grow, we normally think of the advantages of insurance, homes of our own, and the need for retirement income when earnings cease. But we do not live in a vacuum; we are not, after all, a law unto ourselves. We must think of the negative impact of the community upon our financial plans (taxes) and the extent to which we may benefit from community assistance (social security). If we have been fortunate in accumulating modest surpluses, we have an investment problem on our hands and ultimately, since we can take nothing with us when we depart this life, the matter of the fair disposition of our accumulation. This, in brief, is the order we have followed in the development of the subject.

The range of topics covered in this volume is so diverse, detailed, and practical that we felt it essential to consult numerous experts. While any errors that remain are our responsibility, we gladly acknowledge the assistance rendered us by the writings and the cooperation shown us by those versed in the various specialized topics. Hundreds of requests have gone forth from us for permission to use the fruits of their labor. Practically without exception we have been granted enthusiastic assistance. So many experts in their own specialties have given advice or constructive criticism that it is impossible to mention them all in the brief space available here, much as we should like to do it. Some of them, however, have provided such substantial help that we feel impelled to make specific acknowledgment.

We are especially indebted to Dr. Harlan B. Miller, Education Director, Mr. Arthur C. Daniels, Vice-President, and Mr. Alfred Cranwill, C.L.U., all of the Institute of Life Insurance; to Mr. G. Victor Hallman, C.L.U., Director of Educational Publications, The American College of Life Underwriters; Mr. Louis Engel and Miss Janet K. Low of Merrill Lynch, Pierce, Fenner & Smith, Inc.; Dr. Charles Lininger, Senior Study Director, Survey Research Center, University of Michigan; Mr. Lewis Schellbach, Vice-President, Standard & Poor's Corporation; Mr. Fred H. Brockett, President, Dun & Bradstreet, Inc.; Mr. Robert Waldron of The Health Insurance Institute; Dr. Earl G.

Nicks of The Insurance Information Institute; Messrs. Herbert W. Nannen, Charles F. Metz, Thomas J. Tyler, Vincent Nunziato, and Walter J. Hassett of The Chemical Bank New York Trust Co.; Mr. Robert F. Marchant, Executive Vice-President of The New York Bank for Savings; Mr. Fred C. Cohn of Hugh Johnson & Co.; Mr. Sidney Vickers of Vickers Associates; Mr. Rudolph R. Fichtel, Deputy Manager, and Mrs. Helene Duffy of The American Bankers Association; to Dr. Ernst A. Dauer, Director of Consumer Credit Studies of the Household Finance Corporation; to Mr. Robert W. Harvey, Managing Editor and John W. Hazard, Senior Editor, of *Changing Times,* the Kiplinger magazine; to Mr. Louis C. Fieland, Attorney-at-Law, New York; to Mr. Morris Goldstein, Partner-in-Charge of Research, Francis I. duPont & Company; to Dr. Harold Oberg, Director of Research, Investment Company Institute; Mrs. Lucille Tomlinson Wessman, of Arthur Wiesenberger & Co.; Leo Cherne of the Research Institute of America; Mr. Arthur H. Lockard of Arnold Bernhard & Co.; Mr. Arnold E. Chase, Assistant Commissioner, Prices and Living Conditions, U.S. Bureau of Labor Statistics; Mr. Sal R. Nuccio of *The New York Times;* Mr. Thomas G. Campbell of the Systematic Dollar Accumulation Plan; Mr. Robert C. Beetham, Research Director of The Teachers Insurance and Annuity Association; Mr. Antone G. Singsen, Vice-President of The Blue Cross Association; Mr. Ned F. Parish, Assistant Executive Vice-President of The National Association of Blue Shield Plans; Mr. V. G. Phelps of The Government Employees Insurance Company; Mr. Charles K. Reid, II, C.L.U., of The Life Insurance Agency Management Association, Mr. R. F. Kuechenmeister, of The Nationwide Mutual Insurance Company; Dr. Allen O. Felix, Mr. William D. Horgan, Mr. Jonathan A. Brown, and Mr. John LaBarbera of The New York Stock Exchange; Mr. G. Weiner of Forbes, Inc., Mr. R. W. Sterling of M. C. Horsey & Co.; Mr. Daniel J. Ryan of The Boston Fund; Mr. John Burrows and Mr. Cecil Good of Moody's Investors Service; Mr. Donald M. Salsburg of The Prudential Insurance Company; Mr. Francis M. Simon of Kalb, Voorhis & Co.; Mr. Thaddeus Nichols of The Putnam Management Co. of Boston; Mr. Frederic W. Watriss of The Massachusetts Institute of Technology; Mr. Roy L. Swift of the U.S. Department of Health, Education, and Welfare; Mr. B. F. Dunn of The Estate Recording Co.; Mr. William H. Wertz, Health Information Foundation; Dr. S. Lees Booth, Director of Research, National Consumer Finance Association; Mr. Edward B. Burr and Miss Ann V. Galvin of Hugh W. Long and Co.; Mr. K. N. Davis, Jr., Treasurer, International Business Machines

Corp.; Mr. L. B. Gehrke, Treasurer, Minnesota Mining & Manufacturing Corporation.

Adoption and use of our revised edition by 457 colleges and universities encouraged us to undertake another thorough revision and up-dating. We have had the benefit of suggestions for changes and improvements from many of those who have used the book. While the full list of those to whom we are indebted is too long to include here, some must be singled out for a special appreciation: Professor Clyde William Phelps, Department of Economics, University of Southern California, Los Angeles; Dean Nathan A. Baily, School of Business, The American University, Washington, D.C.; Dr. Dorothy Lampen, Hunter College; Professor James Richardson, Director of The Family Finance Workshop, University of Florida; Professor H. W. Hudson, Head, Department of Economics, Kent State University; Professor James R. Kay, Chairman, Department of Finance, Insurance, and Real Estate, University of Texas; Dr. Lawrence V. Conway, Director of Institute Publications, American Savings and Loan Institute, Chicago; Professor Sidney M. Robbins of Columbia University; Professor Joseph F. Bradley, Pennsylvania State College; Dr. Richard L. D. Morse, Head of Department of Economics and Sociology, Kansas State University, Manhattan, Kansas; Professor Avon M. Dreyer, Department of Economics, Central Michigan University; Dr. Ervin K. Zingler, Professor of Economics and Finance, University of Houston; Professor John R. Matthews, Jr., of the Department of Economics of The College of William and Mary; Dr. Truman G. Tracy of The University of Missouri; Professor Gwen J. Bymers of Cornell University; Professor Norman B. Ward, Jr., University of Pittsburgh, and to Professors Leo Barnes and Joseph Taffet of the College of The City of New York.

We are also indebted to Professors Harold H. Cutler of the University of Utah, Conrad Eriksen of Kansas State University, George Preston Martin of the University of Southern California, and Arthur F. Messenger of Purdue University, who read and reviewed the manuscript and offered valuable suggestions.

In the first edition we wrote, "Although the form and content of this volume are, it is hoped, particularly adapted to the work of the college classroom, we have reason to believe that it may lend itself to successful use in adult discussion groups promoted by such organizations as community clubs and by some of the larger banks and stockbrokerage firms. The ordinary adult reader should find in it much information to add to whatever knowledge he already has concerning personal finance; perhaps he will acquire something to sharpen his conversation and debate with his acquaintances and friends." This has been the exact experience and we have had many interesting and some amusing letters as a result.

For college use, this text is designed essentially for a one-semester, fourteen- to seventeen-week course. It may, however, easily be adapted to the two-semester (year) course by the simple expedient of spending one week discussing the principles of a given topic and the following week on the extensive case-problem material on that topic given at the end of each chapter and discussed in the Teacher's Manual. The case problems represent, as closely as possible, real-life situations and may, therefore, play a vital part in any course utilizing this text. Objective tests for each chapter will be found in the Teacher's Manual.

JEROME B. COHEN
ARTHUR W. HANSON

June, 1964

TABLE OF CONTENTS

1   INCOME AND OCCUPATION

Experience keeps a dear school, but Fools will learn in no other.

—Poor Richard's Almanack

YOU HAVE already made the first wise decision in managing your personal finances. You are in college, and experts estimate that the college graduate will receive an average of $180,000 more income during his or her lifetime than will the average high school graduate. There is a very high positive correlation between years of education and average lifetime earnings, as the following figures show:

Years of Education	Average Lifetime Earnings
College graduate	$452,518
One–three years of college	333,581
High school graduate	272,629
Elementary school only	204,530

From the standpoint of maximizing income, it clearly pays to go to college; it also pays even more to graduate. Over his lifetime the average college graduate earns $120,000 more than the student who attends but does not graduate, and $180,000 more than the average high school graduate. Thus the college graduate averages 70 percent more than the high school graduate.

Planning an Adequate Income

"We should all be concerned with the future," Charles F. Kettering once advised, "because we will have to spend the rest of our lives there." Your preparation for the future couldn't start off to better advantage. Personal finance is meaningful only if there is an adequate income to manage. If you pursue your present course, you are probably well on your way to a higher-income bracket, as the following figures indicate:

TABLE 1–1

Family Income by Education of Head of Family, 1963
(Percent of Families in Each Group)

	SCHOOLING COMPLETED					
	ELEMENTARY		HIGH SCHOOL		COLLEGE	
	LESS THAN 8 YEARS	8 YEARS	1 to 3 YEARS	4 YEARS	1 to 3 YEARS	4 YEARS
Number (thousands)	5,471	7,649	7,720	12,548	4,231	5,044
Percent	100.0	100.0	100.0	100.0	100.0	100.0
Under $1,000	7.3	4.2	3.1	1.9	2.3	1.0
$1,000 to $1,999	16.4	8.9	4.5	2.8	2.6	1.4
$2,000 to $2,999	15.6	10.4	6.9	4.2	3.3	2.1
$3,000 to $3,999	12.8	10.4	9.6	6.9	6.1	2.6
$4,000 to $4,999	10.4	10.2	10.3	8.6	7.1	4.7
$5,000 to $5,999	9.1	12.9	12.8	13.0	10.0	6.4
$6,000 to $6,999	7.4	10.3	11.4	12.6	9.9	8.4
$7,000 to $7,999	5.8	8.8	9.8	11.0	9.8	10.6
$8,000 to $9,999	7.0	10.7	15.8	17.0	18.7	13.8
$10,000 to $14,999	6.5	10.6	12.6	17.0	21.8	29.2
$15,000 and over	1.7	2.6	3.2	5.0	8.4	19.8
Median income	$3,837	$5,454	$6,244	$6,997	$7,895	$9,857

SOURCE: Bureau of the Census.

While a college education has many rewards other than monetary benefits, these should not be overlooked. A higher percentage of young people are going to college these days and of those who graduate many are going on to advanced degrees.[1] It has been estimated that each year of graduate work adds $40,000 to average lifetime income. Getting your college degree is step one in sound personal finance. Step two is tied in very closely—deciding what career or profession to pursue as your lifework. That's almost as hard as getting into college these days.

Intelligent Choice of Vocation

In many instances a person finds himself in some occupation more or less by chance and not as the result of some well-thought-out plan. A hunch, a word from some friend, an inviting advertisement in a newspaper, parental advice, a "Help Wanted" sign on a building, or some other small impetus may land a person in a job in which he spends a lifetime. Often it works out pretty well; in other cases the

[1] Herman P. Miller, "Annual and Lifetime Income in Relation to Education," *American Economic Review,* Vol. L, No. 5 (December, 1960), p. 982.

person must wonder whether another calling might not have produced more satisfactory results.

Aids in Choosing a Vocation

Today, progress has been made in devising aptitude and interest tests which can tell you the sorts of things you ought to be able to do satisfactorily and in which you may take a real interest. When we consider that a person sometimes spends on the job nearly half of the hours that he is awake, it certainly seems sensible to strive to find work that will be congenial. We usually like interesting work that we have the ability to perform. Aptitude tests are available in educational institutions and also in commercial testing laboratories in the larger cities throughout the United States.

Every student should consult and spend some time with the *Occupational Outlook Handbook* (830 pages) issued periodically by the U.S. Bureau of Labor Statistics.[2] It not only deals with the employment outlook in over 500 different job categories—ranging from artists and accountants to engineers, teachers, lawyers, and physicians—but also, where data are available, presents information on earnings—past, present, and prospective. Under each occupation listed are sections entitled "Nature of Work," "Where Employed," "Employment Outlook," "Training and Other Qualifications," "Earnings and Working Conditions," and "Where to Go for More Information."

Several abridged examples may give some indication of the usefulness of this volume:

Accountants. "Accounting is the second largest field of professional employment for men. . . . Employment opportunities for accountants are expected to be very good through the mid-1960's. As many as 10,000 accountants may be needed annually during this period to replace those who retire, die, or transfer to other occupations. Provided there is no major drop in the general level of business activity, nearly as many more may be needed each year to fill new positions. Demand for college-trained accountants will rise faster than demand for people without this broad background of training, because of the increased complexity of accounting.

"Starting salaries for new college graduates averaged about $5,300 a year. . . . Salaries of senior accountants with about 5 years' experience are generally about 50 percent higher than starting salaries. . . .

"Information, particularly on CPA's and on the aptitude and achievement tests now given in many high schools and colleges, and by many public accounting firms, may be obtained from:

---

[2] Copies of the 1963–64 edition (sixth revision) may be obtained from the Superintendent of Documents, U.S. Government Printing Office, Washington, D.C., at the cost of $4.75 each. If your college library is a government depository, it has a copy.

American Institute of Certified Public Accountants
666 Fifth Avenue
New York 16, New York"

Home Economists. "About 80,000 persons are employed in home economics occupations. . . . The number of home economists needed in many fields is expected to continue increasing during most of the 1960's. . . . In the field of education, the shortage of home economics teachers is especially critical in public secondary schools. More teachers are needed because of the rising enrollments in secondary schools throughout the country. . . . Moreover, it has been estimated that as many as 5,000 home economics teachers must be recruited annually as replacements. . . . Not enough home economics graduates are entering and remaining in home economics occupations to satisfy current demand. . . . Additional information about home economists and available graduate scholarships may be obtained from:

American Home Economics Association
1600 20th St. N.W.
Washington, D.C. 20006"

Insurance. "Insurance is a multibillion dollar business employing about 1 million people. . . . More than 1,400 life insurance companies and approximately 3,500 property and casualty insurance companies are in operation. . . . Nearly 3 out of every 4 Americans, plus hundreds of thousands of business firms, hold one or more insurance policies. . . . Many thousands of job openings can be expected in the insurance field each year during the 1960's. The number of insurance workers has risen rapidly during recent years, and it will probably continue to mount at a considerably faster rate than employment in many other industries. . . . A beginning agent is usually guaranteed a minimum salary for the first year or two while he is building up a clientele. . . . After 4 or 5 years, a life insurance agent may earn from $7,500 to $10,000 a year; eventually, some highly successful agents may earn as much as $25,000 or more. . . . Information on careers in the insurance field is available from:

Institute of Life Insurance
488 Madison Ave.
New York, N.Y. 10022

Life Insurance Agency Management Association
170 Sigourney St.
Hartford, Conn.

National Association of Life Underwriters
1922 F St., N.W.
Washington, D.C."

Teaching. "Teaching is the largest of all the professions. More than 1¾ million men and women in the United States are full-time teachers, and thousands of others teach on a part-time basis. . . . No other profession offers so many employment opportunities for women; about 1 million women are teachers, more than twice the number employed in nursing—the second largest field of professional employment for women. . . . To staff the new classrooms that must be provided for the rising numbers of students, the Nation's teaching staff will need to be about one-third larger by 1970. In addition, a still greater number will be required to replace teachers who leave the profession. . . . A growing number of secondary school teachers will be needed during the 1960's when enrollments will expand rapidly as a result of the high birth rates following World War II. The great increase in the population reaching high school age, combined with the trend for a growing proportion of young people to enter and graduate from high school, will result in an average annual demand for about 25,000 additional teachers. . . . Openings for new entrants to college teaching will be numerous through the mid-1960's and will increase greatly during the latter part of the decade. . . ."

Particularly helpful to the student who wants to look further into a given occupation is the last section under each job category, "Where to Go for More Information." By writing to or calling on the associations and organizations suggested, a much more detailed picture of the profession or line of business and its earning possibilities can be obtained. Frequently a more precise idea of probable earnings, broken down into entering salary, salary after five years, and so on, may be secured. A relatively small entering salary should not discourage you if it is clear that, with experience, opportunities exist to better your income materially.

Average Income in the United States

Perhaps it would help if you knew what the income of the average family and person in the United States is. Then you can judge your own position and outlook. The U.S. Bureau of the Census reports on family income, while the Survey Research Center of the University of Michigan provides data on spending units.

What is a spending unit? How does it differ from a family? Why does one authority use spending units in attempting to measure changes in income and well-being in the United States, while another bases its analysis on family income?

The Survey Research Center has undertaken and published a very interesting annual survey of consumer finances.[3] Based on a relatively small but carefully selected representative sample, this survey attempts to find out whether consumers feel they are better or worse off than in the previous year; what their average income is; what assets they own and how these have changed from the previous year; how they plan to, and how they do in fact, spend their income; whether and how much they manage to save or whether they must draw upon past savings; what form the savings take, whether in savings banks, govern-

---

[3] See *1962 Survey of Consumer Finances,* Monograph No. 32, Survey Research Center, Institute for Social Research, University of Michigan, Ann Arbor.

ment bonds, stocks, real estate, and so on; whether their debts exceed their assets and what form the debt takes; and whether they use personal loans, mortgages, installment credit, and so on. The survey answers a host of interesting questions and sheds a great deal of light on what consumers get in the way of income and what they do with it.

The annual survey of consumer income conducted by the Bureau of the Census answers such questions as: How many families are there in each income bracket? What is average annual family income? How does family income vary according to urban and rural residence, major source of earnings, color, size of family, type of family, age of head of family, number of children, and so on? The Census Bureau uses the "family" and "unrelated individuals" as units of measurement, while the Survey Research Center uses "spending units."

The term "family" is defined as a group of two or more persons related to one another and living together; all such persons living together are regarded as one family. The term "unrelated individual" is used to refer to a person living alone or with persons not related to him. A "spending unit," on the other hand, consists of all related persons living together *who pool their incomes.*

There may be more than one spending unit in a family, since a spending unit is defined as including all persons living in the same dwelling and belonging to the same family who pool their incomes to meet their major expenses. For example, a grown son who is working and does not pool his income with his parents' income, even though he may pay something for board and room, is treated as a separate spending unit if he retains more than half of his income. Likewise, married children or other relatives who do not pool their incomes with that of the head of the family, even though living in the same dwelling, constitute separate spending units. There are now approximately 58.8 million "spending units" as against 47 million "families" in the United States.[4]

Of the nation's 47 million families, 9.3 million families, or a fifth of the total number, had incomes in 1962 of less than $3,000 (see Fig. 1-1). On the other hand, 17.7 percent had incomes of $10,000 or more. Of these, at the very top of the ladder, 2.3 million families (or 5 percent of the total) received incomes of $15,000 per year or more. Thus the very large middle group, receiving incomes from $3,000 to $10,000, amounted to 29 million families, or 60 percent of the total

---

[4] Families and unattached individuals total 57.5 million.

number. Average (median) family income in the United States in 1962 was $5,956.[5] Over the period from 1947 to 1962, median family income rose by almost $3,000, and the proportion of families with

FIGURE 1–1

Distribution of Money Income of U.S. Families

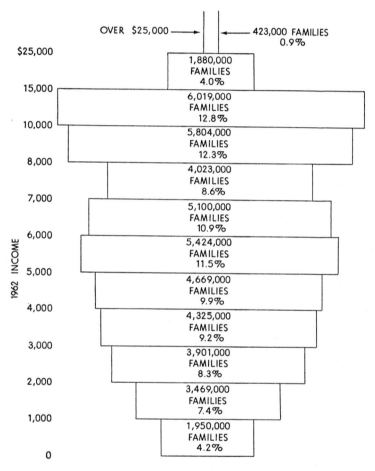

incomes of $6,000 and over increased from 11.7 to 49.5 percent.

Although the median income for all families was $5,956, there was considerable variation, due to a variety of factors. For example, the average income of nonfarm families ($6,126) was higher than that of farm families ($3,418). Marked differences characterized the in-

---

[5] "Median income" may be defined as that income below which (and above which) half of all the units fall. The median is not affected, as is the arithmetic mean (sometimes simply called the "average"), by a few high- (or low-) income units.

come levels of white and nonwhite families. For the country as a whole, the median income of white families ($6,237) was almost twice that received by nonwhite families ($3,330).

Family income varies according to the age of the chief breadwinner and according to who heads the family. The median income rose from $4,276 for families in which the head was under 25 years to $7,040 for families in which the breadwinner was from 45 to 54 years of age. The median then declined to $3,204 for families in which the head was 65 years or older. Thus, middle age, the decade from 45 to 54 years, is the period of peak earnings. Families headed by males received considerably larger incomes ($6,237) than those headed by females ($3,131). This is because families headed by females (widows 58 percent, divorcees 32 percent) represent broken families, where the women did not expect to have to assume the responsibility of providing for the family and may not have been well prepared for it. On the other hand, the increasing tendency of the wife to work outside the home has been one of the major factors boosting family income in recent years. Families with working wives had median incomes of $7,461 as compared to $5,764 for families with nonworking wives.

On a spending-unit basis, the distribution of income may be seen in Table 1–2. In 1962, 26 percent of the total number of spending units had incomes of less than $3,000, while 15 percent had incomes of $10,000 or more. Thus the middle group—the spending units with incomes of $3,000–$10,000—constituted 59 percent of the total. This is, of course, somewhat similar to the family income distribution, and also confirms the Census Bureau with respect to average income. The median annual money income of all spending units was $5,300, while the mean was $6,280. Thus it is apparent that whatever the unit of measurement, average income ranged between these limits.

Differences in the characteristics of spending units are most pronounced at the high and low parts of the income distribution. Spending units with incomes of less than $3,000 tended to have few members, to live in small towns and the open country, and to be headed by persons 55 or more years of age. Retired persons, farm operators, unskilled workers, widows, and students were the occupational groups most frequently found at this income level. Spending units with high incomes ($10,000 or more) were relatively larger in size, lived in metropolitan areas, and were most frequently headed by persons between 35 and 54 years of age who were self-employed, in managerial positions, or in a profession. The intermediate groups tended to progress from one pattern to the other.

TABLE 1–2

Income Grouping of Spending Units and of Total Money Income
(Percentage Distribution)

TOTAL MONEY INCOME BEFORE TAXES	SPENDING UNITS*				SHARE OF TOTAL MONEY INCOME			
	1962	1961	1960	1959	1962	1961	1960	1959
Under $1,000	5	6	6	7	1	1	1	1
$1,000–1,999	10	12	10	12	2	3	2	3
$2,000–2,999	11	10	10	10	5	4	4	4
$3,000–3,999	10	10	10	10	5	6	6	6
$4,000–4,999	10	11	11	12	7	8	9	9
$5,000–5,999	12	12	13	12	10	11	12	12
$6,000–7,499	13	14	15	14	14	15	17	16
$7,500–9,999	14	12	13	11	19	17	19	17
$10,000–14,999	10	9	9	8	20	18	17	16
$15,000 or more	5	4	3	4	17	17	13	16
Total	100	100	100	100	100	100	100	100

Median income †		$5,300	$5,000	$5,170	$4,860
Mean income ‡		6,280	$6,050	$5,830	$5,660

* A Spending Unit consists of all related persons living together who pool their incomes.
† Median income of the middle spending unit in a ranking of all units by size of total money income.
‡ Mean income is obtained by dividing aggregate money income before taxes by number of spending units.
SOURCE: *Survey of Consumer Finances*, Survey Research Center, University of Michigan.

Upper- and Lower-Income Groups—A Contrast

The gap between upper- and lower-income groups in the United States has narrowed somewhat in recent years. Several studies have indicated this. In one[6] Professor Simon Kuznets declares: "The inequality in distribution has narrowed: the percentage shares of the lower income groups have risen and those of the upper income groups have declined."

Families with five-figure incomes are commonplace in America today. The standard of living has been rising more than 1½ percent a year. Average family purchasing power has risen two thirds since 1929 and nearly one third since 1947. There has been a sharp upward shift in families along the income brackets as Table 1–3 shows.

Reading across the top two lines, families with a real income of less than $4,000 plummeted from 70 percent of all families in 1929 to 44 percent in 1947 and to 30 percent in 1962. The last three lines

[6] Simon Kuznets, *Income Distribution and Changes in Consumption*. Paper presented to an Arden House Conference on "The Changing American Population," October 1–3, 1961, p. 9.

TABLE 1–3

Distribution of Money Income of U.S. Families*

	1929	1941	1947	1957	1962
Under $2,000	31%	27%	16%	13%	12%
$2,000–3,999	39	29	28	21	18
$4,000–5,999	15	22	26	24	21
$6,000–7,999	7	12	14	18	19
$8,000–9,999	3	4	7	10	12
$10,000–14,999	5	6	6	9	13
$15,000 plus			3	5	5

* Percents have been rounded.
SOURCE: U.S. Bureau of the Census.

of Table 1–3 show the growth in the proportion of families with a real income of more than $8,000—from a mere 8 percent in 1929 to 30 percent today. Meanwhile, the $10,000 and over families rose from 5 percent to 18 percent of the total. To put it another way, one family in twenty received an income equivalent to $10,000 or over in

TABLE 1–4

The Rich Are Even Richer than Their Income Shows

FAMILY INCOME LEVEL	MEDIAN NET WORTH*	PERCENT OF NET WORTH INVESTED IN					
		STOCK	OTHER FINAN- CIAL ASSETS	EQUITY IN BUSI- NESS	EQUITY IN OWN HOME	LIFE INSUR- ANCE SURRENDER VALUE	OTHER
$ 7,500–10,000	$ 19,000	17%	15%	11%	44%	8%	5%
10,000–15,000	38,000	19	16	21	28	6	9
15,000–25,000	56,000	18	15	31	21	6	9
25,000–40,000	179,000	27	14	32	13	4	11
40,000 and over	386,000	28	13	43	7	2	7

* Net Worth = Sum of value of assets less debts.
DATA: Federal Reserve Board—special survey of 1,200 families in four cities for 1960.
SOURCE: *Business Week*, September 28, 1963.

1929. One family in ten did so in 1947. And now the proportion is one in five. The actual number of families in this bracket has grown from 2 million to 4 million to 11 million. Such families now receive more than 40 percent of all income.[7]

Income doesn't tell the whole story of how well off a family is. Table 1–4 shows what happens when net worth is figured, compared

[7] See "The Dynamic Upper Income Market," *Business in Brief,* Chase Manhattan Bank, New York, September–October, 1963. But see also, "Income Revolution Slows Up," *Business Week,* September 28, 1963.

with income. When stocks, real estate, and other assets are considered, high-income families show up disproportionately richer. For example, families with incomes in the $25,000 to $40,000 brackets typically had more than four times the net worth of families in the $10,000 to $15,000 class. Net worth of the very rich mounts still faster. In 1961, the richest 1 percent of U.S. adults held 28 percent of the nation's total personal wealth.[8]

There is some dissent from the view that the income gap is narrowing and that we are rapidly becoming a middle-income nation. The AFL-CIO Research Department, in a study entitled "The Unequal Sharing of U.S. Wealth," notes that: "The poorest 6.8 million families, with incomes under $2,000 (12 percent of all families), received $7.6 billion of the total (of personal income in the United States in 1961), or about 2 percent. On the other hand, 3.7 million families with incomes in excess of $15,000 (6 percent of all families) received $91 billion— 23 percent of the total."[9] Citing a study by Robert J. Lampman, updated for *Business Week*,[10] the AFL-CIO noted that the richest 1 percent of all adults in the United States owned 36.3 percent of total personal wealth in the U.S. in 1929, 20.8 percent in 1949, and 28.0 percent in 1961. As Bruce Bliven pointed out, however, the family income of workers has increased more than two and a half times since the turn of the century (1900–60), and the total work week has been reduced by 20 hours, or by one third of what it was.[11]

To those of you who aspire, 10 or 15 years from now, to be in the top-income brackets, some of the main facts found in a study of upper-income groups by the National Industrial Conference Board may be of interest. Today, about half of all purchasing power is commanded by families earning between $5,000 and $10,000, but before the decade ends, most buying will be accounted for by families earning over $10,000. By 1970, it is estimated, one out of every three families will be in the top-earning category, and they will consume about three fifths of all goods and services. Currently, that group holds 18 percent of all families and about a third of total spending capacity (see Fig. 1–2). Last year, the upper-earning bracket included 6.5 million families; by 1970 its population will grow to an estimated 15.5 million. The most

---

[8] *Ibid.*, p. 146.

[9] "The Unequal Sharing of U.S. Wealth," *AFL-CIO American Federationist*, November, 1962. See also, "Is the Income Gap Closed? No!" by Herman P. Miller, in *New York Times Magazine*, November 11, 1962, p. 50 *et seq.;* also "Size Distribution of Income," *Survey of Current Business*, April, 1964.

[10] See *Business Week*, January 27, 1962.

[11] "The Revolution of the Joneses," *New York Times Magazine*, October 9, 1960.

FIGURE 1–2

The Growing Importance of Upper Income*

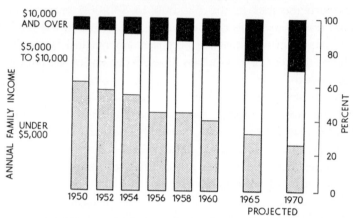

* Total families, each year = 100 percent. All figures based on constant 1960 dollars.
SOURCE: Department of Commerce; the Conference Board.

profound change anticipated in the composition of the group is a sharp rise in the importance of younger families. Currently, roughly one in eight homes earning over $10,000 is headed by a person under 35, and the ratio was about the same a decade ago. By 1970, according to Conference Board projections, the head of one in every four upper-bracket

FIGURE 1–3

Changing Profile of Income Distribution
All Figures in 1960 Dollars*

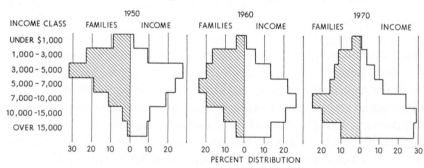

* Reproduced by courtesy of the National Industrial Conference Board.

homes will be under 35. Back in 1950, roughly two thirds of total top-income spending power was wielded by those over 45 years old, but in 1970 that age group will account for only an estimated half of such spending. Young households will achieve an increased prevalence not only generally in our society, but within the upper brackets, specifically. For a view of the changing profile of income distribution, see Fig. 1–3.

What of the lower-income groups? Who are they, and why were they unable, in accordance with the American tradition, to rise at least part way to the top? You will want to know about them. Probably you can avoid some of the pitfalls they encountered. In terms of real income, the poor are shrinking as a class. Families earning less than $3,000 a year have shrunk from 51 percent of the total number in 1929 to 20 percent now. Herman Miller estimates that by 1980, only 12 percent of U.S. families will receive less than $3,000 a year[12] (see Fig. 1–4).

FIGURE 1–4

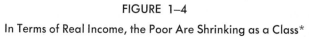

In Terms of Real Income, the Poor Are Shrinking as a Class*

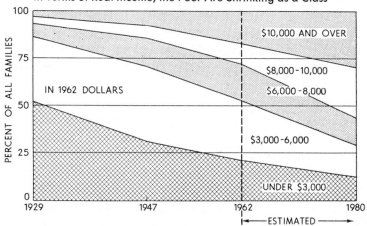

*DATA: Commerce Department; estimates by Herman P. Miller. Reproduced with special permission of *Business Week.*

What are the characteristics of low-income families and what causes their incomes to be low? A study by Robert J. Lampman[13] points to a number of handicapping characteristics. For purposes of his study a "low-income person" was defined as one with an income equivalent to that of a member of a four-person family, with total money income for

[12] Herman P. Miller, *Rich Man, Poor Man* (New York: Thomas Y. Crowell Co., 1964).

[13] Robert J. Lampman, "Low Income Population and Economic Growth," *Study Paper No. 12,* Joint Economic Committee, Congress of The United States, Washington, D.C., December, 1959. See also, "Limited Educational Attainment: Extent and Consequences," by E. W. Brice and E. E. Huyck, in *New Directions in Health, Education and Welfare* (Washington, D.C.: U.S. Department of Health, Education, and Welfare, 1963).

the family of not more than $2,500. Thus an unattached individual would be classified as a low-income person if he had income under $1,157; a member of a six-person family would be so classified if his family had income under $3,236. In line with this definition, it was found that 32.2 million persons were in low-income status. This was 19 percent of all persons. Out of the total of 32.2 million low-income persons, 8 million were 65 years of age or older; 6.4 million were non-white; 8 million were in consumer units headed by women; 21 million were in units headed by a person with educational attainment of eight grades or less. About 70 percent of the low-income population had one or more of these handicapping characteristics.

Lack of education for the better-paying occupations thus appears to be the most important cause of low income. About two thirds of low-income families are headed by persons with no education beyond grammar school. Those with lesser amounts of education are most usually found—when employed at all—in farm, service, and unskilled laboring jobs. Employed workers with an eighth grade education or less have 65 percent of the incomes between $1,000 and $1,500, and 61 percent of the incomes between $1,500 and $2,500. Unskilled workers have the highest rates of unemployment and the lowest average level of education. The rate of unemployment in 1962 among proprietors, managers, and professional and technical personnel was between 1 and 2 percent. Clerical and sales workers were unemployed at the rate of approximately 4 percent. But semiskilled workers were out of work at the rate of 7½ percent and unskilled workers at the rate of about 12 percent. One third of employed heads of families with under $2,500 of income were in agriculture, forestry, and fishing, while industry groups having the highest percent of all families with incomes under $2,500 were agriculture, forestry, fishing, and personal and domestic service.

About 25 percent of all low-income persons were 65 years of age or older. While aged persons were only about 8.5 percent of all persons, they made up one fourth of the low-income population. Of the 15.3 million persons 65 and over:

> 55 percent had less than $1,000 annually
> 23 percent had $1,000 to $2,000 annually
> 9 percent had $2,000 to $3,000 annually
> 13 percent had $3,000 or more.

According to the Census Bureau, of 6.2 million families with the head 65 and older, one half had less than $2,830 in annual income and one fourth had less than $1,620 in annual income. Of 3.6 million aged persons living alone or with nonrelatives, one half had less than $1,000 annually and four fifths had less than $2,000. Using spending-unit data, of the older units (65 and over), 71 percent had a disposable income (after taxes) of less than $3,000, while only 10 percent had more than $5,000. Not only do older units have substantially lower incomes than younger ones, but low incomes may be temporary among younger families but tend to be permanent among the aged.

About one fifth of the 32.2 million low-income persons were nonwhite. Nonwhite families make up 10 percent of all families, but they constitute approximately 22 percent of all families with incomes under $2,000.

One fourth of the low-income persons were in consumer units headed by women. While only 10 percent of all families are headed by women, 24 percent of the families with under $2,000 had women heads. Thirty-eight percent of all families headed by women had less than $2,000 of income. Thus broken homes, in which the male head has died, been divorced, disappeared, or become incapacitated, are characterized by low incomes in many instances.[14]

Income, Occupation, and Education

The foregoing analysis, contrasting upper- and lower-income families, indicated that occupation and education have a good deal to do with determination of level of income. Generally speaking, it appears that heads of low-income families have had little formal education or training and are mainly unskilled workers, whereas heads of upper-income families have had much more formal education, and this seems to have led them into either business or the professions.

"Average family income tends to rise as the educational attainment of the head increases," according to the U.S. Census Bureau. "Families headed by elementary school graduates who had no additional education reported an average income of $4,800 in 1961, as compared with an average of $6,300 reported for families headed by persons who completed high school but went no further, and $9,300 for those headed by college graduates. At each level of schooling, families headed by persons who completed the level reported substantially higher incomes than those who did not. . . . The proportion of families with a head who went to college, whether or not he graduated, was smallest among families with incomes of less than $3,000 (7 percent). This proportion

---

[14] See "Part III, The Low Income Population," in *Income and Welfare in the United States,*" by James N. Morgan, Martin H. David, Wilbur J. Cohen, and Harvey E. Brazer (New York: McGraw-Hill Book Co., Inc., 1962).

rose progressively to about 58 percent for families with incomes in excess of $15,000."[15]

Families headed by professional workers or by managers and officials have higher median incomes ($9,116 and $8,139, respectively) than those headed by other types of workers. Self-employed professionals have the highest average ($13,326). The lowest incomes are received by farm laborers and foremen ($2,700), laborers ($4,732), and private household workers ($1,738). Families headed by persons engaged in finance, insurance, and real estate, where considerable education is necessary, have one of the highest median incomes ($7,686), while those headed by persons engaged in personal services or in agriculture, forestry, and fishing have the lowest median incomes ($3,887 and $3,318 respectively).

An analysis of spending units by occupation of head of spending unit and income group tends to bear out exactly the same conclusion. Two thirds of all spending units having incomes of $8,000 and over are headed by those who fall into either the professional and semiprofessional or managerial and self-employed categories, while spending units having incomes of less than $3,000 consist primarily of unskilled and service workers, farm operators, and retired persons. Spending units in the middle-income categories ($3,000–$8,000) consist primarily of persons falling in the skilled and semiskilled and clerical and sales categories.

Spending-unit data also reveal the marked correlation between extensive formal education and high incomes, on the one hand, and lack of education and low incomes, on the other. The *Survey of Consumer Finances* notes:

> Particularly striking are the differences in the income distribution of educational groups. Of the spending units whose heads went to college, 41 percent were in the highest income quintile. Only 18 percent of those who went to high school, and 6 percent of those who had a grade school education or less had incomes of similar size. . . . The higher the education, the more frequent are income increases and the less frequent is unchanged income.

College Graduates and Professions

Clearly, college graduates predominate among upper-income families and spending units, and the heads of the upper-income groups tend to be either professional men or businessmen. In a study of U.S. college graduates, *Time* concluded: "The fact is that college graduates earn very much more than the average of their fellow Americans," and added, "But at least it must be obvious that a very large proportion of

---

[15] For an extended discussion see *ibid.*, chap. xxiii.

the families in the upper income brackets are college families, and that among the lower brackets a very small proportion of the families have had a higher education."[16]

A fascinating sociological study of the U.S. college graduate begins enthusiastically:

They come from all kinds of places and all kinds of homes; they go to many different types of campuses, meet many breeds of professors, and study everything from Aristotle to zoology, including bait casting and tearoom service. Yet in life after the campus, the college graduates have one trait very much in common. Viewed strictly from a materialistic point of view, they are conspicuously successful. They hold the best jobs, the positions of greatest prestige. They make a great deal more money than their noncollege contemporaries. By all conventional standards of worldly attainment they have made good almost to the man.[17]

A chart (see Fig. 1–5) is used to show the remarkable contrast between the occupations of the college graduates and the fields of employment of nongraduates. The authors declare:

If the line through the center of the chart can be considered the water line, the figures for noncollege men are like an iceberg, with only 16% in the top-ranking positions and all the rest submerged in routine or minor jobs. The college graduates, on the other hand, float up like a high riding ship, with 84% on top and only 16% submerged. There can be no mistaking the import of the table: the college graduates hold the key jobs in our society. The noncollege man who rises to the top is a relative rarity. On the other hand, it is unusual to find an Old Grad who is not at the top.[18]

Most college graduates—over 50 percent of the males and over 80 percent of the females—engage in one of the professions. This compares with something less than 5 percent of the total U.S. adult population who are classified as professional. These figures represent the most extreme variation of the U.S. college bloc from any statistically determined norm for the U.S. adult population as a whole. "One prime characteristic of higher education thus is," the *Time* survey concludes, "that it tends powerfully to lead to the professions."

The professions as a group have been expanding rapidly and will probably continue to grow. The number of women in the professions has grown even more rapidly than that of men. A major reason for the increase in the total number of workers in professional and related occupations has been the development of new professional fields. In 1870 the leading professions were the traditional ones—medicine, the ministry, law, and teaching. Nearly 75 out of every 100 professional work-

---

[16] Reprinted from "The U.S. College Graduate," *Time*, The Weekly Newsmagazine.

[17] Ernest Havemann and Patricia Salter West, *They Went to College: The College Graduate in America Today* (New York: Harcourt, Brace & Co., Inc.), p. 25.

[18] *Ibid.*, p. 26.

FIGURE 1–5

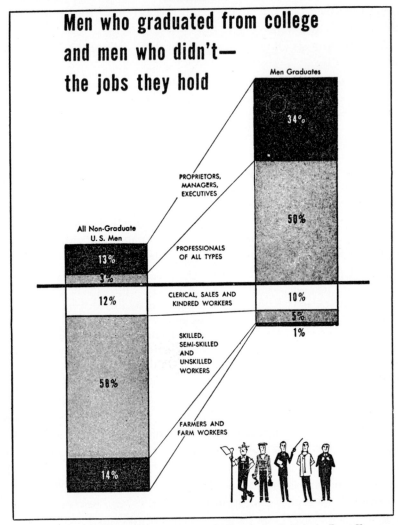

Men who graduated from college and men who didn't— the jobs they hold

Men Graduates

34%

PROPRIETORS, MANAGERS, EXECUTIVES

50%

All Non-Graduate U.S. Men

PROFESSIONALS OF ALL TYPES

13%

3%

12%

CLERICAL, SALES AND KINDRED WORKERS

10%

5%

1%

SKILLED, SEMI-SKILLED AND UNSKILLED WORKERS

58%

FARMERS AND FARM WORKERS

14%

Source: From *They Went to College: The College Graduate in America Today* by Ernest Havemann and Patricia Salter West, copyright by Time, Inc. Used by permission of Harcourt, Brace & Co., Inc.

ers were in these occupations, compared with only about 40 out of 100 today.

The "big four" professions of 1870 have all grown considerably since that time. Today the medical profession employs more than three times as many as in 1870; the ministry and the legal profession employ over four times as many; and teaching about ten times as many. The number of people in scientific, engineering, and closely related professions, however, is a hundred times greater today than in 1870. Other major professions, not recognized as separate occupational fields until the turn of the century, have also developed rapidly—for example, social work, accounting, and personnel work.

The growth of the professions has, of course, been accompanied by a considerable increase in the number of college students (see Table 1–5). Back in 1940 only 15 out of 100 (of the 18–21 age group) went to college. By 1950, the figure had risen to 30 out of 100. In 1960 it was 40 out of 100 and by 1970 it is expected to be 50 out of 100. The number of students in college is expected to rise from an estimated 4.4 million in 1963–64 to 8.3 million in 1973–74.

TABLE 1–5

U.S. Population, College Students, and Graduates, 1900–1970
(In Thousands)

Year	No. of Students Entering College	No. of Students in College	No. of College Graduates That Year*	Total Population (In Millions)
1900	—	238	28	75.9
1920	—	598	49	105.7
1930	337	1,101	123	122.7
1940	418	1,494	187	131.6
1950	516	2,296	384	150.6
1960	923	3,583	392	179.3
1965†	1,415	5,220	534	195.5
1970†	1,569	6,959	726	211.6

* Bachelor's and first professional degree.
† Estimates.
Source: Office of Education, U.S. Department of Health, Education, and Welfare.

In recent years, business has been attracting gradually larger minorities of the men out of college. Most of the high-level administrative and specialized jobs that now exist in business are of fairly recent development. It was only about 75 years ago that really large-scale industrial and commercial establishments such as we have today began to appear. Since 1920, the number of students (male and female) graduating from business administration courses (college) have been increasing very rapidly—from 1,500 in 1920 to 19,000 in 1940 and to 48,000 in 1961–62. Business education is now second only to teacher training as a field of college education; graduates with majors in the various specialties of business administration outnumber those in such large fields as engineering, law, and medicine.

Women college graduates engage predominantly in teaching. Largely because of this, the college woman doesn't, on the average, do as well financially as her male counterpart. Over 60 percent of women college graduates go into teaching, which unfortunately is not one of the higher-paying professions.

More than a third of the women of working age in the United States are employed, compared to less than a fifth in 1890. Between 1930 and 1960, the number of women in the nation's working force rose from 10.4 million to 23.3 million. The number of women who received college degrees rose from 55,000 to 160,000 a year. The number of women pursuing professional careers rose from 1.5 to 2.9 million. Four out of five of today's professional women are concentrated in seven professions: teaching, nursing, social work, library work, music, accounting and auditing, and work as technicians (medical and dental).

In 1940, there were just 4.2 million working wives. By 1950, the number was up to 8.6 million and by 1961, had jumped to 13.3 million. Some of this increase can be explained by the population increase and by the fact that marriages are occurring now at younger ages than previously. But more significant has been the change in social attitudes concerning the employment of married women. Husbands no longer consider it a reflection on their earning ability if their wives have a paying job, and the earnings of these married women have contributed to higher standards of living, including the rise in home ownership and the increase in the number of college-educated youth.[19]

The higher the family income—up to the $15,000 mark—the more likely it is that the wife is working. Thereafter, U.S. families seem more willing to agree that woman's place is in the home—or at the bridge club. In the $7,000 to $15,000 income brackets, more than half of all wives are working. Above $15,000 the proportion declines to one third. The latest survey of the Women's Bureau of the U.S. Department of Labor indicates that 53 percent of all college women graduates work.

> "Whereas woman is the foundation of sin, the weapon of the devil, the cause of man's banishment from Paradise, the University shall be closed to them."
>
> This was the first sentence of the decree issued in 1377 by the faculty of the University in Bologna, Italy, which banished women from its student body. Contrary to general belief, there were women studying at universities, in the Middle Ages. But, after the decree of 1377, in a very short time every university in the world had shut out women. It took exactly 456 years before an institution of higher learning again opened its doors to women . . . in 1833 Oberlin College in Ohio became the first to admit women students.

[19] See Women's Bureau, *15 Years after College: A Study of Alumnae of the Class of 1945,* Bulletin No. 283 (Washington, D.C.: U.S. Department of Labor, 1962).

FIGURE 1–6

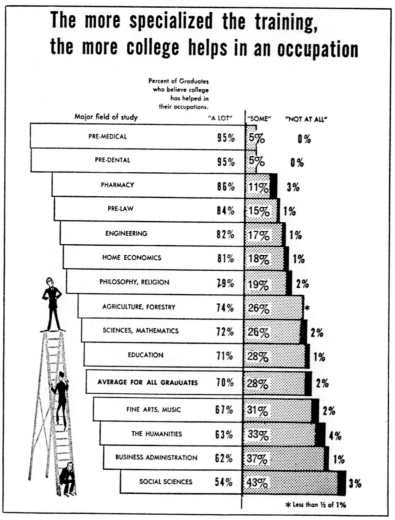

The more specialized the training, the more college helps in an occupation

Percent of Graduates
who believe college
has helped in
their occupations.

Major field of study	"A LOT"	"SOME"	"NOT AT ALL"
PRE-MEDICAL	95%	5%	0%
PRE-DENTAL	95%	5%	0%
PHARMACY	86%	11%	3%
PRE-LAW	84%	15%	1%
ENGINEERING	82%	17%	1%
HOME ECONOMICS	81%	18%	1%
PHILOSOPHY, RELIGION	79%	19%	2%
AGRICULTURE, FORESTRY	74%	26%	*
SCIENCES, MATHEMATICS	72%	26%	2%
EDUCATION	71%	28%	1%
AVERAGE FOR ALL GRADUATES	70%	28%	2%
FINE ARTS, MUSIC	67%	31%	2%
THE HUMANITIES	63%	33%	4%
BUSINESS ADMINISTRATION	62%	37%	1%
SOCIAL SCIENCES	54%	43%	3%

* Less than ½ of 1%

SOURCE: From *They Went to College: The College Graduate in America Today* by Ernest Havemann and Patricia Salter West, copyright by Time, Inc. Used by permission of Harcourt, Brace & Co., Inc.

College provides the essential training necessary to enter the more specialized professions, such as medicine, law, dentistry, and the technical phases of business, such as accounting, finance, and engineering (see Fig. 1–6). By and large, the nongraduate finds himself barred from these fields. And because he can pre-empt highly specialized and technical occupations, the college graduate not only tends to earn more (see Fig. 1–7) even at the outset of his career than the noncollege man, but the cash value of his degree increases with age. When the average

FIGURE 1–7

Family Heads Completing One or More Years of College as a Percent of
All Family Heads, by Family Income in 1963, for the United States

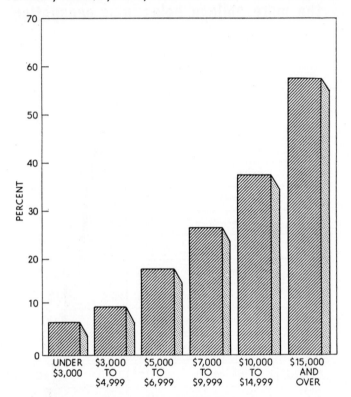

man's income begins to decline as he loses ground after age 50 to younger men, the college graduates are attaining their best returns.

Income in the Professions and in Business

"Judged by earnings, the 3,000,000 professional workers are a fortunate group. Their earnings, though less equally distributed than those of nonprofessional workers, are between two and three times as large." So declare Friedman and Kuznets in their careful statistical study on income from independent professional practice.[20] They further note: "Independent practice of a profession tends to be more lucrative than

---

[20] Milton Friedman and Simon Kuznets, *Income from Independent Professional Practice* (New York: National Bureau of Economic Research, Inc.).

salaried employment; while professional workers, independent and salaried, earn on the average between two and three times as much as all other workers; independent practitioners alone earn about four times as much."

Not all professions pay equally well. As Table 1–6 and Table 1–10

TABLE 1–6

Over a Lifetime, Professionals Do Best

Occupation	Lifetime Earnings (Men, Age 18–64)
Doctors	$717,000
Lawyers	621,000
Managers and proprietors (with college degrees)	593,000
Dentists	589,000
Natural scientists	
Geologists	446,000
Biologists	310,000
Social scientists	
Economists	413,000
Psychologists	335,000
Engineers	
Aeronautical	395,000
Civil	335,000
Teachers	
College	324,000
High school	261,000
Elementary	232,000
Accountants	313,000
Electricians	251,000
Airplane mechanics	248,000
Plumbers	236,000
Carpenters	185,000
Radio and TV mechanics	183,000
Clergymen	175,000

DATA: Estimates by Herman P. Miller from Census Bureau figures. Reprinted by courtesy of *Business Week*.

(see page 26) indicate, medicine and law provide the highest average income. The teachers and the clergy get the least. Business and engineering lie in between. Of course, some corporation executives get handsome incomes running into six figures, but these are the fortunate few—the exceptions, not the average. A survey of administrative salaries in eastern corporations by the Dartnell Corporation of Chicago placed the average executive compensation at levels shown in Table 1–7.[21]

The disparity between a beginner's salary and a seasoned executive's salary in business is much greater than comparable ranges in the professions. For example, a college graduate may start as an apprentice in business at $80 a week and ultimately hope to work his way up to the corporation's top executive ranks with a salary of $26,000 to $50,000

TABLE 1–7

Executive Compensation in U.S. Corporations

POSITION	MEDIAN COMPENSATION*		
	LARGE COMPANIES	INTERMEDIATE COMPANIES	SMALL COMPANIES
Chairman of the board	$66,200	$39,000	$25,000
President	69,200	41,100	25,450
General sales manager	28,225	20,300	15,300
Executive vice-president	48,600	29,850	24,400
Treasurer	26,200	18,000	13,700
Controller	18,800	12,500	10,300
General manager, manufacturing	27,500	18,500	13,800
Secretary	23,100	17,100	13,400
Advertising manager	13,450	10,000	9,200
Industrial relations director	15,600	10,675	9,350
Purchasing agent	13,700	10,050	8,500
Office manager	9,900	8,900	7,800
Credit manager	10,700	8,700	7,300

* Plus Bonus, if any.
SOURCE: The Dartnell Corporation, Chicago.

per year. The dentist or the college professor, on the other hand, will do well if he attains the $15,000 level. In accountancy, the junior may expect to begin at $75 or $80 a week for the first year or two, then earn $6,000 or $7,000 over the next five years, perhaps $8,000–$12,000 the next ten years, and thereafter, as a C.P.A. with a small firm of his own, about $15,000 to $25,000 per annum.[22]

A study of the compensation of "junior executives" indicates that the average starting salaries rose as shown in Table 1–8.

---

[21] Large companies are those with gross sales of over $25 million; intermediate companies have gross sales between $5 million and $25 million; small companies have gross sales under $5 million.

[22] See *Accounting May Be the Right Field for You* (New York: American Institute of Certified Public Accountants, 1961), pp. 18–19.

TABLE 1–8

Average Annual Starting Salaries of Inexperienced Bachelor's Degree
Graduates Recruited by Business and Industry from College Campuses,
1950–1963

Field	1950	1953	1960	1963
Engineering	$3,120	$3,900	$6,120	$6,816
Accounting	2,856	3,564	5,352	6,000
Sales	2,880	3,612	5,280	5,772
General Business	2,808	3,504	5,132	5,736

Source: Frank S. Endicott, *Trends in Employment of College and University Graduates in Business and Industry*, Annual Reports, Northwestern University, Evanston, Illinois.

Some indication of the salary progress of the college graduate in these fields and in teaching five and ten years after graduation is shown in the table which follows:

TABLE 1–9

Average Annual Salaries of Bachelor's Degree Graduates Employed in
Business and in Industry and in Classroom Teaching, by Year of Experience

Years of Experience	Engineering	Accounting	Sales	General Business	Teaching
None	$ 6,648	$ 5,856	$ 5,616	$ 5,592	$4,361
5 years	8,868	8,112	8,436	7,920	5,226
10 years	10,872	10,452	10,800	10,272	6,091
Percent increase—10 years	+63.5	+78.5	+92.3	+83.7	+39.7

Source: *Ibid.*, Seventeenth Annual Report, 1963.

On the average, as Table 1–10 indicates, medicine appears to be the most lucrative of the professions, though it must be remembered that this is, in part, just compensation for much greater preparation than most of the other professions require. As a physician, you would probably not begin practice until you were 27 or 28 years of age because of four years in medical school and one year as an intern. Therefore, the much higher average compensation of physicians is partial payment for the lost years of earnings at the beginning of the career.

Specialization in medicine, as in all the professions, pays a handsome bonus over general practice. In the latest *Medical Economics* survey, general practitioners earned $20,000, while fully specialized doctors averaged 25 percent more. Exotic specializations in medicine, such as neurological surgery, yielded $34,700, plastic surgery yielded $33,300,

TABLE 1–10

Average Income in Five Major Professions, 1929–1962

| | | | | | TEACHERS | |
| | | | | | ELEMENTARY AND | |
YEAR	LAWYERS	DOCTORS	DENTISTS	ENGINEERS	SECONDARY	COLLEGE
1929	$ 5,534	$ 5,224	$ 4,267	$ 3,616	$1,420	$3,050
1939	4,391	4,229	3,096	3,155	1,441	n.a.
1949	8,083	11,744	7,146	6,276	3,010	4,217
1951	8,730	13,150	7,743	7,120	3,450	4,692
1962	12,700	22,100	14,087	10,375	5,921	7,680*

SOURCES: *Lawyers:* "Income of Lawyers, 1929–48," *Survey of Current Business,* August, 1949, and Supplement, July, 1950; also "Incomes of Physicians, Dentists and Lawyers, 1949–1951," *Survey of Current Business,* July, 1952; also "Income of Lawyers in the Postwar Period," *Survey of Current Business,* December, 1956; *Lawyers in the United States: Distribution and Income, Part Two: Income* (Chicago: American Bar Foundation, 1958); also Reginald Heber Smith and E. Blythe Stason, "Income of Lawyers, 1959–1960," *American Bar Association Journal,* Vol. 49 (1963), pp. 732–34.

Doctors: "Income of Physicians, 1929–1949," *Survey of Current Business,* July, 1950, and July, 1952; also *Medical Economics,* 1960.

Dentists: "Income of Dentists, 1929–1948," *Survey of Current Business,* January, 1950, and Supplement, July, 1950 and July, 1952; also *"1962 Survey of Dental Practice"* (Chicago: Bureau of Economic Research and Statistics, American Dental Association).

Engineers: Bureau of Labor Statistics, "Employment Outlook for Engineers," *Occupational Outlook Series,* Bulletin No. 968 (Washington, D.C.: U.S. Department of Labor); also Engineering Manpower Commission, *Professional Income of Engineers—1962* (New York: Engineers Joint Council, January, 1963).

Elementary and secondary school teachers (including principals and supervisors): Economic Status of Teachers in 1962–63 (Washington, D.C.: Research Division, National Education Association, August, 1963).

College teachers: George J. Stigler, *Employment and Compensation in Education,* Occasional Paper No. 33 (New York: National Bureau of Economic Research, Inc., 1950), p. 60.

n.a. = not available.

* For four faculty ranks combined, average faculty salary in four-year undergraduate public and private institutions. The four faculty ranks are instructor, assistant professor, associate professor, and full professor. See *Higher Education Salaries, 1961–62* (Washington, D.C.: Office of Education, U.S. Department of Health, Education, and Welfare, 1962). See also, the annual survey *Economic Status of the Profession,* American Association of University Professors.

while obstetrics and gynecology paid $27,900, and pediatrics averaged $20,700. Among engineers, aeronautical engineers with ten years' experience averaged almost $1,400 a year more than chemical engineers with comparable experience. In dentistry, orthodontists averaged $24,300, oral surgeons $19,964, and periodontists $20,569, as compared to $13,951 for the dentist engaged in general practice.

Compensation for engineers favors the new entrant and is generous to the young practitioner, but then levels off or declines and is not particularly rewarding to the experienced engineer. For example, beginning engineers averaged $6,750 per annum as a starting salary in 1962. The Engineering Manpower Commission Survey showed that, in 1962, those who entered the profession in 1957 were averaging $8,725 a year, those who entered in 1952 were averaging $10,425, those who started in 1942–45 were receiving $12,550, those who began in 1932–36 were averaging $12,725, while those who started in 1927–31 averaged $12,575. Thus the larger-than-average earlier rewards, relative to other fields, fail to expand proportionally as the young engineer gains experience. Of course, we are speaking of averages. Some engineers, especially those who go into management, do very well indeed, much better than the average.

The United States Department of Labor publishes an annual survey of earnings.[23] Chemists and engineers each are surveyed in eight levels. The first is the professional trainee level, typically requiring a B.S. degree. The highest level surveyed involves full responsibility over a very broad and highly complex and diversified engineering or chemical program. In 1961–62, median annual salaries ranged from $6,132 for chemist I to $18,444 for chemist VIII and from $6,696 for engineer I to $19,512 for engineer VIII. In engineering and the sciences it is estimated that a master's degree results in from $800 to $1,400 in higher annual earnings, while the doctorate adds from $2,000 to $4,000 additionally a year.

Lawyers are classified in seven categories in the Labor Department earnings survey. Attorneys classified at level I are trainees with LL.B. degrees and bar membership, who hold positions in companies, other than law firms. Level VII is defined to include attorneys in charge of legal staffs. In 1961–62, median annual earnings ranged from $6,544 for attorney I to $21,768 for attorney VII. The American Bar Association places the average earnings of independent legal practitioners at $12,700. Again age and experience are factors. The young attorney (25–29) may earn about $7,500 a year. Lawyers tend to reach the peak of earning power between 50 and 60 and average $17,500 a year, though incomes of from $25,000 to $50,000 for partners in larger law firms are not unusual.

The National Science Foundation reports periodically on salaries of scientists. A 1962 overall median annual salary of $10,000 was reported by 110,000 full-time employed scientists. This was $1,000 more than the 1960 median. A median annual salary higher than the overall median was reported by selected groups of 1962 registrants—$11,000 for those with PH.D., $12,000 for registrants between the ages of 45 and 65, $12,000 for those working in industry, and $14,000 for those engaged in the management or administration of research and development. Almost two thirds of the employed scientists held advanced degrees—38 percent the PH.D. and 24 percent the master's degree.[24]

Teaching, library work, and nursing are the poorest-paying profes-

[23] "National Survey of Professional, Administrative, Technical and Clerical Pay, Winter 1961–62," Bulletin No. 1346 (Washington, D.C.: Bureau of Labor Statistics, U.S. Department of Labor).

[24] See Scientific Manpower Bulletin, National Science Foundation, No. 19, Washington, D.C., December, 1962.

sions, possibly because of the larger percentage of women who enter these fields, work for a while, and then leave for marriage and a career as a housewife. In 1962, primary and secondary school teachers, including principals and other supervisors, averaged $111 a week; professional registered nurses ranged from $73 to $96 a week; while the median annual salary of professional librarians was $125 per week. Indeed, the value of college preparation for these professions is not apparent when it is seen how many categories of nonprofessional employment requiring little formal education yield as much if not more income. For example, a *New York Times* editorial on "The $92 School Teacher" said, "Why would anyone want to be a teacher, with all the grief that goes with it, when he could be an electrician, who receives $161 for a 30-hour week, and is almost sure to get an extra hour daily of premium overtime to make it $198 a week and maybe if he works a full 8-hour day like most other people he gets $236 a week!"[25]

As Table 1–11 shows, the average salary of all elementary and secondary school teachers, including principals and supervisors, was only slightly better than the average annual earnings of all employed persons in the United States, including dishwashers, ditchdiggers, and other un-

TABLE 1–11

Average Annual Salaries of Teachers Compared with Average Annual Earnings in Other Occupational Groups, 1929–1963

		AVERAGE ANNUAL EARNINGS FOR FULL-TIME EMPLOYEES WORKING FOR WAGES OR SALARIES		
CALENDAR YEAR	AVERAGE ANNUAL EARNINGS OF INSTRUCTIONAL STAFF	ALL PERSONS WORKING FOR WAGES OR SALARIES	EMPLOYEES IN MANUFACTURING	CIVILIAN EMPLOYEES OF FEDERAL GOVERNMENT
1929	$1,400	$1,405	$1,543	$1,933
1930	1,425	1,368	1,488	1,768
1939	1,420	1,264	1,363	1,843
1940	1,450	1,300	1,432	1,894
1949	2,900	2,851	3,092	3,361
1950	3,050	3,008	3,300	3,503
1959	5,017	4,558	5,215	5,682
1960	5,266	4,707	5,342	5,946
1962	5,780	5,013	5,715	6,506
1963	6,002	5,179	5,902	—

SOURCE: *Economic Status of Teachers in 1963–64* (Washington, D.C.: Research Division, National Education Association, 1964), Table 13, p. 19.

[25] "The $92 Schoolteacher," *New York Times,* January 20, 1962.

skilled workers. Recently a high school teacher in Summit, New Jersey, made headlines from coast to coast when he notified the board of education that he was quitting his job, which paid $85 a week ($4,420 annually) to take a job driving a brewery truck for $137.50 a week ($7,150 per annum). It is not strange, therefore, that the country should face a continued shortage of teachers.

Conclusion

The facts presented in this chapter and the additional data available in the sources here utilized should make it possible for you to estimate how much you can expect to earn in a given occupation. For example, if you plan to enter college teaching and obtain a position at a state university, to remain there for life, retiring at age 65, you can expect to earn about $3,000 the first two years as an assistant, approximately $5,900 the next three years as an instructor, about $7,800 the next five years as an assistant professor, approximately $10,000 for the next eight years as an associate professor, and an average of $14,000 thereafter as a full professor until retirement. Assuming you start teaching as an assistant after you receive your master's degree at the age of 23 and teach until you are 65, you will earn approximately $492,700.

If you intend to be a physician, you will probably not begin practice until you are 27 or 28 years of age (because of four years in medical school and one year as an intern). The first year you may earn $5,000; the second year, $8,000; from 30 to 34 years of age as an independent general practitioner, you can expect about $11,000 per annum; from ages 35 through 39, about $17,000; from ages 40 through 44, approximately $19,200; from ages 45 through 49, about $22,000; from ages 50 through 54, about $22,800; from ages 55 through 59, about $18,000; and from ages 60 through 65, about $15,500—at which point retirement can be anticipated. Thus, lifetime income from 38 years of practice would total approximately $656,000. Obviously, if you are equally capable of being either a college professor or a doctor and you choose the former, you are sacrificing $163,300 of income over your lifetime.

While the particular profession or career you choose may have definite advantages in your eyes, you should be aware of the basic financial limitation or advantage and weigh clearly in your own mind all the relative advantages and disadvantages, not neglecting the financial factor. You should, of course, not be unmindful of aptitudes and of nonmaterial and spiritual values in choosing a calling or profession. As you will see in the subsequent pages of this book, however, there are a great many major expenses you will encounter over a lifetime; and as you strive to surmount each financial hurdle, you may some day come to regret that you selected a field of endeavor which yields only two thirds, or a half, of the reward of another and perhaps, on reflection, equally attractive lifetime career.

A pioneering study on the average American "in pursuit of happiness" concluded that happiness depends on the "positive satisfactions" in life. Not unexpectedly, higher income was found to be a "positive satisfaction" and thus closely correlated with happiness.[26]

To those who are fortunate still to have the choice of their life's work before them, calculations of the type described should be useful in helping to eliminate some of the haphazard guesswork and error involved in the difficult and basic decision of choosing an occupation for the rest of their lives. If the perplexities of the choice tend to get you down, do not be discouraged. Remember, "No matter how the statistics are grouped and regrouped, they always lead to just one conclusion: the financial success of the college man is a truly impressive thing."[27]

SUGGESTED READINGS

1. Bureau of Labor Statistics, *Occupational Outlook Handbook*. Bulletin No. 1375. Washington, D.C.: U.S. Department of Labor, 1963–64 ed.

2. *The Occupational Outlook,* issued quarterly by the Bureau of Labor Statistics, U.S. Department of Labor.

3. Herman P. Miller, "Money Value of an Education," *Occupational Outlook Quarterly,* September, 1961, and also "Income in Relation to Education," *American Economic Review,* Vol. L, No. 5 (December, 1960).

4. James N. Morgan, Martin H. David, Wilbur J. Cohen, and Harvey E. Brazer, *Income and Welfare in the United States.* New York: McGraw-Hill Book Co., Inc., 1962.

5. Survey Research Center, *Survey of Consumer Finances.* Current annual survey. University of Michigan, Ann Arbor.

6. Bureau of the Census, "Income of Families and Persons in the United States," in *Current Population Reports, Consumer Income.* Washington, D.C.: U.S. Department of Commerce, latest year.

7. William V. Levy, *How Much Is a College Degree Worth to You?* New York: Macfadden, 1963.

8. Engineering Manpower Commission, *Professional Income of Engineers— 1962.* New York: Engineers Joint Council, January, 1963.

---

[26] See Norman M. Bradburn, *"In Pursuit of Happiness: A Pilot Study of Behavior Related to Mental Health,"* Report No. 92 (Chicago: National Opinion Research Center, University of Chicago, May, 1963).

[27] Havemann and West, *op. cit.,* p. 32.

9. *New Directions in Health, Education and Welfare: Background Papers,* U.S. Department of Health, Education, and Welfare, Washington, D.C., 1963.

10. Women's Bureau, *"15 Years after College: A Study of Alumnae of the Class of 1945,"* Bulletin No. 283. Washington, D.C.: U.S. Department of Labor, 1962.

11. *College Placement Annual* and *Annual Salary Survey of Offerings to College Graduates.* Bethlehem, Pa.: College Placement Council, Inc.

12. *Educational Requirements for Employment in Selected Professional Fields.* Prepared by BLS in co-operation with the Veterans Administration.

   Series of pamphlets providing information on educational requirements for entry and advancement in nine selected professional fields. Describes for each selected field the functions, fields of specialization, and types of employment in relation to the level of educational preparation acquired.
   Actuaries, VA Pamphlet 7–8.1.
   Biological Scientists, VA Pamphlet 7–8.2.
   Chemists, VA Pamphlet 7–8.3.
   Economists, VA Pamphlet 7–8.4.
   Geologists, VA Pamphlet 7–8.5.
   Geophysicists, VA Pamphlet 7–8.6.
   Physicists, VA Pamphlet 7–8.7.
   Sociologists, VA Pamphlet 7–8.8.
   Statisticians, VA Pamphlet 7–8.9.

13. Women's Bureau, *1962 Handbook on Women Workers,* Bulletin 285. Washington, D.C.: U.S. Department of Labor, published biennially. Contains basic information on women's employment and occupations; age and marital status of women workers; their earnings, income, and educational status. See also:
   "Careers for Women as Technicians," Bulletin No. 282, 1961.
   "Careers for Women in the Biological Sciences," Bulletin No. 278, 1961.
   "Careers for Women in the Physical Sciences," Bulletin No. 270, 1959.

14. *"Compensation of Junior Executives,"* Section VIII of The Annual Dartnell Corporation Survey of Executive Compensation. Chicago: Dartnell Corporation.

15. Herman P. Miller, *Rich Man, Poor Man.* New York: Thomas Y. Crowell, Co., 1964.

16. *National Survey of Professional, Administrative, Technical and Clerical Pay,* Bulletin No. 1346. Washington, D.C.: U.S. Department of Labor, Bureau of Labor Statistics, October, 1962.

17. *Changing Times, The Kiplinger Magazine*
   "Careers in Nursing," December, 1962
   "Careers in Running a Business," May, 1962
   "Careers in Planning," February, 1963
   "Wanted—Salesmen," May, 1963
   "11 Ways To Lose a Job," June, 1963

18. J. M. Fitzwilliams, "Size Distribution of Income in 1963," *Survey of Current Business,* April, 1964 (Vol. 44, No. 4).

19. Norman M. Bradburn, *In Pursuit of Happiness; A Pilot Study of Behavior Related to Mental Health,* Report No. 92. Chicago: National Opinion Research Center, University of Chicago, May, 1963.

20. *Economic Status of Teachers,* Annual Report, Research Division, National Education Association, 1201 Sixteenth Street N.W., Washington, D.C. 20036.

21. Career Information Service, *Guide to Career Information.* New York: New York Life Insurance Co. Individual booklets are available free of charge on many careers. They have been prepared on Newspapering, Law, Medicine, Accounting, Teaching, Architecture, Aeronautical Engineering, Electronic Engineering, Public Service, Farming, Chemistry, Selling, Nursing, Starting a Business of Your Own, Pharmacy, Dentistry, Banking, Printing, Home Economics, the Mineral Industry, Personnel Work, Retailing, Atomic Science, Librarianship, the Armed Forces, Engineering, Food Retailing, Medical Technology, Scientific Careers, Traffic Managing, and Secretarial Career. Each is available in booklet form and will be sent to you on request. You'll also find additional help in the free booklet, "The Cost of Four Years at College." Just drop a postcard to: Career Information Service, New York Life Insurance Co., 51 Madison Ave., New York 10, N.Y.

22. *Poverty in the United States,* Committee on Education and Labor, House of Representatives, Eighty-eighth Congress, 2nd Sess., Washington, D.C., 1964.

CASE PROBLEMS

1. Donald has a real aptitude for science. His father is a successful engineer and builder. Donald is having difficulty in deciding whether to become (*a*) a chemist, (*b*) a physicist, (*c*) a chemical engineer, or (*d*) an electrical engineer. Help him develop all the relevant facts on the four alternative fields in order to make a decision. (The Engineers Joint Council is located at 345 East 47 Street, New York 17, N.Y.; The American Institute of Chemical Engineers at 25 West 45 Street, New York 36, N.Y.; The American Institute of Electrical Engineers at 345 East 47 Street, New York 17, N.Y., The American Chemical Society at 1155 16th Street, N.W., Washington 6, D.C.; and The American Institute of Physics at 335 East 45 Street, New York 17, N.Y.)

2. Phil is majoring in political science and thinks he wants to go on to law school. He wonders whether it makes any difference which law school he enters, how much it will cost, and what he can expect to earn as a young attorney. He also wonders whether he should take a first job as a junior in a large law office or apply to the legal department of a large corporation. Help him develop the relevant facts. (The American Bar Association is located at 1155 East Sixteenth Street, Chicago 37, Illinois.)

3. Ed argues that an amazing social revolution has occurred in the United States in the last 25 years, that the income gap is narrowing, and that there is now a much more equitable distribution of income. Dick, whose family runs a retail business in a coal mining town argues that there is still unequal sharing of income and wealth and that the rich are getting richer. With whom do you

side in this debate? Develop the relevant facts to support your side of the argument.

4. John is 32 years old, married, and has four children (ages 1, 3, 5, and 8). He teaches junior-high subjects in a small New England town. He is presently receiving $5,300 per year. The maximum is $7,500 for his present position. For the last two years he had been working the night shift and summers in a local factory. For this he receives $80 per week (40 hours @ $2). In the summer he works a 45-hour week with time and a half for overtime. The school board tells him that he must give up his second job if he wants to keep his teaching position, as they feel that it is lowering the quality of his teaching. John knows that he can get a 45-hour per week job at the factory if he wishes. What are some of the things John should think about when making his decision?

5. Shirley was developing an inferiority complex at college because she thought her family was less well off than most others because her parents insisted she work part time and summers to help pay for tuition, room, and board. Her father owns a book store and earns from $10,000 to $12,500 a year. Her mother is a high school teacher and earns $8,000 annually. What facts and figures can you develop for Shirley to reassure her?

6. Marcia is a junior, majoring in English. She isn't quite certain what she wants to do when she graduates. She seeks your help in analyzing the vocational outlets for an English major. Help her develop the alternatives with respect to field, type of job, remuneration, opportunities for advancement, and where to go for additional information.

7. Joe is a college beatnik. His chief interests are (a) his fraternity, (b) girls, and (c) sports cars and racing. He is finishing his sophomore year and must pick a field in which to specialize in his junior and senior years. He does not come from a wealthy family and will have to earn his way upon graduation, if he graduates. After talking with his advisor he is sent to the Dean of Guidance for specialization and vocational advice. Assume you are the Dean of Guidance, what would you suggest to Joe?

8. Betty and Marie are discussing the respective merits of library work and social work as career fields for women. Betty is introspective and shy. Marie is energetic, outgoing, and vigorous. Help them marshal the facts, including suitability of the field, job opportunities, income to be expected in the first job and after five years, training required, and where to go for more information.

9. In high school, Raymond Durkin took the commercial course. He has had five years' experience as a bookkeeper in San Francisco; his present salary is $90 a week. Raymond knows that he does his present work well. He believes that with proper training he could become a successful certified public accountant. Since he has a wife (age 21) and one child (age 2), he has been able to save only $1,100. Should Raymond consider becoming a certified public accountant? How much different would his work then be? How could he get the training? How long would it take? Could he finance the training? Would it pay him to take it? Where should he go for more information about this field?

10. Carla wants to be a designer of women's or children's clothes. She feels she has had an aptitude for this from childhood. Her mother urges that she go to a four-year liberal arts college and obtain her degree first before trying for a career in designing. Her father feels that she should go to a specialized school to develop her skill. What would you advise?

11. Ben Weintraub's father owned a chain of retail shoe stores. He wanted Ben, who was about to begin his freshman year at the state university, to specialize in business in college and upon graduation to enter the family enterprise and train to take over. Ben, on the other hand, wanted very much to become a doctor, and he wanted his father to finance his four years at medical school after college. If you were Ben, what argument would you use to persuade your father?

2 EXPENDITURE AND BUDGETING

> "What does Grandpa know about hardships? He only did without things . . . He never had to pay for them!"
>
> —*Royal Bank of Canada*

THE OLD truism "You can't take it with you" has a modern counterpart, "You can't keep all you make." Taxes and dollar depreciation take their toll. Because of them it now takes an income of $26,309 to give you as much purchasing power as a $10,-000 income in 1939. As you can see from Figure 2–1, there was a $269 tax bite out of the 1939 $10,000, leaving $9,731. You had to earn $26,309 in 1965 to have $9,731 of purchasing power left because taxes took away $3,395 and depreciation of the dollar cost $12,-183 in lost purchasing power. Even more shockingly, the $25,000-a-year man of 1939 had to earn $73,975 in 1965 to maintain the same standard of living.

Yet despite the sharp rise of prices and taxes, the standard of living of the people of the United States has risen significantly in the last ten years. This has been called "the decade of the discretionary dollar." If you take disposable personal income and subtract necessary expenditures for fixed commitments and essential outlays, you have discretionary income. This is personal income (after taxes) over and above necessary personal expenditure and contractual payments. Disposable personal income rose 60 percent over the last decade while discretionary income increased 62 percent.

On a per capita basis, in constant dollars (adjusted for changes in purchasing power) real disposable personal income rose 18.9 percent over the decade while per capita real discretionary income rose 20 percent. Thus as more and more families rise into middle- and upper-income brackets, they find themselves with larger shares of their income

35

left over after expenditures on essentials, for discretionary spending.
The higher standard of living is reflected in new homes featuring
garbage disposal units, dishwashing machines, electric refrigerators,
electric washing and drying machines, and television sets, which in the
thirties were either nonexistent or available only to the very wealthy.

FIGURE 2–1

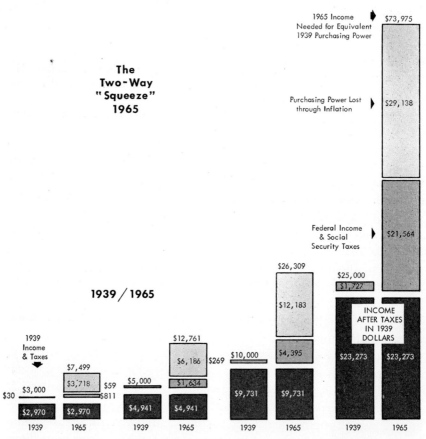

SOURCE: National Industrial Conference Board, *Road Maps of Industry*, No. 1523, June 1, 1965.

About 90 of every 100 homes with electricity have TV sets, 95 have
washing machines, 98 refrigerators, and 94 radios. At present, there
are 55 million TV sets in use in 47 million homes, and the average
home has its set on more than five hours a day.[1]

---

[1] See "Our Spending—It's Different Now," *Changing Times, The Kiplinger Maga-zine,* July, 1962.

It is also manifest by increased expenditures on cars and leisure activities. Total passenger car registrations now exceed 64 million, more than double the car registration of 1950. Seventy-five percent of all American families now own cars. In recent years the increase in automobile registrations has been far more rapid than the increase in the number of households. Fifteen years ago there was one car for every 5.4 persons; today, there is a car for every three persons, and two-car families are no longer an oddity or a sign of great wealth. From just over 1½ million in 1949, the number of families owning more than one car has climbed to 12 million, about one in every five. This is a sevenfold gain from 1949, and a trend that could put two cars in almost every family's garage by 1980. American families now owe over $20 billion on automobiles.

A quarter of a century ago, golf was regarded as a rich man's game. Today, millions of Americans spend almost a half billion dollars a year in pursuit of the little white ball. Twenty years ago, boating was a sport restricted to very few Americans. Today, more than seven million boat owners spend close to a billion dollars a year on this pastime. Spending on foreign travel now exceeds $2.5 billion a year. Fifteen years ago there were only 2,500 private swimming pools in the country, according to the National Swimming Pool Institute. Today, the figure exceeds 250,000, a more than tenfold increase. Personal savings in the last 11 years amounted to $242 billion compared to only $22 billion from the beginning of 1929 through 1939. Over the last decade the net worth of consumers rose by almost 80 percent.

Thus, most families today have more money to spend then ever before, and money management has become a more widespread problem. To handle this matter effectively, many families have taken a page from business, which for a long time has planned not only its production and sales ahead of time but its finances as well. When people realized how well budgeting works for successful business firms, it is not surprising that they thought the same device might be used for planning sensible utilization of a family's money.

Purpose of a Budget

A budget is a financial plan. Too often the purpose of a budget is misunderstood. Budgeting is not a dreary bookkeeping procedure of recording the details of every penny expended. Many people have assumed it to be just this and have quickly grown tired of keeping mountainous records of petty details. Too often the end of budget keeping has occurred abruptly when a husband, coming home exhausted at the end of a trying day, has been asked, "John, now tell me exactly what you spent today."

The Royal Bank of Canada, Montreal, devoted a number of its monthly letters to the subject of family budgets. It stressed the fact that a budget is essentially a matter of planning, not of bookkeeping. Budgeting is a guide to spending and should not be looked upon as an inflexible pattern into which every penny of expenditure has to be fitted. The Bank advised the family not to:

. . . get into the habit of staying home at night, trying to find a missing 23 cents. No one can hope to budget 100% accurately, and only foolish persons try. With all his wizardry at mathematics, Einstein could never make his bank book balance. Let us agree quite cheerfully that there must be some money that disappears as completely as if the mice had eaten it. One husband, going over his wife's records, came, every little while, on an entry: "HOK $1.50" or "HOK $3." He asked what it meant and was told "Heaven Only Knows."

Mindful that most people abandon budgeting when it becomes a matter of penny-hunting record keeping, the Bank suggests an extra category called "OIL" in the budget, amounting to about 2½ percent of the total. It states: "That's for oil for the troubled waters. It will cover mistakes and save personal headaches. It will cover the $10 you lend to a friend and never get back; the $5 you spend on impulse when the budget makes no allowance for it." To discover what happens when a budget becomes a matter of rigid control, one can go back to the famous diarist, Pepys. He tells this sad story: "I and my wife up to her closet to examine her kitchen accounts, and there I took occasion to fall out with her, for buying a laced handkerchief and pinner without my leave. From this we began both to be angry, and so continued till bed."

No family ever has enough money. A budget is simply an application of will power to the management of personal finances. It is a plan for spending, not simply a record of expenditures. It is designed to keep you out of financial trouble, to help you live within what—in terms of your wants and desires—is always an inadequate income. It helps put first things first and enables you to set priorities in spending and to plan to get the most out of your money. If you were given $300,000 tomorrow, you would think very carefully about how best to use it—whether to spend or invest—and, if the choice were the former, on what. You would do some planning about the disposal of the $300,000. Well, if you average $7,500 a year in earnings between the ages of 25 and 65, you will control the spending of $300,000. Even though you obtain the money over a period of time, it would be well to ponder and plan its disposal, just as you would if you received it all at once.

It is not essential to budget, of course. If you live within your income easily, satisfy all your needs and wants, and manage to save in the bargain, then budgeting may be a waste of time for you. Some bright, competent people do their financial planning in their heads and do not stop to put it down on paper to see how it shapes up. But many people (and all responsible governments and successful business firms) estimate their income in advance and carefully plan its disposal —on paper. Because it brings one face to face with reality, the process may not be a pleasant one; but it is better to face facts ahead of time and trim your wants to your income. Some people find this process too onerous. They are the ones who went to debtors' prisons hundreds of years ago and who today have their cars repossessed, their furniture taken back. They pay extra and heavy charges to loan companies, have their salaries garnisheed and their property, if any, attached, and generally slip in and out of side doors to elude creditors' subpoenas and judgments.

Budget planning makes one think about alternatives in spending. With practice, the process of choosing makes you a wiser purchaser, although it may make you a sadder one, too. For example, is it more fun to entertain frequently or to be well dressed? Is laborsaving household equipment more important than the convenience of an automobile? Are temporary luxuries more to be desired than the security of a growing savings account? If drawing up a budget shows you that you may have to make such choices (and this irritates and aggravates you), do not blame it on the budget. Blame it on your income, because that is the real cause of your annoyance and frustration. It is not large enough to meet all your needs. The budget lets you see this fact ahead of time. If you wait to find it out through the spending process, you will be more annoyed later. If you know the facts in advance, you can try to figure out ways and means of increasing your income by working evenings or weekends or by switching into better-paying employment.

A Gallup Poll found that four out of every ten American families keep budgets; and of those that do, one out of three says they fail to stay within it. Gallup interviewers found that nearly half of all persons who have had a college education keep a budget, as compared with less than one third among persons whose education did not extend beyond grade school. This tends to indicate that people with larger incomes and higher standards of living use budgets more frequently than those who live in more modest circumstances. Here is the vote:

	COLLEGE	HIGH SCHOOL	GRADE SCHOOL
Have budgets	48%	47%	31%
Do not have budgets	52	53	69

The two principal reasons given for not keeping a budget were "Not enough money, all spent anyhow" and "Don't need one, can live within means." Those who gave the first reason clearly misunderstood the purpose of budgeting and obviously would benefit from financial planning.

Components of a Budget

The components of a budget are determined wholly by the needs of the individual or family for which it is devised. For example, a college student's budget categories will differ considerably from those of a head of a family. A budget for a college student might have the following breakdowns:

A. Income
   1. From parents
   2. From odd jobs during spring and fall semesters
   3. From summer work
B. Expenditures
   1. Tuition
   2. Fees
   3. Books
   4. Room and board
   5. Clothing, including laundry and cleaning
   6. Transportation or automobile upkeep
   7. Medical and dental care
   8. Donations
   9. Dues (fraternity, clubs, class)
  10. Newspapers, magazines, postage, and cigarettes
  11. Recreation and dates

A budget for a head of a family might be divided into the following categories:

A. Income
   1. From regular employment—salary or wages
   2. From additional employment or commissions → *from largest to smallest*
   3. From dividends, interest, or rent
   4. From bonuses, gifts, government, or other allowances
B. Expenditures
   1. Taxes
   2. Repayment of debt or installment payments

3. Food
4. Rent or mortgage payments
5. Household operation—utilities, supplies, maid
6. Clothing, including laundry and cleaning
7. Insurance
8. Home furnishings and household equipment
9. Medical and dental care
10. Contributions, gifts, subscriptions
11. Transportation or automobile expenses
12. Advancement
13. Personal allowances
14. Entertainment
15. Savings
16. Miscellaneous (OIL or HOK)

How to Budget

Clearly the point of departure in budgeting or financial planning is to estimate your annual income from all sources and then see how well or poorly it covers your estimated annual expenses. If it is apparent that your income will not cover them, then you can seek to increase your income, find ways and means of cutting expenses, or preferably do both. Some people have the idea that budgeting involves buying a large notebook in which each day you put down—to the last penny—every item of expenditure and at the end of some given period total up the various items, by categories perhaps, to see what you have spent. It may perhaps be useful to do this, but it should be realized quite clearly that this alone is not budgeting. There is no financial planning involved in mere record keeping.

Yet you may possibly wish to keep records temporarily for two reasons. You may not be able to estimate one or another of the categories of proposed expenditures precisely enough in drawing up your original budget plan and may therefore wish to keep a record for a week or a month to see what that category of expenditure actually totals as a means of making a more exact annual or pay-period estimate. Or, having drawn up your financial plan (budget), you may wish to check your ability to apply it by keeping an actual record of expenditures as a means of seeing how well you were able to conform to your financial plan.

It is not necessary, however, in budgeting (financial planning) to keep a detailed day-to-day record of expenditures. Many people make this mistake; for a short time they attempt the drudgery of such a procedure, then get disgusted, and finally drop budgeting. Budgeting involves looking ahead—trying to see where you are going financially and whether you are on a safe course. How can you engage in budgeting without bookkeeping? Very simply. Once you have drawn up your annual financial plan, break it down on a per payday basis, and then set up a plan for spending for each pay period. When the pay check is cashed, put the cash in different envelopes, one for rent, one for food, and so on, with the amounts determined by the plan. Then, as you spend over the pay period, there is no need to keep a record of expenditures. If one envelope is consistently exhausted before the end of the period (say the food envelope, for example), you can either draw from the savings envelope to cover the deficit, thus saving less than you had planned, or, if you think your food expenditures have been larger than they might have been, you might try to reduce them by buying cheaper cuts of meat, for example, or by eating veal or pork rather than beef.

Another useful arrangement is to have your monthly pay check sent to your bank and to use checks to pay for all important expenditures. When the checks are returned by the bank with your statement, you can sort them out, total each category, and thus see whether you kept to or exceeded your plan. If you like to operate on a cash basis, you can use the envelope method; if you prefer to use a bank, then you can use your checking account to test your budget and eliminate the deadly record keeping which scares so many people away from budgeting.

Budget Forms

A considerable number of budget forms have been devised to meet varying situations. One of the best comprehensive series of budget forms, designed to emphasize the planning function, is published by the Household Finance Corporation, a large consumer finance company. These forms are found in a 36-page booklet entitled: *Money Management—Your Budget.*[2]

There are seven auxiliary or preliminary forms and two main summary forms. The two main summary forms are shown in Figures 2–2 and 2–3. The starting point is an estimate of income, for which a special form is provided. From income is subtracted "future fixed expenses," such as rent or mortgage payments, insurance, property taxes,

---

[2] This company also publishes a number of other money-management booklets entitled: *Your Food Dollar, Your Clothing Dollar, Your Shelter Dollar, Your Home Furnishings Dollar, Your Health and Recreation Dollar, Your Shopping Dollar, Children's Spending, Your Automobile Dollar, Your Equipment Dollar, Money Management for Young Moderns, Your Savings and Investment Dollar, Your Shopping Dollar,* etc. Information concerning these may be obtained by writing to Money Management Institute, Household Finance Corp., Prudential Plaza, Chicago 1, Ill.

and school tuition. Ask yourself what regular bills must be paid on specific dates over the next year. Everyone has large bills which fall due at certain times throughout the year. Usually it is impossible to pay these fixed expenses out of one pay check. One of the best ways of planning to meet large bills is to chart the dates on which they fall due.

FIGURE 2–2

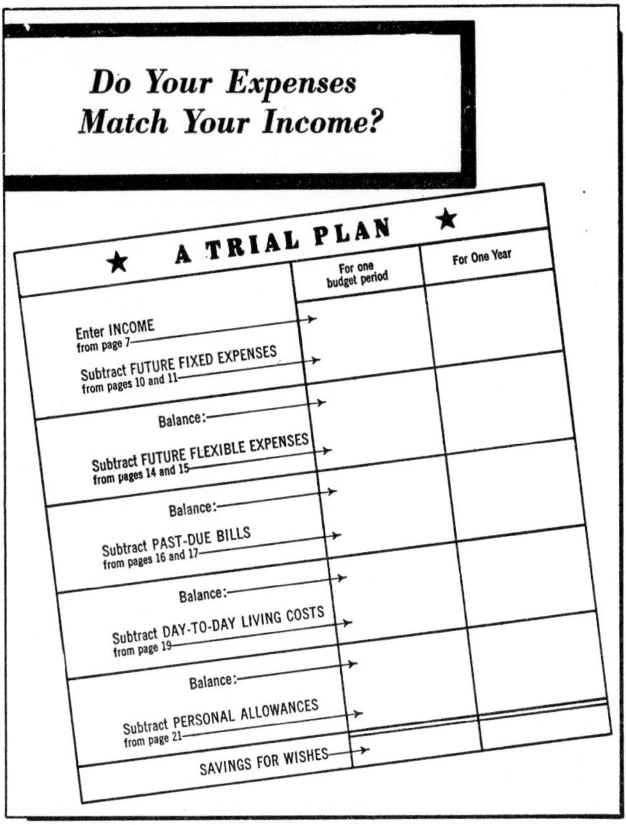

Do Your Expenses Match Your Income?

★ A TRIAL PLAN ★

	For one budget period	For One Year
Enter INCOME from page 7		
Subtract FUTURE FIXED EXPENSES from pages 10 and 11		
Balance:		
Subtract FUTURE FLEXIBLE EXPENSES from pages 14 and 15		
Balance:		
Subtract PAST-DUE BILLS from pages 16 and 17		
Balance:		
Subtract DAY-TO-DAY LIVING COSTS from page 19		
Balance:		
Subtract PERSONAL ALLOWANCES from page 21		
SAVINGS FOR WISHES		

SOURCE: *Money Management—Your Budget* (Chicago: Household Finance Corp.), p. 22.

Then divide the total due into periodic payments and start a reserve fund. For example, if you are starting your budget in October and have a $120 insurance premium due in December, divide the total by three, setting aside $40 in each of the months of October, November, and December. From then on, you need set aside only one twelfth ($10) of the total. There is a separate form provided for future fixed expenses.

The next step is to estimate, list, and subtract "future flexible expenses," such as clothing, household equipment, and home furnishings.

These expenditures are all certain to appear, but they are sufficiently flexible in amount and time of occurrence to offer opportunity to adjust the budget. Next list all past unpaid bills. If you have listed regular payments on loans and installment obligations under future fixed expenses, list, on the special form for unpaid bills, all other un-paid bills or loans, including those from family and friends. You may be able to pay some small bills immediately, some within the next few

FIGURE 2–3

YOUR SPENDING PLAN

This and the following three pages are for charting your spending plan. Use pencil for "planned" figures and pen for "actual" figures. This will become your record for a year.

Your spending plan is divided into 12 or 13 budget periods depending on whether you have a monthly or four-week pay period. If you work out your budget on a weekly basis use 13 columns of four weeks each and divide each section into four parts. If you use a semi-monthly plan, divide each of 12 columns in half.

Budget Period	Planned	Actual	Planned	Actual	Planned	Actual	Planned	Actual	Planned	Actual	Planned	Actual
FUTURE FIXED EXPENSES from pages 10 and 11												
FUTURE FLEXIBLE EXPENSES from pages 14 and 15												
PAST UNPAID BILLS from pages 16 and 17												
PRESENT DAY-TO-DAY LIVING COSTS from page 19												
PERSONAL ALLOWANCES from page 21												
SAVINGS FOR WISHES from page 22												
TOTAL												
INCOME from page 7												

SOURCE: *Money Management—Your Budget* (Chicago: Household Finance Corp.), pp. 26–27.

months. Divide others into payments over six, twelve, or more budget periods. Note the totals which will occur in each month or working period.

There is an additional form for listing your day-to-day living costs, including such items as food, utilities, laundry, car upkeep, and enter-taining. If you do not know these exactly, make rough estimates and then check them against performance over several pay or budget periods. Next comes the form for personal allowances. A personal allowance for every family member is an important part of your spend-ing plan. An allowance gives each person a feeling of independence, of freedom from excessive restraint. Be sure that everyone understands what categories of spending the allowance is to cover and then do not expect an accounting of how each penny is spent. An allowance is a personal "shock absorber," giving each person the right to groan over his or her own expenses and the privilege of figuring out how to meet them.

When personal allowances have been subtracted, the remaining sum, if any, is available for saving or for things you would like to acquire in the future, including vacations. It is at this point that most people have to stop and refigure. If nothing is left for savings, or if you find you have incurred a deficit, take another look at your trial figures. Go over your earlier forms carefully; there may be places where you can tighten your belt. You may be able to cut down temporarily on something. Or you may finally decide that you will have to get additional evening or weekend employment to raise your income. When you have finally adjusted and settled upon your spending plan, then use the form in Figure 2–3.

There are many other sources of budget forms for every need and purpose. The New York Life Insurance Company publishes an excellent *Budget Book* as do The Royal Bank of Canada, The First National City Bank of New York, the Connecticut Mutual Life Insurance Company, and the Union Dime Savings Bank of New York.[3] The Institute of Life Insurance publishes what it calls *The Family Money Manager*.[4] This is shown in Figure 2–4. It involves four basic steps. The first step is the now familiar procedure of estimating total cash income for the year. The second step requires an estimate of fixed expenses. Of this the Institute declares: "The secret of the Money Manager is this: it allows you to 'save ahead' to meet fixed expenses and obligations, so when they come due you will have enough money to pay them." The third step consists of setting aside a sum each week, or each pay period, for an emergency fund to meet unexpected expenditures. The Institute declares:

But you will need something for an emergency fund, if your money manager is going to work properly. You can't estimate in advance all your future ex-

---

[3] Free copies may be obtained upon request in each case. The New York Life Insurance Company address is 51 Madison Ave., New York 10, N.Y.; The Royal Bank of Canada's head office is in Montreal, Canada; the First National City Bank of New York, 55 Wall Street, New York, N.Y., The Connecticut Mutual Life Insurance Company is at 140 Garden St., Hartford 15, Conn.

[4] Copies may be obtained by writing to Institute of Life Insurance, 488 Madison Ave., New York 22, N.Y. See also its *A Discussion of Family Money—How Budgets Work and What They Do*, Women's Division, Institute of Life Insurance, Study No. 3.

FIGURE 2–4

FAMILY MONEY MANAGER

1

ESTIMATE OF OUR TOTAL CASH INCOME

Annual Wages or Income from Farm or Business.................

Interest or Dividends from Bonds and Investments.............

Income from Other Members of Family...............................

Other Income ....

Total ANNUAL Income.. $ _____ a year

Total WEEKLY Income (Divide Annual Income by 52)....... $ _____ a week

This is the money which we have to spend and save during the next 52 weeks.
Enter the amount in the "Family Balance Sheet" at the bottom of the page.

2

ESTIMATE OF OUR FIXED EXPENSES AND OBLIGATIONS

	JAN.	FEB.	MAR.	APRIL	MAY	JUNE	JULY	AUG.	SEPT.	OCT.	NOV.	DEC.	Total 12 Months
FAMILY HOUSING													
Rent, Mortgage Payt.													
Major Fuel Bills													
Other													
FAMILY PROTECTION													
Life Insurance													
Other Insurance													
OUR FAMILY IN THE COMMUNITY													
Church													
Donations													
FAMILY DEBTS AND OBLIGATIONS													
Installments													
Other Debts													
TAXES AND LICENSES													
Taxes													
Licenses													
OTHER MAJOR ITEMS													

This is the Money We Shall Put in a Special Fund Every Week to Meet

Total for the Year

STEP 1

INCOME

Write down in this chart all the cash you expect to receive in the next 12 months. If your income is from wages or salary, include only your "take-home" cash pay. If it is from a business, farm or trade, make the best estimate you can.

Don't forget to include any extra cash income you may receive — interest or dividends from bonds and other investments, money which the children may turn into the family, rent you may get from property you own.

Add up your figures, divide by 52, and you will know what your average weekly income will be for the next 12 months. This is the money your family has to spend and save.

(Remember, you don't have to put your budget on a week-to-week basis unless you want to. If a twice-a-month budget is more desirable, divide by 24 all through your Money Manager whenever it says to divide by 52. If you want a monthly budget, divide by 12.)

STEP 2

FIXED EXPENSES AND OBLIGATIONS

The secret of the Money Manager is this: it allows you to "save ahead" to meet fixed expenses and obligations, so when they come due you will have enough money to pay them.

Here, under Step 2, write down what these fixed expenses and obligations are in your household — rent or mortgage payments, life insurance premiums, taxes other than payroll taxes, church contributions, installment payments and so on. Indicate in what months these outlays will come due.

If you *know* you are going to have a big fuel bill in October or a clothing bill for the children in the Spring or some expensive dentist work for Johnny in the winter, write down these expenses. But *don't* try to guess all your doubtful future expenses, for you'll find it's too difficult. Put down only the major expenses and obligations which you can estimate pretty closely in advance.

Add up all your items, divide by 52, and you will have your *weekly set-aside*. This money goes into a special fund every pay-day. When your fixed expenses and obligations come due later on, they will be paid out of this fund.

STEP 3

EMERGENCY FUND

One of the most important steps, if your Money Manager is to work smoothly, is to provide for an emergency fund.

There are two kinds of savings. Regular family savings is for long-range projects — family security, the children's education, a new house or a new television set or a good vacation. Emergency "set-asides" are something else — it's money you put aside every week to help meet unexpected emergencies or to help you buy things you simply must buy, but haven't provided for.

It is a nice, comfortable feeling to have a lot of extra money left over after you have paid all your bills and met all your other expenses. But most families don't have a lot of extra money. After all, there are other things more important than extra money — good diet and good housing and adequate clothing and the other things which spell out a warm, happy, healthy family life.

But you will need something for an emergency fund all the same, if your Money Manager is going to work properly. You can't estimate in advance all your future expenses; you can't know how much or how little you may have to pay for things like doctor bills and repairs for the car six months or a year in advance. By putting money every week into your emergency fund you will be building up a fund which will help meet these unexpected bills when they come due. So, at this point, set up a *definite* amount which will be placed each pay day in your emergency fund.

An emergency fund should never be allowed to grow too big. When it reaches two or three months' income, put the extra money into regular savings or into something else your family wants and needs.

STEP 4

WEEKLY LIVING ALLOWANCES

How much does it cost you and your family to live? Unless you have kept family books over a period of years you won't be able to tell to the penny. But if you have been moderately careful in the past, you will be able to make a pretty good estimate. Here, under Step 4, is the place to do it.

Exactly how you divide your living expenses into different classifications is up to you. Here, in this chart, they are divided into six sections — how much Mother needs to run the house, how much Father needs to go to and from work, how much the family needs for such items as clothes and ordinary doctor bills, recreation, and how much everybody in the family needs for incidental expenses and allowances. But there are extra lines in the chart for you to use if you want to divide things another way.

There won't be anything final in these estimates of yours — after a month or two, you and your family will probably want to come back and rework everything, according to the lessons you will have learned under your new Money Manager.

Now, you are ready to add all your estimates and find your total expenditures. When you subtract these from your total income have you anything left? If so, this amount may be placed in your regular savings account, in savings bonds or other investments.

SOURCE: Institute of Life Insurance.

OUR WEEKLY SET ASIDE (Divide by 52) _____

ESTIMATE OF OUR EMERGENCY FUND

To meet unexpected expenses we shall put aside each payday....... $

Enter in "Balance Sheet" below.

This fund will be allowed to accumulate until it reaches $_____
after which we shall pay into it merely enough to keep it at that level.

3

ESTIMATE OF OUR WEEKLY LIVING ALLOWANCE

MOTHER'S EXPENDITURES	HOW MUCH A WEEK?
Food	
Household Operation	
Laundry	
TOTAL (Enter Here:)	

PERSONAL ALLOWANCES, Minor Articles of Clothing, Cigarettes, Ice Cream Cones, Etc.	HOW MUCH A WEEK?
Father	
Mother	
Others in Family	
TOTAL (Enter Here:)	

FATHER'S EXPENDITURES	
Car Operation	
Lunches	
TOTAL (Enter Here:)	

OTHER ITEMS AND MISCELLANEOUS	
TOTAL (Enter Here:)	

FAMILY EXPENSES	
Clothing	
Recreation	
Ordinary Medical and Drug Store	
TOTAL (Enter Here:)	

OUR WEEKLY ESTIMATE FOR LIVING EXPENSES _____

This is the amount we shall pay ourselves every week and try to make last until the next week begins. Enter it on the "Balance Sheet."

4

OUR FAMILY "BALANCE SHEET"

OUR WEEKLY INCOME IS	(Step 1)
OUR WEEKLY SET-ASIDES AMOUNT TO	(Step 2)
OUR EMERGENCY FUND	(Step 3)
OUR WEEKLY LIVING ALLOWANCE IS	(Step 4)
AND THIS IS WHAT'S LEFT FOR REGULAR SAVINGS	

penses; you can't know how much or how little you may have to pay for things like doctor bills and repairs for the car six months or a year in advance. By putting money every week into your emergency fund you will be building up a fund which will help meet these unexpected bills when they come due.

The fourth step is the estimate of weekly living allowances. It is not necessary to be able to tell to the penny; a reasonable estimate is adequate. The summation is, of course, made by adding the three expense estimates together and subtracting them from the income estimate. What is left, if anything, is available for saving or investment or for a long-postponed luxury purchase. If your subtraction yields a minus figure, then you are planning to live beyond your income. In that case you must either draw on past accumulated savings to meet the deficit, go into debt, or more intelligently, either cut down on expenditures or seek extra work to raise your income. *The Money Manager* lets you know in advance where you are heading and how you can expect to get along.

Changing Times, the monthly magazine devoted to personal finance, has an excellent "Family Finance Diary," which if used properly can serve as a financial planning guide for any family.[5]

Suggested Expenditure Patterns

Model spending patterns suggested for families at various income levels may be useful in enabling you to make sound decisions concerning your own proposed expenditures. For example, assume you have just graduated from college, gotten married, and, having passed the junior professional assistant, U.S. Civil Service examination, have been offered a position in Washington, D.C. at a salary of $5,235 per annum. You and your wife proceed to Washington and are faced with the problem of renting an apartment. How much can you afford to pay in rent per month? An annual salary of $5,235 approximates $436 per month. But there are monthly income tax deductions (about $59) and also monthly pension retirement deductions (about $31), leaving a take-home sum each month of about $346. How much of this can you afford to spend for rent?

The American Bankers Association has prepared a table showing suggested distribution of income after income taxes (see Fig. 2–5). Looking down the first column, you find that your monthly take-home pay figure falls closest to $350 per month. Then, looking across this line, in the two-in-a-family subdivision, it may be noted that the sug-

---

[5] It can be obtained at nominal cost by writing to The Editor, *Changing Times, The Kiplinger Magazine,* 1729 H Street, N.W., Washington, D.C., 20006.

gested proper expenditure for shelter is about $70 per month. If you spend more than this amount for rent, you will have to spend less in one of the other categories, such as food, clothing, operating (which includes such items as personal expenses, carfare, and recreation), advancement, or savings. In all probability you will not be able to find suitable quarters for $70 per month in a high-cost city like Washington,

FIGURE 2–5

Suggested Distribution of Monthly Income*

These figures are merely suggestions designed to help you work out your own spending and savings plan.

Monthly Income After Taxes	No. in Family	Savings	Food	Shelter	Clothing	Operating (Household)	Advancement and Other†
200	2	$15	$70	$45	$18	$18	$34
	4	7	85	45	20	20	23
250	2	30	75	50	23	20	52
	4	20	95	50	25	22	38
300	2	40	79	65	30	25	61
	4	25	103	65	35	27	45
350	2	50	87	70	35	32	76
	4	35	105	70	45	35	60
400	2	65	97	80	40	38	80
	4	50	120	80	46	39	65
450	2	90	103	85	45	40	87
	4	75	124	85	54	42	70
500	2	100	115	90	55	45	95
	4	90	135	90	65	45	75
600	2	120	125	110	60	55	130
	4	95	145	110	75	55	120
700	2	165	130	125	65	65	150
	4	115	165	125	85	70	140
800	2	185	145	140	80	75	175
	4	135	175	140	100	75	175
900	2	220	160	150	90	85	195
	4	150	205	150	115	85	195
1000	2	250	190	165	110	85	200
	4	170	245	165	130	90	200
YOUR ESTIMATE							

* After taxes and payroll deductions.
† The category "Advancement and Other" includes entertainment, recreation, health, education, transportation, personal care, religious and charitable contributions, gifts, dues, reading matter, and the like.
SOURCE: *Personal Money Management* (New York: Savings Division, American Bankers Association). Your local bank will furnish you with a copy of this 60-page booklet on request.

but will have to pay at least $100. If you do, then you can expect to save $20 per month rather than $50, assuming that you take the $30 difference out of what otherwise would have been savings. If your wife goes to work as a typist, earning $75 a week ($275 a month after taxes and retirement deductions), giving you a combined income of $621 per month, the table indicates that you can afford to pay about $110 per month for rent. Should you wish to pay $25 or $50 more, you will be able to save proportionately less.

Various sources have suggested different annual spending patterns. For example, the Pacific First Federal Savings and Loan Association publishes a slide rule *Family Budget Guide.*[6] You set the scale to the column showing your gross monthly income and the number in your family. Then you read across to find suggested spending patterns. For example, if your family consists of yourself, your wife, and one child, at different levels of income the pattern suggested may be seen in Table 2–1. Suggestions cover families of from two to five members.

A somewhat similar *Slide Guide—Divided Responsibility Family Budget Plan* is available from the National Consumer Finance Association.[7] It also issues a circular family budget guide which appears to be designed to show how loan payments of various sizes can be made at different levels of take-home pay, still leaving funds for food, clothing, and shelter. A stock brokerage house[8] makes available a slide rule family budget guide similar to the Pacific Savings and Loan guide. In the Pacific guide the last item is "savings." In the stock brokerage (and mutual fund) budget guide the last item is "financial progress."

In *The Family in a Money World,* Frances Lomas Feldman presents a table as a guide in budget counseling.[9] It shows a range of acceptable variations for a hypothetical family of four persons—an employed father, a mother at home, a thirteen-year-old boy, and eight-year-old girl. The incomes shown are gross, that is, before tax and other involuntary deductions (see Table 2–2).

Suggested budgets for married couples with incomes varying from $125 to $500 per month and for businesswomen and bachelors with incomes ranging from $100 to $300 per month, drawn up by a leading federal savings and loan association in the District of Columbia, may be seen in Figure 2–6. In terms of present conditions, certainly for urban areas, the suggested allowances for food and for rent are too low, and funds to supplement those categories would have to be drawn by the average family from some of the other categories, probably savings, clothing, or advancement and recreation.

The Heller Committee of the University of California has developed expenditure patterns for a salaried junior professional family earning

---

[6] You can obtain a free copy by writing to the Pacific First Federal Savings and Loan Association, Tacoma, Wash. The Association also has offices in Seattle, Portland, Bellingham, and Eugene.

[7] For a free copy write to Educational Services Division, National Consumer Finance Association, 100 Sixteenth St., N.W., Washington 36, D.C.

[8] Arthur Wiesenberger & Company, 61 Broadway, New York 6, N.Y.

[9] Published by the Family Service Association of America, 44 East 23 St., New York, N.Y., 10010 p. 164.

TABLE 2-1

The Family Budget Guide

	$300	$400	$500	$600	$700	$800	$900	$1,000	$1,100
Gross monthly income	$300	$400	$500	$600	$700	$800	$900	$1,000	$1,100
Number in family	3	3	3	3	3	3	3	3	3
Federal withholding tax	$ 24.00	$ 43.80	$ 61.80	$ 81.60	$ 96.00	$117.60	$132.00	$150.00	$168.00
Social security	10.88	14.50	14.50	14.50	14.50	14.50	14.50	14.50	14.50
Net monthly income	265.12	341.70	423.70	503.90	589.50	667.90	753.50	835.50	917.50
Food	$ 78.18	$ 90.80	$101.75	$112.45	$117.80	$126.40	$130.70	$136.00	$140.50
Shelter	59.50	76.00	94.00	110.00	129.25	145.75	165.00	181.50	192.50
House operation	27.00	34.75	42.50	50.00	59.00	66.50	75.00	82.35	95.00
Clothing	27.89	36.15	43.90	52.85	62.10	69.85	78.55	87.30	96.50
Transportation	24.50	31.50	37.50	44.50	52.00	58.50	66.00	72.25	78.25
Advancement	32.30	44.00	56.55	77.10	94.35	115.90	138.25	153.60	179.75
Savings	15.75	28.50	47.50	57.00	75.00	85.00	100.00	122.50	135.00

Source: Pacific First Federal Savings and Loan Association, 1963.

TABLE 2–2

Range of Acceptable Variations in Budget for Family of Four Persons

| | INCOME | | | |
| | $2,500 | $4,500 | $6,500 | $12,500 |
ITEM	% RANGE	% RANGE	% RANGE	% RANGE
Food	35–45	25–35	20–30	15–25
Clothing	8–12	9–13	9–15	9–15
Housing*	20–30	18–30	15–25	15–25
Transportation	6–9	7–10	7–12	7–15
Taxes	3–5	6–8	12–15	20–30
Health and insurance†	7–10	7–10	7–12	7–15
Savings	....	0–10	0–10	5–15
Advancement‡	3–10	4–10	5–10	5–15
Installment payments	5–15	5–15	5–15	5–15
Household help	....	0–5	0–10	5–15

* Includes household operation.
† Includes current medical costs and payments for prepaid health plans, also social security.
‡ Includes costs for recreation, charity contributions, education, personal needs, gifts, and personal allowances.
SOURCE: Frances Lomas Feldman, *The Family in a Money World* (New York: Family Service Association of America), p. 164.

almost $10,000 and for a wage-earning family with almost $7,000 income. The patterns of expenditure are shown in Table 2–3.

These yardsticks serve only as models. Individual variations are not only necessary but desirable, since few families are exactly like the

TABLE 2–3

Expenditures of Four-Person Family Groups at Two Income Levels

| | SALARIED JUNIOR PROFESSIONAL AND EXECUTIVE | | WAGE EARNER | | | |
| | | | HOMEOWNER | | HOME RENTER | |
ITEM 1	AMOUNT 2	PERCENT 3	AMOUNT 4	PERCENT 5	AMOUNT 6	PERCENT 7
Total budget cost	$9,742	100.0%	$6,875	100.0%	$6,778	100.0%
Income taxes	1,256	12.9	670	9.7	756	11.1
Personal insurance	375	3.9	291	4.2	291	4.3
Recreation	435	4.5	236	3.4	236	3.5
Medical and dental	671	6.9	576	8.4	576	8.5
Clothing	756	7.8	503	7.3	503	7.4
Household operation and furnishing	793	8.1	525	7.7	500	7.4
Transportation	1,004	10.3	588	8.6	588	8.7
Housing	1,378	14.1	1,136	16.5	978	14.4
Food	2,408	24.7	1,831	26.6	1,831	27.0
Other	666	6.8	519	7.6	519	7.7

SOURCE: University of California, Heller Committee for Research in Social Economics, *Quantity and Cost Budgets for Two Income Levels* (Berkeley: University of California Press, 1962), pp. 17, 56, and 57. Copyright 1962 by the Regents of the University of California. Data quoted with permission.

average at a given income level. Costs of living in different communities vary and must be taken into account. Any financial plan, therefore, must be personal and individual. What may be satisfactory for one may prove disturbing to another. The important thing is to have a plan—one that is flexible, and that fits into your scheme of living.

FIGURE 2–6

SUGGESTED BUDGET

NOTE: The following tables are intended to serve only as a guide in making up your own family budgets. The figures given should not necessarily be used as models to follow. Living costs will vary according to the section of the country and size of the town or city in which you reside, the age of your children, the nature of your employment and other such factors. Experience alone will show you the budget plan you must adopt.

BUDGETS FOR COUPLES BASED ON MONTHLY INCOME

Income per month	125	150	175	200	250	300	350	400	450	500
Savings	12	15	18	20	30	40	50	75	90	95
Food	38	42	48	52	60	65	65	70	70	80
Shelter (Rent, etc.)	32	35	45	48	55	60	75	75	80	90
Clothing	14	20	21	24	30	32	35	40	50	50
Operating	14	19	21	28	35	50	60	70	80	95
Advancement & Recreation	15	19	22	28	40	53	65	70	80	90

BUDGETS FOR MAN, WIFE AND CHILD BASED ON MONTHLY INCOME

Income per month	125	150	175	200	250	300	350	400	450	500
Savings	7	12	17	20	25	30	40	50	75	90
Food	42	46	50	55	62	65	70	80	85	85
Shelter (Rent, etc.)	32	35	43	48	55	70	75	80	80	90
Clothing	18	24	26	28	28	35	40	40	50	50
Operating	13	16	17	23	38	48	60	70	80	95
Advancement & Recreation	13	17	22	26	42	52	65	75	80	90

BUDGETS FOR MAN, WIFE AND 2 CHILDREN BASED ON MONTHLY INCOME

Income per month	150	175	200	250	300	350	400	450	500
Savings	7	12	20	28	30	40	55	70	85
Food	50	55	60	65	75	80	80	85	85
Shelter (Rent, etc.)	40	45	50	55	70	75	80	80	90
Clothing	25	30	30	32	40	45	50	55	60
Operating	14	16	18	30	42	55	67	80	90
Advancement & Recreation	14	17	22	40	43	55	68	80	90

BUDGETS FOR MAN, WIFE AND 3 CHILDREN BASED ON MONTHLY INCOME

Income per month	150	175	200	250	300	350	400	450	500
Savings	5	11	15	25	30	40	50	70	80
Food	54	60	65	80	85	85	85	85	85
Shelter (Rent, etc.)	40	45	50	60	70	75	80	80	90
Clothing	25	26	30	35	40	45	50	55	60
Operating	13	16	18	27	35	50	65	75	90
Advancement & Recreation	13	17	22	33	45	55	70	85	95

BUDGETS FOR BUSINESS WOMEN BASED ON MONTHLY INCOME

Income per month	100	125	150	175	200	250
Savings	8	12	15	20	25	35
Food	40	42	42	44	45	45
Shelter (Rent, etc.)	15	20	25	35	40	45
Clothing	12	15	22	22	25	40
Operating	12	18	22	28	35	45
Advancement & Recreation	13	18	24	26	30	40

BUDGETS FOR BACHELORS BASED ON MONTHLY INCOME

Income per month	100	150	200	250	300
Savings	7	15	20	40	50
Food	40	45	45	45	50
Shelter (Rent, etc.)	18	25	35	40	40
Clothing	10	15	20	25	30
Operating	10	25	35	45	60
Advancement & Recreation	15	25	45	55	70

SOURCE: Columbia Federal Savings and Loan Association, Washington, D.C.

Average Consumer Spending

You may also find it helpful in your own financial planning to know what average families in the United States actually spend and how these expenditures are divided among the various major categories, such as food, clothing, and shelter. How does the average family spend its annual income? Budget studies of the Bureau of Labor Statistics, undertaken mainly to provide a continuing accurate basis for its Consumer Price Index, shed a great deal of light on current expenditure patterns of American families at various income levels.

The latest survey, involving representative families in 66 metropolitan areas, showed that personal taxes—federal, state and local—on the average represented 12 percent of money income before taxes for all consumer units. Expenditures for current consumption by all consumer units accounted for about 90 percent of income after taxes, since almost 10 percent was allocated to gifts and contributions and to personal insurance[10] (see Table 2–4). The average family's total expenditures for current consumption came to approximately $5,400 in 1960–61— a more than 40 percent dollar increase and a 17 percent real increase over 1950. With the rise in income, the three basic expenses—food, shelter, and clothing—required a smaller share, declining from 68 to 64 percent.

The national survey is built up from surveys in selected cities and towns in the United States. Table 2–5 presents expenditure patterns for various income level families in New York, N.Y., while Table 2–6 presents similar data for families in San Francisco. Individual reports covering the city or town you are interested in may be obtained by writing to the Bureau of Labor Statistics, U.S. Department of Labor, Washington, D.C.

Food

Food and beverage accounted for 26 percent of the average urban household budget in the BLS survey. This was a significant reduction from the 31.4 percent reported in the 1950 survey. This reflected a rising standard of living. As earnings rise, consumer units spend relatively less for basic necessities and are able to purchase proportionately more of comforts, luxuries, and nonessentials. Witness the report in *Life* magazine that Americans down $425 million of vitamin pills a year and spend $120 million for reducing aids. You will also be fascinated to know, from the same source, that the largest dish prepared regularly anywhere in the world is eaten by Bedouin tribesmen at

---

[10] See BLS Report No. 237–38, *Survey of Consumer Expenditures and Income, Urban United States, 1960–61,* Bureau of Labor Statistics, U.S. Department of Labor, Washington, April, 1964.

wedding feasts. It consists of one whole camel stuffed with one sheep that has been stuffed with several chickens each stuffed with a fish that has been stuffed with an egg.

Consumer preferences for individual foods have changed, both upward and down in the past—sometimes drastically (see Figure 2–7). For example, per capita consumption of frozen fruits and vegetables has more than doubled in the last 15 years. At the same time, consumption of many other foods has declined, sometimes as much as 40–50 percent. Despite all the shifts, the overall caloric intake of Americans has changed very little, dropping from 3,300 calories per person daily in 1935–39 to 3,170 calories in 1962.

If your proposed expenditures for food in your financial plan amount to more than 30 percent of total outlay, then you are about to spend too much on food and should take steps to find ways and means of cutting down. Possibly you can buy in more economical (larger) quantities (perhaps with the help of a home freezer), make better use of leftovers, eat less beef and more poultry or fish, have fewer meals out, do more cooking at home, buy produce at a cash-and-carry market, shop for specials, develop a garden and grow your own vegetables if you own your own home, or use substitutes such as margarine for butter or dried fruits for fresh. With some thought and care most food bills can be reduced.[11]

The cost of one week's food at home is regularly estimated by the U.S. Department of Agriculture at three cost levels. The estimate is available for four regional areas (Northeast, North Central, South and West). The composite U.S. average estimate of cost is shown in Table 2–7.

The American Red Cross, as a guide to its chapter workers in estimating family and individual living costs, suggests the food-cost scale shown in Table 2–8. Because of the many purposes for which chapter workers use the guide, food costs are computed on two levels—one at low cost and the other at moderate cost. The worker may use either schedule, depending on the situation in which the guide is being used, on the individual family problem concerned, or on the range of incomes and living levels. Both plans provide equally good nourishment but with differences in cost. The low-cost food plan places heavier reliance on the less expensive food groups, such as potatoes, legumes (dried beans and peas), flour, and cereals. The moderate-cost food plan per-

---

[11] See *Money Management—Your Food Dollar* (Chicago: Household Finance Corp.).

TABLE 2-4

Average Annual Expenditures, Income, and Savings of All Urban Families and Single Consumers, United States, 1960–61 and 1950

Item	Average per Family				Percent Change, 1950 to 1960–61	Percent of Expenditures for Current Consumption	
	1960–61[1]	1961	1960	1950[2]		1960–61	1950
Expenditures for current consumption[3]	$5,390	$5,381	$5,368	$3,808	41.5	100.0	100.0
Food	1,311	1,306	1,312	1,130	16.0	24.3	29.7
Tobacco	95	93	96	68	39.7	1.8	1.8
Alcoholic beverages	90	87	94	65	38.5	1.7	1.7
Housing, total	1,588	1,585	1,584	1,035	53.4	29.5	27.2
Shelter, fuel, light, refrigeration, and water	992	997	983	596	66.4	18.4	15.6
Household operations	319	317	320	178	79.2	5.9	4.7
Housefurnishings and equipment	277	271	281	261	6.1	5.1	6.9
Clothing, materials, services	558	563	550	437	27.7	10.4	11.5
Personal care	155	156	153	85	82.4	2.9	2.2
Medical care	355	362	345	197	80.2	6.6	5.2
Recreation	217	218	215	168	29.2	4.0	4.4
Reading and education	109	109	111	58	87.9	2.0	1.5
Automobile purchase and operation	700	690	696	443	58.0	13.0	11.6
Other transportation	93	92	94	67	38.8	1.7	1.8
Other expenditures	119	120	118	55	116.4	2.2	1.4
Gifts and contributions	303	298	302	165	83.6	...	...
Personal insurance	324	323	324	177	83.1	...	...
Money income before taxes	6,691	6,756	6,595	4,237	57.9	...	...
Money income after taxes	5,906	5,957	5,829	3,910	51.0	...	...
Other money receipts	82	93	73	49	67.3	...	...

Net change in assets and liabilities[4]	177	219	152	−74	...	...	...
Account balancing difference[5]	−207	−171	−244	−117	...	...	...
Number of families in sample	[1]9,476	4,879	4,463	12,489			
Estimated number of families in universe (000)[6]	40,131	40,131	40,131	31,539			
Average family size	3.1	3.1	3.1	3.0			
Percent nonwhite families	12	13	12	10			
Percent homeowners	53	54	52	48			
Percent auto owners	73	73	72	59			

[1] Includes families surveyed for 1959 in Anchorage, Alaska. Data for Alaska were not included in the columns for 1960 and 1961.

[2] From the Survey of Consumer Expenditures in 1950. See *Study of Consumer Expenditures, Incomes and Savings, Statistical Tables, Urban U.S.—1950* (University of Pennsylvania, 1956–57), Vol. XVIII. See also text footnote 2, p. 1.

[3] The classification of items in the two surveys is not strictly comparable.

[4] The algebraic sum of increases and decreases in assets and liabilities. Net increases in assets or decreases in liabilities represent a net saving (+) during the year. Net decreases in assets or increases in liabilities represent a deficit (−) or net dissaving.

[5] A statistical measure of the net reporting discrepancy of the receipts and disbursements accounts. In this table, the balancing difference is obtained by subtracting current consumption expenditures, gifts and contributions, personal insurance, and the net change in assets and liabilities from the sum of money income after taxes and other money receipts. If reported receipts are less than disbursements (including savings or dissavings), the balancing difference is negative (−).

[6] For derivation of the 1960–61 estimates of the total families in the universe, see p. 8 of BLS Report No. 237–38.

SOURCE: Bureau of Labor Statistics, U.S. Department of Labor.

TABLE 2-5

Summary of Family Expenditures, Income, and Savings, by Income Class
All Urban Families and Single Consumers—New York, N.Y., 1960

	Total	Money Income after Taxes									
		Under $1,000	$1,000 to $1,999	$2,000 to $2,999	$3,000 to $3,999	$4,000 to $4,999	$5,000 to $5,999	$6,000 to $7,499	$7,500 to $9,999	$10,000 to $14,999	$15,000 and Over
Family Characteristics											
Money income before taxes	$7,800	$ 680	$1,598	$2,606	$3,808	$5,081	$6,196	$7,674	$10,061	$13,724	$26,327
Net change in assets and liabilities	—$66	—$1,250	—$90	—$378	—$49	—$517	—$72	—$376	—$103	$223	$2,161
Money income after taxes	$6,708	$ 668	$1,577	$2,569	$3,531	$4,567	$5,590	$6,736	$8,702	$11,582	$20,200
				PERCENT DISTRIBUTION							
Percent Distribution											
Expenditures for current consumption	100.0	100.0	100.0	100.0	100.0	100.0	100.0	100.0	100.0	100.0	100.0
Food, total	25.6	18.9	32.5	31.4	30.3	25.5	27.5	25.3	26.6	24.9	18.9
Food prepared at home	19.4	4.9	28.2	28.8	22.3	20.0	22.5	19.2	19.7	17.5	13.0
Food away from home	6.2	14.0	4.3	2.5	8.0	5.4	4.9	6.1	6.8	7.4	5.9
Tobacco	1.9	0.2	1.5	2.4	2.1	2.5	2.3	2.0	2.0	1.7	0.6
Alcoholic beverages	2.2	2.1	0.9	1.6	3.1	2.0	2.9	2.0	1.9	2.7	2.2
Housing, total	30.4	45.2	46.0	39.3	33.6	30.3	34.9	28.6	27.1	25.7	33.1
Shelter	16.3	39.5	36.8	23.9	21.9	15.9	19.2	15.4	13.6	13.2	15.4
Rented dwelling	9.7	23.7	36.8	18.5	19.4	13.8	10.5	6.9	7.3	8.9	3.6
Owned dwelling	5.7	.0	.0	5.3	2.1	1.5	7.7	7.7	5.4	3.4	10.5
Other shelter	0.9	15.7	.0	.0	0.5	0.6	1.0	0.9	0.9	0.9	1.3
Fuel, light, refrigeration, water	3.0	1.2	3.0	3.9	1.7	2.7	3.8	3.3	3.3	2.1	2.4
Household operations	6.1	2.8	5.0	5.6	6.7	5.8	6.7	6.0	5.8	5.8	6.8
House furnishings and equipment	5.0	1.7	1.2	5.9	3.0	6.0	5.1	3.8	4.4	4.6	8.5

Clothing, clothing materials, services	11.0	8.2	5.8	8.9	10.6	10.7	9.8	10.5	11.6	13.8	10.3
Personal care	2.5	1.3	1.5	3.5	2.8	2.6	2.9	2.3	2.8	2.5	1.7
Medical care	6.8	8.0	3.8	8.9	5.3	5.8	5.2	7.1	6.5	6.5	9.8
Recreation	3.6	2.1	3.5	2.1	2.4	3.6	3.7	4.2	3.4	4.7	3.2
Reading	1.0	0.9	1.3	0.9	1.4	0.9	0.9	1.0	0.9	1.2	1.0
Education	1.1	.0	.0	.0	0.6	0.2	0.1	1.2	1.4	1.9	1.7
Transportation	11.2	13.0	2.6	1.6	6.1	13.5	8.7	12.4	14.5	12.2	8.7
Automobile	8.3	.0	.0	.0	2.1	10.6	6.4	10.5	12.1	8.2	5.3
Other travel and transportation	2.8	13.0	2.6	1.6	4.0	2.9	2.3	1.9	2.4	4.0	3.4
Other expenditures	2.8	.0	0.4	0.4	1.7	2.5	1.1	3.4	1.4	2.1	8.7

SOURCE: Bureau of Labor Statistics.

TABLE 2-6

Summary of Family Expenditures, Income, and Savings, by Income Class All Urban Families and Single Consumers—San Francisco, Calif., 1960

	Total	MONEY INCOME AFTER TAXES									
		Under $1,000	$1,000 to $1,999	$2,000 to $2,999	$3,000 to $3,999	$4,000 to $4,999	$5,000 to $5,999	$6,000 to $7,499	$7,500 to $9,999	$10,000 to $14,999	$15,000 and Over
Family Characteristics											
Money income before taxes	$7,110	$ 662	$1,591	$2,593	$3,762	$4,904	$5,893	$7,688	$10,046	$13,573	$34,214
Net change in assets and liabilities	−$178	−$328	−$552	−$377	−$106	−$357	−$138	−$504	−$190	$515	$3,410
Money income after taxes	$6,154	$ 662	$1,580	$2,493	$3,519	$4,495	$5,339	$6,822	$8,613	$11,808	$21,688
		PERCENT DISTRIBUTION									
Percent Distribution											
Expenditures for current consumption	100.0	100.0	100.0	100.0	100.0	100.0	100.0	100.0	100.0	100.0	100.0
Food, total	24.6	55.4	32.5	27.9	22.6	25.6	26.1	25.3	21.3	24.9	20.3
Food prepared at home	18.8	50.9	25.7	18.6	17.8	15.9	22.2	20.4	16.6	18.4	16.5
Food away from home	5.8	4.5	6.9	9.3	4.8	9.7	3.9	4.9	4.7	6.5	3.8
Tobacco	1.4	0.9	1.0	1.7	2.5	1.6	1.6	1.2	1.3	1.5	0.1
Alcoholic beverages	2.3	0.9	0.6	3.5	1.0	3.6	1.8	1.7	2.6	2.6	3.1
Housing, total	29.0	27.6	29.0	27.6	35.4	31.7	29.6	28.4	30.4	24.5	28.1
Shelter	14.7	23.8	18.8	18.0	20.6	18.2	15.2	13.5	15.2	10.1	11.8
Rented dwelling	7.1	23.8	13.7	15.0	18.6	15.6	8.3	4.0	4.7	2.5	.0
Owned dwelling	6.8	.0	3.5	2.8	1.7	2.2	6.3	8.8	9.1	6.7	10.1
Other shelter	0.8	.0	1.6	0.2	0.3	0.4	0.6	0.7	1.4	0.8	1.7
Fuel, light, refrigeration, water	2.9	.0	2.8	3.7	2.6	2.3	3.3	3.1	3.0	2.6	2.9
Household operations	6.1	3.8	5.4	4.0	6.1	7.0	6.0	5.2	7.0	6.2	6.1
House furnishings and equipment	5.3	.01	1.8								

materials, services	9.2	4.0	4.9	6.6	12.3	8.7	9.8	8.2	9.2	11.7	6.9
Personal care	2.6	2.3	2.4	2.8	3.9	2.5	3.3	2.3	2.6	2.8	1.9
Medical care	6.9	1.6	6.0	8.8	7.9	5.3	9.3	6.5	7.6	5.7	6.3
Recreation	4.9	3.8	7.9	3.9	3.5	3.5	4.0	5.1	4.3	7.6	3.3
Reading	0.9	0.7	1.9	0.7	0.6	0.9	1.1	0.9	1.0	0.7	1.4
Education	1.1	.0	3.0	0.7	0.1	0.6	0.9	0.9	0.8	1.9	3.5
Transportation	15.0	2.4	9.2	14.2	9.8	14.3	11.6	17.1	17.6	13.9	17.0
Automobile	12.9	.0	6.2	11.4	8.2	12.6	10.6	15.5	14.6	12.6	10.9
Other travel and transportation	2.1	2.4	3.0	2.8	1.6	1.7	1.0	1.6	3.0	1.3	6.2
Other expenditures	2.0	0.4	1.4	1.5	0.4	1.6	1.0	2.4	1.3	2.2	8.1

Source: Bureau of Labor Statistics.

FIGURE 2-7

Changes in U.S. per Capita Civilian Food Consumption

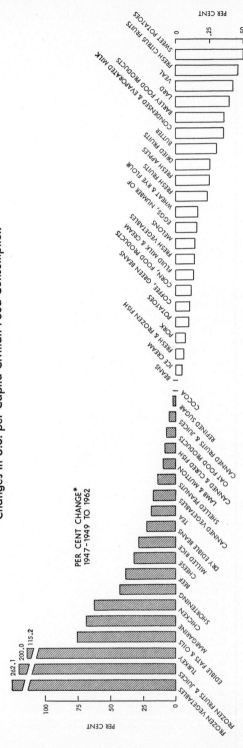

SOURCE: National Industrial Conference Board, *Road Maps of Industry*, No. 1439 (July 26, 1963).

* BASED UPON POUNDS CONSUMED PER YEAR

TABLE 2–7

Cost of One Week's Food at Home* Estimated for Food Plans at Three
Cost Levels, U.S.A. Average

Sex-Age Groups	Low-Cost Plan Dollars	Moderate-Cost Plan Dollars	Liberal Plan Dollars
Families			
Family of two, 20–34 years†	14.40	19.60	22.10
Family of two, 55–74 years†	12.80	17.60	19.70
Family of four, preschool children‡	21.40	28.50	32.50
Family of four, school children§	24.80	33.30	37.90
Individuals‖			
Children, under 1 year	3.10	3.90	4.20
1–3 years	3.80	4.80	5.40
4–6 years	4.50	5.90	7.00
7–9 years	5.40	7.00	8.10
10–12 years	6.30	8.50	9.70
Girls, 13–15 years	6.60	9.00	10.30
16–19 years	6.70	8.90	10.20
Boys, 13–15 years	7.20	9.90	11.30
16–19 years	8.50	11.50	13.10
Women, 20–34 years	5.70	7.80	8.80
35–54 years	5.50	7.60	8.60
55–74 years	5.10	7.10	8.00
75 years and over	5.00	6.60	7.50
Pregnant	7.00	9.20	10.20
Nursing	8.80	11.30	12.50
Men, 20–34 years	7.40	10.00	11.30
35–54 years	6.90	9.30	10.40
55–74 years	6.50	8.90	9.90
75 years and over	6.30	8.50	9.40

* These estimates were computed from quantities in food plans published in USDA Home Economics Research Report No. 20, *Family Food Plans and Food Costs*. The costs of the food plans were first estimated by using the average price per pound of each food group paid by nonfarm survey families at three selected income levels in 1955. These prices were adjusted to current levels by use of *Retail Food Prices by Cities* released periodically by the Bureau of Labor Statistics.

† Ten percent added for family size adjustment.

‡ Man and woman 20 to 34 years; children, 1 to 3 and 4 to 6 years.

§ Man and woman 20 to 34 years; children, 7 to 9 and 10 to 12 years.

‖ The costs given are for individuals in 4-person families. For individuals in other size families, the following adjustments are suggested: 1 person—add 20 percent; 2 person—add 10 percent; 3 person—add 5 percent; 5 person—subtract 5 percent; 6-or-more-person—subtract 10 percent.

Source: U.S. Department of Agriculture, Agricultural Research Service, Consumer and Food Economics Research Division.

mits the use of larger quantities of the more expensive food groups, such as higher-priced cuts of meat, eggs, citrus fruits, and some frozen and convenience foods.

Sometimes the makeup of a family or special conditions in the family make it necessary to provide an allowance in addition to the

TABLE 2–8

A Guide to the Family Food Budget
Cost per Person for Adequate Food at Low and
at Moderate Cost*

Sex-Age Groups	Low Cost		Moderate Cost	
Individuals	Per Week	Per Month†	Per Week	Per Month†
Child under 1 year	$3.15	$13.65	$ 3.90	$16.90
Child 1 through 3 years	3.80	16.45	4.75	20.55
Child 4 through 6 years	4.50	19.50	5.85	25.35
Child 7 through 9 years	5.35	23.15	7.00	30.30
Child 10 through 12 years	6.25	27.05	8.40	36.35
Girl 13 through 15 years	6.55	28.35	8.90	38.55
Girl 16 through 19 years	6.60	28.60	8.85	38.30
Boy 13 through 15 years	7.10	30.75	9.85	42.65
Boy 16 through 19 years	8.40	36.35	11.45	49.60
Woman 20 through 34 years	5.55	24.05	7.75	33.55
Woman 35 through 54 years	5.40	23.40	7.50	32.50
Woman 55 through 74 years	5.10	22.10	7.05	30.55
Woman 75 years and over	4.95	21.45	6.60	28.60
Pregnant woman	6.95	30.10	9.10	39.40
Nursing mother	8.75	37.90	11.20	48.50
Man 20 through 34 years	7.25	31.40	9.95	43.10
Man 35 through 54 years	6.80	29.45	9.30	40.25
Man 55 through 74 years	6.45	27.95	8.80	38.10
Man 75 years and over	6.20	26.85	8.45	36.60

* All costs have been rounded to nearest $0.05.
† Estimated on basis of 4⅓ weeks in a month.
Source: American Red Cross. Based on Bureau of Labor Statistics food prices for 46 cities.

regular budget.[12] The Red Cross chapter worker is told to take note of the following provisions, keeping in mind that it costs more per person to buy food in small amounts.

    1. For a person living alone, add one third (35 percent) to regular allowance.

[12] For further information see:

Family Fare, Home and Garden Bulletin No. 1, Human Nutrition and Home Economics Research, U.S. Department of Agriculture, U.S. Government Printing Office, Washington 25, D.C. A pamphlet giving basic nutrition facts, menus, market orders, and recipes.

Food for the Family with Young Children, Home and Garden Bulletin No. 5, U.S. Department of Agriculture, U.S. Government Printing Office, Washington 25, D.C.

Food for Families with School Children, Home and Garden Bulletin No. 13, U.S. Department of Agriculture, U.S. Government Printing Office, Washington 25, D.C.

Food for the Young Couple, Home and Garden Bulletin No. 85, U.S. Department of Agriculture, U.S. Government Printing Office, Washington 25, D.C.

Planning Your Family Food Supply, PA 425, U.S. Department of Agriculture, U.S. Government Printing Office, Washington 25, D.C.

2. For a family of two, add one fifth (20 percent) to regular allowance.
3. For a family of three, add one tenth (10 percent) to regular allowance.
4. For a child large for his age, use allowance for child in next age group.
5. For extra-nourishment diet, add about $1.85 a week.
6. For specific special diet, add actual cost.
7. For cod-liver oil or another vitamin D preparation for children and nursing and pregnant mothers, add actual cost of the product.
8. For meals away from home, allow about 40 cents per working day for hot soup, milk, or other beverages to go with packed lunch. For lunch at work or school, add actual cost.
9. Additional allowances are usually made for meals on Thanksgiving, Christmas and religious holidays and for other special-occasion meals.
10. If all meals are eaten in a restaurant, allow actual cost.

Housing and Household Operation

Housing and related outlays[13] for the average metropolitan family rose 53 percent over the last decade. Due to cost inflation, a sharp increase in rents, and the rise in home ownership, housing and related outlays rose from 27 to 30 percent of consumer expenditures for current consumption (see Table 2–4). The decade saw an extension of home ownership from 48 percent of all households in 1950 to 54 percent in 1961. The move from rented quarters to houses usually involves an increase in total housing costs. More space means more furniture, more carpeting, additional appliances, more extension telephones, and so on. It has been estimated that this trend will continue and that by 1970 the nation's housing and rent bill will be "over two-thirds bigger than today's."[14] Growth in expenses of household operation are expected to rise even more sharply, doubling by 1970 and requiring about 7.4 percent of the household budget compared with a present 6.0 and 4.7 percent in 1950.

The same declining percentage relationship as income levels rise tends to prevail for housing and rental costs as for food, except with respect to families having incomes in excess of $10,000. Wealthier families tend to spend almost as high a percentage of income for housing and household operation as the lowest-income families, except that the former tend to own while the latter are often forced to rent because they cannot afford ownership.

---

[13] Included in this category are shelter, fuel, light, refrigeration, water, household operation, house furnishings, and equipment. Shelter includes rent and taxes, insurance, interest, repairs, etc. Payments on mortgage principal are not included but are counted as changes in assets and liabilities. See "Workers Wealth and Family Living Standards," *Monthly Labor Review*, June, 1963, p. 680.

[14] See Fabian Linden, "Consumers Choice II: The Decade of the Sixties," in *The Business Record* (New York: National Industrial Conference Board, January, 1962), p. 42.

"Keeping up with the Joneses" is nowhere more manifest than in the purchase of homes the upkeep of which is too expensive in terms of one's income, or in paying too high a rent because of the desire to live in a fashionable neighborhood. Some well-tested rules of thumb are available, but they are not easy to stay with and are more often ignored than observed.

A family should not spend more than one week's net, take-home pay for the monthly rent. Many families probably exceed this limit, but the extra rental cost then comes at the expense of some other category of outlay, such as savings or recreation.

In purchasing a house, you should pay not more than two and a half times your annual income. Thus, if you make $7,000 a year, you can afford a $17,500 house—no higher, though many families do go higher and then have to cut down elsewhere, on food, or clothing, or vacations, or savings, or go into debt more heavily than they should. Then there is the "1 percent rule." The total monthly cost of carrying a house, including all expenses—interest, taxes, repairs, painting, etc. —is about 1 percent of the total cost of the house. Thus, a $20,000 house will involve monthly outlays and expenses of at least $200. If you don't believe it, buy one and see for yourself.

Clothing

Clothing's share of the household budget fell from 11.5 to 10 percent over the decade.[15] This does not mean that clothing expenditures fell. Quite the contrary. They were a fourth larger, but total consumer spending rose proportionately more. Furthermore, since clothing prices rose only half as much as the all-item price index, the consumer had to increase his dollar apparel expenditures less than for other consumer items in order to maintain his accustomed sartorial standards. Women account for three fifths of the total family clothing budget, and their clothing expenditures increased more rapidly than total consumer spending. The poor male, of course, had to offset this, and so he spent only very moderately for clothing. Some $40 billion is likely to be spent by the nation's consumers in 1970 for apparel and footwear, or two fifths more than now, but since expenditures in this category have been expanding by only three fourths the rate of all consumer outlays, they are expected to continue to decline as a relative proportion of the family dollar over the ensuing decade.

There are ways of economizing on family clothing outlays, espe-

---

[15] Fabian Linden, "Family Expenditures Surveyed," in *Business Management Record* (New York: National Industrial Conference Board, August, 1963), p. 58.

cially for the male. Remain a bachelor. Besides, female sizes are very confusing. One source[16] lists the following:

Girls—Size range 7 to 14
Subteen—Size range 8S to 14S
Teen—Size range 10T to 16T
Junior—Size range 7 to 19
Misses'—Size range 8 to 22
Half size—Size range 8½ to 24½
Women's—Size range 28 to 42

It is not clear whether these apply in underdeveloped as well as in mature economies.

Seriously, more utility for money spent can be obtained in good, substantial quality of both materials and workmanship than from either very cheap or very expensive garments. Conservative styles in clothing are more economical than extreme modes or fads. The latter last one season and then become outmoded even though relatively new and unused. The garment may be in perfectly good condition, but you "wouldn't be seen dead in it now" even though last season it was all the rage. Restrain the temptation in shopping to yield to "impulse buying." Buy only the items you set out to buy and don't spend more than your budget or spending plan suggests. Shop several stores first before buying and coordinate the purchase with your existing wardrobe.

Your Automobile

Perhaps one of the most striking observations that emerged from the Bureau of Labor Statistics' budget studies is that the average family, and especially the lower-income family, tends to spend almost twice as much on automobile operation and upkeep as on medical care and more than on clothing. Increased home ownership and the growth of suburban living have greatly extended the use of automobiles. Expenditures for auto purchase and operation accounted for 13 percent of total current consumption expenditures for all consumer units and 14 percent for wage and clerical families, up from 11 percent for both in 1950. Car ownership increased from three in every five households in 1950 to three in every four in the early 1960's. Over the decade expenditures for car operations and maintenance rose by 58 percent, and by 1970 it is estimated that consumers will spend some $60 billion for car purchases, operation, and maintenance, some two thirds more than present outlays.

---

[16] *Money Management—Your Clothing Dollar* (Chicago: Household Finance Corp.), p. 11.

The average person does not realize, when he first buys a car, how much more it takes to operate and maintain an automobile than he anticipates. The American Automobile Association recently made a survey of the cost of car upkeep, and its figures are shown in Table 2–9.

On the national average of 10,000 miles driven per car per year, the variable costs come to $370 a year (3.70 cents per mile of travel); while the fixed costs amount to $792 a year ($2.17 per day), making a total cost of $1,162 per year, or 11.6 cents per mile. On the basis of

TABLE 2–9

National Average Car Costs

VARIABLE COSTS	AVERAGE PER MILE
Gasoline and oil	2.61 cents
Maintenance	0.68 cents
Tires	0.41 cents
Total Variable Costs	3.70 cents per mile
FIXED COSTS	ANNUAL
Fire and theft insurance	$ 30.00
Property damage and liability ($25,000 and $50,000)	117.40
License and registration	23.60
Depreciation	621.00
Total Fixed Costs	$792.00 a year or $2.17 per day

SOURCE: *Your Driving Costs* (Washington, D.C.: American Automobile Association, 1963–64). A free copy may be obtained by writing to the American Automobile Association, 1712 G Street, N.W., Washington 6, D.C.

these figures, the AAA recommends that employers who are paying car allowances to employees grant $2.17 a day for each day that the car is driven *plus* 3.70 cents a mile for each mile driven. This is also a useful basis for computing transportation costs of a personal vacation trip.

The AAA suggests a vacation budget of $31 per day for two people driving 300 miles each day. A breakdown of the daily budget for a couple shows they will spend approximately $7.00 on car operation expenses; $10.50 on meals; $11.00 on lodgings; $2.50 on tips. Amusement, incidentals, souvenirs, tolls, and emergencies are extra. The allowance for driving costs is based on the assumption of averaging 15 miles per gallon of gasoline. No provision is made in this estimate for maintenance or tire costs as it is assumed that the car is in top condition before the trip is started.

The pocketbook appeal of compact cars—both domestic and foreign

—is confirmed by special figures developed by Runzheimer & Co. While these figures apply only to Chicago with 50 to 80 percent stop-and-go driving, they are believed indicative of the ratio of costs as between standard and compact makes throughout the nation.

In the Chicago area, total per mile costs for an eight-cylinder, low-priced standard were computed as 3.80 cents; for a popular domestic compact at 2.70 cents; and for a leading foreign compact at 1.95 cents. The annual fixed costs including depreciation, were reckoned as follows: standard, $877; domestic compact, $739; and foreign compact, $526. Thus, on the basis of 10,000 miles driven annually, total annual costs for the domestic compact would be $248 less than for the standard, and for the foreign compact would be $536 lower.

Medical and Personal Care

Consumer expenditure for medical and personal care rose from 7.4 to 9.5 percent of the average urban household budget over the last decade (see Table 2–4). By the end of the present decade, it is estimated that consumers will be spending $45 billion annually on drugs, doctors, hospitals, dentists, barbers, and beauticians. Outlays in these areas have been rising almost twice as fast as expenditures for all consumer goods and services. Increasing longevity, expanding medical and hospitalization programs, availability of new drugs, and the very sharp rise in the cost of professional services have been partly responsible. On a per capita basis, costs shot up from $57.56 to $109.82 over the ten-year period. Health insurance plans have spread to the point where they cover 73 percent of the population. As a result, 30 cents of every dollar spent on medical care take the form of payments for insurance, compared to only 15 cents in 1950.

A multi-millionaire, being interviewed about his self-made fortune, commented: "I never hesitate to give full credit to my wife for her assistance."

"In what way did she help?" the reporter asked.

"Well, if you want the whole truth," replied the wealthy man, "I was curious to find out if there was any income she couldn't live beyond."

—JOE HARRINGTON in the *Boston Post*

Smoking added another 1.8 percent to the 9.5 percent for medical and personal care. This was the same percentage as a decade earlier.

Because of higher prices and higher taxes, however, smokers had to spend a third more dollars than ten years earlier to maintain the same level of smoking activity.

Education

The very low outlays on education shown in average consumer expenditure figures (2.0 percent for reading and education) reflect the fact that Americans pay for elementary and secondary school education —and, to a limited extent, higher education—through taxes rather than private outlays. Putting a son or daughter through college these days, however, is likely to involve considerable expense and strain on the budget.

The cost of going to college has doubled over the last fifteen years, a recent survey of the U.S. Office of Education indicates. A student attending a typical public college will pay $1,750 for the academic year, while an average private school student must be prepared to pay $2,500. Many colleges now charge from $800 to $1,600 for tuition, compared with half that amount fifteen years ago. Yet, today, the tuition pays for less than 50 percent of the cost to the college of educating a student.

Some Ivy League colleges are now charging more than $1,600 a year for tuition (Princeton, $1,770; Harvard, $1,760; Yale, $1,800). Add to this $1,000 to $1,500 a year for room, board, and personal expenses, such as laundry, haircuts, and dates, and the annual cost rises to $2,700 or over. Attendance at women's colleges is even more costly. According to a survey[17] by the New York Life Insurance Company, entitled "The Cost of Four Years at College," to send a girl through Vassar costs $11,400, through Wellesley $10,000, through Smith, $10,800, and through Sarah Lawrence, $11,800.

College catalogs frequently estimate probable expenses and also list or advise on sources of added income through scholarships and extra employment. The University of Wisconsin, for example, estimates that student expenses for room, board, supplies, laundry, cleaning, and so on, average between $850 and $900 for the academic year. In addition, tuition for state residents is $194 per year, for nonresidents, $574, bringing total annual costs for residents to about $1,200 and for nonresidents to $1,500. In general it can be said that state universities, wherever located, are less expensive than the privately endowed col-

[17] A free copy may be obtained by writing to the New York Life Insurance Company, 51 Madison Ave., New York 10, New York. The survey covers 950 colleges and universities.

leges and that living costs are higher in colleges located in or near the big cities.

Even the state universities, however, require a substantial amount of money for attendance over four years. Tuition[18] and costs for legal residents at the University of California (Berkeley) amount to $4,364;[19] at the University of Florida, to $3,704; at the University of Colorado, to $4,280; at the University of Iowa, to $3,828; at the University of Minnesota, to $4,400; and at Ohio State, to $4,620. Supplementary charges for nonresidents range from $120 to $650 per annum. To become an engineer by attending M.I.T. now requires $10,800 and at California Institute of Technology or Carnegie Tech, approximately $10,000:

Graduate work for professional degrees adds from one to four years of additional cost, depending on the field chosen. Fees for postgraduate work vary considerably as to both the course and the university. At a state university, tuition at the law school for three years is $500–$750 for residents and $1,500–$2,000 for nonresidents. Private universities approximate the latter figures, and the more exclusive ones may charge as much as $2,000 per year. If we assume that room and board cost about $900 per year, a law degree would involve an expenditure of from $4,000 to about $10,000. Since it takes a year longer, or four years, to earn a medical degree, the money cost of becoming a doctor (tuition, room, and board) ranges from $6,000 to $12,000. Tuition at medical schools runs from $500 to $2,000 per year. A master's degree at a two-year graduate school of business will cost about $1,500 in tuition each year and $900 for room and board annually, or a two-year total of $4,800.

All these are substantial sums, and unless a family is well-to-do or begins to make provision long before hand for college costs, it may have to deny this increasingly necessary and valuable privilege to its young.

> A graduate student applying for a scholarship was asked to state his principal reason for needing assistance. "My wife and I are now separated," he wrote, "and this has left me as my sole means of support."

---

[18] For residents of the state. Tuition is usually higher for out-of-state residents.

[19] Tuition is free for residents of the state.

How do people pay for college? A survey[20] at the University of Michigan sheds some interesting light on the subject. The survey found that:

On the average, parents paid about $950, or 60 percent of their children's average annual expenses of $1,550. Scholarships, students' earnings, and "other sources" made up the balance. (Thirteen percent of the unmarried students received no family financial help.)

Although more than half of the students work, few earn enough to pay their own way. Of those who work, 40 percent earned less than $500 annually. Most of the rest earned between $500 and $1,500. Earnings of over $1,500 were rare. Mostly, the parents bear the brunt of paying for their children's education.

Scholarships helped 25 percent of the students. But for most, the grants were not enough to cover full costs. About 60 percent of scholarship recipients received $50 to $500; the others, more than $500.

Of 338 families having children in college in the past five years:

a) Half drew on funds previously set aside.
b) Forty-four percent paid the bills from current income.
c) One out of five mothers took a job.
d) Eight percent of the fathers took on additional work.
e) Eight percent of the families received a gift or inheritance.
f) About 8 percent of the families borrowed money.
g) In addition, 5 percent of the students borrowed.

Parent's plans for financing college for their children were reported as follows:

a) Half of the families with children who may attend college have set aside money for education. This figure is probably larger in the case of those whose children actually will go to college.
b) Endowment insurance appears to be growing in popularity as a means of saving for college. Twelve percent of families who had a child in college recently had endowment insurance, whereas 32 percent of families where the oldest child is seven to twelve and is expected to attend college now carry endowment insurance.
c) One mother in five expects to go to work.
d) Very few fathers plan in advance to do extra work.
e) Parents expect their children to earn about 20 percent of their own educational costs.
f) Very few families expect to borrow money. ("Such borrowing seems to be regarded as not a normal thing to do.")

In recent years as college costs have risen sharply, a variety of financial arrangements has been developed, including loans, insurance, savings plans, and so on. There is now a bewildering variety of solutions to the "Case of the Costly Tassel." Families can finance the spiraling costs of college educations:

a) Out of current income.
b) Out of savings.
c) By insurance.
d) By loans or scholarships.
e) Some combination of these four.

A student could once "work his way through college," but today this is difficult, and part-time employment can at best yield only a part of annual college costs. Meeting college costs out of current income has also become more difficult, since an average family's budget will require considerable rearranging to provide the $2,000 to $3,000 per year for four years now required for college.

Savings and insurance are the two most prudent and foresighted ways to pay, but they are used by only a minority of families. The earlier a family begins to save for college the easier the task. If your child is three years old, you can accumulate $5,000 by the time he or she is eighteen by saving $20.30 a month at 4 percent. If you wait until the child is thirteen, the monthly amount will have to be more than three times as much to reach the same goal.

The monthly cost of reaching three different savings goals when the interest rate is 4 percent compounded semiannually, is as follows:

Years of Saving	Savings Goal		
	$5,000	$7,500	$10,000
15 years	$20.30	$ 30.46	$ 40.74
10 years	33.90	50.86	68.03
5 years	75.23	112.84	150.96

A variety of insurance plans has been developed specially to meet the college cost problem. For example, a 35-year-old father of a child of three who wants to accumulate $7,500 in 15 years might buy an endowment policy (which stresses savings) in that amount, paying about $40 a month. If the father dies before the 15 years are up, the child receives $7,500; if he lives, the father receives it, after having paid about $7,200 in premiums. Or he may buy a less expensive "whole life" policy and use the "cash surrender" value after 15 years to pay for college for his son or daughter.[21] A large savings bank has developed a combination "insured college savings plan," which combines a regular

---

[21] See *"Planning for College Costs,"* by Sidney Sulkin, New York Life Insurance Company; a free copy may be obtained by writing to the company at 51 Madison Ave., N.Y. 10, N.Y. See also *"How To Pay For Your Child's College Education,"* by Sidney Margolius, Public Affairs Committee, 22 E. 38 St., New York 16, N.Y.

FIGURE 2–8A

WHO SPENDS WHAT ON WHAT?

—*this tells how families with the same income as yours spend their money*

income after taxes	$2,000 to $3,000	$3,000 to $4,000	$4,000 to $5,000	$5,000 to $6,000	$6,000 to $7,500	$7,500 to $10,000	$10,000 and over
food	28%	26%	25%	25%	24%	24%	21%
housing and utilities	24%	21%	19%	19%	18%	17%	16%
household operation	6%	6%	6%	6%	6%	6%	7%
furnishings & equipment	4%	5%	5%	5%	6%	5%	5%
total shelter	34%	31%	30%	30%	29%	28%	28%
clothing	8%	9%	10%	10%	10%	11%	12%
automobile	6%	11%	14%	14%	14%	14%	14%
other transportation	2%	2%	2%	1%	1%	2%	2%
medical care	8%	7%	6%	6%	6%	6%	6%
personal care	3%	3%	3%	3%	3%	3%	3%
recreation	3%	3%	4%	4%	4%	4%	5%
tobacco	2%	2%	2%	2%	2%	2%	1%
other expenses	2%	2%	2%	2%	2%	2%	3%
insurance ①	3%	3%	4%	4%	4%	5%	4%
gifts and contributions ①	4%	3%	3%	4%	4%	4%	5%
percent who save	39%	40%	52%	56%	61%	66%	69%
percent with deficit	49%	51%	45%	41%	37%	33%	29%
percent who broke even	13%	10%	4%	3%	2%	1%	1%

note: ① % of total disbursements (other data above are % of expenditures for current consumption)

SOURCE: Reprinted from *Changing Times, The Kiplinger Magazine.* Figures updated.

savings account with a decreasing term insurance policy on the life of the father, in one convenient monthly deposit. As the bank explains the plan:

Let's say you're 30 years old. Your child, age seven, is just entering second grade. You want to make sure he'll have enough money when he's 18 to go through four years of college—$10,000. By depositing $48.30 a month in your insured college savings plan, for a period of 15 years, you'll have that $10,000 available for him in quarterly installments of $625, when he starts college at age 18. Of the $48.30 monthly deposit $45.22 goes into a dividend earning savings account (it is assumed the savings will earn 3½ percent a year, compounded quarterly). The remaining $3.08 buys a low-cost decreasing term insurance policy on your life, so that even if you do not live to completion of the plan, the education fund will still be there when your child starts college.

In recent years loans have come into vogue to pay for part or all of the cost of a college education. Americans borrowed over $600 million

FIGURE 2–8B

YOUR COMPARISON CHART

—use this chart to record your expenses and compare them with the average

your income after taxes **$**   your income group **$**

	your family		your income group	does your budget seem high? about right? low?		
food	$	%	%			
housing facilities $		%	%			
household operation $		%	%			
furnishings & equipment $		%	%			
total shelter	$	%	%			
clothing	$	%	%			
automobile	$	%	%			
other transportation	$	%	%			
medical care	$	%	%			
personal care	$	%	%			
recreation	$	%	%			
tobacco	$	%	%			
other expenses	$	%	%			
insurance	$	%	%			
gifts and contributions	$	%	%			
savings (+) or deficit (—)	$	%	%			
amount of savings	$	%	percent who save %			
			average amount $			
— or —						
amount of deficit	$	%	percent with deficit %			
			average amount $			

SOURCE: Reprinted from *Changing Times, The Kiplinger Magazine.*

last year for college expenses, against $115 million five years earlier. Many colleges have loan funds. Most commercial banks have developed college loan plans. One of the most important developments in the college loan field is the rapid spread of state guaranteed loan programs. Under these plans either the state or a private organization puts up a fund to guarantee long-term low-interest loans usually through banks. In New York, a student can borrow up to $1,500 a year with no interest while he is in college, 3 percent afterward.[22] A number of states

---

[22] For more detail see "Loans for College: Check Your State," in *Changing Times,* May, 1963. See also Douglas Herron, "Student Loan Plans Are Spreading," in *Banking,* American Bankers Association, August, 1960.

have set up Higher Education Assistance Corporations.[23] Many of the guarantee loan plans were stimulated by United Student Aid Funds, Inc., a nonprofit organization that raises reserve funds to underwrite student loans.[24] The sharp rise in loans to students was also aided by the National Defense Education Act under which loans of up to $1,000 a year are permitted. Interest at 3 percent and repayment of principal begin one year after the student leaves college, and he has ten years to repay. If he or she goes into teaching, the loan is reduced by 10 percent each year for five years.

Another combination "package" recently developed is the insurance-bank loan plan. A large insurance company in cooperation with 45 major commercial banks provides financing for college education for children now entering the eighth to tenth grades. The first two years of college are covered by insurance endowment payments. If more funds are needed for the last two years, parents can take advantage of the bank-loan part of the package. The participating banks commit themselves at the time the policy is taken out to make personal loans at the prevailing interest rate. In most states the parents have three years from the date of the son's or daughter's graduation to pay for the loans. With the insurance payments, parents can spread the cost of the college education over eight to twelve years.

Spending Patterns and Your Budget

Now let's tie budget making together with the spending patterns we have explored. Knowing what other people in your income bracket spend, on the average, should make it easier for you to work out your own financial plan. *Changing Times* has worked out a Comparison Chart, shown in Figure 2–8B. Try to fill in the blank spaces. If you succeed you have drawn a financial plan and you can see at a glance how it compares with the national averages (Fig. 2–8A). If it's off here and there, think about the differences, but if you can explain them logically, don't worry about them. Your financial plan is a reflection of your needs and wants and your ability based on your income to fill them. It's a very individual matter, and it would be strange indeed if there weren't some differences.

A Balance Sheet

In addition to the budget and expenditure plan, it is sometimes advisable to draw up a family balance sheet from time to time, just as a business does. This is a statement of assets (things of value belonging

---

[23] See *"Credit for College,"* Educational Information Service, College Life Insurance Company of America, Indianapolis, Ind.

[24] USA Funds, Inc., College Square, Indianapolis 5, Ind.

to the family), liabilities (debts owed by the family), and the family's resulting net worth, all as of a particular time. A family's statement of condition, or balance sheet, might appear as shown in Table 2–10.

Such statements, if compared from year to year, will give some idea of the progress that the family is making (see Fig. 2–9). More elabo-

FIGURE 2–9   *LIFETIME BUDGETING*

PERSONAL BALANCE SHEET			
ASSETS	Five years ago	TODAY	Five years from now
Cash in bank			
Life insurance (paid-in value)			
Annuities (cash value)			
Real estate			
Furniture			
Automobile (trade-in value)			
Money due from others			
Other assets (cash value)			
Security investments:			
Government bonds			
Corporate bonds			
Stocks			
TOTAL ASSETS			
LIABILITIES			
Bills payable			
Loans payable			
Unpaid mortgage			
Other debts			
TOTAL LIABILITIES			
TOTAL ASSETS			
LESS TOTAL LIABILITIES			
NET WORTH			

SOURCE: *How to Invest*, Merrill, Lynch, Pierce, Fenner, and Smith.

TABLE 2-10

Balance Sheet of the Jones Family

Assets		Liabilities	
Cash	$ 261	Owed on home mortgage	$ 7,321
Savings bank books	576	Borrowed against life insurance	629
Cash surrender value of life in-		Total Liabilities	$ 7,950
surance	2,072	Family's net worth	9,622
Furnishings at cost	936		
Cost of home	13,727	Total Liabilities and Net	
Total Assets	$17,572	Worth	$17,572

rate forms are obtainable at local banks, where they are customarily used to give the banker knowledge of the financial strength of those who seek credit from the bank.

If your debts hopelessly exceed your assets, formal bankruptcy may be indicated. Of the 150,000 bankruptcies last year, nine out of ten were personal—as opposed to business bankruptcies. Excessive installment debt, loss of job, and large "medical" expenses were leading causes. Bankruptcies were most numerous in low- and middle-income categories. Leading states in bankruptcies were California, Illinois, Ohio, and Oregon. Unduly stiff laws governing garnishment of wages or salaries, deficiency judgments, and unrelenting collection pressures in some localities account for the drive to bankruptcy. Let's hope you never have to resort to it, however.

SUGGESTED READINGS

1. *Facing Facts about College Costs,* Prudential Life Insurance Company, 1962. A free copy may be obtained on request by writing to Box 36, Education Department, Prudential Insurance Company of America, Newark, N.J., 07101.

2. *Financial Assistance for College Students: Undergraduate,* Office of Education, U.S. Department of Health, Education, and Welfare, Washington, D.C., 1962.

3. *Student Financial Aid,* by Homer D. Babbidge, Jr., American College Personnel Association, Washington, D.C., 1960.

4. *The Family Financial Planner,* The Prudential Insurance Company of America, 1964. A free copy may be obtained by writing to the company at Prudential Plaza, Newark, N.J., 07101.

5. *Study of Consumer Expenditures Incomes and Savings,* University of Pennsylvania, Philadelphia:
   Volume:
   > I—*Summary of Family Accounts* (income, expenditures, savings and other receipts and disbursements), 1956.
   > II—*Summary of Family Expenditures for Current Consumption*
   > III—*Food, Beverages and Tobacco*

IV—*Housing and Household Operations*
V—*Housefurnishings and Equipment*
VI—*Clothing for Women and Girls, and Children under 2 Years*
VII—*Clothing for Men and Boys, Clothing Materials and Clothing Services*
VIII—*Medical Care and Personal Care*
IX—*Recreation, Reading and Education*
X—*Transportation*
XI—*Income, Savings, Insurance and Gifts and Contributions*
XVII—*Ownership of Consumer Durables* (percent of families owning selected consumer durable goods, and distribution of families, by year of purchase and by selected family characteristics)
XVIII—*Summary of Family Income, Expenditures and Savings* (for all urban areas combined), 1957

6. BLS Report No. 237–38, *Consumers Expenditures and Income, Urban United States, 1960–61,* Bureau of Labor Statistics, U.S. Department of Labor, Washington, 1964.

7. *How to Plan Your Spending,* Connecticut Mutual Life Insurance Company. A free copy may be obtained by writing to the company at 140 Garden St., Hartford 15, Conn.

8. *Personal Money Management.* New York: Savings Division, American Bankers Association. A free copy may be obtained on request at your local commercial bank.

9. *The Family Money Manager,* Institute of Life Insurance, 277 Park Ave., New York, N.Y. 10017. A free copy may be obtained on request.

10. *Where Does the Money Go?—Budget and Expense Record,* Union Dime Savings Bank, Avenue of the Americas at 40th St., New York 18, N.Y. A free copy may be obtained on request.

11. *Buying New or Used Cars,* Educational Division, National Better Business Bureau, Chrysler Building, New York 17, N.Y., latest edition.

12. *Money Management—Your Budget,* Household Finance Corp., Prudential Plaza, Chicago 1, Ill. Current. Also *Your Shopping Dollar, The Recreation Dollar, Your Clothing Dollar, The Food Dollar, Children's Spending, The Shelter Dollar, Your Automobile Dollar,* etc. Copies may be obtained at nominal cost.

13. *Facts You Should Know about Budgeting,* Educational Division, National Better Business Bureau, Chrysler Building, New York 17, N.Y.

14. *New York Life Budget Book,* New York Life Insurance Company. A free copy may be obtained upon request by writing to the company at 51 Madison Ave., New York 10, N.Y.

15. *Your Driving Costs,* American Automobile Association, 1712 G Street N.W., Washington 6, D.C., latest annual edition.

16. *"New Spending Guide for Budget-Minded Families,"* First National City Bank of New York. A free copy may be obtained by writing to the Bank at 55 Wall Street, New York, N.Y.

17. *Earn-Money-at-Home Schemes:* Educational Division, National Better Business Bureau, Chrysler Building, New York 17, N.Y., latest ed.

18. *Quantity and Cost Budgets for Two Income Levels.* Berkeley: Heller Committee for Research in Social Economics, University of California.

19. "What Other People Spend on Clothes," *Changing Times, The Kiplinger Magazine,* March, 1962.

20. "Our Spending—It's Different Now," *Changing Times, The Kiplinger Magazine,* July, 1962.

21. Robert Ferber, "Research on Household Behavior," *American Economic Review,* Vol. LII, No. 1 (March, 1962).

22. "Family Budget," *Changing Times, The Kiplinger Magazine,* January, 1963.

CASE PROBLEMS

1. Clara and Edward Fedang had been married six years. They have two children, ages three and five. Ed, an engineer in a large New York City architectural-construction firm, earns $8,040 after taxes. Clara's father, who died some 15 years ago, left her an estate with a yearly income of $2,000 after taxes.

Clara and Ed had lived within their yearly income without budgeting, but they have not increased their savings in the last two years. This past winter they enrolled in an adult education course in Personal Finance. An assignment for one class was to develop a family budget plan. Here is their plan:

THE FEDANG FAMILY BUDGET

Income	Month	Year
Edward's salary (after taxes)	$670	$ 8,040
Clara's income from estate (after taxes)	167	2,000
Total	$837	$10,040

Expenditures
Fixed

	Month	Year
Base rent (co-operative, 7-*room apartment*)	$110	$ 1,320
Utilities (light, gas, telephone, water)	48	576
Household operations	28	336
Food (includes occasional entertaining)	170	2,040
Clothing	85	1,020
Dental and medical care	35	420
Extra life Insurance premium (quarterly $42)		168
Recreation and advancement	30	360
Edward's fare	21	252
	$527	$ 6,492

Variable

	Month	Year
Laundry and dry cleaning	$ 25	$ 300
Edward's personal allowance	60	720
Babysitters	10	120
Church and contributions	8	100
Gifts	12	150
Vacation (3 weeks)		350
	$115	$ 1,740
Total Fixed Expenses	$527	$ 6,492
Total Variable Expenses	115	1,740
	$642	$ 8,232

Income	$10,040
Expense	8,232
	$ 1,808—approximately 15%

Does this appear to be a good financial plan for them? Why? Why not?

2. Lydia Pierce and Florence Ganter, recent college graduates, settled in Seattle. They decided to share an apartment. Lydia, as an assistant to an account executive in an advertising firm, receives $80 take-home pay each week. Florence, who excelled in statistics, works for a utility company on wage and salary scale evaluation. Her initial take-home pay is $75 per week. They prepared the following budget.

THE LYDIA-FLORENCE BUDGET PLAN

INCOMES

Lydia....................$4,160   Florence.................$3,900

COMBINED INCOMES
$8,060

SHARED EXPENDITURES

	Month	Year
Rent (3-room, walk-up apartment, furnished)...........$105		$1,260
Food (breakfast, dinner, plus guests)................... 90		1,080
Utilities (gas, light, and telephone)................... 15		180
Household supplies and repairs........................ 10		120
Newspapers and periodicals........................... 7		84
	$227	$2,724

SEPARATE INCOMES REMAINING

Lydia....................$2,798   Florence.................$2,538

PERSONAL EXPENDITURES

	Month	Annual		Month	Annual
Clothing..................$130		$1,560		$100	$1,200
Dental and medical.......... 12		144		12	144
Transportation.............. 8		96	(within walking distance)		
Allowance:					
Lunch.................... 25		300		20	240
"HOK".................. 10		120		10	120
Contributions.............. 6		72		6	72
Gifts...................... 8		96		8	96
Vacation.................. 20		240		20	240
	$219	$2,628		$176	$2,112

SAVINGS

Lydia..............$170   4%   Florence...........$426   11%

What is your opinion of this spending plan?

3. John Davis and Mary Doe (ages 25 and 22) are engaged to be married. Upon graduating from college, John went to work for a large company. He is now assistant manager of one of their branches at $130 a week. After high school, Mary went to secretarial school. She is now employed as secretary to a lawyer for $70 a week. John has saved $6,000, whereas Mary has saved $500 and has only two more monthly payments of $55 each to make before she will own free and clear a Ford convertible which she bought new two years ago. Mary plans to work for a year or two after they are married in order that they may furnish their home with things they probably could not otherwise afford. Both are anxious to plan carefully for the future. Their wedding is set for next June.

How much would you recommend that a couple of their position should budget for food? Clothing? Shelter? Other necessities? Savings?

What form or forms should they keep in order to compare actual expenditures with budgeted amounts?

They plan to live near to both of their places of employment. Since they are in a moderately large city, what should they plan to do with Mary's automobile?

4. Richard Roberts travels for a company which allows him 10 cents a mile for the use of his car. He drives about 2,000 miles a month on company business. Since he represents a financial organization which wants to make a good impression on its customers, he is expected to drive a relatively new car; but he uses the automobile so much that he figures he must "turn in his old car for a new one about every three years, anyway." In 1963, he turned in his 1960 five-passenger Chevrolet coupe, which cost him $2,200 new, for the same model in the 1963 line, costing $2,800. He was allowed $950 for the old car, which he had run 81,000 miles.

Roberts thinks that his company is not paying him enough for transportation. He wants your assistance in working out a form or forms on which to keep track of all the expenses he incurs in connection with his automobile. What would you suggest? Enter reasonable figures for the various expenses you might expect him to have for the next year and compare the total with the amount he would collect from the company for 24,000 miles. Does it seem that 10 cents a mile is fair reimbursement? Would his expense per mile be different if he traveled only 5,000 miles a year on company business and continued to use his automobile for trips of his own approximating 3,000 miles a year? Would 10 cents a mile be fair reimbursement under these conditions?

5. Ronald Graham, a Junior, was elected treasurer of his college fraternity to serve for the year beginning July 1 and ending June 30. When he took office, the fraternity owned (a) its building, a brick structure, donated by a wealthy alumnus (it had cost $92,000), (b) furnishings which had been bought for $7,800, (c) supplies (chiefly canned goods) amounting to $710 at cost, (d) a bank account with a balance of $3,700, and (e) an endowment fund of stocks and bonds which had been purchased for $16,823. At this time the fraternity owed various accounts payable amounting to $2,613 and a balance of $3,122 on its furniture. Prepare a balance sheet of the fraternity as of that date. Would you say that the fraternity is in a healthy financial condition? Why? Why not?

The previous treasurer presented Graham with a budget for his year in office. It had been adopted by the fraternity at the May meeting. The items it contained are showing in the accompanying table.

Income:

From dues	$ 510
From pledges	75
From rooms	800
From food	1,100
From miscellaneous	1,673
Total Income	$4,158

Expenses:

Food	$ 600
Help	2,700
Miscellaneous	700
Total Expenses	$4,000
Estimated Surplus	$158

How helpful would this budget be? Can it be improved? What records should Graham keep from month to month to know whether the fraternity is keeping within the budget? If the budget for the year is met exactly and there are no other changes except that (a) supplies at the end of the year amount to $525, (b) various accounts payable then total $1,742, and (c) the balance then owing on the furniture is $2,697, what will be the condition of the fraternity as shown by its balance sheet as of that date?

6. Bob and Janet Atkins have been married for four months. Bob has been employed for a year as an engineering salesman, and Janet has just started to teach, following her graduation from college. Their combined income after taxes is $11,500; the savings account contains $800. Because of the city's excellent transportation system, Bob did not need a car previously, but he now needs one for periodic sales trips.

How should the Atkins plan the purchasing and financing of their car, keeping the family budget in mind?

7. Jane, age 24, was trying to decide whether to accept a certain job. The job was just what she had been looking for. The salary was $4,300 a year. The one problem preventing immediate acceptance of the position was transportation. The office was situated just outside the suburbs of the city and there was no public transportation there. Jane investigated all possibilities, and she finally decided that she would either have to take a streetcar as far as she could and then be dependent on a car pool from that point to the factory or she would have to buy a car of her own. Jane was planning to share an apartment in the city with two other school friends. The rent of the apartment would be $150 a month. She had also incurred an educational debt of $320. How would a budget help Jane? What decisions should she make?

8. Sue Miller, age 22, has just graduated from a midwestern college. She has accepted a teaching position, to begin in September, in a small town about 50 miles from her home. After taxes and other deductions her pay is to be $4,020 a year.

Sue is planning to share an apartment with another teacher; her share of the rent would be $50 a month. Since both girls are good cooks, they believe that they can eat well for $40 each per month. During her senior year, it was necessary for Sue to borrow $350 (at 3 percent interest) from her college. According to the terms of the loan, the money should be paid back a year after her graduation date. Because her mother recently underwent an operation, Sue must remain at home during the summer and cannot take a summer job.

Sue is looking forward to buying a car as soon as possible, so that she can make weekend trips home. Being an avid golf enthusiast, she would like to join the local golf club.

How should Sue budget her income to accomplish what she wants to do?

9. Doris Gray and Betty James (ages 27 and 25) both teach kindergarten in a city of 25,000, not far from your home town. They have $250 take-home pay each month. At present they room and board with Mr. and Mrs. Hassler, who treat them just like members of the family, for $85 each per month. They would like a place of their own, so they are considering renting an apartment together.

Prepare a reasonable budget plan for each of them as you think it might be under present conditions. Enter representative figures for a period of a year on a form you consider appropriate. Compare the expenditures for the year with yearly income, not forgetting that both have a summer vacation of approximately three months.

Set up a combined budget for the new conditions. Enter figures and compare with present yearly expenditures, making such assumptions as you think necessary.

Would it probably be financially beneficial to make the change? What other advantages and disadvantages do you see in the contemplated move?

10. Nancy and Robert Zander have an income of $150 a week. They used to live in an apartment for $110 a month. After saving some money and being left some by Nancy's mother, they bought a home for $17,000 in your community and thought they would be free of dwelling expense for life. However, they are beginning to learn that this is far from true.

They ask you to help them devise a form or forms which will enable them to compare how much more or less expensive it is to own their home than to rent one. What is your suggestion? Enter reasonable figures for a year and compare the total with a year's rent at $110 a month. Are there any benefits other than financial from owning one's own home?

3 CHARGE ACCOUNTS, CREDIT CARDS, AND THE INSTALLMENT PLAN

Let us all be happy and live within our means even if we have to borrow the money to do it with.
—*Artemus Ward*

THE CHAIRMAN of the First National Bank of Chicago tells the story of the salesman who was trying to persuade a housewife to buy an electric dishwasher on the installment plan.

"Madam," said the salesman, "if you buy this dishwasher it will help you save the cost of a maid. Don't think of the very small monthly payment. Think of how much you will save on the cost of the maid every month."

"Well," said the housewife, "I'm not sure we can buy it. We bought an automobile to save bus and taxi fares. Then we bought a television set on time, too, to save movie and entertainment expenses. Last week we bought an automatic clothes washer and dryer in order to save laundry bills. You know, I really think we are saving about as much now as we can afford."

The great rise in consumer indebtedness in recent years has been the subject of much debate. "The people who are most responsible for the dangerous increase in mortgage and short-term consumer debt," says William H. Whyte, Jr., writing in *Fortune,* "are younger couples in the $5,000–$7,500 bracket. Sober suburbia is their habitat. No pink Cadillacs, no riotous living. Eminently respectable are the young suburbanites; most of them are salaried members of large organizations; they are homeowners; they go to church; from one third to one half have gone to college; more will send their children to college; and about 65 percent of them vote Republican. And they are the true prodigals."

Fortune summed up: "The young people who some day will run our capitalist economy—how do they run their own? Atrociously. They are so bemused by the rhythm of equal monthly payments, they hardly think about the cost of money at all."

Consumer debt now exceeds $235 billion. Of this, over $170 is mortgage debt on family homes, while over $65 billion is in consumer credit of various forms. It's the young marrieds who are responsible for most of the consumer debt. The *Survey of Consumer Finances* of the Survey Research Center, University of Michigan, found that 61 percent of all spending units headed by those under 35 years of age, had incurred installment debt. Among spending units with incomes of $5,000–7,499 in which the head was under 45 years of age, more than two thirds reported having installment debt. In spending units headed by those from 18 to 34 years of age, 39 percent had installment debts sufficiently large to require the commitment of from 10 to 40 percent of their annual disposable income to the repayment of installment credit. The *Survey of Consumer Finances* declares: "Young people are apparently willing to incur debt regardless of their income level. Furthermore, at each income level the incidence of installment debt declines with increasing age." "A large proportion of credit users in the younger age brackets apparently remain in debt most of the time," the Federal Reserve notes.

Since the odds are now overwhelmingly in favor of your getting into debt shortly after you get married, you ought to know something about the process and the pitfalls. Consumers interviewed for the *Survey of Consumer Finances* were asked whether they thought installment buying was "a good idea." Approximately one half indicated that it was, while a third viewed it unfavorably. The remainder expressed qualifications of their views. For example, 9 percent said "sometimes good, sometimes bad." As might have been expected, the attitude toward installment debt became steadily less favorable in moving up through the age brackets. In the 18–24-year age group, about three fifths viewed installment buying favorably, and about one third expressed unfavorable views.

The Nature of Consumer Debt

The use of consumer credit predominates in the purchase of durable goods. Of the total of $65 billion of consumer credit, some $50 billion is in installment debt and of this over $20 billion is automobile paper. Thus automobiles account for about 40 percent of all consumer installment debt. During the past few years 60 percent of all new cars have been sold on credit. It appears that about 24 percent of all spending units in the United States have incurred installment debt in the purchase of new or used cars. In the case of furniture and household

GRIN AND BEAR IT　　　　　　　　**By Lichty**

Courtesy: George Lichty, Publishers Newspaper Syndicate.

"I stand for more credit, gentlemen! . . . we must give to the people who haven't money, the opportunity to spend it! . . ."

appliances, 48 percent of all spending units making such purchases used credit.

Furniture stores reported that 63 percent of total sales were made on an installment basis, 19 percent on charge accounts, and 18 percent for cash. About 45 percent of television purchasers reported the use of credit, and about 30 percent borrowed more than three quarters of the net price. Credit was used by about 25 percent of the purchasers of television sets who had incomes of $5,000 or more and by about 55 percent of the purchasers having incomes less than $5,000. About 65 percent of the buyers of used cars financed their purchases in part by some form of credit. For household appliance stores, 49 percent of sales were on an installment basis, 27 percent for cash, and 24 percent on charge accounts.

Even in the purchase of certain types of nondurable consumer goods, the use of credit is extensive. Jewelry stores made 52 percent of their sales on an installment basis and 17 percent on charge accounts, compared to 31 percent for cash. Of total men's clothing sales, 49 percent were on charge accounts, 8 percent on an installment basis, and 43 percent for cash. In women's apparel, comparable figures were 46 percent on charge accounts, 4 percent on installments, and 50 percent for cash. Of total department store and mail-order sales, approximately 40 percent were for cash, 20 percent were on the installment basis, and 40 percent were charge accounts or revolving credit.

Consumer credit in recent years has become easier and easier to obtain. Indeed, the consumer's problem is more how to resist it than how to obtain it. Merchants have found that it increases their volume. Customers buy more; and if they are tied to a store by a charge account or an installment contract, they tend to come back to that particular store because their credit is now known—has been established—and the initial red tape involved in opening an account need not be repeated.

THE CHARGE ACCOUNT

Charge accounts not so many years ago were a sign of prestige. Only a limited number enjoyed the privilege of saying, "Charge it, please." The charge account was largely for the "carriage trade." Today charge accounts are a vital part of retail merchandising, and over a third of all retail sales are done on a charge basis. Charge or "open-account" purchases differ in a number of ways from installment purchases. Charge accounts do not call for a down payment; most installment transactions do. To installment prices are added carrying charges, which may or may not be disguised. Charge purchasers do not pay this extra cost for the use of credit; it is merged in the price of the article itself, which is paid by cash customers too. For very slow payment of end-of-the-month bills, a few stores tack on a small carrying charge. On the other hand, many stores allow charges to run up to 90 days without penalty. The average "30-day" account, a retail credit survey revealed, averaged 60–74 days, varying with the line of business. Installment transactions involve contracts whose terms the customer needs to examine very carefully. For the customer who buys on a charge account, however, there is usually no contract to be signed and hence no right of repossession by the dealer should the customer fail to pay. That is, when you purchase on a charge account, you get title to the goods purchased. In most installment sales, title does not pass until the final installment is paid.

Revolving Credit

In recent years the charge account has become a flexible or revolving charge account. When merchants perceived that many customers were slow in paying at the end of 30 days, they decided to capitalize on this situation by imposing a charge and urging customers to add to their balances due by making additional purchases and permitting repayments in installments over ten months. As the balance was reduced, additional purchases could build up the balance due and stretch out the required time to pay. This was, in a way, the adaptation of the "line-of-credit" concept which commercial bankers applied to business customers.

The Sears Revolving Charge Account shown in Figure 3–1 is a good example of a typical arrangement. The customer may either pay the full amount due in 30 days, or he can elect to pay over a ten month period. If he pays at the end of 30 days, he pays only the cash price. If he elects to pay on a monthly basis a "time price" is set based on the cash price plus a differential of 1½ percent of the balance due at the beginning of each monthly billing period. When you need to charge more at any time, your credit limit goes up, within the maximum set by the credit office. When your balance comes down, your monthly payments come down. No down payment is required. You receive a statement each month which shows the unpaid balance, the "time price differential" or "service charge" computed on the balance at the beginning of each monthly billing period, and the amount of the monthly installment due. If the monthly payment is not remitted when due, the seller may stop further purchases and the entire balance becomes due and payable at once.

Opening a Charge Account

To open a charge account is a simple matter. Application is made at the credit office, where a form is filled out giving such information as the name, address, age, husband or wife's name, employer's name and address, position held and length of service, names of other places where a charge account is maintained, and about three references, of which

FIGURE 3–1

AGREEMENT
FOR SEARS REVOLVING
CHARGE ACCOUNT

SEARS, ROEBUCK AND CO., PHILADELPHIA 32, PA.

In consideration of your selling merchandise to me on Sears Revolving CHARGE ACCOUNT, I agree to the following regarding all purchases made by me or on my Sears Revolving CHARGE ACCOUNT Identification:

1. I have the privilege of a 30-day charge account, in which case I will pay the full amount for all merchandise purchased within 30 days from the date of each billing statement.
2. If I do not pay the full amount for all merchandise purchased within 30 days from the date of each billing statement, the following terms shall be in effect:
   (A) I will pay the time sale price for each item purchased consisting of:
      (1) The cash sale price, and
      (2) An amount of time price differential computed at 1½% of the balance at the beginning of each monthly billing period, until the full amount of all purchases and time price differentials thereon are paid in full.
   (B) I will pay for the merchandise purchased in monthly installments which shall be computed according to the following schedule:

If the unpaid balance is:	The scheduled monthly payment will be:
$ .01–$ 10.00	BALANCE
10.01– 100.00	$10.00
100.01– 150.00	15.00
150.01– 200.00	20.00
200.01– 250.00	25.00
250.01– 300.00	30.00
300.01– 350.00	35.00
Over $350.00	1/10 of account balance

I will pay each monthly installment computed according to the schedule at left upon the receipt of each statement. If I fail to pay any installment in full when due, at your option the full balance shall become immediately due.

(C) You are to send me a statement each month which will show the unpaid balance for merchandise purchased, your time price differential computed on the balance at the beginning of each monthly billing period, and the amount of the monthly installment coming due.

(D) I have the right to pay in advance.

_____
(CUSTOMER'S SIGNATURE)

ACCEPTED,
SEARS, ROEBUCK AND CO.

By_____

Date_____

NAME
(PLEASE PRINT)_____

Print names of other members of family authorized to buy on your account. Duplicate identification will be issued.

1_____

ADDRESS_____

CITY_____ZONE_____STATE_____

2_____

| | IS ACCOUNT | DATE FINAL | | AT WHAT |
PREVIOUS SEARS ACCOUNT?_____PAID IN FULL?_____PAYMENT MADE_____SEARS STORE?_____

WIFE'S
AGE?_____MARRIED?_____FIRST NAME_____

NUMBER OF
DEPENDENTS?_____

HOW LONG AT   BOARD ☐   MONTHLY RENT OR
PRESENT ADDRESS?_____OWN ☐ RENT ☐   MORTGAGE PAYMENT $_____PHONE NO._____

FORMER ADDRESS (IF LESS THAN   HOW
2 YEARS AT PRESENT ADDRESS)_____LONG?_____

                              STREET   CITY
EMPLOYER_____ADDRESS_____AND STATE_____

                                                           WEEKLY
HOW LONG?_____OCCUPATION?_____EARNINGS $_____

FORMER EMPLOYER   HOW
(IF LESS THAN 1 YR. WITH PRESENT EMPLOYER)_____LONG?_____

NAME OF   ADDRESS OF   WIFE'S
WIFE'S EMPLOYER_____WIFE'S EMPLOYER_____WEEKLY INCOME $_____

                              STREET   CITY   SAVINGS ☐
NAME OF YOUR BANK_____ADDRESS_____AND STATE_____   CHECKING ☐

IF A FARMER, HOW LARGE IS YOUR FARM?_____ACRES._____HOW MANY ACRES UNDER CULTIVATION?_____

EXPLAIN OTHER INCOME, IF ANY_____

GIVE BELOW THE NAMES AND ADDRESSES OF TWO STORES WITH WHICH YOU HAVE HAD CREDIT DEALINGS OR TWO BUSINESS MEN WHO KNOW YOU

                              STREET   CITY
NAME_____ADDRESS_____AND STATE_____

                              STREET   CITY
NAME_____ADDRESS_____AND STATE_____

The information above will be kept strictly confidential

See charge account information on other side

744 SEARS

one is commonly the applicant's bank. An example of a credit application form may be seen in Figure 3–1. If the applicant is a minor (usually under 21 years of age), he will have to use his parent's or his guardian's account or have his own account guaranteed by his parent or guardian.

The Credit Office and Investigation

The credit office contacts the references, usually by telephone or by sending forms to be completed and returned. In most of the larger cities the retail credit bureau can furnish all needed information about local applicants. Most consumers would be surprised at the extent of information the local credit bureau has or can have about them. In fact, most customers do not even know about the local retail credit bureau. It is a clearing house for the exchange of information among the merchants on the credit experience which each has had with the purchaser. Each firm supplies the bureau with all the details about its dealings with the credit applicant. The bureau is usually maintained by the joint contributions of all its members. If the credit applicant has previously failed to pay, has been slow in paying, or has had his wages subject to garnishment, these facts will be recorded in his folder at the credit bureau.

On the other hand, a person with a good credit record may find that while he is waiting in the store's credit office a phone call to the credit bureau may be sufficient to establish his identity and past good record and permit the credit manager to approve the application without further delay.

If the credit applicant is unknown to the credit bureau, it will, at the store's request, make a detailed investigation of the applicant. Just what it looks for under its four headings—"Identity," "History," "Character," and "Resources"—may be seen in Figure 3–2. If you have just moved from one city to another, the credit bureau in the city in which you are now applying for credit will get in touch with the credit bureau in the city in which you formerly resided via the national organization of credit bureaus, the Associated Credit Bureaus of America, Inc. In this way a person with a bad credit record may find it difficult to obtain credit anywhere in the country. Sometimes persons who fail to pay in one city and then move to another and establish themselves are located by the credit bureau network and are persuaded to pay.

The usual credit investigation is made by phoning the applicant's landlord, employer, bank, and trade references.

FIGURE 3-2

| STANDARD CONSUMER REPORT | CREDIT BUREAU REPORTS, Inc. (Formerly National Consumer Credit Reporting Corporation) | Form 821 64M 2-51 |

1. REPORT ON
   (Surname first)   (Mr.-Mrs.-Miss)   (Given names)   (Wife's or husband's name)   (If single, parent's name)
2. Residence Address
   (Number and Street or R. F. D.)   (City)   (County)   (State)

IDENTITY
3. Time applicant has been known in our files
4. Time applicant has resided at this address and in city
5. Type and condition of residence and neighborhood
6. Is applicant considered a permanent resident?
7. Age (if 21, verify if possible)
8. Nationality, Descent and race
9. Single, married, separated, widowed or divorced
10. Number and identity of dependents

HISTORY
11. Former residence addresses and how long there?
    Note: On reverse side give summary of credit reports received from other towns.
12. Name and address of present employer or business
13. Size and reputation of firm
14. Nature of occupation or business and how long?
15. Name of previous employer, position and how long?
16. Employer's opinion

CHARACTER
17. How regarded as to character, habits, morals, etc.
18. Over-buying
19. Suspicion of liquor or narcotic traffic, if any
20. Steady employment

RESOURCES
21. INCOME—Approximate monthly income
22. Is income steady?   When paid?
23. Prospect of permanency
24. Estimated earnings of wife or others in household
25. Income from other sources, such as investments, rentals, stocks, etc.
26. Applicant owns home   Rooms   Boards
27. Other tangible assets
28. Applicant rents furnished   unfurnished
29. If renting, give amount of rent and paying record
30. Applicant is generally estimated to be worth
31. Bank experience'
32. If financially involved in any way, give details

CREDIT RECORD AND REMARKS:

33 Type of Business Reporting	34 How Long Sold	36 Date of Last Sale	37 Lease or Open Acct.	38 Recent High Credit	39 Owes Now	Amount Past Due and How Long	40 PAYING HABITS Specify 30, 60, 90 days, etc.	41 Remarks

42. USE REVERSE SIDE for suits, judgments, bankruptcies, loans, chattel mortgages, repossessions, domestic troubles, etc. Amplify any unfavorable information given above. Give a brief word picture of the subject, stressing any unusual history or condition. State if radical change has been noted in bills paying habit and give reason.

| 43. Report for | 45. Your File No. |
| 44. Compiled by | 46. Date |

To weed out the weak credit risk, the American Bankers Association suggests that the credit investigator check particularly:

a) Employment. Steady employment may be defined as being employed at one place of business for the past three years or more. Of primary importance is whether it is likely that the applicant will be gainfully employed during the credit period. Of equal importance is the verification of the stated salary.

b) *Bank Account and Previous Trade Experience.* A favorable feature in extending retail credit is a checking account of three figures or more. The two-figure account is an unfavorable indication. Record of prompt payment at other stores is also, of course, a favorable factor.

c) *Residence.* The credit investigator learns a good deal from the applicant's address. He can determine whether the neighborhood is inhabited by a stable, homeowning, regular-income group; whether the section is known to lack sufficient means or represents a prosperous or middle-income community. If the applicant has not been at his present address at least two years, the investigator will check his previous address. Also the amount of rent and promptness of payment, the number of years of residence, and type of section will be reported.

On the basis of the information received, the credit office decides whether to open the account and whether a limit is to be placed on the amount of credit during a given period.[1] The charge customer is given a charge plate as a means of identifying herself.

If you are denied credit find out why. Be persistent. There may have been an error, or a confusion of names. Get it straightened out. Good credit status is too valuable to lose lightly or by error. If you once failed to pay a bill, or are consistently slow in paying when due, this may explain the refusal. Even this can be straightened out and need not remain a blot on your credit record. If you can't pay a bill on time it is always best to get in touch with the seller, explain why, agree on when you can pay and then stick to your promise.

Cost of Charge Accounts

The large volume of business secured through charge accounts and the small losses incurred allow goods to be sold on charge accounts at the same price as for cash sales. The very large department stores and mail-order houses which formerly sold only for cash have in recent years, to meet the competition of credit houses, added various types of credit plans. Credit sales are 60 percent of the total at the typical department store.

Some operate, however, on a two-price system. There is a basic cash price; and if you want credit, you pay for it. Obviously, if you are a consistent cash buyer, these are the best places for you to buy, since no part of your purchase price goes to cover the costs of the credit purchases. In stores which charge cash and credit customers the same price

---

[1] See "How They Size You Up for Credit," *Changing Times, The Kiplinger Magazine,* July, 1960, pp. 29–31.

and make no charge for credit, the cash customers are helping to pay the cost of the credit extended to those who charge.

For example, suppose you find you can buy an item for $100 on a charge which you can stretch to 90 days without any apparent extra charge. But suppose in shopping around you find you can get the identical item for $95 cash. If you buy at the first store you are in effect paying $5 for the use of $95 for three months. This is at the rate of 21 percent interest per annum.

There was considerable controversy at the Douglas Subcommittee hearings on "Truth in Lending" as to what a true annual rate would be for a service charge or time price differential of 1½ percent a month on the beginning monthly balance in a revolving charge account. If the balance does not change for the month it would appear that the annual interest rate is 18 percent (1½ × 12).[2] However, as Professor Johnson points out:

> The dollar finance charge will be entirely dependent upon the customer's habits of payment. Moreover, the maturity of credit would depend on the date of purchase. For example, a customer buying early in the month receives a longer credit term than a customer purchasing shortly before the billing date. On the assumption of a 1½ percent service charge per month, a few sample calculations show a range in the effective annual rate to be from 15 per cent to over 36 per cent.[3]

Small charges may seem high when stated on an annual interest basis. For example, assume that a customer walks into a retail store, picks up a $2.98 item, finds that he has no money, and asks the merchant to send him a bill for it. If the merchant promptly sends his statement and adds only 5 cents to cover the cost of the stamp used, and the customer comes into the store five days later and pays the merchant the $2.98 plus the 5 cents postage, the 5 cent charge represents a simple annual rate of 122 percent.

CREDIT CARDS

You may aspire to the fascinating world of credit cards and expense accounts. Joe Miraglia, a 17-year-old, $75-a-week clerk did. He filed

---

[2] See especially the exchange between Under Secretary of Commerce Edward Gudeman and Senator Wallace F. Bennett of Utah. *Truth in Lending—1962* (Hearings before a Subcommittee of the Committee on Banking and Currency, U.S. Senate, 87th Cong. 2d sess. on S. 1740) (Washington, D.C.: U.S. Government Printing Office, May, 1962), pp. 45–51.

[3] See Robert W. Johnson "Methods of Stating Consumer Finance Charges," *Consumer Finance News,* April, 1961, p. 5.

an application for a Carte Blanche, received one, toured the country, checking into the best hotels, bought $2,000 worth of clothes, all on credit, of course, ran up a close to $10,000 account and then was caught. Carte Blanche, Joe said, seemed to promise to open up a new and magical world, and it did for a short time.[4] Go now and pay later. Eat and charge it. It's a newer way of life and if you become a professional or an organization man, you will probably join the ranks of the 2.5 million who currently carry general-purpose credit cards. The Big Three in this field are Diners' Club, American Express, and Carte Blanche (Hilton). More than a half billion dollars in credit is outstanding at any given time via credit cards.

You can rent a car, stay at a hotel or motel, dine at expense account restaurants, hire an African safari, put your horse up at a Las Vegas horse motel where oats are free, buy anything from a mink coat to a salami, take a plane trip, make a long distance phone call to Tokyo or Teheran or Tallahassee, buy gasoline, or obtain an advance of cash, all on credit cards. You can even play luncheon Russian roulette. A group of businessmen started it. Credit cards are laid face down on the table and the waiter picks one to pay the bill. Even culture comes via the credit card thanks to an arrangement between the American Ballet Theatre and Diners' Club.[5]

In addition to the general-purpose credit cards, there are millions of gasoline cards issued by the big oil companies; telephone credit cards from A.T.&T.; almost a million air travel cards of the Universal Air Travel Plan, which requires a deposit of $425 before you can charge plane tickets; and a quarter of a million railroad travel cards good on almost all U.S. railroads. Paying cash has almost become passé. Sometimes a merchant will examine a bill more carefully to see if it is counterfeit than he will the signature on a credit card to see if it is genuine.

Credit investigations are quite costly to the general-purpose credit card organizations, and they are now requiring a certain income level and upping their rejection rates. They cover costs and earn profits from both the annual fee charged members, now $8.00 for Diners, $10.00 for American Express, and $8.00 for Carte Blanche, and from the percentage deductions on the restaurant and other bills they pay on behalf of cardholders. Approximately three fourths of all general-purpose credit charges are made in restaurants, and this costs the restaurants

[4] "My $10,000 Credit Card Binge," *Life*, October 26, 1959, pp. 53–54.

[5] See Chapter 2, "The Rub in Aladdin's Lamp," in Hillel Black, *Buy Now, Pay Later* (New York: William Morrow & Co., 1961).

from 5 to 7 percent of the amounts billed. The credit card organizations deduct this when making payment. The restaurant which honors credit cards, therefore, is likely to have taken this charge into account in setting its prices. It is likely to be what one might term an "expense account" restaurant, more costly than less pretentious restaurants which do not honor credit cards.

If you lose a credit card it can be costly. The courts have generally been holding that a person losing a credit card is responsible for any bills run up by the finder unless the company is notified of the loss. A man lost his Texaco credit card. He was unaware of the loss. The finder ran up a bill for tires, gas, and oil, for a total of $569, before the card was confiscated by an alert Texaco dealer. Texaco sued the loser of the card for the $569 and won its case.[6]

THE INSTALLMENT PLAN

Commonly about a fifth of all retail sales are made on the installment plan. About one out of every two households has some installment debt. Young households are more likely to have installment debt. Over 70 percent of the households with heads between 18 and 34 years of age have installment debt.

In recent years it has become possible to buy anything from a baby carriage to a tombstone on the installment plan. As one sprightly author declared:

The ordinary life cycle in the United States starts with a lay-away plan in the baby department of a convenient store, wends its way past the diamond counter of a credit jeweler, finds shelter beneath an FHA mortgage and is eventually laid to rest in a time-payment cemetery plot. After that presumably, the terms are strictly cash.[7]

Generally, higher-priced consumer durables, such as automobiles, furniture, radio and television sets, washing machines, and refrigerators, have been the particular object of installment sales promotion, but the practice has now been extended even to clothing. In some

---

[6] For a discussion of legal aspects of credit card transactions see "The Credit Card— Its Legal Implications," in the 1963 *Credit Manual of Commercial Laws,* National Association of Credit Management, and also "The Tripartite Credit Card Transaction: A Legal Infant," by Donald H. Murphy and Alex C. McDonald, *California Law Review,* Vol. 48 (1960), pp. 459–500.

[7] See Penn Kimball, "Cradle to Grave on Easy Terms," *New York Times Sunday Magazine,* June 1, 1952, p. 15.

stores all sales are on installments, and in these so-called "borax houses,"[8] are to be found some of the dubious practices which plague the business. Frequently sellers try to hide the fact that they are engaging in the practice by giving the installment plan some such name as "Budget Plan" or "Thrift Plan."

The Hunt Goes Modern: Ride Now, Pay Later

LONDON, Oct. 19 (AP)—One of Britain's oldest fox hunts put the aristocratic sport of riding to hounds on the installment plan today.

"We feel it's in accord with modern trends," said Col. Sir Ralph Clarke, joint master of the Surrey and Burstow Hunt.

"We're very much against hunting being a rich man's sport," the colonel continued in an interview. "In fact, many of our members have very moderate means."

"Ten years ago," he acknowledged, "dues in installments would have been unthinkable."

Now one can join with very little down and the rest of the £40 ($112) annual membership fee spread out over the months.

The hunt also has started a family plan. For £65 ($182) husband and wife can belong. And children under 17 can come in for as little as £7 10s ($21)—all on the "never-never," as the installment plan is called in Britain.

"Sail Now—Pay Later" was the eye-catching headline in a newspaper,[9] indicative of the wide ranging appeal of installment selling. "Own this boat today . . . ten years sooner than you think." Signs with that intriguing message were displayed on many of the sleek craft, large and small, shown at the National Motor Boat Show at the New York Coliseum. The play-now–pay-later aspect of pleasure boating was a development sponsored by Yacht Finance, Inc., an independent finance company.

---

[8] The word "borax" needs explanation. "In every sizable industry—the American furniture manufacturers are no exception—there is a fringe element that seeks quick profits by shortcut routes. Their product sacrifices quality in order to appear at a low price. In the trade such products are known as 'borax,' which may be defined as 'cheaply built, second rate, sold to the buyer at his own risk.'

"The origin of the word is interesting. Years ago, borax companies asked people to save the wrappers on their products; these—the equivalent of the modern box-top—could be exchanged for furniture. So many hundred wrappers bought a chair; so many a table; so many a bed. The borax companies obtained this premium merchandise from the cheapest sources they could find, and the better factories spoke of it in contempt as 'borax.' The blunt description has persisted." From Max Hess, Jr., *Every Dollar Counts: The Story of the American Department Store* (New York: Fairchild Publications, Inc., 1962), p. 106.

[9] *New York Times,* January 24, 1957. The widespread use of installment buying and its relationship to the American standard of living are discussed in Clyde W. Phelps, *The Role of the Sales Finance Company in the American Economy,* Studies in Consumer Credit, No. 1 (Baltimore: Commercial Credit Co., 1954), pp. 11–31.

Financial Vulnerability

A simple checklist has been devised by Professor Bymers to test the financial vulnerability of installment debtors.[10] There are three questions to answer:

1. How much cash do you have available to meet emergencies?

Add what you have in savings accounts, in government savings bonds, and in your checking account. (You should consider the usual balance just before rather than just after payday.) This sum represents your liquid assets. Place a check in the A or F box.

A	F
More than $200 ☐	$200 or less ☐

2. How long are you committed to your present installment debt?

To figure this, add your outstanding installment debts, and divide the total by the annual installment debt payments. Annual installment debt payments equal the total of current monthly payments multiplied by 12; if you make weekly payments multiply by 52. Example:

$$
\begin{aligned}
\text{Balance due on car} &= \$1,230 \\
\text{Balance due on TV set} &= \underline{\quad 145} \\
\text{Total debt} &= \$1,375
\end{aligned}
$$

$$
\begin{aligned}
\text{Car payments per month} &= \$78 \\
\text{TV set payments per month} &= \underline{\quad 12} \\
\text{Total per month} &= \$90
\end{aligned}
$$

$$\$90 \times 12 = \$1,080$$
$$\$1,375 \div \$1,080 = 1.27+$$

If the result is less than 1 you can be out of debt in less than one year. Check the A box. If the result is more than one, as in the above example, it will take more than one year to liquidate your present installment debts. Check the F box.

A	F
Less than one year ☐	More than one year ☐

---

[10] See Gwen J. Bymers, *A Financial Checkup on the Use of Credit,* Cooperative Extension Service, New York State College of Home Economics, Cornell University, October, 1963. A free copy may be obtained by writing to Professor Bymers at Cornell University, Ithaca, New York.

3. How much of your annual income is committed to installment debt payments?

To obtain this figure, divide the annual installment debt payment total, obtained in 2 above, by your annual income after taxes. If installment debt payments take less than 20 percent, check the A box; if they take 20 percent or more, check the F box.

A   F

Less than 20%   [   ]   20% or more   [   ]

Three F checks mean "very vulnerable." Two F checks indicate vulnerability; either liquid assets are too small, or too large a portion of income is committed to debt repayment, or debt is likely to run too long. One F check may not be serious, while three A checks may indicate that the household can manage its installment debt without great difficulty.[11]

Protection for the Seller

Merchandise sold on the installment plan is usually paid for, with interest, in monthly installments which may range over a period of a year or more. Commonly the seller protects himself until he has received the total payment due by one of three formal written contracts: (a) the conditional sale, (b) the chattel mortgage, or (c) the bailment lease. All have a common purpose—to protect the installment seller against the buyer's general creditors or against innocent third-party purchasers from the buyer. Since a down payment is frequently received, which further protects the seller, sellers commonly allow very liberal terms on installment sales, but these are usually more costly than the buyer realizes.

Conditional Sales

If a conditional sales contract is used, and this is the most common type of arrangement, title remains with the seller until he has received payment in full. In the event that payments are not made when due, the goods may be repossessed. Money already paid may be regarded as rent for the use of the property, or the buyer may receive part of it back, depending on state law.

Installment sales are governed, in a number of states, by the Uniform

---

[11] For a more extended discussion see Gwen J. Bymers, *Time Commitment and Financial Position of Installment Debtors,* H.E.M. Research Report No. 7, Department of Household Economics and Management, Cornell University, February, 1963.

Conditional Sales Act. If the buyer has paid any substantial sum on the price at the time of his default, he is entitled to get that sum back, less the depreciation on the goods caused by wear and tear. The amount of depreciation will ordinarily be estimated by selling the goods a second time, frequently at auction, and seeing what they bring. Depreciation is the difference between what the installment seller sold the goods for originally and what the second, auction, sale brings in. For example, Smith bought a suite of furniture from a dealer on the installment plan for $600. He paid $100 down, got possession of the furniture, and agreed to pay the balance in 20 installments of $25 each. Title to the furniture was to remain with the seller until Smith paid the entire purchase price. After paying $200, Smith took sick, lost his position, and failed to make a payment which was due. The dealer took the furniture back. In a number of states the dealer can keep both the $300 Smith paid and the furniture. But not under the Uniform Conditional Sales Act. If the dealer, in a state in which the act is in force, sold it again at auction for $400, he would have to pay Smith $100, since the $300 he had received from Smith plus the $400 at the auction sale added up to $700, or $100 in excess of the original selling price of $600. Smith would lose $200 of his $300 paid because the furniture, as evidenced by the second sale, had depreciated $200.

An uninformed buyer, however, in the hands of a sharp seller, may not be able to discover what the furniture brings at the second sale; or the second sale may be rigged to establish a low price so that there need be no repayment. Only rarely does the defaulter recover what he has already paid on the conditional sales contract.

When the goods or property which have been sold under the installment plan have been repossessed and resold, the proceeds of resale applied to payment of the debt may not be sufficient to cover the total amount. To satisfy this deficiency, a judgment may be secured against the debtor through court action. Thus the installment buyer may lose not only the cash he has paid and the article purchased but additional amounts as well.

The seller, if he wishes to protect himself against the buyer's creditors and against innocent purchasers from the buyer, is obliged to file his contract in a public office, such as the country clerk's, in certain states. For example, Simpson, a radio dealer, sold Thompson a television set under a conditional sales contract but did not have the contract recorded in a public office, as required by statute. Thompson used the television set for a month and then sold it to Hillman. Hillman received good title to the set because Simpson, through his failure to record the contract, lost his rights in the television set when it came into the hands of an innocent third party.[12]

If the goods are damaged, lost, or destroyed while the conditional buyer is holding them and making his payments, the loss falls upon the buyer, under most contracts, and he must complete his payments. Since under these circumstances the buyer may have no financial means of meeting this obligation, the seller customarily protects himself through insurance, which is paid for by the buyer.

Chattel Mortgages

If a chattel mortgage is used, the buyer signs a promissory note or a series of promissory notes which are secured by the mortgage. In Massachusetts, which follows the old English law, the effect of the mortgage is to convey the legal title to the goods back to the seller for his protection. The seller not only gets back the legal title to the goods but a "power-of-sale" clause in the mortgage gives the seller the right to sell the goods at public auction if the notes are not met in due course. Money received from the sale of the goods is applied to the note or notes; and if it is not sufficient to satisfy them, the buyer (who made the notes) is liable for the deficiency. Upon parting with the legal title to the goods, the buyer retains only an equitable title, which is often called the "right of redemption."

In most of the other states the chattel mortgage does not convey the legal title back to the seller, but it does give the seller an equitable interest in the goods; this enables the seller to go into court and ask the judge to have the goods sold at Sheriff's sale for his benefit. Naturally, the buyer should be sure to receive back all paid notes, and he should also obtain and record a discharge of the mortgage if the mortgage was recorded at the county courthouse. Local newspapers sometimes make a practice of publishing such recordings—often to the discomfort of those who do not like their private business made public.

The Bailment Lease

In the bailment lease, seldom used except in Pennsylvania, title remains with the seller until the last payment has been made and then is purchased for a nominal sum, usually waived by the seller. Until then, the buyer has merely hired the goods for use. If the buyer cannot continue to meet the agreed-upon payments, the seller simply takes back his goods and keeps the previous payments, since legally they were

[12] See "The Things You Buy," in *You and the Law* (New York: Research Institute of America, 1962).

made for the use of the goods for the period. There is no need to return any part of installments previously paid as under the Uniform Conditional Sales Act.

Protection for the Buyer

Unfortunately the average buyer fails to protect himself by reading carefully and understanding thoroughly the papers he signs in many transactions, including installment sales. For no good reason at all, he feels embarrassed to take the necessary time to read a lengthy document in which a lot of important stipulations may appear in very fine print. For his own protection, he should most certainly read and understand before he affixes his signature to anything. It must always be remembered that sellers engage in many transactions of the installment type and obtain the services of able lawyers to see that they are protected to the utmost. The buyer engages in relatively few of these transactions and naturally does not know a great deal about them.

At times installment purchasers sign blank contracts even before the store fills in the amounts and special terms. If most installment purchasers read and understood their contracts, fewer people would buy on this basis, because the contracts often contain harsh provisions which both the sellers and the courts are loath to enforce. Installment sellers expect their customers to fall somewhat behind schedule in their payments. Trade custom usually results in a softening of installment contracts. A rule of thumb often heard in the installment trade is that the average customer will miss about one out of every four payments due. Furthermore, the courts do not look kindly upon the installment house which habitually hauls customers into court. Courts resent being called upon as collection agencies. Nevertheless, the installment contract usually so binds and ties the customer that losses are very low, less than one half of 1 percent of total sales.

Some aspects of installment contracts to watch out for are:

The Add-on Clause. Add-on, or open-end, contracts are something for the individual not to sign. This type of clause or contract is drawn to cover a succession of installment purchases and provides that the seller retains his title or mortgage on each article until the very last one is paid for. A thousand dollars' worth of house furnishings, bought over several years, might be seized because the customer failed to meet a $20 payment on a recently purchased $100 item.

The Wage Assignment. The most drastic form of security in the installment contract may be the wage assignment. An obscure clause may give the dealer power of attorney to collect all or part of the buyer's pay check or envelope if the buyer misses a payment. Most wage assignments are probably signed because the buyer does not know what he is signing. Long contracts in legal verbiage and fine type make it difficult for the buyer to read or understand the contract. The oversight may be encouraged if the document is headed simply "Contract" or "Chattel Mortgage" and fails to call the buyer's attention to the fact that he is signing away future wages. Wage-assignment abuses, like other shady practices, are restricted to a minority of installment dealers. That such abuses threaten the legitimate dealer as well as the unwary customer is indicated by the suggestion of the National Association of Sales Finance Companies that state laws prohibit any wage assignment made before actual default on the installment contract.

Originally the installment contract was used to sell only products for which there was a definite resale market. If an individual lagged behind in his payments on a piano or a car, the dealer could repossess and probably make up the unpaid balance by reselling the item. The merchandise itself was adequate security, until the installment dealers, trying to conquer new markets, made their terms so "easy" that often the unpaid balance exceeded the resale value of the article. At the same time, they went into new fields, selling "soft goods," such as clothing, for which resale value was either low or nil. Resale of a repossessed pair of pants brings little. As added security for deals such as these, the wage assignment came into prominence.

The legal process of attaching the debtor's wage is known as "garnishment" or "garnisheeing wages." By court order, the employer of the debtor is obliged to pay all or a certain percentage of the wages of the debtor (buyer) to the creditor (installment seller) until the debt is paid in full. Some states limit by law the percentage of a wage earner's salary which may thus be taken by a creditor at any given pay period (New York State, 10 percent) or prohibit assignment entirely under certain conditions. Wages below a certain small sum, as, for example, $12 a week, in most states are not subject to garnishment, it being deemed unwise to deprive the individual of the minimum amount necessary for living expenses. In some states, however, the entire pay envelope may be taken by the installment seller. Some employers dislike being bothered with legal forms and with the added bookkeeping routine involved in turning over wages to a creditor. They, therefore, fire employees whose wages are garnisheed.

The Acceleration Clause. This provides that a default in one payment makes all other payments immediately due and payable. If the buyer is dishonest, this drastic safeguard is necessary. But an honest buyer may miss a payment date because of an emergency, perhaps sickness in the family or a temporary layoff from the job. Unscrupulous dealers take advantage of the acceleration clause to swoop down and immediately repossess the car, or refrigerator, or television set, and cart it off for resale without notice.

Sales of repossessed merchandise, especially automobiles, offer an avenue of abuse. Frequently there is no requirement for public sale. Repossession when only one or two payments remain may wipe out the entire equity the purchaser has established. Ethical dealers find ways of avoiding such repossessions, but some firms, particularly in the used-car field, appear to specialize in repossession. They draw up contracts, such as those with "balloon clauses," which encourage delinquency and then, when a payment cannot be met, seize the car without notice and either sell it at a rigged sale or collect excessive fees for its return to the customer. In larger cities, in a number of states, dozens of cars are reported to the police as stolen, though in fact they have been repossessed without notice to the installment purchaser.

In many jurisdictions, collateral can be retaken without notice to the purchaser if it does not involve breach of the peace. Breaching the peace, in this connection, is generally interpreted as breaking into a garage, removing a car from a private driveway, or taking a car from a resisting installment buyer. When a purchaser in default will not surrender a car peacefully, a writ of replevin is served on him by the sheriff. In some states, if the collateral is retaken without notice to the purchaser, he may redeem the collateral within ten days after the retaking by tendering the amount due under the contract, together with any expenses incurred by the seller; but he frequently does not know about this legal right or may not have or be able to obtain the funds to take advantage of it.

The "Balloon Contract." A contract which has as its final installment a payment substantially in excess of the preceding installments is known as a "balloon contract." For example, the contract may call for eleven monthly installments of $25 each and one (the twelfth payment) of $300. This is a highly undesirable type of payment arrangement because total charges paid by the purchaser are higher because of the necessity of refinancing at least once and sometimes two or three times. To illustrate, an example cited by *Business Week* may be used. It should be noted that the balloon contract is usually found in the financing of automobiles.

Business Week stated:

Here's how a typical "$100 down and $40 a month" deal worked in Cleveland:

Advertised price of the car	$1,795.00
But a heater is necessary	60.00
So that the cost now stands at	1,855.00
Add state tax on $1,855	56.65
Add cost of title transfer, etc.	6.36
So the total cost is	1,918.00
The buyer is talked into paying	118.00
Leaving a balance to be financed of	1,800.00
Two years insurance	194.00
Which brings the price back to	1,994.00
Add interest at 6% and carrying charges for two years	269.00
And, as the owner drives away he owes	2,263.00

Notes are $40 a month (as advertised) for 23 months, with a "balloon note" for the balance falling due in the 24th month. So:

The buyer makes 23 monthly payments at $40 each	$ 920.00
And the balloon note amounts to	1,343.00

Meanwhile, the car has depreciated to perhaps $1,450 at the end of the first year, and perhaps in the same proportion during the second. At any rate, the owner can't afford to pay out $1,343 in a lump sum. So he refinances the 24th note for another two years. It works this way:

Amount of the balloon note	$1,343.00
Add another two years' insurance	181.00
Add interest and carrying charges for another two years	200.00
And the buyer starts paying again on	1,724.00

(Remember this is on a two-year-old car that was advertised at $1,795).

And so he makes 23 more payments at $40 each	$ 920.00
And he runs smack up against another balloon note this time for	804.00
(the car is now four years old)	
So he adds another two years insurance	120.30
And another two years interest and carrying charges	146.90
And he starts the fifth year paying on	1,071.60
So he makes 23 more payments of $40 each	920.00

And at the end of six years he finds (if he bothers to add it up) that he has paid out $2,878 in cash, that he still owes $151.60, and that his car is now worth perhaps $150.

Obviously, a balloon contract is something to avoid.

Hidden Clauses. At times an obscure clause in the contract you sign obligates you to buy something which you do not want and cannot possibly use. An example from the *American Legion Magazine* will make clear what is meant:

John and his wife needed a new refrigerator. John knew they needed it, but felt that they couldn't afford it until they had paid off on the car and a couple of other things. One Thursday evening, wifey inveigled John into an appliance store "just to look."

The companion of his joys and sorrows was just showing John one of the new Blank refrigerators, and he was saying that it was swell, but they still couldn't afford it, when Temptation reared its ugly head. Temptation took the form of a smooth-talking, high pressure salesman with a quarter-a-day meter in his hand. He explained that they could have one of these fine new super-de-luxe Blank refrigerators for just twenty-five cents a day. The refrigerator would be delivered with the meter attached, and all they had to do would be to drop a daily two bits into the slot in the meter. Simple. The refrigerator would run as long as the meter was fed, and a man would come around and empty the meter every month until the appliance was paid for.

So John fell. After all a quarter-a-day doesn't sound like much. Ummhmmmm. A quarter-a-day is over seven dollars a month—seven dollars they very definitely did not have to spare. But the things that the salesman didn't tell them (it was in a fine-type clause in the contract) and the thing that really burned John to a crisp when he found out about it, was the fact that along with the refrigerator, they were also buying the meter. Twenty bucks it cost them, about twice what it was actually worth. They didn't have to have a refrigerator, but the meter was absolutely useless after it had served its purpose.

Cost of Installment Financing

In one way or another a seller must be paid for financing the buyer who acquires goods on credit. The various expenses of investigation, collecting, bookkeeping, repossession, reconditioning, reselling, bad debts, and insurance must be covered either by an inflated price for the article sold, by separate fees and charges, or by inclusion in the charge of interest. Although a nominal rate of 5 or 6 percent may be quoted, analysis of the charges will reveal that the real rate is often far in excess —and it must be in order to cover the cost of the service rendered.

Suppose an article selling for $75 is sold with a 20 percent down payment, the balance to be paid in installments over a period of nine months. If a charge of 6 percent of $75 is made for the service rendered, it amounts to $4.50.

```
But the 1st  month the buyer has the use of $60.00
     "  2nd    "      "    "    "    "   "   "   "  53.33
     "  3rd    "      "    "    "    "   "   "   "  46.67
     "  4th    "      "    "    "    "   "   "   "  40.00
     "  5th    "      "    "    "    "   "   "   "  33.33
     "  6th    "      "    "    "    "   "   "   "  26.67
     "  7th    "      "    "    "    "   "   "   "  20.00
     "  8th    "      "    "    "    "   "   "   "  13.33
and  "  9th    "      "    "    "    "   "   "   "   6.67
```

Adding the money column, we find that, all told, the buyer had had the equivalent of the use of $300 a month, which is the equivalent of only $25 for a year. Now $4.50 interest on $25 for a year is $\frac{4.50}{25} \times 100 = 18$ percent, instead of the nominal 6 percent which was quoted.

This result may also be found by using the constant-ratio formula:

$$R = \frac{2mi}{P(n+1)}$$

$$R = \frac{2 \times 12 \times \$4.50}{\$60(9+1)}$$

$$R = \frac{\$108}{\$600} = 0.18 = 18 \text{ percent}$$

where R equals the annual rate charged; m equals the number of payment periods in one year (12 if you are repaying monthly; 52 if you are repaying weekly); i equals the true dollar cost of the credit; P equals the net amount of the balance to be paid; and n equals the number of installment payments you will make.

Another way to look at these figures intelligently is that if the buyer had the use of $60 the first month and only $6.666 during the ninth, he had the use of

$$\frac{\$60 + \$6.66}{2} = \frac{\$66.66}{2} = \$33.33$$

on the average for the nine-month period. Since $4.50 was paid for this accommodation (for nine months), it amounts to paying $6.00 for a year's use of an average amount of $33.33.

Now,

$$\frac{\$6}{\$33.33} \times 100 = \frac{\$600.00}{\$33.33} = 18 \text{ percent .}$$

Variations in Stating the Installment Cost

Broadly speaking, there are four main ways of representing the installment credit charge:[13]

1. There is the familiar "no charge for credit" used by credit jewelers and clothing and furniture houses. In this case the price of credit

---

[13] For further information see Robert W. Johnson, *Methods of Stating Consumer Finance Charges* (New York: Graduate School of Business, Columbia University, 1961).

is included in the price of the goods. A purchaser who offers cash instead of asking for time to pay can get the article for less than the stated price. How is the cost of the credit found in such a case? A piece of jewelry, for example, sells for $79, payable $9.00 down and $10.00 a month for seven months, with "no carrying charge." A cash customer can get the jewelry for $7.00 less, if he asks for the cash price. The cost of credit, therefore, is $7.00. Applying the constant-ratio formula:

$$r = \frac{2 \times 12 \times 7}{63 \times (7+1)} = \frac{1}{3} = 33\frac{1}{3} \text{ percent}.$$

The rate is, therefore, $33\frac{1}{3}$ percent a year as against the stated "no charge for credit."

2. A second method of representing the installment credit charge is merely to apply a nominal percentage charge to the unpaid portion of the price. For example, a jeweler requires a 10 percent down payment and adds a 6 percent charge to the unpaid portion of the price when payment is to be completed in 25 weekly installments. The amount of the down payment is immaterial. The plan is represented as a 6 percent one. Applying the formula:

$$r = \frac{2 \times 52 \times .06}{25 + 1} = 24 \text{ percent}.$$

The rate, therefore, is actually 24 percent rather than 6 percent, as represented.

3. The third method is where a flat charge in dollars is made rather than a percentage. For example, the cash price of a television set is $250; a down payment of $50 is required. There is a flat charge of $16 for the privilege of taking 15 months to pay. What is the rate which the purchaser is paying?

$$r = \frac{2 \times 12 \times 16}{200(15 + 1)} = 12 \text{ percent}.$$

The true annual rate is 12 percent.

4. The fourth method is the most complicated. It is sometimes found in automobile time financing. It calls for interest payable on monthly outstanding balances as well as the usual finance charge. Consider the following example in the case of a car purchase:

Original unpaid balance	$1,600
Charge	112
Note	$1,712

Interest is to be charged at 6 percent per annum, or one half of 1 percent a month on outstanding balances, and there are to be eight monthly payments of $214 plus the interest. The way the eight monthly payments run and the amount still outstanding is shown in the accompanying tabulation. The total cost consists of two items, the $112 charge and $38.52 of interest, or a total of $150.52. Applying the formula to find the true annual rate:

$$r = \frac{2 \times 12 \times 150.52}{1,600(8+1)} = 25 + \text{percent} \,.$$

| | PAYMENTS | | | OUTSTANDING | |
	PRINCIPAL	CHARGE	INTEREST	ON NOTE	ON ADVANCE
1	$ 200	$ 14	$ 8.56	$1,712	$1,600
2	200	14	7.49	1,498	1,400
3	200	14	6.42	1,285	1,200
4	200	14	5.35	1,070	1,000
5	200	14	4.28	856	800
6	200	14	3.21	642	600
7	200	14	2.14	428	400
8	200	14	1.07	214	200
	$1,600	$112	$38.52	....	....

The Time-Honored 6 Percent

Interest rates are often not given at all in installment contracts. When they are given, they are seldom what they seem. Usually they are disguised as forms of the time-honored 6 percent. In the course of the years, 6 percent has come for many people to be synonymous with "fair return." As one merchandiser put it, "Six percent has sex appeal for the customer."

When installment sellers, who are to be repaid in equal installments, state their charge (say 6 percent) as a percentage of the total unpaid balance at the start, since this balance is reduced by installment payments, the average balance outstanding during the term of the installment contract is only about half the original unpaid balance. Therefore, the true rate, in the absence of other manipulations and distortions, when payments are spread over a year, is roughly twice the stated rate.[14]

"One percent a month" appears to be a reasonable charge; but depending on the way it's calculated, it is much more than it seems. It is

[14] See "Beware The Interest Rate," *Reader's Digest*, November, 1963.

12 percent a year if levied on the new reduced unpaid balance each month; but if levied as a percentage of the total unpaid balance at the beginning of the contract, it is about 24 percent, since, over a year, the average balance outstanding is only half the original unpaid balance.

The Federal Trade Commission issued an order against the General Motors Corporation, its subsidiaries, and the Ford Motor Company to cease using the words "six percent," or the symbol "6%" in advertising installment payment plans for purchasing automobiles. The Commissioner found as a fact "that when the term '6%' is used in connection with monthly payments it is understood to mean 6% simple interest per annum, computed on the declining balance as reduced by the monthly payments." In the installment plan advertised, the purchaser paid 6 percent on the total amount originally owed, which resulted in a charge of approximately 11½ percent simple interest per annum on the declining balance instead of 6 percent interest, as was generally implied.

To determine whether credit terms were quoted accurately and whether students understood them, an interesting experiment was undertaken by Dr. Richard L. D. Morse, Professor and Head of the Department of Family Economics at Kansas State University. Students enrolled in the course in family finance were given a standardized problem to finance a used car. They were to contact a bank, a used car dealer, a consumer finance company, and a credit union.

The problem: Your family is buying a $500 used car in your local community.

You have $200 as a down payment, and you wish to finance the $300 in 12 monthly payments.

You have your own car insurance and do not need credit life insurance.

The question: How do credit vendors in your community answer these three basic questions:

What would be the monthly payments? $_____ per month.

What would be the total cost in dollars? $_____ per note.

What would be the credit cost, expressed as a simple annual rate on the money in use? _____% per year on unpaid balance.

Allowing a tolerance of plus or minus 3 percentage points in judging accuracy, 26 percent of the 104 banks and 17 percent of the 88 used car dealers quoted accurate rates: 52 percent of the 63 consumer finance companies and 72 percent of the 43 credit unions were within the tolerance level. Professor Morse found that "banks and used car dealers quoted accurate dollar cost figures but inaccurate rates, while consumer finance companies and credit unions quoted fairly good rate information."

The ability of students to detect errors varied both with their prejudices and with the correctness of the dealers' quotations. For example, only 26 percent of the banks' quotations were accurate within 3 percentage points, and only 14 percent were accurate within 1 percentage point. But because of faith in banks, 83 percent of the students felt that bankers' quotations were correct. The result was that only 38 percent of the students correctly detected the accuracy or inaccuracy of the bankers' quotations.

Dr. Morse drew two broad conclusions: First, those granting credit do not quote percentages or rates as precisely as would be desirable. Second, college students themselves were not as intellectually curious about the correctness of the calculated rates as one might expect.[15]

Hidden Charges

At times the finance charge is clearly and explicitly stated in installment contracts. More often it is only obscurely indicated and is accompanied by a variety of fees—reinstatement fees, adjusters' fees, extension fees, transfer fees, credit life insurance fee, repossession fees, reconditioning fees, etc.—all provided for in obscure clauses in the installment contract, but all equally unknown to the installment purchaser. Perhaps the one which is more often concealed than any other is the "pack" in automobile financing.

The "pack" is an amount arbitrarily added by an automobile dealer to the normal authorized finance charge called for by the finance company. It is kicked back to the car dealer by the finance company when the car buyer has made his last payment. This swollen finance charge is paid by the installment purchaser, who does not know that it is more than he needs to pay for credit and who also does not know that later the finance company will pay (kick) back the extra charge (the pack) to the dealer. The dealer is able to secure this extra charge because he is able to create competition among finance companies and banks for the installment purchaser's note. The dealer may have you sign the note promising to pay in installments to him, and then he may discount the note with the finance company or bank, or he may have you sign the note promising to pay a given finance company or bank. His ability to direct a volume of financing business to a favored finance company enables him to see to it that the favored company pays him back the

---

[15] Richard L. D. Morse and Theresa Courter, *Are Credit Terms Quoted Accurately?* Contribution #225, Department of Family Economics, Kansas Agricultural Experiment Station, Kansas State University, Manhattan, Kansas. See also *Consumer Finance News,* October, 1963.

extra sum, or "pack," which has been added to the regular finance charge. This extra charge or "pack" adds anywhere from 6 to 50 percent to the credit cost of buying cars on the installment plan.

An actual example supplied by *Business Week* of how the "pack" worked out for a Baltimore car buyer who took his case to the AAA follows:

He bought a new Ford custom coupé last year; the total cash price plus delivery was $3,075. He paid down $1,075. He thus owed the $2,000 plus $148.80 for insurance. Added to this was $515.20 in finance charges, bringing his total time balance to $2,664—which he agreed to pay off in 24 monthly instalments of $111 each. Meantime, the dealer had an agreement with the finance company. The company would take this contract, for example, at 6% per year of $2,148.80. For 24 months this came to $257.86. But the buyer was paying $515.20 in finance charges. So, when he paid off his last instalment, the finance company paid back to the dealer the difference between $515.20 and $257.86— or $257.34.

The Role of the Sales Finance Company

You may sign an installment agreement to purchase an automobile from a dealer only to find that you must make your payments to a finance company. Often you are immediately told of the arrangement; sometimes you are not. The reason the dealer utilizes a finance company is that in many cases he does not have sufficient capital of his own to finance the volume of business he can do if he sells on time. Therefore, he uses a finance company, which pays him at the time the car is sold, thus replenishing his capital while, at the same time, financing the extension of credit to the purchaser. The finance company extends the credit and relieves the dealer of this obligation, thus freeing his capital for more rapid turnover.

There is nothing alarming about finding yourself in debt to the finance company rather than to the dealer. There are nearly 6,000 sales finance companies and offices operating throughout the country holding more than one fourth of all consumer installment paper outstanding. They account for more than one half of the total automobile paper and about one tenth of other durable goods paper. The finance company is most prominent in automobile financing. The giants in the field are General Motors Acceptance Corporation, which finances General Motors cars; CIT Financial, which finances Ford cars, grants home-modernization loans, and finances other consumer durable sales; Commercial Credit Corporation, which finances Chrysler cars; and Associates Investment Company, which finances miscellaneous auto paper. Sears Roebuck has established the Sears Roebuck Acceptance Corporation. Some 50 percent of Sears' $5 billion annual sales volume is handled on credit, whereas only 5 percent was a quarter of a century ago. All these companies are well-established, reputable concerns which treat installment debtors fairly and make (as installment costs go) only reasonable charges. It is often better to deal directly with one of these companies than with some unscrupulous dealers.

Finance companies are anxious to have an absolute promise to pay from the purchaser, which cannot be impaired by any disputes or claims between the dealer and the purchaser. Frequently, however, the purchaser will not find servicing or repairs satisfactory, or he will claim he received an inferior or damaged product and will, therefore, refuse to pay. To guard against this, the finance companies have employed a variety of devices. One attempt to deal with the problem has been to provide in the conditional sales contract that the purchaser will settle all claims with the dealer directly and will not set up any such claim in an action brought by the finance company. The courts, however, have been loath to enforce such a clause. Another attempt to deal with it has been the use of the negotiable promissory note, which the purchaser is asked to sign along with the conditional sales contract.

The use of the negotiable note with the conditional sales contract is generally held to cut off defenses and claims which the purchaser might have against the dealer, thus achieving the finance company's purpose. Recently, however, the courts have held against the finance companies where the purchasers had legitimate grievances, and several states have forbidden by law the use of negotiable notes with installment sales contracts. Generally speaking, if the finance company is a legitimate one, the purchaser, by stopping payment when his grievances against the dealer are proper and justifiable, can get the finance company to exert pressure on the dealer to take care of the purchaser's grievances. In this way a time purchaser may often, through the threat of stopping payment, secure better dealer servicing than a cash purchaser. On the other hand, there is the danger of a quick repossession.[16]

---

[16] For more details on the operation of sales finance companies see Clyde W. Phelps, *Installment Sales Financing: Its Services to the Dealer* (Baltimore: Commercial Credit Co., 1953), p. 99, and Walter S. Seidman, *Accounts Receivable and Inventory Financing* (Ann Arbor: Masterco Press, 1957). See also *Financing Small Business* (Report to the Committees on Banking and Currency and the Select Committees on Small Business by the Federal Reserve System, 85th Cong., 2d sess.) (Washington, D.C.: U.S. Government Printing Office, 1958).

Controversy Over the Cost of Credit

For several years Senator Paul H. Douglas of Illinois has been urging Congress to pass a law that would require disclosure of finance charges in connection with extensions of credit. The object seems to be reasonable, but there has been heavy opposition to the bill.

In a speech before Congress, in introducing his bill, Senator Douglas declared:

The consumer is faced with a bewildering and indeed incomprehensible variety of rate statements and charges when he borrows money or buys an article on the installment plan.

For example, a consumer who desires to obtain credit for a $100 purchase to be repaid in monthly installments is usually confronted with one of the following alternatives:

First, no rate is quoted: The borrower is told that the charges will be $10 down and $10 a month. Neither the total finance charges nor the finance rate is disclosed.

Second, the add-on rate: The borrower is told that the finance charge will be $6 on the $100 loan. The lender represents this to the borrower as being a 6 percent rate. This quoted rate is a play on the digit 6. The actual rate is almost 12 percent, or nearly double the stated rate, because a borrower over a period of the year only has the use of approximately $50 credit rather than the $100 face amount.

In other words, the interest rate is quoted on the original amount of the debt and not on the declining or unpaid balance as is the custom in business credit, government loans, or consumer mortgage transactions.

Third, the discount rate: This is a variation of the add-on rate. In the case of the add-on the borrower receives $100 in cash or goods and must pay back $106. In the case of the discount technique the borrower receives $94 but repays $100. The finance charge again is $6 and is often represented as being 6 percent. Again, the actual rate is almost 12 percent, or twice the quoted rate because the borrower is periodically repaying the loan.

Fourth, a simple monthly rate: This rate statement method is usually quoted by small loan companies and by retailers using revolving credit plans. The finance rate is represented as being 1, 2, 3, or 4 percent per month. The simple annual rate in this case is 12 times the quoted figure, or 12, 24, 36, or 48 percent per year.

Fifth, add-on or discount plus fee system: Sometimes lenders compound the camouflaging of credit by loading on all sorts of extraneous fees, such as exorbitant fees for credit life insurance, excessive fees for credit investigation, and all sorts of loan processing fees which rightfully should be included in the percentage rate statement so that any percentage rate quoted is completely meaningless and deceptive.

Looking at these credit practices another way, how many customers are aware that—

The small service charge of 1½ percent per month on department store charge accounts is often a true annual interest rate of 18 percent.

The 3 percent per month plan of small loan companies is really 36 percent per year.

The 4½ percent new car financing plan of some commercial banks is really 9 percent per year.

The advertised 5 percent rate on home improvement loans is not less than a 6 percent first mortgage—but nearly twice as much or about 10 percent per year.

The so-called 6 percent rate for financing used cars offered by some dealers is at least 12 percent per year and sometimes very much higher—18 to 25 percent per year or more.

The cost of teenage credit now being promoted by some retailers as only "pennies per week" is sometimes as high as 80 percent per year.

Senator Douglas' opponents reply that no one objects to having the finance charge stated in dollars and cents but that in some cases, as in revolving charge accounts, it is not possible to state the charge as a simple annual rate without laborious and involved calculations. The First National City Bank of New York[17] noted:

Simple interest is not so simple as it sounds. . . . Mathematicians have devised ways to get closer to a true interest rate equivalent. All these methods are somewhat laborious, and beyond the competence of most people handling installment credit. The closest approach to exactitude can be reached by the calculus of finite differences, a specialized area of mathematics familiar only to professional actuaries, and teachers and students of higher mathematics.

To assist Senator Douglas in his objective of having a simple annual rate stated in installment contracts, the Savings Banks Association of New York State developed a "Quick Credit Cost Computer," a small cardboard slide rule affair which is quite simple to use. Across the top, on both sides, is printed a range of amounts from $100 to $600 on one side, from $600 to $4,000 on the other side, which can be either "Cash You Get When You Borrow" or "Price of Article Less Down Payment." The movable slide rule contains a range of monthly payments, from $8 to $120 on the first side, from $18 to $240 on the other side. You are instructed to pull the slide until the "Monthly Payment" you are asked to make lines up with the appropriate "Price of Article Less Down Payment." Opposite the "months-to-pay" row, which on one side covers 6, 9, 12, 18, and 24 months, and on the other 18, 24, 30, and 36 months, there appears in the appropriate window the "True Interest Rate" you are asked to pay. For example, if you are asked to pay $18.20 a month for the next 12 months and the price of the article you buy less down payment is $200, you move the slide until $18.20 lines up with $200 and you will note that in the 12-months-to-pay row

[17] "The Complexities of Simple Interest," First National City Bank of New York, *Monthly Letter*, March, 1962, pp. 32–35.

17 percent has appeared in the window. This is the approximate true interest rate.[18]

Professor Johnson has argued that if the Douglas Bill were enacted, competition might center on the financing rates offered the consumer. Dealers in automobiles and other consumer durables and those engaged in home repair and modernization, could, he felt, easily drive the finance charge into the cash price of the product or service. As a result they might quote very low financing rates. For example, assume that the cash price of a used car is $800. With a down payment of $200, the principal amount to be financed would be $600. On a two-year contract with an add-on finance charge of 9 percent per year, the dollar finance charge would be $108, and the time balance, $708. The annual rate of charge is about 17.5 percent. With the advent of rate competition, Professor Johnson believes, the dealer would raise his cash price to $887, an increase of 11 percent. A down payment of $200 would leave a principal amount to be financed of $687. The addition of a finance charge of only $21 would bring the time balance to $708, as before. But now the dealer is in a position to advertise low financing rates of less than 3 percent per annum. Given the wide variety in the quality of used cars and allowances granted on trade-in, Professor Johnson feels it would be unlikely for the consumer to detect the additional 11 percent added to the cash price, especially when other dealers may be following the identical practice.[19]

Installment Credit Costs versus Bank Credit Costs

Each semester we have asked our students to sample four installment sellers and one bank. We have suggested that they represent themselves as actual purchasers (as a borrower in the case of the bank) and obtain the actual installment terms in order to compute the exact cost of buying on the installment plan. They have been asked to compare these costs with the cost of a personal loan from a large New York commercial bank. The conclusion which has emerged, inescapably, from such surveys is that in almost all cases it is much less expensive to borrow from the large New York commercial bank and then use the money to make a cash purchase than it is to buy on the installment plan. Over a year, the cost of the bank loan ranges from 8 to 12 percent, depending on the particular bank, while the cost of installment credit runs from

---

[18] To obtain a copy of the "Quick Credit Cost Computer" write to Savings Banks Association of New York State, 200 Park Avenue, New York, N.Y., 10017.

[19] See Robert W. Johnson, "Methods of Stating Consumer Finance Charges," in *Consumer Finance News,* April, 1961, p. 5.

10 to 45 percent, depending on the article and the store.[20] Even in the case of automobile loans financed by a large and legitimate finance company, bank loans may be cheaper.

This conclusion was confirmed by several surveys which found that banks charged the lowest rates; national sales finance companies were a close second; and local finance companies charged the highest rates.[21]

A typical bank or national sales finance company transaction ran somewhat as follows: A man bought a $3,200 car, received a $1,200 trade-in allowance on his old car, and paid $400 down. The amount financed therefore is the unpaid balance of $1,600 plus $34 for "package insurance," or a total of $1,634, and the finance charge for a 24-month contract, on a 6 percent add-on basis, is $196.24, making the amount of the note $1,830.24. Under the constant-ratio method, the effective annual rate would be 11.5 percent, as follows:

$$R = \frac{2\ mi}{P(n + 1)}$$

$$R = \frac{2 \times 12 \times 196.24}{1,634 \times 25}$$

$$= \frac{4,709.76}{40,850.00}$$

$$= 0.1153, \text{ or } 11.53 \text{ percent .}$$

It is least expensive to pay cash; but if you must take time to pay, it is usually less costly to get a bank loan. If you do buy on the installment plan, be sure you ask yourself the questions shown in Figure 3–3.

Credit Life Insurance

A purchaser on the installment plan is often required to buy (a) credit life insurance and (b) credit disability insurance. The purpose is to protect the seller or his finance company in case the buyer dies or becomes disabled and cannot continue to pay off installments due. Credit life insurance is written in two forms, individual policies and group policies. Group now represents 78 percent of all credit life insur-

---

[20] The consumer, of course, needs to compare not only the rates but also the services given for the rates charged. Some two-dozen services which may or may not be offered by a financing service in connection with the rate it charges for installment credit are enumerated in Clyde W. Phelps, *Using Installment Credit,* Studies in Consumer Credit, No. 4 (Baltimore: Commercial Credit Co., 1955), pp. 29–32.

[21] See "Personal Finance: Shopping for Auto Credit," *New York Times,* October 28, 1963, p. 42, and Board of Governors of the Federal Reserve System, "Automobile Installment Credit Terms and Practices," Supplement III, pp. 141–69 in *Consumer Installment Credit,* Part I, Vol. II, "Growth and Import" (Washington, D.C., March, 1957).

ance in force. On group policies, yearly premiums vary from about 39 to 49 cents per $100 of original loan in the first policy year—somewhat lower in policy renewal years. This cost is either (1) passed on to borrowers as a specific charge, (2) passed on to borrowers through an increase in the charge for credit, or (3) absorbed as an operation expense.

FIGURE 3–3

Before You Sign

Here are some of the questions the instalment buyer should ask himself—and the dealer—before he signs on the dotted line:

{1} What will the credit actually cost me in money? What rate of interest is charged?

{2} Are all the dollars and cents figures in the contract correct? Are there any blank spaces to be filled in later?

{3} What are the insurance charges, if any? What insurance is actually provided?

{4} To whom will I owe the payments?

{5} What penalty charges may be imposed for late payment? Are there any other extra charges?

{6} Do I have a right to fair notice before the merchandise can be repossessed? What repossession charges may be collected?

{7} What security have I given? Does the security include other merchandise previously bought? Does it include a wage assignment?

{8} What legal safeguards and guaranties have I waived?

{9} Do terms in fine print commit me to additional obligations?

{10} Is there provision for a fair refund on carrying charges if early payment is made?

In most instances the seller passes the premium cost on to the installment purchaser. In some cases the seller keeps from 40 to 80 percent of the insurance fee he charges the buyer. This is obviously unfair to the buyer and is a sort of "pack," but unless the state law provides protection, there is little the buyer can do about this extra charge. One solution, obviously, is to pay cash. Then no insurance charge can be imposed.

The Discount Houses

A type of retailer who does provide substantial savings for cash has developed over the past decade in the large cities and their suburbs. These retailers are known as "discount houses."

You will find at least one, and often several, of these thriving stores in each of the larger cities. Korvette in New York; Faber Benson in Washington, D.C.; Phil's Distributors in Wilmington, Delaware; Shopper's World in the Chicago area; and Master's Mart in Los Angeles are a few examples. These discount houses sell nationally advertised, first-quality, standard merchandise, especially consumer durables and home appliances. They offer such merchandise as radios, television sets, pressure cookers, photographic equipment, baby carriages and baby furniture, toasters, electric mixers, electric shavers, watches, typewriters, records, sporting equipment, washing machines, air conditioners, refrigerators, and auto equipment and tires at discounts ranging from 15 to 30 percent.

One of our students started his term report, "Discount Houses in New York City," as follows:

This report is quite valuable and worth, at least to one person, $17.95! That amount was saved when I bought this Smith-Corona Silent Portable on which I am now typing.

Seventeen dollars and ninety-five cents represents the difference between the cost of this typewriter at Macy's ($94.70) and Master's Discount House ($76.75). Macy's was the lowest priced department store for this machine. Bloomingdale's and Gimbel's sell it for the regular list price of $100.37. Master's charged only 81% of Macy's price and 77% of the list price.

Prior to my investigation and gathering of material for this report, I was hesitant about the idea of buying from a discount house. Now, however, it seems to me that thousands of bargains are to be bought at a discount under list price if one is willing to go to these places.

Initially you might have found the discount store in a shabby part of town in cheap quarters in a second-story loft. Today there are 2,400 stores, doing $5 billion gross. Many have become huge, luxurious affairs in prime locations. With the elimination of weaker stores, chains such as E. J. Korvette, Kresge's K-Mart, Woolworth's Woolco, Kings, and Zayre's have come to dominate the discount scene. How do these houses manage to sell at from 15 to 30 percent less than regular retailers? They trim costs; they sell at lower margins; they ignore price-fixing stipulations, which usually provide very ample margins; they do a greater volume in fewer items than many department stores and thereby have lower unit costs; they have a large following because of their attractive discounts; they may sell only for cash; and they handle durable, standard, nonperishable, nonstyle-obsolescent, brand merchandise. They carry smaller inventories, reordering as needed more frequently. Basically they operate on a combination of higher volume and lower markups. Some of the larger houses now provide almost all the services of a full-scale department store. The more reputable discount houses usually provide a manufacturers' guaranty on brand items.[22] If there is a legitimate discount house in your town, it is worth investigating.

The Regulation of Installment Selling

Regulation of installment selling falls into two categories: (*a*) federal regulation of unfair practices, and (*b*) state regulation.

Federal regulation of unfair trade practices is largely the responsibility of the Federal Trade Commission. For example, the Commission drafted "trade practice rules covering the automobile 'pack' and related practices." It declared: "The primary purpose of the trade practice rules is to provide for the elimination and prevention of concealed 'packing' and other related practices in the financing of motor vehicles." The rules provide that the seller must furnish the purchaser with the following detailed itemization of his cost in the installment purchase of a motor vehicle:

a) The cash delivered price, including specified extras.
b) The amount allowed in trade-in or down payment or both.
c) The amount unpaid on the cash selling price, which includes item (*a*) less item (*b*).
d) The cost of insurance, the coverage provided, and the party or parties to whom the insurance is payable.
e) The amount of official fees charged.
f) The amount of unpaid balance to be financed (sums of items [*c*], [*d*], [*e*]).
g) The finance charge.
h) The time balance owed by the buyer to the seller (sum of item [*f*] and item [*g*]), the amount and number of installments to be paid, and the time covered.

Under the Commission's rules, it is an unfair trade practice to conceal or to fail or refuse to disclose in a written agreement any of the items enumerated above.[23]

In its regulation of advertising of shell homes the Commission

---

[22] See "What to Expect in Discount Stores," *Changing Times, The Kiplinger Magazine,* April, 1963, p. 6.

[23] For a detailed description of the fair trade practice rules promulgated see *Trade Practice Rules Relating to the Retail Instalment Sale and Financing of Motor Vehicles,* promulgated by the Federal Trade Commission, Washington, D.C., February 6, 1961.

states: "If an interest rate is quoted in advertising, it must be a simple interest per annum calculated on the basis of the unpaid balance due as reduced after crediting installments as paid." It also requires:

If a home is advertised at a quoted price under an installment plan which requires additionally the payment of interest, carrying charges, down payment, or premiums for credit life insurance, the fact that such costs are to be added to the advertised price must be clearly disclosed. If monthly payments are quoted, the duration of the payments must be disclosed. Additionally, if terminal payments are significantly larger than the advertised monthly payments required, this fact must also be clearly disclosed as well as the amount thereof.[24]

Starting with Indiana in 1935, some 31 states have passed legislation concerned with regulating installment selling in the interest of consumers.[25] The Indiana statute applies to all lines of installment selling. Under it, Indiana's State Department of Financial Institutions is empowered to set maximum finance charges for various lines of installment merchandise. Maximum penalties which may be assessed for late payments are prescribed. Minimum rates of rebate for prepayment of installments are required, not only on the finance charge but also on the insurance charge. The "add-on" clause is outlawed. A Wisconsin statute is restricted to the automobile business. Dealers, salesmen, finance companies, and manufacturers' representatives are licensed by the state, and a license is subject to revocation if the dealer wilfully defrauds any retail buyer or if he fails to furnish him with required information. The seller must give the buyer a complete copy of the installment contract, listing the cash sale price, down payment, trade-in allowance, amount of each installment payment, an exact statement of the insurance coverage in force, and the difference between the cash and the time price. Buyers have the right to complain to the State Banking Department if they think their contracts are unfair. Several thousand adjustments have been secured by the Department for installment purchasers.

New York State passed a Motor Vehicle Retail Installment Sales Act, and a Sales Finance Companies' Licensing Act in 1956, and a Retail Installment Sales Act in 1957. Both the Motor Vehicle Law and the Retail Installment Sales Act, which cover all goods other than motor vehicles, set ceilings on credit charges which installment sellers may ask. For example, on cars the credit service charge may not exceed the following per $100 of principal balance:

---

[24] *"Guides for Advertising Shell Homes,"* Federal Trade Commission, Washington, D.C., April 25, 1962.

[25] See *State Statutes Regulating Retail Instalment Sales* (Chicago: Commerce Clearing House, Inc., 1963).

a) For new cars—not more than $7.00 a year.

b) For used cars of the current model year or two previous model years— not more than $10 a year.

c) For all other used cars—not more than $13 a year.

Credit service charges for goods, other than motor vehicles, may not exceed $10 per $100 where the principal balance is $500 or less. Where the principal balance exceeds $500, only $8.00 per $100 can be charged on the excess over $500. In addition to limits on credit charges, the laws also provide for delivery of contracts, full disclosure of all terms and charges, and refunds on prepayments. Examples of full disclosure of the financial terms of the installment transaction as required under the law in the case of a conditional sales contract may be seen in Figure 3–4.

FIGURE 3–4

(For use by retail motor vehicle seller. Cash Sale Price $3,000 or less, non-business use.)

RETAIL INSTALMENT CONTRACT
(CONDITIONAL SALES CONTRACT)

Form MV 1

DATE:

BUYER(S): (Please print or type)

Residence if individual or partner (include town or city) Principal place of business if association or corporation

SELLER(S):

Address (principal place of business)

MOTOR VEHICLE HEREBY SOLD:

Used	Yr.	Make	Body Type Tonnage if Truck	Model No.	Serial No.	Motor No.
New						

......Heater, ...Radio, ...Auto. Transmission, ... Power Steering, ... Power Brakes, Other ......
Location if differs from Buyer(s) above address......
Property described on any att_ched schedule (s) also hereby sold.

STATEMENT OF TRANSACTION

Date of Sale...... 19......

Cash Price . . . . $ ......
Down Payment:
  Cash . . . . . . $ ......
  Trade-in: ...... $ ......
  Total Down Payment . . . . . $ ......

Unpaid Balance to Be Financed . . . $ ......
Insurance Premiums to Be Financed:
  Liab. & Prop. Damage...... mos. $ ......
  Compr. & Coll. $ ...... ded. ...... mos. $ ......
  ...... mos. $ ......
  ...... mos. $ ......
Total Insurance. . . . . . . $ ......
  To be procured by ☐ Buyer, ☐ Seller.
  Agent ......
Other Charges (itemize) Official Fees ...... $ ......
...... $ ......
Total to Be Financed (Principal Balance) . . $ ......
Finance (Credit Service) Charge . . $ ......
Amount Payable (NOTE) (Time Balance) . . $ ......
Time Sale Price (Time Balance plus Total Down Payment) . . . . $ ......

BUYER(S) HEREBY AGREE(S) TO PAY:

$ ...... evidenced by NOTE of even date, payable in ...... equal consecutive monthly installments of
$ ...... each, and ...... installment(s) of
$ ...... each, all payable the same date of each month beginning ......, 19......;
also including obligations described below.
Payable at Seller(s)' address or other address of which notified.

NOTICE TO THE BUYER

1. Do not sign this contract before you read it or if it contains any blank space.
2. You are entitled to a completely filled in copy of this contract when you sign it.
3. Under the law, you have the following rights, among others:
  (a) To pay off in advance the full amount due and to obtain a partial refund of the credit service charge;
  (b) To redeem the property if repossessed for a default;
  (c) To require, under certain conditions, a resale of the property if repossessed.

Liability insurance coverage for bodily injury and property damage caused to others is not included, unless noted.

(Second half of contract omitted.)

Most of the states with laws regulating installment selling require that the installment contract be in writing and that the buyer be given a dollar itemization of price, down payment, finance charges, and insurance or other charges, if any. A number of states require the installment seller to refund a portion of the finance charges whenever the buyer prepays his contract in full.

SUGGESTED READINGS

1. Hillel Black, *Buy Now, Pay Later.* New York: William Morrow & Co., 1961.
2. Robert W. Johnson, *Methods of Stating Consumer Finance Charges.* New York: Graduate School of Business, Columbia University, 1961.
3. *Truth in Lending—1962,* Hearings before a Subcommittee of the Committee on Banking and Currency, U.S. Senate, 87th Cong., 2d sess. Washington, D.C.: U.S. Government Printing Office, May, 1962.
4. "Beware the Interest Rate," *Reader's Digest,* November, 1963.
5. "The Complexities of Simple Interest," First National City Bank of New York, *Monthly Letter,* March, 1962.
6. David Caplovitz, *The Poor Pay More.* New York: Free Press of Glencoe, 1963.
7. Paul Smith, *Cost of Providing Consumer Credit.* National Bureau of Economic Research, 1962.
8. Clyde W. Phelps, *Retail Credit Fundamentals.* 4th ed. St. Louis: International Consumer Credit Association, 1963.
9. E. L. Burland, "Revolving Credit Plans in Retailing," *Proceedings* of the National Consumer Credit Conference, 1959.
10. Lewis E. Davids, "Credit Cards and Consumer Credit," *Consumer Finance News,* Vol. XLVII (April, 1963).
11. Clyde W. Phelps, *Financing the Installment Purchases of the American Family,* Studies in Consumer Credit, No. 3. Baltimore: Commercial Credit Co., 1954.
12. "How They Size You Up For Credit," *Changing Times, The Kiplinger Magazine,* July, 1960.
13. Clyde W. Phelps, *Using Installment Credit,* Studies in Consumer Credit, No. 4. Baltimore: Commercial Credit Co., 1955.
14. *Finance Facts Yearbook,* Educational Services Division, National Consumer Finance Association, Published annually. A free copy may be obtained by writing to the Association at 1000 Sixteenth Street, N.W., Washington 36, D.C.
15. Morris R. Neifeld, *Neifeld's Manual on Consumer Credit.* Easton, Pa.: Mack Publishing Co., 1961.
16. Sarah C. Wang, *Problems in Implementing Full Disclosure of Consumer Credit Cost.* Honolulu: Economic Research Center, University of Hawaii, 1962.
17. Carl A. Dauten, *Financing the American Consumer,* Consumer Credit Monograph No. 1. St. Louis: The American Investment Company, 1956.

18. "All About Credit," *Changing Times, The Kiplinger Magazine,* March, 1963.

19. Gwen J. Bymers, *A Financial Checklist on the Use of Credit.* Ithaca, N.Y.: New York State College of Home Economics, Cornell University, 1963. A free copy may be obtained by writing to Professor Bymers.

20. Richard L. D. Morse and Theresa Courter, *Are Credit Terms Quoted Accurately,* Contribution #225. Manhattan, Kan.: Department of Family Economics, Kansas Agricultural Experiment Station, Kansas State University. See also *Consumer Finance News,* October, 1963.

21. Emil Leffler (ed.), *Proceedings, Fourth Michigan Consumer Credit Conference.* Albion, Mich.: Albion College, 1955.

22. Board of Governors of the Federal Reserve System, *Consumer Installment Credit,* 6 Vols., 4 Parts. Washington, D.C., 1957.

23. *Consumer Credit Guide: Know Your Legal Rights When You Pay on Time,* New York State Banking Department, 100 Church Street, New York 7, N.Y., May, 1963.

CASE PROBLEMS

1. Visit the largest local department store that has a revolving credit plan. Ascertain the price of a household appliance (*a*) if bought for cash, (*b*) if bought under the revolving credit plan. Using the "Quick Credit Cost Computer,"* determine the true annual interest rate being charged. Then visit the store's credit manager and discuss with him whether he agrees with your conclusion as to the true annual rate you are being charged. If he does not agree what are his reasons? Do you think they are sound or not? Why?

2. Visit your local Buick or Chevrolet dealer and obtain enough information on costs for a time purchase to fill out in detail the GMAC form shown below. From the data on this form, compute the true annual cost of the time purchase on a percentage basis. Do you believe you might obtain better terms or service elsewhere?

GMAC MEMO WORK SHEET

CASH SALE PRICE (including Sales Tax, if any)	$ *2244* (1)
INSURANCE TERRITORY CHARGE—Chart No. *2* COLLISION DED. $ *86*	$ *86* (2)
TOTAL (Add Items 1 and 2)	$ *2330* (3)
DOWN PAYMENT, $ *300* (Net Trade-in) , $ *200* (Cash)	$ *500* (4)★
UNPAID BALANCE (Subtract Item 4 from 3)	$ *1830* (5)

	Unpaid Balance	Amt. of Contract	Monthly Payments
Complete from payment charts if Unpaid Balance financed requires the use of $1 to $10 Adjustment Figures.	$_____	$_____	$_____
	$_____	$_____	$_____
	$_____	$_____	$_____
TOTALS	$_____	$_____	$_____

FINANCE CHARGE	$_____ (6)
AMOUNT OF CONTRACT—PAYABLE IN *36* INSTALMENTS $_____ (7-A)★ (Obtain from GMAC Payment Chart)	$_____ (7)★
TOTAL TIME PRICE (Add Items 4 and 7)	$_____ (8)★

GMAC 120 200M-12-49 ★ Copy These Figures on Contract.

---

* A free copy may be obtained by writing to the Savings Bank Association of New York State, 200 Park Avenue, New York, N.Y., 10017.

3. Select either (*a*) a given standard-model television set, or (*b*) a standard-model electric refrigerator, or (*c*) a window air conditioner, and visit 10 stores or dealers, both cash and credit. Ask the basic price, the charge for purchasing under an installment plan, and installation costs for (*a*) or (*b*) or (*c*). Finally, compute the annual cost rate for the installment offers and compare these with the cash offers. What conclusions do you draw from this study?

4. On the purchase of a piano at a price of $485, Carey (the purchaser) makes a down payment of $125 and finances the remainder, $360. He signs a sales contract wherein he agrees to repay the $360 in 20 equal monthly installments of $18 each, plus a "service" charge of $2 per month. What is the real annual installment financing rate? Is this a fair charge for the service rendered?

5. A diamond ring is advertised at a price of $125, $5 down and 24 weekly payments of $5 each, with "no carrying charges." Inquiry by Grant discloses that the ring can be purchased for $100 cash. What is the true annual interest rate? Would you be willing to pay such a rate for the accommodation?

6. The Bon Ton Department Store advertised a standard-make refrigerator for $240 cash. This article may also be purchased on an installment plan, the terms of which are:

a) Down payment—25 percent of cash price.
b) Charges—½ of 1 percent per month on the original balance financed, payable with and in addition to the down payment.
c) Contract terms—balance financed payable in 12 equal monthly payments.

What is the total amount of the credit service charge? What is the annual cost rate? Would you be willing to purchase on such terms?

7. Griffin purchases an automobile costing $2,600 on time. Down payment is to be $500; financing charge is $200. Interest is to be charged in addition at the rate of ½ of 1 percent per month on outstanding balances. Repayment is to be over 30 months. What is the annual cost rate? Would you consider this rate satisfactory?

8. Jim and Mary, newlyweds, are about to buy furniture for their apartment. They can make a substantial down payment, but in addition they need credit amounting to $300. They figure they can pay this balance in 10 months. The store where they plan to make their main purchases figures that the monthly payments will have to be $33. They consider the possibility of borrowing the money and paying cash. A small loan company in the neighborhood offers rates of 2 percent a month. A bank offers such loans at a 6 percent discount with an added $2 fee for investigation. Assuming that they can get the credit at either place, what is your advice to Jim and Mary? Support your conclusions with annual-rate and dollar-cost figures.

9. Clark can discount his note for $500 for a year at a bank at 6 percent. He can buy a television set for $500, no money down, balance to be paid in 15 equal monthly installments of $40. The dealer offers him a discount of 10 percent if he will pay cash. What should he do? Why?

10. Robinson bought a television set for $400. He paid $100 down. The balance was to be paid in 20 monthly installments, each of which amounted to

$19. After he made 10 monthly payments he lost his job. The seller repossessed the set, spent $55 to recondition it, and sold it for $300. Robinson thinks the seller owes him some money. Discuss. If the seller sold the repossessed set for $200, how much do you think he should seek to recover from Robinson as a deficiency? If the seller sold the repossessed set through an agent who charged 25 percent commission, would your answer be different?

4 BORROWING

He who goes a borrowing, goes a sorrowing.
—*Poor Richard's Almanack*

BENJAMIN FRANKLIN'S view of borrowing may have been logical in an age when people went to jail if they could not pay debts, but today we have moved more to the view that a wise and judicious use of credit can materially aid our careers and ease our way. Over half of all the nation's families are in debt, to some extent. Many have borrowed to buy houses and some to buy cars or TV sets; others have gotten loans to meet emergencies such as sudden illness or funeral expenses, or to pay moving expenses to another city to obtain a better income. A number have gone into debt to help put their children through college, and many have borrowed to pay off other debts.

Personal debt exceeds $235 billion, two thirds of it representing mortgage loans which people have obtained to purchase homes. A third consists of "consumer credit," to enable consumers to buy cars, meet doctors' bills, and so on. The funds came from a variety of institutions and individuals—from banks, consumer finance companies, sales finance companies, retailers, insurance companies, savings and loan associations, credit unions, fraternal organizations, loan sharks, pawnbrokers, relatives, and other sources. Indeed, a complete list of sources of small loans would startle you by its diversity, and the complexity of terms and rates is bewildering.

Your credit is probably better than you think. You probably are not aware of the number of lenders who would be glad to help you if you gave them a chance. In fact, millions are spent in advertising each year to persuade you to do just that. And yet the chances are that when you need and want a loan, you will be embarrassed at the prospect of seeking one, become emotionally upset, and lose some of the good judgment you would normally exercise in any other business transaction. The emergency that induces us to borrow may leave us disturbed and troubled and so distracted by the intense need to obtain the money that straight thinking goes by the board.

It would be well, therefore, to become acquainted with the various sources of loans, the services offered, the requirements, and the different rates charged before the emergency or crisis occurs which induces the borrowing. Few want to get into debt; but sooner or later many of us do, and for some it proves to be a very painful lesson which could have been partially avoided if the emergency had been faced coolly because the borrower had previously determined which lenders are reliable, how much could be borrowed, on what terms, etc. The borrower with such knowledge may then calmly apply for the loan as a business transaction, without fear or apology or emotion. Since a wide variety of financial institutions want to make loans, there is no need to approach the lending institution as if seeking a favor. If your credit standing warrants it, most of them will want to lend to you. If it does not, reliable lenders will refuse—and unreliable ones (loan sharks) only spell trouble. Thus, if you need a loan, you should go out and shop for it.

Shopping for a Loan

When you shop for a loan, there are a variety of things to look for; but the two most important are the reliability of the lender and the real total cost of the loan. The former is frequently easier to ascertain than the latter. Any national or state commercial bank with a personal-loan department, any insurance company or mutual savings bank, may be considered a reliable lender. An easy test to use for any other type of lender is whether or not it is licensed by the state in which it operates. If there is no state license then beware! The large personal-loan companies which operate on a national scale are reputable and sound business enterprises, but some of the very small, local companies, even though licensed by the state, may charge concealed and exorbitant rates. The lender who has no office—who just lends at the corner drugstore or barber shop, or who comes around to your home or office or factory gate—is almost invariably a loan shark and someone from whom you should stay away.

How Much Debt Can You Afford?

It's been so easy to get into debt over the past decade that many people have overdone it. If you are in debt, or contemplating the plunge, there are a number of yardsticks you can use to judge your position. First, your total debts should not exceed 20 percent of your annual (take-home) salary. Under this rule, if your annual take-home pay is $5,000, you can incur about $1,000 of debt as a maximum. Second, your total debt should not exceed the amount that you can pay off with 10 percent of your income over 12 to 24 months. Assume your take-home pay is $500 a month. If you used 10 percent, or $50, to pay off what you owe, you could incur a debt of from $600 to $1,200, depending on whether you had one or two years to pay it. Thirdly, what you owe should not exceed a third of your "discretionary" spending (or saving) for the year. By discretionary spending we mean what you have left to spend from your income after you have made essential expenditures such as those for food, shelter, and clothing. For example, assume your take-home pay is $500 a month ($6,000 a year) but that expenditures for rent, food, clothing, essential personal allowances, etc., come to $3,600. This leaves $2,400 for discretionary spending or saving. Taking one third of this would suggest a maximum debt of about $800. Naturally these are flexible rules, but applying them in your own case will give you a range within which to operate.[1]

How Much Will the Loan Cost?

If, in shopping for a loan of $100, repayable in equal monthly installments over a 12-month period, one lender required you to repay $10.07 per month, another $9.75, a third $8.87, and a fourth $8.67, and all other factors were equal, there is little doubt that you would be inclined to borrow from the lender who quoted the lowest rate, namely $8.67. Over the year you would save $16.80 by borrowing from the last rather than the first lender above. These are actual rates. The first lender is a small personal-loan company, the second is a large national consumer finance company, the third is a credit union, and the last is the personal-loan department of a very large commercial bank.[2]

But rates are often not quoted on this simple, comparable basis, and it is frequently difficult to know exactly what comparable costs are. There are different ways of measuring costs. Lenders use varying methods of charging for loans, and in some cases there may be several scattered charges instead of a single one. Fees may be charged for credit investigations, for example. Or if you put up some security, such

---

[1] See "All About Credit," *Changing Times, The Kiplinger Magazine,* March, 1963; also "How Much Credit Can You Afford?" *Good Housekeeping,* April, 1961.

[2] For a survey which reported even wider disparities see Paul Smith, *Cost of Providing Consumer Credit* (National Bureau of Economic Research, Occasional Paper No. 83) (New York, 1962); see also "Why It Pays to Shop for Credit," *Changing Times, The Kiplinger Magazine,* January, 1962.

as an automobile, or insurance, or securities, there may be a legal fee. Generally speaking, legal loan rates on an annual basis range from 4 to 42 percent, though a 42 percent rate will never be quoted as such. It will be stated as a 3½ percent per month rate. Rates may be quoted either on a monthly or an annual basis. Consumer finance companies and credit unions are required to compute rates on a monthly basis, and hence state them in this manner. Rates may be charged either on the full amount of the loan or only on the outstanding balance, the latter, of course, being the more desirable. Rates may be on a discount basis, deducted by the lender in advance from the face amount of the loan, or on an interest basis, added each month to the face amount of the loan repayable.

In many cases the rate will not be clearly stated. The borrower is given a table, such as that shown in Figure 4–1, which indicates the

FIGURE 4–1

Find Here the Cash Loan You Need				
	Choose Your Monthly Payment Here			
	6 payments	12 payments	15 payments	20 payments
$ 50	$ 9.08			
75	13.62	$ 7.31	$ 6.06	
100	18.15	9.75	8.08	$ 6.41
200	36.13	19.33	15.98	12.65
300	54.02	28.82	23.80	18.80
400	71.53	38.00	31.31	24.64
500	88.83	46.94	38.57	30.22

N.Y.

The company's charge is 2½ percent per month on balances of $100 or less, 2 percent per month on that part of the balance in excess of $100 and not in excess of $300, and ½ of 1 percent per month on that part of the balance in excess of $300, up to a maximum of $500.

amount repayable monthly for a given number of months for a stated loan. To find the real dollar cost of his loan, the borrower must multiply the monthly amount repayable by the number of months he is to pay and, from the resulting figure, subtract the amount borrowed. The remaining sum is the true dollar cost of the loan. For example, in Figure 4–1, the borrower will repay $9.75 per month for 12 months if his loan is $100 and he elects to pay it back over a year; 12 × $9.75 = 117 − $100 = $17, the true dollar cost of the loan.

This "true dollar cost" is one of two basic methods of measuring and comparing costs. You add up all the money that you pay the lender from the time you apply for the loan until it is repaid, including all fees, and then subtract the amount of cash you get from the lender. The difference is the true dollar cost. It is the real figure you are looking for, but it affords an accurate comparison only when two loans have the same length and method of repayment. When they do not, then it is better to use the second basic method, the true annual rate. This will enable you to compare costs when loans differ in length and payment plans.

In the dollar-cost illustration given above, you might imagine at first glance that the true annual rate was 17 percent. You paid $17 for a loan of $100 over a period of a year. Offhand, that looks like 17 percent, but it is not. Why? Because you did not have the use of the whole $100 for a complete year. During the second month you would have the use of only $^{11}\!/_{12}$ of the loan, during the third month only $^{10}\!/_{12}$ of the loan, and so on, and during the final month only $^{1}\!/_{12}$, so that, for the whole year, you would have had, on the average, the use of only about $50. To approximate the true annual rate, you need only apply the following formula: $r = \dfrac{2mI}{p(n+1)}$, where

  $r =$ the annual rate charged,
  $m =$ the number of payment periods in one year (12 if you are re-paying monthly, regardless of the number of months you take, and 52 if you are repaying weekly, regardless of the number of weeks you actually take),
  $I =$ true dollar cost of the loan,
  $p =$ the net amount of the loan,
  $n =$ the number of repayments you actually will make.

Applying this formula to the illustration above, of the $100 loan, repayable over a year, which cost $17, we find

$$r = \frac{2 \times 12 \times 17}{100(12 + 1)} = 31+ \text{ percent} .$$

Thus, it is apparent that the annual rate of interest is 31+ percent rather than 17 percent.[3] By applying this formula to each case as one shops for a loan, comparative costs will become clear and evident, and, as will soon be apparent, they will be found to vary considerably.

---

[3] The formula used is known as the "constant-ratio method." It always results in a slightly higher yield than that obtained by the actuarial method, which is recognized as the most accurate but which is much more complicated and cannot be easily computed by the student. For this reason we will use the constant-ratio method, which can be quickly and easily computed, throughout the chapter. Neifeld compares the three methods (constant ratio, direct ratio, and actuarial) and speaks of "the closeness of the results." See Morris R. Neifeld, *Neifeld's Manual on Consumer Credit* (Easton, Pa.: Mack Publishing Co., 1961)

Differences among Lenders

Prospective borrowers will find that lenders differ not only in their charges but in the security or collateral required, in the extent of the credit risks taken, in size of loans, and in length of time allowed for repayment. Some lenders require comakers, or cosigners; others require a specific pledge of collateral, such as the signing of a chattel mortgage on household furniture or an automobile. Others will grant loans merely on the borrower's signature if the credit investigation indicates that there is a reasonable probability that the loan will be repaid. Some will not extend credit to unemployed persons or to those whose income is below a certain level. Most lenders will want to know why you need the money or for what you propose to use it. Some banks will not grant loans where the proceeds are to be used to repay old debts, while, on the other hand, a leading personal finance company reports that 82 percent of its loans are to pay family debts already contracted. Figure 4–2 lists some of the main purposes for which personal loans are granted.

The length of time for which loans are made varies from a few months to as much as three years. Some lenders will not bother with very short-term loans of a month or two. Others will not lend for as long a period as three years even when repayment is on a monthly basis. Personal loans run in size anywhere from $10 to $5,000. Some lenders are limited by law to a maximum amount of $500; others will not wish to bother with a loan of $50 or less. To obtain the kind of loan you want, on the most favorable terms available, requires trying a number of lenders before you make your commitment. You cannot expect to do as well by waiting until the emergency is upon you and then rushing to the first lender within range. Perhaps a survey of different types of lenders and their policies will show you why this is so.

Borrowing on Life Insurance Policies

One of the least expensive ways of obtaining a personal loan is to borrow on your life insurance policy. After the first two or three years, most life policies, except term insurance, accumulate a "cash" or "loan" value, which increases each additional year the policy is in force. This "cash" or "loan" value for each year of the policy's life is shown in a table in your contract. This also tells you at what rate the company will lend you the cash you need against the "loan" value of the policy. You will pay from 4 to 6 percent, depending on the company. On

FIGURE 4–2

Here are some of the useful purposes
for which Personal Loans are made:

FAMILY NEEDS
Medical expenses
Dental bills
Hospital charges
Operation
Household bills
Educational costs
Insurance premium
Clothing
Furniture
House furnishings
Taxes
Vacation and Travel

BUSINESS NEEDS
Goods for inventory
Urgent bills
Additional equipment
Working capital

MOTOR CAR PURPOSES
Purchasing cars and trucks
  – new or used
Using car as collateral
Fire, theft, collision insurance
Public liability insurance

PROPERTY CHARGES
Modernization or improvements
Down payment on home
Taxes or special assessments

MISCELLANEOUS
Consolidating debts
Repaying a friend for a loan
Repaying unsatisfactory loan
Purchase securities for investment

veteran's United States government insurance the rate is 4 percent. Most commercial companies charge 5 or 6 percent, which is as good, if not better, than you can do elsewhere. These are true annual rates, so that the real dollar cost for a loan of $100, borrowed for a whole year and repaid, not in monthly installments, but all at the end of the year, is only from $4.00 to $6.00.

The insurance company cannot turn you down when you ask for a loan within the limit of the "cash" value of your policy. Your right to obtain the loan is part of the contract, and your credit standing, good or bad, has nothing to do with your right to the loan, providing premiums have been paid and the policy is in force. In some states the law permits the company to postpone the loan for a period of from 90 days to six months, but this privilege is rarely invoked. The purpose of this provision is to protect the company against a "run" on its reserves. At a time of crisis or emergency or depression, such a large number of policyholders might, in one short period, ask for funds that the company's liquid assets might become depleted. Apart from this provision, however, you can get your loan at any time merely by requesting it. There is no credit investigation and no extra fee, and the company does not ask, nor has it any control over, what you do with the proceeds of the loan.

Each year insurance companies make new policy loans totaling hundreds of millions and have total loans outstanding of several billion dollars. There is little relationship between new loans made in any year and the total of loans outstanding, because there is no set period of time for repayment of a policy loan. You can take as long or as short a period as you want to repay, and indeed you do not need to repay at all if you so choose. The companies encourage but do not demand that such loans be repaid. If the interest charge is not paid, it is usually added to the loan. Whenever the policy becomes payable, whether due to death or maturity, any outstanding loan is deducted by the company from the amount of the claim it pays. Thus the company is always protected. This unique feature of a policy loan has both advantages and disadvantages. The loan reduces your insurance protection, and there is a constant temptation to postpone repayment because there is an absence of pressure. On the other hand, if you just cannot repay the loan, your salary is not garnisheed, nor is your car or household furniture taken from you.

Personal-Loan Departments of Commercial Banks

At one time commercial banks looked down upon personal loans and would have little to do with them. Today, commercial banks are the largest source of such funds, sharing the field with the small-loan or consumer finance companies. Of total personal loans outstanding, amounting to approximately $14 billion, commercial banks accounted for 34 percent, consumer finance companies for 28 percent, credit unions for 20 percent, sales finance companies for 11 percent, and other financial institutions for 7 percent.[4] Over 10,000 commercial banks in the United States presently have personal-loan departments.

There are two main reasons why the commercial banks have been gaining in the granting of small loans. They are able to make them at rates considerably below those charged by consumer finance companies. Yet they have found the business quite profitable and have, therefore, through advertising, gone after it vigorously.

In recent years, commercial banks have developed several new plans to give them a greater share of the consumer loan market. The two most popular have been charge account banking and revolving personal loans, with the latter now far outdistancing the former. The basic tool of the charge account system is the credit card, issued to those who apply and meet the bank's credit examination. With this card the consumer can charge purchases at any store belonging to the bank's plan. When he makes a purchase, the customer signs a sales slip which, in effect, is a note to the bank. The bank puts a ceiling on his cumulative purchases to prevent him from going on a buying spree, and in addition, purchases over a certain amount have to be cleared through the bank. At the end of the month the customer gets a single bill from the bank covering all his purchases. He then has the choice of either paying in a lump sum or of spreading his payments over a number of months and paying a fee—1 percent or 1½ percent a month—on the unpaid balance. The credit is revolving. As the account is paid down, new purchases may be made.

Revolving personal loans, on the other hand, sometimes called Check-Credit, or Ready-Bank Credit, do not involve a credit card. The customer simply applies for a "line of credit" based on his ability to make monthly repayments. If the bank allows, say, 20 months for repayment, and the borrower can afford to repay $50 per month, then he can apply for a $1,000 "line of credit." Upon approval, after a credit investigation, the borrower gets a special book of checks to use in drawing on the $1,000 account that the bank sets up for him. The borrower is then free to spend the money—write the checks—as he wishes with no need to consult the bank again. Checks drawn under the plan are usable exactly the same as any other checks. The borrower is charged

---

[4] We are referring here only to small personal loans, not to total consumer installment credit. In the latter, which includes retail automobile credit, other consumer goods credit, repair and modernization loans, as well as personal loans, commercial banks account for 46 percent of the total; consumer finance companies for only 10 percent.

only for the amount actually in use. The usual charge is 1 percent a month on the outstanding balance. In addition, some banks have a service charge for each check. As in all revolving plans, the credit is rebuilt, up to the designated ceiling, as the account is repaid. The main advantage of the revolving personal loan plan is that you are not tied down to designated stores. You can buy what you want where you want, and it is for this reason that the revolving personal loan plan has far outdistanced charge account banking.

Banks find the revolving personal loan plan advantageous and can afford to charge only about half the usual small-loan rates. First National Bank of Boston, which pioneered revolving personal loans, is reported to make 50 percent more net profit on such business than on its conventional installment operations, largely because once borrowers are on the books they keep borrowing, on a revolving basis, which cuts down on costs of investigation and "start up."

Banks found that they could handle personal loans at the traditional discount rates charged on commercial loans, since the installment method of repayment for the personal loan made the annual true rate of return on the loan roughly double the stated discount rate. For commercial banks, stated discount rates on the full amount of the loan range from 4.25 to 12 percent. Since loans are repaid in equal monthly installments and only about half of the full amount of the loan is outstanding for the entire repayment period, the true annual rates range from 8 to 24 percent, with 12 or 13 percent as a common average. The very largest banks in urban centers charge but 8 to 12 percent true annual interest. True dollar costs for a $100 loan repayable over 12 months range from $4.25 to $13.00.

One large commercial bank advertises:

LOW IN COST

The Bank deducts in advance $4.25 per year for each $100 of the face amount of the note.

TYPICAL EXAMPLES

Amount of 1-Year Note	Discount	Amount of CASH You Get	Monthly Payment
$ 60	$ 2.55	$ 57.45	$ 5.00
180	7.65	172.35	15.00
300	12.75	287.25	25.00
600	25.50	574.50	50.00
840	35.70	804.30	70.00
1,080	45.90	1,034.10	90.00

HOW MUCH?

You may apply for a single signature loan for any amount of money from $50 to $5,000.

HOW LONG?

You may elect to pay off your personal loan over a term of 12, 18, 24, 30, or 36 months depending on the amount, purpose and credit factors.

The true dollar cost is obviously $4.25 per $100. The true annual rate, for a loan of $300 repayable over one year, can be calculated as follows:

$$r = \frac{2 \times 12 \times 12.75}{287.25(12 + 1)}$$

$$= \frac{306.00}{3,734.25}$$

$$= 0.081+$$

$$= 8.1+ \%$$

Why are many commercial banks able to make personal loans at lower costs to borrowers than most other lenders? They obtain their loan funds from bank depositors at very low cost, whereas the consumer finance companies frequently borrow their funds from the banks. Most of the overhead of the bank's operation is paid for out of earnings on commercial loans, and very little need to be charged to the personal-loan department. Rent is a good example. In the small-loan company, the borrowers carry the entire burden; in the commercial bank, they bear only a very small share. Losses on personal loans of commercial banks are very small, perhaps because they select their credit risks more carefully; perhaps because they prefer secured loans, although they do make single-signature loans; and perhaps because they encourage automobile and home-improvement loans, which run to larger amounts, and tend to shy away from very small loans for short terms.[5] What probably happens is that the better credit risks go to, and are accepted by, the banks, while the poorer risks, knowing their own status, stay away from the banks and go to consumer finance companies initially, with the result that the range of applicants for credit from loan companies is poorer in the first instance than in the case of banks. This suggests, of course, the advisability of trying a commercial bank first, if

---

[5] Commercial banks have found losses on personal loans to be a smaller percentage of total such credit extended than losses on commercial loans are of the total of commercial credit extended.

you want to borrow. If you are accepted, fine; if not, you can always try elsewhere.

Some borrowers avoid the bank and needlessly pay more because they have the erroneous impression that the bank lending officer will treat them coldly and unsympathetically and judge them harshly. Such, of course, is not the case. The bank is in business to make loans, not to refuse them. If it possibly can, it will aid the prospective borrower. It has spent money in advertising to induce him to come into the bank to borrow, and it will certainly, therefore, not turn him away unless his credit record is bad and it feels he will not be able to repay in a reasonable time. Even in such an eventuality, the borrower will be treated pleasantly and sympathetically. It pays to try a bank, if only to test your credit standing.

Are You a Good Risk?

The American Bankers Association *Bank Manual on Personal Loans* sheds interesting light on what banks look for in granting or refusing personal loans. The first question the bank asks itself is "Does the applicant have adequate borrowing capacity?" People frequently want to borrow to "consolidate other debts," and in this case the bank wants to know *all* the other debts; then it will seek to determine whether the borrower's income is sufficient to meet living expenses as well as cover the monthly payments on the consolidated debt. The *Bank Manual* declares: "Income must balance living expenses and the liquidation of all debts. There can be no other deferment of debts while the borrower is liquidating one set of obligations. Only in the rarest instance should the borrower be left with any monthly payments except those to the bank."

If you want a home-improvement loan, the bank will want to be sure that your income is sufficient to meet living expenses, to pay interest and principal on your mortgage, to pay taxes, and to meet the monthly installments on your improvement loan as well. If you are applying for a car loan, the bank will want to be sure that you can make repayments on the debt even when your pocketbook is under the added strain of paying for gasoline, tires, repairs, and the other expenses which a car involves. In short, the bank will in every case ask itself, "Does the applicant have adequate income?" The most common reason for rejecting a loan is lack of income from which repayment can be made. Personal loans are, in a great majority of cases, loans against future income; and if, after careful, down-to-earth calculation, it becomes apparent that future income will not be adequate, the loan application is likely to be rejected. As a rule of thumb, banks tend to limit advances to an amount which will require monthly payments, for the agreed-upon period, no greater than 10 percent of the borrower's income.

The banker is concerned with three important factors: the character of the borrower; his ability to repay, not out of present capital but from future income; and, finally, his capacity for using the money beneficially. In a credit investigation the banker asks himself three questions about the borrower in addition to the income estimation: "Does he work where he says he works?" "Does he live where he says he lives?" and "Does he pay his bills?" He uses various means to check each. The prospective borrower will be asked to fill out an application, and this form is then checked by phone or spot investigation. One side of such an application form is shown in Figure 4–3. This investigation is conducted quickly, and if everything is found to be as the applicant says it was, he will be notified within 24 or 48 hours of the approval of his loan request. When he returns to the bank to obtain his funds, he will be asked to supply additional information. The ABA *Manual* declares:

> With the check in his hand, made payable to the borrower, the banker should ask for information regarding close relatives not living with the borrower, the names of two or three friends, and the names and ages of any of the borrower's children and whether they are in school. . . . The purpose in getting this additional information which is sometimes difficult to obtain at the time the application is being taken (and difficult just because the applicant does not want any one checking with his relatives or his friends), is that such information is necessary in the event of a "skip." Experience will show that a skip can usually be traced if the collector has information regarding two or three friends, two or three relatives, or a child or two in school.[6]

Commercial banks tend to deduct the cost of the loan in advance in the form of a discount, for this is the customary practice of banks. The rate varies from bank to bank, and some will levy different rates according to the credit risk. Most banks, however, have one rate for all acceptable borrowers, and this is frequently 6 percent of the original balance, although several large commercial banks offer personal loans at a stated discount rate of 4.25 percent. On the other hand, some banks charge as much as 12 percent. These are not true annual rates, how-

---

[6] *A Bank Manual on Personal Loans* (New York: Consumer Credit Department, American Bankers Association), pp. 12–13. See also *Analyzing the Cost Factors of Installment Lending* (New York: American Bankers Association).

FIGURE 4–3

APPLICATION FOR PERSONAL LOAN
(INCLUDING DIRECT INSTALMENT SALES FINANCING)

FORM DESIGNED AND APPROVED BY CONSUMER CREDIT DEPT.
AND BANK MANAGEMENT COMMISSION
AMERICAN BANKERS ASSOCIATION

NAME_____

(DATE)

TO_____
(BANK)
(FILL ALL BLANKS, WRITING "NO" OR "NONE" WHERE NECESSARY TO COMPLETE INFORMATION)

AMOUNT OF LOAN APPLIED FOR_____DOLLARS $_____

PURPOSE: PROCEEDS OF THIS LOAN, IF GRANTED, ARE TO BE USED AS FOLLOWS:_____

THE_____DAY OF EACH MONTH IS MOST CONVENIENT FOR MAKING PAYMENTS.

FOR THE PURPOSE OF OBTAINING THE AFOREMENTIONED LOAN, THE UNDERSIGNED MAKES THE FOLLOWING STATEMENT OF_____FINANCIAL CONDITION AS OF THE_____DAY OF_____, 19___. AND CERTIFIES TO THE ABOVE-NAMED BANK THAT THE INFORMATION HEREINAFTER SET FORTH IS IN ALL RESPECTS TRUE, ACCURATE AND COMPLETE AND CORRECTLY REFLECTS THE FINANCIAL CONDITION OF THE UNDERSIGNED ON THE DATE AFOREMENTIONED.

PERSONAL

HOME
ADDRESS_____CITY_____STATE_____PHONE_____
NUMBER OF YEARS   NUMBER OF YEARS   PREVIOUS ADDRESS (IF AT PRESENT
AT THIS ADDRESS_____IN THIS COMMUNITY_____ADDRESS LESS THAN TWO YEARS)_____
                                                 IF YES, NAME   NUMBER OF DEPENDENTS
AGE_____MARRIED—YES ☐   NO ☐   OF SPOUSE_____INCLUDING WIFE_____
NAME OF NEAREST
LOCAL RELATIVE_____ADDRESS_____

EMPLOYMENT

FIRM_____

ADDRESS_____PHONE_____

KIND OF
BUSINESS_____
YOUR
POSITION_____
NAME AND TITLE   HOW LONG WITH
OF SUPERIOR_____THIS EMPLOYER_____
PREVIOUS·   HOW
EMPLOYER_____LONG_____
IF SPOUSE IS
EMPLOYED, WHERE?_____

IF IN BUSINESS FOR SELF, PLEASE STATE

FIRM OR TRADE
NAME_____

ADDRESS_____PHONE_____

KIND OF BUSINESS_____
YOUR INTEREST   HOW
IN THE BUSINESS_____LONG_____
TRADE
REFERENCES_____
PREVIOUS   HOW
EMPLOYER_____LONG_____

MONTHLY INCOME

SALARY, WAGES AND COMMISSIONS_____$_____
SALARY OF SPOUSE (IF EMPLOYED)_____$_____
OTHER INCOME (STATE SOURCE)_____$_____
TOTAL MONTHLY INCOME_____$_____

MONTHLY EXPENSE

RENTAL OR MORTGAGE PAYMENTS_____$_____
ESTIMATED LIVING EXPENSE
(FOOD, UTILITIES, INSURANCE, ETC.)_____$_____
PRESENT CONTRACT OBLIGATIONS_____$_____
TOTAL FIXED EXPENSES_____$_____ $_____

BALANCE,
INCOME OVER
EXPENSE

BANKING

CHECKING
ACCOUNT $_____BANK_____
HAVE YOU HAD A   TYPE
PREVIOUS LOAN WITH US? YES ☐   NO ☐   OF LOAN_____YEAR?_____

SAVINGS
ACCOUNT $_____BANK_____

LIFE INSURANCE

AMOUNT $_____CASH VALUE $_____
COMPANY_____BENEFICIARY_____

AMOUNT BORROWED
ON INSURANCE $_____

SECURITIES

FACE VALUE (BONDS) NUMBER OF SHARES (STOCKS)	DESCRIPTION OF SECURITY	MARKET VALUE	INCOME RECEIVED LAST YEAR
		$	$

ever, since loans are usually repayable in equal monthly installments. If a 6 percent discount rate is charged, deductible in advance, on a loan of $100, repayable in equal monthly installments over a year, the dollar cost and the true annual rate are as follows:

Amount of loan...$100
Dollar cost for one year at 6 percent discount rate.......... 6
Borrower receives.....................................$ 94
Borrower pays..$100

$$r = \frac{2 \times 12 \times 6}{94(12 + 1)} = 11+ \text{ percent} .$$

As a general rule, if the discount rate is an all-inclusive charge and the loan is repaid in equal monthly installments, the interest rate is approximately double the discount rate. In many cases this is the only cost to the borrower, with the exception of a delinquency fee if the installment payments are not made as agreed. Some banks, however, also deduct a small charge in advance in the form of a service or investigation fee. Many banks take out insurance on the borrower's life, thus protecting not only the bank but also the estate of the borrower and his comakers, if any, in the event of the borrower's death. Some banks charge for this credit life insurance, others do not. Some 33 states now regulate rates which can be charged for credit life insurance.

Credit Scoring Systems

A number of financial institutions have experimented with credit scoring systems as a means of more readily discriminating between good and poor credit risks. Weighted values, points, are assigned to various credit characteristics. For example, a homeowner may receive 25 points; a renter who has lived in the same place for five years or more, 15 points; a new renter, 0 points; and a boarder,—10. A man may receive 25 points for having held a position as a foreman for the past five years, a clerk on the job one year, 5 points, a construction worker on a temporary job, 0 points, and an unemployed person,—20. Elaborate studies have been made to develop point scores for identifiable credit characteristics of good borrowers and to detect signs indicative of possible or probable default.

In one scoring system a probability table such as the following was developed:

Credit Risk Probability Table

CREDIT SCORE	No. BAD	No. GOOD	TOTAL	PROBABILITY OF GOING BAD
200–300 pts.	5	1	6	83% (5 ÷ 6)
301–400 "	10	10	20	50 (10 ÷ 20)
401–500 "	13	25	38	34 (13 ÷ 38)
501–600 "	24	115	139	17 (24 ÷ 139)
601–700 "	19	140	159	12 (19 ÷ 159)
701–800 "	19	260	279	7 (19 ÷ 279)
801–900 "	6	200	206	3 (6 ÷ 206)
Over 900 "	4	240	244	2 (4 ÷ 244)

A lender using a scoring system associated with this table might decide to reject all prospective borrowers with scores of 400 or less, thereby sharply increasing the probability that loans granted (to those with scores of 401 or better) would be repaid.[7]

Credit Unions

A credit union is a co-operative association, a group of persons having a common interest banded together to encourage, accumulate, and pool savings and to make loans to each other from the accumulated fund. There are now more than 21,000 credit unions in the United States, whose fourteen million members have saved over $6 billion. Credit unions may be chartered either under the Federal Credit Union Act of 1934 or under state credit union statutes. In the former case, supervision is exercised by the Bureau of Federal Credit Unions of the U.S. Department of Health, Education, and Welfare; in the latter, by the state banking department.

To borrow from a credit union, a person must be a member or become a member. Joining a credit union is easy. Not much money is needed. In fact, credit unions are primarily intended for people who do not have much. The membership entrance fee generally is only 25 cents. A minimum investment of at least one share is required. Shares usually sell for $5.00 each. A credit union is run by its members, and each member is entitled to only one vote regardless of the number of shares held. The $5.00 share may be purchased on the installment plan at terms of 25 cents down and 25 cents a week thereafter. Once you are a member, two kinds of service are available: (1) savings facilities and (2) loan service. Money is deposited in a credit union

---

[7] See "Credit Scoring Systems," *Time Sales Financing,* American Finance Conference, Inc., Vol. 27, No. 5 (September–October, 1963), pp. 3–5; see also "New Credit Scoring System," *Consumer Finance News,* Vol. 46, No. 1 (July, 1961), p. 3.

very much as in a savings bank. The average savings account of members is small, amounting to less than $100. Savings may be used to buy shares on which dividends are paid. These range from 3 to 6 percent a year, with federal credit unions limited to paying the latter as a maximum. Savings may be withdrawn or shares sold very much as money is withdrawn from a bank, that is, at will, although the credit union's board of directors may require two months' notice, as in the case of a savings bank. This provision is seldom invoked.

Out of the funds accumulated from these savings, loans may be made to members. Credit unions will make very small loans, at times for as little as $5.00 or $10.00—loans of a size which other lending institutions tend to avoid. The federal law permits unsecured loans up to $400 and adequately secured loans in larger amounts, depending on the size of the credit union. The board of directors of each federal credit union has authority to fix lower maximum limits for loans and to revise them as the credit union grows. Repayments may be made weekly, semimonthly, monthly, or according to any other agreed-upon schedule, extending up to but not over three years. Applications for loans are passed upon by a credit committee elected by the members. Secured loans, as in the case of other lenders, may be backed by co-makers, assignment of credit union shares, or chattel mortgages on property, household equipment, or an automobile.

The charge on credit union loans may not exceed a maximum of 1 percent per month on unpaid balances, inclusive of all charges and fees. This is a maximum true annual rate of 12 percent a year, or roughly equivalent to 6 percent discounted. Thus the dollar cost is a maximum of $6.50 for $100 for a year, or $12.50 for 24 months. Each credit union fixes its own rate within this limit. Occasionally charges are as low as ½ of 1 percent per month. Rates can be low because, as co-operatives, credit unions usually have little or no expense for rent, salaries, investigations, collections, or federal income taxes. Because the members are usually known to the credit committee, credit investigation is reduced to a minimum. Even if the prospective borrower is not known to the committee, the credit union, since it is formed by people who work together or have a common church or union or fraternal society or live in the same housing project, seldom has difficulty in securing reliable information quickly, with little or no expense. Thus it is usually unnecessary to employ credit men or investigators or to keep elaborate records. Furthermore, the premises on which the credit union locates are often donated by the employer, church, union, etc.; and rent, light, phone and similar expenses are minimized.

Frequently, the employer will regularly deduct the payment due to the credit union from the employee's pay check or salary envelope, thus reducing collection costs to zero. If an employee leaves the firm, his final pay check may be held back until he permits the deduction to pay the credit union advance in full. In this way, the firm becomes a collector, free of charge, for the credit union. In some cases the secretary-treasurer of a credit union may receive a small salary, but usually most officers contribute their services without charge. Little expenditure for advertising is necessary, since knowledge of the credit union travels by word of mouth among those eligible to join. At times, small pamphlets are issued and circulated, but their cost is small. For reasons such as these, credit union costs are relatively low, and it can afford to lend at rates which only large commercial banks can match, or better. Furthermore, losses on loans are quite low. Actual statistics of federal credit unions show that losses charged off because of bad loans amount to less than $\frac{2}{10}$ of 1 percent.

Industrial Banks and Loan Companies

Industrial banks and industrial loan companies, together, are no small factor in the consumer installment loan field. The term "industrial" is a misnomer, for these institutions are not primarily banks for industry. Initially, they were so called mainly because they served wage earners in industry. Today, however, their functions are so mixed that it is difficult to describe them clearly. In many states, industrial banks are hardly distinguishable from commercial banks, and indeed in the Federal Reserve's installment credit statistics they are now included in the commercial bank category. They perform much the same functions except that possibly more emphasis is placed on personal loans. In some states they are not permitted to receive deposits; and thus since they do not perform this essential function of a bank, they are not permitted to use that word in their title but are called instead "industrial loan companies."

The first "industrial" bank in this country, modeled after banks for workers in European countries, was established in 1910 by Arthur J. Morris of Norfolk, Virginia. Thus the name "Morris Plan" banks. The distinctive feature of the Morris Plan bank idea was that the borrower did not repay the bank directly in installments but instead used the regular series of installments of equal amount to purchase an "investment installment certificate" of the same amount as the face value of his loan. This was pledged to back the loan; and when the investment certificate was fully paid up, it was turned over to pay off the loan, and both were then canceled. No interest was paid by the Morris Plan bank on the money paid in to purchase the investment certificate over the same period of time as the loan; while, on the other hand, the bank charged interest on the full amount of the loan, since technically, even though you were paying installments on the certificate, you did not pay off any part of the loan until you turned over the fully paid certificate at the final maturity date of the full loan. This was, of course, merely a device to enable the Morris Plan banks to advertise a nominal charge of "6 percent" but in fact to collect more. Today the investment certificate feature has been dropped in all but a few states, and in most cases loans are now repaid by regular installment payments directly on principal. By and large, industrial bank operations are now not very different from the personal-loan departments of commercial banks, except that the industrial banks tend to charge a little more.

True dollar costs range from $8.00 to $12.00 a year per hundred dollars borrowed, and a usual charge would be about $10.00, including fees. There is frequently, in addition, an investigation fee of 2 percent of the loan. Thus, true interest rates run from 12 to 24 percent, with 16 percent a fair average. For example, if you borrow $100 from a Morris Plan bank and the note is discounted at 6 percent, plus a 2 percent service charge, you would actually receive $92. In return, you agree to make 50 weekly payments of $2.00 each, or a total of $100. At first glance, you might imagine you were paying 8 percent. But you have the use of $92 for only one week; of $90 for a week, of $88 for a week, and so on, which is equal to an average unpaid balance of $41.58. Thus you are paying $8.00 for the use of $41.58 for the year, and this amounts to 19.2 percent interest by the constant-ratio method. Industrial banks and loan companies, then, fall between commercial banks and credit unions, on the one hand, and consumer finance companies, on the other, in the cost of credit. Their credit standards may at times be somewhat more flexible than those of commercial banks, since they may be willing to make more extensive investigations.

Consumer Finance Companies

One out of every five American families is going to borrow some money from a finance company this year. By the year's end, these families will owe the consumer finance companies and personal loan divisions of sales finance companies over $5.5 billion. Small loans are big business. Next to commercial banks, finance companies are second in volume of small loans extended to personal borrowers. They range in size from the nationally known Beneficial Loan Corporation and

Household Finance Corporation to the small, local company which does a strictly neighborhood business. There are some 20 large national chains and about 18,680 licensed loan offices in states which regulate the small-loan business.[8] In 1962, loan companies made over 13 million loans, totaling nearly $7 billion. The outstanding balances at year end exceeded $5 billion. Most states have laws regulating this type of lending, which may be considered effective or relatively effective. Consumer finance companies are legitimate institutions which perform a useful public service. They are not to be confused with loan sharks. Indeed, in many instances, they save a borrower from having to resort to a loan shark. In some states, where overzealous regulation and harsh laws unduly restrict charges, legitimate loan companies have been driven out of the state and the loan sharks have taken over, with such resulting widespread abuses that the state authorities have been glad to amend their statutes and hope for the return of the loan companies.

State statutes legally providing for special companies to make small loans grew out of a report made in New York in 1910 by the Russell Sage Foundation. Impressed with the need for legitimate small loans, and aware of the fact that the poor were being driven into the hands of loan sharks who exacted excessively high rates, the Foundation study pointed up the great need, and the impossibility of filling it by use of then-existing institutions, and suggested that state laws be passed authorizing that lenders be licensed to make small loans at a maximum rate of $3\frac{1}{2}$ percent per month (42 percent a year) on unpaid balances only. While this rate may seem quite high today, it was then much less than the 10–20 percent a month (120–240 percent a year) or more charged by private lenders. The Foundation drew up and secured the adoption in a number of states of the Uniform Small Loan Law. It recognized that personal loans must cost more than commercial loans and that the maximum rates set must permit expenses to be covered and a reasonable profit earned. The Uniform Small Loan Law was revised a number of times over the years and adopted with variations by many states. The National Consumer Finance Association, a trade organization of small-loan companies, published a "Model Consumer Finance Act" in October, 1948. It is significant, and a tribute to the soundness of the Russell Sage Foundation's work, that this Model Act follows the Uniform Small Loan Law closely in all essentials. Like the Uniform Law, it provides for a system of licensing, regulation, and

---

[8] See *Roster of Consumer Finance Companies in the United States* (Washington, D.C.: National Consumer Finance Association, 1963).

supervision. Unlicensed lenders are forbidden, under penalty, to charge interest rates higher than those permitted by the usury laws, while adequate rates are authorized for licensed lenders. Oppressive practices are prevented by detailed requirements as to methods of computing charges, receipts, and so on. By 1962, 44 states had passed effective versions of the law (see Fig. 4–4). Only Arkansas and the District of Columbia were without some form of legislation permitting small loans to be made by finance companies at rates which would attract capital. In about half of the states with small-loan laws, consumer

FIGURE 4–4

Small Loan Map of the United States

Operative Laws
Other Laws—With Major Deficiencies
No Small Loan Laws

finance companies make installment loans under the provisions of other laws commonly known as industrial loan laws or consumer discount acts, and in a few states under general interest laws.

The effective laws generally provide:

a) License. The lender must be licensed, usually after a test of his character, fitness to conduct this business, and financial responsibility; often, also, he must prove that he has sufficient capital and that granting him a license will be for the convenience and advantage of the community.

b) Supervision. State supervision is provided, including annual and special examinations of licensees, annual reports by licensees, revocation of license for violation of the law, and investigation of unlicensed lenders.

c) *Maximum Rate.* Alaska allows 4 percent on the first $300 of the loan, 2½ percent thereafter to $600, and 2 percent thereafter to $1,000. In most other states the maximum rate is 3 or 2½ percent per month. In most states a higher rate is charged on the first $100, $200, or $300 of a loan balance and a lower rate on the rest. For example, in New York the rate is 2½ percent per month on the first $100, 2 percent on the next $200, and ¾ of 1 percent on the amount from $300 to $800. In recent years, there has been a trend for small-loan laws to permit the use of add-on rates, i.e., dollar amounts computed on and added to the original amount lent. Ohio's small-loan law is of this type and provides the following maximum charges: $16 per year per $100 on the original amount of the loan to $500; $9.00 per year per $100 on the original amount between $500 and $1,000; and $7.00 per year per $100 on the original amount between $1,000 and $2,000.

d) *Maximum-Loan Size.* This was originally $300 but now only eight states retain this low maximum and in most of these states finance companies make loans under other laws. In 28 states, the ceiling is $1,000 or more. The maximum is now $5,000 in California;[9] $3,000 in Massachusetts; $2,500 in Georgia, Maine, Nevada, and South Dakota; $2,100 in Kansas; $2,000 in Ohio; and $1,500 in Colorado, Nebraska, New Hampshire, Oregon, and Texas (see Fig. 4–5).

e) *Disclosure.* The loan papers must disclose the amount of the loan, the payment schedule, the security, and the monthly rate of charge. The loan company must give the borrower a written statement disclosing this information.

f) *Prepayment Privilege.* The lender must accept payment in advance of the due date and charge the borrower only for the actual time he has the use of the money.

g) *Judgment Notes Prohibited.* Provisions in a promissory note permitting the lender to obtain judgment against the borrower before giving notice to the borrower or giving him an opportunity to be heard in court are prohibited.

h) *Wage-buying Prevented.* A favorite device used by loan sharks to obtain excessively high returns was to claim that they were not lending money but were buying a man's future wages at a discount. This has been prohibited by defining the purchase of wages as a loan.

---

[9] California's law permits licensees to make loans of more than $5,000, but such larger loans are not subject to rate regulation.

FIGURE 4–5

Summary of Maximum Loan Size

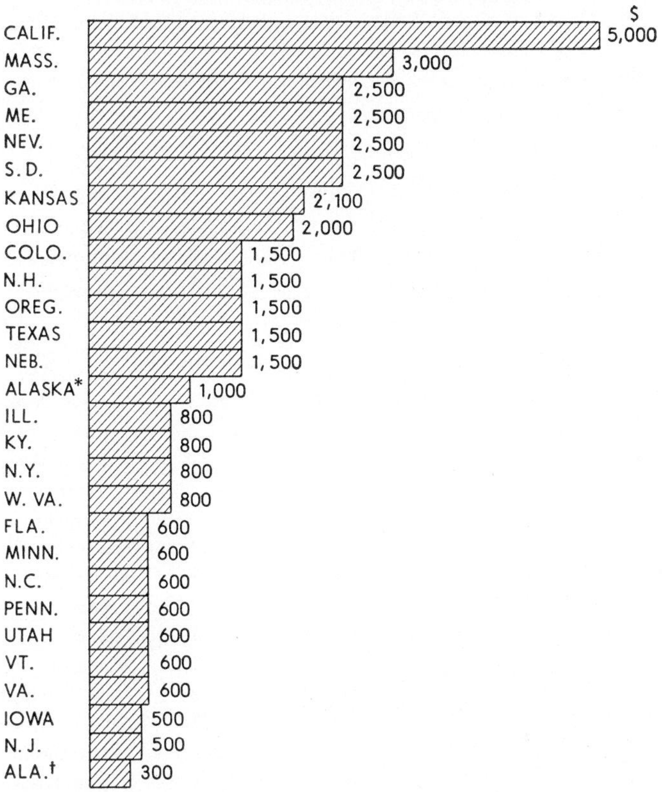

State	Maximum Loan Size
CALIF.	$5,000
MASS.	3,000
GA.	2,500
ME.	2,500
NEV.	2,500
S. D.	2,500
KANSAS	2,100
OHIO	2,000
COLO.	1,500
N.H.	1,500
OREG.	1,500
TEXAS	1,500
NEB.	1,500
ALASKA*	1,000
ILL.	800
KY.	800
N.Y.	800
W. VA.	800
FLA.	600
MINN.	600
N.C.	600
PENN.	600
UTAH	600
VT.	600
VA.	600
IOWA	500
N. J.	500
ALA.†	300

* Also Arizona, Connecticut, Idaho, Indiana, Michigan, Montana, New Mexico, North Dakota, Washington, and Wyoming.
† Also Hawaii, Louisiana, Maryland, Oklahoma, Rhode Island, Tennessee, and Wisconsin.
SOURCE: National Consumer Finance Association.

i) Subterfuges. Subterfuges in the form of concealed or unauthorized charges are prohibited. The state is given the power to investigate any side-line business of the lender, such as insurance, to determine whether it is being used as a subterfuge to secure higher illegal returns.

j) Advertising. False and misleading advertising is prohibited, and the state supervising official has power to require lenders fully to disclose their charges.

k) Penalties. Severe civil and criminal penalties are provided against both illegal nonlicensed lenders and licensees who exceed the limits of the law.

In a majority of states, therefore, licensed small-loan companies are

TABLE 4–1

Summary of State Maximum Small-Loan Rates
(In 44 States with Operative Small-Loan Laws)

Maximum Monthly Rate* (Percent)	Lower Rate on Larger Balances	Number of States	States
4	Yes	1	Alaska
3½	Yes	3	Hawaii, Louisiana, Wyoming
3.1	Yes	1	Nevada
3	Yes	18	Alabama, Arizona, Colorado, Florida, Idaho, Illinois, Indiana, Iowa, Kansas, Kentucky, Maine, New Mexico, Oregon, Pennsylvania, South Dakota, Utah, Washington, West Virginia
3	No	2	Maryland, Rhode Island
2.9	Yes	2	Montana, North Carolina
2.8	Yes	1	Texas
2¾	Yes	1	Minnesota
2.4	Yes	2	New Hampshire, Ohio
2½	Yes	11	California, Connecticut, Massachusetts, Michigan, Nebraska, New Jersey, New York, North Dakota, Vermont, Virginia, Wisconsin
2.218	Yes	1	Missouri
10% a year, plus fee	No	1	Oklahoma

* Connecticut, Montana, Nevada, New Hampshire, North Carolina, Ohio, and Texas set maximum annual add-on rates. These are included at the maximum monthly rate approximated by the highest add-on charge.
Source: National Consumer Finance Association.

legitimate, reputable organizations supervised by the state under a comprehensive law designed to protect the borrower and yet permit the company sufficient scope to operate profitably. While the consumer finance companies lend to all income and occupation groups, their borrowers include a higher proportion of low-income wage earners and salaried people than does the average bank. The small-loan company is specially designed for people without established credit, and its charges are set to cover the costs of extensive investigations and more elaborate collection procedures even on the very small loans. The average size of consumer finance loans is now over $500. Most loans are made to families in the $3,000–7,500 income brackets. Household Finance Corporation recently surveyed its borrowers and found that over 60 percent were industrial or office workers with an average monthly income of $462 (see Table 4–2). The average size of its more

TABLE 4–2
Occupations of 2,045,684 Borrowers

	NUMBER OF LOANS	PERCENT OF TOTAL
Operatives and kindred workers	425,477	20.80
Craftsmen, foremen, and kindred workers	387,172	18.92
Military personnel	254,006	12.42
Clerical and kindred workers	230,319	11.25
Laborers, except farm and mine	184,056	9.00
Proprietors, managers, and officials, excluding farm	151,888	7.42
Service workers, except domestic and protective	136,684	6.68
Professional and semiprofessional workers, except teachers	82,159	4.02
Sales persons	75,625	3.70
Protective service workers	37,772	1.85
Unemployed: pensions or independent income	33,320	1.63
School teachers	25,080	1.23
Farmers and farm managers	9,414	0.46
Farm laborers and foremen	7,884	0.39
Domestic service workers	4,775	0.23
Occupation not reported	53	0.00
Total	2,045,684	100.00

SOURCE: Household Finance Corporation.

than two million loans was $546. It also found that people borrow principally to consolidate other debts (see Table 4–3). The loans are to pay off creditors who will not or cannot wait. The new loan brings order and a respite, in the form of one loan and one monthly installment, to the theretofore harried debtor.

A study comparing personal loans of consumer finance companies with those made by a group of banks found that about half of the bank borrowers were white-collar workers and half blue-collar, whereas only about one quarter of the consumer finance company borrowers were white-collar and three quarters were manual workers. Consumer finance

TABLE 4-3

How 2,045,684 Borrowers Planned to Use Small Loans

	NUMBER OF LOANS	PERCENT OF TOTAL
To Pay Existing Debts and Emergency Expenses:		
Consolidate overdue bills*	603,681	29.51
Medical, dental, and hospital bills	128,060	6.26
Assist relatives	110,058	5.38
Taxes	72,212	3.53
Household repairs	68,326	3.34
Insurance premiums	47,255	2.31
Miscellaneous	38,254	1.87
Moving Expense	24,344	1.19
Payments on real estate loans	21,889	1.07
Rent	16,161	0.79
Funeral expense	10,228	0.50
Food bills	4,296	0.21
Total	1,144,764	55.96
To Buy Durable Goods:		
Automobile purchase or repairs	319,331	15.61
Home furnishings and appliances	110,467	5.40
Miscellaneous equipment	60,348	2.95
Total	490,146	23.96
To Pay for Travel, Business, and Education:		
Travel and vacation expenses	225,025	11.00
Education	23,321	1.14
Business for self	21,684	1.06
Total	270,030	13.20
To Buy Fuel and Clothing:		
Clothing	128,674	6.29
Fuel	12,070	0.59
Total	140,744	6.88
Grand Total	2,045,684	100.00

* All loans were classified under the heading describing the use to which the larger part of the loan was applied. Where several bills were paid and no major purpose appeared, the loan was classified under the heading, "To consolidate overdue bills."

SOURCE: Household Finance Corporation.

company borrowers, in the main, came from somewhat lower-income brackets than did bank borrowers. Fewer bank borrowers were under 30 years of age, and more over 40 years than were consumer finance company borrowers.[10]

---

[10] W. David Robbins, *Consumer Installment Loans* (Columbus: The Bureau of Business Research, The Ohio State University, 1955).

A little more than half of the loans made are on the borrower's signature alone. Most of the remainder are secured by chattel mortgages (see Fig. 4–6) on the borrower's household possessions. This is more a psychological than a material security for the loan company, since it very rarely takes possession of such property; and indeed the legal costs of doing so, in relation to the small secondhand resale value of the furniture, make foreclosure of a chattel mortgage uneconomic. But the average borrower, not knowing this, will try to avoid the ignominy and neighborhood disgrace which the removal of his furniture would entail. A small percentage of loans are secured by pledges of automobiles or insurance or by the added security of a cosigner. A prospective borrower will be asked to fill out a financial statement (see Fig. 4–7), and at the first interview the loan company official will ask questions to enable him to fill out part of the investigation record. When this is checked and completed by the company investigator and it is decided to grant the loan, the applicant will be called in and asked to sign a note (see Fig. 4–8). As indicated above, he may also be asked to sign a chattel mortgage. He will then be given the proceeds of the loan, and a "loan statement and receipt book." The latter is shown in Figure 4–9, page 157.

The charges of consumer finance companies and credit unions are customarily stated as a monthly percentage of the balance of the unpaid principal. Consequently, the effective annual cost to the borrower is twelve times the monthly rate. Two principal methods of setting rates are the "flat" rate and the "graduated" rate. The former approach uses the same monthly rate regardless of the size of the loan extended, but only a minority of states use this method. Most states require lower rates as the size of the loan increases. For example, Illinois has a fairly typical three-step rate: 3 percent per month on the first $150, 2 percent on the amount between $150 and $300, and 1 percent on the amount between $300 and $800. The lower rates do not apply to the entire loan but only to the part above a certain amount. How widely the interest cost can vary for an identical loan in different states because of the differing legal loan rate provisions may be seen in Figure 4–10, page 157.

Taking into account the lower rates on larger amounts of loan balances, true annual rates range from 16 to 42 percent. Dollar costs on a $100 loan, repayable over 12 months, are generally $13–$24 and average about $18 or $19. The larger the loan, the lower will be the cost per $100, since a sliding scale of rates is often used. For example, a $500 loan in New Jersey costs 2½ percent per month on the first

FIGURE 4–6

Chattel Mortgage

CHATTEL MORTGAGE

HOUSEHOLD FINANCE
Corporation
ESTABLISHED 1878
LICENSED PURSUANT TO ARTICLE IX OF THE BANKING LAW
Room 6—Second Floor
1609 Kings Highway—Phone: DEwey 9-5900
BROOKLYN 29, NEW YORK

MORTGAGORS (NAMES AND ADDRESSES):

LOAN NO.

DATE OF NOTE AND THIS CHATTEL MORTGAGE:	FIRST PAYMENT DUE DATE:	OTHERS: SAME DAY OF EACH MONTH	FINAL PAYMENT DUE DATE:

	PRINCIPAL AND INT. PAYABLE	FIRST PAYMENT:	OTHERS:	FINAL PAYMENT EQUAL IN ANY CASE TO UNPAID PRINCIPAL AND INTEREST
PRINCIPAL AMOUNT OF NOTE AND ACTUAL AMOUNT OF LOAN: $	IN MONTHLY PAYMENTS	$	$	

AGREED RATE OF INTEREST: { 2½% PER MONTH ON THAT PART OF THE UNPAID PRINCIPAL BALANCE NOT EXCEEDING $100. 2% PER MONTH ON ANY PART THEREOF EXCEEDING $100. AND NOT EXCEEDING $300. AND ½ OF 1% PER MONTH ON ANY PART THEREOF EXCEEDING $300.

The Mortgagors above named are indebted upon their promissory note above described payable to the order of HOUSEHOLD FINANCE CORPORATION at its above office and evidencing a loan made by said corporation in the actual amount of the principal thereof. By the terms thereof every payment thereon shall be applied first to interest to date of actual payment and remainder to principal; payment may be made in advance in any amount; and default in making any payment shall, at the option of the holder of the note and without notice or demand, render the entire unpaid balance of the principal thereof and accrued interest thereon at once due and payable.

NOW THEREFORE, in consideration of said loan and to further secure the payment of said note, the Mortgagors *hereby convey and mortgage* to said HOUSEHOLD FINANCE CORPORATION, its successors and assigns (hereinafter called Mortgagee), *the goods and chattels hereinafter described;* provided, however, if the Mortgagors well and truly pay and discharge said note according to the terms thereof, then these presents shall cease and be void.

Mortgagors may possess said property until default in making any payment on said note. At any time when such default shall exist and the entire sum remaining unpaid on said note shall be due and payable either by the exercise of the option of acceleration above described or otherwise, this mortgage may be foreclosed; and the Mortgagee may without notice or demand take possession of any or all of said property and with or without notice to the Mortgagors sell the property so taken in accordance with law at public auction or private sale for cash at the best price the seller can obtain. The proceeds of any sale hereunder shall be applied on the indebtedness secured hereby, and any surplus shall be paid to the Mortgagors.

The Mortgagors covenant that they exclusively possess and own said property free and clear of all incumbrances except as otherwise noted, and that they will warrant and defend the same against all persons except the Mortgagee. Any failure of the Mortgagee to enforce any of its rights or remedies hereunder shall not be a waiver of its right to do so thereafter. Whenever the context so requires plural words shall be construed in the singular.

Description of mortgaged property:

All of the household goods now located in or about Mortgagors' residence at their address above set forth.

WITNESS the hands and seals of Mortgagors the day of the date hereof above written.

Signed, sealed and delivered
in the presence of:

....(Seal)

....(Seal)

FORM C. M.—N. Y.—2½.2 (300) ½—REV.7-53

FIGURE 4–7

Financial Statement

Loan Number.......................................

FINANCIAL STATEMENT

The undersigned having applied to HOUSEHOLD FINANCE CORPORATION or one of its subsidiary corporations

for a loan of $..............................., for...................months, for the purpose of showing his, her, or their ability to repay the same, and inducing such corporation to make said loan, hereby represent and warrant that the following is a full, complete, and correct list of all debts and liabilities of and other claims against them and

each of them on..*(If no debts, so state)*
(Month–Day–Year)

	AMOUNT OWED	
	DOLLARS	CENTS
Present loan balance with HOUSEHOLD FINANCE CORPORATION and subsidiaries	$	

APPLICANT(S) MUST LIST ALL DEBTS – DO NOT OMIT ANY DEBTS
(Disputed and so-called outlawed claims must be included.)

Name of creditor Nature of debt		
	$	
	$	
	$	
	$	
	$	
	$	
	$	
	$	
	$	
	$	
	$	
All debts and claims except Real Estate Contracts and Mortgages TOTAL	$	
Real Estate Contracts and Mortgages: (Give name of mortgage or contract holder and unpaid balance)	$	
	$	
	$	

WITNESS our hands and seals the day and year above set forth.

Executed and delivered in the presence of:

....(SEAL)

....(SEAL)

....
Witness

FORM G–REV. 2-56

$300 and ½ of 1 percent on the remainder. This is approximately $11 per $100 borrowed. It should be noted that, under most small-loan laws, the stated rate *must* be calculated on the decreasing periodic balance, not on the entire original credit. Banks are not subject to this regulation, and neither are installment sellers. Small-loan companies and credit unions are, however.

FIGURE 4–8

Note

NOTE

HOUSEHOLD FINANCE *Corporation*
ESTABLISHED 1878
LICENSED PURSUANT TO ARTICLE IX OF THE BANKING LAW
Rooms 304-305 – William F. Kenny Bldg. – 3rd Floor
44-60 East 23rd St. – Phone: GRamercy 3-7553
NEW YORK 10, NEW YORK

BORROWERS (NAMES AND ADDRESSES): LOAN NO.

DATE OF THIS NOTE:	FIRST PAYMENT DUE DATE:	OTHERS: SAME DAY OF EACH MONTH	FINAL PAYMENT DUE DATE:

PRINCIPAL AMOUNT OF NOTE AND ACTUAL AMOUNT OF LOAN: $	PRINCIPAL AND INT. PAYABLE IN MONTHLY PAYMENTS	FIRST PAYMENT: $	OTHERS: $	FINAL PAYMENT EQUAL IN ANY CASE TO UNPAID PRINCIPAL AND INTEREST

AGREED RATE OF INTEREST: 2½% PER MONTH ON THAT PART OF THE UNPAID PRINCIPAL BALANCE NOT EXCEEDING $100. 2% PER MONTH ON ANY PART THEREOF EXCEEDING $100, AND NOT EXCEEDING $300, AND ½ OF 1% PER MONTH ON ANY PART THEREOF EXCEEDING $300.

IN CONSIDERATION of a loan made by **Household Finance Corporation** at its above office in the principal amount above stated, the undersigned jointly and severally promise to pay to the order of said corporation at its above office said principal amount together with interest at the above rate until fully paid.

Payment of principal and interest shall be made in consecutive monthly payments as above indicated beginning on the stated due date for the first payment and continuing on the same day of each succeeding month to and including the stated due date for the final payment except that when any such day is a Sunday or holiday the due date for the payment in that month shall be the next succeeding business day. Payment in advance may be made in any amount. Every payment made hereon shall be applied first to interest to date of actual payment and remainder to principal. Default in making any payment shall, at the option of the holder hereof and without notice or demand, render the entire unpaid balance of the principal hereof and accrued interest thereon at once due and payable.

Cause of action shall arise hereon only with respect to the entire principal and accrued interest remaining unpaid hereunder. The makers, sureties, endorsers, and guarantors hereof severally waive demand for payment, notice of non-payment, protest and notice of protest of this note and consent to extensions of time of payment without notice. A statement of said loan has been delivered to the borrower as required by law. The construction, validity and effect hereof shall be governed by the laws of New York.

Witnesses: ______________ (SEAL)

______________ ______________ (SEAL)

______________ ______________ (SEAL)

FORM NOTE—N. Y.—2½-2 (300) ½—REV. 8-49

Another way in which loan companies state charges is to publish a table showing, for varying loan amounts, what the borrower must pay back, depending upon the repayment period selected. Such a table, published by a large consumer finance company, is shown in Figure 4–11 (p. 158). From the circled figures it may be seen that on a $100 loan, repayable over a year, you pay back $9.75 each month, while on a $300 loan you repay $28.82 per month for 12 months. In the first case, you pay back $117 ($9.75 × 12) for a loan of $100. The true dollar cost is $17, and, using the formula given previously to approximate the true annual rate, it is found to be 31 percent.

$$= \frac{2 \times 12 \times 17}{100\,(12 + 1)} = 31 \text{ percent}.$$

FIGURE 4–9

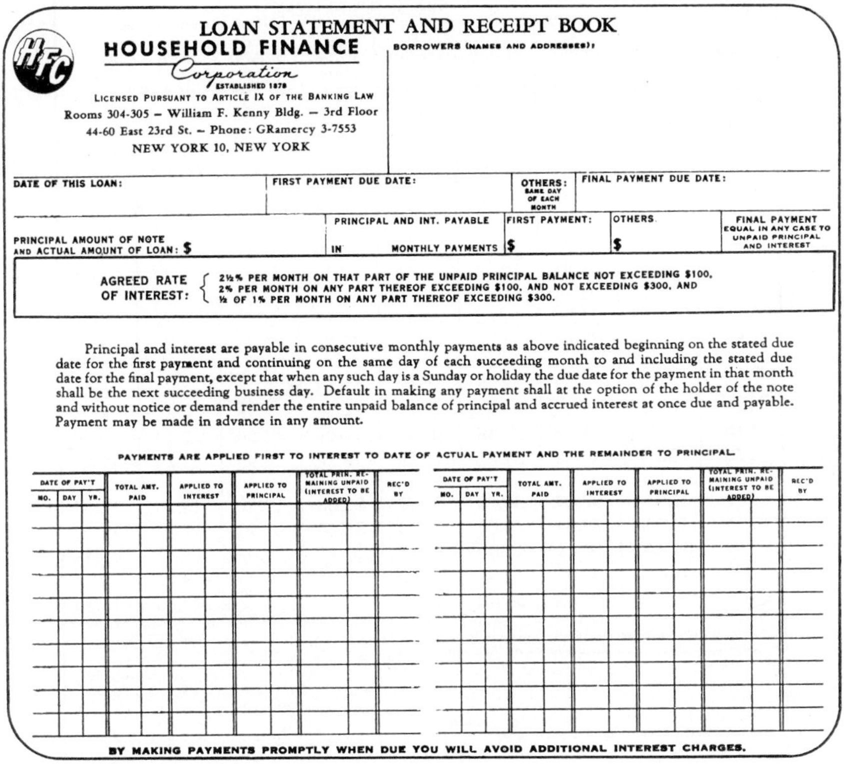

Loan Statement and Receipt Book

LOAN STATEMENT AND RECEIPT BOOK

HOUSEHOLD FINANCE Corporation
ESTABLISHED 1878
LICENSED PURSUANT TO ARTICLE IX OF THE BANKING LAW
Rooms 304-305 – William F. Kenny Bldg. – 3rd Floor
44-60 East 23rd St. – Phone: GRamercy 3-7553
NEW YORK 10, NEW YORK

BORROWERS (NAMES AND ADDRESSES):

DATE OF THIS LOAN: | FIRST PAYMENT DUE DATE: | OTHERS: SAME DAY OF EACH MONTH | FINAL PAYMENT DUE DATE:

PRINCIPAL AMOUNT OF NOTE AND ACTUAL AMOUNT OF LOAN: $ | PRINCIPAL AND INT. PAYABLE IN MONTHLY PAYMENTS | FIRST PAYMENT: $ | OTHERS $ | FINAL PAYMENT EQUAL IN ANY CASE TO UNPAID PRINCIPAL AND INTEREST

AGREED RATE OF INTEREST: 2½% PER MONTH ON THAT PART OF THE UNPAID PRINCIPAL BALANCE NOT EXCEEDING $100, 2% PER MONTH ON ANY PART THEREOF EXCEEDING $100, AND NOT EXCEEDING $300, AND ½ OF 1% PER MONTH ON ANY PART THEREOF EXCEEDING $300.

Principal and interest are payable in consecutive monthly payments as above indicated beginning on the stated due date for the first payment and continuing on the same day of each succeeding month to and including the stated due date for the final payment, except that when any such day is a Sunday or holiday the due date for the payment in that month shall be the next succeeding business day. Default in making any payment shall at the option of the holder of the note and without notice or demand render the entire unpaid balance of principal and accrued interest at once due and payable. Payment may be made in advance in any amount.

PAYMENTS ARE APPLIED FIRST TO INTEREST TO DATE OF ACTUAL PAYMENT AND THE REMAINDER TO PRINCIPAL.

DATE OF PAY'T MO.	DAY	YR.	TOTAL AMT. PAID	APPLIED TO INTEREST	APPLIED TO PRINCIPAL	TOTAL PRIN. REMAINING UNPAID (INTEREST TO BE ADDED)	REC'D BY	DATE OF PAY'T MO.	DAY	YR.	TOTAL AMT. PAID	APPLIED TO INTEREST	APPLIED TO PRINCIPAL	TOTAL PRIN. REMAINING UNPAID (INTEREST TO BE ADDED)	REC'D BY

BY MAKING PAYMENTS PROMPTLY WHEN DUE YOU WILL AVOID ADDITIONAL INTEREST CHARGES.

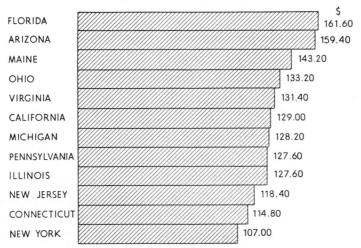

FIGURE 4–10

Interest Charged on a $500, 20-Month Loan in Selected States, October, 1963

$
FLORIDA 161.60
ARIZONA 159.40
MAINE 143.20
OHIO 133.20
VIRGINIA 131.40
CALIFORNIA 129.00
MICHIGAN 128.20
PENNSYLVANIA 127.60
ILLINOIS 127.60
NEW JERSEY 118.40
CONNECTICUT 114.80
NEW YORK 107.00

SOURCE: National Consumer Finance Association.

FIGURE 4–11

CASH LOAN YOU GET ↓	AMOUNT YOU PAY BACK EACH MONTH Including All Charges							
	2 months loan	4 months loan	6 months loan	8 months loan	10 months loan	12 months loan	16 months loan	20 months loan
$ 20	$10.38	$ 5.32	$ 3.63	$ 2.79	$ 2.29	$ 1.95		
25	12.97	6.65	4.54	3.49	2.86	2.44	$20 to $50	
30	15.56	7.97	5.45	4.18	3.43	2.92	loaned only for	
40	20.75	10.63	7.26	5.58	4.57	3.90	12 months or less	
50	25.94	13.29	9.08	6.97	5.71	4.87		
60	31.13	15.95	10.89	8.37	6.86	5.85	$ 4.60	$ 3.85
70	36.32	18.61	12.71	9.76	8.00	6.82	5.36	4.49
75	38.91	19.94	13.62	10.46	8.57	7.31	5.74	4.81
80	41.51	21.27	14.52	11.16	9.14	7.80	6.13	5.13
90	46.69	23.92	16.34	12.55	10.28	8.77	6.89	5.77
100	51.88	26.58	18.15	13.95	11.43	9.75	7.66	6.41
125	64.79	33.20	22.67	17.41	14.26	12.16	9.55	8.00
150	77.70	39.79	27.16	20.85	17.08	14.56	11.43	9.56
175	90.61	46.38	31.65	24.29	19.88	16.95	13.29	11.11
200	103.51	52.97	36.13	27.72	22.68	19.33	15.15	12.65
225	116.39	59.54	40.60	31.14	25.48	21.70	17.00	14.19
250	129.26	66.11	45.08	34.57	28.27	24.08	18.85	15.73
275	142.14	72.69	49.55	37.99	31.06	26.45	20.70	17.26
300	155.02	79.26	54.02	41.41	33.85	28.82	22.55	18.80

WE GUARANTEE the total amount figured by using this table to be the full amount you will pay, when payments are made on schedule. You will pay less if you pay your loan ahead of time since you pay charges only for the actual time you have the money. Payments include charges at Household's rate of 2½% per month on that part of a balance not exceeding $100 and 2% per month on that part of a balance in excess of $100. This rate is less than the maximum prescribed by the Small Loan Law.

B. E. HENDERSON, PRESIDENT

In the second case, the true dollar cost is $45.84 ($28.82 × 12 = $345.84); and, applying the same formula,

$$r = \frac{2 \times 12 \times 45.84}{300\,(12 + 1)} = 28+ \text{ percent}.$$

The approximate annual rate is 28 percent.

Some time ago, teachers in several eastern states received a mail circular from a loan company in a midwestern state. It declared, "Because you are a teacher, you can borrow $50 to $500 by mail on your signature only." Charges were stated thus: "Under our plan, interest is computed on unpaid principal balance at the monthly rate of 3% on that part of the balance not over $150, 2½% on that part of the balance over $150 and not over $300, and ¾ of 1% on any remainder of such balance." The table accompanying this statement of charge is reproduced in Figure 4–12. Referring to the first entry, it is apparent that if you borrowed $100, you would be expected to repay $6.75 per month if you took 20 months to repay. What annual rate does this represent? Using the constant-ratio formula,

$$r = \frac{2 \times 12 \times 35}{100(20 + 1)} = 40 \text{ percent}$$

($6.75 × 20 = $135, which is the total you repay on the $100 loan), it is apparent that the annual rate is 40 percent. If you repaid in 12 months, the rate would be 38 percent:

$$r = \frac{2 \times 12 \times 20.84}{100(12 + 1)} = 38+ \text{ percent}.$$

FIGURE 4–12

	Cash Loan You Get	20* Payments	18* Payments	15* Payments	12 Payments
	$100	$ 6.75	$ 7.29	$ 8.40	$10.07
	150	10.12	10.94	12.60	15.10
SELECT	200	13.43	14.53	16.75	20.09
AMOUNT	250	16.70	18.08	20.85	25.02
YOU WANT	300	19.95	21.60	24.93	29.94
TO	350	23.06	24.99	28.87	34.72
BORROW	400	26.05	28.26	32.70	39.39
	450	28.96	31.46	36.46	43.98
	500	31.83	34.61	40.17	48.54
	*All loans are made in accordance with Government Regulations in effect.				

Ironically, most of the teachers who received this circular, because they have regular jobs with assured incomes, could have borrowed the same amount from banks in their own states at rates ranging from 8 to 12 percent. One can only wonder how many teachers unfamiliar with the simple mathematics of personal loans fell for this expensive lure.

It is difficult to generalize about small-loan companies. Most are considerate and ethical, but some are not. The better ones frequently help borrowers with money management by working out budgets based on total income and all obligations, and they grant only loans which they feel can be repaid within the borrower's income. A small minority are less scrupulous and will take almost any loan that comes along and then hound and harass the borrower until final repayment is secured. Loan company losses are low. They have long ago perfected techniques of collection, as any borrower will discover if he fails to meet the installments. For example, over a period of 13 years (1948–60) consumer finance companies had an average write-off of less than

2 percent (1.81 percent) of the average amount of customers' notes outstanding.

If you have borrowed and find that for reasons beyond your control you just cannot meet an installment that is due, the wisest thing to do is to visit the company and explain your situation. The better company will reschedule your payments by working out a plan you can meet. Other fringe lenders, whether or not you tell them you cannot pay, may call on your neighbors, visit your employer, phone at midnight unless the state law prohibits this, and even annoy you in other ways. In some businesses there are a few companies whose ethics are not up to standard. Generally speaking, loan companies operating in states with effective small-loan laws maintain ethical operations. If you should find you are doing business with a company which engages in unethical practices, see a lawyer or the Legal Aid Society, or visit the local Better Business Bureau.

Loan Sharks

Loan sharks are lenders of money who operate outside the pale of the law. In the field of credit, they are the bootleggers. While occasionally unethical *licensed* lenders will take advantage of an unwary borrower and overcharge him, the term "loan shark" is reserved for those who operate without license or supervision and who violate the letter of the law as well as its social purpose. Loan sharks flourish in states which do not have effective small-loan laws.

If someone offers to lend you $5.00 today if you promise to give him $6.00 a week later, on payday, beware! He is a loan shark. The "five-for-six" racket is an old and lucrative one and still mulcts many an unsuspecting borrower. If you pay one dollar for the use of five for one week, you are being charged interest at the rate of 20 percent a week, or an incredible 1,040 percent per year. No wonder many an industrial worker will find a friendly fellow at the factory gate ready to accommodate him. Borrow $10 from him until payday two weeks later and you will usually pay back $12. A $2.00 charge on $10 for two weeks is 520 percent a year.

Even worse than the exorbitant interest charge is the loan shark's practice of making it difficult, often impossible, for the borrower to repay the principal. The loan shark is glad to have the borrower fall behind in payments of principal, as long as interest is paid; and, indeed, in order to mire the borrower still more deeply, the loan shark may grant another loan to enable the borrower to keep up the interest payments on the first loan. Fantastic cases have come to light of people virtually in bondage to loan sharks as a result of such practices. One cited recently is as follows:

When genial Tony Delotti lent young Mrs. Grace Basso the $50, she never dreamed it was going to cost $4,395. All she had to do was pay him $60 next week. And when next week came, Tony did not press her. She would pay him $72 the following Saturday. Six dollars a week for every five owed; that was his rate.

Mrs. Basso, you will gather, was not very good at arithmetic. Loan shark victims seldom are. Before she realized it, she and the children were going shabby. Tony had a new car and her little debt snowballed into a frightful total. Tony's smile had turned into a scowl and every day he came to ring the doorbell, threatening to tell her husband if she did not pay up.

When her fantastic story recently came to light in court, Mrs. Basso had used up all the family savings, stolen her brother's $1,300 bank account, forged her mother's $2,500 postal certificates, and even pawned her wedding ring, to pay the demands which had sprouted out of that $50 loan with its 1040% annual interest.[11]

Loan-Shark Schemes

The schemes and devices whereby the loan sharks sidestep the law and ensnare victims are myriad. A common device is salary buying. The victim does not borrow; he "sells" the loan shark part or all of his salary. In the middle of the month, for example, the borrower sells $20 of his salary, due at the end of the month, for $18 cash. The loan shark appoints the borrower his agent to collect the salary at the end of the month and deliver it to him. He threatens the borrower with prosecution for embezzlement if he does not deliver. Frequently, no attempt is made to collect the full amount which was "sold," but only the charges are collected and the loan is renewed for another two weeks; and this goes on and on. Many states now have statutes which prohibit salary buying, but a number do not, and it is still widespread.

Another illegal procedure used is to have the borrower sign a note for an amount in excess of the sum actually loaned and then charge interest on the fictitious amount of the signed note. A borrower is frequently so desperate for a loan that he will submit to this. Another technique is endorsement selling. The loan will not be made unless it is endorsed. Luckily, "someone" just happens to be available who, for a fee, will endorse the note. Or two offices, usually run by the same people, claim to be broker and lender. Application for the loan has to be made through the "broker," who then submits it to the "lender." The broker's "commission" is in reality, of course, illegal interest.

---

[11] From *Using Consumer Credit*, Consumer Education Series, Unit No. 9 (Washington, D.C.: National Education Association, latest ed.), pp. 103–4.

Sometimes only one loan shark may be involved in the so-called "brokerage plan." For example, assume you want to borrow $50 in a state which does not have a small-loan law. By means of a card handed to you as you leave work, you are told that a Mr. Smithson arranges loans. When you go to see him, he explains that he does not lend money himself but that he will serve as a broker, for a fee, and arrange a loan for you. For the $50 loan his brokerage fee will be $18.50 and the interest $1.42. If you agree he gives you the $50 and asks you to sign a note for $69.92 payable in eight biweekly installments of $8.74. If you do not stop to calculate, and the average borrower does not, you will have agreed to a loan at a yearly interest rate of more than 260 percent.[12]

A sale of goods—valueless goods—may be tied in to a loan. In this case, the borrower, as a condition of the loan, must buy some valueless ornament or costume jewelry for, say, $25. He will then be granted a $50 loan, with the lender taking a note for $75. An even more vicious variation occurs where the lender gives the borrower who needs cash badly an order on a grocery store for $15 worth of groceries. The store, which is in league with the lender, cashes the order for only $10, but the borrower must repay $15 on the next payday. In some cases, loan sharks will refuse to lend unless the borrower buys costly life, health, and accident insurance, which must be purchased through an agent in league with them and part of the commission on which must be kicked back to the loan shark. Legislative and court records indicate that in some cases over 80 percent of the premiums paid by the borrowers are returned by the agents to the lenders.

The loan-shark jewelry lender has a method all his own, a survey in New York revealed. He solicits business through disarming letters to city employees which make them believe they can borrow with a minimum of red tape. "Just show your badge and your credit is good up to $500," is the appeal. When a city employee swallows the bait and applies for the loan, he is met by the following, according to a report of the Department of Investigation of the City of New York:

"I am sorry I cannot lend you money," says the loan shark, "because I do not have a state license from the Banking Department to do that sort of thing. But I will help you anyway. I have a gorgeous diamond ring here that I could lend you and I don't need a license to do that. You can take the ring down the street to the pawnshop and they'll advance you $200 on it."

The unwary city employee accepts the ring and signs a harmless looking

---

[12] See Wallace P. Mors, *Consumer Credit Facts for You* (Cleveland, Ohio: Bureau of Business Research, Western Reserve University, latest ed.), p. 25.

paper which the lender explains is merely a receipt for the ring. Actually it is a confession of judgment and is used as evidence that the employee purchased a diamond ring for $350. The loan shark claims that the transaction was a bona fide sale and when he sends the execution to the Comptroller's Office for collection of 10% of the employee's wages, there is nothing on the face of the record to indicate that the loan is a swindle. Usually the city employee who has "bought" the ring finds it impossible to borrow more than $50 from a pawnbroker on the ring which has an alleged value of at least $350. After the city employee has made fruitless attempts to get a reasonable loan on the ring he usually returns to the loan shark to protest, but invariably the shark is nowhere to be found, and his clerk is very sorry but knows nothing about the transaction. The victim, in desperation, accepts the largest loan on the ring which he can secure—usually a very small portion of the value suggested by the loan shark. The city employee never knows that his salary is garnisheed until there is a reduction in his pay check.[13]

The jewelry loan sharks, at the time of the survey, had an aggregate claim against city employees which was $75,000 greater than the claims of all the legitimate lending agencies supervised by the State Banking Department. Why did city employees resort to loan sharks when they needed money? The main answer that emerged was that they did not know where money could be borrowed most cheaply. Their municipal credit union and the two largest commercial banks stood ready to grant personal loans at about 6 percent. In addition, they could have borrowed from their retirement system against their cumulated contributions, for 5 percent. Yet, through ignorance, they went to illegal lenders.

This, however, is not the only reason why borrowers resort to unlicensed lenders. Not only do the borrowers feel that they have not much choice but usually they do not know what they are getting into. The borrower usually does not want it known that he is in debt or is taking on a debt, and the illegal lender is well pleased to have the loan kept secret. Everything is done quietly—at first. There is no red tape. No one knows—only borrower and lender. No credit investigation, no cosigners, no calls to employer or landlord to verify job and residence claims. But this initial secrecy boomerangs, for should the borrower fail to pay an installment, the loan shark threatens to tell the borrower's family, or his employer, or the neighbors. He may even appear at the borrower's office and loudly denounce him as a "crook and deadbeat." In more extreme cases, borrowers who are late in payments or who try to pay off the principal entirely are beaten up.

---

[13] "Report to the Mayor on Garnishment Executions against City Employees," A Study by the Department of Investigation and Accounts, City of New York, p. 10.

Loan sharks flourish mainly in those states which have no effective small-loan law or in those where the stringency of the small-loan law, limiting rates to say 10 percent a year, has driven the legitimate small-loan company out of the state because it cannot profitably do business at such a rate. Foster cites several cases where, in battles in state legislatures over whether or not to pass a small-loan law, the agents of the illegal lenders, when it became apparent that their lobbying efforts to prevent the passage of the small-loan law had failed, turned around and lobbied for very stringent regulation, with a low maximum annual rate of 10 percent or less.[14] They knew that the latter would be as effective in insuring their continued operation as the former. Texas, for example, once relied entirely on its 10 percent a year usury law and, as a result, was, for a time, the leading loan-shark state.

The *Dallas Morning News* ran a series of nine articles on loan-shark activities in its state.[15] One article was headlined "$25 Note Grows to $1,500 Debt," while another declared:

The person who borrows $50 in Dallas usually must repay $68 in three months. Ten percent interest? Only 48 cents of the $18 charged represents interest. The rest goes for insurance and fees. A loan company with a credit insurance tie-in likely will make the borrower take two $25 loans instead of one for $50. This is legal. At least no law prohibits the practice in Texas. It permits doubling up on policy and other fees.

With each loan, the borrower in this case must buy life insurance, health and accident insurance, and hospitalization insurance. There is a $1 service charge and 75 cents policy fee, besides what the insurance itself costs. The whole thing adds up to about $9 on each $25 loan. This is $18 for three months —just to get $50.

States which do not have effective small-loan laws include Arkansas, Delaware, Georgia, Mississippi, South Carolina, Tennessee, and the District of Columbia. While exact statistics are, of course, not available, the best estimates are that illegal lenders do in excess of $200 million of business annually in the United States.

The best word of advice that can be given about borrowing from loan sharks is "don't." But if, inadvertently, you do become a victim, go and see the District Attorney, your local Legal Aid Society, or the Better Business Bureau as soon as you realize your predicament.

---

[14] William Trufant Foster, *Loan Sharks and Their Victims,* Public Affairs Pamphlet No. 39 (revised).

[15] Richard M. Morehead, "Loan Shark State," a series of nine articles in the *Dallas Morning News,* April 11–19, 1953. The *Texas Observer* in January–February, 1956, and the *Houston Post* in January–February, 1957, each ran a series of articles on loan-shark practices in Texas.

Pawnbrokers

You will probably never need to resort to a pawnbroker, but for thousands of families he is still an important factor in emergency credit. The role of the pawnbroker has diminished somewhat since the advent of the small-loan company, but there is still no other lender who will let you have $5.00 for a few days at legal rates of interest or who will lend $100 on five minutes' notice, without any investigation of your credit standing or lack of it.

A pawnbroker lends money on the security of personal effects, household or sporting goods, jewelry, furs, etc., left with him by the borrower. The contract by which loans of this description are effected is called a "pawn" or "pledge," and the same terms are also applied to the articles deposited. The pawn or pledge must have resale value, and the pawnbroker, who through long experience has become an expert judge of values, appraises it in terms of the price he can get for it on resale. He will probably lend 60–90 percent of the estimated resale value; that is, he allows a margin of safety in case he is forced to sell the pledged article to recover his loan.

If his offer is accepted, he gives the borrower the money and a ticket which identifies the merchandise and gives the borrower the right to redeem it at any time within a given period by repaying the amount loaned plus interest. The article is left at the pawnshop as security for the loan. If the loan is not repaid within the specified time, or, if no time is specified, then within a reasonable time as defined by state law, the pawnbroker may sell the pledged article and retain the proceeds if this sum does not exceed the amount of the loan plus accumulated interest. If there is, by chance, a surplus, it is supposed to be turned over to the borrower.

A pawnbroker's loan is unlike most others previously described. You never have to pay back a pawnbroker's loan if you do not want to or cannot. You do not even have to pay interest. The pawnbroker cannot force you to do either, nor will he ever try to find you to take you to court or ganishee your salary, for you sign nothing. His security is the article you pledged; and if you fail to repay the loan, he simply sells the article. Even if you repay the loan, you do it in a lump sum, not in installments; and you can pay it back at any time within the over-all period. Interest charges range from 2 percent a month all the way to 10 percent a month, depending upon the state. A common rate is 3 percent per month. Thus you would pay from 20 cents to $1.00 a month (30 cents in the case of a 3 percent rate) on each $10 borrowed.

Who borrows from pawnbrokers? Obviously, only persons in desperate need, those with no cash reserve to fall back on in an emergency and with no certain future income. They want cash quickly and are in no condition to hold out or bargain; if the cash offered for the pledge seems very low, they usually take it, nevertheless. They have very little choice. It is partly for this reason that unscrupulous pawnbrokers were able to take advantage of borrowers at one time, and this subsequently led to regulation. Laws were passed in many states which provided for licensing, set maximum rates, provided for state supervision, and required that a record be kept of all loans, the name of the borrower, the date, the payment, etc.

Remedial Loan Societies

Out of the need to help a poverty-stricken borrower, using his last possessions to get cash before resorting to charity or public relief, and out of the desire of philanthropic citizens to prevent persons in such desperate straits from being subjected to excessive charges, grew the remedial loan society. These are semiphilanthropic pawnshops, the most famous of which is the Provident Loan Society of New York. Formed in 1894, over its first half-century the Society made 20,005,350 loans aggregating $1,055,227,046.[16] It has made loans for as little as 25 cents and for as much as several thousand dollars; currently the Society makes 400,000 loans a year. Its interest rates are the lowest known for pledge loans: 1 percent per month on the amount of the loan that is $100 or less, and ¾ of 1 percent a month on that part of the loan over $100. This is charged only on the outstanding balance for the exact number of days. The loan may be outstanding for a year before the pledge is sold. Interest is not deducted in advance, and loans may be repaid fully or partially at any time during the year at the convenience of the borrower. At any time during the life of the loan, the payment of interest due plus a small reduction of principal will extend the loan for another year. The Society advises the borrower never to destroy an expired loan ticket without first inquiring if a surplus is due. Any surplus realized above the loan amount when the pledge is sold at public auction is paid to the borrower on presentation of the loan ticket. If the sale results in a loss, it is borne by the Society.

Some twenty-one remedial loan societies exist in principal cities in several states, and it is surprising that other pawnbrokers survive in these localities in the face of such competition. The loan societies'

---

[16] See Provident Loan Society of New York, *Fifty Years of Remedial Lending* (New York, 1944) p. 29.

standards are higher, and their charges lower, than those of pawn-brokers. Rates range from 1 to 2 percent a month on unpaid balances. Only ignorance will lead a person to a commercial pawnbroker if the facilities of an organization such as the Provident Loan Society are available.

Miscellaneous Sources of Loans

If you have an account in a savings bank, the bank can, under the law in some states, grant loans against the account. It seems logical to suppose, however, that, if you needed funds, you would use the savings themselves rather than borrow against them, particularly since you normally would pay more as interest on the loan (5 or 6 percent) than you would receive on a savings account (4 or 4½ percent). You can also borrow against shares you may own in a savings and loan association, but the same logic would seem to apply. Why pay 6 percent for the loan when you could use your own money, on which you are getting 4 or 5 percent? The only strong argument in favor of borrowing against savings in either savings banks or savings and loan associations rather than using the savings themselves is that the compulsion to repay the loan will be stronger than the drive to rebuild your expended savings and that you will probably regain your original financial status more quickly and more certainly if you borrow. On the other hand, the financial disadvantage of this in terms of cost is clear.

There is one circumstance where borrowing against a savings deposit or a savings and loan account is clearly justified. Some people borrow against their accumulations shortly before the semiannual dividend-declaration date. By borrowing, the individual continues to receive his dividend for the entire six-month period, whereas he may be paying interest for a much shorter period and may thus come out ahead on the transaction.

Conclusion

Shopping for a loan is a complicated business, but it obviously pays to shop, since it may mean the difference between paying 5, 40, or 520 percent for your money. Generally speaking, an insurance company, commercial bank, or credit union will be your least expensive source of personal credit; industrial banks and consumer finance companies are somewhat more costly, while illegal and unlicensed lenders are simply extortionate. If you shop around for your loan, where you borrow is likely to depend on your credit standing, because if it is good—if your prospective future income is adequate and regular—you will need to

TABLE 4-4

Sources of Personal Loans Compared

Lender	Charge for $100 Repayable in One Year		Range of Loans	Collateral Needed	Other Characteristics
	True Dollar Cost	True Annual Rate			
Insurance company or Veterans Administration	$4–$6*	Range, 4–6%* Common, 6%	Loan value of policy	Insurance policy with cash value	No due date. If interest and principal are not paid, no legal action will be taken, but deductions will be made when policy becomes payable. No questions asked about purpose of loan. No credit investigation. Repayment in lump sum, if at all; usually not on installment basis.
Savings banks or savings and loan associations	$5–$6*	Range, 5–12%* Common, 6%	Up to full value of savings account, or 90% of value of savings and loan assn. shares	Savings account or savings and loan shares	No credit investigation necessary, but must have savings account or loan shares.
Commercial banks, personal-loan department	$4.25–$12.00	Range, 8–24% Common, 12%	$60–$5,000	Varies—single signature; cosigner; chattel mortgages on cars or household goods, etc.	Credit investigation necessary. Loans both installment and single payment. Purpose of loan must be approved. Rate usually quoted on discount basis, and repayment usually on monthly installment basis.
Credit union	$6.50 maximum for federal credit—generally also for state credit unions	Range, 6–12% (Max., 1% per mo.) Common, 12%	$5–$3,000	Anything acceptable to credit committee	Maximum rate is 1% per month on *unpaid balances* for federal credit unions. Repayable in installments. Must be a member of credit union to borrow. Purpose must be approved.
Industrial banks and industrial loan companies	$8–$12	Range, 12–24% Common, 16%	$50–$5,000	Same as commercial bank	Credit investigation necessary. Usually loan repayable in installments, though some single-payment loans made. Purpose must be approved. Investigation fee usually charged. Rates usually quoted on discount basis.
Consumer finance companies	$13–$24	Range, 16–42% Common, 30%	$10–$5,000, varying with the state	Generally, chattel mortgage or signature	Rates quoted on monthly basis, up to a maximum of 3½% on *unpaid balance.* In some states, monthly rate is graduated according to size of loan; thus, in New York State, 2½% on first $100; 2% from $100 to $300; ¾ of 1% from $300 to $800. Purpose of loan must be approved. Repayment on monthly installment basis.
Loan sharks	$50–$1,040	Range, 50–1040% Common, 260%	$5–$1,000	Varies greatly	No credit investigation; purpose of loan of no importance; due date on principal will be ignored if interest paid regularly; frequently strong-arm methods used to collect.
Pawnbroker	$24–$120*	Range, 24–120%* Common, 36%	$1–$500	Pawn or pledge	Rates usually quoted on monthly basis: 2–10% per month. Usually 60–90% of estimated resale value of pledged property is loaned. No credit investigation. Purpose of loan no concern to lender. Single-payment loans usual. Repayment unnecessary.
Remedial Loan Society Pledge loans	$9–$24*	Range, 9–24%* Common, 12%	$1–$500	Pledged property, signature, chattel mortgage, comaker	Rates usually 1% per month on unpaid balances. Loans need not be repaid. Single-payment or installment loans. No credit investigation necessary on pledge loans. Usually one year allowed to repay loan before pledge is sold.
Other loans	$12–$25	Range, 15–30% Common, 18%			

* On the assumption that repayment does not occur in installments but rather in one lump sum at the end of the year and that interest is paid at the time of repayment, not deducted in advance.

go no further than the commercial bank or credit union. If these institutions are reluctant to take you, a consumer finance company or industrial bank may. If you cannot get a loan, however, it means that men skilled at analyzing people's finances have decided you should not borrow, since you have little or no prospect of paying back. If they could with reasonable safety lend to you, they would. If they will not, there is always the pawnbroker; and of these, the best are the remedial loan societies. As between resorting to a loan shark and going to a pawnbroker, it seems quite clear that the latter is preferable. Table 4–4, showing sources of personal loans, may serve to provide a useful comparison and summary.

SUGGESTED READINGS

1. "Quick Credit Cost Computer," Savings Banks Association of New York State. A free copy may be obtained by writing to the Association at 200 Park Avenue, New York, 10017.
2. *Finance Facts Yearbook,* published annually. A free copy may be obtained by writing to the National Consumer Finance Association, 1000 Sixteenth Street, N.W., Washington, D.C., 20036.
3. "Beware The Interest Charge," *Reader's Digest,* November, 1963.
4. M. R. Neifeld, "How To Simplify Use of the Constant Ratio Formula in Computing Annual Finance Rates," in *Personal Finance Law Quarterly Report,* Vol. 17, No. 4 (Fall, 1963), pp. 117–18.
5. National Consumer Finance Association, *The Consumer Finance Industry.* A monograph prepared for the Commission on Money and Credit. Englewood Cliffs, N.J.: Prentice-Hall, Inc., 1962.
6. S. R. Nuccio, "Personal Finance: Borrower Life Insurance," in the *New York Times,* October 14, 1963.
7. Paul Smith, *Cost of Providing Consumer Credit,* Occasional Paper No. 83. New York: National Bureau of Economic Research, 1962.
8. "All About Credit," *Changing Times, The Kiplinger Magazine,* March, 1963.
9. "Why It Pays to Shop for Credit," *Changing Times, The Kiplinger Magazine,* January, 1962.
10. *Facts You Should Know About Borrowing,* Educational Division, National Better Business Bureau, Chrysler Building, New York, latest edition.
11. Wallace P. Mors, *Small Loan Laws.* 13th ed. Cleveland, Ohio: Bureau of Business Research, Western Reserve University, 1961.
12. William Trufant Foster, *Loan Sharks and Their Victims,* Public Affairs Pamphlet No. 39, latest edition.
13. *A Bank Manual on Personal Loans.* New York: American Bankers Association, latest edition.
14. "Credit Scoring Systems," *Time Sales Financing,* American Finance Conference, Vol. 27, No. 5 (September–October, 1963).

15. "Your Legal Rights as a Borrower," *The Credit Union Bridge,* Vol. 21, No. 11 (January, 1957).

16. Wallace P. Mors, *Consumer Credit Facts for You.* Cleveland, Ohio: Bureau of Business Research, Western Reserve University, latest edition.

17. Bureau of Federal Credit Unions, *Report of Operations for the Year 1963.* Washington, D.C.: U.S. Department of Health, Education, and Welfare, 1964 (issued annually).

18. Roger S. Barrett, *Compilation of Consumer Finance Laws.* Washington, D.C.: National Consumer Finance Association, latest edition.

19. *The Computation of Charges for Personal Loan Departments and for Consumer Finance Loans.* Boston: Financial Publishing Co., latest edition. A free copy may be obtained by writing to the company at 82 Brookline Ave., Boston 15, Mass.

20. Board of Governors of the Federal Reserve System, *Consumer Instalment Credit,* Part I, Vol. I, 388 pp. Washington, D.C., 1957.

21. *Consumer Finance Rate and Regulation Chart.* Washington, D.C.: National Consumer Finance Association, latest edition (issued annually). For a copy of this and the latest tabulation of state small-loan laws write to the National Consumer Finance Association, 1000 Sixteenth St., N.W., Washington, D.C., 20036.

22. Credit Union National Association (CUNA), *Credit Union Yearbook.* Madison, Wis., latest edition (issued annually). A free copy may be obtained on request.

CASE PROBLEMS

1. If there is a credit union in your locality, interview the chairman of the loan committee and ascertain:
   a) The general economic status of those who borrow from the credit union.
   b) The credit tests the union uses for loan applicants.
   c) The costs of granting loans.
   d) The loss experience of the union.
   e) The collection procedure followed in case a borrower is late in paying installments.
In your opinion, is this a good place to obtain a loan?

2. If there is a small-loan company in your town, arrange an interview with the manager and ascertain:
   a) The general economic status of the loan company's borrowers. Does the manager think they differ as a group from those who go to a commercial bank for small loans?
   b) The credit tests the company applies to loan applicants.
   c) The cost of granting small loans, both absolute and as a percentage of the rates charged borrowers.
   d) The loss experience of the company.
   e) The collection procedure the company follows if installments are not paid when due.
Would you enjoy doing business with this institution? Why?

3. If there is a commercial bank with a small-loan department in the town in which your school is located, arrange an interview with the manager and ascertain:

a) How an applicant's credit status is investigated and checked.

b) What the loss experience of the bank has been on small loans.

c) What fees, if any, the bank charges on a small loan in addition to the stated interest.

d) What security or collateral the bank requires.

e) What collection procedure the bank follows if the borrower is late in his payments.

For what reasons do you believe that you would or would not like to have a small loan from this bank?

4. The Home Bank agrees to lend you $100 at a discount rate of 6 percent, plus an investigation fee of $3. If the loan is payable in 12 monthly installments, what is the true annual interest rate? In your opinion, is this rate too high?

5. If Timilty borrows $300 at a discount rate of 6 percent and agrees to repay the loan in one payment at the end of a year, what is the true annual interest rate he is paying?

If, on the other hand, he borrows $300 at a discount rate of 6 percent and agrees to pay back the loan in 12 monthly installments of $25 each, what is the true annual interest rate?

6. Jason wants to borrow $250 from a personal-loan company. He has no collateral. He is told that he can have the money only if he can find a satisfactory comaker for his note. He approaches Yarrow, a fellow-worker in an automobile factory. How would you react if you were Yarrow?

7. Barrows has a $10,000 life policy with the John Hancock Mutual Life Insurance Company in Boston. The policy now has a loan value of $3,000. Upon writing to the company, he is told that 6 percent per annum is charged on loans. He also is told that he may surrender the policy for $3,000. He wonders why he should pay any interest at all for the use of his own money. A friend tells him that a local bank will lend $3,000 on the policy, charging only 4.5 percent interest, and that there are other advantages in borrowing from a local bank. Discuss.

8. Lamson works for the Connelly Company, which established a credit union for its employees several years ago; but Lamson knows little about it. He needs to borrow $50 right away. He is about to seek a loan from a local personal finance company when a friend advises that he contact the credit union. Why?

9. Robles meets Gonsalves. They start talking about personal finance companies. Robles says it is always better to deal with one of the giants in the business. What do you suppose are his arguments?

10. Homer, a bachelor, has just been released from the hospital after a serious operation. The doctors have told him that he must spend at least three months recuperating. Homer currently owes $300 to various creditors, and his savings have been depleted by his illness. His company pays all employees on sick leave half their regular salary—or $40 a week in Homer's case. He also has

a $5,000 life insurance policy which has a cash-surrender value of $1,500. What should he do?

11. Lytell and Makepeace meet after having made their payments at a personal finance company. Lytell says next time he will borrow from the local remedial loan association. Makepeace does not agree. He says that he has had dealings there and that he likes dealing at the personal finance company better. What do you suppose their respective arguments are?

5 USING YOUR BANK

A bankbook makes good reading—better than most novels.

—Sir Harry Lauder

A YOUNG couple were talking. "Dear," he said, "you must be more careful. The bank just returned the last check you wrote."

"Oh, darling," she answered, "that's wonderful. What shall we buy with it this time?"

The modern bank is a department store of finance. It performs a wide variety of services for you, but the one you will probably find most useful and convenient, perhaps the first service everyone uses at a bank, is the checking account. Last year in the United States over eleven billion checks, totaling more than $3 trillion, were used.

Why are checking accounts now so universally used? Well, it's a most convenient way to pay. There is a vast saving in time and effort. You can pay by mail, sit at your desk and write out your checks and not have to run from store to store or office to office and possibly stand in line to pay bills. That's eliminated. A check allows you to pay the exact amount due. It represents safety because you don't have to carry or have large sums of cash around. Furthermore it provides an automatic receipt. Your canceled check, which is returned to you after it has been cashed, is a receipt. You can keep your accounts straight through checkbook stubs, the bank's monthly statement to you, and the return canceled checks. A check is simply an order to your bank to pay someone you name an amount of money you have on deposit. Sooner or later everyone needs to write a check, and once you open an account and try it you'll never be without a checking account. It's a tremendous convenience, and it adds prestige. You may frequently be asked to name your bank in connection with transactions involving credit, such as opening a charge account, or renting a house or an apartment.

173

"All I ever get is checks!"

Kinds of Accounts, Balances, and Service Charges

There are regular checking accounts and special checking accounts. The regular checking account requires a minimum balance, sometimes $300, often $500, occasionally $1,000. The special checking account does not require a minimum balance. As one large bank advertises, it requires only $3.00 to open a special checking account, $1.00 to deposit, and $2.00 to buy a book of 20 checks.

Since there are some 23 different operations involved in cashing a check, the expense of handling a checking account is much greater than the average depositor realizes. As a result, most banks today impose service charges, of which there are many variations. The simplest and oldest type is a flat service charge levied at a fixed rate. For example, one bank charges $1.00 on all accounts when the balance falls below $100 at any time during the month; if the balance is between $100 and $300, 75 cents is charged; and if there is a balance above $300 at all times, there is no service charge.

In another case, the service charge takes into account not only the balance maintained but the number of checks cashed as well. If you maintain a minimum balance of $300, you get ten checks free; of $500,

20 free checks, etc. On all checks above the free minimum set by your balance you pay a 5-cent service charge. In most banks, on personal checking accounts there is no service charge if you consistently maintain a minimum balance of $500 and make normal and not excessive use of the account.

Increasingly analysis plans are being used. You pay a fixed amount for type of transaction plus a monthly maintenance fee. For example, you may be charged 6 cents for each check paid, 3 cents for each check deposited, and a 75-cent maintenance fee. The bank assigns you an earnings credit on your balance, say 10 or 13 cents per $100 of average monthly balance. The earnings credit is deducted from the total charges, and you pay the net amount, if any (see Figure 5–1, page 176). The bank maintains an activity card for each account (see Figure 5–2, page 178). Additional charges are levied for other items, such as a 50-cent charge for a check deposited which is returned uncollected, or a $3.00 charge for a check you write which is returned because of insufficient funds (see Figure 5–3, page 179).

You may, of course, open a checking account in which no minimum balance is required. Special checking accounts have been devised over the last two decades to encourage the use of commercial banks by those who find it difficult to maintain a consistent minimum balance. These special accounts are known by various names, such as "Pay-As-You-Go Checkway," "Check-Master," "Chex," "Thrifti-Checks," etc., but there are a number of features common to all (see Fig. 5–4). No minimum balance is required. Each time a check is cashed, a fee, usually 10 cents, is charged. The depositor needs only enough money on deposit to cover any check written. Sometimes a special checkbook, containing 20 checks, is sold in advance by the bank for $2.00. At times a fee, usually smaller than the check fee, is charged for each deposit. Normally there is a monthly 50-cent service or handling charge imposed as well.

The service charge usually does not come to very much each month, and the convenience of having and using a checking account more than compensates for the cost. You should choose the type of account— either special checking account or regular checking account with minimum balance and no fee—best suited to your finances. If you can afford to keep a minimum balance large enough to avoid service charges, it is a good idea to do so. But if you cannot do this, it should not prevent you from enjoying the convenience of a checking account. Over most of the country, the charges on special checking accounts appear to be small and reasonable. If there are a number of banks in your community, shop to see which has the most reasonable service charge consistent with

ACTIVITY COSTS Cost factors are as follows:

Each check paid .... .06
Each check deposited .... .03
Monthly maintenance expense .... .75

THERE IS NO CHARGE FOR DEPOSIT TICKETS

Costs totaling $.25 or less are not charged to you.

Upon request, rates will be supplied for accounts requiring special services or having a large volume of checks paid or deposited.

EARNING ON YOUR MONTHLY AVERAGE BALANCE

A monthly earning credit of $.13 for each $100.00 average balance is allowed on balances maintained as an offset against activity costs.

HOW TO ANALYZE YOUR ACCOUNT

To estimate your monthly activity charge based on average monthly balance maintained, follow these steps:

1. Number of checks drawn ...... [   ] x .06 [$]
2. Number of checks deposited ... [   ] x .03 [   ]
3. Maintenance Expense 75
4. Unusual service (if any):   [$] "A"

   TOTAL EXPENSE   [$] "B"

5. Estimate your average monthly balance

SEE CHART—In first column, locate amount nearest to total expense —"A". Follow chart across to your estimated average balance— —"B". If amount is blank, your account is "Cost Free"—otherwise the amount shown is your activity charge.   [$]

COST FREE ACCOUNT

To determine average monthly balance required to avoid any activity charge see chart—last column—on line with your total expense "A" above.

FIGURE 5-1

Chart for Estimating Charges

Total Ex-pense	Under Min. Bal.	$500 to $599	$600 to $699	$700 to $799	$800 to $899	$900 to $999	$1,000 to $1,099	$1,100 to $1,199	$1,200 to $1,299	$1,300 to $1,399	$1,400 to $1,499	$1,500 to $1,599	$1,600 to $1,699	$1,700 to $1,799	No charge with Avg. Monthly Bal. of
.81															500
.87															500
.93		.28													600
.99		.34													600
1.05		.40	.27												700
1.11		.46	.33												700
1.17		.52	.39	.26											800
1.23		.58	.45	.32											800
1.29		.64	.51	.38											800
1.35		.70	.57	.44	.31										900
1.41		.76	.63	.50	.37										900
1.47		.82	.69	.56	.43	.30									1000
1.53		.88	.75	.62	.49	.36									1000
1.59		.94	.81	.68	.55	.42	.29								1100
1.65		1.00	.87	.74	.61	.48	.35								1100
1.71		1.06	.93	.80	.67	.54	.41	.28							1200
1.77		1.12	.99	.86	.73	.60	.47	.34							1200
1.83		1.18	1.05	.92	.79	.66	.53	.40	.27						1300
1.89		1.24	1.11	.98	.85	.72	.59	.46	.33						1300
1.95		1.30	1.17	1.04	.91	.78	.65	.52	.39	.26					1400
2.01		1.36	1.23	1.10	.97	.84	.71	.58	.45	.32					1400
2.07		1.42	1.29	1.16	1.03	.90	.77	.64	.51	.38					1400
2.13		1.48	1.35	1.22	1.09	.96	.83	.70	.57	.44	.31				1500
2.19		1.54	1.41	1.28	1.15	1.02	.89	.76	.63	.50	.37				1500
2.25		1.60	1.47	1.34	1.21	1.08	.95	.82	.69	.56	.43	.30			1600
2.31	3.06	1.66	1.53	1.40	1.27	1.14	1.01	.88	.75	.62	.49	.36			1600
2.37	3.12	1.72	1.59	1.46	1.33	1.20	1.07	.94	.81	.68	.55	.42	.29		1700
2.43	3.18	1.78	1.65	1.52	1.39	1.26	1.13	1.00	.87	.74	.61	.48	.35		1700
2.49	3.24	1.84	1.71	1.58	1.45	1.32	1.19	1.06	.93	.80	.67	.54	.41	.28	1800
2.55	3.30	1.90	1.77	1.64	1.51	1.38	1.25	1.12	.99	.86	.73	.60	.47	.34	1800
3.15	3.90	2.50	2.37	2.24	2.11	1.98	1.85	1.72	1.59	1.46	1.33	1.20	1.07	.94	2300
3.75	4.50	3.10	2.97	2.84	2.71	2.58	2.45	2.32	2.19	2.06	1.93	1.80	1.67	1.54	2700
4.35	5.10	3.70	3.57	3.44	3.31	3.18	3.05	2.92	2.79	2.66	2.53	2.40	2.27	2.14	3200
4.95	5.70	4.30	4.17	4.04	3.91	3.78	3.65	3.52	3.39	3.26	3.13	3.00	2.87	2.74	3700
5.55	6.30	4.90	4.77	4.64	4.51	4.38	4.25	4.12	3.99	3.86	3.73	3.60	3.47	3.34	4100
6.15	6.90	5.50	5.37	5.24	5.11	4.98	4.85	4.72	4.59	4.46	4.33	4.20	4.07	3.94	4600
6.75	7.50	6.10	5.97	5.84	5.71	5.58	5.45	5.32	5.19	5.06	4.93	4.80	4.67	4.54	5000

(In the "Under Min. Bal." column, a bracket marked ←——$3.00——→ spans the upper rows.)

This chart includes: Earning allowance . . . $.13 per $100 balance

SOURCE: First National Bank of New York.

your financial position and requirements. Figure 5–3 indicates the nature of the service charge.

Opening an Acccount

To open an account is a simple matter and takes only a few minutes. The six steps involved in opening an account may be listed as follows:

1. The necessary information about the new customer—place of birth, address, telephone number, occupation and employer, names of parents and places of birth—is obtained by the bank and later verified.

2. The bank's service charges are explained so that there may be no misunderstanding.

3. Signature cards are made out by the new customer, in the same form that they are to appear on the checks, so that tellers may later verify his signature on all checks until they get to know the customer well.

4. A receipt for the initial deposit, in the form of an official receipt slip, which is a duplicate copy of the deposit slip, is issued. Most banks have now abandoned the passbook in favor of the multiple-copy deposit slip. Some fully automated banks provide multiple-copy deposit slips that have the customer's name imprinted and also have the bank's ABA routing number and the customer's account number in MICR (Magnetic Ink Character Recognition) characters.

5. The customer is supplied with a checkbook, which in the case of fully automated banks has the customer's name printed on each check, as well as the bank's ABA routing number and the customer's account number in MICR characters.

6. The employees of the bank are notified of the new account, and often the new customer is introduced to a teller who will handle his particular account.

Usually an account is opened in the name of one depositor alone. A husband and wife, however, often open a joint account, with right of survivorship. Then each of them can draw checks on the same account. Frequently there is division of labor. He specializes in depositing; she is withdrawing. The service charges are apt to be less than if each had a separate account. In case of the death of a person who has an account in his name alone, no other person, except the legally appointed executor or administrator of his estate, can draw on the account. Sometimes this may tie the account up for months before the court takes action. Usually the survivor or survivors of a joint account can arrange with little difficulty to continue drawing checks on the account; they must merely give the tax authorities assurance that all taxes due will be

FIGURE 5–2

Account Activity Analysis Card

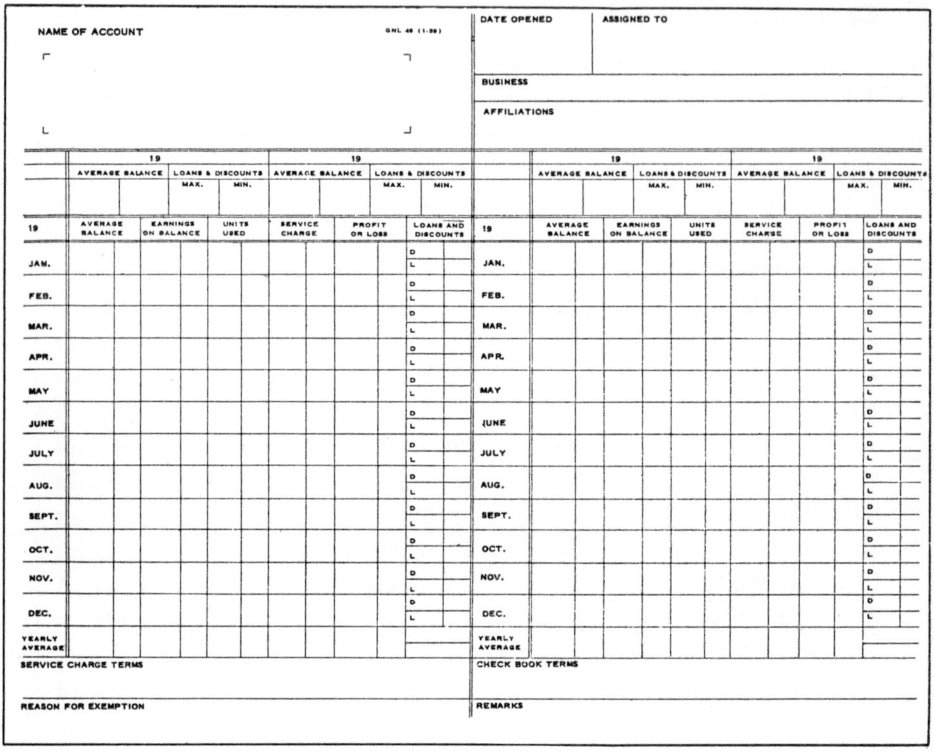

NAME OF ACCOUNT

DATE OPENED | ASSIGNED TO

BUSINESS

AFFILIATIONS

	19				19			
	AVERAGE BALANCE		LOANS & DISCOUNTS		AVERAGE BALANCE		LOANS & DISCOUNTS	
			MAX.	MIN.			MAX.	MIN.

19	AVERAGE BALANCE	EARNINGS ON BALANCE	UNITS USED	SERVICE CHARGE	PROFIT OR LOSS	LOANS AND DISCOUNTS
JAN.						D / L
FEB.						D / L
MAR.						D / L
APR.						D / L
MAY						D / L
JUNE						D / L
JULY						D / L
AUG.						D / L
SEPT.						D / L
OCT.						D / L
NOV.						D / L
DEC.						D / L
YEARLY AVERAGE						

SERVICE CHARGE TERMS | CHECK BOOK TERMS

REASON FOR EXEMPTION | REMARKS

SOURCE: Chemical Bank New York Trust Company.

paid. When two or more persons use the same account, care must be exercised to avoid confusion and not to draw checks for more money than is in the account. Each should keep a full and clear record of every check drawn, and frequently the complete record should be brought together so that both will know just what has been deposited and withdrawn.

Monthly Statements

Customarily, banks prepare monthly statements of each account and submit them, with canceled checks, to the depositors, in person or by mail. They do not necessarily prepare them as of the end of the month; to spread the work, one third may be ready as of the 10th, one third as of the 20th, and the remaining third as of the end of the month. Those that operate on a monthly basis may, in order to get the statements out

Service Charge Rate Schedule

Service		Rate	Service	Rate
Cashing Privilege in other Branch of Bank	Establish	3.00	Mimimum Monthly Charge Business Accounts — a. Under $300 Average Bal.	3.00
Cashing Privilege in other Branch of Bank	Each Review	2.00	b. Under $500 Average Bal. but not under $300	2.00
Checks on us Certified		.50	c. Under $300 Average Bal. (inactive accounts)	1.00
Checks on us Paid (thru Clearings or Deposited by others)		.06	Minimum Monthly Charge Personal Accounts — a. Under $300 Average Bal. Max.	3.00
Checks Deposited – per check		.03	b. Under $300 Average Bal. (inactive accounts)	1.00
Checks Deposited by Correspondent Banks (Also Customers Depositing 100 Checks or more)		.02	Official Checks Purchased	.50
Checks on us Returned (insufficient or uncollected funds)		3.00	Overdrafts & Drawings Against Uncollected Funds (Plus Interest as ordered)	2.00
Checks Deposited Returned: Not Good		.50	Payable Thru Drafts	.03
Deposits – Currency (5¢ minimum)	Per hour	3.00	Payroll Checks Cashed	.15
Collection Items – Cleared		.75	Payrolls Prepared (50¢ minimum) Per Minute	.05
Collection Items – Hand Presentation		1.50	Statements of Account other than Monthly (incl. postage)	1.00
Collection Items – Returned (additional)		.25	Stop Payments	2.00
Coupons Deposited (per envelope)		.50	Transcripts of Account for past period (per sheet)	3.00
Coupons Returned (per envelope)		.50	Transfers (Interior)	.75
Maintenance Charge – Business Accounts		1.00	Transfers (Outside)	1.50
Maintenance Charge – Personal Accounts		.75	Wrapped Coin (Per Roll)	.01½

ACCOUNT ANALYSIS: IF AN ACCOUNT SHOWS A LOSS UNDER $.25, POST LOSS IN THE PROFIT AND LOSS COLUMN OF THE AVERAGE BALANCE CARD (GNL 46) AS OUR MINIMUM CHARGE IS $.25. A LOSS OF $.25 OR MORE SHOULD BE POSTED IN THE SERVICE CHARGE COLUMN.

Earnings Credit Allowance $.10 per $100.00 of Average Balance

FIGURE 5-4

A First National City Special Checking
Account offers you these advantages —

SAFEGUARDS FUNDS

Dispels worry about theft or loss of money. Eliminates the need of keeping large amounts of cash on person or premises. Avoids risk of sending cash by mail.

SAVES TIME AND TROUBLE

Ends necessity of rushing around to pay local bills. Prevents loss of time standing in line; also the aggravation, loss of temper, wear and tear on nerves.

BRINGS NEW CONVENIENCE

Makes it easy to shop, to order by mail —easy to take advantage of bargains. Permits prompt payment of bills when confined to home because of illness or other reasons; or when on vacation, traveling, or visiting out of town. Provides funds for emergencies of every kind. Offers a practical way to send money to relatives or others.

PROMOTES THRIFT

Develops habit of depositing pay regularly. Curbs loose spending of cash on person. Salary check may be mailed direct to bank. Adds to income by releasing funds for investment, through "no minimum balance" feature.

SAVES YOU MONEY

Saves bus or streetcar fares in paying bills. Makes possible the enjoyment of a checking account without carrying large, idle balances. Costs less, on the average, than money orders.

PROVIDES BUSINESSLIKE RECORD

Gives concise, orderly record of current income and expense. Helps prepare income tax returns, as well as to set up personal or household budget. Shows date of last visit to doctor or dentist—when and by whom certain work was performed—when and where a certain article was purchased.

GIVES A PERMANENT RECEIPT

Provides legal receipts in the form of paid checks bearing the actual endorsements of payees. Proves what was paid, when, and to whom. Eliminates need of voluminous files of individual receipts of varying shapes and sizes.

ONLY $3 OPENS AN ACCOUNT

Surprisingly, $3 is all you need to start a special checking account — $1 for your initial deposit; $2 for a book of twenty checks.

Selecting Your Bank At the moment, you may require only a small part of a large bank's complete services. But as your interests grow, your association with a bank of wide resources and facilities can prove a benefit and a satisfaction to you.

promptly, record transactions up to the 25th of the month only, with later transactions appearing on the next month's statements. If all transactions for the month are recorded on the statements, depositors will probably not be able to obtain them till a few days after the beginning of the next month, since preparing statements for distribution takes some time. Many of the larger banks now use computers to speed up the preparation of the monthly statement.

Making Deposits

Deposits are made to regular checking accounts by going to the appropriate counter in the bank and filling out a deposit ticket. After the depositor inserts his name and the date, he then fills in the various amounts which he is depositing. To the right of "bills" or "currency" he inserts the amount of paper money being deposited. The total of coins and silver is entered to the right of these terms, unless the slip calls for "rolled coins" on one line and "loose coin" on another. The amount of each deposited check is listed separately, below. It is good practice to identify the bank on which each check is drawn. Each bank has a number, which appears on its printed checks near its name. This number is good identification of the bank; it is much quicker and easier to write than is the bank's full name. After all items have been listed, the total deposit should be ascertained by addition and entered in the proper space at the bottom of the ticket. The multiple-copy deposit slip should be presented to the receiving teller, along with the items being deposited. The teller will stamp and receipt the multiple-copy deposit ticket and give one copy to the depositor for his record. Of course, the deposit should be entered on the proper stub in the checkbook. This will be useful in balancing your checking account when you receive your monthly statement. Copies of deposit slips should, of course, be saved because in the absence of a passbook they constitute your record of deposits. If you lose your copy of the receipt, it isn't too serious because it only records a deposit and the bank, of course, has a duplicate record. Another person cannot get your money simply because he has your lost receipt. Your signature on a check is the only way money can be withdrawn from your account.

It is a good plan, and often saves difficulty, to deposit promptly all checks received. There is a possible danger that the person who drew the check may die, and the bank will then refuse to pay the check. Or there may no longer be sufficient funds in the account when the check is finally presented for payment.

In addition to cash and checks, other items that may be deposited with the bank for collection include promissory notes, postal money orders, and bond interest coupons. When depositing the latter, it is necessary to fill out an ownership certificate, which is sent to the Federal Reserve Bank in the district in order that the government may see that it receives the income tax on the amount involved. You can bank by mail. After your initial deposit you can handle all transactions—deposits and withdrawals both—by mail. Most banks will provide self-addressed (printed) and franked envelopes, without charge, for this purpose. Frequently, banks have special provisions for receiving deposits outside of regular banking hours. They may provide a small door (to be opened by a key furnished to the depositor, through which the deposit may be dropped into a chute connecting with a vault) or other device.

Certified Checks

Sometimes a person is unwilling to accept an ordinary check in payment. When, for example, in a real estate transaction, the parties meet at the registry of deeds to "pass papers," the seller should deliver a deed to real estate only in exchange for cash or for a check which is certified by a bank. The prospective buyer can make out a check payable to himself, present it at the bank for certification, and then endorse the check to the real estate seller when it is found that everything is in order and the deal is to be consummated. If the deal falls through, it is a simple matter for the disappointed buyer to deposit this check, payable to himself, to his own account again. If the check is made payable to the real estate seller in the first place and is then not used, it is sometimes a bit more troublesome to have it canceled and to have the amount of the certified check credited back to the buyer's account.

When the check is first presented to the bank for certification, the bank ascertains immediately whether there is enough money in the account to cover the check. The check is then stamped "certified" across its face, the stamp also bearing the name of the bank and a space for a proper officer to append his signature. By its certification the bank guarantees that sufficient funds have been set aside to pay the check when presented. In other words, the bank guarantees payment on the check. The amount of the check is immediately subtracted from the depositor's balance, and an offsetting credit is made to the bank's "Certified Checks" account, which thereby records the liability of the bank. A small charge is sometimes made for certification, but usually banks will certify without charge for regular customers. When the certified check is cashed, the bank retains it for its records; and it includes a slip, stating the amount of its charge for certification, when it returns his other canceled checks to the depositor. The recipient (payee) of an ordinary check can also present it to the bank for certification if, for one reason or another, he does not wish to cash it immediately; the effect is that he can then depend on the bank for payment later rather than rely on what may or may not be in the depositor's (maker's) account when he does cash the check.

Why the Bank May Not Honor a Check

As Figure 5–5 indicates, there are some nineteen reasons why a bank

FIGURE 5–5

Returned to...

By

CAMBRIDGE TRUST COMPANY

CAMBRIDGE, MASS.

ACCOUNT CLOSED	INFORMAL
ACCOUNT TRUSTEED	NO ACCOUNT
BANK ENDORSEMENT MISSING	NO FUNDS
CHECK ALTERED	NOT SATISFIED WITH SIGNATURE
DATED AHEAD	NOT SUFFICIENT FUNDS
DRAWN AGAINST UNCOLLECTED FUNDS	PAYMENT STOPPED
ENDORSEMENT MISSING	RECEIPT OF PAYEE
ENDORSEMENT UNSATISFACTORY	SENT US IN ERROR
GUARANTEE OF AMOUNT	SIGNATURE INCOMPLETE
SIGNATURE MISSING	

may not honor a check drawn upon it. Of these, the following seven are the most important:

1. There may not be sufficient funds in the depositor's account to cover the check. Normally, depositors are immediately notified when such checks are presented at the paying teller's window, and the checks are turned back to persons who present them. The person writing a bad check is usually given, by law, a certain number of days to make the check good. If it is not made good, the act becomes an offense under the bad-check law, and the maker becomes subject to prosecution.

2. The check may have been altered. If you make a mistake in writing a check, you cannot erase or cross out. The check will not be honored. It is best to tear up the check on which you made a mistake and write another if you are using a regular checking account. If you have a special checking account and you spoil a check for which you have already paid, the bank will exchange it for a new check without extra charge.

3. The signature may not be genuine. Every bank keeps a file of

signatures of all depositors. The signature card you signed when you opened your account is consulted in case of doubt. The bank must know its depositors' signatures because if a forged check is cashed it cannot be charged against the depositor's account. If the bank pays out money on a forged check, it is paying out its own money and not that of the depositor. Banks protect themselves from such losses by carrying forgery insurance.

4. The check may have been postdated, or the words and figures on the check may not agree. A postdated check cannot be paid until the date specified, although at times a busy bank teller may by accident pay a check which is dated ahead. If the words and figures on a check do not agree, many banks will refuse to cash it, and return it unpaid. Some, however, will pay the written amount, because by law the written amount has precedence over the figure. Upon proper authorization, bank employees sometimes make corrections of such checks.

5. There may be a stop order on the check. This will be discussed later.

6. A check may not be cashed by a bank after it has received notice of the death of the person who wrote it.

7. The party who requests payment must be entitled to receive it; he must be properly identified. Banks will not cash checks for unidentified strangers even when the checks are drawn on the bank and the signature of the person who wrote the check has been verified. Identification satisfactory to the bank is required to cash a check.

If a man's after money, he's money-mad; if he keeps it, he's a capitalist; if he spends it, he's a playboy; if he doesn't get it, he's a ne'er-do-well; if he doesn't try to get it, he lacks ambition. If he gets it without working for it, he's a parasite; and if he accumulates it after a lifetime of hard work, people call him a fool who never got anything out of life.—VICTOR OLIVER

Avoiding Overdrafts

In England it has been an accepted practice to borrow from the bank by overdrawing one's account, being charged interest on the overdraft. Although this practice has not been followed in the United States, overdrafts are common. When a check for which there are insufficient funds on deposit is presented for payment in this country, the bank may refuse payment and return the check to the person tendering it, along with a slip stating that payment is refused because of insufficient funds. An alternative is for the bank to notify the depositor and thereby give him an opportunity to cover the check before payment is refused. Other banks are more lenient and will honor the check, thus making a forced loan. This is done not from choice but because of the fear of injuring the depositor's standing. Many overdrafts result because the customer does not follow his deposits and his drawings; he gets confused as to his balance. These overdrafts are innocently created. However, others are deliberately created because of shortage of funds, and checks are issued against the hope of obtaining funds by the time the check is presented for payment. The practice is so prevalent and so troublesome that it is becoming rather common for banks to penalize offenders by making a charge, such as 50 cents, for each overdraft. You can prevent overdrafts by keeping accurate records. Every time you make a deposit, add it to the previous balance in your own checkbook. Before you write a check, enter the date, number, and payee, and deduct the amount from your balance as shown on your check stub.

Stopping Payment

If you write a check and later for some reason do not want the bank to pay it, you may ask the bank to stop payment. Commonly, you will be asked to fill out a form, giving the number and amount of the check, its date, and the name of the person to whose order it is payable (see Fig. 5–6). This is good procedure when a check is lost. It is also useful if after giving a check you cannot obtain what you were supposed to receive for it, or if what is received is not of the agreed quality or quantity. Payment is occasionally stopped on checks given for illegal gambling debts.

After the bank receives a stop notice from the depositor, it puts a tab or colored flag on the record of the depositor's account and notifies all tellers who might possibly cash the check. If the check should be presented, it will be refused, ordinarily. Most banks insert a clause in the stop-payment form, which must be signed by the drawer of the check to stop it, relieving the bank of any liability if by oversight or error one of its employees pays a check after it has been stopped.[1] With a computerized operation, however, it is practically certain that the check will be stopped.

[1] See *Stop Payment Procedure,* Bank Management Commission, American Bankers Association, latest edition.

FIGURE 5–6

STOP PAYMENT ORDER

OFFICE NO._____   DATE_____

CHEMICAL BANK NEW YORK TRUST COMPANY   ☐ REGULAR
☐ SPECIAL
☐ OTHER

DEAR SIRS:
PLEASE STOP PAYMENT OF CHECK ^(ACCEPTANCE) _(NOTE) DRAWN BY THE UNDERSIGNED
ON OR PAYABLE AT YOUR OFFICE.

NO.   DATED OR DUE

FOR $ PAYABLE TO THE ORDER OF

IT IS EXPRESSLY UNDERSTOOD AND AGREED THAT SHOULD THIS ITEM BE CERTIFIED
AND/OR PAID THROUGH INADVERTENCY OR OVERSIGHT, YOU WILL IN NO WAY BE HELD
RESPONSIBLE.
A DUPLICATE ^(WILL) _(WILL NOT) BE ISSUED UPON RECEIPT OF YOUR ADVICE.

YOURS VERY TRULY,

TELEPHONE ORDER		
	TIME	BY
RECEIVED		
TO AUDIT DEPT.		

ACCOUNT NUMBER

(PRINT NAME OF ACCOUNT)

ADDRESS

AUTHORIZED SIGNATURE

Do not write below line — for Bank use only

Noted by:
P & R TELLERS

DATE RECEIVED_____

TIME RECEIVED_____

VOUCHERS AND
CURRENT WORK
CHECKED_____

CERTIFICATION CLERK_____

ADJUSTER_____   BOOKKEEPER_____

Wall Street Journal

"Wonderful for your wife. It will write on anything except checks."

Automation, Computers and MICR

To clear, collect and process the billions of checks we write each year, banks have had to resort to automation. Computers and MICR have come into vogue as the answer. The funny-looking numbers at the bottom of checks serve a very useful purpose. They allow checks to be read and sorted automatically by new electronic machines and permit accounts to be posted and statements rendered by computer.

The four initials—MICR—which stand for Magnetic Ink Character Recognition—signalize these new developments in banking. These funny numbers at the bottom of checks are readable both by humans and by magnetic sensing devices. They are printed on checks using an ink containing iron oxide, like the coating of magnetic recording tapes. A permanent magnet on the machine magnetizes the iron oxide in the ink on the checks, making the numbers ready to be read by the reading head on the machine. Each numeral gives off a different electrical impulse. The signals given off by the magnetized characters can be used to operate such equipment as sorting machines.

Checks carry two sets of figures at the bottom: the first at the left is the ABA routing symbol, the number of the bank on which the check is drawn and the city and Federal Reserve district in which it is located. This is the same as the printed number in the upper right hand corner of the check. Thus, for example,

$$\frac{1-12}{210}$$

where the 1 stands for New York, N.Y., 12 for the Chemical Bank, and 210 for the New York Federal Reserve Bank (2 for 2nd district), (1 for head office, not branch), (and 0 for immediate availability), becomes in MICR:

⑆0210⑈00121⑉

After this, there follows, next, the number of your account at the bank. Thus the check can be automatically sorted and sent back to the right bank and to the right account. In addition, when the check is presented for collection, additional figures may be added by the use of an inscriber, a machine by which MICR characters may be inscribed on deposit slips or on checks. For example, it is customary now to inscribe the code amount of the check in MICR. This permits processing by a computer which can then adjust accounts and issue daily statements. In large banks there are delivered each morning, before the bank opens for business, computer compiled sheets showing the closing balance in each account at a given branch as of the close of the most recent clearing the night before. Thus the teller knows how much is in every account and does not need to call the head office to find out. Also the monthly statement is put together by the computer.

In this age of intercontinental ballistic missiles, the larger urban banks now each have a depository in more remote locations, where duplicate sets of account records, statements, deposit slips, etc., are available in case of atomic attack. Daily computer tabulations are sent to these depositories to keep accounts up to date, and officials of one bank estimate that the bank could open for banking transactions at the remote location with a complete, up-to-date set of records within 48 hours after an atomic attack. Whether anyone would or could show up to make a deposit or withdrawal is another question.

How to Reconcile Your Balance

Once a month the depositor usually receives his bank statement and canceled checks. The statement shows his balance at the beginning of the month, all individual charges for checks and notes paid and service charges, and the balance at the end of the month. For several reasons, the ending balance on the bank's statement usually will not be in agreement with the depositor's checkbook stub balance as of the same date. Therefore, it is necessary to reconcile the two balances. All checks drawn, if the depositor has been keeping his record correctly, have been deducted by the depositor from his balance at the bank. Some of these checks have, however, probably not yet been presented to the depositor's bank for payment; they are therefore said to be "outstanding." Since these checks, nevertheless, were given by the depositor in payment for something, the proper procedure is to deduct them from the bank's balance on the reconciliation statement, for which the depositor can use any spare piece of paper or a form frequently provided for the purpose on the reverse side of the bank statement. The bank has already deducted service charges, and in that respect is nearer to the true cash balance than is the balance shown on the checkbook stubs. The checkbook, moreover, may show credits for deposits which are still "in transit," i.e., have not yet been credited by the bank. Therefore, if deposits in transit are added to the bank's final balance and outstanding checks are deducted from it, we should usually be able to ascertain the true cash balance.

The depositor has two objectives: (1) he wants to prove that the story told by his checkbook stubs is in agreement (reconciles) with the same story as told by the bank statement and (2) he wants the checkbook stubs to reveal the true cash balance with which he enters the ensuing period. It is important to you to keep your checkbook in agreement with the balance in your account at the bank. Be sure to enter each check on the check stub and subtract that amount from the balance in your checkbook. In this way you can avoid overdrawing your account and having your checks returned unpaid.

As soon as you receive a statement of your account and your canceled checks from the bank, look them over carefully. If no errors are reported, the account will be considered correct by the bank. The following procedure is recommended to balance your record with the bank's statement of your account:

1. Sort checks numerically or by date issued.
2. Reduce your checkbook balance by the amount of any service charges not previously recorded.
3. Enter statement balance here....................$..........
4. Check back each paid check to your checkbook stubs and make a list of all checks issued but not yet paid

by the bank. Enter and subtract the total of these unpaid
checks here...$..........
$..........

5. Enter and add any deposit in transit by mail or
made later than the date of this statement.............$..........

6. This balance should be the same as your checkbook
balance...$..........

Perhaps a simple illustration will clarify the procedure. Let us suppose that your bank statement reveals a final balance of $1,732.49,
whereas your checkbook stubs show that you ended the month with
$1,536.29. When you compare the canceled checks returned by the
bank with the record of checks drawn according to the stubs, you find
that check No. 62 for $88.29 and check No. 67 for $109.45 are still
outstanding. Inspection of the bank statement shows service charges of
$1.54 not yet recorded on the checkbook stubs. You can arrive at the
true cash balance by two independent methods, as follows:

Balance on bank statement......$1,732.49		Balance on checkbook stubs.....$1,536.29	
Less: Outstanding checks:		*Less:* Service charges............	1.54
No. 62...........$ 88.29			
No. 67........... 109.45	197.74		
	$1,534.75		$1,534.75

An alternative method is to start with the bank's balance of $1,732.49
and reconcile it with the checkbook stub balance of $1,536.29:

Balance on bank statement................................$1,732.49		
Less: Outstanding checks: No. 62....................$ 88.29		
No. 67.................... 109.45	197.74	
Total..$1,534.75		
Plus: Service charges....................................... 1.54		
Balance shown on checkbook stubs........................$1,536.29		

Or you can begin with the checkbook stub balance of $1,536.29 and
reconcile it with the balance of $1,732.49 on the bank statement:

Balance on checkbook stubs................................$1,536.29		
Add: Outstanding checks:		
No. 62...$ 88.29		
No. 67... 109.45	197.74	
	$1,734.03	
Less: Service charges....................................... 1.54		
Balance as shown by bank statement........................$1,732.49		

Now that you have reconciled the one story with the other, you
must remember to deduct the services charge of $1.54 from your check-

book stub balance in order that you may begin the next month with your true cash balance of $1,534.75. Canceled checks, bank statements, and checkbook stubs should be retained for a reasonable number of years. The ordinary statute of limitations provides that creditors must bring action for recovery of debts within six years or lose the right to sue for them. In case of dispute as to whether a bill has been paid, a canceled check may prove to be an effective receipt.

How to Write a Check

Checks should be written clearly, completely, and in ink. Make it a practice to fill out your check stub before you write the check itself. There are six different items to be written in ink on the face of the check itself.

1. *The date* should be written first, and it should be the date on which the check is drawn. A check dated as of a Sunday is as good as any other. Since some people may refuse to accept it, however, you might just as well date it the previous day. Ordinarily, checks should not be postdated (dated ahead). Such a check cannot be paid by the bank before the day whose date it bears, unless it is done through oversight. Postdated checks are sometimes issued to creditors when the debtors' accounts do not as yet have enough on deposit to cover them. The creditors are asked not to cash them before the date which they bear, by which time the debtors hope to have enough on deposit to cover them.

2. *The check number* should be filled in next. For your own convenience and use in record keeping, every check you write should be numbered and the same number should be entered on the corresponding stub.

3. *The payee's name* should be written after the printed words "PAY TO THE ORDER OF." (The payee is the person or company or organization to whom the money is to be paid.) Spell the name correctly. Instead of making out checks payable to "Bearer" or "Cash," it is usually better to name a specific person or company as payee. Then the check will bear the endorsement of the payee when it is cashed and will serve as a better receipt for the amount paid. Furthermore, a check drawn to "Cash" can be cashed by anyone, and thus the loss of a check made out to "Cash" is the same as losing currency.

4. *The amount in figures* (after the payee's name) should be written close to the dollar sign to prevent other figures from being inserted between. The correct way to express dollars and cents is: $175⁵⁰⁄₁₀₀.

5. *The amount in words* should be written on the following line. It should be started as far to the left as possible so that no one may insert a word before it and thereby raise the amount. Of course, the two expressions of the amount should be in agreement. The Uniform Negotiable Instruments Law gives preference to the amount written out in words in case they do not agree. The word "dollars" is usually printed on the checks. To prevent anything being inserted between the

FIGURE 5–7

Writing a Check

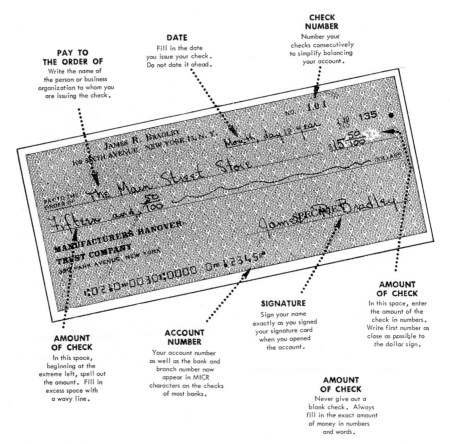

CHECK NUMBER
Number your checks consecutively to simplify balancing your account.

DATE
Fill in the date you issue your check. Do not date it ahead.

PAY TO THE ORDER OF
Write the name of the person or business organization to whom you are issuing the check.

AMOUNT OF CHECK
In this space, enter the amount of the check in numbers. Write first number as close as possible to the dollar sign.

SIGNATURE
Sign your name exactly as you signed your signature card when you opened the account.

AMOUNT OF CHECK
In this space, beginning at the extreme left, spell out the amount. Fill in excess space with a wavy line.

ACCOUNT NUMBER
Your account number as well as the bank and branch number now appear in MICR characters on the checks of most banks.

AMOUNT OF CHECK
Never give out a blank check. Always fill in the exact amount of money in numbers and words.

amount and the word "dollars," it is considered good practice to insert a wavy line, as in Figure 5–7. When the amount is less than $1.00—89 cents for instance—it can be written out as "None $89/100$," or "Eighty-nine cents only." In figures, "$00\,89/100$," "none $89/100$," or "89 cents" can be used.

6. *Your signature* should be written in exactly the same way as you signed it on the signature card which you filled out for the bank. If the signature is reasonably legible, it helps. When signing not in your capacity as an individual but as an agent or officer of a firm, corporation, or association, it is good practice, to avoid personal liability, to sign:

> The Jones Company
> by Peter Jones, President.

Sometimes you may wish to draw a check when you have none of your own bank's checks with you. If you are at the bank, you can use a

---

RANCHER INKS CHECK ON COWHIDE—BANK HONORS IT

Temperatures throughout the Southwest have been high much of the summer. This probably has nothing to do with the fact that Joe M. King, a rancher, spent some time recently inking a $500 check to himself on a six-by-three-foot cowhide.

Equally improbable was Mr. King's explanation: "I didn't have a blank check handy."

Whatever his reason for writing the unusual check, Mr. King presented it last week to be cashed at the downtown Tucson office of the Valley National Bank of Phoenix, Ariz. Jeanne Rudolph, a teller, was a bit taken back. But such checks were nothing new to Gil Bradley, a vice president and manager of the office.

"It is perfectly negotiable, although perhaps unwieldy," he reportedly said.

Mr. Bradley has made a study of unorthodox checks, the bank noted in reporting the event. It disclosed these results of his research:

¶A check written on a paper bag was presented for payment recently at the office of a competitor bank in Tucson.

¶An employer in the Northwest paid off his men with checks written on shingles.

¶A Canadian lumberjack wrote his checks on birchbark peeled from a tree.

Mr. Bradley also found that checks had been written on hard-boiled eggs, watermelons and even boiler plate. In the last instance, the bank cancelled the check with a rented blowtorch.

If a check is worded correctly, has a valid signature and there are sufficient funds in the account upon which it is drawn, Mr. Bradley asserts, it will be honored.

Honored, but perhaps not welcomed. Because of the advent of automatic check sorting and electronic bookkeeping, the American Bankers Association has issued stern injunctions to its members to discourage such oversize and unmanageable checks.

Neither Mr. Bradley nor anyone else at the Valley National explained why they had not made another suggestion to Mr. King—that he use a counter check available in most bank offices.

—SOURCE: *New York Times.*

---

so-called "counter check." Often these forms are not negotiable; they are to be used by depositors only to draw money from their accounts for their own use. At other places, you can use any bank's checks that are at hand by crossing out the city, name, and identifying numbers of the bank printed thereon and inserting the name and city of your own bank. Many stores also have on hand blank check forms on which the name and location of your bank may be written in the appropriate spaces provided.

Your Check Stub

Every deposit you make and every check you write, including blank check forms mentioned above, should be entered on your stub record. This is your only means of keeping an accurate record of your bank account and of reconciling your figures with the bank statement you receive at the end of the month. In fact your stub is so important that it

FIGURE 5–8

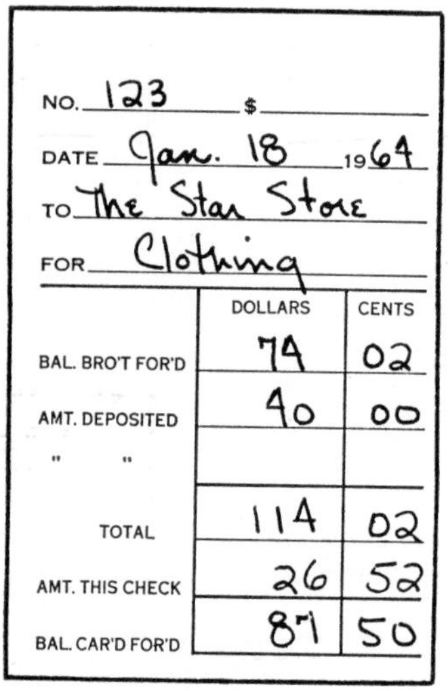

	DOLLARS	CENTS
NO. 123 $		
DATE Jan. 18 19 64		
TO The Star Store		
FOR Clothing		
BAL. BRO'T FOR'D	79	02
AMT. DEPOSITED	40	00
" "		
TOTAL	114	02
AMT. THIS CHECK	26	52
BAL. CAR'D FOR'D	87	50

is advisable to fill out the stub *before* you write the check so that you don't forget it. Enter the check number, the date, the amount of the check, the name of the person or company to whose order the check is payable, and what you are paying for, all in the space on the stub. Then, if a month later you are asked if you paid that particular bill, you can look back over your stubs and see exactly when you did. For one example of the proper way to fill out a check stub see Figure 5–8.

How to Endorse Checks

Before you can cash or deposit a check made out to you, you must sign it on the back, preferably, custom dictates, at the extreme left end. This is known as endorsement. If you want to take a check which has been made out to you and give it to another person in payment for something, you must first endorse it and then the other party must also endorse it before it can be cashed or deposited. If your name is misspelled or incomplete, write your first endorsement in the same way— and then write your correct signature.

You should never endorse a check until you get to a bank. If you endorse a check beforehand and then lose it, the finder may possibly

FIGURE 5–9

A Blank Endorsement

FIGURE 5–10

A Restrictive Endorsement

FIGURE 5–11

A Restrictive Endorsement

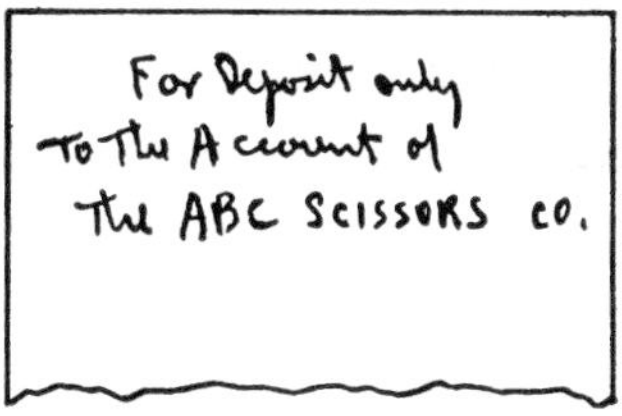

FIGURE 5–12

A Special Endorsement

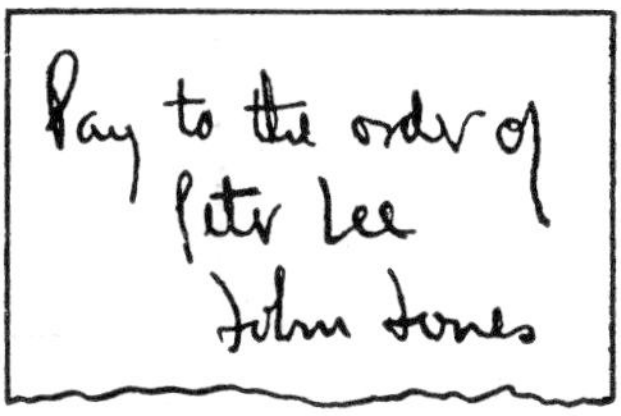

FIGURE 5–13

A Qualified Endorsement

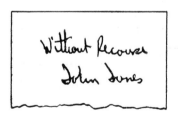

cash it. By endorsement the person to whom the check is made out passes his (or her) title to the check to someone else. If you lose a check made out to you, you may be able to arrange to have payment on it stopped *providing you haven't endorsed it.*

There are several methods of endorsing (see Figs. 5–9, 5–10, 5–11, 5–12, and 5–13). The most common is for you merely to write your name on the back of the instrument across the left-hand end. This is a *blank* endorsement, and since it makes the check payable to bearer, it may be dangerous. With a blank endorsement a check can be transferred from person to person and is payable to anyone holding it. The only time when a blank endorsement is safe is when the check is being cashed in a bank. The blank endorsement should be placed on the check after the endorser arrives at the bank. If a check is made payable to your order and you endorse it and then lose it, whoever picks it up or finds it may be able to cash it. To prevent such a loss, you may resort to the protection of a *restrictive* endorsement or a *special* endorsement. The *restrictive* endorsement,

> For deposit only
> John Jones,

allows the check to be used only for deposit in your account, assuming for the moment that you are Jones. Restrictive endorsements are almost universally used by business firms where it is desirable to prevent loss in case checks are stolen, lost, or fall into the hands of dishonest or irresponsible individuals. This type of endorsement is always recommended when checks are mailed or sent to the bank by messenger to be deposited. The *special* endorsement,

> Pay to the order of Peter Lee
> John Jones,

negotiates the check to Lee, who must, in turn, endorse it in order to pass title to it. The chief advantage of the special endorsement is that the check can be cashed only by the specified party. It is possible to convert a blank endorsement into a special endorsement by inserting the words "Pay to the order of" and a person's name above the blank endorsement. It is also possible to combine the special endorsement and the restrictive endorsement, i.e.,

> Pay to the order of
> The First National Bank of X
> For deposit only
> John Jones.

When the words "without recourse" are inserted above the signature of the endorser, we have a *qualified* endorsement:

> Pay to the order of Peter Lee
> Without Recourse
> John Jones

The qualified endorsement relieves the endorser who uses it of his liability; if the bank on which the check is drawn refuses for any reason to pay it, the holder in due course cannot look to the endorser to do so. The qualified endorsement, however, is rarely used, mainly because few people will accept a check containing a "without-recourse" endorsement, since they then cannot look to the endorser for payment in the event that the maker, whom they may not know, will not make good.

Presentment, Dishonor, and Protest

A check, of course, is a negotiable instrument. It is a draft drawn on a bank, and the rules of presentment, notice of dishonor, and protest apply as in the case of all negotiable instruments. There are three original parties to a check: (*a*) the drawer (maker), (*b*) the payee, and (*c*) the drawee. The drawer or maker of the check is the one who signs it. The payee of the check is the one to whom the check is made payable. The drawee, a bank, is the one who is ordered by the maker to pay the amount of the check to the payee. The drawer (maker) of the check orders the bank (drawee) to make payment to a payee, usually, a third party, though sometimes the drawer. If the third party, the payee, duly presents the check for payment and is refused payment, i.e., the check is not honored, he then makes out a notice of protest, which he sends to the drawer and any endorsers who may have intervened before the check came to him.

After due presentment, if the check is not honored, formal protest follows. The *practical* reason for protest is to give prompt notice to the parties concerned that the instrument has been dishonored. The legal reason is that the endorser has warranted that if the instrument is not paid upon its proper presentation and is dishonored, and the necessary legal steps have been taken upon the dishonor, he will reimburse the holder. Protest consists of having a notary make a record of the fact that the check has been presented and has been refused payment; then formal notices of protest are sent to all endorsers as well as to the drawer. The actual protest notation must be made on the day the presentment and dishonor take place, and the notices of protest must go out within twenty-four hours. The reason in the law for protest is to fasten legal responsibility upon the endorsers, for they warranted payment, provided these steps were properly and promptly taken. Otherwise the endorsers are released. It is aways best to protest to all endorsers and drawer at once and simultaneously, for then there is a chance of collection from one.

How Long Can You Hold a Check before Cashing It?

Theoretically a long time, but it isn't a good idea. Legally, a check is good as long as the Statute of Limitations allows—usually six years. The answer depends more on facts and circumstances, on bank rules and practices. As a practical matter, a check becomes stale after a reasonable length of time has elapsed. In general, banks usually refuse to honor checks more than six months old. "Reasonable time" is as long as the bank feels it can collect the funds. Staleness of a check does not make it bad or void. It merely puts the bank on notice that irregularities may exist . . . that something may be wrong and therefore it shouldn't be paid. Under such circumstances, the bank will not pay the check without obtaining the maker's consent.

Unless a check is presented to the bank for payment within a reasonable time after it is issued, the maker of the check will be relieved of liability on it if the payee suffers a loss by reason of the delay. What constitutes a reasonable time depends on the circumstances in each case. Ordinarily, a reasonable time is determined by the length of time it would take an ordinary prudent person to present the check for payment under similar circumstances. Firestone gives Taffet a check for $100 drawn on the Bankers Bank. Although the bank is a few blocks away, Taffet, being absent-minded, forgets to deposit the check. He remembers it and presents it for payment two weeks later. Meanwhile Bankers Bank has become insolvent. If Firestone had sufficient funds in the bank at the time he made out the check, he is excused from further liability since Taffet's delay caused the loss.

Do's and Don'ts on Checks

Don't write a check in pencil.

Do date the check correctly.

Don't make out a check to "Bearer" or "Cash," unless you are at the bank, where you can cash it yourself.

Don't sign a blank endorsement on a check until you get to the bank to cash or deposit it.

Do cash or deposit checks as soon as possible after you receive them.

Do make sure that the written amount and the amount in figures are the same.

Don't forget to sign the check.

Do keep a record of each check in the stub of your checkbook.

Don't forget to number each check.

If you have a joint account, don't forget to keep a combined, complete record of all checks drawn by *both* parties, so that your balance will be correct.

✓ Do be sure you have sufficient funds in the bank each time you write a large check.

✓ Don't accept checks from strangers or cash checks for strangers.

✓ Don't forget to protest (legally and formally) immediately if you present a check for payment and it is not honored. Notify all endorsers and drawer as well.

✓ Use restrictive or special endorsements whenever possible.

✓ Keep your signature out of circulation. For example, when your monthly bank statement with your canceled checks enclosed is due, take it out of your mailbox as soon as it arrives. The canceled checks offer check thieves and forgers a perfect opportunity to get your signature.

✓ Don't endorse a bearer check if you are passing it on to another party. If there is insistence on endorsement, try a qualified endorsement and see if it is acceptable.

Other Uses of Your Checking Account

There are many other valuable and convenient uses of your checking account. For example, you can arrange, as a permanent matter, to have your salary check sent directly to your bank and deposited automatically to your credit. Thus you can avoid the semimonthly or monthly chore of getting your pay check and taking it to the bank to deposit.

There is now a "dividend deposit plan." Under it your dividend checks on any stock you own will be mailed directly by the disbursing agent to your bank for deposit in your account. This helps avoid the problem of checks going astray or piling up in a mailbox while a family is away on vacation.

On the disbursing side, you can arrange with your bank to have it automatically pay your utility bills or your insurance premiums, or buy a U.S. government bond for you each month, deducting the cost from your account. In the case of utility and insurance bills, the companies are notified to send their bills or notices to your bank and you authorize your bank to pay them as received, deducting the amount from your account, and notifying you, of course, of the payments.

Some banks go even further; there is a monthly payment insurance premium plan. If you have a large annual insurance bill coming due, the bank will pay it for you in one lump sum and you can then repay the bank in equal monthly installments. You can either pay in the cash each month or they will deduct the amount from your account. No assignment of the policy is necessary. A small charge is levied for this service, which is, of course, a loan.

A number of commercial banks have adopted revolving check-loan account plans in the last few years. Most are patterned after plans developed by the First National Bank of Boston and the First National of Dallas. Under these plans a credit limit is set for each borrower, usually twelve times the agreed monthly payment, and he is given a book of special checks which can be used at any time so long as the unpaid balance does not exceed the credit limit. Monthly payments are one twelfth of the line of credit, regardless of the amount of the unpaid balance, as long as some balance is outstanding. These plans involve a service charge, usually 25 cents a check, plus interest on the unpaid balance.

How to Transfer Funds

If you want to transfer funds to someone at a distance who does not know you very well and who will therefore not accept your personal check, there are several alternative possibilities.

1. *A certified check.* Most banks make no charge for certifying a personal check of one of their depositors. You can send a certified check, but the limitation is that you will not have a receipt. The bank assumes liability on the check because of its certification, and it may, therefore, retain the canceled check.

2. *A cashier's check.* This is a check which the bank draws on itself. It is often used by nondepositors. If you do not have a checking account at a bank, you can nevertheless ask for a cashier's check made out payable to the order of the distant party that you want to pay. You give the bank the appropriate amount. They give you a check drawn by the bank on itself payable to the order of the party you name. The charge for this is usually 50 cents per check. The limitation is the same as in the use of the certified check. You have no personal receipt in the form of a canceled check since the bank keeps it. In contrast to the certified check, the cashier's check is used mainly by those who do not have checking accounts.

3. *Bank money order, or register check,* as it is also called, has grown rapidly in use in recent years for domestic transfers of sums up to $250. Bank drafts are used for sums over that amount. The bank money order, or register check, or remittance check, as it is variously called, costs only 20 or 25 cents, depending on the bank for any sum up

to $250 and is therefore one of the least expensive ways of transmitting funds domestically.

The register check contains a space for the sender's name and has a detachable stub or record copy which serves as a receipt and bears (for identification) the same serial number as the main part of the money order itself (see Fig. 5–14).

FIGURE 5–14

For sums from 0.01 cents to $10 the bank money order costs the same as a postal money order. For all sums above $10 it costs less. Just why anyone therefore uses postal money orders for sums above $10 is not clear, except possibly that the post office may be nearer than the bank or they may not know about the low cost and convenience of the bank money order. Why pay 35 cents for a $100 postal money order, for example, when a bank money order for the same amount will cost you only 20 cents?

4. *U.S. Postal and American Express money orders.* Both the U.S. post office and the American Express Company sell money orders, though at somewhat more expensive rates than the banks. The rates for postal money orders are as follows:

> For orders from $0.01 to $10.................20 cents
> For orders from $10.01 to $50................30 cents
> For orders from $50.01 to $100...............35 cents

American Express domestic money orders cost:

> For orders from $0.01 to $1.99...............15 cents
> For orders from $2.00 to $4.99...............20 cents
> For orders from $5.00 to $49.99..............30 cents
> For orders from $50 to $100..................35 cents

Postal money orders, of course, are for sale at any U.S. post office. Less widely known is the fact that American Express money orders are for sale not only at the company's own offices but at all Western Union Telegraph Company offices. This is a convenience because frequently Western Union offices are open on Sundays or holidays when the banks and the post offices are closed.

Postal money orders must be presented for payment within a year of the date of issue. After that time they will not be honored, but substitutes will be issued for an additional fee equal to that originally paid. There are no time limits on American Express money orders, and unlike postal money orders there is also no limit to the number of times they may be endorsed. If postal money orders are presented for payment in a city other than that of issue or the city upon which they are drawn, they must be presented for payment within 30 days of their issue date and a fee equal to that originally paid must be tendered. American Express money orders can be cashed anywhere at banks or other places that cash checks. The highest amount for which a single U.S. postal money order is issued is $100. To remit more than this you must purchase an additional order. For example, if you want to send $250 you will have to buy three postal money orders, two $100 orders and one $50 order. The cost will be $1.00. A bank money order for $250 will cost you just 50 cents.

5. *Telegraphic transfers of funds.* If you want to transfer money in a hurry, you can do so by telegram. Money orders, of course, are sent by mail and this takes time. If the need to transfer funds is urgent, then you can go to the nearest Western Union office, pay the clerk the amount to be transferred, the fee involved, and the cost of the telegram.

The clerk will then send a telegram to the company's office nearest to where the person you want to pay lives, instructing that office to pay the amount. The check drawn is either delivered to the payee by a company messenger or the payee is reached by telephone and asked to come to the telegraph office to receive payment.

The cost of a telegraphic money order, which is naturally much more than either a bank or a postal money order, depends on (*a*) the amount of money sent, (*b*) the distance over which the telegram must be sent, and (*c*) the amount of traffic between the sending and paying locations. In addition there is a federal tax on the transaction.

6. *Sending money abroad.* You can use either international postal money orders or bank drafts. For small amounts the postal money order is less expensive. The rates are

For orders from—

$0.01 to $10	40 cents
$10.01 to $50	60 cents
$50.01 to $100	70 cents

The maximum amount for which an international money order may be drawn is $100. You can send more, of course, but it will take two or more money orders. If you want to send $150, for example, you will have to buy one money order for $100 and another for $50.

In transmitting larger sums than $100 the bank draft is much more convenient. While rates will vary somewhat from bank to bank, the following is typical of current charges:

For amounts—

Up to $10	50 cents
$10 to $300	$1.00
$300 to $500	1.50
$500 to $1,000	2.00
For sums over $1,000	⅛ of 1% with a minimum of $2.50 and a maximum of $25

As Figure 5–15 shows, a remittance abroad can be sent by cable, air mail, or regular mail, depending on the speed with which it is desired to effect the transfer. You, of course, pay the cable or air mail costs.

Traveler's Checks

If you are going on a trip, you will find many opportunities to make use of traveler's checks. It is, of course, hazardous to carry large amounts of money with you. Your personal checks are not generally acceptable. Traveler's checks usually cost $1.00 per $100 and are issued in de-

FIGURE 5–15

We Handle Remittances To All Parts of the World

BY CABLE • AIR MAIL • REGULAR MAIL • CHECK

By Cable and Mail:

This bank can quickly and easily arrange your overseas payments to friends, relatives, or commercial creditors. You simply come to our Teller's Window and order the remittance. At this time, you pay the amount you wish sent abroad, plus our charge for the service. You receive our receipt for this payment. We then send an order—either by cable, air mail or regular mail, as you stipulate—instructing the proper one of many foreign correspondent banks to pay the specified amount to whomever you name as payee.

The payee's receipt for the money is sent to us, and you may inspect this receipt at any time.

By Check:

You may also, if you prefer, send money abroad by check, following this simple procedure:

Upon receiving from you the proper amount, plus our charge, we issue to you our check, payable to whomever you name and drawn on a foreign correspondent bank abroad—usually a bank located right in the city where the payee lives.

You then send this check overseas, via either air mail or regular mail. If it is your intention to send the check by air mail, this should be indicated to our Teller. Payee, upon receiving the check either arranges encashment at his local bank or presents it at the bank on which it is drawn and, upon proper identification, receives immediate payment.

These services are available to you at very reasonable charges. Any of our tellers will be glad to outline these rates to you and answer any additional questions you may have about this quick, easy method of making overseas payments.

---

nominations of $10, $20, $50, $100, and $500. The banks are glad to issue these checks, not so much because of the charge of $1.00 per $100, which they give in part or in full to their agents who sell the checks for them, but rather because of "the large float": the use of the money which they have for the period that elapses between the time the checks are sold and the date they are cashed. When the checks are purchased, the buyer signs each check with his usual signature at the upper left. Later, for identification, he signs the same signature at the lower left in the presence of the person cashing the check for him. The checks are generally sold to the buyer in a folder, which contains a form on which to record the serial numbers and the places and dates where each was cashed. Uncashed checks can be replaced if lost or stolen. American Express Company, Bank of America, Cook's, First National City Bank of Chicago, First National City Bank of New York, and Republic National Bank of Dallas, among others, all issue traveler's checks. You will find that hotels, motels, restaurants, gas stations, and large stores are universally acquainted with traveler's checks and accept them readily. They are a real convenience in traveling. You may keep your traveler's checks as long as you like. They are good until used, and there is no time limit on them.

Some of you may have trouble obtaining traveler's checks. American Express and other issuers will not sell traveler's checks to persons who cannot sign their names. They also insist that countersigning be done in the presence of the person accepting the check. On occasion the double signature requirement has presented difficulties. In one instance the countersignature of an American abroad was questioned. He agreed that the original signature was much more shaky, but observed that he had purchased the checks after imbibing rather freely of cognac. To obtain a comparable signature, he suggested, in all seriousness, that the prospective acceptor of his checks take him to a nearby bistro for a few cognacs.

To have available large sums in traveling, people often avail themselves of *traveler's letters of credit*. These are issued by a bank to a customer preparing for an extended trip. The customer pays for the letter of credit, and the bank issues it for a specified period of time in the amount purchased. The bank furnishes a list of its foreign offices and its correspondent banks, where drafts drawn against the letter of credit will be honored. The bank also identifies the customer by exhibiting a specimen signature of the purchaser on the folder enclosing the list of correspondent banks. The purchaser may go to any bank listed, draw a draft against the letter of credit, and receive payment. The letter of credit then operates like a mobile checking account, letting you cash checks or drafts as you travel. Each bank that honors a draft endorses on the letter of credit: the date a payment was made, its name, and the amount it paid out against the letter of credit.

Promissory Notes and Drafts

When buying a house, borrowing from a bank or other institution, or buying on credit, one often signs a promissory note. Although checks and drafts are orders to pay, notes are promises to pay. To a note there are two parties: the maker and the payee, in addition to any endorsers who appear thereon. In the case of drafts, however, there are usually three parties: A orders B (the bank, when a check is involved) to pay C. Notes may be due on demand or at a fixed and determinable future time. In order to hold the maker, the note must be presented for payment before it is barred by the statute of limitations, time of which differs among the various states. The safest course is to present it promptly when due. In order to hold endorsers, a time note must be presented to the maker for payment on the due date, whereas a demand note must be presented within a reasonable time. Notice of dishonor must be given or be in transit to the endorser by the day following dishonor. Each endorser has a like period in which to notify previous endorsers. Endorsers of notes are liable in the same order as was mentioned in the case of checks. Likewise, they may endorse in the same ways (blank, special, restrictive, or qualified), and their liabilities are similar.

Drafts and notes are governed by the Uniform Negotiable Instruments Law. As we have seen in the case of the check, a draft is an order drawn by one party (drawer) on another party (the drawee), ordering payment to a payee, who may be the drawer or another party. Drafts drawn and payable in the United States are domestic drafts, whereas drafts drawn in this country and payable in a foreign country (or vice versa) are foreign drafts. Foreign drafts are sometimes called "bills of exchange." When a bank draws a draft (check) on another bank, the instrument is called a "bank draft." A draft drawn by a seller to obtain payment for his merchandise is known as a "trade acceptance"—the buyer obtains the merchandise when he "accepts" the draft. He accepts the draft by writing his acceptance and signature on the face of the instrument, very much as a bank certifies a check and thereby promises to pay it. A "sight draft" is payable at sight or presentation, whereas a "time draft" is payable in a given number of days after date or acceptance.

Drafts are used by sellers to expedite payment. The initiative comes from the sellers. Frequently, a seller will not part with the goods until the buyer accepts the draft drawn on him. Sometimes a draft, with an order bill of lading attached, is given to the seller's bank with instructions to have the bill of lading handed to the buyer (through a correspondent bank) only after he has accepted the draft drawn on him. It is even more satisfactory for the seller if the arrangement is for the buyer's bank to accept (and promise to pay) the draft. A draft drawn on a bank and accepted by it is known as a "banker's acceptance." Accepted drafts, being the equivalent of promissory notes, can be discounted (sold) to banks and are, therefore, a source of ready money even before the due dates. The discount is the amount of money deducted from the face value of the note or draft by the bank. Illustrations of promissory notes and drafts may be seen in Figures 5–16 and 5–17.

Sometimes a borrower can obtain money only if he secures a comaker to sign his note with him. In other cases, the lender will require that the maker secure the endorsement of some financially able person. Persons who lend their signatures as accommodation comakers or endorsers often live to regret the act; a comaker will have to pay the amount of the note if the maker fails to do so, just as an accommodation

FIGURE 5–16

Promissory Note

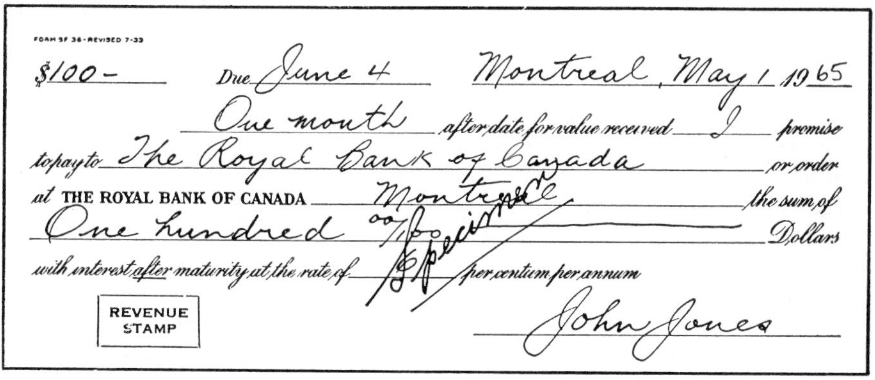
FORM SF 38-REVISED 7-33

$100— Due June 4 Montreal, May 1 1965

One month after date for value received I promise to pay to The Royal Bank of Canada or order at THE ROYAL BANK OF CANADA Montreal the sum of One hundred 00/100 Dollars with interest after maturity at the rate of 6 per centum per annum

REVENUE STAMP

Specimen

John Jones

FIGURE 5–17

Sight Draft

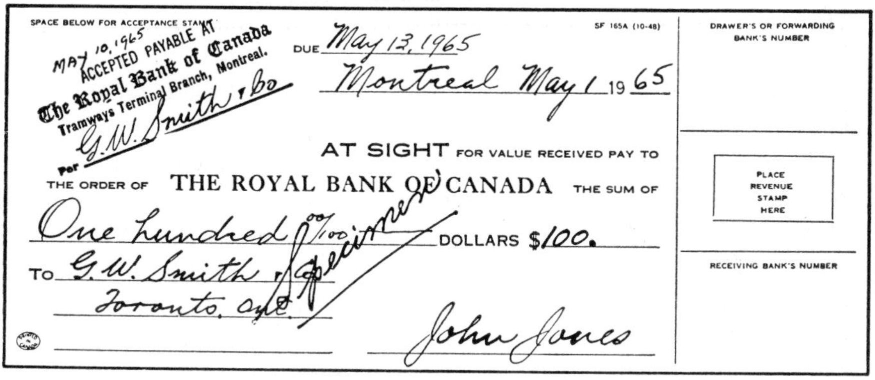
SPACE BELOW FOR ACCEPTANCE STAMP

May 10, 1965 ACCEPTED PAYABLE AT The Royal Bank of Canada Tramways Terminal Branch, Montreal. G.W. Smith & Co Per G.W. Smith

SF 165A (10-48)

DUE May 13, 1965

Montreal May 1 1965

AT SIGHT FOR VALUE RECEIVED PAY TO THE ORDER OF THE ROYAL BANK OF CANADA THE SUM OF One hundred 00/100 DOLLARS $100.

TO G.W. Smith & Co Toronto, Ont.

Specimen

John Jones

DRAWER'S OR FORWARDING BANK'S NUMBER

PLACE REVENUE STAMP HERE

RECEIVING BANK'S NUMBER

endorser can be called upon to pay it upon due presentment and due notice of dishonor.

Safe Deposit Boxes

The safe deposit box is a metal container kept under lock and key in a section of a bank's vault for customers' use. The boxes are kept in small compartments, each with a separate lock. These boxes are rented with the compartment to depositors and other customers for an annual rental, varying with the size of the box but ranging from $7.00 per annum for the smallest-size box to $60 for the largest (plus 10 percent federal tax in all cases). A typical small box is 2 × 5 × 24, that is two inches deep, five inches wide, and twenty-four inches long. A very large one is 10 × 10 × 24. Each customer has an individual key to the safe deposit box that he rents. The bank also has a separate key to each box. The box cannot be opened unless both keys are used, the customer's key opening one set of tumblers, and the bank's key opening another set to release the lock.

A safe deposit box is an excellent place in which to keep a variety of valuable papers, such as insurance policies, savings bank passbooks, stock certificates, bonds, real estate deeds, car titles, wills, valuable receipts, and even unused jewelry. Just how unbusinesslike and costly it may be not to have a safe deposit box may be seen from the following example. A man has 100 shares of General Motors common stock, which he loses through his failure to rent a safe deposit box. To replace it, the General Motors Corporation will require that the stockholder buy and turn over a surety bond for the market value of the stock. At present prices, the bond would be about $8,000, and the insurance premium would be approximately $400. This bond insures the company against the reappearance of the stock in the hands of innocent holders. The cost of the bond would equal the rent of a small safe deposit box for about 50 years.

Every precaution is taken by a bank to safeguard the contents of a box. Carefully constructed steel vaults are guarded by alarms and police protection. Every entrant to a safe deposit department is carefully identified. In addition, insurance policies are carried to protect boxholders against possible loss because of fire, flood, burglary, etc. Bank employees cannot get into your box because when the box is rented the bank loses possession of one of the two keys necessary to open the box, and the bank has no master key which will open every box. If you lose your key, it is usually necessary to destroy the lock by drilling into it. Sometimes, however, it is possible to bring a factory representative to the bank to open the box. One is reminded of the classic story of the man who rented a box with a key lock and another with a combination lock (now rare). He kept the keys for the former in the latter and a record of the combination in the former. Then he forgot the combination!

If the renter of the box dies and the key is not found, the box is opened, either by drilling or by a factory man, in the presence of authorized legal officers and the executors. If the box is in the joint names of husband and wife, the latter, of course, has access to the box on the death of the husband, although the box is immediately and temporarily sealed when the bank receives notice of death and may not be reopened until a tax officer is present to take an inventory of the contents of the box for estate and inheritance tax purposes.

SUGGESTED READINGS

1. *Using Bank Services,* Banking Education Committee, American Bankers Association, New York, 1961. A free copy may be obtained from your local bank.
2. *Personal Money Management,* American Bankers Association, latest edition. A free copy may be obtained from your local bank.
3. *The Commercial Banking Industry,* Commission on Money and Credit. Englewood Cliffs, N.J.: Prentice-Hall, Inc., 1962.
4. "Save Money on Your Checking Account," *Changing Times, The Kiplinger Magazine,* September, 1962.
5. "Paper That Passes for Money," Vol. III of *You and the Law.* New York: Research Institute of America, 1963.
6. Robert Metz, "Personal Finance: 300,000 Checks Bounce Every Day," in the New York Times, September 30, 1963.
7. "Write Way to Write a Check," *Changing Times, The Kiplinger Magazine,* October, 1960.
8. *Banking Forms and Their Uses.* Montreal: Royal Bank of Canada, latest edition.
9. "The Law and Your Safe Deposit Box," *Changing Times, The Kiplinger Magazine,* March, 1964.
10. "The Story of Checks," Federal Reserve Bank of New York, latest edition. A free copy may be obtained by writing to the Bank at 33 Liberty Street, New York 45, N.Y.
11. *Bank Terminology.* Dayton, Ohio: National Cash Register Company, latest edition. A free copy may be obtained upon request.

CASE PROBLEMS

1. John and Sally Yates are a young married couple who believe they should have a checking account. Should the account be opened in the name of John, or Sally, or in the names of both jointly? Why? What are the various advantages and disadvantages?

2. Elizabeth and Benjamin Lake have a joint checking account. The checkbook is kept by Elizabeth at home. She is always careful to record all deposits she makes and all checks that she draws. The checkbook shows a balance of $200 and she is about to draw a check for $180. Unknown to her, Benjamin, while on a business trip away from home, mailed in deposits to the bank in the amounts of $150, $175, and $200. He also, using checks he had taken along from the checkbook, drew checks of $125, $105, $100, and $280 on the joint account. What is the correct balance of this account at present before Elizabeth draws her check?

3. John Jamison has acquired enough money so that he feels he should have some sort of checking account. He wants to pay about five bills a month by check. What are the relative merits of a regular checking account as against a special checking account for him?

4. Helen Ford secured work with a television studio in New York at $90 a week. She opened a checking account at the Broadway Bank. At the end of a month, her checkbook showed a balance of $222.16. She compared this with the balance ($283.17) on her bank statement, which she had just asked for and received at the bank. Before leaving the bank, she asked a teller what the probable reasons were for the discrepancy. What do you suppose he told her? Before noting the balance of $222.16 in her checkbook, Helen had just added a deposit of $50 and had cashed a check for $22. When she arrived at her rooming house, she looked over the canceled checks returned by the bank and found that three of the checks she had drawn during the month (for $20, $27, and $43.44) were missing. From the bank statement she learned that the bank had made a service charge for the month of $1.43. Reconcile the balances. How much money has she in the bank at the present moment?

5. When Peter Green completed graduate school, he accepted a position with the Bisco Corporation, which was located about 300 miles from his home town, where he had had a checking account for over five years in a large commercial bank. The Bisco Corporation is located ten miles from a town whose population is 5,000 and which has two old but small commercial banks. Green wants your advice as to whether to retain the checking account he now has or to close it out and open a new one in one of the banks in the town. Would you give him the same advice if he were running a grocery store doing both a charge and a cash business? Would the large bank be safer than the small ones? Why?

6. Grace Smith, a student in college in New York City, maintains a checking account in the Chase Manhattan Bank. Being short of funds for the spring formal, she writes to her father in San Francisco for financial assistance. About a week later, she receives from him a check for $400, which she immediately deposits. Grace and the receiving teller at the bank both overlook the fact that Grace has failed to endorse the check, which is payable to her order. Since the spring formal is to occur in less than a week, Grace makes several purchases in the next few days, giving checks which she believes will be charged almost entirely against the $400 received from her father. Comment.

7. James Donnelly received a check for $450 from Peter Lyons, drawn on a local bank. James took the check to the bank on which it was drawn and had it certified so that he could use it to pay for some land he was going to purchase in a couple of months. In the interim, the bank, which was not insured by the Federal Deposit Insurance Corporation, failed. How do the parties stand?

8. When Janet Sheridan graduated from college and left home, she made it a practice to send her mother $100 on the first of every month. Janet mailed her mother a check for $100 on May 1, 1964. On May 20 the mother wrote that she had not yet received the check and was worried because she had not yet paid her rent, which was due on the first of the month. Janet lived 200 miles from her mother. What could Janet do to remedy the situation?

9. Edward Downing runs a small business which he owns. At the beginning of the month, both his checkbook and his bank statement showed a balance of $1,522.63. During the month he made deposits totaling $1,732.63, and he also left at the bank for collection three promissory notes (for $392.63, $282.71, and $26.28) which he did not enter in his checkbook (preferring to wait until he received a notice from the bank that they had been collected). Checks drawn during the month totaled $2,264.13. The bank statement at the end of the month showed a balance of $1,995.46 after a service charge of $3.52 had been deducted. Four of the checks he drew (for $90, $67.14, $82.51, and $92.86) were not among the canceled checks returned by the bank. At that time, the checkbook showed a balance of $991.13. Reconcile the balances. How much does Downing have available to spend? Did the bank collect the notes?

10. Gordon went into his bank and bought 10 traveler's checks, each of $10 denomination, for which he paid the bank $101. He noticed that the clerk spent quite a little time explaining the checks to him, making out forms, etc. He wondered how his bank and the bank that issued the traveler's checks could afford to give all the required service for only $1. It was eight months later before he cashed half of the checks. Discuss.

6 SAVINGS AND SAVINGS OUTLETS

> Money makes money
> And the money
> That money makes
> Makes more money.
>
> —*Poor Richard's Almanack*

BENJAMIN FRANKLIN provided one of the most dramatic examples of the ability of money to multiply itself under the impetus of compound interest. In 1791 Franklin bequeathed the sum of $5,000 to the inhabitants of Boston with the proviso that the sum be allowed to accumulate for 200 years. By 1891 the fund had grown to $322,000. From it the Franklin Union Building for a technical school in Boston was paid for, and the remainder was set aside for a second hundred years of accumulation. By 1962 this second century fund had reached $17 million.[1]

Over the years, Americans have rather consistently adhered to the habits of thrift suggested and advanced by their ancestors, and the consequent enormous capital accumulation channeled into productive facilities has made the United States the most advanced industrial country in the world. If there is any one single factor which distinguishes advanced from underdeveloped countries, it is the ability of the former to accumulate savings and funnel them into productive economic activity. Most individuals find, likewise, that unless and until they can accumulate a fund to fall back upon in emergencies or use to take advantage of opportunities for personal advancement, business success, or investment profit, progress in economic status comes but slowly.

---

[1] *The New York Times*, April 21, 1962.

212

Forms of Savings

Savings can take many forms, can be held and used in many different ways. From simple to complex, the range includes keeping cash under the mattress; accumulating cash balances in bank demand deposits; holding savings deposits, accounts in credit unions, or shares in savings and loan associations; building equities in pension funds, annuities, or life insurance; buying savings bonds or other government securities; using the postal savings system; buying capital assets such as homes, personal small business enterprises, or corporate stocks or bonds. While this chapter deals primarily with "liquid" forms of savings (deposits, savings accounts, savings bonds, etc.), it is worth noting that an individual who pays for a home in monthly installments on a mortgage is saving just as effectively as one who puts comparable sums in a savings bank. Most life insurance policies involve not only the purchase of protection but a large element of savings as well.[2]

A Savings Plan

One can save haphazardly, putting aside any surplus that seems to be left over after essential expenditures of the moment have been made, or one can draw up and try to stay with a savings plan (long-term, short-term, or both). The latter usually results in more systematic and consistent and therefore larger savings, just as spending is made more efficient by the use of a plan. But there is no perfect savings plan, and there is no plan that will fit every family. A good savings plan will involve at least five elements. In order of priority these are:

1. A decision, and it should be a realistic one, as to how much of annual, monthly, or weekly income may really be considered surplus, over essential needs, and therefore set aside for savings. It should be remembered that the average family is probably engaged in a considerable amount of contractual saving—paying premiums on life insurance, contributing to a pension fund each month via payroll deduction, etc., and this may leave less room for voluntary saving.

2. How large a cash reserve can you and should you maintain? No matter how well ordered one's life may be, there are always emergencies that strain one's finances; and when they come, it is better to

---

[2] Savings, of course, are a dynamic factor in our economy and have featured importantly in our economic literature in recent years. Two basic surveys made in the 1950's are Raymond W. Goldsmith *et al., A Study of Savings in the United States* (3 vols.; Princeton: Princeton University Press, 1956); and Irwin Friend, *Individuals Saving* (New York: John Wiley & Sons, Inc., 1954).

It Pays to Save!

A husband and wife were arguing about money.

"You're a spendthrift and I can't stand it any longer . . . you're driving us to the poorhouse," he said.

"Drive nothing," the wife answered, "you'll have to walk. The finance company took the car away this morning. Besides, what do we need a car for? That pay-as-you-go budget you put us on is sure working fine . . . we just don't go anywhere anymore."

"How can I possibly estimate our cost of living?" she added.

"That's simple," he retorted, "take our income and add 50 per cent. I'm having a hard time meeting expenses in business," he complained.

"Why that's odd," the wife said, "at home I meet them at every turn. You're so inconsistent. You keep on saying money isn't worth anything these days and then you make a fuss when I spend some of it. Furthermore, why should we try so hard to save?" she asked. "If we miss two payments on the washing machine and one on the refrigerator, we'll have enough for a down payment on a television set."

"Save!" the husband snorted, "why we could take the money we've been able to save toward a house so far and blow it in on a show."

As they moved away the last of the wife's comments to be heard was, "All right, I admit I like to spend money. But just name one other extravagance."

The husband had the last word. In resignation he said, "Yes, dear."

---

be able to fall back on a cash reserve in the bank—or in other forms of savings that can be readily liquidated—than to have to borrow at once. By rule of thumb, the American family has decided that an adequate emergency fund should be the equivalent of three months' salary.[3] This would work out as follows:

Annual Salary	Emergency Fund
$2,500	$ 600
3,200	800
4,000	1,000
5,000	1,200
7,200	1,800

3. How much life insurance (not just a policy, but an insurance plan) will provide reasonable security for your dependents? Can you afford this? Will you have any surplus left over after providing for this?

---

[3] See Personal Money Management, American Bankers Association. A free copy may be obtained from your local bank.

It may be that (2) and (3), or (2) alone, will be your only form of savings. About 86 percent of American families have some life insurance. They own $675 billion of life insurance averaging $11,400 per family.[4]

4. Is your surplus large enough to permit you to meet (2) and (3) and, in addition, buy a home—assuming, of course, you want to own your own home? If you live in a very large city or have no children, you may prefer to rent. This will be discussed in a later chapter.

5. After meeting (2), (3), and (4), do you have any money left over for other forms of savings, such as investments? If so, what are your objectives?

One can look in vain for a place to put savings that will be safe, liquid, inflation-resistant, and yield a large return. There is no such place. One or more of these elements must be sacrificed in whole or in part to achieve the others; and in the formulation of a savings plan, considered judgments must be made.

Various Savings Instruments Meet Different Objectives

There are various savings instruments to meet different objectives. If you want a high return on your savings, you cannot expect safety of principal. If you want safety of principal, you cannot expect the same instrument to provide a good hedge against inflation. Under most conditions, if you want liquidity, you cannot hope for long-term growth. If you want certainty of continued income, you cannot expect a high yield. There is presented in Table 6–1 a comparison of the various outlets for savings, showing their varying characteristics, advantages, and disadvantages.

Quite clearly, no one instrument or institution combines all savings objectives successfully. From a study of Table 6–1 it is apparent that those instruments which combine safety and liquidity sacrifice return and possibility of growth, while for a number of instruments the reverse is true. Your income level and your savings objectives should determine your choice. If you need a reserve against financial trouble or loss of a job, you will want a very different type of savings instrument than if you are trying to protect yourself against long-run (secular) inflation and loss of purchasing power. If you can spare the money for a period of years, you will want a different medium than if you expect to use the fund as a down payment on a house a year or two from now. Many families have several objectives and therefore spread their funds, choosing several rather than one form of savings.

---

[4] *Life Insurance Fact Book,* 1963 (New York: Institute of Life Insurance, 1963), p. 5.

TABLE 6-1
Some Comparative Uses of Savings

Savings Instrument	Principal	Inflation	Rate of Return (Percent)	Certainty of Continued Return	Smallness or Lack of Selling Charge or Other Fees	Liquidity under All Conditions	Chance for Long-Term Growth
Cash	Excellent	Poor	0	. . .	. . .	Excellent	None
Life insurance	Excellent	Poor	3¾	Excellent	Fair	Excellent	Poor
United States savings bonds	Excellent	Poor	3¾	Excellent	Excellent	Excellent	Poor
Savings account in commercial bank*	Excellent	Poor	3–4	Excellent	Excellent	Excellent	Poor
Postal savings	Excellent	Poor	2	Excellent	Excellent	Excellent	Poor
Mutual savings bank*	Excellent	Poor	3½–4¼	Excellent	Excellent	Excellent	Poor
Federal savings and loan association *	Excellent	Poor	4½–5	Excellent	Excellent	Excellent	Poor
Credit union	Excellent	Poor	4–5	Excellent	Excellent	Good	Poor
Corporate bonds	Good	Excellent	4–4½	Good	Fair	Good	Poor
Corporate stock	Fair	Excellent	3½–5	Fair	Fair	Fair	Good
Growth common stocks	Good	Excellent	1–2½	Fair	Fair	Fair	Excellent
High-grade preferred stocks	Good	Poor	4½–5	Good	Fair	Fair	Poor
High-grade convertible preferreds	Good	Good	4–4½	Good	Fair	Fair	Good
Convertible bonds	Good	Good	3–4½	Good	Fair	Good	Good
Investment companies (mutual funds)	Fair	Good	3½–5	Poor	Poor	Good	Good
Common trust funds	Fair	Fair	2–3	Fair	Fair	Good	Good
Real estate mortgages (as investments)	Fair	Poor	5½–6	Poor	Poor	Poor	Fair
Unimproved real estate	Good	Excellent	. . .	Poor	Poor	Poor	Excellent
Your own home	Good	Good	0	. . .	Poor	Poor	Good

* Insured up to $10,000.

Source: Adapted from "What to Do with Your Savings," *Changing Times*, *The Kiplinger Magazine*.

Savings Patterns

Empirical studies undertaken over the past fifteen years have shed a good deal of light on consumer choices in savings and investment. They are valuable in indicating what individuals have tended to do with their savings, and to some extent, reasons have been advanced for this behavior. According to the University of Michigan Survey Research Center's *Survey of Consumer Finances,* 76 percent, of all spending units owned some liquid assets. Only 24 percent of the nation's spending units had no liquid assets. Medium holdings for the 76 percent with savings were $900.[5] For spending units with incomes under $5,000, 39 percent had no liquid assets. For the 61 percent in this income category that did have liquid assets, average holdings were $700. In the case of spending units with incomes of $7,500 or more per annum only 2 percent did not possess liquid assets. For the 98 percent in this income category that did have liquid assets, average holdings amounted to $6,400.

The *Survey* notes that different stages of the life cycle of the family bring significant variations in saving and dissaving. Saving by young, single persons, while frequent, is generally limited by insufficiency of income. Marriage and the setting up of a household are usually accompanied by numerous expenditures for durable goods and a high frequency of dissaving. Several years after children are born, positive saving begins again, particularly as purchases of life insurance and houses tend, at this stage, to increase the importance of contractual savings. Savings reach a peak after the children have left home, but then there develops less incentive to save and, with retirement, less income. At this latter stage, relatively low income and limited access to credit tend to increase the number with zero savings.

How Much Do We Save?

It's not easy to answer this question. Why? Well, because different federal agencies define savings in varying ways. The most complete coverage, the personal savings estimates of the U.S. Department of Commerce, are derived as the difference between personal income and expenditure, obtained in the national income estimates. In recent years the Commerce savings figures (in billions of dollars) have been as follows:

---

[5] *1960 Survey of Consumer Finances,* Survey Research Center, Institute for Social Research, University of Michigan, Ann Arbor.

Year	Disposable Personal Income	Consumer Spending	Personal Saving	Saving as % of Disposable Income
1951	$227.5	$209.8	$17.7	7.8
1953	252.5	232.6	19.8	7.8
1955	274.4	256.9	17.5	6.4
1957	308.8	285.2	23.6	7.6
1959	337.1	313.5	23.6	7.0
1961	364.4	336.8	27.6	7.6
1962	384.4	355.4	29.1	7.6
1963	402.6	373.2	29.4	7.3

Source: U.S. Department of Commerce.

Each year the Securities and Exchange Commission estimates gross (and net) annual financial savings of individuals. This is defined very broadly to include currency, demand and time deposits, accounts in savings and loan associations, increase in private and government insurance reserves, pension funds, all types of securities, purchases of consumer durables, less the increase in mortgage and other consumer debt. For 1963, the SEC's figure was $20.4 billion net (gross $93.7 billion) as compared to the Commerce figure of $29.4 billion.[6] The difficulty is that "savings of individuals," in addition to personal holdings, cover savings of unincorporated business, trust and pension funds, and nonprofit institutions in the SEC data (see Table 6–2).

While Table 6–2 shows SEC data on net annual additions to financial savings less annual increases in individuals' debts, the SEC also compiles data on total financial assets and liabilities of individuals in the United States. These data are perhaps the most comprehensive available reflecting total assets and liabilities (see Table 6–3). On this basis individuals held net assets of $997 billion, distributed as shown in Table 6–3.

Perhaps the most useful series, for our purposes, is the more restricted estimate compiled by the Federal Home Loan Bank Board, entitled *Investments of Individuals in Savings Accounts, U.S. Savings Bonds and Life Insurance Reserves*. It covers savings and loan associations, deposits in mutual savings banks, savings accounts in commercial

---

[6] See Securities and Exchange Commission, *Volume and Composition of Individuals' Saving*, Statistical Series, Release No. 1964 (Washington, D.C., April 1, 1964). Conceptually the SEC and the Department of Commerce savings series differ. The personal savings estimate of the Department of Commerce is derived as the difference between personal income (after taxes) and expenditures. A reconciliation of the SEC and Commerce Department series appears annually in the July issue of the *Statistical Bulletin* of the SEC and in the *Survey of Current Business* (Commerce).

TABLE 6-2

Savings by Individuals in the United States

1946–1963

(Billions of Dollars)

Type of Savings	1946	1950	1954	1958	1960	1962	1963
1. Currency and deposits	10.6	3.5	5.4	10.2	2.8	19.1	17.0
2. Savings shares	1.2	1.7	4.7	6.3	8.3	10.1	11.8
3. Securities	− 1.4	0.9	0.2	1.3	− 0.1	− 0.7	*
a) U.S. savings bonds	1.0	0.3	0.6	− 0.5	− 0.2	0.4	1.2
b) Other U.S. government	− 2.4	− 0.5	− 1.7	− 1.6	− 2.7	0.5	− 0.2
c) State and local government	− 0.2	0.5	0.7	0.8	1.7	− 0.1	1.1
d) Corporate and other	0.2	0.7	0.6	2.6	1.1	− 1.5	− 2.1
4. Private insurance and pension reserves	3.7	4.8	7.3	8.4	9.2	10.2	10.7
5. Government insurance and pension reserves	3.5	1.1	2.6	0.6	3.4	2.8	4.5
6. Increase in individuals' debts	3.2	10.7	10.7	10.0	15.4	21.9	23.6
7. Net financial saving (1 + 2 + 3 + 4 + 5 − 6)	14.5	1.3	9.5	16.9	8.1	19.6	20.4
8. Nonfarm homes	3.8	11.8	13.5	15.3	18.4	17.6	18.0
9. Construction and equipment of nonprofit institutions	0.5	1.4	1.9	2.7	3.2	3.6	3.7
10. Consumer durable goods	15.9	30.4	32.4	37.3	44.8	47.5	51.6
11. Gross savings (7 + 8 + 9 + 10)	34.6	44.9	57.3	72.3	74.5	88.4	93.7

*Indicates less than $50 million.

Source: Securities and Exchange Commission.

TABLE 6–3

Financial Assets and Liabilities of Individuals in the United States
Year-End, 1954–1963
(Billions of Dollars)

FINANCIAL ASSETS	1954	1956	1958	1960	1962	1963
1. Currency and deposits	151.1	159.1	174.3	181.2	209.6	226.6
a) Currency	24.3	24.7	25.0	25.7	27.2	28.8
b) Demand deposits	55.2	55.8	56.7	54.1	57.2	62.1
c) Time and saving deposits	71.6	78.6	92.6	101.5	125.3	135.8
2. Savings shares	28.9	39.6	51.1	66.5	86.0	97.7
3. Securities	336.9	405.5	472.6	501.0	587.7	652.7
a) U.S. savings bonds	50.0	50.1	47.7	45.6	46.9	48.0
b) Other U.S. government*	18.5	20.2	21.3	27.0	26.6	26.8
c) State and local government	18.2	21.5	24.5	31.0	31.8	32.9
d) Corporate and other†	250.2	313.7	379.1	397.4	482.4	544.9
(1) Bonds and notes	20.5	19.3	21.0	21.9	22.9	22.9
(2) Investment company shares	9.5	13.1	17.9	22.8	29.7	34.2
(3) Other preferred and common shares	220.2	281.3	340.2	352.7	429.8	487.8
4. Private insurance and pension reserves	96.7	112.3	130.7	149.9	171.1	186.3
a) Insurance reserves	72.3	81.0	88.6	96.4	106.0	111.9
b) Insured pension reserves	10.0	12.4	15.6	18.8	21.6	23.0
c) Noninsured pension reserves	14.4	18.9	26.5	34.7	43.5	51.3
5. Government insurance and pension reserves	54.3	61.1	64.9	70.6	74.5	79.0
6. Total financial assets (1 through 5)	667.9	777.6	893.7	969.2	1,128.9	1,242.3
LIABILITIES						
7. Mortgage debt	65.6	88.2	105.4	129.6	157.5	174.2
8. Consumer debt	28.0	37.4	40.1	50.5	57.3	63.2
9. Securities loans	4.4	4.3	4.6	5.0	7.2	8.1
10. Total liabilities (7 + 8 + 9)	98.1	129.8	150.1	185.1	222.0	245.5
11. Total individuals' net equity‡ (6–10)	569.9	647.8	743.6	784.1	906.9	996.8

* Estimated market value. Includes nonguaranteed federal agency issues.
† Rough estimates of market value.
‡ The year-to-year changes in the above data are not equivalent to net financial saving which does not reflect revaluations in certain of the components.
SOURCE: Securities and Exchange Commission.

banks, postal savings, United States savings bonds, and current equities in or savings accumulated behind life insurance policies rather than the protection value of the face amount of such policies. It reveals that Americans had a "nest egg" in the form of tangible savings of this type amounting to $402 billion as of the end of 1963. See Table 6–4.[7] This was equivalent to about $7,700 for every American household, as compared with some $3,600 per household in 1945, approximately

[7] *Investments of Individuals in Savings Accounts, U.S. Savings Bonds and Life Insurance Reserves,* Operating Analysis Division, Federal Home Loan Bank Board, latest data.

TABLE 6–4

Investments of Individuals in Savings Accounts,
U.S. Savings Bonds and Life Insurance Reserves
Percent Distribution

	1963	1962	1961	1960	1959	1958	1957
Savings accounts							
Savings and loan associations	22.7	21.7	21.0	19.9	18.5	17.0	16.0
Mutual savings banks	11.1	11.2	11.4	11.6	11.8	12.1	12.1
Commercial banks	24.9	24.1	22.2	21.4	21.3	21.3	20.5
Postal savings	0.1	0.1	0.2	0.3	0.4	0.4	0.5
Credit unions	1.8	1.7	1.7	1.6	1.5	1.4	1.3
Savings bonds—U.S. government							
E & H	11.6	12.2	13.1	13.7	14.3	15.1	15.8
All other	0.4	0.5	0.7	0.9	1.2	1.9	2.5
Reserves of life insurance							
companies	27.4	28.5	29.7	30.6	31.0	30.8	31.3
Total	100.0	100.0	100.0	100.0	100.0	100.0	100.0

SOURCE: Federal Home Loan Bank Board.

$1,700 in 1940, and less than $1,000 in 1920. Thus, over the years, accumulated savings have shown a much greater rate of growth than that of the population or the rise in living costs.

Savings Institutions

Thus far we have seen that the American people have accumulated a greater volume of savings than any other people in recorded history. They have chosen a variety of forms and institutions in which to place these savings. Apparently seven out of ten prefer safety to maximum return, but the inflationary pressures of the forties and fifties increased the popularity of savings forms, such as stocks and real estate, in which the risk of fluctuating principal is present. On the other hand, some individuals are still so cautious and distrustful of financial institutions that they prefer to keep their savings in the form of cash, which they hoard on their persons or hide in their houses. This is certainly the most liquid form of savings, but it is hardly the safest.

From time to time, stories appear in the newspapers telling of eccentric persons, old recluses, the uneducated, and the slightly insane, who upon death are found to have on their persons or premises anywhere from $1,000 to $250,000 in cash. Now and than one reads of old immigrant couples whose life savings were lost or stolen because they kept the cash wrapped in newspaper in their rooms.[8] For every case that reaches the press, there are doubtless dozens that do not. There is, of course, no way of knowing how much of the $31 billion of currency "in circulation" is being hoarded by savers, how much distrustful people have hidden beneath mattresses, or how much gamblers and racketeers keep in safe-deposit boxes because they do not wish it to become a matter of record through a deposit; but the total must be considerable.

The disadvantages of cash as a form of savings are quite apparent. The money is lost or stolen much too easily, and it earns no income. One is reminded of the eccentric old lady who confided to her neighbor

---

Hid Life Savings, Thief Takes All

Associated Press

DALLAS, Tex., April 16 — A. C. Mallory, 44, last night reported his life savings of $7,800 taken from its hiding place under his house. Mallory said the money was in two pint fruit jars suspended in a pillow case under a hallway trap door. He said he had been saving the money since he was 12 and never kept it in a bank.

---

that she kept her money at home, hidden in a coffee can. "But," reminded the neighbor, "you're losing interest." "Oh, no, I'm not," the old lady insisted serenely; "I'm putting away a little extra, just for that." With deposit insurance covering commercial banks, savings banks,

---

[8] From a newspaper article entitled "Life Savings":

"Newspapers recently reported the sad plight of Mr. and Mrs. Albert E. White of Dayton, Ohio. Twenty-five years ago when they were married, they decided to live frugally so they would have something for their old age.

"To economize, they lived in a $12 a month house. They didn't smoke or drink, and seldom saw a movie. Both worked, he as a machinist, she in the Five and Ten. They saved and saved and changed their money into $100 bills. These they would tuck into a muslin bag tied to Mrs. White's slip.

"After 25 years, they again counted their hoard. There was $43,500 consisting of 435 one-hundred dollar bills. 'Perhaps we ought to put the money in the bank where it will be safe,' theorized Mr. White. Agreed, they decided to do so the next day.

"Come next day, they looked for their money. It was gone. After searching, and searching, they came to the conclusion that it had dropped into the trash that Mrs. White had gathered and it had been burned. All that was left of twenty-five years of hard work and skimping was a small pile of black and gray ashes."

and savings and loan associations, and with postal savings and government savings bonds available, there is no longer need to "put away a little extra" to achieve safety. A survey of commercial banks, savings banks, savings and loan associations, postal savings, savings bonds, and credit unions, as savings media, will indicate this. Life insurance, real estate, and securities will be discussed in later chapters.

Save at a Commercial Bank?

The commercial bank has frequently been called a "department store of finance" because it performs so many financial functions. It grants commercial, personal, mortgage, and other types of loans. It receives demand and time deposits (that is, it has both checking and savings accounts); it rents safe-deposit boxes, performs investment services and gives investment advice, handles collections, issues letters of credit and traveler's checks, sells and redeems United States savings bonds, performs trust functions, and provides Christmas Club and other systematic savings schemes.

At one time, commercial banks paid interest on demand deposits. They no longer do so because the law no longer allows it. Indeed, with the rise in costs of bank operations in recent years, service charges have been imposed upon the demand deposit or checking account. These vary from bank to bank and even within a bank according to the activity of the account. Since no interest is paid, most people do not use checking accounts or demand deposits for saving purposes; and indeed, where they maintain a minimum balance, they try to see to it that their account neither falls below nor rises too much above the required level. Funds kept in a checking account materially in excess of the required minimum balance earn no income for the owner, nor, of course, does the minimum balance. The bank keeps the income from the minimum balance to cover the cost of the checking service rendered and to yield a reasonable profit.

Over 12,000 commercial banks located throughout the United States, however, also maintain "savings," "thrift," "special-interest," or "compound-interest" accounts, as they are variously called. These are time deposits, and to them some 45,000,000 depositors have entrusted some $90 billion. In some communities the commercial bank is the only available institution where an individual may deposit savings and receive interest. On these time deposits, commercial banks pay interest rates which range as follows:[9]

---

[9] *Results of 1962 Savings Survey*, Savings Division, American Bankers Association. Vol. 1, p. 11.

INTEREST RATE	PERCENTAGE OF BANKS
Under 2.0%	12.6%
2.0% to 3.0%	54.7%
3.5%	21.6%
3.5% first year, 4% thereafter	11.1%

Checks may not be drawn on time deposits. A time deposit differs from a demand deposit in that the bank, in the case of the former, may require the depositor to wait a period of time, usually 30–60 days, to receive his money from the day he asks to withdraw it. Virtually all banks refrain from exercising this privilege in normal times; they invoke it only when necessary, in times of panic or crisis, when a run on the bank is threatened. In the case of a demand deposit, on the other hand,

HUBERT

Reproduced by permission of King Features Syndicate

"We pay 2½% interest and allow you to fill your fountain pen twice a week."

the bank does not have this privilege and must pay out funds as depositors ask for them; otherwise the bank is regarded as insolvent and is closed.

Savings depositors in a commercial bank are creditors of the bank, in contrast, as we shall see, to depositors in a mutual savings bank, who, in effect, are also owners of the bank. This usually results in the savings depositor in the commercial bank receiving a lower rate of return than the depositor in the mutual savings bank. The reasons are simple. When the commercial bank invests or lends its savings depositors' money, the return it obtains must not only cover the costs of the bank's operations and required reserves but it must also yield a profit to the stockholders or owners of the bank as well as pay interest on the savings depositors' accounts.

In a mutual savings bank, on the other hand, there are no stockholders, and therefore the entire return from investing or lending the depositors' funds may, after banking costs and required reserves are covered, be paid out to the depositors. Since there are no stockholders, none of the return need be set aside for dividends on invested capital. It is partly for this reason that the average return paid by commercial banks on savings accounts is lower than the average paid by mutual savings banks. Furthermore, commercial banks invest their funds in highly liquid, short-term assets and are more restricted in their ability to invest in higher-yielding, less liquid, long-term mortgages than are the savings banks. They tend, therefore, to average a smaller rate of return than do the savings banks, which have a larger percentage of their funds in 5½ and 6 percent mortgages.

Do You Know How Interest Is Computed on Your Savings Deposit?

Not only do banks vary according to the basic rate of interest they pay but they differ as to the method and timing used in computing interest on savings accounts. You will be amazed to know that a Committee of the American Bankers Association found that over one hundred different methods were used. The Committee declared:

Surveys made years ago emphasized the fantastic variations in interest paid on identical accounts by the use of different methods. If a sum of money is on deposit throughout an interest period, the amount of interest at any given rate would not vary regardless of method. The variation in the amount of interest payable depends on the method of determining the balance on which interest should be paid. The activity in savings accounts is the basis for over 100 methods of computing interest.

Of the 100 methods, six are frequently used. In fact, 89.5% of the banks of the country use one of the following six methods:

Method #1—Used by 31.5% of banks: Effective rate[10] .89% (median).

Interest is credited semiannually each year. Interest commences first of the month following a deposit, and on amounts withdrawn ceases at the beginning of the semiannual period in which withdrawn, *withdrawals being charged against the beginning balance of the period or first deposits.*

Method #2—Used by 20% of banks: Effective rate .87% (median).

Interest is credited semiannually each year. Interest commences at the beginning of the semiannual period, and funds must be on deposit for full six months. This method of paying interest *on the minimum balance* for six months has become increasingly popular with banks. Most methods penalize activity in savings accounts but this method appears to levy a greater penalty than most others. Partly for this reason and partly because of ease of computation it has grown in popularity.

Method #3—Used by 13.3% of banks: Effective rate .90% (median).

Interest is credited semiannually each year. Interest commences first of the month following a deposit, and on amounts withdrawn ceases at the beginning of the semiannual period, *withdrawals being charged against the most recent deposits of the current interest period, if any.* This method, by which withdrawals are deducted from the latest deposits, is prescribed by law for all federal savings and loan associations.

Method #4—Used by 11.5% of banks: Effective rate .89% (median).

Interest *commences at the beginning of the next quarter* following a deposit, and on amounts withdrawn *ceases at the beginning of the quarter* in which withdrawn, withdrawals being charged to most recent deposits of quarterly period, if any.

Method #5—Used by 10.0% of the banks: Effective rate .94% (median).

Interest is computed *on lowest monthly balance.* Interest *commences first of the month* following a deposit and on amounts withdrawn *ceases on the first of the month* in which withdrawn.

Method #6—Used by 3.0% of banks: Effective rate .85% (median).

Interest *commences at the beginning of the next quarter* following a deposit, and on amounts withdrawn *ceases at the beginning of the semiannual period in which withdrawn,* withdrawals being charged against *most recent deposits* of period, if any.

Now what does all of this mean? It may seem confusing at first, but it's important to you as a saver. You ought to avoid banks that use Methods #2 and #6 and favor those, if you can find them, that use Method #5. One aspect ought to be quite clear. In Method #2 the bank doesn't start paying interest on your deposit until the beginning of the *new* semiannual period. The funds must be on deposit a whole six months to earn any interest. In Method #5, the bank starts paying

---

[10] The effective rate of interest may be obtained by dividing the total amount of interest paid during the year by the *average* total amount of savings on deposit for the year. This *average* figure would be the month-end total for each of the twelve months added together and divided by twelve.

interest the first of the month following a deposit. Suppose you deposited $100 on January 20 of any given year. Under Method #2, your deposit *would not start earning interest until the following July 1,* and would earn interest for only the last half of the year. It would earn nothing from January 20 to July 1. Under Method #5, your deposit on January 20 would start earning interest commencing February 1. Thus under Method #5, you would earn interest for 11 months of the year as against only six months under Method #2.

The method of treating withdrawals is also very important. You, as a saver, are favored by a method which charges withdrawals against the most recent deposit, and you are hurt by one which charges them against the beginning balance of the period or first deposits. Let's go back to the previous example. Your first deposit of $100 was on January 20. You deposit another $100 on August 10, a third $100 on October 1, and then you withdraw $100 on December 1. Assuming the bank is paying interest from the first of the semiannual period and they charge the $100 withdrawal against the January 20 deposit, you lose all interest on that deposit even though it has been in the bank for over ten months. If, on the other hand, it's charged against the last deposit, the one made on October 1, you lose nothing since interest on that would not start until the following January 1.

In the ABA Survey, for purposes of comparison, a sample account was taken, with an initial balance of $2,736 on July 1. Various withdrawals and deposits left a net balance of $1,044 on November 18. The actual interest in dollars to be credited to the account for the six months' period was computed for each of the methods.[11] The variation in results was surprising, as may be seen in the accompanying tabulation:

Method	Average Balance on Which Interest Is Computed for Six Months' Period	Actual Interest Credited at Rate of 1 Percent per Annum for Six Months
#1	$ 901	$4.50½
#2	792	3.96
#3	917	4.58½
#4	917	4.58½
#5	1,576	7.88
#6	917	4.58½

SOURCE: American Bankers Association, *Methods and Procedures in Computing Interest on Savings Deposits.*

[11] American Bankers Association, *Methods and Procedures in Computing Interest on Savings Deposits.*

Obviously, therefore, six different banks could state that they pay interest at the rate of 1 percent per annum, but, depending on how they compute your minimum balance or the amount to be used for crediting interest, the variations in what you actually got might be as extreme as $3.96 to $7.88 for a half-year. It would pay, therefore, to deposit savings funds in a bank which uses Method #5. You would do well to study the various methods banks use and then choose the bank using the method most favorable to you. The average person unfortunately either does not care or finds it too difficult to understand the various methods. An examination of the methods now in use reveals that most of them penalize the overactive or in-and-out saver. Indirectly, this benefits the true saver, in that these methods reduce to a minimum the number of accounts on which a bank takes a loss, thus leaving more of the bank's earnings to be distributed to the real savers.

Is Your Deposit Insured?

Of the 13,588 commercial banks operating in the United States, 13,189 are members of the Federal Deposit Insurance Corporation. Thus over 90 percent of the commercial banks in the country are insured. Each depositor is protected to an upper limit of $10,000 if the bank should fail. For this insurance, each bank contributes semiannually to the Deposit Insurance Fund based on its total deposits. When an insured bank fails, the Insurance Fund either pays the depositor in cash or opens another account in his or her name for the same amount in a solvent, going bank. The money in this new account may be withdrawn at once.

The $10,000 protection limit applies to a single depositor in a given bank, regardless of the number of accounts he may have. A person who has a $2,000 balance in his checking account in a given bank, as well as a savings account with a $9,000 balance in the same bank, would receive $10,000 (not $11,000) if the bank failed. If he had only the savings account, he would be fully insured for the $9,000. If his savings-account balance were $12,000, he would be insured for only $10,000. The insurance coverage is based upon deposits maintained by a person at a single insured bank, not upon his total deposits throughout the banking system. If you are fortunate enough to possess $30,000, you can, by depositing $10,000 in each of three different banks, be fully insured for the $30,000.

The law limits insurance to $10,000 for any one depositor in any one bank but does not prohibit you from splitting your funds among a number of banks. Moreover, if you are married, your own deposit, your wife's separate deposit account, as well as your joint deposit, *with right of survivorship,* are each separately insured to the maximum of $10,000, even though they are all in the same bank. If the joint account is, however, a tenancy in common (without right of survivorship), it is not separately insured, and the interest of each owner in the common account would be added to the individual deposit of each in computing the insurance coverage. If you have accounts in the main office and a branch or in several branches of one insured bank, the accounts will be added together in determining your insurance, since the FDIC considers the main office and all branches as one bank.[12]

Deposits of a partnership are insured separately from the individual deposits of each of the partners. If you act as a trustee, guardian, administrator, executor, agent, or in some other fiduciary capacity, deposit accounts which you open and maintain in any or all of these capacities are insured separately from the deposits in your individual account. In fact, you can maintain deposits in an insured bank in each of the following rights and capacities and be separately insured to the maximum of $10,000 on each of the accounts shown below:

John Doe	$10,000
Mary Doe	10,000
John Doe and Mary Doe, joint account with right of survivorship	10,000
John Doe, Mary Doe, and Richard Doe, joint account with right of survivorship	10,000
John Doe and Mary Doe, community funds (in community property state)	10,000
John Doe, executor of estate of (name) deceased	10,000
John Doe, administrator of estate of (name) deceased	10,000
John Doe, trustee of (name) estate	10,000

Except to the extent that the annual assessment which the insured bank pays to the Insurance Fund adds to the cost of banking operations and thereby reduces the income available for payment to depositors and stockholders, there is no direct charge to the savings-account depositor for deposit insurance. If you should, therefore, ever have a choice between placing funds in an insured bank or depositing in one that is not insured, your decision should not be difficult. The 400-odd small, state-chartered, noninsured banks (all national banks must be members of the FDIC) are, however, able to survive in their noninsured status largely because they are, in almost all cases, the only bank in the small

---

[12] A copy of *Your Deposit Is Insured,* issued by the Federal Deposit Insurance Corporation, giving all essential facts about insurance coverage, may be obtained by writing to the Federal Deposit Insurance Corporation, National Press Building, Washington 25, D.C.

town in which they are located, and inhabitants of the town thus have no choice.

Savings Banks

From the organization of the first savings bank 148 years ago, these institutions have successfully weathered panics, wars, and depressions and have grown in size and importance in the American economy until today they hold deposits of more than $44 billion, representing the savings of over 22 million depositors. Of the 509 mutual savings banks located in 18 states,[13] 134 are over 100 years old, and 100 have deposits in excess of $100,000,000 each.

In 1816, a number of public-spirited citizens drew plans for and established the Philadelphia Savings Fund Society in that city and the Provident Institution for Savings in Boston to encourage thrift and to provide safe places for the poorer citizens of the community to save. The plans devised have continued to serve as models for all savings banks in the United States.

In contrast to commercial banks, there are no stockholders in mutual savings banks. All earnings, after operating expenses are met, go to benefit depositors either directly, in the form of dividends, or indirectly, as additions to surplus which increase depositors' protection. The United States Supreme Court has defined a mutual savings bank as "an institution in the hands of disinterested persons, the profits of which, after deducting the necessary expenses of conducting the business, inure wholly to the benefit of the depositors, in dividends or in reserve surplus for their greater security."[14]

Your deposit in a savings bank is evidenced by a passbook, in which the bank enters all deposits and withdrawals. This you keep in your possession, and it is a duplicate of the bank's own record of your account. As a depositor, you are an owner of the bank and are entitled to withdraw your money at any time, although if you read the rules of the bank carefully, you will find that the bank has the right to require a reasonable notice of from 30 to 90 days, varying by state, of your intention to withdraw. A typical clause on the bank's rights in withdrawals reads:

The Bank shall not be liable to pay any money to depositors, except on sixty days' previous notice to the Comptroller at the Bank, but moneys may

---

[13] Alaska, Connecticut, Delaware, Indiana, Maine, Maryland, Massachusetts, Minnesota, New Hampshire, New Jersey, New York, Ohio, Oregon, Pennsylvania, Rhode Island, Vermont, Washington, and Wisconsin.

[14] *Huntington* v. *National Savings Bank,* 96 U.S. 388, 395.

voluntarily be paid by the Bank daily, and without such notice, and without thereby waiving the right of the Bank to such notice from any one or more persons seeking to withdraw. Upon the expiration of the sixty days after notice is so given the money will be payable, but if not withdrawn within fifteen days thereafter, such notice shall be void and a new notice may be required.

In practice, savings banks do not exercise this right but pay immediately, reserving the privilege for essential use in periods of crisis. Additional protection of depositors' funds is provided by careful supervision of savings banks' investments by state banking authorities and by the provision requiring banks to set aside a part of earnings as a reserve or surplus. In most states the reserve or surplus must be built up to at least 10 percent of deposit liabilities. The average surplus for all mutual savings banks in the country today equals 9.6 percent of deposits. This means that for every $1.00 of deposits, the banks have about $1.10 in assets. Furthermore, 331 of the mutual savings banks are insured by the Federal Deposit Insurance Corporation in exactly the same way as are both demand and time deposits of commercial banks. In the event of default, savings bank time deposits in the 331 insured banks would be paid off in just the same way as both demand and time deposits in commercial banks. The insured deposit, up to a maximum of $10,000, would be paid in cash within ten days after the date of final closing of the failed bank, or the insured depositor would have his account transferred to a solvent, insured banking institution.[15]

Most mutual savings banks now pay 4 or 4¼ percent on deposits. The latest survey of the National Association of Mutual Savings Banks shows that 4.3 percent of the banks pay less than 4 percent; 42.8 percent pay 4 percent; and 52.8 percent pay over 4 percent (Table 6–5).[16]

To open a savings account is a very simple procedure. The prospective depositor walks into the bank; steps up to the reception desk where accounts are opened; fills out a signature card, which also contains space for his address and other information which will help to identify him, such as the names of his mother and father; makes an initial deposit, which often need not be more than $1.00; and receives a passbook in which deposits, withdrawals, and interest credits are entered by the bank

---

[15] In Massachusetts, the Mutual Savings Central Fund, Inc., insures all accounts in full in all savings banks under Massachusetts law. The Savings Banks' Deposit Guaranty Fund of Connecticut guarantees all deposits in full in most of the savings banks in Connecticut under provisions of the state banking law. The savings banks of New Hampshire maintain a mutual protective organization for the protection of their depositors.

[16] See *Savings Bank Journal*, March, 1964, National Association of Mutual Savings Banks.

or a record folder in which he can enter these transactions himself. The passbook must be presented along with a deposit slip or withdrawal slip, duly filled out, every time that a deposit or withdrawal is made. Forms are available which may be sent to the bank with the passbook if the depositor wishes to do business by mail. Care should be taken not to lose the passbook. The depositor may have to bear the expense of advertising its loss in a newspaper and/or also give an indemnity bond for the bank's protection before another passbook will be issued to him.

TABLE 6–5

Distribution of Mutual Savings Banks by Rates of Interest on Deposits

December 31, 1963

		(Amounts in Thousands)	
Interest Rates	Number of Banks	Total Deposits	Percentage Distribution of Total Deposits
4⅞%	1	$ 49,682	.11%
4¾	1	7,064	.02
4½	4	144,781	.33
4¼	104	22,761,841	51.02
4⅛	6	622,898	1.40
4	345	19,098,045	42.82
3⅞	1	59,200	.13
3¾	27	1,527,880	3.42
3½	14	258,525	.58
3	5	75,068	.17
2½	1	1,368	*
	509	$44,606,352	100.00%

* Less than .01 percent.
Source: National Association of Mutual Savings Banks.

Some of the accounts that may be opened at a savings bank are:

Individual Accounts. Owned only by one person, adult or minor. You are the sole owner, and the money is payable only to your order. It can be opened with a small amount, usually as little as $1.00, and can be increased to the limit prescribed by law.

Joint Accounts. May be opened by two persons, most frequently by a husband and wife. Either may deposit or withdraw. In case of the death of one of them, the balance is payable to the survivor. Such an account is opened "Richard Doe—Jane Doe—payable to either or the survivor."

Voluntary Trust Accounts. Can be opened by you in trust for a child or other person. The account is controlled by you during your life; after your death, it is payable to the person named as beneficiary. The trust is revocable in the sense that you have the right to change the beneficiary at any time. Such an account is opened "Richard Doe in trust for Mary Doe."

Fiduciary Accounts. If you are appointed as executor or administrator of an estate or as guardian for a minor or for an "incompetent" person, you may open an account, called "fiduciary," for the funds entrusted to you.

Organization Accounts. These are accounts in the names of non-profit organizations, such as churches, lodges, clubs, fraternal organizations, etc.

School Savings Accounts. Over two million savings bank accounts are owned by students, who deposit and withdraw in schools co-operating with the savings banks. Thus habits of thrift are learned directly at an early age.

Payroll-Deduction Accounts. May be opened by any business firm for the convenience of its employees. The employee authorizes his company to deduct from his wage each payday a stated amount and to deposit it directly in his savings bank account.

Special Accounts. If you wish to accumulate funds for a special purpose—such as insurance, taxes, travel, United States savings bonds—the bank book can be marked accordingly. These are regular accounts on which dividends are paid. Funds may be withdrawn at any time, but the banks ask that a small balance be left if you intend to save for the same purpose the next year. This avoids the expense and inconvenience of having to open a new account each year.

Christmas Club Accounts. You accumulate extra money for Christmas by depositing a fixed amount—50 cents to $10 a week—and in 50 weeks you receive a check by mail for the total you have deposited. Dividends are *not* paid on Christmas Club accounts.

Vacation Club Accounts. These are similar to the Christmas Club accounts but are opened in June. You deposit $1.00 or more each week for 50 weeks, and a check is mailed to you the following May. Dividends are *not* paid on Vacation Club accounts.

In addition to these services, savings banks perform a variety of others. The average regular account in a mutual savings bank amounts to $2,281. Service charges are not common in mutual savings banks. Less than 30 banks impose them, and apparently all feel that their imposition causes customer relations problems. If a passbook has not been presented for 15 years, an account is legally deemed abandoned in most cases. If the depositor is not then located by advertising, banking law requires that the balance be turned over to the comptroller of the state. Even then, the balance may be reclaimed by the depositor from the comptroller. To guard against this, it is best to have dividends entered at least once a year and to keep the bank informed of all changes of address. Change-of-address cards can be secured free of charge at your local post office.

Savings and Loan Associations

In recent years, savings and loan associations have offered more competition to savings banks, principally because, on the average, they have been able to pay slightly higher dividend rates. When most savings banks were paying 3 percent, savings and loan associations averaged 3½ percent. When savings banks began to raise their rate to 4 percent, savings and loan associations increased their average rate to 4½ percent. This is possible because savings and loan associations tend to place about 85 percent or more of their funds in first mortgages on real estate, whereas savings banks commonly invest only about 65 percent in real estate mortgages. Since savings and loan associations invest a larger percentage of total assets in high-yielding mortgages than do savings banks, they can afford to pay a slightly higher return. Presently the associations pay from 4 to 5 percent.

A savings and loan association is a locally owned and privately managed thrift and home-financing institution. It gathers together the savings of individuals and uses these savings to make long-term amortized loans (that is, loans whose principal is reduced regularly) to purchasers of homes. These loans are made for purposes of construction, repair, purchase, or refinancing of houses, and their repayment is secured by first mortgages. There are now about 6,277 savings and loan associations in the United States, of which some 4,336 are state chartered and 1,941 federally chartered.[17] Of total savings and loan associations 93 percent are mutually owned. The remaining 7 percent operate as stock companies.

The first association was established in 1831 in a suburb of Philadelphia with 37 members. Each member agreed to save a certain amount each month. As funds accumulated, they were loaned to one of the

---

[17] Known also as "savings associations," "building and loan associations," "co-operative banks" (New England), and "homestead associations" (Louisiana). See *Handbook of Savings and Loan* (Chicago: American Savings and Loan Institute, latest edition). A free copy may be obtained by writing to the Institute at 221 North LaSalle St., Chicago, Ill. 60601.

members to build a home. Since the funds were limited, some members of the group had to postpone their homeownership plans while waiting for adequate funds to accumulate. It soon became apparent that to provide a regular flow of funds for steady home financing it was essential to invite other savers to join the association. This was done, and the number of savers came to outnumber the borrowers. Today some 32 million savers have contributed more than $80 billion, which in turn has been loaned, for the most part, to over 10 million mortgage borrowers.

Most savings and loan associations are mutual corporations which distribute their earnings to those who save or invest in them. All savers in these mutual institutions are legally shareholders and part owners; they are not creditors. From their own number they elect boards of directors to guide the associations. All federally chartered associations must be members of the Federal Home Loan Bank System and the Federal Savings and Loan Insurance Corporation. Federal charters are granted by the Home Loan Bank Board, an agency of the federal government. Application to establish a state-chartered association is usually made to the state banking department. In many of the states, membership in the Federal Home Loan Bank System and in the Federal Savings and Loan Insurance Corporation is required by authorities issuing new state charters.

In 1932 Congress passed the Federal Home Loan Bank Act, creating a system of regional Federal Home Loan Banks, of which there are eleven. State-chartered savings and loan associations, which constitute the majority, may or may not be members of the Home Loan Bank System; but federally chartered associations must join. Advantages of membership in this reserve banking system have proved so great that the institutions now affiliated with the Home Loan Bank System represent 97 percent of all the assets of operating savings and loan associations. The liquidity of the associations is advanced, since they may borrow from the Home Loan Bank on the security of mortgages which they pledge.

The Federal Savings and Loan Insurance Corporation, a federal agency, which insures savings accounts in covered associations up to a maximum of $10,000, was established in 1934.[18] It provides the same

---

[18] In March, 1934, four months before Congress authorized the Federal Savings and Loan Insurance Corporation, the state of Massachusetts enacted legislation establishing its own fund for the insurance of share accounts in "co-operative banks," as savings and loan associations are termed in Massachusetts. This is a compulsory program for all co-operative banks in that state, and under an assessment arrangement all accounts are fully insured.

kind of protection to savers in covered savings and loan associations as the FDIC does for depositors in banks. All federally chartered associations must be members, and about 2,000 of the state-chartered associations have elected to join. Some 4,332 of the 6,277 are insured. In case of default, savings-account holders are now paid off in the same way as are depositors under the FDIC. The FSLIC law reads:

> In the event of a default by any insured institution, payment of each insured account in such insured institution which is surrendered and transferred to the Corporation shall be made by the Corporation as soon as possible either (1) by cash or (2) by making available to each insured member a transferred account in a new insured institution in the same community or in another insured institution in an amount equal to the insured account of such insured member. . . .

The insured association pays an annual premium to the FSLIC of $\frac{1}{12}$ of 1 percent per annum on its savings accounts to meet the cost of this insurance. There is no direct cost to the individual saver, however. Just as in the case of the FDIC coverage, one person may have insured accounts in more than one insured association and may receive $10,000 of insurance protection on each account.

A savings account in a savings and loan association may not usually be called a deposit, and as a result, a variety of different names and types of accounts have developed. The two most common types of accounts are:

The Savings Account. This may be opened with a small starting sum, and additional savings may usually be added or withdrawn at the saver's convenience. A passbook is issued, and dividends, as declared, are customarily entered in the passbook when presented. Savings accounts, then, are, in almost all respects, similar to savings bank deposits.

The Investment Savings Account. The individual buys certificates in $100 units or multiples thereof for lump sums of cash, and periodically, as dividends are declared, the holder of the investment certificate receives dividend checks by mail.

In addition, some state-chartered associations offer *installment savings accounts,* which require the customer to save regularly each month. Failure to save regularly, as agreed upon in the savings contract, may result in a lower rate of dividend; and thus failure to save systematically is penalized. The more modern approach, however, is to encourage regular savings through a *bonus account.* Under this plan, the saver opens the usual type of savings account but also agrees to save a stated amount each month for a specified period of time. If the savings agreement is carried out as agreed, an additional bonus dividend is added to the regular dividend as a reward for systematic savings. Although the bonus dividend varies according to state and federal law, it may be as much as 1 percent, and the required period to qualify may vary from five to 15 years.

In contrast to savings banks, savings and loan associations in most cases are not limited by law to any maximum-sized amount that can be accepted, although some associations, as a matter of management policy, do fix such limits, and others from time to time refuse to accept additional funds until new mortgage loan outlets can be found.

As savings institutions, the savings and loan associations, like savings banks, are not required to pay withdrawal requests on demand, although they customarily do. If a period of acute emergency arises, they may require a 30–90-day written notice of withdrawal. Unlike savings banks, however, they are not required to pay out the full amount of the savings account at the expiration of the notice period. This provision permits the continual operation of the association in periods of economic distress and provides for orderly liquidation of long-term assets. On the other hand, the saver may be able to get his funds back in full only over a period of time. When the notice requirement is invoked, withdrawal requests are numbered and are paid, in order of filing, as funds are available. When a person's name is reached on the list, he is entitled to a part of a third of all receipts. Ordinarily, the laws require that at least a third of all receipts must be applied in payment of withdrawal requests. If a saver has more than $1,000 invested, however, he must go to the foot of the list and start over again each time he receives $1,000. Meanwhile, no dividends may be paid on this account from the date he files his application. Federal Savings and Loan Insurance does not become effective until the savings association is placed in receivership by the public supervisory authorities, and since the association does not guarantee to pay withdrawals or to pay dividends until it is able to do so, it may not for these reasons be forced into receivership or insolvency.[19]

It should be stressed that the elaborate procedures with respect to orderly withdrawals are usually not invoked except in crisis periods and that normally the associations will pay out savings and repurchase shares on demand. Furthermore, the safety of the savings and loan association is ultimately assured by (a) its ability to borrow from the Home Loan Bank in time of need, (b) its reserves, (c) its holdings of cash and government bonds, (d) the amortized nature of its

---

[19] For more elaborate treatment see *Savings and Loan Principles*, edited by Lawrence V. Conway (Chicago: American Savings and Loan Institute Press, latest edition).

mortgages, which usually insures an adequate margin of safety should it have to foreclose property and sell it, (e) the regular monthly repayments of principal which flow in on amortized mortgages, (f) the VA and FHA guaranties on a considerable share of its mortgage holdings, and (g) the insurance of accounts up to a maximum of $10,000 each.

From the safety viewpoint, the record of the savings and loan associations is a remarkable one over a period of nearly a century and a quarter. Local management of the institutions, the excellence of homeowners as moral and credit risks, the simplicity of the savings and loan plan of operation, the reserves of the associations, whose adequacy ranks high among financial institutions, all make for the essential safety of this type of savings institution. In addition, the return paid on the savings at work in those associations is often larger than that paid by other savings institutions. The overhead of an association is traditionally small; and, most important, it has larger earnings to distribute because of the simple fact that the major part of its funds are in mortgage loans, which, being long term, command a higher rate of interest than many short-term investments.[20]

Credit Unions

A credit union is a co-operative association organized to promote thrift among its members and to accumulate savings out of which loans are made at reasonable rates of interest, to members only, for useful purposes. Credit unions are not new. The credit union movement in the United States is usually dated from 1909, when Massachusetts passed the first state credit union law. Since then, most of the states, as well as the District of Columbia, have passed similar laws. The Federal Credit Union Act, providing for the chartering and supervision of federal credit unions, was passed in 1934. There are thus today both state and federally chartered credit unions numbering over 21,050 and having over 13 million members. Of these, federal credit unions number 10,632 and have seven million members. Assets of all credit unions exceed $7.0 billion, of which federally chartered unions account for $3.5 billion.

Membership in a federal credit union is limited to persons having a common bond of occupation or association and to groups within a well-defined neighborhood, community, or rural district. Savings by

---

[20] For more information see *Savings and Loan Fact Book,* issued annually by the United States Savings and Loan League. A free copy may be obtained by writing to the League at 221 North LaSalle St., Chicago, Ill. 60601.

members are made in the form of share purchases, each share being valued at $5.00. Savings may be made in amounts as small as 25 cents per month and may be withdrawn at will, although the credit union's board of directors may require two months' notice for withdrawal of funds, as in a savings bank. This provision is seldom invoked. Regular saving of small sums by members is encouraged; the cultivation of the habit of systematic thrift is a basic purpose of credit unions. Average shareholding (savings) per member of federal credit unions amount to $303.

The term "shares" is used to designate members' savings in their federal credit union. Technically, a share is defined as a $5.00 unit of savings. Although this unit is used in computing dividends, it has little significance in the day-to-day operation of a credit union. The term is well chosen, however, because members' savings in a credit union are equity capital in the corporate sense of the term. As in savings and loan associations, savers are owners, not creditors. Sums due members comprise over 90 percent of the liabilities of federal credit unions. Many people join a credit union to obtain a loan. In these cases, it is the usual practice for the officials of the credit union to specify that the member should make payments on shares as he repays his loan. By the time the loan is repaid, the member has learned that he can save also.

Because most officers and all directors serve without compensation; because operating expenses are usually very low, due to donation of premises, electricity, etc., by the business firm or organization within which the credit union is established; because credit unions pay no income taxes; and for other reasons, these co-operative organizations frequently pay a higher rate of return than do savings banks or even savings and loan associations. Of the operating federal credit unions 78.1 percent pay 4 percent or more, while only 11.1 percent pay less than 4 percent. Approximately 8.7 percent paid from 3.0 to 3.9 percent; 45.3 percent paid from 4.0 to 4.9 percent; 26.7 percent paid from 5.0 to 5.9 percent; and 6.1 percent paid a flat 6 percent. All federal bylaws specify that dividends may not exceed 6 percent. Some 10.8 percent of federal credit unions, however, paid no dividends.[21]

Earnings come largely from loans to members. These amounted to $3.5 billion, of which a little more than $2.5 billion was outstanding at the end of the year. The size of the average loan was $701.

---

[21] See Bureau of Federal Credit Unions, *Federal Credit Unions: Report of Operations for the Year 1962* (Washington, D.C.: U.S. Department of Health, Education and Welfare, 1963).

Although savings in credit unions are not insured, safety is achieved in a number of ways:

1. Credit unions are required to set aside a reserve against losses. Federal credit unions are required to transfer to the legal reserve 20 percent of each year's net earnings until the amount of the reserve is equal to or exceeds 10 percent of the amount paid in on shares.

2. The limitation of membership to fellow-employees, to members of the same church, lodge, labor union, or other organization, or to neighbors in a community group, and the further limitation that loans may be made only to members, help prevent the making of unwise loans and tend to give the borrower a strong sense of responsibility to the group.

3. The treasurer and all persons handling or having custody of credit union funds must be bonded for faithful performance of duties.

4. The affairs of the credit union and the records of the treasurer are subject to frequent audits by a supervisory committee responsible directly to the members.

5. Adequate security is required on all loans in excess of $400.

6. Officers and directors of federal credit unions are not permitted to borrow from their associations in excess of their shareholdings.

7. The surplus funds of the federal credit union may be invested only in obligations of the federal government, in loans to other credit unions, and in shares or accounts of federal savings and loan associations.

8. All federal credit unions are periodically examined and supervised by the Bureau of Federal Credit Unions of the U.S. Department of Health, Education and Welfare.

9. Funds of a federal credit union must be deposited promptly in a bank whose deposits are insured by the Federal Deposit Insurance Corporation.

Losses on bad loans have been surprisingly low, amounting to less than two tenths of 1 percent of all loans made. The only study made of federal credit union liquidations, for all causes, including predominantly voluntary liquidations, indicated only minute losses. From 1935 through 1951, 7,579 federal credit union charters were issued; of these, 1,993, or 26.2 percent, were canceled. Of those canceled, the study declares:

Omitting from further analysis 153 "revocations," conversions, and mergers of charters, the 1,840 remaining liquidated credit unions paid to shareholders at liquidation 103.2% of total shareholdings, or a net gain of $327,000; 1,065 credit unions paid more than 100%; 403 credit unions paid exactly 100%;

and 372 credit unions paid less than 100% of the amount due. . . . Total losses in liquidations were amazingly small, only $111,117, or about twenty-five one-thousandths of one percent of the share balances in all federal credit unions, at the end of 1951, an infinitesimally small percentage of the total amounted intrusted to the care of federal credit unions since 1934.[22]

Postal Savings

The U.S. postal savings system was established by an act of Congress approved June 25, 1910. It was intended mainly to provide immigrants with a place for savings in which they would have complete trust. For this reason, the full faith of the United States was and is solemnly pledged to the payment of postal savings deposits, and the funds are almost entirely invested in U.S. government bonds.

At present, 1,164,634 depositors have balances to their credit of $483 million, or an average deposit of $416. The system received a special impetus during the Great Depression, when funds on deposit in the system rose from $153 million in 1929 to $1.2 billion in 1933. A peak was reached in 1947, when 4.2 million depositors owned $3.4 billion of deposits.[23] Since that time there has, however, been a steady decline in the use of the system. As interest rates in alternative savings outlets have risen, the 2 percent paid by the postal savings system has come to seem unattractive.

Any competent person, ten years of age or over, can open an account in his or her own name, but no person may have more than one account either at the same post office or at different post offices. Deposits are accepted only from individuals, and *no* account will be opened in the name of any corporation, association, society, firm, or partnership, or in the names of two or more persons jointly; neither will an account be opened in the name of one person in trust for, or on behalf of, another person or persons.

No account may be opened for less than a dollar, nor may fractions of a dollar be deposited in an existing account. Deposits are evidenced by certificates, which are issued in denominations of $1.00, $2.00, $10, $20, $50, $100, $200, and $500. The certificates are made out in the name of the depositor, serve as receipts, and are valid until paid. There is no passbook. Certificates are not negotiable or transferable. No

---

[22] John T. Croteau, "Federal Credit Union Liquidations, 1935–1951," *Journal of Business of the University of Chicago,* Vol. XXV, No. 3 (July, 1952), p. 203. For more information on credit unions see *The Credit Union Yearbook,* issued annually by Credit Union National Association (CUNA). A free copy of the latest issue may be obtained by writing to the Association at Filene House, 1617 Sherman Ave., Madison 1, Wis.

[23] See *Report of Operations of the Postal Savings System, 1963,* 88th Cong., 2d sess., House Doc. No. 261 (January 7, 1964).

depositor may have more than $2,500 to his credit, exclusive of accumulated interest. The certificates may be cashed at any time, and the depositor may at any time withdraw all or any part of his deposit from the post office where the deposits were made. There is no waiting period.

Postal savings deposits earn interest at the rate of 2 percent a year, except in Mississippi, where the rate is 1½ percent. A deposit made on any day of the month begins to earn interest on the first day of the next-succeeding month, which date is entered on the certificate evidencing the deposit. To earn interest, however, you must leave the money in for at least three months. Interest is compounded annually.

The postal savings system also provides for postal savings stamps, which may be purchased in denominations of 10 cents, 25 cents, 50 cents, $1.00, and $5.00. No interest is paid on stamps, but they may be used to purchase postal savings certificates or United States savings bonds. Postal savings stamps are not made out in the depositor's name, as are postal savings certificates, nor are they numbered serially—the post office keeps no record of them. They cannot, therefore, be replaced if lost or destroyed, as can the certificates; and anyone finding or stealing them can cash them, which is not possible in the case of the certificates. Certificates lost or stolen will be replaced upon identification, and this is rendered easier if the postal savings depositor keeps a separate record of the serial numbers of the certificates.

United States Government Savings Bonds

This form of savings grew remarkably in the years after the outbreak of World War II. The volume outstanding rose from $6 billion in December, 1941, to $48 billion in December, 1945. Thereafter there was a slow rise in the total volume outstanding until a peak of $58 billion was reached in December, 1950. Thereafter the total declined, and now about $48 billion are outstanding. It is estimated that these are held by slightly more than 40 million persons. The "Survey of Consumer Finances" reports a substantial decline in investor preference for savings bonds. Whereas in 1946, 63 percent of all spending units held some savings bonds, this has now declined to about 25 percent.

United States savings bonds were first offered in March, 1935, and began to mature in March, 1945. Series A–D were sold between March, 1935, and the end of April, 1941. They were patterned after the old postal savings bonds. Since postal savings were limited to a $2,500 maximum, persons who were at or approaching this limit were allowed to buy postal savings bonds on which 2½ percent interest was paid, in denominations of $20–$500, with a 20-year maturity. These were discontinued, however, in 1935, at which time United States savings bonds were first introduced. Series E, F, and G were first offered in May, 1941, and began to mature from May, 1951, on. A number of important changes were made effective May 1, 1952. The rate of interest on Series E was increased, with corresponding changes in extended Series E; Series F and G were replaced by two new issues, Series J and K, also at higher rates of interest; and a new current income bond, Series H, similar in interest return to Series E, was offered beginning June 1, 1952. Again in 1957 (effective February 1, 1957) basic changes were made. The interest payable on all unmatured bonds and on all newly issued after February 1, 1957, was raised to 3¼ percent. Maturities were shortened for the E bonds and lengthened for the H bonds. In 1959 the interest rate on Series E and H bonds was raised (effective June 1, 1959) to 3¾ percent. This was accomplished for the E bonds by further reducing their maturity to seven years and nine months. The H bond maturity remained at ten years. The increase applied not only to new bonds issued. All outstanding E and H bonds received the same benefit. Simultaneously with the interest rate increase in 1959, the Treasury announced a definite policy on the automatic extension privilege for E bonds. Since Series J and K are no longer for sale,[24] only E and H bonds will be considered.

Series E

These are appreciation rather than current income bonds. That is, they are purchased at 75 percent of the maturity (par) value and increase in value by the accretion of interest periodically, so that, over a period of time, the inherent value gradually rises to the full par value at final maturity. In contrast, the current income bond (Series H, for example) requires full payment initially of the par value; interest is paid directly to the holder by check every six months; and at maturity the bondholder receives back the same amount that he paid originally.

Series E bonds now mature in seven years, nine months, and pay 3¾ percent interest, compounded semiannually. Originally, the old Series E bonds ran for ten years and paid 2.9 percent if held to maturity. Then this was changed to nine years and eight months and to 3 percent if held to maturity. Then the period was further shortened

---

[24] They were discontinued April 30, 1957.

to eight years and eleven months with the rate raised to 3¼ percent, and finally to seven years, nine months for a 3¾ percent rate.

Effective June 1, 1959 an automatic ten-year extension was declared on all E bonds which had not yet matured by that date as well as on all new issues of E bonds. In 1961 a second ten-year extension period was granted on all E bonds issued between May 1, 1941, and May 1, 1949. Such bonds may now be held for a total of 30 years. During the second extension period all these bonds earn a straight 3¾ percent per year, compounded semiannually, on the first extended maturity value.[25]

The rate of interest paid on E bonds has always been staggered, with lower rates paid in the earlier years and higher rates in the latter years, to provide a financial incentive for individuals to retain their bonds to maturity rather than cash them in at an earlier date. If held six months, new E bonds yield 1.71 percent; if held one year, 2.33 percent; if held two years, 3.00 percent; five years, 3.59 percent; to maturity, 3¾ percent.

Present Series E bonds are issued in denominations of $25, $50, $100, $200, $500, $1,000, and $10,000 (maturity value).[26] For these you pay $18.75, $37.50, $75, $150, $375, $750, and $7,500, respectively. To buy a bond which will pay $100 in seven years and nine months, you pay $75; to buy one which will pay $500, you pay $375. Purchases are limited to $10,000 maturity value, or $7,500 issue price, for each calendar year.

A notable feature of all United States savings bonds, apart from their unquestioned safety, is the redemption provision. In contrast to all other government and corporate securities, which will be paid off by issuers in cash only at maturity, United States savings bonds may be redeemed at any time, after two months from issue date, without advance notice, at any financial institution which is an authorized paying agent, at any Federal Reserve Bank or branch, or at the office of the Treasurer of the United States. Not only is there no penalty attached (the full amount originally paid is given back) but accumulated interest is also paid to the date of redemption from the date of issuance. Furthermore, United States savings bonds are not callable by the Treasury prior to maturity. Redemption values at different stages are shown in Table 6–6. It should be noted that no interest as such is paid on appreciation bonds. The return comes to the saver in the form of the

[25] See *History of United States Savings Bonds*, United States Savings Bonds Division, Treasury Department, Washington, D.C. A free copy may obtained on request.

[26] There is a $100,000 denomination for trustees of employers' savings plans.

difference between what he paid for the bond originally ($18.75, for example) and what he gets when he redeems it before maturity ($22.40, for example if held five years), or the sum he receives when he cashes it in at maturity ($25.00).

TABLE 6–6

Revised Series E Bond
(Effective June 1, 1959)
Schedule of Redemption Values and Investment Yields
(Based on $25 Bond-Maturity Value)

	REDEMPTION VALUE DURING EACH PERIOD	APPROXIMATE INVESTMENT YIELDS*	
		ON ISSUE PRICE TO BEGINNING OF EACH PERIOD	ON CURRENT REDEMPTION VALUE FROM BEGINNING OF EACH PERIOD TO MATURITY
Issue price	$18.75	. . .	. . .
Maturity value	25.00	. . .	. . .
First ½ year	18.75	0.00%	3.75%
½ to 1 year	18.91	1.71	3.89
1 to 1½ years	19.19	2.33	3.96
1½ to 2 years	19.51	2.67	4.01
2 to 2½ years	19.90	3.00	4.01
2½ to 3 years	20.28	3.16	4.03
3 to 3½ years	20.66	3.26	4.05
3½ to 4 years	21.07	3.36	4.06
4 to 4½ years	21.50	3.45	4.06
4½ to 5 years	21.95	3.53	4.04
5 to 5½ years	22.40	3.59	4.03
5½ to 6 years	22.86	3.64	4.02
6 to 6½ years	23.32	3.67	4.01
6½ to 7 years	23.79	3.70	4.01
7 to 7½ years	24.27	3.72	3.99
7½ years to 7 years and 9 months	24.75	3.74	4.06
Maturity value (7 years and 9 months from issue date)	$25.00	3.75	. . .

* Compounded semiannually.

Series H

This is a current income, not an appreciation, bond, for *individuals only,* bearing an investment yield approximately equal to that of the E bond. It is issued in denominations of $500, $1,000, $5,000, and $10,000, and these are the amounts the saver pays when he buys the bond. The original purchase price and the amount payable at maturity are the same. The return (interest) is paid by the government by check semiannually beginning six months after issue date. Beginning with the fourth check, the interest stabilizes at 4 percent annually; it is somewhat lower than that on the first three checks. The yield over the

TABLE 6–7

Revised Series H Bond
(Effective June 1, 1959)
Schedule of Semiannual Interest Checks and Investment Yields
(Based on $1,000 Bond)

| | | APPROXIMATE INVESTMENT YIELD ON FACE VALUE | |
PERIOD OF TIME BOND IS HELD AFTER ISSUE DATE	CHECK ISSUED AT BEGINNING OF PERIOD	FROM ISSUE DATE TO EACH INTEREST PAYMENT DATE	FROM EACH INTEREST PAYMENT DATE TO MATURITY*
½ year	$ 8.00	1.60%	3.88%
1 year	14.50	2.25	3.95
1½ years	16.00	2.56	4.00
2 years	20.00	2.91	4.00
2½ years	20.00	3.12	4.00
3 years	20.00	3.26	4.00
3½ years	20.00	3.36	4.00
4 years	20.00	3.44	4.00
4½ years	20.00	3.49	4.00
5 years	20.00	3.54	4.00
5½ years	20.00	3.58	4.00
6 years	20.00	3.61	4.00
6½ years	20.00	3.64	4.00
7 years	20.00	3.66	4.00
7½ years	20.00	3.68	4.00
8 years	20.00	3.70	4.00
8½ years	20.00	3.71	4.00
9 years	20.00	3.72	4.00
9½ years	20.00	3.74	4.00
10 years (maturity)	20.00	3.75	4.00

* Approximate investment yield for entire period from issuance to maturity is 3.75 percent per annum.

entire life of the bond, however, averages out to 3¾ percent; (see Table 6–7). Series H bonds are redeemable *at par* any time after six months from issue date on one month's written notice. This is a most unusual feature in a current income bond. Usually, corporate bonds of this type will not be redeemed by the issuer until call or maturity, and if in the interim the investor wants his money, he must sell the bond in the market, finding someone who will buy it at a price which may be less than par. Thus, the Series H bond provides a safe investment with no risk of market fluctuations. It is sold at par and is cashable at par at any time after six months from issue date. It offers an ideal savings plan for the individual who wants a bond that pays interest by check every six months. Compare the H bond with the E bond in this respect. The annual limit on the purchase of H bonds by any single individual is $10,000.

Other Aspects of Savings Bonds

E and H bonds may be purchased by individuals and registered in one of three ways: (*a*) in the name of one person, e.g., "Richard Roe, 418 Main Street, Sunrise, Iowa"; (*b*) in the name of two persons as co-owners, e.g., "Richard Roe *or* Mrs. Mary L. Roe, 418 Main Street, Sunrise, Iowa"; or (*c*) in the name of one person, with one beneficiary, e.g., "Richard Roe, 418 Main Street, Sunrise, Iowa; payable on death to Carla Lee Roe." In the case of co-ownership, (*b*) either co-owner, whichever has possession of the bond, can cash it by endorsement without the consent or endorsement of the other. At times this may be an advantage, at times a disadvantage, depending on circumstances. In case of the death of one of the co-owners, it is an advantage, since the other is then the sole owner of the bond without establishing proof of death or having it transferred to his name. In (*c*) only one beneficiary may be named; and to eliminate or change the beneficiary, the owner of the bond would have to cash it and have a new one issued in the form desired. The beneficiary, upon death of the registered owner, may keep the bond until maturity or have it reissued in his name alone or with a designated beneficiary. All United States savings bonds are issued only in registered form, not as bearer bonds.

Savings bonds will be held in safekeeping without charge by the Secretary of the Treasury, if the holder so desires; in such connection, the facilities of the Federal Reserve banks, as fiscal agents of the United States, and those of the Treasurer of the United States will be utilized. Postmasters generally will assist holders in arranging for safekeeping but will not act as safekeeping agents. Banking institutions generally offer safekeeping facilities at no or small cost.

There is probably no security available to savers or investors that is as safe as a United States savings bond. It is actually safer than cash. Your dollars can be lost or stolen, but if savings bonds are lost, stolen, or destroyed, owners may obtain substitute bonds, under provisions of the law and regulations, upon filing proper proof of loss or theft or destruction. For such a contingency, it is a good idea to keep a record of the bonds you own, by serial number, amount, and issue date. Keep the list separate from the bonds, so that you will have one if the other is lost. Then, if your bonds disappear, write to the Bureau of the Public Debt, Division of Loans and Currency, 536 South Clark Street, Chicago 5, Illinois, stating the serial number (with prefix and suffix letters), the issue dates (month and year), and your name and address. The Division will then send you a special form to fill out in order to obtain the issuance of substitute bonds. The Division keeps records of savings bonds by both names of owners and serial numbers; so even if you do not have the serial numbers or issue dates, they may be able to help you. Since this takes much longer and there is greater difficulty involved, it is much wiser to keep a record separate from the bonds themselves.

Savings Bonds—Advantages and Disadvantages

The savings bond offers investors and savers some very valuable features. There is an advantageous combination of safety and yield. The 3¾ percent paid compares favorably with other savings media, and the safety is unequaled elsewhere. The option to redeem before maturity is a unique privilege in a bond. You get compound interest, and the income from your bond is exempt from state and local taxation. You can name a co-owner or beneficiary. The bonds are registered; and if they are lost, stolen, or destroyed, they will be replaced by the Treasury. Thus, small investors are saved a considerable amount of day-to-day worry over the physical safety of their holdings.

Unlike other stocks and bonds, United States savings bonds are purchasable without payment of any commission. Banks sell or redeem them free of charge, and you can buy or redeem them at any time. There is no problem of marketability, no pricing problem, no unfortunate experience of buying high and selling low. You can always get your money back at any time you want it—not only the amount you put in but interest on your money to the date of redemption as well. There are no problems of runs on banks, closings and failures, frozen assets and frozen funds; if and when you need your money, all you have to do is ask for it.

A complaint frequently voiced is that in an inflationary period, while you may be sure of getting back the money you put into savings bonds, the money is worth much less in purchasing power, and had you put it into stocks or real estate you would more successfully have avoided loss of purchasing power. This argument has been advanced widely by

FIGURE 6–1

mutual fund salesmen in an attempt to persuade people to channel savings into investment companies rather than into savings bonds. They will produce charts to show that a $100 E bond purchased for $75 was, upon maturity worth not $100 but only about $65, largely because of loss in purchasing power due to the decline in the value of the dollar. This is a criticism, however, which might be directed, by those who raise it, against holding cash, bank deposits, savings accounts, life insurance, pensions and annuities, or anything payable in a fixed, rather than a varying, sum of money. Critics of savings bonds would hardly argue that all holders of any of the monied assets mentioned should immediately give them up and get into stocks, commodities, or real estate! An appropriate balance of assets is desirable.

Systematic Savings Plans

Different financial institutions have developed a variety of systematic savings plans. The country's largest savings bank has come up with an ingenious "Packaged Savings" plan. Under it one deposit a week brings you a threeway package: (*a*) a constantly increasing bank balance, (*b*) a steadily growing number of United States savings bonds, and (*c*) savings bank life insurance. You can arrange to pay in $3.00,

FIGURE 6–2

The Packaged Savings Plan

$5 a Week For 10 Years Brings You All Three!

Starting Age	Cash* In the Bank	U. S. Savings Bonds (Face Value)	Low-Cost Savings Bank Life Insurance** For 10 Years
20	$1490	$500	$5000
25	1380	500	5000
30	1250	500	5000
35	1080	500	5000
40	1360	500	3000
45	1190	500	3000
50	980	500	3000
55	690	500	3000

(This plan is available for ages 1 month to 70 years)

* The cash-in-bank figure does not include cash dividends which will be paid to you by The Bowery on your account.

** In addition, you will receive yearly cash dividends, as earned, on your policy. Your straight life insurance policy, of course, may be kept in force after 10 years with no increase in premium. Or you may convert your insurance into its cash value, or accept a reduced amount of paid-up insurance.

$10 a Week For 10 Years Brings You All Three!

Starting Age	Cash* In the Bank	U. S. Savings Bonds (Face Value)	Low-Cost Savings Bank Life Insurance** For 10 Years
20	$3390	$500	$10,000
25	3170	500	10,000
30	2900	500	10,000
35	2570	500	10,000
40	2130	500	10,000
45	3190	500	5,000
50	2830	500	5,000
55	2340	500	5,000

(This plan is available for ages 1 month to 70 years)

* The cash-in-bank figure does not include cash dividends which will be paid to you by The Bowery on your account.

* * In addition, you will receive yearly cash dividends, as earned, on your policy. Your straight life insurance policy, of course, may be kept in force after 10 years with no increase in premium. Or you may convert your insurance into its cash value, or accept a reduced amount of paid-up insurance.

SOURCE: The Bowery Savings Bank.

or $5.00, or $10.00 a week for five years, or ten years, or twenty years. The bank publishes tables to show what each amount will accumulate over a stated period in each of the three resource categories. Figure 6–2 shows one page from the bank's descriptive booklet which contains a whole range of other tables for varying amounts over varying periods.[27]

Another savings bank has developed a "Do-It-Yourself Calculator," containing a number of interesting tables on savings. One shows how to save systematically for a child's college education (see Table 6–8). The bank declares:

TABLE 6–8

ANNUAL SAVINGS THAT WILL MAKE $10,000 AVAILABLE TO PAY FOR A 4-YEAR COLLEGE EDUCATION FROM AGE 18 THRU 22. INTEREST RATE OF 4% COMPOUNDED QUARTERLY			
Present Age Of Child	No. Years To 1st College Year	Annual Savings To Create College Fund	Cumulative Value Of Fund 4th Year Of College
1	17	$369	$10,000
2	16	399	10,000
3	15	433	10,000
4	14	472	10,000
5	13	514	10,000
6	12	567	10,000
7	11	627	10,000
8	10	698	10,000
9	9	782	10,000
10	8	886	10,000
11	7	1,015	10,000
12	6	1,181	10,000
13	5	1,403	10,000
14	4	1,715	10,000

SOURCE: Reproduced by courtesy of Thomas G. Campbell and the New York Bank for Savings.

If you intend to put a child through college, you should begin to save right now towards accumulating the estimated $10,000 cost. For example, if a child is now 3 years of age, you have 15 years to save for his first year's cost, 16 for the second, 17 for the third and 18 for the fourth. Annual savings of $433 will assure you achieving your objective. When the child is ready to enter college at 18, you will have accumulated approximately $8,700 and by the time he is ready to graduate, you will have the required total of $10,000. Your total savings will have amounted to $7,794, thereby saving you $2,206 of the total cost of $10,000 or almost enough to cover when pro-rated, a single year's cost of $2,500.

[27] A free copy of the booklet *Packaged Savings* may be obtained by writing to the Bowery Savings Bank, 110 East 42nd Street, New York 10017, attention: Packaged Savings Department.

The "Do-It-Yourself Calculator" also shows how to create your own retirement fund and supplemental pension (see Table 6–9). It is explained that: "When you retire at 65, social security benefits plus your company pension cannot be expected to equal your present annual earnings. To make up the difference you can establish your own retirement fund and build up a supplemental pension." For example, at age 24, savings of $5.00 per week over 50 weeks a year and continued each

TABLE 6–9

PRINCIPAL ACCUMULATED FROM SAVINGS OF $5.00 PER WEEK FOR 50 WEEKS A YEAR, AT INTEREST RATE OF 4% COMPOUNDED QUARTERLY				
Age Now	No. of Years To Age 65	Total Savings Over No. Of Years Shown	Cumulative Value Of Principal	Cash Available Each Year For 25 Years
24	41	$10,250	$25,700	$1,650
26	39	9,750	23,200	1,500
28	37	9,250	21,000	1,350
30	35	8,750	18,900	1,220
32	33	8,250	17,000	1,090
34	31	7,750	15,200	965
36	29	7,250	13,550	870
38	27	6,750	12,050	775
40	25	6,250	10,650	680
42	23	5,750	9,350	600
44	21	5,250	8,200	525
46	19	4,750	7,010	450
48	17	4,250	6,020	380
50	15	3,750	5,100	325

SOURCE: Reproduced by courtesy of Thomas G. Campbell and the New York Bank for Savings.

year until you reach 65 will involve total deposits of $10,250. Based on an average interest rate of 4 percent being earned and compounded quarterly, the power of money at work under a systematic savings plan will increase your own savings to a cumulative principal amount of $25,700. In each of the 25 years succeeding your retirement, you will be able to withdraw from the bank $1,650 and can continue to do so until you reach 90. Should you die before reaching that age, the balance remaining in your savings account will accrue to your beneficiaries. Over the 25 retirement years, withdrawals will total $41,250 compared to the $10,250 you paid in!

Save for What?

It helps to save if you have some definite purpose or goal in mind, one preferably which is realizable. Bought that engagement ring yet? Let's assume she picks out one that costs $250. Don't gasp! That's modest. You're getting off easy. How much would you have to set aside, for how long, to pay for it? Well, if you can afford $40 a month, it will take you only six months and one week. If that's too much per month, scaling it down to $25 will mean ten months. Or how about saving to pay for a vacation? Many banks now have Vacation Clubs. Here's a typical plan:

Vacation Club—25 Payments

Number of Payments	Amount of Each Payment	Total Accumulated
25	$ 2	$ 50
25	5	125
25	10	250
25	20	500

Conclusion

Sooner or later, at one time or another, every family or individual sets out to save. It may be the result of a New Year's resolution and may last but two days, or, because of the nature of one's personality, it may take hold and last a lifetime. Some people can save and some people can't. It takes will power, self-denial, patience, and perseverance, and these qualities are not present in everyone. Level of income is not of overriding importance. There are some who can set aside something out of $2,500-a-year income, while others find it difficult to make ends meet on $10,000 a year. If you can save, it makes life smoother. If you lose your job, you have a cushion to fall back on and can take longer to look around and perhaps get a better job than if you have to take the first thing that comes along. If there is sudden illness or operation, financial tragedy does not accompany the physical distress. Vacations, automobiles, better furnishings, a home—all are more easily within your reach. You may be able to accumulate a modest financial beginning for a small business which in time may develop into a bigger one. You may be able to provide security and self-support for your old age instead of having to depend on the charity of others. It is surprising how small sums set aside regularly cumulate rapidly into substantial and usable surpluses.

The power of compound interest alone will at 3 percent double your capital in 23½ years, at 4 percent in 17½ years, at 5 percent in 14½ years, and at 6 percent in just 12 years. The following table shows what you will have, over varying periods at different rates of interest, if you save as little as $100 a year:

| | | ANNUAL RATE | | |
AT END OF—	3%	4%	5%	6%
Five years	$ 546	$ 563	$ 580	$ 598
Ten years	1,181	1,248	1,321	1,397
Fifteen years	1,916	2,082	2,266	2,467
Twenty years	2,767	3,096	3,472	3,899
Twenty-five years	3,755	4,331	5,011	5,816

If you are one of those who find it difficult to save, there are a number of ways which will help make it easier. Your firm, if you so request, will probably deduct a specified sum from your pay check and send it directly to your bank. You can have your firm deduct for savings bonds, too, or have your bank buy one a month for you from your account. You can open a Vacation Club or Christmas Club account at a savings bank, or start the bonus savings plan at a savings and loan association. Or you can resort to the very familiar device of saving one kind of coin—a dime, a quarter, or a half-dollar. Every time you get one in change, you put it apart from the rest of your change in a separate pocket and then, when you get home, drop it in a milk bottle set aside for savings.

If you do not trust yourself with the milk bottle, some savings institutions will supply their customers with small metal banks to which the institution retains the key. You fill it up, and they empty it into your savings account. Next time you make that New Year's resolution, try one of these methods. It may work. It has for many. We have the most productive economy in the world today because we save more than any other nation, and we save more because we produce more and therefore have more. It is a circle, but *not* a vicious one.

SUGGESTED READINGS

1. George Hanc, *The United States Savings Bond Program in The Postwar Period*. National Bureau of Economic Research, Occasional Paper No. 81, 1962.
2. T. A. Wise, "Growing Rewards For Prudent Money," *Fortune,* October, 1961.

3. National Association of Mutual Savings Banks for the Commission on Money and Credit, *Mutual Savings Banking*. Englewood Cliffs, N.J.: Prentice-Hall, Inc., 1962.

4. Leon T. Kendall, *The Savings and Loan Business,* United States Savings and Loan League for the Commission on Money and Credit. Englewood Cliffs, N.J.: Prentice-Hall, Inc., 1962.

5. Savings Division, American Bankers Association, *Results of 1962 Savings Survey*. 4 vols. New York, 1963.

6. *Facts You Should Know about Saving Money,* National Better Business Bureau, Chrysler Building, New York 17, N.Y., latest edition.

7. "Must You Try To Save" in "Money Talk for Newlyweds," *Changing Times, The Kiplinger Magazine,* June, 1963.

8. "Savings Banking in 1963," in *Mutual Savings Banking,* published by the National Association of Mutual Savings Banks, February, 1964.

9. *Handbook of Savings and Loan.* Chicago: American Savings and Loan Institute, latest edition. A free copy may be obtained by writing to the Institute at 221 North LaSalle St., Chicago, Illinois 60601.

10. *Savings and Loan Fact Book,* United States Savings and Loan League, issued annually. A free copy may be obtained by writing to the League at 221 North LaSalle St., Chicago, Illinois 60601.

11. *Savings and Home Financing Chart Book,* Federal Home Loan Bank Board, Washington, D.C., latest edition.

12. *The Credit Union Yearbook,* issued annually, Credit Union National Association. A free copy may be obtained by writing to the Association at Filene House, 1617 Sherman Ave., Madison 1, Wis.

13. Bureau of Federal Credit Unions, *Report of Operations, Federal Credit Unions.* Washington, D.C.: U.S. Department of Health, Education and Welfare, issued annually.

CASE PROBLEMS

1. Letitia Church, a recent college graduate, earns $450 a month. She is anxious to save money for a trip to Europe two years hence, but she never seems to have any money left over to save. When she cashes her check on payday, she has an irresistible urge to buy new clothes, and she barely manages to pay for rent and food. She works for a company which has a credit union, a bond-a-month plan, Christmas club, and an arrangement with a local bank for depositing employees' checks directly in the bank. What savings plan would you suggest for Letitia?

2. Carroll Robinson and his wife Doris (both age 30) have bought and furnished a home. They have two children (ages 8 and 2). After providing for all regular expenses, they have about $50 left over each month for emergencies and capital expenditures. How would you advise them to invest the money? Why?

3. Mabel and James (both age 25) were married a year ago. They live in a five-room apartment which they rent for $85 a month. Both are working, their total income being $500 a month, of which they are just beginning to save $100 through careful budgeting. They want to accumulate their savings as a down payment on their own home. Where would you advise them to put their savings? Why? How expensive a house do you think they should plan to buy? Why? If everything goes along smoothly, how long will it take to accumulate the down payment? While they are saving up for the down payment, should they put any funds elsewhere for emergencies? Why?

4. John Sullivan is a construction engineer who lives in a community which has a long, cold winter, during which he is often without work for a couple of months. He is age 48, and Kathleen, his wife, is age 45. Their three children are ages 8, 13, and 19. When he works, John finds he has about $120 a week after taxes, of which they manage to save about $15. Where can they put it to best advantage? Is it enough for their needs, considering that they own their home?

5. John and Lydia have accounts in a savings and loan association which they expect will be worth $8,200 when the next dividend ($150) is paid. Lydia has just gone to the hospital because of a serious illness; she may be there for a long time. John thinks he should have $2,000 at hand immediately and is about to make a withdrawal to yield that amount. Should he? What other alternatives does he have?

6. Alice and Lawrence Toddhunter have been investing about $25 or $50 a month for years in Series E bonds and have been taking advantage of the extended maturities. They now believe that future savings should be invested in something which will provide a cash income every year. They own their own home, believe that they have adequate insurance, and have no children. They do not believe that they have the knowledge and experience to invest in other than government issues. What investment would you advise?

7. The Dandis family came to this country only a few years ago. They have saved $2,000, which they keep at home. What are the advantages and disadvantages of this method of handling their savings?

8. For the last 15 years, Belle and Raymond Lynch and their three children (ages 14, 8, and 6) have been able to save nothing except what was necessary to furnish their rented apartment ($70 monthly, heated). On the death of Raymond's mother, they were left $10,000. How should they invest this money? Why?

9. John Smith is a printer who works for Art Crafts, Inc., which makes and sells calendars on a large scale. His company is sponsoring a new credit union, to which it offers free quarters and $500 a year toward expenses. John is popular among the employees and is elected to be the operating head of the credit union at a salary of $500 a year. In what respects do you think he may or may not be qualified for the job? Should he take it? What will his duties be? The company will pay him for his duties at the credit union and will free him from his regular work to the extent necessary. So far, 150 employees have joined the credit union

out of a total of 700. Should the others join? How much time per week would you expect John to have to spend on the new job? What sort of records would he have to keep? Where would you advise him to keep credit-union cash? What furnishings will be necessary for the credit union? Of what advantage will the credit union be to the sponsoring company?

10. Besides the post office, the only place for savings in your fairly large community is the time-deposit department of the People's Bank, which pays 3 percent per annum and which has always given the impression that it is not anxious for business. You are asked to join a group of persons who are interested in establishing a federal savings and loan association in your community. You are a graduate of a collegiate school of business administration and work as chief accountant for a local factory, where you earn $7,000 a year and feel that the future is anything but bright for you. The community is thriving and growing. What advantages or disadvantages for the community do you see in establishing the federal savings and loan association? Should you join the group? Are there personal reasons why it might be advantageous for you to join? Others in the community argue that what is needed is a good credit union. Why? Is there room for both? Why?

7 LIFE INSURANCE

"A Man's Dying Is More the Survivors' Affair than His Own."

—*Thomas Mann*

IN 1850 conditions were such that the expectation of life at birth in the United States was only about 40 years. As a result of a century of scientific, social, and economic progress, which probably has no counterpart in all human history, the baby born today can be expected, on the average, to live to age 67, if it's a boy, to 74, if it's a girl. Thus, within four generations, the expectation of life has risen by about 27 years, or by two thirds, and is steadily rising (see Table 7–1). If you are 20 years old now (and male), having survived

TABLE 7–1

The Lengthening Life Span
Comparison of Life Expectancy at Various Ages in the United States, 1850–1975

If in—	You Are Male and				You Are Female and			
	Just Born	Age			Just Born	Age		
		20	40	60		20	40	60
1850	40.4	40.1	27.1	15.3	43.0	41.7	29.9	16.7
1900	47.9	42.0	27.6	14.3	50.7	43.6	29.1	15.2
1960	67.4	50.1	31.6	15.9	74.1	56.2	37.1	19.7
1975	70.9	52.9	34.3	17.8	77.0	58.5	39.3	21.5

SOURCE: Institute of Life Insurance.

the extra hazards and perils of the teen ages, you can expect to live another 50 years. As for the girls, they are obviously anything but the "weaker sex." On the average, they can expect to live to 74, or seven years longer than the average male. A girl of 20, today, can look forward to another 56 years.

The Money Value of a Man

In a very interesting book entitled *The Money Value of a Man*, Dr. Louis I. Dublin, a vice president and chief statistician of the Metropolitan Life Insurance Company, attempted to estimate the amount of the present worth of a man's future earnings, in excess of expenditures on his own person, assuming the man is subject to existing mortality conditions. While his grim purpose was to find the amounts which the family of a deceased person would have to have at its disposal to replace its share of his earnings if he had not died, his interesting calculations may be presented in a somewhat cheerier frame. If a young lady of age 20 (the average age at which females in the United States marry) marries a young man of 22 (the average age at which males in the United States marry) and he is earning $3,000 a year, she is acquiring $150,500 of future income. If he is earning $5,000 a year, she is getting $220,000. As Dr. Dublin notes: "Little do we ordinarily realize how great these amounts are even in the case of relatively small income."[1]

To put the matter a bit differently, if the average return on a safe investment is 3 percent, then one may say that a young man earning $3,000 a year is about as well off as an elderly retired person who, having accumulated $100,000 during his working lifetime, is now living on the $3,000 annual income from this $100,000. Or one may say that a man's money value to his family is the capitalized value of his current annual income. Capitalizing income is a very simple mathematical process. Assuming a going rate of return of 3 percent, the annual income, $3,000, is to 3 percent as x (the capitalized value) is to 100 percent:

$$\$3,000 \div 3 = x \div 100;$$
$$3x = \$300,000;$$
$$x = \$100,000.$$

Or, if the annual income is $6,000, to use another example, and equals 3 percent; then 100 percent equals $200,000 (100/3 × $6,000), the capitalized value of the earning ability.

Since the purpose of *The Money Value of a Man* was to estimate how much insurance a man would have to carry to enable his family to continue its level of living unchanged in the event of his death, it as-

---

[1] Louis I. Dublin and Alfred J. Lotka, *The Money Value of a Man* (rev. ed.; New York: Ronald Press Co., 1946), p. 147.

sumed various levels of income per annum, and a simplified version of this concept may be seen in Figure 7–1. Of course, not many of us can afford enough life insurance fully to replace our lifetime earnings

FIGURE 7–1

ONE HUNDRED AVERAGE MEN AT AGE 25	FORTY YEARS LATER AT AGE 65	
Looking forward with enthusiasm to 40 years of living, earning and — Ultimate Financial Independence	Gone _____ 36 Still working _____ 5 Dependent—unable to work _____ 54 FINANCIALLY INDEPENDENT _____ 5 _____ 100	

Figures from U. S. Treasury Dept.

THE MONEY VALUE OF LIFE

AGE	YEARS OF EARNINGS TO 65	AVERAGE MONTHLY EARNINGS				
		$200	$300	$400	$500	$600
25	40	$ 96,000	$144,000	$192,000	$240,000	$288,000
30	35	84,000	126,000	168,000	210,000	252,000
35	30	72,000	108,000	144,000	180,000	216,000
40	25	60,000	90,000	120,000	150,000	180,000
45	20	48,000	72,000	96,000	120,000	144,000
50	15	36,000	54,000	72,000	90,000	108,000
55	10	24,000	36,000	48,000	60,000	72,000
60	5	12,000	18,000	24,000	30,000	36,000
65	0	0	0	0	0	0

How much of this money will you have at 65?

Courtesy: United States Life Insurance Company, New York

should we be taken away prematurely, but life insurance is now recognized as the quickest way for a young person to build an estate to provide adequate protection for a family.

Who Owns Life Insurance?

Almost everyone sooner or later. The number of people in the United States who own some form of life insurance now totals 132 million. This means that 70 percent of the adult population held insurance. On a family basis, a study by the Survey Research Center found that 86 percent of all families owned some life insurance. In families headed by college graduates, 76 percent held life insurance. Where family income was $7,500 and over, 94 percent of the families owned some form of life insurance. There are over 290 million life policies in force in the United States, amounting to more than $675 billion of protection. The size of the average ordinary policy is $3,930, and the average amount of life insurance owned per family is $11,400.[2] Families with incomes of less than $5,000 spent about 4 percent of their incomes for

[2] For greater detail, see *Life Insurance Fact Book,* latest ed. (New York: Institute of Life Insurance). Free copies may be obtained by writing to the Institute at 277 Park Ave., New York, N.Y. 10017.

insurance. Those who made $5,000 and over spent approximately 5 percent for this purpose.

Sharing Risks by Insurance

Insurance is a plan by which large numbers of people, each in some danger of possible loss, the time of which he cannot foresee or prevent, are brought together for mutual protection so that when one of the group suffers a loss, it will be made good, partly or wholly, from the contributions of the entire group. In other words, all members of the group contribute small sums regularly and beforehand in order to make good particular losses to the individuals who suffer them.

Perhaps the best way to understand this is to look at fire insurance first. Only a few houses in each community are damaged or destroyed by fire each year. This rate of destruction can be determined from past experience, so that it is possible to estimate approximately the cost that all must pay in order that those who suffer losses can be compensated. The only other question is: "Will past experience be a reliable guide to future losses?" The same principles apply to life insurance. But while a house may never catch fire, everyone must someday die.

Insurance is possible because of the law of probability, or the law of averages. If you toss a penny just once, you have no way of knowing whether you will get head or tails; but if you tossed it a million times, you could be pretty sure of getting very close to 500,000 of each. Insurance companies have skilled mathematicians, known as "actuaries," who study the proportion of people who die at various ages. These actuaries calculate rates of mortality based on hundreds of thousands of cases, and the results are compiled in mortality tables, which insurance companies use as the basis for calculating the rate to charge for insuring any particular person.

Mortality Tables and Premium Rates

A very basic mortality table, the Commissioners Standard Ordinary Table of Mortality, compiled by the National Association of Insurance Commissioners, shown in Figure 7–3, is based on the experience of life insurance companies. It starts with 10 million cases at birth. It follows them through to age 99. For each year it shows how many of the original 10 million will still be living and how many will die; it calculates the death rate per 1,000 at that age.

For example, at age 20, of the original group 9,664,994 are still alive. Seventeen thousand three hundred may be expected to die that year,

FIGURE 7–2

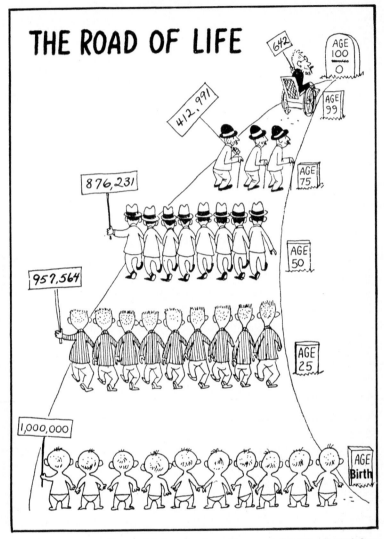

Courtesy: Life Insurance Agency Management Association, Hartford, Conn.

The story of the Road of Life is depicted in the CSO Table of Mortality shown on the next page. Visualize a million people at birth, starting down this road. By age 25, there are 957,564 living. By age 50, 876,231 remain. Only 412,991 are alive at age 75, and there are only 642 left at age 99.

which means that the death rate is 1.79 per thousand.[3] That is, out of 10,000 people at age 20, 1.79 per 1,000, or approximately 18, will die before reaching age 21. Thus, 10,000 college students, all age 20, could easily figure out how to insure themselves and what to pay, *for*

---

[3] The rate is figured not on the original 10,000,000 but on the 9,664,994 still alive.

FIGURE 7–3

1958 CSO Mortality Table
Commissioners Standard Ordinary

Age	Number Living	Number Dying	Death Rate per 1,000	Expectancy, Years	Age	Number Living	Number Dying	Death Rate per 1,000	Expectancy, Years
0	10,000,000	70,800	7.08	68.30	50	8,762,306	72,902	8.32	23.63
1	9,929,200	17,475	1.76	67.78	51	8,689,404	79,160	9.11	22.82
2	9,911,725	15,066	1.52	66.90	52	8,610,244	85,758	9.96	22.03
3	9,896,659	14,449	1.46	66.00	53	8,524,486	92,832	10.89	21.25
4	9,882,210	13,835	1.40	65.10	54	8,431,654	100,337	11.90	20.47
5	9,868,375	13,322	1.35	64.19	55	8,331,317	108,307	13.00	19.71
6	9,855,053	12,812	1.30	63.27	56	8,223,010	116,849	14.21	18.97
7	9,842,241	12,401	1.26	62.35	57	8,106,161	125,970	15.54	18.23
8	9,829,840	12,091	1.23	61.43	58	7,980,191	135,663	17.00	17.51
9	9,817,749	11,879	1.21	60.51	59	7,844,528	145,830	18.59	16.81
10	9,805,870	11,865	1.21	59.58	60	7,698,698	156,592	20.34	16.12
11	9,794,005	12,047	1.23	58.65	61	7,542,106	167,736	22.24	15.44
12	9,781,958	12,325	1.26	57.72	62	7,374,370	179,271	24.31	14.78
13	9,769,633	12,896	1.32	56.80	63	7,195,099	191,174	26.57	14.14
14	9,756,737	13,562	1.39	55.87	64	7,003,925	203,394	29.04	13.51
15	9,743,175	14,225	1.46	54.95	65	6,800,531	215,917	31.75	12.90
16	9,728,950	14,983	1.54	54.03	66	6,584,614	228,749	34.74	12.31
17	9,713,967	15,737	1.62	53.11	67	6,355,865	241,777	38.04	11.73
18	9,698,230	16,390	1.69	52.19	68	6,114,088	254,835	41.68	11.17
19	9,681,840	16,846	1.74	51.28	69	5,859,253	267,241	45.61	10.64
20	9,664,994	17,300	1.79	50.37	70	5,592,012	278,426	49.79	10.12
21	9,647,694	17,655	1.83	49.46	71	5,313,586	287,731	54.15	9.63
22	9,630,039	17,912	1.86	48.55	72	5,025,855	294,766	58.65	9.15
23	9,612,127	18,167	1.89	47.64	73	4,731,089	299,289	63.26	8.69
24	9,593,960	18,324	1.91	46.73	74	4,431,800	301,894	68.12	8.24
25	9,575,636	18,481	1.93	45.82	75	4,129,906	303,011	73.73	7.81
26	9,557,155	18,732	1.96	44.90	76	3,826,895	303,014	79.18	7.39
27	9,538,423	18,981	1.99	43.99	77	3,523,881	301,997	85.70	6.98
28	9,519,442	19,324	2.03	43.08	78	3,221,884	299,829	93.06	6.59
29	9,500,118	19,760	2.08	42.16	79	2,922,055	295,683	101.19	6.21
30	9,480,358	20,193	2.13	41.25	80	2,626,372	288,848	109.98	5.85
31	9,460,165	20,718	2.19	40.34	81	2,337,524	278,983	119.35	5.51
32	9,439,447	21,239	2.25	39.43	82	2,058,541	265,902	129.17	5.19
33	9,418,208	21,850	2.32	38.51	83	1,792,639	249,858	139.38	4.89
34	9,396,358	22,551	2.40	37.60	84	1,542,781	231,433	150.01	4.60
35	9,373,807	23,528	2.51	36.69	85	1,311,348	211,311	161.14	4.32
36	9,350,279	24,685	2.64	35.78	86	1,100,037	190,108	172.82	4.06
37	9,325,594	26,112	2.80	34.88	87	909,929	168,455	185.13	3.80
38	9,299,482	27,991	3.01	33.97	88	741,474	146,997	198.25	3.55
39	9,271,491	30,132	3.25	33.07	89	594,477	126,303	212.46	3.31
40	9,241,359	32,622	3.53	32.18	90	468,174	106,809	228.14	3.06
41	9,208,737	35,362	3.84	31.29	91	361,365	88,813	245.77	2.82
42	9,173,375	38,253	4.17	30.41	92	272,552	72,480	265.93	2.58
43	9,135,122	41,382	4.53	29.54	93	200,072	57,881	289.30	2.33
44	9,093,740	44,741	4.92	28.67	94	142,191	45,026	316.66	2.07
45	9,048,999	48,412	5.35	27.81	95	97,165	34,128	351.24	1.80
46	9,000,587	52,473	5.83	26.95	96	63,037	25,250	400.56	1.51
47	8,948,114	56,910	6.36	26.11	97	37,787	18,456	488.42	1.18
48	8,891,204	61,794	6.95	25.27	98	19,331	12,916	688.15	.83
49	8,829,410	67,104	7.60	24.45	99	6,415	6,415	1,000.00	.50

Source: National Association of (State) Insurance Commissioners.

one year. They can be reasonably certain that 18 of them will die within the year, but, of course, they do not know which 18. If they wanted to be certain that the families of each of the 18 who died would receive a payment of $1,000, they could each (10,000) contribute $1.80, thus establishing a fund of $18,000, out of which $1,000 could be paid to the families of each of the unfortunate 18 who were to die. Each student would be paying for pure protection, and there would be nothing left over from the insurance fund at the end of the year. If the same group, now 9,982, wanted to insure in the same way, the next year, from age 21 to age 22, each would have to contribute a little more than the $1.80 of the year before, first, because there are fewer contributors and, second, because 18 more of them will die the second year. More and more will die in succeeding years. The group left to contribute each year will become progressively smaller. The payments to be made each year will grow larger. Thus, the cost of insurance will rise steadily. By age 60, of the original 10,000, 20-year-old college students, 2,034 will have died, leaving 7,966 living. In the 61st year, 162 more will die. To pay the estates of each the sum of $1,000 would require $162,000. Thus, each of the 7,966 survivors at age 60 would have to contribute $20.34. And each year thereafter, fewer survivors would have to pay steeply increasing amounts. This approximates the simplest form of insurance—term insurance—which will be described later. Rates are low when the average age of the insured is low, but they climb steadily, until old surviving members can hardly pay the premiums (see Fig. 7–4).

Level Premium Policies and Reserves

But the insurance company faces a somewhat different problem. It will be asked, say, to insure the 10,000 for life, and they will want to pay the same amount each year. Sooner or later all will die, and each estate will receive $1,000. How much must the company charge? There will be a total of 10,000 payments by policyholders of the group to the company the first year, plus 9,982 the second year, and so on. According to the mortality table, these add up to a total number of annual payments made by this group, over all the years, of 508,703.

A total of $10,000,000 must be paid by the insurance company; and since the company will collect 508,703 equal installments from policyholders, simple division indicates that the annual payment (premium) will be $19.66. Under this plan, the group will pay the insurance company more than is necessary to meet the claims in the early years, and the extra amount will be available for investment. The money which is accumulated to help pay future claims is known as the "reserve." It is only partly made up of the premiums paid. The rest comes from interest earned on the company's investment of this reserve. These earnings can be used to help pay claims. This reduces what the policyholder

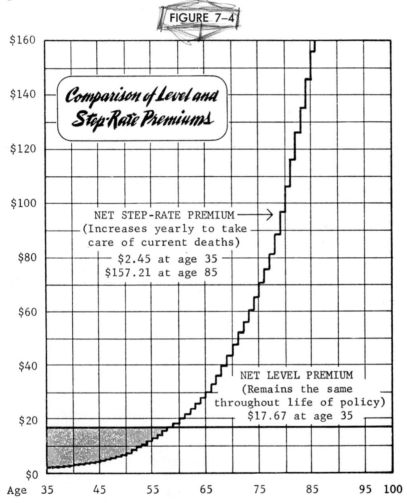

FIGURE 7–4

Comparison of Level and Step-Rate Premiums

NET STEP-RATE PREMIUM →
(Increases yearly to take care of current deaths)
$2.45 at age 35
$157.21 at age 85

NET LEVEL PREMIUM
(Remains the same throughout life of policy)
$17.67 at age 35

Age 35   45   55   65   75   85   95   100

$160 $140 $120 $100 $80 $60 $40 $20 $0

By paying the difference indicated by shaded portion below the level premium line, the company accumulates funds which offset the yearly increases occurring in later years.

SOURCE: Life Insurance Agency Management Association.

would otherwise have to pay. Therefore, the company, before it can determine the premium rate, must estimate the interest rate it can expect to earn on its reserve funds. Generally, in recent years, this has been calculated at 3 percent.

For example, if 3 percent interest is earned, each member of the group need pay a premium of only $9.56 a year instead of $19.66. In other words, the total payments over the years for everybody need be only $4,863,201 instead of $10,000,000, in that an average of $10.10 a year for each member is paid toward the cost of insurance by interest earnings, or a total for everybody of $5,136,799.[4]

Legal Reserves and Premium Rates

In the level premium policies, one pays more than the current cost of insurance in the early years but less in the later years. Consequently, a reserve fund accumulates to one's credit. This, together with future premium payments and interest earnings, makes it possible to pay death benefits in later years when level premiums alone would be insufficient because of increasing death rates. The difference between the level premium and the old step-rate premium may be seen in Figure 7–4. The policyholder can borrow against his pro-rata share of the reserve fund; or if he wishes, he can surrender the policy and collect it as cash value. Thus, level premium insurance provides a savings or investment feature along with pure protection or insurance. Collecting more funds than are needed in the earlier years of life creates definite obligations on the part of the company to its policyholders. These obligations are called "policyholders' reserves" or "legal reserves" and are carefully supervised by the state, for on the ownership of assets equal to these reserves (which are really liabilities) depends the company's solvency. The reserve is separate from surplus and is not available for distribution as dividends.

When basic premium rates are set, something must be added to cover the cost of running the insurance company. This charge is known as the "loading." Efficient companies hold expenses low. Thus the premium charged you for life insurance depends on three factors: (a) the real cost of insurance based on mortality experience, (b) the return earned on the reserve accumulated under level premium policies, and (c) the costs of running the insurance company.

How Much Insurance Should I Buy?

A student once asked his professor, "Skipping all the details, how much insurance should I carry and what's the best policy for me?" The professor thought for a moment and then said, "Skipping all the details,

---

[4] For a more detailed explanation, see R. Wilfred Kelsey and Arthur C. Daniels, *Handbook of Life Insurance* (New York: Institute of Life Insurance, latest ed.). A free copy may be obtained by writing to the Institute at 277 Park Ave., New York, N.Y., 10017.

just tell me when you are going to die and whether you'll have any dependents or not at the time. Then I'll answer your question."

How much life insurance is enough? Men of all ages and responsibilities have puzzled over this question for a long time. You can answer it, however, if you examine your needs. In fact, you can list them and come to a pretty definite answer. Naturally, a college student at 18 or 20 isn't thinking about death and, consequently, your first and most immediate need may not even occur to you. It's—

1. *Cleanup Expenses.* The high cost of your dying will hit your family. There will be medical bills, hospital bills, funeral costs. There may also be bills and loans to pay as well as your final tax remittance. Based on the experience of others, these costs will range from $1,000 to a half-year's income.

2. *Family-Period Income.* The second essential need you face is to provide a minimum monthly income for your dependents, if you have any. If there are two or three young children, it will be difficult, if not impossible, for the wife to go off to work to support them. To stay home and take care of them, she needs a minimum monthly income. It's been estimated that the surviving family can live three quarters as well as before on half the income. You won't be able to duplicate your present income, but you won't need to because part of your present budget involves your own expenses. If you are covered under social security, then your wife and children will receive monthly survivors benefit payments until the youngest child is 18. In estimating the need for minimum monthly income until the little ones grow up, figure from one third to one half of your present monthly income.

3. *Pay Off the Mortgage.* If you live in a house which you "own," but on which the bank has made a substantial mortgage loan, this is your next need to be taken care of by insurance. There is no need for estimating here. You know the exact monthly cost of interest and principal repayment on your mortgage. And there's a special insurance policy designed just to handle this situation. If your wife wants to keep the house and continue to live in it, you can buy a policy—reducing term insurance—which will pay off the mortgage. On the other hand, if she is likely to want to sell the house and move back with her parents, then all you need is enough insurance to enable her to meet the mortgage payments for six months or a year so that she doesn't have to sell the house under pressure.

4. *An Emergency Fund.* Savings may provide this, but if not, you'll have to use insurance to set it up, provided of course, you can afford the cost. Every family needs an emergency fund in case of major

illness, an accident, sudden hospitalization, etc. It's a sort of "reserve for contingencies," and for young families something between $500 and $1,000 is about right.

5. *Income for the Wife's Middle Age.*   Remember social security payments to your family cease when the youngest child reaches 18. They don't resume again until your widow reaches 62. This gap is known as the "blackout period" in the insurance man's jargon. Perhaps you can provide a monthly income for your wife during this blackout period until social security payments resume at 62.

6. *Income for the Wife's Old Age.*   When social security payments resume, they will range from $40 to $104.80 per month for the rest of her life, depending on what your earnings were. You may be able to supplement this by monthly insurance payments, but as the head of a young family, it isn't likely that you'll be able to afford the cost of reaching this far into the future.

7. *A College Fund for the Children.*   This is your next goal, and we use the term "goal" advisedly. Paying for your child's college education is a goal; buying groceries for the family when the youngster is in first grade is a need. If your income permits the extra insurance cost involved, by all means buy the special kinds of policies devised to cover the costs of four years at college. This is a cost which is not difficult to approximate in your planning.

8. *Retirement Income.*   Almost all the insurance you buy to cover the previous expenses can be converted, as you will see, to provide retirement income if you are lucky enough to live that long. But you may find you want a higher monthly retirement income even after you take into account social security benefits. If so, insurance, using endowment policies perhaps, or annuities can provide it. As your income rises and your children grow older, you'll want to look into this possibility, but right now it's probably the most expendable goal on the list.

Changing Times, The Kiplinger Magazine, has devised a table (shown in Fig. 7–5) to enable you to pin down your insurance needs in money terms and to offset against each need the cash resources you may already have accumulated to meet it.[5] You'll probably need an insurance agent to help you with this form, but it's the way a skilled agent would go about helping you figure out how much insurance you need.

Can you afford what you need? Perhaps not. Then, having listed the needs in order of priority and essentiality, you do the best you can

---

[5] See "How Much Life Insurance Do You Need?" *Changing Times, The Kiplinger Magazine,* February, 1956.

FIGURE 7-5

HOW MUCH INSURANCE? *Use this form to estimate your needs.*

cleanup expenses

				cash available		
medical care	$			savings	$	
funeral				social security		
debts & bills				group insurance		
taxes				other		
insurance loans				other		
estate settlement						**needed from life insurance** ⬇
extra family expense						
total needed	$	less		total available	$	= $

mortgage

				cash available		
				savings	$	**needed from life insurance** ⬇
balance outstanding, or payments pending sale	$	less		other		
				total available	$	= $

family's monthly expenses

				monthly income available		
housing	$			social security	$	
utilities & household operation				investments		
				earnings		
food				other		
clothing				other		
medical care						**needed monthly from life insurance** ⬇
incidentals (car, personal, recreation)						
total needed	$	less		total available	$	= $

emergency fund

				cash available		
				savings	$	
				investments		
				group insurance		**needed from life insurance** ⬇
				other		
estimated need	$	less		total available	$	= $

wife's monthly expenses to age 65

				monthly income available		
				investments	$	**needed monthly from life insurance** ⬇
				earnings		
estimated budget (follow family-period headings)	$	less		other		
				total available	$	= $

wife's monthly expenses after age 65

				monthly income available		
				investments	$	**needed monthly from life insurance** ⬇
				social security		
estimated budget (follow family-period headings)	$	less		other		
				total available	$	= $

special funds

				cash available		
for	$			investments	$	**wanted from life insurance** ⬇
for				other		
total wanted	$	less		total available	$	= $

SOURCE: *Changing Times, The Kiplinger Magazine.*

within your financial capacity. Remember the average family spends about 5 percent of its income on life insurance. This is about what you can afford. It's a good bench mark to stay close to in paring your list of needs to your financial ability.

What Kind of Policy Shall I Buy?

If you have only a certain limited amount of money to spend on life insurance and you find that for one type of policy you have to pay $5.00 per $1,000 of insurance protection, while for another you have to pay $46 per $1,000, or that for a given expenditure of $100, one policy you can buy provides $19,500 worth of protection while another provides only $2,200 of insurance, you'll begin to think about the kinds of policies available and the differences among them (see Table 7–4). Naturally you may wonder at these large differences and the reasons for them. Various kinds of policies offer differing advantages and limitations. To be able to buy insurance intelligently, you'll need to examine and understand the basic differences.

Kinds of Life Insurance

Life insurance may conveniently be grouped as follows:

1. Ordinary
    a) Term
    b) Straight or whole life
    c) Limited payment (20 or 30 years) life
    d) Endowment
    e) Combination plans
2. Group
3. Industrial
4. Credit life insurance

When you buy life insurance, you receive a *policy* which is the contract between you and the company. The money you send to the company at regular intervals to pay for your life insurance is known as the *premium*. The person you name to receive the money from the policy if you should die is the *beneficiary*. A *contingent beneficiary* may also be named to receive the money if the beneficiary dies before you do. The *face value* of the policy is the amount stated on the first page of the contract that will be paid in case of death, or in the case of an endowment policy at maturity. As you pay premiums on your policy, a certain amount of reserve accumulates to its credit. This is called its *cash value*. The *loan value* is the amount you may borrow on your policy while it is still in force. Usually, this matches the cash value.

Ordinary Life Insurance

Ordinary insurance is sold on an individual basis for larger amounts than industrial insurance, and premiums are usually paid by check or at the insurance company office on a quarterly, semiannual, or annual basis. Although a minority of the total number of policies issued are ordinary policies, ordinary insurance accounts for more than half of the total value of life insurance in force in the United States today and bought from insurance companies. Generally, the smallest amount for which an ordinary policy is written is $1,000; the average of such policies is in excess of $2,800. When we remember that many of these policies are written for $5,000, $10,000, $25,000, and $50,000, it is not difficult to see why they all add up to a very substantial amount of insurance. They are usually written with level premiums (premiums fixed in amount and continuing at the fixed amount throughout the life of the policy), and in most cases provide both living and death benefits.

By "living benefits" we mean the values which exist in most life insurance policies which enable you to benefit while you are still alive. These living benefits include the ability to convert an ordinary policy to retirement income at 65, the ability to surrender the policy for cash, the ability to borrow against it, matured endowments, disability benefits, dividends, and the "nonforfeiture" provisions, which will be explained subsequently. Life insurance companies pay more money to living policyholders than to families of policyholders who have died. Last year 56 percent of insurance company payments were "living benefits." Death benefits, of course, are the sums paid to beneficiaries upon the death of the insured. The various ways in which the death benefits can be paid are known as "settlement options." They too will be explained later.

Term Insurance

When you buy term insurance, you buy pure insurance protection and nothing else. Everyone seems to know that if he buys a policy from a fire insurance company and does not cancel the policy, he will collect nothing from the company unless he has a fire; the policy will be worthless when the time for which it has been written has expired. Exactly the same sort of situation exists for a person who buys term insurance from a life insurance company. If he dies within the term for which he is insured, the company will pay his beneficiary the face of the policy; but if he is still living at the expiration of the time for which the policy was written, then the policy is of no value. Term policies are usually issued at level premiums for terms of 1, 5, 10, 15, or 20 years;

sometimes they are written to expire at age 65. Some companies write one-year term policies which are renewable one year at a time for a given number of years—perhaps five or ten—without further medical examination. The insured pays the lowest premium the first year, when he is youngest, and pays a higher premium each succeeding year that he renews, because by then he is older. Such a policy has the lowest possible premium in the first year, because it is not averaged up for later years, when the age of the insured will be greater. A five-year policy with a level premium would tend to have a premium equivalent to what would be paid in the third year of renewal of a one-year term policy. It is usually advisable to purchase a term policy which is renewable, without another medical examination, for a fairly large number of years, if it can be obtained, since you may later want the protection longer than you had originally planned. Many term policies are convertible into the more permanent types of life insurance policies; but on the policies into which you convert, you must pay premiums based on your age at time of conversion, which premiums will naturally be higher than they would have been if these policies had been taken earlier. The chief advantage of the conversion feature is that you know that you can have the policy if you want it; you need take no medical examination at time of conversion.

If you buy straight life or endowment insurance, you not only buy protection but in addition pay enough so that for all practical purposes you have a savings account with the insurance company. This is the reason your policy has a cash surrender value or loan value. Since term policies have no savings or investment feature, they are accordingly the least expensive form of insurance to buy in the short run and at young ages. Another way to express it is that a given amount of money will buy a larger face amount of term insurance than of straight life or endowment. For example, as Figure 7–6 shows, if you can spend (at age 20) only $100 annually for insurance, this amount will provide $15,220 of term insurance protection as against only $6,835 of straight life, or $6,373 of limited payment life, or $5,640 of endowment (at age 65) insurance.

It should be clear, therefore, that term insurance may be, temporarily, the most convenient insurance for a young family to buy when it needs a maximum amount of protection but cannot afford to pay the larger annual premiums which other forms of insurance require. To generalize: at the younger ages, term insurance costs only about a third of the cost of straight life insurance and less than a fifth of what 20-year endowment insurance costs. But remember that term insurance

FIGURE 7–6

What Insurance $100 a Year Will Buy
(Policies Bought at Age 20)

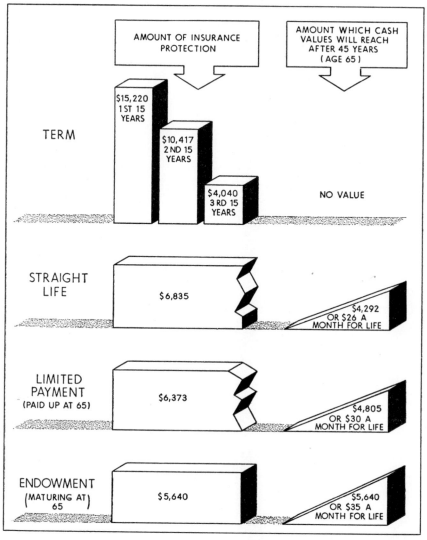

These are the four basic kinds of life insurance policies. Straight life insurance and limited payment policies can give lifetime protection. Term insurance cannot be purchased after age 65; the term insurance rates shown here are for a term policy which will call for a new physical examination every 15 years. Figures are approximate.

SOURCE: Institute of Life Insurance.

FIGURE 7-7

Comparative Costs of Different Types of Insurance

Annual and Monthly Premium Rates per $1,000 for Policies of $2,000 or More*

KIND OF POLICY		Age nearest birthday:	15	16	17	18	19	20	21	22	23	24	25	26	27	28	29	30
STRAIGHT LIFE	Annual	$ 2,000 to $ 4,999	$12.79	$13.07	$13.36	$13.65	$13.96	$14.32	$14.62	$14.97	$15.34	$15.72	$16.12	$16.55	$16.99	$17.46	$17.95	$18.46
		5,000 to 9,999	11.29	11.57	11.86	12.15	12.46	12.79	13.12	13.47	13.84	14.22	14.62	15.05	15.49	15.96	16.45	16.96
		10,000 or more	11.04	11.32	11.61	11.90	12.21	12.54	12.87	13.22	13.59	13.97	14.37	14.80	15.24	15.71	16.20	16.71
		Waiver of Premium	.23	.23	.24	.25	.26	.27	.28	.29	.30	.31	.32	.34	.35	.37	.39	.40
	Monthly	2,000 to 4,999	1.15	1.18	1.20	1.23	1.26	1.29	1.32	1.35	1.38	1.41	1.45	1.49	1.53	1.57	1.62	1.66
		5,000 to 9,999	1.02	1.04	1.07	1.09	1.12	1.15	1.18	1.21	1.25	1.28	1.32	1.35	1.39	1.44	1.48	1.53
		10,000 or more	.99	1.02	1.04	1.07	1.10	1.13	1.16	1.19	1.22	1.26	1.29	1.33	1.37	1.41	1.46	1.50
		Waiver of Premium	.02	.02	.02	.02	.02	.02	.03	.03	.03	.03	.03	.03	.03	.03	.04	.04
20 PAYMENT LIFE	Annual	2,000 to 4,999	19.46	19.84	20.24	20.64	21.05	21.47	21.91	22.35	22.81	23.29	23.78	24.29	24.82	25.36	25.92	26.51
		5,000 to 9,999	17.96	18.34	18.74	19.14	19.55	19.97	20.41	20.85	21.31	21.79	22.28	22.79	23.32	23.86	24.42	25.01
		10,000 or more	17.71	18.09	18.49	18.89	19.30	19.72	20.16	20.60	21.06	21.54	22.03	22.54	23.07	23.61	24.17	24.76
		Waiver of Premium	.15	.15	.16	.16	.16	.17	.17	.17	.18	.18	.19	.19	.20	.21	.22	.23
	Monthly	2,000 to 4,999	1.75	1.79	1.82	1.86	1.89	1.93	1.97	2.01	2.05	2.10	2.14	2.19	2.23	2.28	2.33	2.39
		5,000 to 9,999	1.62	1.65	1.69	1.72	1.76	1.80	1.84	1.88	1.92	1.96	2.01	2.05	2.10	2.15	2.20	2.25
		10,000 or more	1.59	1.63	1.66	1.70	1.74	1.77	1.81	1.85	1.90	1.94	1.98	2.03	2.08	2.12	2.18	2.23
		Waiver of Premium	.01	.01	.01	.01	.01	.02	.02	.02	.02	.02	.02	.02	.02	.02	.02	.02
20 YEAR ENDOWMENT	Annual	2,000 to 4,999	42.82	42.85	42.88	42.91	42.93	42.96	42.99	43.02	43.06	43.10	43.15	43.21	43.27	43.35	43.44	43.54
		5,000 to 9,999	41.32	41.35	41.38	41.41	41.43	41.46	41.49	41.52	41.56	41.60	41.65	41.71	41.77	41.85	41.94	42.04
		10,000 or more	41.07	41.10	41.13	41.16	41.18	41.21	41.24	41.27	41.31	41.35	41.40	41.46	41.52	41.60	41.69	41.79
		Waiver of Premium	.21	.21	.22	.22	.23	.23	.24	.24	.25	.25	.26	.27	.28	.29	.30	.31
	Monthly	2,000 to 4,999	3.85	3.86	3.86	3.86	3.86	3.87	3.87	3.87	3.88	3.88	3.88	3.89	3.89	3.90	3.91	3.92
		5,000 to 9,999	3.72	3.70	3.72	3.73	3.73	3.73	3.73	3.74	3.74	3.74	3.75	3.75	3.76	3.77	3.77	3.78
		10,000 or more	3.70	3.70	3.70	3.70	3.71	3.71	3.71	3.71	3.72	3.72	3.73	3.73	3.74	3.74	3.75	3.76
		Waiver of Premium	.02	.02	.02	.02	.02	.02	.02	.02	.02	.02	.02	.02	.03	.03	.03	.03
5 YEAR TERM	Annual	2,000 to 4,999	4.30	4.37	4.42	4.47	4.52	4.55	4.58	4.61	4.63	4.66	4.70	4.74	4.78	4.84	4.90	4.96
		5,000 to 9,999	4.05	4.12	4.17	4.22	4.27	4.30	4.33	4.36	4.38	4.41	4.45	4.49	4.53	4.59	4.65	4.71
		10,000 or more																
		Waiver of Premium	.31	.33	.34	.35	.37	.38	.40	.41	.42	.44	.45	.48	.50	.52	.53	.57
	Monthly	2,000 to 4,999	.39	.39	.40	.40	.41	.41	.41	.42	.42	.42	.42	.43	.43	.44	.44	.45
		5,000 to 9,999	.36	.37	.38	.38	.38	.39	.39	.39	.39	.40	.40	.40	.41	.41	.42	.42
		Waiver of Premium	.03	.03	.03	.03	.03	.03	.04	.04	.04	.04	.04	.04	.05	.05	.05	.05

STRAIGHT LIFE — Lowest cost form of permanent protection. Cash and loan values. By leaving in dividends, policy can become fully paid-up.

20 PAYMENT LIFE — Becomes paid-up in only 20 years . . . sooner if dividends are left in. A good choice for those who want early paid-up insurance. Cash and loan values.

20 YEAR ENDOWMENT — Cash payable to you in 20 years (earlier if dividends are left in) or to your beneficiary if death occurs earlier. Cash and loan values.

5 YEAR TERM — Automatically renewable every five years at increased rate up to age 65. Convertible. No cash or loan values. Minimum policy $5,000.

LIFE PAID-UP AT 65

Provides protection for life, but premiums stop at age 65 (sooner if dividends are left in). Cash and loan values.

ENDOWMENT AT AGE 65

Cash payable to you at 65 (earlier if dividends are left in) or to your beneficiary if death occurs earlier. Cash and loan values.

20 YR. DECREASING TERM—POLICY; Home Protector Plan

To cover a mortgage or to provide maximum protection at very low cost. Minimum policy $5,000.

20 YR. DECREASING TERM—RIDER

This rider may be attached to new permanent policies of $3,000 or more in amounts of $5,000 or more.

Plan	Mode	Amount	15	16	17	18	19	20	21	22	23	24	25	26	27	28	29	30
LIFE PAID-UP AT 65	Annual	2,000 to 4,999	13.36	13.68	14.01	14.36	14.72	15.10	15.50	15.92	16.36	16.83	17.32	17.85	18.40	18.99	19.62	20.28
		5,000 to 9,999	11.86	12.18	12.51	12.86	13.22	13.60	14.00	14.42	14.86	15.33	15.82	16.35	16.90	17.49	18.12	18.78
		10,000 or more	11.61	11.93	12.26	12.61	12.97	13.35	13.75	14.17	14.61	15.08	15.57	16.10	16.65	17.24	17.87	18.53
		Waiver of Premium	.21	.21	.22	.23	.23	.24	.25	.26	.27	.28	.29	.30	.31	.33	.34	.36
	Monthly	2,000 to 4,999	1.20	1.23	1.26	1.29	1.32	1.36	1.40	1.43	1.47	1.51	1.56	1.61	1.66	1.71	1.77	1.83
		5,000 to 9,999	1.07	1.10	1.13	1.16	1.19	1.22	1.26	1.30	1.34	1.38	1.42	1.47	1.52	1.57	1.63	1.69
		10,000 or more	1.04	1.07	1.10	1.13	1.17	1.20	1.24	1.28	1.31	1.36	1.40	1.45	1.50	1.55	1.61	1.67
		Waiver of Premium	.02	.02	.02	.02	.02	.02	.02	.02	.02	.03	.03	.03	.03	.03	.03	.03
ENDOWMENT AT AGE 65	Annual	2,000 to 4,999	15.34	15.74	16.16	16.60	17.06	17.54	18.05	18.58	19.14	19.73	20.36	21.03	21.73	22.48	23.28	24.12
		5,000 to 9,999	13.84	14.24	14.66	15.10	15.56	16.04	16.55	17.08	17.64	18.23	18.86	19.53	20.23	20.98	21.78	22.62
		10,000 or more	13.59	13.99	14.41	14.85	15.31	15.79	16.30	16.83	17.39	17.98	18.61	19.28	19.98	20.73	21.53	22.37
		Waiver of Premium	.22	.23	.24	.25	.25	.26	.27	.28	.30	.31	.32	.34	.35	.37	.39	.41
	Monthly	2,000 to 4,999	1.38	1.42	1.45	1.49	1.54	1.58	1.62	1.67	1.72	1.78	1.83	1.89	1.96	2.02	2.10	2.17
		5,000 to 9,999	1.25	1.28	1.32	1.36	1.40	1.44	1.49	1.54	1.59	1.64	1.70	1.76	1.82	1.89	1.96	2.04
		10,000 or more	1.22	1.26	1.30	1.34	1.38	1.42	1.47	1.51	1.57	1.62	1.67	1.74	1.80	1.87	1.94	2.01
		Waiver of Premium	.02	.02	.02	.02	.02	.02	.02	.03	.03	.03	.03	.03	.03	.03	.04	.04
20 YR. DECREASING TERM—POLICY; Home Protector Plan	Annual	5,000 to 9,999	3.39	3.43	3.47	3.50	3.53	3.57	3.61	3.65	3.70	3.75	3.82	3.89	3.98	4.07	4.19	4.31
		10,000 to 30,000	2.89	2.93	2.97	3.00	3.03	3.07	3.11	3.15	3.20	3.25	3.32	3.39	3.48	3.57	3.69	3.81
		Waiver of Premium	.06	.06	.06	.06	.06	.06	.06	.06	.06	.06	.06	.07	.07	.07	.07	.07
	Monthly	5,000 to 9,999	.31	.31	.31	.32	.32	.32	.32	.33	.33	.34	.34	.35	.36	.37	.38	.39
		10,000 to 30,000	.26	.26	.27	.27	.27	.28	.28	.28	.29	.29	.30	.31	.31	.32	.33	.34
		Waiver of Premium	.01	.01	.01	.01	.01	.01	.01	.01	.01	.01	.01	.01	.01	.01	.01	.01
20 YR. DECREASING TERM—RIDER	Annual	5,000 to 9,999	2.94	2.98	3.02	3.05	3.08	3.12	3.16	3.20	3.25	3.30	3.37	3.44	3.53	3.62	3.74	3.86
		10,000 to 30,000	2.44	2.48	2.52	2.55	2.58	2.62	2.66	2.70	2.75	2.80	2.87	2.94	3.03	3.12	3.24	3.36
		Waiver of Premium	.06	.06	.06	.06	.06	.06	.06	.06	.06	.06	.06	.07	.07	.07	.07	.07
	Monthly	5,000 to 9,999	.26	.27	.27	.27	.28	.28	.28	.29	.29	.30	.30	.31	.32	.33	.34	.35
		10,000 to 27,000	.22	.22	.23	.23	.23	.24	.24	.24	.25	.25	.26	.26	.27	.28	.29	.30
		Waiver of Premium	.01	.01	.01	.01	.01	.01	.01	.01	.01	.01	.01	.01	.01	.01	.01	.01

* For policies under $2,000, add $2. per $1,000 to the annual premiums and 18¢ per $1,000 to the monthly premiums shown above. (Waiver of Premium rates for policies under $2,000 same as above.)

SOURCE: The New York Bank for Savings.

provides no "living benefits." Since most younger men with families simply can't afford as much protection as they need, their choice narrows down to the lower premium forms of policies which provide the greatest protection for what they can afford to spend. Older men, whose family responsibilities may be less, may wish less emphasis on protection and more on an income at retirement.

Study of Figure 7–7 will give a good idea of comparative costs. While the rates quoted are based on savings bank life insurance and are somewhat lower than for commerical companies, the purpose is to compare the cost of a term policy with other types of insurance, and, consequently, Figure 7–7 serves this purpose very well. It will be seen that, at age 25, buying a $10,000 term insurance policy will cost you an annual premium of $44.50, while the comparative cost of $10,000 of straight life will be $143.70 and that of $10,000 of endowment insurance (payable at age 65) will be $186.10.

Advantages and Limitations of Term Insurance

Since term policies provide the largest amount of protection for the lowest immediate cost, they are useful, temporarily, for young married couples when the husband is earning a small salary and offspring are expected. Suppose $150 a year is all that can be spared for insurance on the husband. As you can see from the following figures, your $150-a-year achieves maximum protection through term insurance:

Approximate Amounts of Insurance Protection That $150 per Year Will Purchase under Varying Policies at Three Ages

Type of Policy	Age 25	Age 35	Age 45
20-year endowment	$ 3,800	$ 3,700	$ 3,500
Endowment at 65	8,900	6,000	3,500
20-payment life	6,400	5,400	4,200
Payments to 65	10,700	7,200	4,200
Straight life	12,100	8,800	6,000
5-year convertible and renewable term	35,000	25,800	14,300
10-year convertible and renewable term	35,500	23,300	11,600
20-year convertible term	39,500	21,700	10,200

Source: *Changing Times, The Kiplinger Magazine.*

Whenever protection, and protection alone, is needed, and at low cost, term insurance may be the answer or a combination of term and straight life in the form of a family income policy, which combines temporary and lifetime protection and provides "living" as well as "death" benefits. This will be discussed shortly. If the sole need is protection while the children are growing up, term insurance will provide it at lower cost than other ordinary policies. Another typical use of term insurance is to protect your family against mortgage foreclosure in the event of your death. You can buy a decreasing term policy where the amount and premium on the insurance will decline at exactly the same rate as the amount of the mortgage which you are paying off month after month. If you should die at any time during the mortgage term, the amount of insurance payable under the policy will cover the remaining amount of the mortgage. Frequently, term insurance is combined with straight life (permanent) insurance in one policy, called a "family income" or "family maintenance" policy (to be described later), designed not only to protect the wife and children from loss of the home but to provide additional protection as well.

It should be remembered, however, in the case of term insurance that if the insured lives beyond the term of the policy, he will have nothing—no income in old age, no paid-up insurance, no cash surrender or loan value. Other types of ordinary policies provide all these features. Term insurance only provides death benefits provided you die within the stated term or an extension thereof. Term policies have no "living benefits." The term policy accumulates no reserve funds from which you can get cash or a loan. Furthermore, renewal rates get very high as you grow older. For short periods, term insurance costs less than other insurance; for a longer period—as for life—it costs more. Term insurance does not help in an investment or savings program, nor is it the best kind of insurance to carry as one grows older, because the premiums become so large as to be prohibitive for most people. Since the premium for a term policy pays only the cost of protection during the term of the policy, the policy seldom has any *nonforfeiture* values, which permanent policies have. Thus, if unemployment or sickness make it impossible to keep up the premiums, since there is no reserve, the policy will terminate at the end of the grace period, usually 30 days from premium due date.

Some term policies have *renewal* privileges, which give the right to renew the policy for another term, at a higher rate, without proving one's insurability at the end of the original policy term. Some term policies, also, can be converted into a permanent form of insurance within a definite period of years specified in the contract, generally without a medical examination. You should never buy a term policy which does not have these two features: renewability and convertibility, both without requiring a medical examination. This is important, because there may come a time when you may not be able to pass an insurance examination or when rates on your renewable term policy become quite high. You may then want to convert to a permanent plan, and you should be sure that your term policy permits you to do so even if you are not in good health.

The variation in rates among the various types of term insurance may be seen in the following tabulation:

Rates for Various Types of Term, Modified, and Straight Life per $1,000 of Insurance

KIND OF POLICY	AGE WHEN BOUGHT 25	35
One-year term, convertible and renewable	$ 5.45	$ 6.36
Five-year term, convertible	5.48	6.81
Ten-year term, convertible	5.64	7.50
Five-year term, convertible and renewable	6.21	7.66
Ten-year term, convertible and renewable	6.37	8.35
Term to age 70	12.74	15.90
Modified life, first five years	8.89	11.88
thereafter	17.78	23.76
Ordinary life	15.64	21.08

SOURCE: *Changing Times, The Kiplinger Magazine.*

Straight Life Insurance

A straight or ordinary life policy is a plan of insurance for the whole of life with premiums payable until death. It has the lowest premium rate of any permanent policy on the level premium plan. It is the most widely used, and it is a good all-purpose policy, which meets many different needs and family situations. A level premium is paid throughout life (with premiums stopping sometimes at a ripe old age), and the face of the policy is payable to the beneficiary upon the death of the insured.

This type of policy combines protection with saving; but since the premium, and therefore the saving, is moderate, the cash surrender or loan value also grows at a moderate rate. It fits the needs of those who wish to secure protection for beneficiaries and do some saving in addition. It provides both "living" and "death" benefits. If the death of the insured occurs, the beneficiary is paid the face of the insurance policy. On the other hand, if the insured lives, he can borrow against the straight life policy or cash it in. The loan value is the amount which may be borrowed with the policy as sole collateral. But he cannot eat his cake and have it too: if he surrenders the policy for its cash value, the protection will be gone; if he borrows on the policy, his beneficiary will receive on his death only the face value of the policy reduced by the amount of the loan and interest thereon.

If, some day, the holder of a straight life policy wishes, say upon retirement, to discontinue premium payments, he can select any one or, if his policy is large enough, a combination of the following alternatives:

1. Continue the protection at a reduced amount for the balance of his lifetime.
2. Continue the full amount of protection for a definite period of time.
3. Cancel the policy entirely in return for a cash settlement of guaranteed amount.
4. Discontinue life insurance protection and, if the policy permits, elect to receive an income from the policy for a certain limited period of time or for life.

In the next chapter it will be shown that social security provides something for the old age of many people but that in many cases it must be supplemented to provide reasonable retirement comforts. Savings built up through life insurance can help in supplementing social security benefits, and indeed, modern insurance programming builds from the social security base to meet family needs more adequately.

Whole or straight life combines protection, savings, and retirement income at a minimum yearly cost. It has the lowest premium rate of any permanent policy on the level premium, legal reserve plan. The premium rate, however, is higher than the rate on a term policy because, if the policy is continued, it must some day be paid as a claim; whereas a term policy is paid only if the insured dies within the term. In the straight life policy, the increasing risk of death is averaged over the years at a level premium. For example, as Figure 7–8 indicates, if you buy $1,000 worth of whole life insurance at age 20, you will pay a level premium of $15.30 per annum over the ensuing years until death. A renewable five-year term policy for the same amount would cost you $5.30. But if you kept renewing the term policy every five years, at age 50 you would pay $16.75 per annum, more than the whole life policyholder; and when you renewed at age 60 (the last time you would be permitted to renew), you would pay $35.25 a year for the next five years. At age 65, your term policy would expire and could not be renewed again. You would have no accumulation to show for your 45 years of payments, although, of course, you had protection

FIGURE 7–8

The Four Kinds of Life Insurance

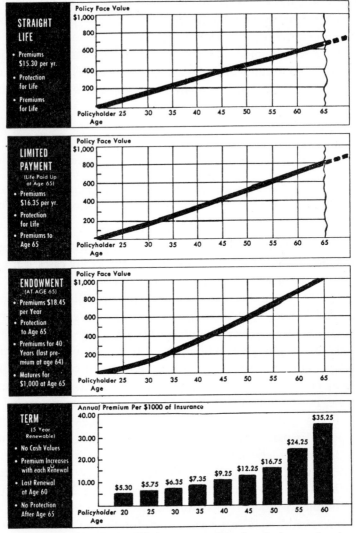

Here are four $1,000 life insurance policies bought by people who are 20 years old. Approximate cash values and premiums are shown in this chart. The limited payment policy becomes "paid up" at age 65, and the endowment "matures" at age 65.

SOURCE: Institute of Life Insurance.

over this period. The holder of the straight life policy, however, if he wished to stop paying premiums at age 65—and any whole life policyholder can exercise this privilege—could give up the policy and receive $628 (the cash surrender value) in cash or as income over a period.

What Happens if You Can't Pay Your Premium?

In a permanent policy, where a cash value has been built up, you don't usually lose the policy. The nonforfeiture provisions come into play. If you are temporarily unable to meet your premium payments, you can borrow against the cash value of your policy and thus continue payments through the loan. If it looks as if you will be unable to resume payments again, or if you become 65 and you don't want to continue to pay premiums, you can choose one of the various nonforfeiture options.

Every permanent policy, of which the whole or straight life policy is the most popular, has the built-in "nonforfeiture values." There are three kinds of nonforfeiture or guaranteed values:

1. *Cash Value.* This is the money you will get if you give up your permanent life insurance policy. A policyholder who has purchased life insurance on the level premium plan has paid premiums which were more than needed to pay claims in the earlier years, thus building up a fund of assets with which to meet claims in later years. It follows that if he withdraws, there is an accumulation of assets out of the premiums paid by him to which he is entitled.

The cash value is his share of this accumulation. It will be paid to him as guaranteed in his insurance contract and as required by law. It may be taken in a lump sum or in a series of regularly recurring payments over a period of years providing it amounts to $1,000 or more. The longer you have your policy, the more your cash value will be (see Table 7–2). Today, many people reaching retirement ar-

TABLE 7–2

Table of Approximate Cash, Loan, and Nonforfeiture Values for Straight Life Policy Issued at Age 20*

Premiums Paid to Age—	Paid-up Insurance (Participating)	Cash Value (Loan Values, Subject to the "Loans" Clause)	Extended Term Insurance (Participating)	
			Years	Days
25	$105	$ 39.11	12	215
30	250	113.60	23	101
35	365	178.33	25	205
40	480	247.93	25	302
60	785	553.34	19	237
65	833	627.62	17	166

* For each $1,000 of the face amount of the policy free from indebtedness and without dividend accumulations or paid-up additions. Paid-up insurance will be adjusted to the nearest dollar.
Source: Institute of Life Insurance.

Straight life (whole life

PERSONAL FINANCE

range to take their cash value in the form of income that will be paid for life over the retirement period. Some requests for cash reflect an upset in family finances as a result of unexpected illnesses or loss of a job. Though life insurance is not designed as a way of preparing to meet such financial difficulties, it may help more in this way, in some cases, than it would if kept in force to fill primary needs.

You can borrow against your cash values at any time; if you die before the loan is repaid, the payments to your beneficiaries will be reduced by the amount of the loan. In an emergency, then, the loan provision of your life insurance policy can be used to secure money or to pay premiums due. Some policies have a special provision for the latter, called the "automatic premium loan." If this provision is in your policy, your company will automatically pay any premium that is not paid when due. The company will charge such premiums as loans against your policy to the extent of the available loan values. The policy continues in force until such time as the total loan against the policy equals the cash value. At that time the policy terminates without further value.

2. *Reduced Paid-up Life Insurance.* This is a nonforfeiture or guaranteed value you can use if you want to keep some protection but are not in a position to or do not wish to pay any more premiums. The amount of your insurance will be reduced, as may be seen in Table 7–2. For example, if you bought a $1,000 policy at age 20 and at age 60, because of illness, were unable to continue paying premiums, you could arrange to have $785 of paid-up insurance as long as you lived without any further payments of premiums. That is, if you have a permanent life policy, the paid-up insurance feature will protect you for life without further premium payments, but the insurance is reduced in amount to what your net cash value will buy as a single payment at your attained age.

3. *Extended Term Insurance.* Suppose you can no longer pay premiums on your policy but want to continue the maximum amount of protection as long as possible. Extended term insurance gives you continued protection for the full face value of your policy (less any loan outstanding) for a limited length of time. As Table 7–2 indicates, if, at age 60, you were unable to continue to pay premiums on the $1,000 policy you bought at age 20, you could continue to enjoy the protection of the full face value of your policy, without paying any more premiums, for an additional 19 years and 237 days. The time is determined by what your net cash value will purchase when used as a single payment to buy the extended term protection at your attained age.

Combination Policies

The straight life policy has many variants—in fact, the insurance companies are constantly trying to devise new contracts which meet the needs of certain people better than the older forms. Thus we hear of *family income* and *family maintenance* policies, of *family* policies and of *modified life.* These are combinations of whole life and term policies. A 20-year *family income* policy provides that if the policyholder dies within 20 years after he takes out a policy, his beneficiary will be paid $10 a month for each $1,000 of the policy for the balance of the 20 years *after the policy was taken out.* At death or at the end of the twentieth year, depending upon the contract, the beneficiary receives, in addition, the face value of the policy or its equivalent in the form of income. If the insured lives on beyond the 20-year term, he can continue the whole life portion of the policy at the rate for straight life in effect when he bought the policy. The premiums on these combination policies run only a little higher than those for ordinary life policies, and for families with young children they are often excellent.

For example, if a man who has a wife and a one-year-old baby takes out a 20-year, $10,000 family income policy and dies three years later, the policy will assure the widow and child of $100 a month income until the child is age 21. Then the face of the policy will become due and payable to the widow, either as a lump sum or as income. If the man had lived, he could have continued paying on the policy as an ordinary whole life policy after the 20-year period was up.

The way in which the family income policy combines permanent life insurance and term insurance is shown in Table 7–3, where $5,000 straight life is combined with enough decreasing term insurance to provide $50, $75, or $100 per month for a period of 20 years from the date of purchase. The policy provides that if the head of the family dies during the family protection period, then the monthly income will be paid until the end of the term or family period. At that time, the $5,000 of permanent protection will be paid in a lump sum or may be taken in the form of an income. If the insured outlives the family protection period, he has simply a straight life policy for $5,000 —the term portion having run out. At or near the end of this 20-year period, his policy generally provides for a reduction in premium to that of the $5,000 straight life policy.

Family maintenance policies are similar, except that a 20-year policy of this kind would pay its monthly income for 20 years *after the death of the insured,* should he die within 20 years after purchase of the policy.

To illustrate the difference: suppose that two men buy policies of the two types in 1960 and that both die in 1970; the beneficiaries under the family income policy will receive a monthly income until 1980 and will then receive the face of the policy, while the beneficiaries under the family maintenance policy will receive a monthly income until 1990 and will then receive the face of the policy. Naturally, therefore, family maintenance policies cost more, since the company faces the possibility of having to extend the monthly income payment over a longer

TABLE 7–3

Illustration of Family Income Policy, Insured Age 30
(Basic Policy, $5,000 Straight Life)

	FAMILY INCOME		
	$50 per Month (1% Benefit)	$75 per Month (1½% Benefit)	$100 per Month (2% Benefit)
APPROXIMATE ANNUAL PREMIUMS			
For $5,000 straight life	$ 100	$ 100	$ 100
For family income rider (20 years)	26	41	56
Total	$ 126	$ 141	$ 156
TERM INSURANCE PROVIDED IN ADDITION TO $5,000 STRAIGHT LIFE			
Year 1	$7,900	$12,750	$17,595
2	7,585	12,235	16,890
3	7,260	11,715	16,165
4	-6,930	11,180	15,430
5	6,590	10,630	14,675
6	6,245	10,070	13,900
7	5,890	9,500	13,115
8	5,525	8,915	12,305
9	5,155	8,320	11,480
10	4,775	7,705	10,635
11	4,390	7,080	9,775
12	3,995	6,440	8,890
13	3,590	5,790	7,990
14	3,175	5,120	7,065
15	2,750	4,435	6,125
16	2,320	3,740	5,160
17	1,875	3,025	4,175
18	1,420	2,295	3,165
19	960	1,545	2,135
20	485	785	1,080

SOURCE: Institute of Life Insurance.

period. Both kinds of insurance are available in ten-year and 15-year as well as 20-year policies.

Modified life is a type of policy which starts as term insurance and then after a stated period, usually five years, automatically changes to whole life at a higher premium. During the first five years the low term premium rate prevails. The basic purpose of modified life, of course, is to provide permanent insurance for young people who aren't yet in a position to pay for it. It is therefore a very useful policy for newlyweds or for the young family.

The *family* policy (not to be confused with family income or family maintenance) is one of the insurance industry's combinations of term and straight life. It provides a "package" of insurance coverage for the whole family—husband, wife, and children. The policy is issued in $5,000 units with each unit providing $5,000 of whole life insurance for the husband, $1,250 of term insurance for the wife, if she is the same age as her husband, and $1,000 of term insurance for each covered child. The wife's insurance coverage is more if she is younger than the husband and less if she is older. The premium is not affected by the number of children covered. Children born after the plan is issued are automatically eligible for children's coverage when they are 15 days old, at no extra premium.

Extra protection policies also combine term and ordinary life. There are "double," "triple," and even "quadruple" protection policies. The double protection policy, for example, may be $1,000 of straight life with $1,000 of term tacked on. Triple protection adds $2,000 of term to the $1,000 of whole life, and so on. The term portion usually runs until age 60 or 65 and then expires leaving the straight life protection only. These policies give less "extra" protection in the early years than a comparable premium expenditure on a family income policy, but the "extra" protection lasts longer—to 60 or 65.

Preferred risk policies are regular policies issued at specially reduced rates to those who are in very good health, in safe occupations, and who will buy a large minimum amount of insurance, usually $5,000 or $10,000. The rate is significantly less than for an ordinary whole life policy. If you are going into the professions and enjoy excellent health, inquire about the preferred risk policy. For those who qualify, it means buying regular insurance at very favorable rates.

Limited Payment Life Policies

Limited payment life policies are straight life policies with the one difference that premium payments are not made for life but for a limited term, such as 20 or 30 years. They have been called "hurried-up" ordinary life policies. Since the insured contracts to make fewer premium payments, naturally those that he does make will have to be larger; for the insurance company is obligated to insure him for his lifetime. Since the insured makes larger payments and makes them during the first 20 or 30 years the policy is in force, the cash (and loan) value accumulates faster than it does in the straight life policy.

The limited payment life policy is attractive to those who for one reason or another want to cut short the burden of paying premiums. Often the insured wishes to complete premium payments before earnings start to decline. He may have a "life-begins-at-forty" philosophy and aim to have many of his obligations squared away by middle age so that he will have less to encumber a free and easy existence from his forties or fifties to the end of his days. Of course, this puts a larger burden on his most active working years than if he spread the load over a longer span. Sometimes, fear that work will not be available later leads to the decision to strike while the iron is hot and pay while earnings are at their peak. This is particularly true of professional athletes, movie stars, etc.

For a young person, especially with family responsibilities, limited payment life is not the best plan. You get less protection for your premium dollar than you would if you bought ordinary life. A 22-year-old with $200 a year to spend on insurance would get about $14,000 of straight life protection. He'd get only $8,200 if he bought 20-payment life. Of course, if you can afford it and if you outlive the premium-paying period, there is a big advantage. Your insurance is paid up. You are insured for life, but you need make no more premium payments. A life-paid-up-at-65 policy makes a good deal more sense than a 20-pay life if you are under 30 and insist on a limited payment plan. It's less costly for one thing. At age 22, life paid up at 65 will cost only $16 per $1,000 compared to $24.40 for 20-pay life and $14.30 for straight life. Since your highest earning period may be from 40 to 65, there is no need to try and pay off your insurance by 40, although there is a good deal more sense in trying to get it paid up by 65.

Endowment and Retirement Income Policies

Both of these policies place the emphasis on savings rather than on protection. Both cost more than any other type of policy. An endowment policy is one that is written for a given period of time and for a stated face value. Endowment at 65 and 20-year endowments are the most common types. If you die before the stated period is up, your beneficiary receives the full face value. If you live until the maturity of the policy, you receive the full face value. Once you have received the full face value on maturity, however, you are no longer insured. The company has paid off under the contract, and the policy terminates.

Naturally, since the cash value must build up to the face value by the time the contract period is up, an endowment premium is very much higher, that is much more costly than any other type of policy. As you can see from Table 7–4, a 20-year endowment would cost $45.60 per

TABLE 7–4

What $100 a Year Premium Will Buy in Life Insurance*
(Male Age 22)

Type of Policy	Annual Rate per $1,000 of Insurance	Amount of Insurance $100 a Year Will Buy†	Cash Value at Age 65 per $100 Annual Premium	Monthly Life Income at Age 65, Men (10 Years Certain)
1. Term (5-year renewable and convertible)	$ 5.12	$19,500	None	None
2. Term (10-year convertible, nonrenewable)	5.18	19,300	None	None
3. Straight life	14.30	7,000	4,200	26.50
4. Life-paid-up-at-65	16.00	6,250	4,475	28.20
5. Modified life (5 years)	16.65	6,000	3,510	22.15
6. Family income (20 years)	17.75	5,600	3,360	21.20
7. Endowment at 65	18.35	5,400	5,400	34.00
8. 20-payment life	24.40	4,100	2,935	18.50
9. Retirement income at 65	25.25	3,960	6,555	41.30
10. 20-year endowment	45.60	2,200	Matured (age 42)	13.90‡

* Approximate amounts
† Most policies are issued in $1,000 units or in multiples of $500.
‡ If matured amount is left at interest with the company until age 65.
Source: Institute of Life Insurance.

$1,000 face value for a 22-year-old as compared with $14.30 for straight life and $24.40 for 20-payment life.

There is a great difference, of course, between a limited payment life and an endowment policy.[6] When you are finished paying on a

[6] See Davis W. Gregg, *Life and Health Insurance Handbook* (2d ed.; Homewood, Illinois: Richard D. Irwin, Inc., 1964).

limited payment life policy, you are insured for life but you collect nothing, although your cash value has built up to about three fifths of the face value. On the other hand, in the case of the endowment, once you have finished paying (a) you are no longer insured, (b) you collect the face amount of the policy, and (c) the policy terminates.

For young people, endowments are not very sensible. As insurance protection, it's very expensive and as savings it's costly.[7] You can see from the figures above that $1,000 of protection at age 22 costs $31.30 more if you buy it as an endowment than if you buy it as straight life. Ah, yes, you say, but I'm saving the difference. Perhaps you are, perhaps you're not. Suppose you have a 20-year endowment and you die in the nineteenth year. What your beneficiary receives is 95 percent your savings and almost no insurance. Had you bought straight life, or a family income policy, and saved the difference in premiums, your beneficiary would have gotten both the full face amount of the insurance and your savings as well. Every young family needs life insurance, but they don't need the most expensive kind. If you must buy an endowment, the endowment at age 65 is much less costly ($18.35 per $1,000 when purchased at age 22, see Table 7–4) than a 20-year endowment, and makes more sense for a younger man.

The retirement income policy differs from the endowment in that it pays a monthly income from the date of its maturity rather than a lump-sum cash amount. It is, of course, an insurance policy and therefore has a stated face value and pays a death benefit of this amount to your beneficiary if you should die before the maturity date. However, to build cash value to pay the retirement income, the reserve behind the policy builds up very rapidly and in time exceeds the face value. If you die after that has happened, your beneficiary will receive more than the face value of the policy. He or she will receive the full cash value which is now greater than the face value. It's no sudden windfall, though. It's your accumulated savings. A retirement income policy is expensive; less expensive than a 20-year endowment, more expensive than an endowment at age 65.

Sometimes parents take out endowment policies, maturing at ages 17 or 18, on children, to provide funds for a college education. Generally speaking, in families of moderate income, practically all life insurance should be placed on the wage earner, without whose income the family finances would be sadly crippled. Only enough insurance

---

[7] Clyde S. Cassady, *A Buyer's Guide to Life Insurance* (rev. ed.; Boston: Savings Bank Life Insurance Council).

should be carried on the other family members to finance their burial if other sufficient funds are not available to meet such emergencies. Money for a college education can be accumulated, if the parent lives, with less outlay (because nothing is paid to buy protection) by saving the money in a savings bank or savings and loan association, provided the latter can pay as good a return in interest or dividends as a life insurance company can, which is usually the case. If it is desired to combine protection with saving for a college education through life insurance, the policy should be taken out on the life of the parent, the child being thus assured of cash for an education if the parent dies; whereas, if the insurance were on the life of the child, the parent's death might result in the policy's lapsing before a sufficient sum had accumulated for the desired education. (For a small extra premium, however, a clause can usually be added to a child's policy waiving further premiums should the head of the family die or become disabled before the child reaches a certain age.) If the parent lives, the cash surrender or loan value of his policy can be used, if necessary, to meet college costs. Thus, in insuring to cover the costs of a college education, as well as in other general life insurance situations, the best principle to follow is to have the insurance placed on the life of the breadwinner rather than on that of a dependent.

Some Comparisons

The many different kinds of policies described thus far may be a bit puzzling. Stop then and try to put all this together, to compare and contrast. Study Table 7–4. The range of policies is from those with maximum protection and minimum (or no) savings to those with less protection (per premium dollar) and more savings. The term policy provides maximum protection and no savings for your premium money. The 20-year endowment provides the least protection and the maximum savings for your premium dollar. Generally speaking, the more costly the insurance, the faster it's building a cash value and, therefore, the more it is emphasizing savings. This may be all right for the established man of 40–45 with married children, but for the young man of 20–25, the emphasis should be placed on protection.

Insure Your Insurability

A new kind of rider is now available to add to a regular insurance policy. Designed primarily for young people who can purchase only a limited amount of insurance at first, it gives you the right to purchase additional insurance later at standard premiums, within certain limits, even if your health should become impaired making you uninsurable under ordinary circumstances.

The rider, which can generally be purchased up to age 37, gives you the right to buy more insurance at specified intervals, without a medical examination, in amounts equal to the face value of the basic policy. The number of option dates depends on your age when you buy the basic policy. For example, on a policy purchased up to age 29, you can buy up to $10,000 more (if the face value of your basic policy is $10,000 or more) at ages 25, 28, 31, 34, 37 and 40. Thus you could buy an additional $60,000 of insurance, until age 40, regardless of the condition of your health or the type of job you hold. At age 23, for example, the rider would cost approximately $1.15 a year for each $1,000 of insurance you add at any option date. The rider doesn't buy the insurance for you. It simply gives you the right to buy the insurance regardless of health. You pay the standard premium for your age each time you buy an extra policy. The rider is an option to buy insurance tomorrow. It doesn't add to your insurance today.

Group Insurance

Would $5,000 of life insurance offered to you for an annual premium of $25 interest you? It should. It's quite a bargain, and it may well be your introduction to life insurance. It's group insurance, of course, the kind a firm might make available to you when you start your first career job. Increasingly, responsible firms are providing employees with group life insurance. Usually, the employer pays at least half, sometimes all, of the premium cost. Usually, the amount of group insurance you can buy is equal to one year's salary.

Group insurance is usually term insurance written under a blanket (master) policy issued to an employer or sponsoring association on all or some of the members of the group. Group insurance usually costs less per $1,000 of protection than ordinary insurance. Since the groups are frequently large—often running into the thousands—with all being covered by one sale, the selling cost is low per thousand dollars face value of insurance, even though considerable effort may be expended in arranging the details so that the needs of the group will be satisfied. Another factor making for lower costs is that the employer does much of the bookkeeping, since he makes collection through payroll deductions from employees of their share of the premium and pays the insurance company one sum covering the premium for the whole group. In many ways it resembles a wholesale operation rather than a retailing of insurance. Costs of group insurance are so low that eligible employees who can use the added insurance protection should think twice before passing up the opportunity to obtain it. Group insurance generally is written for one year, renewable.

One of the chief advantages of group insurance is that no medical examination is required of the members of the group. Risk is spread sufficiently because of the very size of the group itself—varying perhaps from a low of about fifty persons to a high of thousands in some of the larger organizations. By means of group insurance, some persons obtain life insurance protection who, because of the status of their health, might otherwise be unable to obtain it.

It is generally required that the employer pay some part of the premium cost. His contribution may be reduced if because of favorable experience a dividend on the master policy is returned to him. Each member of the group is given an individual certificate indicating his rights in the group contract. Generally, regardless of age, each employee pays the same amount per $1,000 of protection.

Group insurance is usually a form of term insurance, although in some cases it is now being written as a combination of term and straight life. Therefore, it may carry no cash surrender or loan provisions. It customarily terminates when the employee leaves his job with the employer, whether before or at retirement age. It is, however, a common provision to allow employees covered by group insurance to convert it into the standard forms of straight life or endowment within 30 days after severing their employment. Since group insurance usually does not cover retired employees—or at least to a smaller extent than when they were actively employed—this very fact cuts down claims against the insurance company and is a further reason for the low cost of this type of insurance.

If your first job offers group insurance, don't turn it down. It protects a new family, the cost is very low, the employer pays all or part of the premium, you won't need to take a medical examination, and you can convert to ordinary insurance, in most cases, if and when you leave the company. There are over 48 million individual certificates under 193,000 master group life insurance policies outstanding in the United States. The average amount per employee is $4,320. One half of all employees in the country are now covered by group life insurance.

Industrial Insurance

Industrial insurance, which is sold in small sums of less than $1,000, involves weekly premiums (usually of small amounts—5 cents, 10 cents, or 25 cents) collected at the home by the insurance agent. Since the agents must visit the home, write receipts for very small sums, enter amounts in their record books, possibly chat briefly with the family, and often find people out and have to come back again, it can readily be seen that this type of insurance must be relatively expensive.

One large company pays the policyholders 10 percent of the premiums for each full year that they make payments at the company's offices instead of depending on the agent to call at the residence to collect. Of course, the contact at the homes frequently leads to sales of insurance that might otherwise not be made. The name of this insurance is derived from the fact that it is usually sold to industrial workers who are paid weekly and, therefore, find it convenient to pay for insurance weekly.

Industrial policies are only rarely written for as much as $1,000 of protection; policies of $500 or less are much more common. The average size policy is $420. Because of their small weekly cash premiums, more policies of this type have been written than any other sort. The little protection they afford, however, makes all of them together amount to but a small fraction of total life insurance protection in force. These policies are particularly useful to pay funeral expenses, and it is not unusual to find a half-dozen of them in force in a single family (covering both parents and children).

Although the straight life contract was the first sort to be sold in the industrial insurance form, other types, particularly endowment, are now sold widely; but term insurance is not written on an industrial basis. The Metropolitan Life Insurance Company, the Prudential Insurance Company, and the John Hancock Mutual Life Insurance Company do a large volume of business with industrial insurance, these three firms together accounting for perhaps three fourths of the total. More than 95 million industrial policies are in force today, amounting to $40 billion; this compares with total life insurance outstanding of $675 billion (290 million policies). Death benefits payable annually on industrial policies now run to $358 million a year. Because of the small amount of protection under each policy, medical examinations are sometimes (particularly on children) not required.

Usually, industrial policies are issued on the basis of the soliciting agent's recommendation and the applicant's own statements as to his medical history and present condition of health. If the insured warrants that he is in "sound health," receives a policy, and then dies within a year or two, the company may investigate, find that the state of health had been misrepresented, and reject the insurance claim. If an examination is required, it may be less thorough than in ordinary policies, in order to keep the cost in line with the small premium. These facts produce rather high mortality experience (20 percent higher for industrial policyholders than for others)—another factor making for high cost of industrial insurance.[8]

Policy lapses are large, sometimes amounting to as much as new policies written, in spite of the fact that the agent is penalized for allowing policies on which he is collecting (technically, "in his debit") to lapse. Thus the life of these policies is short. Moreover, the cost of writing the policies and salesmen's commissions must be absorbed so soon that we have another of the causes of high cost.

In spite of high costs and low cash surrender and loan values, these industrial policies appear to be necessary, since altogether too many people would have no insurance at all if it were not possible to pay low weekly premiums to an agent obligated to call at the residence of the insured to collect. If you can afford the lower-cost ordinary insurance, you will find it wise to avoid industrial insurance, which, through no fault of the insurance companies, must sell at substantially higher rates.

Credit Life Insurance

There has been a phenomenal growth in credit life insurance over the last decade paralleling the growth of consumer credit. Credit life insurance is written through lenders on the lives of borrowers and installment purchasers. It assures full payment of loans in the event of death, thus leaving survivors in the debtor's family free of his indebtedness. More than 47 million policies are outstanding for a total of $38 billion. The average amount covered per policy or certificate under credit life insurance amounts to $800.

Most credit life insurance (five sixths) is written on a group basis and is, therefore, relatively inexpensive. However, there have been repeated instances of abuse all over the country with some lenders or installment dealers adding on from 50 to 100 percent of the actual cost of the premium as a "pack," thus overcharging the unsuspecting borrower.

Payment of Premiums

It is preferable, if possible, to pay premiums on an annual basis. However, arrangements can usually be made to pay semiannually, quarterly, or even monthly. In the latter cases, the company does not

[8] See "Cost and Coverage of Industrial Life Insurance," *Yale Law Review*, Vol. LXI, No. 1, pp. 46–75.

obtain the total premium so soon, and it must, therefore, be paid interest for the delay. In addition, several payments in each year rather than one single premium payment increase the costs of sending out notices and keeping the records, so that it may cost you 10–15 percent extra to avail yourself of the privilege of making partial payments. Of course, the average person is paid weekly or monthly; and it is somewhat of a hardship to pay a large insurance premium at one time, just as it is to pay a large real estate or income tax bill. One way out of the difficulty is to take out several smaller policies, instead of one larger one, having each payable in a different month, providing, of course, that you stay with ordinary insurance and do not resort to industrial. Each of the smaller policies can be paid on an annual basis, with staggered due dates, thus achieving the economies of annual payment for the policyholder.

How Life Insurance Policies Pay Off

If you married a showgirl with maximum figure and minimum brain, better study the "settlement options" in your life insurance contract carefully. It just wouldn't make sense to leave her $10,000 or $20,000 in a lump sum. If, on the other hand, your wife has the family's Phi Beta Kappa key, makes out the budget, pays the bills, fills out the income tax forms, etc., you may not have to read the following section so carefully.

Apart from a lump-sum cash settlement, there are four settlement options, as Table 7–5 shows. All four are explained in your life insurance policy. If the *interest* option is chosen, the company holds and invests the money until the beneficiary needs it; in the meantime, it sends him regular checks for the interest which his money has earned. If an *amount* option is chosen, a regular income of as much money as you want per month will be paid until the money and interest are gone; for example, if you have a $10,000 policy and want $100 a month, the company will be able to pay you this amount for nine years and three months. If you chose a *time* option, the company will pay, for the period you specify, a monthly amount fixed to last for the period selected; for example, if you wish some income for at least 20 years, the company will pay $51 a month for the 20 years. If the *lifetime income* option is chosen, a regular income is paid as long as the person named to receive it lives; the monthly amount will be less for a younger person, more for an older person.

If the insurance company has contracted to pay monthly installments for a certain number of years and the beneficiary dies before payments are completed, remaining payments will be made to the estate of the insured in the absence of a second, named beneficiary. You, as the insured, may either choose the plan by which settlement is to be made or leave the choice of settlement options to your beneficiary. Some people have their insurance payable to a bank as trustee

TABLE 7–5

The Four Optional Settlements

This table shows what a person can do if he has $10,000 coming to him from a life insurance policy and if he wants to receive this money as income rather than in a single cash payment.

WHAT $10,000 WILL PROVIDE UNDER THE FOUR SETTLEMENT OPTIONS:

THE INTEREST OPTION: Money left at interest until the family asks for it	$250 a year at 2½% interest, until the money is withdrawn
THE AMOUNT OPTION: A regular income of as much money as you want, paid until money and interest are gone	$100 a month for 9 years and 3 months, or $200 a month for 4 years and 4 months
THE TIME OPTION: A monthly income to last as many years as you want, paid until money and interest are gone	10 years income of $92 a month, or 20 years income of $51 a month
THE LIFETIME INCOME OPTION: A regular income guaranteed for the person's lifetime	$57.60 a month for life (for a woman 65 years old) $67.25 a month for life (for a man 65 years old)

SOURCE: Institute of Life Insurance.

and indicate in a trust agreement how the money is to be used. The method you select should take into consideration the financial capacity of your beneficiary and his or her needs.

Beneficiaries

When you take out a policy, you have the right to name a beneficiary to whom the policy is payable in case of your death. You may also retain the right to change the beneficiary later, if you deem it wise to do so. A wife designated as beneficiary must ordinarily consent to a change of beneficiary in community-property states.

If a beneficiary is not named, the proceeds will be paid to the insured's estate, where they will be subject to creditors' claims and to inheritance and estate taxes. In some states, the proceeds are subject to inheritance taxes, even when there is a named beneficiary; but sometimes amounts of less than about $10,000 escape this tax if left to immediate relatives. A federal estate tax applies to estates where there is a net value over $60,000. It also applies when the proceeds go to a named beneficiary if the insured retained such incidents of ownership in the policy as the right to change beneficiaries, to borrow with the policy as sole security, or to surrender the policy for cash.

At times it is sensible to name a contingent beneficiary to receive the proceeds if the primary beneficiary should predecease the insured. Frequently, children are named *contingent* beneficiaries. If the children are young, money for them may perhaps be better left to a trustee, to be administered for their benefit. Possible future children should be included in the wording. In the event that one child dies, his share may be left to his children or be divided among his brothers and sisters. Since this is all very technical, the average person will have to depend for guidance on his life insurance agent, who, after a few years of experience, is well versed in these complexities and usually can render good advice or can obtain it from others in his company. If you get to the point where your estate is substantial, then it will be advisable to obtain the services of a competent attorney who knows a good deal about estate planning.

What's in Your Life Insurance Policy?

"The big print gives it to you, the fine print takes it away," a lawyer once remarked in reading a contract. In the case of your insurance policy, however, the fine print confers many more benefits than it takes away.[9]

Have you ever taken the time to read your life insurance policy? Do you know the benefits it offers to you and to those for whom you bought the protection?

Most likely your policy came to you carefully folded. On its back you will notice your name, your policy number, its amount, and the date it was issued. The amount of your premiums and the type of policy are also written here.

---

[9] The Institute of Life Insurance, 277 Park Ave., New York, N.Y., 10017, will send you, gratis, a specimen "Institute Life Company" contract to enable you to see what a representative policy is like. It will also send you a copy of its booklet *What's in Your Life Insurance Policy?* Both of these publications, especially when read together, are very useful.

Open your policy. On the first page you will find the main part of the contract. Your policy states that the XYZ Life Insurance Company insures your life. You are called the *insured.* The company agrees to pay $_____, the *face amount,* to the person you have named, called the *beneficiary.* In return, you promise to make a periodic payment, called a *premium,* to the company. If you fail to make the premium payment within the *grace period* (usually 31 days after a premium is due), your policy *lapses,* which means that the policy comes to an end, unless it can be kept in force on a different basis by *nonforfeiture provisions,* such as *policy loan* against *cash value, reduced paid-up* insurance, *extended term* insurance, or *automatic premium* loan, all previously described. Sometimes, after your policy has lapsed, you may put it into full effect again (*reinstate it*), provided (*a*) you have not turned it in for cash, (*b*) that you again qualify as a good risk (*are insurable*), and (*c*) that, of course, you pay the back, overdue premiums. Your policy will be *incontestable* after either one or two years, usually two. During this initial period the company has the opportunity to check the information you gave in your application. After the period of contestability, the company cannot withdraw from the contract or contest it.

Your policy will probably have a number of special clauses. Life insurance policies will not pay off for death by suicide if it occurs during a stated period, usually the first year or two of the contract. The *suicide clause* states that the company will return the premiums paid in case of suicide during this period. There are occasionally other *limitations of coverage,* which at times exclude payment when death results from abnormal risks, such as travel in dangerous places or by dangerous means of conveyance, or death due to war, if there is a *war clause.*

In some states, the law permits you to include in the settlement arrangements a so-called *spendthrift clause,* which protects your beneficiaries from the claims of their own creditors. In most states, your life insurance, if payable to named beneficiaries rather than to your estate, is already protected from the claims of your own creditors, unless it can be shown that funds were purposely diverted in order to bypass the creditors.

Your policy may contain *waiver-of-premium* and *double indemnity* clauses. Under the former clause, any premiums which fall due after the beginning of total and permanent disability will be waived. In effect, the company will pay them. Disability must occur before you reach a certain age, usually 60, and before the policy matures, if it is an endowment. The disability must last for at least six months before premiums will be waived.

The accidental death benefit, or *double indemnity,* provides that an additional sum, equal to the face of the policy, will be paid if death occurs by accidental means. Accidental death must occur within a certain time after the injury, usually 90 days, and before a certain age, usually 60 or 65. The double indemnity clause usually says that certain causes of death are not covered.

Both clauses require small additions to the premium to cover the extra cost to the company, but both enjoy wide favor, especially the waiver of premium, without which many incapacitated insured persons would be forced to drop their policies. Life insurance thus protects against "economic death," whether casket or disability. The latter, however, must be total and permanent. Partial or temporary disability comes under *casualty insurance.*

Commissions, Dividends, and Reserves

A number of questions always come up in class discussion on these three points. The first one invariably is: "How much of my premium goes to the insurance agent as his commission?" The answer depends on the type of policy and on whether you mean first-year commission or that on your premium payments in subsequent years. Naturally, since a greater effort is involved in initially selling the policy, the first-year commission is higher than those of subsequent years. On an ordinary whole life policy, the average agent receives from 40 to 55 percent of your first year's premium. Thus, if you buy $10,000 of whole life at say age 23 and pay a $200 annual premium, the agent will get about half of this the first year. On term insurance policies, he gets a smaller percentage on, of course, a smaller premium. On one-year renewable term, he will get about 20 percent; on five- or ten-year renewable term about 30 percent. For the next nine years, after the first, they receive 5 percent on most policies.

"Why do some companies pay 'dividends' on policies, while others do not?" First of all, the term "dividends" as used in insurance parlance does not mean the same thing as it does in finance and investments. In insurance, a dividend is a partial return of your own money; it is a *refund* of part of the premium you paid. To make this clear, a number of other things need to be explained first.

Insurance companies are of two kinds: stock and mutual. Policies are of two kinds: participating and nonparticipating. A stock company is similar in its corporate organization to any other corporation. The stockholders own the capital and surplus. They take the risk of loss and are entitled to any profits. The stock company sells life insurance at guaranteed rates, guaranteed neither to increase nor decrease. Because of competition, the premium rates are kept as low as possible. If they are too low, the stockholders take a loss; if they are more than is exactly sufficient, there is a profit.

A mutual company, on the other hand, is "a co-operative association of persons established for the purpose of insuring their own lives." There are no stockholders to receive any profits nor to absorb losses. Hence, the gross premium rates in mutual companies may be higher than stock company rates to cover all contingencies. Mutual company rates are usually set high enough so that there is usually a refund, which the insurance salesman calls a dividend, to the policyowner, after his policy has been in force for a certain time.

Policies sold with a higher gross premium and a subsequent refund (dividend) are called participating policies. Those sold on a lower guaranteed rate without refund are called nonparticipating. The Institute of Life Insurance declares:

> Life insurance dividends are a return to policyholders of the unused portion of premiums paid. They are refunds given after actual costs have been determined. Premiums on participating policies are purposely set at a higher rate than would normally be necessary in order to provide funds which might be needed for unforeseen emergencies. At the end of each year, the company totals the amount actually paid for death claims and operating expenses, and determines the amount of money earned on investments. After the amount required by law has been added to the policy reserve fund, another portion may be added to supplementary reserves for the policyholders benefit. The excess is then returned as policy dividends. Since non-participating policies do not pay dividends, the premiums you pay represent the actual cost of your policy.[10]

Premiums do vary from company to company, though not too much. If you do "shop" for insurance, then, be sure that when comparing rates of a stock and a mutual company, you compare net premium rates, not gross. That is, ask for the rate after the refund dividend, not before.

Just as the term "dividend" when used in the insurance sense is misunderstood, generally so is the word "reserves." There is a misconception that the term "reserves" maintained by insurance companies represents surplus or accumulated profits. It does not. U.S. insurance

---

[10] *Your Life Insurance and How It Works,* Institute of Life Insurance, New York. A free copy may be obtained by writing to the Institute at 277 Park Ave., New York, N.Y., 10017.

companies are "legal reserve" companies, that is, they are required by law to set aside part of the premium you pay in a reserve fund to meet their future liability to your beneficiary. Thus, the reserve does not represent either earned surplus or profit but is the amount of money which together with future premiums and interest earnings will insure the ability of the company to carry out policy obligations whenever they mature. This is the primary reason why reserves are required by law. The way in which the reserve behind your policy builds up as you continue to pay premiums may be seen in Tables 7–6 and 7–7 and in

TABLE 7–6

Approximate Cash Values, Whole Life ($1,000) (CSO 2½%)

	At End of Year							At Age	
Age	2	3	4	5	10	15	20	60	65
20	$ 4	$ 16	$ 28	$ 40	$105	$167	$236	$546	$623
25	8	21	35	49	124	196	274	523	603
30	12	28	44	60	146	229	316	493	578
35	18	36	55	73	171	264	360	455	547
40	23	44	66	87	198	302	406	406	506
45	30	54	79	103	227	342	453	342	453
50	37	65	93	120	259	384	499	259	384
55	45	77	108	140	292	425	542	140	292
60	54	89	125	159	324	462	585	..	159
65	63	102	141	178	352	501	622	..	..

Source: *Flitcraft Compend* (New York: Flitcraft Corp.).

TABLE 7–7

Cash Values, 20-Year Endowment
per $1,000 (CSO 2½%)

	At End of Year							At Age	
Age	2	3	4	5	10	15	20	60	65
20	$63	$106	$149	$194	$434	$698	$1000	..	..
25	63	106	149	194	434	698	1000	..	..
30	64	106	150	195	435	698	1000	..	..
35	65	107	151	196	435	697	1000	..	..
40	65	108	152	196	435	695	1000	1000	..
45	66	109	152	197	434	692	1000	692	1000
50	66	109	153	198	432	687	1000	432	687
55	68	111	155	199	430	679	1000	..	430
60	69	111	155	199	428	669	1000	..	199
65	70	112	156	199	425	660	1000	..	..

Source: *Flitcraft Compend* (New York: Flitcraft Corp.).

Figures 7–9 and 7–10. The "net amount which the company has at risk" decreases as the reserve behind the policy builds up. Another way of looking at this is that increasingly your savings (cash value) are accumulating to enable the company to pay its liability to your beneficiary. The longer your policy runs (assuming it is permanent insurance and not term), the more the cumulation of your savings reduces the company's "risk."

FIGURE 7–9

AS THE CASH VALUES INCREASE . . .
THE NET AMOUNT AT RISK DECREASES

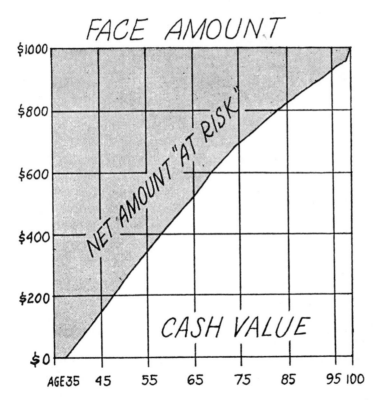

A **Policy Picture** of a hypothetical ordinary life contract written at age 35. Note that the cash value builds up until age 100, when it equals the face amount. Thus, as the cash value increases, the net amount at risk decreases.

Observe there is no cash value in this particular policy until the end of the second year because the expenses incurred by the company in writing the policy are greater than the total of the premiums paid by the policyowner. Some special policy forms provide a first-year cash value.

SOURCE: Life Insurance Agency Management Association.

FIGURE 7–10

How Cash Values Build Up for $10,000 of Insurance for Each of Four Types of Life Insurance Policies Taken Out at Age 22*

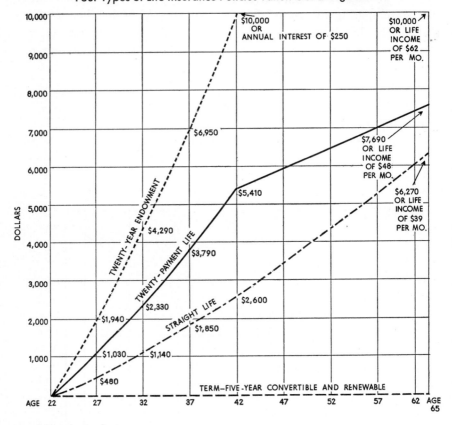

* Approximate values.
SOURCE: Institute of Life Insurance.

Pointers for Policyholders

As a policyholder, be sure to do these five things, which will help you and your beneficiaries:

1. *Read Your Life Insurance Policy.* Be sure you understand its basic provisions and benefits, as well as its limitations and restrictions. If you have any questions, do not hesitate to ask your agent; or write to the company or to your state insurance department.

2. *Keep Your Policy in a Safe Place.* Actually your policy has no value to a stranger who might find or take it. Moreover, your company will issue a duplicate policy if yours should be lost or destroyed by fire. A safe deposit box is a good place to keep the policy, but it has the disadvantage that, after the death of the insured, the box may not be

opened except by court order. Let your beneficiaries or attorney know where your policies are, for, in order to obtain payment, your beneficiary must turn the policy over to the company or give reasonable proof of loss.

3. *Keep Your Company Informed of Your Address.* Each year a number of policyholders move without either leaving a forwarding address or notifying their insurance companies. There may be dividend checks to be mailed to you; or if you let your policy lapse, the company will want to mail you a form on which to indicate your choice of nonforfeiture options.

4. *Discuss Your Insurance Program with Your Family or Other Beneficiaries.* It is usually advisable to have them share in the planning from the outset and to discuss with them each addition to or change in the program. It is a good idea also to leave a letter outlining your insurance policies and indicating any choices the beneficiary may have in the settlement of the policies. It may be well to point out (*a*) that no outside assistance is needed in order to collect the insurance money and (*b*) that your life insurance agent will help your beneficiary fill out the "proof-of-claim" papers and assist in selecting a settlement option if the choice is left to the beneficiary.

5. *Review Your Insurance Program Periodically.* We live in a changing world. A program for insurance which is sensible for any of us when we are 20 years old may no longer fit our needs when we are age 40 and may be ridiculous when we are 60 years of age. Consequently, the wise person will review his insurance periodically, perhaps every five or ten years, and consider its adequacy, not only alone but in connection with his other assets and the persons who look to him for protection. Able insurance men, bank trust officers, investment counsel, and attorneys are often helpful in assisting the ordinary person to rearrange his total financial program so that it will reasonably meet the apparent needs.

Government Insurance

During World War I, the United States government made life insurance available for members of the armed forces. Veterans of World War I, in good health, may still obtain it (total limit $10,000). Known as "United States Government Life Insurance," it was issued as five-year renewable term, straight life, 20-payment life, 30-payment life, 20-year endowment, 30-year endowment, and endowment at age 62.

Insurance sold by the government to servicemen in World War II and those who served thereafter up until April 25, 1951, is known as "National Service Life Insurance." NSLI was issued to eligible persons in any amount from $1,000 to $10,000 in multiples of $500. Originally, five-year, level premium, participating, term insurance was sold. All five-year term policies applied for and issued before January 1, 1946, were automatically extended for an additional period of three years at the same premium rates by an act of Congress in 1945. Presently, the term insurance may be renewed, prior to expiration of the term, for new terms, every five years, without a physical examination, at the premium rate for the then-attained age. It may also be converted into any one of six permanent plans: ordinary life, 30-payment life, 20-payment life, 20-year endowment, endowment at age 60, or endowment at age 65.

NSLI insurance was one of the best insurance buys ever offered, and those who have it should retain it. The cost was and is very low, for a variety of reasons. There was no loading charge, that is, the government paid the costs of the insurance operation out of budgetary funds, with no charge by way of premiums. Veterans who died in service, or later, as a result of service-connected disabilities, had death benefits paid from government appropriations rather than from insurance reserves. Dividends have been very generous. It has been reported that 67 cents has been paid out in dividends for every dollar collected in National Service Life Insurance premiums. The dividend windfall resulted primarily because fewer World War II veterans died than experience had indicated. There are many favorable clauses and features, as, for example, settlement option No. 4, refund life income, which, for the NSLI low rate, no commerical insurance company can match. The advantage of refund life income is that, not only may the beneficiary choose to receive the proceeds of the policy in monthly installments as long as he or she lives, but if, upon his or her death, the amount paid out in these monthly installments has not equaled the face amount of the policy, the remainder is paid to the contingent beneficiary.

Veterans of the Korean conflict, that is, all those called to active duty for 31 days or more on and after June 27, 1950, as well as those who served after the war, until January 1, 1957, were treated differently under the Servicemen's Indemnity and Insurance Acts of 1951, which became effective April 25, 1951. They were automatically covered by a free indemnity against death in active service for $10,000, less any NSLI or USGLI in force at time of death. This free indemnity protection, at no charge to the servicemen, continued for 120 days after separation from service. The insurance was payable only to surviving spouse, child or children, parent, brother, or sister; and the insured could name one or more beneficiaries within this permitted class. The $10,000 indemnity was payable in 120 equal installments of $92.90 per month.

Within 120 days after they were released from active service, but before January 1, 1957, veterans who were *not disabled* could apply for a five-year level premium term policy that could be renewed every five years at the premium rate for the then-attained age. This insurance was at first not convertible to any other form of government life insurance, nor did it pay dividends. No physical examination was needed to obtain it, only payment of the first premium. A veteran was allowed to take out from $1,000 to $10,000 of this term insurance, less any other government life insurance in force at the time of application. In 1958 the law was changed to permit conversion to any of a variety of permanent plans.

Today, anyone entering military service is protected in two ways; by what is called a "six-month's death gratuity," and by "in-service guaranty of commerical insurance premiums." Under the death gratuity a serviceman's beneficiaries may be entitled to a sum equal to six months' pay if a veteran's death occurs while he is on active duty, active duty for training or inactive duty training, or if he dies of a service-connected cause within 120 days after discharge or release from duty. The minimum gratuity payable is $800, the maximum is $3,000, regardless of the monthly service pay of the deceased.

Under the in-service guaranty, if a commercial insurance policy has been in effect for 180 days or more, the United States will guarantee the payment of premiums for the period of active service and for two years thereafter on policies not exceeding $10,000. Any money which the Veterans Administration is required to pay to an insurance company must be repaid by the serviceman. When he leaves active duty he has two years to resume regular premium payments and to repay any premiums which the government has paid plus interest.

For the present-day serviceman, unless he incurs a service-connected disability, GI life insurance is not available in any form.

SUGGESTED READINGS

1. J. B. MacLean, *Life Insurance*. 9th ed. New York: McGraw-Hill Book Co., Inc., 1962.
2. Clyde S. Cassady, *A Buyer's Guide to Life Insurance*. Latest rev. ed. Boston:

Savings Bank Life Insurance Council. A Free copy may be obtained by writing to the Council at 47 Franklin Street, Boston, Mass., 02110.

3. R. Wilfred Kelsey and Arthur C. Daniels, *Handbook of Life Insurance.* New York: Institute of Life Insurance, latest edition. A free copy may be obtained by writing to the Institute at 277 Park Ave., New York, N.Y., 10017.

4. Davis W. Gregg, *Life and Health Insurance Handbook.* 2d ed. Homewood, Ill.: Richard D. Irwin, Inc., 1964.

5. W. J. Matteson and E. C. Harwood, *Life Insurance and Annuities from the Buyer's Point of View.* Great Barrington, Mass.: American Institute for Economic Research, latest edition.

6. *Life Insurance Fact Book,* Institute of Life Insurance, New York. Latest annual number. A free copy may be obtained by writing to the Institute at 277 Park Ave., New York, N.Y., 10017.

7. *Decade of Decision,* a life and health insurance primer for college students. New York: Institute of Life Insurance. A free copy may be obtained by writing to the Institute.

8. *Facts You Should Know about Life Insurance,* Educational Division, National Better Business Bureau, Chrysler Building, New York, N.Y., 10017, latest edition.

9. Robert I. Mehr and Robert W. Osler, *Modern Life Insurance.* 3d ed. New York: Macmillan Co., 1961.

10. Davis W. Gregg, *Group Life Insurance.* 3d ed. Homewood, Ill.: Richard D. Irwin, Inc., 1962.

11. *What's in Your Life Insurance Policy?* New York: Institute of Life Insurance, latest edition. A free copy may be obtained by writing to the Institute.

12. Janice E. Greider and William T. Beadles, *Law and the Life Insurance Contract.* Homewood, Ill.: Richard D. Irwin, Inc., 1960.

13. Barbara H. Hathaway, *Your Life Insurance.* New York: Doubleday & Co., Inc., 1962.

14. Life Insurance Association of America for Commission on Money and Credit, *Life Insurance Companies as Financial Institutions.* Englewood Cliffs, N.J.: Prentice-Hall, Inc., 1962.

15. *How Much and What Kind of Life Insurance Should I Own?* Hartford: The Connecticut Mutual Life Insurance Co. A free copy may be obtained by writing to the company.

16. In *Changing Times, The Kiplinger Magazine:*
"Is Your Life Insurance Up To Date?" May, 1964.
"Life Insurance—With Dividends or Without?" April, 1964.
"Straight Life: Best All-Around Policy," July, 1963.
"Your GI Insurance Today," June, 1963.
"Buy Term Insurance and Invest the Difference?" October, 1962.
"Trade in Your Life Insurance Policy?" December, 1961.
"Life Insurance: The Pay-Off," May, 1961.
"How to Buy Life Insurance," November, 1960.
"Borrowing on Your Life Insurance," March, 1960.
"Insure Your Insurability," January, 1960.

"The New 'Family Plan' Life Insurance," April, 1958.

"Group Life Insurance," December, 1957.

"Life Insurance, Yes—But What Kind?" September, 1957.

"How They Bought Their Life Insurance," May, 1957.

"How to Settle an Insurance Claim," May, 1956.

"How Much Life Insurance Do You Need," February, 1956.

"Your Life Insurance: How to Plan It Right," September, 1954.

"Should You Buy Term Insurance?" April, 1953.

"How Life Insurance Policies Pay Off," October, 1952.

"Which Kind of Life Insurance Policy?" December, 1951.

17. Donald R. Johnson, *Savings Bank Life Insurance*. Homewood, Ill.: Richard D. Irwin, Inc., 1963.

CASE PROBLEMS

1. Sally and Charles Donaldson, 30 and 32 years old respectively, are working for the same concern. Together, they earn about $8,500 per year after taxes, but Charles has chronic heart trouble and is frequently ill. They have one child.

They have a five-year term policy with no conversion clause which expires next year. They also have Blue Cross and Blue Shield coverage. Their employer is now offering group insurance, and they are wondering if they should take it. What is your advice?

2. Jack Jamison, age 35, is earning $10,000 annually. He and his wife, Mary, have no children. Jack's company provides for early retirement at age 60 on a pension amounting to about ⅓ of average salary for the prior ten years, and he plans to take advantage of this opportunity. With this in mind Jack decides to purchase a $20,000, 20-payment life insurance policy. Is he wise?

3. Daniel and Helen Smith (three children, ages 2, 5, and 7) have $25,000 of straight life insurance (cash-surrender value, $7,200). They own their home and an automobile; there are no other assets. They have been living comfortably on his salary of $160 a week. Now his employer transfers his business from Boston to Los Angeles. Daniel and Helen want to remain in Boston. Another suitable job may be hard to find. Daniel's health is not as good as it used to be. What should they do?

4. Martin Skoler is 25 years old. He lives with his widowed mother and is just about to set up a law practice. Martin's mother is self-supporting and her home is paid for. Now he is thinking of buying some life insurance and is trying to decide which kind would be best for him. What would you suggest?

5. Samuel Becker is a 40-year-old businessman with an income of $10,000–$12,000 a year. He is married and has four children ranging from 1–10 years old. Samuel already carries a $10,000 straight life insurance policy and would now like to take out enough insurance to protect his wife and children until the youngest child reaches 21. What insurance program would you suggest for him?

6. John Allison is planning to buy some life insurance. He notices that different companies charge different rates for the same types of insurance. He wonders why this is so. Advise him.

7. Grace Robinson (age 26) is a kindergarten teacher. She is single; her father, mother, and two older brothers are living. An agent tries to sell her $5,000 of 5-year term insurance. Should she buy it? Why? Why not?

8. John Sullivan (wife and two children, ages 6 and 9) has a $20,000 term policy which is expiring. It is convertible into straight life (cost, $25 per $1,000) or endowment (cost, $40 per $1,000). The family has been able to save little. Every month they have had difficulty paying $15 on the term policy. What should John do?

9. Peter Quirk's job pays well ($150 a week), but it is not steady. Sometimes he is out of work for three months at a time. He has a wife and three small children (ages 2, 4, and 5). As long as he has work, the family feels that it can spend about $250 a year for insurance. The agent tells him he ought to buy a $10,000 straight life policy. Do you agree?

10. Joseph, Patrick, and Michael are three brothers. Joseph took out a $10,-000 term policy. Patrick bought a $10,000 straight life policy. Michael bought a $10,000 10-year endowment policy. Three years later they were all killed in one automobile accident. Each left a wife and two small children; their other assets were negligible. Comment.

11. Jack Gunnison is 22 years old. He and his wife have decided to take out a $10,000 straight life policy on him. The cost is $20 annually per $1,000 of insurance. After necessary expenses of running the home, they have $400 left over each year for other things. They are expecting a baby. Gunnison is strong and healthy and drives a truck for a living. The agent advises them to take a 30-payment life policy which will cost $5 extra per $1,000 per annum. What are the arguments pro and con? Do you think the limited-payment life policy is preferable in their case?

12. Lawrence and Martha Washington have three children (ages 4, 6, and 7). They own their home and have sufficient insurance for current protection and old age. Their principal worry is concerned with their children's education. An agent tries to sell them a $10,000, 10-year endowment policy on each of the children. Should they buy? Why?

13. Ronald Smithers (two children, ages 19 and 23) works for the Jonas Corporation. He and his wife think that, with $20,000 of straight life insurance, they have enough insurance. What they have costs $400 a year, which seems to be large in relation to what he earns ($80 a week). The Jonas Company offers Smithers a group participation of $4,000 of insurance for 60 cents per month per $1,000. Smithers is 50 years old, and his health is beginning to fail. Should he take the group insurance?

14. Frank Jackson (age 57) has paid his premiums faithfully on his straight life policy for 30 years. Now he is in ill health and has retired. His company has pensioned him, and the pension is just enough to support him and his wife. They live in a rented flat. He can no longer afford to pay the insurance premiums. What should he do?

15. While the family was growing up, James Colson and his wife paid premiums on $20,000 of endowment insurance, which has matured, and on

$30,000 of straight life insurance, with annual premiums of $600. The children are now grown up and prosperous. James's wife has just died. He is 67 years old, is worth $80,000, and wonders what to do about the straight life insurance. Does he need it? What would you advise?

8

SOCIAL SECURITY, ANNUITIES, AND PENSIONS*

The essence of social insurance is bringing the magic of averages to the rescue of the millions.
—*Winston Churchill*

YOUR little white and blue social security card represents a combination of retirement pension, life insurance, and disability protection which may be worth more than $100,000 to you and your dependents.

To Tom Linen of Columbia, South Carolina, social security was something you collected when you were old and could no longer work. Or benefits your wife and children received after your death. So the money that was taken out of his wages at the paper mill each payday for social security did not have much relevancy to his young, healthy, everyday life.

On July 10, 1962, Tom had a serious accident while working and suffered a spinal cord injury that caused him to become completely paralyzed. Neither Tom nor his wife thought of social security while trying to make plans to repair their shattered lives. Then, many months later, a friend casually remarked to Mrs. Linen, "Of course, Tom's social security disability benefits must be a big help. . . ."

Mrs. Linen lost no time in applying for social security disability insurance benefits on Tom's behalf, and for herself and their four minor children as dependents. Tom's doctor supplied the medical evidence that showed the Social Security Administration that he had a severe, long-term disability that qualified him for payments.

But even with the delay in making application, there was no loss in benefits. Social security can be paid retroactively for up to 12 months. Tom and his family received just over $1,500 in their first benefit checks. They will receive $254 a month while the children are still young and his condition remains disabling. Tom will receive $119 a

---

* For 1965 legislation on social security, see "The New Medicare and Social Security Provisions" following p. 850.

month for himself after all the children have reached age 18. Mrs. Linen can again become a beneficiary when she attains age 62. Total benefits may add up over their lifetime to more than $100,000.

Mrs. Ronnie Armstrong, age 17, of Greencastle, Pennsylvania, knew that social security paid old-age, survivors, and disability insurance benefits. But when her 18-year old husband was killed at work on April 13, 1963, she was pretty sure that there would be no payments for her—Ronnie Armstrong had been employed but a short time under social security before his tragic death. However, a call at the social security office brought out the news that the law had a special provision to cover cases such as hers, and that benefits could be paid if the worker had a minimum of a year and a half in covered employment.

Ronnie had that much covered work and a little more. Mrs. Armstrong was paid a lump-sum death payment shortly after making application. When a posthumous child was born a few months later, she and the child qualified for monthly payments of $103.60. Ronnie's wages as a beginning worker had been modest, which had a lowering effect on the benefit rate. Even so, the payments over the next 18 years could amount to more than $22,000, contributing importantly to the support of the mother and child.

If you were told that you had inherited $73,000—free from income and estate taxes—you would be interested, wouldn't you? You would want to know more about it. Well, social security can yield this amount and more. How?

If a father of two children, age one and two, dies in 1964 after having earned an annual salary of at least $3,600 in covered employment each year 1951 through 1954; $4200 annually 1955 through 1958; and $4800 in each following year through the year of his death in 1964:

a) His widow will receive a lump-sum death payment of $255.
b) His two children and their mother will receive payments of $254 a month until the two-year-old reaches age 18. Over a 16-year period this amounts to $48,768.
c) His younger child and the mother will then receive a benefit payment of $190.60 until the second child reaches age 18. This amounts to $2,287.20.

The young mother's benefit stops when there is no longer a child eligible for payments. However, she will begin receiving widow's benefits when she reaches age 62. She will then draw $104.80 a month for the rest of her life. Assuming that she lives to age 80, she will receive $22,636.80, making a grand total of $73,947, all tax free.

The Social Security Act

Congress first passed the Social Security Act in 1935, but it has been amended a number of times since. So many changes have been made over the years that the discussion which follows will be only in terms of the Act as it now stands. The work of nine out of ten Americans is now covered by social security.

Although the Social Security Act covers a wide variety of social insurance, unemployment insurance, public assistance, and health and welfare services, the federal government administers only the old-age and survivors insurance (OASI) program, and our discussion will be confined to this. Under it, those who work in employment or self-employment covered by the law make social security tax contributions during their working years to provide, as a matter of right and not as a matter of need, an income for themselves and their families when earnings cease in old age, and for their families in case of their death. Some 90 million living persons in the United States are fully insured under OASI, and over 18 million are already receiving monthly benefits. Of the 18 million persons receiving benefits, 12.5 million are retired workers and dependents, 5.0 are survivors of insured workers, and 950,000 are disabled workers. Payments to all beneficiaries now amount to more than $14 billion a year!

Kinds of Benefits

Broadly speaking, there are now three different kinds of benefits under OASI, namely, "retirement" benefits (or what we previously called "living" benefits), "survivors" (or "death") benefits, and "disability payments." When you become age 62 and retire, you and certain members of your family can become eligible for monthly insurance payments if you are fully insured. After you reach age 72, the payments may be made even if you have not retired. In the event of your death at any age, certain members of your family may receive insurance payments if you were either fully or currently insured at time of death.

If you become totally disabled and are unable to work, you may become eligible for monthly payments if you have social security credit for at least five years in the ten-year period ending when you become disabled. The different kinds of payments under the three major categories and the ways in which you must be insured for each are shown in the accompanying tabulation. You will notice that you are eligible for retirement benefits only if you are fully insured, whereas most survivors benefits are payable to your family if you are only currently insured.

Types of Payments

This table shows the different types of payments and how you must be insured for each.

RETIREMENT

Monthly payment to—	*If you are—*
You as a retired worker and your wife and child	Fully insured.

SURVIVORS

Monthly payments to your—	*If at death you are—*
Widow 62 or over	Fully insured
Widow (regardless of age) if caring for your child who is entitled to benefits	Either fully or currently insured.
Dependent child	Either fully or currently insured.
Dependent widower 62 or over ...	*Both* fully and currently insured.
Dependent parent 62 or over	Fully insured.
Dependent divorced wife (regardless of age) if caring for your child who is entitled to benefits .	Either fully or currently insured.
Lump-sum death payment	Either fully or currently insured.

DISABILITY

Monthly payments to—	*If you meet specified work requirements.*
You and your dependents if you are totally disabled for work	

What is the difference between being fully and currently insured, and how do you become insured?

Becoming Insured

To become eligible for monthly payments for yourself and your family, or for your survivors to get payments in case of your death, you must first have credit for a certain amount of work under social security. Social security credits are called "quarters of coverage." You can get social security credit for up to four quarters in a year. You may have earned social security credit (quarters of coverage) by working in employment covered by the law at any time after 1936 and in self-employment covered by the law after 1950.

Most people who work for someone else get one quarter of coverage for each calendar quarter in which they are paid total wages of $50 or more including the cash value of wages in kind.[1] If you receive wages of

---

[1] Wages in kind (such as meals or a room) do not count, however, if they are paid for work in private households, on farms, or in the Armed Forces.

$4,800 or more during a year, you get credit for all four quarters of that year even if you receive no wages in some of the quarters. If you are self-employed, you get social security credit for four calendar quarters for each taxable year in which you have net profit of $400 or more from self-employment covered by the law. If your net profit is less than $400 for any year, it does not count for social security.

There is no age limit. You get social security for work covered by the social security law no matter how young or how old you are. Most jobs, businesses, and professions are now covered by social security. Active duty in military service is also under social security. Your base pay is credited to your social security record. If you should stop working under social security before you have earned sufficient credit to become insured, no benefits will be payable to you. If you should later return to work covered by social security, regardless of your age, both your past earnings and any additional earnings will be combined in determining whether you qualify for benefits.

Fully Insured. For monthly benefits to be payable to you and your wife (or husband) in your old age, or to your aged widow (or widower) or aged dependent parents in case of your death, you must have worked under social security long enough to become "fully insured."

Just how much credit you must have to be fully insured depends upon the year you reach 65 if you are a man, or 62 if you are a woman, or upon the date of your death or disability if you die or become disabled before reaching that age.

You are fully insured if you have credit for at least as many years as shown on the appropriate line of Table 8–1.

TABLE 8–1

A worker who reaches 65 (62 for women) or dies:	Will need credit for no more than this much work:
In 1964	3¼ years
1965	3½
1966	3¾
1967	4
1968	4¼
1969	4½
1970	4¾
1971	5
1975	6
1979	7
1983	8
1987	9
1991 or later	10

Currently Insured. You will be currently insured if you have social security credit for at least 1½ years work within the three years before you die or become entitled to retirement benefits.[2]

How to Estimate Your Benefits

The exact amount of old-age and survivors or disability insurance benefits payable on your social security account can't be figured until a claim for benefits is made by you upon your retirement, or by your family in case of your death. This is because the benefits must be figured from the record of your earnings right up until the year that you retire or die.

But it's not hard to estimate how much would be payable to you and your dependents if you were now 65[3] and retired, and also how much would be payable to your family in the event of your death at this time.

Benefits are based on *average* monthly earnings. If your earnings in the future are higher than they have been up to now, your actual benefits may turn out to be higher than this estimate. If your earnings go down or if you are out of work for any long period of time, your actual benefits may be lower.

Old-Age Retirement Payments.[4] If you are fully insured, you and certain members of your family can be paid monthly benefits when you are 65 or over (benefits are payable as early as age 62 if the worker is fully insured, but in a reduced amount to take account of the longer period over which benefits will be paid.) It is not necessary to stop work completely to get benefits.[5]

The amount of your payments is figured from your average earnings under social security. The more regularly you work under social security and the higher your earnings, the higher your benefits will be.

Most people may figure their average yearly earnings by:

1. Counting the number of years after 1955 and up to, but not including, the year they reach 65 (62 for women). (If the result is less than 5, increase it to 5.)
2. Selecting an equal number of years after 1950 in which their earnings

---

[2] See *Your Social Security,* OASI–35, Social Security Administration, U.S. Department of Health, Education, and Welfare, Washington, D.C.

[3] You may choose to retire between age 62 and 65 and take reduced benefits (see Table 8–2).

[4] *Social Security Benefits—How You Earn Them—How Much Credit You Need,* OASI–855, Social Security Administration, U.S. Department of Health, Education, and Welfare, Washington, D.C.

[5] *You Don't Have to Retire Completely to Get Social Security Benefits,* OASI–23c, Social Security Administration, U.S. Department of Health, Education, and Welfare, Washington, D.C.

were highest. (Do not count more than: $3,600 a year for 1951–1954; $4,200 a year for 1955–1958; $4,800 a year for 1959 and after.)

3. Averaging their earnings in the selected years.

If you decide to start receiving benefits before you are 65, the amount of your monthly benefit will be reduced according to the number of months you are under 65. The closer you are to 65 when you start receiving payments, the smaller the reduction will be. A man who elects to retire at age 62 will receive roughly 80 percent of what he would get if he waited until age 65 to retire. Are you better off financially retiring at 62 or at 65? It depends, among other things, on how long you expect to live! If you die before 75, you'd come out ahead if you had begun at 62. If you die after 75, you'd probably have been better off waiting until 65 to retire.

You can estimate your average yearly earnings and find about what your benefit will be from Table 8–2.

Family Payments

Monthly payments can be made to certain of your dependents:

a) When you are receiving old-age or disability insurance benefits.
b) When you die.

These dependents are:

a) Unmarried children under 18 years of age.
b) Unmarried children 18 or over who were severely disabled before they reached 18 and have remained so since.
c) A wife or widow, regardless of her age, if she is caring for a child who is getting payments based on the worker's social security account.
d) A wife or widow 62 or older even if there are no children entitled to payments.
e) A dependent husband or widower 62 or over.

After the death of an insured worker, benefits may *also* be paid to:

f) Dependent parents at 62.
g) A divorced wife, if, before the worker's death, she is dependent on him for her support pursuant to a court order or agreement, and if she has in her care his child who is also entitled to payments.

If a person becomes entitled to monthly benefits based on the social security account of more than one worker, he will receive each month no more than the largest benefit. For example, a woman who is eligible for benefits based on her own earnings and also for wife's benefits based on the earnings of her husband will receive an amount equal to the larger of the two benefits. She will not receive both.

Amount of Your Family's Benefits. If you receive old-age or disability insurance benefits, the monthly payments to your wife, child, or

TABLE 8–2

Examples of Social Security Monthly Payments

AVERAGE YEARLY EARNINGS AFTER 1950	$800 OR LESS	$1,200	$1,800	$2,400	$3,000	$3,600	$4,200	$4,800
Retirement								
Retirement at 65 or later	$ 40.00	$ 59.00	$ 73.00	$ 84.00	$ 95.00	$105.00	$116.00	$127.00
Disability benefits								
Retirement at 64	37.40	55.10	68.20	78.40	88.70	98.00	108.30	118.60
Retirement at 63	34.70	51.20	63.30	72.80	82.40	91.00	100.60	110.10
Retirement at 62	32.00	47.20	58.40	67.20	76.00	84.00	92.80	101.60
Wife's benefit at 65 or with child in her care	20.00	29.50	36.50	42.00	47.50	52.50	58.00	63.50
Wife's benefit at 64	18.40	27.10	33.50	38.50	43.60	48.20	53.20	58.30
Wife's benefit at 63	16.70	24.60	30.50	35.00	39.60	43.80	48.40	53.00
Wife's benefit at 62	15.00	22.20	27.40	31.50	35.70	39.40	43.50	47.70
Survivors								
Widow 62 or over	40.00	48.70	60.30	69.30	78.40	86.70	95.70	104.80
Widow under 62 and 1 child	60.00	88.50	109.60	126.00	142.60	157.60	174.00	190.60
Widow under 62 and 2 children	60.00	88.50	120.00	161.60	202.40	236.40	254.00	254.00
One surviving child	40.00	44.30	54.80	63.00	71.30	78.80	87.00	95.30
Two surviving children	60.00	88.50	109.60	126.00	142.60	157.60	174.00	190.60
Maximum family payment	60.00	88.50	120.00	161.60	202.40	240.00	254.00	254.00
Lump-sum death payment	120.00	177.00	219.00	252.00	255.00	255.00	255.00	255.00

SOURCE: Social Security Administration.

dependent husband will be one half the amount of the benefit you receive. In the event of your death, your widow while under 62, and your children and parents (if both parents survive) will receive three fourths of your benefit amount. Your widow or widower over 62, or your parent, if only one parent is eligible, will receive 82½ percent of your benefit amount. However, benefits may be less than these amounts when they must be reduced to keep the total family payments within the maximum provided in the law.

If the wife of a living worker chooses to start getting payments before she reaches 65, she gets a reduced amount for as long as she receives wife's benefits unless she is caring for a child who is getting payments on her husband's account. However, full benefits are payable to a widow, at 62.

Lump-Sum Payments

After your death, in addition to regular monthly survivor payments to your wife and children under age 18, a lump sum of three times the amount of your monthly benefit may be paid to your widow or widower if you were living together. If there is no widow or widower, the person who paid the burial expenses can be repaid up to the amount of the lump sum. The payment may be three times the monthly insurance benefit, but not more than $255.

Who Pays for It?

Federal old-age and survivors insurance is paid for by a contribution (or tax) on the employee's wages and on the self-employed person's earnings from his trade or business. If you are employed, you and your employer will share equally in the tax. If you are self-employed, you pay three fourths as much as the total payment of employee and employer would on the same amount of earnings.

How Social Security Taxes Are Paid. If you are employed, your contribution is deducted from your wages each payday. The employer sends your contribution and his own matching contribution to the Director of Internal Revenue, with a report made out on Form 941. Employers of household workers may use a special envelope report, Form 942. If you are self-employed, you must report your earnings and pay your contribution each year when you file your individual income tax return. Schedule C-a of your income tax return Form 1040 should be used for this purpose. As long as you have earnings that are covered by the law, you continue to pay the social security tax regardless of your age.

The following tabulation shows the tax rates and the scheduled increases:

CALENDAR YEAR	EMPLOYEE (PERCENT)	EMPLOYER (PERCENT)	SELF-EMPLOYED (PERCENT)
1963–65	3⅝	3⅝	5.4
1966–67	4⅛	4⅛	6.2
1968 and after	4⅝	4⅝	6.9

Since January 1, 1959, earnings from employment or self-employment up to a total of $4,800 a year have been subject to the social security tax. Those who have earnings from both employment and self-employment pay contributions on their wages from employment. If these wages amount to less than $4,800, they also pay contributions on that part of their self-employment income necessary to bring the total up to $4,800 for a year.

From the social security tax report your wages and self-employment income are posted to your individual record by the Social Security Administration. This record of your earnings will be used to determine your eligibility for benefits and the amount you will receive.

The Social Security Trust Funds. The Old-Age and Survivors Insurance Trust Fund, the older and larger of the two social security trust funds, was set up in 1939 to finance the payments of old-age and survivors insurance benefits.

The newer of the two funds is the Disability Insurance Trust Fund. This fund was set up in 1956 to finance the benefits payable to persons who become totally disabled for any substantial work before they reach 65. Under amendments to the law, benefits are also payable from this fund to the dependents of disabled persons. A fixed part of the social security tax is earmarked to pay these disability benefits.

By law, the assets in these two trust funds can be used only for the payment of benefits and administrative expenses. The money in the funds not needed currently for the payment of benefits and operating expenses is invested in interest-bearing U.S. government bonds. The interest earned on these investments is added to the trust funds.

Special Refunds. Your social security taxes apply only to the first $4,800 of your earnings in any calendar year. However, if you have more than one employer, each different employer must deduct the tax from the first $4,800 of the wages he pays you in a year. You should keep a record of your employers' names and addresses and of the wages paid by each. If you pay the tax on total wages of more than $4,800 for any year, you may claim the excess tax (tax on that portion of the wages over $4,800) as credit on your income tax return for that year.

Claiming Benefits

Benefit payments, whether retirement, disability, or survivors, monthly or lump sum, are not made automatically. *An application for benefits must be filed before monthly payments or the lump sum can be paid.* The application should be filed promptly. Only 12 months of back payments can be made when an application is filed late; years of payments may be lost. The lump sum may be paid only if an application is filed within two years after the death of an insured person. Benefits payable to a child or to an incompetent adult are usually paid for his use to a parent or near relative. The place to file a claim is the nearest Social Security Administration field office. There you and your family will receive, free of charge, any help you need to make out the claim papers. If, because of sickness or distance, you cannot go to the social security office, you may write or telephone. The local post office will furnish the address of the nearest social security office.

Four Times for Action

There are four times when it is especially important to consult the social security office:

If a Worker in Your Family Dies. Some member of his family should inquire promptly at the social security office to learn if survivors insurance benefits are payable.

If You Become Disabled. If you become disabled after you have been in work covered by social security, you should get in touch with your social security office. You and your dependents may be eligible for monthly payments.

When You Are Near Retirement Age. When you approach 65 (62 if not working or working for low earnings), get in touch with your social security district office. Application for benefits may be filed in advance of retirement age, but even if you do not plan immediate retirement, you should get information about your social security rights. You need not be completely retired to get social security benefits.

When You Are 72. When you reach 72, if not receiving benefits, get in touch with your social security office. If you are insured, benefits may be payable to you even if you are working full time.

Many young people assume that social security is only for the elderly.

In fact, there are a broad number of payments, particularly for dependents, at varying ages in case of death of the primary insured or in case of total disability. For example, a young mother in California died, leaving three children under 18. Her husband did not apply for social security because he thought children could collect benefits only in the case of their father's death. His wife had worked as a nurse. He didn't know that benefits are payable to children under 18 if the mother had worked under social security coverage for at least 1½ years of the three years prior to her death. When he did apply, the children got the maximum family benefit of $254 a month, plus $3,048 for the previous 12 months.[6]

When Payments Stop

When you become entitled to monthly old-age or survivors insurance payments, you will receive a check each month unless certain events occur. The law lists some events that will stop the payment of monthly checks for only one or two months or for some longer period, and some that end your right to receive payments. These events are listed below. You must report promptly to the Social Security Administration if any of them happens in your case.

If You Work after Payments Start.[7]—If you are under 72 years of age and are receiving monthly payments as a retired worker and you earn more than $1,200 in a year, benefits will be affected as follows:

If you earn more than $1,200 in a year while under 72, $1.00 in your benefits (or your family benefits) may be withheld for each $2.00 you earn from $1,200 to $1,700.

For every $1.00 you earn over $1,700, $1.00 in benefits may be withheld.

EXAMPLE: You work throughout a year and earn a total of $1,750. Three hundred dollars (one-half of the first $500 over $1,200, plus the $50 over $1,700) in benefits would then be withheld for that year. If your monthly benefit rate (or the monthly family benefit rate) is $100, checks for the months of January, February, and March of that year would be held back to make up for the amount of benefits not due you.

EXCEPTION: Regardless of your total earnings for a year, however, benefits will be payable for any month in which you neither earn wages

---

[6] See Michael Belloise, "Are You Missing Out on Social Security Payments?" *Reader's Digest*, June, 1963.

[7] See *If You Work While You Get Social Security Payments*, OASI–23, Social Security Administration, U.S. Department of Health, Education, and Welfare, Washington, D.C.

of more than $100 nor perform substantial services in self-employment.

The decision as to whether you are performing substantial services in self-employment depends on the amount of time you devote to your business, the kind of services you perform, how your services compare with the services performed in past years, and other circumstances of your particular case.

Earnings from work of any kind, whether or not it is covered by the social security law, must be counted in figuring the amount of benefits due for a year. Total wages (not just take-home pay) and all net earnings from self-employment must be added together in figuring up your earnings for the year. However, income from savings, investments, pensions, and insurance does not affect your old-age or survivors insurance.

In the year in which you first become entitled to benefits, you must count your total earnings for the entire year in determining the amount of benefits that can be paid to you.

After you reach 72, you can earn any amount and still get payments for the months in which you are 72 or over.

Investment Income Does Not Affect Benefit Payments. People who don't get benefit checks because their earnings from work are too high sometimes wonder why others, with good incomes from stocks, bonds, or real estate, are nevertheless paid benefits. The reason is that the purpose of the program is to insure against loss of earnings from work.

Social security is not intended as a substitute for private savings, pension plans, and insurance protection. It is, rather, intended as a foundation upon which these other forms of protection can be built. If benefits were withheld from people who have income from savings, there would be less incentive for people to save to provide for a more comfortable life in their old age than social security benefits alone can provide.

Events That End Payments. If any person receiving monthly benefit payments as a dependent or as a survivor gets married, his or her right to payments stops. However, if a widow remarries and her second husband dies within a year after their marriage and she has no child by her second husband, she may regain her right to any benefits payable to her at age 62 under the social security account of her first husband.

Payments to a wife or dependent husband are ended if a divorce is granted.

A wife or widow under 62 or the divorced wife of an insured person may receive payments only while she has in her care a child who is also entitled to monthly payments.

Payments to a child stop when the child marries.

When a child entitled to benefits reaches age 18, his payments are stopped unless he is disabled. When the child of a deceased insured person is adopted, his payments end unless the adopting person is the child's stepparent, grandparent, aunt, or uncle.

When any person receiving monthly benefits dies, his or her payments are ended. The last payment in such cases is for the month immediately before the month of death.

If a person receiving disability benefits recovers or returns to work, his payments (and any payments to his dependents) will stop, but not right away—he will be given a chance to test his ability to work and to adjust. If he goes to work despite a severe handicap, he can continue to be paid benefits for as long as 12 months. If a beneficiary recovers from his disability, his benefits will continue to be paid for three months.

Military Service [8]

After 1956. Members of the Armed Forces have been covered by social security in the same way as people in civilian employment since January 1, 1957, under the Servicemen's and Veterans' Survivor Benefits Act of 1956. They receive social security credit for their base pay for active duty (and active duty for training), and their share of the social security tax is deducted from their base pay, just as the social security tax of civilian workers is deducted from their wages. Service described as inactive duty for training, such as drill duty of reservists, is not covered by social security.

NOTE: Military service since January 1, 1957, appears on the serviceman's social security earnings record and can be counted toward both military retirement pay and social security benefits.

Before 1957. Since 1950, the Congress has enacted laws giving *free* social security wage credits of $160 for each month of active military service from September 16, 1940, to December 31, 1956. These credits count the same as actual earnings of $160 a month in determining whether a veteran has enough credits for a social security benefit and in figuring the amounts a veteran and his family can receive in social security benefits.

To get these free wage credits of $160 for each month of active duty he served between September 16, 1940, and December 31, 1956, a veteran must have been discharged or released from service under conditions that were other than dishonorable. In addition, he must have had at least 90 days of active service or, if he had less, he must have been

---

[8] See *Social Security for Servicemen and Veterans*, OASI–31a, Social Security Administration, U.S. Department of Health, Education, and Welfare, Washington, D.C.

discharged or released because of disability or injury caused by or made worse in line of duty.

NOTE: Free credits are not entered in your social security earnings record, but are computed when you or your survivors file a claim for benefits and submit evidence of all your military service. Consequently, they are not entered on the form you receive from the Social Security Administration when you request an accounting of your earnings record.

If You Become Disabled [9]

If you become disabled before age 65, you may qualify for monthly disability benefits, and certain members of your family may also be paid monthly benefits. The time element is very important in applying for disability benefits—a delay in making an application may result in your losing benefits.

How Disabled Must You Be? To be found disabled under the social security law, you must have a condition so severe that, in the words of the law, it makes you unable to "engage in any substantial gainful activity." If you can't do your regular work, but can do other substantial gainful work, you cannot qualify under these disability provisions. Your education, training, and work experience are considered in determining whether you are able to do other substantial work.

Your disability must have lasted for at least six months and be expected to continue for a long and indefinite time. Payments start with the month following the six-month waiting period.

How Much Work Is Required? In general, if you have social security credit for at least five years in the ten-year period ending when you become disabled, you have enough work to qualify for disability insurance benefits.

Proof of Your Disability. When you apply for disability insurance benefits, your social security office will give you a medical report form to have filled in by your doctor or by a hospital or clinic where you have had treatment. You are responsible for whatever charges the doctor or the hospital may make for these services.

The Amount of Your Disability Benefit. The amount of your monthly disability insurance payment is the same as the amount of the old-age insurance benefit you would get if you were already 65. Figure your average earnings as if you reached 65 (62 if a woman) at the time you became disabled.

---

[9] See *If You Become Disabled*, OASI–29, Social Security Administration, U.S. Department of Health, Education, and Welfare, Washington, D.C. Also OASI–29d, *How Disabled Must You Be;* and *The Social Security Disability Insurance Program*, OASI–29g.

Account-Number Cards

If you are employed or self-employed in any kind of work covered by the Social Security Act, you must have a social security card. Your card shows your account number, which is used to keep a record of your earnings. You should use the same account number all your life, for the number on your social security card distinguishes your account from the social security accounts of other people who have names similar to or exactly like yours. Both your name and account number are needed to make sure you get full credit for your earnings. Show your card to each employer so that when reporting your wages he may use your name and account number exactly as they appear on the card.

Your nearest social security office will issue a social security card or a duplicate card to replace one that has been lost. If there is no social security office in your town, ask at the post office for an application blank. If your name has been changed, ask your social security office for a new card showing the same account number and your new name.

Your card is a symbol of your social security account. The benefits payable to you or to your family are figured from the earnings recorded in your social security account.

Checking Your Account

Each employer is required by law to give you receipts for the social security taxes he has deducted from your pay. He must do this at the end of each year and also when you stop working for him. These receipts will help you check on your social security account because they show not only the amount deducted from your pay but also the wages paid you.

You may check your own record as often as once a year by writing to the Social Security Administration, Baltimore, Maryland, 21203, and asking for a statement of your account. You can get an addressed post-card form at any field office for use in requesting wage information (see Fig. 8–1).

If an error has been made in your account, the field office will help you get it corrected. You should check on your account at least each three years, since there is a limit to the period within which certain corrections can be made.[10]

The Adequacy of Social Security

The foregoing discussion of social security does not pretend to be an exhaustive treatment of all ramifications of the subject. It should, how-

---

[10] See *Your Social Security Earnings Record*, OASI–93, Social Security Administration, U.S. Department of Health, Education, and Welfare. Washington, D C.

ever, give you a fairly good indication of your future stake in the program. A family may receive benefits from social security which could otherwise be obtained only by having saved thousands of dollars or by having insurance policies upon which thousands of dollars of premiums had been paid.

In view of the fact that high living costs and high taxes are making it difficult for many families to save adequately in order to have reasonable income for survivors in case of the wage earner's death or for the wage earner and his wife in retirement, the forced saving of social security may indeed prove a blessing to many who, in its absence, would be forced into the humiliation of going on relief roles.

FIGURE 8–1

REQUEST FOR STATEMENT OF EARNINGS

| | | ACCOUNT NUMBER | | | |
| | | DATE OF BIRTH | MONTH | DAY | YEAR |

Please send me a statement of the amount of earnings recorded in my social security account.

NAME { MISS MRS. MR. } _____ Print Name and Address In Ink Or Use Typewriter

STREET & NUMBER _____

CITY, P.O., ZONE & STATE _____

SIGN YOUR NAME AS YOU USUALLY WRITE IT _____

Sign your own name only. Under the law, information in your social security record is confidential and anyone who signs someone else's name can be prosecuted.

If your name has been changed from that shown on your social security account number card, please copy your name below exactly as it appears on that card.

Social Security and Insurance Programing for Death or Retirement

One insurance broker tries to get families to think about retirement and death by showing a chart entitled "A Financial Forecast for Age 65." "Take 100 men starting out at age 25," he declares; "40 years later, nine out of ten are either dead—or dead broke!" While the figures are not accurate, the chart does get people to stop and think.

Today it is possible to have a skilled insurance man sit down with you and show you, by simple charts and tables, how to build a considered program, within your resources and capabilities, for family financial security in the event of your untimely death or for your own benefit when retirement is at hand.

Modern insurance programing builds on a social security base and adds to meet felt needs—within the limit of financial capacity, of course. Even those insurance men who were originally opposed to social security now recognize that it was one of the best things that could have happened to their industry. Why? Simply because without social security the average middle-income family could not afford sufficient insurance to provide for essential needs in case of either premature death or retirement. Now, with part of the burden met by social security, it is easier to show the average family that the amount of insurance it requires for meeting minimum needs is, coupled with social security benefits, financially attainable. As a result, insurance is sold more easily—and more intelligently; and, what is most important, the average family is closer to financial security than it ever was previously.

In the following pages are presented case studies of four relatively young families with continuing responsibilities for raising children. The insurance programs worked out for them are shown, and the tie-up with social security. These are from the files of the Institute of Life Insurance. Were the families a little older or a little better off, annuity programs could be linked with insurance and social security, looking toward comfortable retirement. It should be remembered, however, that it is usually possible to take the cash value of ordinary life insurance at retirement and use it for monthly payments.

Each situation is different, and a program prepared for one family will hardly fit the needs or resources of any other. You can have a plan tailored to your situation, developed by the agent of any good insurance company. He will figure out your social security payments due in the event of death, will show you how to make the best use of your government life insurance, if you have retained it, and then will point out the gaps and indicate how much it would cost to fill them, in whole or in part. You can build a program gradually, as your resources and earning power grow; but if you have a program, you will be able to see where you are going and plan wisely instead of either ignoring your responsibilities or trying to meet them in a hit-or-miss, illogical way.

FOUR LIFE INSURANCE PROGRAMS WITH A SOCIAL SECURITY BASE

The following are case studies of typical owners of life insurance, and you will be interested to see what these life insurance programs are like. The programs were tailor-made by these families with the help of their life insurance agents. They will not fit just anybody. But they will help you to see how families are using life insurance, along with social security, to provide for their financial needs.[11]

1. The George Kents

George Kent, 28; his wife, Mary, 25; and their three children— Roger, four, Billy, two, and Virginia, one—live in Minneapolis, where George is employed by a public bus line. George earns a weekly salary of $105. This is the total income for the family.

They own $14,800 of life insurance, including one industrial 20-payment life, two ordinary straight life, and two renewable and convertible term insurance policies. Their premiums total about $187 a year. Their policies, each on Mr. Kent's life, are as follows:

POLICY NUMBER	AGE AT PURCHASE	AMOUNT AND KIND	PREMIUMS
1	9*	$ 800 20-payment life, industrial	$ 0.50 cents a week ($26 a year)
2	21	1,000 straight life	16.50
3	23	3,000 straight life	52.05
4	26	5,000 10-year term	44.88
5	28	5,000 10-year term	47.28

* Bought by George's parents and paid for by them until he was 21.

Figure 8–2 shows the combined social security and insurance income for the Kent family in the event (a) that George Kent dies now (this is shown in the lower portion of the diagram) or (b) that George Kent lives through a normal retirement period (shown in the retirement-income box in the upper right of the diagram).

If George Kent Should Die Now. George's program is intended, first of all, to care for his family until the youngsters are grown. If George dies now, his life insurance and social security will furnish an income $275.50 monthly until Billy is age 18. Then Mrs. Kent will receive $207.50 monthly until Virginia is 18, when the income drops to $67, which is the income from the life insurance being held at interest until Mrs. Kent is age 42. The $67-a-month insurance payment will run from the time Mrs. Kent is 42 until she is 62, the "blackout" period during which she does not receive social security payments.

[11] Based on social security payments at 1964 levels.

FIGURE 8–2

Income Distribution
The Kents' Life Insurance Program

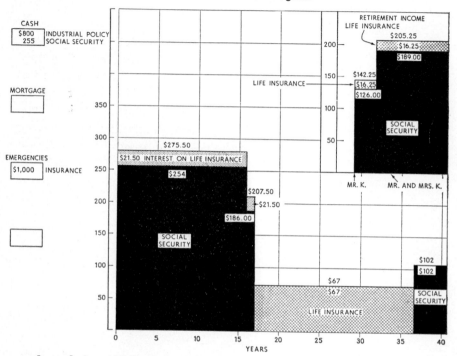

SOURCE: Institute of Life Insurance.

The industrial policy (Policy 1) is to be used to pay the bills at the time George dies. In addition, social security will pay a lump sum of $255 at that time.

When Virginia is 18, social security stops; the balance of the life insurance proceeds will provide some income ($67 per month) for Mrs. Kent, which she will need to supplement by working. When she is 62, she will receive $102 monthly for as long as she lives from George's social security. She and George know there will be at least enough to care for the children through the critical years.

At Retirement Time. When George is 65 years old, he can stop working. His social security will pay $126 a month; and when his wife reaches 65, this social security income will increase to $189 for as long as they both are living. To supplement this, he can use the cash values of his two whole life policies. From them he will receive an income of $16.25 a month. Figure 8–2 shows how his life insurance and social security benefits combine to take care of the minimum needs of his family.

2. The Dawsons

The Dawsons live in California, where Mr. Dawson is a mechanic. They have two children—Jack, who is eight, and Margaret, four. Mr. Dawson is now 30 years old, and his wife is 28. Their annual income amounts to $6,000, but this will probably increase. They own their own home, on which there is a $2,500 mortgage at the present time.

Mr Dawson has taken particular care in planning his life insurance program. The company he works for does not offer any group life or retirement insurance plan, but he is covered by federal social security.

An inventory of their life insurance shows that they own a total of $28,000 of insurance, all on Mr. Dawson's life, as follows:

Policy Number	Taken at Age	Amount and Kind	Annual Premium
1	22	$ 5,000 straight life	$ 84.50
2	23	10,000 straight life	173.50
3	26	7,500 family maintenance	189.40
4	28	1,000 straight life	19.90
5	29	4,500 10-year term	43.70

If Mr. Dawson Dies Now. The graph (Fig. 8–3) shows what Mr. Dawson's life insurance will do should he die now. There will be a monthly income of $103 from life insurance until Margaret is age 18. Added to that will be an income from Mr. Dawson's social security ($254 until Jack is age 18 and then dropping to $186 until Margaret is age 18).

Because the social security income stops when Margaret is 18, Mr. Dawson has arranged for the bulk of his life insurance to provide income until his wife becomes 62. When Mrs. Dawson is age 62, the social security income will start again and pay her $102 a month as long as she lives. Added to that will be $45 a month from his insurance, thus increasing her monthly income to $147.

Policy 5 is a ten-year term. It was purchased to pay off the mortgage, and $2,000 of the insurance will be used for family income needs. Mr. Dawson expects to change part of the term insurance to whole life later on, when his salary increases. Policy 4 plus a $255 lump sum from social security will be used to pay Mr. Dawson's final expenses.

FIGURE 8–3

Income Distribution
The Dawsons' Life Insurance Program

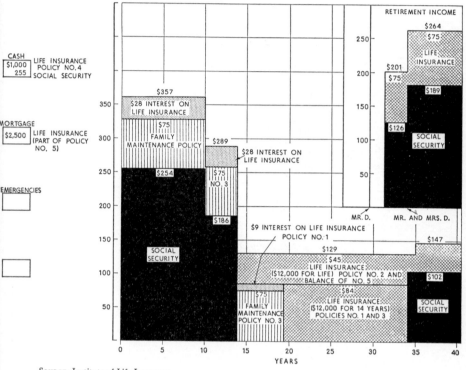

SOURCE: Institute of Life Insurance.

Of course, the mortgage will decrease annually, and it will be paid off completely by the time Mr. Dawson's term policy expires. That is why he selected term insurance for the mortgage cancellation. Later in the term period, the mortgage will be considerably less than the insurance covering it; and if he should die then, the extra money can be used to help the family over the first few months following his death.

At Retirement Time. Chances are that Mr. Dawson will live to see his children grown and with families of their own. Then this program will provide a retirement income for him and his wife. At age 65 his policies will have a total cash value of about $14,000. If he converts the term policy to permanent insurance before he is 65, the cash value will be somewhat larger. Mr. Dawson will continue about $2,000 of his insurance. The cash values of the balance will be used for retirement. This will be sufficient to pay them a monthly income of $75 for as long as they both are living. From Mr. Dawson's social security there will be an income of $126. When they both are 65, the income from social security will be $189 a month. Thus, for the first three years of his retirement, he will have a combined (insurance plus social security) monthly income of $201 and thereafter it will rise to $264.

3. The Crawfords

Bill Crawford is age 30. He and his wife Jean, age 28, have a little boy, four years old. Bill is a pharmacist and earns $7,500 a year. He is covered by social security, and he owns his own home, which has only a small mortgage.

The Crawfords' resources are the home which cost $10,000 and is worth more now; four life insurance policies totaling $24,000; and

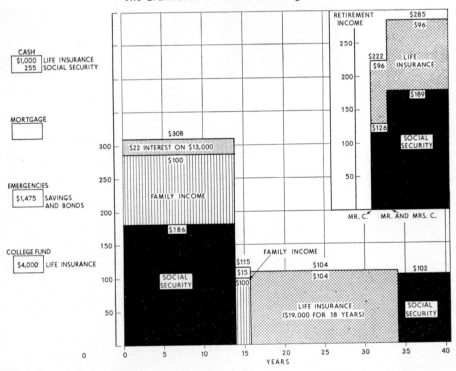

FIGURE 8–4

Income Distribution
The Crawfords' Life Insurance Program

SOURCE: Institute of Life Insurance.

$825 in savings in the bank and $650 in government bonds. Their life insurance policies are as follows:

Amount and Kind	Taken at Age	Annual Premiums	Retirement Values at Age 65
$ 1,000 straight life	20	$ 13.95	$593 or $3.80 a month for life
$ 5,000 straight life	25	81.75	$3,031 or $18 a month for life
$10,000 family income (20-year)	26	206.80	$6,014 or $37 a month for life
$ 8,000 30-payment life	30	182.55	$6,029 or $37.12 a month for life

Use of Resources if Bill Should Die. There would be $1,255 in cash, consisting of $1,000 from life insurance and $255 from social security. This would take care of the funeral and other last expenses. The $1,475 in savings and bonds would remain for subsequent emergencies. As may be seen in the diagram in Figure 8–4, Mrs. Crawford would receive $308 a month until Bill, Jr., is 18 ($186 from social security and $122 from insurance). The life insurance is so arranged as to provide $115 a month for the next two years, i.e., until Bill, Jr., is age 20. He will be receiving $1,000 a year from life insurance to pay his college expenses for four years, starting when he is 18. After Bill is 20 years old, Mrs. Crawford will receive $104 a month until she becomes age 62; then she will get $102 from social security.

Use of Resources if Bill Lives. If Bill lives to retire, the combined insurance policies (monthly income from cash values) will provide $96 a month for life. Social security will provide $126 for Bill alone; then, when Mrs. Crawford becomes age 65, the combined social security payment will rise to $189 and total monthly income to $285. Thus they will be fairly well protected in their old age, apart from any other savings or investments which they may accumulate.

4. The Lawrences

Tom and Nancy Lawrence are both 27 years old and have a brand-new baby girl. Tom owns a young and struggling business, a general store in a middle-western town. His income was around $4,000 last year and will be $4,300 this year; everything else he has earned he has plowed back into the store. Also, Tom is now covered by social security.

The Lawrences' resources are a home which cost $11,000, with a $4,000 mortgage; five life insurance policies totaling $16,500; their savings, which are invested in the store. The store is worth $15,000, but $6,000 is still owed on the purchase price, payable in ten years. Their life insurance policies are as follows:

Amount and Kind	Taken at Age	Annual Premiums	Retirement Values at Age 65
$1,000 straight life	20	$13.95	$593 or $3.80 a month for life
$1,500 straight life	22	21.55	$915 or $5.72 a month for life
$6,000 10-year term	25	52.44	None
$4,000 paid-up at age 65	26	79.44	$3,060 or $18.85 a month for life
$4,000 reducing term (20-year)	27	16.88	None

Use of Resources if Tom Should Die. Most of Tom's insurance would be taken in cash to pay off debts on the store and on the house. The 20-year reducing term policy, which decreases over the years as the mortgage decreases, will pay off the mortgage, leaving the house free and clear. The $6,000, ten-year convertible and renewable term policy will pay off the debt on the store. This was the purpose for which it was purchased. The $1,000 and the $1,500 straight life

FIGURE 8–5

Income Distribution
The Lawrences' Life Insurance Program

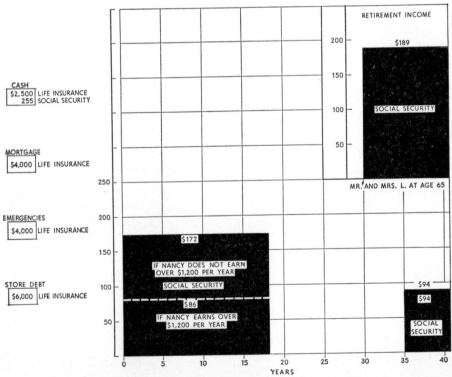

SOURCE: Institute of Life Insurance.

policies, as well as the $255 social security lump-sum payment, will be taken in cash to cover burial expenses and other costs, such as doctor's bills, and to clear up bills at the store. The last $4,000 life policy will be left at interest with the insurance company for an emergency fund. Nancy will run the store for income, which should improve, since the store will now be free of debt. Social security will provide $172 a month, as Figure 8–5 shows, until the baby is 18 years old; and although it stops then, it will resume again for Nancy when she is age 62 and will pay $94 a month for life.

Use of Resources if Tom Lives. The Lawrences look to their store for most of their family income when they retire. Social security will contribute $189 a month when they reach age 65. They may sell the store, or lease it, or have employees run it. As the value of their store increases, they will probably increase their other kinds of savings and will be able to raise their life insurance ownership.

ANNUITIES (FIXED AND VARIABLE)

You may look at some of these cases of retirement income in old age and say to yourself "the total combined income from social security and insurance may be enough for some but it's not enough for me." Those of you who don't feel that way can skip the rest of this chapter. But all prospective entrants into the upper-income brackets read on. You'll learn a bit about "annuities," a subject of interest to upper-middle income (and on up) groups. At 20 you may not find the subject all-absorbing; at 40 you'll be much more interested, especially if your income exceeds $20,000 a year, as it undoubtedly will—either due to your own competence or to inflation.

The word "annuity" comes from the Latin word *annus,* meaning "year." Thus, in origin, an annuity is an annual payment. Today, however, any fixed, periodic payment (weekly, monthly, quarterly, or yearly) for a given period of time or for life is an annuity. So, for example, a bank that advanced $5,000 on mortgage and agreed that it could be paid off (principal and interest) in equal monthly installments of $50 in 12 years would, in fact, be buying an annuity of $50 a month for 12 years.

An annuity is a contract that provides an income for a specified period of time, such as a number of years or life. A life annuity is a way of taking a certain sum of money, or building up a fund, and then using it up month by month, year by year, principal as well as interest thereon, and yet being absolutely sure that you will not run out of money as long as you live. That is the reason why anyone who is planning to retire some day, whether soon or in the distant future, ought to know something about annuities.

Insurance provides protection against dying too soon. An annuity, strange as it sounds, provides protection against living too long. Annuities may be bought by payment of a lump sum or by installment payments. The same companies that sell life insurance also sell annuities; the same care in choosing a company from which to buy insurance should be used in choosing a company from which to buy an annuity.

The Annuity Principle

Annuities are based on the principle of a group of people getting together and sharing risks. Individually, these people could not spend their savings without fear of outliving their principal. Some would die before their principal was exhausted, but others would live long after their money had disappeared. As members of a group of annuitants, however, each of these people can turn all or part of his savings over to a life insurance company and secure in exchange a promise that the company will pay him a regular income as long as he lives. While a life insurance company does not know how long any individual member of the group will live, it does know approximately how many in a group will be alive at the end of each successive year. A company can thus calculate the amount of annuity payments for each member of the group. The annuitant receives a certain income each year. Moreover, if he is over 50 years of age, he would have a greater assured income for life than he could safely obtain by investing the same amount otherwise. For example, a man of age 65 can obtain an income equal to 8 percent of his investment in a straight life annuity. In general, no medical examination is required for any annuity unless it includes insurance features.

Payments for Annuities

Suppose a person of age 40 has $20,000. He could, if he wished, give the $20,000 to an insurance company in return for the promise of the company to give him a small monthly payment for life, to begin immediately. Or, if he needed no immediate income from his money, he would get a much larger monthly payment if he allowed the $20,000 to grow at interest with the company and began to receive the monthly payments for life when he became 60, 65, or 70 years of age. The later the payments begin, the greater each one will be. If he had no such lump sum to give the company, he could build an equivalent accumulation through regular installments over a period of years and in return obtain monthly payments later on.

Who Is Protected

The ordinary life insurance policy gives protection primarily to beneficiaries in the event the insured dies and secondarily builds up cash surrender (and loan) values for the insured; the annuity policy is primarily for the benefit of the insured (the annuitant) and only secondarily of benefit to others. Since life insurance gives protection to others in the event the insured dies and annuity policies are primarily for the benefit of the insured (the annuitant), their purposes and use are therefore very different. To put it briefly, life insurance is primarily to protect others; annuities are to protect oneself. It should be remembered, however, that the proceeds of life insurance policies are often paid out to beneficiaries in the form of annuities. Or the insured may take the cash value of his policy—or, in the case of an endowment, the maturity value—and elect to receive his money in the form of an annuity.

Effects of Rates of Interest upon Income

As you get older, you will begin to think of the time when you will no longer be able to earn an income. If you are fortunate, you may perhaps have saved some money, which may be earning interest in banks, be coming to you from insurance companies, or be invested in securities or in real estate. It is only natural to ask yourself whether you will be able to live in retirement on the income which your accumulated assets will provide. These days it takes $100,000 (a rather large sum of money for most of us) to provide an annual income of $4,000 or $4,500. Suppose you manage to accumulate $100,000 but you feel that you must have $6,000 a year; you will perhaps conclude that you will have to sell some of your assets, as time passes, to supplement your income. Such a procedure will naturally leave less assets to produce income, and you will probably envisage yourself selling more and more assets as the years go by and then you will begin to worry that you will be destitute before you die.

Annuities Assure a Maximum Income

It is in such a situation that an annuity comes to the rescue. If you turn your money over to an insurance company in return for an annuity policy that guarantees you a given monthly income for life, you can be sure that you cannot possibly outlive your money, unless perchance you make a poor choice of an insurance company which fails. Of course, you may also worry lest you give the insurance company $100,000 today and die after receiving only a few monthly payments. In that case the insurance company would retain the balance of what you paid (plus earnings thereon) so that it could pay other annuitants who lived beyond expectation. We shall see later that there are ways, at a price, to avoid such a worry. In fact, annuities remove so much worry that this is often said to be the reason that annuitants live longer than others.

Kinds of Annuities

Annuities are sold both to individuals and on a group basis. Group annuities are for pension plans and are outside the scope of this book.[12] Group or individual, the same kinds of contracts are available, and an employer has about the same array to choose from when setting up a pension plan that you have when you shop for an annuity.

Every annuity has three variables: how you pay for it, when you collect, and how you collect. In the same fashion, every annuity contract has a three-part name. One part specifies when you collect; one, how you pay; and one, how you collect. For example, a single premium, deferred, straight life annuity is one (a) for which you pay a lump sum in a single premium; (b) on which the company starts paying you a periodic income at a future date, e.g., when you become age 65; (c) with an income for as long as you live, but all payments stop at your death. Figure 8–6 sets out these three classification points for quick reference and shows you the various types of annuities available.

Immediate Annuities

When a person pays the insurance company a lump sum and wants his annuity payments to begin without delay, we have an immediate annuity. We also have smaller periodic payments than if payments were to begin later. To obtain such an annuity of $100 a month at age 40, a man would have to spend over $30,000. By the time he was 65 he could probably buy it for a little over half that amount. Ordinarily, people buy immediate annuities just about the time they want to have payments to them begin, i.e., when they are older and approaching retirement. They want this income to begin almost at once and to continue as long as they live.

---

12 For a discussion of group annuities see *Handbook of Life Insurance*, Institute of Life Insurance, New York, pp. 28–30.

FIGURE 8–6

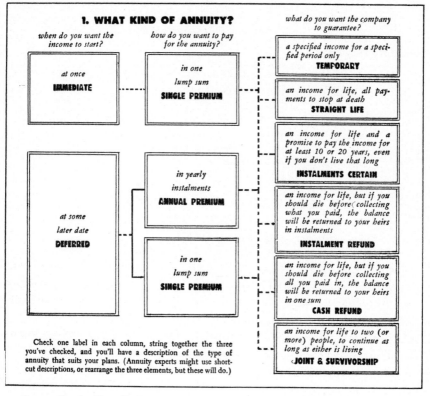

1. WHAT KIND OF ANNUITY?

when do you want the income to start?

how do you want to pay for the annuity?

what do you want the company to guarantee?

at once
IMMEDIATE

in one lump sum
SINGLE PREMIUM

a specified income for a specified period only
TEMPORARY

an income for life, all payments to stop at death
STRAIGHT LIFE

an income for life and a promise to pay the income for at least 10 or 20 years, even if you don't live that long
INSTALMENTS CERTAIN

at some later date
DEFERRED

in yearly instalments
ANNUAL PREMIUM

an income for life, but if you should die before collecting what you paid, the balance will be returned to your heirs in instalments
INSTALMENT REFUND

in one lump sum
SINGLE PREMIUM

an income for life, but if you should die before collecting all you paid in, the balance will be returned to your heirs in one sum
CASH REFUND

Check one label in each column, string together the three you've checked, and you'll have a description of the type of annuity that suits your plans. (Annuity experts might use short-cut descriptions, or rearrange the three elements, but these will do.)

an income for life to two (or more) people, to continue as long as either is living
JOINT & SURVIVORSHIP

SOURCE: *Changing Times, The Kiplinger Magazine.*

Deferred Annuities

Payments on deferred annuities begin at some time in the future, whether they are paid for in a lump sum or by a series of installments. If paid for in a lump sum, the person who buys such an annuity must ordinarily have saved and invested the money in some other way. He must, therefore, have assumed the risks involved in accumulating the money. When paid for in installments, the company assumes the burden of investing the money as received and paying the annuitant beginning with the arrival of the contracted date for payments to start. Naturally, more people can undertake to buy annuities on the installment plan than can produce a lump sum with which to buy them. In many company pension plans, employer and employee co-operate to pay the installments, which eventually produce an accumulation that provides a retirement income for the employee. The younger man is likely to prefer the annual (or installment) payment deferred annuity, while the older man is more likely to prefer the single premium, immediate annuity. If you think about it, you'll realize why this is so.

Annuity Payments

Annuitants have various options as to how they will receive annuity payments. The following are usual:

    A. Types of immediate annuities
        1. Straight life annuity
        2. Life annuity with installments certain
        3. The installment refund annuity
        4. The cash refund annuity
    B. Variations of deferred annuities
        1. The retirement income annuity
        2. The retirement income policy
    C. Joint and survivorship annuities

Although we have spoken of the annuity payments as being made monthly—on the theory that most people need frequent payments, just as while working they need their pay on a weekly or monthly basis—it is, of course, possible to contract to have payments made quarterly, semiannually, or annually. The more often the company must make payments, the more costly it is because of mailing, bookkeeping, and clerical expense and, furthermore, because of loss of interest involved in making payments sooner. Another factor making the cost of monthly annuity payments more than that of quarterly, semiannual, or annual payments is that some people live long enough in the year they die to collect some monthly payments, whereas their death would eliminate payments to be made at the end of a following quarter, half, or full year.

The Straight Life Annuity

The straight life annuity is the original and basic type of annuity. It is purchased for a lump-sum premium, and annuity payments are immediate. It does not have a cash value. Payments cease, and there is no value left in the policy, upon the annuitant's death, no matter how soon he dies. This type of annuity (returning to the annuitant both principal and interest) provides the annuitant with the largest possible payments, but there is no value left in his policy should he die even a month or two after buying the policy. Notice that this type of annuity protects the annuitant only and provides nothing for his dependents beyond what they obtain out of the payments made to the annuitant. It is something like a pension for life: when the pensioner dies, the pension ceases, regardless of how many dependents the pensioner leaves. An indication of the cost of a straight life annuity at different ages may be seen in Table 8–3.

TABLE 8–3

Immediate Annuities—Nonparticipating

Age Last Birthday	Single Premium Purchase Price for Annuity of:			
	$100 Annually	$50 Semiannually	$25 Quarterly	$10 Monthly
		LIFE—MALE		
30	$2217.62	$2244.22	$2257.51	$2716.65
35	2096.91	2123.51	2136.80	2571.80
40	1960.78	1987.38	2000.67	2408.44
45	1809.14	1835.74	1849.03	2226.48
50	1647.47	1674.07	1687.36	2032.47
55	1479.29	1505.89	1519.18	1830.66
60	1304.45	1331.05	1344.34	1620.85
65	1121.62	1148.22	1161.51	1401.45
70	935.35	961.95	975.24	1177.93
75	754.37	780.97	794.26	960.75
80	590.77	617.37	630.66	764.43
85	452.10	478.70	491.99	598.03
		LIFE—FEMALE		
30	2328.25	2354.85	2368.14	2849.40
35	2223.49	2250.09	2263.38	2723.70
40	2105.74	2132.34	2145.63	2582.40
45	1974.01	2000.61	2013.90	2424.32
50	1827.53	1854.13	1867.42	2248.54
55	1665.31	1691.91	1705.20	2053.88
60	1486.56	1513.16	1526.45	1839.39
65	1293.04	1319.64	1332.93	1607.16
70	1089.53	1116.13	1129.42	1362.94
75	884.74	911.34	924.63	1117.20
80	692.58	719.18	732.47	886.60
85	524.14	550.74	564.03	684.48

Source: Metropolitan Life Insurance Company.

Life Annuity with Installments Certain

The straight life annuity is not favored by some people, who dislike the idea of a contract that might pay them an income for only a few months and then stop if they died at that time. These people feel that they would like some close relative to get something out of their purchase money besides the few payments they received. Actually, of course, the company does not get the apparently unused part of the purchase money. This money, according to the risk-sharing principle, goes to other annuitants who live a long time and receive much more than their purchase money.

To meet the objection to the straight life annuity, however, a life annuity with installments certain was developed. This not only pays an income to the annuitant for life but if he dies within the guaranty period, the income payments for the balance of the guaranty period are paid to a beneficiary selected by the annuitant. This period is usually from 10–20 years and is often expressed as 120 or 240 months. The company is obligated to pay income benefits, in any case, for ten or 20 years. There is no risk-sharing or life-annuity principle involved until after the end of that time.

Since, on this type of annuity, the company cannot benefit from the very early death of the annuitant, payments to the annuitant must be less than those on a straight life annuity. If the annuitant lives and receives payments for four years and payments have been guaranteed for ten years, the beneficiary receives the payments for six more years, making, together, four and six—the ten years certain. The beneficiary may elect to receive the six years' payments in one lump sum, which will, however, be smaller than the total amount he would have collected had he waited to receive it in installments over the six years. Should the annuitant live and collect for a longer period than ten years, the policy would terminate on his death, and no value would remain for the beneficiary.

The Installment Refund Annuity

The installment refund annuity also pays an income to the annuitant for life. But if the annuitant dies before he has received as much money as he paid for the annuity, income payments are continued, in installments, to his beneficiary until total payments equal the amount paid.

The Cash Refund Annuity

A cash refund annuity is also a life annuity, but the company guarantees to pay out (all told) a sum equivalent to the cost of the annuity policy, either to the annuitant if he lives or to the annuitant and his beneficiaries in the event that he does not live long enough to collect it all. If $10,000 is paid for such a policy and the annuitant dies after receiving $2,000 in payments, $8,000 would still be due the beneficiaries, making a total of $10,000 to be paid out by the company. A policy of this type assures the annuitant that no part of his principal (but not interest) will be lost to him or his beneficiaries. For this guaranty the annuitant must pay by accepting smaller annuity payments (sometimes as much as 20 percent smaller) than he could get without it. In contrast to the installment-certain annuity, where the beneficiary is paid for the remainder of the guaranteed installment periods, under the cash refund annuity the beneficiary is paid the remainder of the total amount of the annuity in one lump sum.

A straight life annuity is advisable for the person who wishes to receive the largest possible income for his money. A life annuity with installments certain or a cash refund annuity is advisable for the person who not only wants a lifetime income but who also wishes to provide some payment to his beneficiary in the event of his early death. The income to the annuitant is less, it should be remembered, under the installment refund and cash refund than under the straight life annuity, since additional benefits are provided.

Variations of the Deferred Annuity

All deferred annuities have initial payments which begin at a stipulated time in the future, i.e., payment is deferred. A deferred life annuity begins paying at some date after that of original purchase; and when it starts, it pays for life. This annuity may be purchased by a single premium. More often, it is paid for over a period of years. Deferred annuities are usually bought by people who do not need or who already have adequate life insurance protection.

Any annuity under which the income payments are deferred is commonly called a "deferred annuity." A true deferred annuity has no cash value and no death benefit. For example, assume you start buying a deferred annuity, on the installment plan, at age 35 and that you pay in $500 a year. Payment to you on this annuity is to start at age 65 under the terms of your contract. If you should become unemployed at age 60 and should wish to draw out the funds accumulated under the annuity, you cannot do so. It has no cash surrender value. If you should die at age 60, after having made payments of $500 a year for 25 years (for a total of $12,500), your estate would receive nothing from this annuity, since there is no death benefit. Offsetting this, it has the advantage of providing maximum income per dollar of premium to those surviving beyond the deferred period. Because so many people misunderstand the "all or nothing" nature of the benefits and because it fits the needs of so few people, only occasionally do life insurance companies sell this annuity contract.

Most individual retirement plans that are popularly known as deferred annuities are actually savings plans. These generally include some insurance but no annuity element during the deferred period. These contracts build up a fund which is used at the end of the deferred period to buy an immediate annuity. The two most popular plans of this type are (a) the retirement income annuity and (b) the retirement income policy.

The Retirement Income Annuity

The companies give various names to this plan, which is issued to meet the needs of people who want to save regularly for a life income but who need no insurance protection. This contract is really an accumulation at interest of premiums paid, less expenses. The amount accumulated by the end of the deferred period is used to buy a life annuity of the straight life, or more often of the refund, type. The usual unit for this contract is $10 of monthly retirement income at the selected age, which is generally 65.

Added to each unit of retirement income is a very small amount of life insurance protection—just enough, in fact, to provide a death benefit during the early years of the policy equal to all premiums paid. After that time, the savings accumulation exceeds the total of premiums paid and becomes the death benefit, the insurance element ceasing. As the savings accumulation builds up, the death benefit likewise increases.

Prior to the maturity date, the policy has a cash surrender value and also a loan privilege equal to the savings accumulations. During the early years of the policy, due to sales expenses and insurance costs, the cash and loan values will be less than the total of premiums paid.

A retirement income annuity enables you to set aside funds regularly for retirement. Your beneficiary will receive at least the amount of the premiums you paid if you die before the retirement age. You can borrow on the accumulated fund in case of need. You can cash the policy in if your situation changes, and, except for the early years, you will get back at least what you paid in.

The Retirement Income Policy

This is a variation of the retirement income annuity. It includes a substantial insurance element coupled with each unit of $10 of monthly income at the retirement age selected. The insurance element ranges from $1,000 to $1,500. In all other respects this contract is identical in principal to the retirement income annuity.

The retirement income policy fits the needs of many types of people. Single persons often find that the insurance furnishes them all the protection they need, while the policy directs their premium dollars principally toward filling retirement needs. People with dependents who have purchased nearly all the insurance protection that they want and now wish to strengthen their retirement program find this policy helpful. It adds to their insurance protection, which is an advantage, while it lays principal stress on building a retirement income.

The Joint and Survivorship Annuity

Joint and survivorship annuities are especially useful where it is desired to have a retirement income for both husband and wife. They receive the annuity jointly during the life of both of them, and then payments of like (or lesser—often one half) amounts are made to the survivor as long as he or she (probably she) lives. This type of annuity may meet the needs of an elderly couple with no dependents.

A larger monthly payment can usually be obtained by stipulating that the survivor (usually wife) is to receive two thirds of what was received while both were living, rather than the full amount.

There are deferred joint and survivorship annuities, similar to joint and survivorship annuities, except that annuity payments do not begin immediately. While the immediate joint and survivorship annuity must be purchased on a single premium basis, the deferred joint and survivorship annuity is often purchased on an annual premium (installment) basis. As in the case of the true deferred annuity, the deferred joint and survivorship annuity is rarely sold, because death of either before the "maturity" date would terminate the contract and provide no benefit to the survivor.

One of the principal advantages of an immediate joint life and survivorship annuity is that much of the need for life insurance is eliminated. For example, if a man and a wife have such an annuity, providing sufficient income for their needs, the husband would have to carry insurance sufficient only to cover cash for final expenses and one year's readjustment income, because the wife will be supported by the annuity income even after his death.

Life insurance policies can be and are paid off in joint and survivorship annuities. The way to look at a life insurance policy, in this connection, is not in terms of the face amount but rather in terms of the amount of income it will produce. More people use life insurance policies with their annuity income options to provide joint and survivorship income than use the joint and survivorship annuity contract to accomplish the same result. The cost of a single-payment, immediate, joint and survivorship annuity of $10 monthly is shown in Table 8–4.

TABLE 8–4

Joint and Survivor Annuity—Nonparticipating
Single Premium Price for an Annuity of $10 Monthly

	FEMALE AGE			
MALE AGE	10 YRS. YOUNGER	5 YRS. YOUNGER	SAME AGE	5 YRS. OLDER
45	$2713.89	$2615.74	$2521.69	$2436.50
46	2688.72	2588.09	2491.71	2404.43
47	2662.94	2559.81	2461.05	2371.65
48	2636.54	2530.85	2429.68	2338.14
49	2609.50	2501.22	2397.62	2303.90
50	2581.81	2470.90	2364.85	2268.92
51	2553.48	2439.89	2331.35	2233.20
52	2524.47	2408.18	2297.12	2196.73
53	2494.79	2375.75	2262.13	2159.51
54	2464.41	2342.60	2226.39	2121.53
55	2433.34	2308.71	2189.86	2082.78
56	2401.55	2274.07	2152.54	2043.25
57	2369.04	2238.65	2114.43	2002.93
58	2335.79	2202.44	2075.51	1961.85
59	2301.78	2165.43	2035.78	1919.98
60	2267.02	2127.59	1995.21	1877.34
61	2231.48	2088.92	1953.82	1833.92
62	2195.14	2049.41	1911.60	1789.75
63	2157.97	2009.07	1868.58	1744.87
64	2119.98	1967.89	1824.77	1699.32
65	2081.17	1925.87	1780.20	1653.14
66	2041.53	1883.05	1734.90	1606.38
67	2001.06	1839.42	1688.92	1559.14
68	1959.76	1795.04	1642.30	1511.50
69	1917.66	1749.92	1595.12	1463.52

SOURCE: Metropolitan Life Insurance Company.

The Cost of Annuities

The price of an annuity is based on the amount of income it will pay. You can look at price in two ways: you can take the amount you can pay and see what income it will buy, or you can take the income you want and see what it will cost. Figure 8–7 gives some averages of annuity costs from both points of view. The amount you will pay for a

FIGURE 8–7

The Cost of Annuities

Annuity rates are usually quoted in two ways: the amount of income you get per unit of premium or the amount you pay per unit of income. Figures given below are only approximate, being based on rounded averages of several companies' rates. Nonparticipating rates are shown for single-premium annuities, participating rates for the annual-premium annuities.

IMMEDIATE SINGLE-PREMIUM ANNUITIES
(Income to Begin at Once)

Age		EACH $1,000 BUYS THIS MONTHLY INCOME			EACH $10 OF MONTHLY INCOME COSTS		
Male	Female	Life Only	10 Years Certain	Refund	Life Only	10 Years Certain	Refund
50	55	$4.20	$4.10	$3.70	$2,400	$2,450	$2,750
55	60	4.75	4.50	4.00	2,100	2,200	2,500
60	65	5.50	5.15	4.50	1,850	1,950	2,300
65	70	6.40	5.80	5.00	1,575	1,725	2,100
70	75	7.70	6.50	5.60	1,300	1,550	1,800

DEFERRED ANNUAL-PREMIUM ANNUITIES
(Assuming Income Starts at Age 60 for Men, Age 65 for Women)

Age at Issue		EACH $100 A YEAR BUYS THIS MONTHLY INCOME			EACH $10 OF MONTHLY INCOME COSTS THIS MUCH A YEAR		
Male	Female	Life Only	10 Years Certain	Refund	Life Only	10 Years Certain	Refund
20	25	$35.00	$33.25	$30.75	$31.00	$33.00	$35.00
25	30	29.00	27.00	25.00	37.00	39.00	42.00
30	35	23.00	21.75	20.00	47.00	49.00	52.00
35	40	18.00	17.00	15.50	60.00	63.00	70.00
40	45	13.50	12.50	11.50	79.00	84.00	90.00

SOURCE: *Changing Times, The Kiplinger Magazine.*

given income—say, $100 a month—depends on what income plan you select, how old you are when payments begin, and whether you are a man or a woman.

Things to remember about costs are:

1. The older you are when the income is to start, the less you will pay. In the case of an immediate annuity, the older you are when you buy, the less your cost will be.

2. With a deferred annuity, the younger you are when you sign up, the less your annual premium cost will be. The lower premiums result

from spreading payments over a longer period and from the interest your payments can earn.

3. The total of annual premiums paid for an annuity of so much a month will be less than the single premium you will pay for an immediate annuity of the same amount beginning at the same age. All of the latter comes out of your pocket, whereas the annual premiums are built up with compound interest of between 2 and 3 percent.

4. At the same age, a woman pays more than a man for the same income, because women, on the average, live longer and collect more.

5. For each dollar of income, you pay least if you take a straight life plan, most if you take a cash refund joint and survivorship plan.

Life insurance premiums are based on age at nearest birthday. Annuity premiums, however, change with each quarter-year. Life insurance premiums increase as one gets older; premiums for immediate annuities decrease the older one is and the shorter the time for which the company contracts to make payments. It is sensible for one to buy life insurance just before his age changes and to buy a life annuity just after he has attained a higher age. Annuity rates for women are higher than for men of equal age because women have a longer expectation of life. For life annuities it is customary to charge women the same rates that are charged men who are five years younger, since this measures approximately the difference in length of life.

Most immediate annuities are nonparticipating, whereas more and more deferred annuities are being written on a participating basis. Medical examinations are not required for annuities that combine with them no insurance protection: the poorer one's health, the less likelihood there is that the company will have to pay for a long time. Various combinations of annuities and insurance have been worked out by insurance companies to fit particular needs.

Annuities and Investments

The major limitation of annuities is that they provide a fixed dollar income, which is not protected from shrinkage in purchasing power due to inflation. On the other hand, putting all one's retirement funds into investments might be too risky; or if safety is desired and a more conservative investment policy is therefore pursued, the resultant income might not be sufficient to meet needs. Assume, for example, that a couple (man age 66; wife age 64), who are not covered under social security, have accumulated $40,000 on which to retire. Assume further that, under present conditions, their minimum income requirements are $2,500 annually. If the $40,000 fund were conservatively invested and averaged a 4 percent return, the couple would receive only $1,600; if somewhat more risk were taken and 5 percent were averaged, the return of $2,000 would still be insufficient.

By a judicious combination of annuities and investments, however, a greater fixed income could be obtained, along with a hedge to protect against inflation. The $40,000 might be divided as follows:

	ANNUAL INCOME
$12,000 for straight life annuity for man (at age 66)	$ 975
$15,000 for straight life annuity for wife (at age 64)	962
$13,000 in common stock (at yield of 5 percent)	650
	$2,587

Such a program is safer than the investment program, even at a conservative 4 percent, and yields a very much larger income.[13]

Figure 8–8 presents the alternatives between buying an annuity or investing your funds directly. People choose annuities for all sorts of reasons, ranging from taxes to timidity. The tax advantage is that money put into annuities during your working years earns interest, but you do not need to pay income taxes on the interest until you actually collect it; and then your income and your tax bracket will presumably be much lower. Timidity enters because people mistrust their ability to invest wisely, especially their ability to handle the somewhat complicated operation of continuing to invest while using up capital gradually over the retirement period. They cannot live on earnings alone; their capital fund to start with is not large enough; and they must, therefore, gradually draw on principal, but there is the danger that they may use it up too rapidly, live longer than they anticipated, and thus face destitution. The annuity relieves them of such worries.

In the annuity-versus-investment debate, you will find that annuities gain in popularity in recession or depression, when investments lose their luster, whereas, in boom and inflation, when the fixed-dollar income from annuities purchases less and less and stock investments are rising in value and yielding capital gains, the annuity looks less attractive.

---

[13] See chap. xvi, "Use of Annuities," in *Life Insurance and Annuities from the Buyer's Point of View,* by American Institute for Economic Research, Great Barrington, Mass.

FIGURE 8–8

Annuities: To Buy or Not to Buy

Here are the figures and vital statistics as they might confront a person thinking of retirement and seeking to choose among annuities, other investments, or a combination of the two. Take a man and a woman needing at age 65 an income of $1,200 a year on top of Social Security. Let's say that each will have between $15,000 and $20,000, from life savings and the sale of a house, to work with.

Read across from left to right. First, there are the average lifetimes they can look forward to, plus the chances of living at least 20 years. Then there's the cost of an annuity—guaranteeing an income but involving the risk of loss in case of early death. Then the rate of interest which would allow them to draw about $1,200 a year without touching their principal. Next, the approximate length of time their money would last if they put it in the bank or into savings and loan shares and withdrew about $1,200 a year, using up interest and principal both. And, finally, the average years of life remaining if they should outlive their capital.

You can see, for example, how the annuity offers the only assurance of income but that it also means that all the money will be gone at death. And you can see how other plans involve investment risks or the danger of outliving capital but offer the chance of preserving some capital for heirs.

Start with You		Suppose You Buy an Annuity	Suppose You Invest the Same Amount and Take $100 a Month to Live on		
If You Are	Your Life-Expectancy Is	$100 a Month, Guaranteed for Life, but All Payments Stopping at Death, Costs	You Can Live on Interest Only If Your Money Earns about	With Lower Interest Rates, You Can Tap Both Interest and Principal and Your Money Will Last	And If Still Living, Your Life-Expectancy Will Then Be
A woman aged 65	17½ years (41% live at least 20 yrs.)	$18,500	6½%	At 2%, 18 years At 3%, 21 years At 4%, 24 years	At 83, 8 years At 86, 7 years At 89, 6 years
A man aged 65	14½ years (27% live at least 20 yrs.)	$15,750	7½%	At 2%, 15 years At 3%, 17 years At 4%, 18 years	At 80, 7 years At 82, 6 years At 83, 6 years

Source: *Changing Times, The Kiplinger Magazine.*

Variable Annuities

To combine the safety advantages of fixed annuities with the inflation-hedging protection of common stock investment, the "variable" annuity has been developed. The variable annuity is an annuity providing a life income, not of a fixed number of dollars but of variable amounts keyed to an underlying common stock investment portfolio. Under a variable annuity your premiums are invested in common stocks and provide a retirement income that increases as stock prices and dividends increase, and decreases as they decline. A fixed annuity, on the other hand, invests your premiums primarily in bonds and mortgages and provides a guaranteed fixed-dollar annuity income that does not change in amount from year to year, except as extra dividends are added.

In the words of a former President of the Metropolitan Life Insurance Company: "The so-called variable annuity is similar to a true annuity in that premiums are paid to the issuing company by the annuitant, presumably during his working years. At retirement the company makes payments periodically to the annuitant—generally speaking over the remaining years of his life. The difference, however, and a vast difference it is, is that in the variable annuity type of contract the premium payments to the company are to be invested in equities, which to all intents and purposes, means common stock, and the issuing company makes *no* commitment as to any dollar amount that will be paid to the annuitant during the period of retirement. The issuing company merely undertakes to make payments based on the annuitant's pro rata share of the then market value of the common stock fund in which his payments have been invested."

How the Variable Annuity Developed

Inflation has reduced the purchasing power of the dollar by 50 percent over the past 25 years. It was fear of inflation and its debilitating impact on retirement income which gave rise to the variable annuity.

The modern variable annuity was first developed by the Teachers Insurance and Annuity Association of America. It established the College Retirement Equities Fund (CREF) in 1952 to enable college teachers who were contributing to the TIAA retirement system (buying an individual fixed-dollar annuity) to have up to one half of their contribution (including the college's contribution) go toward the purchase of a CREF variable annuity, with the balance going to TIAA to purchase the fixed-dollar annuity.

Based on careful studies of investment and price trends over a previous 70-year period, the TIAA concluded:

1. It is unwise to commit *all* of one's retirement savings to fixed-dollar obligations, since decreases in the purchasing power of the dollar can seriously reduce the value of a fixed income annuity. Increases in the purchasing power of the dollar, on the other hand, improve the status of the owner of a fixed income annuity.

2. It is equally unwise to commit *all* of one's retirement savings to equity investments, since variations in prices of common stocks are

much too pronounced to permit full reliance on them for the stable income needed during retirement. Changes in the value of common stocks and other equities are by no means perfectly correlated with cost of living changes, but they have provided a considerably better protection against inflation than debt obligations.

3. Substantial problems exist whenever an individual has the option to invest a large single payment in *either* an equities fund or a fixed-dollar fund. If he had invested $10,000 in common stocks in 1929, he would have seen it drop in value to $2,600 in 1932. (Since the price level also fell, the purchasing power would have been $3,250.) Likewise, if he had invested $10,000 in government bonds, a savings account, or a life insurance fund in 1914, it would have declined *in purchasing-power value* to $5,000 in 1920. (Both figures exclude interest and dividend additions.)

4. Therefore, the TIAA concluded, contributions to a retirement plan which are invested partly in fixed-dollar obligations, such as bonds and mortgages, and partly in common stocks offer promise of providing retirement income which is at once reasonably free from violent fluctuations in amount and from serious depreciation through price-level changes.[14]

Over 100,000 college teachers are now contributing to the College Retirement Equities Fund,[15] two insurance companies were formed for the special purpose of selling variable annuities—The Variable Annuity Life Insurance Company of Washington, D.C., and Equity Annuity Life Insurance Company also of Washington, D.C. In addition, a growing number of employers have plans for providing variable pensions for their employees, including Bristol-Myers Company; Long Island Lighting Company; Warner Lambert; Jersey Central Power and Light; New Jersey Power and Light; Boeing Airplane Company; Pan American Airlines; Delta Airlines; Kidder, Peabody & Company; Smith, Barney & Company; etc. Among the major life insurance companies, the Prudential is pioneering the idea of making variable annuities available to the public on both an individual and a group basis. Metropolitan Life, on the other hand, has been steadfastly opposing the idea.

How the Variable Annuity Works

Suppose you decide to set aside $50 a month over a period of years for a variable annuity. (1) The funds you pay in would be placed in

---

[14] Adapted from William C. Greenough, *A New Approach to Retirement Income,* Teachers Insurance and Annuity Association of America, 730 Third Ave., New York, N.Y., 10017, latest edition.

[15] A prospectus of this Fund may be obtained by writing to the TIAA.

the insurance company's variable contract account and invested separately, from the company's regular insurance or annuity funds, in common stocks. (2) Each $50 monthly payment, after deduction of a specified allowance for expenses, would be applied to credit you with a number of Variable Contract Account Units, determined by the current dollar value of an accumulation unit. The dollar value of an accumulation unit would go up and down depending on changes in the value of the assets in the account. Each $50 that you paid might buy a different number of units. The dollar value of the units credited to you would change each month. The company makes no dollar guarantees. Its liabilities for the variable annuity are always in terms of the current value of its assets.

(3) When you retire, all of your Variable Contract Account Units would be converted, on a basis set forth in your contract, into a fixed number of annuity units. As in a straight life annuity you are guaranteed a payment each month for as long as you live. But instead of providing for the payment each month of a fixed number of dollars, your variable annuity contract will provide for the payment each month of the current value of the fixed number of annuity units credited to you.[16] Thus the dollar amount of each payment would depend on the dollar value of an annuity unit when the payment is made. The dollar value of an annuity unit would change from month to month, according to the investment results of the account, in much the same way as the Variable Contract Account Units. For example, if you were entitled to a payment of ten annuity units each month and the dollar value of the common stock assets behind each annuity unit fell from $10.00 to $9.50 and then rose to $11.00, with change in market trends, your retirement income over the three months would be $100, $95, and $110 for each month, respectively.

You may find of interest the trend in CREF annuity unit values since they were first made available in 1952. The performance is shown in Figure 8–9.

Why Not Invest in Common Stock Directly?

Why not buy common stock directly and provide this variable income in retirement by a systematic liquidation of your investments over your retirement period? There is one big reason why you can't. You can set up an investment program, but you can't predict how long

---

[16] See *The Aims, Background and Case for a Variable Annuity Contract*, The Prudential Insurance Company of America, September 21, 1955.

FIGURE 8–9.

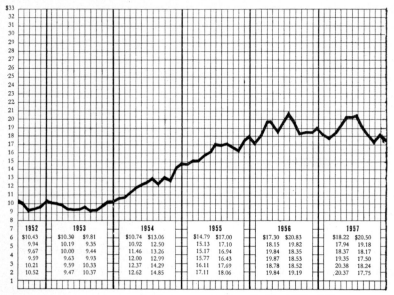

Monthly Value of the CREF Accumulation Unit, 1952-1963

CREF Annuity Unit Values Since 1952

Annuity Year May through April	Annuity Unit Value
Initial Value	$10.00
1953-54	9.46
1954-55	10.74
1955-56	14.11
1956-57	18.51
1957-58	16.88
1958-59	16.71
1959-60	22.03
1960-61	22.18
1961-62	26.25
1962-63	26.13
1963-64	22.68

SOURCE: *Teachers Insurance and Annuity Association (College Retirement Equities Fund)*

FIGURE 8–9 (Continued)

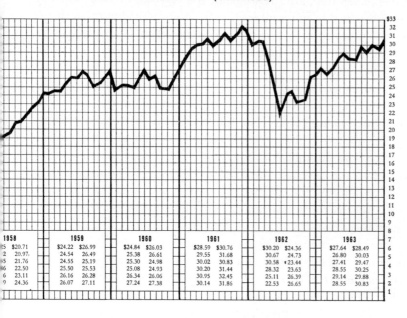

1958		1959		1960		1961		1962		1963	
?5	$20.71	$24.22	$26.99	$24.84	$26.03	$28.59	$30.76	$30.20	$24.36	$27.64	$28.49
2	20.97	24.54	26.49	25.38	26.61	29.55	31.68	30.67	24.73	26.80	30.03
?5	21.76	24.55	25.19	25.30	24.98	30.02	30.83	30.58	?23.44	27.41	29.47
?6	22.50	25.50	25.53	25.08	24.93	30.20	31.44	28.32	23.63	28.55	30.25
6	23.11	26.16	26.28	26.34	26.06	30.95	32.45	25.11	26.39	29.14	29.88
9	24.36	26.07	27.11	27.24	27.38	30.14	31.86	22.53	26.65	28.55	30.83

Experience of $50 a Month Paid to CREF

*YEAR-END DOLLAR VALUES OF CREF ACCUMULATIONS
UNDER FOUR DIFFERENT PERIODS OF PARTICIPATION*

This table shows successive year-end CREF accumulations for persons starting a $50 level monthly premium to CREF on four different dates. For example, the person starting January 1, 1957, had a $4,205 accumulation value at the end of 1962 after paying $3,600 in premiums to CREF, and an accumulation of $5,611 at the end of 1963 after paying $600 more in premiums. CREF accumulation amounts are reported to each participant annually on the CREF Yellow Slip.

Date of First $50 Monthly Premium to CREF

Year Ending December 31	July 1, 1952	January 1, 1957	January 1, 1959	January 1, 1961
1952	$ 304			
1953	931			
1954	2,085			
1955	3,261			
1956	4,160			
1957	4,516	$ 552		
1958	7,086	1,488		
1959	8,691	2,316	$ 621	
1960	9,613	3,023	1,272	
1961	12,016	4,201	2,124	$ 616
1962	10,899	4,205	2,426	1,135
1963	13,533	5,611	3,506	1,977

you will live. Therefore, after retirement, you can't know how much of your principal it is safe to spend each year. You might figure on drawing down your money over say 15 years—and then live only half as long. Or you might still be hale and hearty after 20 years—but with all your money gone.

Only an insurance company, spreading the mortality risk on a sound actuarial basis over a large group of people can guarantee you a distribution of your savings over your full retirement lifetime no matter how long you may live. The insurance company can do this because, dealing with a large number of annuitants, the "losses" on those who live longer than the "average" will be offset by "gains" on those who do not live as long as the average. By enabling you to use up your principal as well as the return on it, over the retirement period with income guaranteed for life no matter how long you may live, annuities generally provide a higher monthly return than comparable forms of direct investment. The purchase of a $100,000 fixed annuity is a much better arrangement *for retirement* than say the direct ownership of $100,000 of high-grade bonds. The purchase of a $100,000 variable annuity is a much better arrangement *for retirement* than the ownership of $100,000 of either common stock directly or of such ownership through the intermediary of mutual funds.

Conclusion

The chief advantage of the variable annuity from the purchaser's point of view is that it helps to provide a hedge against retirement income being diminished in purchasing power due to continuing inflation. The chief disadvantage, on the other hand, is that it subjects retirement income to the vagaries of the stock market and may result in a diminution of retirement income in a period of stock-market decline.

Your Company Pension Plan

When you graduate and are deciding which job to take, check the pension plan of each of the companies that have made you an offer. Today most medium and large corporations provide attractive retirement plans. A generous plan will enable you to use funds that you might otherwise husband for retirement.

Will you contribute to the plan or does the company pay all the cost? Practice varies. When you contribute, by payroll deduction, benefits may be larger. At any event all the income the money earns during your working years is tax-free until your retirement. In some companies there is no payroll deduction on the first $5,000 or $10,000 of income but a significant contribution from higher compensation. Plans vary widely in this respect.

How much will you get? Here, too, it is hard to generalize. Some plans are tied to profit sharing; others use formulas and pay benefits without any formal relationship to profit. Pensions may be based on length of service or on level of salary, or on both. The company, for example, may pay 1 percent for each year's service. The 1 percent may be on your average salary or it may be on your salary for the five years prior to retirement. The latter would probably be more advantageous since your last five years' salary is likely to be higher than your average salary with the firm. Almost all corporate pensions are in addition to or on top of social security benefits.

Is the plan vested? What happens if you serve for a number of years but leave the company for another job, prior to the official retirement age? Vesting is your right to share in some or all of the money your employer has contributed to the pension fund in your behalf, even if you leave before retirement. Many plans are not vested. If you leave before retirement you get only the return of any contributions you made plus interest on these. Where vesting occurs you may get either a lump-sum payment on leaving, or more usually, the money is retained in the pension fund and paid out to you as a pension only after you reach the company's retirement age. If the pension is not vested, and you lose all rights if you quit, you may become tied to the company because of this, after some years of service.

The company's pension fund may be invested by a bank or trust company, in which case when you retire, your pension benefits are paid directly from the trust fund. Or the pension fund may be handled by an insurance company, in which case pension funds are in effect used to purchase annuities payable to you upon your retirement.

What form will the pension take? Usually you receive a monthly check for as long as you live. Widows and survivors get nothing after the death of the pensioner. However, some plans offer other options. One is the "years certain" option. You can elect to receive a somewhat smaller monthly payment with the assurance that whether you live or not it will be paid to you or to your widow for five, ten, or fifteen years, that is, for a certain specified period. Or you can choose the "joint and survivor" option. If you die, the same or reduced payment is made regularly to your widow for as long as she may live.

Clearly there are many variations and ramifications of corporate pension funds—many more than have been explored here. And plans and provisions change over time. You will want to examine the pension and retirement provisions of a company job offer as one of the important features, just as you certainly will weigh salary, location, type of work, and opportunities for advancement.

Pensions for the Self-Employed

If, instead of going to work for a company, you set up your own small business or enter one of the professions, the provisions of the Self-Employed Individuals Tax Retirement Act of 1962, popularly known as the Keogh Act, will interest you. The act permits self-employed persons to establish tax-favored retirement plans for themselves.

If you are self-employed as an accountant, architect, author, decorator, dentist, doctor, farmer, lawyer, etc., or are an owner or partner in an unincorporated business and receive self-employment income from personal services rendered, you can set up a retirement plan and be eligible for tax benefits under the act.

You can contribute up to 10 percent of your earned income to your retirement fund but no more than $2,500 in any one year. For example, a dentist earning $20,000 a year, can contribute 10 percent or $2,000 to his plan. A doctor, netting $30,000 a year, may contribute only the maximum, $2,500, not $3,000.

The tax advantage you receive is that you can deduct one half of your annual contribution to your retirement plan from your taxable income. In the two examples above, the dentist can deduct $1,000, the doctor $1,250. Furthermore, the income or capital gains from your invested fund are free from taxes until withdrawn. You will not be taxed until you actually receive distributions upon retirement. By that time your tax rate may be lower than in your active earning period.

There are some limitations, of course. You cannot withdraw funds until you reach age 59½ without incurring tax penalties. However, earlier distribution is permitted in case of permanent disability. Also your beneficiaries can receive benefits upon your death, even though that occurs before age 59½. If you set up a plan for yourself, you must also set up a plan for all employees of yours who have completed three years of continuous service at the date of the plan's adoption. Full tax deduction is permitted, however, for contributions made on behalf of "regular" employees. Also, you are restricted as to how you can invest the money. You have four main choices:

a) You may put the money into a trust.
b) You may purchase annuity contracts from an insurance company.
c) You may open a special "custodial" account with a bank, which account

can be invested wholly in mutual fund shares, or wholly in annuity, endowment, or life insurance contracts issued by an insurance company.

d) You may purchase special U.S. government "retirement" bonds. These bonds pay 3¾ percent and can't be cashed until you are 59½, unless you die or become disabled earlier.

To set up a plan you have to write out a formal document and have it approved by the Internal Revenue Service. Most large banks and insurance companies have master and model plans already approved. Also, many trade and professional associations have developed group plans involving, for example, group annuity contracts, or mutual fund plans.

Setting up a self-employed retirement plan isn't simple. The act is more complicated than has been indicated above. If and when you decide to take advantage of the act, consult a lawyer, or an accountant, or your insurance man, or your local banker. They will know about details and all changes which are likely to occur in this area between now and the time you may want to act.

SUGGESTED READINGS

1. *Social Security Handbook.* 2d ed. Social Security Administration, U.S. Department of Health, Education, and Welfare, Washington, D.C., 1963.
2. Michael Belloise, "Are You Missing Out on Social Security Payments?" *Reader's Digest,* June, 1963.
3. "Check Up On Your Social Security," *Changing Times, The Kiplinger Magazine,* December, 1963.
4. Dan M. McGill, *Fundamentals of Private Pensions.* 2d ed. Homewood, Ill.: Richard D. Irwin, Inc., 1964.
5. *The Older American,* President's Council on Aging, Washington, D.C., 1963.
6. *Facts on Aging—Living Arrangements of Older Persons,* U.S. Department of Health, Education, and Welfare, Washington, D.C., 1963.
7. *Aging.* Issued monthly by the U.S. Department of Health, Education, and Welfare. Reports current activities, programs, and publications in the field of aging.
8. *Your Social Security,* OASI-35. Social Security Administration, U.S. Department of Health, Education, and Welfare, Washington, D.C., latest edition.
9. *Social Security Benefits,* OASI-855, Social Security Administration, U.S. Department of Health, Education, and Welfare, Washington, D.C.
10. *If You Become Disabled,* OASI-29. Social Security Administration, U.S. Department of Health, Education, and Welfare, Washington, D.C., latest edition.
11. *If You Work While You Get Social Security Payments,* OASI-23, Social Security Administration, U.S. Department of Health, Education, and Welfare, Washington, D.C., latest edition.

12. "Your Company Pension Plan," *Changing Times, The Kiplinger Magazine,* May, 1962.

13. *Now That You Are Retiring,* OASI-853. Social Security Administration, U.S. Department of Health, Education, and Welfare, Washington, D.C., latest edition.

14. "Your Questions Answered About Social Security," *Changing Times, The Kiplinger Magazine,* August, 1963.

15. "Pensions For the Self-Employed," *Changing Times, The Kiplinger Magazine,* May, 1963.

16. *What You Need to Know About Social Security Disability Insurance-Benefits,* OASI-29a. Social Security Administration, U.S. Department of Health, Education, and Welfare, Washington, D.C., latest edition.

17. *Facts on Aging.* Office of Aging, U.S. Department of Health, Education, and Welfare, Washington, D.C.

18. *Farm People and Old-Age, Survivors and Disability Insurance in the United States,* OASI-868. Social Security Administration, U.S. Department of Health, Education, and Welfare, Washington, D.C., latest edition.

19. *Social Security Information for Self-Employed Farmers,* OASI-864. Social Security Administration, U.S. Department of Health, Education, and Welfare, Washington, D.C., latest edition.

CASE PROBLEMS

1. Joan Gale is trying to decide between two job offers. One job is with a large oil company. The starting salary is $4,000 per year, with good prospects of promotion over ten years to a salary of $9,000. Among the fringe benefits is a noncontributory life insurance and pension plan. The rate of pension is 50 percent of the employee's average annual salary in the last five years of employment.

The second job is with a small research firm sponsored jointly by a large university and leading business firms in the area. The starting salary is $4,500 with prospects of promotion over ten years to $10,000. The fringe benefits are much the same as those of the oil company except that there is no pension plan.

Miss Gale is 24. She has no one dependent on her now or in the foreseeable future. Neither can she foresee any substantial inheritance coming her way.

How is Miss Gale to weigh these alternative jobs?

2. Joseph Caine is a bachelor who has just turned 37. He has a choice of two jobs; one is covered by social security and the other is not. Retirement is mandatory at 65 in both jobs. The covered job pays $310 a month and Caine will be unable to save if he takes it. The other job will enable him to save $50 each month, since it pays $360. Caine is a healthy man and has no dependents or relations. Which job should he take? Why?

3. Johnson and his wife reason that they will need $350 a month to live comfortably when they retire in four years. Of this they expect social security to provide $190. They own a home worth $10,000 and have cash in the bank and cash surrender values of insurance policies amounting to $25,000. Johnson is being paid $8,000 a year. His company has no pension plan. The Johnson chil-

dren are grown up and self-supporting. What would be a good financial plan for the future?

4. Malcolm Watson earns $5,350 from his own business. Must he pay for social security? How much? When and how does he make a return?

5. Joe Bartlett first became covered by social security on January 1, 1956. He is now 59 and will retire July 1, 1969 at age 65. His average earnings are $500 a month. When he retires, how much will his total payments into social security be, and how large will his monthly benefits be? His wife is now age 56. Will she receive benefits? How much? His children are ages 17 and 24. Will they receive benefits? How much?

6. When George McNair (annual earnings, $12,000) received his monthly wage statement under social security, he found that $22.50 had been deducted as his social security payment. He figured that this was too much because at that rate he would be paying $270 a year, and he knew that the most an employee must pay is $174 (3⅝ percent of $4,800). Advise him.

7. Raph Vinal now earns $95 a month. Do his present earnings cancel his social security benefits? Ralph will be 73 years old next week. He is offered a job paying $200 monthly, but he is afraid to take it because he does not want to lose his social security. Comment.

8. Francis O'Connor was covered by social security from July 1, 1954. His average wages amounted to $250 a month. He died in November, 1964. What benefits should his wife (age 29) and his two children (ages 2 and 7) have received? For how long?

9. When Peter Robbins died at age 54, he left a net estate of about $600,000. He had first married at age 42 and had no children, but he did leave a sister and brother, in comfortable circumstances, a niece, and a nephew and also his wife's mother, sister, and the sister's two children. Robbins' will directed his executors to buy annuities of the cash refund type for his widow (age 44) and specified how any money payable after his wife's death should be divided among his and her relatives. Do you think Robbins used good judgment?

10. When John Spangler retired at age 65, his wife was 57 years old. They owned their home and had $10,000 in the bank. Installment payments made on a deferred annuity would provide a monthly annuity of $200 for his life, but the annuity contract he owned gave him also the options of choosing to take payments either (*a*) on the cash refund plan; (*b*) on his life, with installments certain; or (*c*) on the joint and survivorship plan. Which plan would best meet their needs?

11. Arnold Nickerson started to accumulate money for retirement years ago, when he could safely earn 4 percent on his money. He hoped to be able to accumulate $100,000 by the time he reached age 65. With that amount of money he expected to be able to buy an annuity which would make him comfortable for life. He is now 60 years old and has accumulated a total of $55,000. To what extent will he have to change his retirement plans if he cannot do any better these next five years?

12. Mary Anne Hearn (age 23) teaches in a private school. She is covered only by social security. At present she earns $250 a month, from which taxes and other deductions amount to $40. How could an annuity help provide for her retirement? How much would it cost? How much retirement income would she receive? When?

9 HEALTH, PROPERTY, AND AUTOMOBILE INSURANCE*

The reason there were fewer wrecks in the old horse and buggy days was because the driver didn't depend wholly on his own intelligence.

—Anon.

ONE NIGHT Freddy Johnson, aged three, began to fret. When his eyes turned puffy and his skin turned gray, the Johnsons became alarmed. The doctor's diagnosis was nephrosis, a kidney disease. Thus began a nightmare which lasted three years and cost the Johnsons not only great anxiety but $8,691 as well. They were soon in trouble financially because Freddy's father earned only $3,500 a year. Fortunately, Freddy recovered, but the Johnsons were saddled with a huge debt which took years to pay off.

Fiction? Not at all. A real life story! Fortunately, as medical costs have risen, the insurance device has been adapted to meet them. It is now possible to obtain insurance to meet the two essential needs in any accident or illness: (*a*) to provide for the continuance of income while a breadwinner is ill or disabled, and (*b*) to provide funds to pay the medical and hospital bills involved.

HEALTH INSURANCE

Medical needs for the individual are unpredictable. One severe illness, or a number of minor ones in a short period, can wreck the family budget and bring on indebtedness. A hospitalized illness "involves a severe physical shock, a high emotional crisis, and a large economic expenditure." In one year illness cost families of the United States $21.9 billion. The average hospitalized illness costs in the neighborhood of $280, apart from loss of income, and in some cases the cost rises to several thousand dollars. Last year one out of every eight

---

* For 1965 legislation on medicare, see "The New Medicare and Social Security Provisions" following p. 850.

persons in the United States was hospitalized. Each average-sized family has at least three sicknesses a year needing treatment. Doctors in the United States treat more people in their offices in two days than all the undertakers bury in a year. Every minute 76 Americans are injured or become ill.

The Public Health Service reports that on an average winter day, six million persons are unable to work, attend school, or pursue their usual activities. Of that number 2.5 million suffer from chronic diseases, 1.5 million from colds, flu, or pneumonia, and 250,000 from diseases of the stomach and intestines. Statisticians report that every year in the United States about 21 percent of the population can expect to be accidentally injured in some way. Of these injuries, 17 percent are sufficiently serious to require professional medical attention. About ten million people are temporarily disabled each year. Almost 100,000 persons are accidentally killed each year. About 300,000 persons are permanently disabled.[1] Although the toll of automobile accidents is great, more than three times as many persons are disabled by accidents in their own homes each year. Last year, for example, 1.5 million were disabled by auto accidents, but 4.3 million were injured by accidents in the home.

The economic cost of accidents add up to $15.5 billion—a dollar amount required to pay for property damage, legal, medical, surgical and hospital costs, the administrative costs of insurance and loss of income resulting from absence from work.[2]

Among currently employed persons an average of 5.6 days per person were lost from work because of illness or injury. This caused a loss in wages and salaries of about $5.8 million. More work-loss days per person were reported among lower-income than higher-income persons. Those from families with an income of $4,000 or more reported 4.8 days per person lost from work. Those from families with an income between $2,000 and $3,999 lost 6.5 days, and those with less than $2,000 lost 8.4 days each.[3] Those least able to afford illness suffered more.

Professional people and skilled workers spend proportionately more for medical care than the semiskilled, unskilled, or other occupational types.

---

[1] See *Handbook of Health Insurance* (rev. ed.: Cincinnati, Ohio: The National Underwriter Co.), 1962.

[2] *Insurance Facts, 1963.* Insurance Information Institute, 110 William St., New York, N.Y., 10038.

[3] *Progress in Health Services,* Health Information Foundation, University of Chicago, Vol. XII, No. 2 (March–April, 1963).

Small, growing families earmark a larger share of their available dollars for health than do large families.

Expenditures for medical purposes vary tremendously in different areas.

These facts emerge from a study of the Bureau of Labor Statistics *Survey of Consumer Expenditures.* About every ten years the BLS conducts such a survey, the latest in 1961 and 1962. Analysis by the Health Insurance Institute shows:

In 21 cities ranging in size from Orlando, Florida, to New York, *professional people and skilled workers* spent for medical care an average 6.2 percent of all expenditures. A sampling of all active occupations in the same 21 cities put at 5.3–5.9 percent the range of average expenditures for medical care as a percentage of all expenditures.

Smaller families apparently are more health conscious than larger families. A family with one or two children commonly spends a greater percentage of its expenditures for medical care than the family with four or more children.

Even in terms of average, there is a great variability of health outlays according to geographic area. Average expenditures for medical care by all families in Baltimore, for example, were only $278, while comparable figures were 41 percent higher at $393 in San Francisco and 55 percent higher at $431 in New York.

For individual families the variability is much greater, the Institute said, pointing out that other studies have shown that one family in twenty has no medical expense whatsoever in a given year, while three in a hundred experience very high medical costs exceeding $1,000 and ranging to many thousands of dollars.[4]

Accident and sickness can (1) cut off family income, (2) quickly wipe out savings slowly accumulated over a long period, or (3) leave a hopeless muddle of debt, or (4) be so large that a family cannot afford all the medical service it needs. For these reasons, increasing millions have turned to prepayment insurance plans to ease the monetary pains of heavy hospital, surgical, and medical bills.

A simple appendectomy will cost, in all, about $450 ($190 for the surgeon, $40 for the anesthetist and operating room, $100 for hospital room at the rate of $20 a day for five days in a semiprivate room, $21 for drugs in the hospital, and about $100 in fees for diagnosis and for visits to the general practitioner before and after the operation)—in addition to loss of income for a month. Further, if you need special nursing care, a registered nurse charges $22 for an eight-hour shift, and sometimes necessity requires special-duty private nurses in the hospital on a

---

[4] *Survey of Health Economics,* Health Insurance Institute, New York, N.Y., June 26, 1963.

round-the-clock, 24-hour basis. If you should need a practical nurse (one who has not received a diploma but has either [a] completed about a year of study toward the R.N. or [b] has studied at one of the practical-nursing schools) at home after the operation, it will cost about

---

Star's Illness Costs Insurers $2 Million

ELIZABETH TAYLOR, the sultry movie queen who is among the industry's biggest box-office attractions, has no fans among the men operating in the international insurance market.

This became apparent this week when a group of 40 insurance companies and 90 syndicates of Lloyd's underwriters in London agreed to a $2 million out-of-court settlement with 20th Century-Fox Film Corp. Fox had brought suit against the insurance consortium for losses involved in production of its film, *Cleopatra,* starring Elizabeth Taylor.

Fox, which had insured both the film and the actress, asked for $3 million when production was delayed after she got sick in London last year. At first, the insurers denied any liability, then offered $1.3 million. Fox felt this was inadequate, and took legal action.

$28 for a 12-hour day. When the less-than-$6,000-income family is confronted with such costs, it is in trouble.

Prepaid Voluntary Medical Care Insurance

Accident and sickness (health) insurance has usually been used broadly to provide two very different kinds of protection: (*a*) "health" or "medical care" insurance plans, including the cost of hospitalization, surgical, limited medical, major medical catastrophes, and comprehensive medical care; and (*b*) "disability" insurance plans, compensating injured persons for the loss of a part or parts of the body, such as an arm or a leg or an eye, *or* for the loss of earnings through disability.

The former type now covers some 141 million persons in the United States, the latter some 45 million. There has been a striking increase in recent years in the number of people in the United States who have been covered by voluntary insurance, especially group insurance, against some part of the costs of medical care. The number of those who have some protection against the costs of hospital care, for example, rose from less than 6 million in 1939 to more than 141 million today (see Fig. 9–1). Thus more than three fourths of our population are now covered by some form of voluntary medical care insurance.

While disability insurance was the more popular type prior to World War II, medical care insurance has now superseded it in importance, as more and more people have come to realize that the chances of their losing an eye, or an arm, or a leg are infinitesimal compared to the prospect that they will, at some point, land in a hospital to have an appendix removed or some infectious disease cured. Health insurance,

FIGURE 9–1

Growth of Hospital, Surgical, and Regular Medical
Expense Protection in U.S., 1940–1962

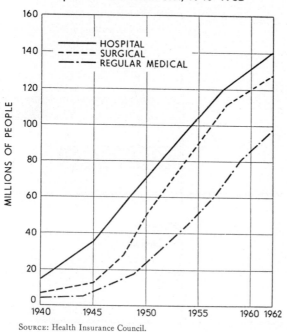

SOURCE: Health Insurance Council.

then, can be considered in six categories: (a) disability insurance, (b) hospital expense insurance, (c) surgical expense insurance, (d) limited medical care insurance, (e) major medical expense insurance, and (f) comprehensive coverage.

Loss of Income or Disability Insurance

Protection against loss of income resulting from sickness or accident is the oldest form of voluntary health insurance. This type of insurance pays benefits when you are unable to work because of sickness or accident. Developed more than 70 years ago, this kind of insurance is now held by some 45 million persons, as Figure 9–2 shows. The problem which looms large in illness or accident is the loss of wages or salary during the period needed to regain one's health.

Policies of this type provide as much as 75 percent of wage earners' normal earnings for a specified period of disability. Usually a company will not pay more than three quarters of the regular weekly or monthly income for a very good reason. If a person were able to buy a policy which paid as much or more than he earned while working, there would be strong incentive toward feigned illnesses and continued accidents. The companies would have their hands full trying to prevent fraud.

FIGURE 9–2

Extent of Loss of Income Protection in U.S.
December 31, 1962

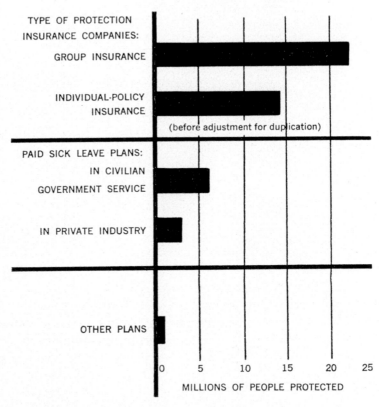

SOURCE: Health Insurance Council.

The longer the waiting period—the more inexpensive the insurance. To avoid small claims which cost the insurance companies money in paper work and overhead, they pass the benefit to the insured person in either larger monthly income or longer coverage. The best policy is the longest, noncancellable and guaranteed renewable until the day the policyholder retires.

The number of persons protected by group loss of income plans through private industry and government is greater than those covered by individual policies. This is true also of other forms of health insurance since most of the people who have health insurance today obtain it as members of employed groups. Self-employed people have to choose their coverage, but even they can frequently find some group—such as fraternal organizations—to cover them.

Since policies in this category are legion, consider two actual cases. Mary O'Brien graduated from State Teachers two years ago. She is 24 now, teaching school in Illinois, earning $4,500 a year. Since she is single and has no dependents, all she needs to do is take care of herself until she finds some male willing to take over this task in return for a promise to "love, honor, and obey." As part of her health insurance protection, she has purchased a policy which, at an annual premium cost of only $58.40, will pay her a weekly income of $40 for five years in case she is disabled by an accident or $40 weekly for two years in case sickness prevents her from earning a living.

Since Mary rooms with another teacher her rent is low, and she feels she can save enough money from her salary to cover her possible expenses if she buys the policy with a 90-day waiting period rather than one with a 7-day waiting period. This will reduce her premium costs by 45 percent.

Our second case is a young bachelor attorney, Harlan Farmer, Jr. He's 26, graduated from Yale Law School, earns $8,200 a year. At a premium cost of $68 a year, he recently purchased a policy through his bar association which, if he becomes totally disabled as a result of an accident, will pay him $50 a week for 260 weeks starting the first day of the accident, or $50 a week from the eighth day of sickness, or of hospital confinement, for 104 weeks.

If Harlan wanted to, for an additional annual premium of $9.00, he could extend the $50 weekly benefit for sickness from 104 to 260 weeks (five years). This would bring the total annual cost of his policy to $77. Also, if he wanted to receive a benefit of $75 a week, rather than $50, for five years for accident and for two years for sickness, he could simply pay a premium of $85 a year. If he wanted to raise this $75 a week for sickness from a maximum period of two years to a maximum of five years, he could do so by paying an additional premium of $19.25, bringing his total payment under the $75-a-week benefit policy to $104.25 per annum. Thus, you can see that loss-of-income insurance can be tailored both to individual financial needs and to individual financial resources.

Hospital Expense Protection

More than three out of four persons in the entire population of the United States are now protected through voluntary programs against the costs of hospital care in the event of accident or illness. This represents the biggest single form of coverage in the field of health protection. The total number with this form of protection now equals 141 million, as Table 9–1 reveals. Insurance companies provide somewhat more than

TABLE 9–1

Distribution of Hospital, Surgical, and Regular Medical Expense Coverage by Type of Insuring Organization, December 31, 1962

	NUMBER OF PEOPLE PROTECTED (000 OMITTED)		
TYPE OF INSURING ORGANIZATION	HOSPITAL EXPENSE	SURGICAL EXPENSE	REGULAR MEDICAL EXPENSE
INSURANCE COMPANIES:			
Group insurance	59,153	59,787	40,012
Individual-policy insurance	36,061	31,443	10,974
Unadjusted total	95,214	91,230	50,986
Deduction for duplication in persons with insurance-company protection	10,040	9,247	3,976
Net total for insurance companies	85,174	81,983	47,010
BLUE CROSS, BLUE SHIELD AND MEDICAL SOCIETY PLANS:	60,566	51,769	48,093
INDEPENDENT PLANS:			
Industrial plans	4,696	4,688	4,290
Community plans	1,837	3,010	2,904
Private group clinics	60	243	249
College health plans	400	300	900
Total for independent plans	6,993	8,241	8,343
DEDUCTION FOR DUPLICATION:			
Persons protected by more than one type of insuring organization	11,296	10,808	5,242
NET TOTAL PERSONS PROTECTED	141,437	131,185	98,204

SOURCE: Health Insurance Council.

half the coverage. Hospital expense protection provides benefits toward the payment of hospital charges for room, board, and miscellaneous services. Benefits have been steadily liberalized and expanded since this form of coverage began its major growth some two decades ago. Present-day coverage usually includes payment for use of an operating room and for laboratory and X-ray examination, medicines, and all other services incidental to medical care and treatment which are furnished by the hospital.

You are allowed so much per day up to a maximum number of days, usually 70 to 120. Hospital expense insurance is the most widely held of all types of health insurance. Pioneered by Blue Cross, hospital expense insurance is now sold by all the major insurance companies as part of their total health insurance package.

Surgical Expense Protection

The next largest form of protection in the field of voluntary accident and health coverage is surgical expense protection. The number of persons with this form of coverage now totals more that 131 million. A later development than coverage for hospital care, surgical expense protection has shown the more rapid growth over recent years. Most persons with surgical expense protection are covered either by insurance companies or by Blue Shield. If the services of a surgeon are needed, the protection provides payments in accordance with a schedule of fees fixing maximum reimbursement for each type of operation.

A small part of a surgical expense allowance schedule runs as follows:

| | ALLOWANCES | | |
DESCRIPTION OF OPERATION	AFTER-CARE	SURGICAL	ANESTHESIA
Appendectomy (I.P.)	3 weeks	$175.00	$ 35.00
Pericardiectomy	3 weeks	500.00	100.00
Lobectomy	3 weeks	500.00	100.00
Laparotomy	3 weeks	175.00	35.00
Cataract	6 weeks	275.00	55.00
Removal of kidney	3 weeks	275.00	55.00
Pancreatectomy, local, partial, or subtotal	3 weeks	350.00	70.00
Hysterectomy	3 weeks	175.00	35.00
Large bowel resection	6 weeks	350.00	70.00

The policy you buy prescribes the maximum the insurance company, or Blue Shield, will pay according to the schedule. If an operation costs more than the sum the company will pay under the schedule, you pay the extra amount. The cost of the policy bears a direct relationship to the maximum the company contracts to pay. The higher the maximum, naturally the higher the cost; the lower the maximum, the lower the cost.

Regular Medical Expense Protection

In the development of voluntary accident and health coverage, limited or regular medical expense protection came third, following the growth of hospital and surgical benefits. Its growth has been essentially a post-World War II phenomenon. In 1941 it was estimated that there were only about 3 million persons with regular medical expense protection. Today more than 98 million carry this type of coverage.

This type of coverage pays for visits to a doctor's office or for his visits to you at your home or in a hospital. The maximum number of calls for each sickness or injury is usually specified in the policy, so the patient won't be tempted to demand undue service. Some companies will not write this type of policy because they feel it is a cost that should be budgeted rather than insured. They will, however, provide for it in combination policies, either surgical-medical, or comprehensive. The Blue Shield organizations will sell different kinds of general medical policies.

Major Medical Expense Coverage

Major medical expense coverage, a relatively new addition to voluntary health protection plans, is designed to help meet the catastrophic costs resulting from very serious illnesses and from prolonged disability. Broadly speaking, this type of coverage takes up where the customary forms of health protection—hospital, surgical, and medical care—leave off.

It is designed to meet the needs of those who may be hospitalized for long periods, or those who require extensive treatment by medical specialists. It is a form of protection against large medical bills not covered by the usual type of hospital and surgical plans. As one authority put it: "Major medical takes up where the basic health plans stop." Major medical expense insurance ordinarily pays benefits whether hospitalization is involved or not. Major medical policies, furthermore, insure against expense arising from almost any conceivable medical cause, not just rarities like polio, spinal meningitis, or a selected list of diseases. A few policies exclude mental illness, but most in group insurance don't. The very rapid growth of major medical in recent years may be seen in Figure 9–3. Over 38 million persons are now covered under this type of policy.

There are three distinguishing features to major medical insurance: (1) There are high maximum limits, ranging from $5,000 to $20,000 or more. The maximum may apply to any one illness, or the total may apply to a policy year. (2) A deductible provision, similar to that found in most automobile collision policies, is used in major medical. This is to eliminate what would otherwise be an undue burden of many small claims, excessive in number and costly to handle and process. The deductible is the beginning amount of medical expense which the policyholder himself must pay before insurance coverage takes effect. The deductible amounts commonly range from $200 to $1,000. The

FIGURE 9–3

Growth of Major Medical Expense Coverage
in U.S., 1951–1962

MILLIONS OF PEOPLE PROTECTED AT END OF YEAR

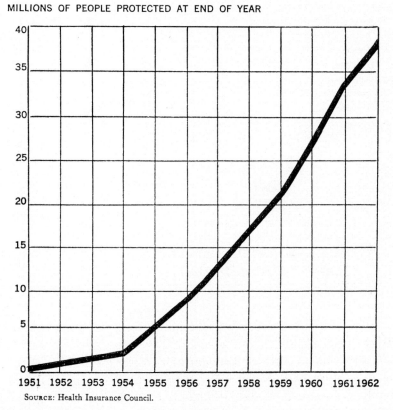

Source: Health Insurance Council.

higher the deductible, the lower the premium. (3) The third feature is the "coinsurance" clause. This requires the policyholder to pay part of the total bill, over and above the deductible. The purpose is to prevent demands for excessive medical service.

What does major medical cost? Most major medical policies are sold under group plans. Harlan Farmer purchased a major medical policy through his bar association. It had a $10,000 maximum benefit, a

$500-deductible clause, and a 20 percent coinsurance provision. It cost but $36 per annum.

Let's see how major medical works. Don Thomas developed a severe case of hepatitis which necessitated an extended period of hospitalization followed by a long convalescence at home. He is covered by a basic plan and by major medical insurance. His expenses are shown in the following table:

	TOTAL CHARGES	COVERED BY BASE PLAN*	COVERED BY MAJOR MEDICAL
Hospital room and board:			
50 days @ $15 per day	$ 750	$350	$ 400
Other hospital charges:			
X-rays, blood tests,			
medicines, etc.	325	150	175
Registered nurses:			
$15 per day for 20 days	300	...	$ 300
Physicians' fees	700	150	550
Totals	$2,075	$650	$1,425
Less deductible of $100			−100
Balance Subject to Co-insurance			$1,325
Less Co-insurance at 20%			−265
Amount Paid by Major Medical			$1,060
Summary:			
Paid by Base Plan*	$ 650		
Paid by major medical	1,060		
Paid by patient	365		
Total	$2,075		

* Hospital room and board and general medical expense.
SOURCE: Health Insurance Institute.

As you can see, of a total bill of $2,075 Don paid only $365; major medical paid $1,060, half the bill.

It is possible to purchase supplementary major medical coverage—to add to existing basic hospital and surgical plans as an alternative to comprehensive major medical. Both have high maximums ranging from $5,000 to $20,000 or more for an accident or illness.

Comprehensive Medical

A newer and growing type of health insurance is a combination which ties together the basic plans (hospitalization, surgical, regular medical) and major medical in one big package policy called "comprehensive." It began in 1954. About 100 policies were issued in that year. It has grown so fast, however, that today over ten million policies are outstanding.

What is "comprehensive"? Well, as its name implies, like Blue Cross–Blue Shield, it covers the hospital, surgical, and medical services normally required during *short-term* illness in the hospital. It also covers home and office medical care, private-duty nursing, and prescriptions too. And, like major medical expense insurance, it also covers most services required during *long-term* illness, up to liberal limits. Like major medical, it has a deductible feature, though usually somewhat lower than major medical, and it also has the coinsurance provision.

The Federal Employees Program written by an insurance company is the largest group comprehensive major medical plan in force. It has a $40,000 maximum a year for each enrollee and each member of his family, with exhausted benefits automatically restored by an amount not exceeding $1,000 a year until the top limit is again reached. Hospital benefits are for semiprivate room and board charges up to $1,000 per person per year plus 80 percent of any balance.

The insurance company pays 80 percent of the hospital costs after a $25 deductible. Surgical, medical and para-medical costs are 80–20 percent coinsurance after a $50 deductible. The policy covers 50 percent of out-patient psychiatric treatment limited to an annual maximum of $250 per patient. Maternity benefits are also provided under the comprehensive plan the same as regular hospital, medical and surgical benefits. The premium total is $227.76 yearly—of which the government pays $81.12 and the family $146.64.

Dental Insurance Growing

The number of persons covered by group dental insurance has more than doubled since 1960.

According to the U.S. Public Health Service, about 1.15 million persons were covered by dental insurance by the end of 1962, up from 550,000 in 1960. The number of plans offering coverage for dental work more than doubled over the same period, from 128 to 296.

Group dental insurance programs help pay the costs of such items as oral examinations, fillings, extractions, inlays, bridgework, dentures, oral surgery, anesthesia, treatment of gum diseases, root canal therapy, and orthodontics.

—*Health Insurance Institute, Oct. 31, 1963*

Types of Organizations Which Provide Voluntary Medical Care Insurance Protection

Medical care insurance at present is provided by three large groups of organizations: (*a*) the nonprofit Blue Cross and Blue Shield plans; (*b*) the casualty, life, and other commercial insurance companies; (*c*) a number of organizations independent of the first two groups, including industrial and labor union plans, consumer co-operatives, programs under the auspices of private medical groups, some medical societies, community organizations, and others. Blue Cross is concerned primarily with hospital insurance, Blue Shield with surgical, limited, and general medical-service insurance; while the independent organizations provide either hospital, surgical, or group service medical care. None of the Blue Shield plans provides for group practice of medicine, while many of the independent plans do.

The commercial insurance companies and the nonprofit Blue Cross largely share the coverage held for hospital insurance; but in the field of surgical insurance, the commercial insurance companies have written three fifths of the coverage. Blue Shield leads the medical-protection field, but the 8 million people who have group service medical care coverage obtain it mainly from independent, unaffiliated plans (see Figures 9–4a and 9–4b).

FIGURE 9–4a

**Health Insurance Benefit Payments
in the U.S. by Type of Insurer
and by Type of Coverage
1957 and 1962**

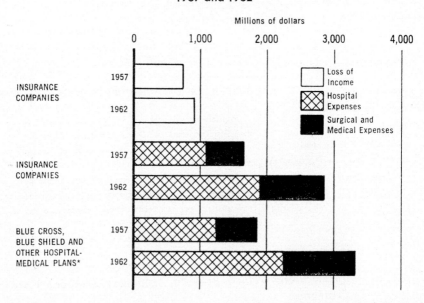

*Includes payments by Independent and Medical Society-approved or-sponsored plans.

Source: Health Insurance Council.

In 1929 a group of teachers in Dallas, Texas, realized that *individually* a serious illness requiring hospitalization would impose a cost upon any one of them beyond their resources. Millions of other Americans had found themselves in this plight but had done nothing about it; these Dallas teachers did. They figured that, as a *group,* they could easily pay all the hospital bills they were likely to incur. So they

FIGURE 9–4b

Health Insurance Benefit Payments
of Insurance Companies*

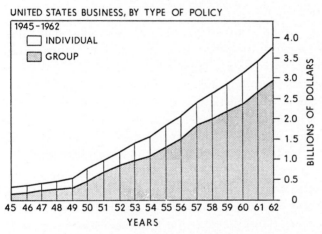

UNITED STATES BUSINESS, BY TYPE OF POLICY

1945–1962
☐ INDIVIDUAL
▨ GROUP

BILLIONS OF DOLLARS

45 46 47 48 49 50 51 52 53 54 55 56 57 58 59 60 61 62

YEARS

* Includes loss of income and excludes accidental death and dismemberment benefits.
    Source: *Accident and Sickness Review, Spectator Health Insurance Index,* Health Insurance Council, and Health Insurance Association of America.

worked out an arrangement with Baylor University Hospital to provide, for $3.00 per teacher per school semester, 21 days of hospital care to any one of them who needed such care. This was the beginning of Blue Cross. By 1938, Blue Cross membership had reached half a million. Today it is over 62 million, with 77 Blue Cross plans, plus 4 associate plans in Canada and one in Jamaica.

Blue Shield was established in 1946 by a group of nine predecessor plans known as "Associated Medical Care Plans." It was designed to provide insurance for costs of surgical and limited medical care. It now has 71 plans with an aggregate enrollment of over 50 million members. It was sponsored by the American Medical Association and is known as the "Doctors' Plan." Stress is placed on the fact that under it the subscriber has free choice of physician.

Through arrangements other than Blue Cross, Blue Shield, or commercial accident and health insurance, more than 800 plans provide medical care and hospitalization protection to some 8 million people on a prepayment basis. These prepayment medical care organizations have no national affiliation (with few exceptions), so that they may properly be characterized as independent plans. While they are greater in number than the Blue Cross and Blue Shield plans, their membership is nevertheless much smaller. Their significance is derived from the fact that some of them provide a wider range of insurance benefits and medical care than do the plans classified as Blue Cross, Blue Shield, or commercial insurance.

Blue Cross

Rates. More than 40 percent of those who held some form of insurance against the costs of hospital care were insured through the 77 nonprofit, tax-free, autonomous Blue Cross plans. A majority of these plans contract with hospitals to provide most or all of their services in semiprivate accommodations with a minimum of additional charges. If you are a member of Blue Cross, the rate you pay depends on the type of plan you select and where you live and work. There are contracts for individuals or for a family (including all unmarried children under 19), enrolled either through a group or separately. Group enrollment costs you less. Rates vary from plan to plan, largely because of the variation in hospital costs in different areas and different benefits offered. In general, hospital protection in semiprivate accommodations for 70 or 120 days will cost an individual from $36 to $84 a year and from $96 to $190 for a family. Table 9–2 shows rates under a 120-day Blue Cross plan.

TABLE 9–2

Rates for 120 Day Blue Cross Plan

Type of Contract	Group Enrollment		Nongroup Enrollment	
	Monthly	Annually	Quarterly	Annually
Individual	$ 4.40	$ 52.80	$18.00	$ 72.00
Family	11.72	140.64	39.30	157.20

Benefits. Benefits differ somewhat but follow a general pattern. Some provide more care than others, and some allow more special services. Most of the standard contracts provide full hospitalization benefits for 70 or more days in a year, or for each admission. In most areas it is customary to provide bed, board, general nursing care, customary drugs, special diets, use of operating room, anesthesia, laboratory tests, special equipment, such as oxygen tents, X-ray examinations, etc., as part of the semiprivate service.

Room and board coverage provided by the plans varies from coverage in full in semiprivate accommodations to per diem allowances. Over 70 percent of the participants are entitled to full coverage in semiprivate accommodations regardless of the cost, the remainder having either ward coverage or indemnity allowances, which are continually being modified to keep them close to the prevailing cost of hospital rooms. In private accommodations, nearly half of the plans provide an indemnity amount, usually ranging between $10 to $20 per day. The remaining plans provide an allowance, equal to the hospital's average semiprivate charge, toward the cost of a private room. Dependents are entitled to the same benefits as the subscriber with rare exceptions.

Typical Limitations. Contracts usually exclude admissions for diagnostic care, rest cures, and blood, blood-plasma, or blood-donor services. Mental care in a general hospital is covered by 61 plans. Only 9 of the 77 plans exclude all dental care with most allowing benefits when such care is necessitated by accident. Maternity hospital costs are usually given only after a membership of 8 to 10 months.

Organization. The plans co-ordinate enrollment, public relations, and statistical research through the Blue Cross Association, but each Blue Cross plan exercises complete local independence over the benefits and rates included in its contracts. The plans arrange with local member hospitals (some 6,000) to furnish care to subscribers, and they pay for the hospitalization according to the contract agreement. Almost all Blue Cross plans have a working agreement which allows for transfer of their subscribers from one plan to another when a subscriber moves to another community. A second agreement gives benefits to a subscriber hospitalized in any community serviced by Blue Cross, whether or not it is his home area. Although most of the emphasis is on group enrollment, all the plans enroll individual subscribers. Approximately one out of every three persons in the United States now belongs to Blue Cross.

Blue Shield

While Blue Cross is entirely a hospitalization insurance plan, mostly on a service basis, its allied Blue Shield plan covers the costs of physicians' services, mostly on a cash-indemnity basis.

Over 50 million subscribers received payments of about $950 million against some of the costs of physicians' services (mostly surgery and nonsurgical treatment in the hospitals) under the 77 nonprofit Blue Shield plans last year.

There are three principal types of programs which Blue Shield offers. The largest number of Blue Shield subscribers, some 70 percent, are enrolled under service programs, in which participating doctors accept the Blue Shield allowances as full payment for subscribers whose incomes are within predetermined levels. Full service benefits, which provide full payment for covered services without regard to income are available to another 6 percent of total Blue Shield membership. Fifteen plans, which account for 24 percent of the total membership offer primarily cash indemnity benefits. The service programs are for families with limited incomes; the cash indemnity programs for those of higher incomes. In recent years, Blue Shield service plans have developed higher income ceilings to keep pace with rising income levels. For example, at the end of 1956, service income ceiling averaged $5,500, while for 1963 the average was $7,200.

The Blue Shield plans contract with local physicians to accept payment according to a standard fee schedule. If your income is above the ceiling set by the medical plan in your area, you may be charged the difference between the participating physician's regular fee and the amount set in the Blue Shield fee schedule. If you select a non-participating physician, you are allowed cash indemnity up to the amount stated in the Blue Shield schedule, and you make your own financial arrangements with the physician. Blue Shield plans are either sponsored directly by a medical society or are officially approved by it. Generally speaking, the majority of Blue Shield surgical-medical coverage is added to a Blue Cross hospitalization enrollment. Like the Blue Cross, Blue Shield plans provide for transfer from plan to plan without a waiting period. Each plan designs its own local program.

Blue Shield generally offers three kinds of coverage:

a) Surgical
b) Surgical-medical
c) General medical

The surgical only contracts are being discontinued. The surgical-medical coverage includes allowances toward doctors' fees for surgery performed in the hospital, or in the doctor's office, or in your home, and maternity allowances under family enrollment *plus* medical care in the hospital when no surgery is involved. The general medical care coverage provides all the benefits given in the surgical-medical plan *plus* home and office medical care and specialists' consultation. Supplemental major medical is also offered in a majority of the Plans.

What You Get. For each of the types of coverage mentioned above there are two plans. The first, which for convenience we can call the *"basic"* plan, involves a "$2,500–$4,000 service contract." The second, which we will call the "expanded benefit" plan is a "$4,000–$7,200 service contract." Naturally, the second costs more than the first and provides greater benefits. Let's take the general medical coverage and compare the benefits under the basic and expanded plans. Surgical allowances are larger under the expanded plan, and there is an additional allowance for anesthesia. The contrast may be seen in the following:

Basic Plan (New York area)

Description of Operation	After-Care	Allowance
Gynecology:		
Dilation and curettage (I.P.), (nonpuerperal)	3 weeks	$ 40.00
Hysterectomy:		
Not including cervix	3 weeks	$150.00
Including cervix	3 weeks	200.00
Myomectomy, abdominal approach	3 weeks	125.00
Radical hysterectomy for cancer, including lymph glands and adnexa (complete pelvic viscera)	4 weeks	250.00

Expanded Plan (New York area)

Description of Operation	After-Care	Allowances	
		Surgical	Anesthesia
Gynecology:			
Dilation and curettage (I.P.), (nonpuerperal)	3 weeks	$ 75.00	$20.00
Hysterectomy:			
Not including cervix	3 weeks	175.00	35.00
Including cervix	3 weeks	275.00	55.00
Myomectomy, abdominal approach	3 weeks	175.00	35.00
Radical hysterectomy for cancer, including lymph glands and adnexa (complete pelvic viscera)	4 weeks	350.00	70.00

Source: United Medical Service of New York.

Under this basic plan, the maximum allowance for a single operative procedure during the course of an operation is $250. If there are two or more distinctly different procedures during any one disability, the maximum allowance is $500. Under the expanded benefits plan, the maximum for a single operative procedure is $350, for a combination, $700.

For medical care in a hospital, when no surgical procedure is involved, under the basic plan the maximum allowance totals $452, whereas under the expanded plan, it is $895. For home and office medical care the basic plan allows $4.00 a visit if the doctor comes to your home, $3.00 a visit if you go to the doctor's office. Under the expanded plan $5.00 a visit is allowed if the doctor comes to you, but $3.00 if you go to the doctor's office. Under both plans you are allowed a maximum of 30 visits in each contract year. There are other differences as well which your regional Blue Shield organization will be happy to explain.

What You Pay. The cost of Blue Shield coverage varies with the scope of covered services, local medical economics, and local patterns of utilization. As an indication of the range involved, monthly rates for most-widely-held group service benefit medical-surgical programs ranged from $1.10 to $4.85 for individuals, and from $2.70 to $9.80 for family coverage. The median rates for such programs were $1.65 for individuals and $5.16 for families. You will want to check your local organization to determine the current rates in your area.

Independent Organizations

There are 800 nonaffiliated plans, which range in membership from fewer than 100 to over 500,000 and which bring benefits from a few dollars a day for hospitalization to complete medical care. Some 8.5 million persons who had comprehensive voluntary medical care insurance belong to 516 of these plans.[5] These independent plans either developed within a community, an industry, among consumers, or through a prepayment arrangement by private group clinics. Figure 9–5 shows five different types of groups, comparing and contrasting sponsorship, benefits, exceptions, membership, and costs. Each membership has been able to obtain that type of plan which meets its own particular needs, although, generally, the plans provide comprehensive medical care in home, doctor's office, group clinic, or hospital, as required.

All but six of the 50 states had one or more independent plans but the concentration of membership—nearly 47 percent of the total enrollment—was in New York and California. Three plans—with a combined enrollment of 2.2 million—the Kaiser Foundation Health Plans of California, Oregon, and Hawaii; Group Health Insurance of New York; and the Health Insurance Plan of Greater New York constituted 70 percent of the enrollment in all community plans.

---

[5] Donald G. Hay, "Independent Health Insurance Plans," *Social Security Bulletin,* February, 1963.

Among the employer-employee union plans, the eleven with 50,000 or more members had 55 percent of the total enrollment. Four plans—the United Mine Workers of America, the International Ladies Garment Workers Union, the National Association of Letter Carriers, and the United Federation of Postal Clerks—enrolled 2 million or 43 percent of enrollment in all employer-employee-union groups.

The majority of the independent groups are co-operative organizations controlled in their financial, economic, and general policy by the members. However, in the medical sphere and in the relationship between the doctor and his patients, the professional medical staff has complete control. Most of the member plans provide direct service to covered individuals, while others offer cash-indemnity payments. Some plans provide hospitalization to their members through Blue Cross; others have made their own arrangements with hospitals.

Commercial Insurance Company Plans

Over 85 million people now hold hospital expense policies issued by the insurance companies: 59 million under group policies and 36 million under individual insurance payable in cash indemnities to be applied against hospital bills. In a recent year, insurance companies paid hospital bills of their policyholders, whether under group or individual enrollment, equal to an estimated $1.9 billion (see Table 9–3).

TABLE 9–3

Voluntary Health Insurance Benefits Paid
(Millions of Dollars)

	Type of Insurance Organization			
Type of Benefit	Insurance Companies	Blue Cross– Blue Shield	Independent	Total
Hospital expense*	$1,899	$2,081	$178	$4,158
Surgical and medical expense*	958	820	235	2,012
Loss of income	906	. . .	. . .	906
Total	$3,763	$2,901	$413	$7,077

* Including major medical expense.
Source: Health Insurance Council.

About 82 million persons now hold commercial insurance policies (approximately 60 million under group coverage) against costs of surgery. Some 47 million were covered by insurance companies for regular medical expense protection. And some 35 million persons obtained major medical expense protection through insurance com-

FIGURE 9-5

Comparison of Five Comprehensive Medical Care Plans in the United States

SPONSORSHIP

	Consolidated Edison Company of New York	Labor Health Institute	Health Insurance Plan of Greater New York	Ross Loos Group of Los Angeles	Group Health Association, Washington, D.C.
Area served	Employer-employee, New York City and vicinity.	Greater St. Louis	Community, Greater New York	Greater Los Angeles area	Washington metropolitan area including the counties of Montgomery and Prince George in Maryland and the cities of Alexandria and Falls Church, Virginia, and the counties of Arlington and Fairfax, Virginia.
Type of benefit	Service	Service	Service	Service	Service
Method of operation	Medical group practice in plant. District physician for home calls. Specialists for consultation.	Medical group practice in medical center	32 medical groups—and centers, group affiliated with hospital	Medical group practice in medical center and branch offices	Medical group practice in medical center
Enrollment	21,600 employees	16,000 employees and dependents	630,000	135,000	48,000
Eligibility for enrollment	Employees only, 3 mos. service. Mutual Aid Soc. membership. Physical examination. Hourly or weekly payroll.	Group enrollment only. Union members of Warehouse & Distrib. Workers Union, Teamsters, Local 688.	Individual and group. Employed persons and their dependents. Individual—health statements.	Various group and individual Plans. Group-Employee, Union, Association-Member/Employee and Dependents. Individual-Subscriber to age 55 when applying, plus dependents. Physical exam.	Individual and group enrollment. Enrollees over 60 at time of joining: med. care at cost. Individual enrollment: physical exam. Federal employees enrollment; accepted without physical exam, no restriction for pre-existing conditions, no restrictions because of age.
Benefits Hospital care	Room and board, semi-private, no time limit. Special reimbursement for out-of-area care as per established schedule.	90 days, $15.00 per day, add'l 6 mos. semiprivate with ⅓ rate covered. Covers operating-room charge and allowance of $100 for special services.	Not included. Required coverage by hospital insurance.	Varying selected insurance benefits provided by the Independence Life Insurance Company of America.	No limit on days, semiprivate accommodations. High option; medical or surgical, GHA pays all hospital expenses exclusive of personal comfort items. Maternity, patient pays first $50 of hospital expenses. Low option; member pays 50% of first $150 of hospital expenses exclusive of personal comfort items. Maternity; patient pays first $125 of hospital expenses.
Extras	Excludes only special-duty nursing and appliances	Included in the $100 allowance		Included. See "Benefits, Hospital care" above	Included (see Benefit Hospital care)
Surgical care (major and minor)	Included	Included	Included	Included for subscribers and dependents. Some Plans—$25 maximum fee including postoperative care.	Included
General medical care	Included, at clinic, office, home, and hospital. For home calls out of area employee receives $6.00 indemnity.	At clinic, home, and hospital	Included, at office, home, and hospital	Included at office, home and hospital. (Some plans $1.25 fee for office call, $5.00 fee for home call).	Included—home, office, and hospital. $5.00 for first home call in each illness.
Specialists' care	Included, as well as referrals to other specialists	Included, all major specialties, plus psychiatry, consultation with those not on staff	Included, all major specialties. Panel of superspecialists also provided.	Included	Included. Major specialists on staff. Consultation with specialists outside.

	Consolidated Edison Company of New York	Labor Health Institute	Health Insurance Plan of Greater New York	Ross Loos Group of Los Angeles	Group Health Association, Washington, D.C.
Maternity care	Not included	9 months' wait hosp. included for individuals after initial group enrollment.	Included	Included for subscribers and dependents. Some plans $50 fee for delivery, pre- and postnatal care.	Individual enrollment—included after 10 months enrollment. Enrollment under Federal Employees Health Benefits Program—no waiting period.
Preventative care	Included. Periodic health exams and immunizations	Included. Periodic health exams and immunizations	Included. Periodic health exams and immunizations.	Included and recommended.	Included. Periodical exams and immunization.
Home nursing	Not included	Included	Included—visiting-nurse services	Not included	Not included
Dental care	Included—oral surgery. Dentures after 2-yr. membership.	Patient pays for material and drugs. Patient pays laboratory cost for dentures and bridges.	Not included	Not included	At cost. Prepayment plan for maintenance care only at $3.00 per month for adults; $2.50 for the first two children and $2.25 for each additional child under 13.
X rays (diagnostic and therapeutic)	Included. Therapeutic not included	Included	Included	Included	High option included, low option $5 per film or treatment.
Laboratory and tests	Included	Included	Included	Included	High option, included, low option, included with additional minimum charge.
Drugs and medicine	If prescribed by physician	At reduced rates	Immunization agents.	Available at pharmacies.	Sold at discount
Appliances	Not included	Not included	Not included	Included as insured benefit in some plans.	Not included
Physical therapy	Included	Included	Included	Included	High option, included. Low option, included except first 20 treatments at $1.50 per treatment.
Ambulance service	Included	Included	Included	Included as insured benefit	Included
Other benefits	Financial assistance for convalescent care for needy	Out-of-area service for acute or emergency care while on vacation.	Out-of-area service up to $350.	Emergency Accident ($50) and Travel ($250–$500) Benefits included as insured benefits. Are in addition to hospital coverage.	Out-of-area hosp. up to 180 days at semiprivate room rates. Patient pays first $75 of hospital charges. GHA pays all other medically needed services and items.
Exclusions	Hosp. for acute alcoholism, mental illness, drugs. Dependents not covered. $6.00 reimbursement for night emergency home calls.	Mental illness over 30 days; above $100 for T.B. Fourteen-day diagnostic care for T.B., venereal, drug, and alcoholic diseases in a general hospital, or up to $100 in any membership year in a private or government sanitarium.	Alcoholism, drugs, cosmetic surgery, T.B., and mental illness	Alcoholism, drug addiction, insanity.	Psychiatric care, congenital conditions, alcoholism, T.B. after institutionalization recommended. Cosmetic surgery, limited to repair of injuries sustained in an accident. Treatment and/or hospitalization for those conditions for which the patient is covered under Workmen's Compensation Laws and/or other state or federal laws.
Cost	50/50—employee/employer, approximately 1.5 percent of weekly base pay to a maximum of $144.00 matched by company.	Employer contributes 5 percent of employee's gross pay to cover employee and dependents. 3½ percent covers employee only.	Employee groups at least 50%. One person $54, two person $108, families $162. Individuals: one person $59.88, two persons $119.76, families $179.64.	Rates vary from $60 per year single group member to $260 per year broadest coverage for a family.	Changes being processed. Write for latest cost information.

SOURCE: Originally from *Health Insurance Plans in the United States*, U.S. Senate Report No. 359, Part I (82d Cong., 1st sess.), May, 1951. Revised, 1964.

panies. Benefits payable by the companies to cover these three types of health insurance amounted to almost $1 billion, which was approximately 50 percent of total benefits paid for these three types of coverage.

In recent years the insurance companies have increased their share of health protection coverage. For example, the insurance companies now provide 60 percent of the grand total of hospital expense protection. They account for 62 percent of all surgical expense insurance. They provided only 47 percent, however, of regular medical expense protection, but accounted for almost all of the major medical, comprehensive, and loss of income (disability) policies. Of the $7.0 billion of voluntary health insurance benefits paid, the insurance companies accounted for $3.7 billion, or 50 percent.

Types of Commercial Policies

There are so many varieties, shapes, and sizes of policies that for the most part generalization is useless. Two $10,000 face value policies which purport to pay this amount if you or some member of your family contracts one of a number of dread diseases may be as different as day and night. The list of diseases may differ. One list may contain many no longer widespread in the United States. One policy may pay only if you contract the disease in the United States and have a specific exclusion for travel abroad. One may cover members of the family from the ages of 21 through 65 only, while the other covers both children and older members as well. Usually it not only pays to read the policy you contemplate buying very carefully, it's essential. Generally, the lower the cost the greater the limitations, exclusions, and exceptions and therefore the less potentially useful is the policy.

The cost of any commercial health insurance policy depends upon the extent of benefits provided. You may pay $10 a year for very limited benefits or larger sums for contracts that offer much more. Those which pay many claims on small illnesses are expensive. Others which pay large benefits on types of claims which do not occur often cost the company less. You can buy a program which covers only the extremes of loss of limb or accidental death; and since these are rare occurrences, the cost is little, and the odds that you will ever use the policy are greatly in favor of the company. At the other end of the scale you can, for a substantial premium, buy a comprehensive policy providing $25,000 or more in various medical benefits, guaranteed renewable for life.

Over the last decade insurance companies have made a number of real advances in broadening their coverage in the health insurance field.

They now write policies covering not only the customary loss of income, hospital expense, surgical expense, and general medical expense insurance, but they have expanded into major medical expense, guaranteed renewable for life policies, and special health insurance policies for the aged.[6]

"It says, 'If you can read this the contract will have to be renegotiated'."

Major medical insurance is now provided by 255 companies—ranging from high benefit maximums of $5,000 to $20,000 or more. Of the group policies issued, 99 percent now provide some coverage for nervous or mental disorders. Guaranteed renewable health insurance policies are now offered to the public by more than 300 insurance companies. These cannot be terminated by the insurance company prior to the age limit stated in the policy, and premiums can only be modified

---

[6] See *Outline of Health Insurance,* Health Insurance Institute, New York, 1963. A free copy may be obtained by writing to the Institute at 488 Madison Avenue, New York, N.Y., 10022.

on a policyholder class basis. Increasingly, hospital, surgical and major medical policies guaranteed for lifetime are being made available. Some 170 insurance companies now issue new individual health insurance policies to persons 65 years of age and over.

Older Age Health Coverage

People over 65 traditionally had found health insurance difficult to buy. Policies already held lapsed or were not renewable. However, there is a new trend which since 1960 has enrolled more than 10 million persons in a drive to provide private health coverage for the aged. Blue Cross, Blue Shield, and commercial insurance companies have extended coverage to provide nongroup policies for persons over 65 years of age—or the right of conversion when an employee retires.

Group type health insurance plans through a mass enrollment program for a specified period have been offered on a state, regional, or nationwide basis. Hospital, surgical, and major medical plans are so issued at various benefit levels with varying premiums (see Figure 9–6).

FIGURE 9–6

Extent of Voluntary Health Insurance Protection
for Persons Age 65* and over and Persons
under 65

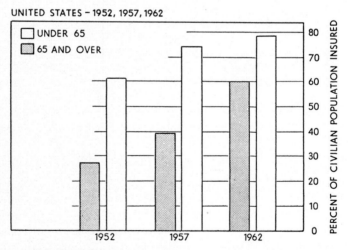

UNITED STATES – 1952, 1957, 1962

* Noninstitutionalized aged population.
Source: Health Insurance Association of America, Health Insurance Council.

State-wide programs, such as New York 65—Connecticut 65— Texas 65—Western 65, have been offered through a pooling of resources of insurance companies.

Aged persons are being enrolled through community, professional, fraternal groups and Golden Age Clubs.[7]

At the end of 1963 almost 100 insurance companies were offering guaranteed for life health insurance plans to persons in or near retirement. Included are catastrophic hospital expense plans which pay up to $10,000, after a deductible—and coinsurance—for prolonged hospitalization.

The federal government has begun a program of medical assistance for the aged under the Kerr-Mills law which matches state funds to cover all kinds of medical needs including physicians' and surgeons' fees as well as hospital and nursing home care for the medically indigent. This law is limited to those 65 and over who can demonstrate to their state welfare agencies that they need help in meeting their medical bills.

Check Your Policy

Read your policy carefully; note the limitations, the maximum number of days of hospitalization paid for, and the amount of hospital benefits specified. Use the following questions as a guide to help understand the terms of your policy:[8]

When does the policy or contract go in force?

Are there other benefits besides payment for loss of income, such as payment of hospital bills? Medical fees? Nursing fees? In what amounts?

Are benefits for diagnostic services included? Are any of these services included: maternity, common operations and illnesses? What other services?

Are the first seven days (or more) excluded in benefit payments? Is there a "deductible clause" requiring you to pay your initial medical bill? If so, how much must you pay before benefits can be obtained?

How long will you receive benefits? Are the benefits reduced if the illness does not require continuous confinement to the house?

What requirements are set for payments for accident and sickness benefits? Does the policy or contract provide benefits for partial as well as total disability?

What will you receive each week or month when disabled?

What will your beneficiary receive in case of your accidental death?

Are benefits reduced at certain ages? Does the premium remain fixed as long as the policy or contract is in force, or are there reductions in benefits or increases in premiums in the older ages?

Are you covered while in other countries besides your own? Does it cover travel in chartered or private planes?

Are there occupational restrictions?

---

[7] "Health Insurance for Older Folks—A Company by Company List of What's Available," *Changing Times, The Kiplinger Magazine*, April, 1962.

[8] *Money Management: The Health Dollar* (Chicago: Household Finance Corp.), pp. 28–29.

Are exceptions made in the policy or contract or in any papers attached to them for certain illnesses or conditions? If so, exactly what are they?

The answers to the above questions should give you full knowledge of the exceptions, reductions, and limitations of your commercial policy and of important clauses which are sometimes the most difficult to understand. A person gets about what he pays for in insurance, and policies which purport to offer a great deal for little or nothing are usually deceptive.

Conclusion on Health Insurance

The various voluntary medical care insurance plans have made it possible for millions of people to buy protection ahead of time for unforeseen illnesses, operations, and hospital costs. Prepaid voluntary insurance provides a way to create group purchasing power for health needs and to replace some of the unpredictable costs for the individual with predictable costs for the group—at a saving to the individual. Just as most Americans have decided that life insurance is good protection for their families against death, they also appear to be concluding, in increasing numbers, that a voluntary prepaid medical care insurance arrangement is a useful and sensible way to meet the inevitable hazards and often catastrophic expenses of illness, accidents, and hospitalization. For the average lower- and middle-income family, it makes a lot of sense.

INSURANCE ON THE HOME

Every 27 seconds a fire breaks out somewhere in the United States. Annual losses due to fire now amount to $1.5 billion. Every homeowner knows that he needs fire insurance. Some time back it was customary to buy fire insurance as a separate policy, perhaps add extended coverage or additional extended coverage, buy a separate personal liability policy, etc. Today the trend is to purchase a package policy covering a large number of risks and perils.

This is a complicated insurance area, and you need to understand certain terms to know what the insurance agent means. *Property* insurance provides financial protection against loss or damage to property caused by such perils as fire, windstorm, hail, explosion, riot, aircraft, motor vehicles, vandalism and malicious mischief, riot and civil commotion, smoke, etc. *Liability* insurance affords financial protection for injury to persons or property of others for which you may be held liable. *Burglary and theft* insurance protects financially against loss of property due to burglary, robbery, or larceny. *Comprehensive personal liability* insurance reimburses the policyholder if he becomes liable to pay money for damage or injury he has caused to others. *Fire* insurance covers losses caused by fire and lightning, as well as the resultant damage caused by smoke and water. *Extended coverage* insurance protects you against loss or damage to your property caused by windstorm, hail, smoke, explosion, riot, vehicles or falling aircraft. It is provided in conjunction with the fire insurance policy. A *homeowner's* insurance policy is a package type which includes fire and extended coverage, theft and personal liability coverages in a single policy. *Multiple peril insurance* policies combine many perils previously covered by individual policies of fire and casualty companies. The homeowner's policy is one example. Others are the commercial property policy, the tenant's policy, the farm owner's policy, etc.[9]

The Homeowners' Policy

This package policy comes in several forms, standard, broad or comprehensive. The nature of the perils covered in each case may be seen in Figure 9–7. The advantage to the homeowner is obvious. You have only one policy and one premium to worry about, and by packaging a number of perils in one policy, the insurance companies are able to offer the policy at 20 to 30 percent less than that of separately purchased coverages.

The homeowner's policy provides both property insurance and liability coverage. As to property, your house, or dwelling, is covered. This includes your garage. Your personal property is covered including household contents and other personal belongings used, owned, worn, or carried by you or your family. The protection applies both at home and away from home. If you wish, this coverage may apply to the personal belongings of your friends while they are on your premises. Certain limits are set on the amount of coverage on money, stamps, jewelry, and furs. If you want to recover full value for loss or damage to such items, you should have them covered under separate policies. You are also insured for additional living expense when damage to your home requires you to live elsewhere, in a hotel, for example, while a house damaged by fire is being repaired.

[9] See *"Insurance Facts,"* latest annual edition, Insurance Information Institute. A free copy may be obtained by writing to the Institute at 110 William Street, New York, N.Y., 10038.

FIGURE 9-7

Your Homeowners Policy
Summary of Coverage—Standard, Broad, and Comprehensive Forms

PROPERTY COVERAGE	POLICY FORM	PERILS INSURED AGAINST	LIABILITY COVERAGE
Property coverages include: 1. Dwelling 2. Private Structures 3. Personal Property 4. Additional Living Expense Property coverage is the same for all forms of a homeowners policy	C O M P R E H E N S I V E B R O A D S T A N D A R D	1. fire and lightning 2. loss or damage to property removed from premises endangered by fire 3. windstorm or hail 4. explosion 5. riot, riot attending a strike, and civil commotion 6. aircraft 12. falling objects 13. weight of ice, snow, or sleet 14. collapse of building or any part thereof 15. accidental discharge, leakage or overflow of water or steam from within a plumbing, heating, or air-conditioning system 16. sudden and accidental tearing asunder, cracking, burning, or bulging of a steam or hot water heating system **All perils except:** earthquake, landslide, flood, surface water, waves, tidal water or tidal wave, backing up of sewers, seepage, war, and nuclear radiation	**All members of the family have the following coverages:** 1. **Comprehensive Personal Liability** 2. **Medical Payments** 3. **Physical Damage to the Property of Others** Liability coverage is the same for all forms of a homeowners policy.
		7. vehicles, if not owned or operated by an occupant of the premises 8. smoke or smudge caused by sudden, unusual, or faulty operations of a cooking or heating unit 9. vandalism and malicious mischief 10. theft 11. breaking of glass constituting a part of the building 17. sudden and accidental tearing asunder, cracking, burning, or bulging of appliances for heating water for domestic consumption 18. freezing of plumbing, heating and air-conditioning systems and domestic appliances 19. sudden and accidental injury to electrical appliances, devices, fixtures, and wiring. (TV picture tube not included)	

Against what perils is your property insured under the homeowners policy? It depends on the form. The *Standard Form* insures against eleven named perils. The *Broad Form,* which is the most popular, covers nineteen perils (see Fig. 9–7). The Comprehensive Form is a so-called "all-risks" contract. Actually, no policy gives you protection against every possible peril. Generally speaking, an "all-risks" contract is one that covers you for everything except—and then it lists the exceptions. In the *Comprehensive Form,* as Figure 9–7 indicates, perils excluded are earthquake, flood, landslide, surface water, tidal wave, etc., the major difference between the Comprehensive Form and the other forms of the homeowners policy is that the Comprehensive Form lists the perils you are *not* insured against while the other policies list the perils you *are* insured against. The former names the exclusions; the latter names the perils.

As to liability coverage, all three forms of the homeowners policy have three insuring agreements, comprehensive personal liability, medical payments, and physical damage to the property of others. *Comprehensive personal liability* protects you against claims arising from bodily injury to others or damage to their property. For example, suppose your neighbor slips and falls on your icy steps, suffers a head injury which impairs his sight, and files suit for damages. Your insurance company will represent you in court, and if the court verdict goes against you, damages will be paid by your insurance company up to the limit of your policy. A note of caution: in states where workmen's compensation insurance is required by law, the personal liability coverages under the homeowners policy do not provide coverage if a cook, housekeeper, maid, etc., is injured.

Medical payments coverage protects you when persons are accidentally injured on or away from your premises if the injury is caused by you, members of your family, or your animals. The insurance company reimburses the injured party, regardless of who is at fault, for medical and surgical services incurred within one year of the accident. The basic amount of this protection under the homeowners policy is $500 for each person. Unlike medical payments in the case of automobile insurance, the coverage in the homeowners policy applies only to outsiders—not to you or members of your family. *Physical damage to the property of others* is easy to understand. A child kicks a football through the neighbor's picture window. Under the father's homeowners policy the insurance company will pay the damages up to the limit of the policy, which is usually $250 for each such occurrence.

If you live in an apartment, rented house, or co-op you will now find widely available the same sort of insurance package offered to home-owners. It's called the Residence Contents Broad Form, or Tenants Form. It protects your furniture and your personal belongings against loss or damage from the 19 perils shown on Figure 9–7. It also provides the three liability coverages as well. For $15,000 worth of personal property in a city apartment, the cost of such a policy will range from $200 to $400 for three years, depending on city, neighborhood, construction type, fire protection.

How Much Property and Liability Insurance Do You Need?

For liability insurance coverage it is difficult to estimate needs because you cannot know ahead of time how large the claim or suit against you may be. Even against persons of average means jury awards may be very high. Therefore, most people, especially those who have assets, salaries, or other income to protect, should carry at least $25,000 of liability insurance. As to property insurance, the amount you need depends on the replacement value of your house and personal property. If your home burned to the ground, how much would it cost, at today's prices, to replace it? Replacement cost is the basis for determining how much property insurance is enough.

Assume your house would cost $20,000 to rebuild and that your household contents are valued at $6,400. To receive full payment (replacement cost) for partial loss or damage to your house under the homeowners policy, you need insure it for only 80 percent of replace-ment value. Eighty percent of $20,000 is $16,000, and it is the basis for determining the amount of the other property coverages under a homeowners policy. In the case of a Broad Form homeowners policy, the property and liability protection would be as follows:

Property*

House	$16,000 (80% of full value)
Appurtenant private structures	1,600 (10% of dwelling)
Personal property	6,400 (40% of dwelling)†
Additional living expenses	3,200 (20% of dwelling)

Liability

Comprehensive personal liability	25,000 (each occurrence)†
Medical payments	500 (each person)†
Physical damage to property of others	250 (each occurrence)

* Illustration from *A Family Guide to Property and Liability Insurance*, Insurance In-formation Institute. A free copy may be obtained by writing to the Institute at 110 Wil-liam Street, New York, N.Y., 10038.
† May be increased.

What would such coverage cost? Based on a frame house in a specific midwestern town, a comparison of costs for Standard, Broad, and Comprehensive Forms of the homeowners policy would be as follows:

Coverage	Cost for 3 Years
Standard Form (11 perils)	$136* ($3.78 per mo.)
Broad Form (19 perils)	174* ($4.83 per mo.)
Comprehensive Form ("all risks")	361† ($10.03 per mo.)

* $50 deductible on wind and hail only.
† $100 deductible on all perils except fire and lightning. If loss is $500 or more, this deductible does not apply.

Keep in mind that these figures are only an example of what one person might pay for this coverage. For various reasons your coverage may cost more, or less. Costs vary according to territory, water supply available for fire fighting, efficiency of fire department, type of construction, and other factors.

Separate Policies

You may be the old-fashioned type and prefer to buy your coverages in individual policies, as the need appears to develop. Or you may feel you do not need protection against as many perils as the homeowners policy covers. You may just want to get down to basics and buy fire insurance, for example, and nothing else. In that case read on. If you are mainly interested in cars, however, skip to page 405.

Fire Insurance Policies

Fire insurance reimburses for the replacement value (less depreciation) of property destroyed, not for its original cost. Ordinarily, fire insurance policies are written for one, three, and five years. The three-year policy may be obtained for two and one-half times the annual rate, and the five-year policy costs four times the annual premium. Mathematically, the three-year policy is, by a hair, a better bargain than the five-year policy. An example of the standard fire policy used in most states and territories may be seen in Figure 9–8.

When you buy fire insurance, a "form" or "endorsement" is attached to the standard contract by the company. It contains all the personal details of the contract, the amount of insurance, for example, a description of the property covered, its location, the owner, etc. The "form" or "endorsement" becomes part of the contract. In fact, without it the standard policy insures nothing. Basically all provisions fall into two categories:

FIGURE 9–8

A Standard Fire Insurance Policy

1 **Concealment,** This entire policy shall be void if, whether
2 **fraud.** before or after a loss, the insured has wil-
3 fully concealed or misrepresented any ma-
4 terial fact or circumstance concerning this insurance or the
5 subject thereof, or the interest of the insured therein, or in case
6 of any fraud or false swearing by the insured relating thereto.
7 **Uninsurable** This policy shall not cover accounts, bills,
8 **and** currency, deeds, evidences of debt, money or
9 **excepted property.** securities; nor, unless specifically named
10 hereon in writing, bullion or manuscripts.
11 **Perils not** This Company shall not be liable for loss by
12 **included.** fire or other perils insured against in this
13 policy caused, directly or indirectly, by: (a)
14 enemy attack by armed forces, including action taken by mili-
15 tary, naval or air forces in resisting an actual or an immediately
16 impending enemy attack; (b) invasion; (c) insurrection; (d)
17 rebellion; (e) revolution; (f) civil war; (g) usurped power; (h)
18 order of any civil authority except acts of destruction at the time
19 of and for the purpose of preventing the spread of fire, provided
20 that such fire did not originate from any of the perils excluded
21 by this policy; (i) neglect of the insured to use all reasonable
22 means to save and preserve the property at and after a loss, or
23 when the property is endangered by fire in neighboring prem-
24 ises; (j) nor shall this Company be liable for loss by theft.
25 **Other insurance.** Other insurance may be prohibited or the
26 amount of insurance may be limited by en-
27 dorsement attached hereto.
28 **Conditions suspending or restricting insurance. Unless other-**
29 **wise provided in writing added hereto this Company shall not**
30 **be liable for loss occurring**
31 (a) while the hazard is increased by any means within the con-
32 trol or knowledge of the insured; or
33 (b) while a described building, whether intended for occupancy
34 by owner or tenant, is vacant or unoccupied beyond a period of
35 sixty consecutive days; or
36 (c) as a result of explosion or riot, unless fire ensue, and in
37 that event for loss by fire only.
38 **Other perils** Any other peril to be insured against or sub-
39 **or subjects.** ject of insurance to be covered in this policy
40 shall be by endorsement in writing hereon or
41 added hereto.
42 **Added provisions.** The extent of the application of insurance
43 under this policy and of the contribution to
44 be made by this Company in case of loss, and any other pro-
45 vision or agreement not inconsistent with the provisions of this
46 policy, may be provided for in writing added hereto, but no pro-
47 vision may be waived except such as by the terms of this policy
48 is subject to change.
49 **Waiver** No permission affecting this insurance shall
50 **provisions.** exist, or waiver of any provision be valid,
51 unless granted herein or expressed in writing
52 added hereto. No provision, stipulation or forfeiture shall be
53 held to be waived by any requirement or proceeding on the part
54 of this Company relating to appraisal or to any examination
55 provided for herein.
56 **Cancellation** This policy shall be cancelled at any time
57 **of policy.** at the request of the insured, in which case
58 this Company shall, upon demand and sur-
59 render of this policy, refund the excess of paid premium above
60 the customary short rates for the expired time. This pol-
61 icy may be cancelled at any time by this Company by giving
62 to the insured a five days' written notice of cancellation with
63 or without tender of the excess of paid premium above the pro
64 rata premium for the expired time, which excess, if not ten-
65 dered, shall be refunded on demand. Notice of cancellation shall
66 state that said excess premium (if not tendered) will be re-
67 funded on demand.
68 **Mortgage** If loss hereunder is made payable, in whole
69 **interests and** or in part, to a designated mortgagee not
70 **obligations.** named herein as the insured, such interest in
71 this policy may be cancelled by giving to such
72 mortgagee a ten days' written notice of can-
73 cellation.
74 If the insured fails to render proof of loss such mortgagee, upon
75 notice, shall render proof of loss in the form herein specified
76 within sixty (60) days thereafter and shall be subject to the pro-
77 visions hereof relating to appraisal and time of payment and of
78 bringing suit. If this Company shall claim that no liability ex-
79 isted as to the mortgagor or owner, it shall, to the extent of pay-
80 ment of loss to the mortgagee, be subrogated to all the mort-
81 gagee's rights of recovery, but without impairing mortgagee's
82 right to sue; or it may pay off the mortgage debt and require
83 an assignment thereof and of the mortgage. Other provisions

84 relating to the interests and obligations of such mortgagee may
85 be added hereto by agreement in writing.
86 **Pro rata liability.** This Company shall not be liable for a greater
87 proportion of any loss than the amount
88 hereby insured shall bear to the whole insurance covering the
89 property against the peril involved, whether collectible or not.
90 **Requirements in** The insured shall give immediate written
91 **case loss occurs.** notice to this Company of any loss, protect
92 the property from further damage, forthwith
93 separate the damaged and undamaged personal property, put
94 it in the best possible order, furnish a complete inventory of
95 the destroyed, damaged and undamaged property, showing in
96 detail quantities, costs, actual cash value and amount of loss
97 claimed; and within sixty days after the loss, unless such time
98 is extended in writing by this Company, the insured shall render
99 to this Company a proof of loss, signed and sworn to by the
100 insured, stating the knowledge and belief of the insured as to
101 the following: the time and origin of the loss, the interest of the
102 insured and of all others in the property, the actual cash value of
103 each item thereof and the amount of loss thereto, all encum-
104 brances thereon, all other contracts of insurance, whether valid
105 or not, covering any of said property, any changes in the title,
106 use, occupation, location, possession or exposures of said prop-
107 erty since the issuing of this policy, by whom and for what
108 purpose any building herein described and the several parts
109 thereof were occupied at the time of loss and whether or not it
110 then stood on leased ground, and shall furnish a copy of all the
111 descriptions and schedules in all policies and, if required, verified
112 plans and specifications of any building, fixtures or machinery
113 destroyed or damaged. The insured, as often as may be reason-
114 ably required, shall exhibit to any person designated by this
115 Company all that remains of any property herein described, and
116 submit to examinations under oath by any person named by this
117 Company, and subscribe the same; and, as often as may be
118 reasonably required, shall produce for examination all books of
119 account, bills, invoices and other vouchers, or certified copies
120 thereof if originals be lost, at such reasonable time and place as
121 may be designated by this Company or its representative, and
122 shall permit extracts and copies thereof to be made.
123 **Appraisal.** In case the insured and this Company shall
124 fail to agree as to the actual cash value or
125 the amount of loss, then, on the written demand of either, each
126 shall select a competent and disinterested appraiser and notify
127 the other of the appraiser selected within twenty days of such
128 demand. The appraisers shall first select a competent and dis-
129 interested umpire; and failing for fifteen days to agree upon
130 such umpire, then, on request of the insured or this Company,
131 such umpire shall be selected by a judge of a court of record in
132 the state in which the property covered is located. The ap-
133 praisers shall then appraise the loss, stating separately actual
134 cash value and loss to each item; and, failing to agree, shall
135 submit their differences, only, to the umpire. An award in writ-
136 ing, so itemized, of any two when filed with this Company shall
137 determine the amount of actual cash value and loss. Each
138 appraiser shall be paid by the party selecting him and the ex-
139 penses of appraisal and umpire shall be paid by the parties
140 equally.
141 **Company's** It shall be optional with this Company to
142 **options.** take all, or any part, of the property at the
143 agreed or appraised value, and also to re-
144 pair, rebuild or replace the property destroyed or damaged with
145 other of like kind and quality within a reasonable time, on giv-
146 ing notice of its intention so to do within thirty days after the
147 receipt of the proof of loss herein required.
148 **Abandonment.** There can be no abandonment to this Com-
149 pany of any property.
150 **When loss** The amount of loss for which this Company
151 **payable.** may be liable shall be payable sixty days
152 after proof of loss, as herein provided, is
153 received by this Company and ascertainment of the loss is made
154 either by agreement between the insured and this Company ex-
155 pressed in writing or by the filing with this Company of an
156 award as herein provided.
157 **Suit.** No suit or action on this policy for the recov-
158 ery of any claim shall be sustainable in any
159 court of law or equity unless all the requirements of this policy
160 shall have been complied with, and unless commenced within
161 twelve months next after inception of the loss.
162 **Subrogation.** This Company may require from the insured
163 an assignment of all right of recovery against
164 any party for loss to the extent that payment therefor is made
165 by this Company.

IN WITNESS WHEREOF, this Company has executed and attested these presents; but this policy shall not be valid unless counter-signed by the duly authorized Agent of this Company at the agency hereinbefore mentioned.

JGlendenning
Secretary

Harvey W Smith
President

1. The provisions that explain the risks covered and the risks excluded.
2. The provisions that should be considered before a loss occurs and those that should be considered after a fire.[10]

Annual Fire Premiums

Annual premiums for fire insurance vary widely, depending on construction, use, location, nearness to a hydrant, adequacy of water supply, fire-fighting facilities, etc. Fire insurance rates are customarily expressed as the number of dollars or cents which would be charged for $100 of insurance for one year. Thus a rate of 20 cents means that you pay 20 cents for each $100 of fire insurance protection. An $8,000 policy would thus cost $16. Under the best conditions an annual rate approaching 10 cents per $100, or $1.00 per $1,000, of insurance may be expected, whereas the rate can be as much as $8.00 per $1,000 under extremely adverse conditions. A rate in the neighborhood of $1.50 per $1,000 has been fairly typical for an ordinary frame house, but, like everything else, there is a tendency for rates to go up.

Extended Coverage on Fire Policies

Since fire insurance is designed only to reimburse the loss resulting from fire or lightning, it is sensible to consider whether additional insurance should be carried to protect against other hazards. *Extended coverage* offering protection against damage by cyclone, tornado, hurricanes, hailstorms, windstorm, and such unrelated things as damage caused by a motor vehicle or an airplane, or explosion, riot, or smoke damage is often added to fire policies. The fee for extended coverage is small, ranging from 6 to 8 cents per $100 of protection for one year. The fire insurance companies have also developed another "endorsement" or "clause" which may also be added to your fire policy. This is called *additional extended coverage* and protects against water damage from plumbing and heating systems; vandalism and malicious mischief; glass breakage; ice, snow, and freezing; fall of trees; and collapse. The rate for additional extended coverage is 4 cents for $100 of protection for one year. Most extended coverage policies and all additional extended coverage policies are sold only with $50-deductible clauses.

In the suburbs of a large city, where fire-fighting facilities are adequate, the cost of $20,000 of fire insurance would be about $120 for

---

[10] For details see *Risks We Face, an Introduction to Property Insurance* (rev. ed.; New York: National Board of Fire Underwriters). A free copy of this 130-page book may be obtained by writing to the National Board of Fire Underwriters at 465 California St., San Francisco 4, Calif.; or 222 West Adams St., Chicago 6, Ill.; or 85 John St., New York 38, N.Y.

five years; extended coverage would cost another $64, and additional extended coverage $32 more. Rates vary so greatly from area to area, from city to city, and for different types and construction of buildings that it is dangerous to generalize. Check your local rates with two or three companies. They should be the same per $100 of protection desired for your particular piece of property.

Cancellation and Reduced Protection

There are two commonly misunderstood facts that deserve mention. The first is that if one buys a fire policy and wants to cancel it, he will probably not receive a pro-rata refund of his premium but will receive a refund based on a short-rate table contained in or on the policy. The effect is to return to him considerably less than the pro-rata amount which the company will refund if it decides to cancel the policy. If the company wishes to cancel, it must give you written notice five days (in some states ten days) before the insurance is to be terminated. The purpose is to give you a few days to seek protection from some other company.

The second is that if a payment is made under a fire policy, the protection afforded by the policy may be reduced to that extent for the balance of its life. Suppose, therefore, that X bought a $5,000 fire policy with a five-year life and, because of a fire, collected $1,000 from the company after the policy had run one year. The policy would now afford only $4,000 of protection for the next four years, unless an extra premium were paid to restore the other $1,000 of protection. This was the old procedure. Many new policies being written provide for automatic reinstatement of the full amount of the policy without any additional premium. Such newer policies generally cover whatever losses occur during the term of the policy up to the policy amount in any one loss. Check your company to see which kind of policy it's selling.

Coinsurance

Many people underinsure their properties either because they expect a fire loss, if it occurs, to be only a small percentage of the total value of the property, or because, having bought the property and originally taken out the fire insurance some years back, they have not taken into consideration the subsequent appreciation in value of property due to inflation.

In those states having a "coinsurance" clause in the standard fire insurance contract, the underinsurer is often surprised and shocked to find that he can recover only part of the amount of his fire loss from the insurance company, even though the face amount of his policy actually exceeds the amount of the fire loss. This sounds surprising and complicated, but it is really easy to understand.

A coinsurance clause, which most people do not bother to read, or, if they do read, do not understand, might appear as follows:

It is a part of the consideration of this policy, and the basis upon which the rate of premium is fixed, that the insured shall at all times maintain insurance on each item of property insured by this policy of not less than 80 (the rate may vary from state to state) percent of the actual cash value thereof, and that failing to do so, the insured shall be an insurer to the extent of such deficit, and in that event shall bear his, her or their proportion of any loss.

What does this mean? It merely says that if you fail to carry insurance amounting to 80 percent of the value of the property, in the event of a loss you must share the loss with the insurance company and may collect only that proportion of the loss which the amount of insurance you actually have bears to the amount of insurance you should have under the coinsurance clause. For example, if you own a property valued at $10,000, you should, under a typical coinsurance provision, carry $8,000 worth of fire insurance. Suppose that you carry only $4,000 of fire insurance and that a fire occurs, causing a $4,000 loss. You will be surprised to find that you cannot collect the whole $4,000 from the insurance company. You are a coinsurer with the company for one half the loss, since you were carrying only one half ($4,000) of the insurance you should have been carrying ($8,000); and you will collect only $4,000/$8,000, or one half of the loss, namely, $2,000.

If you have a coinsurance clause in your fire policy, then the following simple formula will apply:

$$\frac{\text{Amount of Insurance Carried}}{\text{Amount of Insurance Required}} \times \text{Amount of Loss} = \text{Amount Collectible.}$$

Some people believe that in the event of any loss, either partial or total, the property owner is entitled to collect only that percentage of his loss which is stated in the coinsurance clause. For example, they think that if a man owns a building worth $10,000 and carries $8,000 of insurance with an 80 percent coinsurance clause, he will collect only 80 percent of any loss. Thus, if he has a $1,000 loss, they believe he would collect only $800. This impression is incorrect. He would collect $1,000. He will collect in full any loss up to $8,000 since he has purchased the full protection required, namely, 80 percent of the value.

The true purpose of the coinsurance clause is to distribute the cost of fire insurance equitably among property owners, and it has been widely adopted by insurance companies. For example, North and West each own buildings valued at $10,000. North, gambling on the fact that most fires result in partial losses, purchases only $2,000 of fire insurance. West, the more sensible property owner, carries $8,000 of coverage. If both men call on their insurance company to reimburse them in the event of $2,000 fire losses each, North, the property owner who gambled, would in effect be seeking the same indemnity as West, although he has paid only one quarter of the premium West paid. Because of coinsurance North would collect only $500, while West would be paid $2,000.

The fairness of coinsurance is demonstrated by the companies' willingness to grant a reduction in the rate or cost of insurance for the acceptance of this clause. It provides an incentive to the owner to insure his property fully and to increase his insurance when there is an appreciation in values. Fire insurance rates would be higher were it not for this clause. Coinsurance is generally considered the fairest method yet devised for equalizing the cost of insurance between those who carry complete coverage and those who attempt to get away with only enough to cover small losses.

Things to Watch in Fire Policies

Fire policies may be unknowingly voided for various reasons stated in the policy. You will not know about these unless you read your policy carefully. For example, if you leave your house unoccupied for more than 60 consecutive days, you may void your policy. If you add a room, you may need more insurance. Does your policy cover your household furnishings as well as the house itself? If so, do you have an inventory of the furnishings, so that you can prove your loss in the event of fire? Your insurance broker can give you a room-by-room form which makes inventory taking easier. Put the completed inventory in your safe-deposit box. Some homeowners take their inventories with a camera, photographing each room and then putting the pictures in a safe-deposit box. If household furnishings are covered, you may also have a 10 percent off-premises clause in the policy, protecting your personal property away from your home. You may not know about this, suffer a fire loss while traveling, and fail to collect. Policies cover losses due to damage by water used to extinguish the fire. They also cover the cost of removing debris.

The 10 percent provision is important in four instances. (a) It applies to the cost of renting a hotel room or apartment if you are forced to do this temporarily because your dwelling was destroyed by fire. The insurance company will cover the cost of your actual expense for rental of temporary quarters up to a maximum of 10 percent of the insurance on the dwelling. You cannot, however, receive more than one twelfth of the 10 percent for rental expense for any one month. For example, you have insured your house for $12,000. A fire breaks out and you are forced to live in a hotel for three months while repairs are being made. The insurance company will not pay more than $100 a month toward your hotel bill (10 percent of $12,000 is $1,200, $\frac{1}{12}$ of $1,200 is $100 maximum per month).

(*b*) Ten percent of the insurance on your dwelling can be applied to cover losses on other buildings on your premises. Suppose your house is insured for $12,000. Your garage burns down. The company will pay up to 10 percent of $12,000, or $1,200 on the loss of the garage. If the garage was worth $1,200, the 10 percent clause would pay for it in full. If it was worth $1,000, that is the amount the insurance company would pay. If the garage was worth $1,500, you could collect only $1,200.

(*c*) Up to 10 percent of the household contents coverage can be applied to any additions, alterations, or improvements you may make should they be destroyed by fire. For example, you live in a rented apartment. Since the landlord won't paint it you do. If fire should break out and ruin the apartment, you can collect not only for your household contents but for the cost of your paint job as well.

(*d*) Finally, the 10 percent protection on household contents covers your personal property even though away from home. You are traveling. Fire breaks out in the hotel where you are staying. You flee to the street. Your luggage is destroyed by fire. You can collect up to a maximum of 10 percent of your fire insurance coverage.

When You Have a Fire Loss. There are four things to do:

1. Report the loss to the company at once.
2. Safeguard the remaining property.
3. Prepare an inventory of lost or damaged property.
4. Submit "proof of loss" supported wherever possible by bills, vouchers, cancelled checks, etc., showing how much you paid for things lost. It is an excellent idea to call your insurance agent right away and to sign nothing until you have discussed your loss with him. A loss is payable, as a rule, sixty days after the property owner's sworn statement, called the "proof-of-loss," is received by the company. Most companies pay claims in much less time, however. The company will probably send its adjuster to inspect your loss.

In large cities there are licensed "public adjusters," who persuade the harassed and excited homeowner who has just suffered a fire loss to sign a paper authorizing the "public adjuster" to represent the homeowner in dealing with the insurance company. The homeowner may initially be glad to have someone else handle the problem for him, until he finds that the public adjuster gets 10 percent or more of everything the insurance company pays. Either deal with the insurance company adjuster, who will be sent around to inspect your loss, yourself or have your agent do it for you. There is no need to hire a public adjuster.

If you and the company adjuster cannot agree on the value of what was lost, take the matter to your agent. If he agrees with you, he can ask the insurance company for a special investigation. You may get a better settlement. If, however, you still cannot agree, your policy provides that the dispute may be settled by two appraisers, one selected by you and the other by the company. These two then select a competent and disinterested umpire, and the dispute is then arbitrated. But you pay half the costs of appraisal and arbitration (see lines 123–40 in Fig. 9–8). While you may not want to go this far because of the expense, do not settle for an unsatisfactory sum simply because you are in a hurry to get your check. The adjuster, while normally fair, may perceive this or count on it, and you may get less than you would have received if you had been more determined.

Do not underinsure. Remember the coinsurance clause. On the other hand, don't overinsure. It doesn't help. For example, your property is worth $22,000. You insure it for $30,000. A fire causes a total loss. You can collect only $22,000, the value of the property destroyed, not $30,000. Read your policy carefully. Ask your broker to explain those things that you do not understand. Find out how coinsurance affects you. Know what your policy covers. Make an inventory, and keep it somewhere other than on the insured premises, preferably in a safe-deposit box. Do not settle hastily. When you have done all this, you will have reasonable protection.

Other Separate Policies on the Home

A householder, transplanting a shrub, hadn't finished when darkness came. That night a neighbor started across the lawn, fell into the hole and broke a leg. He sued and was awarded $7,500 damages. As a homeowner, you may want separate policies for your protection. If someone visiting you slips on the porch steps and falls and breaks his back, you may find yourself facing a costly lawsuit for damages, even though you had nothing to do with the accident. It was on your property, and you may thus be liable.

1. *A comprehensive personal liability policy* covering your legal liability for bodily injury, illness, death, or property damages suffered on your property by a nonmember of your family may be purchased for a small premium. A $10,000 policy, paying damages up to the face value and medical bills up to $250, may be purchased for an annual premium of $10. A $25,000 policy (with $250 for medical payments) costs only $12. If you want to increase the medical payments to $500, the cost of the $10,000 goes up to $12.50 and of the $25,000 policy to $14.50. You can buy larger policies, of course, for slightly higher annual premiums. The *comprehensive personal liability policy* is well worth its small cost and is a must not only for the homeowner but for the apartment tenant as well. If you live ten stories up and your air conditioner falls out of the window and kills someone, or if your bathtub or washing machine runs over due to your negligence and ruins the neighbor's paint job down below, *comprehensive personal liability* is a very useful policy to have.

2. A *personal property floater* is very useful. If you are going to insure your household contents and personal property against fire, there are lots of additional things that can happen to them. For example, you can spill ink on an expensive rug; someone you invited to dinner, but never will ask again, drops the eclair he's eating for dessert on your well-upholstered dining room chair; your maid breaks the $5,000 Ming dynasty vase which was your pride and joy, etc. The *personal property floater* insures furniture, clothing, sporting goods, cameras, linens, rugs, silverware, luggage, furs, books, etc., both in the home and away from it against almost all risks of loss or damage with a few minor exceptions such as moths, vermin, dampness, etc.

A "personal property floater" policy is a good idea for valuables costing $300 or more—with each article appraised and listed separately. There's no geographical limitation—the property is covered no matter where you take it. Rates vary depending on where you live and the items insured. Furs, for example, take about 50 cents a year for each $100 of value in most places. In Chicago, however, where fur thefts have been heavy, they go up to $2.40 for mink. Jewelry across the country runs nearly $1.50 per $100, but in New York, where jewelry thefts have been numerous, the rate is up to $2.25. You can get a lower insurance rate for jewelry normally kept in a bank vault; however, this doesn't apply to furs kept in storage. A reputable insurance agent can give you all the essential facts.

3. *Theft* insurance covers burglary, robbery, and larceny. You will want residential theft insurance covering both the stealing of property from your home and also damage to home and property by thieves. This

will cost from $15 to $21 per $1,000 of protection for one year. You'll want your theft insurance to cover not only burglary, robbery, and larceny but also "mysterious disappearance" (it's just gone but you don't know how!) and also "theft damage." The last is important. Often burglars will twist, shatter, and break far more than they steal. A "broad form" theft policy will cover all this whereas the "limited" form is more restricted.

FIGURE 9–9

The Homeowners Policy

Here's what you get in this new 1 Policy Plan

Under Policy A, you are insured against the following perils

FIRE

LIGHTNING

EXPLOSION

SMOKE

RIOT AND CIVIL COMMOTION

HAIL

LIABILITY ON PREMISES

LIABILITY OFF PREMISES

TORNADO AND WINDSTORM

VANDALISM AND MALICIOUS MISCHIEF

VEHICLES

AIRCRAFT

HOLD-UP

BURGLARY ON PREMISES

Policy B offers the same protection as Policy A, but also covers loss from these additional perils

GLASS BREAKAGE

FALL OF TREES

COLLAPSE OF FLOORS, WALLS OR ROOFS

COLLAPSE FROM ICE, SNOW & FREEZING

WATER ESCAPE

RUPTURE OF STEAM OR HOT WATER HEATING SYSTEMS

Policies A and B insure the dwelling, household and personal effects, other private structures on premises, personal property off premises and additional living expenses.

Both policies cover against loss by fire, lightning, extended coverage, vandalism and malicious mischief, theft, burglary and holdup, comprehensive personal liability and medical payments.

Policy B also covers against loss caused by perils included in the Additional Extended Coverage endorsement. A Special Building Endorsement may be attached to Policy B changing the coverage on the dwelling and other private structures on premises, to that of ALL RISKS OF PHYSICAL LOSS excluding certain uninsurable perils.

Policy C insures not only the building and appurtenant private structures but also household and personal effects against "All Risks of Physical Loss" excluding certain uninsurable perils. Policy C provides coverage for additional living expenses and also includes comprehensive personal liability and medical payments.

AUTOMOBILE INSURANCE

In San Francisco recently, a jury awarded $155,000 for a fractured back suffered in an automobile accident. In New York a woman received $86,000 for a broken hip. In Richmond a jury sat sadly as a lawyer pleaded for an adequate settlement for his client, a teen-age lad, facing the painful and humiliating prospect of being a cripple for life as a result of an automobile accident. The jury awarded $98,000. Three months later the boy was playing on the high school football team. No wonder with high awards like these and with the number of accidents rising yearly, automobile insurance rates have risen sharply in the last five years; yet some insurance companies are still losing money on auto insurance.

Next to the home and its contents, the automobile is typically the most expensive family possession. Some states, such as Massachusetts and New York, have laws which require that liability insurance be carried as a prerequisite to obtaining license plates and registration for the car. It is common, however, to find a "financial-responsibility" provision in the laws of the other states. Such a provision says that if one is not covered by minimum public liability insurance, and perhaps property damage insurance, and has an accident, he must be able to post a bond of perhaps $5,000 or its equivalent or lose his registration. Whether or not one must have liability insurance to obtain registration for his automobile, the average person should carry such insurance for his own protection and peace of mind.

Kinds of Automobile Insurance

Last year more than 40,000 people died in automobile accidents and 3.5 million more were injured. There were more than twice as many casualties in traffic accidents last year as in our Armed Forces during all the years of World War I and World War II. Half the automobile accidents occur on weekends. Death struck every nine minutes last year, and every ten seconds someone suffered an injury in an automobile accident.

There are six basic automobile insurance coverages. They include:

a) Bodily injury liability
b) Property damage liability
c) Medical payments
d) Comprehensive physical damage
e) Collision
f) Protection against uninsured motorists

See Figure 9–10. These coverages are available in many combinations and for varying amounts. In some cases they can be purchased separately, but large numbers of owners of private passenger cars prefer a package policy, either in the form of the Family Automobile Policy or the Special Automobile Policy. Experienced drivers and insurance experts will tell you that the basic coverages of bodily injury and property damage are an

FIGURE 9–10

Automobile Insurance
A Summary Chart—Six Basic Coverages

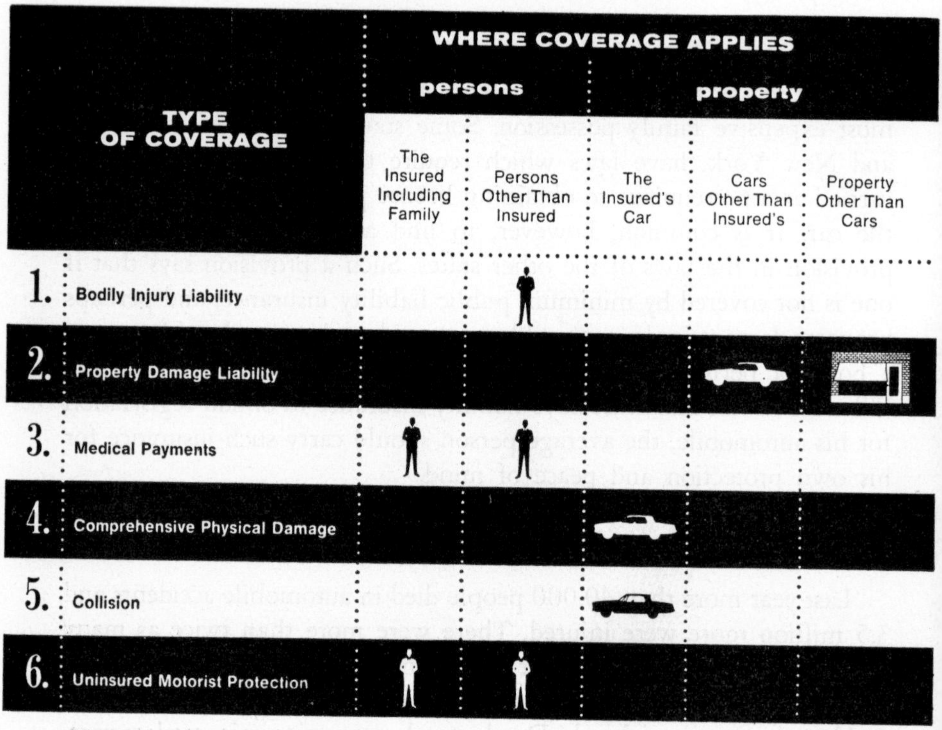

TYPE OF COVERAGE	WHERE COVERAGE APPLIES				
	persons		property		
	The Insured Including Family	Persons Other Than Insured	The Insured's Car	Cars Other Than Insured's	Property Other Than Cars
1. Bodily Injury Liability		●			
2. Property Damage Liability				●	●
3. Medical Payments	●	●			
4. Comprehensive Physical Damage			●		
5. Collision			●		
6. Uninsured Motorist Protection	●	●			

Source: Insurance Information Institute.

absolute must. To be without these is to run the risk of financial disaster. Think of having to pay a damage award of $155,000 over your lifetime out of earnings.

Bodily Injury Liability Insurance

This pays for injury, sickness, disease, or death of others for which you may be legally liable, including claims for damages for care and loss

TABLE 9—4

Table of Automobile Insurance Rates*

Coverage Available	New York "A"	New York "B"	Washington "A"	Washington "B"	Chicago "A"	Chicago "B"	Dallas "A"	Dallas "B"	San Francisco "A"	San Francisco "B"
A—Bodily injury liability										
$10,000 and $20,000	$139.20	$289.90	$40.55	$113.85	$70.20	$197.95	$37.00	$85.00	$76.75	$216.50
$20,000 and $40,000	154.30	321.35	46.55	130.70	81.00	228.40	43.00	96.00	88.10	248.50
$25,000 and $50,000	157.75	328.60	48.30	135.65	83.15	234.45	45.00	99.00	91.45	257.80
$50,000 and $100,000	168.20	350.30	52.90	148.50	90.20	254.25	49.00	107.00	100.15	282.40
B—Property damage liability										
$5,000	$26.40	$56.00	$21.75	$60.75	$21.75	$60.75	$22.00	$51.00	$31.50	$88.50
$10,000	29.05	61.60	23.95	66.85	23.95	66.85	24.00	56.00	34.65	97.35
$25,000	31.70	67.20	26.10	72.90	26.10	72.90	26.00	61.00	37.80	106.20
C—Automobile medical payments										
$1,000	$12.80	$12.80	$6.75	$10.50	$9.00	$15.00	$11.00	$13.00	$13.50	$20.25
$2,000	13.60	13.60	8.25	12.00	10.50	16.50	13.00	15.00	15.00	21.75
$3,000	14.40	14.40	9.00	12.75	11.25	17.25	14.00	16.00	15.75	22.50
$5,000	16.00	16.00	10.50	14.25	12.75	18.75	16.00	18.00	17.25	24.00
J—Uninsured motorists										
$10,000 and $20,000	(1)(2) $2.00 $3.00	(1)(2) $2.00 $3.00	$5.25	$5.25	$3.75	$3.75	$4.00	$4.00	$4.50	$4.50
H—Fire, theft-comprehensive										
Non-deductible			$16.25	$16.25	$22.40	$22.40	$38.00	$38.00	$21.00	$21.00
$50 deductible	$4.20	$4.20	7.15	7.15	10.50	10.50	13.00	13.00	9.10	9.10
E—Collision or upset										
$25 deductible	$123.20	$231.85	$71.20	$159.90	$88.50	$199.35	$68.00	$170.00	$117.60	$264.60
$50 deductible	77.00	144.90	47.45	106.60	55.30	124.60	59.00	148.00	78.40	176.40
$100 deductible	56.00	105.00	35.75	80.60	32.20	72.80	40.00	100.00	57.40	129.50
I—Towing and labor costs										
$10	$1.75	$1.75	$1.30	$1.30	$1.75	$1.75	$.75	$.75	$3.50	$3.50
$25										

SOURCE: Government Employees Insurance Company.
NOTES: "A"—For a car driven to and from work with no male drivers under age 25.
"B"—For a single, under age 25 male driver having principal use of the car.
* —All Quotations are based on a 1964 Ford Galaxie, 4-door sedan.
(1) —New York State only.
(2) —New York State plus country-wide.

of services, because of accidents involving your automobile, up to the limits of the policy. The New York law requires at least "ten-twenty and five" coverage. This means that the insurance company agrees to protect the insured up to $10,000 for bodily injuries to or death of any one person, and, subject to the same limit for each person, up to $20,000 for bodily injuries or death involving two or more persons in a single accident and $5,000 for property damage. Premium rates for such protection vary greatly from place to place. In rural areas, where the chance of hitting people is considerably less, 10/20 bodily injury liability protection may be obtained for as little as $25 per year, whereas in the larger cities its cost may amount to five or six times as much.

Who is protected? You, all other members of your family, and all those who may on occasion drive your car with your permission. Members of your family are covered even when driving someone else's car, as long as the owner has given them permission. What is covered? Bodily injury liability insurance protects you when claims or suits are brought against you by or on behalf of people injured or killed by your automobile.

Costs of Bodily Injury Liability Insurance

Amounts of bodily injury coverage are usually spoken of in such terms as: "ten, twenty," "twenty-five, fifty," or "one hundred, three hundred." They are usually written 10/20, 25/50, 100/300, etc. In each case the first number refers to the limit, in thousands of dollars, that the insurance company will pay for injury to any one person. The second number is the limit they will pay for all of the injuries resulting from any one accident. Often you will hear insurance men refer to bodily injury and property damage limit, combined, as "ten, twenty, and five." The first two numbers refer to bodily injury liability and the last one to property damage insurance in thousands of dollars. Actual costs for varying limits for five large cities in the United States are shown in Table 9–4.

It's not uncommon for a jury to award an injured person $25,000— or more. If this happened to you and you had 10/20/5 coverage, your insurance company would pay only $10,000 and you would be personally liable for the remaining $15,000. It doesn't cost very much more in the way of an additional premium to increase your bodily injury and property damage coverage. If we assume that 10/20/5 costs $100, then the following comparative cost relationships would prevail:

Comparative Costs of Bodily Injury and Property Damage Liability Coverage

Assume that	10/20/5 costs you	$100
then	25/50/5 would cost about	$112
then	50/100/5 would cost about	$120
then	50/100/10 would cost about	$123
then	100/300/10 would cost about	$130
then	100/300/25 would cost about	$134

Note that in the third assumption bodily injury coverage is five times as great as in the first assumption, but the increase in cost is only 20 percent or $20 on each $100 of premium. In the last example the bodily injury coverage is ten to fifteen times as great and the property damage coverage is increased fivefold, yet the increase in premium is only 34 percent.

Thus the extra protection can be gained at relatively little extra cost. Juries, of course, take no notice of and are in no way bound by your insurance limits in any damage suit against you. You may carry 10/20 and a jury may award $50,000 damages, if you gravely injure or cripple someone. The insurance company will pay $10,000 if there is only one person injured. You will have to pay the remaining $40,000 either out of savings or future income. It is thus well worth the small added cost to buy all the bodily injury liability coverage you can afford.

The Cost of Being Young and Irresponsible

Automobile insurance rates are based, principally, on the dollar amount of claims paid out over a period of three years. The more insured accidents you and your friends have, the more claims insurance companies must pay. The more claims paid, the higher the cost of your automobile insurance. The highest rate is paid by the unmarried male under 25 years of age who owns or is the principal driver of the car. The cost of his liability insurance is more than three times that of the basic classification (see Fig. 9–11). This chart shows the relative cost of bodily injury liability insurance in large cities by driver classification. Classification 1A is used as a base for comparison. Note that coverage for a car used for business, classification 3, costs 50 percent more than does one not used for business nor driven to work. Classification 2C shows the rate for the unmarried male driver under 25 who owns or is the principal driver of the car. The reason his rate is three times the basic rate is that over a period of years statistics compiled by insurance companies show that the cost of settling claims against drivers in classification 2C was more than three times that of drivers in classification 1A. Last year persons under 25 were involved in 30 percent of all accidents even though they accounted for only 18 percent of all drivers.

Insurance Companies and Lawsuits

When the average person is involved in an automobile accident, he is apt to feel helpless. He finds himself faced with a possible suit for a staggering sum of money and does not know how to go about conducting an adequate defense. In such a situation it is comforting to

FIGURE 9–11

A Comparison of Liability Rates by Driver Classifications in Large Cities

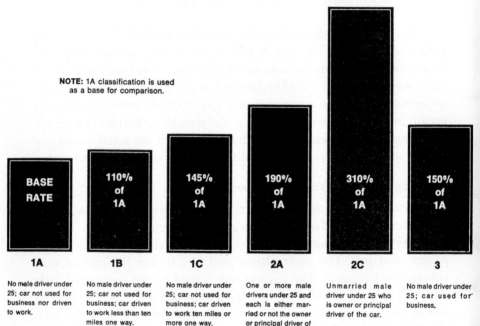

NOTE: 1A classification is used as a base for comparison.

1A	1B	1C	2A	2C	3
BASE RATE	110% of 1A	145% of 1A	190% of 1A	310% of 1A	150% of 1A
No male driver under 25; car not used for business nor driven to work.	No male driver under 25; car not used for business; car driven to work less than ten miles one way.	No male driver under 25; car not used for business; car driven to work ten miles or more one way.	One or more male drivers under 25 and each is either married or not the owner or principal driver of the car.	Unmarried male driver under 25 who is owner or principal driver of the car.	No male driver under 25; car used for business.

SOURCE: Insurance Information Institute.

have the protection of liability insurance because the insurance company at its own expense will defend the insured. Since insurance companies are constantly defending suits, they are therefore expert in knowing what to do and which attorneys to engage in order to bring the suits to a successful conclusion. The insured must hold themselves ready to appear in court, but every move they make is guided by experienced lawyers provided by the insurance companies; one often feels that this defense is worth the total cost of the insurance. As the insurance company states in Figure 9–12, bodily injury liability insurance is "your

FIGURE 9–12

GOVERNMENT EMPLOYEES INSURANCE COMPANY

A Capital Stock Company—Not Affiliated with the U.S. Government

GOVERNMENT EMPLOYEES INSURANCE BUILDING
WASHINGTON 5, D. C.

TO ORDER YOUR POLICY
1. Insert all missing automobile and registration information.
2. Check below each coverage desired and compute the total premium.
3. Select payment terms.
4. Answer all questions on the reverse side.
5. Mail application with your payment in postage-paid return envelope.

OFFICE USE ONLY	STATE	SOURCE	TERR.	CITY CODE	POLICY NO.
	04	001	51		

3194 JP

Name and Address

Rated location, if not City and State shown in mailing address: **SAN FRANCISCO, CALIF.**

PLEASE FILL IN ALL MISSING INFORMATION

Year	Make (Trade Name)		# Cyl.	OFFICE USE
				Symbol / Class
64	Ford		8	J1 / 1BC

Model (Spl., Bel Air, Fairlane, etc.)		Body Style (4 Dr., Hard Top, Sta. Wgn., etc.)
	Galaxie 500	4Dr. Sed.

Serial or Identification Number Recorded on Your Registration Card	State of Car Registration

Cost	Purchase Date	
$	(mo.) (day) (yr.)	New ☐ / Used ☐

COMPACT & FOREIGN CARS—Additional Rating Information			Port of Entry Price (Foreign Cars Only)
Length (ft)	Weight (lbs)	Horsepower	$

COVERAGES AVAILABLE
Coverage descriptions and insurance ordered are subject to policy terms and conditions.

	LIMITS OF COVERAGE (Limits Recommended as Minimum are printed in red below)	ANNUAL PREMIUM (Limits or Coverage unavailable if premium not quoted)		PREMIUM OF COVERAGE SELECTED
A — BODILY INJURY LIABILITY Not available without Coverage B. Your protection against loss of home, income and life savings should your car injure or kill others and you be held liable— includes bail bond expenses, defense of all suits, court and other costs. Pays up to the first limit for any one person and up to the second limit for two or more persons injured or killed.	$10,000 and $20,000	$ 76.75	☐	
	$20,000 and $40,000	$ 88.10	☐	
	$25,000 and $50,000	$ 91.45	☐	$................
	$50,000 and $100,000	$100.15	☐	
Other limits available if desired.	$........M and $........M	$	☐	
B — PROPERTY DAMAGE LIABILITY Not available without Coverage A. Your protection against financial loss should your car damage the property of others and you be held liable. Pays for damages caused by your car to the property of others up to the limit you select.	$ 5,000	$ 31.50	☐	
	$10,000	$ 34.65	☐	$................
	$25,000	$ 37.80	☐	
Other limits available if desired.	$................	$	☐	
C — AUTOMOBILE MEDICAL PAYMENTS Not available without Coverages A & B. Pays expenses for Medical, Dental, Surgical, Hospital, Funeral, etc., to each person for injury or death caused by accident. Protects everyone in your automobile. Also protects you and household relatives in other automobiles or through being struck by an automobile.	$ 1,000	$ 13.50	☐	
	$ 2,000	$ 15.00	☐	$................
	$ 3,000	$ 15.75	☐	
	$ 5,000	$ 17.25	☐	
J — UNINSURED MOTORISTS Not available without Coverages A & B. The "Family Protection" coverage which pays damages that you, household relatives and passengers in the insured automobiles are legally entitled to recover because of bodily injury or death caused by uninsured or hit-and-run automobiles. Pays up to the first limit for one person and up to the second limit for two or more persons injured or killed.	$ 5,000 and $10,000	$	☐	
	$10,000 and $20,000	$ 4.50	☐	$................
Only quoted limit is available.				
H — FIRE, THEFT — COMPREHENSIVE Not available without either Coverage E or Coverages A & B. Broad form protection for loss caused other than by Collision. Includes fire, theft, glass breakage, riot, windstorm, hail, etc. The deductible applies to all damage except by fire and total theft.	Actual Cash Value less Non-Deductible	$ 21.00	☐	
	$50 Deductible	$ 9.10	☐	$................
D — FIRE, THEFT — Combined Additional Not available without either Coverage E or Coverages A & B. Same as described in "H" above except glass breakage not covered and a $25 deductible amount applies to loss by malicious mischief or vandalism. Written on older model cars, trailers and truck type vehicles used commercially.	Actual Cash Value, or $................ (Stated Amount applies only if inserted herein)	$	☐	$................
E — COLLISION OR UPSET Protection for loss or damage to YOUR CAR caused by collision with another object or by upset of your automobile, for the amount of each loss in excess of the deductible amount.	Actual Cash Value less $ 25 Deductible	$117.60	☐	
	$ 50 Deductible	$ 78.40	☐	$................
	$100 Deductible	$ 57.40	☐	
I — TOWING & LABOR COSTS Not available without other Coverages. Pays up to the limits indicated per claim for disablement of your car. Includes labor cost at place of disablement and towing costs. Parts not covered.	$10.00	$	☐	
	$25.00	$ 3.50	☐	$................
Only quoted limit is available.				

PAYMENT TERMS: (Check One)
☐ Payment in full (due with application); or
☐ 3-Payment Plan — 1st payment (40% of total plus $1.50 Deferred Payment Charge) due with application. Balance is billed in two equal installments at the end of 3 and 6 months.
(If no premium is quoted, a $15.00 minimum payment must be enclosed.)

ENCLOSED IS
$................
☐ Check ☐ Money Order
Please do not send Currency, Coin or Stamps.

TOTAL ANNUAL POLICY PREMIUM $................

U-15-A (5-63)

protection against loss of home, income and life savings should your car injure or kill others and you be held liable—includes bail bond expenses, defense of all suits, court and other costs." The insurance company, thus, will pay all legal costs as well as bail bond premiums of up to $100 if you are involved in a bodily injury or property damage suit.

Property Damage Insurance

Property damage liability insurance is your protection against financial loss should your car damage the property of others and you be held liable. This second important type of automobile insurance pays for damages caused to the property of others, for which you are legally liable, up to the limits of the policy. It includes damage to another automobile, damage to or destruction of another's property of any description, and the loss of the use of the property damaged. It is customary to write property damage and bodily injury liability insurance together.

Bear in mind that damage to your own car is *not* covered under property damage liability. This insurance is available in amounts ranging from $5,000 to $100,000. Either $5,000 or $10,000 is generally purchased and, as Table 9–4 shows, rates range from $20 to approximately $100 depending on age of drivers, location, and use of car.

Both property damage insurance and bodily injury insurance cover you if you are driving someone else's car. It also covers anyone driving your car with your permission. Your policies, of course, cover anyone you invite to ride with you.

Automobile Medical Payments

Under this coverage the insuring company agrees to pay, up to the limits of the policy, medical expenses resulting from accidental injury. It applies to you and your immediate family whether in your car, someone else's, or if struck while walking. Passengers and guests riding in your car are covered also. The insurance company agrees to pay all reasonable expenses incurred within one year from the date of the accident for necessary medical, surgical, X-ray, and dental services, ambulance, hospital, professional nursing and even funeral services, up to the limits declared in the policy. Payment is made regardless of who is at fault, or if no one is at fault. Amounts available range from $500 to $5,000. These limits apply to each individual injured. Typical costs are shown in Table 9–4.

Premiums vary according to the dollar amount of claims paid in each locality. The range of rates might run as follows in a small town:

Comparative Costs of Medical Payments Coverage

Assume that	$500 costs you $6
then	$1,000 would cost about $8
then	$2,000 " " " $10
then	$5,000 " " " $13

Collision Insurance

Collision insurance provides reimbursement for damage done to *your own automobile* through collision or upset. It doesn't cover damage done to the other fellow's car. That's covered by the property damage insurance you carry, assuming the accident was your fault. Put it this way. If the accident was the other fellow's fault, his property damage insurance will pay your damages. His own collision insurance will pay his own damages. If he had no insurance, your collision insurance can cover your car, but your company has the right of subrogation, the legal right to proceed against him to recover the sums it paid to you. If the accident was your fault, your property damage insurance pays the other fellow, and your collision insurance pays you. Clear?

More people would doubtless have this protection if it did not cost so much. The cost varies with the protection provided, the type of automobile insured, and the locality. On a new automobile of average worth in one of our larger cities it may amount to $100 a year, whereas half that sum would secure it in a smaller place. One common device used to reduce the cost of this insurance is for the insured to agree to pay for the first $50 or $100 of the damage out of his own pocket, the insurance company being responsible only for the balance. This is known as "deductible collision." Insurance companies are able to write policies with such "deductible" clauses at lower premiums because such a clause saves them from having to pay for a host of accidents each of which involves little damage. Devices of this sort are rather common in insurance; the insured can buy protection more cheaply if he will bear a small initial part of the risk himself. Because of the cost of collision insurance, many automobile owners decide to try to avoid accidents and if they have one, bear the cost themselves; often, however, one is forced to provide collision insurance when he must finance the purchase of a car by borrowing. The cost of $50-deductible collision insurance (the most usual type written) varies from $35 to $250, depending upon type of car and locality. Straight collision insurance without a deductible clause is prohibitive; and the rate goes down sharply, as the sums quoted for $25-, $50-, and $100-deductible insurance in the following tabulation for Washington, D.C., indicate:

POLICY	APPROXIMATE PREMIUM
$25-deductible	$80
$50-deductible	50
$100-deductible	38
$250-deductible	23
$1,000-deductible	8

Comprehensive Physical Damage Insurance

Careful owners almost always insure their automobiles against fire and theft. The annual premium amounts to only a few dollars. In fact, a comprehensive policy affording protection against malicious damage, vandalism, glass breakage, windstorm, or anything except collision and upset, in addition to fire and theft, can be purchased for $10–$30 per annum, depending on location. Reimbursement is made on the basis of the actual cash value of the vehicle when the loss or damage is incurred. In some of the larger cities, losses to companies on this type of insurance have been so large due to petty thefts and vandalism that a number of the companies have either refused to write such policies for cars that are not garaged, or have introduced a $50-deductible clause. If the theft or vandal's damage amounts to less than $50, the car owner cannot collect from the insurance company. This relieves the companies of thousands of small claims which are costly to service and permits them to write the insurance less expensively. If the cost of repairing the damage is more than $50, the first $50 is paid by the insured.

If your automobile is stolen, your comprehensive policy will compensate you for the cost of substitute transportation, whether rented car or taxi. Usually you cannot collect more than $5.00 a day for this, and there is an overall limit. The theft of the car must have been reported to the police and, of course, to the insurance company. Your insurance does not cover things you leave in the car, only the car itself or parts thereof such as tires, battery, etc.

Protection against Uninsured Motorists

This coverage applies to bodily injuries for which an uninsured motorist, or a hit-and-run driver, is legally liable. It applies to the policyholder and family whether occupying their car, someone else's, or while walking. It also applies to guests occupying the policyholder's car. The insuring company agrees to pay damages to injured persons to the same extent that it would if it had carried insurance on the uninsured or unknown motorist.

The advantage of protection against uninsured motorists is immediate payment from your insurance company for hospital bills and medical costs. Assuming the uninsured motorist is at fault, it may take some time before an agreement can be reached on the amount you should receive for your injury. Furthermore, the uninsured motorist may have little or no property or money and may never be able to pay. The amount of protection you can purchase under this coverage is limited to the liability required under the financial responsibility laws of your state. Cost of this protection is so small that automobile owners who know about it are seldom without it.

Total Costs of Automobile Insurance

Think carefully about the cost of automobile insurance. Today, it is not unusual for the premiums on the various sorts of insurance which you should have to total $100 in a small town and $150–$600 a year in a large city (see Table 9–5). A moment's thought may reveal that insurance costs alone may equal or exceed the annual expense of travel by public transportation. If you decide to cut down on the kinds of automobile insurance you wish to carry, remember that, most importantly, you need protection against disastrous lawsuits for bodily injury, medical payments and property damage to others. These types of policies are essential. Coverage for fire, theft (or comprehensive), and collision is a secondary matter, since these items can hardly wreck you financially. All you can lose here is the total value of your own car.

Preferred Risks and Assigned Risks

Here we have the extremes of driving performance. The preferred risk is a person with an excellent safety record, unmarred by accidents, who because of his fine driving ability and caution and maturity at the wheel will be given the lowest premium rate by some insurance companies or a 10 to 20 percent rebate by others from their standard rates. The preferred risk rate is a monetary reward for safe driving and is thus designed to encourage more of it.

The assigned risk, on the other hand, is one whose driving record is so bad that he finds it difficult, if not impossible, to obtain the various automobile insurance coverages through regular channels. Sometimes, as in the case of males under 25, it is the high accident rate of the whole group which makes it difficult for the new applicant in this age category

TABLE 9–5

Nonfarm, Annual Premiums for a 1964 Four Door Ford Galaxie 500

TERRITORY	COVERAGE	PLEASURE	MALE OVER 25 — MILES TO WORK — LESS THAN 10*	MALE OVER 25 — MILES TO WORK — 10* or MORE	BUSINESS	MALE UNDER 25 — OCCASIONAL OPERATOR OF FAMILY CAR	MALE UNDER 25 — MARRIED OPERATOR OR OWNER	MALE UNDER 25 — UNMARRIED PRINCIPAL OPERATOR OR OWNER
New York (Manhattan)	Full Coverage Comprehensive	$ 30.00	$ 30.00	$ 30.00	$ 30.00	$ 30.00	$ 30.00	$ 30.00
	$100 Deductible Collision	63.00	63.00	63.00	78.80	110.20	94.60	157.60
	10/20 BI; $10,000 PD	155.80†	179.20†	202.60†	210.40†	305.20‡	288.20‡	395.40‡
	$1,000 Medical Payments	12.00	12.00	12.00	12.00	14.00	14.00	14.00
	Statutory Uninsured Motorist	3.00	3.00	3.00	3.00	3.00	3.00	3.00
	Voluntary Uninsured Motorist	1.00	1.00	1.00	1.00	1.00	1.00	1.00
	Combined	$264.80	$288.20	$311.60	$335.20	$463.40	$430.80	$601.00
Chicago	Full Coverage Comprehensive	$ 20.00	$ 20.00	$ 20.00	$ 20.00	$ 20.00	$ 20.00	$ 20.00
	$100 Deductible Collision	29.80	29.80	29.80	29.80	59.60	44.80	89.40
	10/20 BI; $10,000 PD	75.20†	90.20†	112.80†	112.80†	210.60†	142.80‡	315.80‡
	$1,000 Medical Payments	7.00	7.00	7.00	7.00	7.00	7.00	7.00
	Voluntary Uninsured Motorist	4.00	4.00	4.00	4.00	4.00	4.00	4.00
	Combined	$136.00	$151.00	$173.60	$173.60	$301.20	$218.60	$436.20
Washington, D.C.	Full Coverage Comprehensive	$ 16.80	$ 16.80	$ 16.80	$ 16.80	$ 16.80	$ 16.80	$ 16.80
	$100 Deductible Collision	38.60	38.60	38.60	38.60	58.00	58.00	77.20
	10/20 BI; $10,000 PD	52.60†	63.20†	79.00†	79.00†	131.60‡	110.40‡	221.00‡
	$1,000 Medical Payments	9.00	9.00	9.00	9.00	9.00	9.00	9.00
	Voluntary Uninsured Motorist	6.00	6.00	6.00	6.00	6.00	6.00	6.00
	Combined	$123.00	$133.60	$149.40	$149.40	$221.40	$200.20	$330.00

*Twenty miles in Illinois.
†Surcharge for female operators under 25: 10 percent in New York; 15 percent in Illinois and District of Columbia.
‡15 percent discount if all male operators under 25 have completed an accredited driver training course.

SOURCE: Nationwide Mutual Insurance Company.

to obtain any insurance at all even though he himself has no accident record as yet. Companies cannot be compelled to accept applicants, and where they anticipate they will lose more in loss payments than the premiums they receive, they will refuse to write insurance. Some companies will withdraw from a high-risk territory. In some states an assigned risk pool has been set up by all auto insurance companies licensed to and doing business in the state. Each company agrees to accept a proportionate share of the "poor risks." A person who is so classified by reason of having been rejected by at least three companies within sixty days applies to the assigned risk pool, pays an application fee, and is usually assigned to one of the companies. He will probably have to pay the highest rate the company charges because of his assigned risk status. This insurance is only for one year, and if his record continues bad, he may find that thereafter no company will accept him even as an assigned risk.

Choice of Companies and Policies

Automobile insurance policies vary in cost from company to company. Shop for yours. Ask four or five companies to send you their quotations. Remember that mutual (as compared with stock) companies belong to their policyholders and distribute net earnings to the policyholders as dividends, thus decreasing the cost of the insurance. In the insurance of automobiles, it is not uncommon to find that mutual companies save their policyholders from 20 to 40 percent of the cost. Some persons claim that mutual companies can do this only because they are not liberal in settling claims and that an insurance broker who places your insurance with a stock company can obtain a much better settlement for you. Others, however, say that there is nothing to this —that settlements are fair, and that the savings are brought about by the selection of good risks and because there are no stockholders (owners of the company other than the policyholders) to whom dividends must be paid. Once in a while policyholders in mutual companies find that they are assessed, perhaps as much as an additional premium, because the company cannot meet its liabilities. Careful reading of a policy may reveal whether or not it is assessable. Generally speaking, assessable policies should be avoided.

Most companies will grant 10 to 20 percent discounts if you own two or more passenger cars. Farmers can usually qualify for a 30 percent discount. Owners of compact cars can obtain a 10 percent discount, provided the compact isn't a "sports car". The company you choose should offer the "economy-type special automobile policy". This is a "package" policy affording bodily injury liability, medical payments, collision, comprehensive and other automobile insurance coverages designed to meet the needs of the average motorist at a lower cost than if the same coverages were bought separately. The savings range from 10 to 20 percent.

SUGGESTED READINGS

1. *Facts You Should Know about Accident and Health Insurance,* Educational Division, Better Business Bureau, latest edition.

2. *Source Book of Health Insurance Data,* Health Insurance Institute, latest annual edition. A free copy may be obtained by writing to the Institute at 277 Park Ave., New York, N.Y., 10017.

3. *Handbook of Health Insurance.* Cincinnati: The National Underwriter Company, latest edition.

4. Louis S. Reed and Dorothy P. Rice, "Private Consumer Expenditures for Medical Care and Voluntary Health Insurance, 1948–1962," *Social Security Bulletin,* U.S. Department of Health, Education, and Welfare, Social Security Administration, Vol. 26, No. 12 (December, 1963) Washington, D.C.

5. Donald G. Hay, "Independent Health Insurance Plans," *Social Security Bulletin,* February, 1963.

6. "Medical Assistance For The Aged," *Management Record,* National Industrial Conference Board, New York, Vol. XXIV, No. 3 (March, 1962).

7. "Health Insurance For Older Folks," *Changing Times, The Kiplinger Magazine,* April, 1962.

8. "Health Insurance In Force For Life," *Changing Times, The Kiplinger Magazine,* August, 1962.

9. H. Ashley Weeks, *Family Spending Patterns and Health Care.* Cambridge: Harvard University Press, 1961.

10. Duncan M. MacIntyre, *Voluntary Health Insurance and Rate Making.* Ithaca, N.Y.: Cornell University Press, 1962.

11. Ethel Shanos, *The Health of Older People, A Social Survey.* Cambridge: Harvard University Press, 1962.

12. O. D. Dickerson, *Health Insurance.* Rev. ed., Homewood, Ill.: Richard D. Irwin, Inc., 1963.

13. J. F. Follmann, Jr., *Medical Care and Health Insurance.* Homewood, Ill.: Richard D. Irwin, Inc., 1963.

14. Davis W. Gregg, *Life and Health Insurance Handbook.* 2d ed., Homewood, Ill.: Richard D. Irwin, Inc., 1964.

15. Calvin H. Brainard, *Automobile Insurance.* Homewood, Ill.: Richard D. Irwin, Inc., 1961.

16. Jesse F. Pickrell, *Group Health Insurance.* Homewood, Ill.: Richard D. Irwin, Inc., 1961.

17. Robert D. Eilers, *Regulation of Blue Cross and Blue Shield Plans.* Homewood, Ill.: Richard D. Irwin, Inc., 1963.

18. *Property and Casualty Insurance Companies: Their Role as Financial Intermediaries,* American Mutual Insurance Alliance and Association of Casualty Companies for the Commission on Money and Credit. Englewood Cliffs, N.J.: Prentice-Hall, Inc., 1962.

19. "Trouble Getting Auto Insurance," *Changing Times, The Kiplinger Magazine,* November, 1962.

20. *Insurance Facts* (Relating to Property and Liability Insurance), latest annual edition, Insurance Information Institute, 110 William Street, New York, N.Y., 10038.

21. Richard M. Heins, *Fundamentals of Property and Casualty Insurance.* Rev. ed. Bryn Mawr, Pa.: The American College of Life Underwriters, 1960.

22. Ralph H. Wherry and Monroe Newman, *Insurance and Risk.* New York: Holt, Rinehart & Winston, Inc., 1964.

23. Gayle E. Richardson, *Behind The Fine Print.* Indianapolis: David-Stewart Publishing Co., 1961.

24. "Blue Cross and Blue Shield," *Changing Times, The Kiplinger Magazine,* January, 1963.

25. "Price of Fire Insurance," *Changing Times, The Kiplinger Magazine,* February, 1961.

26. "For Auto Accident Victims: A New Kind of Insurance," *Reader's Digest,* May, 1961.

27. "Do You Have The Right Insurance for Your Home," *American Home,* December, 1961.

28. Frank J. Angell, *Health Insurance.* New York: Ronald Press, 1963.

CASE PROBLEMS

1. John Sing bought a home for $20,000. John and his wife were very insurance conscious and wanted their house to be fully protected by fire insurance. They purchased an insurance policy in the amount of $20,000, with extended coverage and additional extended coverage. For reasons of health, he and his wife closed the house last winter and went to Florida. The necessary precautions to prevent freezing of pipes were taken. However, upon their return from Florida, they found that the pipes had burst and there was much water damage to the house. Floors were swollen and ceilings damaged. He notified the insurance company and an adjustor was sent to investigate the damage. John was amazed to hear the adjustor say he was sorry but he could not compensate them for the damage. Explain.

2. Rita and Olaf were married a year ago. They have just bought a frame house for $18,500. He earns $8,500 a year. She keeps house. What essential insurance coverages should they have for their home? What kind of policy would you advise? At what cost? They ask you to write to three insurance companies for them, get examples of policies, and rates and advise them which one to purchase.

3. Mr. Brown bought fire insurance with an 80 percent coinsurance clause some years ago, when the value of his property was $10,000. His insurance agent now suggests purchasing additional insurance. What should Mr. Brown do?

4. Brooks Elliott is a young lawyer, aged 27. He is still a bachelor. He earns $9,500 a year. His small law firm does not provide any fringe benefits—no hospitalization or health insurance of any sort. He feels a vague need for some sort of medical insurance protection. Since he is busy and has no time to investigate he asks you to suggest a program for him—policies, coverages, costs. What definitive program would you prepare for him? By phone calls or letters to appropriate companies or organizations determine costs and benefits.

5. Clara has just started teaching. She's 24, not married—yet. Because she wasn't able to find housing near the school where she teaches, she bought a car —a new Ford Galaxie and now drives back and forth to work (7 miles each way). Assuming she works in a town in your state, what basic insurance coverages should she have for her car? Prescribe an automobile insurance policy or policies for her and determine how much it will cost her annually.

6. Rogers had formerly worked for a company which provided Blue Cross and Blue Shield for its employees. When he left the company, he paid for his family certificate individually ($120 a year). On his new job he is offered the opportunity to take $5,000 of group life insurance in combination with hospital and surgical benefits similar to those provided by Blue Cross and Blue Shield, at a cost to him of $132 a year. Rogers is married, has two children (ages 8 and 10), and earns $12,000 a year. He wonders whether he should drop Blue Cross and Blue Shield. Advise him.

7. Worthen has a wife and three children (ages 8, 14, and 19). He earns $11,000 annually. He carries family membership in Blue Cross and Blue Shield. His eldest son, John, has just become 19 years old and will no longer be covered by the family membership. Upon inquiry he is told that it will cost him $7.50 per quarter for Blue Cross and $6.40 quarterly for Blue Shield in a separate member-ship for John—a total of $13.90 a quarter, or $55.60 a year. Should he take the separate membership for John?

8. Eames is earning $72 a week. He is 48 years old, has a wife (age 43) and two children (ages 16 and 18). The family has always been frugal, with the result that they own their home, and automobile, and $6,782 in a savings bank. In addition, a $10,000 straight life-insurance policy has been carried on Eames for the last 20 years. Eames's employer now makes Blue Cross and Blue Shield available to his employees. A family membership including both sorts of benefits will cost Eames $8 a month. He hesitates whether to avail himself of the opportunity. What do you advise?

9. In Mandell's town, bus fares have just been advanced to 20 cents a ride. He lives in a state with a financial-responsibility provision in the law. Mandell has been married five years and has a child of three years. He works in a grocery store five miles from his home, earning $63 a week. It is his opinion that, if he bought an old car, it would be cheaper to commute to work in it than it now costs on the bus and that the automobile would be available for

use evenings and week ends. He could park it in the yard behind his flat. Should he get the car?

10. Halley had just bought a home. It is worth $12,000 and the land $3,000. The Halley family consists of Halley (age 38), his wife (age 33), and three children (ages 12, 8, and 5). Halley is a dentist and averages a net income of $10,500 a year. He carries $22,000 of straight life insurance, owns securities worth $14,386, and has $3,800 in savings accounts and $1,183 in his checking account. Since he has noticed that most fires in connection with residences cause damage amounting to from $500 to $2,000, he believes that if he carries $3,000 of fire insurance on the house he will be amply protected. Do you agree with him? Why? Why not?

11. King, a salesman who travels by automobile, owns his home and has $1,800 in the bank. He buys a new Plymouth for $2,400, using $800 of his funds for a down payment. When the bank (from which he borrows the balance of the money necessary to acquire the automobile) gives him a statement of the total amount he owes to it, he notices that he is being charged $90 for a year's collision insurance. He argues that he does not want the collision insurance, but the bank insists that he must have it. How do you react? Why?

12. George and Nancy Green have budgeted $60 a month to run their new Chevrolet. George uses it to commute to work each day (48 miles each way), and the two of them use it evenings and for week-end travel to their camp (180 miles away), which is good for winter sports as well as summer activities. Insurance costs average $10 a month. Is the budget sufficient?

10 BUYING A HOME

> I never saw an oft-removed tree nor yet an oft-re-
> moved family that throve so well as those that settled
> be.
>
> —*Poor Richard's Almanack*

WHEN YOU look into a new field, it's useful to get your terms straight right at the beginning. Here are some expressions that you will encounter whenever you set out to buy a home:

GLOSSARY FOR HOME BUYERS

One of the preliminaries in buying a house is the reading of real-estate ads. This can be a confusing process. So to help the prospective home buyer, this magazine has compiled its own handy glossary of real-estate terms and phrases. It follows (even if all the definitions don't —quite):

OWNER LEAVING TOWN—He's hoping to retire to Florida on the proceeds.

SELDOM HAVE WE BEEN PRIVILEGED TO OFFER SUCH A BUY—A white elephant, the kind with eight bedrooms and a 1908 bath.

MAGNIFICENT VIEW—The nearest bus stop is at least five miles away.

IMMEDIATE OCCUPANCY—You'll get in sometime between the date set by the builder and the next Christmas.

PRICED WELL BELOW THE MARKET —Been trying to unload this one for some time.

TWENTY MINUTES FROM TOWN— Forty minutes from town unless you have a police escort.

SPACIOUS DINING ROOM—Will hold a table.

A SETTING OF NATURAL CHARM— You get rid of the poison ivy yourself.

NEEDS SOME REDECORATING—It will take the Army Engineers to fix this one up.

RAMBLER—Anything under three stories.

SEMIDETACHED—Semiattached.

ALL MODERN IMPROVEMENTS—Has inside plumbing.

LOT BEAUTIFULLY LANDSCAPED— Has a tree on it that looks like a buggy whip.

SUBSTANTIAL CASH REQUIRED— You couldn't afford it.

ONLY TWO LEFT—There were three originally.

SOURCE: *Changing Times, The Kiplinger Magazine.*

To Buy or to Rent?

The old argument whether to rent or to buy is almost never resolved on the basis of a careful financial investigation. For one thing, the

FIGURE 10–1

HOUSING STATUS BY INCOME CLASS, 1962
(NONFARM FAMILIES)

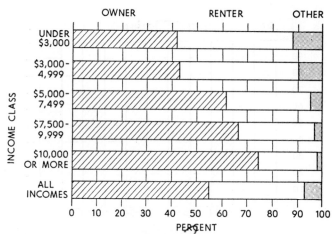

SOURCE: Survey Research Center, University of Michigan, and National Industrial Conference Board.

essay ⬭

average home buyer couldn't make the detailed comparison even if his inclination were not to be content with a superficial contrast. Even when the experts try, they have to use a contrived, artificial example which doesn't reflect real facts and which provides only a very hedged answer with a lot of "ifs" and "buts."

In the first place, you are comparing two dissimilar things. When a young couple rent an apartment, they usually have two or three rooms. When, in due course, they buy a house, it usually has six or seven rooms, a bit of land around it, and a garage. Secondly, the difference between short and long run is ignored. The fact is that buying a home may cost more over the *short run,* whereas over the *long run,* renting may cost more. Thirdly, after the removal of rent controls all over the country, rents rose sharply, and the rise was clear and obvious. The purchase price of new homes also has risen sharply, but changes in methods of financing have been used to conceal it. For example, if rents of three-room apartments rise from $100 to $150 a month, the tenant knows and feels it. If the cost of a given type of new house rises from $10,000 to $15,000, it can be made to appear that the purchaser at $15,000 is not paying much more per month than an earlier purchaser at $10,000. How? By lengthening the terms of the mortgage debt. For example, if you buy a $10,000 house, put $2,000 down and take out a 6 percent, 20-year mortgage for $8,000, the monthly payment is $57.32. If, later, the same house costs $15,000 and is bought with

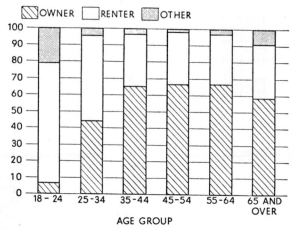

FIGURE 10–2

HOUSING STATUS BY AGE GROUP, 1962
(NONFARM FAMILIES)

SOURCE: Survey Research Center, University of Michigan, and National Industrial Conference Board.

$2,000 down and a $13,000 mortgage for 35 years, the monthly payment goes up only to $74.13. The increase from $57 to $74 a month doesn't seem as if you are paying $17,377.80 *more* for your $15,000 house than the earlier purchaser paid for the same $10,000 house.

You don't believe it? How can the difference between $57.32 a month and $74.13 a month come out to $17,377.80, you ask? Well, figure it out for yourself. On the $10,000 house you pay $57.32 a month for 240 months (20 × 12 = 240), which amounts to $13,756.80. On the $15,000 house you pay $74.13 for 420 months (35 × 12 = 420), which comes out to $31,134.60. An apparent difference of some $17 a month thus works out to a total difference of $17,377.80!

The decision to buy or to rent is usually made on the basis of needs and wants, not financial comparisons. A young couple, recently married, may prefer to rent for a variety of reasons. They may both work and they want to be within easy transportation range of their jobs. In a city this may mean rental housing. His career isn't set yet. He may change jobs several times, or be transferred by the company. More than 55 percent of American families have plans to move, according to findings of the University of Michigan Survey Research Center based on a national sampling. The most mobile group are predominantly renters and younger people. More than half of all renters plan to move within the next five years, but only one out of five homeowners do. Later, when he is set in his job and when she has decided to stay home and raise children,

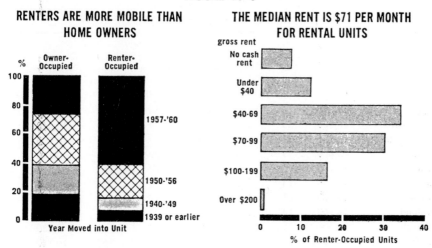

FIGURE 10–3

RENTERS ARE MORE MOBILE THAN HOME OWNERS

THE MEDIAN RENT IS $71 PER MONTH FOR RENTAL UNITS

Source: Chase Manhattan Bank.

there is need for more space, safer and more pleasant surroundings in suburbia or exurbia for the children. He becomes a commuter, and they buy the house even though over the first few years—the short run—it may cost them much more than renting did.

The important thing, once the decision to buy a house has been made, is to know how much house can you afford?

Why People Buy the Houses They Do

More than 50 percent of American families now own their own homes, subject to mortgage debts, of course. Thus the old debate as to whether it is better to buy or to rent seems to be resolving itself, slowly, in favor of buying. Why do people decide to buy rather than rent? Table 10–1 provides a partial answer. It is interesting that a fourth of the home buyers felt that ownership is cheaper than renting.

TABLE 10–1

Why Buyers Decided Not to Rent*

	Percentage
Buying is an investment	24
Rents too high: ownership cheaper	24
Ideal of homeownership	22
Forced to buy: could find no place to rent	19
Desire for independence: security	11
"Found just the right place"	4
Reasons of location	2
Other reasons	

* From "Why People Buy the Houses They Do," *Housing Research*, Housing and Home Finance Agency, Washington, D.C.

TABLE 10–2

Home Ownership Costs and Family Income Required

	Minimum Selling Price	Utilities per Month	Taxes per Year	Debt Service per Month*	Insurance & Maintenance per Month†	Total Housing Cost per Month	Annual Income Required‡	Percent of all Families Able to Buy§
Chicago	$16,250	$40	$250	$95	$30	$186	$11,160	12.9
New Haven	16,000	35	400	94	29	191	11,460	12.1
San Francisco	15,950	18	375	94	29	172	10,320	16.3
Fall River	15,600	35	150	92	29	169	10,140	16.9
Honolulu	15,180	20	120	90	28	148	8,880	23.1
New Orleans	15,050	13	60	89	28	135	8,100	28.7
Milwaukee	14,980	27	438	89	27	180	10,800	14.4
Cleveland	14,960	14	180	89	27	145	8,700	24.3
Pittsburgh	14,600	31	228	86	27	163	9,780	18.2
New York	14,300	25	400	85	26	169	10,140	16.9
Los Angeles	12,995	30	300	77	24	156	9,360	20.3
Denver	12,500	20	200	72	23	132	7,920	30.3
Gary	12,500	25	250	72	23	142	8,460	26.0
Washington	12,500	20	175	72	23	130	7,800	31.3
Minneapolis	12,250	35	200	72	22	146	8,760	23.9
Norfolk	12,000	30	255	70	21	142	8,520	25.5
Baltimore	11,850	25	285	69	21	132	7,920	30.3
Providence	11,300	18	250	67	21	134	8,040	29.1
Philadelphia	11,250	25	168	65	20	124	7,440	34.6
Detroit	10,990	25	171	64	20	122	7,320	35.7
Charlotte	10,850	24	180	62	19	126	7,560	33.4
St. Louis	10,500	30	96	59	18	105	6,300	45.8
Louisville	10,000	20	75	59	18	98	5,880	49.5
Atlanta	10,000	15	132	59	18	103	6,180	47.1
Dallas	9,900	15	84	58	18	105	6,300	45.8
Wilmington, Del.	9,850	22	240	57	18	120	7,200	36.9
Boston	9,625	25	125	57	18	110	6,600	42.6
Little Rock	9,600	25	60	53	17	90	5,400	55.2
Birmingham	9,000	15	265	53	17	114	6,840	40.3
Phoenix	8,990	22	165	50	16	94	5,640	52.3
Memphis	8,550	14	180	52	22	103	6,180	47.1

* Debt service (rounded to nearest dollar) is figured on a 30-year basis with the maximum mortgage (97 percent of the fir $15,000, 90 percent of the next $5,000, and 75 percent of the balance). This is $5.68 monthly per $1,000, plus 41¢ for insuran

† Hazard insurance is figured at 0.2 percent of value annually and maintenance at 2 percent of value annually.

‡ Annual income required is five times the total cost of the maximum mortgage, taxes, utilities (including heat), insuranc and maintenance.

§ The percentages are estimated on a nationwide basis from the Census Bureau's reports on family incomes in 1961, p jected to 1962. Incomes tend to be higher in the North than in the South, and higher in urban areas than in rural areas. Hence actual percentages would be higher than shown in northern states and in urban areas—and lower in southern states and in ru areas.

Source: *The Housing Yearbook, 1963* (Washington, D.C.: The National Housing Conference).

How Much Can You Afford for a House?

Less than one third of the families living in American cities have enough income to justify the purchase of a new house, according to the National Housing Conference. It reported that a survey of 31 cities had shown that the *minimum* price of new one-family houses ranged from $8,500 in Memphis to $16,250 in Chicago. The median was $12,000. The Conference estimated that a family would have to have an annual income of $7,980 to meet the costs of a $12,000 house. This is based on estimated monthly expenses of $133 for amortization, taxes, insurance, maintenance, utilities, and heat. The Conference applied the rule that housing costs should not exceed one fifth of income.

TABLE 10–3
Housing Medians for 1961–1963

	1963 MEDIAN	1962 MEDIAN	1961 MEDIAN
Minimum price of house	$12,000	$11,800	$12,300
Monthly housing costs*	$ 133	$ 131	$ 136
Annual income required	$ 7,980	$ 7,860	$ 8,142
Size of house (gross sq. ft.)	1,000	1,000	980
Size of lot (sq. ft.)	6,000	7,200	6,600
Taxes per year	$ 180	$ 200	$ 210
Utilities per month	$ 25	$ 23	$ 23
Miles from city center	6	8	10
Ratio of selling price to annual income required	1.5	1.5	1.5
Percent of families able to buy	29.8	29.6	23.6

* Amortization of maximum mortgage, maintenance, insurance, taxes, and utilities. Taxes and utilities are the national medians.
SOURCE: National Housing Conference, 1963.

This study offers one possible approach to provide answers to the question: "How much can you afford for a home?" You can use Table 10–2 to ascertain what annual income you should have (next-to-last column) to enable you to carry the minimum price house (first column). For example, if you are thinking of buying a $16,250 house, looking across to the next-to-last column, you should have an income of $11,160 a year, for monthly costs will amount to $186. Another way to use the table is to look down the "annual income required" column until you find the figure closest to your annual income and then look across to the first column to see what you can afford to pay for a house. You will notice that costs vary from city to city.

There is a second method for figuring out how much of your income you can devote either to renting or to buying a home. List your expenses and income—either on a monthly or a yearly basis—as follows:

What is your total income?*......$_8250_ Monthly savings budget.........$_600_
What are your withholdings for Food and clothing..............$_1680_
  income taxes, retirement, so- Medical care....................$_180_
  cial security benefits, hospital- Life insurance..................$_300_
  ization insurance, and any other Recreation.....................$_960_
  deductions from your wage or Utilities and fuel...............$_600_
  salary.....................$_2062_ Automobile expenses...........$_600_
Subtract the second figure from All other expenses (membership
  the first.   dues, contributions, charge ac-
Your TOTAL "TAKE-HOME   counts, installment pur-
  PAY" is....................$_6187_   chases, etc.)..................$_950_
  _____ Add these up.
  Your TOTAL EXPENSES are.....$_820_

* Omit wife's income from this computation.

Now subtract TOTAL EXPENSES from TOTAL "TAKE-HOME PAY." You get the figure, $_____, which is the amount of money you can afford to pay for a roof over your head. This figure is referred to as your *income for housing.*

Now that you have your income for housing either on a yearly or monthly basis, consult Table 10–4. Find your housing income in the table to learn the amount of the loan you can afford. The figures in this table include not only principal and interest charges on a mortgage but also estimate an allowance for taxes, maintenance, and insurance as well.[1] Suppose you have found that your income for housing is $100 a month. According to Table 10–4 this would, for example, permit you to afford a home loan of $9,590 at 5½ percent for 20 years. This figure represents what you should be able to finance from your current income. It does not, of course, include your down payment. If you can afford a down payment of $2,000, then you will be able to buy a house selling for about $11,500.

A House Built to Specifications

Naturally, if a family has a home built to its specifications, it should expect to be able to get a house meeting those specifications; but it is

---

[1] Taxes, maintenance, and property insurance will vary in each community and geographical area. For the purposes of this table, taxes have been estimated at $18.00 annually, insurance at $3.00 annually, and upkeep at $20.00 annually for every $1,000 loaned on the home. These figures may need adjustment to bring them into conformity with your location.

TABLE 10-4
How Much of a Mortgage Can You Afford?

Amount of Loan Which Income for Housing Will Finance

INCOME FOR HOUSING		At 4 Per Cent			At 5 Per Cent			At 5½ Per Cent			At 6 Per Cent		
Monthly	Annual	10 Yrs.	15 Yrs.	20 Yrs.	10 Yrs.	15 Yrs.	20 Yrs.	10 Yrs.	15 Yrs.	20 Yrs.	10 Yrs.	15 Yrs.	20 Yrs.
$ 15	$ 180	$1110	$1380	$1580	$1070	$1320	$1500	$1050	$1280	$1440	$1030	$1240	$1395
20	240	1470	1850	2110	1430	1760	2000	1400	1700	1920	1635	1645	1845
25	300	1840	2310	2630	1790	2210	2500	1750	2140	2400	1720	2110	2360
30	360	2210	2770	3160	2140	2650	3000	2090	2570	2880	2070	2540	2830
35	420	2580	3230	3680	2500	3090	3500	2440	2990	3360	2410	2960	3310
40	480	2940	3690	4210	2860	3530	4000	2800	3420	3840	2760	3380	3780
50	600	3680	4620	5260	3570	4410	5000	3490	4270	4800	3450	4230	4720
60	720	4420	5540	6320	4290	5290	6000	4200	5120	5760	4140	5070	5670
80	960	5890	7380	8420	5710	7060	8000	5580	6840	7670	5520	6760	7560
100	1200	7360	9230	10530	7140	8820	10000	6980	8540	9590	6700	8450	9450
125	1500	9200	11540	13160	8930	11030	12500	8730	10680	11990	8620	10560	11810
150	1800	11025	13520	15400	10620	13200	14970	10380	12780	14360	10230	12590	14150
175	2100	12860	15775	17970	12390	15400	17460	12110	14910	16760	11940	14690	16510
200	2400	14700	18030	20530	14160	17600	19960	13850	17050	19150	13650	16790	18870
225	2700	16530	20280	23100	15930	19800	22450	15580	19180	21540	15350	18890	21230
250	3000	18370	22540	25670	17700	22000	24950	17310	21300	23940	17060	20980	23590

Source: United States Savings and Loan League.

common for persons not used to reading blueprints to get quite a surprise when they see the house which was built from them. Sometimes it is far different from what they imagined it would be. As they see the house going up, it is not unusual for them to discover things that they want changed to make them (in the family's opinion) what they visualized them to be. To make these changes, much more expense may be involved than can be comfortably financed.[2] In a great many cases it is wise to secure the services of a competent architect, who may charge from 12 to 15 percent of the total construction cost, to draw plans that will suit the family's needs and wants and to see that the contractor is building according to specifications. Honest and able architects and builders can do much to smooth the path of the unwary person who for the first time is having a house built.

Building your own home is usually a long, costly, and often bitter process; and if your funds are limited and your patience short, it is not a good idea. Figure 10–4 shows a few of the construction features of a house, and you can see at a glance how much study and time it will take to acquire enough information to talk intelligently with your architect and contractor. If you do decide to build, a construction loan can be obtained.

The House Already Built

In most cases it is better to buy a house already built—preferably a new house; at least you can see what you are getting. A new house is usually easier to finance. The down payment may be as little as 5 percent of the house price—occasionally less—whereas an old house may require between 20–33 percent. You may need $3,000 in cash to buy a $15,000 old house—a probably good buy in more space for your dollars, although you will also need money for repairs and perhaps modernization. Where you merely add modern equipment, such as rewiring, plumbing, heating-cooling, or are doing inside alteration, such as installing a bathroom or kitchen, a contractor is adequate. But if you want to create new space instead of altering the old, an architect is needed to save money and prevent mistakes. His fee ranges from 12 percent to 15 percent of construction costs.[3]

If you are going to buy a used house which requires extensive

---

[2] See Eric Hodgins, *Mr. Blanding Builds His Dream House* (New York: Simon & Schuster, Inc., latest edition).

[3] For further details, see Arthur M. Watkins, *How Much House Can You Afford*, New York Life Insurance Company, 1963.

FIGURE 10-4

remodeling to make it suit your needs, it may ultimately cost more than a new house. Things which have already cost money have to be removed and scrapped, and substitutes have to be installed at further expense. Then, again, there is always the danger that the remodeled home will be a hodgepodge, inferior to one built from scratch to a carefully drawn plan. Some houses built in former days, however, have materials and workmanship that can be duplicated today only with difficulty. They are apt to be large, with big rooms, and, in some climates, high heating expense. Of course, any house more than five or ten years old requires more in the line of repairs than most of those which have just been built. Older houses, however, may be cheaper and perhaps better buys for those who are content to live in them as they are and not undertake extensive remodeling.

A Limit to Cost

If a family is going to buy a home, it is most important to buy one which can be paid for comfortably. The usual rule is that the family should buy a house whose price does not exceed 2½ times the family's annual income. This means that a family with annual earnings of $5,000 should try to be content with a home costing about $12,500. Since in many parts of the country this ($5,000) is a fairly typical family income today, and since it is not easy to find suitable housing costing $12,500 or less, it is obvious that many families just do not earn enough money to become homeowners without making substantial sacrifices of other things they would like to have. To a greater or lesser degree, we can have one thing only by abstaining from something else that we would like to have. Our thoughts and feelings are changeable, however. We may decide to buy a house even when it is obvious that we can do so only by dispensing with other things we want. Later we may decide that the burden of homeownership is costing us other pleasures which we crave. It is, therefore, probably wise for most families to limit the price for a home to about 2½ times the family's annual income.

Another useful rule is that rent or housing costs per month should not exceed more than one week's take-home pay. Since the monthly housing cost is usually roughly 1 percent of the total purchase price of the house, a $16,000 house is likely to cost $160 a month to carry (this will vary somewhat, depending on size of mortgage and cash down payment). Obviously, if your take-home pay is $85 a week, this is too expensive a house for you.

Assume you wanted to buy it anyway and went to a bank to help finance it, since you were able to put up $5,000 of the purchase price and therefore needed an $11,000 mortgage loan (at 5¾ percent) for 20 years. The bank would examine your loan application in the light of your income, along the lines shown in Figure 10–5. Under this procedure, which is used by a number of banks and insurance companies, your application would be turned down because your monthly carrying charges (limited here to three items only) exceed 20 percent of your effective weighted annual income. In the computation of your weighted annual income, the analysis considers your full salary but only half of your investment income, which may fluctuate and decline, and only a third of your income from a second job, because the chances are that you

FIGURE 10–5

Credit Pattern for Residential Loan Application

Determine weighted annual income as follows:

Regular wages or commissions.....................5,200 × 1	=	$5,200
Income on investments............................ 200 × ½ =		100
Secondary job..................................... 900 × ⅓ =		300
Wife's earnings if under 32 years.................3,000 × 0 =		0
Wife's earnings if from 32 to 38 years.............. × ½ =		
Wife's earnings if over 38 years.................... × 1 =		
Wife's earnings if professional and under 32 years.... × ½ =		
Wife's earnings if professional and over 32 years..... × 1 =		
Gross weighted annual income...............................		$5,600
Less installment debts..		800
Effective annual weighted income.............................		$4,800

Carrying Charges (*for $11,000 mortgage at 5¾%, 20 years on $16,000 home*)

Mortgage.........$77.23 *per mo.*
Taxes............ 33.00 " "
Insurance........ 3.00 " "
_____
$113.23 " "   × 12 = $1,358.76
Percentage to carry (acceptable maximum: 20%)   = 28 + %

will find it too burdensome to hold this for long. If your wife is under 32 years of age, her earnings are not counted, on the assumption that she may not retain her job for long, since you may wish to raise a family. Finally, from your gross weighted annual income the bank subtracts the $800 installment debt you owe on your car in order to arrive at the effective annual weighted income. When the bank denied your application because the proposed monthly carrying charges exceeded 20 percent of the effective weighted annual income, it would tell you that if you could lower the proposed monthly carrying charges by putting up more cash and taking a smaller mortgage, it might finance the transaction. Otherwise, you would be told that you ought to buy a less expensive house.

You may wonder why the $800 installment debt is deducted in arriving at the effective annual weighted income, since you expect to pay it off in two years or so. The bank knows, however, that buying a house entails a number of unexpected expenses which the purchaser either does not anticipate or does not consider important, but which do add up and may increase installment debts and make it difficult to pay them off. For example, a new home usually results in purchase of additional furniture, or new furniture. Then there are moving expenses and other miscellaneous expenses you never thought of, such as storm doors and storm windows ($500–$700); a fence ($200); landscaping ($400–$1,000); gardening tools, hose, and lawn mower ($150–$250); work tools ($100); etc. Furthermore, the monthly carrying charges listed in Figure 10–5 are not complete. To the $113.23 must be added $20 a month for heating, $20 for repairs and painting, possibly a charge for garbage removal, and, if you are calculating accurately, $30 for depreciation (assuming a 40-year life for your $16,000 house). Usually the total monthly carrying costs of a modest house are much larger than the average family calculates or expects when they lightly and cheerfully assume the burden.

One bank has developed a very simple form for quickly estimating whether or not to grant a proposed mortgage loan. This is shown in Figure 10–6. In the bottom half of this form, if the ratio of income to carrying charges is less than 20 percent, the loan will be granted. If it exceeds 25 percent, it will be rejected. If it falls between 20 and 25 percent, it will be studied carefully by the mortgage loan officer and becomes a matter for his critical judgment. In a period of tight money, it would probably be rejected. In a period of easier money, it might well be granted.

Location and Transportation

Land cost is a variable factor which is closely related to both location and convenience. The same house that would cost $35,000 within a 15-mile radius of Times Square in New York City might sell for $14,000 fifty miles away. It has been found that the cost of land declines to the extent that people must pay extra and higher transportation costs to get to and from it. Builders found, over the last decade, that if they pushed too far out, the land and house built on it brought less than they estimated. The land cost in the average cost of a house rose from 10 percent in 1950 to just under 25 percent in the mid-1960's. A house that is conveniently near to good bus or train service has a considerable advantage for most families. Railroad commuting fares were once small enough to occasion little comment, but they are now an important expense. The cost of transportation, which for a typical move from city to suburb may add from $25 to $50 to previous monthly transportation costs, should not be overlooked in computing future estimated total monthly housing costs.

FIGURE 10–6

Credit Analysis for a Mortage Loan

CREDIT ANALYSIS

Servicer _____ FHA. _____ VA. _____

Subdivision _____ Sales Price _____
                          VA. Value
Property _____
                          FHA. Value _____

                          FSB. Commitment _____
Borrower _____
                          Mortgage Amount _____

                          VA. Guaranty _____
Commitment Date _____
                                    Term _____

                                    Int. Rate _____

APPROVED

_____   _____

(A) MORTGAGORS MONTHLY INCOME	(B) MONTHLY CARRYING CHARGE	RATIO-INCOME TO CARRYING CHARGES
1. Mortgagor $_____	1. Princ. & Int. $_____	B to A-1 _____ %
2. Other Income _____	2. Taxes _____	B to A-1-2 _____ %
_____	3. Insurance _____	B to A-1-2-3 _____ %
_____	4. Water Rent _____	INCLUDING (4) _____ %
3. Co-Mortgagor _____	5. M.I.P. _____	
4. Co-Bondsman _____	TOTAL $_____	
TOTAL $_____		

Schools

If there are children in the family, it becomes necessary to consider whether a house is conveniently situated, not only as to elementary schools but also as to junior high schools and high schools as well. It can be both expensive and burdensome to transport children to school and back several times a day. Investigate the present school tax and the prospects for the future. If a new school is badly needed and the community quite properly authorizes it, you may find your school tax suddenly doubled. If you are considering a new development, most likely populated by young families, this will be especially true.

Stores

As a result of high labor and transportation costs, grocery and meat stores no longer make a practice of delivering orders to the extent that they did in former years. The high cost of living has also caused more and more people to take advantage of the lower prices charged by chain stores and supermarkets. A home which is conveniently situated so that daily shopping can be accomplished with a minimum of time and effort will, because of this advantage, be found to merit serious attention.

Other Conveniences

Proximity to churches and synagogues, clubs, lodges, and other community activities are also things to be remembered when choosing a home site. The lay of the land (topography) in the immediate vicinity of the home is also important. The view from a home on a high hill can be an inspiring sight, but it takes effort to climb the hill. When one is young, the trip may not be difficult in a car or even on foot, but in later years age may make the journey troublesome. In some of our climates, coping with slippery, icy streets may cause trouble for those still young and able. Therefore, consider well the location of the proposed home site; view it carefully by day and by night, in all seasons, and try to imagine how suitable it will prove to be for your family at present and in the future. It is a human failing to enthuse over the first view of a given spot; but sometimes familiarity with it may breed contempt. Remember, once you choose a location you may be stuck with it—it may be hard to change.

Environment

Whether the neighborhood is populated with families that probably would prove to be congenial is worth noting. There are young people's neighborhoods, where older persons feel out of place; and there are neighborhoods filled with older persons, where growing children find it hard to meet suitable playmates. Everything may be fine about some location except for the absence of a suitable place for the children to play. Remembering Alfred Marshall's remark that it is common for things to have a period of growth, a period of leveling off, and a period of decline, one should give thought to the present status of a proposed home site. Does it appear to be one that will increase in value and draw in more people who would be acceptable to the family, or has it reached its zenith, or is it already on the downgrade? Are there local building codes determining zoning, lot size, and sidewalks and curbs which would keep property values more stable? The house you buy should conform in price and size to the other houses around. A $25,000 house in a $15,000 neighborhood has less resale value. This matter of choosing a place in which to live is not one for quick, offhand decision. A chart showing the more important points you should check before buying is shown in Figure 10–7.

The Lot

For most purposes, a level, rectangular lot of reasonable size is preferred by most people. Blasting away cliffs, digging garages into hillside cellars, and getting automobiles out of sunken garages on icy pavements can be expensive and provoking. Corner lots may seem attractive from some points of view, but to some of us they mean extra sidewalks from which to remove snow. More land than the family can reasonably use and service involves a useless financial burden. A lot with 100 feet of frontage and a like depth—a little less than a quarter-acre—should prove ample for most families, unless they want a vegetable or flower garden. More than this can lead to quite a chore of lawn mowing and, in some localities, a considerable expense for water. Presence of sheltering trees may mean freedom from oppressive heat in summer or blistering winds in winter. Whether the lot faces in a certain direction may have large bearing on the comfort of the residence on it. A southern exposure for the main living quarters is considered the most desirable, offering the greatest amount of light and sun for most of the day.

Other Exterior Features

Is the design standard? Unusual styling may be very interesting and attractive, but it may also narrow your market for resale at a later date. A man built a strikingly modernistic home at a cost of $110,000 in a small, conservative Ohio city. It was a most unusual and very attractive house. A few years later he accepted an offer of a much better position in another city. After commuting (week ends) for two years between the two cities while trying to sell the house for what it cost him, he finally let it go for $54,000.

Has the lot been graded away from the house? This is to permit proper drainage of surface water. Have dry wells or splash blocks been provided at the drainpipes to carry roof rain water away from the foundation walls assuring a warm, dry basement?

Another thing to check is the landscaping of the grounds around the house. Is there shrubbery circling along the perimeter of the property to provide privacy? How is the lawn? If it needs redoing, it's a costly business. Have concrete walks and curbing been installed? Also, is there

FIGURE 10–7

POINTS

TO CHECK

BEFORE

YOU BUY

Here are 20 points to consider about any neighborhood.
To compare two different
houses or neighborhoods, rate
one in column a, the other
in column b. Use check
marks; then figure the scores
as indicated below. Don't be
discouraged if you don't have
a lot of "good" checks. This
is a tough test.

a b

"Good" checks × 3 ___ ___
"Fair" checks × 2 ___ ___
"Poor" checks × 1 ___ ___

Total scores ___ ___

		GOOD	a	b
	shopping	Local shopping center within walking distance; major shopping area within 4 miles.		
	churches & amusements	Available within 2 miles.		
	community pride	Well-kept lawns and gardens. Houses in good repair, painted and neat.		
	neighbors	Mostly people not much better off nor much worse off than you, most of whom are likely to share some of your tastes and interests.		
	police & fire protection	Well-trained, adequately equipped, full-time paid forces in the locality.		
	schools	Good schools within ½ mile, off important thoroughfares.		
	playgrounds	Within 15-minute walk. Separate facilities for preschool and older groups.		
	trash & garbage disposal	Several public or private collections weekly.		
	street layout	Streets gradually curved to slow traffic, fitted to land contours, intersections at right angles or close to it.		
	transportation	Convenient bus or car stop, frequent service, less than 30 minutes' ride to work.		
	growth trend	In direct path of growth of city's most desirable residential areas.		
	lay of the land	Moderately sloping, rolling land, readily drained.		
	trees	Numerous scattered trees, well developed, likely to remain healthy because original land level has not been changed.		
	water	Public water supply with mains in place.		
	sewerage	Public sanitary sewer system.		
	protection against encroachment	Area zoned against undesirable uses like railroad tracks, cemeteries, cheaper residential areas. Restrictions rigidly enforced.		
	traffic	No thoroughfare through neighborhood, existing or potential. Lot on dead-end street.		
	hazards	No hazards—such as airport, gas or oil storage tanks—for considerable distance.		
	privacy	Spacious lots with houses arranged to give maximum seclusion to each.		
	nuisances	Nothing in vicinity to produce noise, smoke, soot, dust or odors.		
	ADD CHECK MARKS			

SOURCE: *Changing Times, The Kiplinger Magazine.*

FIGURE 10–7 (Continued)

FAIR	a	b	POOR	a	b
Local shopping within 1 mile; major shopping area within 4 miles.			More than 1 mile to any store; major shopping area more than 4 miles away.		
Available within 3½ miles.			More than 3½ miles away.		
Mostly a well-kept neighborhood but with a few exceptions.			Well-kept property exceptional. Numerous overgrown, littered vacant lots.		
Mostly people of somewhat higher, or lower, economic and social standing than yours, but a few in your bracket, too.			Everybody a few steps above, or below, your rung on the ladder. You'd be a novelty in the neighborhood.		
Part-time or volunteer forces maintained by community organization.			Protections skimpily provided for or absent.		
Good schools up to 3 miles away, with school bus or other transportation provided.			More than 3 miles to nearest schools.		
Available, but it takes more than 15 minutes to get there.			None provided.		
Public or private collection once a week.			None provided.		
Mostly curved, limited traffic streets—including yours—but some through streets.			Rigid waffle squares unrelated to traffic flow or land contours.		
Adequate service at rush hours, 30 to 45 minutes to work.			Infrequent service, more than 45 minutes to work.		
Not directly in path of growth of most desirable sections but far enough out to avoid encroachment by undesirable development.			Not in path of desirable development, close to existing and undesirable development		
Steep but accessible land or flat land that is well drained.			Very flat, low-lying land that may have drainage or sewerage problems. Filled land.		
Few mature trees or nothing but newly planted trees.			Barren land, land overgrown with brush, or deep fill that will kill existing trees.		
Community water system.			Individual wells.		
Community sewer system, installed by developer with provision for continued operation.			Individual septic tanks or cesspools.		
Shielded from undesirable uses by buffer areas like golf courses, parks, stream valleys.			Adjacent undesirable areas, zoning inadequate or lacking.		
Neighborhood split by street carrying through traffic, but it's not your street.			Lot located directly on heavily traveled street.		
One or more hazards in vicinity but at some distance.			Nearby hazards.		
Medium-sized lots but with houses located to give as much seclusion as possible to each.			Small lots with houses lined up in rows, staring at each other.		
Only possible sources of nuisances considerable distance away. Prevailing winds blow in opposite direction.			Nuisance sources nearby and to windward.		

a finished driveway, either concrete or asphalt? You'll need them to avoid dust and dirt, and if they are not there, it's another expense to add them.

Are you so far out in exurbia that sewerage, water, garbage disposal, etc., are continuing headaches and expenses? In other words, does the property have a public sewer system, community water, and garbage and refuse collections? Are there adequate street lighting facilities? Have the streets been surfaced and deeded to the municipality so that they are a community responsibility? Absence of such utilities or community services is likely to involve future assessments, or higher taxes to provide for their installation and upkeep.

Appraising the Lot

Since the investment involves so much money for the average family, whether one has a house built to his order or buys an existing one, he must be sure that he is getting reasonable value for his money. The person who plans to build must first select a lot which will suit his needs. How is he to know that the price being asked for it is fair? There are at least two things that he can do to assure himself. First, he can use the comparison or market method, commonly used by real estate appraisers. This consists of comparing the price asked for the particular lot with the prices at which other comparable lots are being offered. Such a procedure takes time and effort; but if it is carried out intelligently, it prevents paying a price far out of line from what other people are paying for such properties.

Most families have to borrow from some financial institution a large part (sometimes 70 or 80 percent) of what they pay for a home. The bank will, through its investment or mortgage committee, usually composed of persons of long experience in the real estate field, assure itself of the value of the property which is to serve as security for the loan. The prospective homeowner can profit from the advice obtained from such an institution as to the value of the lot (and buildings, if any). Experienced bank mortgage loan officers know more about the value of a lot than the average person can learn in a reasonable time. Since financial institutions which make a business of lending on home mortgages often charge a modest fee for appraising property (so that they can state how much they feel able to lend with it as security), it is often advisable to pay for this service even though it is not certain that you will have to borrow in order to buy. Some careful persons submit applications to two or more institutions, and pay the required fees, simply to secure assurance that the price to be paid is not excessive.

The family, therefore, which independently does a reasonably competent job of deciding whether the price at which a lot is offered is fair, and then gets support for its decision by obtaining the opinion of impartial experts, should not pay an unduly high price. However, it must be remembered that sellers who ask a certain price for a given property are frequently ready to do business, if necessary, at a lower price; bargaining as to real estate prices is rather common, especially at times when real estate is not selling readily.

Appraising the House

The fair price for having a house built can be obtained by having a few contractors bid independently for the privilege of building a house for which plans and specifications drawn by an architect are presented for the contractors' study. Care should be taken to secure the services of a competent and honest architect to prepare the plans and specifications and to allow only contractors of good general reputation to bid. The financial inability of many contractors, who are frequently mere carpenters who have decided to go into business for themselves, is so notorious that it is only common sense to make sufficient investigation to determine that the contractor can and will perform the work competently for the agreed price.

The National Established Repair, Service, and Improvement Contractors Association suggests you check bank references; contact at least two wholesale suppliers who sell materials to the contractor and talk with at least three homeowners whose remodeling jobs have been finished within the last year. It is wise to be sure that the contractor has public liability insurance—a protection to you in case of property damage or injury to third persons.

A detailed written contract covering brands and quality grades of materials, room by room, is vital for your protection. The contract should also include a provision for sketches (subject to your approval) and a starting and finishing date.

If an old house is being considered, there are other things, besides using the comparison method, which a family can do to assure itself of the value of the property. Banks and dealers in builders' supplies can give information as to present building costs per cubic foot and per square foot of living space for houses of various sorts (frame, brick, etc.). A typical family of four requires a house with at least 1,300–1,400 square feet of living area. Generally speaking, development houses are merchandised at prices ranging from $10–$16 a square foot. At the upper end of this figure there should be some special finishing items such as de luxe door and window hardware, better bathroom tiling, or finer lighting fixtures.

From $16 a square foot to about $20 a square foot, the extra unit cost should reflect nonspace extras such as a large or beautiful parcel of land, extra large garage, or a fireplace.

Above $20 a square foot lies the custom-building range at which individual preferences are taken into account. Sometimes it is cheaper in the long run to consider a more expensive house per unit cost, than to plan to add the extras to an inexpensive one at what will be a higher cost later. For example, insulating walls will cost about six to eight cents a square foot during construction, yet the same installation done after the walls are closed in will cost twenty to twenty-five cents a square foot.

With such information it is possible to approximate how much a house would cost to build new. If we deduct from this cost an allowance for the fact that the building is no longer new but is partially worn out, we can get a figure (cost less depreciation) for the value of the building which may prove of some help in knowing whether the price being asked for it is reasonable. Of course, the figure for the building would be added to a reasonable figure for the lot in order to arrive at a valuation for the complete property.

Another useful method, although more usually applied to commercial or business property, is to find the valuation of the property by capitalizing the net income. A simple way to approximate this method is to decide how much a property should rent for, as compared with what other, similar properties are commanding. If we think that the property should rent for $100 a month, application of the 1 percent rule will tell us that the property in question should be worth something like $10,000. If we wish to make a more detailed and careful study, we can start with the $100 rent figure, which we think is about right, convert it to a $1,200 annual basis, and subtract the estimated yearly expenses (depreciation, taxes, repairs, insurance, interest, etc.), to try to find the net annual income. Suppose the expenses, as best we can judge them, will amount to $600. Then we expect the net income to be $600 ($1,200–$600). If we think the net income ($600) should be 5 percent of the value of the property, we divide $600 by 5 and multiply this result ($120) by 100 to get 100 percent or $12,000, the value of the property by this method. The hardest thing about this method is to decide at what rate (we used 5 percent) to capitalize the net income. Using 8 percent would give $7,500 as the value of the property. A rate of 6 percent would lead to the $10,000 value indicated by the 1 percent rule.

Generally, it will be found helpful to try to obtain a value figure by two or three methods (comparison, cost less depreciation, and capitalization of income). If they lead to different results, they give you something to think about. You can compromise here and there while you try to arrive at the one figure which in your judgment best expresses the real value of the property. Armed with such an estimate and fortified by what you can learn from others, you should have a much better understanding of the value of the property you are considering than has the average buyer.

Examining the House

You have never bought a house before, and when the real estate agent ushers you into the gleaming new house, aside from your wife's noting with approval the lavender-and-black décor of the bathroom and the spick-and-span white kitchen, with its dishwasher and garbage-disposal machine, refrigerator and washing machine, electric mangler and dryer, etc., all of which will probably require a weekly visit from a mechanic to service, how do you tell whether or not the house is soundly constructed? What do you look for, and how will you know what is right and what is not right?

A check list for your guidance is presented in Figure 10–8. Merely glancing at it will indicate what a complicated job you face. Floors, doors, machines, walls, electrical outlets, windows, heating unit, insulation, fans or ventilators, basement, storage, plumbing, roofing, sewage disposal, etc., all must be considered and examined. You cannot possibly know whether the strip flooring is good or bad; whether the doors will warp; whether good or bad "dry-wall" "Sheetrock" board, or "fiber" board, or plastered wall has been used and finished properly; whether the windows will continue to open and close a month hence or after a heavy rain; whether the heating system is adequate or not; whether the basement-less house has adequate crawl space and foundation vent openings or, if there is a basement, whether it is going to drain properly if it leaks a little or a lot; whether insulation thickness in the attic is adequate or not; or whether the plumbing is designed to hold up for 12 months or 12 years. Since you know little or nothing about such things and it is very costly to learn the hard way by buying, moving in, and waiting to see, the best suggestion we can offer is to get expert advice.

The time and expense of getting expert advice is well worthwhile; you do not want to buy a house with termites, a leaky roof, a wet basement, a poor foundation, or defective floors, walls, or ceilings without knowing exactly what you are getting into. Extensive repairs to

FIGURE 10-8

Checklist for Use in Buying or Building a Home

This checklist is offered to aid you in selecting your home. The list does not cover everything but does include the principal items which you should consider.

CHARACTERISTICS OF PROPERTY (Proposed or existing construction)

Neighborhood

Consider each of the following to determine whether the location of the property will satisfy your personal needs and preferences:

Remarks

Convenience of public transportation ☐
Stores conveniently located ☐
Elementary school conveniently located ☐
Absence of excessive traffic noise ☐
Absence of smoke and unpleasant odors ☐
Play area available for children ☐
Fire and police protection provided ☐
Residential usage safeguarded by adequate zoning ☐

Lot

Consider each of the following to determine whether the lot is sufficiently large and properly improved:

Size of front yard satisfactory ☐
Size of rear and side yards satisfactory ☐
Walks provide access to front and service entrances ☐
Drive provides easy access to garage ☐
Lot appears to drain satisfactorily ☐
Lawn and planting satisfactory ☐
Septic tank (if any) in good operating condition ☐

Exterior Detail

Observe the exterior detail of neighboring houses and determine whether the house being considered is as good or better in respect to each of the following features:

Porches ☐
Terraces ☐
Garage ☐
Gutters ☐
Storm sash ☐
Weather stripping ☐
Screens ☐

Interior Detail

Consider each of the following to determine whether the house will afford living accomodations which are sufficient to the needs and comfort of your family:

Rooms will accommodate desired furniture ☐
Dining space sufficiently large ☐
At least one closet in each bedroom ☐
At least one coat closet and one linen closet ☐

Source: Veterans Administration.

FIGURE 10–8 (Continued)

Remarks

Convenient access to bathroom ☐

Sufficient and convenient storage space (screens, trunks, boxes, off-season clothes, luggage, baby carriage, bicycle, wheel toys, etc.) ☐

Kitchen well arranged and equipped ☐

Laundry space ample and well located ☐

Windows provide sufficient light and air ☐

Sufficient number of electrical outlets ☐

CONDITION OF EXISTING CONSTRUCTION

Exterior Construction

The following appear to be in acceptable condition:

Wood porch floors and steps ☐

Windows, doors, and screens ☐

Gutters and wood cornice ☐

Wood siding ☐

Mortar joints ☐

Roofing ☐

Chimneys ☐

Paint on exterior woodwork ☐

Interior Construction

Plaster is free of excessive cracks ☐

Plaster is free of stains caused by leaking roof or sidewalls ☐

Door locks in operating condition ☐

Windows move freely ☐

Fireplace works properly ☐

Basement is dry and will resist moisture penetration ☐

Mechanical equipment and electrical wiring and switches adequate and in operating condition ☐

Type of heating equipment suitable ☐

Adequate insulation in walls, floor, ceiling or roof ☐

The following appear to be in acceptable condition:

Wood floor finish ☐

Linoleum floors ☐

Sink top ☐

Kitchen range ☐

Bathroom fixtures ☐

Painting and papering ☐

Exposed joists and beams ☐

Are You Sure . . .

That the basement will stay dry after heavy rains?

That the foundations are sound?

That there has been no TERMITE damage?

You'd better get EXPERT ADVICE on the condition of existing construction, if you want to *be sure* the house is a good buy.

correct such defects may be very costly. Hire an expert to look the house over for you if you think you are interested in it; go out to the house with him when he examines it; have him explain his observations to you. And if he notes a number of things that need to be corrected, and you do want to buy the house, insist that the builder or seller agree *in writing* to make the necessary changes or corrections. Do not be content with oral assent. Get it in writing. Then you can be half-sure that it will be done. Many a naïve and unsuspecting purchaser has taken a builder's word for it that a leaky basement would be fixed and has then waded around in hip boots for six months while waiting for the contractor to get around to the repair work. Before you take title, insist that the seller agree in writing to do the repairs, and specify that they be done before you move in.

Financing the Home

Once you have selected the house you think you want to buy, your next step is to arrange for financing. If you are in the position of most, you will be able to make only a modest down payment, 25 percent or less, and will need to get the rest of the purchase price by mortgage from a financial institution. When contemplating making a down payment, no family should thoughtlessly decide to part with all of its cash resources for this purpose. It should always strive to retain something in the bank for meeting emergencies.

Where to Go for a Mortgage Loan

Most home loans on mortgages today are made by savings and loan associations, savings banks, commercial banks, insurance companies, and individuals. Of these, only the savings and loan associations specialize exclusively in lending on mortgages. They (including co-operative banks in Massachusetts, homestead associations in Louisiana, and building and loan associations generally) make a business of obtaining savings from the public and putting this money to work earning interest by lending it out on mortgages, largely on residences. They have from 80 to 95 percent of their funds invested in mortgages. Savings banks invest about 70 percent of their funds, on the average, in real estate mortgages; commercial banks, as their name implies, endeavor to put most of their money to work in commercial loans and place only relatively small percentages of assets in mortgages; insurance companies have large bond portfolios and have only recently gone actively into the market for residential mortgages. Many persons like to do business with a local institution if it offers terms and advantages comparable with those that can be obtained elsewhere. It is not unnatural, therefore, that he who seeks a mortgage loan often drops in to the local savings and loan association, savings bank, or commercial bank to talk it over. If he wishes to do business with an insurance company, he will have to deal with a local real estate broker who acts as loan correspondent for one or more insurance companies. Real estate mortgage loans may also be obtained from individuals, but they usually cost more than if secured from a financial institution.

The Old-Type Straight Mortgage

When a loan is made on the security of a mortgage, the mortgagee—the lender—makes the loan to the mortgagor—the homeowner or borrower—in return for a promissory note secured by the mortgage of the property and adequate insurance thereon. The promissory note can be payable in any number of years, depending on agreement. Formerly it was customary to write these promissory notes for three or five years. They were known as "straight mortgages" because there was no provision for partial payment of the principal of the loan during the period for which the note was written; customarily, only the interest was paid periodically—every quarter, every half-year, or every year. At the end of the note's term, it really became a demand instrument, full payment of which could be demanded immediately. Many borrowers would forget about the principal until the full amount of the note was due and payable when the note matured, and then they would attempt to renew the loan for another term of years. Many promissory notes were permitted to run for years, in some cases for 15 or 25, with only interest payments made during the interim. If the note came due in a prosperity period, there might not be any difficulty in renewing it; but if it came due in a depression, the borrower usually lost his property.

For several reasons the straight mortgage is now thought to be disadvantageous. The lender, on the one hand, continues to have just as much money at risk throughout the years in spite of the fact that the security for the loan (the house on the land) is depreciating year after year. The borrower, on the other hand, goes through the period of the note paying merely interest till maturity, at which time he is to pay off the full amount of the note, and this is generally impossible. It is doubtful whether the average family was ever able to accumulate enough money to pay off the full face value of the loan at one time. In case the loan was called at the maturity of the note or later, the borrower would have to refund the loan (get a second loan to pay off the first) or run the danger of having his mortgage foreclosed (property sold to secure whatever money it would provide, to apply on the note). In event of foreclosure, if the note was not satisfied fully by the sale of the property, there was a good chance that the borrower could be held for the deficiency, since he had not made good on his promise as evidenced in the note. Another difficulty with the straight mortgage, from the point of view of the borrower, was that he frequently could not borrow enough on one mortgage of this type (the risk to the lender being what it was) and was forced to borrow the balance on a second mortgage, which, because of the greater risk, commanded a high rate of interest.

Under the straight mortgage, the borrower had to accumulate the funds to pay off his total obligation. If he went to a savings and loan association, the borrower obtained a favorable straight mortgage, in that the period for which the promissory note was written was long enough to permit him to build up share value (he was obliged, as a condition of the loan, to buy shares of the association on the installment plan; he received dividends on his share investment) sufficient to pay off his note at maturity. The way it worked amounted to borrowing in one place, saving in the same place, and finally using the savings to pay off the borrowings. Usually he paid a higher rate on his borrowings than he earned on his savings. And he owed the full amount of his borrowings till the day when he had saved enough to pay off the loan in full at one time; his payments (savings) meantime did nothing to reduce his borrowings.

It is easy to see how disadvantageous such a loan could be for a borrower. Suppose $10,000 were borrowed at 6 percent per annum, the interest, therefore, being $600 a year. When the borrower had saved, say, $6,000, on which we shall assume that he was earning 3 percent per annum, i.e., $180, it was really costing him $420 net a year to have the use of $4,000 net, which is a cost of over 10 percent. The larger his savings became, the higher would be the effective rate of interest which he was paying.

The Amortized or Direct-Reduction Mortgage

The old straight-type mortgage has gone out of favor today because both government and private mortgage financing agencies insist on the amortized mortgage. They want the loans paid off in the foreseeable future—during the economic life of the building. The direct-reduction or amortized mortgage is thus named because the borrower makes a fixed monthly payment which not only includes interest (and perhaps taxes and insurance) but also reduces the principal of the mortgage debt.

The earlier monthly installments include primarily interest and only small amounts of principal repayment. As the principal is gradually reduced, a larger and larger percentage of the monthly payment is applied to repayment of principal, until the loan is entirely repaid. Under this plan, interest at the stipulated rate is figured on the reducing unpaid balance of your loan. Thus, as the regular payments of the fixed monthly amount are made, the part of the payment needed to pay

TABLE 10–5

PAYMENTS INCLUDING AMORTIZATION AND INTEREST REQUIRED
TO LIQUIDATE A LOAN OF $1000.

PAYMENT PERIOD	INTEREST RATE						
	4%	4½%	5%	5½%	6%	6½%	7%
10 Yrs.	$10.12	$10.36	$10.61	$10.85	$11.10	$11.35	$11.61
15	7.40	7.65	7.91	8.17	8.44	8.71	8.99
20	6.06	6.33	6.60	6.88	7.16	7.46	7.75
25	5.28	5.56	5.85	6.14	6.44	6.75	7.07
30	4.77	5.07	5.37	5.68	6.00	6.32	6.65

SOURCE: American Bankers Association.

interest becomes less, and the part applied to reducing the loan becomes greater.

As compared with the old-type straight mortgage, the amortized mortgage requires a higher monthly payment but results in a very large saving in interest costs. For example:

Under the old-type straight mortgage:
    You make a mortgage loan of $10,000.
    You do not make payments to reduce the principal of the mortgage.
    You make 240 monthly payments of $47.91.
    You pay in interest, in 20 years at 5¾ percent per annum, $11,500.
    You still owe the original mortgage of $10,000.
Under the amortized mortgage:
    You make monthly payments of $70.21 to pay both interest and reduce the principal.
    You pay in interest, in 20 years at 5¾ percent per annum, $6,850.40.
    Thus you save $4,649.60 in interest costs and the principal is entirely paid off at the end of the 20th year.

Obviously, the amortized mortgage is a much better arrangement for the borrower.

In the 1930's it was often found that borrowers had not kept up their tax and insurance payments; today, to prevent trouble from this source, it is common practice for borrowers to give the lending institution one twelfth of estimated yearly tax and insurance payments each month.

Taxes in arrears for one or more years seriously shrink the security (property value pledged for the loan), since the government has a first lien for property taxes.

Perhaps an illustration is in order. Let us suppose that Jones owns a house valued at $15,000 and borrows $10,000, with the house mortgaged as security for his promissory note. After the direct-reduction loan has been reduced to $6,000, Jones loses his job, so that he can no longer keep up his payments. After giving due notice of the default in the newspapers, the lending institution proceeds to have the property auctioned off at a foreclosure sale (expense, $150) and bids the property in, itself, at the sale for $5,000. If it is then found that real estate taxes are in arrears in the amount of $1,000, the bank will have to pay this sum to the local political subdivision (city or town) to clear the title. To the borrower's obligation for $6,000 the bank can add the foreclosure expense of $150 and the tax payment of $1,000, making the total amount due from the borrower, $7,150. If the $5,000 received from the sale of the property is credited against the total due, there is a deficiency of $2,150 for which the borrower is still technically liable; but since Jones is out of a job, it will probably be difficult to collect anything from him, and the bank will accordingly have to take a loss of $2,150. If Jones had kept his taxes paid to date, the bank's loss would have been $1,000 less; learning from experience, therefore, banks are today, in many cases, requiring that tax payments be made to them monthly, together with interest and principal payments.

Mathematics of Direct-Reduction Loans

The mathematics of direct-reduction mortgage loans of 15, 20, or 25 years, payable in monthly installments, are too complicated for the average borrower to comprehend; and indeed, lenders use mathematical tables to determine quickly the monthly payment required to amortize a given loan at a certain percentage for a fixed period. Your local bank or savings and loan association will undoubtedly have a copy of *Extended Payment Tables for Monthly Mortgage Loans,* published by the Financial Publishing Company of Boston. One page of this 126-page table is shown in Table 10–6. From it you can see, if you look down the first column (on page 452), that to amortize a loan of $10,000 at 5¾ percent over a 25-year period, a monthly payment of $62.92 is required. To pay off the same loan over a 30-year period, look across the $10,000 line to the seventh column, and you will see that a monthly payment of $58.36 is required. Table 10–7 may be more useful to you, since it shows the annual payment necessary to amortize a loan of $1,000 over any pe-

TABLE 10–6

Monthly Payment Necessary to Amortize a Loan at 5¾ Percent

TERM	25	26	27	28	29	30	35	40
AMOUNT	YEARS	YEARS	YEARS	YEARS	YEARS	YEARS	YEARS	YEARS
5600	35.23	34.63	34.08	33.57	33.11	32.69	31.00	29.85
5700	35.86	35.25	34.69	34.17	33.70	33.27	31.55	30.38
5800	36.49	35.87	35.30	34.77	34.29	33.85	32.11	30.91
5900	37.12	36.49	35.90	35.37	34.88	34.44	32.66	31.45
6000	37.75	37.10	36.51	35.97	35.48	35.02	33.22	31.98
6100	38.38	37.72	37.12	36.57	36.07	35.60	33.77	32.51
6200	39.01	38.34	37.73	37.17	36.66	36.19	34.32	33.04
6300	39.64	38.96	38.34	37.77	37.25	36.77	34.88	33.58
6400	40.27	39.58	38.95	38.37	37.84	37.35	35.43	34.11
6500	40.90	40.20	39.56	38.97	38.43	37.94	35.98	34.64
6600	41.53	40.81	40.16	39.57	39.02	38.52	36.54	35.18
6700	42.16	41.43	40.77	40.17	39.61	39.10	37.09	35.71
6800	42.78	42.05	41.38	40.77	40.21	39.69	37.64	36.24
6900	43.41	42.67	41.99	41.37	40.80	40.27	38.20	36.77
7000	44.04	43.29	42.60	41.97	41.39	40.86	38.75	37.31
7100	44.67	43.91	43.21	42.57	41.98	41.44	39.30	37.84
7200	45.30	44.52	43.81	43.17	42.57	42.02	39.86	38.37
7300	45.93	45.14	44.42	43.76	43.16	42.61	40.41	38.91
7400	46.56	45.76	45.03	44.36	43.75	43.19	40.96	39.44
7500	47.19	46.38	45.64	44.96	44.34	43.77	41.52	39.97
7600	47.82	47.00	46.25	45.56	44.93	44.36	42.07	40.50
7700	48.45	47.62	46.86	46.16	45.53	44.94	42.62	41.04
7800	49.08	48.23	47.47	46.76	46.12	45.52	43.18	41.57
7900	49.70	48.85	48.07	47.36	46.71	46.11	43.73	42.10
8000	50.33	49.47	48.68	47.96	47.30	46.69	44.29	42.64
8100	50.96	50.09	49.29	48.56	47.89	47.27	44.84	43.17
8200	51.59	50.71	49.90	49.16	48.48	47.86	45.39	43.70
8300	52.22	51.33	50.51	49.76	49.07	48.44	45.95	44.23
8400	52.85	51.94	51.12	50.36	49.66	49.03	46.50	44.77
8500	53.48	52.56	51.72	50.96	50.26	49.61	47.05	45.30
8600	54.11	53.18	52.33	51.56	50.85	50.19	47.61	45.83
8700	54.74	53.80	52.94	52.16	51.44	50.78	48.16	46.37
8800	55.37	54.42	53.55	52.76	52.03	51.36	48.71	46.90
8900	56.00	55.04	54.16	53.36	52.62	51.94	49.27	47.43
9000	56.62	55.65	54.77	53.96	53.21	52.53	49.82	47.96
9100	57.25	56.27	55.38	54.56	53.80	53.11	50.37	48.50
9200	57.88	56.89	55.98	55.15	54.39	53.69	50.93	49.03
9300	58.51	57.51	56.59	55.75	54.98	54.28	51.48	49.56
9400	59.14	58.13	57.20	56.35	55.58	54.86	52.03	50.10
9500	59.77	58.75	57.81	56.95	56.17	55.44	52.59	50.63

TABLE 10–6 (Continued)

TERM AMOUNT	25 YEARS	26 YEARS	27 YEARS	28 YEARS	29 YEARS	30 YEARS	35 YEARS	40 YEARS
9600	60.40	59.36	58.42	57.55	56.76	56.03	53.14	51.16
9700	61.03	59.98	59.03	58.15	57.35	56.61	53.69	51.70
9800	61.66	60.60	59.63	58.75	57.94	57.20	54.25	52.23
9900	62.29	61.22	60.24	59.35	58.53	57.78	54.80	52.76
10000	62.92	61.84	60.85	59.95	59.12	58.36	55.36	53.29
10100	63.54	62.46	61.46	60.55	59.71	58.95	55.91	53.83
10200	64.17	63.07	62.07	61.15	60.31	59.53	56.46	54.36
10300	64.80	63.69	62.68	61.75	60.90	60.11	57.02	54.89
10400	65.43	64.31	63.29	62.35	61.49	60.70	57.57	55.43
10500	66.06	64.93	63.89	62.95	62.08	61.28	58.12	55.96
10600	66.69	65.55	64.50	63.55	62.67	61.86	58.68	56.49
10700	67.32	66.17	65.11	64.15	63.26	62.45	59.23	57.02
10800	67.95	66.78	65.72	64.75	63.85	63.03	59.78	57.56
10900	68.58	67.40	66.33	65.35	64.44	63.61	60.34	58.09
11000	69.21	68.02	66.94	65.94	65.03	64.20	60.89	58.62

Courtesy: Financial Publishing Company, Boston.

riod from 1 to 40 years and at any rate from 5 to 7 percent. By dividing the annual payment by 12, you can get the approximate monthly payment required; and then, if your loan is a multiple of $1,000, you can multiply the monthly figure by the number of times $1,000 goes into your loan to get your approximate monthly payment. For example, a loan of $1,000 at 5 percent amortized over 20 years will require an annual payment of $80.25, or a monthly payment of $6.6875. A $10,000 loan at 5 percent amortized over 20 years would mean an annual payment of $802.50, or a monthly payment of $66.875.

For each mortgage loan that is made, an individual amortization schedule is prepared and given to the borrower. An example of such a schedule is shown in Table 10–8. As you can see, this covers a loan of $3,300 at 6 percent for five years. The required monthly payment is $63.80, and the schedule shows each of the 60 monthly payments that must be made, indicating how much goes to interest, how much to repay principal, and what the balance of the loan is.

What You Should Know about Mortgages

Do you know the difference between an open-end and a closed mortgage; between a quitclaim and a warranty deed; between escheat and escrow; between dower and curtesy; between encroachment and encumbrance; between joint tenancy and tenancy in common? Probably not! But you ought to before you buy a house!

TABLE 10–7

Annual Payment Necessary to Amortize a
Loan of $1,000

TERM IN YEARS	INTEREST RATE						
	5	5¼	5½	5¾	6	6½	7
2	537.81	539.72	541.62	543.53	545.44	549.27	553.10
3	367.21	368.94	370.66	372.39	374.11	377.58	381.06
4	282.02	283.66	285.30	286.95	288.60	291.91	295.23
5	230.98	232.58	234.18	235.79	237.40	240.64	243.90
6	197.02	198.60	200.18	201.77	203.37	206.57	209.80
7	172.82	174.39	175.97	177.55	179.14	182.34	185.56
8	154.73	156.29	157.87	159.45	161.04	164.24	167.47
9	140.70	142.27	143.84	145.43	147.03	150.24	153.49
10	129.51	131.09	132.67	134.27	135.87	139.11	142.38
11	120.39	121.98	123.58	125.18	126.80	130.06	133.36
12	112.83	114.43	116.03	117.65	119.28	122.57	125.91
13	106.46	108.07	109.69	111.32	112.97	116.29	119.66
14	101.03	102.65	104.28	105.93	107.59	110.95	114.35
15	96.35	97.98	99.63	101.29	102.97	106.36	109.80
16	92.27	93.92	95.59	97.27	98.96	102.38	105.86
17	88.70	90.37	92.05	93.74	95.45	98.91	102.43
18	85.55	87.23	88.92	90.64	92.36	95.86	99.42
19	82.75	84.44	86.16	87.88	89.63	93.16	96.76
20	80.25	81.96	83.68	85.43	87.19	90.76	94.40
21	78.00	79.73	81.47	83.23	85.01	88.62	92.29
22	75.98	77.72	79.48	81.25	83.05	86.70	90.41
23	74.14	75.90	77.67	79.47	81.28	84.97	88.72
24	72.48	74.25	76.04	77.85	79.68	83.40	87.19
25	70.96	72.75	74.55	76.38	78.23	81.99	85.82
26	69.57	71.37	73.20	75.04	76.91	80.70	84.57
27	68.30	70.12	71.96	73.82	75.70	79.53	83.43
28	67.13	68.96	70.82	72.70	74.60	78.46	82.40
29	66.05	67.90	69.77	71.67	73.58	77.48	81.45
30	65.06	66.92	68.81	70.72	72.65	76.58	80.59
32	63.29	65.18	67.10	69.04	71.01	75.00	79.08
35	61.08	63.02	64.98	66.97	68.98	73.07	77.24
40	58.28	60.29	62.33	64.38	66.47	70.70	75.01

Courtesy: Financial Publishing Company, Boston

It is unfortunate that the average person or family buying a home must necessarily have had so little contact with and understanding of mortgages. Bank mortgage-loan officers have long and varied experience with these documents, and much knowledge may be learned from them if they are patient and helpful. The prospective homeowner should therefore carefully seek out one who can guide him to satisfactory decisions. Lending institutions want, above everything else, to get back

TABLE 10–8

An Amortization Schedule

Starting with the payment as shown herewith, an amortization schedule can be constructed showing the allocation of each payment into interest and principal; also the balance outstanding after each payment has been made. Proceed by (1) computing the interest on the previous balance; (2) deducting this from the payment; and (3) crediting the remainder as a repayment of principal. As a specimen, in the table below, we give the amortization schedule for a loan of $3,300 at 6 percent payable over 5 years by monthly payments of $63.80.

Note that the final payment is usually several cents smaller than the regular payment. This is because the tabulated payment is always a fraction of a cent too large. (If, however, the payment were 1 cent less, the final payment would be slightly larger.)

Amortization schedules for loans of any amount, interest rate, and term of payment may be obtained from the Financial Publishing Company of Boston.

SCHEDULE OF DIRECT-REDUCTION LOAN

```
Loan........................$3,300.00
Rate........................ 6 per cent
Term........................ 5 years
No. of payments.............. 60
Amount of monthly payment....$63.80
```

Time			Payment on—		Balance of Loan	Time			Payment on—		Balance of Loan
Yrs.	Mos.	Periods	Interest	Principal		Yrs.	Mos.	Periods	Interest	Principal	
0	1	1	16.50	47.30	3,252.70	2	7	31	8.87	54.93	1,718.23
0	2	2	16.26	47.54	3,205.16	2	8	32	8.59	55.21	1,663.02
0	3	3	16.03	47.77	3,157.39	2	9	33	8.32	55.48	1,607.54
0	4	4	15.79	48.01	3,109.38	2	10	34	8.04	55.76	1,551.78
0	5	5	15.55	48.25	3,061.13	2	11	35	7.76	56.04	1,495.74
0	6	6	15.31	48.49	3,012.64	3	0	36	7.48	56.32	1,439.42
0	7	7	15.06	48.74	2,963.90	3	1	37	7.20	56.60	1,382.82
0	8	8	14.82	48.98	2,914.92	3	2	38	6.91	56.89	1,325.93
0	9	9	14.57	49.23	2,865.69	3	3	39	6.63	57.17	1,268.76
0	10	10	14.33	49.47	2,816.22	3	4	40	6.34	57.46	1,211.30
0	11	11	14.08	49.72	2,766.50	3	5	41	6.06	57.74	1,153.56
1	0	12	13.83	49.97	2,716.53	3	6	42	5.77	58.03	1,095.53
1	1	13	13.58	50.22	2,666.31	3	7	43	5.48	58.32	1,037.21
1	2	14	13.33	50.47	2,615.84	3	8	44	5.19	58.61	978.60
1	3	15	13.08	50.72	2,565.12	3	9	45	4.89	58.91	919.69
1	4	16	12.83	50.97	2,514.15	3	10	46	4.60	59.20	860.49
1	5	17	12.57	51.23	2,462.92	3	11	47	4.30	59.50	800.99
1	6	18	12.31	51.49	2,411.43	4	0	48	4.00	59.80	741.19
1	7	19	12.06	51.74	2,359.69	4	1	49	3.71	60.09	681.10
1	8	20	11.80	52.00	2,307.69	4	2	50	3.41	60.39	620.71
1	9	21	11.54	52.26	2,255.43	4	3	51	3.10	60.70	560.01
1	10	22	11.28	52.52	2,202.91	4	4	52	2.80	61.00	499.01
1	11	23	11.01	52.79	2,150.12	4	5	53	2.50	61.30	437.71
2	0	24	10.75	53.05	2,097.07	4	6	54	2.19	61.61	376.10
2	1	25	10.49	53.31	2,043.76	4	7	55	1.88	61.92	314.18
2	2	26	10.22	53.58	1,990.18	4	8	56	1.57	62.23	251.95
2	3	27	9.95	53.85	1,936.33	4	9	57	1.26	62.54	189.41
2	4	28	9.68	54.12	1,882.21	4	10	58	0.95	62.85	126.56
2	5	29	9.41	54.39	1,827.82	4	11	59	0.63	63.17	63.39
2	6	30	9.14	54.66	1,773.16	5	0	60	0.32	63.39	0.00
									FINAL PAYMENT, 63.71		

(with interest and with as little bother as possible) the sums that they lend. There is, therefore, every reason for them to advise a prospective borrower (homeowner) to sign a mortgage whose terms he should be able to meet with no great difficulty in normal course, unless he loses his health or his job—contingencies which no one can foresee.

Down Payment

The size of the mortgage loan is of great importance, since the bigger it is, the larger the interest charges must be. Interest costs are reduced by a large down payment. For example, assume you are buying a $15,000 house. If you can pay $7,500 in cash and take a $7,500 mortgage for 20 years at 5¾ percent, the total interest cost over the 20 years will be $5,138.40. If, however, you make only a $2,000 down payment and must have a mortgage for $13,000 at 5¾ percent for 20 years, then the interest cost totals $8,913.20, or $3,774.80 more. See Figure 10–9.

But it is foolish to make such a large down payment in cash that there is little or nothing left in the bank with which to meet emergencies. Temporary unemployment, sickness, need to replace a leaking roof, sudden breakdown of the heating system, and other possibilities too numerous to mention make it very desirable to have an emergency fund of several hundred dollars in the bank. If your mortgage payments are not met on time, the loan is in default; after a few months of default (generally about three or four), the lending institution, under the terms of the mortgage contract, has the right to begin proceedings (foreclosure) to sell the property and apply the proceeds from the sale (cash received) to the debt. Unless you have the wherewithal to keep up your mortgage payments, you may lose your home. While worrying about your inability to meet mortgage payments, you will (in the absence of ready cash) also be worrying about where food and other necessities are to be obtained. If a reasonable down payment cannot be made without leaving the family stripped of adequate reserves for the unexpected, it is doubtless better to defer acquiring a home until more money has been saved.

Monthly Payments

The longer the period (years) for which a loan is written, the smaller the monthly payments must be to pay it off, other things being equal. To pay off a $10,000 amortized mortgage loan over five years would require (assuming a conventional loan at 6 percent) a monthly payment of $193.33. Relatively few people can afford so large a monthly payment. To pay off the same mortgage over a 20-year period

FIGURE 10–9

Total Payment for $15,000 House under Six Methods of Financing

A. $7,500 DOWN PAYMENT, 5 3/4 %, 20-YEAR MATURITY

PRINCIPAL	INTEREST
$15,000	$5,138.40

$7,500	$7,500
DOWN	BALANCE

B. $2,000 DOWN PAYMENT, 5 3/4 %, 20-YEAR MATURITY

PRINCIPAL	INTEREST
$15,000	$8,913.20

$2,000	$13,000
DOWN	BALANCE

C. $2,000 DOWN PAYMENT, 5 3/4%, 30-YEAR MATURITY

PRINCIPAL	INTEREST
$15,000	$14,313.20

$2,000	$13,000
DOWN	BALANCE

D. $7,500 DOWN PAYMENT, 4 1/2 %, 20-YEAR MATURITY

PRINCIPAL	INTEREST
$15,000	$3,888.00

$7,500	$7,500
DOWN	BALANCE

E. $2,000 DOWN PAYMENT, 4 1/2 %, 20-YEAR MATURITY

PRINCIPAL	INTEREST
$15,000	$6,740.00

$2,000	$13,000
DOWN	BALANCE

F. $2,000 DOWN PAYMENT, 4 1/2%, 30-YEAR MATURITY

PRINCIPAL	INTEREST
$15,000	$10,713.20

$2,000	$13,000
DOWN	BALANCE

requires a monthly payment (for principal and interest) of only $71.65. If the maturity is 30 years, the monthly payment becomes $59.96. Thus you can see why, with the trend to the amortized mortgage and the sharp increase in the prices of houses, the tendency has been to write mortgages with longer and longer maturities so as to bring the required monthly payment within financial reach of the average family. Formerly, the straight mortgage ran for five years on the average, and mortgages for more than 15 years were virtually unknown. Today, however, savings banks and savings and loan associations are making 30- and 35-year loans. With today's high real estate prices, few persons can afford the large monthly payments necessary to pay off a large mortgage in as short a period of time as five or ten years.

It must be realized that although longer mortgages require smaller monthly payments, they cost the borrower more in interest than those running for a shorter term. This seems reasonable: he has borrowed and had the use of the money for a longer term, and, naturally, he must pay more interest. As we have seen, if he borrowed $10,000 at 6 percent for five years, his monthly payments would be $193.33. In the five years he would make 60 payments of this amount: $193.33 × 60 = $11,-599.80. This $11,599.80 would pay off the $10,000.00 of principal and provide $1,599.80 for interest.

If $10,000 were borrowed at 6 percent for 20 years, monthly payments would be only $71.65 each, but there would be 240 (20 × 12) of them: $71.65 × 240 = $17,196. After paying off the $10,000 principal, there would be $7,196 remaining for interest. Compare the two interest totals: $1,599.80 in the case of the five-year loan and $7,196 in the 20-year loan; the 20-year loan costs $5,596.20 more for interest than the corresponding loan written for only five years. Now consider the 30-year maturity. If $10,000 were borrowed at 6 percent for 30 years, monthly payments would be only $59.96 each, but there would be 360 (30 × 12) of them: $59.96 × 360 = $21,585.60. Not only would you be paying $21,585.60 for a $10,000 house but the total interest of $11,585.60 would be $9,985.80 more than if you had been able to pay off the loan in five years. The chief justification for the longer period is that it makes the monthly payments small enough so that the borrower can meet his obligations. It might be impossible for the average person to make monthly payments of $193.33, whereas many persons could pay $59.96 monthly without spending more than a reasonable portion of income for payments on the house.

The larger the down payment the lower the interest cost will be, as Table 10–9 indicates. For example, in the purchase of a $15,000 house, if the down payment is only $2,000 and a $13,000 mortgage loan is obtained at 6 percent for a 25-year period, the total interest cost amounts to $12,128. If, however, you can raise an additional $4,000 for a down payment, bringing the total down payment to $6,000 and the mortgage loan is held to $9,000, then the interest cost for the same 25-year, 6 percent loan amounts to $8,397, and you save $3,731 in interest charges.

The Contract of Purchase

When you have selected the house, given some thought to the financing, and decided to buy, the builder or seller will usually require a cash deposit as evidence that you really intend to go through with the deal. Make certain when you hand over the deposit that you get a signed agreement from the seller providing for a refund of your deposit if you are unable to obtain financing or if the builder or seller fails to go through with his part of the agreement. You may also expect to be requested to agree that if you fail to comply with your pledges, you will forfeit your deposit. Such clauses are customary and usual in sales

TABLE 10-9

Purchase of $15,000 Home and Interest Paid for Various Amounts Borrowed at 6 Percent

Down Payment	Mortgage Amount Borrowed	Monthly Payment for 20 Yrs.	Monthly Payment for 25 Yrs.	Total Interest Paid Over 20 Yrs.	Total Interest Paid Over 25 Yrs.
$2,000	$13,000	$93.13	$83.76	$9,351	$12,128
3,000	12,000	85.97	77.32	8,633	11,196
4,000	11,000	78.80	70.87	7,912	10,261
5,000	10,000	71.64	64.43	7,194	9,329
6,000	9,000	64.48	57.99	6,475	8,397

Source: American Bankers Association.

agreements. Try to be sure that the person to whom you are making the payment is reliable. Some prospective purchasers have lost their deposits to persons who were dishonest or who went bankrupt.

The seller will also expect you to sign a contract of purchase. This sales contract is a legal agreement containing legal terms with which the average person is unfamiliar. Under the statutes of frauds in all the states, any contract of sale of lands, tenements, or hereditaments, or any interest in them, must be evidenced by a memorandum signed by the party whom one seeks to hold to the agreement. Therefore, one cannot be held to an agreement to buy real property (or to sell it) until one signs a memorandum of the agreement.

Commonly, it is good to have an attorney draw an agreement which properly expresses the intentions of the parties. If an agreement is drawn by the other side to the deal, have it carefully studied by your own attorney before your signature is appended. Once you bind yourself to the agreement, you must abide by its consequences. Before you sign anything, be sure that you know to what you are agreeing and that you are able to comply with the financial arrangements.

The sales contract should cover the following points:

1. The sales price should be specified in the contract. For your protection, it is usually best if the contract states that the sales price is not subject to change. Some contracts contain a so-called "escalator"

clause which permits the builder to increase the price because of future cost increases. Such clauses should be avoided, but some builders may insist upon them. If they do, and you agree, you should insist upon a maximum beyond which you will not go just to protect your financial status.

2. The sales contract will state the amount of cash payment which will be required from you and the method of financing the balance. If the contract requires that you must arrange to obtain a loan for the balance due, it should provide that any cash deposit you make will be refunded to you if you cannot obtain appropriate financing.

3. The contract should require the seller to deliver the property to you on or before an agreed date and should set forth your right to withdraw and get your deposit back if the property is not delivered on time.

4. If you are buying a new house, it is desirable to have indicated in the contract (or by separate written agreement) what responsibility the builder will assume after you move in. You will want him to agree in writing to correct any defects due to poor material or workmanship within a limited period after you move in, without any cost to you. If he was unable to complete the landscaping and seeding before you took possession, you may find that you will have to do it yourself unless he is obligated in writing to complete the work.

5. In the case of new construction, the contract should provide that the builder will complete the home in accordance with definite plans and specifications, which you should either review or have reviewed for you by an expert for a small fee. Furthermore, you should be provided with a copy of the plans and specifications for your retention.

6. You should not sign any contract containing a so-called "safety" or "escape" clause which would enable the builder or seller to back out of the contract any time he wants to unless you also have similar rights. If you do sign such a paper, be sure it specifies that the builder or seller must advise you in writing on or before a definite date that he will accept or that your offer will expire and you will be free to get your money back.

7. Be sure you have protection against mechanics' liens. Have a seller agree to indemnify you for any losses due to unpaid bills for labor or materials. Unlike other purchases, the buying of a home often carries with it a liability for unpaid claims on the part of those who supplied labor or materials for the house. If the bills for labor or materials are unpaid when one takes title, craftsmen or tradesmen holding the unsatisfied bills can under certain circumstances file liens (mechanics' liens) against the house and collect from the purchaser.

8. There should be a clause protecting you against a defective title and providing for the return of the down payment or for clearing the title in case the search should prove the title to be defective.

These are just a few of the items to check. Legal documents are complicated things, and your best bet will be to retain a lawyer. His small fee may save you a large loss or an unhappy experience.

Final Settlement, or Closing the Loan

After the house is ready and financing has been arranged, the lender will set a date for "settlement" or "closing." Settlement day is the occasion when the property officially becomes yours. You will also remember it as the "paper-signing" day. Among the papers you sign is the *note* or *bond* or other evidence of debt which is used in your area. This document is your promise to repay the loan with interest within a specified period of time, and it will show the repayment terms by means of an amortization schedule. Another paper you will sign is the *mortgage* or *deed of trust,* which is a conditional lien and serves as security for the note or other evidence of the debt. Most of this document is devoted to outlining the rights of the lender in enforcing payment on the debt, including his right to "foreclose the mortgage" (take over the property) should you fail to make prompt payment of interest, principal, taxes, and insurance, or neglect the property so that it is not in a good state of repair. The mortgage is recorded with the county clerk (or other proper official) in the county, town, or city in which your property is located. It remains on record there as a lien or claim against your property until the loan has been paid off.

A *title search* will have been made and you will probably have purchased a *title insurance policy* to protect you from any loss as a result of any defect in the title.[4] You will receive a copy of this policy. A *survey* will also perhaps have been made showing the exact boundaries of your property, and you will receive a copy of this. You should also receive a copy of the bond, the mortgage, and the deed—the legal document conveying title to you. The original will probably have been sent to the proper local official for recording. Thus you should receive five documents: the *bond,* the *mortgage,* the *deed,* the *survey,* and the *title insurance policy,* as well as receipts for all payments you make. Ask for

---

[4] The so-called "Torrens system" of registering titles to land is in force in some of our states. Under this system, one who wishes to have his title to land registered may have the title examined by an official examiner of titles. If this examiner finds that the title is valid, he issues a certificate of title. All later transfers of the property are noted on this certificate and in later transactions affecting the property search back of this registration need not be undertaken.

copies of all papers. Ordinarily they will be provided. Obviously, closing is a complicated business involving a number of legal documents which you have probably never seen before. Do not be afraid to ask questions about any or all of them; but even if you do ask many questions, you probably will not know or cover all the angles, and therefore it is a very good idea to have your lawyer along with you. His fee for this service will be well worth it in the reassurance and peace of mind that comes from knowing that everything is being arranged properly.

Closing costs will probably run higher than you anticipated. These are the fees which you will have to pay at the settlement for all the various documents that have been drawn and services rendered in connection with your buying the house, borrowing, and taking title. An example of closing costs provided by the American Bankers Association for a $20,000 home purchase involving a $12,000 mortgage loan is as follows:

Expenses:		
Legal fees		$200.00
Recording fees		9.30
Survey		25.00
Appraisal		20.00
Mortgage and title policy fee		107.50
Total closing costs		$361.80
Funds Collected for Delivery to Mortgagee (the Bank)		
Taxes (3 months at $35.00)	$105.00	
Interest	22.00	
Hazard insurance premiums (2 months)	9.80	
Total other funds to be in hand at closing	136.80	136.80
Total		$498.60

These closing costs are only an example. Exact costs will vary among the localities and should be investigated carefully.

Approximate closing costs on purchases of houses[5] ranging in price from $20,000 to $40,000 may run as follows:

Survey	$25 to $200
Title fee	$75 to $200
Mortgage tax	$100 to $200
Recording fees	$5 to $20
Bank's lawyer	$75 to $150
Buyer's lawyer	$50 to $400
Engineer	$35 to $55
Advance real estate taxes	up to ½ year
Advance insurance	up to 3 years

---

[5] Robert Metz, "Advice to Home Buyers," *New York Times,* October 21, 1963.

Closing costs

Closing costs involved in a mortgage takeover may run $200 below those involved on a new mortgage.

The Federal Housing Authority figures show that closing costs for new mortgages are $200 to $300 on two out of every five mortgages. On about a fourth of both existing and new mortgages, closing costs varied between $300–$400. For less than 10 percent of the mortgages closing costs run over $500.

Deeds and Titles

A *deed* is a written instrument which is used for the purpose of transferring the title to real estate from one party to another. The one who transfers the title to the real property by means of the deed is called the *grantor;* the one to whom the title is transferred is called the *grantee.* There are two principal kinds of deeds: (*a*) *quitclaim deeds* and (*b*) *warranty deeds.*[6] The quitclaim deed (sometimes called a "release deed") conveys to the grantee whatever title the grantor may have had in the property and throws upon the grantee the risk as to whether there is good or bad title to the property or no title at all. A warrany deed conveys title, and, in addition, the grantor warrants that his title to the property and his right to transfer it are unencumbered and not defective. If property is transferred by a warranty deed and it is later discovered that the title was defective—that the seller did not have good title to the property—the purchaser may proceed at law to recover from the seller for breach of the warranty. Obviously, if the seller has means, this is the best type of deed to obtain from him. However, if he dies, or loses his wealth, or leaves the area and cannot be traced, the warranty deed may be no better than the quitclaim deed.

Naturally, when you make as large a purchase as a house (and the land on which it stands), you will want to be as sure as you can that you really own it, that no one with a prior, unsettled claim will come along and dispute your title. This quest for certainty has, therefore, led people to want something more than the deed. By and large, it only conveys whatever title the seller had to the property. He believes and says he had

---

[6] There are also *special warranty deeds* and *deeds of bargain and sale.* In the former case, the grantor simply warrants that he did not at any time in the past execute any deed or mortgage or place an encumbrance on the property, not mentioned in the present deed. His warranty and liability extends only to this, therefore, and if it later develops that some prior owner had granted some claim and had not transferred a clear title, the grantor of the special warranty deed cannot be held liable. In the bargain and sale deed the consideration for which the property is transferred is recited and one or more warranties may also be explicitly stated. If such is the case, the bargain and sale deed falls midway between the quitclaim and the warranty deeds. If not, the bargain and sale deed resembles a quitclaim deed. It is best to demand and get a regular warranty deed. If the seller does not want to grant it, then don't buy!

an unimpaired title. But to try and make sure, prudent and cautious people have devised four techniques for checking the safety of their titles.

The first method used is the *abstract*. This involves having someone, usually a lawyer or a title guarantee company, trace and write up the history of the ownership of the property. The resulting legal document, the abstract, indicates if there are any liens or claims still outstanding, and if so, states just what they are. All legal transactions, deeds, mortgages, sales, etc., which involved the property in the past are recorded in the abstract, which may therefore be quite lengthy. It does *not* evidence or guarantee title, but if the search has been careful and thorough and no unsettled claims appear, it provides reassurance.

A *certificate of title* may be used in some areas in place of the abstract. It is merely a certification by an attorney that he has examined all the records affecting the property and that in his opinion there appear to be no unsettled or prior liens or claims. Thus he is in effect certifying that in his opinion the purchaser is receiving a valid title. But he is not guaranteeing this, and if his search has been made with due care, he cannot be held liable if in fact some obscure claim does arise to impair title.

The *Torrens certificate* is one issued by a governmental unit evidencing and registering title to real property. In the United States it is used mainly in large cities. It is a safer and faster method than either the abstract or certificate of title since an official recorder or registrar issues a certificate stating ownership after all those who could possibly have a claim or lien are notified and invited to sue. If no suit develops, as is usually the case, then a court orders the registrar to record the title in the new owner's name and issue a certificate to this effect.

Fourthly, there is *title insurance.* A title guarantee company searches the records and having established to its own satisfaction that a clear title is being transferred, writes a policy in favor of the new owner, for a fee, insuring him against any loss from the possibility of defects in the title, other than those which may be stated in the policy. If a lawsuit should arise the title company will defend for the owner and pay the expenses and costs involved. While title insurance is now found mainly in the larger cities, its use is growing.

To protect himself, therefore, from a defective title, the prospective purchaser should always have the title searched either by a competent lawyer or by a title guarantee company. If he is borrowing to finance the purchase, the lender may insist on this and will, in addition, take out title insurance up to the amount of the loan for protection. The purchaser, too, will find it a good idea to buy title insurance covering not the amount of the loan but the full cost of the house, so as to protect his equity in the property. Title insurance taken by the lender protects only the lender. It does not protect the equity of the borrower-owner.

It is customary to have deeds and mortgages recorded in the registry in some public office, such as a county courthouse. Failure to do so may result in a later-recorded deed or mortgage taking precedence over an earlier unrecorded deed or mortgage. The theory is that the public is entitled to rely on the status of titles as revealed by the public records. Thus the seller's title, and that of those who sold to him, can be examined and traced back to insure that the present purchaser is receiving a valid, nondefective title.

Title to real property may be held by one person alone or by two or more persons together. If it is held by one person, it is said to be an *estate in severalty*. Persons holding real property jointly may have taken title as *joint tenants* or as *tenants in common*. Under the common law, if two or more persons took title to real property together under the same instrument, it was interpreted to be joint tenancy, the principal feature of which was that if one of the joint tenants died the survivor took the whole property, and nothing passed to the heirs of the deceased joint tenant. Most states have now superseded the common law by statutes which provide for *joint tenancy with rights of survivorship* or *tenancy by the entirety* (limited to husbands and wives only; neither spouse can transfer any interest during their joint lives without consent of the other). Both have the same essential feature as did the common-law joint tenancy. If one of the joint tenants dies, the survivor takes the whole property, and no part of it passes to other legal heirs. If you are buying property jointly with your spouse and both wish to have it all fall to one on the death of the other, you may take title in this fashion. Depending on the laws of your state, it can be arranged by your lawyer at the closing.

Tenancy in common is different. When two or more persons hold shares in property under separate instruments or under one instrument which shows that each has a separate or individual interest in it, there is *tenancy in common*. On the death of one of the tenants in common, his share goes to his heirs and not to the surviving tenants in common. If ownership of real property involves a corporation as one of several

---

[7] Neither, acting alone, can dispose of his or her interest to a third party. Tenancy by the entirety, which is a form of joint tenancy limited to husbands and wives only, is not recognized in community property states since it is not necessary. See Robert Kratovil, *Real Estate Law* (New York: Prentice-Hall, Inc., latest edition).

owners, then there must be a tenancy in common, since a corporation cannot be a joint tenant. The statutes now generally provide that all conveyances or devises to two or more persons shall be deemed to be tenancies in common unless specifically expressed to be joint tenancies, and that heirs shall receive the land as tenants in common. For wealthy persons the tax aspects of how title is taken and passed become quite important.

Even though a married man or woman owns real estate in his or her own right, in some states he or she cannot pass good title to it to another person without having wife or husband join in the deed to release *dower* or *curtesy*. By common law, dower is the wife's right to a life interest in one third of her husband's real property in the event of his death. Dower and curtesy (the husband's right in his deceased wife's property, providing the couple had a child, even though the child may have predeceased the mother) still exist unimpaired in some states. In most states, these rights have been much modified by statute; and if you are acquiring real property, it would be worthwhile to find out about the law in your state.

In many states a *homestead status* can be placed upon the house you buy. Under these state statutes, the property is declared to be the home of the parties and is then protected from seizure for liability for debts. The amount of property exempted under the right of homestead differs in the several states; and in the same states, more is allowed in the country than in a city. Some states fix this amount by area, some by value, and some by both. It is usually provided that a husband cannot transfer a homestead estate without his wife's consent. In many states, on the death of the husband, the widow or minor children succeed to the homestead right.

Tax Savings for the Homeowner

The homeowner, in contrast to the renter, does have a definite tax advantage. The homeowner may deduct from adjusted gross income in computing net taxable income (*a*) interest paid on a mortgage loan, (*b*) real estate taxes, and (*c*) any casualty losses in excess of those compensated for by insurance.

Assume A rents an apartment and B owns a house, both have $10,000 incomes, and both have $650 of deductions for contributions, medical expenses, etc. B, however, pays $370 in real estate taxes and $530 interest on a mortgage. When A comes to take his deductions in computing his tax he finds that it is better for him to take the standard 10 percent deduction. On an income of $10,000 this gives him a $1,000 deduction rather than $650 if he itemizes. B, on the other hand, finds it better to itemize. He gets a larger deduction—$1,550 ($650 + $370 + $530)—by doing so than by taking the standard 10 percent deduction which is limited to a maximum of $1,000. It can, of course, be argued that A is better off than B because A gets a windfall of $350 in his deductions, being allowed to take $1,000 as against the $650 he actually spent. On the other hand, B's net taxable income will be lower than A's by $550.

If you are a professional—doctor, lawyer, dentist—and use part of your home as an office, you can deduct additionally that proportion of depreciation, heat, painting, insurance, repairs, etc., as the space used for an office bears to total household space. For example, suppose a doctor uses one room for an office and another for a waiting room. If his home has a total of six rooms, he can deduct two sixths or one third of expenses of maintaining the house. A doctor who rented a six-room apartment could, of course, do the same thing, that is, deduct one third of the rent as a business expense. Both the homeowner and the renter could also take as a legitimate deduction a proportion of a maid's pay if she cleaned and took care of the two rooms used for business along with her other household duties.

Ordinarily if you sell your house at a higher price than you paid for it, you will be taxed (at capital gains rates) on the profit. If you buy another house within a year of the sale of the old one, and the new house costs at least as much or more than you received for the old one, you can avoid the capital gains tax on the profit from the old house. This is explained in more detail in the tax chapter which follows.

If you sell your old house and build a new one, the one-year rule is extended. You have 18 months following the sale to build and move in. Furthermore, you can start construction 12 months before you sell. The one year or 18 months rule where you buy or build applies only to your "principal residence." It doesn't apply to a summer house, for example.

It also applies, however, when you sell and then buy a co-op apartment or a condominium apartment.

If instead of realizing a profit on the sale of your old house you take a loss, you cannot deduct the loss either from other capital gains or from regular income.

An individual who is 65 or older is permitted to exclude from gross income any capital gain up to $20,000 of the sale price of his personal residence provided the property had been owned and used by him as his principal residence for at least five years during the eight-year period preceding the sale. This once-in-a-lifetime exclusion applies to sales from 1964 on.

If you sell your old house at a profit and don't buy another house you can minimize your capital gains tax by adding to the original cost of the house all capital improvements put into it during your ownership. Also, you can add your initial buying costs such as attorney's fees, title search charges, etc. Finally, you can subtract from the price received all sales costs such as attorney's fees, broker's commission, cost of advertising, and so on.

FHA Insurance

Your lender may ask you if you wish FHA insurance on your loan, or he may insist that you apply for it through him for his protection. Under an FHA insured mortgage, you borrow from your lending agency, and then the U.S. government, through the Federal Housing Administration, insures the lending agency against any loss of principal if you fail to meet the terms and conditions of your mortgage. Under the FHA plan, you pay an "insurance fee" of ½ of 1 percent, computed monthly, on the outstanding amount of the principal for the full term of your loan. This is in addition to the normal interest on your loan. You also pay an FHA "processing or application fee" when you apply for the loan. This FHA insurance fee, which you and millions of other home buyers contribute, is used to build up a fund to take care of the losses when homeowners default on their mortgages and foreclosures become necessary. It protects the lender, not you; but you do derive some benefits from FHA insurance. You can, for example, probably borrow more on a new house than would otherwise be possible—up to 97 percent of appraised value. Normally, a lending institution could not give you so large a loan in relation to appraised value; but since, under FHA insurance, its risk is transferred to the FHA, it can do so. This 97 percent applies only on loans not exceeding $15,000. On loans above this amount the percentage is gradually reduced to 83⅓ percent. The FHA will not insure loans of more than $30,000 on one- or two-family dwellings (see Table 10–10).

Another advantage of an FHA insured loan is that the property is inspected carefully by an FHA appraiser; and if he thinks it is not worth what you expect to pay for it, you will learn of his judgment in time to avoid an unwise commitment. If you are building you own house, or if the builder from whom you expect to buy has an FHA construction loan, the FHA will supervise each step in the building of your house, and the builder or contractor will have to comply with the exacting standards of the FHA. The FHA staff will check the construction several times while it is under way to see that its specifications and conditions are met. It may thus be worth the extra ½ of 1 percent to be reassured that your house is being constructed properly and checked by an impartial outside agency. There is also a negative sort of benefit, in that if you did not apply for FHA insurance, your lender might, because of the greater risk he was assuming, be forced to charge you a higher rate of interest. If you are not a veteran and are buying a home, it will probably pay to apply for FHA

TABLE 10–10

FHA MAXIMUM MORTGAGE AMOUNTS MINIMUM DOWN PAYMENTS, AND MONTHLY MORTGAGE PAYMENTS

PROPOSED AND EXISTING CONSTRUCTION[1]

(FHA Limits and Requirements Effective July 7, 1961)

FHA Value	Maximum Mortgage Amount[2]	Loan-Value Ratio[3]	Monthly Payment[4]	Minimum Down Payment
$6,000	$5,800	96.7%	$32.63	$200
7,000	6,750	96.4	37.97	250
8,000	7,750	96.9	43.59	250
9,000	8,700	96.7	48.94	300
10,000	9,700	97.0	54.56	300
11,000	10,650	96.8	59.91	350
12,000	11,600	96.7	65.25	400
13,000	12,600	96.9	70.88	400
14,000	13,550	96.8	76.22	450
15,000	14,550	97.0	81.84	450
16,000	15,400	96.3	86.62	600
17,000	16,300	95.9	91.68	700
18,000	17,200	95.6	96.74	800
19,000	18,100	95.3	101.81	900
20,000	19,000	95.0	106.87	1,000
21,000	19,800	94.3	111.37	1,200
22,000	20,500	93.2	115.31	1,500
23,000	21,300	92.6	119.80	1,700
24,000	22,000	91.7	123.74	2,000
25,000	22,800	91.2	128.25	2,200
26,000	23,500	90.4	132.19	2,500
27,000	24,300	90.0	136.68	2,700
28,000	25,000	89.3	140.62	3,000
29,000	25,000	86.2	140.62	4,000
30,000	25,000	83.3	140.62	5,000

[1] Limits and requirements are shown for home mortgages insured under Sec. 203(b) of the National Housing Act, as amended.

[2] Mortgage amount limited to 97 percent of the first $15,000 of value plus 90 percent of next $5,000, plus 75 percent of value in excess of $20,000 to a maximum mortgage of $25,000.

[3] After adjustment to the next lower multiple of $50 for mortgage amounts up to $15,000, and $100 for mortgage amounts in excess of $15,000.

[4] For the maximum term of 35 years. Monthly payment includes principal, interest at 5¼ percent per annum, and 1/12th the first annual mortgage insurance premium at ½ percent per annum.

SOURCE: Mortgage Finance Committee—American Bankers Association.

insurance. If you are building your own home, it will be especially valuable and useful to do so.

FHA Insured Home-Improvement Loans

Want to borrow to install air conditioning, wall-to-wall carpeting, or a swimming pool in the back yard? The FHA won't help you do this. But it will help if you want to add a room, or bath, or redo the porch, or roof, or put in a new heating system or septic tank. The FHA has a program for *insuring,* not making, loans for home improvements.

You can obtain FHA insured loans to enlarge your house, for new flooring, plumbing, wiring, painting, plastering, fences, driveways, sewerage, pumps, insulation, landscaping, lawn-sprinkling systems, etc. You cannot secure them for swimming pools, barbeque pits, TV antennas, tree surgery, furniture, fixtures, appliances, etc. The purpose of the loan must be for a permanent, structural improvement. The FHA insures your lender for up to 90 percent of the loan. For this the FHA collects a premium of 0.50 percent of the net proceeds of the loan. The insurance, by protecting the lender, helps you get the loan, because the lender is encouraged to make what is, to him, a virtually riskless loan. You can, of course, obtain a non-FHA insured home-improvement loan from various commercial lenders, but it will cost you more, because the lender is taking the whole risk.

There are three principal methods by which home-improvement loans can be financed under the FHA system. There are Title I loans up to $3,500; Section 203 (k) loans of from $2,500 to $10,000; and Section 203 (b) refinancing mortgages.

Title I loans are for minor repairs and improvements. Section 203 (k) loans are for major improvements from $2,500 to $10,000. The financing charge on the smaller loans (Title I), which includes an FHA insurance premium, is $5.00 discount per $100 per year on the first $2,500 and $4.00 per $100 per year on the amount above $2,500. On a simple interest basis this is equivalent to an interest rate ranging from 8.54 percent to 9.58 percent. The interest rate ceiling on the larger, 203 (k) loans is 6 percent plus an FHA insurance premium of ½ of 1 percent.

A decision as to which financing method to use in a given situation is not one that can or should be made arbitrarily. From the standpoint of the borrower the determination depends on a number of factors, some of the most important being the kind and amount of indebtedness already existing on the property, the borrower's own financial condition, and the type and extent of improvements to be made.

Generally speaking, a Title I loan would be best for minor improvements and a 203 (k) loan for major improvements. Sometimes, however, depending on circumstances, it might be more advantageous to refinance and include the cost of the improvements in a new mortgage.

When a choice between Title I and 203 (k) is to be made, consideration should be given to how much of a loan it will take to do the job. If more than $3,500 is required, Title I, which has a top limit of $3,500, cannot be used; and if less than $2,500 is required, Section 203 (k), which ordinarily has a floor of $2,500 cannot be used. Currently, the average Title I loan is in the neighborhood of $1,000 and the 203 (k) loan averages about $5,500.

Just what an FHA home-improvement loan will cost may be seen in Table 10–11.

TABLE 10–11

Home-improvement loans: the little, old ones & the big, new ones

if you need	1 yr.	1½ yrs.	2 yrs.	2½ yrs.	3 yrs.	5 yrs.
$ 100	$ 8.78	$ 5.99	$ 4.59	$ 3.76	$ 3.20	$ 2.08
200	17.55	11.97	9.18	7.51	6.39	4.16
300	26.32	17.95	13.77	11.26	9.59	6.24
400	35.09	23.94	18.36	15.01	12.78	8.32
500	43.86	29.92	22.95	18.76	15.97	10.40
600	52.64	35.90	27.54	22.52	19.17	12.47
700	61.41	41.89	32.12	26.27	22.36	14.55
800	70.18	47.87	36.71	30.02	25.56	16.63
900	78.95	53.85	41.30	33.77	28.75	18.71
1,000	87.72	59.83	45.89	37.52	31.94	20.79
2,000	175.44	119.66	91.77	75.04	63.88	41.57

These are the old FHA home-improvement loans, still available. Payments calculated on basis of 5% discount (about 9.4% true interest).

if you need	3 yrs.	5 yrs.	7 yrs.	10 yrs.	12 yrs.	15 yrs.	17 yrs.	20 yrs.
2,500	76.97	49.31	$ 37.52	$ 28.79	$ 25.41	$22.12	$20.63	$18.96
3,500	107.76	69.03	52.52	40.30	35.58	30.97	28.88	26.54
5,000	153.94	98.62	75.02	57.56	50.83	44.24	41.25	37.91
7,500	230.91	147.92	112.54	86.35	76.24	66.37	61.88	56.87
10,000	307.87	197.23	150.04	115.12	101.66	88.49	82.50	75.82

These are the new, jumbo loans. Payments at 6% interest, plus FHA insurance.

SOURCE: *Changing Times, The Kiplinger Magazine,* February, 1962.

Thousands of homeowners have been victimized by glib, fast-talking salesmen who sell shoddy, third-rate repair materials and home-improvement services at excessive prices. They appear to offer "something for nothing," and you know that in this world that never happens. How can you avoid being taken? Easy. Deal only with local, well-established, reputable contractors, plumbers, electricians, etc. Check with your local real estate board and with your bank. They will quickly be able to tell you whether the firm you propose to deal with is established and reputable or fly-by-night and dubious.

Death, Mortgages, and Insurance

Will you live to pay off the 20-year mortgage on your home? One out of four homeowners aged 40 will not. One out of ten aged 25 will not. One out of six aged 35 will not. But statistics do not really matter when *you* are the one. What will happen to your family if you die prematurely and there is an unpaid mortgage? In a way, a mortgage is a one-sided contract. It protects the lender and his investment in every possible way. For his protection he has:

1. A mortgage on your home
2. A bond signed by you and your wife
3. A fire insurance policy
4. A title insurance policy
5. Monthly payments from your income

But unless you tie your insurance program to your mortgage, you have no protection against death or adversity, such as unemployment or financial reverses. The leading insurance companies have all developed plans which, by the use of decreasing term insurance (on top of ordinary life) over the life of the mortgage, matching the decreasing principal owed, guarantee your family the home free and clear of debt if you should die. In addition, they provide a reserve fund that you can draw upon if financial reverses hit during your lifetime and threaten your ownership of the house. Any good insurance agent will explain what one company calls its "assured homeownership plan." It is a sound idea and well worth investigating when you buy a home and obtain a mortgage loan. FHA insurance is designed primarily to protect the lending institution. Mortgage-redemption insurance protects the widow.

POLICY LIFTS MORTGAGE

Denver, Nov. 6 (AP)—A widow paid off a $9,000 mortgage on her home at a cost of $9.46.

Her husband, George Smart, 31, applied for life insurance to pay the mortgage last Saturday. He had passed the necessary physical examination the day before. He died Sunday.

Courtesy: New York Post

Do You Want to Sell?

As the seller you pay the brokerage commission—5 or 6 percent of the price. In return you get a number of services. There are several kinds of agreements to be made with brokers.

Sole Contract. Just one broker has the right to work on selling the house. But if the owner sells it himself, the broker gets no commission.

Exclusive Right to Sell. Same as above, except that the broker gets a commission even if you sell the house. Both types have very limited exposure to possible buyers.

Open Listing. You simply have as many brokers as you wish list your house. But who will bother—if he has no special advantage?

Multiple Listing. All local brokers included in the listing can handle the house. Brokers in other areas may forward customers. You deal with one broker, but have the selling efforts of all.

The Co-op

The purchaser of a co-operative apartment buys an interest in a nonprofit corporation which will own and run the buildings that form the co-operative. In this sense the owner of a co-op apartment is a landlord, but in his responsibility to the board of directors of the co-op, he is also a tenant.[8]

Co-op vs. Leasing. Carrying charges for a co-op are usually lower than the rental prices for a similar apartment. Also, the co-op owner has income tax benefits because of his share in real estate. He may deduct his share of the interest on the co-op's mortgage and his share of the real estate taxes the co-op pays.

The tenant has the advantage of using his capital in any investment venture, since it is not frozen into the cost of the apartment. He need not worry about the sale of his apartment in the future, nor whether he can recoup his investment. While he knows his rent may go up, he does not have to share increased maintenance costs with other co-op owners if there is a high vacancy rate or unexpected repair expense.

The co-op buyer should check whether the maintenance budget includes adequate reserves for major repairs or replacements.

He should compare the total cost and valuation of the prospective co-op building with similar buildings in the same or comparable neighborhoods.

---

[8] Varying number of shares in the corporation are allocated to the apartments according to respective values. Mortgage charges, real estate taxes, cost of maintenance, repairs, replacements, and administration are budgeted annually and divided among the owners in proportion to the number of shares of stock allocated to the apartment and are payable by each owner in monthly installments as rent.

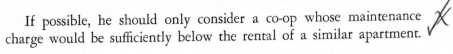

If possible, he should only consider a co-op whose maintenance charge would be sufficiently below the rental of a similar apartment.

Type of Co-op

The Leasehold Co-op. Where the building and not the land is owned by the co-operators. In this case the down payment is lower than in the fee co-op because the organization doesn't have to buy the land. Its maintenance is higher because the co-op must pay for the use of the land and profit to the owner.

The Fee Co-op. Owns both land and building, and pays interest and amortization on a mortgage covering both. These tenant owners can deduct for tax purposes the interest on both, which is higher than the deduction allowed the leasehold co-op tenant, which is only for interest paid on the mortgage of the building and not on the mortgage of the land.

Co-op or Condominium?

The condominium is closer to true ownership. The purchaser actually gets a deed to his own apartment, plus an undivided share in the halls, elevators, heating equipment, and other common facilities. Condominium housing is not the same as co-operative housing. The chief differences between the two are:

1. In condominiums, individuals take title to their units; in co-operatives, an individual has a stock ownership in the co-operative and the right of occupancy to a specific unit.

2. In condominiums, individuals vote on a proportionate basis; in co-operatives, each individual has one vote regardless of the size of his unit.

3. In condominiums, individuals are taxed separately on their units; in co-operatives, individuals pay their share of taxes on the project in their monthly carrying charges.

4. In condominiums, individuals are responsible only for mortgage indebtedness and taxes involving their own property and their proportionate share of the expenses of operating the common property, and have no mortgage indebtedness, tax, or other liability for the other properties; in co-operatives, each individual is dependent upon the solvency of the entire project.

5. The condominium owner can sell his apartment to whomever he chooses—more freely than the co-op owner, who is bound by the need to have the purchaser approved by the board of directors. A prospective purchaser of a co-op must pay cash for the equity and assume the seller's

pro-rata share of the unpaid indebtedness under the blanket mortgage. Therefore, a co-op seller must find a buyer with enough cash. The would-be purchaser of the condominium, on the other hand, can mortgage his unit to finance his purchase—like any other home buyer.

The FHA has been authorized to provide mortgage insurance—under the National Housing Act of 1961—for condominiums which provide ownership of apartments in multiple dwellings.

The condominium apartment is treated like a separate parcel of real estate—even separately assessed and taxed. In the co-operative apartment, if an owner does not pay his share of the charges as rent, they must eventually be distributed among the owners. But this is not the case in the condominium.

If a stockholder-tenant (co-operative) violates the terms of his agreement (lease), he may be dispossessed in the same manner as a defaulting tenant (renter). The condominium owner cannot, in absence of special statutory authorization, be ousted from possession for infraction of the bylaws or regulations.[9]

Conclusion

Surveys indicate that people who become dissatisfied with the homes they have purchased and sell them or who find themselves unable to meet monthly charges and thus face foreclosure find themselves in this predicament for one of the following reasons:

1. Insufficient funds to begin with
2. Buying a more expensive home than one can afford
3. Selecting a poorly built house
4. Picking an unsuitable neighborhood
5. Decline in property values over a period of years
6. Decreased income
7. Not sufficient investigation of all facts and costs involved

Earlier in the chapter you were shown a check list for both neighborhood and physical condition of the house. You can use these to guard against errors 3, 4, and 7 above. To judge your financial ability, and avoid errors 1, 2, and possibly 6, use the following financial check list:

---

[9] Arthur E. Warner and Alvin G. Becker, "Condominium," *Business Topics,* Michigan State University, Graduate School of Business Administration, Autumn, 1963. See also *FHA Mortgage Insurance on Condominiums,* FHA No. 491, FHA Fact Sheet, Federal Housing Administration, Washington, D.C., 1963.

Down payment	————	Add these to
Closing charges:		get your
Title search and clearance	————	TOTAL INITIAL
Various legal fees		
Other charges	————	CASH
TOTAL INITIAL COST	- - - - - - -	OUTLAY

Size of monthly payment on mortgage	————	Add these to
Monthly payments on taxes and assessments	————	
Monthly payments on insurance	————	get your
Probable fuel cost (average per month)	————	
Probable monthly utility cost (lights, water, gas, etc.)	————	TOTAL
Estimated monthly upkeep and repair expenses	————	MONTHLY
TOTAL MONTHLY COST	- - - - - - -	COST

The total initial cash outlay should be judged in the light of your savings. If it exhausts them or does not leave an adequate margin for emergency expenditures and for the extra costs of a new home, such as moving, new furniture, garden tools, etc., then you ought not go ahead with the purchase. The total monthly cost (if you have new expenses, such as an automobile which you did not own before, or new monthly railroad commutation costs, or both, these should be added) should not exceed your take-home pay for one week. If it does, work out a realistic budget for a month and see if you can really cut down elsewhere sufficiently to carry the extra housing cost, as you will be forced to do if you buy this house. Be realistic. Face the facts now rather than face financial difficulties later.

SUGGESTED READINGS

1. Arthur M. Watkins, *How Much House Can You Afford.* New York: New York Life Insurance Company, latest edition. A free copy may be obtained by writing to the company at Box 10, Madison Square Station, New York, N.Y., 10010.
2. *You, Your Bank and Your Mortgage.* New York: American Bankers Association, latest edition.
3. "Turning Your House Into Cash—Refinancing a Mortgage," *Changing Times, The Kiplinger Magazine,* November, 1963.
4. "It's a Good Time to Buy a House," *Changing Times, The Kiplinger Magazine,* April, 1963.
5. "So It's Your First House," *Changing Times, The Kiplinger Magazine,* March, 1962.

6. "Good News for House Buyers," *Changing Times, The Kiplinger Magazine,* March, 1964.

7. "Home Improvement Loans," *Changing Times, The Kiplinger Magazine,* February, 1962.

8. *Facts You Should Know about Buying or Building a Home,* Educational Division, National Better Business Bureau, Chrysler Building, New York, N.Y., 10017, latest edition.

9. *Extended Payment Tables for Monthly Mortgage Loans.* Boston: Financial Publishing Co., latest edition.

10. *The Housing Yearbook.* Washington, D.C.: The National Housing Conference, latest edition.

11. A. F. Jung, "Terms on Conventional Mortgage Loans on Existing Houses," *Journal of Finance,* September, 1962.

12. *You and the Law,* Vol. I: Research Institute of America, 1962. See sections on "When You Are Buying a House"; "When You Are Selling a House"; "When You Rent."

13. "Why Are Your Closing Costs So High," *American Home,* January, 1961.

14. "What to Consider When You Buy an Old House," *American Home,* April, 1961.

15. A. E. Warner, and A. G. Becker, "Condominium" in *Business Topics,* Michigan State University, Graduate School of Business Administration, Autumn, 1963.

16. Harold N. Vogel, *The Co-op Apartment,* Libra, 1960.

17. Henry E. Hoagland, and Leo D. Stone, *Real Estate Finance.* Rev. ed., Homewood, Ill.: Richard D. Irwin, Inc., 1961.

18. Eugene M. Mortlock, "The Home For You and How To Select It," First Federal Savings and Loan Association of New York, N.Y., 1962.

19. "Could Houses Cost Less," Symposium, D. Jordan, *Better Homes and Gardens,* March, 1963.

20. "What You Should Know Before You Buy a Home," United States Savings and Loan League, Chicago, Ill., 1962.

21. William K. Kerr, "Analysis of Condominium Ownership," *St. John's Law Review,* December, 1963.

22. Publications on FHA Programs. (Available upon request from the Office of Public Information, Federal Housing Administration, Washington, 25, D.C.)

FHA-206   *FHA's New Home Improvement Programs.*

FHA-208   *FHA Home Mortgage Insurance.*

FHA-219   *FHA Mortgage Insurance on Low Cost Homes.*

FHA-221   *FHA Mortgage Insurance for Rental and Cooperative Housing for Families of Low and Moderate Income.*

FHA-232   *How to Do Business with the FHA . . . A Message to Builders.*

FHA-246   *FHA Experimental Housing Program.*

FHA-247   *FHA Mortgage Insurance on Housing for the Elderly.*

FHA-313   *Improving Your Property with Title I Insured Loans.*

FHA–428   *FHA Financing for Home Purchases and Home Improvements —A Guide to Financing Costs and Home Buying Ability.*
FHA–467   *FHA Forbearance Provisions.*
FHA–491   *FHA Mortgage Insurance on Condominiums.*
FHA–492   *FHA Low Cost Housing for Small Towns and Outlying Areas.*
FHA–528   *FHA Mortgage Insurance for Urban Renewal.*
FHA–770   *A Comparison of FHA Home Improvement Programs.*
FHA–3239 *Summary Statement on Cooperative Housing.*

CASE PROBLEMS

1. Ellen and John are both graduating college in June. They are to be married the day after commencement. They have both been offered positions in Chicago. He will be earning $110 a week. She will be earning $85 a week. They have surveyed housing possibilities and have narrowed down their choices to three alternatives. They can rent a three-room apartment in the heart of town for $160 a month. They can buy a new five-room house in a suburban development for $18,900 ($3,500 down, 5¾ percent, 30-year mortgage for balance), or they can purchase a co-op apartment (four rooms) for $24,000 (monthly carrying charge $170). Which would you choose? Why?

2. Ring earns $6,000 a year. He has a wife and two children (ages 2 and 4). Since he and his wife are good savers, they already have $8,000 in the bank. They decide to buy a $15,000 home ($3,000 down). The bank informs them that they may borrow $12,000 for 10 years at 5 percent or for 20 years at 5½ percent. Ring and his wife do not like having a debt hanging over their heads, and they naturally prefer the lower interest rate; so they are inclined to borrow for 10 years at 5 percent. Are they wise?

3. Martin earns $350 a month. He is paying $85 rent. He can buy a suitable home for $10,000, all of which he can borrow on a 20-year mortgage at 5¾ percent. This, he figures, is cheaper than renting. What do you think?

4. Link used all his savings ($2,000) as a down payment on a farm costing $10,000, borrowing the balance at 5½ percent for 20 years on a direct-reduction mortgage. He owns his furniture and $20,000 of straight life insurance (two years old) and has a wife (age 43) and two children (ages 11 and 13). His job pays him $3,300 a year. After he had succeeded in accumulating $500 more in the bank, he was approached by a digger of artesian wells who told him that he could dig a well for him (the water supply had never been satisfactory) for $6 a foot and that they ought to strike five gallons of water a minute at 80 feet. Link told the digger to go ahead. At 80 feet the digger had found no water. What should Link do?

5. Rollins borrowed $7,500 on his $10,000 home from the local savings and loan association. A fire caused $2,000 damage to the property, which sum the insurance company paid to the association. Rollins wants to repair the property, but he has no money. Can anything be done?

6. Jane and William Carleton have been married three years. The birth of their daughter, Linda (now 7 months), made them decide to give up living in an apartment in town and instead buy a house in the suburbs. They have decided on a $20,000 house. In shopping for financing they have received the following offers:

a) $2,000 down, $18,000 mortgage at 6 percent for 30 years.
b) $2,000 down, $18,000 mortgage at 6 percent for 25 years.
c) $2,000 down, $18,000 mortgage at 5¼ plus ½ percent FHA insurance fee, for 25 years.
d) $2,000 down, $18,000 mortgage at 5½ percent for 20 years.
Which should they choose? Why?

7. Martha and Sam Winkler decide to buy a $35,000 house. They are offered the following financing possibilities:

a) $5,000 down, $30,000 mortgage for 30 years at 5¾ percent.
b) $10,000 down, $25,000 mortgage for 30 years at 5¾ percent.
c) $15,000 down, $20,000 mortgage for 30 years at 5¾ percent.
d) $17,500 down, $17,500 mortgage for 20 years at 5¾ percent.
Assuming they have the savings to make up to a $20,000 down payment what should they do? Why?

8. In the town of X, the only lawyer is young and inexperienced. He gives his opinion that the title to the home Young is buying from Bright is good and is in Bright's name, but Young hates to trust him entirely in the matter of this $40,000 deal. What can Young do?

9. Ralph and Ethel Gould are 28 and 26 years of age. They live in Minnesota. A 10-room house, 30 years old, which they like, comes to their attention. It is common knowledge that houses cost $2,000 a room to build in their town, and ordinary rooms are nowhere near as large as the rooms in the house in question. They feel that they have an opportunity to make a very attractive purchase for $8,000. Comment.

10. When Jones was in the Navy, he was assigned to Northwestern University in Evanston, Illinois, adjacent to Chicago. To assure his family (wife and two children, ages 3 and 5) of a comfortable dwelling, he bought a home for $18,000. At the termination of his work at Northwestern, he was sent to the Pacific Coast. Inquiry showed that he could then probably sell his home for about $15,000. Comment.

11. Raymond and Ruth Wilkes have three children (ages 2, 5, and 7). Raymond is a lawyer earning $7,000 net a year. They have been living in a house which was rented to them for $85 a month, but this house has been sold and they must move. In their town, properties for sale are hard to find. One that is available has four bedrooms, is 30 years old, and is being offered for $12,000. A new house large enough for the family would cost at least $18,000. No rental property is vacant. Outside of $10,000 of straight life insurance which Raymond has carried, the family has been able to do little saving. What should they do?

12. Jane and Frank Prince have been married three years. He earns $70 a week; she earns $50. They have saved enough money to buy furniture for five

rooms, and they have $2,600 in the bank. Recently they have become interested in buying a home. They have discovered a Cape Cod cottage which is three years old, in good condition, and whose price seems right ($12,000). It can be bought for $2,000 down on a 20-year mortgage at 5½ percent. Would you advise them to buy? Why? Why not?

11   TAXES

I'm proud to pay taxes in the United States. Only thing is—I could be just as proud for half the money.
—*Arthur Godfrey*

MARK TWAIN, once asked what the difference was between a taxidermist and a tax collector, answered, "The taxidermist takes only your skin." We don't know who it was who said that the taxpayer is the only varmint expected to yield a pelt every year, but we do know you'd like to meet the mild little man who walked into the income tax collector's office, sat down, and beamed at everyone. "What can we do for you?" asked the receptionist. "Nothing, thank you," replied the little man, "I just wanted to meet the people I'm working for." If you stop to reflect, you do work for the government three or more months out of every year.

Today, the chief source of federal revenue is the income tax. It was originally introduced as a means of helping to finance the Civil War, but in its modern form it dates only from 1913. At first, its rates were very moderate; but two world wars and the sorry state of the world today have caused the rates to rise to very high levels. The growth in the burden of the personal income tax may be seen from the fact that in 1915 a single person, with no dependents, earning $10,000 a year paid a federal income tax of but $70. In 1929 the tax was $90. Today the tax is approximately $2,200. A married couple, with no dependents, earning $10,000 a year, paid $60 in 1915, $52 in 1929, and $1,800 today. For the married couple with two dependents, comparable payments on a $10,000 income were $60 in 1915, $40 in 1929, and $1,400 today.

Or, to put it another way, the married couple, if the husband earned $100,000 a year, had $97,500 left over after taxes in 1915; they had $85,000 after taxes in 1929, and less than $55,000 today. The single person earning $25,000 was able to retain $24,730 after taxes in 1915, $24,100 in 1929, $17,000 today.

As a result of high taxes and high prices, the married man (with two children) who made a $5,000 income would have to earn over $12,500 today to have the same purchasing power and to be as well off as he was in 1939. The $10,000 man must, to maintain his status, earn about $26,000 today, while the $25,000-a-year man has to think in terms of an income over three times as large. Even at the small-income end of the scale, a $3,000 income in 1939 has to be raised today to over $7,000 in order to have the same net purchasing power, for out of the $7,000 income today must come over $800 in personal income taxes, and there is a purchasing-power shrinkage of more than $3,500 due to the decline in the purchasing power of the dollar since 1939.

"We're not questioning your tips and donations - it wasn't necessary to bring proof!"

Courtesy: *Jeff Keate and Chicago Tribune—New York News Syndicate, Inc.*

There is really no "average" American taxpayer. Over 14 million Americans who filed income tax returns either earned so little that they paid no tax or reported adjusted gross incomes of less than $1,000 a year. About half of American taxpayers earn less than $5,000 a year. Over the last decade the number in this category shrank steadily. The largest gains were in the $5,000 to $10,000 category and this group represents more than one third of the total returns. The largest single taxpaying group is composed of persons in the $5,000 to $6,000 a year bracket. There are over 6 million such returns. At the top of the scale, the number earning and reporting incomes of over $10,000 increased from 1 million to more than 7 million over the decade. If you are making $10,000 a year, you are in the top 10 percent of all taxpayers. If you are earning $25,000 you are in the top 1 percent, and if you are making more than $50,000 you are in the top two tenths of 1 percent.

THE FEDERAL INCOME TAX LAW

Since practically everyone who works or has any income is subject to the federal income tax law, it is of the utmost importance that everybody have knowledge of at least its main provisions. Unfortunately, it has grown so complex that only those persons who devote most of their time and attention to it (tax experts) can really be fully conversant with it; and even they constantly run into troublesome situations where final decisions must be left to the courts.

Just how complex it has become can be seen from the fact that in a recent year one out of every five of the more than 60 million federal income tax returns filed was in error. Some 14 million returns were incorrect; nine out of ten paid too little, one out of ten paid too much. Approximately $100 million was overpaid; $1.4 billion was underpaid. The Bureau of Internal Revenue has time and staff to examine only about 8 percent of all returns filed, and it does this largely on a sampling basis—except for the larger returns, all of which are examined. The larger your return, the more likely it is that you will face an audit. If you itemize your deductions rather than take the standard 10 percent deduction, this increases the chance of an audit, especially if you take any large or unusual deductions. If you are self-employed, your chances of being investigated increase, and if you earn more than $10,000 in self-employment, there is more than a 50 percent chance of an examination. Usually about six out of every ten returns examined are found to be wrong.

Automatic data processing (ADP) is now being extended nationwide. Performing arithmetic checks at speeds up to 250,000 numbers a second, this electronic computer system detects errors, discloses proper refunds and credits, and maintains a continuing account of your individual tax records. IRS keeps track of you by your tax identification number (social security number). Also information returns are taking on an expanded role. Banks, brokers, and other businesses paying you $10 or more a year in dividends must report them to the Internal Revenue Service. Each information return contains your taxpayers identification number.

The Pay-as-You-Go Plan—Withholding

Much of the income tax is collected through the withholding system. Under this system, the employer deducts part of your pay as tax and turns it over to the District Director of Internal Revenue or to a depositary bank. The tax owed by you is determined after the close of your taxable year when you file your income tax return. You are then given full credit for the amounts withheld from your pay as shown by your withholding statement (Form W-2).

Wages subject to withholding include salaries, fees, bonuses, commissions, vacation allowances, dismissal and severance pay. Certain kinds of income such as tips, payments for odd jobs, retirement and pension payments, etc., are not subject to withholding. Amounts received as scholarship and fellowship grants are not subject to withholding.

Two things determine how much tax your employer withholds from you. These are the amount of your salary and the number of withholding exemptions you claimed in a statement you are required to file with your employer on a Withholding Exemption Certificate. You are entitled to receive from your employer on or before January 31, *two* copies of a "withholding statement" Form W-2. This statement shows the total wages paid and the income tax and the social security tax withheld, if any, during the previous calendar year. One copy of the W-2 Form should accompany your tax return. The remaining copy is for your personal records.

Declarations of Estimated Tax

Because the withholding tax on wages is not sufficient to keep many taxpayers—particularly business owners, professional people, investors, and landlords—paid up on their income tax, they are required to file a declaration of estimated tax and to make quarterly payments in advance of the annual income tax return. This declaration is required of you if your estimated tax is $40 or more and

a) You can reasonably expect to receive more than $200 from sources other than wages subject to withholding, or
b) You can reasonably expect gross income exceeding—
  1. $5,000 and you are single;
  2. $10,000 and you are a head of household, or a widower (or widow);

3. $5,000 for a married person not entitled to file a joint declaration;
4. $5,000 for a married person entitled to file a joint declaration, where the combined income of both husband and wife can reasonably be expected to exceed $10,000.[1]

Normally, you file your declaration (Form 1040 ES) on or before April 15, along with your annual tax return. The return covers the previous year's income. The declaration estimates the current year's anticipated income. It must be accompanied by your first quarterly installment payment of the estimated tax. Payments are due April 15, June 15, September 15, and January 15.

If you do not expect any considerable change in income from last year to this one, the whole estimating process can be simplified by using last year's income and last year's tax as your current year's estimate. If you do this you will not be subject to any penalty even though your income and tax finally turns out to be much greater than the amount used in your declaration. Estimates do not have to be absolutely accurate. You are allowed a 30 percent margin of error before a penalty is imposed, and you are given an opportunity to change your estimate from quarter to quarter. You are liable for an additional charge of 6 percent a year for each underpayment. The addition is computed on the difference between 70 percent (66⅔ percent in the case of farmers) of the amount which you should have paid and the amount actually paid. For example, suppose you should have paid $1,000 but you only paid $600. Seventy percent of $1,000 is $700. Take 6 percent of the difference between $600 (what you paid) and $700 (70 percent of what you should have paid) and the penalty comes to $6.00. If your situation calls for a difficult estimate (for example, if last year's income was abnormally high), secure a Form 2210 from your District Director. It should be of considerable help in making your calculations.

Who Must File a Tax Return

Every citizen or resident of the United States, whether adult (under 65) *or minor,* who has a gross income of $600 or more in the taxable year ($11.54 a week) must file a federal income tax return. Minors earning less than $600 and having tax withheld will do well to file a return in order to claim the withheld tax. The fact that you are under 21 does not exempt you from filing a return. If you are 65 or over on the last day of the taxable year, you are not required to file a return unless you

---

[1] If this isn't clear, what follows won't be either. You have three possible choices (*a*) go find an accountant, (*b*) call or write your nearest U.S. Internal Revenue office, or (*c*) resign from the course.

have gross income of $1,200 or more during the taxable year. The United States is divided into 64 collection districts; returns should be filed with the District Director of Internal Revenue in the district where the taxpayer has his legal residence or conducts his business.

"Do we get employee's discount?"

Tax Forms

To fit tax returns to the differing needs of the more than 60 million people who file, the government has provided two types of returns for reporting income of individuals:

Form 1040
Form 1040A (card form)

You can use the simpler Form 1040A, printed on a punchcard, if:

1. Your income was less than $10,000, and
2. It consisted of wages reported on withholding statements (Forms W-2) and not more than $200 total of other wages, interest, and dividends, and
3. You wish to take the standard deduction (about 10 percent of your income) instead of itemizing deductions.

One of the special features of the form is that if your income is less than $5,000 you can choose to have the Internal Revenue Service figure your tax for you.

If your income was more than $10,000, or if it was less but you received more than $200 of income from interest, dividends, rents, royalties, etc., you must use Form 1040. If your income was entirely from salary and wages you will need only the two-page Form 1040. If you have other types of income you may need one or more of the following forms:

> Schedule B for income from dividends, interest, rents, royalties, pensions, annuities, partnerships, trusts, estates, etc.;
> Schedule C for income from a personally owned business;
> Schedule D for income from the sale or exchange of property; and
> Schedule F for income from farming.

Form W-2 is not a tax return. It is a receipt which shows how much tax has been withheld from your salary. It must accompany your return, whether Form 1040 or Form 1040A, as evidence of taxes withheld. If you work for more than one employer during the year you will have more than one Form W-2. Copy B of *each* Form W-2 must accompany your return.

> An income tax form is like a laundry list—either way you lose your shirt.
> —Fred Allen

Married Persons—Joint or Separate Return

Marital status is determined as of the last day of the taxable year. For tax purposes, a person is considered to be married for the entire calendar year if he or she is married on December 31, regardless of the date of the wedding. If you are divorced or legally separated on or before December 31, you are single for the entire calendar year for income tax purposes.

If either the wife or the husband dies before the close of the survivor's taxable year, the survivor is considered, for tax purposes, as having been married for the entire year. Thus, if the survivor did not remarry before the close of the taxable year, a joint return may be filed—except under certain limited circumstances—for both taxpayers by the surviving spouse.

In some states, which are known as "community-property states" (Arizona, California, Idaho, Louisiana, Nevada, New Mexico, Texas, and Washington), the earnings of a married couple belong one half to

Shooting the Rapids Again

Courtesy: Newspaper Enterprise Association

As taxes took a bigger bite, exemptions and loopholes multiplied, and the forms became increasingly complicated.

the husband and one half to the wife, irrespective of who earned it. If,
therefore, a husband and wife in a community-property state file separate
returns, it is mandatory that each shall report one half of the combined
community income. Taxpayers domiciled in these states have always
divided their income for federal income tax purposes.

Although married couples in noncommunity-property states cannot
divide their income under state law, they can now "split" their income
for purposes of federal income taxation in joint returns. This equalizes
federal income taxes on married couples in all states.

Married taxpayers may make a joint return and include all the
exemptions, income, and deductions of both husband and wife. Even
though one spouse had no income, husband and wife may still file a joint
return. Ordinarily it will be to your advantage, if you are married, to file
a joint return using the "split-income" method of computing the tax. It
usually results in a lower tax than would result from the use of separate

returns. This is because the tax is computed at the lower surtax rate which applies to each half of the income rather than at the higher surtax rate which would apply to the combined or total income. The surtax on one half of the taxable income when multiplied by two results in a total tax considerably less than if it had been computed on the total income as one sum.

Usually, but not always, the tax on a joint return is lower than the total tax of separate returns. Before making your decision as to which to use, you would do well to compute the total tax liability both ways and select the method resulting in the lower total tax.

If You Are under 21

You are subject to the same requirements for filing returns and paying tax on your income as anyone else. A minor (you are a "minor" or "child" in the eyes of the law if you are under 21) is subject to tax on his own earnings and income even though his parent may, under local law, have the right to it and might actually have received the money. The income of a minor child is not required to be included in the return of the parent. As a minor you are entitled to a personal exemption of $600 on your own return.

If you are under 19 or a student, your parent may also claim an exemption for you as a dependent if he furnishes more than half of your support even though you earn more than $600. For example, Carla is 20, a junior at Swathmore. She works for one of the deans as a part-time secretary and earns $800. She saves $350 and spends $450 for clothes, beauty parlor, etc. Her father pays her tuition and her room and board, transportation, etc. Since he pays for more than half her expenses he may claim her as a dependent and obtain a $600 exemption for her. Carla, in turn, when she files her income tax return may claim a $600 exemption for herself. Thus, two exemptions are allowed for Carla.

A minor who has a gross income of less than $600, and whose wages have been subject to withholding, is entitled to a refund. This can be obtained by filing Form 1040A accompanied by the withholding statement (Form W-2).

Unmarried Persons as Head of Household

Any unmarried person required to maintain a household for the benefit of others is given a special tax concession of about one half the benefit that a married couple filing a joint return enjoys by reason of the split-income computation. If you are not married (or are legally separated) at the end of the taxable year, you qualify as a "head of household," provided you furnish over half of the cost of maintaining a home which, during the entire taxable year, except for temporary absences, was occupied as a principal residence both by yourself and by (*a*) any related person for whom you are entitled to an exemption or (*b*) your unmarried child, grandchild, or stepchild, even though such child is not a dependent. If your mother or your father, or both, qualify as your dependent and you maintain a home for one or the other or both, it is *not* necessary that you live in the same household to qualify as head of household. You may live in separate homes and still meet this test. However, paying the entire expense of maintaining a parent in a home for the aged is *not* maintaining a household for your parent. You are considered as maintaining a household only if you pay more than one half of such items as mortgage interest, rent, taxes, insurance on the dwelling, upkeep and repairs, utilities, and food consumed in the home.

When to File a Return

For most individuals, April 15 is the date when federal income tax returns must be filed. Returns, in most cases, can be filed at any time after the close of the taxable year up until midnight April 15. The April 15 deadline results from the fact that the Internal Revenue Code provides that income tax returns must be made on or before the fifteenth day of the fourth month following the close of the taxable year. For most persons filing individual income tax returns, the taxable year is the calendar year ending December 31. Therefore, the fifteenth day of the fourth month thereafter is April 15.

Under unusual circumstances a taxpayer may be granted an extension of time within which to file a return. You must apply by letter or Form 2688 to the district director for the extension and explain your reasons, which must be substantial and persuasive. If the extension is granted, however, interest at the rate of 6 percent per annum on the unpaid taxes will be added from the original date due until they are paid.

How to Claim Your Exemptions

You, as the taxpayer, are always entitled to at least one exemption for yourself. If, at the end of your taxable year, you were blind or were age 65 or older, you get two exemptions for yourself. If you were both blind and age 65 or over, you get three exemptions. You get exemptions for your wife (or husband) if you and she are filing a joint return. If you file a separate return, you may claim her exemptions only if she had no income and was not claimed as a dependent on another taxpayer's return for the taxable year. Otherwise your wife's (or husband's) exemptions are like your own—one, if she was neither blind nor age 65; two, if she was either blind or age 65; three, if she was both blind and age 65 or over.

You are entitled to one exemption for each child (including a stepchild, or legally adopted child), if during the taxable year, that child:

1. Received more than one half of his or her support from you (or from your husband or wife if this is a joint return), and
2. Had not attained the age of 19 or was a student (if the child is 19 or over and not a student, he must have received less than $600 gross income), and
3. Did not file a joint return with her husband (or his wife), and
4. Was either a citizen or resident of the United States or a resident of Canada, Mexico, the Republic of Panama or the Canal Zone.

You are entitled to one exemption for each other dependent who meets all the following requirements for the year:

1. Received less than $600 gross income, and
2. Received more than one half of his or her support from you (or from husband or wife if this is a joint return), and
3. Did not file a joint return with her husband (or his wife), and
4. Was either a citizen or resident of the United States or a resident of Canada, Mexico, the Republic of Panama or the Canal Zone, and
5. (a) Either was related to you (or to husband or wife if this is a joint return) in one of the following ways:

Mother	Stepbrother	Son-in-law
Father	Stepsister	Daughter-in-law
Grandmother	Stepmother	*The following if*
Grandfather	Stepfather	*related by blood:*
Brother	Mother-in-law	Uncle—
Sister	Father-in-law	Aunt—
Grandson	Brother-in-law	Nephew—
Granddaughter	Sister-in-law	Niece—

or, (b) had as his principal place of abode your home and was a member of your household, even if not related to you.

Some men never appreciate their children so much as when making out their income tax. —MORTON GOWDY

Information Returns

In case you are ever tempted not to report part or all of your income, remember that the Bureau of Internal Revenue has, by statutory authority, many sources which can be checked for information about your income. The "information-at-source" provision of the Internal

Revenue Code requires every individual, partnership, or corporation to report certain payments to the Director of Internal Revenue.

In addition to Form W-2, which is filed for wages from which taxes have been withheld, there is another information return—Form 1099—which must be filed under certain circumstances. It is required when total compensation from sources of income such as rents, royalties, interest, alimony, annuities, wages not covered by withholding, etc., is equal to or exceeds $600.

What Income Is Taxable

If you win the Nobel or Pulitzer prize, you won't have to pay tax on the income from it! The law says that all kinds of income are subject to tax, with specific exceptions. This means that all income which is not specifically exempt must be included in your return, even though it may be offset by expenses and other deductions. Exempt income should be omitted entirely from your return.

The following are examples of income which *must* be reported:

Wages, salaries, bonuses, and commissions
Tips and gratuities for services rendered
Dividends and other earnings from investments
Interest from bank deposits, bonds, and notes
Industrial, civil service, and other pensions, annuities, and endowments
Rents and royalties from property, patents, copyrights
Profits from business or profession
Profit from sale of real estate, securities, automobiles
Your share of partnership profits
Your share of estate or trust income
Contest prizes
Gambling winnings
Military pay

These are merely examples. The list is not all-inclusive, since all income, unless specifically exempt, must be reported.

The following are examples of income which should *not* be reported:

Scholarship and fellowship grants
All government payments and benefits to veterans and their families, with a few minor exceptions
Dividends on veterans' government insurance
Federal social security benefits
Unemployment Compensation
Railroad Retirement Act benefits
Gifts, inheritances, bequests
Workmen's compensation, insurance, damages, etc., for bodily injury or sickness

Interest on state and municipal bonds
Accident and health insurance proceeds
Casualty insurance proceeds
Disability and death payments
Life insurance proceeds upon death of the insured

Even though tax has been withheld by your employer, the law requires you to report all your wages, salaries, fees, commissions, bonuses, and all other payments for your personal services. When your employer deducts taxes, insurance, union dues, savings-bond subscriptions, social security, pension-fund contributions, etc., from your pay, these amounts are still part of your wages, and you are required to report the total amount of your wages as if your employer had not made any deductions. You must also include in your wages all tips, gratuities, bonuses, and similar payments, whether you get them from a customer or from your employer. Legally these are not "gifts," even though people sometimes mistakenly call them by that name. If your employer pays part or all of your wages in merchandise, services, stock, or other things of value, you must determine the fair market value of such items and include it in your wages. Taxpayers who receive meals and lodging as part of their salaries must include in income the fair market value of the meals and lodging.

Adjusted Gross Income

Adjusted gross income is the balance remaining after deducting from gross income the following:

1. Expenses of a trade or business.
2. Expenses of a property yielding rents or royalties.
3. Expenses of travel, meals, and lodging while away from home at least overnight in the service of one's employer. You may also deduct transportation expenses incurred in connection with the performance of service as an employee even though you are not away from home.
4. Reimbursed expenses (other than those for travel, meals, and lodging while away from home overnight) incurred in the service of one's employer.
5. Allowable losses from a sale or exchange of property.
6. Sick pay. If you have sick pay included in your gross income, a certain proportion of it may be deducted in arriving at adjusted gross income.
7. Fifty percent of capital gains. You may also deduct 50 percent of the excess of net long-term capital gains over net short-term capital losses in determining adjusted gross income.

Adjusted gross income is the amount you enter on line 9, page 1, of Form 1040. Some deductions are subtracted from gross income to determine the amount of adjusted gross income. Other deductions are subtracted only from adjusted gross income in arriving at the amount of taxable income.

The importance of adjusted gross income as a factor in determining your tax liability cannot be overemphasized. It governs the amount of the standard deduction you may claim if you do not itemize your deductions. It is used to determine the limitation on deductions for contributions and medical expenses if you do itemize your deductions. It is the basic figure used in determining your tax by the use of the tax table. If you are an employee working for a straight salary or wage and have no other income, your gross income and your adjusted gross income will usually be the same.

Dividends

Dividends representing distributions of earnings and profits by corporations and associations are taxable income. Those which are merely a return to the taxpayer of part of his investment are nontaxable. Among taxable dividends, the following are included:

1. Dividends in cash
2. Dividends in property (to be valued at market)
3. Stock chosen by the taxpayer in lieu of a cash dividend
4. Dividends which the taxpayer has consented to report as income
5. Any payments supposed to be expenses but which are really dividends

The following are exempt from tax as dividends:

1. Returns of capital (principal)
2. So-called "dividends" (partial return of premiums) of mutual life or accident insurance companies or on government insurance[2]
3. Payments out of depletion reserves of oil, mining, or lumber companies, etc.
4. Stock dividends or stock rights which do not increase the stockholder's proportionate interest in the corporation

In some cases, a corporation distributes both a dividend and a repayment of capital at the same time. When the mixed distributions are made, the check or notice will usually show the dividends and the capital repayment separately. In any case, you must report the dividend portion as income. If you are the owner of stock held in the name of your broker, the dividend must be reported on your return.

You may exclude from your income $100 of dividends received from

---

[2] So-called dividends from mutual savings banks, building and loan associations, savings and loan associations, credit unions, etc., are considered *interest* for federal income tax purposes and should be reported as *interest*.

domestic corporations during your taxable year. If a joint return is filed and securities are held jointly, $200 of dividends may be excluded. If securities are held individually, each one may exclude $100 of dividends received from qualifying corporations, but one may not use any portion of the $100 exclusion not used by the other. For example, if the husband had $200 in dividends, and the wife had $20, only a total of $120 may be excluded on a joint return. You may obtain both the $100 exclusion whether you itemize deductions, or whether you use the standard deduction or the tax table.

Interest

Interest income is usually taxable. You must include in your return any interest you receive or which is credited to your account (whether entered in your passbook or not) and can be withdrawn by you. All interest on bonds, debentures, notes, savings accounts, or loans is taxable, except for certain governmental issues. For example, some of the interest which is fully exempt from tax is (*a*) interest from state and municipal bonds and securities (including political instrumentalities or subdivisions thereof, such as Port of New York Authority, the Indiana Toll Road Commission, State Industrial Development Boards, Oklahoma County Utility Services Authority, etc.) and (*b*) interest on up to $5,000 principal value of Treasury bonds issued before March 1, 1941.

If you own United States savings discount bonds and are on a cash basis, you have a choice as to when you may report the interest: (*a*) You may elect to report the interest each year. If you do, the amount of interest to be included in income each year is shown on the table on the bond as the increase in redemption value, or (*b*) you may defer reporting the interest until the bonds are matured or cashed, in which case the interest must be included as income for that year. In most cases this is the more convenient way. It is especially useful if your income fluctuates from year to year because then you can plan to cash your bond and report the appreciation proceeds as income in a year in which your income is lower than usual, thereby minimizing taxes.

If you elect, however, to report the interest each year, you must continue to do so as to *all* bonds owned and those subsequently acquired. You may not change to another method unless you first receive permission to do so. If you are deferring the reporting of interest and wish to change to reporting the interest each year, you may do so without obtaining permission. However, in the year of change, you must report *all* interest on *all* such bonds which you own which was not previously reported.

Where interest on savings bonds is paid by check at stated intervals, the interest income thus received must be reported in the year in which it is received under the cash method.

Business or Profession

Profits from an unincorporated business or profession are taxable to the individual as income and therefore must be included in your personal income tax return.[3] A separate Schedule C, entitled "Profit (or Loss) from Business or Profession," is provided to enable you to subtract your costs from your receipts to arrive at net profit.

Generally, the costs you can deduct are the ordinary and necessary expenses of doing business—cost of merchandise, salaries, interest, taxes, rent, repairs, and incidental supplies. In the case of capital investments and improvements in depreciable property, such as buildings, machines, fixtures, and similar items having a useful life of more than one year, the law provides an annual depreciation allowance as the method of recovering the original capital cost tax-free. If some of your expenses are part business and part personal, you can deduct the business portion but not the personal portion. For instance, a doctor who uses his car half for business can deduct only half the operating expenses of the car and take depreciation on half the original cost of the car.

A partnership or similar business firm (not a corporation) does not pay income tax in the firm's name. Therefore, each partner must report in his personal tax return his share of his partnership's income and pay tax on it. As a partner you must include in income on your Form 1040 your distributive share of partnership earnings which may be more or less than withdrawals. The partnership is required to file a Form 1065, which is an information return showing the results of its operations for the taxable year and the items of income, gain, loss, deduction, or credit affecting its partners' individual income tax returns. The partnership pays no income tax unless it has elected to be taxed as a corporation. Your distributive share of the partnerships' income is your part of the partnerships' business results whether distributed to you or not.

If, in the current taxable year, your business or profession lost money instead of making a profit or you had a casualty loss, you can apply these losses against your other income. If these losses exceed your other income, the excess, or "net operating loss," may be carried backward to offset your income for the three previous taxable years, and any remaining excess may be carried over to any or all of the five taxable years

---

[3] See *Tax Guide for Small Business*, Internal Revenue Service Publication No. 334. It may be obtained from your District Director of Internal Revenue or from the Superintendent of Documents, U.S. Government Printing Office, Washington, D.C., for 40 cents.

following the current one. If a carry-back entitles you to refund on either of the three previous year's taxes, you file Form 1045.

The social security tax for those who are self-employed is reported and paid as part of Schedule C of the personal income tax. The computation of your self-employment tax is made on the separate Schedule C, which, with attached Schedule C-3, should be filed with your income tax return on Form 1040. The self-employment tax is a part of your income tax and applies to every self-employed individual if he has at least $400 of net earnings from self-employment in a taxable year.

Sale and Exchange of Property

If you sell your house, car, furniture, stocks or bonds, real estate, or any other kind of property, the law requires you to report any profit in your tax return. Because of the many special rules for taxing the profit and deducting the loss from such transactions, a special form, Schedule D, is provided. Capital gains and losses will be considered in more detail later.

Annuities and Pensions

The government has granted a series of extra benefits in the tax law to older persons (65 and over). Yet the Internal Revenue Service seems determined to minimize these benefits by driving the recipients to an early grave through two of the most complex parts of the tax form. If an elderly person feels that senility has come upon him when he tries to understand and comprehend either the "Pension and Annuities" section of the tax law or the "Retirement Income Credit" schedule, let him be reassured. It's just about as difficult at 25 or 45 as it is at 65.

The monthly payments you receive from social security when you retire are *not* taxable income, nor are veterans' pensions. If you receive any other kind of pension or annuity, however, it must be reported in Schedule B.

If your pension did not cost you anything and it was fully paid for by your employer, you must pay tax on the full amount you receive each year. If you and your employer each contributed a part of the cost of your annuity or pension and you will recover your contributions completely within three years from the date of your first pension payment, the amounts you receive are *not* taxed as income *until* you have recovered your contribution in full. All amounts received after you have fully recovered your cost are included in taxable income.

If you will not recover your cost within three years after your pension starts, your pension or annuity will be treated under the general rule for annuities. To understand this, take two aspirins, and then try and read the "simple" explanation of the "General Rule for Annuities" in the instructions accompanying Form 1040. We'll give odds that you won't follow it, but at the end there is a cute clause: "For other types of annuities which are not covered by these rules and for more detailed information, call or visit your Internal Revenue Service office." The whole thing makes you shudder at the prospect of living to 65.

Now take a deep breath and let's plunge into the "general rule for annuities." Each annuity or pension payment received consists of two parts: (1) a return of cost, and (2) taxable income. The method of making this division is based on two factors: (a) your investment in the contract, which is your net cost of the annuity; and (b) your expected return, that is the total amount you will receive, or the amount it is estimated you will receive, under the contract.

Investment in the contract is, in general, your net cost of the contract as of the annuity starting date. To compute the amount of your investment determine the total amount of premiums paid. This includes the amounts, if any, your employer contributed, and which you were required to include in income at the time, as well as the amounts you actually contributed.

The second factor in the computation is the expected return. If you will receive annuity payments for a fixed number of years, without regard to your life expectancy, the expected return is the total amount you or your beneficiary will receive after the annuity starting date. If you are to receive annuity payments for the rest of your life, the expected return is found by multiplying the amount of the annual payment by a multiple which is based on your life expectancy as of the annuity starting date. These multiples are set out in tables provided by the Internal Revenue Service.

After you determine your net investment in the contract and your expected return, you are ready to figure how much of each annuity payment is a return of your investment and how much is taxable income. First, you obtain the percentage of the annuity to be excluded by dividing your net investment in the contract by your expected return. Once this percentage is found it will remain the same as long as you draw the annuity. Next, multiply the amount of the annuity received during the year by this percentage. This will give you the amount of the annuity payment which is a return of your investment and thus not included in income. Finally, you subtract this amount from the total amount you receive during the year. The remainder is the amount of your annuity which is taxable income.

Let's take a simple example. Suppose you have an annuity paying you

$1,000 a year for life. Your net investment in the annuity is $9,000. The multiple you use is 15.0 as shown in the Internal Revenue Service actuarial tables for your age (male age 65), and your expected return is $15,000 (15 × $1,000). Your net investment of $9,000 divided by your expected return of $15,000 equals 60 percent, the percentage you will exclude. Each year you will exclude $600 (60 percent of $1,000) and $400 will be taxable income, as long as payments are received.

The Retirement Income Credit

This is the second, even less excusable horror, which the tax law inflicts on elderly retired persons. Cheer up, however, for you have until retirement to understand what follows, and if you read and study it once a year for the next 40 years, you may begin to understand the retirement income credit.

If you are retired, or if you are 65 or over, and receive taxable pension or annuity payments, or have income from rents, interest, or dividends, you may be entitled to a credit against your tax for a certain percentage of your retirement income. The retirement income credit is 15 percent of your taxable retirement income. To claim it you must fill out Part VIII of Schedule B, Form 1040. To do that you must have at least a Ph.D. in actuarial math, accountancy, tax law, and higher logic!

To qualify for the retirement income credit you must meet the age requirement, the prior earned income test, and have retirement income. (*a*) The prior earned income test—you must have had more than $600 of earned income in each year for any ten calendar years before the current year. It doesn't matter which years they were, and they need not have been consecutive years. (*b*) Retirement income—if you meet the prior earned income test, your next step is to determine whether you had any retirement income during the year which entitles you to the credit. Different rules apply for people under 65 and people over 65 years old.

If you are under 65, retirement income includes only a pension received from a public retirement system. Only the taxable portion of the pension is considered retirement income in computing the credit. If you are over 65 before the end of your taxable year, your retirement income includes all your taxable income from pensions, annuities, interest, dividends, and rents.

After you determine that you have received eligible retirement income, your next step is to determine how much, if any, is to be used in computing the credit. It is often possible under the rules to have retirement income and not be entitled to the credit. The credit is 15 percent of the lesser of:

a) The retirement income you received during the year; or
b) $2,286 minus the total of certain pensions and annuities and current earned income.*

If you are under 62, you must reduce the amount in (*b*) above by your earned income received during the year which is in excess of $900. If you are 62 or over but not yet 72, reduce the amount in (*b*) above by your earned income which is in excess of $1,200, but which is not in excess of $1,700, plus the total amount over $1,700. If you are 72 or over by the end of the year, do not reduce the amount in (*b*) above by earned income regardless of the amount earned. You must also reduce the $2,286 referred to in (*b*) above by the amount of any pension and annuity that you receive which is *not* taxed. This includes the amount you receive as a social security pension. Thus, if you receive social security benefits of $2,286 or more during the year, you *cannot* claim the credit.

Unless you have already decided that upon retirement you will emigrate to Canada rather than face this ordeal, let's take a case example and compute the retirement income credit.

Assume you are 67 years old and have met the prior earnings requirement. You have the following income for the year:

Dividends (after $100 exclusion).............................	$ 240
Social Security retirement pension (nontaxable).................	500
Disability benefits under Workmen's Compensation Act (nontaxable)..	400
Rental income (gross rents).................................	900
Purchased annuity ($600 minus return of investment of $140).....	460
Earned income from odd jobs................................	2,000

You would compute the credit as follows:

Retirement income includes:		
Dividends..		$ 240
Rents...		900
Annuity...		460
Total Retirement Income............................		$1,600
But the retirement income is limited to......................		$2,286*
Less:		
Social Security retirement pension.........................$500		
50% of $500 (earned income over $1,200 but not over $1,700)... 250		
Earned income over $1,700 ($2,000 minus $1,700)	300	1,050
Base for computing credit.................................		$1,236

Fifteen† percent of $1,236 equals the retirement income credit of $185.40 which is the amount you may deduct from the income tax payable.

---

* The amount of $2,286 may be used where a joint return is filed by husband and wife and *both* are 65 years of age or over. In all other instances the amount will be $1,524.

† Rate effective for tax years beginning January 1, 1965.

Rents and Royalties

The term "rents" includes income from real estate and the income from any other property. Royalties are received by authors and composers and for the use of property. People owning rented property must incur costs in connection with it. Ordinary expenses and repairs are deductible expenses. Capital expenditures or improvements must be added to the cost of the rented property and depreciated over its remaining life.

If a taxpayer occupies a portion of a dwelling and rents out the balance of it, only those expenses chargeable against the rented portion are deductible. Rents and royalties are reported on Part IV of Schedule B of Form 1040.

Miscellaneous Income

If you cannot find any specific place on your tax return to list some type of income, you should put it in Part V of Schedule B of Form 1040. This is the proper place to report amounts received as alimony or separate maintenance under a court decree; rewards or prizes; recoveries of bad debts, losses, etc., which reduced your tax in a prior year; and health and accident insurance benefit payments received by you as reimbursements for medical expenses which reduced your tax in a prior year.

DEDUCTIONS

Apart from the deductions which you may take from gross income to arrive at adjusted gross income, other deductions fall into two broad categories: the standard deduction and itemized nonbusiness deductions. The standard deduction may be taken in lieu of the itemized nonbusiness deductions. If the taxpayer is single, the standard deduction is equal to 10 percent of the adjusted gross income but cannot amount to more than $1,000. The Tax Act of 1964 provided that the minimum standard deduction shall not be less than $300 plus $100 for each exemption over one.*

If the taxpayers are a married couple filing a joint return, the standard deduction is also equal to 10 percent of the adjusted gross income and may not be more than $1,000. If husband and wife file separate returns, two cases are possible. If each has an adjusted gross income of $5,000 or more, the standard deduction is a flat $500 in each return. It may be more advantageous in this case for each to itemize his

---

* This means that a single person without dependents will have no tax liability until income reaches $900 ($675 under prior law).

deductions, since these may amount to much more than $500 in each return.

If the adjusted gross income for the husband is $5,000 or more and for the wife who is filing a separate return is less than $5,000, the husband is entitled, in his return, to a standard deduction of not more than $500; while the wife, using Form 1040A, gets a standard deduction of 10 percent of the adjusted gross income (say 10 percent of $3,400, or $340). If the husband had itemized his deductions he might have had, let us say, $900 of deductions. But he cannot itemize his deductions if his wife does not; and if she files a separate return on Form 1040A, she is not allowed to itemize her deductions.

It may be, from her individual point of view, that the standard deduction is better for her, since under it she is allowed $340; whereas her actual deductions, if itemized, come to only $250. From the point of view of their joint income, however, the filing of separate returns and the use of the standard deduction results in a smaller aggregate standard deduction ($500 + $340 = $840) than in a joint return. If they used the standard deduction in a joint return (assuming his adjusted gross income was $7,500), they could have deducted $1,000 (10 percent of the total adjusted gross income—in this case, $7,500 plus $3,400, equaling $10,900—or a maximum of $1,000). Had the couple filed a joint return and itemized deductions rather than taken the standard deduction, they would have had a total deduction of $1,150 ($900 for the husband and $250 for the wife). Obviously, it pays to stop and actually figure out how to take your deductions.

How to Figure Depreciation

In the case of capital investments and improvements in depreciable property having a useful life of more than a year and owned for the purpose of making a profit from rents, royalties, business, or a profession, the tax law provides an annual depreciation allowance as the method of recovering the original capital cost tax-free. This means that you can spread the cost over as many years as the property is expected to be useful. These rules apply to a profession as well as to a business. For instance, a lawyer can deduct the cost of his law books and a doctor can deduct the cost of his instruments *only* through the depreciation allowance.

The first step in figuring depreciation is to determine the useful life of each asset to be depreciated. The useful life of an asset depends on how long you expect to use it, its age when acquired, your policy as to repairs, upkeep and replacement, and other conditions. There is no average useful life which is applicable in all situations. Useful lives prescribed by the Internal Revenue Service, for depreciation purposes, are applicable to all assets used in a particular industry or business rather than to individual assets.[4]

Once you have made a reasonable estimate of the useful life of your property, you may divide its cost, less salvage value, if any, by the number of years of such useful life, and that is the amount you can deduct during each of these years. For example, suppose you own a house which has an estimated useful life of 40 years. If you rent the house to someone else, you can deduct from your rental income 2½ percent of its cost (excluding the land cost) each year for 40 years. If you use the house as your own residence, you may *not* deduct depreciation. Depreciation may not be taken on property used for personal purposes exclusively, such as a taxpayer's automobile or home.

In addition to the "straight-line" depreciation method described above, there are two others that may be used for property acquired from January 1, 1954, on: (*a*) the "double-declining-balance" method, and (*b*) the "sum-of-the-years-digits" method.

Under the double-declining-balance method a uniform rate of *twice* the straight-line depreciation rate is applied each year to the *remaining* cost of the property (without adjustment for salvage value). The amount of depreciation taken each year is subtracted from the basis of the property before figuring the next year's depreciation, so that the same depreciation rate is applied to a smaller or declining balance each year.

In the sum-of-the-years-digits method, you apply a different fraction each year to the basis of the property less its estimated salvage value. The denominator or bottom of the fraction is the total of the numbers representing the years of useful life of the property. Thus, if the useful life is five years, the denominator is 15 $(1 + 2 + 3 + 4 + 5 = 15)$. The numerator, or top of the fraction, is the number of years of life remaining at the beginning of the year for which the computation is made. Thus, if the useful life is five years, the fraction to be applied to the cost minus salvage to figure depreciation for the first year is $\frac{5}{15}$. The fraction for the second year is $\frac{4}{15}$ and so on.

Take an example: Suppose a doctor buys a second car to use exclusively to make calls and not for personal use. He pays $3,500. The car has an estimated useful life of five years at the end of which its salvage (or trade-in) value is estimated to be $500.

---

[4] For more detailed information see IRS Publication No. 456, *Depreciation Guidelines and Rules*, obtainable from the U.S. Government Printing Office, Washington, D.C. This will also explain "additional first year depreciation."

Under the straight-line method the annual depreciation is $600, computed as follows: Deduct $500 (salvage value) from $3,500 (cost of automobile), leaving $3,000. Then divide $3,000 by five (the number of years of useful life) to arrive at the annual depreciation of $600.

Under the double-declining-balance method the rate of depreciation may not exceed 40 percent, that is twice the straight-line rate of 20 percent above. The depreciation the first year is $1,400 (40 percent of the $3,500 cost). The depreciation for the second year is $840 (40 percent of $2,100, the unrecovered cost; that is $3,500 minus the first year's $1,400 depreciation).

Under the sum-of-the-years-digits method, the depreciation would be $1,000 the first year. This is $5/15$ of $3,000 (cost of $3,500 less salvage value of $500). The depreciation the second year would be $4/15$ of $3,000, or $800, the third year, $3/15$ of $3,000, or $600, and so on.

A detailed comparison of the three methods may be seen in the following table:

	ANNUAL DEPRECIATION		
YEAR	STRAIGHT-LINE (20 PERCENT)	DOUBLE-DECLINING-BALANCE (40 PERCENT)	SUM-OF-THE-YEARS-DIGITS
1................................	$ 600	$1,400.00	$1,000
2................................	600	840.00	800
3................................	600	504.00	600
4................................	600	302.40*	400
5................................	600	181.44*	200
Total......................	$3,000	$3,227.84	$3,000
Salvage value or unrecovered cost.....	$ 500	$ 227.84	$ 500

* Under the double-declining-balance method, depreciation must stop when the unrecovered cost is reduced to salvage value. Therefore, the fourth year only $211.68 of the $302.40 could be taken in depreciation and no depreciation could be taken the fifth year.

MODEL TAX RULING HOLDS BEAUTY IS NEVER OBSOLETE

Washington, Nov. 13—The Internal Revenue Bureau told a group of models today that wrinkles were not tax deductible.

The girls had asked the bureau if they could make allowances on their income tax returns for bodily depreciation. They said that they were subject to "age, exhaustion and obsolescence." The bureau replied:

"Charm, beauty and talent, while undoubtedly of great value in your profession, are not generally recognized as depreciable for tax purposes. American beauty never becomes obsolete."

How to Deduct Bad Debts

Bad debts, with certain exceptions, are deductible if they become worthless during the year. But they must meet specific requirements in order to be deductible, and they must always be satisfactorily explained by the taxpayer. The explanation, if required, must show:

1. The nature of the debt
2. The name of the debtor, and the debtor's relationship to the taxpayer, if any
3. When the debt was created
4. When the debt became due
5. The effort made by the taxpayer to collect the debt
6. How the debt was determined to be worthless

For a debt to be worthless, it must not only be uncollectible but must also appear to be uncollectible at any time in the future. The taxpayer must take reasonable steps to collect the debt. He does not have to go to court, however, if it can be shown that a judgment, once obtained, would also be worthless. If a debtor, as lawyers say, is "judgment proof," then the judgment would be of no value. Bad debts must be shown to have existed in fact and in law. A taxpayer cannot, for example, claim a bad-debt deduction for a debt which cannot be enforced in the courts. A gambling debt is a good example of an unenforceable debt.

Advances to relatives to tide them over financial difficulties may not be legally collectible debts, since they may be made without any fixed understanding as to repayment and may therefore be legally considered a gift rather than a loan. Deductions of bad debts resulting from trade, business, or professional activity must always be deductions of amounts which the taxpayer has or is reporting as income in his tax return. For example, a lawyer cannot deduct an unpaid fee as a bad debt, nor can a landlord claim a tenant's unpaid rent as a bad debt.

How to Deduct for Contributions

If you itemize deductions, you can deduct gifts to religious, charitable, educational, scientific, or literary organizations, and organizations for the prevention of cruelty to children and animals, *unless* the organization is operated for personal profit, or conducts propaganda, or otherwise attempts to influence legislation. You can deduct gifts to fraternal organizations if they are to be used for charitable, religious, etc., purposes. You can also deduct gifts to veterans' organizations, or to a governmental agency which will use the gifts for public purposes. The law does *not* allow for gifts to individuals, or to other types of organizations, however worthy.

In general, the deduction for contributions may not exceed 20 percent of your adjusted gross income. However, you may increase this limitation to 30 percent if the extra 10 percent consists of contributions made to churches, to public organizations such as the Red Cross, libraries, symphony orchestras, to tax-exempt educational institutions, tax-exempt hospitals, or certain medical research organizations. Of course, the entire 30 percent contribution deduction allowance could be made to these institutions.

A contribution may be made in money or property (but not services). If in property, it is measured by the fair market value of the property at the time of contribution. For example, if you give $50 in old clothes to your church, it's as much a deductible contribution as if you had given cash. While you can deduct for gifts to organizations mentioned previously, you cannot deduct for dues or other payments to them for which you receive personal benefits. For example, you can deduct gifts to a YWCA but not dues.

You CAN deduct gifts to:

Churches and temples
Salvation Army
Red Cross, Community Chests, and United Funds
Nonprofit schools and hospitals
Veterans organizations
Boy Scouts, Girl Scouts, and other similar organizations
Nonprofit organizations primarily engaged in conducting research or education for the alleviation and care of diseases such as tuberculosis, cancer, multiple sclerosis, muscular dystrophy, cerebral palsy, polio, diseases of the heart, etc.

You CANNOT deduct gifts to:

Relatives, friends, other individuals
Political organizations or candidates
Social clubs
Labor unions
Chamber of commerce
Propaganda organizations

Interest as a Deduction

In general, interest on indebtedness is deductible if you itemize your deductions. Interest on mortgages, judgments, delinquent taxes, personal loans, and installment payments is deductible. Discount (interest paid in advance by being deducted from principal of the loan) is deductible on a cash basis only when the loan is fully paid, but taxpayers on the accrual basis may take the deductions as they accrue.

Probably the most common type of interest deducted is the interest paid on home mortgages. Monthly mortgage payments usually consist of repayment of principal and of interest. The former is not deductible, the latter is. If your records do not clearly show these two components, ask the lender to give you the exact breakdown. If you prepay your mortgage, any fee charged by the bank for this privilege is deductible as interest. If you purchase a co-operative apartment, you are entitled to deduct your portion of the interest payments on the indebtedness of the co-operative.

When you buy items such as an automobile, television set, etc., on the installment plan under a contract in which the carrying charges are separately stated but the interest charges cannot be determined, you are allowed to treat a portion of the payments made under such a contract as interest. This deduction is equal to 6 percent of the average unpaid monthly balance under the contract.

Interest payments are not deductible if made:

1. For another person for whom taxpayer has no legal obligation to make payment.
2. On indebtedness entered into to purchase or carry tax-exempt securities.
3. On indebtedness entered into to purchase single premium life insurance or endowment contracts.
4. On a life insurance loan, if interest is added to the loan and you report on a cash basis.
5. On a gambling debt or other nonenforceable obligation.

Deductible interest must be paid or accrued in the year of the deduction. Interest on debts incurred to produce rents or royalties and interest on obligations in connection with a trade or business are deductions in the computation of adjusted gross income.

Taxes as Deductions

Nonfederal taxes are generally deductible. They include state and local income taxes, personal property taxes, and real estate taxes (except those assessed for pavements, sewers, or other local improvements which tend to increase the value of your property). You can deduct state or local retail sales taxes if under the laws of your state they are imposed directly on the consumer, or if they are imposed on the retailer (or wholesaler, in the case of gasoline taxes) and the amount of the tax is separately stated by the retailer to the consumer.

Taxes chargeable to rents and royalties and taxes on property used in business may be deducted as business expenses in computing adjusted gross income. State income taxes are not deductible in computing adjusted gross income but may be taken as nonbusiness deductions.

Social security taxes paid by an employer are deducted as business expenses, but the social security tax which you pay as an employee you are not permitted to deduct. Social security taxes paid by an employer on wages of domestic employees are not deductible, since in this case they are not business expenses but are considered federal excise taxes, whose deduction as a tax is prohibited by law.

In general, you cannot deduct any federal excise taxes on your personal expenditures, such as taxes on theater admissions, furs, jewelry, cosmetics, railroad tickets, telephone, etc.

Taxes imposed on a previous owner of a property and paid by the taxpayer as part of the contracted purchase price should be included in the cost of purchased property. Municipal water bills, parking-meter charges, service fees, etc., are nondeductible as personal expenses but may be deducted as expenses of those in business. Real property and personal property taxes, state capitation or poll taxes, and state gasoline taxes are deductible.

Federal income taxes, excess-profits taxes, gift taxes, estate taxes, and excise taxes are not deductible, nor are taxes paid by you for another person.

Casualties and Thefts

Whether arising from business or not, deductions may be taken for actual net property lost because of war; because of casualties such as, for example, accident, fire, shipwreck, or storm; or because of theft. Only the actual net loss may be claimed; to the extent that the loss is reimbursed by insurance or otherwise, the allowable deduction is reduced. Casualty and theft losses sustained in business are deducted in the computation of adjusted gross income. Damage to your car by collision or accident can be deducted if due merely to faulty driving but cannot be deducted if due to your willful act or negligence.

You can deduct losses on:

1. Property—such as your home, clothing, or automobile—destroyed or damaged by fire
2. Loss or damage of property by flood, lightning, storm, explosion, or freezing
3. Property, including cash, which is stolen from you
4. Damage to your automobile by accident if not due to your willful act or negligence

You cannot deduct losses on:

1. Personal injury to yourself or another person
2. Accidental loss by you of cash or other personal property

3. Property lost in storage or in transit
4. Damage by insects, rust, or gradual erosion
5. Animals or plants damaged or destroyed by disease

Sentimental values are excluded from consideration when determining the amount of loss. The amount of the loss to be deducted is measured by the fair market value of the property just before the casualty less its fair market value immediately after the casualty (but not more than the cost or other adjusted basis of the property), reduced by any insurance or compensation received.

Dental, Hospital, and Medical Expenses

If you itemize deductions, you can take limited deductions for the amounts you paid during the year (not compensated by hospital, health, or accident insurance) for medical or dental expense for yourself, your wife, or any dependent who received over half his support from you. Ordinarily, the limit of deductions for dental and medical expenses is the amount by which they exceed 3 percent of your adjusted gross income; but if the taxpayer or his wife is 65 years old, he may deduct all medical expenses for himself and wife plus the usual deduction (expenses in excess of 3 percent of adjusted gross income) for his dependents. Any reimbursement (insurance or otherwise) reduces the allowable deduction.

There is a maximum limit to medical and dental deductions. Your deduction for medical and dental expenses may not exceed $5,000 multiplied by the number of your exemptions, exclusive of exemptions for age or blindness. In no case may you claim more than: (*a*) $10,000 if you are single and not head of a household; (*b*) $10,000 if you are married but file a separate return; or (*c*) $20,000 if you file a joint return or are head of a household. In figuring the limitations, do not count the added exemptions for age and blindness.

You can deduct payments to doctors, dentists, nurses, hospitals, etc. Allowable deductions are limited to those expenses which are sustained "primarily for the prevention or alleviation of a physical or mental defect or illness." They include hospital, nursing, medical, laboratory, surgical, and dental services, eyeglasses, hearing aids, seeing-eye dog and its maintenance, supplies (including false teeth and artificial eyes and limbs), ambulance hire, and necessary travel for medical care. The amount paid for medicine and drugs may be taken into account only to the extent it exceeds 1 percent of your adjusted gross income but for a taxpayer 65 or over that 1 percent floor does not apply. A prescription is *not* required as long as the medicine and drugs are legally obtained. You may not include the cost of toothpaste, toiletries, cosmetics, etc., in medicines and drugs. Medical expenses include sums paid for hospitalization, membership in certain associations which furnish medical service, and clinical care. Premiums for accident and health insurance which indemnifies for medical care of a specific injury are classed as medical expenses.

Burial and funeral expenses are not medical expenses, nor can you deduct for an illegal operation or for drugs or travel ordered or suggested by your doctor merely for rest or for change.

If medical expenses are deducted in one year and reimbursement is received in a later year, the reimbursement must be reported as income in the year when received, but only to the extent that the reimbursement equals the deduction. Reimbursement to a taxpayer who took a standard deduction and did not take a specific medical deduction is not considered to be income. Insurance premiums paid to provide indemnification for loss of earnings are not a deductible medical expense, and any amount received under such a policy for loss of earnings is not taxable income.

An example will serve to make clear the medical deduction. Assume your adjusted gross income is $6,000. Your medical expenses for the year total $475. Three percent of $6,000 is $180. The first $180 of your $475 medical expense is *not* deductible. The remaining $295 *is* deductible.

Care of Children and Other Dependents

If deductions are itemized, a woman or widower (including men who are divorced or legally separated under a decree and have not remarried) may deduct expenses paid,[5] for the care of (*a*) dependent children under 13 years of age; or (*b*) dependent persons physically or mentally incapable of caring for themselves, if such care is to enable the taxpayer to be gainfully employed or actively to seek gainful employment. The maximum deduction is $600 annually where there is only one dependent, but is increased to $900 if there are two or more.

In the case of a woman who is married, the deduction is allowed if: (*a*) she filed a separate return because she has been deserted by her husband, did not know his whereabouts at any time during the year, and has applied to a court to compel him to pay support; or (*b*) she files a joint return with her husband, in which case, the deduction is reduced by the amount (if any) by which their adjusted gross income exceeds $6,000. If the husband is incapable of self-support because he is

[5] A husband whose wife is incapacitated for at least 90 days will qualify.

mentally or physically defective, this income limitation does not apply.

If the person who receives the payment also performs duties not related to dependent care, only that part of the payment which is for the dependent's care may be deducted. You may not claim any child care payments to a person for whom you claim an exemption.

Expenses of Earning Nonbusiness Income

Taxpayers who itemize nonbusiness deductions may deduct nonbusiness expenses incurred in earning nonbusiness income, such as the income from securities and real estate. Such expenses must be necessary to the collection of income from, or to the conservation, maintenance, or management of, the property held to produce the income. For example, if you subscribe to an investment advisory service such as Standard and Poor's or Moody's, or if you pay a fee to an investment counselor, you may deduct the expense. You can deduct the rental cost of a safe-deposit box in which you keep securities but not the cost of a box used merely for jewelry and other valuables.

Expenses for Education

Expenses for education may be deducted if primarily for the purpose of: (a) maintaining or improving skills required in your employment or other trade or business, or (b) meeting the express requirements of your employer, or the requirements of applicable law or regulations, imposed as a condition to the retention of your salary, status, or employment.

Expenses incurred for obtaining a new position, for meeting minimum requirements, a substantial advancement in position, or for personal purposes, are not deductible.[6]

Most scholarship grants and some grants for doctoral research are tax-free but the rulings and court decisions in this area have been changing, and you will want to check the tax status of your grant or fellowship with a tax authority on your campus, or with your Internal Revenue Office.

Alimony Payments

Alimony or separate-maintenance payments are expenses deductible by the husband when his wife or ex-wife must include them in income. If you are divorced or legally separated and are making periodic payments of alimony or separate maintenance under a court decree, you can deduct

---

[6] For more detail see Chapter 12, "Educational Expenses," in *Your Federal Income Tax*, latest annual edition, U.S. Government Printing Office, Washington, D.C., 20402.

these amounts. Such payments must be included in the wife's taxable income.

However, you may not deduct lump-sum settlements, specific maintenance payments for support of children, or any voluntary payments not under a court order or a written separation agreement. Any alimony payment for which the ex-husband is allowed a deduction must be reported by the ex-wife as income.

If the decree, or some incidental legal instrument, specifies the total sum of husband's alimony obligation and makes the total payable within ten years, no deduction is allowed. If the pay period is over ten years, each installment is a periodic payment and may be deducted, but not more than 10 percent of the total sum may be deducted in any one year. Where no total sum is specified but the court orders periodic payments for life or until the ex-wife remarries, the payments are deductible.

If a taxpayer pays medical expenses of his former wife by the terms of a separation agreement which is part of a divorce decree, he may deduct them as alimony; she must include them in gross income, but, to the extent allowable, she may deduct them as medical expenses. When the wife is irrevocable beneficiary and absolute assignee of a policy on her husband's life under a property-settlement agreement approved by a divorce decree, premiums paid by him thereafter under the agreement are deductible from his income and includable in her gross income. Obviously, from a tax viewpoint, how alimony payments are to be made is an important consideration.

Automobile Expenses

The expense of running an automobile may be a business expense, a personal expense, or a combination of both. It depends on how the automobile is used. The costs of gasoline, oil, repairs, garage rent, insurance, and any other necessary operation and upkeep expenses are deductible for an automobile used in a trade, business, or profession but not for one used personally. Deductions are also allowable for damages paid as a result of accidents which result from business use, provided, of course, that the taxpayer is not reimbursed by insurance, or otherwise, for the damages for which he is liable. Such deductions are not allowable if the car is used for personal purposes. Depreciation on the cost of an automobile used in trade, business, or a profession is also deductible, but it is not deductible if the automobile is used for personal pleasure. Taxpayers who use their automobiles to look after income-producing properties, yielding either rents or royalties, can deduct their automobile expenses from such income.

If you use your car for both business and for personal travel, you must apportion your expenses appropriately. To illustrate, suppose you are a consulting engineer and drove your car 20,000 miles during this year. Upon checking your records you find that 12,000 miles was for business travel and 8,000 for personal use. In this case 12,000/20,000, or 60 percent, of the total cost of operating your car may be claimed as a business or employment expense.

A simple alternate method is available for claiming automobile expenses. For business use of a family car you may take 10 cents a mile for the first 15,000 business miles and 7 cents a mile for any in excess of 15,000. Where you use a car for charitable work or for medical expenses such as trips to a hospital for treatments you can claim expenses of 5 cents a mile.

Keep in mind that automobile business expenses are deductible from gross income to arrive at adjusted gross income (line 9 on page 1 of Form 1040) rather than being a deduction from adjusted gross income to arrive at net income (page 2 of Form 1040). This means that automobile business expenses may be used to reduce your gross income whether or not you itemize deductions.[7]

As far as personal expenses are concerned, taxpayers who itemize nonbusiness deductions may claim the following nonbusiness automobile deductions:

1. State and municipal property taxes on automobiles
2. Interest on money borrowed on the security of an automobile
3. Losses from fire, accident, storm, or theft not compensated for by insurance or otherwise
4. Annual registration fees
5. Damages to an automobile not compensated by insurance and not from a willful act of negligence of the taxpayer
6. State and municipal sales taxes on the purchase of a car, accessories, or replacement parts
7. State gasoline taxes

Miscellaneous Deductions

Many people pass up tax savings because they overlook obscure deductions, do not know about them, and do not take them. You are going to be paying income taxes for the rest of your life—a good many years—and it will pay you to familiarize yourself with present-day complications of tax forms and tax rulings as early as possible in your career. Sooner or later, if you procrastinate, you will learn the hard way.

---

[7] For more detail see *"Automobile Income Tax Deductions,"* latest annual revision, American Automobile Association. A free copy may be obtained by writing to the Association at 1712 G Street, N.W., Washington 6, D.C.

It is really much more simple to spend a few hours now and straighten yourself out on a matter which will affect you all your life.

For example, Tom Dobbins came back from two years' service in the Army. He weighed 158 pounds, whereas he had weighed 179 when he was drafted. He gave away all his old clothes to the Salvation Army because they did not fit. He could have deducted the fair market value of these, but he did not know about it. Then he got a job which required that he furnish small tools and a uniform at his own expense. He could have deducted for this, too, but he did not know that if you work for wages or a salary, you can deduct the ordinary and necessary expenses which you incur for your employer's benefit. He joined a union, because he had to as a condition of keeping his job; and he had to pay union dues, which he could have deducted. He had paid a fee to an employment agency for getting him a job, but he did not deduct that either, though he could have. His boss sent him to a neighboring town to do some repair work. He used the company car to get there and back, but he had to stay over two nights. He could have deducted for meals and room, since he was not reimbursed for these outlays; but no one told him, and he had never read anything about taxes.

Generally speaking, if you operate a business or engage in a trade or profession, you can take a lot more deductions than if you are a wage earner. If you are an executive, the cost of a chauffeur to drive your car, used in business, is deductible; but a working wife may not deduct wages paid to a part-time cleaning woman. If you are a businessman and entertain customers at dinner, you can deduct the cost of the dinners—yours and your customers—but an allowance paid by a husband to his wife for cooking dinner for him is not deductible, nor is the cost of the dinner. Traveling expenses, such as railroad fares, meals, lodgings, tips, etc., incurred while away from home in the pursuit of your regular trade or business are deductible (in computing your adjusted gross income). But no deduction is allowable for traveling expenses that are personal in nature; this includes traveling to seek a position and commuter's fares and similar costs of traveling between home and place of employment or business.

If you own your own home and use it solely for your personal residence, its depreciation, the cost of its restoration by repainting, the cost of insurance, or any loss on its sale represent personal expenses which are not deductible. If you own the house and rent it for income, all these expenses are deductible. Even maintenance costs of idle property, when you are attempting to rent or sell the property, are deductible. If you rent part of your house, you may deduct a proportionate part of the expense of running the house against rental income. If you are a businessman and your firm pays the expense of a membership in Kiwanis or Rotary, this is deductible; but if you pay your personal dues, it is not deductible. If your business moves its office to another city, the cost of moving is a deductible business expense; but if you relocate to find employment your moving expenses are not deductible. In business you can deduct the cost of training new employees, but students cannot deduct educational expenses. The legal expenses of a business are deductible, but you may not deduct legal fees paid for the preparation of a will or for securing a divorce.

The law specifically provides that no deduction shall be allowed for "personal living or family expenses, except extraordinary medical expenses." They are not part of the cost of operating a business or of producing income from investment property. The basic principle covering deductions applies to all taxpayers: he who seeks a deduction must point to some specific provision of law or regulations authorizing that deduction, and he must be able to prove that he is entitled to such a deduction. It is very important to keep records and receipts in case you are called upon for such proof.

CAPITAL GAINS OR LOSSES

In general, capital gains are profits from selling or exchanging any kind of property, except certain kinds when they are used or held in your trade or business. The capital assets you hold may be of two types: income producing and nonincome producing. Stocks and bonds purchased as investments are normally income producing; the house in which you live and your pleasure car are nonincome-producing assets. The law requires that you report and pay a tax on any gains from the sale or exchange of either of these two types of capital assets and allows you to claim a loss and deduct in the case of the sale or exchange of income-producing property, such as stocks or bonds, but not in the case of nonincome-producing capital assets (such as the home in which you live or the pleasure car you drive). In the latter case, you pay a tax on the capital gain, if any, but can take no deduction for the capital loss, if any.

Capital and Noncapital Assets

Although most property is classified by the law as capital assets, there are certain kinds which are not so considered, including:

1. Stock in trade
2. Real or other property of a kind includable in inventory

3. Property held for sale to customers
4. Depreciable property used in trade or business
5. Real property used in trade or business
6. A copyright; a literary, musical, or artistic composition; or similar property held by a taxpayer who personally created such property or acquired it from such creator by gift or transfer in trust
7. Accounts or notes receivable acquired in the ordinary course of business
8. Certain short-term federal, state, and municipal obligations

Accordingly, stocks and bonds are capital assets when held by individual taxpayers but are not when held for sale by a securities dealer. One's personal residence is a capital asset, but houses held for sale by a real estate dealer are not. A pleasure automobile is a capital asset, but one used in business is not, since it comes under category four, above.

If a capital asset is held six months or less, the gain or loss resulting from sale or exchange is short-term. In general, any such profit is fully taxable and any loss is deductible in full. If a capital asset is held longer than six months, gain or loss resulting from its sale is long-term. Short-term capital gains and losses will be merged to obtain the net short-term capital gain or loss. Long-term capital gains and losses (taken into account at 100 percent) will be merged to obtain the net long-term capital gain or loss. If the net short-term capital gain exceeds the net long-term capital loss, 100 percent of such excess shall be included in income. If the net long-term capital gain exceeds the net short-term capital loss, 50 percent of such excess shall be included in income. If your capital transactions result in a net loss for the year, this may be deducted from ordinary income to the extent of $1,000. If your ordinary income is less than $1,000, you may deduct the capital loss only to the extent of the ordinary income. If the capital loss exceeds $1,000, the excess of loss to the extent of $1,000 annually may be carried over to succeeding years, until it is absorbed.

The tax on net long-term capital gains will not normally exceed 25 percent because of the alternatives available to the taxpayer. He may either take half of his net long-term capital gain and add it to his ordinary income and pay the customary income tax on the total, or he may pay a tax of 25 percent of the full net long-term capital gain. He is permitted to choose whichever method gives him the lower tax. Persons filing separate returns will find that the 25 percent alternative is less costly for them only when their net income exceeds $18,000; on a joint return, using the 25 percent alternative does not become advantageous unless the combined income is more than $36,000. In the case of net short-term capital gains there is no alternative, nor is there any halving of the gain. The full gain is added to ordinary income, and the total is taxed at regular income tax rates.

Taxpayers who operate businesses deduct losses on sales or exchanges of stock in trade or property held for sale and pay income tax on any profits from such sales or exchanges. Generally, the length of time such property is held is of no importance; gains are taxed in full; all losses are deductible.

It should be remembered that sales or exchanges of any property which is not used for business or held for the purpose of producing income may result in taxable profit, but losses cannot be deducted. This is the rule which requires one to pay a tax if he sells his home or television set for a profit, but does not allow him to deduct a loss thereon. The gain, however, is a capital gain; and if the property has been held for more than six months, it is a long-term gain, and therefore only half of it need be added to ordinary income.

Cost or Other Basis

Taxpayers who sold or exchanged any property during the taxable year must fill in Schedule D of Form 1040. One of the most important items used in computing capital gain or loss in this schedule is that shown in the column headed, in part, "Cost or Other Basis." To fill in this schedule properly, you must understand the meaning of two terms: *the basis of the property* and *the adjusted basis.*

What is meant by the "basis" for determining capital gain or loss? Taxpayers who sell or exchange property at a profit receive, in return, their capital, which is tax-free, of course, and a taxable gain, which is sometimes loosely referred to as "profit." Some taxpayers think of the gain as merely the difference between their purchase price and the selling price. If, on the other hand, their purchase price exceeds the selling price, they believe they have sustained a loss. However, this is sometimes not the case for income tax purposes.

The basis of property is in most cases the cost or purchase price. By the time the property is sold, however, this basis may have been changed, either by depreciation or by improvements or alterations. It is this depreciated or enhanced value that is called the "adjusted basis." It is the adjusted basis of the property that must be compared with the selling price to arrive at capital gain or loss. If the property is purchased by rendering services, its fair market value at the time received represents taxable compensation and becomes the basis of the property. If the taxpayer exchanges property, the basis of the newly acquired property is its fair market value at the time of the exchange.

In order to determine the adjusted basis of the property, it is necessary to know what must be added to or subtracted from the original cost or other basis. Taxpayers should add to the basis the cost of all improvements and betterments to the property, together with any other costs which were incurred during the time it was held, such as purchase commissions, cost of defending and protecting titles, and other similar costs. The basis is reduced by subtracting the receipts, which represent, in whole or in part, a return of capital, or by subtracting any losses properly applicable to capital accounts, resulting from storms or other casualties. Allowable depreciation is perhaps the main subtraction.

If a taxpayer owns and lives in a residence, depreciation cannot be deducted for income tax purposes, since depreciation on such property is not permitted. Any improvements or betterments which are made on the home must, however, be added to the cost in order to determine the adjusted basis, and they thus influence the amount of capital gain.

Securities and Capital Gains

Obviously, it pays to hold your securities long enough to establish long-term rather than short-term capital gains, since the tax advantage is considerable. The holding period of six months, necessary to establish the long-term gain, includes the day of sale but not the day of purchase. Every other day in the period—Sundays, holidays, business days, etc.—is counted. Remember that *only one half* of your net long-term capital gain need be added to ordinary income for tax purposes. The wealthier person, who may be taxed at 50 or 60 percent on the income tax scale, will prefer, in investments, to aim at capital gains rather than recurrent income, because the income will be taxed at 50 or 60 percent, but the long-term capital gains will be taxed at a maximum of 25 percent. Frequently, investors sell some securities from their portfolio toward the end of the year to establish capital losses to offset earlier capital gains. They then buy back (after 30 days have elapsed) the securities at not very different prices, having by this means minimized their tax and yet not having changed their investment position materially. The tax law does not recognize losses, however, if the same stock is acquired either within 30 days before or 30 days after the tax-loss sale—a total of 61 days.

When You Sell Your Home

The tax law has a special provision for homeowners who sell one house and buy another. If a taxpayer sells his principal residence at a gain and buys within one year another dwelling which he uses as his principal residence, the gain is not taxable if the cost of the new dwelling equals or exceeds the sale price of the old one, but such gain is subtracted from the basis of the new home. You are allowed additional time in case of (*a*) construction of the new residence or (*b*) military service. If you begin construction of a residence, either before the sale of your old residence or within one year after the sale, and occupy it not later than 18 months after the sale, you will be considered to have purchased a new residence, and the nonrecognition of gain rule applies. The running of the one-year period or the 18-month period after the sale of your old residence will be suspended during the time you serve on active duty in the armed forces. This suspension applies only where your service begins before the end of the one-year or the 18-month period, and it cannot be extended for more than four years after the date of sale.

The rule provides that no tax is payable if a new residence is purchased and occupied within one year before or after the sale of the former residence at a profit, provided the cost of the new home equals or exceeds the selling price of the former home. The law takes the position that the new residence is in substance a continuation of the former investment in a home. To the extent that the former residence, however, sells for more than the cost of the new property, the gain is, therefore, taxable. A loss from the sale of one's residence is not deductible. The rule as to gains applies also, under certain conditions, to exchanges of one residence for another, to construction of a new residence, and to the acquisition of a new residence on which work must be done to make it fit for occupancy.

If an old residence costing $8,000 is sold for $15,000 (at a profit of $7,000), and a new residence is acquired for $17,000, the new residence takes as its basis (on which to compute later gain) the $17,000 cost diminished by the $7,000 profit on the former residence, or an adjusted basis of $10,000. This amounts to the cost of the old home increased by the additional investment ($2,000) in the new home. The apparent gain of $7,000 on the sale of the old home is not taxed but instead is used to reduce the cost of acquisition (basis) of the new house from $17,000 to $10,000. If, a few years later, you sell the new house for $20,000 and do not buy another, you will have a $10,000 capital gain, not a $3,000 gain.

If, to take another example, the taxpayer sells the original old home for $15,000 (at a profit of $7,000) and buys a new home for $12,000, he does not invest $3,000 of the $7,000 profit made on the sale of the old home when he buys the new home; this part ($3,000) of the gain on the sale of the old property is taxable. In this case, the basis taken by the new home is $12,000 (cost) less $4,000 of nontaxable profit, or

$8,000. That is, if the sale price of your old residence exceeds the cost of your new residence, the gain on the sale is taxable to the extent of such excess.

Should you sell your new residence, to determine the gain on its sale, reduce its cost by the gain from the sale of your old residence which was not taxable. For example, if you sell your new residence—which cost, say, $14,000—for $16,000, and the nontaxable gain on your old residence was $4,000, your gain on the sale of the new residence is $6,000.

The Tax Act of 1964 provided a special benefit for older persons. If a person 65 or over sells his residence for a gain it is tax-free if the adjusted sales price is $20,000 or less. The adjusted sales price is the amount realized less "fixing up" expenses, that is, those incurred within 90 days prior to sale. This tax relief applies only if the taxpayer used the property as his principal residence for at least five of the eight years before sale.

If the sales price is more than $20,000, the gain is tax-free in the ratio that $20,000 is to the selling price. Assume the adjusted selling price is $30,000, for example, and the gain is $9,000. Only $6,000 of the gain is tax-free [$9,000 × ($20,000/$30,000)].

OTHER PROVISIONS

Cash or Accrual Accounting

Your return must be on a cash basis unless you keep accounts on the accrual basis. "Cash basis" means that all items of taxable income actually or constructively received during the year (whether in cash or property or services) and only those amounts actually paid during the year for deductible expenses are shown. Income is "constructively" received when the amount is credited to your account, or set aside for you, and may be drawn upon by you at any time. Thus, such income includes uncashed salary or dividend checks, bank interest credited to your account, matured bond coupons, and similar items which you can immediately turn into cash. The "accrual basis" means that you report income when earned, even though not received, and deduct expenses when incurred, even though not paid within the taxable period. Most people find it more convenient to use the cash basis.

How to Figure Your Tax

To save arithmetic for the average taxpayer, the law provides a table which shows the correct tax for any income up to $5,000. If you file

Form 1040A, the district director uses this table to determine your tax for you.

If your income is $5,000 or more you must compute your own tax. Form 1040 may be filed by anyone regardless of the source or amount of income. You can use it whether you take the standard deduction or itemize deductions. If you have less than $5,000 adjusted gross income and use Form 1040, you may either itemize your deductions and compute your tax from the tax schedule, or use the tax table. If you use the tax table you cannot itemize your deductions. The tax table allows for an exemption of $600 for each person claimed as a dependent, and charitable contributions, interest, taxes, etc., approximating 10 percent of your income. It may only be used if your income is under $5,000. It must be used if your income is less than $5,000 and you do not itemize your deductions.

If you have $5,000 or more of adjusted gross income you may file Form 1040 and compute your tax from the appropriate tax schedule. Table 11–1 shows a tax schedule for taxable years beginning after December 31, 1964. You will note that rates range from 14 to 70 percent. Before the 1964 tax reduction they ranged from 20 to 91 percent. Table 11–2 shows the savings resulting from the tax act of 1964.

The standard deduction is an allowance in lieu of itemized deductions and certain credits. Its use relieves you of substantiating your itemized deductions. But you still may claim any deduction which is allowable in determining adjusted gross income.

To obtain the standard deduction, if your adjusted gross income is $5,000 or more, take 10 percent of it. The standard deduction is limited, however, to $1,000 ($500 for a married taxpayer who files a separate return). As between the two ways of taking deductions (a) by itemizing them on page two of Form 1040 or (b) by taking the standard deduction, use the method which will produce the lower tax. If your itemized deductions total less than 10 percent of your adjusted gross income it will usually be to your advantage to claim the standard deduction.

You may pay your tax by cash, check, or money order. Check or money order are more advisable, since you have a receipt if you use the mail to file your return. Never send cash through the mail unregistered.

You have not filed a legal return unless you sign it. If you and your wife are filing a joint return, both of you must sign. You do not need to have your return notarized, since your signature has the same legal effect as swearing to the truthfulness of your return.

TABLE 11–1

TAX RATE SCHEDULES

INDIVIDUALS

(Other Than Head of Household or Surviving Spouse)

Taxable Years Beginning After December 31, 1964

TAXABLE INCOME	TAX
Not over $500	14% of the taxable income.
$ 500 to $ 1,000	$ 70 plus 15% of excess over $ 500
1,000 to 1,500	145 plus 16% of excess over 1,000
1,500 to 2,000	225 plus 17% of excess over 1,500
2,000 to 4,000	310 plus 19% of excess over 2,000
4,000 to 6,000	690 plus 22% of excess over 4,000
6,000 to 8,000	1,130 plus 25% of excess over 6,000
8,000 to 10,000	1,630 plus 28% of excess over 8,000
10,000 to 12,000	2,190 plus 32% of excess over 10,000
12,000 to 14,000	2,830 plus 36% of excess over 12,000
14,000 to 16,000	3,550 plus 39% of excess over 14,000
16,000 to 18,000	4,330 plus 42% of excess over 16,000
18,000 to 20,000	5,170 plus 45% of excess over 18,000
20,000 to 22,000	6,070 plus 48% of excess over 20,000
22,000 to 26,000	7,030 plus 50% of excess over 22,000
26,000 to 32,000	9,030 plus 53% of excess over 26,000
32,000 to 38,000	12,210 plus 55% of excess over 32,000
38,000 to 44,000	15,510 plus 58% of excess over 38,000
44,000 to 50,000	18,990 plus 60% of excess over 44,000
50,000 to 60,000	22,590 plus 62% of excess over 50,000
60,000 to 70,000	28,790 plus 64% of excess over 60,000
70,000 to 80,000	35,190 plus 66% of excess over 70,000
80,000 to 90,000	41,790 plus 68% of excess over 80,000
90,000 to 100,000	48,590 plus 69% of excess over 90,000
Over $100,000	55,490 plus 70% of excess over 100,000

MARRIED TAXPAYERS FILING JOINT RETURNS AND CERTAIN WIDOWS AND WIDOWERS

Taxable Years Beginning After December 31, 1964

TAXABLE INCOME	TAX
Not over $1,000	14% of the taxable income.
$ 1,000 to $ 2,000	$ 140 plus 15% of excess over $ 1,000
2,000 to 3,000	290 plus 16% of excess over 2,000
3,000 to 4,000	450 plus 17% of excess over 3,000
4,000 to 8,000	620 plus 19% of excess over 4,000
8,000 to 12,000	1,380 plus 22% of excess over 8,000
12,000 to 16,000	2,260 plus 25% of excess over 12,000
16,000 to 20,000	3,260 plus 28% of excess over 16,000
20,000 to 24,000	4,380 plus 32% of excess over 20,000
24,000 to 28,000	5,660 plus 36% of excess over 24,000
28,000 to 32,000	7,100 plus 39% of excess over 28,000
32,000 to 36,000	8,660 plus 42% of excess over 32,000
36,000 to 40,000	10,340 plus 45% of excess over 36,000
40,000 to 44,000	12,140 plus 48% of excess over 40,000
44,000 to 52,000	14,060 plus 50% of excess over 44,000
52,000 to 64,000	18,060 plus 53% of excess over 52,000
64,000 to 76,000	24,420 plus 55% of excess over 64,000
76,000 to 88,000	31,020 plus 58% of excess over 76,000
88,000 to 100,000	37,980 plus 60% of excess over 88,000
100,000 to 120,000	45,180 plus 62% of excess over 100,000
120,000 to 140,000	57,580 plus 64% of excess over 120,000
140,000 to 160,000	70,380 plus 66% of excess over 140,000
160,000 to 180,000	83,580 plus 68% of excess over 160,000
180,000 to 200,000	97,180 plus 69% of excess over 180,000
Over $200,000	110,980 plus 70% of excess over 200,000

SOURCE: U.S. Treasury Department.

TABLE 11–2

Savings Due to the Tax Act of 1964

Individuals Filing Separately

Years	Taxable Income						
	$10,000	$15,000	$20,000	$25,000	$30,000	$50,000	$100,000
1963	$2,640	$4,730	$7,260	$10,150	$13,220	$26,820	$67,320
1964	$2,360	$4,200	$6,450	$9,065	$11,840	$23,940	$59,340
1965	$2,190	$3,940	$6,070	$8,530	$11,150	$22,590	$55,490
Savings '64 over '63	$280	$530	$810	$1,085	$1,380	$2,880	$7,980
Savings '65 over '63	$450	$790	$1,190	$1,620	$2,070	$4,230	$11,830

Married Couple Filing Jointly

Years	Taxable Income						
	$10,000	$15,000	$20,000	$25,000	$30,000	$50,000	$100,000
1963	$2,200	$3,620	$5,280	$7,230	$9,460	$20,300	$53,640
1964	$1,950	$3,230	$4,720	$6,455	$8,400	$18,130	$47,880
1965	$1,820	$3,010	$4,380	$6,020	$7,880	$17,060	$45,180
Savings '64 over '63	$250	$390	$560	$775	$1,060	$2,170	$5,760
Savings '65 over '63	$380	$610	$900	$1,210	$1,580	$3,240	$8,460

SOURCE: Financial Planning Study Series: Kalb Voorhis & Co., 1964. Reproduced through the courtesy of Francis M. Simon, LL.M., Editor-in-Chief.

Examination of Returns

In filing your return, you determine the amount of tax you owe the government according to your own calculation. The return must, however, be examined by the government before the amount of tax liability is officially determined. If the government finds that more tax is due, you have the right to appeal. More than 95 percent of such disputes are settled by agreements between taxpayers and field offices of the Bureau of Internal Revenue. If they cannot agree, the taxpayer may appeal to the tax court or to the federal district court, circuit court, court of claims, or, finally, to the U.S. Supreme Court.

The government is allowed (by the applicable statute of limitations) three years from the filing of the return in which to examine it. This general rule is subject to three exceptions:

1. If a fraudulent return is filed, there is no limit to the time which the government may take to examine the return.
2. When no return is filed, the government may levy the amount it determines to be due at any time.
3. If more than 25 percent of total gross income reported is omitted from a return, the government has five years in which to assess a tax or to start court proceedings to collect.

Penalties

There are a whole series of penalties provided for in the tax law. There is a penalty for failing to file a declaration on time. A penalty is imposed if returns are not filed when originally due or within a period of extension, deferment, or postponement. A penalty in the form of interest at the rate of 6 percent must be paid on taxes not paid by their due date. A similar penalty is charged if a declaration is filed but installments are not paid on time. When the taxpayer is able to satisfy the Bureau of Internal Revenue that the delay was not caused by willful neglect but was the result of a reasonable cause, neither of these two penalties will be levied.

If a taxpayer underestimates his tax by more than 30 percent (33⅓ percent for farmers), a penalty may be levied. This penalty is not applicable if the taxpayer applied the current rates and exemptions to an amount not less than his previous year's income. There is, of course, no penalty if the sole reason for underestimation is an increase in tax rates. Severe fines and jail sentences may be imposed by the courts in cases involving large frauds.[8]

Minimizing Taxes

The higher your income, the more numerous are the ingenious techniques devised by clever tax lawyers to enable wealthy clients to minimize taxes. The methods are fascinating to read about, but they can seldom be used by people of moderate income and are usually of little use to those who depend primarily on wages or salaries for income.

Just for future reference when you climb up into the $25,000 and over annual income bracket, let's look at a few of them. First, you can arrange to divide your income among members of your family. How? By gifts, by family trusts, and by family corporations. A married man earning $30,000 pays about $10,000 in taxes. Assume his father dies and leaves him $50,000 (after estate taxes). If he invests it at 4 percent, he can keep less than half of the $2,000 income he would receive. He doesn't need the income and he feels it would be wasteful to receive it and then have to pay most of it in taxes. He has four children. They are young now, ages 1, 2, 3, and 4. Putting all four through college some day, he figures, will cost him about $10,000 each. He decides to create irrevocable trusts of $12,500 for each. Each will receive $500 a year income (at 4 percent) from his $12,500 trust until age 18 when the proceeds of the trusts will be paid to each over a four-year period to

---

[8] See E. L. Irey and W. J. Slocum, *The Tax Dodgers* (New York, 1948).

finance the costs of a college education. Thus the father, by turning over his $50,000 inheritance to his children in irrevocable trusts, saves the taxes on the annual $2,000 income. Since $500 annually goes to each of the children, they pay no tax on it because each has a $600 exemption. They remain $600 exemptions for the father since he continues to provide more than half their support.

A device, which is now being used by moderate income families, is the bunching of deductions in alternate years. In one year you take the standard 10 percent deduction. Deductions are then maximized by bunching into the second year the contributions, doctor's bills, property taxes, etc., which you would normally pay each year. Assume, for example, you normally give $100 to the Community Chest in December. You postpone this contribution until the next month, that is January of the following year, and then at the end of the year in December you give again as you normally do. Thus in the first year when you took the 10 percent standard deduction you make no contributions. In the following year you make your donations both at the beginning and end of the year. By doing this with as many deductions as you can, you maximize your legitimate deductions.

When you are in the upper brackets, capital gains look much more attractive than income. That's why many a corporate executive prefers a stock-option plan to a boost in salary. If you are in the 60 percent bracket a $10,000 increase in salary leaves you only $4,000, whereas an ability to buy shares of the company's stock and then sell them in the open market realizing a $10,000 gain will net the executive $7,500.

As an actual example, consider the option granted in 1956 to Mr. Thomas J. Watson, Jr., the president of the International Business Machines Corporation, giving him the right, *for ten years,* to buy a total of 11,464 shares of the company's stock at $91.80 per share. Subsequently the stock soared to $600 per share. Assume Mr. Watson exercised his rights and bought the 11,464 shares. They would have cost about $1,000,000. Had he sold them at $600 a share, he would have had a total profit of $5.8 million on which he would be taxed at the 25 percent capital gains rate. Had he exercised his rights but not sold the shares and held them until his death he would not pay any income or capital gains tax on this considerable profit.[9]

It is for this reason that many corporations in which insiders have large holdings deliberately keep dividend payments low. Plowing back earnings enhances the value of the company's stock and ultimately

---

[9] See Philip M. Stern, *The Great Treasury Raid,* Random House, New York, 1964.

means a handsome capital gain taxable only at 25 percent. If you fly down to the Virgin Islands and establish legal residence and thereafter buy and sell your securities through a Virgin Islands bank, the capital gains tax is only 12½ percent. It is surprising how many wealthy Americans are legal residents of the Virgin Islands. The fact that their wealth can be bequeathed with only a 5 percent estate tax is another powerful motivating factor.

Fortune reported that Mrs. Horace Dodge invested the entire estate her husband left her—$56,000,000—in tax-exempt state and municipal bonds and, assuming a return of 3½ percent, had an annual tax-free income of $1,960,000.

The corporate expense account has often in the past been a favorite device for shifting personal expenses which would otherwise be nondeductible to corporate deductible business expenses. Under the guise of "business," for example, corporate officials have gone to Florida in the winter and Europe in the summer, have had their liquor, theater, restaurant, medical, dental, hospital, insurance, pension and annuity, and country club bills paid by their companies. Taxwise it has paid to be an "organization man." The Internal Revenue Bureau has been clamping down on these corporate "fringe" benefits.

There are a good many other devices and techniques but by the time you get to the $25,000 bracket, some of the old loopholes will have been plugged and new ones opened.[10]

Conclusion

As you have undoubtedly gathered by now, taxes are a very complicated subject; and, aside from studying the instructions and forms carefully, you should get expert advice if you are in doubt. The district director's office will be glad to give you help at any time on a specific problem involving your own situation. Either visit the office or write. A hypothetical or theoretic question will not be answered, however. If you have a complicated tax situation, you would do well to consult a lawyer or an accountant with experience in handling tax matters. Their advice and suggestions may save you time, trouble, and money. Do not ever hesitate, however, to take the deductions and exemptions to which you feel you are really entitled. It is not fraud to become involved in a legitimate disagreement with the Internal Revenue Bureau. As Justice Learned Hand once held: "Nobody owes any public duty to pay more than the law demands."

---

[10] For a fascinating account see Philip M. Stern, *The Great Treasury Raid*, Random House, New York, 1964.

SUGGESTED READINGS

1. Treasury Department, Bureau of Internal Revenue, *Your Federal Income Tax—for Individuals,* Publication No. 17. Washington, D.C., latest edition. A copy may be obtained by writing to the Superintendent of Documents, U.S. Government Printing Office, Washington, D.C. 20402, and enclosing 40 cents.

2. Treasury Department, Bureau of Internal Revenue, *U.S. Income Tax Form 1040 and Instructions for [Year].* Washington, D.C., latest year. Free.

3. In *Changing Times, The Kiplinger Magazine:*
   a) "Income Taxes: Stick up for Your Rights," April, 1964.
   b) "Your Income Tax," March, 1964.
   c) "Your Income Tax," February, 1964.
   d) "Tax Help for Single People," March, 1963.
   e) "Yes, You *Can* Save on Taxes," February, 1963.
   f) "Do You *Really* Know the Tax Rules?" September, 1963.
   g) "Your Income Tax," January, 1963.
   h) "If the Tax Agent Calls You," April, 1962.

4. Philip M. Stern, *The Great Treasury Raid.* Random House, New York, 1964.

5. *Federal Tax Course.* New Jersey: Prentice-Hall, Inc., latest year.

6. *Tax Ideas.* New Jersey: Prentice-Hall, Inc., latest year.

7. *Individual Federal Income Tax Specimen Returns, Completely Worked Out for Filing in [Year].* New Jersey: Prentice-Hall, Inc., latest year.

8. *Automobile Income Tax Deductions,* latest annual edition, American Automobile Association. A free copy may be obtained by writing to the Association at 1712 G Street, N.W., Washington, D.C. 20406.

9. "The Deductibility of Expenses: A Professor's Research and a Study in His Home," William W. Oliver, *AAUP* Bulletin, Vol. 50, No. 1, March, 1964.

10. *Explanation of the Revenue Act of 1964.* Prentice-Hall, Executive Report, 1964.

11. *Travel, Entertainment, and Gift Expenses,* Internal Revenue Service Publication No. 463. Washington, D.C., latest edition. A copy may be obtained by writing to the Superintendent of Documents, U.S. Government Printing Office, Washington, D.C. 20402 and enclosing 15 cents.

12. *How to Prepare Your Personal Income Tax Return.* New Jersey: Prentice-Hall, Inc., issued annually.

13. *Investor's Tax Guide,* issued annually by Merrill Lynch, Pierce, Fenner & Smith. A free copy may be obtained by writing to this firm at 70 Pine Street, New York, N.Y. 10005.

14. *How to Prepare Your [Year] Tax Returns.* New York: Research Institute of America, latest year.

15. Practising Law Institute Monographs, New York. Current monographs:
    Introduction to the Income Tax, by Freeman and Levinson.
    Items of Gross Income, by Riggs and Levinson.

Deductions, Exemptions and Credits, by Molloy and Warren.
Capital Gains and Losses, by Moroney, Moser, and Hornett.
Gain or Loss on Sales and Exchanges, by Moroney, Colgan, and Anthoine.

16. *Tax Guide for Small Business,* Internal Revenue Service Publication No. 334. Washington, D.C.: U.S. Government Printing Office, latest edition. Price 40 cents.

17. *Farmer's Tax Guide,* Internal Revenue Service Publication No. 225. Washington, D.C.: U.S. Treasury Department. Free.

CASE PROBLEMS

1. John Daly sells magazines on commission in the city of Chicago and its suburbs. He finds it necessary to use his automobile a good deal in order to reach favorable areas in which to sell. Only infrequently is it possible for him to eat his luncheons at home during the week; occasionally he is forced to have dinner at a restaurant or hotel when he stays on his job until it becomes dark. To what extent may he deduct these expenses on his income-tax return?

2. Roswell traded his Chevrolet club coupé for a new Ford Galaxie. The dealer allowed $1,175 for the old car toward the purchase of the new automobile, which cost $2,600. Roswell had driven the Chevrolet 21,962 miles during the three years he owned it, traveling between home and work and for general family use. What are the income-tax implications?

3. Stanlaw earns $8,000 a year. He owns a camp on an island in a lake. Heavy rains cause the water in the lake to rise so high that damage of $2,500 is done to his boathouse and dock. Insurance which he has been carrying reimburses him the next year to the extent of $500. Which of these items enters into his income-tax calculations? Why?

4. When Maddox and his wife were 64 years of age and had an adjusted gross income of $6,500, their medical expenses were $5,200 and those of their daughter, a junior in college, were $256.

The following year, with an adjusted gross income of $6,100, their medical expenses amounted to $3,200 and those of their daughter were $186.

How much could they deduct for medical expenses in each year?

5. Mary Jane Hancock is a widow with two children (ages 3 and 5). To help support her family, she works as a secretary at $100 a week. She finds it necessary to employ a housekeeper at $40 a week. In her estimation, the housekeeper costs her at least $5 more a week because of the food she eats. To what extent does the federal income-tax law make provision for the housekeeper?

6. Biddle bought a six-acre tract of land for $2,400. He divided the tract into 24 house lots. Improvements (roads, sewers, sidewalks, etc.) cost him $7,200. By November of the first year, he was ready to begin selling lots, but he had to wait for the selling season in the following spring. From June to August, he sold 16 lots—all he sold during the year. These lots were sold for

$1,200 each. Biddle paid salesmen commissions of 25 percent for effecting the sales. What was the taxable profit? What can you tell about the tax?

7. Kerensky bought a two-family frame house for $12,000 as of January 2. He estimated that the lot was worth $2,000. During the year he paid interest of $450, real estate taxes of $380, and fire insurance of $38. Miscellaneous painting cost him $24, and carpentry work for repairing the front steps amounted to $37. A new roof, guaranteed for 15 years, was installed for $693. The upper part of the house was rented throughout the year to Mrs. Kerensky's brother and his family at $70 a month. How should these facts appear on the joint tax return of the Kerenskys?

8. Kirkland earns $10,000 a year and lives with his wife and two children (ages 13 and 17). In computing his estimated tax for the year, Kirkland took an exemption of $600 for each of the children. By December 31, it is learned that the younger child earned $18 for baby sitting (for which no tax was withheld) and that the 17-year-old boy earned $728 (from which $15.60 was withheld) for his work as a caddy. Now what must be done?

9. In January, Dirksen estimates that he will earn $6,500 in the current year. During the prior three years he was desperately ill and used up all his savings, but he is now fully recovered and back on the job. He calculates that the total tax on his earnings will be $1,430, but at the rate at which his employer is withholding for taxes from his salary, the total amount withheld for the year will be $1,280. The balance of $150 which he will have to pay as tax is brought about largely through his earnings from outside work on which no tax is withheld. Dirksen, because of his illness, feels out of touch with the federal income tax law. He asks you to refresh his memory as to his obligations under that law.

10. Putman is a teacher earning $4,200 a year. He lives in a Southern community with his wife and two children (ages 2 and 4). His summer vacation period was spent at a school 1,000 miles from home, where he earned $800. Expenses of $382 were incurred by him for travel, meals, and lodging in connection with this employment. Should he use Form 1040A or Form 1040? How should the above facts be entered on the return?

11. In March, 1964, Smith bought a house as a residence for himself and his family at a cost of $15,000. During the next two years, he spent $1,000 for improvements to the house. In March, 1966, he sold the house for $18,000. Six months later, in September, 1966, he bought another home for $22,000. What are the income-tax implications?

12 INTRODUCTION TO INVESTMENTS

> A bull can make money in Wall Street; a bear can
> make money in Wall Street; but a hog never can.
> —Not Confucius

THRIFT IS a wonderful virtue, especially in an ancestor," someone said. If your father or grandfather had the foresight to buy 300 shares of Minnesota Mining and Manufacturing in 1913 at $1.00 a share, then 300 shares would have become 57,600 shares as a result of successive stock splits. Each share is worth about $65 at current market prices, bringing the value of the original modest investment of $300 up to $3,700,000. What's more, the investment would also now yield $57,600 a year in dividends.

Or perhaps one of your ancestors bought 100 shares of International Business Machines (IBM) in 1914 at a cost of $2,750. Without further cash investment, as a result of stock splits and stock dividends, this would now amount to 15,433 shares with a market value of $9,051,454. In addition, cash dividends of $398,200 were paid through March, 1964, and the proceeds from the sale of stock rights during the period amounted to $54,900. Over the past decade, the market price of IBM zoomed from around $33 to $607 at its peak.[1]

Nor are investment opportunities of this type a matter of the past. They have been available in recent years as well. For example, to cite four cases: (*a*) A $1,000 investment in Food Machinery stock in 1932 was worth $100,000 by 1946. (*b*) The old Homestake Mining gold stock rose from 81 in 1931 to 544 in 1936. (*c*) The stock of the Cross Company soared from $1.00 a share in 1950 to $80 in 1955. (*d*) Control Data rose from 37½ cents a share (adjusted for a stock split) in 1958 to a high of $113 in 1963. Now if you'd like to know more about

---

[1] Had all rights been exercised total investment through 1963 would have amounted to $225,704. Present shareholdings would be 25,938 with a market value of $15,212,637. Cash dividends paid through March, 1964, would have totalled $644,300.

the fascinating subject of investments, the next few chapters offer a brief introduction.

Single Proprietorships

In general, business is organized as (*a*) single proprietorships, (*b*) partnerships, and (*c*) corporations. A business operated by an individual as a single proprietorship does not issue stocks and bonds. Ordinarily, such a business has no piece of paper which evidences ownership in it (unless there is a bill of sale). It belongs to its owner just as his house, clothing, or dog belongs to him. He merely uses his property, or part of it, in conducting a business. If there are debts of the business, they are also his debts, for which he is liable without limit. These debts are usually accounts payable (evidenced by no formal paper) or notes payable (secured or unsecured).

Partnerships

A partnership is a business operated under an agreement by two or more individuals (partners). It does not issue stocks and bonds. The only formal evidence of ownership that is commonly found in such an organization is a written partnership agreement which sets forth the various interests and rights of the partners. Partnerships are governed by special laws applicable to partnerships, but in general the partners are liable without limit for the debts of the partnership.

Corporations; Common and Preferred Stocks

It is only the corporation which issues stocks and bonds. When we are stockholders, we own part or all of a corporation; when we are bondholders, we are creditors of a corporation. A corporation in the eyes of the law is a legal entity apart from its owners. It is itself a legal person brought into existence under an act of the legislature. In legal language, a corporation is an artificial (not natural) entity (being) existing only in contemplation of law. This artificial person (the corporation) has only the rights and privileges which its creator (the legislature or lawmaking body) gives it. Ordinarily it has such rights as the power to own property in its own name, incur obligations to others (debts), sue, and be sued. This artificial person, which commonly is the possessor of valuable properties, is owned by its stockholders. As evidence of their ownership, they hold printed or engraved certificates of ownership known as "stock certificates." An individual certificate may show ownership of one or more shares or interests in the corporation. When all shares have the same rights in the corporation, they are known as "common shares" or "common stocks." If some of the shares have superior rights (as compared with other shares) to dividends or assets in event of liquidation (termination) of the corporation, they are "preferred shares."

Federal and State Charters

Both the federal legislature (Congress) and our state legislatures can create corporations, but most, nowadays, are given their charters by the states. Formerly the legislatures voted in each case whether or not to charter an individual corporation. If they persisted in this practice today, when so many corporations are formed, they would have little time for anything else. At present, therefore, it is customary for a legislature to pass an enabling act, a general incorporation law, whereby those who follow the provisions in the act may apply to the designated authorities for a charter. This makes application for a charter a fairly straightforward procedure; but since some states are more generous toward corporations than others, there is always the question of determining in which state to apply. The corporate charter dictates the amount of stock, common and preferred, which is authorized. That part of the authorized stock which is issued and outstanding (usually in return for cash, property, or services) constitutes the ownership of the corporation.

Limited Liability

When we discussed single proprietors and partners, it was said that ordinarily they are liable for debts of their businesses without limit. In the case of the single proprietor, this means that if the business cannot pay its debts, the proprietor must pay them with other private funds if he has them. Whenever a partnership cannot pay its bills, the partners can be compelled to pay them out of any other of their personal resources. The stockholders of a corporation are in a happier position. Remember that the law regards the corporation itself as a person; if the corporation cannot pay its bills, nobody else has to pay its bills for it. Thus, the shareholders have limited liability; they can lose only what they have invested in the corporation. It is for this reason that after a corporate name in England and Canada we find the word "Limited," usually abbreviated to "Ltd." (for example, British Empire Steel Corporation, Ltd.).

Classes of Common Stock

Occasionally one finds common stock divided into two classes—A and B, for example. Although common stock generally has voting power, it may be found that one class has voting control and the other is denied it. When the Dodge brothers sold their automobile company, a new company was formed to buy the business. The latter sold securities of several types to the public (including nonvoting common stock) to raise money for the purchase. Finally, a relatively small block of voting common stock was sold to the Chrysler Corporation, thus giving Chrysler the control of the Dodge operation which permitted Chrysler to consider Dodge cars a product of Chrysler. This is not the only instance of nonvoting common stock in the automobile business. Henry Ford died in 1947, at which time he owned about 1,900,000 shares in the Ford Motor Company. He left most of his holdings (1,805,000 shares) as a tax-free gift to a charity, the Ford Foundation, but this stock had no voting power. The rest of his stock (95,000) had all the voting power and was bequeathed to his heirs; it vested control of the company in them. The net result was that the Ford family was saved the difficulty of trying to raise a huge sum for taxes, although it retained control of the business, and the world got the benefit of a large part of the wealth which the free-enterprise system allowed Henry Ford to accumulate.

Despite its occasional use, nonvoting common stock is frowned upon as a general proposition. It is felt that if common stock is residual with respect to income (gets only what is left), it should, at least, have the power to vote. Since 1926, nonvoting common stock has not been eligible for listing on the New York Stock Exchange, and it is not often encountered today in the United States, though it is quite usual in Canada.

Par and No-Par Stock

Prior to 1912, when New York State first permitted the issue of no-par stock, all stock issued had to have a face or par value. This was the value mentioned in the stock certificate. To creditors it was supposed to mean that that much money or its equivalent had been given by the stockholders to the corporation in return for the stock (as a fund for creditors' protection), or that the creditors could sue to have the deficiency paid to the corporation if it sold the stock for less than par (at a discount).

Although the par value may have meant something at or about the time the stock was issued originally, after a while it became practically meaningless; few stocks continued to sell at anything like their par value. In fact, some people were deceived into thinking that a stock selling for $45 must be worth more because a par value of the more or less customary amount of $100 was mentioned on the stock certificate.

Today, most states provide for the issue of no-par-value shares. They can be sold for whatever they will bring in the market. There is at present a fairly widespread view that par value is only a legal fiction. Thus it is recognized that no-par stock represents a share of ownership which is valued from time to time at whatever investors estimate it is worth. In contrast, par-value stock is tagged with an artificial fixed value, which seldom remains the market's valuation for long. For example, E. I. du Pont has a par value of 5 for its common, which has ranged in the market from a low of 22 to a high of 278. Coca-Cola common has no par value; the market price has ranged from 18 to 121. No-par stock may be sold initially at whatever the market will bring.

In many cases today, primarily for tax purposes, corporations assign a nominal stated value of $5.00 or $10.00 a share to their stock when initially issued, regardless of the price at which stock is first sold. The investor today is generally little concerned whether stock has par value or no-par value or stated value. Market value is the important consideration.

Book Value, Market Value, Earnings Value

What is a given share of common stock worth? This is a key question which has been discussed and written about extensively. It is clearly not related to par value. Is it book value? Book value may be defined as the total assets (using values carried on the company's books) of the company less its debts and preferred stock. It is the value at which the common shares are carried on the company's books together with the surplus and reserves. It is largely an accounting concept and usually not too useful.

Market value is the price set in the market as a result of the forces of supply and demand at work. It's what one person is willing to pay for a share and what another person is willing to sell it for—one man's bid, another man's asking price. Market value or market price, however, doesn't tell you whether the stock is a good buy or a poor buy; whether it is expensive or cheap. The price of a certain company's share may be high because few shares are outstanding. Superior Oil Company's shares sell from $1,200 to $1,500 per share. Another company's shares may sell at low prices because there are a great many shares outstanding.

What is more important in determining the value of the shares of a company over the long run? The answer is earnings and dividends. To state it, at this point, as simply as possible, shares tend to sell over the longer run at a multiple of earnings. For example, if the company is likely to earn $3.00 a share next year and stocks tend to sell at 15 times earnings, then the shares should be worth and sell at $45 a share. For certain growth stocks whose earnings are expected to grow rapidly from year to year, a higher multiple may be regarded as appropriate—25 times prospective earnings, for example. In that case the stock should sell at $75 a share based on prospective earnings of $3.00 a share next year.[2]

Common Stocks as an Investment

Since common stocks are residual as to assets and earnings, the common stockholders may, in the event of reorganization or liquidation, receive what is left after ordinary creditors, bonds, and preferred stocks have had their rights satisfied. Furthermore, common stocks are subject to risk and fluctuations in value varying with the earnings and profits of the corporation and with the business cycle.

The three chief advantages of common stock, however, which have had a strong appeal to investors are (a) ability to participate financially in the economic growth of the country over the next few decades, (b) capital gains, and (c) a hedge against inflation.

Common stock investment is likely to be one of the most effective financial means of participating in the coming enormous growth and change in the American economy over the next generation. It is estimated that our present population will have grown to 245 million by 1980 and to 331 million by the year 2000. We will produce four times as much by 2000. GNP will have grown from $500 billion in 1960 to $1,000 billion in 1980 and to $2,200 billion in 2000. Consumers bought 7 million cars per year in the early 1960's. In 1980 they are likely to buy 14 million cars and by the year 2000 some 28 million a year.[3] Financial sharing in the economic rewards of such growth can be obtained by judicious investment in common stock.

By judicious investment substantial capital gains can be realized in common stocks. Such gains are not possible, of course, in fixed-dollar obligations, such as bonds, savings accounts, etc. For example, you could have picked up shares of the common stock of Northern Pacific Railroad, before World War II, for a low of $3.75 and a dozen years

---

[2] It's more complicated than this, but this gives you an idea of the method of valuing common stocks. For more detail see Chapter 6, "Common Stocks," in William C. Freund and Murray G. Lee, *Investment Fundamentals* (New York: The American Bankers Association, 1960); also Part Four, "The Valuation of Common Stock" in Benjamin Graham, David L. Dodd, and Sidney Cottle, *Security Analysis: Principles and Techniques* (New York: McGraw-Hill Book Co., Inc., 1962).

[3] See Henry Steele Commager, "The Nation: A Visit in the Year 2000," *The New York Times Magazine*, April 16, 1964, p. 88.

later sold them for as much as $94.37. In the case of Du Pont, it could have been purchased in the late thirties for $22 (adjusted for stock split) and sold in recent years as high as $278 per share. Minnesota Mining and Manufacturing went from 50 cents (adjusted) per share to $88; International Business Machines from $40 a share to over $600; and Amerada Petroleum from $2.00 (adjusted) a share to $81. You have to exercise careful judgment to find and time these capital gains correctly. Some people bought A. T. & T. at $310 a share in 1929 and had to sell it at $70 a share in 1933. More recently, others may have bought United Dye and Chemical at $35 a share and later had to sell it at $2.00 a share. Certain types of investors who are interested in capital gains rather than steady or high income look for "special situations" or for "growth stocks," both of which are especially conducive to yielding capital gains. This will be discussed subsequently.

Common Stocks as a Hedge against Inflation

Common stocks are usually regarded as a good hedge against inflation. From time to time in our history, the rise in the price level has reduced the purchasing power of the dollar, so that those who have to live on fixed, or relatively fixed, dollar incomes find themselves seriously pinched. It has become customary to speak of a 50-cent dollar. What is meant, of course, is that because of the rise in the price level and the decline in the value of the dollar, the dollar now buys only 50 percent as much goods as did a dollar in 1939 or 1940. Thus you need more dollars if you want to buy the same amount of food, clothing, shelter, entertainment, etc., i.e., maintain your standard of living. The decline in the purchasing power of the dollar over the last century and a half may be seen in Figure 12–1. Stock prices, however, rose as commodity prices advanced; and while there were occasional setbacks in both, as in 1929–33, the secular (long-term) trend of the two series since 1900 has been upward.

One's purchasing power would, by *average* common stock investment, have been preserved; and that is why we speak of common stocks as being a hedge against inflation. The long-term, secular, upward trend of common stock prices may be seen in Figure 12–2. Occasionally a long-term, common stock investment will do considerably more than protect against secular inflation. An investment of 100 shares of Eastman Kodak, bought for $10,000 in 1901, would now be worth, with dividends, about $2.4 million, while 100 shares of Sears, Roebuck bought in 1906 at $5,700 would now be worth about $2.5 million. Consider this in another light. In 1914 the French franc was worth

FIGURE 12–1

PURCHASING POWER OF THE DOLLAR

1939 DOLLAR EQUALS 100 CENTS

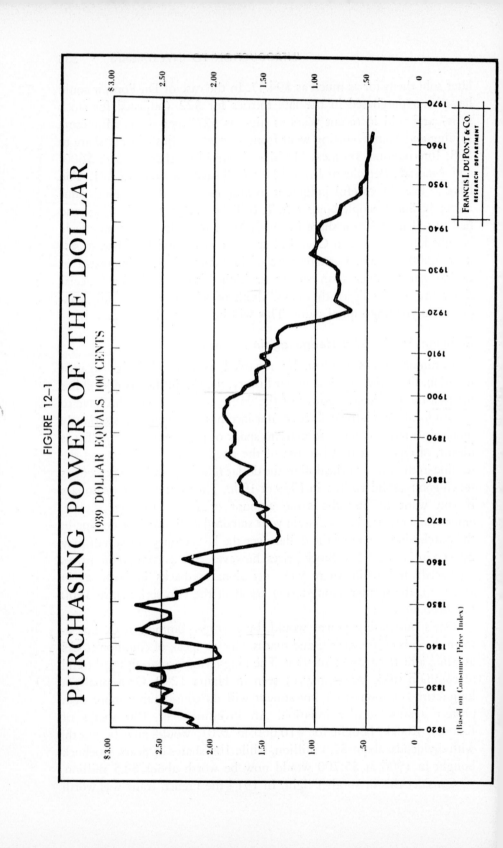

(Based on Consumer Price Index)

FRANCIS I. DU PONT & CO.
RESEARCH DEPARTMENT

Trading Range of Dow-Jones Industrial Stock Average

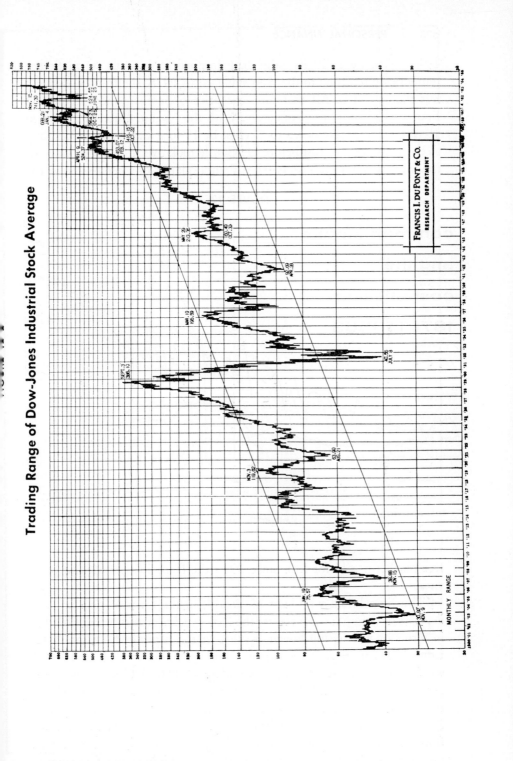

19½ cents; by 1920 its value had dropped to 7 cents; when France temporarily returned to the gold standard in 1928, the franc was worth less than 4 cents. All that time the price of stocks (and of gold) in France was rising proportionately. With the Nazi invasion of France in 1940 the franc went down to 2 cents; by 1946 it was down to less than a cent (0.84 cent). Just before De Gaulle took over the official value of the franc was but 0.23 cents—less than a quarter of a cent—and in the

FIGURE 12–3

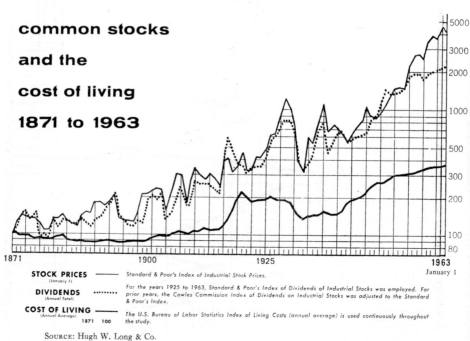

common stocks

and the

cost of living

1871 to 1963

STOCK PRICES ———— Standard & Poor's Index of Industrial Stock Prices.
(January 1)

DIVIDENDS ·········· For the years 1925 to 1963, Standard & Poor's Index of Dividends of Industrial Stocks was employed. For
(Annual Total) prior years, the Cowles Commission Index of Dividends on Industrial Stocks was adjusted to the Standard
& Poor's Index.

COST OF LIVING ————
(Annual Average) The U.S. Bureau of Labor Statistics Index of Living Costs (annual average) is used continuously throughout
1871 100 the study.

SOURCE: Hugh W. Long & Co.

free market it sold for less. Since 1914 the franc lost 99 percent of its value.

The Frenchman who kept his wealth in the form of cash or bank deposits or savings accounts over the last 40 years probably had little left in terms of purchasing power because of the continued decline in the value of his money. If he owned a million francs in cash in 1914, it would have bought what approximately $200,000 U.S. dollars could purchase at that time. If he had kept his million francs in cash and spent them just before the revaluation of the franc, they would buy only what $2,380 U.S. dollars can purchase today. But if he had put his million francs in select common stocks or in gold in 1914, he would have preserved his purchasing power over the years. Living costs, for example, rose 1,800 percent in France during and after World War II; common stock prices almost kept pace—they rose 1,600 percent.

Clearly, common stock prices more than keep pace with the rise in the price level and provide an excellent hedge against inflation.[4] This may be seen in Figure 12–3.

A study by Hugh Long & Co. indicates that living costs rose in 58 percent of the one-year periods since 1871 and in 61 percent of the ten-year periods. When longer periods were tabulated, it was found that living costs increased in 60 percent of the fifteen-year periods, 77 percent of the twenty-year periods and in 94 percent of the thirty-year spans. Whether they have invested for one year or longer, investors have had inflation in store for them more than half the time since 1871. Over twenty-year spans they have experienced inflation three quarters of the time; over thirty-year spans, nearly all this time. Stock prices rose in 66 percent of the one-year inflationary periods and in 9 out of 10 of the longer periods of rising prices. Since 1871 common stock prices have increased in value in 95 percent of the twenty-year periods and in all thirty-year periods of rising living costs. Increases in stock prices matched or bettered increases in the cost of living in 68 percent of all ten-year periods, 77 percent of the fifteen-year periods, 89 percent of all twenty-year periods, and 90 percent of all thirty-year periods of inflation and rising stock prices.

But Stocks Can Go Down Too

Two limitations should be noted. First, the results shown for the past are not necessarily indicative of results to be expected in the future. The next decade may not be as inflationary as the last. If there is deflation, of course, common stock values shrink. The investor who has bought common stock outright (not on margin) in sound companies and who can afford to hold (is not forced by need for funds to sell) may not be hurt at all by a short-period deflation, but one who is forced to sell may be hurt severely. Table 12–1 shows what happened to the unlucky investor who went into the market in 1929, picked a dozen sound stocks, but was forced to sell in 1932 to obtain funds on which to live.[5] Obviously, as good as common stocks are as a hedge against long-

---

[4] See *Common Stocks and the Cost of Living, 1871–1963* (Elizabeth, N.J.: Hugh W. Long & Co.).

[5] For a fascinating account of the stock-market boom of the late twenties, the 1929 crash, and the immediate aftermath see Frederick Lewis Allen, *Only Yesterday* (New York: Harper & Bros., 1931), and Edward Angly, *Oh, Yeah* (New York: Viking Press, 1931). See also John Kenneth Galbraith, *The Great Crash, 1929* (Boston: Houghton Mifflin Co., 1955).

TABLE 12–1

A Dozen Good Common Stocks, 1929–32

COMPANY	1929	1932
Anaconda Copper	174⅞	3
A. T. & T.	310¼	70¼
Chrysler Corporation	87	5
Du Pont	503	22
General Motors	224	7⅝
Montgomery Ward	156⅞	3½
New York Central	256½	8¾
Standard Oil of New Jersey	83	19⅞
Standard Oil of California	81⅞	15⅛
Sears, Roebuck	197½	9⅞
U.S. Steel	261¾	21¼
Western Union	272¼	12⅜

term secular inflation, the investor who may be forced to sell in a shorter-term deflation hardly finds this an advantage.

The second limitation is that, even in an inflationary decade, some stocks do not move up; and if you are not careful and selective, you may acquire some of these. Table 12–2 shows how some well-known issues, after one of the most inflationary decades in U.S. history, were, in 1950, selling at or below their 1940 average prices and were paying prewar dividend rates or less.

TABLE 12–2

Market Laggards, 1940–50

	AVERAGE PRICE		DIVIDEND	
STOCK	1940	1950	1940	1950
Air Reduction	47	25	$1.75	$1.00
A. T. & T.	160	154	9.00	9.00
American Tobacco	78	70	5.00	4.00
Chesapeake & Ohio R. R.	37	30	3.50	1.50
North American Aviation	21	15	1.25	1.25
Standard Brands	22	22	2.00	1.70
United Aircraft	31	26	3.33	1.67
United Shoe Machinery	54	45	4.00	2.50
U.S. Tobacco	26	20	1.50	1.35

SOURCE: Robert D. Merritt, *Financial Independence through Common Stocks* (Boston: United Business Service, 1952), p. 278.

Who Owns Common Stock

Wall Street and its counterparts in other American cities—La Salle Street in Chicago, Montgomery Street in San Francisco, Marietta Street in Atlanta, and State Street in Boston—now teem with investors.

There are now more than 17 million shareholders. This represented an increase of more than 10 million over the decade. See Table 12–3. Nearly one out of six adults is now a shareowner as compared with one out of sixteen a decade ago. Women shareholders outnumber men—51 percent female, 49 percent male. The average shareholder has an annual household income of $8,600. Of the 17 million shareowners 63.6 percent had household incomes of under $10,000, while 36.4 percent

TABLE 12–3

Highlights of Four NYSE Shareowner Census Surveys

		ESTIMATED		
	1952	1956	1959	1962
No. of Individual Shareowners (Thous.)	6,490	8,630	12,490	17,010
No. Owning Shares Listed on NYSE (Thous.)	n.a.	6,880	8,510	11,015
Shareowner Incidence to Adult Population	1 in 16	1 in 12	1 in 8	1 in 6
Median Household Income	$7,100	$6,200	$7,000	$8,600
No. of Shareowners With Household Income:				
Under $7,500** (Thous.)	n.a.	5,438	6,720	6,666
Over $7,500** (Thous.)	n.a.	3,042	5,564	10,040
No. of Adult Female Shareowners + (Thous.)	3,140	4,260	6,347	8,291
No. of Adult Male Shareowners + (Thous.)	3,210	4,020	5,740	7,965
Median Age	51	48	49	48
No. of Issues Owned by Average Shareowner	4.1	4.25	3.5	3.4

** 304,000 shareowners not classified by income in 1962; 206,000 in 1959; and 150,000 in 1956.

+ 304,000 shareowners not classified as to sex in 1962; 206,000 in 1959; 350,000 in 1956; and 140,000 in 1952.

n.a. not available.

SOURCE: New York Stock Exchange.

had incomes of $10,000 or more. Only 4.8 percent had household incomes of $25,000 or more. The median age of the shareholder population is 48 compared with 39 for those who have become shareholders for the first time since 1959. Four out of five shareowners are high school graduates. One out of three is a college graduate. The average shareholder lives in a middle-sized city. If his home is in a metropolis, however, it is more likely to be San Francisco than Chicago or New York (26.6 percent of San Francisco's residents hold stock, as against 14.4 percent in New York, and 13.8 percent in Chicago). Among the states, Connecticut has the highest shareowner density (18.1 percent). Nearly 5.5 million housewives comprise the largest single group of shareowners; 15 percent of all housewives own stock. Approximately 36 percent of all professional men, 33 percent of managers and proprietors, and 25 percent of all sales and clerical workers own shares.[6]

Investment Objectives and Common Stocks

You would not think of going into a drugstore and asking for a dollar's worth of medicine. You would want a certain kind of medicine to treat a particular condition or illness. In just the same fashion, you do not buy $1,000 worth of securities. You want a certain type of security to meet a particular aim or objective. Generally, three major objectives are discernible in investments: growth (or capital gains or appreciation), income (either high or moderate with stability), and safety (no dollar loss of capital invested). The largest brokerage house in the country, Merrill Lynch, Pierce, Fenner & Smith, classifies the three major kinds of securities in terms of these objectives as shown in the accompanying tabulation:[7]

TYPE OF SECURITY	GROWTH	INCOME	SAFETY
Common stock	Best	Variable	Least
Preferred stock	Variable	Steady	Good
Bonds	Generally none	Very steady	Best

---

[6] For more detail see Michael D. Reagan, "What 17 Million Shareholders Share," *The New York Times Magazine*, February 23, 1964; see also *The 17 Million: 1962 Census of Shareowners in America*, New York Stock Exchange, 1962. A free copy of this and of the annual *Fact Book* may be obtained by writing to the Exchange at 11 Wall Street, New York, N.Y., 10005.

[7] From *How to Invest*, published by Merrill Lynch, Pierce, Fenner & Smith, New York (latest edition). A free copy may be obtained on request by writing to this company at 70 Pine St., New York, N.Y., 10005.

But there are important qualifications to this table. Not all stocks are growth stocks, as we shall see. Common stocks are, on the average, better for growth than are other types of securities, because they reflect the earning power and the prospects of a company. Common stocks are called "equities" because they receive what is left out of earnings after the companies' fixed charges are paid. Since what is left over goes to common stockholders, when a company prospers and its earnings rise, almost all the increase goes to benefit the common stock.

Another qualification is that while, for the whole range of common stocks, income is characterized as variable, some common stocks have paid regular dividends for decades and have been a steadier source of income than many of the railroad bonds which went into default over the first half of the century. But some common stocks have not done so well. Judgment and selection play an important role, and that is why we speak of common stock income as "variable."

Again, to say that common stocks are "least" safe, using a term of comparison, may perhaps give the impression that they are *not* safe. This is not what is meant. Many common stocks are not only good, safe investments; they have survived more business setbacks than many bonds, which, though originally considered safe, subsequently went into default. The common stock of the Bank of New York, which has paid dividends uninterruptedly for more than 175 years, is a much safer investment than were the bonds of the Missouri Pacific Railroad. Generally speaking, though, common stocks vary more in price than either preferred stocks or bonds. If by "safety" is meant the assured return of the same number of dollars one put into an investment, then there is no certainty that a given common stock will, if sold next year, bring in the same number of dollars paid for it today. If you must sell in the downward phase of the business and price cycle, then common stocks may not return the same number of dollars, but the fixed-value security (bonds) faces an inflation hazard in the upward phase of the cycle.

Common stock price appreciation preserves purchasing power in the inflationary phase, whereas the fixed-value security, even though it may return the same number of dollars, shrinks in real terms. This may be seen in Figure 12–4. Furthermore, the same disability attaches to the income of fixed-value securities (see Fig. 12–5). Therefore, one must conclude that, in investments, safety is a relative term; that in seeking safety or protection against certain hazards, such as price decline, you necessarily expose yourself to hazards of other types, such as loss of purchasing power due to inflation. There is, then, in investments, never absolute safety.

FIGURE 12-4

Stocks vs Bonds—for Preserving Real Capital Value

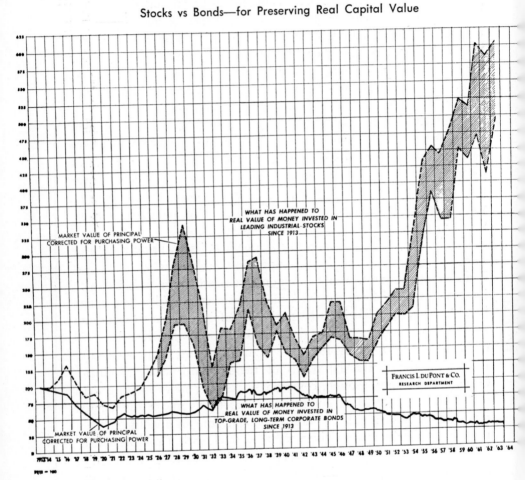

Objectives and Types of Common Stock

A young man, with good earning power, who has surplus funds to invest will seek a very different kind of investment than an elderly couple who must live on the income from a $100,000 lifetime accumulation which they have invested. The young man will either seek speculative gains, or, if he is wiser, will invest in growth stocks, which, over the years, will yield substantial capital gains, though current income may be low. The elderly couple will seek as high an income as they can attain consistent with stability and relative safety.

"Growth stocks" are those of companies usually, though not always,

FIGURE 12–5

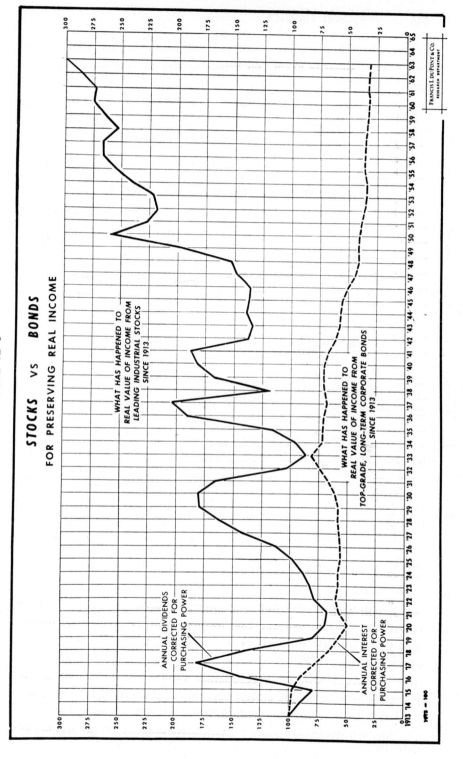

STOCKS vs BONDS
FOR PRESERVING REAL INCOME

WHAT HAS HAPPENED TO
REAL VALUE OF INCOME FROM
LEADING INDUSTRIAL STOCKS
SINCE 1913

WHAT HAS HAPPENED TO
REAL VALUE OF INCOME FROM
TOP-GRADE, LONG-TERM CORPORATE BONDS
SINCE 1913

ANNUAL DIVIDENDS
CORRECTED FOR
PURCHASING POWER

ANNUAL INTEREST
CORRECTED FOR
PURCHASING POWER

1913 '14 '15 '16 '17 '18 '19 '20 '21 '22 '23 '24 '25 '26 '27 '28 '29 '30 '31 '32 '33 '34 '35 '36 '37 '38 '39 '40 '41 '42 '43 '44 '45 '46 '47 '48 '49 '50 '51 '52 '53 '54 '55 '56 '57 '58 '59 '60 '61 '62 '63 '64 '65

1913 = 100

FRANCIS I. DU PONT & CO.
RESEARCH DEPARTMENT

paying relatively low current returns because earnings are being plowed back. They are considered attractive because of future prospects. In earnings they have been doing better than the industry average or are expected to do so. The rate of growth must be greater than the rate of population increase. Furthermore, earnings tend to move forward from cycle to cycle and are only temporarily interrupted by business recessions.

TABLE 12-4

HOW GROWTH STOCKS GROW

	1953	1963
American Cyanamid	$1,000	$ 2,615
Bristol-Myers	1,000	15,671
Caterpillar Tractor	1,000	5,356
Corning Glass Works	1,000	5,548
Factor (Max)	1,000	23,484
General Electric	1,000	3,320
Grumman Aircraft	1,000	2,540
Gulf Life Insurance	1,000	4,336
International Business Machines	1,000	14,557
Magnavox	1,000	18,556
Minneapolis-Honeywell	1,000	3,500
Minnesota Mining & Manufacturing	1,000	7,235
Pacific Gas & Electric	1,000	2,601
Pitney-Bowes	1,000	7,557
Polaroid	1,000	33,777
Procter & Gamble	1,000	5,071
Radio Corporation of America	1,000	3,106
Safeway Stores	1,000	4,857
Texaco	1,000	5,646
Union Bank (Los Angeles)	1,000	8,681

The adjacent table shows how a $1,000 cash investment in any of 20 different stocks would have grown since mid-1953. Most of these issues were regarded as growth stocks ten years ago; all of them are so regarded now.

Thanks in part to a very strong market, a number of these equities sell at or very close to their all-time highs, including such well known companies as American Cyanamid, Corning Glass, Safeway Stores, and Texaco.

On the other hand, despite the historic levels of the stock market and the peak prices for many issues, there are some exceptionally well known growth stocks selling well below their highs. These include IBM, Minneapolis-Honeywell, Minnesota Mining and Polaroid, all of which currently are selling at least 20% below their highs. Even so, this merely emphasizes the fact that profits, while accruing in growth stocks almost without regard to market swings, can be maximized through careful selection and timing of purchases.

Note: Full adjustment has been made in this tabulation for splits and stock dividends. No account has been taken of cash dividends or rights offerings, nor any allowance made for brokerage fees.

Source: Merrill Lynch, Pierce, Fenner & Smith, Inc.

The growth company suffers less of a setback than the average company, recovers more quickly, and moves forward more rapidly.[8] Today certain aluminum, electric utilities, electronic, plastics, instrument, cosmetic, pharmaceutical, office equipment, etc., companies are regarded as "growth" companies. An example of 20 selected growth stocks and their performance over the 1953–1963 period may be seen in Table 12–4.

The elderly couple seeking maximum return consistent with the

[8] See "Why Buy Growth Stocks?", *Changing Times, The Kiplinger Magazine,* February, 1964.

greatest stability and least risk, and willing to forego growth possibilities, might invest in what one large brokerage house calls *"heirloom stocks,"* i.e., those that have paid dividends uninterruptedly for from 35 to 180 years.[9] Table 12–5 shows the "blue chips," as these high-grade, relatively safe stocks are called, that were selected from the list to provide good return and stability. All of the companies shown in Table 12–5 had paid dividends uninterruptedly for over 60 years.

Or our elderly couple could have picked "defensive" stocks of equally high quality and almost as long an uninterrupted dividend record. By "defensive" stocks are meant shares of a company which is likely to do better than average, from an earnings and dividend point of view, in a

TABLE 12–5

Selected Blue-Chip (*Heirloom*) Stocks

COMPANY	DIVIDENDS PAID UNINTERRUPTEDLY FOR AT LEAST—	PRICE RANGE 1936–1964
Chesebrough-Pond's	81 years	5¾*–62¾
E. I. du Pont de Nemours	60	22⅜*–278¾
General Electric	65	7⅛*–99⅞
First National Bank of Boston	180	20½*–103½
New England Tel. & Tel. Co.	78	15¾*–57¾
Eastman-Kodak	62	9*–136¼
Travelers Insurance Co.	100	6½*–207
Norfolk & Western R. R.	63	33¼*–125
A. T. & T.	83	33¾*–148⅝
Texaco	61	3¾*–74½

* Adjusted for stock split.

period of deteriorating business. If a business recession is feared, a growing interest tends to develop in these recession-resistant companies. While these stocks lack the glamor of certain market leaders, they are characterized by a relatively high degree of stability, an attribute much to be desired when the economy faces a period of uncertainty. Utility stocks are usually regarded as the best defensive issues, and Table 12–6 shows what a portfolio for our retired couple might look like. All have paid dividends uninterruptedly for at least 40 years.

In addition to utilities, the shares of gold-mining companies theoretically are ideal defensive issues. The price of gold remains stationary, while the cost of mining it decreases due to the lower cost of supplies,

[9] See *Heirloom Stocks,* latest edition (New York: Paine, Webber, Jackson, & Curtis). See also "101 Growth Stocks," Merrill Lynch, Pierce, Fenner & Smith, New York, 1963.

cheaper labor, and a better availability of manpower. No salesmen are needed and no customers are lost, since the whole output can be sold to the Treasury. In bear markets, gold shares usually rise and pay higher dividends. The so-called "habit-forming-product" companies also suffer relatively little even in a fairly severe business adjustment. This makes the shares of tobacco, snuff, soft-drink, gum, candy-bar, and similar companies "defensive." Also, with social security and unemployment insurance, the earnings of packaged-foods and grocery-chain companies tend to be maintained under less favorable business conditions.

TABLE 12–6

Selected Defensive Stocks

COMPANY	DIVIDENDS PAID UNINTERRUPTEDLY FOR AT LEAST—	STANDARD & POOR'S RATING	PRICE RANGE 1936–1964
American Electric Power	65 years	A	2¼*–42⅜
Boston Edison	74	A+	7¾*–43⅞
Cleveland Electric Illuminating Co.	63	A+	5¼*–36⅞
Commonwealth Edison Co.	74	A+	8¾*–54¼
Consolidated Edison of New York	79	A	11⅝ –90¾
Cincinnati Gas & Electric Co.	111	A	5½*–28¼
Houston Light & Power	42	A+	3⅜*–49⅜
Hartford Electric Light	63	A+	19*–50½
Central Hudson Gas & Electric	61	A	5⅜ –38⅛
Pacific Gas & Electric	45	A	5⅛*–34⅝
Potomac Electric Power Corp.	60	A	6¼*–25
San Diego Gas & Electric	55	A	8¼ –49½
Southern California Edison	57	A	5*–34½
Texas Utilities	47	A+	4¾*–59⅝
Tampa Electric	64	A+	1½*–26¼

* Adjusted for stock split.

At the opposite pole from "defensive" stocks are the "cyclical" stocks—those which often furnish impressive rewards when business conditions are improving rapidly but which suffer most when business conditions are falling off. As may be seen from Figure 12–6, the pre-eminently cyclical stocks are found in the automobile, steel, cement, machinery, building-materials, coal, railroad, and railroad-equipment industries. This is shown in the lower right-hand corner of Figure 12–6. U.S. Steel, New York Central, General Motors, and Anaconda Copper are examples of stocks which would be classified as cyclical. Such stocks may pay excellent dividends and may go up in price sharply in the prosperity phase of the business cycle but will tend to decline in

Basic Investment Character of Stock Groups

	Superior Growth Groups	Good Growth Groups	Average or Nongrowth Groups	
Comparatively Stable or Cyclically Resistant Groups	Publishing-Book Drugs Cosmetics	Convenience Foods Bus Lines Household and Industrial Cleansers Life Insurance Soft Drinks	Baking and Biscuits Banks Cigarettes Cigars Dairy Products Glass-Container	Electric Power Grocery Chains Natural Gas-Distribution and Transmission Variety Chains
Moderately Cyclical Groups	Office Equipment	Apparel Chemicals-Light Discount Stores Electronics Oil Plastics Synthetic Fibers Truck Lines Natural Gas-production Radio-TV Broadcasting	Can Manufacturing Department Stores Chemicals-Heavy Finance Brewing Liquor	Paints Sulphur Restaurants Shoes Telephone
Cyclical Groups		Air Transportation Aluminum Electrical Equipment Radio-TV Manufacturing Tire and Rubber Transportation Leasing	Coal Cement Autos-Passenger Agricultural Implements	Food-Canning Meat Packing Paper Containers Paper and Paperboard Railroads Textiles
Highly Cyclical Groups		Toys	Auto-Accessories Aircraft Manufacturing Building Materials Floor Coverings Glass-Flat Machinery	Metals (nonferrous) Movies Railroad Equipment Steel Trucks Machine Tools

Source: Moody's Investors Service, Inc.

price and reduce or even pass dividends during the downward phase. They are, therefore, somewhat speculative in nature.

"Speculative" common stocks may be grouped in four broad categories. (1) In the first category are very low-priced common stocks which in a major bull market advance more than the averages.

Dr. Leo Barnes notes that historically, low-priced shares often move much faster in the market than high-priced issues.[10] One study shows that over a 35-year period, stocks which sold for less than $5.00 a share at the beginning of an advance rose an average of 241 percent; those selling between $5.00 and $10 rose 146 percent; between $20 and $30, 94 percent; between $70 and $100, 43 percent; over $100, 36 percent.

TABLE 12–7

Assuming You Purchased 100 Shares at the 1942 Low and Still Maintained Your Original Position—

	Your Cost per 100 Shares	Shares Now Held after Stock Splits and Stock Dividends	Mkt. Price Close 3/25/64	Mkt. Value of Original Purchase
Cities Service	212.50	276	65⅜	$18,043
Eason Oil	37.50	100	21 bid	2,100
Empire State Oil	10.00	100	21	2,100
Louisiana Land & Expl.	312.50	300	86¼	25,875
Shamrock Oil & Gas	187.50	310	34⅝	10,733
Texas Gulf Producing	200.00	377	57¼	21,583
Wilcox Oil & Gas	150.00	236	33½	8,107

The lowest priced shares rose almost seven times as fast as did the most expensive ones. Note, however, that they tend to drop faster, too, in declining markets. (2) In the second category are stocks which offer potential growth possibilities, or as one brokerage house called them— "Today's Speculation . . . Tomorrow's Investment." Only by diligent search is one able to discover a company that, due either to indifference or ignorance of the investing public, is selling well below its price potential. Some of today's younger oil and gas companies, for example, are successfully providing their original investors with unusually large capital gains. See Table 12–7. In the third and fourth category are: (3) Those which are purchased because of, and which pay, *very high yields* (the high yields are the result of the risk involved; the yields

[10] See *Your Investments* by Dr. Leo Barnes, American Research Council, Larchmont, 1964.

may or may not continue); and (4) *pure gambles,* such as "penny" Canadian oil and uranium stocks, which pay nothing at the time of purchase and which, in most cases, will never pay anything.

A leading brokerage house defines speculative stocks as "stocks of lower quality which will probably fluctuate over a fairly broad price range for a number of reasons such as the unstable character of the business engaged in or because of the large amounts of debt and/or preferred stocks ahead of the common." One who buys stocks to obtain 6 percent yields is properly classed as a "speculator," i.e., one who takes a

TABLE 12–8

Some Common Stocks Which Yield 6 Percent or More

Name of Company	Yield	Dividends Paid Each Year since—
South Puerto Rico Sugar Co.	8.6	1924
Union Stock Yards of Omaha	6.2	1884
Fedders Corp.	6.2	1949
Shoe Corp. of America	6.3	1929
Sterling Brewers	6.0	1941
D. C. Transit System, Class A	7.4	1957
Bralorne-Pioneer Mines	10.4	1955
Great Northern Iron Ore	8.5	1934
O'okiep Copper (American shares)	9.6	1946
Sheaffer (W.A.) Pen Co.	8.9	1935
Longhorn Portland Cement	6.0	1937
Huttig Sash & Door Co.	6.1	1939
Continental Steel Co.	6.1	1936
Rhodesian Selection Trust (American shares)	10.6	1943
Arden Farms Co.	6.3	1944

big chance to obtain a big return. An "investor," on the other hand, is one who takes but moderate risks to obtain moderate returns—which, in the case of common stock, would be 3 or 4 percent.

Table 12–8 shows some common stocks which yield 6 percent or more.

The only term appropriate for those who buy penny oil and mining shares is "gambler." The lure that, perhaps once in 2,000 cases, a small outlay will pay incredible dividends, draws people in; but most of these wildcat fly-by-nights have as much prospect as Cheyenne Oil Ventures (sold by the now defunct Tellier & Co. of New Jersey for 15 cents a share), of which, in its offering circular, it was stated: "The U.S.

Geological Survey has prepared a map which indicates that the immediate area of this structure is not considered by it as favorable with respect
to its relative likelihood of yielding commercial quantities of oil as those
areas of the United States which have yielded oil in commercial
quantities." Thus the prospective purchaser was, in effect, told—if he
took the trouble to read the fine print in the offering circular—that no
oil of commercial value was likely to be found; but this apparently did
not deter those who wanted to get in on a "good thing" on the "ground
floor."

Common Stocks and Institutional Investors

Common stock investment, then, can range from buying shares in
the First National Bank of Boston, which has paid dividends uninterruptedly for the past 175 years, to paying 15 cents a share for Cheyenne
Oil Ventures, Inc. Obviously, with so wide a diversity in common stocks,
generalizations are both difficult and hazardous. One thing is quite clear,
however. In recent years, institutional investors, under the guidance of
skilled investment managers, have been turning more and more to
common stock investment for part or all of their funds. They have been
doing this both to obtain capital gains and as a hedge against inflation.

A survey of 1,900 institutional investors, summarized in *The Exchange,* indicated that these skilled investors tended strongly to favor
the blue chips. See Table 12–9.

TABLE 12–9

Wall Street's Favorite 50*

In Order of Popularity	Number of Inst. Holdings Mar., 1963
1. General Motors (2)	983
2. Standard Oil (N.J.) (1)	939
3. American Tel. & Tel. (3)	839
4. General Electric (4)	830
5. Texaco (6)	725
6. du Pont de Nemours (5)	698
7. Int'l Business Machines (9)	659
8. Union Carbide (7)	639
9. Socony Mobil (10)	573
10. Phillips Petroleum (11)	545
11. U.S. Steel (8)	524
12. Gulf Oil (13)	497

TABLE 12–9—Continued

In Order of Popularity	Number of Institutional Holdings Mar., 1963
13. Eastman Kodak (16)	482
14. Standard Oil (Calif.) (12)	479
15. Sears, Roebuck (14)	472
16. Ford Motor (17t)	464
17. International Paper (19)	432
18. American Electric Power (17t)	410
19. Standard Oil (Ind.) (20)	408
20. Dow Chemical (21)	405
21. Westinghouse Electric (15)	396
22. National Lead (28)	372
23. Commonwealth Edison (23t)	367
24. Allied Chemical (27)	362
25. General Foods (26)	359
26. Southern Calif. Edison (25)	358
27. Texas Utilities (32)	355
28. Monsanto Chemical Co. (34)	350
29. American Cyanamid (23t)	344
30. Int'l Nickel (37t)	337
31. Southern Co. (39)	335
32. Penney (J. C.) (30)	332
33. Kennecott Copper (22)	328
34. National Dairy Products (33)	323
35. Continental Oil (31)	322
36. Consumers Power (35)	319
37. Virginia Electric & Power (40)	315
38. American Can (29)	310
39. U.S. Gypsum (46)	303
40. Merck (42)	302
41. Pacific Gas & Electric (37t)	302
42. Central & South West (41)	301
43. Goodyear Tire (49)	293
44. Minnesota Mng. & Mfg. (65)	285
45. Reynolds Tobacco (62)	282
46. Continental Can (43)	280
47. Caterpillar (55)	278
48. Public Service E. & G. (53)	278
49. International Harvester (45)	277
50. Johns-Manville (44)	275

(Figures in parentheses after Name of Company Indicate 1962 Ranking)
* Stocks listed on NYSE; Source: Data Digest, Inc.
Reproduced by courtesy of Mr. William D. Horgan, editor of *The Exchange.*

The Boston Fund makes and publishes an annual survey of the investment policies of 65 of the largest college and university endowment funds.[11] It includes, among others, Harvard (total endowment $843 million), Yale ($392 million), MIT ($267 million), Chicago ($233 million), and Princeton ($230 million). On the average 55.8 percent of 65 endowment funds was invested in common stock, 30.4 percent in bonds, only 1.4 percent in preferred stock and 6.1 percent in income-producing real estate and mortgages. Most of the institutions surveyed had between 50 and 70 percent of their funds in common stocks; a few —Ohio State (79.3 percent), Swarthmore (76.6 percent), Washington University (71.3 percent), and Wesleyan University (75.1 percent)

TABLE 12–10

The MIT Endowment Fund: Distribution of Investments by Type
(Percentage of Market Value as of June 30)

	1929	1932	1937	1941	1946	1951	1956	1963
Cash	1.0%	—%	—%	4.7%	7.3%	2.7%	—%	—%
U.S. govt. bonds	—	—	19.6	21.3	41.5	24.3	12.6	14.5
Other bonds	73.5	70.8	28.7	16.2	7.3	9.4*	22.2*	26.2*
Preferred stocks	2.2	2.8	5.1	4.6	2.6	0.3	0.4	0.6
Real estate	5.1†	2.8	2.2	9.7	7.6	17.4	9.3	6.6
Common stocks	18.2	23.6	44.4	43.5	33.7	45.9	55.5	52.1

* Includes commercial paper and interest bearing bank deposits.
† Includes real estate mortgages.

—exceeded 70 percent. The ten largest common stock holdings of all 65 endowment funds were Standard Oil of New Jersey, Texaco, IBM, A.T.&T., General Motors, Gulf Oil, Christiana Securities, Standard Oil of California, Du Pont, and Eastman Kodak. Harvard University, the largest endowment, had 55 percent of its funds in common stock, of which 32.5 percent was in public utilities, 21.7 percent in oils, 29.3 percent in industrials, and 16.5 percent in banks, insurance, and finance company stocks. The growth of common stock in the general investment fund of Massachusetts Institute of Technology may be seen in Table 12–10. The breakdown of the common stock holdings by industries is shown in Table 12–11. The most interesting developments have been the marked increase in holdings of industrial and utility stocks in recent years.

In addition to college endowment funds, savings banks, insurance companies, pension funds, and, of course, mutual funds invest in

[11] See "The 1963 Study of College and University Endowment Funds," Boston Fund, 111 Devonshire Street, Boston, Massachusetts, 02109.

common stocks. Their portfolio holdings and changes in investment choices—what they sell off and what they acquire, from year to year—can be studied, and the individual in his investment choices can

TABLE 12–11

MIT Endowment Fund: Common Stock Breakdown
(At Market, June 30)

	1929	1932	1939	1941	1946	1951	1956	1963
Industrials	60.0%	53.8%	76.0%	69.6%	68.5%	78.3%	81.5%	74.0%
Railroads	20.6	22.2	2.4	1.3	2.7	1.8	1.2	0.7
Public utilities	11.5	14.8	7.4	11.5	6.1	5.5	8.1	14.9
Banks	5.7	7.4	10.9	14.1	13.9	6.1	3.4	4.3
Insurance	—	—	2.7	2.8	8.6	5.4	3.7	3.9
Other	2.2	1.8	0.6	0.7	0.2	2.9	2.1	2.2

thus obtain, without cost, the benefits of skilled investment managers' decisions.

Rights

"Rights" are privileges granted to stockholders to buy new stocks or bonds at a price generally below the prevailing market. By state law or corporate charter, stockholders (generally common stockholders only) are given a pre-emptive right to buy a proportionate part of any new stock issued, or other securities which can be converted into stock, in order that they may retain their proportionate ownership in the company. Suppose that Company A has 100 common shares outstanding, of which Jones owns ten. If the corporation is successful and it is felt that earnings would be even better if the company had more money with which to work, it may be decided to sell 50 additional shares. If Jones has the right to buy five of the new shares (generally expressed as ten rights, i.e., one for each old share), he can, by exercising his right, acquire five shares to add to his old ten, allowing him to retain his 10 percent ownership in the company. Although pre-emptive rights are not so important as they used to be, in the days when corporations were small, and although it is the trend to deny them to stockholders in corporate charters whenever state law does not make them mandatory, some of our biggest and best corporations find corporate rights the instrumentality by which additional corporate funds can often be obtained advantageously.

By way of illustration, the American Telephone and Telegraph

Company has made use of rights for years. Whenever it needs new money, it can offer its stockholders additional shares. If the stock is selling at $140 a share, stockholders feel they are getting a bargain when they are told that they can buy the additional stock at, say, $100 a share. The result is that the company sells practically all of the new issue to its stockholders.

Even though stockholders do not have pre-emptive rights, it is common financial practice to grant them privileged subscription rights. Since the stockholders have had experience with the company's stock, why should they not be among the best customers for an additional issue of the company's stock if the company has been successful? Furthermore, if the new stock is offered at a price materially below the market price of the old stock, the equity of the old stockholders would be diluted if they were not given rights to acquire a proportionate amount of new stock.

What to Do with Rights

A right is a valuable instrument; it is the privilege of being able to buy for less the equivalent of what has been and is selling for more. There are three things that can be done with a right:

1. Do nothing.
2. Exercise it.
3. Sell it.

To do nothing is very foolish, since a right has value only so long as it is used (exercised). Rights are usually issued for only short periods— two weeks or a month. He who does nothing with his rights will find that their value evaporates. In spite of repeated warnings, however, we constantly read of people who, through ignorance, do not take proper action to preserve their interests. Of course, it takes money to exercise rights (you have the right to buy for a certain price, but you must have the price). It is only by exercising rights, however, that a stockholder can end up with as large an interest in the company as he had before the new stock was issued. If one does not have the money to exercise his rights, he should sell them (any stockbrokerage firm can sell them for him) before they lose their value.

The Value of a Right

There is a formula for computing the theoretical value of a right. This formula rests on the assumption that the corporation can earn the same percentage on the money received for new stock as it was earning on the total market value of the old stock. If this is not a fact or if investors do not believe it is a fact, the price at which rights will sell in the market will differ from the theoretical value. The formula is $V = \dfrac{M - S}{N + 1}$, in which:

V = Value of a right;
M = Market value of a share of old stock;
S = Subscription price of new stock;
N = Number of old shares necessary to have the privilege of buying a new share.

This formula is to be used to calculate the theoretical value of a right when the old shares are sold and the rights which attach thereto are sold along with them. In the financial market this condition is expressed by saying that the stock is sold "cum rights" or "rights-on." When the time comes when the stock alone (without the rights) is sold (called "ex-rights" or "rights-off"), we use the formula $\dfrac{M - S}{N}$.

We may illustrate the use of the first formula by a simple illustration. Suppose a company has $1,000,000 of stock outstanding (10,000 shares, each of $100 par) and has been earning $100,000 yearly, so that the stock is selling in the market at $200 a share. Now the company decides that it could earn 10 percent on $1,500,000 of new money, so it decides to give its stockholders the right to buy a new share at $150 for each old share held:

$$V = \frac{M - S}{N + 1},$$

$$V = \frac{\$200 - \$150}{1 + 1},$$

$$V = \frac{\$50}{2},$$

$$V = \$25.$$

Now suppose that Jones had one share of the old stock. It was worth $200 in the market (including the $25 right inherent in it). If he sold the right, he would still have a share worth $175. The share and the $25 in his pocket would keep his $200 intact. If he used (exercised) his right and paid $150 along with it, he would have two shares, each worth $175, or $350 for the two, representing his former investment of $200 and his additional investment of $150 more. We now see that if he failed to do anything with his right, he would end up with merely $175 in his old share and would have suffered a shrinkage in his investment of $25. The $25 should preferably have been received in cash through sale of the right or invested in new stock, rather than have been lost through shrinkage of the investment.

After the old stock sold, ex-rights, it would presumably be worth $175 in the market, other things being equal. The right to buy for $150 the equivalent of what was selling for $175 would surely be worth $25:

$$V = \frac{M - S}{N}$$

or

$$\frac{\$175 - \$150}{1} = \frac{\$25}{1} = \$25$$

The essential thing to note is that, when rights are issued, value leaves the old stock. This value should be turned into cash (by selling the right) or invested in new stock (by exercising the right). If nothing is done, the value is lost. Naturally, it would be better to sell rights than to exercise them if, for any reason, it were felt that it would not be good to make a further investment in the same stock.

Warrants

Warrants are options to buy securities, generally common stock, at a given price. They are at times issued in connection with reorganizations; at other times we find them offered in connection with the initial sale of securities which would not sell satisfactorily without the help of the warrants (to "sweeten" the offering). Nondetachable warrants may be sold only along with the securities to which they are attached; detachable warrants may be sold separately. Rights are relatively short lived, whereas warrants are good either for a period of years or indefinitely until exercised. Warrants fluctuate more than the stock to which they apply, and in this sense they are more speculative.

"$500 to $104,000 in 4 years" is the way an advertisement about warrants begins. It tells the amazing but true story of the R.K.O. warrant. In 1940 the Radio-Keith Orpheum Co. (R.K.O.) reorganized after some years of bad fortune. The old common stockholders seemed to fare badly. For each old share, they received only one sixth of a share of new common stock plus one warrant, good to buy one share of new common stock from the company at $15 per share. In 1942 R.K.O. common was selling at a low of 2½ and with general pessimism rife, the chance of R.K.O. common ever selling above $15, at which point the warrants would begin to have some actual value, seemed slim. R.K.O. warrants were, therefore, selling on the New York Curb Exchange at only one sixteenth, or 6¼ cents, per warrant. But the picture changed in four years. The R.K.O. common stock advanced to a high of 28⅛ on the New York Stock Exchange. The right to buy R.K.O. common at $15 per share from the company when it was selling on the open market at $28 per share was worth $13, and the warrants did sell at exactly $13 on the American Stock Exchange (then the New York Curb Exchange). That is the story of the R.K.O. warrant—$500 invested in these warrants in 1942 was worth $104,000 just four years later.

From this illustration you can see how much more the warrant lends itself to a capital gain than does the common stock itself. Between 1942 and 1946 R.K.O. common stock went from $2.50 a share to $28. Therefore, a $500 investment in the stock appreciated to $5,625. But between 1942 and 1946 R.K.O. warrants went from 6¼ cents to $13. Therefore, a $500 investment appreciated to $104,000. Interesting warrants are now outstanding but this is an area primarily for the sophisticated investor.

Preferred Stock

From an investment point of view, preferred stocks are more like bonds than common stocks. The return on the investment, if one gets it, is fixed and limited. Of course, preferred stock, unlike most bonds, has no maturity, and the preferred stockholder is a stockholder, i.e., he is an owner, not a creditor. Ordinarily a corporation gets into little difficulty by foregoing dividends on its stock, common or preferred. Preferred stocks are issued to attract investors who wish a safer and less changeable income than they could get from common stocks. For the last 30 years, preferred stocks of high grade have tended to yield more income than high-grade bonds, but this extra payment is largely to compensate for extra risk.

The rights of the preferred stockholder are to be found in the corporation's charter. Dividends on preferred stock may be cumulative or noncumulative. Cumulative dividends which are not paid when they should regularly be paid (ordinarily once a quarter) accumulate for the benefit of the preferred stockholder and must be paid, as a matter of law, when earnings of the corporation permit, before dividends can be paid on the common. If the preferred is noncumulative, the stockholder has no special claim for dividends which have been passed.

Ordinarily, the return on preferred stock is definite, and the owner of preferred stock does not share in earnings beyond his stated 4 or 5 percent. In some cases, however, a special type of preferred stock is issued, known as "participating preferred." In the case of participating preferred, the stock is permitted to share in earnings, if they are large enough to so warrant, in excess of the stated rate of dividend. Such a stock is entitled to its regular dividend and then, after the common shares receive a similar rate of dividend, participates with the common stock in the balance of the earnings distributed as dividends.

Some preferred stock is callable, that is, the issuing company can retire the stock, usually at a premium of 5 percent or more. Only when market conditions make it impossible to issue callable preferred stock will preferred stock without a call provision be issued.

Although preferred stock represents ownership and cannot be secured like a debt, there have been instances where a fund has been provided to assure future dividend payments. There have also been sinking funds used to provide for retirement of preferred stock. Such devices may make the preferred stock easier to sell. Sometimes preferred stock is issued with a conversion feature which allows it to be exchanged for common stock at a given ratio. Convertible preferreds have been popular because they give the cautious investor a steady return but also provide him with a hedge against inflation, since conversion into common is possible. Such conversion proves advantageous when earnings increase and common stock rises in price.

Ideally, the best preferred to buy would be a cumulative, participating, convertible preferred, but there are few such animals. The entrance of savings banks, pension funds, and similar types of institutional and corporate investors into the market for high-grade preferred stocks has caused prices for most of these stocks to rise to levels where, so far as the individual is concerned, they no longer may be considered attractive.

Bonds and the Individual Investor

A bond is a formal evidence of a debt in which the borrower promises to pay the lender a specified amount, with interest at a fixed rate, payable on specified dates. It differs from a stock in that it constitutes a debt of the issuing corporation rather than a share in the ownership of the business. Interest on bonds is a fixed charge which the borrowing corporation must pay, whether it has sufficient income or not. If it misses an interest payment, it is said to be "in default," and reorganization or bankruptcy will follow.

The volume of bonds, listed and unlisted, outstanding in the United States is greater than all stock issues, but most of the bonds are held by institutional investors, such as insurance companies, banks, etc. Relatively few individuals—and then only the wealthier ones—own corporate bonds. Indeed, for the investor of average means, the amount of time and energy that would be necessary to obtain a good grasp of the complexities of bond investment, and the relatively small differential at present in the return on high-grade corporate bonds as compared to U.S. savings bonds, may make investment in U.S. savings bonds preferable. A savings account yielding 4 to 4½ percent may also be a better alternative.

The Case for Bonds

The purchaser of a bond limits his income return and foregoes all prospect of capital gain, appreciation, or speculative profit. If, despite these sacrifices, he must still subject himself to serious risk of loss, as is the case when he buys a corporate bond, particularly if it is not of the highest grade, is it worth it?

Mr. George Wanders, editor of the *Bond Buyer,* in stating the case for bonds, tells a fable:

Once upon a time a stock hare and a bond tortoise set out on an investment race. The hare had all the best of it for a while, what with fat dividends, good business prospects, and a boom on the New York Stock Exchange. The tortoise merely plugged along, paying a stipulated rate of interest. Almost everyone cheered the hare and bet on it, but there were a few who favored the tortoise, partly because as trustees of savings banks they had no alternative under state law.

This fable ends in the traditional way. The stock hare lagged after a time and took a dividend nap. The bond tortoise kept going and in the end paid the investors rather handsomely and also returned to them the entire original investment.

There is nothing far fetched in this approach to the investment problem. It reflects the theory that stocks have the better of it in prosperity, while bonds come into their own and are really appreciated in recession or depression. The rule is not invariable, for there are corporations in which a stock investment has proved, over the years, a better proposition than almost any bond investment. Some of our leading corporations have no bonded debt, and an equity, representing ownership, is the only possible way of investment in such cases. Du Pont, for example, has no bonded indebtedness.

The wealthier investor, whose financial needs require that a portion of his capital be subjected to no more than minimum risk, may turn to high-grade bonds. Common stocks, even those of investment grade, may represent a greater risk than do high-grade bonds because they represent a share of ownership in a business, whose profits will necessarily vary with changes over time.

There are at least five reasons for favoring high-grade bonds. (a) When the economic going gets rough and dividends on stock may be omitted, interest payments on high-grade bonds may continue. (b) If it gets too rough, and a company ends in the bankruptcy court, the bondholder ends up with the assets and the stockholder gets little or nothing. (c) In a depression, the prices of high-grade bonds tend to go up. This is because investor demand now concentrates upon those securities which continue to pay interest and which appear to be able to weather the storm. The increased demand concentrated on a limited supply sends the price up. The opposite is true, of course, in a prosperity period, when investor interest turns away from the fixed and limited returns on a high-grade bond. There is also a lessening of investor interest because the purchasing power of the fixed and limited return is diminishing. The bond offers no hedge against inflation. The really high-grade bond, however, is a hedge against deflation. (d) There are numerous individuals of substantial means whose requirements for fixed-income securities cannot be met solely by U.S. savings bonds. (e) Wealthier investors find that the tax-exempt features of state and municipal bonds are quite attractive.

If you or your parents are in this category there is a simple formula which will show you the percentage yield which a bond or other security with fully taxable income must give in order to provide an after-tax yield equivalent to a given tax-exempt yield. Find your tax bracket and then apply this formula:

Tax-exempt yield ÷ (100% − tax bracket %) = Taxable equivalent yield

Assume you are in the 55 percent tax bracket. If you can buy a 3 percent tax-exempt bond what would an alternate investment with fully taxable income have to yield to provide 3 percent after taxes?

$$3.00\% \div (100\% - 55\%) = ?$$

$$\frac{3.00\%}{45\%} = 6.66\%$$

Your fully taxable investment would have to yield 6.66 percent to give an after tax return of 3 percent for someone in the 55 percent tax bracket.

The way in which Merrill Lynch, Pierce, Fenner & Smith advise that bonds fit into the investment pattern may be seen from Table 12–12.

TABLE 12–12

Securities for Different Investment Objectives

For greatest safety, least income
 Short-term governments
 Short-term, best-grade bonds

For safety and tax exemption
 Municipal bonds
 State bonds

For safety, moderate income
 Long-term governments
 High-grade bonds

For reasonable safety, fair income
 Good-grade bonds
 High-grade preferreds

For good income
 Good-grade preferreds
 High-grade commons

For income and growth
 Convertible preferreds
 Convertible bonds
 Good dividend-paying common stocks

For growth—speculative
 Speculative-grade bonds and preferred stocks
 Good-to-speculative common stocks

Bond Ratings

When you first become interested in a particular bond, an initial step in finding out something about it is to go to one of the financial services, such as Standard & Poor's, Moody's, etc., and see what rating they have assigned to the bond. While these financial services are not infallible, their experts are accustomed to judging the relative merits of fixed-income securities, and the rating will give you a clear idea of the approximate quality of the bond. It is a useful orientation for looking further into the merits, or lack of them, of the proposed purchase. It may be that when you see the rating assigned, you will no longer be interested in the bond, since it may be classed as speculative; and you would have little interest in buying a speculative bond, which is really a contradiction in terms. The Standard & Poor's Bond Ratings are as shown in Figure 12–7. The other services have similar classifications; they differ only in the symbols assigned and vary little in the method of classification. While these services can be obtained in banks, brokerage houses, or large libraries, Standard & Poor's publishes a *Monthly Bond Guide,* which provides, among other information, the bond ratings.

A sample half-page from this *Bond Guide* is shown in Figure 12–8. You will note that bonds are described by:

1. The name of the company
2. The type of bond or security
3. The interest paid
4. The maturity date

FIGURE 12-7

STANDARD & POOR'S BOND RATINGS

In the Standard & Poor's bond quality ratings system, interest-paying bonds are graded into eight classifications ranging from AAA for the highest quality designation through AA, A, BBB, BB, B, CCC to CC for the lowest. Bonds on which no interest is being paid, either because of default or because of "income" characteristics, are given C, DDD, DD and D ratings. Rating symbols are the same for corporate and municipal bonds, and every effort has been made to keep the two systems on a comparable basis. United States Government bonds are not rated, but are considered as a yardstick against which to measure all other issues.

BANK QUALITY BONDS

Under present commercial bank regulations bonds rated in the top four categories (AAA, AA, A, BBB or their equivalent) generally are regarded as eligible for bank investment.

AAA Bonds rated AAA are highest grade obligations. They possess the ultimate degree of protection as to principal and interest. Marketwise, they move with interest rates, and hence provide the maximum safety on all counts.

AA Bonds rated AA also qualify as high grade obligations, and in the majority of instances differ from AAA issues only in small degree. Here, too, prices move with the long term money market.

A Bonds rated A are regarded as upper medium grade. They have considerable investment strength but are not entirely free from adverse effects of changes in economic and trade conditions. Interest and principal are regarded as safe. They predominantly reflect money rates in their market behavior, but to some extent, also economic conditions.

BBB The BBB, or medium grade category is borderline between definitely sound obligations and those where the speculative element begins to predominate. These bonds have adequate asset coverage and normally are protected by satisfactory earnings. Their susceptibility to changing conditions, particularly to depressions, necessitates constant watching. Marketwise, the bonds are more responsive to business and trade conditions than to interest rates. This group is the lowest which qualifies for commercial bank investment.

SUB-STANDARD BONDS

As we move down the rating scale, beginning with BB, investment characteristics weaken and the speculative elements become progressively stronger. The fortunes of the obligors change rapidly with economic and trade conditions and in adverse periods interest requirements may not be earned. Investment in bonds in this group must be under constant surveillance. Prices fluctuate widely with changing business conditions and with little regard for the money market.

BB Bonds given a BB rating are regarded as lower medium grade. They have only minor investment characteristics. In the case of utilities, interest is earned consistently but by narrow margins. In the case of other types of obligors, charges are earned on average by a fair margin, but in poor periods deficit operations are possible.

B Bonds rated as low as B are speculative. Payment of interest cannot be assured under difficult economic conditions.

CCC-CC Bonds rated CCC and CC are outright speculations, with the lower rating denoting the more speculative. Interest is paid, but continuation is questionable in periods of poor trade conditions. In the case of CC ratings the bonds may be on an income basis and the payment may be small.

C The rating of C is reserved for income bonds on which no interest is being paid.

DDD-D All bonds rated DDD, DD and D are in default, with the rating indicating the relative salvage value.

CANADIAN BONDS

Canadian corporate bonds are rated on the same basis as American corporate issues. The ratings measure the intrinsic value of the bonds, but they do not take into account exchange and other uncertainties.

FOREIGN BONDS

Foreign bonds carry the same rating symbols as domestic bonds, but in all cases they are preceded by a ★ to denote a conditional rating. This is applied because the obligor is a foreign body and the bonds are sometimes affected by other than economic factors.

FIGURE 12–8

STANDARD & POOR'S CORPORATION

INDEX	Exchange	BONDS Name and Description of Issue	Description, Interest Rate, Due	Interest Dates	S&P Quality Rating	Eligibility	LEGALITY Conn.	Me.	Mass.	N.H.	N.J.	N.J. tr	N.Y.	CALL PRICE For S.F.	Regular	Ref. Start	PRICE RANGE 1960-62 High	1960-62 Low	1963 High	1963 Low	1964 High	1964 Low	LAST SALE or Bid s=Sale	Yield to Mty.
1		New England Power Co.	1st I 4⅝s '91	mN	AA	X	√	√	√	√	√	√	√	†101.66	†105.91		104	100⅞	105½	101½	102¾	101	102½	4.48
2		do	1st J 4⅜s '92	jD	AA	X	√	√	√	√	√	√	√	†101.41	†105.61		102	101⅜	102⅝	99	99½	98½	98¾	4.45
3		do	1st K 4½s '93	mN	AA	X	√	√	√	√	√	√	–	101.14 '65	†105.66		....	....	100½	100⅛	101½	100⅜	100¾	4.45
4	•	New England Tel. & Tel.	Deb 3s '74	Ms15	AAA	X	√	√	√	√	√	√	√	....	†101.17		88¾	79	89	86⅜	87⅞	87	87⅞	4.20
5		do	Deb 3¼s '77	jD15	AAA	X	√	√	√	√	√	√	√	....	†102.66		88½	78	90½	86¾	88½	87⅝	88½	4.35
6	•	do	Deb 3s '82	aO	AAA	X	√	√	√	√	√	√	√	....	†102.49		84	72½	85¼	80	80⅝	80½	80½	4.54
7		do	Deb 3⅛s '88	jD15	AAA	X	√	√	√	√	√	√	√	....	†104.18		80¾	74½	82½	80	81⅜	80⅛	81⅜	4.37
8		do	Deb 3¼s '91	mN15	AAA	X	√	√	√	√	√	√	√	....	†103.46		84⅝	76	83½	81⅛	82¼	81¼	82¼	4.35
9		do	Deb 4s '93	Ao	AAA	X	√	√	√	√	√	√	√	....	†106.60		94	80¼	95¾	93½	94⅛	92¾	94⅛	4.35
10		do	Deb 4⅝s '99	Ao	AAA	X	√	√	√	√	√	√	√	....	104	'66	107¼	98¾	105	101¾	103⅞	102	103⅞	4.41
11		do	Deb 4½s 2002	jJ	AAA	X	√	√	√	√	√	√	√	....	104.43	'67	103¾	98⅞	104	100	101⅜	100¼	101⅜	4.43
12		New Hampshire Electric	1st A 3s '75	mS	A	X	√	√	√	√	–	√	√	†101.01	†102.19		87	76¼	88⅛	86⅛	86⅞	85⅞	86⅞	4.40
13		New Jersey Bell Telephone	Deb 3¼s '84	Mn	AAA	X	√	√	√	√	√	√	√	....	†104.05		84¾	73	86½	84	84⅞	83¾	84⅞	4.35
14	•	do	Deb 3⅛s '88	jJ15	AAA	X	√	√	√	√	√	√	√	....	†103.95		85	73¼	83¾	81½	78	77⅛	77⅛	4.67
15		do	Deb 3s '89	Mn	AAA	X	√	√	√	√	√	√	√	....	†103.23		80	72	81	78⅜	79⅛	77⅞	79⅛	4.34
16		do	Deb 2¾s '90	Ms15	AAA	X	√	√	√	√	√	√	√	....	†103.70		75	70	86½	75⅜	74⅜	73½	74⅜	4.36
17		do	Deb 3⅞s '93	Ao	AAA	X	√	√	√	√	√	√	√	....	†103.74		93¼	85	92¾	90	91⅝	90⅝	91⅝	4.37
18		do	Deb 3⅜s '95	jD	AAA	X	√	√	√	√	√	√	√	....	†103.48		85⅛	75	83¾	81⅝	82¾	81⅞	82¾	4.38
19		do	Deb 4⅞s 2000	mN	AAA	X	√	√	√	√	√	√	√	....	†106⅞		107	101⅞	108	105	103⅞	103⅝	103⅝	4.67
20	•	New Jersey Junct. RR.	1st Curr 4s '86	Fa	BBB	X	–	–	–	–	–	–	–	....	NC		78¼	69	69⅛	69	No Sale		68	6.75
21	•	New Jersey Power & Light	1st 3s '74	Ms	AA	X	√	√	√	√	√	√	√	....	†103⅜		87½	75⅛	88	83	86	83¼	88	4.45
22		do	1st 3s '78	Jd	AA	X	√	√	√	√	√	√	√	101¼	†103⅛		86¼	72	87⅛	83¼	85⅜	84⅛	85¼	4.38
23		do	1st 2⅞s '79	Jd	AA	X	√	√	√	√	√	√	√	†101.61	†102.87		83	74½	84⅞	82	83¾	82⅛	83¾	4.30
24		do	1st 3⅛s '84	fA	AA	X	√	√	√	√	√	√	√	†101.01	†103.28		82⅜	73	84¾	82	82⅞	81⅝	82⅞	4.37
25		do	1st 4⅛s '88	Mn	AA	X	√	√	√	√	√	√	√	†101.97	†105.22		98	91½	97⅞	94½	96¼	94¾	95⅞	4.40
26		do	1st 4⅞s '90	jJ	AA	X	√	√	√	√	√	√	√	†101.13	†105.44		107¾	101⅛	108	103¼	105⅜	103	104⅞	4.57
27		New Orleans Gr. Nor. Ry.	Inc Deb 5s 2032	jJ	B	Y	–	–	–	–	–	–	–	....	100		68½	53	83	67	81	78	78	Flat
28		New Orleans Public Service	1st 3⅛s '74	jJ	A	X	√	√	√	√	–	√	√	†102⅛	†102⅜		89½	81½	90½	86	89¼	88¼	89¼	4.40
29		do	1st 3¼s '78	aO	A	X	√	√	√	√	–	√	√	†101.31	†102.48		86½	82	89	86	87⅛	86	87⅛	4.43
30		do	1st 4⅛s '83	Ao	A	X	√	√	√	√	–	√	√	†102.28	†103.73		96¼	91	98	95½	95⅞	94¾	95⅞	4.45
31		do	1st 3¼s '84	jD	A	X	√	–	√	√	–	√	√	†102.15	†103.95		83½	78	85¾	83⅝	83⅝	82¾	83⅜	4.47
32		do	1st 4½s '87	Ao	A	X	√	√	√	√	–	√	√	†100.72	†104.04		100	91½	102½	99	100¾	99⅞	100¾	4.45
33		do	1st 5s '91	Jd	A	X	√	√	√	√	–	√	√	†100.91	†105.53		105½	99⅞	104½	101	105	104¼	104⅝	4.70
34		do	1st 4½s '92	Ao	A	X	√	√	√	√	–	√	√	†100.97	†105.13		101½	96½	104	97	100⅝	99⅞	100⅝	4.47
35	•	New Orleans Terminal Co.	1st 3¾s '77	mN	A	X	√	√	–	√	–	√	√	100⅛	†102		No Sale		No Sale		No Sale		88	4.95
36	•	N.Y. Cent. & Hudson Riv. RR.	3½s '97	jJ	BB	Y	–	–	–	–	–	–	√	....	NC		63	51½	70½	60⅝	70¾	67⅝	s70¼	5.40
37	•	do Michigan Central	CT 3½s '98	Fa	B	Y	–	–	–	–	–	–	–	....	NC		57	47	63½	52¾	65½	60	64½	5.93
38	•	do Lake Shore	CT 3½s '98	Fa	B	Y	–	–	–	–	–	–	–	....	NC		56	47	59⅞	52½	63	58	62½	6.13
39	•	New York Central RR.	Con A 4s '98	Fa	B	Y	–	–	–	–	–	–	–	....	NC		60⅝	42	65	55½	69¼	63⅝	s68⅜	6.23
40	•	do	Ref & Imp A 4½s 2013	aO	B	Y	–	–	–	–	–	–	–	....	*110		63⅞	45¼	71	59½	74½	69¼	s74	6.21
41	•	do	Ref & Imp C 5s 2013	aO	B	Y	–	–	–	–	–	–	–	....	*105		71¾	48½	78	65½	82½	76⅞	s81¼	6.20

Thus, "New Jersey Power & Light 1st 3s '74" means the first-mortgage bond issue of the New Jersey Power & Light Company paying 3 percent interest per annum and maturing in 1974.

Bond Prices, Coupons, and Yields

Usually, though not always, bonds are issued in denominations of $1,000. This is the par or face value stated on the bond, and it is the amount on which interest is computed. The bond rate, sometimes called the "coupon" rate in the case of coupon bonds, is the simple interest rate, stated in the bond, at which the interest payment is computed. If you buy a bond for a $1,000 par value and the stated rate of interest is 3 percent, you will be paid $30 a year interest, or $15 every six months if interest is paid semiannually. The price quoted for bonds is usually expressed as a percentage rate of the par value. That is, a year after you have purchased your $1,000 bond, you may find it quoted in the newspaper at 96. This does *not* mean it is worth only $96. It means that the bond may be purchased for 96 percent of par value: $960 for a $1,000 bond, or $96,000 for a $100,000 bond.

If you needed funds at the time and decided to sell your bond for $960, the person who bought it would receive $30 a year from the corporation whose obligation it was. When you received $30 a year on an investment of $1,000, your return—3 percent—was the same as the stated interest rate in the bond; but the new purchaser, assuming he holds it just one year and then resells it to someone for $960, has received $30 for one year on an investment of $960. Clearly, he has received a return of more than 3 percent. His current yield, not the stated rate (coupon rate), on the bond was:

$$\begin{array}{r} .03125 \\ \hline 960\overline{)30.00000} \\ 28\ 80 \\ \hline 1\ 200 \\ 960 \\ \hline 2400 \\ 1920 \\ \hline 4800 \\ 4800 \end{array},$$

or 3.125 percent, or 3⅛ percent. "Yield" is not to be confused with "stated" or "coupon" rate. The latter is fixed once and for all when the bond is originally issued and governs the fixed amount which the corporation pays each year to whoever happens to own the bond. The former (the yield) is determined by the price you pay for the bond. If you pay less than par for the bond, the yield will be more than the coupon rate. If you pay more than par, the yield will be less than the coupon rate. To state it in another way: yield varies inversely with price. The lower the price you pay for the bond, the higher the yield; the higher the price you pay, the lower the yield.

But the current yield does not tell the whole story with respect to returns on bonds. When you buy a bond below par (at a discount) and hold it to maturity, you receive not only the current yield, as described above, but also the difference between your purchase price ($960) and the par value ($1,000) at which the corporation will redeem the bond at maturity. This extra $40 must be added to your income from the bond over the period you hold it to determine the true yield to maturity. In the same fashion, if you pay more than par for the bond (assume $1,040) and hold it until maturity, you will get back only $1,000 from the company. Thus you will lose $40, which must be subtracted from your income from the bond over the period you hold it in order to arrive at the true yield.

If the bond is bought at a discount, the difference between the purchase price and the redemption value is a gain for the investor. If you divide this difference by the number of years in the remaining life of the bond, you may consider the result an average annual gain. If the bond were bought at a premium, this result would be an average annual loss. Now, if you add this average annual gain to, or subtract the average annual loss from, the total interest payment received in a year, you get the average annual income from the investment. The investment at the time of purchase is the price paid; but the investment at the time of redemption is the redemption value; so the average of these two could be considered as an average investment. The average annual income divided by the average investment gives the approximate true yield.

An illustration may clarify this. Take the previous case of the 3 percent bond purchased for $960 in the market and assume that it has ten years to run to maturity and that you hold it for the ten years. You saw that the current yield was 3⅛ percent (3.125 percent), but you realize that this is not the true yield because, over the ten years, you will receive a $40 gain. Your average investment was $960 + $1,000 ÷ 2, or $980. If you divide the $40 gain over ten years, you received an extra $4.00 a year. Add this to the $30 you received in interest from the company each year, and you have an average annual income of $34 on an average investment of $980. Your approximate yield is then:

$$
\begin{array}{r}
.03469 \\
980\overline{)34.00000} \\
29\ 40 \\
\hline
4\ 600 \\
3\ 920 \\
\hline
6800 \\
5880 \\
\hline
9200 \\
8820 \\
\hline
\end{array}
$$

or 3.47 percent.

To take an example of a bond purchased at a premium, assume that you bought the bond at $1,040 and that it has ten years to run, at which time you will receive $1,000 for it. Thus you will lose $40 over the ten years, or $4.00 a year, which you must deduct each year from the $30 interest you receive in order to arrive at your real average annual income, which is thus, of course, $26. Your average investment over the ten years was $1,040 + $1,000 ÷ 2, or $1,020. Thus your return—your approximate yield—is:

$$
\begin{array}{r}
.02549 \\
1020\overline{)26.00000} \\
20\ 40 \\
\hline
5\ 600 \\
5\ 100 \\
\hline
5000 \\
4080 \\
\hline
9200 \\
9180 \\
\hline
\end{array}
$$

or 2.55 percent.

The rates in both these examples are approximate and not mathematically exact, for reasons too complicated to explain here. For this reason, investment officers of financial institutions and others dealing with bonds use an elaborate book of bond tables to determine the true yield when they know the coupon rate, maturity, and proposed purchase price of a bond. A page of a standard bond table is shown in Figure 12–9.

Assume you purchased a bond with a 3 percent coupon which has 13 years to run to maturity for a price of $890. If you had purchased the bond for $1,000, the coupon and the yield would have been identical—3 percent—as the table indicates; but since you purchased the bond at a considerable discount, your yield must obviously be higher than 3

FIGURE 12–9

A Page of a Standard Bond Yield Table

3 Percent Coupon

PERCENT PER ANNUM	12½	13	13½	14	14½	15	15½	16
				YEARS TO MATURITY				
2.00	111.011578	111.397602	111.779804	112.158222	112.532893	112.903854	113.271143	113.634795
2.10	109.849442	110.192422	110.531838	110.867727	111.200125	111.529070	111.854597	112.176741
2⅛	109.561107	109.893488	110.222375	110.547805	110.869813	111.188436	111.503709	111.815668
2.15	109.273644	109.595492	109.913918	110.228957	110.540645	110.849018	111.154111	111.455959
2.20	108.701328	109.002303	109.300003	109.594464	109.885721	110.173809	110.458762	110.740616
2¼	108.132472	108.412828	108.690065	108.964217	109.235320	109.503407	109.768511	110.030666
2.30	107.567054	107.827043	108.084076	108.338187	108.589409	108.837775	109.083316	109.326067
2.35	107.005052	107.244924	107.482010	107.716343	107.947955	108.176876	108.403139	108.626775
2⅜	106.725324	106.655231	107.182439	107.406981	107.628888	107.848191	108.064920	108.279106
2.40	106.446442	106.666445	106.883839	107.098655	107.310924	107.520676	107.727941	107.932748
2.45	105.891205	106.091583	106.289536	106.485094	106.678285	106.869138	107.057681	107.243943
2½	105.339317	105.520313	105.699075	105.875629	106.050004	106.222227	106.392323	106.560319
2.55	104.790758	104.952612	105.112428	105.270233	105.426051	105.579907	105.731826	105.881833
2.60	104.245505	104.388455	104.529571	104.668875	104.806392	104.942144	105.076154	105.208444
2⅝	103.974112	104.107698	104.239554	104.369702	104.498164	104.624961	104.750116	104.873649
2.65	103.703538	103.827819	103.950475	104.071528	104.190997	104.308904	104.425269	104.540113
2.70	103.164835	103.270681	103.375116	103.478161	103.579834	103.680152	103.779133	103.876796
2¾	102.629375	102.717016	102.803468	102.888748	102.972871	103.055853	103.137710	103.218456
2.80	102.097138	102.166803	102.235505	102.303260	102.370079	102.435975	102.500962	102.565051
2.85	101.568102	101.620017	101.671202	101.721669	101.771426	101.820484	101.868853	101.916542
2⅞	101.304779	101.347902	101.390415	101.432326	101.473642	101.514373.	101.554526	101.594111
2.90	101.042248	101.076636	101.110534	101.143946	101.176882	101.209346	101.241347	101.272890
2.95	100.519554	100.536638	100.553475	100.570066	100.586416	100.602529	100.618408	100.634055
3.00	100.000000	100.000000	100.000000	100.000000	100.000000	100.000000	100.000000	100.000000
3.05	99.483566	99.466699	99.450085	99.433721	99.417603	99.401726	99.386089	99.370686
3.10	98.970233	98.936714	98.903706	98.871203	98.839195	98.807676	98.776638	98.746074
3⅛	98.714722	98.672957	98.631835	98.591345	98.551478	98.512225	98.473575	98.435520
3.15	98.459979	98.410022	98.360838	98.312418	98.264748	98.217817	98.171614	98.126128
3.20	97.952786	97.886601	97.821457	97.757340	97.694232	97.632118	97.570983	97.510810
3¼	97.448634	97.366430	97.285540	97.205943	97.127619	97.050548	96.974709	96.900082
3.30	96.947503	96.849486	96.753061	96.658201	96.564882	96.473074	96.382759	96.293909
3.35	96.449374	96.335750	96.223998	96.114087	96.005987	95.899667	95.795099	95.692254
3⅜	96.201429	96.080077	95.960740	95.843383	95.727973	95.614479	95.502868	95.393109
3.40	95.954227	95.825198	95.698327	95.573576	95.450911	95.330296	95.211697	95.095080
3.45	95.462043	95.317811	95.176025	95.036643	94.899624	94.764929	94.632518	94.502353
3½	94.972805	94.813567	94.657068	94.503261	94.352100	94.203538	94.057531	93.914035
3.55	94.486491	94.312445	94.141435	93.973407	93.808309	93.646091	93.486702	93.330093
3.60	94.003085	93.814425	93.629101	93.447054	93.268226	93.092560	92.920000	92.750491
3⅝	93.762466	93.566572	93.374165	93.185183	92.999566	92 817254	92.638186	92.462307
3.65	93.522566	93.319486	93.120045	92.924179	92.731823	92.542915	92.357392	92.175195
3.70	93.044918	92.827607	92.614244	92.404756	92.199073	91.997126	91.798847	91.604170
3¾	92.570121	92.338769	92.111675	91.888761	91.669949	91.455165	91.244334	91.037383
3.80	92.098157	91.852951	91.612317	91.376170	91.144425	90.917002	90.693820	90.474799.
3.85	91.629008	91.370133	91.116147	90.866958	90.622475	90.382610	90.147275	89.916385
3⅞	91.395483	91.129843	90.869251	90.613612	90.362832	90.116819	89.875482	89.638731
3.90	91.162656	90.890295	90.623144	90.361102	90.104073	89.851960	89.604669	89.362108
3.95	90.699083	90.413418	90.133286	89.858579	89.589192	89.325023	89.065970	88.811934
4.00	90.238272	89.939482	89.646551	89.359364	89.077808	88.801772	88.531149	88.265833
4.05	89.780204	89.468468	89.162919	88.863434	88.569894	88.282180	88.000176	87.723770
4.10	89.324863	89.000356	88.682367	88.370766	88.065425	87.766218	87.473021	87.185714
4⅛	89.098209	88.767382	88.443240	88.125648	87.814475	87.509590	87.210866	86.918178
4.15	88.872230	88.535126	88.204875	87.881337	87.564377	87.253859	86.949654	86.651632
4.20	88.422289	88.072761	87.730422	87.395125	87.066724	86.745077	86.430046	86.121495
4¼	87.975023	87.613241	87.258988	86.912106	86.572441	86.239845	85.914168	85.595269
4.30	87.530414	87.156548	86.790551	86.432257	86.081505	85.738135	85.401992	85.072924
4.35	87.088445	86.702662	86.325091	85.955558	85.593891	85.239922	84.893489	84.554430

SOURCE: "Acme Table of Bond Values," Financial Publishing Company, Boston.

percent. Looking down the 13-year column, you come to the figure $89.000356 near the bottom. Looking across to the left, you find the exact yield—4.10 percent. In similar fashion, somewhere in the 627 pages of this particular set of tables, you would be able to find the effective yield of any bond with a maturity of from six months to 50 years bearing a coupon rate of from 3 to 8 percent. Other sets of tables cover rates below 3 percent, still others cover maturities of from 50 to 100 years, and there is a special set of tables covering maturities of less than six months. There is, therefore, no need to be concerned with the exact details of computations of bond yields, since it is much more accurate and easier to use prepared bond tables. Bond experts and investment specialists do, and there is no reason why you should not do likewise.

Bond Prices and Interest Rates

The principal risk in high-grade bonds is not related so much to the course of business activity as it is to the trend of interest rates. If you hold high-grade bonds and interest rates, which had been low, start to rise, and you cannot hold your bonds until maturity but are forced to sell them because you need funds, you can suffer a capital loss. Why is this, and how does it work? If interest rates start to rise (because the Federal Reserve raises the discount rate, for example), the 3½ percent rate on the bond, bought at par several years back, will no longer look so attractive as it once did to some holders of the issue, who now become aware of the fact that they can get 4 or 4½ percent in more recent issues. They, therefore, sell the old issue to free their funds for investment in better-yielding issues. This selling pressure forces the price of the old issue down, and it will continue to fall until its price in the market yields the new purchaser the same rate of return as the average new, higher level of rates in the market. Thus as the boom progresses and the demand for money grows and interest rates rise, high-grade bond prices will fall as stock prices rise.

At the top of a boom when the central banking authorities are enforcing a tight-money policy which has driven interest rates up and bond prices down, if your timing is good, switch from common stocks to high-grade bonds just as the boom turns into recession. Tight money will be relaxed, interest rates will be allowed to fall, and high-grade bond prices will rise. In fact the deeper the recession, the higher will go the prices of high-grade bonds as investment demand switches to them and bids up their prices.

The Security behind Bonds

Bonds may be either secured or unsecured and may range from first-mortgage or collateral-trust bonds, on the one hand, to debentures or income bonds, on the other. The security behind the bond, while important, is not necessarily the governing factor, however. The earning power, financial status, and reputation of one company may result in its unsecured bonds being rated higher than the secured bonds of another company. For example, the debentures of A. T. & T. are rated higher than the first-mortgage bonds of Indianapolis Power & Light. The debentures of Commonwealth Edison have a higher rating than the first-mortgage bonds of Missouri Power & Light Company.

In the case of secured bonds, the issuing corporation backs up its promise to pay interest and repay principal by a pledge of specific property, as evidenced by a mortgage bond, a collateral-trust note, or an equipment trust certificate. In the case of unsecured bonds, such as debentures or income bonds, on the other hand, the issuing corporation merely promises to pay interest and repay principal, but there is no specific pledge of security to back up its promise.

Mortgage Bonds

Mortgage bonds are secured by a mortgage on part or all of a company's property. If the company defaults (fails to pay interest or repay principal), the bondholders, through the trustee appointed to represent them and look after their rights, may foreclose the mortgage and take over the pledged property.

When we discussed homeownership and home mortgages, it was stated that the mortgagee gets title (in such states as Massachusetts) or a lien (in other states) on the real estate to secure the promissory note which is given to him. Bond issues are usually large. It would be impossible to give every bondholder title to or a lien on part of the specific property used to secure the bonds. It is much more convenient to transfer the security to a trustee (often a bank) which will represent the bondholders and see that the issuing company does what it has agreed to do. The agreement of the issuing company with the bondholders is contained in a legal instrument called an *indenture*.

Some corporate mortgages have what is known as an *"after-acquired"* clause, which provides that all property thereafter acquired will become subject to the mortgage and automatically be pledged to secure the bond issue. This is so favorable a feature for the investor that it is not widely found. When there is an "after-acquired" property clause and the company wishes to put out another bond issue secured by a mortgage on its property, this second mortgage will be a *junior lien,* subordinate to the first mortgage, or *senior lien,* on the property. Usually, when corporations float junior issues, secured by junior liens, they do not clearly label them as such. They call them "general" or "consolidated" or some other ambiguous name, and the only way you can determine the security status of the bonds exactly is to read the bond indenture carefully—something which the average bondholder, unfortunately, usually never does.

When more bonds may be issued with the same security or under the same mortgage deed, the mortgage is said to be "open"; additional bonds will naturally dilute the security available for each bond. If the mortgage is "closed," no additional bonds may be issued with the same security, and each bond has, therefore, better protection.

Collateral-Trust Bonds

Security for bonds need not be real estate, as in the case of mortgage bonds. Just as we may borrow at a bank and put up securities of one sort or another as collateral for the loan, it is possible for a corporation to issue bonds secured by the pledge of other stocks and bonds which it owns. A bond secured by a pledge of specific securities is known as a "collateral-trust bond." Collateral-trust bonds are issued mainly by holding companies, investment companies, and finance companies, which do not have much real property, as would a utility or a railroad, to pledge.

The securities or notes pledged are transferred to the trustee who acts for the bondholders. The income from these assets goes to the corporation as long as it continues to pay interest on the collateral-trust bonds (or "notes," as they are sometimes called). If it should default on interest payments, the trustee can use the income from the securities held to reimburse the bondholders. The investor should realize, however, that if the securities pledged as collateral are mainly common stock, the superior safety of a bond is, in this case, merely an illusion. Investment experts tell us, however, that the strength of a collateral-trust bond lies not so much in the type of securities pledged as in the general financial standing of the companies whose securities are used as collateral.

Equipment Trust Obligations

A relatively safe type of bond investment is the equipment trust certificate, which is used to finance the purchase of rolling stock by railroads. Approximately one seventh of railroad debt is represented by these certificates. They owe their strength to the fact that they are secured by railroad rolling stock, which can be moved anywhere in the country. If the certificates are in default, the equipment may be sold to another railroad.

Under the Philadelphia Plan, title to equipment (freight cars, locomotives, passenger coaches, etc.) being bought by a railroad vests in a trustee who holds it for the benefit of certificate-holders. The railroad makes a down payment (perhaps 20 percent), and the trustee issues equipment trust certificates to cover the balance of the purchase price of the equipment. The trustee then leases the equipment to the railroad under an agreement whereby the railroad obtains title to the equipment only when all obligations have been met. Sometime when you are at a railroad station, it may interest you to note that each piece of equipment financed by such an arrangement has a plate attached to it stating where the ownership lies (temporarily in the trustee).

Debentures

Debentures are unsecured bonds protected only by the general credit of the borrowing corporation. If there are no mortgage bonds, and debentures are the senior issues, they may rate very high. A. T. & T., for example, has only debentures outstanding. There are no bonds senior to these. Debentures may contain a "covenant of equal coverage," which means that if any mortgage bond is issued in the future, which ordinarily would take precedence over the debentures, the issuer agrees to secure the debentures equally. In some states the law requires that this be done.

All direct domestic obligations of federal, state, and municipal governments in the United States are debentures. Since this type of security is protected only by the general promise to pay and, in the event of default, the debenture-holder is merely a general creditor, debentures can usually be sold only by corporations enjoying very high credit standings. The value of a debenture must be judged wholly in terms of the overall financial status and earnings outlook of the issuer, which is the best basis for evaluating any bond.

Income or Adjustment Bonds

Income or adjustment bonds are bonds on which interest is not mandatory but is paid only when earned and declared. Usually, income or adjustment bonds result from corporate reorganizations, under which it is desired to reduce fixed interest charges to a level which can be reasonably expected to be met. Former holders of junior liens are, therefore, as a result of the reorganization, given income or adjustment bonds to replace their former holdings. Several examples of income bonds are (*a*) the Atchison, Topeka, & Santa Fe Railroad adjustment 4s of 1995, issued in the railroad's reorganization of 1895; (*b*) the Erie Railroad 5s of 2020; and (*c*) the Lehigh Valley income 4s of 2003. The Atchison 4s are rated AA, while the latter two are rated C. The Atchison issue is an exception. Most income bonds are rated in the C category, because, as a group, they are regarded as speculative. In a few instances they are secured by general mortgages, but not in most cases. Some income bonds, as the Atchison issue, are cumulative, in that interest not paid on the due date accrues as a charge against future earnings and must be paid before any dividends may be paid on stock. In this sense they resemble cumulative preferred stock.

Guaranteed or Assumed Bonds

Particularly in the case of railroads and railroad terminals, you find one company guaranteeing the bonds of another. In the railroad consolidations of the last half of the nineteenth century there was much guaranteeing or assuming of bonds. For example, the Pennsylvania Railroad Company technically operates only from Philadelphia to Pittsburgh, but the Pennsylvania Railroad System includes many leased lines, such as the United New Jersey (New York to Philadelphia) and the Pittsburgh, Fort Wayne, & Chicago (Pittsburgh to Chicago). The Pennsylvania Railroad Company guarantees the outstanding bonds of these leased lines.

Terminal companies generally have their bonds guaranteed by the railroad companies principally using the terminal. For example, the Terminal Railroad Associates of St. Louis' Refunding and Improvement 2⅞s of 1985, rated Aaa by Moody's, are guaranteed by 15 railroads. The value of a guaranteed bond is determined not only by the credit of the guaranteeing company but also by the value, essentiality, and usefulness of its own property to the guaranteeing company. Leases are sometimes not renewed, and guaranties are allowed to lapse, in cases where the value of the underlying property proves to be less than anticipated.

Convertible Bonds

Convertible bonds are bonds which may be exchanged, at the option of the holder, for a specified amount of other securities (usually common stock) of the issuing corporation. Theoretically, this would appear to be an ideal security, since it affords, on the one hand, the safety of a fixed-income creditor obligation and, on the other, an opportunity to share in the prospective profits of the company. Thus it would seem, at one and the same time, to provide safety as well as a hedge against inflation. See Figure 12–10.

The value of convertible bonds in the market tends to rise as the price of the common into which they are convertible rises. On the other hand, in a declining market, the price declines until the conversion parity point is reached; that is, the conversion feature no longer has any value, and the bond, therefore, sells solely on the basis of its fixed-income, safety status. Thus you may conclude that there are two considerations

FIGURE 12–10

CONVERTIBLE SECURITIES

Convertible securities appeal primarily to investors who seek the relative income safety of senior securities plus some of the speculative qualities of common stocks. Risk is cushioned by the level at which such securities might be expected to sell should the conversion feature be of no immediate importance or should common stock prices decline. Usually, where the conversion feature is of value, convertibles sell at premiums over that value. In some instances, the conversion feature may never become of actual value; in the case of others, the risk of call must be considered.

Security	Moody's Rating	Approximate Amount Outstanding (Millions)	Convertible into Com. at Rate of (Per $1,000 Bond)	Current Call Price§	Approximate Price 2-12-64 Bond	Approximate Price 2-12-64 Common Stock	Com. Price Needed for Profitable Conversion	Yield on Bond or Preferred#
BONDS:								
American Distilling Conv. Sub. Deb. 4⅜s, 1986	Ba	$ 9.5	23.15 shs. through 10-31-71	103⅞	103	32	45	4.17
Am. Mach. & Found. Cv. Sub. Deb. 4¼s, 1981	Ba	39.9	16.77 shs. through 3-1-71†	103½	90	18	54	5.14
Amer. Optical Cv. Sub. Deb. 4.40s, 1980	Baa	8.0	17.97 shs. through 10-1-70†	104	129	68	72	2.23
Bausch & Lomb Conv. Sub. Deb. 4½s, 1979	Baa	6.8	27.78 shs. through 6-1-79	103.55[1]	118	36	43	3.00
Baxter Labs. Conv. Sub. Deb. 4s, 1982□	Baa	10.0	26.32 shs. at any time	105¾[2]	110	26	42	3.26
Broadway-Hale Conv. Sub. Deb. 5s, 1979	Ba	9.1	30 shs. through 7-31-69	104[3]	117	30	40	3.53
Carrier Corp. Conv. Sub. Deb. 4⅛s, 1982	Baa	17.0	16.40 shs. through 2-1-67	103.575	102	47	63	3.97
City Products Conv. Sub. Deb. 5s, 1982	Ba	15.0	31.93 shs. at any time	104½[1]	118	35	37	3.63
Cons. Electrodynamics Conv. Sub. Deb. 4½s, 1984	Ba	7.1	25.63 shs. through 5-31-69†	104.20[1]	102	22	40	4.35
Fruehauf Trailer. Conv. Sub Deb. 4s, 1976	Ba	26.9	38.11 shs. at any time	103¾	114	29	30	2.63
Hooker Chem. Conv. Sub. Deb. 5s, 1984	Baa	24.4	23.29 shs. at any time	104	123	40	53	3.40
Hunt Foods & Ind. Conv. Sub. Deb. 4⅜s, 1986	Ba	38.8	20.40 shs. through 6-30-66†	103⅞[4]	97	27	48	4.59
International Silver Conv. Sub. Deb. 5s, 1981	Ba	6.9	36.95 shs. at any time	104½[3]	155	42	42	1.37
Keystone Steel & Wire Conv. Sub. Deb. 4½s, 1981	Baa	20.0	25 shs. at any time	105½	109	38	44	3.78
National Cylinder Gas Conv. Sub. Deb. 5⅛s, 1977	Ba	17.5	25.72 shs. through 9-1-67	103½	109	26	43	4.22
Northrop Corp. Conv. Sub. Deb. 5s, 1979	Ba	8.7	51.95 shs. at any time	104[4]	116	20	23	3.61
Olin Mathieson Conv. Sub. Deb. 5½s, 1982	Ba	60.0	20 shs. through 11-15-72†	104½	121	46	61	3.87
Rohr Aircraft Conv. Sub. Deb. 5¼s, 1977	Ba	5.8	54.05 shs. at any time	103.41	108	16	20	4.43
Stouffer Foods Conv. Sub. Deb. 4¼s, 1981Ⓢ□	Ba	7.5	21.65 shs. at any time	103¾	105	29	49	3.85
Union Oil Conv. Sub. Deb. 4¼s, 1991	Baa	59.3	16.33 shs. through 6-1-66†	104¼	133	81	82	2.56
Vendo Co. Conv. Sub. Deb. 4½s, 1980	Ba	5.2	21.05 shs. at any time	103¾	91	16	44	5.34
PREFERRED STOCKS:		Thousand Shares	(Per Pfd. Share)		Pfd. Stock			
Consolidated Edison 4.12% Cum. Conv. (Series A)		911.7	1.25 shs. at any time	102½[5]	108	82	87	3.81
Emerson Electric $1 Cum. Conv. ($5 Par)		188.1	0.16 shs. at any time	27½[9]	35	39	22	2.86
International Pipe & Ceramics 5% Cum. Conv.		334.2	2.625 shs. at any time	110[6]	104	23	40	4.81
Kaiser Alum. 4¾% Cum. Conv. (1957 Series)		299.5	2.11 shs. through 5-31-67†	103	103	36	49	4.61
Permanente Cement 5% Cum. Conv. ($50 par)		365.0	2.17 shs. at any time	54½	54	16	25	4.63
Pittston Co. $3.50 Cum. Conv. ($75 Par)		286.2	1.93 shs. through 12-31-81	80	105	55	55	3.33
Purex $1.35 Cum. Conv. ($5 Par)		432.6	1.2 shs. at any time	37½[10]	40	27	34	3.38
Reynolds Metals 4½% 2nd. Conv.		616.1	2.0 shs. at any time	103	107	36	54	4.21
Std. Packaging 6% Cum. Conv. ($20 Par)		789.2	1.0 shs. at any time	40	23	11	24	5.22
Texas Eastern Trans. $5.125 Sub. Cum. Conv.		200.0	5.0 shs. through 7-31-66†	104.64[7]	111	20	23	4.62
Warner Lambert $4 Cum. Conv.		345.7	3.0 shs. at any time	104[8]	107	25	36	3.74
Whirlpool 4¼% Cum. Conv. ($80 Par)		215.5	1.45 shs. at any time	80	91	61	63	3.74

§—Lowest effective call price over next six months. †—Fewer shares thereafter. #—Maturity yield on all bonds. [1]—Through May 31, 1964; lower thereafter. [2]—Through March 31, 1964; lower thereafter. [3]—Through July 31, 1964; lower thereafter. [4]—Through June 30, 1964; lower thereafter. [5]—Through April 30, 1964; lower thereafter. [6]—Beginning August 1, 1972. [7]—Through August 1, 1964; lower thereafter. [8]—Beginning December 1, 1965. [9]—Beginning July 1, 1968. [10]—Beginning October 31, 1968. Ⓢ—Merrill Lynch, Pierce, Fenner & Smith Incorporated, for its own account, and/or its officers or voting stockholders, on February 3, 1964 had a small direct and/or indirect beneficial interest (less than $50,000) in this security. □—Merrill Lynch, Pierce, Fenner & Smith Incorporated was recently, or is expected shortly to be, a manager of a public offering of securities of this corporation.

SOURCE: Merrill Lynch, Pierce, Fenner & Smith, Inc.

affecting the market value of a convertible bond: (*a*) its actual value as a fixed-income obligation and (*b*) its potential value in terms of the stock into which it may be converted.

BUSINESS BUZZ

The Commercial and Financial Chronicle

"Well, if you consider a four hour briefing on convertible subordinated debentures a good time—then I had a good time!"

Callable Bonds

Callable bonds are bonds which may be redeemed by the issuing company prior to the maturity date. Usually the bonds require the company to pay a premium over their face value when called before maturity. Why should a corporation, when it has borrowed for a term of, say, 20 years, decide to retire its debt in a shorter period of time? Usually it does so because it finds that, due to a decline in interest rates, it can borrow more cheaply now. It therefore calls the old issue with the higher coupon rate and sells a new one at a lower rate. Some bonds are noncallable. Back in 1886 the West Shore Railroad issued 475-year noncallable 4 percent bonds which cannot be paid off before the year 2361.

Because bonds are likely to be called when it is advantageous to the issuer and, therefore, disadvantageous to the bondholder, there is usually a premium paid over and above the maturity price if the bond is called. The call price may be 105, for example, if the redemption value at maturity is 100. Frequently, also, the premiums are on a sliding scale, with higher premiums paid for calls in the early life of the bond, when it has a long period to run, and lower premiums if the bond is called later in its existence.

Serial Bonds, Series Bonds, and Sinking Funds

Usually, all bonds of the same issue mature and are retired at the same time out of a sinking fund set up for that purpose. Some issues, however, are retired serially, some in series, and some (perpetual bonds) are never retired at all. When all the bonds of a given issue are to be retired simultaneously at maturity, it is customary and good financial practice for the corporation to set aside a definite sum out of earnings each year to accumulate in a sinking fund, out of the cumulated proceeds of which the bond issue will be paid off at maturity. Actually, the sinking fund is almost never held in cash but (a) is used to buy up or redeem some of the outstanding bonds, either by call or in the open market, each year, or (b) is invested in other securities to earn a return. The sinking-fund arrangement is of definite value to the bondholder because his position is strengthened by the accumulation of funds toward the redemption of the issue, or, if bonds are bought up and retired, by the diminution in the company's liability at the final maturity date. Furthermore, the purchase of the bonds in the market tends to support the price of the remainder of the issue and thus enhances its marketability.

When serial bonds are issued, the maturities of segments of the entire issue are staggered; some bonds of the issue will mature in five years, some in seven and one half, some in ten, etc. The interest rate may or may not vary; but if it does, lower rates will be paid on the near maturities and higher rates on the more distant maturities.

Series bonds, in contrast to serial bonds, not only have different maturities, but they are not issued at the same time. Each series, under the same mortgage, is issued at a different time, with an interval of as much as a year or two between individual series. Usually designated by letter, such as "Series A," "Series B," "Series C," etc., each has its own distinctive features, such as date of issue, coupon rate, call price, date of maturity, etc. The one feature in common is the same mortgage.

Perpetual bonds are interest-bearing creditor obligations which have no maturity date. They run on forever; and if you want to get your money back, you must find someone to sell them to—someone who wants to buy them. Thus there is no fixed maturity or redemption value, and what you realize for them will depend on the market price at time of sale. Both governments and private corporations have issued perpetual bonds; British Government "Consols," French "Rentes," and the Canadian Pacific Railroad perpetual 4s. Some corporations have issued bonds with maturity dates so fantastically far in the future as to be, for all practical purposes, perpetual bonds. The Elmira & Williamsport Railroad, for example, issued a 5 percent income bond due in the year 2862. It is rated "A" by Standard & Poor's.

Financial Analysis and Bond Evaluation

While all the technical aspects of bonds which have been described thus far are useful in judging the quality and soundness of an issue, the real basis for evaluation lies in the financial status and earning power of the borrowing corporation or government. The farsightedness and efficiency of the management, the outlook for the industry, the position of the particular firm in the industry, and the soundness of the company's internal finances as reflected in its balance sheet and income account, all must be carefully considered.

The security behind a bond is, in itself, no guaranty of soundness, since the value of pledged property is often dependent on the earning power of the corporation. If the corporation fails, its fixed assets may prove to be worth very little. A good example is the Seaboard—All Florida Railway's first-mortgage 6s, which sold in 1931 at 1 cent on the dollar, soon after completion of the road. In selecting bonds, it is best to try and choose a company which will avoid trouble rather than seek to protect yourself in the event of trouble.

The use of certain financial standards, which will be described in Chapter 14, are of value in judging the financial position of a company. For example, a company's average earnings before taxes should, over a period of seven–ten years, have covered total fixed charges—at least four times in the case of public utilities, five times for a railroad, and seven times for an industrial company. If earnings have not provided this coverage, on the average, then you ought not to think of buying the company's bonds. If you do—if you ignore or overlook these and similar tests which experts have worked out—you may find the company defaulting on interest payments in poor years and ultimately involved in a reorganization.

Real Estate Investment

The lures of tax-free income, high returns ranging from 10 to 15 percent, substantial capital gains, and, in addition, an excellent hedge against inflation, have combined to heighten interest over the last decade in real estate investment and speculation.

There are a wide and unfortunately bewildering variety of ways to invest or speculate in real estate. Generally, the main channels are buying your own home or apartment, investing in raw land or in mortgages, participating in real estate syndicates, buying shares in real estate companies, or investing in real estate investment trusts.

Raw Land

As cities grow and the urban pattern encroaches upon suburbia, land in the path of the expansion increases in value. Over time the sheer growth of population tends to enhance the value of raw land. Seemingly all you have to do is follow the bus line out, see where the vacant lots start and buy a few. It isn't this easy, however. Towns don't necessarily grow in all directions and you may pick the wrong end of town. You can't borrow money on land from banks, insurance companies, or savings and loan associations. You either sink your own cash or you put up a down payment and give the seller a purchase money mortgage for the main amount. In Florida, for example, it is customary to put up 29 percent of the cost in cash and give a purchase money mortgage for the remainder. But you have to pay interest on the mortgage, of course, and usually at a rate of at least 6 percent. And you have to pay taxes on the idle, vacant land, and a 10 percent sales commission to the real estate broker through whom you made the purchase. And you lose the return you could otherwise have earned by investing the money you put up as a cash down payment. Therefore if you have to hold the lot or lots for a while waiting for the growth of population and enhancement of values to occur, it can cost you a good sum each year without any return. Some experts estimate that your lots must increase in value 12 to 15 percent a year to provide a gain equal to that you could obtain in other, more conventional, forms of investment. Also you may be locked in. You may want to sell and find no one who wants to buy. Or, on the other hand, you may be one of the fortunate ones, and double or triple your money in a few years. It's a tricky operation.

Real Estate Syndicates

In the real estate syndicate you obtain the benefit of professional real estate judgment, at least in theory. The real estate syndicate is a limited partnership formed to offer participations to numerous nonprofessional investors. It was very popular in the 1950's and enabled the smaller investor to participate in ventures involving higher cost, higher yielding properties that otherwise would have been available only to wealthier investors. Partnership shares were sold in units of from $500 to $5,000 and even higher in semiprivate syndicates. Yields ranged from 8 to 15 percent, much higher usually than returns on stocks and bonds. The key advantage of the syndicate was the tax-free cash flow through accelerated depreciation. Usually, half or more of syndicate yields came from depreciation and were a return of capital and not taxable as income. This advantage needs to be understood clearly because it lies at the bottom of the attractiveness of much real estate investment.

Changing Times cites an example, given in a speech before the New York Society of Security Analysts, to show how depreciation is used to achieve tax-free income.[12]

Assume that property has been bought for $1,000,000—$900,000 for the building and $100,000 for the land. Cash payment was $400,-000 and a 6 percent mortgage was secured for the balance, or $600,-000. Annual payments on the mortgage are $45,000 including principal and interest. Rent comes in at $100,000 a year, and operating expenses, including insurance, repairs, real estate taxes, and management, are $19,000. Here are two statements showing how a tax-free income of $36,000 a year could be paid to owners of the building.

PROFIT AND LOSS FOR INCOME TAX PURPOSES

Rent income		$100,000
Expenses:		
Mortgage interest	$36,000	
Depreciation (5%)	45,000	
Operating expenses	19,000	
Total expenses		100,000
Net profit or loss		–0–

CASH FLOW

Rent		$100,000
Cash disbursements:		
Mortgage (principal and interest)	$45,000	
Operating expenses	19,000	
Total expenses		64,000
Balance for distribution		$ 36,000

As you can see, here is a property that made no profit, and therefore paid no income tax, but was able to give its owners a 9 percent return on

---

[12] *Changing Times, The Kiplinger Magazine,* January, 1962, p. 29.

the cash investment of $400,000. This technique can be carried even further. If a faster rate of depreciation is used, the owners may not only get a tax-free distribution but receive a tax loss in addition, which they may use to reduce their other income.

The syndicate appeared to be a way a small investor could participate in a high-return, tax-free real estate investment and avoid the headaches of property management and be in partnership with professional operators. While some of the earlier syndicates worked out well, later ones paid excessively high prices for properties, underestimated maintenance, overestimated income and after the first few years when the accelerated depreciation fell off, proved disappointing. The syndicates that were offered to the public, and required extensive sales efforts and numerous small investors, were likely to be the least attractive, because if they had really excellent prospects they would have been absorbed by big professional investors and never offered to the public.

Disadvantages of Syndicates

Most syndicates owned a single property which no matter how well chosen was more risky than diversified real estate investment. Also for the individual participant there was little liquidity. No formal market existed for the sale of a participating unit of the syndicate. Usually the contract made no provision for the repurchase or retirement of the participation. Furthermore, the property share in the syndicate could not be used for loans. Syndicators took much of the profit with little financial investment. One proposed syndicate listed in its prospectus the following details: For forming the syndicate and financing the estimated $50,000 organizational expenses, the promoters were to collect $612,-350 in profit. An additional $265,650 in sales commission would go to their sales subsidiary. The subsidiary had agreed to hire the sellers of the building as "management consultants" at an annual fee of $20,000 for 25 years or $500,000. The prospectus conceded, "The services of the consultants may not be required more than one day each month nor more than 12 times in any fiscal year. No representation is made that there is any relationship between the consultants' services and the compensation they are to receive." Even if the sellers worked their full 12 days a year, their pay would be at the rate of $1,600 a day. The prospective investors shunned the deal and the prospectus was revised.[13] Supervision by the SEC was avoided by limiting investment eligibility to residents of a single state. Only a very few states regulate intrastate syndicates.

---

[13] *Forbes,* August 1, 1962.

A number of highly speculative syndicates collapsed in scandalous fashion in the early sixties and made investors wary.

Real Estate Companies

A number of real estate syndicates converted subsequently into publicly held companies to finance large property acquisitions. The owner of stock in a real estate corporation has all the advantages of the usual stockholder, liquidity, marketability, limited liability, plus that which accrues to him because his funds are invested in a diversified portfolio representing various properties whose blend of earnings are combined in a single earnings package.

There are a number of different types of real estate companies from which to choose. There are diversified real estate companies such as City Investing, Webb & Knapp, converted syndication corporations such as Basic Properties, First National Realty, Kratter, Tenney, etc., construction firms such as Tishman and Uris, hotel-motel firms as Hilton, Sheraton, Loew's, garage and parking lot operators such as Kinney, Airport Parking, etc., and land development firms as General Development, Del Webb, Gulf American Land. While the returns, which investment in such companies yield, are less than for syndicates, such investments provide greater diversification, marketability, and flexibility. You can buy small or large amounts of stock depending on your financial ability.

In evaluating such companies it is more important to look to their cash flow before taxes than to their net income after taxes. Cash flow is depreciation plus net income. Depreciation in industrial firms is plowed back to replace old and worn equipment, but in real estate operations, well-constructed and well-maintained buildings have actually increased rather than decreased in value. Thus the depreciation allowed on them represents nontaxable earnings which can be paid out to investors. This results in large tax-sheltered earnings and at times high dividends.

Real Estate Investment Trusts

Since 1960 interest has shifted to the real estate investment trust primarily for tax purposes. The concept of the real estate investment trust goes back to 1886. But the trusts, which are unincorporated, increased rapidly in numbers as a result of a 1960 law which permits them to operate without paying taxes if they pay out 90 percent of their income to shareholders and meet certain other restrictions on operations and investments. The trusts, of which there are now over 60, are set up along the same lines as closed end investment companies—pooling money of small investors for placement in real estate ventures. They avoid making any promise on their return to shareholders and operate at a lower, and, theoretically, safer yield than syndicates. Trusts now yield anywhere from 3 to 8 percent.

To qualify as a real estate investment trust there must be at least 100 shareholders and not more than 50 percent of the shares may be owned by five or fewer persons. These provisions are designed to insure that every trust will be broadly owned and not serve as a personal holding company for a few investors. At least 75 percent of gross income must be from investments related to real estate and not more than 25 percent of the total assets can be invested in other than real estate.

The trusts may not manage any property they own. Nor may they engage in developing or selling land. Capital gains on securities held less than six months and on properties held less than four years must constitute less than 30 percent of the trusts gross income. Thus the trust must place its emphasis on longer term investments in office buildings, apartments, shopping centers, leases, mortgages, etc. The law discourages it from engaging in the kind of wheeling and dealing operations characteristic of big real estate operators and syndicators.

Types of Trusts

There are several different kinds of trusts.

Blank-Check Trusts—so called because they sell their shares to investors and then seek properties in which to invest.

Purchase Trusts—go to the public seeking funds to buy specified properties. Sometimes these are properties in which the promoters have interests. The SEC requires the offering prospectus to include a full description of the properties. This must be done whenever a trust offers new shares to the public.

Exchange Trusts—offer their shares in exchange for properties. This enables property owners to diversify their holdings and postpone any capital gains tax until they sell their shares of the trust.

Mortgage Trusts—do not buy properties but invest in mortgages and construction loans. They are, therefore, competing with all other financial institutions trying to invest mortgage money.

Procedures

All the trusts are users of borrowed capital. Some are permitted to mortgage up to two thirds of their total properties' market value. Others have set lower limits for themselves.

The trusts also vary in their treatment of depreciation. Some use accelerated depreciation but not for the same reason corporations do—i.e., to defer taxes. The trusts, which are not taxed on distributed earnings, do it to protect their shareholders from taxation. Because any distribution paid out of depreciation instead of net income is a return of capital, the shareholder owes no tax on it until he recovers the full cost of his shares or sells them—at which point he pays a capital gains tax instead of straight income taxes.

Those who favor straight-line depreciation feel that the other method may lead to a cash bind since principal payments get bigger as the years go by, while depreciation allowances, under an accelerated schedule, get smaller and eventually no longer cover the mortgage amortization.

The Ten Largest Real Estate Investment Trusts

Trust	Assets ($000)	Debt ($000)	Net Cash Flow*	Net Income	Payout	Price $	Indicated Yield (%)
			$ per Share, Latest Quarter			Nov. 20, 1963	
Continental Mortgage Investors	54,870	30,329	.273	.273	.25	14¾	6.8
First Mortgage Investors	51,800	36,450	.254	.242	.24	15⅝	6.1
First Union Realty	46,042	24,486	.206	.069	.195	13½	5.8
R.E.I.T. of America	37,922	10,963	.344	.310	.30	21⅜	5.6
U.S. Realty Investments	33,951	23,691	.195	.020	.175	9¼	7.6
First Natl. Real Estate Trust	28,929	14,477	.184	.061	.175	9¼	7.6
National Realty Investors	22,694	10,068	.212	.122	.15	10	6.0
Pennsylvania R.E.I.T.	22,567	15,980	.233	.140	.20	10⅜	7.7
Greenfield R.E.I.T.	20,392	10,661	.225	.112	.225	14⅝	6.2
Franklin Realty	20,258	13,271	.109	.087	.075	9⅝	3.1

The ten largest trusts operate with dissimilar financial strategies. Some, like Pennsylvania R.E.I.T., have heavy debt burdens and a lot of leverage; some others, notably R.E.I.T. of America, have low debt ratios. The trusts that use straight-line depreciation, such as R.E.I.T. of America and Franklin Realty, show high net incomes in proportion to cash flow. Their payouts to stockholders are usually made out of net income and are thus fully taxable, while the distributions of the trusts that use accelerated deprication are, in varying degrees, tax-sheltered returns of capital. (The two mortgage trusts have no properties and thus no depreciation allowances.) To figure yields, Fortune multiplied the latest quarterly payout by four; however, the payouts of some trusts are likely to be higher because their distributions are still in a rising trend.

* After deducting principal payments on mortgages.
Source: Fortune, January, 1964.

The advocates of accelerated depreciation feel this can be handled by refinancing mortgages or by selling properties and buying different ones in order to acquire new depreciation bases.

Real estate trusts usually have but one class of stock. Management responsibility is vested in trustees. The shareholder has no voice in policy. In some cases he is allowed to elect trustees each year. Elsewhere he may only have the right to remove a trustee by two-thirds vote or three-quarters vote and elect a replacement. Sometimes he has no vote at all.

As compared to the real estate syndicate, the real estate investment trust provides much greater liquidity for the investor. Usually shares can be sold either on organized exchanges or over-the-counter. It also usually provides greater diversification. It usually invests in a number of properties, not just one or two as in the case of the syndicate. As compared to real estate companies, the real estate investment trust must pay out 90 percent of its net income. The real estate company does not have to do this. The R.E.I.T. is not subject to the corporate income tax whereas the real estate company is.

As compared to direct investment in common stock or shares of investment companies, investing in real estate investment trusts raises some difficult questions. Are insiders unloading properties at inflated prices on the trust? Is the trust paying a reasonable price for the properties it acquires or in which it invests? Real estate values are harder to measure than values in securities. What kind of management fee is being charged? Is this fair and reasonable? Who are the trustees? Are they competent, experienced in real estate investment, and honest? You should have answers to all these questions before you invest in a real estate investment trust.

SUGGESTED READINGS

1. *Fortune's Guide to Personal Investing,* by the Editors of *Fortune.* New York: McGraw-Hill Book Co., Inc., 1963.

2. Janet Low, *The Investor's Dictionary.* New York: Simon & Schuster, Inc., 1964.

3. Louis Engel, *How to Buy Stocks.* New York: Bantam Books, paperbound. A free copy may be obtained by writing to Mr. Engel, who is a Vice President of Merrill Lynch, Pierce, Fenner & Smith, at 70 Pine Street, New York, N.Y., 10005.

4. Benjamin Graham, David L. Dodd, and Sidney Cottle, *Security Analysis: Principles and Techniques.* 4th ed. New York: McGraw-Hill Book Co., Inc., 1962.

5. William C. Freund and Murray G. Lee, *Investment Fundamentals.* New York: The American Bankers Association, 1960.

6. Joseph E. Granville, *A Strategy for Daily Stock Market Timing for Maximum Profit* (1961) and *New Key to Stock Market Profits* (1963), Englewood Cliffs, N.J.: Prentice-Hall, Inc.

7. *How to Invest,* published by Merrill Lynch, Pierce, Fenner & Smith, New York. A free copy may be obtained by writing to this firm at 70 Pine Street, New York, N.Y., 10005.

8. *The Exchange,* monthly magazine published by the New York Stock Exchange. For a sample copy write to New York Stock Exchange, 11 Wall Street, New York, N.Y., 10005.

9. William L. Jiler, *How Charts Can Help You in the Stock Market.* New York: Commodity Research Publications Corp., 1962.

10. Douglas H. Bellemore, *Investments: Principles and Practice.* 2d ed. New York: Simmons-Boardman Books, 1960.

11. John W. Hazard and Lew G. Coit, *The Kiplinger Book on Investing for the Years Ahead.* New York: Doubleday & Company, Inc., 1962.

12. Leo Barnes, *Your Investments.* Issued annually. Larchmont, New York: American Research Council.

13. Walter K. Gutman, *You Only Have to Get Rich Once.* New York: E. P. Dutton & Co., Inc., 1961.

14. *101 Growth Stocks.* New York: Merrill Lynch, Pierce, Fenner & Smith, October, 1955. A free copy may be obtained by writing to the firm at 70 Pine Street, New York, N.Y., 10005.

15. *Heirloom Stocks.* Issued annually. New York: Paine, Webber, Jackson & Curtis. A free copy may be obtained by writing to the firm at 25 Broad Street, New York, N.Y., 10004; or 24 Federal Street, Boston, Mass.; 209 South LaSalle Street, Chicago, Illinois; or 204 W. 7th Street, Los Angeles, Calif.

16. *Senior Securities.* New York: Merrill Lynch, Pierce, Fenner & Smith. A free copy may be obtained by writing to the firm at 70 Pine Street, New York, N.Y., 10005.

17. Richard H. Rush, *A Strategy of Investing for Higher Returns.* Englewood Cliffs, N.J.: Prentice-Hall, Inc., 1962.

18. "Real Estate Speculation," *Changing Times, The Kiplinger Magazine,* January, 1964.

19. "Real Estate Investment Trusts," *Changing Times, The Kiplinger Magazine,* January, 1962.

20. "The Prudent Play in Real Estate," *Business Week,* March 28, 1964.

21. "A New Road into Real Estate," *Fortune,* January, 1964.

CASE PROBLEMS

1. Jane and Bob, a young married couple, are both working. She intends to continue to do so for another three or four years. They have been living on his salary, placing most of her $3,500 a year take-home pay in their savings account, in which they have about $5,000. They now plan to invest about $2,000 and her current income in securities. Bob is buying a 20-payment life insurance policy and their Blue Cross–Blue Shield insurance out of his salary. What kind of an investment program would you suggest for them?

2. Jack Rothwell, a lawyer, age 45, is married and has three children (ages 12, 14, and 15). He has a current income of $25,000 a year. During the years he has built up considerable savings through insurance and investments (in stocks). He decided to buy some bonds, primarily as a hedge against downward fluctuations in the business cycle, and partly to round out his investment program. What types of bonds would best meet his needs?

3. Paul and Dorothy have been married a year. Paul is studying for his doctorate in history, which he expects to receive in two years, and has just been hired at a neighboring institution as a half-time instructor. His wife has a full-time job. They have been living on Dorothy's salary and have been able to add $30 to their savings bank account each month. They rent a small apartment, are covered by Blue Cross–Blue Shield, and have a small amount of life insurance. Should they consider investing the additional income from Paul's new position in stocks? Why? Why not?

4. John Blake is 55 years old; his wife is 50. Their two sons have graduated from college and have good jobs. Blake is earning $10,000 and hopes to retire after another 10 years, at which time he will receive a pension of $5,000 a year. He owns his home and has sufficient life, health, and general insurance. They have emergency funds in the savings bank. He has just inherited $50,000 which he wishes to invest, along with some additional money he believes he can save, since he will no longer have any college bills for his boys. He thinks he knows a good deal about investing, although he has never actually done any himself. He asks for your suggestions.

5. Tom and Polly are a young married couple with two children (ages 2 and 4). Thus far the family has lived on his salary; he feels that he has enough health insurance protection which he obtained through his company. In addition he is covered by a $20,000 straight life insurance policy (paid up at age 65), which seems adequate. He has just received a $25,000 inheritance from his uncle and wants to invest it in growth stocks. Help him select five growth stocks and justify your choices.

6. Terry and Judy have recently moved to Scarsdale with their two young children, since Terry has been transferred to the New York office of his company. He has group life and health insurance through his firm and a tidy sum in the bank. They have just bought a house, but do not know how long his firm will want him to remain at the home office. They feel they can afford to invest about $1,200–$1,300 a year and have heard that stock brokerage firms are encouraging small investors. What suggestions can you give them?

7. The Dew Drop Inn Company, Inc., is a chain of restaurants in a large

city. It is a family-held corporation, and its capitalization consists of 1,000 shares of common stock divided equally among five brothers. The stock is not for sale on the market but is valued on the books at $100 per share. All the owners agree that this price represents a fair value. Business opportunities look good. The company wishes to expand and finance this expansion by offering rights in the ratio of 5 to 1 at $80 for each new share. One brother, Larry, cannot afford to retain his equity in the company. He wants to know how much he should receive when he offers to sell his rights to his brothers and what percentage of the business he will retain.

8. Bryan has been buying the common stocks of companies which, after careful study, he expected would experience a healthy growth. He is now worth $50,000. In two more years, he must retire without pension from his $10,000-a-year job. Although his three children are grown up and independent, his wife (age 62) is bedridden, thus causing large medical expenses. Under the circumstances, would you advise any change in his investment practices? Explain and justify.

9. When Timothy Lingham finally had $5,000 which he felt he could invest in securities, it was toward the end of a long period of prosperity which Lingham thought could only be followed by several years of poor business conditions. Under the circumstances, what investment policy would be most suitable for his consideration?

10. Amos and Natalie Hopkins have just made the final payment on their home. They have three children (ages 9, 14, and 17). Amos runs the local hardware store (he owns the stock of merchandise and the building) and has kept about $5,000 on deposit for several years to meet the needs of the business. For several years he has been carrying $50,000 of straight life insurance on his life. Now he feels that they can invest about $3,000 yearly in stocks and bonds. If you were in his position, what kind of an investment program would you develop?

11. Samuel Lincoln is a trustee. He is to pay the income of a $250,000 estate annually to John Brown for life. Upon Brown's death he is to turn over the principal of the estate to a designated college. Lincoln has an opportunity to invest the $250,000 in high-grade 3 percent bonds, which he can buy to yield 4 percent. Should he do so? Why, why not?

12. Saul Levine is 30, married, and earns $11,000 a year. His wife has inherited $75,000 and they are debating how to invest it. He favors real estate. She prefers blue chip common stocks for their safety and marketability. He argues that returns over time are higher in real estate and that it is a better hedge against inflation. With whom would you side in this debate? Why? How would you suggest investing the $75,000?

13. Kickham, age 32, has a wife (age 30) and three children (ages 3, 4, and 6). He is the manager of a local factory, where he earns $9,000 a year. He owns his home and an automobile, in addition to having saved $7,000 in the local savings and loan association. On his savings he is now earning 4½ percent per annum. He has been reading about common stocks and real estate as a hedge against inflation. Do you believe that he should invest part or all of his savings in common stocks or real estate? If so, what kind of investment program do you think would suit his needs?

13 HOW TO BUY AND SELL SECURITIES

The Public is always wrong.
—*Wall Street maxim*

IF YOU want to make your pile, you have got to be in style," wrote Eldon Grimm of Walston & Company in the *Security Analysts Journal*. Styles in common stock, he pointed out, change almost as rapidly as women's fashions. You have to be alert to changing fancies in the market if you would do well in common stocks, he concluded after a fascinating review of some extremes of mass emotion in the market. For example, during World War I, Bethlehem Steel was in high fashion. It soared from $10 a share in 1914 to $200 just one year later. In the twenties, talking pictures and radio absorbed the country. Warner Bros. Pictures (your parents may remember Al Jolson in "The Singing Fool") skyrocketed from 9¾ in 1927 to 138 in 1928. RCA rose from 12½ in 1922 to 573 in 1929. Airplane stocks boomed with the first trans-Atlantic flight. Wright Aeronautical rose from 9⅝ in 1924 to 289 in 1928. Ever hear of the Auburn car? Its stock rose from 78 in 1928 to 514 in 1929 and then dropped to 60 in 1930.

During the Great Depression and the early New Deal days, gold and liquor stocks were in high style. The price of the old Homestake Mining stock went from 81 in 1931 to 544 in 1936. Alaska Juneau rose from 4½ in 1930 to 33 in 1933. With the repeal of Prohibition, National Distillers zoomed from 13 in 1932 to 124 a year later.

During World War II airline shares boomed. The old stock of American Airlines rose from 7½ in 1937 to 94½ eight years later. Eastern Airlines increased from 16¾ to 134 in some seven years. TWA went up from 7⅝ in 1942 to 79 in 1945.

The post–World War II period saw television, electronics, aircraft, and aluminum, among others, rise to great popularity. Motorola went from 8¾ in 1946 to 57 in 1950. General Dynamics, which had ranged from 1 to 11 between 1929 and 1949, rose from 4 in 1949 to 68⅝ in 1957. Over the same period Minnesota Mining and Manufacturing jumped from 8¼ to 101. Aluminum Company of America rose from 46 in 1949 to the equivalent of 352 in 1955, and Reynolds Metals moved up from 19 to the equivalent of $300 over the same period. More recently the ephemeral popularity of metrecal as a dieting fad sent Mead Johnson shares from $40 to over $200. The advent of the computer age pushed IBM from $40 to $600 and Control Data from $2 to over $100. The profitability of the jets sent airline stocks soaring—Pan American from 15 to 85 and Northwest Airlines from 23 to 99.

Now lest performances of this type cause you to rush into the market, a word of caution. It's a rare investor who was able to pick more than a few of these successes. And even more rare was the investor who timed

Drawing by Robert Day; © 1964 the New Yorker Magazine, Inc.

"Don't laugh. Did *you* buy Control Data at eight?"

his or her style changes correctly. It's just about impossible to buy at the low and sell at the high. You're not that omniscient. Don't try. Some wise rules for successful investment were offered by Mr. Edgar Scott, formerly president of the Philadelphia Stock Exchange and a governor of the New York Stock Exchange. His list of Do's and Don'ts includes:

1. Don't pay attention to irresponsible tips. Tipsters have surprisingly little money of their own and if they are convinced that they know of a stock that will go up 10 points in 10 days, let them lose their own money, not yours.

2. Don't open an account with a brokerage house until you have satisfied yourself that it is thoroughly reputable. Member firms of the New York Stock Exchange now observe the highest standards of business conduct and financial responsibility.

3. Don't approach the market with the hallucination that you can buy at the bottom and sell at the top. That is as rare as a hole in one, even for the most experienced brains in the business. Wise investing consists of selecting securities which represent real present and *future* values, then buying them at some reasonable stage in their price cycle.

4. Don't be stubborn about your own errors of judgment. If a stock fails to fulfill the promise you thought you saw in it, sell it—at a loss if necessary. Quick action in such cases often cuts losses which would otherwise grow larger.

5. Don't become blindly attached to a stock because it has done well for you. Take your profits and find a new, better situation. You seldom lose money taking a profit.

6. Don't be swayed by a loquacious salesman peddling an unseasoned stock. Of course, you would have made millions if you had gone in with Henry Ford, but you might also have bought Stutz, Hupmobile or one of the other 20-odd automobile companies which disappeared in the twenties.

7. Do take your time. Check up on all the available facts about a contemplated investment.

8. Do be clear about your particular purpose. What is your objective? Until you know what you are looking for, there is little chance of finding it.

9. Get in the habit of reading the financial section of a newspaper, or other good financial publication.

10. Do, in the process of forming your considered judgment, seek information and ideas from qualified people and sources of financial information.

11. Do remember that not every transaction will be successful. That is true of any business. If an investor or trader in securities tells you he never takes a loss, pay him no heed, for the truth is not in him.

Diversification

There is an old adage that it is never wise to put all one's eggs in one basket; this is an excellent rule to follow in investment. It means much more, however, than simply investing in several companies rather than in one. It means, first of all, a proper blending of common stocks, preferreds, and bonds in the light of your investment objectives and of the business cycle. For example, if yours is a young family, after you have provided adequately for insurance and after you have established an emergency fund to fall back on by a savings bank deposit or by government savings bond purchases, then your surplus savings can to a large extent go into good growth (common) stocks and convertible bonds in the upward phase of the business cycle and then, toward the top of the cycle, be shifted gradually, in part, to high-grade bonds.

An elderly couple, to take a second example, dependent upon the income from a savings accumulation of a lifetime, might put 75 percent of their fund in good-grade income stocks (common) and 25 percent in bonds in the upward phase of the cycle and then shift the proportion increasingly to high-grade bonds as it became apparent that the down-trend either would soon begin or had begun, until the percentages were reversed: 75 percent in high-grade bonds, 25 percent in common stock. Diversification of this sort among types of securities involves close attention to the trend of the business cycle and a nice precision in investment timing. As we shall see, if the individual is too busy or too unsure of himself to feel reasonably confident and competent in judging trends, there are mechanical formulas for investment which help to do it for him.

The second phase of diversification is selecting and differentiating among industries. Few young people today elect to become blacksmiths or wheelwrights, yet some people buy stock in snuff or traction companies. Industry selection, as practiced by an increasing group of investors and investment managers, recognizes that "the market" is composed of many industrial groups of securities and that economic pressures and influences bear unequally on the various industries at any given period, resulting in dissimilar and often divergent market action. For example, if you had invested 1,000 in shipping and coal stocks in August, 1939, and had held the stocks through the period ending July, 1952, your capital would have grown to $6,570—a 557 percent gain. But had you invested the same $1,000 in shipping and coal stocks, then switched into printing and publishing and radio broadcasting, and then into petroleum and chemical stocks, your capital would have increased to $38,260, or a 3,726 percent gain in the same period. This illustration, employing hindsight, covers a period in which the market advanced. In a declining period, your experience could easily be one that showed a percentage gain by shifting as against a percentage loss by sitting tight.

The third aspect of diversification is to pick the best companies within the industry. In any industry, whether it is declining or advancing, there are a few companies doing better than average. For proper diversification you will want to find which companies these are and then invest in them.

Investment Timing

One of the most difficult aspects of investments is to know when to buy and when to sell. There are three broad approaches to this problem:

a) Fundamental value approaches
b) Technical indicators of market timing
c) Mechanical formulas

At the outset, however, you should be aware of objective studies of stock market forecasting, which have indicated that stock prices cannot be successfully forecast consistently based on any recurrent pattern. Market movements are random and most stock market "experts" have been wrong more often than right. Almost no one, for example, forecast the stock market setback in the Spring of 1962. But forecasting or evaluation techniques have a certain usefulness even if they are correct only 60 or 70 percent of the time. They provide a kind of blurry radar which prevents flying blind.

Fundamental value approaches depend on earnings, yields, and the relationship of both to prices. While basic economic factors such as business conditions, government fiscal and tax policies, interest rates, and so forth, are taken into consideration, analysis centers on price-earnings ratios, yields, profits, cash flow, etc.

The yield on a share of common stock is the effective return to the investor and is based on two factors: the price he paid for the share, and the dividend paid to him. For example, if he bought A. T. & T. stock at $140 per share and received a $5.00 per year dividend per share, the yield would be:

$$
\begin{array}{r}
.035 \\
\hline
140)\overline{5.00} \\
4\ 20 \\
\hline
800 \\
700 \\
\hline
100
\end{array}
$$

or 3.5 percent per annum. When stock prices go up, unless dividends are raised proportionately, yields fall. Conversely, when stock prices fall, unless dividends are reduced as fast or faster, yields increase. In past bull markets, whenever stock prices rose to a point where stock yields came down close to 3 percent, bull market peaks have been reached and stock prices tended subsequently to come down. In bear markets, when stock prices fall and yields on stocks rise, when they go above 5 percent, buying has generally proved worthwhile. Low points in bear markets seem to have been reached in the past when common stock yields were 5 to 6 percent. In the same fashion price-earnings ratios can be used as broad-gauged indicators of market levels. When the price-earnings ratio gets close to or goes above 20 bull market peaks have been reached or have been close at hand. Conversely when the price-earnings ratio falls below 15 buying may be advisable. These are not absolute but merely approximate indicators. They suggest general buying or general selling ranges. They are not precise timing devices. See Figures 13–1, 13–2, and 13–3.

In the attempt to find more precise and less vague timing indicators, a bewildering variety of technical approaches have been developed, starting way back with the Dow theory which has been found to be far from infallible, and including everything from odd-lot indexes, breadth of trading and volume of trading indicators, to Barron's "smart-money" Confidence Index and the Elliot Wave Theory.[1] Since individual indicators have given false signals from time to time in the past, the idea occurred to use a consensus of indicators for greater reliability. There are now a number of services using the consensus technique. One of the most interesting is the Indicator Digest, which achieved some prominence as a result of the "sell" signal which it gave in January, 1962, thereby anticipating correctly the subsequent sharp drop in the market later in the Spring of 1962.

Indicator Digest uses a consensus of 12 technical indicators at any one time, varying several of them depending on whether a bull or bear market is under way. These are then given weights of 1 or ½ for a total weight of 9. Whenever the composite total is 5 or more, a favorable signal is being given and stocks should be purchased. If the score sinks to 4½ or less, this is an unfavorable signal and stocks should be sold. The buy and sell signals given by such composite indicators over the 22 years (1942–1963) are shown in Figure 13–4. They were quite good in working the turns. The action of the composite indicator index over recent years is shown in the bottom part of Figure 13–5. The top part of this figure shows the range of closing prices of the Dow-Jones Industrial Stock Price Index. There are several

---

[1] For explanations of these technical approaches see Joseph E. Granville, *Strategy of Daily Stock Market Timing for Maximum Profit* (Englewood Cliffs, N.J.: Prentice-Hall, Inc., 1961) and *New Key to Stock Market Profits* (Englewood Cliffs, N.J.: Prentice-Hall, Inc., 1963). See also Leo Barnes, *Your Investments*, Chapter 30, "Technical Approaches to Timing Market Shifts," American Research Council, 1964.

FIGURE 13–1

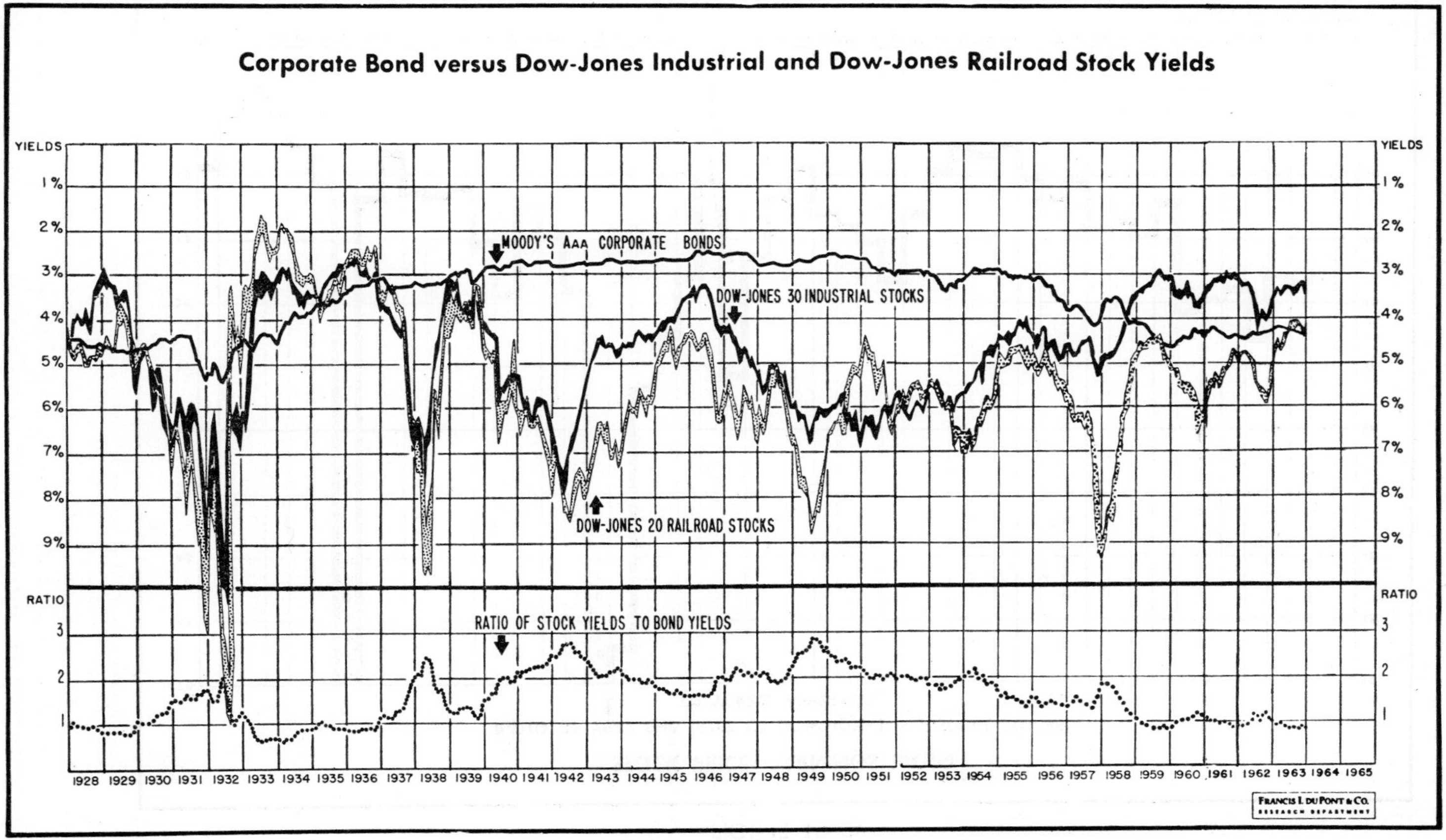
Corporate Bond versus Dow-Jones Industrial and Dow-Jones Railroad Stock Yields
YIELDS
1%
2%
3%
4%
5%
6%
7%
8%
9%
RATIO
3
2
1
MOODY'S AAA CORPORATE BONDS
DOW-JONES 30 INDUSTRIAL STOCKS
DOW-JONES 20 RAILROAD STOCKS
RATIO OF STOCK YIELDS TO BOND YIELDS
1928 1929 1930 1931 1932 1933 1934 1935 1936 1937 1938 1939 1940 1941 1942 1943 1944 1945 1946 1947 1948 1949 1950 1951 1952 1953 1954 1955 1956 1957 1958 1959 1960 1961 1962 1963 1964 1965
FRANCIS I. DU PONT & CO.
RESEARCH DEPARTMENT

FIGURE 13-2

STOCK PRICE - EARNINGS RATIO

RATIO OF YEAR END PRICE OF DOW-JONES INDUSTRIAL STOCKS
TO YEARLY EARNINGS

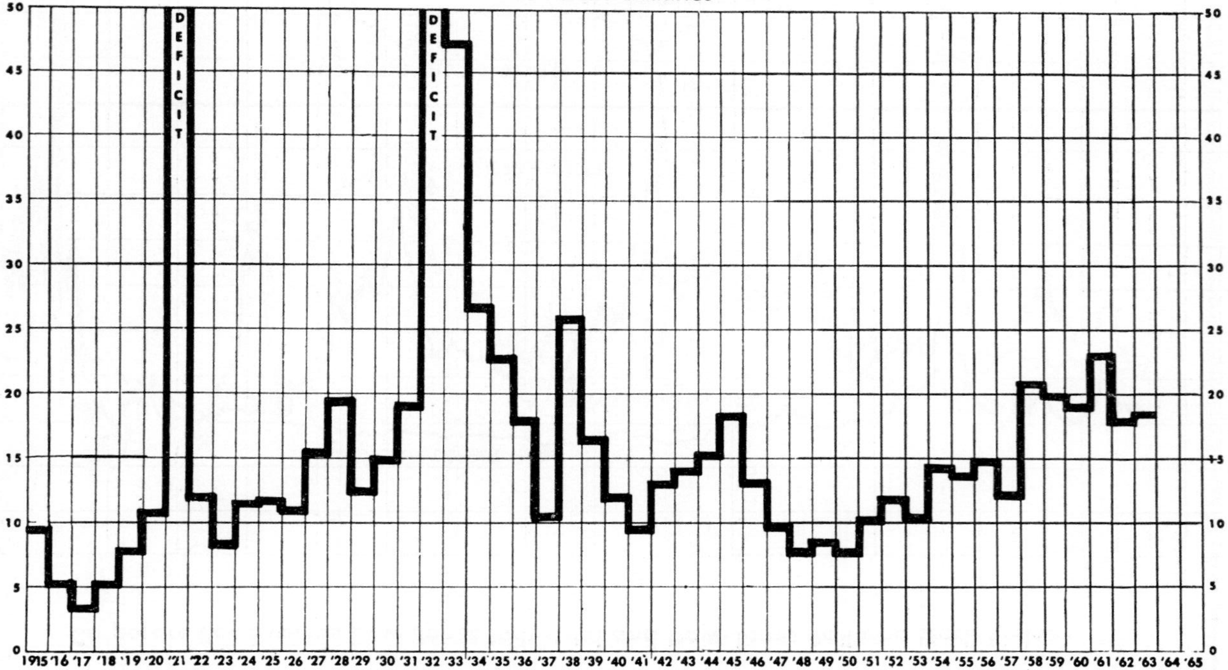

FRANCIS I. DU PONT & CO.
RESEARCH DEPARTMENT

FIGURE 13–3

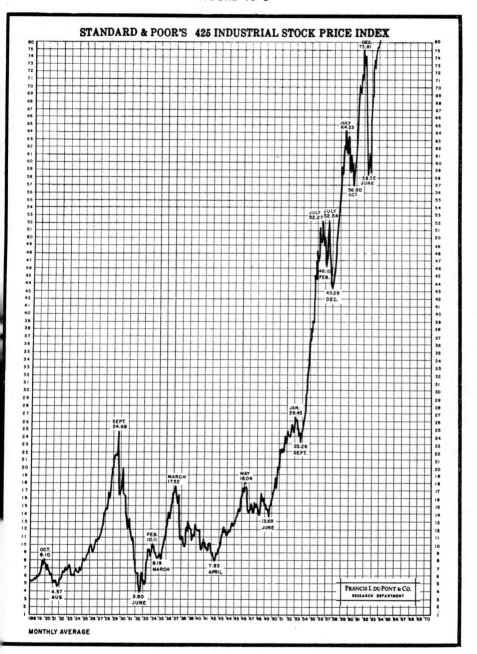

STANDARD & POOR'S 425 INDUSTRIAL STOCK PRICE INDEX

MONTHLY AVERAGE

FIGURE 13–4

22-Year Chart (1942–1963) of Indicator Digest's Composite Indicator Index

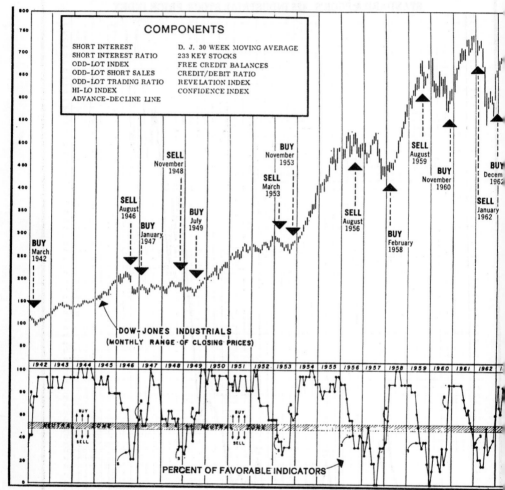

SOURCE: The Composite Indicator Index has been a copyright feature of Indicator Digest, Inc., since publication began in May, 1961.

FIGURE 13–5

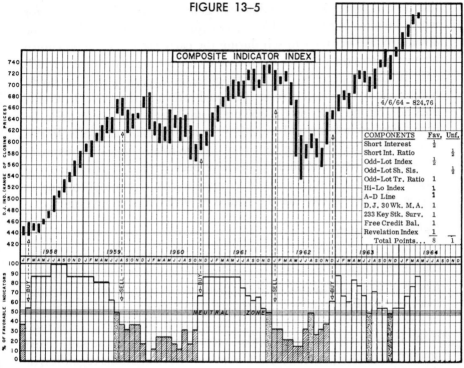

SOURCE: The Composite Indicator Index has been a copyright feature of Indicator Digest, Inc., since publication began in May, 1961.

services using somewhat similar consensus techniques but they are not always in agreement. Thus it's still a very difficult investment problem to know when to buy and when to sell.

Some solve this dilemma by resorting to mechanical formula plans which provide in advance for automatic buying and selling action. Dr. Barnes declares:

In most forms, they compel caution in bull markets and bravery in bear markets. They automatically (even if only partially) achieve the investment target of buying cheap and selling dear. They impel you to sell as prices rise and force you to buy as prices decline. Formula plans can definitely improve the batting average of most investors. While they deliberately avoid maximum theoretical profits, they more than make up for this by substantially cutting potential losses. Only the exceptional investor or speculator can hope to outperform a good formula plan in the long run.[2]

Formula-Plan Investing

In the uptrend of the market, the average person hates to sell and take his profit because he is afraid the market will continue to rise and

_____
[2] Barnes, *op. cit.,* 171.

that he will, by selling, miss additional gain. Thus he misses the top, for which he aims but never achieves, and continues to hold well into the downturn. He hesitates to sell during the early stages of the downturn because he sees the profit he has missed by not selling at the peak (which only hindsight permits him to recognize as a peak), and he holds, hoping the market will reverse itself and return to the peak. It usually does not, but he holds on the downturn until, well on the downside, he grows tired of holding and watching the retrogression and sells. In this way emotion and bad judgment play a large role in lack of investment success. A variety of formula plans have been devised to overcome to a large extent this human element in investing. A description of one or two will suffice to indicate the nature of formula-plan investing.

Dollar Averaging

This is the simplest type of formula plan. It is nothing more than the regular purchase of securities in equal dollar amounts, but the potential results of strict compliance with the plan are startling. The very obvious fact that the same amount of money will buy a greater number of shares of any stock when the price is low than it will when the price is high is the basis of the success of dollar averaging. You put the same fixed amount of money periodically into the same stock or stocks regardless of the price of the stock. Your fixed amount of money buys more shares when the stock is low, less shares when it is high. The important thing is to stick to your schedule—to buy, even though the price keeps falling, which, psychologically, is usually hard to do. This brings your average cost down, and any subsequent rise will yield a handsome profit.

Dollar averaging over a period of time will result in the average *cost* of all shares purchased being *lower* than the average *price* at which the shares were bought. An example may serve to show why this is so. Assume that $500 is invested at quarterly intervals in a certain stock and that the first two purchases are made at prices of 100 and 50, as shown in the accompanying tabulation. Thus the average price is $75, but the

Price	Shares Purchased Each Time	Total Shares Purchased	Average Price	Average Cost of Shares Purchased
100	5	5	100	100.00
50	10	15	75	66.66

average cost is $66.66. More shares were bought at 50, and that is why average cost is lower than average price.

An excellent example of dollar-cost averaging is given by Louis Engel in his interesting book.[3] He asks you to assume that you buy $500 worth of a given stock when it is selling at $10 a share, another $500 worth six months later when it is $9.00, another $500 worth at $8.00, and so on while the stock falls to $5.00, then rises to $15, and settles back to $10. If you sold out at this point, you would have a profit of about 10 percent, despite the fact that you paid an average price of $10 and sold out at exactly the same price. In case you do not believe it, here are the figures (Table 13–1), assuming that, since you cannot buy

TABLE 13–1

An Example of Dollar-Cost Averaging in Buying Stocks

Price per Share	Number of Shares Purchased	Cost of Shares	Number of Shares Owned	Cumulative Cost of Shares	Total Value of Shares
$10	50	$500	50	$ 500	$ 500
9	55	495	105	995	945
8	63	504	168	1,499	1,344
7	71	497	239	1,996	1,673
6	84	504	323	2,500	1,938
5	100	500	423	3,000	2,115
6	84	504	507	3,504	3,042
7	71	497	578	4,001	4,046
8	63	504	641	4,505	5,128
9	55	495	696	5,000	6,264
10	50	500	746	5,500	7,460
11	45	495	791	5,995	8,701
12	42	504	833	6,499	9,996
13	38	494	871	6,993	11,323
14	36	504	907	7,497	12,698
15	33	495	940	7,992	14,100
14	36	504	976	8,496	13,664
13	38	494	1,014	8,990	13,182
12	42	504	1,056	9,494	12,672
11	45	495	1,101	9,989	12,111
10	50	500	1,151	10,489	11,510

Source: Louis Engel, *How to Buy Stocks—a Guide to Successful Investing* (paperbound ed.; New York: Bantam Books).

fractional shares, you buy whatever number of shares yields a total cost nearest $500. As shown in the table, you paid $10,489, but your shares are worth $11,510, for a profit of $1,021. If you had sold out at 15,

[3] Louis Engel, *How to Buy Stocks—a Guide to Successful Investing* (paperbound ed.; New York: Bantam Books, latest edition). A free copy may be obtained by writing to Mr. Engel at Merrill Lynch, Pierce, Fenner & Smith, 70 Pine St., New York, N.Y., 10005.

your profit would have been $6,108. Even if you had undertaken only the first half of the purchases, and the price had fallen to 5 and then returned to 10, at which point you closed out, you would have had a profit of $1,960, or almost 35 percent on your money. Clearly, dollar-cost averaging is a very useful technique if it enables you to make a 35 percent profit on a stock which declines after you start buying it and then merely returns but does not go above the price you originally paid for it. You must, however, have both the courage and the funds to continue buying in a declining market.

What to Buy

Even if you use a formula plan or dollar-cost averaging to solve the problem of when to buy, you still face the problem of what to buy. The first approach to the solution of this problem is to pick the industries or industry whose outlook seems most attractive. After that you can give attention to the problem of what companies or company within the industry to choose. Most of the large stockbrokerage houses and all of the large financial services devote considerable effort to the problem of industry selection and analysis. For example, the *Security and Industry Survey* of the largest brokerage house, Merrill Lynch, Pierce, Fenner & Smith, is organized largely on an industry-analysis basis. The bulk of the *Security and Industry Survey* consists of a page devoted to each industry.[4] There is a statement of the position and outlook for the industry and a tabulation of the stocks of individual companies in the industry classified according to whether the stock is considered "investment type," "liberal income," "good quality," or "speculative" (see Fig. 13–6). This *Survey* is of considerable value in enabling an investor to make an informed judgment on the outlook and prospects for a given industry.

Choosing the Industry

Some industries over a period of time do better than the market; some do less well. For example, soft-drink stocks ever since 1949 have done less well than the market average. This may be seen in Figure 13–7. This has been true of tobacco stocks too. Oil and paper stocks, on the other hand, have done very much better than the market average, ever since 1944 (see Fig. 13–8). This is also true, for example, of tire and rubber goods stocks. A third category, as represented by electrical equipment stocks (see Fig. 13–9), appears to move with the market.

---

[4] A free copy of the latest *Security and Industry Review* may be obtained by writing to Merrill Lynch, Pierce, Fenner & Smith at 70 Pine St., New York, N.Y., 10005.

FIGURE 13–6

NATURAL GAS

Distributing and integrated companies should show a more rapid earnings growth than the pipelines

Most stocks of the natural gas distributing companies and integrated systems with major distribution facilities do not appear to reflect the probability that both first quarter and full year earnings will show impressive improvement over 1963 comparable levels. Pipeline companies, too, should register profit gains in both periods; but it is unlikely that the rates of increase will match those of the distribution companies. It must be remembered that virtually the entire operation of a pipeline is subject to the more rigid regulation of the Federal Power Commission. Looking beyond the immediate future, we believe the use of natural gas as a fuel, not only for heating but for the creation of other forms of energy including electricity, will expand. Purchases of stocks at present relatively modest price levels should, in our opinion, prove highly profitable over the longer term. Meanwhile, most of these issues provide yields which are attractive in the broad area of utility issues. We believe stocks of such companies as Lone Star Gas, Pacific Lighting, United Gas, Peoples Gas Light & Coke, and Brooklyn Union Gas are suitable for participation in the long-range growth of the natural gas industry. The pipeline systems still face major

Pipeline is laid on Texas Eastern system

regulatory problems at the Federal Power Commission level. Following what appears to have been a short-lived truce, the spirit of cooperation, which existed between the regulatory agency and the major pipeline companies, now seems dissipated. A ruling by the Commission earlier this year which involved a wholly-owned producing subsidiary of a major system undoubtedly will not be resolved until tested in the

NATURAL GAS	Fiscal Year Ends	†Earnings—$ a Share 1963	1962	Interim Period	Interim 1963	Interim 1962	Consec. Years Divs. Paid	Divs.-$ a Share Paid 1963	Paid or Decl. Last 12 Mo.	Price Range 1953-62 High	1953-62 Low	1963-64 High	1963-64 Low	Approximate Price 2-13-64	Yield %
INVESTMENT TYPE: GROWTH															
Amer. Nat. Gas	Dec.	2.22[40]	2.08[40]	12 mo. 9-30	2.38	2.11	61	1.45	1.60[4]	55¼	11⅜	45⅝	39⅛	42	3.8[4]
Peoples Gas Lt. & C.	Dec.	2.67[35]	2.45	—	—	—	28	1.69	1.84	58¾	15⅞	56½	46	53	3.5
INVESTMENT TYPE: STABILITY															
Cons. Nat. Gas	Dec.	3.14[40]	2.85[40]	12 mo. 9-30	3.60	3.08	21	2.30	2.30	67½	24¼	68¼	56¾	62	3.7
*Pacific Lighting	Dec.	3.27	3.50	—	—	—	56	2.40	2.40	65¼	27¾	63¾	53⅝	55	4.4
United Gas Imp.	Dec.	1.41	1.32	—	—	—	80	0.88	1.00[4]	27¼	10⅛	28	21¼	25	4.0[4]
LIBERAL INCOME															
Alabama Gas	Sept.	2.36[40]	2.17[40]	12 mo. 12-31	2.11	2.10	22	1.70	1.70	41¾	13¼	38¾	34⅛	35	4.9
Columbia Gas System	Dec.	1.63[40]	1.55[40]	12 mo. 9-30	1.81	1.49	22	1.16	1.22[4]	30⅛	12½	30½	26⅝	29	4.2[4]
Equitable Gas	Dec.	2.35[40]	2.48[40]	12 mo. 9-30	2.47	2.29	15	1.85	1.85[14]	48⅜	20⅜	45⅜	38	40	4.6[14]
Nat. Fuel Gas	Dec.	2.15[40]	1.84[40]	12 mo. 9-30	2.38	2.03	62	1.30	1.36[4]	33¼	13⅞	36⅞	29¼	33	4.1[4]
Southern Nat. Gas	Dec.	2.97[40]	2.76[40]	12 mo. 9-30	3.15	2.95	29	2.10	2.20[4]	50	23	53½	43	50	4.4[4]
GOOD QUALITY: WIDER PRICE MOVEMENT															
Brooklyn Union Gas	Dec.	1.98	1.99	—	—	—	16	1.29	1.32	45	10¼	46	36½	40	3.3
Colo. Interst. Gas	Dec.	2.17	2.04[1]	—	—	—	15[16]	0.89	1.25[4]	41½	15¼	45	28¼	30	4.2[4]
Laclede Gas	Sept.	1.45	1.48	—	—	—	19	1.00	1.05[4]	31¼	7⅜	32⅛	22⅝	25	4.2[4]
*Lone Star Gas	Dec.	1.18[40]	1.07[40]	12 mo. 9-30	1.22	1.15	39	1.00	1.00	29¼	11⅝	24¼	22	23	4.3
‡Northern Nat. Gas	Dec.	2.70	2.52	—	—	—	30	1.75	1.80[4]	48⅛	17¼	58	43	51	3.5[4]
Southern Union	Dec.	1.53[40]	1.48[40]	12 mo. 9-30	1.66	1.56	22	1.02	1.06[4]	30⅝	13⅝	35	24	35	3.0[4]
Texas Gas Trans.	Dec.	2.56[40]	2.38[40]	12 mo. 9-30	2.73	2.57	12	1.65	1.70[4]	45¾	14⅝	49¼	41	41	4.1[4]
*United Gas Corp.	Dec.	2.36[35]	2.27	—	—	—	20	1.60	1.60	42⅞	23½	39⅞	34	34	4.7
SPECULATIVE															
*Florida Gas Co.	Dec.	0.32[23,40]	0.04[23,40]	9 mo. 9-30	0.19[23]	0.25[23]	—	Nil	Nil	23⅝[12]	8½[12]	15	9¼	11	—
*Texas East. Trans.	Dec.	1.27[10,35]	1.12[10]	—	—	—	15	0.83	0.90[4]	20⅛	7½	20⅝	16¼	20	4.5[4]
‡Transcontl. Gas P.L.	Dec.	1.21[40]	1.08[40]	12 mo. 9-30	1.23	1.20	13	0.96	1.00	22¼	8	25¼	21⅝	22	4.5
Transwestern Pipeline	Dec.	0.34[40]	0.32[40]	9 mo. 9-30	0.27	0.23	—	Nil	Nil	20⅜[12]	8½[12]	12⅜	9⅜	9⅞	—

Source: Merrill Lynch, Pierce, Fenner & Smith, Inc.

FIGURE 13–7

Soft Drink Stocks Compared with Composite Industrial Shares

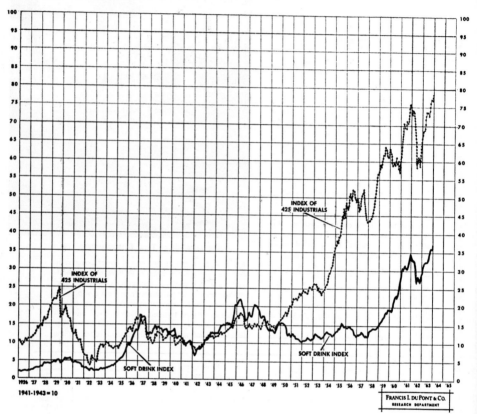

The successful investor learns how to avoid the lower-than-market-average stocks and chooses the above-market-average industry groups. Discrimination in this respect makes a very big difference in your investment experience. Standard & Poor's believes that the industry approach is the greatest single factor in investment success. The "Fan" chart, shown in Figure 13–10, indicates how various industry groups performed price-wise during the period of the big bull market which started in April, 1942, and ended in May, 1946. Which industrial group would you have picked in April, 1942? Probably aircraft, since you would have expected aircraft manufacturers to benefit most from the war. You would probably never have given a thought to printing and publishing. Yet aircraft had the worst comparative performance, as the "Fan" chart shows: you would have gained only 50 percent; while printing and publishing had the best: you would have gained over 1,000

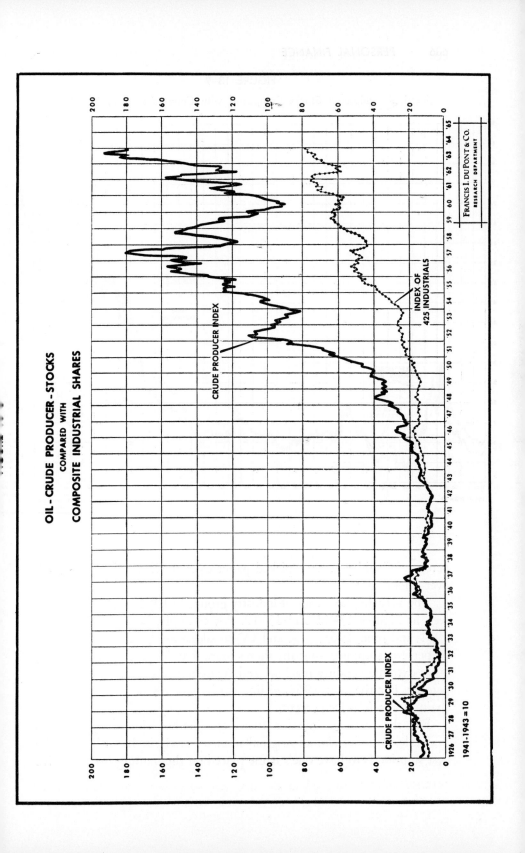

OIL-CRUDE PRODUCER-STOCKS
COMPARED WITH
COMPOSITE INDUSTRIAL SHARES

CRUDE PRODUCER INDEX

CRUDE PRODUCER INDEX

INDEX OF
425 INDUSTRIALS

1941-1943 = 10

FRANCIS I. DU PONT & CO.
RESEARCH DEPARTMENT

FIGURE 13–9

Electrical Equipment Stocks Compared with Composite Industrial Shares

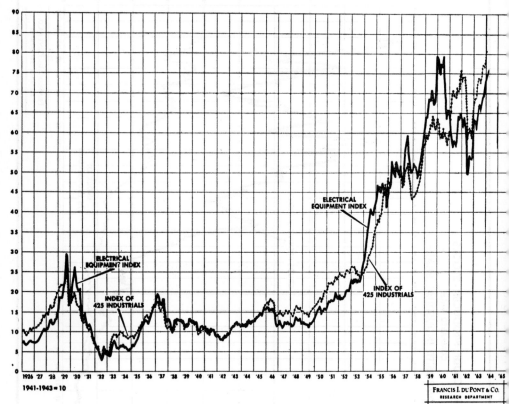

1941-1943 = 10

FRANCIS I. DU PONT & CO.
RESEARCH DEPARTMENT

percent. Would you have picked paper over steel? Or floor coverings over chemicals?

The very diverse trends of industry groups in 1962 and 1963 may be seen in Figures 13–11 and 13–12. For example, between December, 1961, and June, 1963, radio and TV broadcasting shares rose more than 60 percent, shipping company shares more than 50 percent, while at the other extreme vending machine and cigarette shares fell more than 40 percent. For the year 1963, airline stocks rose 88 percent while shoe chain stores fell 18 percent.

For the average investor there are neither time nor resources available to undertake an original industry analysis. In such cases the best solution is to have one's name placed on the mailing list to receive

FIGURE 13–10

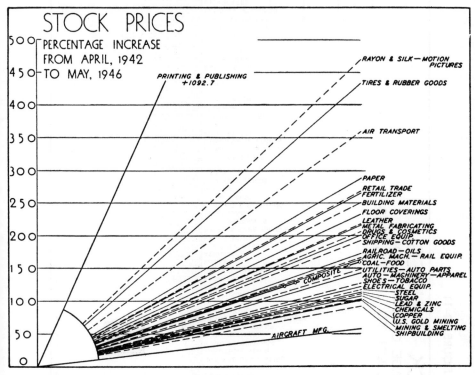

SOURCE: Standard & Poor's.

the publications of three or four of the leading brokerage houses which have large research departments competent to make industry analyses. Also, such an investor can consult one or more of the large financial services—Moody's, Standard & Poor's, Value Line—in any library and carefully read their industry outlook summaries.

From time to time Standard & Poor's publishes "Price Movements of Leading Stock Groups" shown in Figure 13–13, and also "Appeal of Stock Groups Measured against the Market." If you read enough of these special studies and industry analyses, you will in a short time acquire a "feel" for the contrasting patterns and soon be able to select the industry or industries in which you want to invest.

Choosing the Company

Your next step, once you have chosen the industry, is to select the company or companies. Again the average investor has neither the time nor the technical know-how to study and analyze a large number of

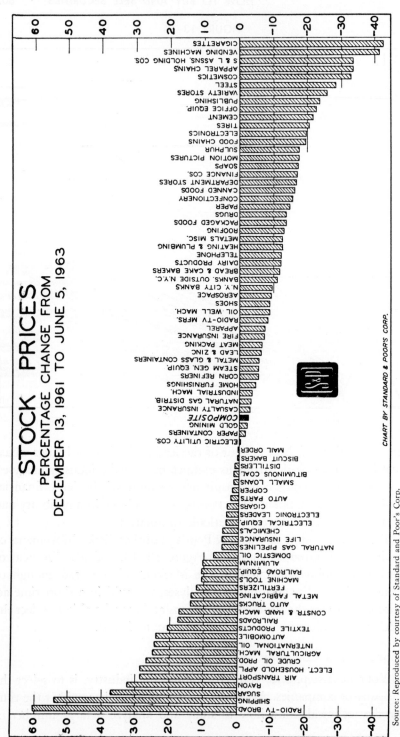

FIGURE 13-11

STOCK PRICES
PERCENTAGE CHANGE FROM
DECEMBER 13, 1961 TO JUNE 5, 1963

CHART BY STANDARD & POOR'S CORP.

Source: Reproduced by courtesy of Standard and Poor's Corp.

FIGURE 13–12

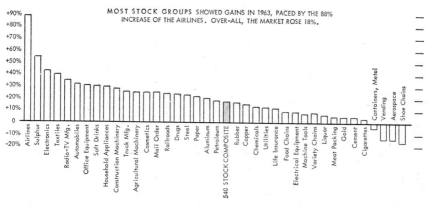

© 1964 by Merrill Lynch, Pierce, Fenner & Smith, Inc.

individual companies in order to choose two or three. If by chance you do have the time and the accounting competence to look into balance sheets and income accounts, then you can engage in ratio and financial analysis, described in a modest way in the following chapter, and come up with your own conclusions. Then you can check these against the opinions of the leading services in arriving at a final decision. But if you are the average investor, a balance sheet or an income account will frighten you away, while a 10K (the annual detailed financial report the company files with the SEC) will horrify you. Under these circumstances, you can do several things. You can rely on the company analyses and recommendations of the leading services (to be described in the next chapter), or you can find out what the big institutional investors, such as insurance companies, savings banks, mutual funds, and college endowment funds, are buying and selling, and pick and choose from among their most frequent selections. For example, one financial house publishes a semiannual survey of "The Favorite Fifty," the 50 listed stocks most popular with investment company managers. The first ten were International Business Machines, Standard Oil of New Jersey, Texaco, General Motors, A. T. & T., Royal Dutch Petroleum, Ford, Gulf Oil, Xerox, and General Electric. By dollar value 31 percent of total funds were in oil and natural gas stocks, 13 percent in utilities, 11 percent in office equipment, 9 percent in chemicals and drugs, 9 percent in motors, etc. Other tabulations are available of the investment preferences of insurance companies, trust companies, savings banks, endowment funds, etc. It is always useful to check your own judgment, however derived, against these lists.

FIGURE 13-13

Price Movements of Leading Stock Groups
on Different Sections of Same Logarithmic Scale (1941–43 = 10)

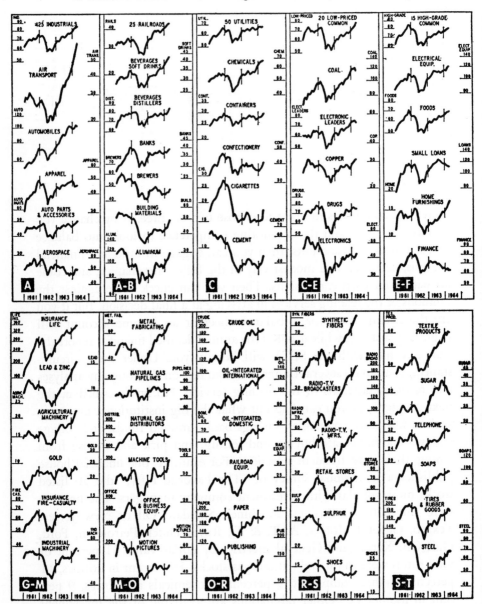

SOURCE: Standard and Poor's.

Special Situations

Most institutional investors have concentrated their holdings in 70 to 100 of the so-called "blue chips," and the disadvantage at times of following this lead is that, often, better appreciation values and opportunities are found among the overlooked and less popular common stocks. For example, 50 years ago, the New York, New Haven & Hartford Railroad was one of the popular "blue chips," considered a fine investment for "widows and orphans." At the same time, little-known General Motors was a new, speculative venture, well beyond the pale of respectability. One thousand dollars invested in New Haven common 50 years ago would be worth nothing now, while the same sum put into General Motors would now be worth over $50,000.

One method of investment which avoids this disadvantage is to look for and take advantage of "special situations." This involves finding a clearly undervalued situation before the general public does; or profiting from possibilities inherent in a merger or reorganization, a recapitalization or liquidation; or finding a cumulative preferred with large back dividends whose earnings are just about to increase sufficiently to pay off the accumulation.

Of special situations, one leading expert declares:

Special situations are investments in stocks or bonds that reflect *Corporate Action,* meaning activities occurring within the administrative scope of the corporation rather than at the business level. Their built-in potential for capital gains is the hallmark distinguishing true special situations from run of the mill investments. Apart from Corporate Action, which is the common denominator of all special situations, we can usually find the following identifying characteristics:

1. Profits develop independently of the trend of the securities market.
2. Risks are at a minimum (reflecting prior knowledge of anticipated profit).
3. Corporate action is in the development stage.
4. The securities are undervalued.
5. Information is available inviting comprehensive analysis.

In short, a true special situation is an investment in securities . . . where risks are at a minimum and achievement of the expected profit a calculated probability, regardless of the trend of the securities market.[5]

Most analysts regard undervalued and special situations in the same category. Northern Pacific Railroad common was so recommended several years back. Before World War II it had sold as low as 3¾. By

---

[5] Maurece Schiller, *Fortunes in Special Situations in the Stock Market,* American Research Council, Larchmont, N.Y., 1961.

1949 it reached 17; in 1951 it was 31¼; and then, in a little more than a year, it rose to a high of 94. This last spurt was due to the fact that oil was discovered in the Williston Basin, which stretches from the Dakotas and eastern Montana into Manitoba and Saskatchewan. Northern Pacific had large landholdings in the Basin.

Philadelphia and Reading in the early fifties was losing money in anthracite coal. Its sales and earnings dropped, reaching a deficit of $2.60 a share. The common stock sold at from $6.00 to $10.00 a share (adjusted). New management took out in 1955 and began a major acquisition and diversification program. The stock rose from 17 in 1956 to 131½ in 1959.

A service recommended U.S Foil Company, Class "B" common stock as a special, undervalued situation. It was pointed out that U.S Foil is a holding company whose chief investment is 48 percent of the shares of the common stock of Reynolds Metal Corporation. If the value of its other assets were disregarded, U.S. Foil held, after deduction of the value of its own preferred stock, approximately one share of Reynolds for each share of its own common. At the price at the time of the recommendation, the investor could have acquired an equity in Reynolds at about 28 percent below the market price. When its whole portfolio was considered, U.S. Foil "B" was selling at a discount from its net asset value per share of about 40 percent. Over the years U.S. Foil, Class B stock went from 25 cents a share (adjusted) to a high of $60.75.[6]

An example of the Forbes special situation survey is shown in summary form in Figure 13–14 and in chart form in Figure 13–15. On the chart notice the estimated earnings per share. The full write-up of this special situation recommendation covered some 10 pages.

Markets, Exchanges, and Brokers

Although stocks and bonds are usually sold initially to the investing public by investment bankers, they are later bought and sold by investors in the over-the-counter market or on the organized stock exchanges. The person who wishes to buy or sell such securities should seek out a reliable stockbroker who, for a modest commission, will act as his agent and handle the details of the transaction for him. Whereas an investment banker is a dealer who buys securities in the hope that he can resell them

---

[6] Two investment services, Forbes and Value Line, issue periodic special situation recommendations. See "Over-the-Counter Special Situation Service," The Value Line Investment Survey, New York. See also "Forbes Special Situation Survey," 70 Fifth Ave., New York, N.Y., 10011.

FIGURE 13–14

FORBES
Special Situation Survey

Published by INVESTORS ADVISORY INSTITUTE INC., *Subsidiary of Forbes Inc.*, 70 FIFTH AVE., NEW YORK, N.Y.

American Metal Products Company (APS)

LISTED N.Y.S.E.

IN BRIEF	
	ESTIMATED 1964 EARNINGS $2.75
	PRICE EARNINGS RATIO 7.3
BUYING RANGE 20-24	INDICATED CASH DIVIDEND $1.00
RECENT PRICE 20	CURRENT YIELD 5.0%

American Metal Products is an automotive parts manufacturer whose earning power has increased sharply under new leadership in recent years. Until 1964, the recovery in earning power has been masked by heavy losses on an experimental program. Now that program has been abandoned. We estimate earnings this year at $2.75 a share, sufficient to warrant a price at least 50% above the current level within 18 months even assuming no improvement in the present low earnings multiple applied to the stock. Moreover, there are reasons to believe that the multiple may be improved in the year ahead, in which case the shares might double in price.

Reproduced by courtesy of Investors Advisory Institute, Inc. (Forbes, Inc.)

at a profit, the broker, as such, buys no securities himself but merely earns commissions by representing other persons who wish to buy or sell securities. Stockbrokers are, therefore, often called "commission brokers."

The Over-the-Counter Market

The over-the-counter market has no one place in which buyers and sellers of securities (or their agents) make it a practice to meet to transact business. It has no common meeting place and is not housed in any one location; yet it is national in scope and local as well. Its segments are tied together by a vast system of telephone and telegraph connections. All securities transactions that are not made on stock exchanges take place in the over-the-counter securities markets. In this market, buyers and sellers contact each other commonly by telephone or telegraph. Buyers, through their brokers, telephone likely prospective sellers, concentrate on the seller offering to sell at the lowest price, and negotiate with him in the hope of obtaining a still lower price. Sellers, on the other hand, contact prospective buyers, concentrate on the buyer bidding the highest price, and endeavor to obtain an even higher price

FIGURE 13–15

American Metal Products Company (APS)

LISTED N.Y.S.E.

FORBES INVESTOGRAPHS

INCOME STATEMENT

($MILLIONS)	1950	1951	1952	1953	1954	1955	1956	1957	1958	1959	1960	1961	1962	1963	1964	1965	1966	1967
NET SALES	30.8	28.0	28.4	37.5	41.4	63.5	65.2	72.5	46.4	57.4	57.7	56.5	62.4	64.0				
GROSS OPERATING MARGIN (per cent)	19.2	16.8	20.8	13.9	14.5	17.0	16.2	16.9	11.0	9.2	7.6	7.9	9.1	11.2				
DEPRECIATION	0.3	0.3	0.4	0.4	0.8	1.8	2.1	2.4	1.8	1.8	1.9	1.8	2.1	2.1				
OPERATING PROFIT (see chart)	5.6	4.4	5.5	4.8	5.2	9.0	7.8	9.9	3.3	3.5	2.5	3.1	3.6	5.1				
OTHER INCOME	0.1	0.1	0.7	0.5	0.1	0.4	0.6	0.5	0.5	0.7	0.5	0.3	0.5	0.3				
PRETAX PROFIT	5.6	4.6	5.6	4.8	5.3	9.3	8.3	10.4	3.5	4.2	3.7	3.6	4.0	5.1				
PRETAX PROFIT MARGIN (per cent)	18.2	16.4	19.7	12.9	14.5	17.0	15.9	17.6	7.5	7.3	6.3	6.3	8.4	8.0				
NET INCOME FOR COMMON	3.0	2.2	2.4	2.2	2.5	4.2	3.6	4.6	1.6	1.9	1.7	1.6	2.0	2.4				
AVERAGE PRICE/EARNINGS RATIO	5.0	6.5	5.1	6.3	6.6	8.2	8.5	6.9	18.7	20.1	16.0	14.9	10.8	10.5				
AVERAGE YIELD	11.0	9.1	10.6	9.1	8.1	5.1	5.8	6.7	7.1	8.0	5.8	5.8	6.3	5.5				
COMMON EQUITY PER SHARE	12.05	13.08	14.71	15.81	17.20	19.11	20.94	24.59	22.03	21.74	21.94	23.18	22.53	22.90				

OPERATING PROFIT MARGIN (AFTER DEPRECIATION)

24.2% 18.1 15.9 19.2 12.8 12.6 14.2 12.0 13.7 7.2 6.1 8.2 5.6 5.8 7.9%

PRICE PERFORMANCE RELATIVE TO DOW-JONES

CAPITALIZATION
AS OF 12/31/63

	AMOUNT OUTSTANDING ($ MILLIONS)	INTEREST OR DIVIDENDS ($MILLIONS)
DEBT	None	
PREFERRED	None	
COMMON	1,390,364	

SHARES OUTSTANDING ISSUED LAST PERIOD 23.49

*Before non-recurring loss on sale of assets equal to 57¢ a share.

SALES PER SHARE

31 3/8   46.04

13 3/4   13 1/2

BUYING RANGE

MONTHLY PRICE RANGES

CASH FLOW PER SHARE
3.52 3.45 2.75 2.60 2.77 3.26 3.01 3.49 2.75est.

EARNED PER SHARE
1.90 2.53 1.50 1.50 1.50 1.60 1.21 1.40 1.15 1.24 1.16 1.47 1.72*
1.25 1.60

1.00 1.00

CASH DIVIDENDS PER SHARE

BALANCE SHEET

	1929-35	1936-42	1943-49	1950	1951	1952	1953	1954	1955	1956	1957	1958	1959	1960	1961	1962	1963	1964	1965	1966	1967
CASH AND EQUIVALENT				4.4	5.4	8.0	6.7	2.8	6.2	8.7	4.8	6.2	4.4	4.8	5.7	3.9	2.9				
INVENTORIES				1.7	1.9	1.5	3.7	3.4	6.8	8.7	8.7	6.7	8.4	7.4	7.0	6.4	8.9				
TOTAL CURRENT ASSETS				9.1	8.7	13.1	13.7	12.8	18.7	19.4	23.2	20.5	22.5	18.8	19.1	17.7	21.6				
TOTAL CURRENT LIABILITIES				4.3	3.7	5.5	6.2	6.3	8.3	8.4	8.5	5.0	7.2	5.1	7.2	6.1	7.7				
WORKING CAPITAL				4.8	5.0	7.6	7.5	6.6	10.4	11.0	14.7	15.5	15.3	13.7	11.9	11.6	14.0				
GROSS PLANT ACCOUNT				6.1	6.9	7.0	8.2	13.1	21.2	23.2	23.0	23.4	24.4	26.6	26.1	26.5	29.3				
NET PLANT ACCOUNT (after depreciation)				4.5	5.2	4.9	5.9	8.2	14.2	15.2	13.6	12.7	13.2	15.6	15.0	14.5	14.2				
OTHER TANGIBLE ASSETS				1.0	1.0	3.2	1.9	5.1	2.9	2.2	2.2	2.0	1.7	1.0	4.1	5.4	3.4				
LONG TERM DEBT				0	0	0	0	2.4	1.2	0.6	0	0	0	0	0	0	0				
CURRENT ASSETS/CURRENT LIABILITIES				2.1	2.4	2.4	2.5	2.0	2.3	2.3	2.7	4.1	3.1	3.6	2.6	2.9	2.8				
WORKING CAPITAL/SALES RATIO				.16	.18	.27	.17	.16	.16	.17	.20	.11	.12	.24	.21	.19	.22				
COMMON EQUITY % OF CAPITALIZATION				100	100	100	100	77	91	94	98	98	100	100	100	100	100				

SOURCE: Reproduced by courtesy of Forbes, Inc.

from him. In the over-the-counter market, securities are traded whether or not they have been listed or accepted for trading on the organized stock exchanges.

Buyers and sellers consist of securities dealers, institutions, estates, corporations, wealthy individuals, and people in all walks of life. Today the over-the-counter securities market consists of more than 2,500 securities houses and over 1,500 branch offices. The over-the-counter market is primarily a "negotiation" market. Buyers and sellers seek each other out and negotiate prices.[7]

Of the 500,000 corporations in the United States it is estimated that about 10 percent, or 50,000, have stock in the public's hands. In a year's time, the National Quotation Bureau, which collects and publishes over-the-counter securities prices, quotes prices on about 25,000 issues. It quotes prices daily on about 5,000 over-the-counter stocks—a larger number than are listed on the country's major exchanges. All bank stocks are traded over the counter, as are many insurance company shares, and state and municipal securities. Companies range from Space Age Materials Corp., whose stock sells at about $4.00 a share, to General Aniline & Film, whose shares are priced at around $375 each.

The Organized Stock Exchanges

The stock exchange, on the other hand, is an "auction" market. Trading is conducted in the manner of a two-sided auction, with competition among both buyers and sellers. The buyer making the highest bid buys, and the seller with the lowest offer sells, when the two agree on price. Stock exchanges are centers for trading in securities that are listed with them.

On the organized stock exchanges, only those securities are traded which have been listed. To secure the privileges of listing, the company issuing the securities must fill out an application to list the securities and must satisfy the particular exchange that the security is one which should properly be traded there. Only members of the exchange are permitted to trade on its "floor." To become a member, one buys a "seat" on the exchange. A seat, or membership, on the New York Stock Exchange has sold for as high as $625,000 (1929) and for as low as $17,000 (1942). The current price is about $150,000 to $200,000. In addition to the price of membership, the initiation fee is $4,000, and dues are $750 annually. The second largest exchange is the American Stock

---

[7] For further information write to OTC Market Information Bureau, 342 Madison Ave., New York, N.Y., 10017. A bulletin "Selected Over-the-Counter Stocks" may be obtained from Carl M. Loeb, Rhoades & Co., 42 Wall St., New York, N.Y., 10005.

Exchange. Trading is governed by the rules of the exchange. It is carried on by means of a method which is sometimes called "double auction" because of the fact that buyers compete among themselves, and sellers compete among themselves; whereas, in the usual simple auction, one auctioneer puts up goods for sale, and the buyers compete for the goods through their offers.

Types of Members

There are now 1,366 members of the New York Stock Exchange. A member may be a partner or officer in one of the brokerage concerns which, by virtue of his Exchange membership, is known as a "member firm." Today there are 667 such firms. From the founding of the Exchange in 1792 until May, 1953, membership in the Exchange was limited to individuals, and member firms were limited to partnerships. Then the Exchange Constitution was amended to permit corporations to become member firms, provided the corporation is engaged primarily in the securities business as a dealer or broker. There are now 122 member corporations.

About half the members are partners or officers in firms doing business with the public—so-called "commission houses." These members execute customers' orders to buy and sell on the Exchange, and their firms receive the commissions on those transactions. Many firms have more than one member.

About one third of all members are specialists—so called because they specialize in "making a market" for one or more stocks. Carrying out his function of "making a market," the specialist must often risk his own capital by buying at a higher price than the public may be willing to pay at that moment. For instance: let us say that the best offer to sell XYZ stock is at $35 a share and that the best bid to buy is at $34. The specialist would be expected, under normal conditions, to bid 34½ in order to narrow the temporary spread between supply and demand. In a rising market the specialist may be expected to sell stock from his own account at a price lower than that at which the public will sell.

A specialist restricts his business to a particular stock or group of stocks at one trading post on the floor of the Exchange. Primarily he acts as agent for other brokers who cannot remain at one post until prices specified by their customers' buy and sell orders—either below or above prevailing prices—are reached. Part of the commission the customer pays his own broker goes to the specialist for his services. Much of the specialist's earnings comes from commissions on orders executed for other brokers.

The Exchange sets specific requirements for specialists regarding market experience and the amount of capital they must have. The specialist must assume full responsibility for all orders turned over to him. He is expected to maintain a fair and orderly market in the stocks in which he specializes. This function is essential to the smooth operation of a national securities exchange. He must always subordinate his personal interests in the market to that of his customers. The specialist cannot buy or sell in the Exchange market at any price for his own account until he has executed all public orders held by him at that price.

Some members are odd-lot dealers. They serve investors who purchase or sell a few shares at a time rather than in the conventional 100-share unit, known as a "round lot." The odd-lot member acts as a dealer, not as a broker. He buys odd lots of stock from, or sells odd lots of stock to, other members doing a public business. In most stocks, an "odd lot" is any number of shares from 1 to 99. The price at which the odd-lot dealer fills an order is determined by the price of the next round-lot sale on the floor. Odd-lot dealers do not deal directly with the public.

Then there are floor brokers, whose function is to assist the commission brokers. Floor brokers are still popularly known as "$2.00 brokers," although the commission they receive for their services has long been above that amount.

All members—whatever their function—must, of course, own a "seat" on the Exchange—a term that traces back to early years, when the brokers did remain seated while the president called the list of securities. The price of a Stock Exchange membership is determined by how much a candidate will pay and the amount the owner of the membership will accept. The Board of Governors maintains complete control over admissions of new members.

Pay Cash or Buy on Margin?

Transactions in securities may be for cash or on margin. Although securities (like merchandise) can be bought for cash, it is commonly the practice for one who wishes to deal in securities to open an account with a stockbroker in much the same manner as he opens an account with a commercial bank. Then he gives orders for securities to be bought and/or sold and charged or credited to his account, whether or not the transactions are for cash or on margin.

Margin transactions involve credit. The buyer of securities on margin puts up part of the necessary cash himself and borrows from his broker the balance necessary to pay for the securities bought. The broker may in turn borrow from a commercial bank. The Federal Reserve Board has authority to specify how much of the total purchase price the buyer must himself provide (and, consequently, how much of it may be borrowed both by the customer and by the broker). Lately the Board has required the buyer to pay from his own funds at least 50 percent of the total purchase price. This means that the buyer may borrow half of the price of the securities acquired. By thus restricting the amount of credit (borrowing) permitted, a control or brake is applied to the amount of gain or loss to which a given investor may expose himself. In other words, foolish excesses in the quest for gain are discouraged. Prior to the

TABLE 13–2

Relative Gain or Loss under Different Margin Requirements

Requirement for Margin	Funds Advanced by Buyer	Amount of Credit Needed	Number of Shares Purchased at $50 Each	Per-Share Change in Market Value	Profit (+) and Loss (−) Involved
10%	$1,000	$9,000.00	200.00	±$5	±$1,000.00
20	1,000	4,000.00	100.00	± 5	± 500.00
50	1,000	1,000.00	40.00	± 5	± 200.00
75	1,000	333.33	26.67	± 5	± 133.33
100	1,000	0.00	20.00	± 5	± 100.00

crash in the stock market in 1929, it was usual to buy stocks with a margin payment of 10 or 20 percent. The chance for substantial gain (or loss) under those circumstances was much greater than it is today, as can be seen from Table 13–2.

Only one tenth of the profit or loss is possible when one uses only his own money, as compared with the possibilities when his own money is merely one tenth of the total funds used. By operating with other people's money, the opportunity for profit or loss is greatly magnified, especially with the very low margins. With a 50 percent margin, the chance for profit or loss is only twice what it would be if only one's own money were used; as the margin is reduced below 50 percent, the possible profit or loss is expanded several times. Of course, borrowed money generally has an interest expense connected with it.

How an Order is Handled

How does a transaction take place on the floor of the New York Stock Exchange? Here are four considerations to keep in mind:

1. When you buy, you buy from another person.
2. When you sell, you sell to another person.

3. The Stock Exchange itself neither buys nor sells, nor sets prices.
4. The Exchange provides the market place.

Let us say that a Dr. R. J. Phillips of Baltimore has sold his summer place. After talking things over with a Stock Exchange member firm, he decides to buy common shares in U.S. Steel Corporation. He asks the member firm's registered representative to find out for him what U.S. Steel shares are selling for on the Exchange.

Over a wire to his New York office the representative asks for a "quote" on U.S. Steel. His request is telephoned to the quotation department at the Exchange, where current quotations on all listed securities are received by direct wires to each trading post on the floor. Each stock is assigned a particular location at one of the 18 posts on the trading floor, and all transactions in a stock must take place at its assigned location.

Almost immediately one of the operators tells the New York office, which relays the information to Baltimore, that U.S. Steel common is quoted "65 to a quarter." This means that, at the moment, the highest bid to buy U.S. Steel stock is $65 a share, and the lowest offer to sell is $65.25 a share.

Dr. Phillips learns that 100 shares will cost him approximately $6,500, plus a commission of $41.50.

The Order Enters the Market

He tells the registered representative to go ahead. The latter writes out an order to buy 100 shares of U.S. Steel "at the market" and has it wired to his firm's partner on the floor of the Exchange. "At the market" means at the best price possible at that time. The floor partner hurries over to the trading post where U.S. Steel shares are traded.

About the same time, a Seattle hardware man, let us say his name is James Greenway, decided he would sell his 100 shares of U.S. Steel to get funds to enlarge his store. He called his broker, got a "quote," and told his broker to sell. That order, too, was relayed to the floor over a direct wire. Greenway's broker also hurried to the Steel post. Just as he entered the Steel "crowd," he heard Phillips' broker calling out, "How's Steel?" Someone answers, "65 bid, offered at a quarter."

Phillips' broker could, without further thought, buy the 100 Steel offered at $65.25, and Greenway's broker could sell his 100 at $65. In that event, if their customers had been looking over their shoulders, the customers probably would have said, "Why didn't you try to get a better price for us?" The customers would have been right. That's what a broker is expected to do. Every broker is charged with the responsibility of getting the best possible price for his customer. He must exercise his experience, knowledge, and brokerage skill. He must make split-second decisions. Here's how Phillips' and Greenway's brokers might figure as each tries to get the best price for his customer.

PHILLIP'S BROKER: "I can't buy my 100 at 65. Someone has already bid 65, and no one will sell at that price. Guess I'd better bid 65⅛."

GREENWAY'S BROKER: "Looks like I can't sell my 100 at 65¼; someone has already tried to get that price. I'd better try to get 65⅛."

Greenway's broker hears Phillips' broker bid 65⅛ and instantly shouts, "Sold 100 at 65⅛." They have agreed on a price, and the transaction takes place.

Here is the auction market in operation. This procedure is repeated over and over again every day on the floor of the Exchange.

The two brokers complete their verbal agreement by noting each other's names and reporting the transaction back to their phone clerks so that their customers can be notified. In the meantime, an Exchange employee had sent a record of the transaction to the ticker department for transmission over a nationwide ticker network. The transaction is printed simultaneously on 2,096 tickers in 361 cities in 50 states, and in Canada. It appears like this: X 65⅛—"X" being the ticker symbol of U.S. Steel. The number of shares in a round-lot transaction is specified only when more than 100 shares are involved.

Thus, within a few minutes, Dr. Phillips has arranged to exchange the proceeds from the sale of his summer cottage for 100 shares in the world's largest steel company; Jim Greenway has sold his shares in that company for money to expand his own business.[8]

Less than 100 Shares—Odd Lots

But, you may ask, what if Dr. Phillips had only $1,000 to invest in U.S. Steel stock rather than $6,500? In other words, could he buy only 15 shares instead of 100?

Yes, he could buy only one share, if he wanted to. In most stocks, an order to buy or sell less than 100 shares is an odd-lot order. These orders are serviced by odd-lot members, who act as dealers in odd lots on the floor of the Exchange. The mere fact that most stocks on the Exchange are traded in units of 100 shares does not prevent the investor of modest means from buying or selling any number of shares he desires.

---

[8] See *Understanding the New York Stock Exchange* (New York: New York Stock Exchange). A free copy may be obtained by writing to the Publications Division, New York Stock Exchange, 11 Wall St., New York, N.Y., 10005.

If Dr. Phillips had ordered only 15 shares of U.S. Steel common, his broker would have given the order to an odd-lot dealer at the Steel trading post. There is at least one odd-lot dealer at each post. The dealer would fill the order at a price based on the next round-lot transaction in Steel common. Assuming this next round-lot trade is made at 65⅛ a share, the odd-lot dealer would sell 15 shares of Steel from his own inventory to Dr. Phillips' broker at 65⅜. The additional one-quarter point, or 25 cents per share, is designed to cover expenses incident to the odd-lot dealer's operations. If the round-lot price had been less than $40, the odd-lot differential would have been ⅛, or 12½ cents a share, above the round-lot price on purchases and below on sales.

Much the same procedure would have been followed if Jim Greenway had had only 15 or 28 or 99 shares of Steel common to sell. His broker, too, would have given the sell order to an odd-lot dealer. If the next 100-share transaction in Steel were at 65⅛ a share, the dealer would have bought Jim's stock for 64⅞ a share. In neither instance could the odd-lot dealer refuse either to sell 15 shares to Dr. Phillips' broker or to buy the odd lot offered by Greenway's broker.

Pay-as-You-Go Investing

Every investor faces two basic problems: when to buy and what to buy? The Monthly Investment Plan of the member firms of the New York Stock Exchange, by affording the investor a way to buy common stock systematically by the dollars' worth and to average costs over a period, provides a practical, though somewhat costly, approach to the problem of when to buy.

You can invest any amount from $40 to $1,000 per month or per quarter to purchase any one stock. Your money is invested promptly no matter whether you are buying shares at $180 or at $18 each. The exact number of shares (and fraction of a share figured to four decimal places) bought for you with each payment is credited to your account by your stock broker. For example, if Dr. Phillips decides to invest $100 a month in U.S. Steel and it is selling for $65 a share, his $100 (at the odd-lot price) buys 1.4514 shares. Dividends paid by the company apply to his full shares and any fractional share. He can have the dividends mailed to him or automatically reinvested in U.S. Steel and his account charged for the commissions.

The plan is noncontractual, which means that he is at liberty to stop his payments whenever he chooses without penalty. Since he is buying only a $100 worth of stock each month, his transaction is an odd-lot purchase and he is charged a commission of 6 percent plus the regular odd-lot differential. This is, of course, a costly way to buy stock. It would be much less expensive for him to buy a 100 shares at a time, if he could afford it. It's like buying anything on the installment plan. It costs more than if you buy it outright.

Since he is buying shares by the dollar's worth—putting in the same amount each month—he is engaging in dollar cost averaging. If the market price of U.S. Steel declines, his $100 buys more shares; if the price advances, his $100 buys fewer shares. Under this theory, as we have seen, investors may benefit from a temporary decline in the price of the stock they are accumulating, provided its long-range price trend is upward and periodic purchases are continued in good times and bad.

"MIP"—the Monthly Investment Plan—was inaugurated in January, 1954, by member firms of the New York Stock Exchange to meet the needs of individuals who wish to invest in NYSE listed stocks regularly out of current income. A total of over 6 million shares have been purchased, representing an investment of over $270 million.[9]

The 50 stocks most popular with Monthly Investment Plan buyers are shown in Table 13–3. The investment experience of MIP investors over a 10-year period in 20 of the most popular stocks is shown in Table 13–4.

Types of Orders

Dr. Phillips, as we have seen, gave the registered representative a market order to buy U.S. Steel. And Jim Greenway placed a market order when he wanted to sell Steel. This is the procedure used by most investors. Some other kinds of orders are:

A *limit order* specifies a price. If an order is entered to buy a stock at $35, for example, it cannot be executed at a price higher than $35. If an order is entered to sell at $35, it cannot be executed below that price. In all cases the broker will, of course, do his best to get a better price.

Stop orders, sometimes known as "stop-loss orders," are designed to limit losses or protect profits. To illustrate: if you bought stock at $35 a share, you could enter an order to sell at "30 stop." In the event the stock should decline to $30, your order automatically becomes a market order and is executed at about $30, depending upon the market in the stock at that time.

---

[9] A descriptive pamphlet on the Monthly Investment Plan may be obtained by writing to the Publications Division, New York Stock Exchange, 11 Wall St., New York, N.Y., 10005.

TABLE 13-3

The 50 STOCKS most popular with MONTHLY INVESTMENT PLAN buyers

Under the Monthly Investment Plan there are some 1200 stocks on the New York Stock Exchange from which to choose. Here's the latest list of the 50 most popular with MIP buyers.

Symbol	In order of popularity as of November 29, 1963	Year Consecutive Annual Dividend Payments Began	Latest 12 Months Cash Dividends (Incl. Extras)	Closing Price Per Share 12/6/63	Yield**	Symbol	In order of popularity as of November 29, 1963	Year Consecutive Annual Dividend Payments Began	Latest 12 Months Cash Dividends (Incl. Extras)	Closing Price Per Share 12/6/63	Yield**
GM	General Motors Corp. Cars, trucks, appliances	1915	$3.50	$77⅞	4.5%	UK	Union Carbide Corp. Chem., plastics, metal alloys	1918	$3.60	$115¾	3.1%
T	American Tel. & Tel. Co. Bell Telephone System	1881	3.60	140	2.6*	LIT	Litton Industries, Inc. Electronic equip., bus. mach.	—	—	81½	—
IBM	Int'l Business Machines Corp. Sells, leases bus. machines	1916	3.75	484½	0.8*	CG	Columbia Gas System, Inc. Natural gas pipelines	1943	1.16	29⅜	3.9
GEN	General Telephone & El. Corp. Tel. hldg. co., electronics	1936	0.82	31⅝	2.6*	IT	Int'l Tel. & Tel. Corp. Electronic & communic. equip.	1951	1.00	53⅜	1.9
TY	Tri-Continental Corp. Closed-end investment co.	1945	1.53e	46⅞	3.3	AL	Aluminium Ltd. Aluminum	1939	0.60t	25¼	2.4
MMM	Minnesota Mining & Mfg. Co. Adhesives, abrasives	1916	0.88	65½	1.3*	WX	Westinghouse Electric Corp. Elec. equip., atomic energy	1935	1.20	33⅝	3.6
GE	General Electric Co. Electrical equip., jet engines	1899	2.00	83⅛	2.4*	F	Ford Motor Co. Cars, trucks, parts, service	1947	1.80	50⅜	3.6
J	Standard Oil Co. (N.J.) Petroleum products	1883	2.65	72¾	3.6*	MAD	Madison Fund, Inc. Closed-end investment co.	1939	0.45e	21	2.1
DOW	Dow Chemical Co. Industrial chemicals	1911	1.58a	65⅞	2.4*	ELG	El Paso Natural Gas Co. Natural gas pipelines	1936	1.00	18⅜	5.3
PFE	Pfizer (Chas.) & Co., Inc. Drugs, chemicals	1901	1.05	49¾	2.1	LLT	Long Island Lighting Co. Operating public utility	1950	0.85a	30	2.8*
RCA	Radio Corp. of America Electronics, TV, radio brdcast.	1937	1.30a	97⅞	1.3*	X	U. S. Steel Corp. Basic & finished steel, cement	1940	2.00	53⅜	3.7
S	Sears, Roebuck & Co. Mail order & retail stores	1935	1.65	98¾	1.7*	BS	Bethlehem Steel Corp. Steel, shipbuilding	1939	1.50	30¼	5.0
SD	Standard Oil Co. of Calif. Petroleum products	1912	1.98a	59¾	3.3*	BC	Brunswick Corporation Bowling equip., pleasure boats	1937	0.45	10½	D
SA	Safeway Stores, Inc. Chain grocery stores	1927	1.60	59¼	2.7*	MRK	Merck & Co., Inc. Medicinal chem., drugs	1935	2.00	106	1.9*
PCG	Pacific Gas & Electric Co. Operating public utility	1919	1.00	31¼	3.2	AV	Avco Corporation Aircraft parts, electronics	1957	0.80	22⅞	3.5
SY	Sperry Rand Corp. Electronic controls, bus. mach.	—	—	18¾	—	AC	American Can Co. Cans & containers	1923	2.00	42	4.8
EK	Eastman Kodak Co. Photo equip., synthetic fibres	1902	2.55	119⅛	2.1	XRX	Xerox Corporation Photocopy, photographic prods.	1930	1.00	367⅛	0.3*
GO	Gulf Oil Corp. Petroleum products	1936	1.60	47½	3.4	AMF	American Machine & Foundry Co Recreational eq., indust. mach.	1927	0.90	17¾	5.1
P	Phillips Petroleum Co. Petroleum products	1934	1.98	48¾	4.1*	CFG	Corn Products Co. Corn refiner, grocery products	1919	1.40	59¼	2.4
LEM	Lehman Corp. Closed-end investment co.	1930	0.51e	30¾	1.7	GF	General Foods Corp. Food processor & distributor	1922	1.95	86⅜	2.3*
SPP	Scott Paper Co. Paper towels, tissues	1915	0.80	37⅝	2.1*	RLM	Reynolds Metals Co. Aluminum producer	1942	0.50	31	1.6
MTC	Monsanto Chemical Co. Chem., synthetic fibers	1925	1.17a	58⅝	2.0*	WIN	Winn-Dixie Stores, Inc. Chain grocery stores	1934	1.01	31	3.3*
ACY	American Cyanamid Co. Pharmaceuticals, chemicals	1934	1.80	57⅛	3.2	GT	Goodyear Tire & Rubber Co. Tires, rubber, chem. prods.	1937	1.00	42	2.4
DD	duPont de Nemours (E.I.) & Co. Nylon, chemicals	1904	7.50	246	3.0	LCE	Lone Star Gas Co. Natural gas pipelines	1926	1.00	22⅝	4.4
TX	Texaco Inc. Petroleum products	1903	2.00	66⅜	3.0*	OLM	Olin Mathieson Chemical Corp. Chemicals, drugs, metals	1926	1.00	45⅛	2.2

**Yield based on dividends paid in latest 12 months (including extras) and December 6, 1963 price.
a—Adjusted for stock dividends and splits.
e —Excludes dividends paid from security profits.

*—Dividend rate increased since December 7, 1962.
D—Dividend rate decreased since December 7, 1962.
t—Subject to tax withheld by a state, territory or foreign government.
Sources: Wall Street Journal; Standard & Poor's Dividend Record.

SOURCE: New York Stock Exchange.

Stop orders are also used to protect profits after a stock has risen in price. If stock bought at $35 a share should rise to $55, for example, the customer could enter a stop order to sell at $50. Should the stock decline to $50 or below, the stop order would automatically become a market order, and the stock would be sold at the best-obtainable price.[10]

When he gives his broker a limit order or stop order, the customer can specify that it is to be good for only one day; this is known as a *day order.* Or he can give a *week order* or a *month order.* If the order is not executed during the period designated, it automatically expires.

If the customer wants his order to hold good indefinitely, he gives his

[10] See "The Stop Order," New York Stock Exchange. A free copy of this booklet may be obtained by writing to the Exchange.

TABLE 13–4

The Monthly Investment Plan in Retrospect
January, 1954—January, 1964

How an investor would have stood on January 24, 1964, if he had invested $100 each month in any of the 20 stocks presently most popular with Merrill Lynch's MIP investors. Starting in Jan 1954 (the month the MIP was inaugurated) and continuing through January 24, 1964, the performance of the present 20 most popular stocks is shown below. These stocks are not necessarily all presently suggested for purchase. Those stocks that Merrill Lynch, Pierce, Fenner & Smith does suggest for long-term investment are listed in the latest issue of "20 Stocks for Long-Term Growth."

Stock	Without Reinvestment of Dividends				With Reinvestment of Dividends		
	Total Invested	Shares Owned	Market Value	Total Dividends Received	Total Invested	Shares Owned	Market Value
American Cyanamid Company	$12,000	283.87	$17,564	$2,602	$14,949	343.77	$21,271
American Telephone & Telegraph	12,000	150.31	21,908	3,327	15,973	192.52	28,060
Dow Chemical	12,000	197.65	13,786	1,458	13,473	220.86	15,492
Eastman Kodak	12,000	206.77	24,011	2,474	14,723	238.54	27,700
General Electric	12,000	178.64	15,296	1,989	14,086	207.98	17,922
General Motors	12,000	262.71	20,721	3,856	16,611	346.19	27,306
General Telephone & Electronics	12,000	701.30	23,142	3,109	15,571	860.77	28,405
Gulf Oil	12,000	393.72	19,883	2,448	14,717	464.85	23,475
International Business Machines	12,000	84.95	46,383	1,435	13,503	90.66	49,501
Minnesota Mining & Manufacturing	12,000	403.06	26,501	1,569	13,658	437.86	28,789
Monsanto Chemical	12,000	306.22	19,904	1,623	13,759	345.35	22,448
Pfizer (Charles)	12,000	505.31	25,707	2,667	14,979	592.72	30,154
Phillips Petroleum	12,000	252.91	12,266	2,387	14,700	305.32	14,808
Radio Corporation of America	12,000	264.53	22,463	1,838	13,897	304.08	34,003
Safeway	12,000	418.81	25,338	3,467	15,922	505.93	30,608
Sears Roebuck	12,000	295.24	30,299	2,580	14,888	346.68	35,578
Sperry Rand	12,000	651.74	13,360	1,403	13,541	723.35	14,828
Standard Oil of California	12,000	260.74	16,557	2,597	14,959	317.74	20,176
Standard Oil of New Jersey	12,000	235.68	18,501	2,978	15,465	298.11	23,402
Tri-Continental	12,000	344.51	15,890	3,275	15,910	444.63	20,508

The above table shows for each stock the number of shares an investor would have owned at January 24, 1964, and the market price of such shares on that day (1) if dividends had not been reinvested and (2) if dividends had been reinvested. Dividends received and dividends reinvested are before deduction for income taxes. Brokerage commissions on all purchases have been deducted.

The table illustrates how an investment through MIP can work out over a period of years. It is, of course, no indication as to future performance of any of the 20 stocks or of any other stock which might be purchased under MIP. Accordingly, the investor should take into account his financial ability to continue purchases through periods of low price levels. An investor should understand that he will incur a loss if he discontinues his purchases or sells when the market price of his shares is less than his average cost and that the MIP does not protect against loss in value in declining markets. The Monthly Investment Plan is designed to take advantage of temporary fluctuations in the market price and its advantages depend upon continuous, regular investment.

Source: Merrill Lynch, Pierce, Fenner & Smith, Inc., February 15, 1964, published twice yearly.

broker a *good-till-canceled order*. This type of order is carried as an open order—until the broker is able to execute it at the specified price, or until the customer cancels it.

Long and Short

A person may be long on certain securities which he holds and short on certain securities which he has sold before he has acquired them. If he sells from his holdings, we have a *long sale*, according to the terminology of the market. If he sells shares that he does not have (and through his broker borrows the shares to make delivery to the buyer), he is engaged in a *short sale*. Margin requirements of the Federal Reserve Board apply to both long and short sales. Short sales are now subject to certain restrictions.

Short Selling

Short selling in the securities market is selling shares you do not own and borrowing the number of shares you sell in order to make delivery to the purchaser. When you buy the stock later to return to the lender, you hope to do so at a lower price, thus making a profit. Short selling may not be used as a device to depress security prices artificially, and there are rigid rules to enforce this prohibition. No short sale of a stock is permitted except on a rising price. For instance, there might be six separate transactions in a given stock at a price of $45 a share. However, no stock could be sold short at $45 unless the price before the six transactions at $45 had been $44⅞ or less. Essentially, of course, short selling is a normal business transaction, as old at the first wheat crop ever planted. Yet, to some uninformed persons it still seems to be a sinister operation.

A market in which people may buy in the hope of a rise but in which others expecting a decline may not sell would cease to be a true market. Such a market would give a distorted reflection of the public's opinion of values and could not function properly. A true market allows full freedom of expression.

Delivery

Delivery of securities to buyers must, according to the rules and practices of the business, be made with dispatch. On transactions which are designated as "cash," delivery must be made to the purchaser's broker on the very day of the transaction. However, the usual, or "regular" way, of making delivery requires transmission to the buyer's broker by the fourth full business day following the transaction.

Quotations

Stocks are usually quoted at eighths of a point (28⅛, 28¼, 28⅜, 28½, 28⅝, 28¾, etc.). Bonds are quoted in a like manner, except that there is an addition of "and interest," meaning that the buyer must pay the interest accrued since the date when the bond last paid interest, along with the quoted price. Of course, the buyer gets this interest back when he collects from the issuer the next installment of interest. Some bonds (income bonds, adjustment bonds, bonds in default, etc.) are traded flat—with no "and interest." In the case of obligations of the United States government, the spread between quotations is reduced from the usual ⅛ to ⅟₃₂.

Why Stock Prices Change

It is rare indeed when an active issue does not change in price during the day, even if only an eighth of a point, or 12½ cents a share. Why should a share of stock change in value so frequently? A share of stock represents part ownership in, say, a giant utility which supplies a metropolis with power, or a railroad which daily hauls thousands of tons of freight and thousands of passengers. It seems unlikely that Commonwealth Edison Company or Pacific Gas & Electric, to name two corporations, becomes any more or any less valuable from one day to the next. But shares in them do. The answer is supply and demand.

A corporation has just so many shares outstanding. If you want to buy 25, 100, 500, or 5,000 shares of any stock listed on the New York Stock Exchange, you must buy them from someone who owns that number of shares. If you want to sell, you must find someone who wants to buy your shares. The Exchange brings together those who want to buy and those who want to sell.

An investor's decision to buy or sell a stock reflects his opinion of its value in relation to his personal investment needs and his financial position. His opinion may be influenced, literally, by anything from the state of his digestion to a crisis abroad. Facts sway him; so do fears, hopes, his appraisal of the future, and the past. Earnings reports and prospects may disturb him or elate him. An increased or an omitted dividend may clinch his decision. These opinions—of investors all over the nation—are reflected hour by hour, day by day, on the trading floor of the New York Stock Exchange.

Every day nearly 600 newspapers across the country publish a price record of stocks traded on the New York Stock Exchange, or tell about the market's action in a news column. Many papers do both. Eighty percent of all dailies in large United States cities regularly publish stock-market news.

When most people want to buy, the general market will rise. When most people want to sell, the market will decline. Individual stocks, of course, may move independently of the main body of shares. And they frequently do, reflecting developments peculiar to a company or an industry. When it is reported that the market "advanced," it means really that a majority of issues went up—not every stock.

What Are Bull and Bear Markets?

Sometimes a great many people will decide, more or less at the same time, perhaps just on the basis of the general business outlook, that it is a good idea to buy stocks—all kinds of stocks. Such general buying action raises the average price of all stocks. If the price rise is big enough and lasts long enough, we have what is called a "bull market." A "bear market" is just the opposite. The average price of all stocks drops because of widespread selling. To be "bullish" or "bearish" simply means to believe that stocks are going up or down.

Incidentally, it is a simple business to keep track of whether the market as a whole is moving up or down, because almost every major newspaper in the country publishes daily the average price of some group of key stocks and reports whether that average is moving up or down. The Dow-Jones averages are the best known of these indexes, but certainly not the most accurate.

Marketability and Organized Exchanges

Investment of liquid funds in both short- and long-term capital commitments is enhanced if there is a wide market for both new and seasoned securities. Most people are unable to invest their money and forget it, even though, in the case of a few foolish ones, that may be their wish. They never know when a need may arise for current funds. Unless they can readily sell investments and convert back to a liquid (cash) position, intelligent persons hesitate to part with their money for investments, no matter how sound. The great function of the organized exchange is that it provides the marketability and liquidity desired. You never have to worry about being able to sell a security listed on an organized exchange. Even if no other person wants to buy your shares, the specialist usually will.

The speed with which orders are executed is extraordinary. It takes only a few seconds to send a customer's order from any branch office to the broker's main office located in the same city as the exchange. A few minutes suffice to put through an order either on the floor of the exchange or, for that matter, in the over-the-counter market. An hour or two will usually suffice to make all the records necessary for a transaction. Contrast this speed with a sale of real estate, where months or even years may elapse before a deal can be consummated.

Customers' Accounts

To open an account at a stockbrokerage firm is a procedure which is comparable to opening an account at a commercial bank. Having opened his account and deposited a sufficient amount of money with the broker, orders may be given in person or by mail, telephone, telegraph, or cable. The customer receives a confirmation from the broker for each order completed. Monthly statements are sent to customers showing the details of all transactions and any other facts, such as dividends collected for and credited to customers' accounts, interest charges on borrowings, and customers' deposits and withdrawals.

Services of Securities Houses

Securities houses perform a vast variety of services for their customers. They open branches in communities where large numbers of investors and speculators reside. They stand ready to supply current quotations on securities and to put through transactions promptly. It is common practice for them to furnish news of, and opinions about, happenings in the world of finance. Inquiries concerning investment and tax problems of individuals are cheerfully answered. Recommendations for the inclusion or exclusion of specific securities in portfolios of individual investors are offered as part of ordinary, everyday services. Research departments which study financial facts about individual businesses and which make and publish studies of industries and companies are common. They disseminate facts concerning the workings of the securities markets and the methods of making investments therein. Some of them publish instructional material on the financial structure of corporations and the interpretation of published financial statements. Some brokerage houses even go so far as to conduct formal educational courses for customers and prospective customers on various phases of the financial world. The New York Stock Exchange supports the efforts of its members in these respects by publishing a monthly magazine and running educational advertisements in the press. It has produced and makes available for free distribution color films, which describe the investment process and the operation of the Exchange.[11] Also, any visitor who applies at the Visitors' Gallery entrance to the Exchange, at 20 Broad Street, will be taken on a guided tour of Exchange facilities and be permitted to watch operations on the floor of the Exchange from the second-floor balcony.

Commission Rates and Transfer Taxes

Commissions charged by Stock Exchange members are among the lowest for the transfer of any property—on average, about 1 percent of the value of the transaction. Commissions are figured on the following basis for each 100 shares:

NEW YORK STOCK EXCHANGE COMMISSION RATES
Selling at $1.00 a Share and Above
Round-Lot Charges

Money Value	Minimum Commission
under $100.00	as Mutually Agreed
$100.00 to $399.99	2% plus $ 3.00
$400.00 to $2,399.00	1% plus $ 7.00
$2,400.00 to $5,000	$\frac{1}{2}$% plus $19.00
over $5,000	$\frac{1}{10}$% plus $39.00

Thus a customer of a Stock Exchange firm who buys 100 shares of a stock at, say, $18.75 a share, or $1,875, would pay a commission of $25.75, or 1.3 percent of the purchase price. The commission on the purchase or sale of 100 shares of a $50 stock, or a total value of $5,000, would be $44, or 0.8 of 1 percent. On an odd-lot purchase or sale, the commission is the same as in the above schedule, less $2.00. On a purchase or sale involving less than $100, the commission can be any amount agreed upon by the firm and the customer. See Table 13–5.

The federal government collects a transfer tax of 4 cents per $100 actual value on stocks selling below $200 a share and 8 cents per share on stocks selling at $200 and over. New York State imposes a transfer tax of from 1 to 4 cents a share, based on selling price of the stock. Federal and state transfer taxes are paid by the sellers. In odd-lot transactions, the federal tax is also paid by the buyer.

Your broker will provide you with a more detailed explanation of commissions charged on the New York Stock Exchange for both round and odd lots.

---

[11] Requests for films, which are available free of charge, should be sent to the local office of any member firm of the New York Stock Exchange.

TABLE 13–5

MINIMUM COMMISSION CHARGES ON STOCKS

For stock transactions on the New York Stock Exchange involving $100 or more, the minimum commission charge ranges between $6 and $75 per transaction, provided the number of shares involved in the transaction does not exceed 100. Also, within these limits, the minimum charge shall not exceed $1.50 per share. (If the money involved is less than $100, the commission is as mutually agreed upon between the customer and broker.)

Commissions are basically calculated as a per cent of the money involved plus a stated dollar amount per transaction. A simplified method of computing commissions is as follows:

| | MINIMUM COMMISSION PER TRANSACTION | | |
| | | Plus Stated Amount: | |
Money Involved	Per Cent of Money Involved	For 100 Shares	For Less Than 100 Shares
$100 to $400	2%	$3 *	$1 *
$400 to $2,400	1%	7	5
$2,400 to $5,000	1/2%	19	17
Over $5,000	1/10%	39	37

* Minimum $6

The following examples show how these commission rates may be applied:

Examples

| Money Involved | COMMISSION PER TRANSACTION OF: | |
	100 Shares	Less Than 100 Shares†
$ 100	$6 (minimum)	$6 (minimum)
400	11 ($3 + 2%)	9 ($1 + 2%)
2,000	27 ($7 + 1%)	25 ($5 + 1%)
4,000	39 ($19 + 1/2%)	37 ($17 + 1/2%)
10,000	49 ($39 + 1/10%)	47 ($37 + 1/10%)
25,000	64 ($39 + 1/10%)	62 ($37 + 1/10%)
50,000	75 (top minimum)	75 (top minimum)

† Subject to the top minimum of $1.50 per share.

For transactions in excess of 100 shares, each 100 shares or fraction thereof is considered separately.

SOURCE: New York Stock Exchange.

Stock Gifts to Minors

It is now possible in most states and the District of Columbia to make stock gifts to minors. The Uniform Gifts to Minors Act, adopted by the National Conference of Commissioners on Uniform State Laws provides:

—The donor registers the securities either in his own name, the name of an adult member of the child's family, or the name of the child's guardian, as custodian for the minor.

—The gift to the minor is irrevocable.

—The custodian may buy, sell, collect dividends or reinvest, subject only to the restrictions of normal prudence.

—The gift is exempt from gift tax up to the donor's annual exclusion of $3,000 (or $6,000 for a married couple).

—The income from the gift will be taxable to the child. No income tax is payable on the first $600 of the child's income. If any income from such a gift is used to relieve a person's legal obligation to support the child, it will be taxable to that person.

Previously gifts of stock and other securities to minors were subject to severe legal restrictions. An adult could, it was true, simply register an issue in a child's name—but once done the action was irrevocable. The security had to remain untouched until junior reached 21. Not even parents (or junior) could sell, exchange, or otherwise dispose of the security to take advantage of changing market conditions. Legally, dividends also could not be touched but accrued to the minor.

The Uniform Act now makes possible an outright gift to a minor by registering the security in the name of an adult (parent, for example) as "custodian for a minor." Of crucial importance is the fact that the custodian has the right to sell the stock, reinvest the proceeds, collect dividends, and in general manage the investment until the owner becomes 21. The gift is still irrevocable, but the securities are no longer frozen but may be traded.[12]

Controls—from Within

Over the years, the Exchange—largely through experience—has evolved a complex system of rules for self-control. But the underlying principles have remained the same, namely, (1) securities may be bought and sold on the Exchange only at prices openly and fairly arrived at; (2) regulations for trading on the floor of the Exchange repeatedly stress the importance of the open market—"open" in the sense that

---

[12] See *Gifts of Securities or Money to Minors—A Guide to Laws in 50 States,* Association of Stock Exchange Firms, 120 Broadway, New York, N.Y., 10005.

secret deals are prohibited; (3) bids and offers are made in multiples of the unit of trading (ordinarily 100 shares), and the highest bid and the lowest offer have precedence. Bids and offers must be called out loud. Transactions are immediately reported across the country. No trades are allowed on the Exchange floor before or after trading hours, which are from 10 A.M. to 3:30 P.M., Monday through Friday.

The relations of Stock Exchange member firms and corporations and their clients must meet a rigid set of requirements. Member firms must inform their customers, monthly or at other set periods, of the condition of their accounts, and all customers of a Stock Exchange member firm must be supplied with copies of the firm's financial statement upon request.[13] Member firms must have adequate capital and must answer at least three financial questionnaires of the Exchange every year. One of these reports is based on a surprise audit by independent public accountants. In addition, Stock Exchange examiners visit member firms' offices and spot check their books and records to see that Exchange, federal, and state regulations are being followed. Member firms also must report weekly on their positions as underwriters of securities and must disclose borrowings or loans by the firm or by individual partners.

Controls—from Without

The Securities Acts of 1933 and 1934 ushered in a new era in American finance. The 1933 Act provides for full and fair disclosure of the character of new issues of securities publicly offered in interstate and foreign commerce and through the mails, and for the prevention of fraud in the sale of such securities. The 1934 Act provides for the regulation of securities exchanges and of over-the-counter markets operating in interstate and foreign commerce and through the mails, to prevent inequitable and unfair practices. The Securities and Exchange Commission, with headquarters in Washington and offices in other cities, administers the Acts.

The 1934 Act makes mandatory:

1. Adequate disclosure of information about a listed security
2. Registration with the SEC of all securities listed on national securities exchanges
3. The banning of all manipulative operations, such as pools, wash or faked sales, false and misleading statements, etc.
4. The prohibition of "actual or apparent active trading in any security, or raising or depressing the price for the purpose of inducing the purchase or sale of it by others"

---

[13] For further details see George L. Leffler and Loring C. Farwell, *The Stock Market* (3d ed.; New York: Ronald Press Co., 1963).

In addition, the SEC prescribes rules for periodic reports covering dealings in their stock by officers, directors, and principal stockholders of companies whose securities are listed on an exchange.

Government controls also regulate the flow of credit into the securities market. This section of the Securities Exchange Act of 1934 is administered by the Federal Reserve Board, as this agency has jurisdiction over the use of credit and regulates the flow of credit in the banking system. Brokers may borrow only from a source approved by the Federal Reserve, which also determines how much credit a broker may extend to a customer to purchase or carry listed securities.

SUGGESTED READINGS

1. Louis Engel, *How to Buy Stocks—a Guide to Successful Investing.* Paperbound edition. New York: Bantam Books. A free copy may be obtained upon request to Mr. Engel at Merrill Lynch, Pierce, Fenner & Smith, 70 Pine St., New York, N.Y., 10005.

2. *Over-the-Counter Securities.* New York: Merrill Lynch, Pierce, Fenner & Smith. A free copy may be obtained by writing to the firm at 70 Pine St., New York, N.Y., 10005.

3. *New York Stock Exchange Fact Book,* NYSE, annual. A free copy of the latest edition may be obtained by writing to the Publications Division, New York Stock Exchange, 11 Wall St., New York, N.Y., 10005.

4. G. L. Leffler and Loring C. Farwell, *The Stock Market.* 3d ed. New York: The Ronald Press Company, 1963.

5. B. E. Shulz and A. P. Squier, *The Securities Market and How It Works,* Rev. ed. New York: Harper & Row Publishers, 1963.

6. *Encyclopedia of Stock Market Techniques.* Larchmont, N.Y.: Investors Intelligence, Inc., 1963.

7. Mark Weaver, *The Technique of Short Selling.* Rev. ed. New Jersey: Investors Library, Inc., 1963.

8. Maurece Schiller, *Special Situations.* Larchmont, N.Y.: American Research Council. 1961.

9. Hillel Black, *The Watchdogs of Wall Street.* New York: William Morrow & Co., Inc., 1962.

10. Philip A. Fisher, *Common Stocks and Uncommon Profits.* Rev. ed. New York: Harper & Row Publishers, 1960.

11. Raymond Trigger, *How to Run a Successful Investment Club.* Rev. ed. New York: Harper & Row, Publishers, 1960.

12. David Jenkins, *How to Profit from Formula Plans in the Stock Market.* Larchmont, N.Y.: American Research Council, 1961.

13. Helen J. McLane and Patricia Hutar, *The Investment Club Way to Stock Market Success.* Garden City, N.Y.: Doubleday & Company, Inc., 1963.

14. *The Financial Analysts Journal,* published by the New York Society of Security Analysts, Inc. New York.

15. *Security and Industry Survey,* issued quarterly by Merrill Lynch, Pierce, Fenner & Smith. A free copy may be obtained by writing to this firm at 70 Pine St., New York, N.Y., 10005.

16. *Odd Lots,* published by Carlisle & Jacquelin, New York. A free copy may be obtained by writing to this firm at 120 Broadway, New York, N.Y., 10005.

17. Robert D. Merritt, *Financial Independence through Common Stocks.* 7th ed. New York: Simon and Schuster, Inc., 1963.

18. Richard H. Rush, *The Techniques of Becoming Wealthy.* Englewood Cliffs, N.J.: Prentice-Hall, Inc., 1963.

19. *Facts You Should Know about Securities.* Latest edition. Educational Division, Better Business Bureau, Chrysler Building, New York, N.Y., 10017.

20. *Facts You Should Know about Security and Commodity Exchanges.* Latest edition. Educational Division, Better Business Bureau, Chrysler Building, New York, N.Y., 10017.

21. Publications and Films available from the New York Stock Exchange:
Single Copies Free on Request:*
Dividends over the Years—A guide to common stock investment, containing data on some 500 long dividend-paying stocks listed on the NYSE. Includes special groupings of stocks by yield, dividend payment, and other common yardsticks.

Investment Facts—Tabulation of NYSE listed common stocks which have paid cash dividends every three months for 20 years or more, with key data on dividends, recent prices, and yields.

How to Invest on a Budget—Describes the story of the Monthly Investment Plan, how it works, what it costs, how to start a plan. Contains current list of top 50 stocks favored by MIP investors—with price and dividend information.

Investments Clubs . . . What Are They? . . . How Are They Started?—Information on the organization and operation of investment clubs.

Understanding the New York Stock Exchange—Comprehensive and easy-to-read description of the functions of the Stock Exchange and Member Firms.

Now, About the Specialist—Tells about the activities and responsibilities of the specialist, and Exchange regulations and policies governing his operations.

The Language of Investing, A Glossary—Definitions of stock market terms.

How to Understand Financial Statements—Comprehensive 32-page booklet for educators, students, and investors. Explains basic techniques used in investment analysis.

Does It Make Sense for Me to Buy Stocks?—Answers nine questions most often asked about investing.

Marketing Methods for Your Block of Stock—A handbook for investment managers of financial institutions.

---

* Requests for free single copies of publications should be sent to: New York Stock Exchange, Publications Division, 11 Wall St., New York, N.Y., 10005.

Subscription Publications:

The Exchange—Monthly magazine of the NYSE provides, in every-day language, facts, figures, and articles of current interest to present and potential shareowners. ($1.50 per year; $3.50 for 36 monthly issues.)

New York Stock Exchange Monthly Review—A compilation of current business and financial statistics, including record highs and lows for each series. ($1.00 for 12 issues.)

Films:*

The Lady and the Stock Exchange—An amusing drama produced in color by Paramount and starring Janet Blair. Emphasizes the right versus the wrong way to start investing. (27 minutes)

Your Share in Tomorrow—The role of the shareowner in the past, present, and future. Eastman color. (27 minutes)

What Makes Us Tick—An animated Technicolor short about the investment process, the NYSE, listed corporations and their stockholders. (12 minutes)

Working Dollars—A cartoon film in full color, showing how Fred Finchley puts his dollars to work through MIP. (13 minutes)

The Big Board (13 minutes) and *Bid and Asked* (15 minutes)—Designed for the professional investment manager. In color.†

CASE PROBLEMS

1. Nancy is a recent college graduate. She has a good job with a firm in the San Francisco area. Her salary allows her to make small weekly contributions to her savings account, which by now, with the help of a graduation gift from her parents, is equal to a year's salary. She feels that she would like to invest part of it in securities. What things should she consider? What would you advise her to do?

2. Bert (35), an alumnus of a graduate school of business, has a secure job with a manufacturing firm. He is married and has two children (ages 5 and 3). His home and automobile are paid for. Ten years ago Bert inherited a dryland wheat farm, which for years, because of drought and poor crops, barely produced a sufficient income to cover taxes and cost of operation. Three years ago oil was discovered on his farm and it is now yielding an annual net income of $25,000. Bert wants to invest this extra income in securities. What would you advise him to do?

3. Winters has just received a promotion with a substantial increase in salary. He feels that the time has come to begin to build an investment fund. In his opinion he can afford to invest $500 every three months. Since he does not have enough capital to secure the services of an investment counselor, and

---

* Requests for these films should be sent to the local office of any Member Firm of the NYSE or to Modern Talking Picture Service, with offices in major cities. Films loaned free of charge.

† Available, free of charge, through any Member Firm, or contact Institutional Investor Information Office, New York Stock Exchange, 11 Wall St., New York, N.Y., 10005.

since the idea of a mutual fund does not appeal to him, he has decided to try the dollar-averaging formula plan. While this plan helps him to decide *how* to invest, it does not tell him in *what* stocks he should invest. How can he obtain this information?

4. Lyons and his wife have been married six years. They live in a rented, furnished apartment and carry no insurance. They have saved about $3,000. Both work and are covered by social security and pension plans. Lyons wants to invest their savings in shares of the stock of the American Telephone and Telegraph Company. What do you think about it?

5. Mandel started his own business 10 years ago. By now he owns the business (including buildings), his home, an automobile, and savings accounts of $8,000. He is currently earning about $9,000 a year. His family consists of a wife and two young children. Now he thinks that he should invest $5,000 of his savings in good common stocks. Do you agree?

6. Robbins is 32 years old. He lives with his wife (age 30) and two children (ages 6 and 8). For the last few years the family has been living comfortably on his income (average, $10,000 a year) from a small business which he owns and which has taken all of his time and attention. At his mother's death he inherits $50,000, which he would like to invest in securities. What advice can you give him concerning the investment of this money at present?

7. Corcoran knows by experience that it is not good to "put all of one's eggs into one basket." Having $75,000 to invest, he decides to buy approximately $1,000 worth of each of 75 "blue-chip" stocks, selected pretty much at random. Can you improve upon his plan?

8. Archer has accumulated $25,000 in savings banks and savings and loan associations. He was always afraid of investing in stocks because he thought the stock market was subject to such abuses that investment therein was unsafe. He has been led to believe, however, that most of the abuses have now been eliminated by regulation. Now he is beginning to think that his money would be about as safe in securities as it would be in savings banks. He is a married man in his 40's with four children (ages 12, 14, 17, and 19). His job pays him, steadily, $15,000 a year. He thinks that hereafter he will invest $2,000 a year ($500 a quarter) in common stocks, leaving his already accumulated $25,000 and the earnings thereon where they are. What is your opinion of this plan?

9. Balcom has $1,800 of surplus savings. With this money he can buy shares in a small local company or shares in a large company, national in scope. At the present rate of dividends, he will receive 4 percent on his investment in either company. Does one investment look better to you than the other?

10. Zettelli is a real estate broker whose earnings fluctuate widely from year to year, although they have averaged $8,000 annually over the last 10 years. He and his wife live comfortably on $5,000 a year. They own their home and have a nest egg of $10,000 in the bank. He is intrigued by dollar averaging, believing that he could not fail to be successful if he followed it in the stock market. However, he thinks that his fluctuating earnings bar his using it. What advice would you give him?

11. After Bisbee, an average married man, had $2,000 for emergencies, he decided to invest his remaining savings, $1,000, in a common stock selling at $100 a share. Since he realized that his $1,000 would permit him to buy only 10 shares outright and he believed strongly that shares in this company would advance sharply in price, he decided to buy 20 shares on a 50 percent margin. Do you agree with him?

14 OBTAINING INVESTMENT INFORMATION

> Investigate before you invest.
> —*Better Business Bureau*

BACK IN 1925, *Barron's* published an article suggesting how $100,000 might be well invested in securities for a widow with two small children. The plan was based on a set of ten rules for investors.

The securities (both stocks and bonds), all hand-picked in accordance with the rules, are today worth $524,000. The stocks are worth $473,000—over nine times their original value of $51,000. Average annual income, for the entire 39 years, has exceeded $8,900. Income for 1963 was $16,491.

Barron's ten rules were:

Rule One. Own only bonds and stocks of leading companies in sound and essential industries.

Rule Two. Except for bank and insurance stocks, own only stocks listed on a National Securities Exchange.

Rule Three. Own only stocks which can boast an earnings or a dividend record—or both—unbroken for at least 10 years.

Rule Four. Own stocks in at least five different industries.

Rule Five. Own stocks in fairly equal amounts in at least eight or ten different companies.

Rule Six. Own a few low-yield stocks as a means of building up capital and future income.

Rule Seven. Buy bonds below par to reduce the likelihood of spending capital.

Rule Eight. Once a year sell at least one stock, choosing the weakest on the list with no consideration whatever for its original cost. Replace it by a more attractive stock.

Rule Nine. Do not be disturbed by losses on individual risks, but keep an eye open for a gain or a loss on the aggregate.

638

Rule Ten. Subscribe to at least one high-grade financial publication and read it regularly and thoroughly.[1]

Rule ten is our main concern in this chapter.

Before buying stocks and bonds, an intelligent investor should accumulate a good deal of information concerning the securities in which he is interested. It is common to undertake the inquiry in three steps: (1) Are general business conditions such that it is a propitious time to invest? Should one buy or sell short? (2) What is the condition and what are the prospects of the industry in which one proposes to invest? Which are the best growth industries? Which are the best defensive industries? (3) What is the status of, and what has the future in store for, the particular company in the industry in which the investor is interested? Or which is the company with the best prospects in the industry? Although the job may be too extensive for the average person to do it adequately, a general outline of where to look and what to look for may be given if one has the time, the patience, and the intelligence to do it.

Large Investors

Large investors, such as investment companies, banks, and insurance companies, have extensive research organizations which study all available facts before a commitment is made in a given security. They keep track of conditions pertaining to specific securities as long as they hold those securities; they continue to hold the securities only because the facts indicate that it is the wise thing to do. When conditions develop which indicate that securities should be sold, the decision to sell is based on facts. Research is kept constantly up to date. Experience proves that it is not satisfactory to buy a security (after investigation), put it away in a vault, and forget about it. Such a procedure almost invariably ends in a result which is less advantageous than constant watchfulness would have produced. The larger organizations can afford to buy and read the services published by specialists. While these services may be too expensive for the average small investor to buy, any good public library or university business school library will have them available for reference and use.

Typical Investors

Unfortunately, most small investors expect to obtain for nothing the facts on which to form a judgment. Sometimes they act on the basis of

[1] From A. Vere Shaw, *Ten Rules for Investors* (New York: Barron's Publishing Co., 1963).

tips, without even finding out whether there is any merit in the tip. Often they rely on offhand information received from a banker or somebody in a stockbrokerage house. Even though the individuals who give the information may be able persons, the casual, offhand remark or advice may not fit the particular investment problem of the listener. Banks or brokerage houses may give some useful information and advice as to where more can be found, but the individual must expect to do a lot of digging himself. The broker, as his name implies, earns his living by bringing buyers and sellers together, effecting purchases and sales. Most of the large brokerage houses have competent research departments. It is to their advantage to make sound recommendations, for they will not long retain a customer who loses money acting on their advice, and they know it. Also, the more farsighted brokerage houses know that the younger, small investor of today may become the larger investor of tomorrow, and some of these houses are now actively catering to the small investor. He, therefore, need no longer feel that because he does not have $50,000 to invest, the brokerage house will have no interest in him. One difficulty that the small investor may encounter is that while brokers often advise persons what to buy and when to buy, less often do they give adequate advice as to when to sell.

Use an Investment Counselor?

For the investor with $50,000 or more who feels that investing is too much of a job for him personally, the investment counselor is available to furnish necessary information and make decisions as to buying and selling. For a relatively small percentage of the market value of a list of investments, usually one half of 1 percent annually, one may hire an investment counsel who maintains a staff and makes a business of furnishing advice for a fee. Since they cannot afford to furnish much information for little compensation, they usually cannot afford to work for clients who do not have at least $50,000 to invest, and they are therefore not available to the smaller investor. However, some of the smaller investment-counseling firms will take accounts of $10,000 size. The fee involved is usually worth the cost because investment counselors today must register with and are regulated by the SEC. This does not guarantee, of course, that the advice they give is good, but it does insure that it is not fraudulent; and the investment counselor usually obtains business by recommendations of satisfied and pleased clients. Leading investment-counseling firms include Scudder-Stevens & Clark, Calvin Bullock, Loomis-Sayles, Lehman Brothers, and Lionel Edie. Also, the leading financial services—Moody's, Standard & Poor's, and Value Line—all have investment-counseling departments.[2]

General Business Conditions

To keep abreast of general business conditions and be informed on trends and developments is not at all difficult. The financial section of a good newspaper, such as the *New York Times,* or a magazine, such as *Business Week,* will, if read regularly, build a feeling of awareness of what is happening and a background to understand it. The *Survey of Current Business,* published monthly by the U.S. Department of Commerce, is also helpful. Specialized daily or weekly financial newspapers, such as the *Wall Street Journal, Journal of Commerce, Commercial and Financial Chronicle,* and *Barron's* are invaluable. The Federal Reserve System publishes a "National Summary of Business Conditions" each month in its *Federal Reserve Bulletin.* Upon request, a mimeographed copy of this summary will be mailed in advance of publication. There is no charge for this. Your name will be placed on the Federal Reserve's mailing list for this summary if you write to the Publications Division, Board of Governors, Federal Reserve System, Washington, D.C. Each month the U.S. Government's Council of Economic Advisers prepares and issues *Economic Indicators.* This may be obtained from the Superintendent of Documents, U.S. Government Printing Office, Washington, D.C. The Council also prepares the very useful annual *Economic Report of the President,* analyzing current economic trends in the country.

There are many other publications which are useful to a person who is attempting to keep abreast of general business conditions. *Sources of Business Information* (2d rev. ed.), by Edwin R. Coman, Jr., may assist the student in locating some of these; *Business Service Checklist* of the U.S. Department of Commerce and the *List of Selected U.S. Government Publications* (appearing twice a month), obtainable from the Superintendent of Documents, Washington, D.C., are also worth knowing about. Once the student becomes acquainted with some of these sources of information, he will inevitably be led by them to others. After he has been studying business information for a time, he will probably be bothered not so much by the difficulty of obtaining information but rather by the difficulty of making intelligent choice as to what part of the mass of available material should receive his attention and what part should be dismissed from consideration.

---

[2] See H. C. Walter (ed.), *Investment Information and Advice: A Handbook and Directory* (Whittier, Calif.: FIR Publishing Co., 1964).

Industry Information

As to the essentials of an industry, much can be learned from the *Industry Surveys* of Standard & Poor's. These are excellent, brief, yet comprehensive studies, revised annually. Trade associations are sources of information about the various industries; a list of them may be found in *National Organizations of the United States,* Vol. I of the Encyclopedia of Associations. The *Industry Record* of the National Industrial Conference Board publishes excellent studies on particular industries. There are a large number of industry journals, some issued by the trade associations, some published commercially. Each usually issues an annual or review-of-the-year number, which provides much useful information. Examples are *Coal Age, Electrical World, Iron Age, Oil and Gas Journal, Paper Trade Journal, Farm Implement News, Printing, Railway Age, Canner,* etc. The student who wishes further information and does not know how to acquire it can usually obtain help from the librarians at any good public or university library.

Information about Particular Companies

The various financial services, such as Moody's, Standard & Poor's, and Value Line (to be described later), publish a wealth of information about particular companies, and there is no excuse for anyone investing in a corporation without first having looked it up in one of the services and learned all the basic facts about its finances, operations, and outlook. In most cases, the services not only provide the basic financial and economic facts about the company but also give a recommendation as to whether the company's stock (or bond) should be bought, sold, or held. An example of a company analysis is shown in Figure 14–1. Loose-leaf volumes, arranged alphabetically, of these company analyses issued by the various services are available in any good business or financial library.

Whenever a company floats a new issue of securities, it is required (with certain exceptions) by law to file a *registration statement* and *prospectus* with the Securities and Exchange Commission. The *registration statement* contains all the pertinent financial, economic, and legal information about the company, its officers, and its operations that any investor might need and want to know in arriving at a decision as to whether to buy the company's securities. A copy of the *registration statement* may either be examined at the nearest SEC office or a photostatic copy may be purchased at cost. The *prospectus* is a summarized or abridged version of the information contained in the

FIGURE 14–1

T[1]   182

American Tel. & Tel.

Stock—	Approx. Price	Dividend	Yield
CAPITAL	142½	[2] $4.00	[2]2.8%

RECOMMENDATION: The company has a dominant position in the communications field, not only through its telephone subsidiaries but also through Western Electric, Bell Telephone Laboratories, and the numerous wire services provided. While current prices in part reflect the rights offering of common shares and the proposed 2-for-1 stock split, rather than the near-term earnings outlook, this top-grade stock merits retention for secure income and the company's promising growth potential.

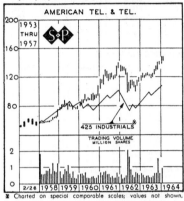

[※] Charted on special comparable scales; values not shown.

[3]OPERATING REVENUES (Million $)

Quarter:	1963	1962	1961	1960	1959
Feb.	2,295	2,174	2,029	1,908	1,775
May	2,378	2,242	2,083	1,971	1,837
Aug.	2,401	2,256	2,106	1,991	1,863
Nov.	2,432	2,269	2,150	2,010	1,877

For 1963, total operating revenues exceeded those of the previous year by 6.6%, reflecting gains of 5.9% and 7.6% in local and toll receipts, respectively. Despite higher maintenance-depreciation allowances, the operating ratio dropped to 82.1%, from 82.5%, thereby extending the rise in operating income to 8.8%. With a greater charge to other income offsetting the investment tax credit and with 9.2% heavier interest requir :nents, the gain in net income was pared to 6.6%. The lesser rise in earnings to $6.06 an average share from $5.79 in 1962, reflected the increased average number of outstanding shares. Credits for interest charged to construction amounted to $0.13 and $0.12 a share, respectively.

[34] CAPITAL SHARE EARNINGS ($)

Quarter:	1963	1962	1961	1960	1959	1958
Feb.	1.43	1.42	1.36	1.32	1.21	1.07
May	1.49	1.47	1.37	1.41	1.32	1.16
Aug.	1.57	1.47	1.36	1.40	1.30	1.19
Nov.	1.55	1.43	1.40	1.40	1.33	1.21

PROSPECTS

Near Term—While the company's steadily improving operating ratio demonstrates management's ability to offset rising costs, the anticipated added expense resulting from new labor contracts is bound to exert some restraint on earnings expansion this year. Thus, considering the possibility of lower federal income tax rates and the effect of the current common stock rights offering, profits for 1964 are tentatively estimated at $6.15-$6.20 an average share, up from $6.06 in 1963. Dividends have been raised to $1.00 quarterly, from $0.90, effective with the April payment. Shareholders will vote April 15, 1964, on a proposed 2-for-1 split. Dividends on the new shares would be at $0.50 quarterly, equal to the present rate.

Long Term— The outlook for continued growth in all phases of operations is highly promising. While new telephone installations can be expected to fluctuate from year-to-year, increasing usage and new communication services point to further revenue growth for some time ahead. Areas in which the full potential is far from realized include overseas calling, educational television networks and industrial applications of data communication systems. Moreover, further mechanization should enhance margins. While over 99% of System telephones are dial operated and almost 80% are equipped for Direct Distance Dialing, the introduction of electronic switching centers in coming years should yield additional benefits.

RECENT DEVELOPMENTS

On July 31, 1963, the FCC ruled that tax savings from the 3% investment credit should flow through to earnings. Company has petitioned for reconsideration of the ruling. This item equaled $0.23 and $0.20 a share in 1963 and 1962, respectively.

DIVIDEND DATA

Dividends in the past 12 months were:

Amt. of Divd. $	Date Decl.	Ex-divd. Date	Stock of Record	Payment Date
0.90...	May 15	May 27	May 31	Jul. 1'63
0.90...	Aug. 21	Aug. 27	Aug. 30	Oct. 1'63
0.90...	Nov. 20	Nov. 25	Nov. 29	Jan. 2'64
1.00...	Feb. 11	Feb. 25	Feb. 28	Apr. 1'64
Stkhldrs. vote Apr. 15, 1964 on 2-for-1 split.				

[1]Listed N.Y.S.E., Boston, Phila.-Balt.-Wash., Midwest, and Pacific Coast S.Es. and Paris Bourse; also traded Cincinnati, Detroit, and Pitts. S.Es.   [2]Rate indicated by latest quarterly.   [3]Consol.; earns. based on average shares outstanding.   [4]Adj. for 3-for-1 split in May, 1959.

Vol. 31, No. 38   Wednesday, February 26, 1964   Sec. 3

SOURCE: Standard & Poor's Corp.

FIGURE 14–1—*Continued*

182 AMERICAN TELEPHONE & TELEGRAPH COMPANY

INCOME STATISTICS (Million $) AND PER SHARE ($) DATA

Year Ended Dec. 31	Revenues: Local	Revenues: Toll	Revenues: Gross	²Oper. Ratio	% of Gr. Revs.: Taxes	% of Gr. Revs.: Dep. & Maint.	Net Inc.	⁵Capital Share ($) Data: ⁴Earns.	Divs. Paid	Price Range
1964--	-----	-----	-----	---	---	---	-----	---	1.90	----------
1963--	5,389.7	3,737.1	9,569.0	82.1	23.5	31.0	1,479.5	6.06	3.60	141⅜–114½
1962--	5,088.5	3,471.8	8,980.2	82.5	23.4	30.6	1,388.2	5.79	3.60	136¼ – 98⅛
1961--	4,797.5	3,217.3	8,414.4	83.0	23.4	30.1	1,284.6	5.52	3.45	139⅞–103⅛
1960--	4,547.4	2,996.4	7,920.5	83.4	23.3	30.1	1,213.0	5.53	3.30	103½ – 79⅞
1959--	4,250.8	2,786.1	7,393.0	83.4	22.9	30.0	1,113.2	5.22	3.15	89 – 74⅞
1958--	3,944.4	2,490.6	6,771.4	84.4	21.9	30.4	952.3	4.67	3.00	75⅝ – 55⅞
1957--	3,647.6	2,357.7	6,313.8	86.1	20.1	31.2	829.8	4.33	3.00	59⅞ – 53⅜
1956--	3,368.6	2,176.2	5,825.3	86.4	19.8	30.5	755.9	4.39	3.00	62⅛ – 55
1955--	3,086.5	1,959.7	5,297.0	86.4	19.7	30.0	664.2	4.37	3.00	6[illegible]½ – 57⅝
1954--	2,837.0	1,720.7	4,784.5	87.2	18.5	30.2	549.9	3.97	3.00	59⅜ – 52

¹ PERTINENT BALANCE SHEET STATISTICS (Million $)

Dec. 31	Gross Prop.	% Depr. of Gross Prop.	³% Earn. on Net Prop.	Net Workg. Cap.	Funded Debt	% Fund. Debt of Net Prop.	% Fund. Debt of Gross Rev.	Total Invest. Cap.	% Earn. on Inv. Cap	Net Inc. per Tel.	⁵($) Book Val. Cap. Sh.
1963--	30,306	21.3	7.2	151.1	8,579	36.2	89.7	25,584	7.2	21.54	65.75
1962--	27,914	21.3	7.2	549.1	8,224	37.5	91.6	24,221	7.1	21.04	62.66
1961--	25,893	21.6	7.0	351.2	7,271	35.8	86.4	22,299	7.1	20.33	59.82
1960--	24,072	21.8	7.0	128.9	7,232	38.4	91.3	20,452	7.3	19.97	56.50
1959--	22,205	22.2	7.1	271.0	6,432	37.3	87.0	18,832	7.2	19.20	54.48
1958--	20,646	22.4	6.6	372.8	6,042	37.7	89.2	17,651	6.6	17.41	52.57
1957--	19,117	22.8	6.0	27.7	5,688	38.6	90.1	15,945	6.2	15.88	51.24
1956--	17,074	24.1	6.1	497.5	4,618	35.6	79.3	14,487	6.2	15.29	49.87
1955--	15,344	25.4	6.3	524.0	4,376	38.2	82.6	12,844	6.2	14.37	50.14
1954--	14,136	25.9	5.8	266.3	4,001	38.2	83.6	11,485	5.9	12.69	48.87

¹Consol. ²After depr. ³Based on oper. inc. ⁴Based on aver. shs. outstg. ⁵Adj. for 3-for-1 split in 1959.

Fundamental Position

A holding and operating company, American Telephone & Telegraph, through its operating telephone subsidiaries comprising the Bell System, controls 68,639,837 telephones, about 82% of country's total. Substantial, but not controlling, stock interests are held in other telephone operating companies, including Bell Telephone of Canada, which are not now considered part of the Bell System. The parent company directly operates long distance lines connecting regional units and independent systems. Approximately 56% of system revenues is from local service.

Equipment is purchased largely from the Western Electric Company, 99.8% owned, which has been a substantial contributor to earnings in recent years. Research, development and engineering work is conducted for the company and Western Electric on a nonprofit basis by Bell Telephone Laboratories, a wholly owned subsidiary.

Auxiliary services of the company include teletypewriter exchange service (recently converted to dial operation on a national basis); private line telephone and teletypewriter services; and facilities for transmission of television and radio programs. By means of cable and radio circuits overseas service is provided, and interconnections are maintained between telephone systems in the United States and those in 175 countries and territories.

On August 31, 1962, a law was passed authorizing the establishment of a satellite communications corporation. Through its leadership in this field, AT&T will obviously play an important role in the development of this new company which is to be jointly owned by the public and certain communications companies.

Dividends have been paid each year since 1885. The increase in 1959 was the first since 1922.

Employees: 733,138. Shareholders: about 2,250,000.

Finances

Planned outlays in 1964 of $3.25 billion will be financed in part by a 1-for-20 rights offering of common stock to holders of record February 18, 1964, at a subscription price of $100 a share. The rights expire April 6, 1964. Additional security sales by the parent should not be necessary this year.

In 1963, funds for expenditures of about $3.1 billion were provided by internal sources, a $250 million debenture sale by the parent, $332 million from employee stock sales and subsidiary financings.

CAPITALIZATION
(12/31/63)

FUNDED DEBT: Parent......*$3,498,618,000
Subs. $5,080,000,000

*Includes $8,618,000 4¼% debentures convertible into 3 shares of stock for each $100 debenture and $42 cash.

SUBSIDIARY PFD. STOCKS: $17,904,300
MINORITY INTEREST........ $567,884,000
CAPITAL STOCK: 244,729,744 shares ($33-1/3 par).

Incorporated in N. Y. in 1885. **Office**—195 Broadway, NYC 10007. **Pres**—E. J. McNeely. **VP-Secy**—C. E. Wampler. **VP-Treas**—J. J. Scanlon. **Dirs**—F. R. Kappel (Chrmn), L. D. Brace, E. B. Hanify, H. T. Heald, J. V. Herd, W. A. Hewitt, J. R. Killian, Jr., J. L. McCaffrey, J. J. McCloy, E. J. McNeely, J. I. Miller, W. B. Murphy, T. F. Patton, M. J. Rathbone, H. I. Romnes, G. F. Smith, J. Taylor, W. White. **Transfer Agents**—Company's offices; 195 Broadway, NYC 7; New England Tel. & Tel. Co., Boston; Illinois Bell Telephone Co., Chicago; Pacific Tel. & Tel., San Francisco. **Registrars**—Bankers Trust Co., NYC; Old Colony Trust Co., Boston; First National Bank, Chicago; Wells Fargo Bank, San Francisco.

registration statement. A copy must be given to every prospective purchaser of the company's new issue of securities. Frequently, in seeking information about a company, if there has been a recent new issue, examination of the *registration statement* and *prospectus* at the nearest SEC office will yield a wealth of information about the company and its operations.

If you have the technical competence, the best way, of course, to find out about a company's financial status and position is to analyze its balance sheet and income account yourself. You can usually obtain copies of the latest balance sheet and income account by writing to the company itself. Normally, unless it is a closed or family corporation, it will make its balance sheet and income account public. All corporations whose securities are listed on organized exchanges are required to make their financial statements available. They, and all corporations which have issued new securities, have registered them with the SEC, and have at least a million dollars worth of such securities still outstanding, must file *Form 10K* with the SEC. This is a detailed financial statement, prepared annually in accordance with SEC specifications. It can be consulted either at the office of the exchange on which the company is listed or at the local branch of the SEC.

Brokerage Houses

Most of the leading brokerage houses not only publish a wealth of information in the form of analyses worked up by their own research departments but also distribute free of charge, on request by customers, company analyses prepared by the standard financial services. They also have available in their offices, for examination and use by customers, the various manuals and compilations of the leading financial services.

The following large brokerage houses all have competent research departments and will make available studies, reports, and analyses upon request:

1. Merrill Lynch, Pierce, Fenner & Smith
   70 Pine St.
   New York, N.Y.
2. Bache & Co.
   36 Wall St.
   New York, N.Y.
3. Paine, Webber, Jackson & Curtis
   25 Broad St.
   New York, N.Y.
4. Kidder, Peabody & Co.
   20 Exchange Place
   New York, N.Y.
5. Shearson Hammill & Co.
   14 Wall St.
   New York, N.Y.
6. Hornblower & Weeks
   One Chase Manhattan Plaza
   New York, N.Y.
7. Walston & Co.
   75 Wall St.
   New York, N.Y.

8. Francis I. du Pont & Co.
   One Wall St.
   New York, N.Y.
9. E. F. Hutton & Co.
   61 Broadway
   New York, N.Y.
10. Hirsch & Co.
    25 Broad St.
    New York, N.Y.
11. Carl M. Loeb, Rhoades & Co.
    42 Wall St.
    New York, N.Y.
12. Smith, Barney & Co.
    20 Broad St.
    New York, N.Y.
13. Van Alstyne Noel & Co.
    52 Wall St.
    New York, N.Y.
14. Goodbody & Co.
    2 Broadway
    New York, N.Y.

These and many other brokerage houses are glad either to answer specific questions or to send their weekly or monthly publications upon request.

The Financial Services

In recent years so many financial and investment services have sprung up that it is almost as difficult to know which to use for what as it is to pick the right stock at the right time. The three leaders in the field are:

Standard & Poor's Corporation, 345 Hudson St., New York, N.Y., 10014
Moody's Investors Service, 99 Church St., New York, N.Y., 10007
The Value Line Investment Survey, 5 East 44th St., New York, N.Y., 10017

They publish a wide variety of financial and investment data, some of it so expensive and technical, such as the bond service, that the average investor seldom sees or hears of it. Basic, however, are the reference books—Standard & Poor's *Corporation Records* and Moody's *Manuals.* These are big, thick volumes for each year and by fields—industrials, rails, utilities, governments, etc. Each volume contains reports on thousands of corporations (or governmental bodies), giving the history and full financial data for a period of years. These volumes are kept up to date by current supplements—Standard & Poor's six-volume *Corporation Records* are supplemented with a daily bulletin, while five Moody's *Manuals* are kept up to date by a biweekly report. A good library or a brokerage office will have both the basic volumes and the supplements.

All of the agencies have a bulletin service on all the leading companies. On one page (both sides) is condensed all the pertinent financial information about the company, its outlook, and prospects for its stock. An example of the Standard & Poor's bulletin is shown in Figure 14–1. Standard & Poor's has a special survey reviewing conditions industry by industry. The larger brokerage houses subscribe to at least one of these services and make them available to customers or prospective customers.

The Standard & Poor's *Stock Guide* is a pocket-size condensed handbook, issued monthly, containing a thumbnail sketch of essential facts about a given stock. Two pages of one of these handbooks are shown in Figure 14–2. They are given away free of charge by some brokerage houses as a service to customers.

Both Moody's and Standard & Poor's publish weekly or monthly bond guides. Moody's, for example, issues a weekly *Bond Survey,* a bimonthly *Bond Record;* and one-page summaries of individual bond situations.

Some parts of both the Standard & Poor's and Moody's service are aimed primarily at the smaller investor. Standard & Poor's issues a weekly magazine, the *Outlook,* a daily *Facts and Forecast Service,* and an *Investment Advisory Survey,* which consists of a confidential bulletin featuring a supervised list of recommended investments. In addition, subscribers are offered an inquiry and consultation service. Moody's *Stock Survey,* a weekly letter, reviews market conditions and analyzes various investment opportunities. *Moody's Handbook of Widely Held Common Stocks,* first published in 1964, contains charts and summary reports on 879 common stocks. It contains a 12-year "Price Action Profile" chart, with earnings and dividends, for each of the stocks; 11-year comparative statistics (income, profit margins, payout, price-earnings ratio, yield, etc.); a brief description of the company's history and its products, and Moody's analytical characterization of the stock. The Handbook is published quarterly. It also has an Investors' Advisory Service, offering subscribers a review of their present holdings plus recommendations about what to buy or sell.

Both Moody's and Standard & Poor's now use computers in investment analysis and investment information retrieval. Moody's calls its computer work *"Creative Analysis."* It provides data for over 700 companies in 59 industry groups on a uniform per share basis, showing year to year changes and 5-year rates of growth compounded annually, with adjustments made for splits and stock dividends. Any company's record can be directly compared with the record of any other company in its industry group, with the industry group as a whole, with any other industry group, or with any other company in the *"Creative Analysis"* computer program.

Standard & Poor's now publishes as a monthly supplement to the *Outlook,* the "S & P 200 Rapid Growth Stocks," screened and selected from nearly 6,000 stocks, by an electronic computer program. The

FIGURE 14–2

STANDARD & POOR'S CORPORATION

INDEX	Ticker Symbol	STOCKS NAME OF ISSUE (Call Price of Pfd. Stocks)	Market	S&P Rating	Par Val.	★ Inst. Hold Cos	Shs. (000)	STOCK CHARACTERISTICS Principal Business	PRICE RANGE 1936-62 High	1936-62 Low	1963 High	1963 Low	1964 High	1964 Low	Feb. Sales in 100s	February, 1964 O-C Monthend High	Low	Last	% Div. Yield
1	GM	General Motors	²NYS, De, MW	A	1⅔	1077	9168	Automobiles and commercial	59⅝	a4¼	91⅜	57⅞	80⅞	77¼	8722	80¼	77¾	80	5.8
2		$5 cm Pfd (120)	NYS, MW, PB, PC	AAA	No	134	351	trucks; diesel engines;	132	100⅜	118¾	114	116¾	114¼	53	116¾	115	115¾	4.3
3		$3.75 cm Pfd (102 '66)	NYS	AAA	No	126	272	electric appliances	109	75¼	95½	87	89	88	74	88⅞	88	88⅜	4.2
4	GPY	General Plywood Corp.	ASE	C	50¢	....	....	Plywd flush doors; Microseal	27¼	1⅜	24¾	12¼	16½	12¾	613	15½	13⅜	15	....
5	GPT	General Portland Cement	NYS, MSE	B+	1	82	830	Low-cost cement producer	43⅞	a3¼	23¼	17½	25½	22⅜	521	25¼	23¾	24⅝	4.9
6	GPE	General Precision Equipment	NYS	B	1	31	275	Electronic equip; liquid con-	78	7¾	43⅝	27½	32⅜	28	759	31¼	28⅝	29⅝	4.1
7		$4.75 cm Pfd (104 '65; SF 100) vtg.	UNL	BB	No	3	2	trol systems; theatre, motel	100	70½	99½	94	95	94	....	....	95B	100A	4.8
8		$1.60 cm Cv Pref (42) vtg	NYS•	B	No	...	....	eqp; Graflex cameras; etc.	52	27	39½	33⅝	36½	34	3.7	36½	35	36½	4.4
9	GPV	General Public Service	NYS, PB, PC	NR	10¢	3	2	Closed-end management type	8	¼	6	5½	5¾	5½	976	5⅝	5½	5½	‡3.1
10	GUY	General Public Utilities	³NYS	A	2½	230	2773	Controls public utility cos	38	a5½	34⅞	31¼	34	31½	1380	33¼	31½	32⅛	4.0
11	GRX	General Refractories Co.	NYS, PBS	B	5	3	11	Fire-brick for steel industry	39¾	a2¾	16¾	11¼	15⅞	13¾	351	15	13¾	14¾	†4.4
12		General Reinsurance Corp.	UNL	NR	10	26	165	Reinsurance exclusively	225	a11⅜	241	200	237	228	....	....	228B	238A	0.8
13		General Shale Products	UNL	B+	No	2	1	Face brick & concrete blocks	19¾	10¼	21¾	14½	20⅜	18⅜	....	....	19⅞B	21⅜A	†4.9
14	GSX	General Signal Corp.	NYS, PB	A–	6.67	9	108	Railway signaling devices	54¾	a3	34	25⅜	31½	28	238	31½	30⅜	30⅞	3.9
15	GSI	General Steel Industries	NYS	B	1	10	180	Heavy duty castings; RR cars	a20¾	a2	31½	a17½	27¼	23¼	467	27	24⅛	24⅛	5.0
16	GSW	General Steel Wares, Ltd.	TS, MS	B–	No	1	5	Heating, plumbing, other eqp	23	3	13¾	7½	13¼	12¾	41	13¼	12⅞	13	....
17		General Stone & Materials	UNL	NR	5	...	....	Terrazzo & quartz aggregates	....	....	7¼	6¾	8⅝	7⅛	....	....	8½B	9¼A	3.2
18	GSC	General Stores Corp.	ASE	NR	1	...	....	Subsids operate drug stores	a28½	a⅜	1⅜	15/16	1⅝	1⅛	309	1⅝	1⅛	1½	....
19	GNS	General Super Markets	ASE	NR	8¢	1	10	Shop-Rite stores in N.J.	20	6¾	16⅞	8¼	19⅞	16⅜	326	19⅞	16½	17¾	....
20		Gen. Tel. of Calif., 4½% Pfd (23½) vtg.	UNL	A	20	37	121	Largest sub Gen Tel system	28	15¼	20¼	19	19¼	19⅛	....	....	19¼B	20⅝A	4.4
21	GLF	Gen. Tel. of Fla., ⁴$1.30 cm B Pfd.	NYS	A	25	18	87	Tel. service in Fla., Tampa	28	24	28⅛	26½	28	26⅝	22	27¾	26⅝	27¾	4.7
22		$1.25 cm Pfd (27½ '66)	NYS	A	25	32	211	largest community served	28	24¾	27½	26	27¼	26⅛	25	26⅞	26¼	26⅝	4.7
23	GEN	General Tel. & Electronics	³NYS	A	3⅓	234	4190	2d largest telephone system;	34⅛	a1¼	32	22⅞	34⅛	31⅜	3901	33⅜	32	32⅞	2.7
24		5.28% cm Cv Pfd (56 '67) vtg	UNL	A	50	6	6	Sylvania radio & TV tubes,	109	49	93½	70¼	99	93½	....	....	98B	....	2.7
25		4.36% cm Cv Pfd (53½) vtg	UNL	A	50	11	23	electronics, lights	82½	45	75½	55	79	76	....	....	78B	83A	2.6
26	GLI	General Time Corp.	NYS, PB	B	2½	3	34	Clocks; time recording devices	33⅛	a2	15½	9⅝	14¼	11⅝	704	13⅝	11⅝	11¾	2.1
27	GY	General Tire & Rubber	¹NYS, MW	A–	30¢	62	1400	Replacement and fleet tires;	a33¾	a⅜	27⅞	20⅝	23¾	21⅜	2233	22⅞	21⅜	22⅜	2.2
28		$5 cm Pref (101½ '65; SF 100) vtg.	NYS•	BBB	100	5	9	plastics; a leader in rockets	102½	74½	103⅛	100	103	100½	4.7	103	101¼	102¾	4.9
29		5½% cm Pref (100½) vtg	NYS•	BBB	100	13	29	and propellants; owns 81%	107	83½	107¾	101¼	107¾	105	0.6	107	106¾	106¾	5.2
30		Warrants (Purch 3 Com at $26.43)	UNL	NR	....	...	....	A.M. Byers; 8½% Aerojet.	74	5½	56	39	45	40½	....	....	41½B	45A	....
31		General Waterworks	UNL	NR	1	1	81	Waterworks system, tele cos;	28⅜	6	30	24	30½	27¾	....	....	29⅝B	31⅞A	‡...
32		$2 cm Cv 2nd Pfd (⁶40) vtg	UNL	NR	1	...	....	mfr subsids prov most rev	46	37	43½	39	45¼	43½	....	....	44¼B	46½A	4.3
33	GCO	Genesco Inc.	NYS, MW	A–	1	16	241	Shoe mfr, retailer; prestige	42⅜	a4¼	38⅞	34	38½	36	368	37¾	36½	36⅞	4.3
34		$4.50 cm Cv Pfd (104½)	NYS, MW	A	No	3	8	apparel stores; apparel mfr	....	....	104¾	99½	103⅜	102	23	103	102½	102½	4.4
35	GES	Genisco Technology	ASE, PC	B–	1	...	....	Missile test eq; flight instr	17	7	9½	7¾	10¾	8⅛	157	10¾	8⅛	8⅛	3.7
36		Genuine Parts Co.	UNL	NR	5	7	172	Distri auto replacement parts	35	a1⅝	26½	21¼	27	23¾	....	....	25¼B	27¼A	2.6
37	GNG	Genung's Incorporated	ASE	B	1	1	1	Dept store chain; NY-Conn	15⅜	7⅛	12¾	11¼	12⅛	11	56	11¾	11	11¾	6.0
38	GCA	Geophysics Corp. of Amer.	ASE	NR	60¢	...	....	Measuring eqp; research; etc	58	9	22½	13	28	21	119	28	23¼	25	....
39	GP	Georgia-Pacific Corp.	¹NYS	A	80¢	32	306	Plywood products, lumber	75¼	a1⅝	55⅞	43½	60⅜	51½	1927	60⅜	53⅞	60⅛	‡1.7
40	GOW	Georgia Power, $5 cm Pfd (110)	ASE•	A	No	8	2	Operates entirely in Ga.;	111⅜	54¾	110	102	108	106½	0.2	108	106½	106½	4.7
41		$4.60 cm Pfd (108 '64)	ASE♦	A	No	40	72	owned by Southern Co.	111	85	101¾	96½	99½	97	12.3	99½	98	99½	4.6

Uniform Footnote Explanations—See Page 6. Other: ‡Net invest income only. [1]Bo, De, PB, PC. [2]Bo, Ci, MS, PB, PC, TS. [3]Bo, Ci, De, MW, PB, PC. [4]Callable at 27½, '64 [5]Fewer shrs thereafter. [6]From 1-1-70. [7]With Automobile Parts Co. q—Incl $0.33 spec cr. r—‡$0.17, 64; $0.12, '63. s—Yrs Oct. t—Excl spec cr $0.30, '62 & $2.50, '63.

FIGURE 14–2—*Continued*

COMMON AND PREFERRED STOCKS

INDEX	Some Divs. Ea. Yr. Since	DIVIDENDS — Latest Payment — Per. $	Date	Ex. Div.	$ So Far 1964	Total Ind. Rate	$ Paid 1963	FINANCIAL POSITION Mil-$ — Cash & Equiv.	Curr. Assets	Curr. Liabs.	Balance Sheet Date	CAPITALIZATION Long Term Debt Mil-$	Shs. 000 Pfd.	Com.	Yrs. End.	ANNUAL EARNINGS $—Per Share—$ ▼ 1959	1960	1961	1962	1963	INTERIM EARNINGS OR REMARKS Period	$—Per Share—$ 1962	1963	INDEX
1	1915	0.65	3-10-64	2-7	0.65	4.60	4.00	1891	5363	1635	12-31-63	261	2836	284653	Dec	3.05	3.35	3.10	n5.09	5.55				1
2	1930	Q1.25	5-1-64	4-1	2.50		5.00						1836		Dec	307.9	338.2	314.9	514.6	561.4				2
3	1947	Q0.93¾	5-1-64	4-1	1.87½		3.75						1000		Dec	307.9	338.2	314.9	514.6	561.4				3
4	......	0.10	7-20-48	7-6	....	Nil	....	0.11	7.34	7.90	10-31-63	....	....	1199	Oct	d0.58	d1.36	nd0.42	d0.15	d0.52				4
5	1947	Q0.30	3-31-64	3-9	0.30	1.20	1.20	12.0	24.2	6.46	12-31-62	9.49	....	5297	Dec[16]	2.27	1.87	1.60	1.47	1.50				5
6	1936	Q0.30	3-15-64	2-25	0.30	1.20	1.20	8.85	121	39.6	12-31-62	35.1	128	1643	Dec	2.63	3.46	2.94	2.40	1.42				6
7	1955	Q1.18¾	6-15-64	*5-29	2.37½		4.75						79		Dec	48.27	62.26	65.14	63.53					7
8	1956	Q0.40	3-15-64	2-25	0.40		1.60	Each shr conv into ⅔ common					59		Dec	6.10	7.91	83.53	68.40					8
9	1946	‡0.09	1-15-64	12-10	r0.09		r0.16	Net Asset Val $660			12-31-63	....	....	12822	Dec	#6.18	#6.49	#6.80	#6.12	#6.60				9
10	1942	Q0.32	2-25-64	1-21	0.32	1.28	1.22	NR	63.1	67.1	9-30-63	492	....	23836	Dec[16]	1.57	1.61	1.60	1.64	E1.77	12 Mo Sep	1.78	1.75	10
11	1939	†0.20	12-27-63	12-5	....	0.65	†0.65	11.4	42.7	8.44	9-30-63	17.7	....	2937	Dec[16]	1.62	1.52	1.34	0.85	E1.40	9 Mo Sep	0.45	1.11	11
12	1934	Q0.50	12-18-63	*12-16	....	2.00	2.00	Equity per sh $138.69			9-30-63	....	....	726	Dec	X5.52	X6.34	X6.90	X7.63					12
13	1951	†0.43	1-4-64	*12-20	†0.43	1.03	†0.86	2.49	4.76	1.43	12-31-62	1.59	....	514	Dec	2.31	1.72	1.66	2.11	2.65				13
14	1940	Q0.30	4-1-64	3-4	0.30	1.20	1.20	6.21	23.8	6.05	12-31-62	0.72	....	1459	Dec	2.02	2.25	n2.45	n1.70	E1.70	9 Mo Sep	1.21	1.21	14
15	1952	Q0.30	3-31-64	3-17	0.30	1.20	1.00	3.41	41.6	22.4	12-31-62	5.50	....	2015	Dec[15]	a1.24	a1.05	a1.73	a1.79	2.45				15
16	......	g0.05	12-30-61	12-15	....	Nil	....	0.25	16.1	9.18	j12-31-62	4.45	39	479	Dec	q1.08	d1.62	0.35	d2.69					16
17	1964	Q0.07½	3-16-64	*3-2	0.07½	0.30	0.07½	0.33	2.82	1.10	p6-30-63	1.00	....	415	Jun	p0.22	p0.03	p0.39	p0.50	kp1.21	6 Mo Dec	k0.42	0.47	17
18	......	0.10	10-24-47	10-6	....	Nil	....	0.62	6.41	3.22	9-28-63	1.45	....	2612	Sep[14]	0.15	0.05	0.03	d0.07	nd0.03				18
19	......	None paid			....	Nil	....	1.94	3.83	3.11	11-2-63	0.94	....	762	Oct	0.01	0.21	0.37	0.68	1.06				19
20	1945	Q0.22½	2-1-64	*1-8	0.22½		0.90	3.52	30.3	56.9	6-30-63	227	*3249	7850	Dec	5.97	6.02	5.89	6.51	7.54				20
21	1959	Q0.32½	2-15-64	1-21	0.32½		1.30	1.77	13.2	25.3	12-31-62	‡81.0	*908	1772	Dec	9.58	9.70	4.94	5.68		12 Mo Sep	4.82	6.83	21
22	1961	Q0.31¼	2-15-64	1-21	0.31¼		1.25						400		Dec	....	....	4.94	5.68					22
23	1936	Q0.22	4-1-64	2-20	0.22	0.88	0.84	68.6	480	363	12-31-62	‡1039	185	76079	Dec[11]	a1.08	1.02	1.00	1.14	1.38				23
24	1957	Q0.66	4-1-64	*2-26	1.32		2.64	Conv into 3 shrs of common					26		Dec	....	....	296.6	467.2					24
25	1959	Q0.54½	4-1-64	*2-26	1.09		2.18	[5]Conv into 2.4 com to 6-30-64					149		Dec	....	....	296.6	467.2					25
26	1963	0.06¼	1-8-64	12-13	0.06¼	0.25	0.25	3.03	32.9	10.7	12-31-62	8.16	....	2054	Dec[13]	a0.91	d0.36	0.23	0.53	0.69				26
27	1937	Q0.12½	2-29-64	2-11	0.12½	0.50	0.42½	15.5	325	168	11-30-63	134	182	16685	Nov[19]	a1.61	a1.36	a1.62	1.55	2.02				27
28	1956	Q1.25	12-31-63	12-11	....		5.00						98		Nov	130.4	117.0	142.4	143.3	190.7				28
29	1954	Q1.37½	12-31-63	12-11	....		5.50						84		Nov	130.4	117.0	142.4	143.3	190.7				29
30	......	....	....	....	....		....	Warrants expire 10-1-67				....	....	341	Nov	....	....	....	....					30
31	......	3% Stk	11-1-63	*10-18	....		6% Stk	13.9	42.0	16.7	9-30-63	79.3	445	1454	Dec	1.33	1.82	1.42	1.53		12 Mo Sep	t1.26	t1.27	31
32	1959	Q0.50	3-15-64	*2-28	0.50		2.00	Cv into 1½ com thru 1-1-71					308		Dec	5.37	9.56	8.16	8.70					32
33	1934	Q0.40	1-31-64	1-10	0.40	1.60	1.60	22.3	160	22.1	7-31-63	47.0	296	3944	Jul	s2.66	2.12	2.06	1.94	1.80	6 Mo Jan '64	1.13	1.52	33
34	1963	Q1.12½	1-31-64	1-10	1.12½		3.56¼	Each shr conv into 2¼ common					277		Jul	....	....	....	....	27.23				34
35	1957	Q0.07½	2-29-64	*2-15	0.07½	0.30	0.30	0.14	3.02	1.61	9-30-63	0.44	....	408	Sep	0.10	0.45	0.56	0.82	0.48	3 Mo Dec	0.20	0.13	35
36	⊙'48	Q0.17½	4-1-64	*3-7	0.32½	0.70	0.58½	[7]Merger plan ratified				1.47	....	2307	Dec[20]	a1.24	a1.16	a1.30	1.44		6 Mo Jun	0.61	0.60	36
37	1940	Q0.17½	4-1-64	3-10	0.35	0.70	0.70	1.29	16.1	5.88	1-31-63	5.00	....	428	Jan	0.95	0.90	0.96	1.37		12 Mo Oct	0.75	1.23	37
38	......	None paid			....	Nil	....	0.17	2.53	1.63	9-30-63	0.05	....	482	Sep	0.21	0.17	0.10	0.35	0.52				38
39	1927	‡Q0.25	3-21-64	2-4	‡0.25	1.00	‡1.00	34.8	163	65.4	p12-31-62	255	200	9505	Dec[12]	p2.73	p2.59	p2.21	p2.67	2.90				39
40	1929	Q1.25	4-1-64	3-6	2.50		5.00	4.22	31.2	59.0	9-30-63	‡334	758	6082	Dec	38.46	40.40	33.63	35.53	40.67	12 Mo Jan'64	36.00	41.13	40
41	1955	Q1.15	4-1-64	3-6	2.30		4.60						434		Dec	38.46	40.40	33.63	35.53	40.67				41

▼Stock Splits & Divs: [11]3-for-1, '60. [12]5-for-4, '59. [13]4-for-1, '60. [14]Reverse 1-for-3, '59. [15]100%, '63. [16]2-for-1, '59. [19]3-for-1, '62. [20]2-for-1, '59; 200%, '62.

major criteria employed in the selection process are: (1) if growth in share earnings over the past five years has been steady, it must have amounted to at least 7 percent per annum, compounded; (2) if growth has been interrupted in only one year and the decline has been less than 5 percent, annual growth must have been at least 10 percent; (3) if growth has been interrupted in more than one year, or in one year has declined more than 5 percent, the annual growth rate must have been at least 12 percent.

The Value Line (5 East 44th St., New York, N.Y., 10017) has an interesting technique, which may be seen in Figures 14–3 and 14–4. It

FIGURE 14–3

THE VALUE LINE INVESTMENT SURVEY ANSWERS THESE QUESTIONS ABOUT GENERAL MOTORS AND EACH OF 1100 COMPANIES

(1) What is the recent price of this stock?

(2) What is the company's business? What are its products? Who are its chief executives? Where is it located?

(3) What is the statistical background—annual sales volume, profit margin, plant account, working capital, book value per share, cash flow per share, earnings per share, pay-out ratio based on cash earnings, price/earnings ratio, dividend yield?

(4) How do current quarterly sales and earnings compare with previous years' results?

(5) What is happening to the company currently?

(6) What will be the sales, earnings and dividends in the current year, as estimated by the Value Line staff of analysts, statisticians and economists?

(7) What are the estimated average sales, earnings and dividends 3 to 5 years hence?

(8) How do current price/earnings ratios and dividend yields compare with past averages?

(9) What is the company's growth index? Its stability index?

(10) What is the investment quality of this company's stock?

 . . . and much more, as you will see from your own reading.

FIGURE 14–4

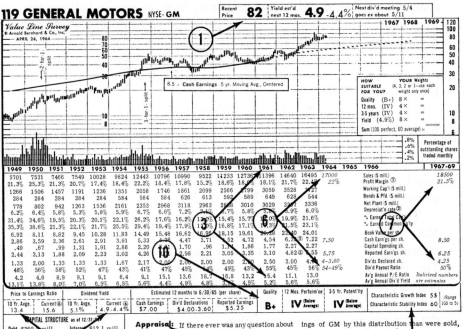

119 GENERAL MOTORS NYSE-GM

| Recent Price | **82** | Yield est'd next 12 mos. | **4.9** -4.4% | Next div'd meeting 5/4 goes ex about 5/11 |

Value Line Survey
© Arnold Bernhard & Co., Inc.
— APRIL 24, 1964 —

HOW SUITABLE FOR YOU? / YOUR Weights (4, 3, 2 or 1—use each weight only once)

Quality	(B+)	8× =
12 mos.	(IV)	4× =
3-5 years	(IV)	4× =
Yield	(4.9%)	8× =

Sum (100 perfect, 60 average) =

Percentage of outstanding shares traded monthly

	1949	1950	1951	1952	1953	1954	1955	1956	1957	1958	1959	1960	1961	1962	1963	1964	1965	1966	1967-69
Sales ($ mill.)	5701	7531	7466	7549	10028	9824	12443	10796	10990	9522	14233	12736	11396	14640	16495	17000			18500
Profit Margin ①	21.3%	25.3%	21.3%	20.7%	17.4%	18.4%	22.2%	18.4%	17.8%	15.2%	18.6%	18.7%	18.1%	21.7%	22.4%	22%			21.5%
Working Cap'l ($ mill.)	1266	1506	1457	1191	1236	1351	2058	1746	1861	2099	2566	1799	3059	3528	3427				
Bonds & Pfd. ($ mill.)	284	284	284	284	284	584	584	584	626	613	592	589	649	628	544				
Net Plant ($ mill.)	778	802	942	1263	1536	2161	2353	2968	3118	2963	2868	3010	3029	3271	3336				
Deprecia'tn rate ②	6.2%	6.4%	5.8%	5.3%	5.8%	5.9%	6.7%	6.6%	7.2%	6.7%	5.8%	5.9%	5.8%	6.0%					
% Earn'd Total Cap'l	31.4%	34.6%	19.5%	20.3%	20.1%	22.1%	26.2%	17.6%	16.2%	12.0%	15.4%	15.7%	15.0%	19.9%	21.6%				
% Earn'd Common Equity	35.3%	38.6%	21.3%	22.1%	21.7%	25.5%	29.4%	19.4%	17.9%	13.1%	16.8%	17.1%	13.7%	21.5%	23.1%				
Book Value per sh.	6.92	8.11	8.82	9.45	10.28	11.83	14.49	15.48	16.62	16.86	18.15	19.61	20.28	22.40	24.01				
Cash Earn'gs per sh.	2.86	3.59	2.36	2.61	2.91	3.91	5.33	4.47	3.71	3.52	4.72	4.54	6.32	7.22	7.50				8.50
Capital Spending per sh.	.49	.67	.99	1.31	1.91	2.88	2.20	1.70	.96	1.14	1.86	1.77	2.27	2.27					
Reported Earn'gs sh.	2.44	3.13	1.88	2.09	2.23	3.02	4.26	2.98	2.21	3.05	3.35	3.10	4.82	5.55	5.75				6.25
Div'ds Declared sh.	1.33	2.00	1.33	1.33	1.33	1.67	2.17	2.00	2.00	2.00	2.00	2.00	2.50	3.00	4-3.60				4.25
Div'd Payout Ratio	48%	56%	58%	52%	47%	43%	41%	47%	45%	52%	48%	43%	55%	56%	54-49%				50%
Avg Annual P/E Ratio	4.2	4.6	8.9	9.1	9.1	8.4	9.1	15.1	13.6	18.7	16.8	13.2	15.4	11.1	13.0				Italicized numbers are estimates
Av'g Annual Div'd Yield	13.1%	13.8%	8.0%	7.0%	6.5%	6.5%	5.6%	4.4%	4.9%	4.8%	4.3%	5.2%	5.6%	5.6%					

Price to Earnings Ratio				Dividend Yield			Estimated 12 months to 6/30/65 (per share)			Quality	12 Mos. Perform'ce	3-5 Yr. Potent'ly	Characteristic Growth Index 55 (Range
10 Yr. Avge.	Current⑥	10 Yr. Avge.	Current⑥	Cash Earnings	Div'd Declarations	Reported Earnings	B+	IV (Below Average)	IV (Below Average)	Characteristic Stability Index 60 100 to 5)
13.4	15.6	5.1%	4.9-4.4%	$7.00	$4.00-3.60	$5.25				

CAPITAL STRUCTURE as of 12/31/63

Debt $260.5 mill. Interest $12.1 mill.
(Includes $12.6 mill. debt of foreign subsidiaries)

Pfd Stock $283.6 mill. Div'd $12.9 mill.
1,000,000 shares $3.75 cum. (no par)
1,835,644 shares $5.00 cum. (no par)
Common Stock 284,652,505 shares④

Cal- endar	Mar. 31	June 30	Sept. 30	Dec. 31	Full Year
1959	3206	3306	2345	2376	11233
1960	3658	3451	2201	3426	12736
1961	2724	3088	1968	3616	11396
1962	3665	4026	2760	4189	14640
1963	4147	4517	3017	4814	16495
1964					17000
1965					

QUARTERLY SALES ($ Millions)

Cal- endar	Mar. 31	June 30	Sept. 30	Dec. 31	Full Year
1959	1.03	1.04	.47	.51	3.05
1960	1.13	1.01	.31	.90	3.35
1961	.65	.88	.30	1.27	3.10
1962	1.23	1.40	.64	1.55	4.82③
1963	1.44	1.62	.72	1.77	5.55
1964					5.75
1965					

QUARTERLY EARNINGS (Per Share)

Cal- endar	Mar. 31	June 30	Sept. 30	Dec. 31	Full Year
1959	.50	.50	.50	.50	2.00
1960	.50	.50	.50	.50	2.00
1961	.50	.50	.50	1.00	2.50
1962	.50	.50	.50	1.50	3.00
1963	.50	1.00	.50	2.00	4.00
1964	.65				
1965					

QUARTERLY DIVIDENDS PAID ③

Appraisal: If there ever was any question about General Motors' competitive vigor, the events of the 1964 auto year should resolve any doubts. In a determined effort to find a market for all the cars it could produce, GM returned this year to the sales contest philosophy of promoting merchandise. High-pressure selling does not really mean much economic sense for this manufacturer, as it can not possibly add enough to its volume to offset the lower profit per unit; but it is a technique for keeping the assembly lines humming. And the whole auto market is strong enough this year to permit GM to make more money even if it earns less profit per car. But now that this company has unleashed its full sales strength, where can it go next year? Its wide profit margin is an inviting target for large union demands. Another year of robust auto sales seems highly dubious indeed. Even for General Motors, lower volume plus increased costs still means curtailed profits. On this basis, we do not recommend GM to capital-oriented accounts at this time. However, investors seeking large and dependable income from an issue of unimpeachable quality might still find a place for GM in their portfolios now.. Heavy Fund selling of GM shares was reported during the fourth quarter of last year. Much of this liquidation, however, appears to be traceable to Du Pont's distribution of GM stock to its own stockholders - more shares were added to Fund holdings of GM by this distribution than were sold, on balance, during the period.

Analysis: One of the most notable aspects of GM's record 1963 performance was the company's strength in foreign markets. For the year as a whole, overseas unit volume showed a 30% increase, vs. only a 10% gain in this country. The fourth quarter improvement was especially dramatic. Through the first nine months of the year, GM's increases abroad had just about kept pace with Ford's - a 20% advance for each company. Ford held on to this rate of gain in the fourth quarter, but GM's shipments climbed 45% above their year-earlier figure. The obvious implication of these figures is that GM is enhancing its market penetration abroad, as well as in this country.

We look for foreign markets to provide the principal stimulus to further improvement for GM this year. Domestic activity, while running well ahead of last year's rate currently, may not hold on to this pace for the full year, especially if labor negotiations lead to a production slowdown or strike this Fall. The status of these discussions could also have an effect on the company's dividend policy - if contract negotiations should still be underway on Nov. 1st, GM's directors might feel a large year-end dividend declaration to be inconsistent with the company's best bargaining interests. E.P.S.

BUSINESS: General Motors is the world's largest automobile manufacturer; 1963 output 53% of U.S. total. Makes Chevrolet-Corvair, Pontiac-Tempest, Buick-Special, Oldsmobile-F-85, and Cadillac cars; Chevrolet and GMC trucks; Frigidaire and Delco appliances; GM Diesel locomotives and engines; Allison aircraft engines; and Euclid earth-moving equipment. Plants in 19 foreign countries make Vauxhall cars and Bedford trucks (England), Opel cars and trucks (Germany), and Holden cars and trucks (Australia). Defense business 3% of 1963 sales; foreign, about 15%. Since 1947-49, sales have increased 248% (GNP, 133%). Labor costs, 29% of 1963 sales; materials costs, 46%. Has 640,073, employees, about 1,068,000 stockholders. Directors own 1.4% of common; E.I. duPont, 8%. Chrmn.: F. G. Donner. Pres.: J. F. Gordon, Inc.: Del. Add.: 2044 W. Grand Blvd., Detroit 2, Mich.

①-Operating Profit Margin before Interest, Depreciation, Tax.
②-Annual Depreciation to Gross Plant Account.
②-Dividend payment dates: Mar. 10, June 10, Sept. 10, Dec. 10.
④-Excludes 2,000,502 treasury shs.
⑤-Excl. extraordinary income from Ethyl Corp., equal to 27¢ a share.
⑥-Based on current price related to earns. and div'd next 12 months.

SOURCE: Value Line Investment Survey.

publishes standard charts showing the stock performance of the leading companies and then adds a line indicating how the service believes the stock is likely to move over the next three to five years. The charts are revised quarterly. In addition, this service supplies reports recommending "special situations," a fortnightly letter of market comment and advice, a report on the Value Line's model fund, and a recommended list of stocks to buy.

The Investograph Service (31 Gibbs St., Rochester, N.Y.) issues a weekly investment letter and also charts (*Investographs*) which present all the essential facts about a stock necessary to judge its value and to estimate its trend. In addition, there is a complicated technical service, called *Stock Appraisals and Forecasts,* by which recommendations of when to buy and when to sell are reached.

The American Institute for Economic Research (Great Barrington, Mass.) in the investment field publishes a weekly *Research Report,* a semimonthly *Investment Bulletin,* and special studies from time to time. The *Investment Bulletin* covers three typical investment plans, all designed for the long term, although with different objectives. It recommends purchases or sales of securities for each plan and explains the reasons for its recommendation.

Babson's Reports (Wellesley Hills, Mass.) are designed for the investor who has at least $10,000, half of which he is interested in investing in common stock. The weekly *Babson Report* comments on market trends, but, in addition, the subscriber's investment situation is analyzed and purchases or sales are suggested. The subscriber gets a one-page report on each company whose stock he owns—a red-bordered report if Babson's thinks it is not particularly sound, a green border if it is all right.

Indicator Digest, Inc. (Palisades Park, New Jersey) covers stock market timing by reviewing and interpreting a large number of stock market indicators. It also, in its bimonthly review, covers industry group selection in relation to market timing and occasionally has individual company selections related to phase of the market.

America's Fastest Growing Companies, published by John S. Herold, Inc. (25 Greenwich Avenue, Greenwich, Connecticut) provides a constantly revised list of growth companies, together with relevant, factual data and comment. Some 150 companies are selected and listed based solely on growth in net income per common share. Companies are delisted when earnings decline or fail to measure up to expectations. Two programs of growth stock investment operations are reported each month showing changes and resulting profits or losses.

The United Business and Investment Service (210 Newbury St., Boston, Mass., 02116) issues a comprehensive *Weekly Report* on business, investment, and stock-market conditions. In addition, regular reports are issued on all stocks on the Service's supervised lists. A summary of the opinion of eight other advisory services is given, and subscribers are offered an inquiry and advisory service.

The International Statistical Bureau (350 Fifth Ave., New York, N.Y., 10001) publishes a weekly *Selected Securities Guide and Market Timer,* which suggests what to buy and when to buy and sell. A variety of novel timing measures are provided, including a "Market Sentiment Index." The Bureau publishes a variety of other weekly services in such fields as general business, textiles, commodities, housing, etc. The subscriber also receives quarterly a supervised list of securities.

There are a number of chart services, of which three leading ones are:

M. C. Horsey & Co., 37 Wall St., New York, N.Y., 10005
F. W. Stephens, 87 Nassau St., New York, N.Y., 10038
Chartcraft, Inc., Larchmont, N.Y.

These companies publish chart books, which portray graphically, by means of a separate chart for each stock, the monthly movement of prices and sales volume over a period of years for individual stocks. Horsey issues *The Stock Picture,* a book of over 1,200 charts. Twice a year it also publishes *Selected Stocks,* which gives added detail and 25-year coverage of some 224 stocks. See Figure 14–5. Chartcraft, Inc., publishes a monthly chart book containing over 1,500 point and figure charts. See Figure 14–6. A point and figure chart shows only one thing, price movement. It does not take into account volume of trading, or time in the usual sense. Unless the price of the stock changes, by one point, or three points, no entry is made on the chart even though weeks and months may go by. X's are used when the price is going up and O's when the price is going down. When the stock changes price direction, a new column is started. Figure 14–6 is a three-unit point and figure chart. The trend lines are drawn at 45° angles (not connecting particular points on the chart).[3]

These are but some of the sources of information for the investor who would be informed. The annual cost of any of these services can be deducted from investors' income under the personal income tax.

---

[3] For more detail see "Can Charts and Graphs Predict the Stock Market," *Changing Times, The Kiplinger Magazine,* February, 1962.

FIGURE 14-5

From the 25-Year Picture—A Book of Special Long-Range Charts

INTERNATIONAL BUSINESS MACHINES

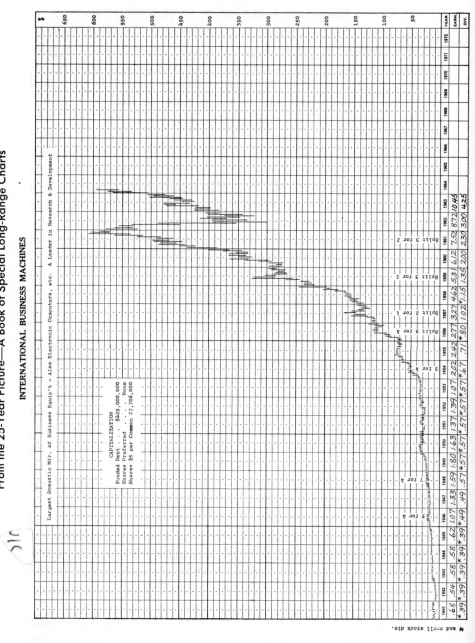

FIGURE 14–6

Example of Point and Figure Chart

S. H. KRESS (KSC)

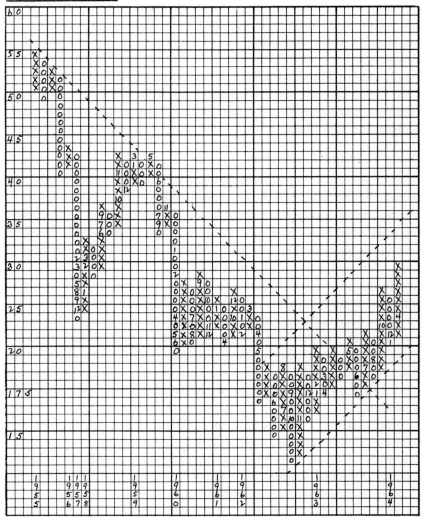

SOURCE: Chartcraft, Inc.

Choosing the Company

Once you have decided on the industry or industries in which you want to invest, you have done only half the job. Even within a given industry selecting a company is a difficult and trying task. Assume you picked a given industry a decade ago, say office equipment. Over the decade IBM rose 1493 percent, Royal McBee fell 24 percent. Perhaps you picked something more stable as food chain stores: Winn-Dixie rose 441 percent, First National Stores fell 5 percent. In plumbing and heating you might have bought Trane Co. (+559 percent) or Holland Furnace (−61 percent). In paper, Scott Paper (+219 percent) or Great Northern Paper (−14 percent). In foods, General Foods (+500 percent) or General Baking (−13 percent); in home furnishings, Armstrong Cork (+456 percent) or Congoleum-Nairn (−57 percent); in agricultural machinery, Deere & Co. (+197 percent) or J. I. Case (−26 percent) were all possibilities. Even if you feel reasonably certain of your industry choice, selecting the company requires additional competence and effort.

Direct Financial Information

To the average person who has not had an accounting course, the mere sight of a balance sheet or income statement inspires awe and fear. Yet, to invest wisely, you should know how to read and understand a financial statement. It is not difficult at all, and the mathematics involved is no more than one learns in grade school. This ability to read and understand a financial report is a "must" today for anyone going into business; and for the average investor, putting in a few hours to study the subject will pay handsome dividends in the future.

If you have had a year of accounting, the following pages may not be for you; they will doubtless seem simple and very elementary, with the possible exception of the specific applications to investment analysis. But if you have not had accounting, then resolve that this is the time and place to obtain a working idea of the balance sheet and the income statement.

You may ask, "What good is a balance sheet, since assets and liabilities are always equal whether it is a good company or a poor one?" It is true that, on an overall basis, the balance sheet must balance; but by looking at the relationship of the parts to each other and by comparing changes in categories over periods of time, one can learn a great deal about the operations and status of a given company from its balance sheet.[4]

THE BALANCE SHEET AND INCOME STATEMENT

The two most common financial statements that a potential investor studies are the balance sheet and income statement. A balance sheet

---

[4] A free copy of *How to Read a Financial Report* may be obtained by writting to Merrill Lynch, Pierce, Fenner & Smith, 70 Pine St., New York, N.Y., 10005. For greater detail, see Roy A. Foulke, *Practical Financial Statement Analysis* (5th ed.; New York: McGraw-Hill Book Co., Inc., 1961).

attempts to show the condition of a business as of a given moment of time. It is sometimes described, rather inadequately, as a "financial snapshot." In this country it is the custom to list the assets of a company on the left and the liabilities and capital on the right, in a balancing statement—hence the name "balance sheet." At times, however, space limitations require that liabilities and capital be shown below the assets.

Assets

Assets are the things of value, of all sorts, belonging to a business. It is customary to divide them into four groups: current assets, investments, fixed assets, and other assets, such as "goodwill."

Current Assets

Current assets are cash, accounts receivable, inventory, and any other assets which are expected to become cash in the ordinary course of business *within a year.* They represent current power to pay; they constitute the ability to meet ordinary debts which must soon be paid. Therefore, any cash which has already been designated to meet a specific need should not be considered a current asset. It is rather common to find cash, marketable securities, receivables, and inventories listed as current assets.

Cash and Cash Equivalents

Cash is paying power now. Ordinarily, marketable securities may quickly be sold for cash; for this reason they are considered as the practical equivalent of cash. Sometimes they are looked upon as cash at work earning income, as contrasted with cash in the drawer or cash in a commercial checking account. A block of securities otherwise marketable but which is so large that it could not be sold immediately without depressing the market (selling at an unduly low price) is not the equivalent of cash. Any company that owns stock of another company to insure control or necessary and continuing business relationships cannot maintain this condition and part with the stock, even though there may be a market for it. Such holdings also are better classed as investments.

Valuation of Current Assets

Marketable securities classified as current assets should usually be valued at what they could be sold for on the date of the balance sheet, since we think of current assets as paying power. Such a figure would adequately express their ability to provide the funds to pay current debt. In fact, it is often said that current assets should be valued at cost or market, whichever is lower. For most purposes, this seems to be a sensible rule. Cost is the upper limit at which assets ordinarily should be valued. We may buy assets at a given price (cost) and believe that they are worth more later on; but to write them up and take a profit before actually having sold them above cost would be similar to "counting our chickens before they are hatched"—it would not be conservative.

When we think of paying power, cost may at times, however, be an excessive figure to use. If we bought marketable securities for $10,000 and they are worth $5,000 on the date of the balance sheet, cost would give little indication of the extent to which these securities can now aid us in meeting pressing obligations. If the present market price of these securities is $5,000, this figure is a better indication of what they are worth to the business at the moment. According to accounting conventions, then, current assets should be stated at cost, and at no more than cost, unless, at the balance sheet date, they are worth less than cost in the market, in which case they should be shown at the market value.

Receivables

Receivables may be notes receivable; promissory notes on which the business is to collect principal, with or without interest; or mere unwritten rights to collect on open account. When we buy something in a store and say "Charge it," there is thereby created an account receivable for the store; the store expects to collect its cash within a month or so. This is an example of an open account. Receivables which arise from deals which are not "at arm's length," i.e., those due from company officials or affiliated companies, are often not paid as soon as ordinary receivables are; for this reason they should not be classed with the current assets. They may be shown as investments or be included with the "other assets."

Obviously, the face amount of receivables may not represent paying power; some of the receivables will not be collected. In attempting to apply the rule of cost or market, whichever is lower, to receivables, the common practice is to deduct a reserve or allowance for bad debts from the receivables in order to show the expected realizable value, i.e., what the receivables are probably worth, to what extent we may expect the receivables to be able to pay our current liabilities.

The uninitiated often believe that accounting is an exact science and that the statements (balance sheets, for example) which it produces are exactly correct in all respects. We have already seen that this is not so. When a reasonable allowance for bad debts is deducted from receivables, it should be obvious that the amount deducted is the result of judgment; some persons might think that the amount deducted should be a little more or a little less.

It is not enough to note merely the amount of receivables. The thoughtful analyst will ask himself whether the amount shown is reasonable or excessive—whether he can deduce from the amount shown that the company appears to be in good shape or bad. Suppose that in a given line of business, sales are made on terms of 2/10, net 30. This means that if the customer pays within ten days, he may take a 2 percent discount; but if he delays longer, he must pay the full amount in 30 days. Most customers would not feel that they could afford to throw away the opportunity to take such an attractive discount (remember that it amounts to 36 percent a year). With this thought in mind, we would expect to find something like ten days' credit sales on the books as receivables. If the income statement (to be discussed later) should show that the year's credit sales were $300,000, we might say to ourselves that the year has about 300 business days in it (Sundays and holidays omitted) and that average sales amounted to $1,000 a day. If the balance sheet showed receivables of $10,000, the amount would accord with expectations; but if we saw $50,000 of them there, then we would be justified in supposing that collections were not as good as they should be.

In many cases it is best not to depend too much on one single statement. If we use comparative statements for the last five or ten years, we may be able to extract far more useful information about a company's affairs. The year's credit sales divided by 300 may give us a good indication of an average day's credit sales. If we divide the receivables on the books by the average day's credit sales, we find the number of days' sales on the books (in the form of receivables). Suppose we look at the last five balance sheets of a given company and find that, in order, they show receivables equivalent to 10, 12, 14, 16, and 18 days' credit sales. Here we would most certainly conclude that, with the passage of time, the company is finding its collections slowing down, unless there has been a change in credit terms. Perhaps times are becoming harder (customers are finding it more difficult to pay on time), or perhaps the store is dealing increasingly with an inferior class of customers as time goes on.

It is also useful to compare the receivables on one company's statements with those of competitors in the same line of business. Other things being equal, they should be about the same. Differences may be accounted for by different business policies (one company may sell for cash and another on time; one may sell on one set of terms and another on terms more or less favorable to the customer) or by different degrees of success in collecting from customers within a reasonable time. It is an old axiom that the longer receivables are on the books, the more difficult it is to collect them. If you conclude that the receivables on the books are too large, you may well ask next whether the allowance for bad debts is adequate.

The turnover of receivables (sales divided by receivables) is one of several useful ratios of which the analyst may sometimes make good use. It shows how much sales volume is being produced with a given amount of resulting receivables. When this ratio rises, it indicates better collections. When the ratio declines (for the amount of business done, more is uncollected), collections are slowing down. When the ratio is expressed as a ratio of receivables to sales (receivables divided by sales), then the smaller the ratio, the better. A gradual lowering of this ratio over the years would usually be an indication of constantly improving collections. One must be ever on the alert, however, when trying to draw conclusions. The latter result might have been caused because the company had increasingly indulged in the practice of discounting receivables; only in this sense were collections really improving. It is generally considered legitimate to discount notes receivable, and it usually can be done at some such reasonable rate as 5 or 6 percent per annum; but discounting of accounts receivable is often regarded as a sign of financial weakness, except in certain industries, such as textiles. The financial institutions willing to discount accounts receivable generally find that they must charge something like 1 percent a month for their services; few companies would be willing to pay such a high rate if they were not in need of help.

Inventories

Inventories represent stocks of merchandise (goods for sale) on hand. It is sometimes said that they are two steps removed from cash and are therefore the least current of the current assets. First (and often with great expenditure of time and effort), they must be sold and turned into receivables; second, the receivables must be converted into cash. Unless the inventories will convert into cash in ordinary course within a year, the inventories are really not current assets. In manufacturing industries, inventories may be classified as raw materials and manufacturing supplies, goods in process, and finished goods. Of these, the raw materials and manufacturing supplies are the least current, in that they have to be manufactured (which may take some time) before they can be sold and converted into cash. Since they may be useful for several purposes, however, they may be more salable than finished or manufactured goods for which there is no ready market. Inventories of manufacturing companies are usually (perhaps by trade practice) included in current assets even though they may not be converted into cash in the ordinary course of business in a year.

In applying cost or market, whichever is lower, to inventories, we must remember especially that when we think of current assets we think of paying power. When we speak of "market" in this connection we are not talking about the price for which the goods would sell in the market; we are talking about what the goods would cost if they were acquired on the balance sheet date. When, therefore, we mention "cost or market, whichever is lower," in connection with inventories, we mean that goods should be valued at what they cost unless they would cost less if bought on the date of the balance sheet; in this case, what they would cost on the balance sheet date is the value to be used for the balance sheet. This is a figure (cost) at which we can still hope to sell the goods at a profit, if selling price bears any relation to cost. By using this price, we express a conservative figure as to the paying power of inventories as of the date of the balance sheet.

Cost

People speak glibly of "cost" as though it were a definite and exact figure. As a matter of fact, when inventories are taken and costed, the cost will vary according to the method used. Usually, various items will be on hand, some of which were bought at one time at one price, and others of which were bought at other times at other prices. Specific identification of the various items and the actual prices paid for them is often impossible. Usually some assumption is made. As long as the same assumption is made consistently, year after year, it makes little difference over a business cycle which assumption is adopted, although it may have important effects on individual balance sheets and income statements. Three of the assumptions that are often used are (1) the assumption that the first goods purchased and brought into the plant were the first goods to be sold and go out (FIFO, or first-in, first-out), (2) the assumption that the goods sold were made up of an average of early and late purchases, known as "average cost," and (3) the assumption that the last goods to be bought and come in were the first goods to be sold and go out (LIFO, or last-in, first-out). The ordinary person who speaks more or less thoughtlessly of "cost or market, whichever is lower," probably is unconsciously using a FIFO basis.

FIFO

To operate on a FIFO basis in a constantly rising market means that by the time the goods are sold, some inventory advantage is obtained from the rising market; finished products are sold at a good profit. The cost of goods in the inventory (at which they are valued) is less than would be required to buy them on the balance sheet date; no loss (writing down to a lower market) must be taken on these inventories. The combination of these two facts makes for large profits (and large income taxes) as long as the market continues to advance.

In a falling market, FIFO means that goods which cost us more have had to be sold later for less. When we take inventories, market is usually lower than cost, and a loss is taken by writing the inventories down to what they would cost on the date of the balance sheet. Just how the loss is taken may be illustrated by a simple illustration from retailing. If we start the year with an inventory of $40,000 and purchase $110,000 of goods, the total goods available for sale stand us $150,000. The usual practice is to subtract from the $150,000 the value of the ending inventory in order to arrive at the cost of the goods sold. If the goods still on hand cost us $50,000, we could figure that since all the goods cost us $150,000, the cost of the goods sold was $100,000. If these goods sold for $90,000 on a falling market, our gross (explained later in connection with the income statement) profit would be a minus or loss figure of $10,000. If, however, we said that the ending inventory, in spite of its $50,000 cost, was worth only $30,000 on the balance sheet date (because it could have been bought for $30,000 on that date), we would subtract only $30,000 from the cost of $150,000 of the total goods handled and find that the cost of goods sold was increased to $120,000. If then we sold for $90,000 goods to which we ascribed a cost of $120,-000, our gross profit would now be a minus or loss figure of $30,000. By showing the ending inventory at a lower figure (writing it down), we load a bigger cost on the goods sold and thereby cut the profit (if there is one) or increase the loss when the goods are sold. The ending inventory of one year is the beginning inventory of the next year; if the ending inventory is written down, it is inherited by the next year at the same lower figure. To the extent that the first year takes the loss, the first year frees the next year from the necessity of taking a loss. In a falling market, the combination of losses on sales and losses on inventories on the FIFO assumption leads to large losses. There is generally partial income tax relief from these losses available (through loss carryovers, forward and backward). This FIFO assumption, therefore, almost always results in sensible and conservative balance sheet values for inventories on balance sheets and leads to big profits in good times and big losses in bad times on income statements.

Average Cost

Those who use an average-cost assumption for inventories in a rising market show inventories at a lower figure than the goods would cost on the balance sheet date (since they average lower earlier costs with the higher costs of the balance sheet date). The reverse would be true in a falling market. If the volume of sales and inventories continued about the same over the years, there would be no appreciable effect of the assumption on the income statements, since the conservatism or lack of it in the beginning inventory with which a year was charged or burdened would be offset by the conservatism or lack of it in the ending inventory with which that year was credited and the following year was charged.

LIFO

To cushion the impact of rapid price changes, the last-in, first-out method (LIFO) of inventory valuation has been adopted by many companies. It rests on the view that current sales are made from current purchases. By matching the cost of current purchases against the selling price of current sales, there is little opportunity and time for rising prices to inflate profits or for falling prices to enhance losses. Sales are costed on the basis of inventory acquired most recently, or last-in, while first-in inventory is regarded as unsold. Consequently in a period of rising prices, LIFO results in the application of a higher unit cost to items sold and a lower unit cost to inventory still unsold. The converse is true in a period of falling prices. This assumption, then, tends to result in more moderate profits (and lower average income taxes) over all the years of the business cycle. This is permissible for income tax calculations.

Thus it should be apparent, in this brief discussion of current assets, that what financial statements show depends to a large extent on the methods, conventions, and accounting principles employed. The intelligent investor must be on the alert to note the methods used and the effect of those methods.

A Balance Sheet

In the simple balance sheet, for the Work Horse Manufacturing Company of America, Inc., shown below, the various categories of assets in the upper half of the balance sheet may be seen. Current assets have already been described. Fixed assets and other assets remain to be explained.

WORK HORSE MANUFACTURING COMPANY OF AMERICA, INC.

BALANCE SHEET

January 1, 196X

ASSETS

Current Assets:

Cash..		$ 50,000	
Accounts receivable........................	$100,000		
Less: Allowance for bad debts..........	5,000	95,000	
Inventories (at			
FIFO cost or market, whichever is lower)			
Raw materials...........................	$ 20,000		
Goods in process.......................	30,000		
Finished goods.........................	35,000	85,000	
Total Current Assets............			$230,000

Fixed Assets:

Land..		$ 25,000	
Buildings....................................	$100,000		
Less: Reserve for depreciation.........	25,000	75,000	
Machinery...................................	$175,000		
Less: Reserve for depreciation.........	35,000	140,000	
Total Fixed Assets..............			240,000

Other Assets:

Goodwill....................................			200,000
Total Assets...................			$670,000

LIABILITIES

Current Liabilities:

Accounts payable...........................	$ 25,000		
Notes payable..............................	50,000		
Total Current Liabilities........		$ 75,000	

Fixed Liabilities:

Twenty-year, 5 percent, first-mortgage bonds maturing in 1970	$100,000		
Total Fixed Liabilities...........		100,000	

Net Worth or Capital:

Common stock, 2,000 shares, each of $100 par value	$200,000		
Surplus.....................................	255,000		
Reserve for contingencies...................	40,000	495,000	
Total Liabilities and Net Worth....		$670,000	

Fixed Assets

The fixed assets consist of such things as land, buildings, machinery, and equipment used in the business. It is particularly important to note that, according to the best accounting practice, these assets should be carried at cost as long as they remain with the business.

Often there is no ready market for most of a company's fixed assets, so it is not possible to give market value. A good balance sheet will indicate what has been included under fixed assets and how they have been valued. If the value has been increased by a "write-up" or decreased by a "write-down," a footnote explanation is usually given. A write-up might occur, for instance, if the value of real estate increased substantially. A write-down might follow the invention of a new machine that put an important part of the company's equipment out of date.

To allow for the fact that most fixed assets wear out (depreciate or become obsolete), it is customary to take depreciation as an expense on the income statement (on a straight-line or sum-of-the-digits basis over their useful life) and to show the cumulative deduction from cost on the balance sheet as a reserve or allowance for depreciation.

If a truck costs $4,500 and is expected to last six years, it will be depreciated at the rate of $750 per year. At the end of the fourth year, the balance sheet will list the truck as worth $4,500, less $3,000 reserve for depreciation, or a net of $1,500. The income account for that same year would show a deduction of $750 as depreciation expense.

If we see a plant costing $100,000 on a balance sheet accompanied by a reserve for depreciation of $50,000, we may say that the depreciated cost is $50,000 (the difference between the two). It is very unusual for the cost (after the asset has been with the company for some years) or the depreciated cost to bear any close relation to what the asset is actually worth in the market. It will be remembered that current assets are shown at their ability to pay off current obligations; this means, also, that they are shown at that amount of cash which it is expected they can produce in the ordinary course of business. How different this is from what we find as to the fixed assets: they are shown on an historical-cost basis. In fact, it is often said that since the company must retain fixed assets to carry on its business, the market (or cash) value of them is of little practical importance. Sometimes, when the market value is far in excess of depreciated cost, the market value is shown parenthetically or in a footnote as additional information for the reader of the balance sheet; but the depreciated cost figure is usually the one used in the balance sheet itself.

Two other terms also frequently occur in connection with depreciation—"depletion" and "obsolescence." Companies may lump depreciation, depletion, or obsolescence under a single title or may list them separately. "Depletion" is a term used primarily by lumber, mining, and oil companies (or any of the so-called "extractive" industries). To "deplete" means to use up or to exhaust. As the oil or other natural resource is used up, a reserve is set up to compensate for the disappearance of natural wealth that the company no longer owns. This is a recognition of the fact that as the company sells its natural product, it must get back not only the cost of extracting but also the original cost of the natural resource. "Obsolescence" represents the loss in value because a piece of property goes out of date before it wears out. A good example is the modern airlines situation, where DC-6's and DC-7's (gasoline-powered propeller planes) had to be scrapped by the companies long before their useful life was up because jets came into vogue.

Edgar Allen, Jr., *The Commercial and Financial Chronicle*

"No annual report, no net earnings, no dividends—what a chance to get in on the ground floor!"

Other Assets

This is the category usually reserved for intangibles, such as patents, copyrights, and goodwill. Intangibles of both old and new companies are often of considerable but generally unmeasurable worth. Company practice varies considerably in assigning value to intangibles. Procter &

Gamble, despite the substantial goodwill that has been built up for many of its products, such as Ivory Soap, has reduced all of its intangibles to the nominal $1.00. Some of the big cigarette companies, on the other hand, place a high dollar value on the goodwill their brand names enjoy. American Tobacco carries goodwill at over $50 million; U.S. Steel puts it at $1.00. Companies that spend a good deal for research and the development of new products are more inclined than others to reflect this fact in the value assigned to patents, license agreements, etc. Du Pont carries goodwill, patents, etc., at almost $50 million.

Other assets also include "deferred charges" and "prepayments." "Deferred charges" refer to items which will be expenses in the future; they may be carried as assets until the time comes when they should be charged off as expenses. Bond discount and costs of organization are examples of this type of asset. If these extraordinary and nonrecurring items were charged off in their first year, it would result in burdening that year unduly. It is much more equitable to charge them off ratably over the years which benefit from them. Prepaid assets are assets which are paid for in the beginning and which are not exhausted in the first year. For example, suppose a three-year fire insurance policy is bought for $30. In the beginning, the whole policy is an asset, else one would not have paid $30 for it. At the end of a year, one third of it is exhausted and is charged to expense, but two thirds ($20) represents coverage for the next two years and is still a prepaid asset.

Current Liabilities

Usually the right-hand side of the balance sheet is for liabilities (current and fixed), reserves, capital, and surplus. Current liabilities are obligations which must be paid in a comparatively short period, such as a year. They usually consist of debts on open account for merchandise (accounts payable), short-term notes payable (often owed to banks), accrued liabilities for such things as taxes and wages, and the part (if any) of long-term debt maturing within a year. The accrual for income taxes is often called a "Reserve for Income Tax."

Current assets are compared with current liabilities in order to convey an idea of the company's financial ability to meet its current liabilities. In the balance sheet presented previously, the current assets totaled $230,000, and the current liabilities were $75,000. Thus the current assets amounted to over three times the current liabilities, resulting in a current ratio of 3.07. This really means that there was over $3.00 of ability to pay for each $1.00 of debt that had to be paid. This current ratio used to be about the only evidence some bankers required before they were ready to grant a loan. As long as the current ratio was two to one or better, they felt satisfied. Today, most companies try to have a current ratio higher than two to one. It is not unusual to find current ratios of three to one, four to one, or five to one.

Today we realize that a good current ratio is only one evidence of financial strength, i.e., a company may have a satisfactory current ratio and still have important financial weaknesses. Since cash, marketable securities, and receivables can usually be counted upon to convert themselves in the ordinary course of business into paying power, whereas inventories have to be sold before they produce the wherewithal to pay off current obligations, it is common practice to compute a quick ratio (current assets less inventories divided by current liabilities). To assure reasonable freedom from financial difficulties, the quick ratio should be one to one or better.

What "Capital" Means

The beginner (and the experienced accountant also, for that matter) may have a good deal of trouble with accounting terminology. For this there are several reasons. The peculiar or technical way in which a term (word) is used may give trouble to the uninitiated, but even more confusion results from the fact that occasionally a word is used in different ways with different meanings. One of the words which sometimes causes confusion is "capital." When the statement is made that "dividends should not be paid out of capital," it means that a stockholder should not be given back part of his investment as a dividend or return on his investment. Bonds not due within a year are frequently added to net worth (stocks, surplus, etc.) to give another version of the capital (or capitalization) of a company. A company is overcapitalized when it has more bonds and stocks outstanding than it is able to earn a reasonable return on; it is undercapitalized when it has not been able to sell sufficient bonds and stocks to provide the necessary funds for the operation of the business.

Another very different meaning of "capital" occurs when it is used to refer to the assets; sometimes one speaks of the assets of a business as its capital. If, with this definition in mind, we divide the assets into those which will be with the business more or less permanently and those which are constantly turning over in the attempt to earn profits, we may call the former "fixed capital" and the latter "working capital." From this point of view, the current assets are working capital. Now the current assets are not all provided to a business by its stockholders. Banks which make short-term loans and suppliers who furnish inventory on credit may, for example, be said to have furnished part of the working capital. If we subtract the current liabilities from the current assets, we may be said to have arrived at the current assets provided to the business by the stockholders, or the net working capital. It is important to notice whether the stake of the stockholders in the current assets is sufficient and whether it is growing or decreasing with the passage of time, regardless of what the current ratio may be. If the ratio of net working capital to sales has been dropping, perhaps as the result of dividends paid, the company may find it difficult to finance future business.

Fixed Liabilities

Bonded indebtedness is the most usual type of fixed or long-term liability. On the assumption that most fixed or long-term liabilities are incurred to help provide the fixed assets which often serve as security for such debts, the net fixed assets (fixed assets less long-term liabilities) may be regarded as net fixed capital, or the contribution of the stockholders to the fixed assets. Thus we can see the contribution of the stockholders to the net working capital and to the net fixed capital and can judge whether the two are in fair balance for the particular company.

Reserves

Doubtless as a reader of balance sheets you will be confused at times by the term "reserve." Sometimes it means a liability, e.g., "Reserve for Income Taxes," which might more clearly be shown as "Estimated Liability for Income Taxes." We have seen that the reserve for depreciation is a deduction from the cost of fixed assets (a valuation reserve) to allow for the fact that the fixed assets are wearing out. On the balance sheets of banks, reserves (appearing as plus items on the asset side) mean cash (at the Federal Reserve Bank) being used to secure deposit liability; this is the only case in which a reserve signifies cash. Reserves for general contingencies are really a part of surplus; they are set off by themselves, as shown earlier, in the balance sheet of the Work Horse Manufacturing Company of America, Inc., to prevent their being used as the basis for a dividend. Reserves which have been set aside from surplus to meet specific contingencies which appear about to flower into liabilities are often carried on balance sheets in suspense by showing them between the liabilities and net worth. If the liabilities for which the reserves are created eventuate, these reserves can be moved up among the liabilities to show this fact; if the liabilities do not arise, the reserves can be added back to surplus.

A very large reserve for contingencies or a sharp increase in this figure from the previous year should be examined closely by the investor. At times, in the past, companies tried to hide their true earnings by transfers into a contingency reserve. As a reserve looks somewhat like a true liability, stockholders may be confused about the real value of their securities. When a reserve is considerably in excess of a probable loss or expenditure, it should be regarded by the investor as part of surplus.

Deferred Credits

Deferred and prepaid items are sometimes shown in a group on the right-hand side of the balance sheet between the liabilities and capital. These amounts received and not yet earned appear under such titles as "Deferred Income," "Deferred Credits," or "Unearned Income." If rent is collected in advance, it represents a liability until it is earned. Ordinarily, there is no liability to return the cash, so the item is not classed as a current or fixed liability; the liability is to render a service (to allow the tenant to occupy the premises for which he has paid rent). As soon as the service is rendered, the liability is extinguished and the rent is earned; it then becomes part of the surplus, where all net earnings come to rest on a balance sheet.

Contingent Liabilities

Frequently, balance sheets show contingent liabilities as footnotes, perhaps because of the impossibility of attaching a definite figure to them. If you read that a company is being sued for $10 million, you should remember that a court may rule that the company must pay little or nothing. You will have to use your own judgment as to the seriousness of the liability mentioned.

Net Worth, Surplus, and Book Value

The net worth section of the balance sheet consists of the capital stock of all sorts, surplus, and reserves which are merely allocations of surplus. The capital stock accounts show the stockholders' claims against the assets because of investment, whereas the surplus account indicates claims against assets that have arisen in favor of stockholders because of the profitable operation of the business. Two different kinds of surplus frequently appear on company balance sheets: "earned surplus" and "capital surplus." Earned surplus is that part of net income which has not been paid to stockholders as dividends. It still "belongs" to the stockholders, but the directors have decided that it is best for the company and the stockholders to keep it in the business. The surplus may be invested in the plant, just as you might invest part of your savings in your home. It may also be in cash or securities. Capital surplus, on the other hand, may arise from selling stock at a higher amount per share than its par value.

The value of the common stock plus the surplus belonging to it may be divided by the number of common shares to ascertain the book value of a share of common stock. Book value is calculated by subtracting from total assets all liabilities ranking prior to the common stock and dividing by the number of common shares outstanding. Earnings per share compared with book value per share may give some indication of what the company has been able to earn on the common stockholders' investment. The price at which common shares sell in the market, however, commonly bears little resemblance to their book value. At times, common shares of companies for which the earnings outlook is unfavorable sell for much less than the book value per share.

One must not make the mistake of believing that surplus is cash. We have seen that a balance sheet derives its name from the fact that the two sides balance. The left side shows all the assets of the company, including all its cash. On the right-hand side we find liabilities and capital or net worth; these are claims of outsiders (creditors) and insiders (stockholders) against the assets. Stockholders' claims are sometimes called "equities." The reason the statement balances is that there are no assets (things of value) that someone does not claim; hence, the assets are equal to the claims. In fact, the fundamental equation of double-entry bookkeeping says that assets are equal to liabilities and capital (or net worth),

$$A = L + C.$$

In business, books of account are kept in accordance with this principle.

What the Balance Sheet Shows

Now that the essential components of a balance sheet are apparent, what can you, as an investor, expect to learn from an analysis of the balance sheet? Only some general indications can be provided here, for the subject is vast and at times complicated.[5] Graham and Dodd point to six types of information which the investor may obtain for his guidance from a study of the balance sheet.

1. It shows in nearly all cases how much capital is actually invested in the business and how the capital structure is divided between senior issues and common stock.

[5] For a detailed, competent discussion see Benjamin Graham, David L. Dodd, and Sidney Cottle, "Balance Sheet Analysis," in *Security Analysis* (4th rev. ed.; New York: McGraw-Hill Book Co., Inc., 1962), chap. 16.

2. It reveals the strength or weakness of the working-capital position.
3. It provides a check upon the validity of the earnings reported in the income account.
4. It supplies data to test the true success or prosperity of the business— viz., the amount earned on invested capital.
5. It supplies the basis for analyzing the sources of income.
6. It supplies the basis for a long-term study of the relationship between earning power and asset values and of the development of the financial structure over the years.

An example or two must suffice to indicate the nature of this type of analysis. Before investing, you will want to know the proportion in the capital account of senior liens to common stock equity. A high proportion of bonds reduces the attractiveness of both the preferred and common stock, while too large an amount of preferred shares detracts from the value of the common. The bond ratio is found by dividing the face value of the bonds by the total value of the bonds, preferred stock, common stock, reserves, and surplus. The preferred stock ratio is found in the same way, only the stated value of the preferred stock is divided by the total of the other five items. The common stock ratio is the difference between 100 percent and the totals of the bond and preferred stock ratios. Based on certain standards established by experience, investment analysts believe that for an *industrial* company, funded debt (bonds) should not exceed 25 percent of total capitalization, or that stock should be at least 75 percent of total capitalization, and that common stock should total at least as much as all senior securities (bonds and preferred issues). When this is not the case, companies may find it difficult to raise new capital. In the case of utility companies it is customary for debt to be about 50 percent of total capitalization.

There are a number of similar ratio tests and standards, but since many of them depend on income-account items, it is best to defer a discussion of them until the income (or profit and loss) statement has been presented and explained.

The Income Statement

The income statement is often called an "operating statement" or a "statement of profit and loss." It shows which income items during the year caused an increase in the stockholders' claim against the business (surplus) and which expense items brought about a decrease in the same claim. Although one form is not uniformly used, the accompanying illustration gives a general understanding of its content.

In this statement, Net Sales of $102,000 and Other Income of $6,000 brought $108,000 of assets into the business during the year.

These assets would appear on the balance sheet, balanced by an increase of $108,000 in Surplus. In other words, the stockholders have an increased claim of $108,000 against the business because of the increase in the assets to be claimed. On the other hand, Cost of Sales of $49,000, Selling and Administrative Expenses of $31,000, Other Expenses of $3,000, and Estimated Income Taxes of $16,000—a total of

THE YO-YO DISTRIBUTION COMPANY OF NORTH AMERICA, INC.

INCOME STATEMENT FOR THE YEAR 196X

Net sales	$102,000
Cost of sales	49,000
Gross Profit	$ 53,000
Selling and administrative expenses	31,000
Net operating profit	$ 22,000
Add: Other income	6,000
Total Income	$ 28,000
Deduct: Other expenses	3,000
Net income before income taxes	$ 25,000
Deduct: Estimated income taxes	16,000
Net Profit Added to Surplus	$ 9,000

$99,000—will sooner or later take $99,000 of assets out of the business, if they have not already done so. Since the stockholders no longer can claim these $99,000 of assets, their claim (surplus) is reduced by $99,000. Therefore, all the items on the income statement had the effect of increasing assets and surplus by $108,000, and of decreasing assets (or increasing liabilities) and surplus by $99,000, making a net increase of assets and surplus of $9,000, which is the figure on the income statement for the Net Profit Added to Surplus.

Income and Expense Items Are Additions to and Subtractions from Surplus

It is the purpose of the income statement to bring together in one orderly array all the transactions (in summary) during a given period which increase or decrease the stockholders' claim against the business. The balance sheet is kept simple by adding to the surplus (or subtracting from it) merely the net result of what the income statement shows. Our final figure on the income statement (Net Profit Added to Surplus, $9,000) might, therefore, have been called "Net Addition to Surplus." The items on the income statement are, then, merely increases and decreases in the Surplus (as shown on the balance sheet) arranged in orderly form. We can accordingly say that the income statement explains how it came about that the mathematical difference between assets and liabilities (capital, net worth, or proprietorship) changed during the fiscal period. Remember that Assets = Liabilities + Capital (or Net Worth). Therefore, Assets — Liabilities = Capital. If net assets (Assets — Liabilities) or assets belonging to shareholders increase, the claim of the shareholders (Surplus) must also increase, else the balance sheet would not balance. A decrease in net assets is correspondingly matched by a decrease in the Surplus account.

The Items of the Income Statement

"Net sales" is the result of having deducted such things as returns, allowances, sales discounts, and outward freight from the gross sales figure. "Cost of goods sold" is found by adding to the beginning inventory (of merchandise for sale) the cost of the purchases for the period, to arrive at the total cost of goods handled, and then deducting from this total the ending inventory; the assumption is that, except for the goods still on hand, the total goods handled have been sold. "Gross profit" (or "gross margin") is merely the difference between net sales and the cost of goods sold. Some people object to this term, saying that it is really not a profit at all, since other expenses (expenses of selling and administration, for example) must be deducted from it before we know whether we have actually made a profit or a loss on the period's transactions. However, it is sometimes useful to relate the gross profit of a company over a period of years to its sales in order to see whether the company has been successful in maintaining its markup (sales prices as compared with product costs). It is often helpful to express all other figures on the income statement as a percentage of net sales (100 percent) and see how these percentages behave over several years in a company's life. We may learn, for example, that sales have been maintained only by incurring increasing percentage expenses for selling and administration.

"Other income" represents income arising from sources other than the business itself, such as income from investments. "Other expenses" are expenses, such as financial expenses, which have little to do with the operations of a company's business. We may regard the business itself as the main tent of a circus with its own income and expenses leading to the "net operating income." Then the "other income" and the "other expenses" can be considered the results of operating the side shows. The net result of operating all activities is the net income from all sources.

Consolidated Statements

When a business enterprise with a setup which includes a main company organized as a corporation and subsidiary companies incorporated as separate corporations reports to its stockholders, it is the custom to combine the balance sheets of the different corporations into one consolidated balance sheet for the group of companies and to combine the individual income statements into a consolidated income statement. In consolidation, intercompany items are eliminated. Consolidated statements are useful summaries for the family of corporations which together constitute the business enterprise, but they may hide some details which may only be learned from a study of the individual statements before consolidation.

What the Income Account Shows

An analysis of a company's income account, either over a number of periods or by comparing its figures with those of other companies in the industry, as in the case of balance sheet analysis, will reveal a good deal about the nature of the company's operations and its status as an investment risk. For example, before you select a company for investment, you will want to know something of its "margin of profit"—how this figure has changed over the years, and how it compares with figures for comparable companies and with the average for the industry in which the company operates. Finding the "margin of profit" is not difficult. You divide the net profit from operations by net sales. The resultant figure shows what percentage of profit the company made from its operations. For example, if net profits from operations were $15,000 for the year based on net sales of $100,000, the margin of profit would be 15 percent. If the average margin of profit for the industry was 10 percent, one could say, based on this measure alone, that this was a superior company.

The significance of the current year's figure can be established in two ways: (1) it can be compared with previous years, and you can determine whether the company has been gaining or losing in efficiency; and (2) you can also compare it with figures for other companies engaged in the same type of business. If it is low in comparison, it is an unhealthy sign. A good comparison to make is that between (a) the margin of profit of a given company and (b) the average for the industry. If there is a marked disparity, then you can look further for the causes before deciding whether or not to invest.

Analysts also frequently use the "operating ratio" to ascertain the efficiency of a company over a period of time or to compare companies within an industry to the industry average. The operating ratio is obtained by dividing total operating costs by net sales. A high operating ratio means a low margin of profit and is unfavorable. A lower operating ratio means a higher margin of profit and is more favorable.

Ratios, Standards, and Investment Judgment

There are a considerable number of ratios used in investment analysis which combine items from both the balance sheet and the income account. Standards of average or acceptable performance have been established for many of these ratios, and a study and knowledge of them, if time affords, will provide the prospective investor with useful tools of analysis.

Consider briefly nine basic financial relationships derived from balance sheets or income accounts. These you should understand.

1. *Net Income to net worth, or rate of return on stockholders' equity.* You divide net income after taxes by the total of preferred stock, common stock, and surplus accounts. This is one of the most significant of all the financial ratios. It tells you how much the company is earning on the stockholders' investment. The higher the ratio, the more favorable. On the average, U.S. corporations tend to earn 9–10 percent on stockholders' equity. Comparable figures for a large number of industries are provided quarterly by the government[6] and annually by the First National City Bank of New York.[7] By using these two sources you can compare figures of companies you are interested in with the average for the industry or for other industries.

2. *Times fixed charges earned or interest coverage.* You divide net income before taxes by the annual interest requirements (fixed charges). Sometimes interest coverage after taxes is shown but since interest is a claim prior to income taxes, it is therefore better practice to compute interest coverage before provision for income taxes. This ratio shows how well protected by earnings—or how poorly—is the bondholders' interest. Ordinarily, a manufacturing company's interest coverage is regarded as satisfactory at 5 times; among public utilities a 3 to 4 times coverage is satisfactory.

3. *Earnings per share—preferred stock.* This ratio is found by merely dividing the net income by the number of shares of preferred stock. You use net income after interest and after taxes. This ratio shows the earnings protection for the preferred dividend. A coverage of 4 times is usually considered adequate for industrial companies.

4. *Combined or overall coverage.* You divide the adjusted operating profit (net income before interest but after taxes) by the total of

---

[6] See *Quarterly Financial Report for Manufacturing Corporations,* Federal Trade Commission—Securities and Exchange Commission, Washington, D.C.: U.S. Government Printing Office.

[7] See "Review of Corporate Profits in (year)," in the April issue each year of *The Monthly Economic Letter,* First National Bank of New York. A free copy may be obtained by writing to the Bank at 399 Park Avenue, New York, N.Y., 10022.

interest and preferred dividends. This is a more conservative method than merely considering the net income available for the preferred stock. A preferred stock of an industrial company with average earnings (before interest on bonds but after taxes) for five years of not less than 4 times the combined interest and preferred dividend requirements is usually regarded as satisfactory. For a public utility preferred, earnings of around 3 times the combined requirements make the stock high grade.

5. *Earnings per share—common stock, or yield on common stock.* The buyer of common stock is often more concerned with the earnings per share of his stock than he is with the dividend. It is usually earnings per share, or rather, prospective earnings per share, that influence stock prices. The income statement does not show the earnings available for common stock, if a company has preferred stock outstanding. You must subtract the preferred dividend from net income after taxes. You then divide this residual net income by the number of shares of common stock outstanding. This gives you earnings per share. For example, net income after taxes amounts to $5,000,000. The preferred dividend requires $1,000,000. Thus $4,000,000 remains for the 500,000 common shares outstanding. Earnings per share are thus $8.00 ($4,000,000 divided by 500,000 shares). See Figure 14–7.

6. *Dividends per share—common stock.* This, too, is a simple computation. You divide the dividends paid on the common stock by the number of shares. In the example above, assume the company pays $2,000,000 of the $4,000,000 available. With 500,000 shares outstanding each share receives a dividend of $4.00. Dividend payout varies from company to company depending on stability of earnings, need for new capital, the directors' judgment as to the outlook for earnings, etc. On the average, industrial companies pay out between 50 and 60 percent of earnings as dividends. Growth companies pay out less because of their greater need for capital for expansion. Utilities pay out more because of their stability of earnings and because they depend more on debt.

7. *Book value per share of common stock.* This is found by adding the stated or par value of the common stock to the surplus accounts and dividing the total by the number of shares. To continue the illustration:

Common stock	$ 5,000,000
Capital surplus	1,000,000
Earned surplus	14,000,000
Total	$20,000,000
Number of shares	500,000
Book value per share =	$40

FIGURE 14–7

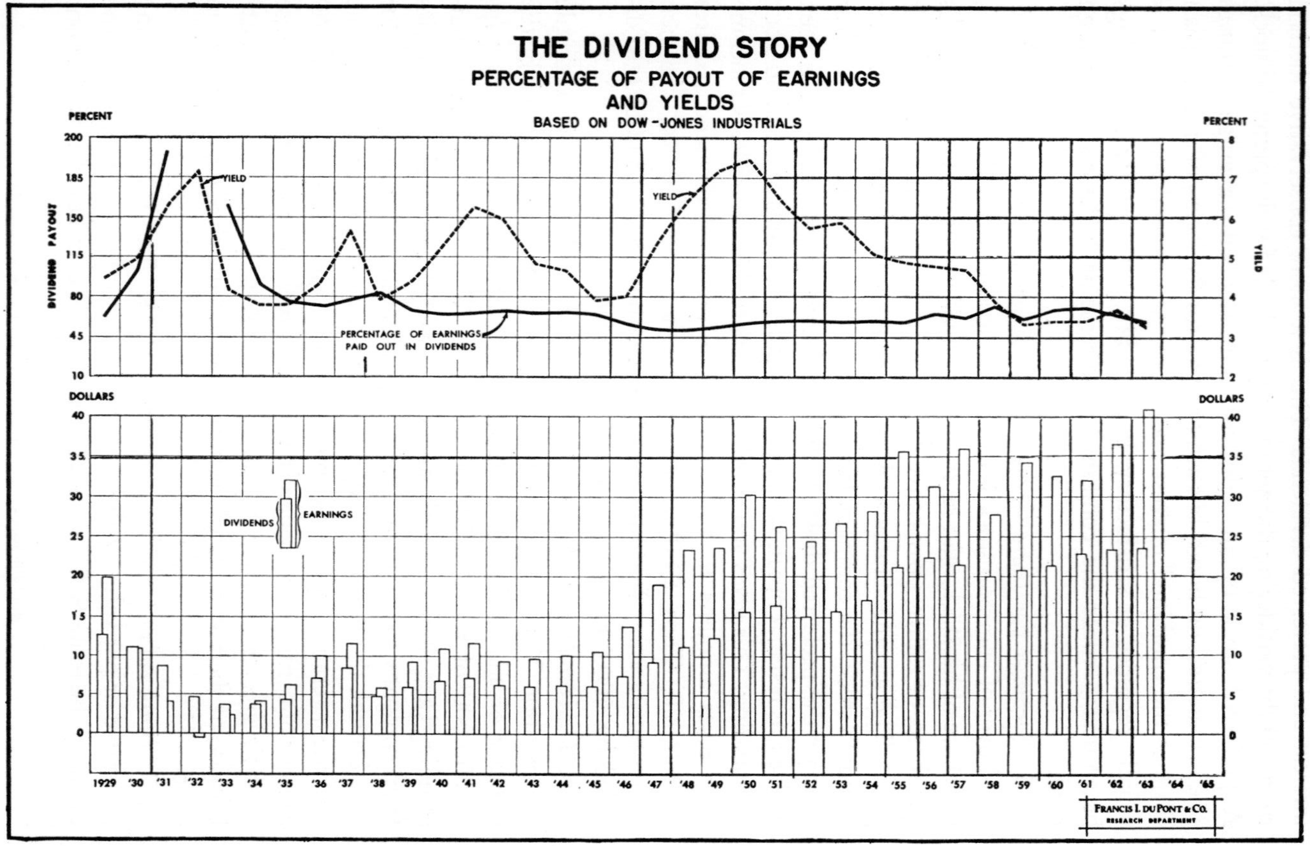
THE DIVIDEND STORY
PERCENTAGE OF PAYOUT OF EARNINGS
AND YIELDS
BASED ON DOW-JONES INDUSTRIALS
PERCENT
DIVIDEND PAYOUT
YIELD
PERCENTAGE OF EARNINGS PAID OUT IN DIVIDENDS
DOLLARS
DIVIDENDS
EARNINGS
1929 '30 '31 '32 '33 '34 '35 '36 '37 '38 '39 '40 '41 '42 '43 '44 '45 '46 '47 '48 '49 '50 '51 '52 '53 '54 '55 '56 '57 '58 '59 '60 '61 '62 '63 '64 '65
FRANCIS I. DU PONT & CO.
RESEARCH DEPARTMENT

Another method of calculating book value, called the long way, is to deduct from total assets (exclusive of such intangibles as goodwill and patents) all liabilities and preferred stock, if any. The remainder is divided by the number of common shares and the result is the book value per share or net tangible assets per share of common stock.

For industrial companies, book value per share does not mean very much. It is not as important as earnings and prospective earnings. Usually the largest category of assets is plant and equipment and aside from salvage value, such assets are worth only what they can earn.

On the other hand, the book value of the common stock of such money corporations as banks, insurance companies, and investment companies is more significant. The assets of these companies are in securities or in other forms that can usually be readily turned into cash. The book value of public utility common stock is also important, since these regulated companies are entitled by law to earn a fair return on their investment, which is made up largely of fixed assets. Their rates, and hence, earnings are based on the value of their investment in plant and equipment.

8. *Price-earnings ratio.* This is simply the earnings per share of the common stock divided into the market price. For example, if the company earns $8.00 per share and the stock sells for 96, the price-earnings ratio is 12. The stock is selling at 12 times earnings. What is the right price-earnings ratio? No one can really say. All we can do is study trends over time, and average levels. It used to be said that a stock should sell at 10 times earnings but this is now regarded as rather low. An average level today would be closer to 15 to 18 times earnings. Some growth stocks sell at 40 to 50 times earnings. Buyers are anticipating and paying for sharply higher expected or projected earnings.

9. *Dividend return (dividend yield or income).* This is determined by dividing the annual dividend per share by the price of the stock. For example, if there is a $4.00 per share dividend on common which sells for $96, the dividend return is 4.1+% ($4.00 divided by $96).

Some of the more important ratios[8] used by leading security analysts in forming judgments and making investment decisions follow.

Profitability ratios include:

1. Earnings per dollar of capital funds (return on capital).
2. Sales per dollar of capital funds (sales ratio).
3. Profit per dollar of sales (return on sales).

---

[8] For a discussion of these frequently used financial ratios, see "Key Ratios in Security Analysis" in Benjamin Graham, David L. Dodd, and Sidney Cottle, *Security Analysis* (4th ed.; New York: McGraw-Hill Book Co., Inc., 1962), pp. 231–38.

The best gauge of the success of a company is the percentage earned (though not necessarily paid out) on its invested capital.

Credit ratios include:

4. The working-capital ratio—current assets to current liabilities.
5. The common stock ratio—the total capital fund at book value to the common stock component thereof.
6. Senior-charge coverage ratio—the balance of earnings available for senior charges divided by the fixed charges.

Ratios which help to judge the *growth* of a company over a period of time include:

7. Dollar sales—annual rate of growth.
8. Net profits in dollars to total capital.
9. Earnings per share.

Ratios which indicate the *stability* of earnings of a company over a period of years include:

10. Minimum coverage of senior charges—times earnings cover senior charges in poorest years.
11. Maximum earnings decline—percentage decline in income in given poor years to average income in a normal base period. This is very useful in comparing the volatility of earnings as among companies.

The percentage of available earnings paid out in common dividends affects the market's evaluation of the stock. This ratio is the

12. Pay-out ratio: divide earnings per share into the dividend paid per share.

Then there are a number of ratios which are useful in judging the *price of an issue*—whether it is too high or too low. These include:

13. Sales per dollar of common, at market.
14. Earnings per dollar of common, at market (earnings yield).
15. Dividends per dollar of common, at market (dividend yield).
16. Net assets (equity) per dollar of common at market (asset ratio).

While the use of all of the ratios may be too difficult for the average investor, the application of three or four of the more significant ones to a given stock or bond investment possibility will provide safeguards and permit the avoidance of costly mistakes. If you have no time at all or cannot understand balance sheets, income accounts, and ratio analysis, then at least you can consult one or more of the financial services which do understand and use these tools. They will give you the essence of their judgment, boiled down in a few simple words. Thus you save time and profit from the hours of work which their skilled analysts devote to the task. You need not even buy the service, since one or more will be found in any good library. There is really no excuse for hit-or-miss investing based on tips, rumor, or flights of fancy and imagination.

SUGGESTED READINGS

1. *How to Read a Financial Report.* New York: Merrill Lynch, Pierce, Fenner & Smith, latest edition. A free copy can be obtained by writing to this firm at 70 Pine St., New York, N.Y., 10005.

2. *How to Understand Financial Statements,* New York Stock Exchange. A free copy may be obtained from Publications Division, New York Stock Exchange, 11 Wall Street, New York, N.Y., 10005.

3. *The Outlook,* published weekly by Standard & Poor's Corporation, 345 Hudson St., New York, N.Y., 10014. A free sample copy will be sent on request.

4. *Moody's Stock Survey,* published weekly by Moody's Investor's Survey, 99 Church St., New York, N.Y., 10007. A free sample copy will be sent on request.

5. Eugene Lerner (ed.), *Readings in Financial Analysis and Investment Management.* Homewood, Ill.: Richard D. Irwin, Inc., 1963.

6. Benjamin Graham, David L. Dodd, Sidney Cottle, *Security Analysis, Principles and Technique.* 4th ed. New York: McGraw-Hill Book Co., Inc., 1962.

7. Roy A. Foulke, *Practical Financial Statement Analysis.* 5th ed. New York: McGraw-Hill Book Co., Inc., 1961.

8. C. Norman Stabler, *How to Read the Financial News.* New York: Harper & Bros., latest edition. See also *Financial News: How to Read and Interpret It,* John G. Forrest, *New York Times,* latest edition.

9. H. C. Walter (ed.), *Investment Information and Advice: A Handbook and Directory.* Whittier, Calif. FIR Publishing Company, 1964.

10. In *Changing Times, The Kiplinger Magazine:*
    (*a*) "How to Look Up a Stock," May, 1963.
    (*b*) "A Family Financial Program—When You're Starting Out," August, 1963.
    (*c*) "A Family Financial Program for the Middle Years," September, 1963.
    (*d*) "A Family Financial Program—Getting Ready for Retirement," October, 1963.
    (*e*) "A Family Financial Program—The Retirement Years," November, 1963.
    (*f*) Why Buy Growth Stocks," February, 1964.
    (*g*) "Growth Stocks: How Have They Fared," November, 1962.

11. William Chambless, *Behind the Annual Report.* New York: Simon & Schuster, 1963.

12. *Securities and Industries Review,* issued quarterly by Merrill Lynch, Pierce, Fenner & Smith. A free copy may be obtained by writing to 70 Pine St., New York, N.Y., 10005.

13. John C. Clendenin, *Introduction to Investments.* 3rd ed. New York: McGraw-Hill Book Co., Inc., 1960.

14. John W. Hazard and Milton Chrystie, *The Investment Business.* New York: Harper & Row, 1964.

15. R. D. Kennedy and S. McMullen, *Financial Statements: Form, Analysis and Interpretation.* 4th ed. Homewood, Ill.: Richard D. Irwin, Inc., 1962.

CASE PROBLEMS

1. Max Kugelfuss is a young bachelor, a teacher with a Ph.D., and a man earning a moderately good income. Since he has no outstanding financial obligations, he decides to invest some of his savings. He hears about some oil stock in a Canadian company which is for sale at five cents a share. Before he decides to buy 1,000 shares, what facts do you think he should consider? How can he find out more facts about the company?

2. Jim Jefferson, age 23, is advised by his father to buy a few shares in the stock market in order to learn about investments. He recently graduated from college and is earning $5,000 per year. In school he majored in liberal arts and had no investment training. His savings are such that he feels that he can invest $1,000 initially in stock. He asks you to advise him how he should proceed. What would you suggest?

3. A friend tells you that he has just heard that Mattel, Inc. (NYSE) and Tonka Toys (ASE) are "sleeper stocks," that he is going to buy shares in both and that you should do likewise. Research these stocks, using at least five sources of information. Evaluate them. Do you agree with your friend or not? Why?

4. Your barber tells you that he has heard from a customer of his that Amerline Corporation (O-T-C) and Pueblo Supermarkets, Inc. (O-T-C) are "hot buys." With your usual judicious skepticism you decide to look into the situation, to investigate before you invest. What sources of information will you use? After using them, what conclusions do you come to regarding these "tips"?

5. Your mother-in-law to be wants to give her daughter a gift of $25,000 of stock as a wedding gift for choosing such an attractive and intelligent son-in-law. To be polite she asks your advice as to what stocks she should buy for your fiancee. She indicates that she is quite conservative and favors only the bluest of the blue chips. Write her a letter giving your suggestions for this $25,000 blue chip investment program, citing facts, figures, and sources to back your choices.

6. Bush has been a college professor for ten years. His retirement fund is with the Teachers Insurance and Annuity Association in New York and has been invested (along with the funds of other teachers) in bonds. The Association has also set up an organization (CREF) which invests its funds in common stock. Bush is asked whether he wants part of his past and future retirement payments handed to that organization or whether he prefers to have his entire retirement fund invested in bonds as heretofore. What are your thoughts on the subject?

7. Aaron Rudstein has been asked to invest $10,000 in the common stock of the Better Homes Mortgage Corporation, which buys old houses, restores them,

and then endeavors to sell them at a profit. To persuade him to invest, he is given the financial statements of the company for the last five years. His study of these statements reveals that the company's inventory of houses for sale was carried at cost for the first four years but that in the latter year the company carried this inventory at the total figure for which the company expected to sell them. How should Aaron react to this change? Why?

8. A wealthy man, Louis Potter, made a loan of $10,000 to the Pawtucket Company for the period of one year. The loan was made primarily because he was on friendly terms with the officers of the company. Since he was asked to consider the possibility of buying stock in the company, he began to learn something about its method of operations and to study its recent financial statements. He learned that the company bought lumber, piled it in its yards, and removed boards from the top of the piles whenever lumber was needed in the plant. The company carried its inventory of lumber (approximately $50,000) on its statements at cost. The total assets of the company amounted to about $100,000. Current liabilities of the company were $35,000 as against total current assets of $55,000. The plant had recently been mortgaged for $30,000 (10-year direct-

APPENDIX 14–A

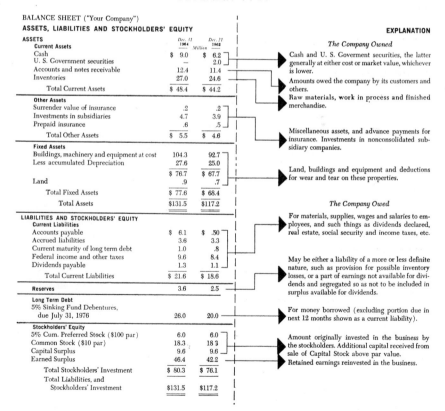

BALANCE SHEET ("Your Company") ASSETS, LIABILITIES AND STOCKHOLDERS' EQUITY			EXPLANATION
ASSETS	Dec. 31 1964	Dec. 31 1963	The Company Owned
Current Assets		*Million*	
Cash	$ 9.0	$ 6.2	Cash and U. S. Goverment securities, the latter generally at either cost or market value, whichever is lower.
U. S. Government securities	—	2.0	
Accounts and notes receivable	12.4	11.4	
Inventories	27.0	24.6	Amounts owed the company by its customers and others.
Total Current Assets	$ 48.4	$ 44.2	
Other Assets			Raw materials, work in process and finished merchandise.
Surrender value of insurance	.2	.2	
Investments in subsidiaries	4.7	3.9	
Prepaid insurance	.6	.5	
Total Other Assets	$ 5.5	$ 4.6	Miscellaneous assets, and advance payments for insurance. Investments in nonconsolidated subsidiary companies.
Fixed Assets			
Buildings, machinery and equipment at cost	104.3	92.7	
Less accumulated Depreciation	27.6	25.0	
	$ 76.7	$ 67.7	Land, buildings and equipment and deductions for wear and tear on these properties.
Land	.9	.7	
Total Fixed Assets	$ 77.6	$ 68.4	
Total Assets	$131.5	$117.2	The Company Owed
LIABILITIES AND STOCKHOLDERS' EQUITY			For materials, supplies, wages and salaries to employees, and such things as dividends declared, real estate, social security and income taxes, etc.
Current Liabilities			
Accounts payable	$ 6.1	$ .50	
Accrued liabilities	3.6	3.3	
Current maturity of long term debt	1.0	.8	
Federal income and other taxes	9.6	8.4	May be either a liability of a more or less definite nature, such as provision for possible inventory losses, or a part of earnings not available for dividends and segregated so as not to be included in surplus available for dividends.
Dividends payable	1.3	1.1	
Total Current Liabilities	$ 21.6	$ 18.6	
Reserves	3.6	2.5	
Long Term Debt			
5% Sinking Fund Debentures, due July 31, 1976	26.0	20.0	For money borrowed (excluding portion due in next 12 months shown as a current liability).
Stockholders' Equity			
5% Cum. Preferred Stock ($100 par)	6.0	6.0	Amount originally invested in the business by the stockholders. Additional capital received from sale of Capital Stock above par value. Retained earnings reinvested in the business.
Common Stock ($10 par)	18.3	18 3	
Capital Surplus	9.6	9.6	
Earned Surplus	46.4	42.2	
Total Stockholders' Investment	$ 80.3	$ 76.1	
Total Liabilities, and Stockholders' Investment	$131.5	$117.2	

SOURCE: New York Stock Exchange.

reduction mortgage at 4½ percent interest per annum). After 28 years of operation the company had an earned surplus of $3,000. Recent earnings had averaged about 8 percent of net worth. Potter gives you these facts only and asks you to advise him.

9. Arthur Byron's $2,000 endowment policy has matured. He is 45 years of age and has a wife (age 43) and one child (age 15). His other assets are a home (cost, $12,000 but probably worth $20,000), subject to a mortgage of $4,000, and $2,000 in banks. He is principal of the local high school, at a salary of $7,500 a year. He asks you to advise him as to the most effective use of the proceeds of the endowment policy. Develop an investment portfolio or program for him, supplying facts, figures, and sources.

10. Using the Balance Sheet and Income Account of Your Company, shown in Appendix 14–A and 14–B, compute *ten* significant financial relationships or ratios for each of the years given, and evaluate the company from an investment viewpoint.

APPENDIX 14–B

STATEMENT OF INCOME	Year Ended December 31		EXPLANATION
	1964	1963	
	— Million —		
SALES	$115.8	$110.0	Amount received or receivable from customers.
Less:			Part of income used for wages, salaries, raw materials, fuel and supplies and certain taxes.
Costs and Expenses:			Part of income used for salesmen's commissions, advertising, officers' salaries and other general expenses.
Cost of goods sold	74.8	73.2	
Selling, general and administrative expenses	14.2	13.0	
Depreciation and depletion	4.2	3.5	Provision from income for the reduction of the service life of machinery and buildings and the use of minerals in mines.
	$ 93.2	$ 89.7	The remainder after deducting the foregoing expenses from sales, but before providing for interest charges and taxes.
Operating Profit	$ 22.6	$ 20.3	
Interest Charges	1.3	1.0	Amount required for interest on borrowed funds.
Earnings before Income Taxes	$ 21.3	$ 19.3	
Provision for Federal and State Taxes on Income	11.4	9.8	Amount paid or payable for taxes.
Net Income for the Year	$ 9.9	$ 9.5	This amount was earned for stockholders.
Dividend on Preferred Stock	.3	.3	Amount paid to preferred stockholders.
Balance of Net Income Available for Common Stock	$ 9.6	$ 9.2	Amount remaining for common stockholders.

STATEMENT OF EARNED SURPLUS	Year Ended December 31		
	1962	1961	
	— Million —		
Balance at beginning of year	$ 42.2	$ 37.6	Surplus or retained earnings reinvested in the business. Usually not all of the year's earnings can be paid out in dividends, a part being retained in the business for expansion or other purposes.
Add — Net Income for the year	9.9	9.5	
	52.1	47.1	
Less Dividends Paid on			
Preferred Stock	.3	.3	
Common Stock	5.4	4.6	
Balance at End of Year	$ 46.4	$ 42.2	

SOURCE: New York Stock Exchange.

15 INVESTMENT COMPANIES— MUTUAL FUNDS

An investment trust is known by the companies it keeps.

—Herbert Prochnow

⪡DELMONICO'S⪢

RESTAURANT.
494·PEARL·STREET.

BILL OF FARE.

Cup Tea or Coffee,	1	Pork Chops,		4
Bowl " "	2	Pork and Beans,		4
Crullers,	1	Sausages,		4
Soup,	2	Puddings,		4
Fried or Stewed Liver,	3	Liver and Bacon,		5
" " Heart,	3	Roast Beef or Veal,		5
Hash,	3	Roast Mutton,		5
Pies,	4	Veal Cutlet,		5
Half Pie,	2	Chicken Stew,		5
Beef or Mutton Stew,	4	Fried Eggs,		5
Corn Beef and Cabbage,	4	Ham and Eggs,		10
Pigs Head " "	4	Hamburger Steak,		10
Fried Fish,	4	Roast Chicken,		10
Beef Steak,	4			

Regular Dinner 12 Cents.

Smith & Handford Printers 23 and 25 Day St N. Y.

THIS IS a pre-Civil War menu of a once-famous restaurant. When dinner cost 12 cents, an average weekly wage was $6.00. Secular (long-run) inflation has carried us very far from the 12-cent dinner and the $6.00 wage. If we project from the $3.00 dinner and $85 weekly wage of today, what will prices and wages be in the year 2065?

"If you are afraid of inflation, buy mutual fund shares." This is the basic appeal which has sold two million investors almost $25 billion of mutual fund shares over the last 20 years. So great is the versatility of the funds' appeals that they have also been able to persuade people to buy mutual fund shares instead of life insurance, to cash bonds and withdraw savings in order to buy mutual fund shares for "safety of principal in old age and retirement." Probably no other financial institution has had so rapid a growth in recent years as the open-end investment company, as the mutual fund is technically called. Are the extravagant claims of the mutual fund salesmen justified?

Kinds of Investment Companies

An investment company is simply a financial institution whose aim is to gather the savings of many individuals and invest them in a diversified portfolio of securities. If the investments were made chiefly in bonds and mortgages, the portfolio would not be unlike that of mutual savings banks, savings and loan associations, or life insurance companies. However, investment companies typically invest far more extensively in common stocks than do these other institutions.

It cannot be emphasized too much that all sorts of investment companies exist. Some of them, such as the American Research and Development Corporation, have as their prime purpose investment in new and untried undertakings, which by their very nature can be only speculative. At the other extreme, some investment companies invest only in high-grade bonds. If he will but seek them out, the investor can find investment companies which limit their investments to the type or types of securities in which he wishes to participate, be they blue-chip common stocks, speculative common stocks, high-grade preferred stocks, speculative preferred stocks, high-grade bonds, more-speculative bonds, or a balanced fund of stocks and bonds. Companies can be found which emphasize as objectives high income or capital appreciation; others stress primarily the preservation of principal. Of course, preservation of principal may be sought either from the point of view of maintaining the number of dollars in the original investment or from the point of view of maintaining the purchasing power of the original investment.

The Investment Companies Act of 1940 requires a statement by each company of its basic investment policies. Once stated, policies may not be changed without stockholder approval. Thus the investor can tell fairly quickly the aim and investment objective of any company in which he is interested. For example, one of the more successful mutual funds, Fundamental Investors, has as its objective: "Long-term growth of capital and income." Its policy is to invest in "principally common stocks but other securities or cash may be held under flexible policy." The fund with one of the best capital-gains records over the last decade, Keystone Custodian Funds—S4, has as its objective: "Capital growth in rising markets." Its policy is stated as "widely diversified, fast moving, lower-priced common stocks with wide variations in dividends." On the other hand, Wellington Fund has as its objective: "To pay reasonable dividends: to secure profits and to conserve principal." It is a balanced fund, holding bonds and preferred and common stock.

Not only do investment companies vary widely according to objectives and policy, but very great disparities exist in investment results. In many cases the management more than earns its fee; in some others, it would seem as though the managers should pay the investors for the privilege of learning how to invest with the use of public funds. Indeed, the most difficult problem for the small investor is to learn how to distinguish the competent, ably managed funds from the less effective ones.

How Investment Companies Obtain Their Funds

Like other corporations, investment companies obtain the money with which to operate by selling their securities—common stock, preferred stock, and bonds—to the public. Before 1940, bonds were sold more commonly than they are today. Since 1940 the Federal Investment Company Act of 1940 has required open-end companies, the ones which are growing most rapidly at the present time, to have a single capital structure—only one class of security outstanding, usually common stock. See Appendix B to this chapter.

Open-End Investment Companies

There are two principal types of investment companies—open end and closed end. An open-end investment company is one whose shares are redeemable at any time at approximate asset value. In most cases, new shares are offered for sale continuously at asset value plus a fixed percentage as selling charge.

Open-end investment companies offer additional shares of their stock for sale at all times, and, furthermore, they will repurchase previously issued stock from investors at any time. They are usually called "mutual funds." They sell their own shares at prices which will net the fund an amount equal to the net asset value of each share outstanding at the time of sale. This means that the investor must pay 6–9 percent more than the net asset value to buy shares, since, of course, it costs money to get the shares sold.

The large majority of open-end investment companies appraise the market value of portfolios twice daily—at 1:00 P.M. and 3:30 P.M., New York time—and thus arrive at a figure for net asset value per share on which the published bid and offered prices are based. Net asset value is then the worth of a mutual fund share as determined by dividing the total market value of its portfolio by the number of its own shares outstanding.

The surcharge of 6–9 percent is worthy of comment. Usually it is the only cost the investor incurs in making this type of investment; when he sells, he usually receives the net asset value of his shares without deduction. But even this slight cost will wipe out earnings of 3–4½ percent per year for a couple of years, should the investor decide not to retain the investment. If there is doubt as to whether the investment can be retained for at least five years, the investor might well consider whether it might not be more profitable to accept 4 or 4½ percent per annum from a savings bank or savings and loan association than to buy shares in an open-end investment company. It is the surcharge of 6–9 percent which encourages stockbrokerage firms to push the sales of open-end investment company shares to the extent which is prevalent today.

If a mutual fund has a surcharge—or "loading charge," as it is usually called in the trade—of, say, 8 percent, this means that if you invest $10,000 in a fund, you get only $9,200 of net asset value, while $800 of your money goes to the broker or other financial middleman who solicited and obtained your order. Some have held that this contrasts unfavorably with New York Stock Exchange commission rates, which are less than 1 percent, on the average, when a "round lot" (usually 100 shares of stock) is purchased. Proponents of mutual funds reply that this is a fallacious and misleading comparison because two entirely unlike things are being compared. A share in an investment company, they hold, is not an ordinary "security." In addition to representing a prorata share of ownership in a fund, it is in effect, they contend, a service contract. But, of course, you also pay, out of dividends earned and due you, an annual management fee for this service. A number of funds, such as Scudder, Stevens and Clark, and also Loomis-

Sayles, both of Boston, the Rittenhouse Fund of Philadelphia, the De Vegh Fund of New York, have no loading charge at all. See Table 15–1. They are, however, as a result, not very popular with brokerage

TABLE 15–1
No Load Funds

COMMON STOCK FUNDS

American Enterprise Fund
American Investors Fund
Continental Mutual Investment
De Vegh Mutual Fund
Energy Fund
Fairfield Securities
Guardian Mutual Fund
The Johnston Mutual Fund
Mairs & Power Growth Fund
National Industries Fund
Nelson Fund
Northeast Investor Trust
Penn Square Mutual Fund
Rowe Price New Horizons Fund
T. Rowe Price Growth Stock Fund
The Regency Fund
Scudder, Stevens & Clark Common Stock Fund
Stein Roe & Farnham Stock Fund

Trans-American Fund
Variable Stock Fund
Wade Fund

BALANCED FUNDS

Counselors Investment Fund
Dodge & Cox Fund
Loomis-Sayles Mutual Fund
Mutual Shares Corp.
The Nassau Fund
Newton Fund
The Prudential Fund of Boston
Rittenhouse Fund
Scudder, Stevens & Clark Balanced Fund
Stein Roe & Farnham Balanced Fund

FUNDS FOR INVESTING ABROAD

Loomis-Sayles Canadian and International Fund
New York Capital Fund
Scudder Fund of Canada

houses which push mutual funds.

A comparison of the mutual fund "loading" charge and New York Stock Exchange Commission rates is as follows:

AMOUNT OF PURCHASE Less than—	MOST COMMON MUTUAL FUND SALES COMMISSION	NEW YORK STOCK EXCHANGE COMMISSION ON PURCHASES AND SALES
$100	8%	6%
$500	8	2½
$1,000	8	1.8
$2,000	8	1.4
$5,000	8	0.8

In a useful and interesting book, *How to Buy Stocks*, a Merrill Lynch partner points out that a dealer who sells $2,000 of mutual fund shares, where the loading charge is 8 percent, keeps about two thirds of this, or

$120, whereas if he had sold the same dollar amount of a listed stock, his commission would be only $25.

Obligatory repurchase of its shares by a corporation is relatively uncommon. Savings and loan associations and credit unions indulge in the practice, but investment companies, as far as is known, provide the only other corporate example. Savings and loan associations always repurchase without penalty (except for unearned dividends or interest), and investment companies usually do; but the potential investor in an investment company will do well to check to see whether any redemption fee will be charged by his company if he wishes to sell. Since open-end investment companies repurchase their shares on demand, they must constantly be selling at least as many shares as are redeemed in order to have the necessary redemption money; otherwise they will be forced to liquidate some of the investments they hold to obtain it, perhaps at an unauspicious time.

It is these open-end investment companies which have enjoyed the greatest growth in the last dozen years. By 1964 there were over 350 open-end investment companies, with combined assets of over $25 billion and three million shareholders. See Table 15–2. The largest of these investment companies has assets in excess of $1 billion, and the average company has about $25,000,000 of assets.

The Mutual Fund Shareholder—A Profile

A recent survey by the Investment Company Institute has shed light on who buys mutual funds and what their financial status is. The study divides mutual fund holders into two categories, namely, regular account holders (i.e., those who have bought mutual fund shares as a "lump-sum" investment to which they may or may not add), and accumulation plan holders (including both voluntary and contractual plan holders).[1] Accumulation plan holders are those who are investing new money in additional shares on a monthly or quarterly schedule.

There is solid evidence, the survey indicates, that mutual fund shares are used, by both regular account and accumulation plan holders, as part of overall financial plans, and not as a single investment means. Mutual fund shareholders had life insurance coverage, savings accounts and savings bonds, and individual securities held directly, in addition to their mutual fund investment.

The regular account holder had larger financial holdings in each area

---

[1] See *The Mutual Fund Shareholder: A Comprehensive Study*, Investment Company Institute, New York, 1963. A free copy may be obtained by writing to the Institute at 61 Broadway, New York, N.Y., 10006.

TABLE 15–2

Shareholder Accounts and Total Net Assets, 1940–1963
(Assets in 000's of Dollars)

CALENDAR YEAR END	No. of Cos.	No. of ACCOUNTS	ASSETS
1963	165	6,151,935	$25,214,436
1962	169	5,910,455	21,270,735
1961	170	5,319,201	22,788,812
1960	161	4,897,600	17,025,684
1959	155	4,276,077	15,817,962
1958	151	3,630,096	13,242,388
1957	143	3,110,392	8,714,143
1956	135	2,580,049	9,046,431
1955	125	2,085,325	7,837,524
1954	115	1,703,846	6,109,390
1953	110	1,537,250	4,146,061
1952	110	1,359,000	3,931,407
1951	103	1,110,432	3,129,629
1950	98	938,651	2,530,563
1949	91	842,198	1,973,547
1948	87	722,118	1,505,762
1947	80	672,543	1,409,165
1946	74	580,221	1,311,108
1945	73	497,875	1,284,185
1944	68	421,675	882,191
1943	68	341,435	653,653
1942	68	312,609	486,850
1941	68	293,251	401,611
1940	68	296,056	447,959

NOTE: Figures for shareholder accounts represent combined totals for member companies. Duplications have not been eliminated. Figures are only for member companies of the Investment Company Institute.
SOURCE: Investment Company Institute.

analyzed than had the accumulation plan holder. It would appear that regular account holders have already created estates whereas the average accumulation plan investor is younger and is just building an estate. As Tables 15–3 and 15–4 show, the regular account holder is older and has larger financial assets. He is more inclined to own shares of more than one mutual fund and has a larger proportion of his total financial assets in individual corporate stocks held directly. However, his insurance coverage is lower than the younger accumulation plan holder, who has generally broader family and financial responsibilities. Approximately 38 percent of regular account shareholders are age 60 and over, whereas only less than 8 percent of the accumulation plan holders fall in this age category. See Table 15–4.

TABLE 15–3

The Mutual Fund Shareholder—A Profile

MEDIAN* FIGURES	1963		1958	
	REGULAR ACCOUNT HOLDER	ACCUMULATION PLAN HOLDER	REGULAR ACCOUNT HOLDER	ACCUMULATION PLAN HOLDER
AGE OF RESPONDENTS	54.8 yrs.	42.8 yrs.	55.0 yrs.	42.3 yrs.
FAMILY INCOME IN A RECENT YEAR	$8,122	$ 9,045	$6,542	$ 7,034
VALUE OF MUTUAL FUND HOLDINGS	$5,591	$ 2,386	$4,171	$ 1,890
NUMBER OF FUNDS HELD	1.2	1.0	1.2	1.0
AMOUNT OF MOST RECENT FUND PURCHASE	$1,140	$ 72 (Under Plan)	$ 963	$ 58 (Under Plan)
Other Assets:				
NUMBER OF CORPORATE STOCKS OWNED DIRECTLY	2.7	1.3	3.7	1.1
VALUE OF CORPORATE STOCK HOLDINGS	$6,115	$ 2,428	$8,187	$ 1,696
BANK ACCOUNTS AND U. S. SAVINGS BONDS	$3,846	$ 1,886	$3,344	$ 1,970
LIFE INSURANCE IN FORCE	$8,671	$14,542	$8,497	$11,950

* The median is the middle figure in the series, with an equal number of people represented on either side.

SOURCE: Investment Company Institute.

Types of Open-End Companies

There are, broadly, five types of open-end investment companies (mutual funds): diversified bond-stock funds; diversified common stock funds; bond funds; preferred stock funds; and specialized common stock funds. Diversified bond-stock funds normally invest some portion of their assets in bonds or preferred stocks, or both, in addition to a portion which is invested in common stocks. On the average, the funds in the bond-stock classification follow more conservative investment policies than do those which normally limit their holdings to common stocks. They tend to have a lower average return, less capital gain in a rising market, less volatility, better defenses in a falling market, more stability of income, and greater safety of principal than do the stock funds.

The most common type of bond-stock fund is the *balanced* fund. This has been described as any fund which at all times holds at least 20–25 percent (although never more than 75–80 percent) of its assets in cash and good-grade or high-grade senior securities for defensive purposes and which invests the remainder in common stocks or other equity-type securities. Balanced funds appear suitable for investors who want to turn over to investment company management fairly complete

TABLE 15–4

Characteristics of Mutual Fund Shareholders

	REGULAR ACCOUNT HOLDER	ACCUMULATION PLAN HOLDER
Age:		
UNDER 30	4.7%	13.2%
30-39	11.6	27.2
40-49	19.7	30.6
50-59	26.2	21.3
60-64	11.7	4.7
65 AND OVER	26.1	3.0
	100.0%	100.0%
Occupation:		
PROFESSIONAL	24.5%	33.0%
EXECUTIVE-ADMINISTRATIVE	16.5	18.5
CLERICAL	6.9	7.8
SALES	5.3	9.3
SKILLED & SEMI-SKILLED	8.1	10.5
CIVIL SERVICE & MILITARY	3.9	10.6
HOUSEWIVES	12.0	4.7
RETIRED	17.7	2.5
OTHER (NOT ANALYZED)	5.1	3.1
	100.0%	100.0%
Family Income:		
UNDER $3,500	11.7%	3.9%
$3,500 UP TO $5,000	12.9	8.9
$5,000 UP TO $7,500	20.8	23.4
$7,500 UP TO $10,000	18.5	22.3
$10,000 UP TO $15,000	18.6	25.1
$15,000 UP TO $20,000	7.3	8.1
$20,000 UP TO $30,000	6.1	4.7
$30,000 AND OVER	4.1	3.6
	100.0%	100.0%
Value of Mutual Fund Holdings:		
UNDER $1,000	13.2%	29.7%
$1,000 UP TO $2,500	16.3	21.9
$2,500 UP TO $5,000	18.1	18.5
$5,000 UP TO $10,000	19.8	14.7
$10,000 UP TO $25,000	19.2	10.7
$25,000 AND OVER	13.4	4.5
	100.0%	100.0%

SOURCE: Investment Company Institute.

responsibility for their invested capital and who prefer a "middle-of-the-road" course to one that assumes greater risks in the hope of greater profits or higher income. Examples are Wellington Fund, Eaton & Howard Balanced Fund, the George Putnam Fund of Boston, etc.

The largest group of funds—over 50 percent by net assets—are the diversified common stock funds. These have all, or almost all, of the money they hold in common stock, but they are by no means alike, either in investment objective or in performance. Some invest primarily in the better-known stocks of large corporations—the standard type of good-quality shares frequently described as "blue chips." Others may specialize in "growth-company" shares. Some concentrate on shares of less well-known firms, where greater opportunities for profits or income are believed to exist. Some funds provide a means of buying into a diversified list of low-priced or highly volatile shares. Some place greater stress on income, while others emphasize capital appreciation. Generally they appeal to those investors who concentrate funds in common stock, taking risks to achieve either capital growth or better income, or both. Examples are Affiliated Fund; Dreyfus Fund; Fundamental Investors; Keystone Custodian Funds S1 (high grade), Keystone S2 (income common stocks), Keystone S3 (appreciation), and Keystone S4 (lower priced); Massachusetts Investors Growth Stock Fund; Investors Stock Fund; Massachusetts Investors Trust.

There are relatively few bond funds or preferred stock funds. They are designed for diversification in senior securities and continuous professional supervision. Examples of bond funds are the Keystone Custodian Funds B1 (high grade), Keystone B2 (medium grade), Keystone B3 (low priced), Keystone B4 (discount bonds), etc. Preferred stock funds include Franklin Custodian Funds—Preferred Series; National Securities Preferred Stock Series; etc.

The specialized common stock funds provide diversification only within a single industry. The holdings of each fund are restricted to securities related to a particular industry, such as aviation, chemicals, electronics, railroads, utilities, etc. Almost every industry group represented on the New York Stock Exchange is available in the form of a separate mutual fund. The advantage of industry specialization has been proven only in a very few fields. In numerous areas it is an unfortunate restriction, which vitiates one of the chief advantages of the mutual fund, namely, broad diversification for the small investor. Examples of single-industry common stock funds include Chemical Fund, Inc., Life Insurance Stock Fund, Medical Securities Fund, Television-Electronics Fund, etc.

Closed-End Investment Companies

The closed-end investment company is one with a relatively fixed amount of capital, generally all raised at formation, whose securities are traded on an organized securities exchange or in the over-the-counter market in the same way as ordinary corporate securities. They issue authorized stock at a given time and wait before they float another issue, if at all. Stock is not usually redeemed by them for their shareholders. Investors who wish to purchase issued shares of closed-end companies must purchase them from those who are already stockholders, through their brokers on the exchanges (if it is listed) or on the over-the-counter market. Tri-Continental Corp., The Lehman Corp., Adams Express, etc., are examples of leading closed-end investment companies.

Shares of closed-end companies differ from those of open-end companies in the way they are priced. Open-end company shares are bought and sold on the basis of their net asset value, whereas the prices of closed-end shares are governed entirely by the supply and demand of the shares in the open market. Closed-end company shares are usually traded at discounts from their asset value, although a few command premiums.

The resale market for shares of open-end investment companies lies primarily in the companies themselves, for they are pledged to redeem their shares. In good times, when the sale of their new shares to the public is producing more money than is needed to buy in old shares offered for redemption, there is apt to be no problem; but in times when investment company shares are difficult to sell, the only way that open-end investment companies can secure money with which to redeem their own outstanding shares is by selling the investments in their portfolio. To sell at such times may upset dollar averaging and automatic formula timing. In addition, wholesale selling of good securities by many investment companies can only serve to depress the price at which they can be sold.

The closed-end investment companies do not have this problem, because they do not, and cannot be required to, repurchase their shares. Many closed-end investment companies have their shares listed on the security exchanges, where active trading secures for them a wide market.

Many closed-end companies have a multiple capital structure. Besides common stock, they often have preferred stocks, bonds, or bank loans (or all three) outstanding. In such cases, the common stock, possesses a special quality generally known as "leverage." To understand the closed-end investment company, it is important to understand clearly the meaning of this term.

Leverage

"Leverage" is the special force created by the use of borrowed money or other senior capital which magnifies changes in the assets and earnings available for junior issues. More simply, it is just a case of making money with the use of other people's (low-cost) money. The degree of leverage depends on the ratio of senior securities and bank borrowings to the total resources of the corporation and the relationship of the rate of interest paid on senior securities and bank borrowings to the rate of return which is earned on all the assets of the corporation. If the common stockholders have the use of a lot of money furnished by others at a low rate of return and can earn a high rate of return on all the money, including their own, the earnings of the common shareholders will be magnified as compared with what they would be if only their own money were used. The important thing for the potential investor in an investment company to remember is that he has the possibility of greater earnings (and also greater loss) if leverage is present. Such leverage is rarely found in open-end investment companies.

A few examples may serve to make more apparent what is meant by leverage. If a closed-end, nonleverage company has a capitalization consisting of $5,000,000 of common stock only, with no senior securities or bank loans, and it earns 5 percent net on its money, the common stockholders, assuming all earnings are paid out, would earn a return of just 5 percent. A second company also has a total capitalization of $5,000,000, but this consists of $2,000,000 of 3 percent bonds and $3,000,000 of common stock. It, too, earns 5 percent net on its total capitalization; thus earnings are $250,000 (5 percent of $5,000,000), of which $60,000 must go to pay interest on the $2,000,000 of 3 percent bonds, leaving $190,000 of earnings to be paid out on the $3,000,000 of common stock, or a return of 6⅓ percent. Thus the leverage in this second company has increased the return to its common stockholders over and above that going to the common stockholders of the first company, even though total earnings of the two companies are the same. By using borrowed low-cost money, part of the higher return on this money can be siphoned off to benefit the common stockholders.

Just as the good earnings of prosperous times enhance the earnings of common stockholders in a leverage company, the reduced earnings in depressed periods cut back their earnings below that which a nonleverage company stockholder would realize. This is because a much larger proportion of total (reduced) earnings must now go to meet fixed charges on the bonds. Take the same two companies and assume that net earnings fall to 2 percent, or $100,000, on the total capitalizations of $5,000,000. In the case of the nonleverage company, all of the $100,000 would be available for common stockholders, and they would, therefore, have a 2 percent return. In the case of the second company, however, of the $100,000 total earnings, $60,000 (3 percent of $2,000,000) would have to go to the bondholders, leaving only $40,000 for the $3,000,000 of common stock investment, or a return of only $1\frac{1}{3}$ percent. Leverage company stocks will rise more sharply than nonleverages shares in a bull market and will fall more precipitously in a bear market.

Types of Closed-end Investment Companies

At one time a number of closed-end investment companies were highly leveraged and therefore speculative. In recent years leverage has declined in importance as closed-end companies have reduced or eliminated senior capital. About the only remaining large closed-end company which can be classed as leveraged is the Tri-Continental Corporation.

Most of the larger closed-end companies, such as Lehman Corp., Madison Fund, U.S. & Foreign Securities, now have only common stock outstanding. They are also diversified in their investment policy in that they do not specialize in any one industry or field. There are a few specialized closed-end companies such as National Aviation Corp. and the Petroleum Corporation of America. Then there are venture capital investment companies such as American Research and Development Corp., Electro-Science Investors, Inc. Some closed-end companies concentrate their investments in specific areas of the world as American–South African Investment Company, Eurofund, and Japan Fund.

Two newer types of closed-end investment companies are the real estate investment trust (REIT), discussed in a previous chapter, and the small business investment company (SBIC). There are now well over 600 SBIC's in operation, of which about 50 are publicly owned. These will be considered in the next chapter.

Methods of Purchase

There are three basic ways to purchase mutual fund shares: regular account, accumulation plan, and contractual plan.

Regular Account. This is a lump-sum purchase. A specific amount of money is invested at one time. The sales fee, or "loading charge" of

7½ or 8 percent is assessed against your total purchase. Thus, if you invest $10,000, $800 goes to dealers or distributors, and you buy $9,200 worth of shares. Most funds now reduce the loading charge for larger purchases. One fund, for example, has the following schedule:

Amount of Purchase	Sales Charge as Percentage of Offering Price
Less than $25,000	8½%
$ 25,000 or more but less than $50,000	6
$ 50,000 " " " " " $100,000	5
$100,000 " " " " " $250,000	4
$250,000 " " " " " $500,000	3
$500,000 " " " " " $1,000,000	2
$1,000,000 and over	1

A few days after you place the order you should receive a certificate in your name for the proper number of shares. Dividend checks are sent to you in the mail, usually quarterly, though some funds will arrange to pay monthly dividends. Or you can arrange to reinvest your dividends to purchase additional shares. If the fund distributes realized capital gains, as many do from time to time, you can either take them as cash or you can reinvest them in additional shares.

Accumulation Plans. These are of two types, informal or voluntary and contractual. The informal or voluntary plan starts with an application stating the amount of the initial purchase, which must be from $100 to $500, depending on the particular fund, and an indication of the amounts to be invested periodically thereafter and the dates on which payments will be made. There is usually a minimum of $25 or $50 required for the periodic payment, but there is no compulsion to adhere to the amount stated in the application, provided the payment tendered does not fall below the minimum required. A confirmation of each purchase is sent to the investor but stock certificates are not sent unless specifically requested.

An informal accumulation plan differs in many respects from the contractual plan to be described. Each purchase is an entity in itself. There is no specified duration of the plan. It lasts as long as the purchaser wishes to continue making further payments. There is no built-in element of compulsion to continue payments in order to minimize the effect of the sales charge. In the voluntary accumulation plan the load is based only on the individual payment and is deducted from each payment. Thus the voluntary plan combines the advantage of the dollar cost averaging principle with the "load" arrangements of the regular account. It does not have the penalty arrangement of the contractual plan. The investor can liquidate his account, if he wishes, just as he can in the case of shares bought the regular way. In many funds the informal accumulation plan can be used as an open account by investors, who instead of making regular payments of stated amounts at indicated future dates, prefer to make irregular additions at varying times. The voluntary accumulation plan allows the investor maximum flexibility in contrast to the contractual plan.

The Contractual Plan. There has been a very rapid growth in contractual plans over the last decade partly because they are exceedingly favorable to the salesmen. They are accumulation plans with a built-in financial incentive to carry out the agreed-upon future purchases and payments. Under a contractual plan, the purchaser agrees to make regular monthly or quarterly payments toward the purchase of mutual fund shares, over a period of years, usually 10. The plan is set up in such a way as to discourage the purchaser from discontinuing payments, especially in the early years. This is achieved by providing that a substantial part of the total sales commission on the entire plan be deducted in the first year. Under the Investment Company Act the specific provisions with respect to contractual plans limit the sales charge on them to a maximum of 9 percent of the total investment over the life of the plan, but permit the deduction for sales charges of up to 50 percent of the first year's investment. Thus, if you purchase a 10-year, $10,000 plan and pay in $1,000 the first year, assuming the "load" is 8 percent, or $800 on the $10,000, your $1,000 the first year will bring only $500 worth of shares because $500 of the $800 commission will be deducted from the first year's $1,000 investment. The balance of the sales charge, amounting to $300, must be apportioned evenly over the remaining installments.

You can easily see the great disadvantage of discontinuing the plan in any early year. If you discontinue the plan at the end of the first year, for example, assuming the price of the shares have not changed, you would receive back only $500 of your $1,000 investment. The remaining $500 went to the distribution organization. How sharply must the shares rise and how much capital gain and dividend distribution must there be to enable your $500, which was all that was actually put to work of your first year's $1,000, to double itself? It is quite unlikely to double within a year or two. Thus the financial pressure of the contractual plan. For this reason it has sometimes been called a "penalty plan" or a "front-end load plan." The more polite term, preferred by the mutual funds, is, however, "contractual" plan, because it formalizes the buyer's agreement to make periodic payments.

Capital gains and dividend distributions paid on the shares owned are automatically reinvested and thus used to purchase additional shares, an important factor in adding to the longer term value of the accumulation. Keep in mind, however, that such capital gains and dividends, even though they are reinvested, are taxable annually to the shareholder.

A useful form of insurance has been developed to provide, in the case of the purchaser's death before completion of the plan, the funds to cover the difference between the intended total investment and the amount already paid. Known as "plan-completion insurance" the maximum coverage with any plan company is usually $30,000. The cost of the insurance is deducted from the investor's regular monthly payments. Investors must be able to prove insurability. A medical examination is usually required. Insurance rates charged are usually low, based on group term policies and partly on the age of the investor.

Bear in mind that the insurance does not guarantee the purchaser's estate any fixed sum of money. All it does is provide for the fulfilment of the plan and therefore the delivery of the number of shares that could be bought based on the agreed-upon investment and the net asset value of the shares at time of purchase. The value of the shares delivered to the estate may be more or less than the total amount invested, depending on market conditions at the time of the purchaser's death.

Contractual plans may not be sold in some states such as California, Illinois, New Hampshire, Ohio, and Wisconsin. Plan completion insurance is not available in a few states.[2]

The Portfolio

Since 1940 in the open-end company, management has had wide discretion as to the securities to be carried in the portfolio. This is known as the "management" type of operation, and the managers deduct an annual fee from accumulated earnings to cover their services. The fee is usually stated as a percentage of asset value. For example, if a fund charges 1 percent per year of asset value and its assets are $20 million, the management fee is $200,000. If the fund earned a 5 percent return on its $20 million of assets, or $1 million, then the management fee would be 20 percent of annual income. It is usually never stated in this fashion, however, the funds preferring to state it as a percentage of asset value, not of annual income.

---

[2] For further information on contractual plans, see Chapter VII, "Contractual Plan—Road to a Goal," in *Investment Companies*, by Arthur Wiesenberger, latest annual edition, New York.

Most mutual funds publish, quarterly, a list showing their holdings of securities; and perhaps more than any other type of financial institution their portfolio and their operations are largely open to public scrutiny. The securities they hold, as of the last quarter, can usually be easily ascertained, either by writing to the fund itself or by consulting such sources as the annual edition of *Investment Companies,* published each year by Arthur Wiesenberger and Company, or *Vickers Guide to Investment Company Portfolios.* Observation of changes in portfolios over a period of years will provide interesting insights into changing patterns of investment and will tell the small, amateur investor what the investment managers are thinking and doing. For example, industry preferences over a period of time by investment company managers may be seen from Tables 15–5 and 15–6.

Earnings

From their investments, both closed- and open-end companies have two sorts of income. In addition to the ordinary interest and dividends earned, there is often a profit secured by selling securities at more than their cost. These latter profits (capital gains) are often thought of as a nice, juicy melon to be cut and enjoyed. Income taxes on capital gains (25 percent) are much less for many wealthier investors than the taxes they have to pay on ordinary income; the result is that some managements feel an especial urge to attempt to achieve them.

This is especially true since for many funds expenses run quite high. For example, according to the "Tablistics" section of *Johnson's Charts,* expenses expressed as a percent of income, rather than as a percent of asset value (Johnson shows it both ways), run from a low of 5.9 percent (for the Massachusetts Investors Trust) to a high of 349 percent (for the Samson Fund, Inc.). A goodly number of funds have expenses running in excess of 50 percent of income. This seems quite high and before investing in high expense funds you should investigate the causes for the high charges, since they eat into prospective dividend distributions and in due course affect capital gains.

Payments from both sources are made to the investor in the same way, and frequently in the same check. The companies are required by law, however, to state the source of distributions from anything other than net investment income. The distinction between dividends from net investment income and distributions from capital gains is important and should be thoroughly understood. Investment companies differ in their view of how shareholders should regard capital-gains distributions; some maintain that they should never be thought of as spendable income, while others believe it is all right to consider small payments

TABLE 15-5

Vickers Favorite Fifty

RANK BY $ VALUE					STOCKS	$ Value (Millions)	§ No. Fds. Holding	Number Shares Held	% Outst. Stk. Held by Fds.
Dec.31 1960	Dec.31 1961	Dec.31 1962	Sept.30 1963	Dec.31 1963					
1	1	1	1	1	INTL. BUSINESS MACHINES	820	192	1,617,000	5.8
7	8	3	3	2	STANDARD OIL (NEW JERSEY)	587	164	7,720,900	3.6
2	2	2	2	3	TEXACO INC.	518	148	7,396,700	5.8
14	5	4	4	4	GENERAL MOTORS CORP.	472	175	6,007,600	2.0
3	3	5	5	5	AMERICAN TEL. & TEL.	343	153	2,466,500	1.0
20	31	8	7	6	ROYAL DUTCH PETROLEUM	286	119	5,832,500	7.2
24	4	6	6	7	FORD MOTOR CO.	273	109	5,473,700	5.0
15	11	13	8	8	GULF OIL CORP.	219	108	4,651,000	4.5
-	-	25	14	9	XEROX, INC. (New)	215	67	2,533,600	13.1
R.	16	11	11	10	GENERAL ELECTRIC CO.	197	95	2,262,000	2.5
-	-	20	10	11	SOCONY MOBIL OIL	194	94	2,673,800	5.4
6	7	7	9	12	DU PONT (E. I.)	187	94	781,500	1.7
5	6	10	12	13	INTL. NICKEL OF CANADA	186	106	2,713,100	9.2
17	23	12	18	14	EASTMAN KODAK CO.	173	74	1,495,600	3.7
42	26	18	13	15	AMERADA PETROLEUM	161	49	2,305,800	18.3
13	13	14	17	16	SOUTHERN CO.	160	59	2,922,700	12.6
21	12	15	19	17	FLORIDA POWER & LIGHT	156	54	2,140,200	15.7
-	39	31	22	18	INTERNATIONAL TEL. & TEL.	156	69	2,820,700	15.7
11	18	17	15	19	CONTINENTAL OIL CO.	153	61	2,533,700	11.8
-	-	-	20	20	COLUMBIA BRDCSTNG.SYS.(New)	144	47	3,762,600	19.3
25	24	9	16	21	STANDARD OIL OF CALIF.	144	75	2,418,600	3.5
23	21	16	21	22	TEXAS UTILITIES CO.	141	57	2,480,800	9.9
49	42	39	33	23	MONSANTO CHEMICAL	138	87	2,202,400	7.2
12	20	26	25	24	ARMCO STEEL CORP.	133	64	2,017,000	13.6
18	25	19	27	25	CENTRAL & SOUTH WEST	132	54	2,856,400	13.4
9	15	28	26	26	GOODYEAR TIRE & RUBBER	131	53	3,159,800	8.9
-	47	30	30	27	SOUTHERN PACIFIC CO.	129	73	3,520,800	13.0
10	22	23	28	28	MINNESOTA MINING & MFG.	129	67	1,990,100	3.8
19	27	35	31	29	UNION CARBIDE	124	89	1,032,200	3.4
33	28	21	32	30	AMERICAN ELECTRIC POWER	124	54	3,077,000	6.8
38	19	24	23	31	SEARS, ROEBUCK & CO.	124	63	1,265,400	1.7
16	17	29	24	32	INTERNATIONAL PAPER	121	70	3,782,500	8.7
26	40	32	34	33	ALLIED CHEMICAL CORP.	114	70	2,081,200	7.9
-	-	-	47	34	RADIO CORP. OF AMERICA	109	71	1,125,700	6.5
41	43	38	35	35	STANDARD OIL (INDIANA)	107	66	1,671,300	4.6
31	29	27	29	36	LOUISIANA LAND & EXPLOR.	106	41	1,314,900	14.6
-	-	-	43	37	GENERAL TEL. & ELECTRONICS	104	43	3,297,700	4.4
28	35	41	39	38	MERCK & CO.	102	53	932,200	8.7
-	-	-	40	39	MARATHON OIL	99	40	1,758,400	11.8
34	14	36	46	40	REYNOLDS TOBACCO	93	72	2,206,400	5.4
-	-	37	42	41	LOCKHEED AIRCRAFT	93	70	2,608,000	24.6
43	34	34	41	42	GENERAL FOODS	92	37	1,021,300	4.1
37	-	-	44	43	SHELL OIL CO.	86	37	1,841,100	3.0
-	-	-	38	44	NORFOLK & WESTERN RWY.	86	55	728,100	9.8
-	-	-	-	45	*CORNING GLASS WORKS	84	44	399,000	5.9
-	-	47	-	46	**GRACE (W. R.) & CO.	81	51	1,618,700	14.1
-	49	-	50	47	FEDERATED DEPT. STORES	78	44	1,436,100	8.3
46	-	-	-	48	**DOW CHEMICAL	78	57	1,130,700	3.8
-	-	48	45	49	HOUSTON LIGHTING & POWER	78	33	1,798,000	8.9
-	-	-	-	50	**ILLINOIS POWER CO.	77	25	1,877,700	14.6

DISPLACED: Chrysler Corp.   -   Gillette Co.   -   Pfizer (Chas.) & Co., Inc.   -   Polaroid Corp.
* NEWCOMER   ** RETURNEE:

§ The figures in this column have been adjusted for late reporting funds and may not agree completely with RANK BY NUMBER OF INVESTMENT COMPANIES.

SUMMARY OF FAVORITE FIFTY BY INDUSTRY

dollar value of stocks by industry to total dollar value of favorite fifty

	12/31/63	9/30/63	12/31/62	12/31/61	12/31/60
Oils & Natural Gas	30.1%	31.0%	29.7%	21.7%	23.8%
Utilities	13.7	13.2	16.7	12.9	15.2
Office Equipment	11.7	10.5	9.8	11.8	11.1
Chemicals & Drugs	9.3	8.3	9.9	12.9	11.2
Motors	8.4	9.8	8.0	7.3	3.9
Electric & Electronics	6.4	5.7	3.5	4.2	5.4
Leisure	3.6	4.6	3.2	3.0	2.0
Rails	2.5	2.4	2.3	1.0	-
Miscellaneous	14.3	14.5	16.9	25.2	27.4
	100.0%	100.0%	100.0%	100.0%	100.0%

SOURCE: *Vickers Guide to Investment Company Portfolios.* Reproduction hereof permitted by courtesy of Vickers Associates, Inc.

TABLE 15–6

100 STOCKS RANKED BY
NUMBER OF INVESTMENT COMPANIES

Rank	Stock	No.of Inv.Cos. Holding	Rank	Stock	No.of Inv.Cos. Holding	Rank	Stock	No.of Inv.Cos. Holding	Rank	Stock	No.of Inv.Cos. Holding
1.	I.B.M.	190	26.	Xerox	67	51.	Alum.Co.of Amer.	49	76.	Unilever N.V.	42
2.	General Motors	174	27.	Allied Chem.	64	52.	Anaconda	49	77.	Union Bag–Camp	42
3.	Std. Oil (N.J.)	168	28.	Armco Steel	64	53.	Ark. La. Gas	49	78.	F.M.C.	41
4.	A.T. & T.	152	29.	No.Amer.Avia.	63	54.	Gillette	49	79.	La.Land & Explor.	41
5.	Texaco	147	30.	Sears Roebuck	63	55.	Phillips Petrol.	49	80.	Marathon Oil	41
6.	Royal Dutch	121	31.	Continental Oil	61	56.	Genl.Public Util.	48	81.	United Air Lines	41
7.	Intl. Nickel	106	32.	Litton Industries	61	57.	Goodrich (B.F.)	48	82.	Air Prods.& Chem.	40
8.	Ford Motor	104	33.	Southern Co.	60	58.	Am.Metal Climax	47	83.	American Airlines	39
9.	Gulf Oil	102	34.	Westinghouse El.	58	59.	C.B.S.	47	84.	Bethlehem Steel	39
10.	Monsanto Chem.	102	35.	Dow Chemical	57	60.	So.Calif.Edison	47	85.	Chrysler	39
11.	duPont (E.I.)	95	36.	Texas Utilities	57	61.	Va. Elec. Pwr.	47	86.	Natl.Cash Reg.	39
12.	Genl. Electric	95	37.	Fla.Pwr. & Lt.	56	62.	Bristol Myers	46	87.	Pepsi–Cola	39
13.	Socony Mobil	92	38.	Pfizer (Chas.)	56	63.	Phelps Dodge	46	88.	Transamerica	39
14.	Union Carbide	89	39.	Amer.Elec.Pwr.	54	64.	Union Pacific	46	89.	Consol. Edison	38
15.	Aluminium Ltd.	82	40.	Caterpillar Tr.	54	65.	Intl. Harvester	45	90.	Financial Fed.	38
16.	Std. Oil, Calif.	77	41.	Central & S.West	54	66.	Polaroid	45	91.	Hercules Powder	38
17.	Eastman Kodak	74	42.	Merck	53	67.	Burlington Ind.	44	92.	Jones & Laughlin	38
18.	Southern Pacific	73	43.	Norfolk & Wstrn.	53	68.	Cities Service	44	93.	Martin–Marietta	38
19.	Intl. Paper	71	44.	Goodyear	52	69.	Corning Glass	44	94.	Reynolds Metals	38
20.	Lockheed	71	45.	U.S. Steel	52	70.	Fed.Dept.Stores	44	95.	Sinclair	38
21.	R.C.A.	70	46.	Amerada	51	71.	Genl.Tel.& El.	43	96.	Tenn. Gas Transm.	38
22.	Reynolds Tobacco	69	47.	National Lead	51	72.	Minn.–Honeywell	43	97.	Coastal States Gas	37
23.	I.T. & T.	67	48.	Southern Rwy.	51	73.	Pan Am.World	43	98.	Continental Can	37
24.	M.M.M.	67	49.	Atch.Top.& S.F.	50	74.	St. Regis Paper	43	99.	General Foods	37
25.	Std. Oil (Indiana)	67	50.	Grace (W.R.)	50	75.	Kennecott Copper	42	100.	Great No'n. Rwy.	37

SOURCE: *Vickers Guide to Investment Company Portfolios.*

from that source as an earned addition to dividend income. The more conservative view is that capital gains realized in rising markets must be conserved to offset capital losses which are inevitable in falling markets.

Measuring Performance

There are generally two views of the performance record of investment companies, especially of the mutual funds. One is the salesman's view, which makes mutuals appear incomparable. The exhibit is usually a formidable-looking chart that shows the 10-year rise in per-share asset value. This is normally unaccompanied by an explanation that rising stock prices over the 1954–64 period caused a swelling book value for virtually all investment portfolios. Nor is there any indication that a given sum of money, such as $10,000, invested at compound interest over a decade would appreciate significantly solely by reason of the compounding process. See Figure 15–1.

The second, more sober, view was expressed by *Forbes Magazine* when it declared: "The real truth lies somewhere between these two extremes and it varies widely from fund to fund. Some mutuals have achieved results far better than the average small investor could

FIGURE 15–1

Quarterly Compounding Table

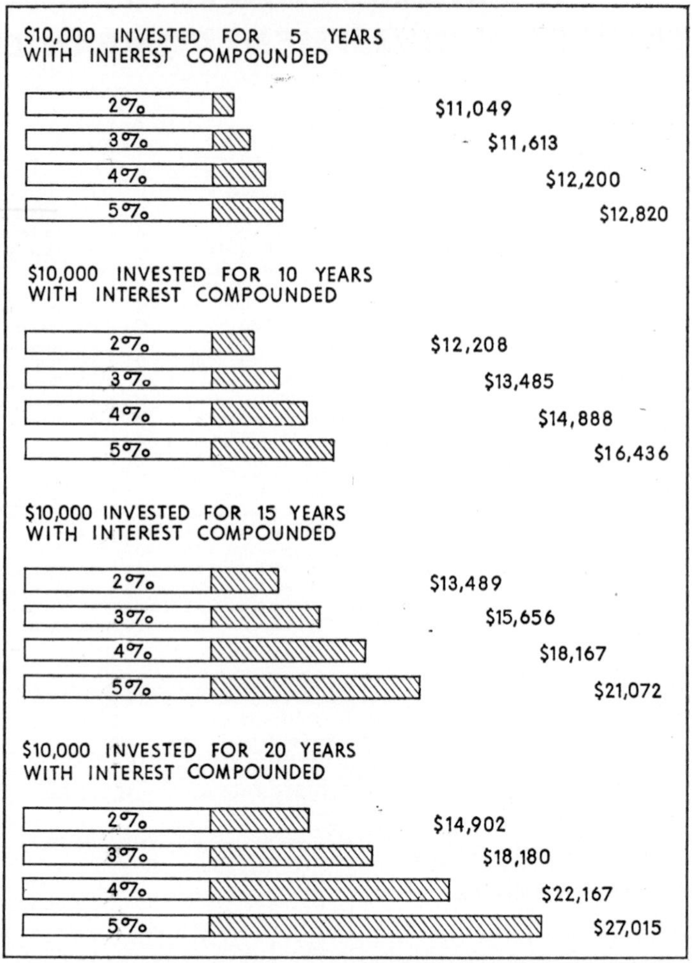

$10,000 INVESTED FOR 5 YEARS
WITH INTEREST COMPOUNDED

2%	$11,049
3%	$11,613
4%	$12,200
5%	$12,820

$10,000 INVESTED FOR 10 YEARS
WITH INTEREST COMPOUNDED

2%	$12,208
3%	$13,485
4%	$14,888
5%	$16,436

$10,000 INVESTED FOR 15 YEARS
WITH INTEREST COMPOUNDED

2%	$13,489
3%	$15,656
4%	$18,167
5%	$21,072

$10,000 INVESTED FOR 20 YEARS
WITH INTEREST COMPOUNDED

2%	$14,902
3%	$18,180
4%	$22,167
5%	$27,015

accomplish for himself. Others just equal blind chance. And a third and sizeable group show few results but expensive managements."

In support of the first view it is customary to assume that $10,000 was invested in a given fund 10 or 15 years back and then show what happened to the investment by the end of the selected period. In many cases the results are truly impressive. For example, in the case of Fundamental Investors, an assumed investment of $10,000 made in 1949 would by the end of 1963, with dividends reinvested and with security profits distributions accepted in additional shares, have amounted to $65,744. Over the 10-year period, January 1, 1954, though December 31, 1963, the $10,000 investment, under the same assumptions, would have grown to $33,850. See Figure 15–2. This is, of course, a fine performance, and it is the use of statistics such as these that have brought total investment in mutual funds from $400 million in 1941 to over $25 billion today. But Fundamental Investors turned in one of the better performances. A good many funds did not do as well,

FIGURE 15–2

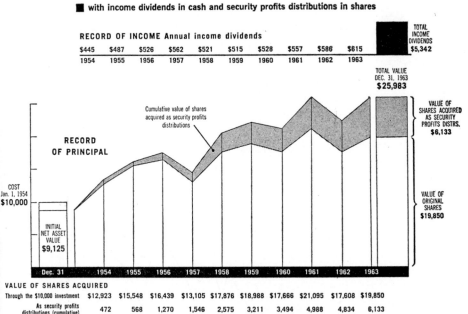

■ with income dividends in cash and security profits distributions in shares

										TOTAL INCOME DIVIDENDS
RECORD OF INCOME Annual income dividends										
$445	$487	$526	$562	$521	$515	$528	$557	$586	$615	$5,342
1954	1955	1956	1957	1958	1959	1960	1961	1962	1963	

TOTAL VALUE
DEC. 31. 1963
$25,983

Cumulative value of shares acquired as security profits distributions

RECORD OF PRINCIPAL

VALUE OF SHARES ACQUIRED AS SECURITY PROFITS DISTRS.
$6,133

COST
Jan. 1, 1954
$10,000

VALUE OF ORIGINAL SHARES
$19,850

INITIAL NET ASSET VALUE
$9,125

Dec. 31	1954	1955	1956	1957	1958	1959	1960	1961	1962	1963

VALUE OF SHARES ACQUIRED										
Through the $10,000 investment	$12,923	$15,548	$16,439	$13,105	$17,876	$18,988	$17,666	$21,095	$17,608	$19,850
As security profits distributions (cumulative)	472	568	1,270	1,546	2,575	3,211	3,494	4,988	4,834	6,133
TOTAL VALUE	$13,395	$16,116	$17,709	$14,651	$20,451	$22,199	$21,160	$26,083	$22,442	$25,983

Initial net asset value is the amount received by the Fund after deducting from the cost of the investment the sales charge as described in the prospectus. The dollar amounts of security profits distributions accepted in shares were: 1954 - $450, 1955 - None, 1956 - $596, 1957 - $640, 1958 - $332, 1959 - $438, 1960 - $538, 1961 - $665, 1962 - $782, 1963 - $586 — Total - $5,027.

SOURCE: Fundamental Investors, Inc.

and a number did not match the capital appreciation of standard stock indexes, such as Dow-Jones or Standard & Poor's. It is this type of comparison which brings us to the second view.

The second view compares the performance of a given fund with the investment results which would have followed had the same amount of money been placed across the board directly in the stocks comprising, say, the Dow-Jones industrial average. In 1949 one of the longest and greatest bull markets in U.S. history began. From December 31, 1949, to April, 1964, the Dow-Jones industrial average rose from 200 to 830, a rise of 315 percent. Only a minority of the funds equaled or exceeded this performance. Many of the funds, despite their professional management, did not do as well.

This type of comparison—contrasting, for example, the Standard & Poor's stock index performance with that of any given fund—can be undertaken at a glance by using *Johnson's Charts,* published annually by Hugh A. Johnson, Buffalo, New York. This volume has a chart for each fund and also overlays of the Standard & Poor's index and of the performance of the stock of many individual companies, such as Du Pont, Sears Roebuck, etc. You simply place the overlay on the chart of a given fund, and you can see a comparison or contrast of performance at a glance. It is a very useful volume, and any prospective investor in mutual funds should study it carefully before buying. It helps materially in the difficult process of deciding which fund to select. Individual funds can be compared to the average of all balanced funds or the average of all stock funds.

The variety of ways by which *Johnson's Charts* enable you to

FIGURE 15–3

Johnson Stock Fund Average*

January 1, 1954—December 31, 1963

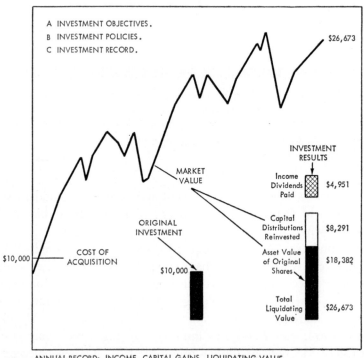

A INVESTMENT OBJECTIVES.
B INVESTMENT POLICIES.
C INVESTMENT RECORD.

$26,673

INVESTMENT RESULTS

MARKET VALUE

Income Dividends Paid — $4,951

ORIGINAL INVESTMENT

Capital Distributions Reinvested — $8,291

COST OF ACQUISITION

$10,000

$10,000

Asset Value of Original Shares — $18,382

Total Liquidating Value — $26,673

ANNUAL RECORD: INCOME, CAPITAL GAINS, LIQUIDATING VALUE.

* Chart represents an assumed investment of $10,000 in the fund with realized capital gains taken in additional shares.
Source: Reproduced by permission of *Johnson's Investment Company Charts.*

compare and measure market performance may be seen by reviewing Figures 15–3 through 15–6. Figure 15–3 shows the 10-year performance of the Johnson stock fund average. You can compare any individual fund performance with the average. For example, Figure 15–4 shows the comparable results for the Dreyfus Fund. Clearly this fund performed much better than the average. Tables are also provided

FIGURE 15–4

Dreyfus Fund, Inc.

January 1, 1954—December 31, 1963

OBJECTIVES: Growth of capital and income, with emphasis on capital appreciation.
POLICY: Generally fully invested position in common stocks, but management policy is flexible.

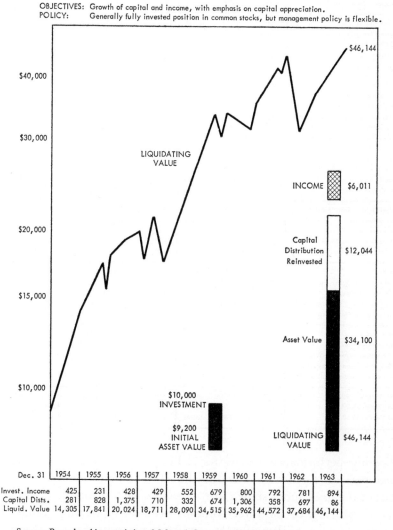

Dec. 31	1954	1955	1956	1957	1958	1959	1960	1961	1962	1963
Invest. Income	425	231	428	429	552	679	800	792	781	894
Capital Dists.	281	828	1,375	710	332	674	1,306	358	697	86
Liquid. Value	14,305	17,841	20,024	18,711	28,090	34,515	35,962	44,572	37,684	46,144

SOURCE: Reproduced by permission of *Johnson's Investment Company Charts.*

FIGURE 15–5

10–Year Summary Table—Stock Funds

January 1, 1954—December 31, 1963

($10,000 Initial Investment)

FUND	ALL DISTRIBUTIONS TAKEN IN CASH			CAPITAL DISTRIBUTIONS REINVESTED IN STOCK			CAPITAL DISTRIBUTIONS AND INVESTMENT INCOME REINVESTED IN STOCK		
	Investment Income	Capital Dists.	Liquidating Value	Investment Income	Cap. Dists. Reinvested(1)	Liquidating Value	Income Reinvested(2)	Cap. Dists. Reinvested	Liquidating Value
Aberdeen Fund, Inc.	$ 3,400	$ 3,500	$23,900	$ 3,827	$ 3,904	$29,230	$ 4,277	$ 4,350	$35,500
Affiliated Fund, Inc.	4,434	5,657	15,576	5,550	7,049	24,086	6,660	8,600	33,101
American Mutual Fund, Inc.	3,862	8,641	15,324	5,509	11,990	29,144	6,483	14,010	38,769
Atomics, Physics & Science Fund	3,201	3,356	13,196	3,549	3,695	16,645	3,967	4,097	20,594
Axe-Houghton Stock Fund, Inc.	3,022	6,066	12,231	3,805	7,741	20,162	4,384	9,066	26,140
Blue Ridge Mutual Fund	3,608	7,588	11,801	5,097	10,394	22,749	6,227	12,159	31,083
Broad Street Investing Corp.	5,511	4,068	18,416	6,335	4,639	24,065	7,651	5,613	33,748
Bullock Fund, Ltd.	4,433	6,903	16,029	5,508	8,673	25,739	6,509	10,270	34,282
Canada General Fund, Ltd.	503	—	23,063	503	—	23,063	508	—	23,545
Canadian Fund, Inc.	3,444	3,766	14,132	3,871	4,250	18,440	4,231	4,837	23,047
Century Shares Trust	2,734	4,007	24,919	3,173	4,603	32,637	3,498	5,102	38,671
Chemical Fund, Inc.	3,605	5,947	23,619	4,257	7,026	32,617	4,748	7,896	39,437
Colonial (The) Fund, Inc.	5,311	5,671	16,332	6,529	6,890	24,351	7,904	8,421	34,256
Colonial Growth & Energy Shares, Inc.	2,993	5,195	11,913	3,722	6,290	17,970	4,177	7,059	22,369
Commonwealth Stock Fund, Inc.	3,210	1,092	21,838	3,562	1,115	23,019	3,993	1,307	28,272
Composite Fund, Inc.	2,671	5,401	12,834	3,692	6,755	20,188	4,211	7,670	25,325
Corporate Leaders Trust Fd.Cer.Ser.B	4,525	3,482	11,636	4,825	3,893	24,841	5,665	4,545	32,656
Crown Western - Diversified Fund	4,124	7,622	12,932	5,053	9,958	22,120	5,970	11,897	30,514
Delaware Fund, Inc.	3,798	6,874	13,450	4,715	8,772	21,898	5,509	10,613	29,635
deVegh Mutual Fund, Inc.	2,461	12,053	16,636	4,020	17,235	35,609	4,375	24,870	41,488
Diversified Growth Stock Fund	2,069	5,934	22,938	2,513	7,058	31,886	2,683	7,527	35,633
Dividend Shares, Inc.	4,379	4,660	17,241	5,137	5,502	24,119	6,038	6,567	32,158
Dreyfus Fund, Inc.	4,829	5,633	34,100	6,011	6,647	46,144	6,931	7,405	58,236
Eaton & Howard Stock Fund	4,284	3,056	22,156	4,739	3,341	26,463	5,397	3,784	33,397
Equity Fund, Inc.	3,417	6,252	17,618	4,272	7,709	26,096	Not Available		
Fidelity Fund, Inc.	5,016	5,561	18,551	5,912	6,574	26,235	6,982	7,935	35,400
Financial Industrial Fund, Inc.	4,336	4,501	16,727	5,003	5,131	22,481	5,917	6,070	30,191
Founders Mutual Fund	5,171	106	30,298	5,171	106	30,404	6,029	116	39,480
Franklin Custodian Funds-Cm.Stk.Ser.	4,517	6,250	18,778	5,811	7,735	28,600	6,909	9,453	38,584
Franklin Custodian Funds-Util. Ser.	3,918	4,767	21,123	4,759	5,753	29,938	5,569	6,835	39,022
Fund of America	3,844	5,709	17,354	4,486	6,792	24,492	5,252	8,181	32,157
Fundamental Investors, Inc.	4,622	4,407	19,266	5,341	5,027	25,953	6,197	5,857	33,850
Group Securities-Aerospace-Science Fd.	4,494	7,589	12,661	4,999	8,755	21,357	5,696	10,389	27,204
Group Securities-Common Stock Fund	5,637	5,647	14,564	7,006	6,865	22,200	8,897	8,754	34,019
Growth Industry Shares, Inc.	4,045	7,831	21,236	4,804	9,631	31,715	5,505	11,295	40,097
Guardian Mutual Fund	4,133	6,765	19,475	5,083	8,323	29,686	5,935	9,850	38,829
Hamilton Funds H-DA	3,778	3,103	15,724	4,328	3,450	19,926	4,984	4,016	26,199
Imperial Capital Fund, Inc.	2,343	5,884	12,393	2,884	7,549	20,138	3,230	8,628	24,730

SOURCE: *Johnson's Investment Company Charts.*

showing performance results for 10-year, 15-year, 20-year, and 25-year periods. Figure 15–5 shows the 10-year performance record for half of the stock funds shown in *Johnson's Charts.* Running your eye up and down each of the three columns headed "liquidating value" will give you a very quick notion of comparative results. Bear in mind that

FIGURE 15–6

Markets of the Period

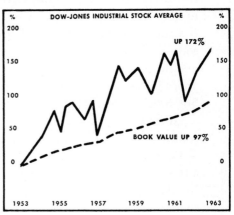

SECURITIES MARKETS
OF THE PERIOD

	January 1, 1954	December 31, 1963	% Change
Cost of Living Index	93.6	107.6	+15.0%
Value of the Dollar	100.0	87.0	−13.0%
Johnson Growth Stock Fund Average (31)	100.0	300.57	+200.6%
Johnson Stock Fund Average (71)	100.0	266.73	+166.7%
Dow-Jones Industrial Average (30)	280.90	762.95	+171.6%
Securities & Exchange Index (300)	51.6	151.5	+193.6%
S & P 500 Stock Index	24.81	75.02	+202.4%
Johnson Balanced Fund Average (38)	100.0	184.58	+84.6%
S & P Preferred Stocks	166.7	161.2	−3.3%
S & P Municipal Bonds	122.1	109.9	−10.0%
S & P Long-Term Government Bonds	103.7	86.95	−16.2%
S & P High-Grade Corporate Bonds	113.7	95.24	−16.2%

PRICE EARNINGS RATIOS AND INVESTMENT YIELDS

	DOW-JONES INDUSTRIAL AVERAGE					──INVESTMENT YIELDS──			
	Year End Average	Book Value	Earnings	Dividends	P/E Ratio	D-J Stocks	High Grade Bonds	Municipal Bonds	Government Bonds
1963	762.95	$441.06(E)	$41.00(E)	$23.41	18.6	3.07%	4.36%	3.32%	4.18%
1962	652.10	400.97	36.43	23.30	17.9	3.57	4.20	3.11	3.85
1961	731.14	365.33	31.91	22.71	22.9	3.11	4.44	3.44	4.11
1960	615.89	346.74	32.21	21.36	19.1	3.47	4.41	3.73	4.02
1959	679.36	339.02	34.31	20.74	19.8	3.05	4.38	3.95	4.08
1958	583.65	310.97	27.95	20.00	20.9	3.43	3.80	3.56	3.43
1957	435.69	298.69	36.08	21.61	12.1	4.96	3.91	3.60	3.47
1956	499.47	284.78	33.34	22.99	15.0	4.60	3.38	2.93	3.08
1955	488.40	271.77	35.78	21.58	13.7	4.42	3.04	2.53	2.84
1954	404.39	248.98	28.40	17.47	14.2	4.32	2.87	2.37	2.55
1953	280.90	$224.26	$27.23	$16.11	10.3	5.74%	3.18%	2.72%	2.94%
% Change	172%	97%	51%	45%					

Note again, that despite the irregularities in market prices, earnings and dividends, there is a continuous build-up in the book-value of the Dow-Jones Industrial Stock Average. This basic value is constantly "filling-in" behind stock prices and pushing them on to higher market appraisals.

SOURCE: *Johnson's Investment Company Charts.*

while these are all stock funds (there are separate tables and charts for balanced funds), the objectives may vary and thus you should turn to the "tablistics" section, which tabulates the essential characteristics and facts about each fund covered. An interesting set of comparisons is also provided for the Johnson Growth Stock Fund Average, and the Stock Fund Average with the three leading stock indexes, Dow-Jones Industrials, the SEC 300 Stock Index, and the Standard & Poor's 500-Stock Index. This comparison is shown in Figure 15–6.

Wiesenberger's *Investment Companies* annual also compares and contrasts funds according to their performance record in a variety of ways. Funds are classified by objective and a 10-year illustration of a $10,000 investment is developed on a basis which permits comparison. In addition the approximate percent net change in net asset value per share with capital gains (reinvested) plus income dividends (received in cash) is calculated for varying periods of time for both open-end and closed-end investment companies.[3] A 10-year performance chart for each individual fund listed is also presented. Finally, Wiesenberger computes composite indexes of mutual fund performance by type of fund. These are shown in Figure 15–7.

Each year *Forbes Magazine* publishes a special report on mutual fund performance. It asks and answers such questions as "How well did the fund do in keeping up with (or ahead of) the stock market? How big is the fund? How much income? How do its costs compare? What have you done for me lately?" *Forbes* compares the performance of each mutual fund over (*a*) the long bull market and (*b*) the more recent rise since 1962, with the performance of the Standard & Poor's 500-stock average and with the *Forbes* index of 10 stock funds. The results are shown in Appendix A to this chapter. An investment of $100 in the Standard & Poor's 500 stocks in 1953 increased to $297 by mid-1963. The average of the 10 stock funds rose to $279. The Standard & Poor's stocks paid a dividend return of 3.9 percent while the 10-fund average was 3.1 percent. Some individual funds performed much better than the 10-stock fund average. You can determine which ones by looking down the first column under "Management Results."

Forbes declares: "The survey demonstrates the nature of mutual funds in general. A glance down the columns shows clearly that no one has made a killing in the funds. Over the past decade, only 21 percent of all stock funds outperformed the Standard & Poor's 500, and almost half

---

[3] See Chapter XI "Appraisal of Management," *Investment Companies, op. cit.*

FIGURE 15-7

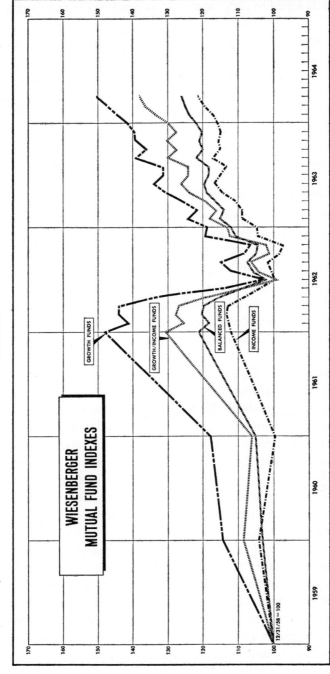

SOURCE: *Investment Companies*, Arthur Wiesenberger & Co.

of the others failed to come within 15 percent of the Standard & Poor's showing."[4]

Note especially the section on the last page of Appendix A entitled "The Funds vs. the Big Twenty." This compares individual stock performance over the 1953–63 period with both the Standard & Poor's average and the 10-stock fund average. While $100 invested in Standard & Poor's stocks rose to $297, in the 10-stock fund average to $279, $100 invested in General Electric rose to $324, in General Motors to $377, in General Telephone and Electronics to $750, in Sears Roebuck to $485, in Texaco to $592, and in IBM to $1,465.

Investment Company Act of 1940

Because of the abuses to which investment companies were subject prior to the stock-market crash of 1929, Congress, after an exhaustive five-year study by the SEC, passed the Investment Company Act of 1940. This Act required full disclosure and aimed to prevent the speculation and manipulation by management which had been prevalent. Since the Act requires a minimum capital of $100,000 before the stock of an investment company may be offered for sale to the public, it serves to discourage companies without some potential financial strength from trying to come into existence.

The law provides for more conservative capital structures for investment companies. Under the rules of the Securities and Exchange Commission, open-end investment companies incorporated after 1940 may issue only common stock, but they may enjoy limited leverage through the medium of bank borrowings. Assets must, however, cover bank loans at least three times. With the exception of refunding operations, the Act provides that funded debt (or bank loans) created after 1940 by closed-end companies must be covered by assets at least three times as large, and their new issues of preferred stocks must be covered twice by assets.

According to the Act, investment policies of an investment company must be stated clearly and specifically, and policies once declared cannot be changed without the stockholders' consent. This effectively prevents the sudden conversion of a diversified list of marketable securities into a nondiversified list. The law requires semiannual reports on investment company operations, but the majority of companies publish quarterly statements. Sale of management contracts is discouraged by a provision of the Act that such contracts are automatically terminated if transferred.

---

[4] See *Special Report: Forbes Mutual Fund Survey: 1963*, p. 4.

Many regulations govern investment companies' boards of directors, sales of securities, advertising, etc., and such safeguards have helped greatly to strengthen public respect for and confidence in investment companies. See Appendix B to this chapter.

Income Taxes

Earnings of ordinary corporations are subject to income tax. Then the persons who receive dividends out of corporate earnings are also taxed. This is double taxation—the same income taxed twice. If an investment company received this already taxed dividend income, paid a tax on it, and paid dividends to its own shareholders, who were again taxed, we would have triple taxation of the same income.

The Internal Revenue Law permits investment companies which are irrevocably registered as regulated investment companies, and which agree to distribute at least 90 percent of the dividends and interest received from the securities they own, to avoid triple taxation on the earnings distributed, although they must pay the ordinary corporate income tax on any such earnings retained. They enjoy a like exemption on long-term capital gains distributed, but they are subject to the usual 25 percent tax on such gains retained. The latter provision may be harmful in that capital gains cannot be retained (without incurring the 25 percent tax) to offset capital losses, which are bound to occur sooner or later.

Thus, under the Internal Revenue Code, investment companies which qualify as such are *not* taxed on any of their income or capital gains which they pay out. The investor in shares of open- or closed-end investment companies is taxed at the same rates as if he had realized the income and capital gains—paid him by the investment company—from his own direct investments.

Invest in Common Stock Directly or Buy Mutual Fund Shares?

Well-managed investment companies may be in a position to handle the problems of selection, timing, and diversification of security purchases and sales more effectively than an individual with moderate resources. Which securities to buy and which to sell are difficult problems which can perhaps best be answered by analysts who have had sufficient training in such areas as accounting, economics, and finance and who have had years of experience. Not only do investment companies have their own staffs, skilled in such work, but they can employ outside counsel whenever it is deemed necessary. With the best of resources at one's command, wise selection of securities is not easy; for the individual with few of these resources at hand, it is quite difficult. Not only is it necessary to choose the right securities to buy or sell but it is equally as important to time the purchases and sales correctly. If the individual feels unable to do this for himself, he can pass the problem along to an investment company to do it for him. In this way he may secure the advantages of such techniques as dollar averaging and automatic formula timing, which he may not understand.

But even if he turns to the investment company to solve his investment problems, there still remains one major problem which he cannot unload in this fashion. He must make at least one judgment and one decision—and it is a major one—himself: he must decide which of the many and diverse investment companies, with their very different objectives and unequal performances, he wishes to choose. This is a decision which you should not let a salesman make for you. It is a most important judgment and should only be arrived at after considerable investigation and study. If you do decide to buy mutual fund shares, don't let yourself be sold; decide for yourself after you have all the facts.

Forbes declared:

Nevertheless, in the light of events the average investor can draw some useful conclusions. Probably the most basic lesson is simply this: mutual fund investing is not the simple procedure that many salesmen try to make it. The funds, obviously, differ radically from one another in investment slant and management dexterity.

To invest intelligently, therefore, the investor must make a choice. Does he want a "growth" stock for the long pull? A diversified commitment in a single promising industry? A changing approach which gives management full power to switch money around as conditions change? Or a low-geared stake in stocks through a balanced fund?

If you are smart enough, however, to pick and choose intelligently from among the many investment companies now on the market, you are smart enough to pick and choose common stocks directly. It wouldn't have been very difficult 5, 10, or 15 years ago to decide that Du Pont, General Electric, General Motors, IBM, Sears Roebuck, or Texaco were good common stocks to buy, and if you had you would have done better financially and saved money in expenses as compared with investment in most mutual funds.

Mutual Funds and Insurance

Occasionally one hears of an unscrupulous mutual fund salesman who attempts to persuade elderly persons to cash in their life insurance and use the proceeds to buy mutual fund shares. While there is a place in a total financial program for both life insurance and investment company shares, the latter are no substitute for the former when matters of death, family security, and protection of dependents are involved. Insurance is the quickest way for a young man to create an estate. It provides the older man with income should he live or death benefits that are certain for his dependents should he die. Insurance should be the keystone for meeting the basic needs of your family in case of your death. Mutual fund investment based on the fluctuating market price of common stock is too uncertain where maximum security is required. It would be most unwise to liquidate a basic insurance protection program to permit investment in mutual shares. If and when resources permit expansion and diversification in a financial program, then common stock investment can be undertaken, either directly or through mutual funds. A well-rounded financial program has room for fixed dollar as well as variable dollar investment outlets. But if there is not enough to go around, life insurance should receive priority.[5]

---

[5] For more detailed discussion see "Buy Term Insurance and Invest the Difference?," *Changing Times, The Kiplinger Magazine,* October, 1962.

Forbes Comparative Mutual Fund Performance

1963

MUTUAL FUND REPORT

	OTHER DATA.			FORBES PERFORMANCE RATING*		MANAGEMENT RESULTS		
Assets in Millions	Sales Charge %	Annual Expenses (Cents per $100)		In Rising Markets	In Declining Markets	In the 1953-1963 Bull Market	In the 1962-1963 Market Rise	Dividend Return %
						$100 Ended as . .		
			Standard & Poor's 500 Stock Average	—	—	$297.09	$126.70	3.9%
			Average of 10 stock funds in FORBES Index	— 1	+ 1	$279.15	$124.53	3.1%

COMMON STOCK FUNDS

$25.2	8.5%	$0.76	Aberdeen Fund	+ 4	— 4	$324.57	$127.61	2.2%
1.8	8.75	0.85	Advisers Fund	—10	+ 3	199.52	125.04	3.0
858.7	7.5	0.41	Affiliated Fund	— 5	+ 5	260.24	124.29	3.7
1.7	1.0	1.64	Leon B. Allen Fund	— 1	+ 3	328.58	118.29	2.6
0.5	none	2.43	American Enterprise Fund (started 9/58)	—	— 3	—	120.00	1.2
3.5	7.5	1.03	American Growth Fund (started 8/58)	—	+ 1	—	128.81	2.4
8.9	none	1.37	American Investors Fund (started 1/58)	—	— 1	—	145.47	none
205.4	8.5	0.69	American Mutual Fund	+ 2	+ 1	311.80	126.37	3.3
1.0	7.5	1.50	Apache Fund (started 9/56)	— 1	— 3	—	117.00	1.4
51.0	8.5	0.75	Associated Fund Trust	—11	+ 2	203.50	116.66	3.8
2.9	2.0	0.96	Associations Investment Fund (started 3/60)	—	—	—	123.20	2.3
44.5	8.25	0.74	Atomics, Physics & Science Fund (started 12/53)	—11	— 3	175.87△	118.37	3.0
8.9	8.5	0.97	Axe-Houghton Stock Fund	— 8	+ 6	225.65	127.12	2.6
21.8	8.0	1.03	Axe Science & Electronics Corp. (started 2/55)	— 4	+ 2	—	116.30	1.9
36.3	8.5	0.79	Blue Ridge Mutual Fund	— 5	+ 1	258.19	123.20	3.1
3.3	8.5	1.22	Bondstock Corp.	— 1	— 5	235.23	115.54	2.3
277.9	7.5	0.23	Broad Street Investing Corp.	— 5	+ 3	266.85	126.67	3.9
80.7	8.67	0.45	Bullock Fund	— 3	+ 2	284.01	125.74	3.7
2.9	8.5	1.00	California Fund (started 1/54)	— 7	— 1	205.52△	127.18	1.2
0.2	8.75	1.00	Cambridge Growth Fund (started 4/61)	—	—	—	101.09	0.4
112.0	8.75	0.94	Capital Life Insurance Shares (started 1/60)	—	—	—	137.11	0.3
0.8	8.5	0.46	Cardinal Investors Fund (started 2/59)	—	+ 2	—	135.22	1.3
116.8	8.5	0.36	Century Shares Trust	+ 6	0	361.73	138.67	1.5
30.6	8.5	0.68	The Chase Fund of Boston (started 7/58)	—	— 2	—	114.08	1.1
265.9	8.0	0.43	Chemical Fund	+ 5	— 2	327.90	128.28	2.2
111.1	8.5	0.64	The Colonial Fund	— 5	+ 3	274.02	121.27	3.7
48.5	8.5	0.76	Colonial Growth & Energy Shares	— 7	— 3	206.27	125.19	2.0
1.3	8.0	NA	Common Stock Fund of State Bond & Mortage Co. (started 5/62)	—	—	—	130.55	1.2
0.8	7.5	1.60	Commonwealth Fund for Growth (started 9/61)	—	—	—	117.17	0.6
35.4	8.5	0.61	Commonwealth Income Fund (started 11/57)	—	+ 6	—	113.91	4.8
21.1	8.5	0.65	Commonwealth Stock Fund	— 2	— 2	263.58	120.94	2.3
17.1	8.0	0.91	Composite Fund	—10	+ 7	223.71	117.47	2.8
1.3	8.0	0.75	Consumers Investment Fund (started 5/58)	—	+ 3	—	121.48	2.4
1.2	none	1.29	Continental Mutual Investment (started 11/59)	—	+ 1	—	138.86	none
74.7	7.5	0.25	Corporate Leaders Trust—Series "B"	— 4	+ 3	263.23	124.72	3.5
			Crown Western Investments					
1.6	8.5	0.83	Dallas Fund (started 2/54)	— 1	— 4	236.84△	118.87	1.2
8.4	8.5	0.92	Diversified Fund	— 3	— 1	259.45	117.12	3.1
142.5	8.5	0.67	Delaware Fund	— 2	— 3	249.30	128.55	2.7
18.4	8.5	0.81	Delaware Income Fund (started 3 57)	— 7	+ 7	—	117.64	5.3
21.5	none	1.25	De Vegh Mutual Fund	+ 3	— 3	374.82	124.98	2.2
117.0	8.75	0.69	Diversified Growth Stock Fund	+ 7	— 4	356.15	125.33	1.2

△Fund was not operating for full period. NA—Not available.

Explanation of Column Headings

Only funds in existence for most of the measured periods are given a FORBES Performance Rating.
"In the 1953-1963 Bull Market" covers the period from Sept. 30, 1953 to June 30, 1963.
"In the 1962-1963 Market Rise" extends from June 30, 1962 to June 30, 1963.
All capital gains distributions have been plowed back into more stock but regular dividends have not.
All ratings are based on investments at net asset value and do not allow for sales charges.
Dividend Return based on June 30, 1962 prices and succeeding 12-month payout.
Annual Expenses include management fee and operating expenses as a percentage of average net assets.

* If a fund betters the Standard & Poor's average by 1 to 4.99 percent, *Forbes* allows the fund plus 1 for the period. Topping the Standard & Poor's by 5 to 9.99 percent earns a fund plus 2. The ranges climb at 5-point intervals up to 50 percentage points; above this upper figure no fund is given more than plus 13. The same range in reverse applies to subpar performance. If a fund has tended to climb faster than the Standard & Poor's, it shows a plus rating; if not, a minus.

APPENDIX A TO CHAPTER 15 (Continued)

Forbes Comparative Mutual Fund Performance

1963

MUTUAL FUND REPORT

OTHER DATA				FORBES PERFORMANCE RATING		MANAGEMENT RESULTS		
Assets in Millions	Sales Charge %	Annual Expenses (Cents per $100)		In Rising Markets	In Declining Markets	In the 1953-1963 Bull Market	In the 1962-1963 Market Rise	Dividend Return %
						$100 Ended as. .		
			Standard & Poor's 500 Stock Average	—	—	$297.09	$126.70	3.9%
			Average of 10 stock funds in FORBES Index	— 1	+ 1	$279.15	$124.53	3.1%
			COMMON STOCK FUNDS					
$327.1	8.67%	$0.52	Dividend Shares.......................	— 6	+ 4	$263.23	$125.26	3.4%
441.7	8.0	0.64	Dreyfus Fund.........................	+ 7	0	476.53	126.00	2.7
199.0	7.0	0.55	Eaton & Howard Stock Fund.............	— 2	— 1	290.97	124.18	2.7
29.8	8.5	0.89	Electronics Investment Corp. (started 5/55)..........	+ 2	— 2	—	110.77	1.6
31.6	none	1.02	Energy Fund (started 10/55)............	+ 5	— 3	—	130.54	1.3
24.2	3.5	1.19	Equity Fund...........................	— 1	+ 2	284.85	122.62	2.5
3.7	none	1.00	Fairfield Securities (started 10/60).....			—	132.94	none
8.0	8.5	1.04	Federated Growth Fund (started 11/55)....	0	— 3	—	115.93	1.4
151.2	8.0	0.71	Fidelity Capital Fund (started 5/58).................	—	+ 3	—	123.45	1.7
453.6	7.5	0.53	Fidelity Fund........................	0	— 2	280.02	125.48	3.2
71.8	8.0	0.78	Fidelity Trend Fund (started 6/58).......	—	+ 5	—	128.28	1.6
255.5	8.5	0.66	Financial Industrial Fund..............	— 1	— 5	249.19	123.30	2.8
5.3	8.5	0.98	Florida Growth Fund (started 2/57).......	— 4	+ 6	—	115.79	2.3
3.7	8.5	1.45	Florida Mutual Fund (started 1/54).......	— 8	— 3	154.48△	129.27	3.4
0.5	8.5	0.02	Foundation Stock Fund (started 10/59).....	—	— 3	—	129.84	2.2
99.1	8.0	0.72	Founders Mutual Fund...................	+ 3	— 1	322.68	126.34	3.0
5.0	8.5	NA	Foursquare Fund (started 4/62)..........	—	—	—	124.79	2.7
			Franklin Custodian Funds					
4.7	8.75	0.99	Common Stock Series...............	+ 1	— 1	325.34	129.46	1.8
8.9	8.75	0.89	Utilities Series..................	— 2	+ 8	350.50	126.87	1.6
4.9	8.0	1.00	Fund of America......................	— 6	+ 6	271.11	122.95	2.0
708.5	8.75	0.57	Fundamental Investors.................	0	— 3	297.06	125.80	3.0
1.7	8.5	1.00	General Securities....................	— 4	— 1	220.34	133.52	1.5
			Group Securities					
13.1	8.5	0.74	Aerospace-Science Fund.............	+ 6	— 4	257.64	116.22	1.3
184.4	8.5	0.72	Common Stock Fund.................	— 7	+ 4	242.49	120.54	4.4
32.4	2.91	0.49	Growth Industry Shares.............	+ 5	— 3	341.21	123.57	2.4
20.0	none	0.75	Guardian Mutual Fund.................	— 5	+ 4	287.77	123.62	2.8
120.3	8.5	0.74	Hamilton Funds—Series H-C7..........	— 6	0	221.90	119.80	3.2
23.0	8.0	1.20	Imperial Capital Fund.................	— 5	0	217.57	122.05	2.1
149.0	8.5	0.45	Incorporated Income Fund (started 10/54)...........	—12	+ 6	—	112.83	4.8
266.8	8.5	0.51	Incorporated Investors................	+ 1	— 7	239.13	121.25	2.7
0.2	8.5	0.68	Industry Fund of America (started 4/61)............	—	—	—	124.18	0.7
			Institutional Shares					
133.5	8.5	0.69	Growth Fund.......................	0	— 5	249.39	126.08	1.8
38.0	8.5	0.71	Income Fund.......................	—13	+ 5	192.98	120.86	5.3
3.1	8.5	0.70	Insurance & Bank Stock Fund (started 1/60)........	—	—	—	134.71	0.6
6.1	8.8	1.03	Insurance Investors Fund (started 6/57)............	+ 6	+ 3	—	125.17	2.3
277.9	8.5	0.57	Investment Co. of America...............	+ 1	— 1	330.50	124.21	2.9
73.6	8.5	0.58	Investment Trust of Boston.............	— 2	— 1	276.92	124.89	3.3
2.3	8.5	1.00	Investors Research Fund (started 4/59)..............	—	— 2	—	128.97	1.5
1117.0	7.5	0.55	Investors Stock Fund..................	0	— 2	276.61	125.46	2.8
304.0	7.5	0.53	Investors Variable Payment Fund (started 5/57)......	+ 4	— 3	—	128.73	1.6
28.9	1.96	0.82	Istel Fund (started 1/54).....................	— 7	+ 6	269.54△	122.11	3.9

△Fund was not operating for full period. NA—Not available.

Explanation of Column Headings

Only funds in existence for most of the measured periods are given a FORBES Performance Rating.
"In the 1953-1963 Bull Market" covers the period from Sept. 30, 1953 to June 30, 1963.
"In the 1962-1963 Market Rise" extends from June 30, 1962 to June 30, 1963.
All capital gains distributions have been plowed back into more stock but regular dividends have not.
All ratings are based on investments at net asset value and do not allow for sales charges.
Dividend Return based on June 30, 1962 prices and succeeding 12-month payout.
Annual Expenses include management fee and operating expenses as a percentage of average net assets.

APPENDIX A TO CHAPTER 15 (Continued)

Forbes Comparative Mutual Fund Performance

1963

MUTUAL FUND REPORT

OTHER DATA				FORBES PERFORMANCE RATING		MANAGEMENT RESULTS		
Assets in Millions	Sales Charge %	Annual Expenses (Cents per $100)		In Rising Markets	In Declining Markets	In the 1953-1963 Bull Market	In the 1962-1963 Market Rise	Dividend Return %
						$100 Ended as . .		
			Standard & Poor's 500 Stock Average	—	—	$297.09	$126.70	3.9%
			Average of 10 stock funds in FORBES Index	− 1	+ 1	$279.15	$124.53	3.1%
			COMMON STOCK FUNDS					
$1.1	8.5%	$1.70	Ivest Fund (started 1/59)........................	—	+ 7	—	$127.20	none
33.8	none	0.78	The Johnston Mutual Fund........................	−10	+ 5	$239.47	119.87	2.6%
			Keystone Custodian Funds					
90.6	8.3	0.67	K-1	−19	+ 8	133.07	115.80	5.4
110.9	8.3	0.61	K-2	+ 1	− 2	302.83	123.41	1.9
34.4	8.3	0.69	S-1	− 1	0	296.93	122.68	2.5
116.0	8.3	0.62	S-2	− 4	+ 2	265.40	125.25	3.6
79.8	8.3	0.67	S-3	+12	− 6	390.10	131.77	2.4
182.9	8.3	0.72	S-4	+13	− 4	393.26	125.41	2.4
3.2	8.7	1.09	Knickerbocker Growth Fund...................	0	− 5	245.68	130.98	1.0
108.9	*	0.67	Lazard Fund (started 7/58)...................	—	0	—	130.46	2.5
1.4	8.5	0.63	Liberty Fund (started 7/56)...................	0	− 1	—	120.04	2.8
58.2	8.5	0.67	Life Insurance Investors (started 7/57)............	+13	+ 1	—	133.58	0.4
6.5	8.25	0.82	Life Insurance Stock Fund (started 1/55)......	+12	+ 3	—	133.48	none
1.4	none	0.75	Mairs & Power Growth Fund (started 1/58)........	—	+ 2	—	122.42	2.4
			Managed Funds					
41.2	8.5	0.97	General Industries Shares..................	− 4	− 3	238.62	122.42	3.1
7.9	8.5	0.96	Special Investments (started 9/54)...........	0	− 8	—	113.01	0.4
612.9	8.5	0.43	Massachusetts Investors Growth Stock Fund........	+ 9	− 2	398.60	129.14	2.0
1776.8	8.5	0.18	Massachusetts Investors Trust..................	0	0	279.73	127.39	3.4
3.5	8.5	NA	Medical Securities Fund (started 5/62)...........	—	—	—	113.88	0.9
2.6	7.5	0.83	Midamerica Mutual Fund (started 1/61).............	—	—	—	121.33	1.6
			B.C. Morton Funds					
4.3	8.75	0.88	Growth Stock Series (started 2/56).............	+ 1	+ 3	—	120.07	1.1
7.3	8.75	0.88	Insurance Stock Series (started 2/56)...........	+ 7	+ 6	—	130.91	0.6
			Mutual Investing Foundation					
44.9	7.5	0.69	MIF Fund.....................	− 7	+ 3	258.20	118.73	4.6
4.4	7.5	0.75	MIF Growth Fund (started 2/61).................	—	—	—	127.44	2.4
0.6	8.75	1.00	Mutual Investment Co. of America..................	− 1	− 5	246.73	129.94	0.9
37.9	8.5	0.68	Mutual Investment Fund.....................	−12	+ 1	171.10	121.24	3.3
0.5	7.0	1.47	Mutual Securities Fund of Boston (started 7/58)......	—	+ 1	—	123.77	1.8
10.7	2.0	0.90	Mutual Trust........................	−11	+ 1	198.78	119.81	3.3
0.6	none	1.03	National Industries Fund (started 6/60)...........	—	—	—	129.11	1.8
341.7	7.5	0.23	National Investors Corp..........................	+ 5	0	388.63	130.83	2.5
			National Securities					
128.3	8.5	0.71	Growth Stocks Series.........................	+ 6	− 4	330.70	126.78	1.7
224.7	8.5	0.71	Stock Series.........................	− 6	− 2	228.71	117.52	4.6
4.2	none	1.90	Nelson Fund (started 11 58).....................	—	+ 9	—	114.42	0.9
0.2	8.5	1.64	New Jersey Growth Fund (started 10 58)...........	—	+ 3	—	116.15	5.3
11.2	none	0.73	Northeast Investors Trust.........................	−12	+ 8	244.42	111.89	4.9

Fund no longer selling new shares; existing shares traded over-the-counter. NA—Not available.

Explanation of Column Headings

Only funds in existence for most of the measured periods are given a FORBES Performance Rating.
"In the 1953-1963 Bull Market" covers the period from Sept. 30, 1953 to June 30, 1963.
"In the 1962-1963 Market Rise" extends from June 30, 1962 to June 30, 1963.
All capital gains distributions have been plowed back into more stock but regular dividends have not.
All ratings are based on investments at net asset value and do not allow for sales charges.
Dividend Return based on June 30, 1962 prices and succeeding 12-month payout.
Annual Expenses include management fee and operating expenses as a percentage of average net assets.

APPENDIX A TO CHAPTER 15 (Continued)

Forbes Comparative Mutual Fund Performance

1963
MUTUAL FUND REPORT

OTHER DATA				FORBES PERFORMANCE RATING		MANAGEMENT RESULTS		
Assets in Millions	Sales Charge %	Annual Expenses (Cents per $100)		In Rising Markets	In Declining Markets	In the 1953-1963 Bull Market	In the 1962-1963 Market Rise	Dividend Return %
						$100 Ended as..		
			Standard & Poor's 500 Stock Average	—	—	$297.09	$126.70	3.9%
			Average of 10 stock funds in FORBES Index	— 1	+ 1	$279.15	$124.53	3.1%
			COMMON STOCK FUNDS					
$16.6	8.5%	$0.84	Nucleonics, Chemistry & Electronics Shares (started 8/56)	0	+ 2	—	$118.38	2.1%
251.9	8.5	0.59	The One William Street Fund (started 6/58)	—	— 3	—	123.11	2.4
16.3	8.5	0.79	Oppenheimer Fund (started 4/59)	—	+ 2	—	125.66	1.1
0.8	8.0	1.59	Over-the-Counter Securities Fund (started 5/56)	+ 5	+ 3	—	104.44	0.9
3.0	0.5	1.00	Paramount Mutual Fund (started 10/58)	—	— 1	—	127.73	2.3
43.4	none	0.75	Penn Square Mutual Fund (started 11/57)	—	0	—	137.69	2.7
15.1	8.75	0.72	Peoples Securities Corp. (started 12/55)	+ 8	— 4	—	128.36	none
34.3	8.75	0.77	Philadelphia Fund	+ 2	+ 1	$319.70	125.83	2.6
31.2	0.99	0.46	Pine Street Fund	— 5	+ 4	278.56	123.73	4.0
0.2	8.5	1.04	Pioneer Enterprise Fund (started 7/57)	—	— 2	—	122.51	1.0
55.7	8.5	0.78	Pioneer Fund	— 5	+ 2	283.91	122.52	3.6
8.6	none	1.40	Rowe Price New Horizons Fund (started 6/60)	—	—	—	117.22	none
92.1	none	0.72	T. Rowe Price Growth Stock Fund	+ 6	+ 2	407.49	126.15	2.3
279.8	8.5	0.68	Putnam Growth Fund (started 11/57)	—	+ 2	—	122.30	1.4
0.6	none	3.86	The Regency Fund (started 8/57)	—11	— 5	—	116.40	none
5.7	8.5	1.02	Research Investing Corp. (started 6/59)	—	0	—	111.74	2.2
2.9	8.0	1.43	Revere Fund (started 8/59)	—	+ 4	—	116.82	1.1
0.6	8.5	4.89	Samson Fund (started 6/57)	— 3	+ 6	—	114.29	none
61.5	none	0.64	Scudder, Stevens & Clark Common Stock Fund	0	0	303.80	126.62	2.8
122.2	7.5	0.63	Selected American Shares	— 1	— 2	257.57	128.54	3.1
3.0	8.25	1.00	Shares in American Industry (started 12/59)	—	— 1	—	120.78	1.7
8.9	7.5	0.74	Southwestern Investors (started 2/54)	— 8	+ 6	219.69△	124.21	3.5
4.1	8.67	0.82	Sovereign Investors	— 6	0	234.96	121.39	3.9
225.4	*	0.52	State Street Investment Corp.	— 5	+ 1	260.92	126.27	2.6
2.4	7.5	0.85	Steadman Investment Fund (started 8/57)	+ 1	— 1	—	126.30	1.5
37.7	none	0.61	Stein Roe & Farnham Stock Fund (started 7/58)	+ 1	+ 1	—	128.01	2.5
5.5	8.0	1.59	Supervised Shares	— 7	+ 3	242.02	120.03	2.5
0.2	8.5	3.53	Technical Fund (started 11/60)	—	—	—	93.56	2.1
375.5	8.25	0.74	Television Electronics Fund	+ 3	— 2	345.26	120.58	2.2
58.1	8.5	0.65	Texas Fund	0	+ 2	334.28	132.05	2.1
0.2	8.75	0.50	Transwestern Mutual (started 6/61)	—	—	—	128.61	3.0
			Twentieth Century Investors					
6.9	8.5	0.97	Growth Investors (started 10/58)	—	+ 2	—	129.00	0.3
1.3	8.5	0.97	Income Investors (started 10/58)	—	+ 4	—	130.38	1.8
0.4	none	1.10	Trans-American Fund (started 8/60)	—	—	—	117.92	2.9
			United Funds					
697.5	8.5	0.55	Accumulative	— 1	0	312.51	124.64	3.2
38.3	8.5	0.62	Continental	— 3	— 4	224.18	120.76	2.6
407.3	8.5	0.57	Income	— 2	0	289.33	123.52	3.5
191.9	8.5	0.61	Science	+ 5	— 4	327.21	127.64	1.9

△Fund was not operating for full period.
*Fund no longer selling new shares; existing shares traded over-the-counter.

Explanation of Column Headings

Only funds in existence for most of the measured periods are given a FORBES Performance Rating.
"In the 1953-1963 Bull Market" covers the period from Sept. 30, 1953 to June 30, 1963.
"In the 1962-1963 Market Rise" extends from June 30, 1962 to June 30, 1963.
All capital gains distributions have been plowed back into stock but regular dividends have not.
All ratings are based on investments at net asset value and do not allow for sales charges.
Dividend Return based on June 30, 1962 prices and succeeding 12-month payout.
Annual Expenses include management fee and operating expenses as a percentage of average net assets.

APPENDIX A TO CHAPTER 15 (Continued)

Forbes Comparative Mutual Fund Performance

1963
MUTUAL FUND REPORT

	OTHER DATA		MUTUAL FUND REPORT	FORBES PERFORMANCE RATING		MANAGEMENT RESULTS		
Assets in Millions	Sales Charge %	Annual Expenses (Cents per $100)		In Rising Markets	In Declining Markets	In the 1953-1963 Bull Market	In the 1962-1963 Market Rise	Dividend Return %
						$100 Ended as..		
			Standard & Poor's 500 Stock Average	—	—	$297.09	$126.70	3.9%
			Average of 10 stock funds in FORBES Index	—1	+1	$279.15	$124.53	3.1%
			COMMON STOCK FUNDS					
$11.2	8.5%	$1.10	The Value Line Fund	—5	+2	$228.14	$132.17	2.2%
86.9	8.5	0.80	The Value Line Income Fund	—16	+3	148.25	115.18	6.0
18.0	8.5	1.03	The Value Line Special Situations Fund (started 5/56)..	+7	—4	—	118.08	1.2
0.7	8.5	0.76	Vanderbilt Mutual Fund (started 5/57)	—4	+1	—	124.87	3.8
2.5	8.5	1.00	Vanguard Fund (started 12/60)	—	—	—	119.60	1.7
0.9	none	0.73	Variable Stock Fund (started 3/57)	—9	+3	—	123.91	2.1
3.8	8.0	1.06	Varied Industry Plan (started 10/61)	—	—	—	120.21	2.7
0.6	7.5	2.70	Venture Securities Fund (started 8/56)	—5	+3	—	85.61	none
0.5	none	1.89	Wade Fund	—5	—1	226.65	121.23	1.2
12.8	8.5	0.74	Wall Street Investing Corp	—9	+6	234.99	119.55	3.0
46.9	8.5	0.77	Washington Mutual Investors Fund	+1	+2	334.33	124.47	3.9
75.5	8.0	0.74	Wellington Equity Fund (started 10/58)	—	—1	—	124.02	1.3
0.8	8.5	1.01	Western Industrial Shares (started 4/59)	—	+1	—	125.45	1.1
11.5	8.5	0.82	Winfield Growth Industries Fund	+3	0	297.60	133.08	0.4
21.0	7.5	0.67	Wisconsin Fund	—5	+3	251.61	121.81	2.8
0.9	8.3	4.32	Worth Fund (started 5/60)	—	—	—	117.45	0.9
			Average of 10 balanced funds in FORBES Index	—11	+5	$206.22	$118.09	3.8%
			BALANCED FUNDS					
$27.2	7.5%	$0.76	American Business Shares	—15	+9	$175.48	$116.33	3.7%
46.3	8.0	1.01	Axe-Houghton Fund A	—12	+5	196.32	125.87	3.4
198.8	8.0	0.85	Axe-Houghton Fund B	—10	+4	217.93	120.72	3.4
321.7	8.5	0.55	Boston Fund	—10	+7	242.32	117.06	3.4
30.2	7.65	0.66	Commonwealth Fund Indentures of Trust, A & B	—12	+5	201.93	117.49	3.6
164.4	8.5	0.55	Commonwealth Investment Co	—13	+5	196.59	115.50	3.6
10.4	8.0	0.94	Composite Bond & Stock Fund	—15	+9	195.11	111.55	3.4
1.5	none	0.88	Counselors Investment Fund	—12	+6	178.77	120.77	4.6
109.6	8.75	0.64	Diversified Investment Fund	—11	+6	202.42	116.67	4.3
9.7	none	0.63	Dodge & Cox Fund	—10	+4	209.75	120.98	3.0
218.5	7.0	0.55	Eaton & Howard Balanced Fund	—13	+6	206.01	116.36	3.4
12.4	7.5	0.77	Fiduciary Mutual Investing	—11	+6	232.33	119.21	3.2
4.4	8.5	0.56	Financial Industrial Income Fund (started 7/60)	—	—	—	120.92	5.4
1.3	8.75	0.85	Franklin Custodian—Income Series Shares	—11	+4	207.95	114.31	4.8
18.3	8.0	0.69	General Investors Trust	—14	+7	198.81	116.49	4.6
17.2	8.5	0.77	Group Securities—Fully Administered Fund	—13	+7	189.48	114.49	4.3
26.2	8.5	0.97	Income Foundation Fund	—11	+5	215.64	111.79	2.7
49.6	8.5	0.68	Income Fund of Boston (started 2/55)	—12	+4	—	118.40	5.7
66.5	8.5	0.68	Institutional Foundation Fund	—10	+4	224.93	119.60	3.9
2106.8	7.5	0.54	Investors Mutual	—12	+7	196.33	115.92	3.9
13.2	8.7	1.10	The Knickerbocker Fund	—10	+1	165.97	128.82	3.6

Explanation of Column Headings

Only funds in existence for most of the measured periods are given a FORBES Performance Rating.
"In the 1953-1963 Bull Market" covers the period from Sept. 30, 1953 to June 30, 1963.
"In the 1962-1963 Market Rise" extends from June 30, 1962 to June 30, 1963.
All capital gains distributions have been plowed back into more stock but regular dividends have not.
All ratings are based on investments at net asset value and do not allow for sales charges.
Dividend Return based on June 30, 1962 prices and succeeding 12-month payout.
Annual Expenses include management fee and operating expenses as a percentage of average net assets.

APPENDIX A TO CHAPTER 15 (Continued)
Forbes Comparative Mutual Fund Performance

1963

OTHER DATA			MUTUAL FUND REPORT	FORBES PERFORMANCE RATING		MANAGEMENT RESULTS		
Assets in Millions	Sales Charge %	Annual Expenses (Cents per $100)		In Rising Markets	In Declining Markets	In the 1953-1963 Bull Market	In the 1962-1963 Market Rise	Dividend Return %
						$100 Ended as. .		
			Average of 10 balanced funds in FORBES Index	—11	+ 5	$206.22	$118.09	3.8%
			BALANCED FUNDS					
$6.6	8.5%	$1.00	Lexington Income Trust	—16	+ 6	$172.90	$112.14	2.8%
107.4	none	0.66	Loomis-Sayles Mutual Fund	—14	+ 6	191.99	115.92	3.1
5.3	7.5	0.61	Horace Mann Fund (started 12/57)	—	+ 4	—	122.22	3.5
95.7	8.5	0.54	Massachusetts Life Fund	—13	+ 6	192.74	115.38	3.5
0.9	8.75	0.87	B. C. Morton—Income Series (started 7/57)	—13	+ 8	—	112.40	5.8
2.5	none	1.56	Mutual Shares Corp.	—10	+ 7	254.71	123.21	2.1
4.7	none	0.81	The Nassau Fund (started 10/57)	—	+ 5	—	121.80	3.3
			National Securities					
4.3	8.5	0.73	Balanced Series	—16	+ 7	157.25	116.06	4.4
87.1	8.5	0.73	Dividend Series	—12	0	161.84	126.44	5.8
88.4	8.5	0.72	Income Series	—13	+ 5	174.77	115.56	5.2
53.4	7.5	0.48	Nation-Wide Securities Co.	—13	+ 9	206.18	118.09	4.0
20.8	7.5	0.74	New England Fund	—14	+ 9	188.24	114.10	3.6
1.6	none	0.77	Newton Fund (started 8/60)	—	—	—	110.77	3.9
11.3	8.5	0.40	Provident Fund for Income (started 8/60)	—	—	—	113.98	5.9
1.5	none	0.72	The Prudential Fund of Boston	—14	+ 6	182.34	115.28	3.0
165.5	7.5	0.51	Puritan Fund	— 6	+ 4	236.84	121.41	5.0
311.5	8.5	0.45	The George Putnam Fund of Boston	— 8	+ 5	241.99	118.37	3.3
7.9	8.5	0.96	Quarterly Distribution Shares	—12	+ 3	184.20	116.57	4.1
7.0	none	0.64	Rittenhouse Fund	—12	+ 4	188.95	115.47	3.0
99.9	none	0.56	Scudder, Stevens & Clark Balanced Fund	—13	+ 5	194.23	119.13	3.4
3.4	8.5	0.84	Securities Fund	— 9	+ 5	238.05	117.59	2.8
2.5	7.5	0.69	Security Diversified Shares (started 6/60)	—	—	—	114.20	3.5
72.0	8.5	0.44	Shareholders' Trust of Boston	—13	+ 6	203.75	116.63	4.5
85.5	none	0.58	Stein Roe & Farnham Balanced Fund	— 8	+ 6	249.02	119.34	2.9
4.8	7.5	0.72	Sterling Investment Fund	—15	+ 5	164.56	117.94	4.3
1538.1	8.0	0.35	Wellington Fund	—11	+ 5	202.57	114.74	3.6
15.4	7.5	0.34	Whitehall Fund	—13	+ 7	207.46	115.24	3.7
			BONDS AND PREFERRED STOCK FUNDS					
$0.2	3.0%	NA	Atlantic Fund for Investment in U. S. Government Securities (started 8/61)	—	—	—	$100.19	2.7%
			Franklin Custodian Funds					
2.0	8.75	$1.00	Bond Series	—24	+ 8	$90.31	120.00	5.8
0.6	8.75	1.00	Preferred Series	—23	+ 6	107.65	112.87	6.4
33.4	6.5	0.47	Investors Selective Fund	—24	+13	114.10	102.85	5.0
			Keystone Custodian Funds					
5.9	4.15	0.33	B-1	—29	+16	94.51	100.90	4.1
11.3	8.3	0.65	B-2	—25	+13	98.54	108.58	5.1
50.9	8.3	0.65	B-3	—25	+12	103.10	113.76	6.4
78.8	8.3	0.65	B-4	—22	+ 5	111.92	117.50	6.6
			National Securities					
2.3	8.5	0.72	Bond Series	—24	+ 9	100.57	117.40	6.1
11.3	8.5	0.72	Preferred Stock Series	—24	+ 9	108.34	107.41	5.2

NA—Not available.

Explanation of Column Headings

Only funds in existence for most of the measured periods are given a FORBES Performance Rating.
"In the 1953-1963 Bull Market" covers the period from Sept. 30, 1953 to June 30, 1963.
"In the 1962-1963 Market Rise" extends from June 30, 1962 to June 30, 1963.
All capital gains distributions have been plowed back into more stock but regular dividends have not.
All ratings are based on investments at net asset value and do not allow for sales charges.
Dividend Return based on June 30, 1962 prices and succeeding 12-month payout.
Annual Expenses include management fee and operating expenses as a percentage of average net assets.

APPENDIX A TO CHAPTER 15 (Continued)

Forbes Comparative Mutual Fund Performance

1963 MUTUAL FUND REPORT

OTHER DATA				FORBES PERFORMANCE RATING		MANAGEMENT RESULTS		
Assets in Millions	Sales Charge %	Annual Expenses (Cents per $100)		In Rising Markets	In Declining Markets	In the 1953-1963 Bull Market	In the 1962-1963 Market Rise	Dividend Return %
						$100 Ended as . .		

FUNDS FOR INVESTING ABROAD

Assets in Millions	Sales Charge %	Annual Expenses	Fund	In Rising Markets	In Declining Markets	In the 1953-1963 Bull Market	In the 1962-1963 Market Rise	Dividend Return %
$55.4	8.5%	$0.62	Canada General Fund (started 8/54)	− 6	− 1	—	$123.81	†
34.1	7.5	0.75	Canadian Fund	− 8	0	$207.76	115.14	2.7%
7.8	8.5	1.00	Canadian International Growth Fund (started 6/56)	− 3	+ 2	—	119.12	†
2.4	8.5	0.70	Commonwealth International & General Fund (started 5/61)	—	—	—	111.33	1.9
1.5	8.75	0.91	International Investors (started 8/55)	− 4	+10	—	108.68	2.7
19.2	8.5	1.02	International Resources Fund	− 7	+ 1	272.21	118.81	2.3
65.0	7.5	0.56	Investors Inter-Continental Fund (started 5/55)	− 6	− 4	—	119.76	†
10.8	7.5	0.75	Keystone International Fund (started 10/54)	− 3	− 1	—	114.19	†
17.9	none	0.93	Loomis-Sayles Canadian and International Fund (started 4/61)	—	—	—	115.67	†
24.9	none	0.74	New York Capital Fund (started 8/54)	− 4	+ 1	—	118.43	†
39.5	none	0.69	Scudder Fund of Canada (started 6/54)	− 5	− 1	—	117.26	†
4.3	8.5	0.88	Templeton Growth Fund of Canada (started 10/54)	− 5	+ 8	—	107.76	†
4.2	8.5	1.00	UBS Fund of Canada (started 11/60)	—	—	—	121.76	†
10.1	8.0	0.79	United Funds of Canada (started 8/54)	−11	− 1	—	115.15	†
15.9	8.8	1.00	United International Fund (started 4/61)	—	—	—	105.53	†

THE FUNDS vs. THE BIG TWENTY

It is possible to rate individual stocks on the same bases as FORBES rates the funds. Below are comparable figures for 20 of the most widely held U.S. stocks. Several did far better than the average mutual funds, several far worse.

Stock	In Rising Markets	In Declining Markets	In the 1953-1963 Bull Market	In the 1962-1963 Market Rise	Dividend Return %
American Telephone & Telegraph	− 9	+ 9	$234.22	$116.27	3.5%
Bank of America	− 2	+ 1	224.12	133.77	4.2
Bethlehem Steel	− 2	− 4	264.52	90.11	5.1
Cities Service	− 3	+ 4	254.34	133.76	5.5
Columbia Gas System	−11	+ 8	228.57	115.94	4.4
Consolidated Edison	−13	+10	209.69	120.04	4.4
Du Pont**	+ 5	− 2	272.98	141.62	4.3
Ford Motor	+18	−10	—	134.95	4.7
General Electric	+ 4	− 2	324.10	132.77	3.4
General Motors	+ 6	+ 2	377.18	145.22	7.2
General Telephone & Electronics	+15	+ 2	750.00	124.53	4.0
International Business Machines	+29	+ 2	1465.89	128.59	1.0
Sears, Roebuck	+14	+ 4	485.05	139.73	2.6
Socony Mobil	− 8	+ 5	211.97	140.05	5.2
Sperry Rand	− 8	− 9	—	102.70	none
Standard Oil (Calif.)	− 3	+ 5	300.58	120.79	3.7††
Standard Oil (N. J.)	− 3	+ 2	297.28	136.75	5.2
Texaco	+13	+ 3	592.44	144.99	4.0
U. S. Steel	+ 8	−12	274.29	108.78	5.1
Westinghouse Electric	−11	− 2	160.39	132.55	4.5

†All dividends automatically reinvested; Canada General paid out for latest six months.
**Prices adjusted for distribution of one-half share of General Motors stock.   ††Plus stock.

Explanation of Column Headings

Only funds in existence for most of the measured periods are given a FORBES Performance Rating.
"In the 1953-1963 Bull Market" covers the period from Sept. 30, 1953 to June 30, 1963.
"In the 1962-1963 Market Rise" extends from June 30, 1962 to June 30, 1963.
All capital gains distributions have been plowed back into more stock but regular dividends have not.
All ratings are based on investments at net asset value and do not allow for sales charges.
Dividend Return based on June 30, 1962 prices and succeeding 12-month payout.
Annual Expenses include management fee and operating expenses as a percentage of average net assets.

Source: Reprinted from August 15, 1963 FORBES Magazine, 70 Fifth Avenue, New York, N.Y. 10011

APPENDIX B TO CHAPTER 15

Principal Provisions
of the
Investment Company Act of 1940:

REGISTRATION: All investment companies with 100 or more shareholders must register with the Securities and Exchange Commission. A company must have a minimum capital of $100,000 before it may publicly offer securities.

DIVERSIFICATION: The registration statement must clearly define the kind and quality of securities eligible under the investment policy. At least 75 percent of assets must be in cash or securities, and no individual investment of a diversified company can exceed 5 percent of its assets or 10 percent of the controlling stock of any company.

INVESTMENT POLICY: Important investment practices and policies, as well as specific investment objectives, must be detailed in the registration statement and cannot be altered in any way without the approval of a majority of shareholders. The charters of most mutual funds explicitly prohibit such speculative practices as buying securities on margin, selling short, or participating in joint trading accounts with others.

MANAGEMENT: All contracts with investment advisers must be approved by the shareholders and cannot be altered without the approval of a majority of the shareholders. The board of directors, or trustees as the case may be, is always subject to the approval of shareholders. Investment bankers, brokers, or others connected with the sale of securities must be in the minority. No more than 60 percent of the board may be officers or employees, or affiliated with the investment advisers of the fund. Directors, officers, trustees, or sponsors cannot sell general market securities to, or buy them from, the fund.

DIVIDENDS: The sources of all distributions must be accurately described to shareholders. Supplement Q of the Revenue Act of 1942 specifically exempts mutual funds from corporate taxes on all income and profits paid to shareholders, provided such payments represent at least 90 percent of net investment income and security profits.

REPORTS: Full disclosure of all investment activity, financial condition, income, expenses, salaries or fees of management, and current status of investments must be reported to shareholders at least twice each year and certified by independent auditors approved annually by shareholders. With few exceptions, these reports are issued quarterly.

SHARES: Each share represents an equal and proportionate claim on all assets, and no security can ever be subsequently issued with a prior claim to assets.

MARKETABILITY: Shares may be redeemed without cost at asset value on any business day. There may be small redemption fees charged, but these are very isolated exceptions. The value of shares upon redemption may, of course, be more or less, than the investor's cost depending upon the market value of all assets.

PROSPECTUS: The prospectus fulfills the purpose of the Securities Act of 1933 and the Investment Company Act of 1940 by making available to prospective investors the information required for an intelligent appraisal of the investment company.

SAFEKEEPING: All assets must be deposited in a bank or trust company, or other company subject to all regulations of the Securities and Exchange Commission. Such bank may also act as dividend disbursing agent and transfer agent of fund shares, but cannot participate in the management policies or practices of an investment company.

REGULATION: While federal and state statutes are extensive and thoroughly designed in the best interests of the public, they do not, however, provide for any governmental supervision of the investment policies and practices of management.

LITERATURE: All sales literature and representations of past investment results must comply with the Securities Act of 1933, the Investment Company Act of 1940, and the Statement of Policy of 1950 (as amended November 5, 1957) and must in no way be deemed to be misleading in an accurate appraisal of a particular company.

SOURCE: *Johnson's Investment Company Charts,* Buffalo, N.Y.: Hugh A. Johnson & Co. Reproduced by permission.

SUGGESTED READINGS

1. *Investment Companies.* Latest annual edition. Arthur Wiesenberger & Co., 61 Broadway, New York, N.Y., 10006.

2. *Johnson's Investment Company Charts.* Latest annual edition. Hugh A. Johnson Investment Co., Rand Building, Buffalo, N.Y.

3. In *Changing Times, The Kiplinger Magazine:*
    a) "Mutual Funds: Pick with Care," February, 1963.
    b) "Mutual Funds and How to Pick Them," March, 1962.
    c) "No Load Funds," June, 1960.

4. R. L. Weisman, *Investments Made Easy.* New York: Harper & Row, 1962.

5. R. L. Smith, *The Grim Truth about Mutual Funds.* New York: Putnam, 1963.

6. Stuart B. Mead, *Mutual Fund and Investment Company Performance in the '50's.* Occasional Paper No. 9, Bureau of Business and Economic Research, Graduate School of Business Administration, Michigan State University, East Lansing, Michigan, 1961.

7. *Management Investment Companies.* A monograph prepared for The Commission on Money and Credit by the Investment Company Institute, Prentice-Hall, Englewood Cliffs, N.J., 1962.

8. *Vickers Guide to Investment Company Portfolios.* Latest annual edition. Vickers Associates, Inc., 48 Elm Street, Huntington, New York.

9. T. A. Wise, "It's Getting Hard to Pick a Mutual Fund," Chapter 4, and "The Double Play in Closed-End Funds," Chapter 5, in *Fortune's Guide to Personal Investing.* New York: McGraw-Hill Book Co., Inc., 1963.

10. In *Dun's Review and Modern Industry:*
    a) "Which Mutual Fund?" March, 1962.
    b) "How Good Are No Load Funds?" June, 1961.
    c) "Those Mysterious No Load Funds," May, 1961.

11. *Investment Trusts and Funds from the Investor's Point of View.* Great Barrington, Mass.: American Institute for Economic Research, latest annual edition.

12. *The Mutual Fund Shareholder.* New York: Investment Company Institute. A free copy may be obtained by writing to the Association at 61 Broadway, New York, N.Y., 10006.

13. "Forbes Mutual Fund Survey," issued annually in the August 15 issue of *Forbes Magazine.* A reprint may be obtained by writing to *Forbes* at 70 Fifth Avenue, New York, N.Y., 10011.

CASE PROBLEMS

1. Robert and Alice Quint have one son (age 8), for whose education they are building a college fund. Whenever they can afford it, they buy a share of the capital stock of the American Telephone and Telegraph Company and add it to the fund. What do you think of their plan? Can you suggest a better one?

2. The John Dohertys, who live next door to the Quints, have a daughter (age 6) whom they want to be able to send to college. They make regular monthly payments to a savings and loan association with an eye to building a fund of $6,000 for their daughter's education. Do you like this plan more than that of the Quints? Why? Why not?

3. James Layton received the prospectus of a mutual fund (it happened to be that of a specialized common-stock fund). He read the prospectus and was impressed by the growth in the value of the shares and by the earnings per share which it had achieved in the years since 1945. He thought he would withdraw $12,000 of his savings from the savings department of his local commercial bank and invest the money in these shares. His total savings amounted to $18,000. In two years, Layton was due to retire; he and his wife would have to depend on his savings for much of their support in retirement. Do you think he was making a good move? Why? Why not?

4. Lionel Batson has worked hard all his life. At age 40 he owns his $15,000 home, has $5,000 in savings banks, and has a steady job which now pays $10,000 a year and promises to pay much more. He has a wife (age 38) and two children (ages 16 and 13). Upon the death of his mother, he inherits $25,000 from her. For the first time in his life he thinks that he is in a position to "buy common stocks and make some money," "buy a stake in American industry"; but (not having had any experience) he debates whether to invest directly or through an investment company. One evening while you are at his house, he engages you in conversation on this topic. What advice would you give him?

5. Peter Putnam has just started at his first career job. He is earning $505 a month and since he is still a bachelor, he finds he can save and invest $100 a month. He knows he knows nothing about investments and therefore he decides to buy investment company shares. He asks all his friends what they would recommend. The suggestions include Wellington Fund, T. Rowe Price Growth Stock Fund, Scudder, Stevens & Clark Common Stock Fund, Lehman Corp.,

Samson Fund, Tri-Continental, Dreyfus Fund, Keystone S–4 Fund, The Knicker-bocker Fund, and Keystone B–1. Since you have taken a course in personal finance and are presumably knowledgeable he asks you to help him by evaluating the characteristics and performance trends of each of these funds and selecting the one you think best for his purposes. Help him.

6. Arthur Haskins, Jr., is a bachelor (age 31). He lives in Rio de Janeiro, Brazil, where he has been working for the last eight years for a New York bank. Promotion for him is expected to be rapid. Some of his savings he invests in Brazil, where he gets a very good return. He feels that he is too far away from North America to invest directly in stocks there. What type of mutual fund, if any, do you think he should consider? Which particular one would you recommend? Why?

7. Jonathan Swift is a man (age 30) of little education. He has saved his money and invested it in wholly owned common stocks which he selected by noting what the mutual funds appeared to be buying (from their lists, published quarterly). Once he bought, he continued to hold. He made a practice of never investing more than $1,000 in the stock of any one company. After 8 years of this sort of program, he finds that original investments of $8,000 are now worth $12,000 and that he has averaged a 5.5 percent return on his investments. What is your opinion of his plan?

8. Janet Clarkson is a secretary for a lawyer, who pays her $100 a week. At age 40 she has been in his employment for 22 years. She lives in an apartment with her mother (whom she supports). She has $6,000 in various savings banks and $12,000 of straight life insurance. In addition, she manages to save about $15 a week. It is her desire to retire when she is age 62. She expects to draw a Social Security monthly retirement benefit but no pension. She intends to put future savings into a mutual fund. What sort of fund would you advise her to seek? Why?

9. The Adams family owns its home, has $5,000 in the bank for emergencies, has all the life insurance which it thinks it should carry, and is now considering the investment of $3,000 of other savings. Mr. Adams, who is a research worker in a chemical factory, thinks that it is prudent to buy a few shares of common stock in two or three good companies. Mrs. Adams thinks that it would be better to buy the shares of an investment company. Which of them do you believe is right? Why?

10. John and Elizabeth Raynhauer have just saved their first $1,000 since they were married. John especially fears the results of inflation. He wants to invest their $1,000 emergency fund in the common stock of some good company. Elizabeth, who has had a course in personal finance, feels that it should be put in a savings bank. If it is to be invested in common stock, she feels that this should be done by buying shares in a nonleverage investment company. What would you advise? Why?

11. At age 28 Peter Dane finds himself still single and doing rather well as a loan officer in the commercial bank for which he works. He lives with his mother in the family home. Except for owning the home the mother is without

funds. Since Peter's salary has just been increased to $9,000 annually, he is considering an investment of about $2,500 a year in a mutual fund. He asks you to help him decide whether to invest in a balanced fund, or a diversified common-stock fund. Also he wonders whether an accumulation plan or a contractual plan would be best for him. All of Peter's savings to date ($7,000) are in an account in the savings department of the bank where he works. Advise him.

16 INVESTING IN A SMALL BUSINESS

"If I sold shrouds, no one would die.
If I sold lamps, then in the sky
The sun, for spite,
Would shine all night."

—*Abraham ibn Ezra*
Toledo, Spain circa 1150 A.D.

OF CONSUMER WEALTH, according to the Federal Reserve, about $17 in every $100 is invested in family businesses or in professional practice. Among families with the smallest amounts of net worth—zero to $5,000—5 in 100 had a business interest. Among families with moderate amounts of net worth— $5,000 to $25,000—interest in a family business or profession was reported by 19 families in 100. Where net worth ranged from $25,000 to $100,000, 42 families out of 100 had an interest in a family business or profession. For the wealthiest families, those with net worth of $100,000 or more, 57 families in 100 had an investment in a business firm or profession.[1]

There are now approximately 4.8 million businesses, of which 4.5 million are classed as "small." Each year approximately 430,000 new businesses are started, while some 385,000 are discontinued.

This last fact is food for thought. The survey does not give the reason why there was so big an annual turnover of small business—especially remarkable in a year of prosperity. Nor does it tell how many families were forced out of business by factors that could have been avoided. But it does highlight the large risk in small business.

The success stories make interesting reading,[2] while the failures are

---

[1] See "Survey of Financial Characteristics of Consumers," Federal Reserve Bulletin, March, 1964, p. 287.

[2] For some intriguing ones, see *Opportunities for Growth in Small Business* (New York: Dun & Bradstreet, Inc. A free copy may be obtained by writing to the firm at 99 Church St., New York, N.Y, 10007.

but cold statistics; and since hope springs eternal, each year thousands of people take their life savings and try their hand at a small business. The very fact that so many are inexperienced and enter fields they know little or nothing about makes inevitable a percentage failure rate that brings distressing losses. A profitable small business is the foundation on which the American free-enterprise system has been built. This chapter is designed to be of some small help in giving you an introductory view of the field and its problems so that you can decide whether or not to risk your savings (and credit) in a small business.

Why People Go into Small Business

Reasons given in a recent survey range all the way from "Could not find another job" to "Want to hit the jackpot." Some people find that their personality is such that they cannot hold a job. They do not like to be guided, supervised, or "bossed." Often a person just wants to be independent, on his own, does not want to work for someone else all his life. When he graduated from college, William Black went into business for himself. He rented a 6 by 20 foot space under a stairway in a building in New York and invested all his capital of $250 in nuts. Today Black, chairman of the board of Chock Full O'Nuts, is worth over $20 million.

Jim Ryder started as a bull-shouldered day laborer loading concrete blocks aboard trucks in Miami. He figured driving a truck would be easier than loading one. He put $30 down on a $130 used Model A Ford truck and thereby launched a business that has since grown into a large corporation with annual sales in excess of $50 million and made him, as the head of Ryder System, Inc., a wealthy man.

On a Sunday morning, a three-line classified advertisement in the *Tampa Tribune* offered the shell of a house—complete on the outside but left for the buyer to finish inside—for sale. The ad was spotted by Jim Walter, a newly-wed Navy veteran. He set out to buy the house and became so intrigued with the idea that for a small sum he bought a partnership in the shell house enterprise. Ultimately he bought out his partners and the firm became Jim Walter Corp. His personal fortune now is estimated to exceed $10 million. It is success stories like these that motivate many people. In 1902, for example, J. C. Penney took his savings of $2,000 and started on his own, opening his first "Golden Rule" store in the little town of Kemmerer, Wyoming. Today the average store in his chain does $600,000 annually, and there are 1,630 of them in the 50 states. Total annual sales exceed $1.1 billion.

Are You Qualified to Run Your Own Business?

You will be the biggest asset—or liability—in your business. You will find that running a business, however small, is quite a different thing from working for someone else. You will have a multitude of responsibilities and details to watch, and you will have to think in both imaginatively broad and meticulously precise terms. Can you do it? Can you handle buying, selling, advertising, employer-employee relations, bookkeeping, inventory control, rent, taxes, insurance, etc., and still keep your balance and affability? As a small business owner, you will soon find that hours do not stop at 40 a week. Long after others have gone home, you may have to stay on the job checking odds and ends, getting books in order, going over inventory, rearranging stock, seeing that repairs are made, and looking after a thousand and one other details. You will find, early in the game, that anyone who starts in his own business is not going to be able—for the first 20 years, at least—to keep golf appointments at three in the afternoon.

Ask yourself the following questions:

1. Can I get along with other people and inspire confidence?
2. Can I shoulder the responsibility of meeting a payroll and paying debts on time?
3. Do I like the business I expect to enter so that I will not mind working longer hours and making other personal sacrifices?
4. Do I understand that business involves considerable risk, and am I willing to take the risk involved?
5. Do I like to sell? Can I handle a lot of detail and still keep an amiable disposition?
6. Can I make decisions easily and weather wrong ones?
7. Am I resourceful in emergencies?
8. Am I a good organizer? Can I pull things together without getting flustered?

If you come up with too many "no's," then do not try to run your own business. You will not succeed. The personal element is extremely important. You have to have perseverance—the ability to keep going in rough times. You have to have a certain degree of aggressiveness. That is, you have to be a self-starter. In your own business, no one is going to tell you what to do, how to do it, or when to do it. You have to generate your own decisions and actions. You have to have self-control—the ability to keep a level head and not get pressured into hasty action or, on the other hand, worry so much about decisions that you keep postponing and avoiding them. You also need a moderate degree of optimism and confidence. You have to have stamina and vigor, too, to keep working long hours at a steady pace, day after day, with—certainly at first—little or no vacation.

In addition, studies of small business have indicated that knowing a business from the ground up is an important factor in success. It is often better to obtain a position in the kind of firm you would like to buy or start than to go out on your own initially. It is not essential, but it is helpful; and it may often mean the difference between success and failure. You can see the mistakes being made in the business for which you are working and can avoid making them when you are on your own. You can watch and listen and keep an open mind for useful techniques and procedures. You will learn the importance of record keeping and come to realize how essential it is for the owner-manager to know at all times exactly where he stands. You may pick up a number of the "tricks of the trade." But just being a clerk is not enough; you also need some general managerial experience, and it is better to acquire a little of this before you risk your own capital. Thus, for the young person, even if he knows the field of business in which he wants to establish his own enterprise, it is better initially to work for someone else in the same line before starting on his own.

Is It Better to Start a New Business or to Buy an Existing One?

You may, of course, not have a choice at all. If you have a new idea or a new gadget, and it is really a "first," you will have to start on your own. The first "diaper service," the first "Toni" home permanent, had of necessity to be new enterprises. But if you want a business of your own in any established field, then you do have a choice. It is not impossible, of course, to find an excellent small business, complete with equipment, fixtures, inventory, and even steady customers, ready and waiting for you to walk in, take over, and start making money. The odds are against it. But for all the limitations you will discover in the average existing enterprise up for sale, it probably has less headaches and pitfalls attached to it than starting your own would entail. Some of the poor practices you can correct, and others can be improved if not entirely eliminated. As we shall see, more new businesses fail in the first few years, especially the first year; and if you buy a going business, you avoid many of the initial troubles.

The five most important pitfalls to be avoided during the first years are (1) too lavish expenditure for fixtures; (2) overpurchase of merchandise, especially in slow-moving items; (3) too great variety and wrong types of items for the neighborhood; (4) too heavy expense in relation to the size of the business; and (5) an overly optimistic estimate of anticipated sales. If you purchase a small going business with a past profit record, most of these mistakes have already been made and paid for, and, by and large, you avoid these pitfalls.

Starting a new business may sometimes be advisable, but it is always harder, especially if it means competing with an established firm. To launch a competing firm, you must select a location, rent a building, sign a lease, buy merchandise, hire a staff, and straighten out a tangle of legal problems before you open. And most new businesses operate at a loss for varying periods until they are over the hump. Thus, you make a substantial investment in time and money in the hope of catching up with an established competitor. Not that it cannot be done. But unless your potential competitor has obvious weaknesses that could give a new firm a better-than-average chance to succeed, starting a new business is a bigger gamble than buying a going enterprise.

What to Look for in Buying a Business

There is no infallible way to pick the right business. Every enterprise has an element of risk, but care in selection will cut down that risk; and the more careful you are, the smaller will be your chance of failure. When you set out to buy a business, your biggest problem will be to find out enough about it to judge its value and desirability. You will need the help of a lawyer and of an accountant familiar with the field.

Changing Times, The Kiplinger Magazine, suggests a number of things to look for in either buying or establishing a new business. The first question you will want to ask is why the present owner wants to sell. Sometimes the answer you get here may be legitimate. If they tell you the owner died and his widow cannot run the enterprise by herself, you need hardly do more than check the obituary column. But if it is because the owner is "ill," it may be that he is ill from worry about the financial condition of his business. Or he may be ill because he has just heard that a large, modern, effective competitor has taken a lease on the store across the way and is going to open up in a month or so. Sometimes you will need to do some careful canvassing of the neighborhood, making discreet inquiries, before you learn the true reason for selling.

If you satisfy yourself on this score, then you will want to know whether or not the business is profitable. Here an accountant who knows the particular field of enterprise is indispensable, and his fee may save you a large loss later. Obviously, he will dig into the firm's books, but these are not conclusive. You will want to check the volume of purchases by seeing old bills of suppliers over a period of time. You will want to see copies of the owner's income tax returns for at least the past five years. To check on the volume of business he and his books claim he is doing, you can check his weekly bank deposits back over several years, ask for old bank statements showing his checking-account activity, and look at his sales tax or gross-receipts tax payments. He may tell you that these last two will not give a true picture because he has been "taking something off the top," pocketing and not reporting some percentage (say 10 percent) of cash sales; but this should not deter you from asking for and looking over the sales tax or gross-receipts tax returns, for even if they really are 10 percent short, this will allow for a shrinkage when you take over, since a change of management may lose (as well as gain) some old customers.

Is the business financially sound? Even though it has been making profits, there may be weak points. Is there sufficient working capital? If not, how much will you have to supply, over and above your purchase price, to keep inventory at working levels? Do you have enough savings both to buy the business and to provide the working capital? If not, what is the prospect that you may be able to borrow? In what condition are the assets of the business? Are fixtures new, modern, usable? Or must they be replaced? What will that cost? Is the inventory salable? Has it been turning over adequately, or is what is being left as inventory old, out-of-date, unusable merchandise which has been on the shelves for a long time? Have the fixtures and inventory been paid for fully? If not, what is still due, and who is to assume liability for these debts in the event you do want to buy the business? If debts are large, inventory old, or major repair or replacements of fixtures necessary, you will want to be sure that allowance is made in the purchase price for these limitations.

How much can you expect to realize from the business? Check the seller's claims carefully against Dun & Bradstreet averages for representative small businesses. These are shown in Table 16–1. To estimate how much you can expect to earn in any given line, take the annual net sales figure the seller supplies and apply both the net operating profit percentage and the owner's salary percentage as shown in Table 16–1.

Next, what about accounts receivable? How much of the sales have been for credit? Have they been large or small or average for this type and size of business? How current are the accounts receivable? Have they been on the books a long time? Are they really uncollectible? As a general rule, you can count on getting about 90 cents on every dollar if the accounts are three months old, about 50 cents after six months, and

TABLE 16–1

What Would You Make as an Owner?

Line of Business	Net Operating Profit*	Owner's Salary*
Appliance-radio-television dealers..................	2.6%	3.8%
Auto accessory and parts stores....................	2.4	8.2
Bars and taverns..................................	2.4	10.9
Bookstores..	3.0	9.2
Camera and photographic supply stores............	2.4	9.8
Children's and infant wear stores.................	3.6	8.9
Drugstores..	5.1	8.0
Dry goods and general merchandise stores..........	2.8	8.2
Family clothing stores............................	3.4	8.5
Farm equipment dealers............................	2.6	3.0
Farm supply stores................................	2.0	3.2
Florists..	3.3	12.6
Gasoline service stations.........................	1.9	6.2
Gift, novelty, and souvenir stores................	3.4	13.9
Grocery stores....................................	1.5	6.0
Grocery and meat stores...........................	2.0	3.7
Hardware stores...................................	1.9	7.7
Jewelry stores (primarily cash and open account)...	3.7	15.3
Jewelry stores (primarily installment credit).......	5.8	10.1
Liquor stores (package)...........................	2.6	7.6
Lumber and building materials dealers.............	5.8	4.2
Meat markets.....................................	1.4	6.8
Men's furnishings stores..........................	3.5	9.8
Men's wear stores.................................	2.2	6.0
Office supply and equipment dealers...............	3.8	4.3
Paint and wallpaper stores........................	5.1	6.5
Restaurants.......................................	3.3	7.9
Shoe stores (family)..............................	5.3	7.1
Sporting goods stores.............................	2.0	9.3
Women's accessory and specialty stores............	2.2	11.2
Women's ready-to-wear stores.....................	2.9	8.2

* As percent of annual net sales (in dollars).
SOURCE: Dun & Bradstreet, Inc.

only 30 cents after a year's delinquency. It will pay you to make a spot check of these accounts to determine their age and the credit standing of some of the larger debtors.

The lease and rent situation should be checked. This ties in closely with the question of goodwill. Years of doing business successfully at a given location, on which the owner places a high goodwill price, will be of little value to you if, in the case of a store, for example, the lease has only one year to run and the landlord either will not renew it or will renew it only at a new, higher rental which will wipe out a good part of the profit margin. Thus it is essential to check the lease and the rental. In a retail-store purchase, the lease should have at least five years to run, or longer if more time is required for you to get back your initial investment; and the rent, as we shall see, should be no more than a certain percentage of gross volume, varying in different lines of business. Goodwill is, of course, the difference between the value of tangible assets and the asking price. Only in exceptional cases should you pay heavily for goodwill. It is too difficult to measure. You may find, after taking over, that this so-called "goodwill" was nothing but a bad reputation. Or the goodwill may vanish as soon as the present owner gets out of the business. On the other hand, if you are capable, you may be able to create far more goodwill than was left to you.

Location, parking, and store traffic require consideration. Although this will be considered in more detail later, you should check the neighborhood. Is it a good, growing area, or is it running down, changing rapidly, and in danger of soon becoming a slum area? It makes a big difference. Also, you should double check with city or town officials to be sure that no changes in zoning regulations are planned. You may be buying with the idea of expanding into other, allied lines in the back of your mind; but if this is not legally possible because of regulations, or if parking facilities are not adequate to support the larger volume you expect to build, or if parking regulations are soon to be changed to cut down parking at and around your location, this may make all the difference in your decision.

A similar check of franchises, local codes, ordinances, and licensing regulations is essential, and here you will need a lawyer. If sales depend largely on a wholesaler's or manufacturer's franchise for a fast-selling brand of merchandise, you will want to check with the wholesaler or manufacturer to be certain that the franchise will be continued. You may discover that they had already notified the present owner that it would be discontinued at the end of the term (year) and that this is the real reason he wants to sell a business which has been quite profitable up to this point. He may have neglected to tell you this, however. Most governmental units have the power to make you buy a license to go into a particular business. Some of these licenses are issued almost automatically on payment of a fee, but others require rigid tests, health examinations, or extensive hearings before a licensing authority. For example, you may pay $20,000 for the "key" (goodwill—buying the business as a going operation) to a liquor store (plus dollar for dollar for stock) only to find to your dismay that you cannot get the license renewed at the end of the year because in your youth, in your home town, you were convicted and fined for a petty theft. Even though you have led an honorable and exemplary life since then, this may be sufficient in some states to prevent you from owning and operating a liquor store or a bar and grill.

Checking to see whether back taxes, accounts payable, rent, etc., have been paid up to date is another essential task for you or your accountant or lawyer. Be sure that you know the full extent of any such liabilities. Then have your lawyer draw up a sales contract in such a way as to specify the particular liabilities you will assume, and exclude all others. Be sure, too, that you check the provisions in your state law concerning bulk sales. In most states a proprietor is required to settle with all suppliers and creditors before selling out. If he fails to do so, the new owner may be liable for those debts. You will want to have your lawyer provide in the contract of purchase that a certain amount of the price you are paying is to be set aside and held in escrow for 60 or 90 days to take care of any such debts which may have been overlooked and on which payment may be demanded after the business changes hands.

These are only some, and by no means all, the factors you must take into account when you set out to buy a business. When you think you have all the facts—after you have talked to bankers, suppliers, competing businessmen, customers, city or state licensing or local zoning officials, your accountant, and your lawyer—only then are you prepared to sit down, tie all the facts together, and come to your decision (see Fig. 16–1).

Using a Business Broker

Particularly if you have never bought (or sold) a business before, it is usually well worth the small commission charged to use a business broker. You can easily locate reliable business brokers by the ads they place in the better local newspapers in the larger cities. For example, one small part of the "Business Opportunities" section of the *New York Times* is reproduced in Figure 16–2. As may be seen, businesses offered for sale are grouped by category: drugstores, manufacturing plants, printing plants, garages–gasoline stations, restaurants, etc. The illustration contains a number of listings of business brokers. David Jaret Company is New York's leading business-brokerage firm and handles enterprises throughout the metropolitan area. It carries about 10,000 listings and sells about 350 a year. Charles Ford and Associates is the nation's largest business-brokerage service. It has 260 associated brokers scattered across the United States and in Hawaii. This firm handles about $300 million in business sales a year and, to attain this volume, advertises for buyers and sellers in 1,500 newspapers, 200 trade papers,

FIGURE 16–1

CHECKLIST FOR GOING INTO BUSINESS

By Staff Members of the Small Business Administration, Washington, D. C.

─────── SUMMARY ───────

People sometimes go into business for themselves without being fully aware of what is involved. Sometimes they're lucky and succeed. More often, they fail because they do not consider one or more of the ingredients needed for business success.

This checklist is designed to help you decide whether you are qualified or have considered the various phases of going into business for yourself. Careful thought now may help you to prevent mistakes and to avoid losing your savings and time later. Use this list as a starter. Consider each question as it applies to your situation. Check off each question only after you've made an effort to answer it honestly. Before you omit a question, satisfy yourself that it does not apply to your particular situation.

After each section, you will find a few references. If you have uncovered doubtful areas or weaknesses in your preparation, it is strongly recommended that you obtain these publications and study them. You will find it time well spent. Most of the references are available, free, on request from any SBA field office or the Small Business Administration, Washington 25, D. C. However, the notation "Supt. Docs." means that the item is for sale at the price indicated by the Superintendent of Documents, Washington 25, D. C. (not from SBA).

QUESTIONS TO CONSIDER

Are You the Type?

Yes   No

1. Have you rated your personal traits such as leadership, organizing ability, perseverance, and physical energy?
2. Have you had some friends rate you on them?
3. Have you considered getting an associate whose strong points will compensate for your weak traits?

   REFERENCES: Starting and Managing a Small Business of Your Own (40¢ Supt. Docs.); SM 39, Balanced Skills; Measure of Effective Managers; SM 46, Essential Personal Qualities for Small Store Managers; SM 52, Are You Really Service-Minded?

What Are Your Chances for Success?

4. Have you had any actual business experience?
5. Do you have special technical skills, such as those needed by a plumber, electrician, mechanic, or radio repair man?
6. Have you obtained some basic management experience working for someone else?
7. Have you analyzed the recent trend of business conditions (good or bad)?
8. Have you analyzed business conditions in the city and neighborhood where you want to locate?
9. Have you analyzed conditions in the line of business you are planning?
10. Have you determined what size business you plan to establish (dollar sales per year)?
11. Have you built up a detailed set of figures on how much capital you will need to launch the business?
12. Have you figured how much time you will need until the business income equals the expenses?
13. Have you planned what net profit you believe you should make?

FIGURE 16–1 (Continued)

- 2 -

	Yes	No

14. Will the net profit divided by the investment result in a rate of return which compares favorably with the rate you can obtain from other investment opportunities?
    REFERENCES: Appraise Your Competitive Position to Improve Company Planning, in *Management Aids Annual No. 2* (55¢ Supt. Docs.); Appraising the Market for the Services You Offer, in *Marketers Aids Annual No. 2* (40¢ Supt. Docs.); Practical Business Use of Government Statistics (20¢ Supt. Docs.)

How Much Capital Will You Need?

15. Have you worked out what income from sales or services you can reasonably expect in the first 6 months? The first year? The second year?
16. Do you know what net profit you can expect on these volumes?
17. Have you made a conservative forecast of expenses including a regular salary for yourself?
18. Have you compared this income with what you could make working for someone else?
19. Are you willing to risk uncertain or irregular income for the next year? Two years?
20. Have you counted up how much actual money you have to invest in your business?
21. Do you have other assets which you could sell or on which you could borrow?
22. Have you some other source from which you could borrow money?
23. Have you talked to a banker?
24. Is he favorably impressed with your plan?
25. Do you have a financial reserve for unexpected needs?
26. Does your total capital, from all sources, cover your best estimates of the capital you will need?
    REFERENCES: MA 105, Watch Your Cash; Term Loans in Small Business Financing, in *Marketers Aids Annual No. 2* (40¢ Supt. Docs.); A Handbook of Small Business Finance (30¢ Supt. Docs.)

Should You Share Ownership With Others?

27. Do you lack needed technical or management skills which can be most satisfactorily supplied by one or more partners?
28. Do you need the financial assistance of one or more partners?
29. Have you checked the features of each form or organization (individual proprietorship, partnership, corporation) to see which will best fit your situation?
    REFERENCES: MA 80, Choosing the Legal Structure for Your Firm; MA 111, Steps in Incorporating a Business; Equity Capital and Small Business (35¢ Supt. Docs.)

Where Should You Locate?

30. Do you know how much space you will need?
31. Do you know what type of building you will need?
32. Do you know of any special features you require in lighting, heating, ventilating, air conditioning, or parking facilities?
33. Have you listed the tools and equipment you need room for?
34. If the proposed location does not meet nearly all your requirements, is there a sound reason why you should not wait and continue seeking a more ideal location?
35. Have you checked the U. S. Census Bureau population figures?
    REFERENCES: MA 99, Plant Location Factors for Small Industry; Sizing Up Small Business Locations, in *Marketers Aids Annual No. 1* (45¢ Supt. Docs.); SBB 16, Store Location.

Should You Buy A Going Business?

36. Have you considered the advantages and disadvantages of buying a going business?
37. Have you compared what it would take to equip and stock a new business with the price asked for the business you are considering?
38. Have you learned why the present owner wants to sell?
39. Have you checked the owner's claims about the business with reports from an independent accountant's analysis of the figures?
40. Have you checked with the company's suppliers to obtain their ideas of the value of the business?
41. Do the suppliers think well of the proposition?
42. Is the stock of merchandise a questionable buy? (Would a large proportion of it have to be disposed of at a loss? Is any of it out of date, unsalable, or not usable?)

FIGURE 16–1 (Continued)

- 3 -

	Yes	No

43. Are the physical facilities old or in poor condition and, hence, overvalued?
44. Are you sure the accounts receivable are worth the asking price?
45. Is the present company's good will fairly valued?
46. Are you prepared to assume the liabilities, and are the creditors agreeable?
47. Has your lawyer checked to see if the title is good and if there is any lien against the assets?
48. Are there any back taxes to pay?
49. Have the sales been temporarily increased by conditions which are not likely to continue?

REFERENCES: Key Factors in Starting a New Plant, in *Management Aids Annual No. 5* (45¢ Supt. Docs.); SM 20, Buying a Small Going Concern.

Are You Qualified to Supervise Buying and Selling?

50. Have you estimated your total stock requirements?
51. Do you know in what quantities users buy your product or service?
52. Do you know how often users buy your product or service?
53. Have you made a sales analysis to determine major lines to be carried?
54. Have you decided what characteristics you will require in your goods?
55. Have you set up a model stock assortment to follow in your buying?
56. Have you investigated whether it will be cheaper to buy large quantities infrequently or in small quantities frequently?
57. Have you weighed price differentials for large orders against capital and space tied up?
58. Have you decided what merchandise to buy direct from manufacturers?
59. Will you make your account more valuable to your suppliers by concentrating your buying with a few of them?
60. Have you worked out control plans to insure stocking the right quantities?

REFERENCES: MA 120, Checking Your Marketing Channels; MA 123, Getting the Most From Your Purchasing Dollar; SM 28, Profitable Buying for Small Retailers; SM 56, Advertising for Profit and Prestige; SM 60, Sales Promotion Pointers for Small Retailers; SBB 37, Buying for Retail Stores.

How Will You Price Your Products and Services?

61. Have you determined what prices you will have to charge to cover your costs and obtain profit?
62. Do these prices compare favorably with prices of competitors?

REFERENCES: How to Price a New Product, in *Management Aids Annual No. 3* (45¢ Supt. Docs.); MA 100, Pricing Arithmetic for Small Business Managers; SM 21, Pricing and Profits in Small Stores.

What Selling Methods Will You Use?

63. Have you studied the sales promotional methods used by competitors?
64. Have you outlined your own sales promotion policy?
65. Have you studied why customers buy your product (service, price, quality, distinctive styling, other)?
66. Will you do outside selling?
67. Will you advertise in the newspapers?
68. Will you do direct mail advertising?
69. Will you use posters and handbills?
70. Will you use radio and television advertising?

REFERENCES: SM 16, Improving Personal Selling in Small Business; SM 32, Methods of Improving Off-Season Sales; SM 56, Advertising for Profit and Prestige; SBB 20, Advertising-Retail Store.

How Will You Manage Personnel?

71. Will you be able to hire satisfactory employees, locally, to supply skills you lack?
72. Do you know what skills are necessary?
73. Have you checked the prevailing wage scales?
74. Have you a clear-cut idea of what you plan to pay?
75. Have you considered hiring someone now employed by a competitor?
76. Have you checked on the pros and cons of doing so?
77. Have you planned your training procedures?

REFERENCES: MA 102, Keeping Your Salesmen Enthusiastic; Sales Training for Small Wholesalers, in *Marketers Aids Annual No. 1* (45¢ Supt. Docs.); SBB 23, Training Retail Sales People; Sales Training for the Smaller Manufacturer (20¢ Supt. Docs.)

FIGURE 16–1 (Continued)

- 4 -

What Records Will You Keep?	Yes	No
78. Have you a suitable bookkeeping system ready to operate?	___	___
79. Have you planned a merchandise control system?	___	___
80. Have you obtained standard operating ratios for your type of business to use as guides?	___	___
81. Have you provided for additional records as necessary?	___	___
82. Have you a system to use in keeping a check on costs?	___	___
83. Do you need any special forms?	___	___
84. Have you made adequate provision for having your record keeping done?	___	___

REFERENCES: MA 75, Protecting Your Records Against Disaster in *Management Aids Annual No. 5* (45¢ Supt. Docs.); SM 36, Picking An Auditor For Your Firm; SBB 15, Record Keeping Systems-- Small Store and Service Trade.

What Laws Will Affect You?

85. Have you investigated what, if any, licenses to do business are necessary?	___	___
86. Have you checked the health regulations?	___	___
87. Are your operations subject to interstate commerce regulations?	___	___
88. Have you seen your lawyer for advice on how to meet your legal responsibilities?	___	___

REFERENCES: MA 108, Selecting a Lawyer for Your Business; SM 42, FTC and Guides Against Deceptive Pricing; Small Business and the Federal Trade Commission, in *Marketers Aids Annual 2* (40¢ Supt. Docs.)

What Other Problems Will You Face?

89. Have you worked out a system for handling your tax requirements?	___	___
90. Have you arranged for adequate insurance coverage?	___	___
91. Have you worked out a way of building a management team?	___	___
92. Does your family (if any) agree that your proposed venture is sound?	___	___
93. Do you have enough capital to carry accounts receivable?	___	___
94. Will you sell for credit?	___	___
95. Have you worked out a definite returned goods policy?	___	___
96. Have you considered other management policies which must be established?	___	___
97. Have you planned how you will organize and assign the work?	___	___
98. Have you made a work plan for yourself?	___	___

REFERENCES: MA 103, Organizing the Owner-Manager's Job; MA 113, "Tailor-Make" Your Executive Staff; Building Sound Credit Policies for Small Stores, in *Marketers Aids Annual 1* (45¢ Supt. Docs.); SM 49, Improving Collections from Credit Sales; Business Insurance, in *Management Aids Annual No. 1* (65¢ Supt. Docs.); How Good Records Aid Income Tax Reporting, in *Management Aids Annual No. 3* (45¢ Supt. Docs.); Appeal Procedure for Income Tax Cases, in *Management Aids Annual No. 4* (45¢ Supt. Docs.)

Will You Keep Up To Date?

99. Have you a plan for keeping up with new developments in your line of business?	___	___
100. Have you a small group of qualified advisors from whom you can get help in solving new problems?	___	___

REFERENCES: MA 117, Selecting Marketing Research Services; MA 125, Building Growth-Mindedness Into Your Business; SM 54, Store Modernization Check List

GPO 8 22582

SOURCE: Small Business Administration.

and on some 50 radio stations. Ford publishes a monthly *Business for Sale Directory* that averages more than 300 pages and lists upwards of 2,000 business offerings throughout the United States. The directory goes to 9,000 brokers, realtors, bankers, and prospective buyers. In addition, Ford maintains two files, one that lists some 24,000 businesses for sale and another that contains thousands of names of buyer prospects. These files are constantly cross-checked to match buyers and sellers. No business is listed for sale before it has been inspected and appraised, and approved as a good risk.

A reliable business broker—and you can check on his reliability by

FIGURE 16–2

Business Opportunities

SOURCE: "Business Opportunities" section of the *New York Times* classified ads.

consulting your local chamber of commerce or Better Business Bureau —knows how to size up a business and spot the significant factors quickly. He will be able to provide you with these details with a minimum of effort on your part; and since he hopes to retain you as a satisfied customer who may some day—perhaps in selling the same business—use his services again, he is not likely to attempt to mislead you. You can and should, of course, check the facts independently of him, but he will provide an invaluable orientation as well as a whole series of leads. A business broker ordinarily makes no charge to the buyer for his services; but usually he asks a 1 percent retainer of the seller (1 percent of the asking price) and then, when the business is actually sold, charges a 5–10 percent commission, which includes the 1 percent retainer.

What Should a Business Cost?

Two basic considerations in either starting a new business or buying an existing one are how much capital you need and how can you obtain it. Both vary from line to line, but some guiding generalizations are possible. Generally, for a small retail business the average amount of capital required is $10,000–$15,000. Most or all of this will have to come from your own savings. In retailing, particularly, the percentage of initial capital put up by the owners is quite high. The average is 56 percent, but 70 or 80 percent is not unusual. The smaller the business, the greater the portion of capital that comes from the personal savings of the owner. This may be seen in Table 16–2. Only very rarely is the small

TABLE 16–2

Where Small Business Gets Capital

	Sources of Funds				
Initial Investment	Personal Savings	Capital Stock	Supplier Credit	Bank Loans	Other
Under $10,000	70%	1%	7%	10%	12%
$10,000–$19,999	65	2	9	11	13
$20,000–$49,999	57	8	9	16	10
$50,000 and over	42	11	14	17	16
All retailers	56	7	10	14	13

Source: *Changing Times, The Kiplinger Magazine.*

businessman able to raise capital by selling stock; and in the few cases where it is done, the stock is not sold publicly but is purchased instead by business associates and friends. Borrowing from relatives or friends, while seemingly convenient, is not usually a good idea. The relative may insist that you take his advice and let him help you run your business—his way. The friend, out of kindness, may be helping you make the biggest mistake of your life by enabling you to go into a business proposition which more experienced and less partial commercial lenders would size up quickly as a potential failure and therefore refuse to lend.

Frequently a good business broker will help you finance the purchase of a business by lending one half or one third of the purchase price at bank rates. For example, in the advertisements shown in Figure 16–2, you will note that for the first drugstore listed the complete price is $52,000 but that only $15,000 cash is necessary. In such cases the broker will finance the balance and take a mortgage on the property. Where an advertisement reads "Cash necessary, $20,000"—as in the case of the second drugstore—but no total price is given, the implication is that the full price is higher but that the broker will finance the difference. When the business broker is willing to make a loan and take a mortgage, you may be sure that he has investigated the situation fully.

There are, of course, other sources of financing which the small businessman, current or prospective, can draw upon.[3] For example, suppliers of machinery and equipment may provide credit. If you want to open a new dry-cleaning establishment, the company manufacturing the dry-cleaning units, which cost about $8,000 each, may ask for only $2,000 down and let you finance the rest over a period of time out of the income from the business. Or if the nature of your business lends itself to their type of operation, you may be able to use sales-finance companies or factors. An automobile dealer is a small businessman who would typically resort to a sales-finance company, while a small textile converter would normally use a factor. Both would thereby reduce their need for working capital and make possible a larger volume of business.

A factor is a financial company which performs the specialized service of credit checking and of financing the producer or wholesale (rarely retail) distributor of merchandise. A factor purchases accounts receivable and, in addition, makes loans on inventory and sometimes on fixtures and equipment. A sales-finance company aids in the financing of automobiles and other consumer durable goods by purchasing from the dealers who sell the goods the installment-sales contracts or notes which the dealers receive from their customers. Essentially, though not exclu-

---

[3] See *A Handbook of Small Business Finance,* Small Business Administration, Washington, D.C., 1964.

sively, factors extend credit to manufacturers or wholesalers, while sales-finance companies provide credit for retail distributors. Manufacturers and wholesale distributors usually extend credit themselves to retailers, but it is usually better, when they offer terms, for the retailer to take advantage of the discounts they offer for prompt cash payment.

Commercial banks provide credit for business, of course, but they are seldom prepared to provide long-term venture capital for the initial purchase of a small business. Commercial banks have in a number of instances organized and financed Small Business Investment Companies to undertake such financing.

Let us assume that you set out to buy a business—say, an auto-laundry—and find the price too high for your resources: they ask $40,000 cash, you have only $20,000. You may be able to find a partner who also has $20,000 to invest, and jointly purchase the auto-laundry. A good business broker will at times bring two individuals together to form a partnership to purchase an enterprise which neither alone could afford. The "Business Opportunity" section of a newspaper will feature advertisements of "Capital to Invest" and "Capital Wanted," such as are shown in Figure 16–3.

In forming a partnership to obtain enhanced capital, great care should be exercised in investigation of the background and reputation of the prospective partner; for once the partnership is formed, the acts of either partner in the name of the partnership commit and obligate the other. Since there is unlimited liability in partnerships, such commitments may, if unwise, be financially disastrous, not only to the business itself but to the personal assets of the partners as well, since any property they own—car, house, etc.—may be seized in settlement of their business debts. Thus, if there is the slightest doubt about the reputation or business judgment of your prospective partner, it is better either to drop the deal or to look around for another partner.

A Loan from the Small Business Administration?

One of the fundamental problems of small business concerns is difficulty in obtaining, on reasonable terms, medium- and long-term financing to purchase equipment and materials, to expand and modernize operations, or for working capital.

The Small Business Administration helps here in several ways. It counsels with small business concerns on their financial problems; it helps them obtain credit from private lending sources; and when private credit is not available on reasonable terms, it extends needed financing to qualified small firms.

FIGURE 16–3

Capital Wanted	Capital to Invest

10% - 10 YRS.

REAL ESTATE OPPORTUNITY

to invest in purchase-money mortgages secured by fee title to prime downtown commercial real estate, ready for $300,-000-$500,000 improvement. Self-amortizing over 10 years at 10% interest per annum. Our client is major nationwide corporation with properties coast-to-coast. Brokers invited. Contact

Management Directions, Inc.

Exclusive Real Estate Agents

Box 137, Englewood, N. J.

or call 201—LO 7-4441

PARTNER $100,000

To promote only International copyrighted Star Chart. It encompasses all 180 degrees of Celestial latitude; world wide utility. Has public acceptance. The tremendous interest in this field makes this chart an assured success. Sales outlets—department stores, variety stores as well as scientific equipment shops in U. S. and abroad. Z2503 Times

PARTNER

Or sell outright, want to retire Newark, N.J., invest $15,000.00 good going credit store, men's, ladies, boys, girls jewelry and small appliances, 30 day outstanding accounts receivable $16,000.00 and $28,000.00 in cost price inventory. Z2957 Times.

WORKING PARTNER WANTED

for established drive-in drycleaner. Bergen County N.J. 15 minutes from Geo. Wash bridge. Small cash investment for experienced man. Wonderful opportunity to associate with aggressive company. Weekly salary assured. Write Z2567 Times.

14K JEWELRY mfr. Estab West Coast firm seeks man capable of running office. Competence is most important requisite. Min of $25,000 required with option to buy up to 50% of stock. Firm is well known and distributes nationally to over 2000 outlets. Z3039 Times.

INVESTOR WANTED

To lend up to $20,000 in established art galleries with fashionable following. BONUS 50 pct of stock. Active optional. Inquire
TAURUS ASSOCIATES
1775 Broadway, NYC   CO 5-0225

PARTNER WANTED

with $30,000. For excursion boat. World's Fair package deal. Very high return assured. Investigate now. H155 Times.

$5,000-$20,000 investments in screened selected first and second mortgages & other secured corporate loans. Excellent yields including full servicing.
Warren Funding Co   261 Bw.,
BA 7-7872   Ask for Chas. L Fisher

$500,000 CAPITAL required to establish production & investor opportunity for development of new multi-million dollar industry based upon new United States basic patent grant in building construction field. Z2716 Times.

Working Partner Needed

To buy into fast moving est'd emplymnt agcy. Required bkgd, several yrs personnel exp, ambitious, hard-working. Z3032 Times.

WORLD'S FAIR MONEY MAKER World's first molded plastic brassiere patented and manufactured with amazing result. Seeking investor to finance expansion and promote fantastically high income potential. Z2218 Times

ENGINEER has full developed advanced electronic products (patents pending) & fully equipped & instrumented production facilities. Will sell 50 Pct. equity $30,000 needed for working capital. Princ only. (516) VA 5-2771.

$25,000—new "class" magazine-thoroughbred racing field. 1st issue already out. Reception/sales excellent. Money needed for expansion. Z2396 Times.

GROWING 3 yr. old Conn. photo offset shop needs outside investor with $5,000 or working partner w/sales ability & $2500. Exp. '64 gross at $12,000 as is. Z2147 Times.

LEADING DRESS MFR

With national accounts estab 25 years Seeks active/inactive partner. Principals only. H92 Times.

$100,000 TO EXPAND

business to include drastically needed

CAPITAL TO INVEST
PRINCIPAL WITH
$50,000 TO $1,000,000
AVAILABLE

Any type of construction project-starting, under construction, before C.O., or complete. Z2445 Times

YOUNG Executive seeks active partnership in going business where working capital is limited. Manuf of direct consumer products preferred. Will share administrating responsibility. Immed Capital Avail. All replies confidential. Z2511 Times.

WIG MAKER WANTED

Unlimited financial backing to experienced man to set-up and operate factory for machine made wigs. Must know all phases, sources, etc. Salary + profit sharing plan. Y8861 Times

ATT: BROKERS/DEALERS

Rapidly growing investment brokerage firm interested in acquiring mutual fund &/or brokerage organizations in N. Y., N. J., Conn., & Pa., with retained management. Phone 516—CH 8-6625.

UNLIMITED capital available for meritorious inventions, products & articles, patented or patentable, copyrighted or not, for manufacture & promotion. Write fully for appointment. Y8270 Times.

LONG Term Financing arranged 50M & up, Working capital $500M & up available at competitive rates and terms.
E. L. Wheeler 383 Washington Ave.
201 PL 1-2400 Belleville, NJ

MONEY AVAILABLE

INVESTMENTS OR LOANS ARRANGED
American World Enterprises Ltd
917 2nd Ave   NYC 17,   PL 2-1050

ENERGETIC BUSINESSMAN

$20,000 to invest any profitable business as working partner 40 years old, college graduate. X4390 Times.

DYNAMIC BUSINESSMAN

40, will buy or participate small, expanding enterprise. No retail. H374 Times.

PARTNERSHIP WANTED

Adv. exec. with acct. bkgrnd seeks int. in new or estab. school adv. service, school, empl. agency, management consultant, etc. Z2179 Times

WILL invest $25,000 to $50,000 in a successful manufacturing business. Must stand rigid investigation. Z2208 Times.

MANAGEMENT man, sales and operations, wil purchase or invest and participate in growing business with potential. Rigid investigaton. Y4399 Times.

FINANCIAL Executive with capital to invest seeks active participation in substantial profitable business. Z2941 Times.

SALES MKTG PROM ADV PR EXEC 26 BA, MA several years business exp, will invest capital and services in going business or proposition. Z2384 Times.

INVEST $50-$75,000 in manufacturing or wholsale business. Active participation or purchase considered. Z3116 Times.

PARTNER for retail boys & men's sportswear clothing. Bklyn. Some experience. Part-time or full time. Small investment. Call CL 9-2102.

NEED PARTNER? I have diversified sales + mgmnt exp + cash to invest in going busn. (914) DE 7-6363 Z2366 Times

PARTNER Wanted-growing L.I. ceramic & dental lab seeks merger w/top gold man with accounts to buy in. Z2951 Times.

WILL purchase half interest good going Real estate office; Buy outright; Manhattan, Queens Y 4382 Times

Parking lots wanted—Cash

Must be going business. TFX5641 Times
YOUNG man, 31, sales & busn exp, will invest $10M to 15M with services in sound-est busn. H488 Times

CATERING SITUATIONS

bought/sold—confidential. Write needs CATERCO AGENCY Z2148 TIMES.
WORKING Partner-dry cleaning—expd manager will invest in establ going business. Give details. Z2507 Times.

COLLECTION AGENCY WANTED

Also interested purchasing any type small business, all/part. H271 Times
ESTABLISHED Manufacturer seeks capable person for mail order dept. Will teach (914) OW 3-0330.

$3000 in business notes for sale at discount with

Loans are made by the SBA—

1. To finance business construction, conversion, or expansion;
2. To finance the purchase of equipment, facilities, machinery, supplies or materials; and
3. To supply working capital.

The Agency's loans are of two types, "participation" and "direct." Participation loans are those made jointly by the SBA and banks or other private lending institutions. Direct loans are those made by the Agency alone. The Agency cannot make a direct loan if a private lending institution will participate with it in a loan to the applicant.

To qualify for consideration for either a participation or a direct loan, a firm must be a small business and must meet certain practical credit requirements.

In the Act which created the Small Business Administration, a "small business" is defined as one which is independently owned and operated and which is not dominant in its field. The Act also authorizes the SBA, in making a more detailed definition of small business, to use such criteria as number of employees and dollar volume of business.

In general, the Agency's criteria for determining whether a firm is small, for loan purposes, are as follows:

A *manufacturing* concern is considered small if it employs 250 or fewer persons, including employees of affiliates, and large if it employs more than 1,000 persons; if it employs more than 250, but not more than 1,000 persons, it may be considered either small or large, depending on the employment size standard which the SBA has developed for its particular industry.

Most *wholesale* concerns are classified as small if their yearly sales are $5,000,000 or less.

Most *retail* and *service trades* firms are considered small if their yearly sales or receipts are $1,000,000 or less.

An applicant for a Small Business Administration loan must meet the requirements of the Small Business Act as to independence of ownership and operation and nondominance in its field, as well as the more detailed standards developed by the SBA.

In addition to the "small business" criteria, a loan applicant also must meet certain *practical credit requirements* established by the SBA's Loan Policy Board. This Board, made up of the Secretary of the Treasury, the Secretary of Commerce, and the Administrator of the Small Business Administration, has established these requirements for the Agency's loans:

1. An applicant must be of good character.

2. There must be evidence he has the ability to operate his business successfully.

3. He must have enough capital in the business so that, with loan assistance from the SBA, it will be possible for him to operate on a sound financial basis.

4. The proposed loan must be "of such sound value or so secured as reasonably to assure repayment."

5. The past earnings record and future prospects of the firm must indicate ability to repay a loan out of income from the business.

The amount which may be borrowed from the Small Business Administration depends upon how much is required to carry out the intended purpose of the loan. However, by law the maximum loan which the Agency can have committed or outstanding to any one borrower is $350,000. This limitation applies both to the Agency's share in a participation loan and to a direct SBA loan.

An exception to the $350,000 limitation is a loan made to a corporation formed and capitalized by a group of small business concerns for the purpose of producing or obtaining raw materials or supplies, or to obtain the benefits of research and development. In the case of these loans, called "pool" loans, the maximum loan is $250,000 multiplied by the number of small firms which have formed and capitalized the corporation.

Loan Terms

Small Business Administration business loans generally are repayable in regular installments, usually monthly, including interest on the unpaid balance. Interest is charged only on the actual amount borrowed, and for the actual time the money is outstanding. All or any part of a loan may be repaid without penalty before it is due.

The maximum maturity of an Agency business loan is 10 years, except that working capital loans are limited to 6 years, but pool loans may be for up to 20 years.

The interest rate on the SBA's direct business loans has been set by the Agency's Loan Policy Board at 5½ percent per annum. In loans made jointly by the SBA and a bank or other private lending institution, the private lender may set the rate of interest on its share of the loan, provided the note is legal and reasonable. The interest rate on the Agency's pool loans is 5 percent per annum.

By law, the Small Business Administration can make loans to small firms only when financing is not otherwise available to them on reasonable terms. Before applying to the Agency for a loan, a business-man therefore must first seek the needed funds from his local bank or other local source of financing.

There is also an SBA Limited Loan Participation Plan which provides for loans to small business concerns on a somewhat different basis from the regular participation and direct loans. The Plan is designed especially to assist small retail, wholesale, and service establishments which are unable to pledge as much tangible collateral as is required for SBA's regular business loans. The prospective borrower must, however, have a good earnings record, competent management, and a creditable record with local banks for meeting obligations. The limited loans are made entirely through banks, with the banks participating in and servicing them. The SBA's share of a loan of this type is limited to $25,000 or 75 percent of the total amount of the loan, whichever is the lesser. The maximum maturity of a limited loan is 5 years, with a monthly repayment schedule. The maximum interest rate on the SBA portion of the loan is 5½ percent per annum. Figure 16–4 summarizes the key features of SBA lending programs.[4]

Small Business Investment Companies

More than 600 small business investment companies were formed following the passage of the Small Business Investment Company Act in 1958. Some 50 of the larger ones have "gone public." The purpose of the Act was to encourage the organization of privately-owned investment companies for the purpose of supplying equity capital and long-term loans to small business firms. The SBIC's were to provide long-term capital to small businesses unable to get money from the usual investment channels. SBIC's could lend these companies, generally defined as having total assets under $5 million and net worth below $2.5 million, as much as $500,000 or 20 percent of the SBIC's capital and surplus, whichever was smaller.

Tax incentives and financial leverage through the use of borrowed funds were used to stimulate the growth of the SBIC's. Investors in the stock of small business investment companies are allowed an ordinary loss deduction rather than a capital loss deduction on any losses arising from their holdings of SBIC shares. Profits still get capital gains treatment. Also, the SBIC's themselves are allowed an ordinary loss deduction rather than a capital loss deduction on losses on their investments. SBIC's are incorporated in their respective states with a

---

[4] See also "SBA Loans At Work," Small Business Administration, Washington, D.C., 1962.

FIGURE 16–4

Key Features of SBA's Principal Lending Programs

BUSINESS LOANS

	REGULAR BUSINESS	LIMITED LOAN PARTICIPATION PLAN	SIMPLIFIED BANK PARTICIPATION PLAN	SIMPLIFIED EARLY MATURITY PLAN
WHO IS ELIGIBLE?	Most businesses that are independently owned and operated and non-dominant in their fields; that cannot obtain private financing on reasonable terms and are not eligible for financing from other Government agencies, and that qualify as "small" under SBA's size standards, which generally are based on dollar volume of business or number of employees.	Any business that meets criteria stated under Regular Business Loan Plan. However, Limited Loan Participation Plan is of special interest to small retail, wholesale and service concerns.	Any business that meets criteria stated under Regular Business Loan Plan. However, this plan, under which the businessman deals entirely with his bank, is intended to assist the "stronger credits."	Same as under Simplified Bank Participation Plan. Major distinction between this plan and Simplified Bank Participation Plan is that bank provides at least 50% of loan and is repaid before SBA.
LOAN PURPOSES	Business construction, conversion or expansion; purchase of equipment, facilities, machinery, supplies or materials; and working capital.	Same as under Regular Business Loan Plan.	Same as under Regular Business Loan Plan.	Same as under Regular Business Loan Plan.
MAXIMUM AMOUNT	$350,000 to any one borrower. This is maximum SBA share of "participation loan" - - one made jointly by SBA and private lending institution - - and maximum SBA "direct loan" - - one made entirely by Agency.	Maximum SBA share of $25,000 or 75% of total loan, whichever is lesser; private lending institution's share must equal any outstanding loan to be repaid to it with part of participation loan or must be 25% of participation loan, whichever is larger.	$350,000 to any one borrower, as SBA share of participation loan or SBA direct loan.	Same as under Simplified Bank Participation Plan.
INTEREST RATE	Maximum of 5½% per annum on SBA share of "immediate participation loan" (where SBA and private lending institution each put up part of loan funds immediately) and on SBA direct loan. [1] Where SBA "defers" providing its share of participation loan until asked by lending institution to do so, institution may set "reasonable and legal" rate on entire loan. However, if SBA later provides its share of "deferred participation loan," rate on SBA share then is maximum of 5½%. [1]	Maximum of 5½% per annum on SBA share of loan where Agency puts up its share immediately or where Agency has provided its share of deferred participation loan at request of participating institution. [1] Participating institution may set "legal and reasonable" rate on its share of loan and on SBA share of deferred participation loan until SBA provides its share.	Same as under Limited Loan Participation Plan.	Same as under Limited Loan Participation Plan, but on immediate participation basis only.
MATURITY	Maximum of 10 years as a rule. However, working capital loans generally are limited to 5 years, while construction loans may have maximum of 10 years plus estimated time required to complete construction.	Maximum of 5 years.	Same as under Regular Business Loan Plan.	Same as under Regular Business Loan Plan.
TYPE OF COLLATERAL	Real estate or chattel mortgage; assignment of warehouse receipts for marketable merchandise; assignment of certain types of contracts; guarantees and personal endorsements; in some instances assignment of current receivables, and inventories stored in bonded or otherwise acceptable warehouse.	Real estate or chattel mortgage; assignment of accounts receivable or funds due on contracts; pledges of warehouse receipts; negative pledge agreements; and corporate guarantees or personal endorsements.	Same as under Regular Business Loan Plan.	Same as under Regular Business Loan Plan, except that collateral must be of a type not subject to rapid depreciation or obsolescence.

MARCH 1963   [1] 4% interest charged in areas classified by Federal Government as having substantial unemployment.

minimum of $300,000 of paid-in capital and surplus. The SBA is permitted, by purchase of subordinated debentures, to provide one half the capital up to $400,000 for each SBIC, if private funds are not available. In addition, each SBIC may borrow up to 50 percent of its total capital and surplus, but not more than $4 million, from the SBA in the form of loans if private financing is unavailable. Such borrowed funds carry an interest rate of 5 percent. [See Figure 16–5.]

Commercial banks have played a large role in forming SBIC's. They are permitted to invest up to 2 percent of their capital and surplus in

FIGURE 16–5

Small Business Investment Company Loans

	LOANS TO HELP MEET STARTING CAPITAL REQUIREMENTS	LOANS FOR OPERATING CAPITAL PURPOSES
WHO IS ELIGIBLE?	Any company licensed by SBA under the Small Business Investment Act to provide equity capital and long-term loans to small business concerns.	Same as under loans for starting capital requirements.
LOAN PURPOSES	To enable a company that otherwise is qualified under the Act and SBA regulations to meet initial capital requirements for licensees, as well as growth capital requirements.	To provide a company operating capital for use in financing small businesses.
MAXIMUM AMOUNT	Up to $150,000 in the case of a company which plans to start with the minimum required capital of $300,000, and in the same ratio for companies planning greater starting capital. However, the maximum loan to any one company is $400,000.	Loans totaling 50 percent of company's statutory paid-in capital and surplus, with a maximum of $4 million of loans to any one company.
INTEREST RATE	5% per annum.	5% per annum.
MATURITY	Maximum of 20 years.	Maximum of 20 years, but maturity may be extended at SBA's discretion.
SECURITY	Loan secured by the general credit of the company but subordinate to all other debts of the company.	Small business securities held by investment company and earmarked against SBA loan.

Source: Small Business Administration.

SBIC's. The bank-related SBIC is able to consider loans which the commercial bank itself might find inappropriate to handle.

The SBIC's have supplied some capital to small business by purchasing convertible debentures. This form of financing appeals to speculative investors who seek an opportunity to share in the future growth of small business firms. SBIC's may make loans to smaller firms with minimum terms of 5 years but not more than 20 years. Loans provide the only method of SBIC financing to unincorporated firms. Since the SBIC's have sought the most attractive outlets for their funds, really small business firms have not benefitted greatly from their activities. A significant amount of financing has gone into electronic-science firms and into real estate. As a whole, the SBIC's have had difficulty committing their funds and in many instances were unable to find suitable small business financing opportunities.[5]

How Much Capital Will You Need?

The extent to which the capital needed for a small business varies from line to line may be seen in Table 16–3. A motel will cost from $35,000 to $50,000, and some of the luxury type, with a large number of units, will exceed $100,000. On the other hand, you can open a women's accessory shop for $3,500—$6,000. Do not take the statistics in Table 16–3 lightly. They are probably the closest thing to a guide to costs and returns in small business that you will get to see on a comparative basis. They do not tell the whole story, of course. Your local banker, or chamber of commerce, or business broker can provide more specific information closer to home. When business brokers are called in by a man who has a store to sell and are asked what they think the store will bring, they use a number of variables in the calculation, but one constant is the gross-sales figure. Almost by itself this can determine the selling price.

For example, the average package liquor store would cost $1,500 for each $100 of weekly gross sales. Thus, if the store did $1,000 gross a week, or $52,000 annual volume, it would cost $15,000 (exclusive of stock, which would be sold on a dollar-for-dollar basis). If a substantial part of its sales was in case lots, the price would be lower, because the discount on cases lowers the gross profit. If, on the other hand, a considerable percentage of its total sales was derived from wine rather than liquor, the price would be higher, because the margin of profit on

---

[5] See "Are SBIC's Doing Their Job?" *Harvard Business Review*, March–April, 1963; see also "SBIC's: Rocky Road Looms Ahead," *Business Week*, July 20, 1963.

TABLE 16-3

25 Businesses—and Facts You Should Know about Them

Kind of Business	Minimum Capital to Start (Est.)	No. of Families Needed to Support	Failure Rate per 10,000 Firms	Total No. in Operation (Thousands)	Average No. of Full-Time Employees	Typical Annual Sales Volume
Appliance store..................	$ 7,500–$10,000	1,000	85	29.7	3.5	$ 72,600
Auto parts and accessories store....	10,000– 15,000	1,800	10	20.6	2.4	65,300
Beauty shop....................	2,000– 3,000	600	....	74.5	1.1	5,600
Bakery shop....................	5,000– 8,000	2,400	50	20.1	3.1	36,000
Bookstore......................	7,000– 10,000	12,800	29	2.9	3.8	92,100
Camera and photo supply store....	8,000– 10,000	12,300	40	3.0	2.8	80,800
Drugstore......................	10,000– 15,000	800	22	55.8	3.8	89,800
Dry-goods store.................	10,000– 14,000	1,250	24	29.7	4.3	66,700
Furniture store..................	15,000– 18,000	1,300	53	29.0	5.2	118,000
Frozen-custard stand.............	6,000– 7,500	....	....	....	2.0	21,000
Gas station.....................	5,000– 8,000	500	5	188.3	2.0	34,440
Grocery store...................	6,000– 8,000	250	16	377.9	1.3	139,600
Hardware store..................	7,500– 12,000	1,100	13	34.7	3.1	91,100
Infants' and children's wear store...	6,000– 9,000	5,500	97	6.7	1.4	53,300
Jewelry store...................	10,000– 15,000	1,750	36	21.2	2.7	60,000
Dry-cleaning shop...............	5,000– 7,000	1,300	21	25.5	8.3	111,000
Liquor store....................	5,000– 8,000	1,100	14	33.4	1.3	74,300
Lumber and building supply.......	15,000– 20,000	1,900	31	26.1	7.4	286,600
Men's wear store................	8,000– 12,000	2,500	41	23.7	3.2	74,700
Motel.........................	35,000– 50,000	....	....	20.0	....	20,500
Restaurant.....................	6,000– 8,000	300	26	194.1	5.2	65,800
Shoe store.....................	8,000– 12,000	1,900	50	19.5	2.7	67,500
Sporting-goods store.............	8,000– 10,000	5,400	57	6.8	1.6	45,100
Women's ready-to-wear shop.......	7,500– 10,000	1,200	60	30.6	3.2	60,900
Women's accessory shop..........	3,500– 6,000	4,600	37	13.5	1.6	39,500

wine is higher than that on liquor. A candy and stationery store, with new, modern fixtures and air conditioned, would cost $2,000 for each $100 of weekly gross sales, while a nonair-conditioned store with older fixtures might sell for $1,000 per $100 of weekly gross volume. Similar rules have been developed for capital required for inventory. In the case of a grocery store, for example, the stock which must be carried is roughly five times the weekly gross sales. Thus, if weekly gross sales are $1,000 on the average, a $5,000 inventory would be required.

How Much Rent Should You Pay?

The rent you can afford to pay is limited. It is limited by the volume of business you can expect to do and is thus determined by how many families, population, or customers you can expect to draw on—and their incomes—as well as by the number of other stores competing with you. Let us take a simple example. Suppose you need $50,000 of sales a year in order to make a clothing store pay. Assume that there are about 4,000 families in town, with average family income of about $5,300. Census Bureau or Bureau of Labor Statistics figures indicate that people in this area spend about 10 percent of their income for clothing. This means

Cost of Goods Sold		Typical Operating Expense*		Important Items of Expense						Owner's Salary and Profit Before Taxes	
				Rent and Utilities		Advertising		Wages			
Amount in Dollars	Percentage of Sales	Amount in Dollars	Percentage of Sales	Amount in Dollars	Percentage of Sales	Amount in Dollars	Percentage of Sales	Amount in Dollars	Percentage of Sales	Amount in Dollars	Percentage of Sales
$ 49,950	68.8%	$17,570	24.2%	$1,810	2.5%	$1,960	2.7%	$ 9,570	12.9%	$ 5,080	7.0%
44,990	68.9	13,390	20.5	2,680	4.1	780	1.2	6,460	9.9	6,920	10.6
....	....	3,750	66.9	500	9.0	100	1.7	1,120	20.0	1,850	33.0
14,540	40.4	18,000	50.0	1,300	3.6	400	1.1	11,050	30.7	3,460	9.6
58,200	63.2	27,720	30.1	5,990	6.5	1,470	1.6	9,390	10.2	6,170	6.7
55,670	68.9	15,920	19.7	3,550	4.4	1,530	1.9	6,630	8.2	9,210	11.4
60,530	67.4	16,880	18.8	2,240	2.5	450	0.5	9,880	11.0	12,390	13.8
48,360	72.5	11,000	16.5	2,270	3.4	530	0.8	4,800	7.2	7,340	11.0
75,640	64.1	28,080	23.8	4,720	4.0	2,240	1.9	12,150	10.3	14,280	12.1
8,100	38.5	6,045	28.8	1,300	6.2	....	....	2,000	9.5	6,870	32.7
25,830	75.0	4,650	13.5	1,480	4.3	140	0.4	2,000	5.8	3,960	11.5
116,840	83.7	14,800	10.6	2,650	2.2	560	0.4	7,540	3.1	7,960	5.7
65,230	71.6	15,850	17.4	2,730	3.0	1,000	1.1	7,840	8.6	10,000	11.0
35,980	67.5	10,660	20.0	4,000	7.5	800	1.5	3,140	5.9	6,660	12.5
36,060	60.1	15,180	25.3	2,160	3.6	2,160	3.6	5,220	8.7	8,760	14.6
....	....	98,010	88.3	9,430	8.5	3,330	3.0	36,850	33.2	12,990	11.7
59,440	80.0	7,360	9.9	2,080	2.8	220	0.3	2,750	3.7	7,500	10.1
219,250	76.5	38,690	13.5	5,160	1.8	1,720	0.6	20,630	7.2	28,660	10.0
49,600	66.4	19,050	25.5	3,060	4.1	2,610	3.5	8,520	11.4	6,050	8.1
....	....	13,320	65.0	6,360	31.0	410	2.0	2,460	12.0	7,170	35.0
34,680	52.7	23,750	36.1	4,410	6.7	330	0.5	14,340	21.8	7,370	11.2
43,670	64.7	13,900	20.6	4,390	6.5	1,550	2.3	5,200	7.7	9,920	14.7
30,760	68.2	7,940	17.6	1,890	4.2	900	2.0	3,520	7.8	6,400	14.2
39,590	65.0	16,930	27.8	2,190	3.6	1,520	2.5	7,370	12.1	4,390	7.2
26,700	67.6	7,740	19.6	2,570	6.5	390	1.0	2,530	6.4	5,060	12.8

* Excluding owner's salary.

SOURCE: *Changing Times, The Kiplinger Magazine*. Credit is given to Dun & Bradstreet, Inc., for supplying the figures on failure rates and most of the figures on operating expenses.

that the average family spends a little over $530 a year for the products you propose to sell, or, for the town as a whole, $2.1 million annually. There are already ten clothing stores in town; yours would make the eleventh. Over $190,000 worth of business would thus be your theoretic share, assuming that all firms shared equally. Obviously, there is room for your store, even though this kind of analysis does not mean that you will necessarily succeed. All it does mean is that you are not necessarily doomed to failure before you start. Different types of business require different degrees of population support. Variations are great, as Table 16–4 shows. As these estimates demonstrate, some stores do quite well with less than 1,000 people to draw from, while other types need more than 50,000.

No rental is satisfactory, obviously, if the potential shopping population is not sufficient to meet the requirements of your type of operation. If, however, it is adequate, what rent can you afford? A rough rule of thumb is that rent should not exceed 5 percent of sales unless special circumstances, like a corner location, justify the extra amount. The amount of rent, of course, depends on the kind of business and the size

TABLE 16–4

How Many Customers Do You Need?

Business	Population Required	Business	Population Required
Grocery	500	Jewelry	5,000
Restaurant	800	Florist	7,000
Drugstore	1,200	Appliance store	8,000
Bakery	2,500	Sporting goods	45,000
Hardware	2,700	Photo supplies	60,000
Shoe store	3,400	Toy store	70,000
Women's clothing	4,000		

SOURCE: *Changing Times, The Kiplinger Magazine.*

of the town. The ratios shown in Table 16–5 apply to the average store with $30,000–$50,000 net sales a year.

While most rentals are for a fixed monthly or annual amount under a long-term lease, in some instances percentage leasing has been used. This permits a flexibility useful to both landlord and tenant. It stems from recognition of the fact that success in the retail business is dependent upon an adequate gross volume of sales with sufficient markup to insure a profit after covering all operating costs, including rent. The retailer can, therefore, only afford to pay rent equal to a certain percentage of his gross volume of sales in a particular location. If the percentage is too high, the tenant cannot succeed; if it is too low, the landlord does not receive a fair return. Thus rentals may be written, not in dollar terms, but as a given percentage of gross receipts. It is usually provided, however, that a minimum fixed rental, sufficient to pay the

TABLE 16–5

How Much Rent Should You Pay?

Business	Rent as a Percentage of Net Sale		
	Small Town	Medium-Sized Town	Big City
Grocery	1.9	2.2	1.8
Restaurant	5.0	4.4	5.5
Drugstore	3.6	4.9	5.1
Bakery	4.5	...	5.5
Hardware	3.5	4.0	4.7
Shoe store	5.5	6.6	6.3
Women's clothing	4.7	4.8	5.7
Jewelry	4.6	5.4	8.1
Appliance store	3.0	3.6	2.4

SOURCE: *Changing Times, The Kiplinger Magazine.*

proportion of the owner's overhead applicable to the leased premises, be paid and credited against the percentage. Percentage rates for 39 different lines of business, developed and recommended by the Real Estate Board of New York (and reflecting high land values in Manhattan) are shown in Table 16–6.

What Return Should a Small Business Yield?

The compensation or return in a small business normally includes two elements: the salary to the owner for his time and effort, and a net profit on his invested capital. In most cases, the return (salary and profit) for the average-sized establishment, especially in retailing, is not startling. For all the risk, responsibility, and long hours, the small businessman, on the average (there are, of course, exceptions), makes considerably less than the executive on the payroll of a large corporation. This may be seen in the last column of Table 16–3, which shows owner's salary and profit before taxes. Only in six cases does it exceed $10,000, and in most of these instances substantial capital investment was necessary. There is, however, no real correlation between capital invested and return. This will be clear if you compare motels with dry-cleaning shops. A capital investment of $35,000–$50,000 in a motel, plus his services, paid the owner, on the average, only $7,170 per annum before taxes, whereas $5,000–$7,000 invested in a dry-cleaning shop yielded $12,990 before taxes.

The Merchants Service of the National Cash Register Company publishes a survey of expenses and rates of profit in some 63 lines of retail businesses.[6] Whenever you reach the point where you contemplate buying or starting a business in one of the 63 fields, you can check the figures to see what the average experience has been and how well or poorly you can expect to do if you achieve the average for the particular line. For example, automobile dealers, on the average, can expect a net profit of from 3.5 to 4.0 percent on total sales. Bakeries earn from 11 to 13 percent on sales. Beauty shops provide an average return of 7.19 percent on sales. Garages earn 13 to 17 percent on sales. Grocery stores provide a return of about 5 percent on sales. Liquor stores had an average net profit on sales from 8.5 to 10.5 percent. Net profit of motels, depending on number of units, ranged from 5 to 21 percent. Music stores averaged 14.7 percent. Expenses and profits for retail pharmacies and for prescription pharmacies are shown in Tables 16–7 and 16–8.

---

[6] *Expenses in Retail Businesses,* Merchants Service, National Cash Register Company, Dayton 9, Ohio. A free copy may be obtained on request.

TABLE 16–6

Percentage Leasing Rates for 39 Lines of Business in New York City
(Per Cent of Gross Receipts)

Antiques (including silverware, china)............................ 12–15
Gift shops... 10–12
Bakeries.. 6– 8
Barber shops.. 10–15
Beauty parlors.. 10–15
Books... 9–11
Candy:
    Without soda fountain..................................... 8–10
    With soda fountain and luncheonette....................... 7– 9
Cigars, cigarettes, tobacco, candy, and small package goods.......... 5– 8
Children's ready-to-wear:
    Popular price... 6– 8
    Higher price.. 8–11
Cleaning and dyeing... 10
Department stores...$2\frac{1}{2}$– 3
Department stores (specialty type)............................. 3– 4
Drugstores including fountain and luncheonette, perfumes, cosmetics,
    cigars, etc... 6–10
Five-cent-to-one-dollar stores................................. 5– 7
Florist... 8–12
Furniture (new; household)—cash and credit..................... 6– 8
Garages (storage)... 35–40
Gas stations.. 1– $1\frac{1}{2}$¢
                                         per gal.
Groceries:
    Popular price, self-service................................$2\frac{1}{2}$– $3\frac{1}{2}$
    Popular price, with service...............................$2\frac{1}{2}$– $3\frac{1}{2}$
    Higher price.. 6– 8
Hosiery, lingerie, and women's accessories..................... 8–10
Jewelry:
    Genuine... 8–10
    Novelty... 12–15
Liquor (off premises, package stores).......................... 5– 7
Luggage... 10–12
Luncheonette, soda fountain, candy, etc........................ 8–10
Men's clothing.. 5– 8
Men's haberdashery.. 8–10
Men's hats.. 8–10
Men's shoes:
    Popular price... 5– 8
    Higher price.. 8–10
Millinery... 10–15
Optical store, including cameras, binoculars, hearing aids, etc....... 10–12
Parking lot... 40–60
Pianos and musical instruments................................ 6– 8
Restaurants:
    Self-service, without liquor.............................. 5– 7
    Self-service, with liquor................................. 5– 8
    Service, with liquor...................................... 7–10
Shoe repair... 12–15
Sporting and athletic goods................................... 7–10
Women's ready-to-wear, including dresses, suits, coats:
    Popular price... 6– 8
    Higher price.. 8–10

Source: Real Estate Board of New York.

Knowing Your Costs and Profits

One of the hardest things for the small businessman, but one of the most essential, is knowing where he stands at all times with respect to costs and profits. This involves, among other things, understanding terms of sale, concepts like "markup" and "gross profit," ratios, keeping accurate records, and having an adequate system of inventory control. Where the small businessman has to be his own bookkeeper, stock-control man, and sales analyst, this can become quite a chore; but it must be done if a close check is to be kept on the trend of the business.

Your accountant (and you will need one part-time, to come in at the end of the month for a day or two and at tax time) will be able to set up simple journals and ledgers for you to work with. He will be able to tell you, too, exactly what records you must keep to comply with the tax laws, the labor laws, and other regulations—federal, state, and local. A good, inexpensive manual on record keeping is available from the Superintendent of Documents, Washington, D.C. It is called *Records Management in Smaller Stores.*

Dun & Bradstreet publishes a bulletin called *Terms of Sale,* describing those generally used in 90 lines of business activity. Some standard terms are:

Net 30 = full amount due in 30 days.

2% 10 Net 30
  2–10–30 = 2 percent discount allowed if bill is paid within 10 days,
  2/10/N 30   full amount due in 30 days.

Proximo = Next month. "Net 10th proximo" means full amount due the 10th of next month.

E.O.M. = End of month. "3%, 10 days E.O.M., or net 70 days," means that you can deduct 3 percent if you pay within 10 days after the end of the month (after the 25th is considered the end of the month), but you must pay the full amount by the 70th day.

Your accountant or supplier will explain any other terms to you, as will Dun & Bradstreet, if you write to them.

To understand the relationship of costs, markup, selling prices, and gross profit, you need to know a few retailing concepts and a little business arithmetic. "Cost of goods" is the delivered cost at the store. The first pricing at retail is known as the "initial markup." It represents the difference between the cost of the item to the store and the original selling price. In retailing, it is customary to speak of a "percentage markup." This means something different to the retailer than it does to you. If you bought an item for $100 and sold it for $150, you might

TABLE 16–7

Retail Pharmacies

Items	Average All Stores (2,581 Stores)	Total Sales Under $40,000 (115 Stores)	Total Sales $40,000 to $50,000 (99 Stores)
Average Sales per Store	$139,176	$30,707	$45,346
Sales			
Prescription	35.3%	51.6%	44.2%
Other	64.7	48.4	55.8
Total	100.0	100.0	100.0
Cost of Goods Sold	64.0	61.3	63.4
Gross Margin	36.0	38.7	36.6
Expenses			
Proprietor's or Manager's Salary	8.3	15.2	12.4
Employees' Wages	11.4	4.3	6.0
Rent	2.4	4.3	3.4
Heat, Light, and Power	0.9	1.1	1.2
Taxes (except on buildings, income, and profit) and Licenses	1.1	1.0	1.1
Insurance (except on buildings)	0.6	0.7	0.7
Interest Paid	0.3	0.5	0.4
Repairs	0.3	0.3	0.4
Delivery	0.4	0.7	0.5
Advertising	1.5	1.3	1.3
Depreciation (except on buildings)	1.2	1.4	1.5
Bad Debts Charged Off	0.1	0.2	0.1
Telephone	0.3	0.6	0.5
Miscellaneous	2.0	2.0	2.2
Total Expenses	30.8	33.6	31.7
Net Profit (before taxes)	5.2	5.1	4.9
Add Proprietor's Withdrawals	———	15.2	12.4
Total Income of Self-Employed Proprietor (before taxes on income and profits)	13.5%	20.3%	17.3%
Annual Rate of Turnover of Merchandise Inventory	3.7 times	2.5 times	2.7 times
Size of Area (square feet)			
Prescription	272	237	222
Other	1,639	778	1,045
Total	1,911	1,015	1,267
Sales per Square Foot			
Prescription	$180.53	$66.83	$90.40
Other	54.93	19.12	24.22
Total	$ 72.82	$30.26	$35.78
Number of Prescriptions Filled			
New	7,402	2,738	3,300
Refilled	7,733	2,024	2,789
Total	15,135	4,762	6,089
Prescription Price	$ 3.25	$ 3.32	$ 3.29
Number of Hours per Week			
Pharmacy Was Open	———	64 hours	67 hours
Worked by Proprietor	———	60 hours	61 hours
Worked by Employed Pharmacist(s)	———	5 hours	9 hours

Total Sales $50,000 to $60,000 (125 Stores)	Total Sales $60,000 to $70,000 (180 Stores)	Total Sales $70,000 to $80,000 (168 Stores)	Total Sales $80,000 to $90,000 (174 Stores)	Total Sales $90,000 to $100,000 (176 Stores)	Total Sales $100,000 to $120,000 (305 Stores)
$55,443	$ 65,265	$ 75,074	$ 85,065	$ 94,727	$109,467
41.8%	41.6%	39.9%	37.5%	39.0%	36.9%
58.2	58.4	60.1	62.5	61.0	63.1
100.0	100.0	100.0	100.0	100.0	100.0
63.2	63.8	64.2	64.4	64.5	64.6
36.8	36.2	35.8	35.6	35.5	35.4
12.3	11.4	11.0	10.0	10.1	9.4
7.0	7.6	7.8	8.6	8.7	10.1
3.1	2.9	2.4	2.5	2.3	2.3
1.3	1.1	1.0	1.1	1.1	1.0
1.1	1.1	1.0	1.1	1.1	1.1
0.6	0.6	0.6	0.6	0.6	0.6
0.4	0.4	0.4	0.4	0.4	0.3
0.4	0.4	0.4	0.4	0.3	0.4
0.5	0.5	0.4	0.4	0.4	0.5
1.2	1.3	1.3	1.2	1.5	1.4
1.2	1.3	1.2	1.4	1.3	1.2
0.1	0.2	0.2	0.1	0.1	0.2
0.5	0.4	0.3	0.3	0.4	0.3
1.7	1.7	1.8	1.7	1.7	1.7
31.4	30.9	29.8	29.8	30.0	30.5
5.4	5.3	6.0	5.8	5.5	4.9
12.3	11.4	11.0	10.0	10.1	9.4
17.7%	16.7%	17.0%	15.8%	15.6%	14.3%
2.9 times	3.1 times	3.0 times	3.1 times	3.3 times	3.3 times
241	261	259	224	231	254
1,076	1,206	1,286	1,396	1,331	1,468
1,317	1,467	1,545	1,620	1,562	1,722
$96.03	$104.14	$115.65	$142.77	$160.01	$158.83
30.00	31.58	35.07	38.07	43.42	47.05
$42.10	$ 44.50	$ 48.60	$ 52.50	$ 60.63	$ 63.56
3,548	4,483	4,565	4,879	5,585	6,087
3,665	4,122	4,828	5,479	6,002	6,386
7,211	8,605	9,393	10,358	11,587	12,473
$ 3.21	$ 3.16	$ 3.19	$ 3.08	$ 3.19	$ 3.24
70 hours	71 hours	71 hours	73 hours	75 hours	77 hours
64 hours	62 hours	59 hours	60 hours	59 hours	58 hours
10 hours	13 hours	18 hours	19 hours	26 hours	36 hours

SOURCE: 30th Annual Lilly Digest, Eli Lilly and Company, Indianapolis, Ind.

TABLE 16–8

PRESCRIPTION PHARMACIES

Number of Pharmacies	184
Average Sales per Pharmacy	$168,717
Prescription Sales	67.5%
Net Sales	100.0
Cost of Goods Sold	56.4
GROSS MARGIN	43.6
Operating Expenses:	
Owner's Salary	7.2
Employees' Wages	20.5
Rent, Heat, and Light	3.9
Advertising	1.6
Delivery	1.0
Depreciation	.9
Taxes and Licenses	1.0
Insurance	.7
Telephone	.7
Repairs	.2
Miscellaneous	2.2
TOTAL OPERATING EXPENSES	39.9
NET PROFIT	3.7
Net Profit plus Owner's Salary	10.9%
Average Inventory	$ 28,753
Inventory %	17.0%
Average Number of Prescriptions	32,323
Average Prescription Fee	$ 3.49
Average Deliveries/Pharmacy	44
Average Cost per Delivery	47¢
Average Work Week Pharmacist Employee	43.0 hrs.
Average Weekly Salary Pharmacist Employee	$ 151.20

Note: Prescription pharmacies are those pharmacies whose prescription volume accounts for over 60 per cent of the total volume.

SOURCE: "Tenth Annual Survey of Operating Costs of Prescription Pharmacies," American College of Apothecaries, Hamilton Court, Philadelphia, Pa.

assume that this represented a 50 percent increase over cost. In the common retail view, the increase, or markup, would be one third, not one half. The retail calculation would be:

Cost (including delivery charges)	$100
Selling price	150
Difference between cost and selling price	50
Percentage markup ($50 divided by $150)	33⅓%

Thus, markup can be expressed either as a percentage of cost or as a percentage of selling price. In the example above, the initial markup is $50, which is 33⅓ percent of the selling price ($50/$150), or 50 percent of the cost price ($50/$100).

After experimenting with different markups—sometimes reducing the originally established selling price by a markdown, until the right price is reached to move the item effectively—you arrive at a lowered margin, called the "maintained markup." "Gross margin" is the difference between net sales and cost of goods sold; it is also known as "gross profit," "realized margin," or "maintained margin." It is expressed in dollar amounts and also as a percentage of sales.

The relation between gross margin or profit and maintained markup is that they are two views of the same figure. Both are expressions referring to the difference between the cost of an item and the retail price at which it was actually sold. But the merchandise manager speaks of this "spread" as his "maintained markup," while the controller or bookkeeper calls it "gross margin." For it is from this gross margin or profit that the accountant or bookkeeper subtracts expenses to reach a net profit figure for the month's or year's operation. It is easy to set a selling price if you know the gross profit you want to make. The following tabulation will help you:

IF YOU WANT TO MAKE A GROSS PROFIT OF	ADD TO THE COST PRICE
50%	100%
40	66⅔
35	53⅘
30	42⁹⁄₇
25	33⅓
20	25
15	17⅔
12½	14²⁄₇
10	11⅑
8	8⅔
5	5¼

Just how important the matter of markup is may be seen from the study of 333 women's ready-to-wear stores (most of them located in communities of less than 20,000 people) by Dun & Bradstreet, shown in Table 16–9. You will note that the stores are divided into two categories—profitable and unprofitable. If you try to determine the reason, from this composite profit and loss statement, why some did well and others did not, you will not find the answer in salaries, wages, rent,

TABLE 16–9

Profit and Loss Statement

(In Percentages of Net Sales)

	PROFITABLE STORES	UNPROFITABLE STORES
Number of stores	195	138
Net sales	100.0	100.0
Cost of goods sold	67.4	73.8
Total expense:	27.1	30.9
Salaries—owners or officers	9.3	9.1
Wages—employees	6.5	7.9
Occupancy expense (94% of concerns renting)	5.2	5.7
Advertising	1.1	1.3
Bad-debt losses	0.4	0.4
All other expense	4.6	6.5
Net profit or loss	5.5	−4.7

Merchandise Ratios

Gross margin (percentage of net sales)	32.6	26.2
Realized markup (percent of cost)	48.4	35.5
Inventory turnover (times per year)	3.8	3.5

SOURCE: Dun & Bradstreet, Inc.

advertising, bad debts, or even cost of goods sold. The real difference between the profitable and unprofitable stores is to be found largely in the pricing policies disclosed by the big difference in realized markup. Realized markup indicates the relative success of the merchandising and sales-promotion policies. Where realized markup is low, it might indicate slow-moving merchandise, poor choice of merchandise for the neighborhood, or an unhealthy competitive condition which results in an insufficient margin of gross profit.

The Merchants Service of The National Cash Register Company warns small businessmen of the important difference between margin and markup, and provides a markup table which shows margin as a percent of selling price and the equivalent markup as a percent of cost. [See Figure 16–6.]

Another measuring stick of value is inventory turnover. The term "turnover" is applied to describe the number of times your stock, or a given segment of it, is purchased and then sold in a given period of time, usually a year. In other words, "turnover" refers to the number of times the retail value of your stock at any given moment can go into your total

FIGURE 16–6

Computing MARGIN and MARKUP

Many a business fails to make an expected profit because its owner figures his percentage of margin on the cost of goods. He assumes that the percentages of margin and markup on cost are the same. This confusion is not strange, because margin and markup in dollars are identical. The percentages, however, are different. Both represent the difference between cost of merchandise and selling price.

Selling price covers the cost of merchandise plus all expenses of operation and net profit. The selling price is always 100% because it is the total amount of money we are going to get from the sale.

Margin is always figured on the selling price. It is a percentage of sales.

Example: Suppose we buy an article for $1.20 and sell it for $1.60. The margin would be 40c, which is ¼ or 25% of the selling price. Therefore, our margin on this article would be 25%.

Markup can be computed either as a percentage of cost or of selling price. Although many consider markup a percentage of the selling price, retailing authorities point out that figuring markup on the cost price is easier and less confusing in everyday pricing. The important thing to keep in mind is that when markup is figured on the selling price, a different markup percentage must be used than when figuring the markup on the cost price. Otherwise, the anticipated margin will not be attained.

Example: Suppose we buy an article for $1.20 and wish to sell it on a markup of 25%. What must the selling price be? The markup of 25% times the cost, 1.20, equals 30c. Add 30c to the cost price of $1.20 and we have a selling price of $1.50 with a margin of 30c, or 20%. However, if we want to mark up the article so that we have a 25% margin, we must first determine the percentage that will yield the desired margin when applied to the cost price. Looking at the Markup Table below, we see that a 25% margin is equivalent to a 33⅓% markup on cost. Multiplying 33⅓% times the cost, $1.20, equals 40c. Adding 40c to the cost price gives us a selling price of $1.60, and a margin of 40c, or 25%.

We can readily see from these two examples that on an item costing $1.20 a margin of 25% gives a selling price of $1.60,

BUT

a markup on cost of 25% gives a selling price of $1.50.

Therefore, if we must have a margin of 25% to cover the cost of operation and net profit, we would be losing money by pricing merchandise on the basis of a 25% markup on cost! To realize a 25% margin, we would have to use a markup of 33⅓% on the cost price.

Markup Table

The following table shows what the markup on cost must be to give the desired margin in a number of more common cases. To use this table, find your margin or gross profit percentage in the left-hand column. Multiply the cost of the article by the corresponding percentage in the right-hand or markup column. The result added to the cost gives the correct selling price.

Margin Per Cent of Selling Price	Markup Per Cent of Cost	Margin Per Cent of Selling Price	Markup Per Cent of Cost	Margin Per Cent of Selling Price	Markup Per Cent of Cost
4.8	5.0	18.0	22.0	32.0	47.1
5.0	5.3	18.5	22.7	33.3	50.0
6.0	6.4	19.0	23.5	34.0	51.5
7.0	7.5	20.0	25.0	35.0	53.9
8.0	8.7	21.0	26.6	35.5	55.0
9.0	10.0	22.0	28.2	36.0	56.3
10.0	11.1	22.5	29.0	37.0	58.8
10.7	12.0	23.0	29.9	37.5	60.0
11.0	12.4	23.1	30.0	38.0	61.3
11.1	12.5	24.0	31.6	39.0	64.0
12.0	13.6	25.0	33.3	39.5	65.5
12.5	14.3	26.0	35.0	40.0	66.7
13.0	15.0	27.0	37.0	41.0	70.0
14.0	16.3	27.3	37.5	42.0	72.4
15.0	17.7	28.0	39.0	42.8	75.0
16.0	19.1	28.5	40.0	44.4	80.0
16.7	20.0	29.0	40.9	46.1	85.0
17.0	20.5	30.0	42.9	47.5	90.0
17.5	21.2	31.0	45.0	48.7	95.0
				50.0	100.0

SOURCE: Merchants Service: National Cash Register Company.

sales for a month or year. For example, to find your turnover rate for a year on the basis of a typical month's experience, the estimate can be made as follows:

Beginning inventory, first of month	$ 5,000
Ending inventory, end of month	7,000
	$12,000
Average inventory for month	$ 6,000
Sales for the month	$ 2,500
	× 12
Estimated sales for year	$30,000

Thirty thousand dollars of annual sales divided by $6,000 average inventory equals 5 (annual turnover rate).

This means that on an average inventory investment of $6,000, you can reasonably support annual sales of $30,000. It is apparent at once how turnover rate offsets profits; for if you bought and stocked the full $30,000 of goods at the first of the year, you would be carrying useless stock at great expense for most of the year. By a judicious estimate of turnover, you can reduce inventory investment, storage space, and depreciation of stock to a minimum.

Turnover is extremely important to the lifeblood of a business. In a buyer's market, inventory depreciates with age—rapidly in perishable foods and style-controlled merchandise and slowly in durable items such as utensils, appliances, and hardware. A haberdashery store may show a reasonable net profit by turning over its inventory two and one half times a year, but a women's dress shop must turn over its inventory at least four times. Standards vary from line to line. Meat markets turn over their inventory weekly; filling stations, every fortnight; food stores, once a month or faster; jewelers, only once a year.

With the typical profit margin as small as it is in normal, competitive times, it can be seen how essential are knowledge and experience to the proper control of costs and the pricing policy. When turnover lags, the shrewd and prompt markdown of sluggish inventory is a painful necessity; but it is good economics to sacrifice some profit in order to get working capital back in motion and to make room for faster-moving goods. The ability to recognize and to correct mistakes quickly is the mark of business sense and is part of the know-how of a successful merchandiser.

Ratio Analysis

Dun & Bradstreet, the unique credit rating agency, has made extensive studies of costs and profit margins in many lines of business. Its

"Cost of Doing Business Ratios" provides a guide to the average amount spent by corporations in 185 lines of business for various operating expenses. The section dealing with wholesale and retail corporations is reproduced in Figure 16–7.

FIGURE 16–7

Cost of Doing Business Ratios – Corporations

The following operating ratios for 185 lines of business have been derived to provide a guide as to the average amount spent by corporations for these items. They represent a percentage of business receipts as reported by a representative sample of the total of all Federal Income Tax returns† filed for 1960-1961 or where noted for the 1961-62* year.

Industry (and total number of returns filed)	Cost of Goods Sold %	Gross Margin %	Compen-sation of officers %	Rent paid on Business Property %	Repairs %	Bad Debts %	Interest Paid %	Taxes Paid§ %	Amortiza-tion Deprecia-tion Depletion %	Adver-tising %	Pension & Other Employee Benefit Plans %
*ALL INDUSTRIAL GROUPS (1,190,286)	71.18	28.82	1.86	1.20	.87	.38	1.89	2.72	3.42	1.16	.93
*CONSTRUCTION (83,791)	83.99	16.01	3.28	.53	.48	.16	.51	1.49	1.83	.22	.50
General building contractors (21,672)	89.64	10.36	2.50	.27	.20	.08	.43	.94	.97	.20	.27
Highway & Street construction & heavy construction (9,551)	83.51	16.49	2.25	.43	.98	.15	.61	1.43	4.01	.12	.48
Special trade contractors (38,392)	79.00	21.00	4.75	.63	.28	.22	.32	1.85	1.34	.29	.75
Real estate operators (except developers) & lessors of buildings (149,367)	–	–	3.07	4.44	3.60	.26	15.82	15.06	19.65	.46	.15
Subdividers & developers & operative builders (48,174)	–	–	12.55	.95	.95	.53	12.74	5.50	4.00	4.00	.35
*WHOLESALERS & RETAILERS (364,947)	79.51	20.49	1.75	1.34	.26	.22	.40	1.16	.84	1.04	.26
*RETAILERS (230,243)	73.99	26.01	1.86	2.12	.35	.25	.42	1.36	1.10	1.48	.31
*Food (16,299)	80.06	19.94	.57	1.40	.37	.03	.14	.97	.96	1.11	.41
*General Merchandise (14,979)	64.74	35.26	.71	2.52	.37	.38	.47	1.81	1.37	2.47	.48
Department stores (3,866)	64.79	35.27	.53	2.00	.34	.32	.47	1.82	1.18	2.67	.58
Mail order houses (1,055)	55.53	44.47	1.08	.60	.09	2.29	1.21	.84	.36	9.92	.24
Limited price variety stores (2,053)	61.93	38.07	.56	5.16	.38	.14	.44	1.97	1.64	.95	.26
Merchandise vending machine operators, direct selling organiz. & other general mdse. stores (7,425)	71.05	28.95	2.34	2.34	.36	.20	.40	1.57	2.09	1.12	.16
*Apparel & accessories (27,379)	65.35	34.65	2.73	5.37	.30	.25	.38	1.55	1.04	2.27	.24
*Furniture, home furnishings & equipment (22,370)	66.37	33.63	4.49	2.92	.31	.80	.68	1.54	.89	3.10	.15
*Automotive dealers & gasoline service stations (38,128)	85.35	14.65	1.67	.93	.18	.18	.52	.84	.58	.82	.14
Motor vehicle dealers (25,185)	87.90	12.10	1.41	.72	.12	.17	.54	.60	.42	.85	.11
Tire, battery & accessory dealers, miscellaneous aircraft, marine & automotive dealers (6,844)	73.86	26.14	2.70	1.93	.32	.44	.80	1.20	1.12	1.57	.16
Gasoline service stations (5,917)	77.25	22.75	2.12	1.73	.27	.11	.33	3.74	1.28	.61	.05
*Eating & drinking places (34,498)	50.39	49.61	4.19	4.89	1.12	.06	.53	2.95	2.92	.96	.43
Building materials (14,846)	76.91	23.09	3.36	.68	.32	.59	.56	1.42	1.23	.77	.19
Hardware & farm equipment (10,009)	78.47	21.53	3.84	1.43	.16	.33	.67	1.35	.93	.84	.08
Drug stores & proprietary stores (10,292)	68.04	31.96	3.50	3.05	.31	.28	.22	1.47	1.10	1.35	.28
Liquor stores (4,379)	79.92	20.08	4.32	1.83	.10	.02	.21	1.18	.75	.43	.05
Jewelry stores (4,755)	55.84	44.16	3.95	4.47	.20	1.66	.62	1.97	.93	4.36	.20
*WHOLESALERS (123,412)	85.77	14.83	1.62	.56	.16	.20	.37	.93	.56	.60	.21
*Groceries & related products (14,240)	89.74	10.26	1.05	.38	.15	.12	.20	.54	.45	.35	.14
Meats & meat products (2,110)	91.19	8.81	1.24	.26	.11	.08	.11	.41	.29	.08	.08
Poultry & poultry products, fish & sea foods, & other groceries & related products (11,963)	90.07	9.93	1.02	.37	.13	.12	.21	.49	.47	.38	.12
*Electrical goods, hardware & plumbing & heating equipment & supplies (13,766)	81.84	18.16	2.10	.65	.09	.36	.34	.78	.46	.91	.27
Electrical goods (6,901)	83.45	16.55	1.70	.60	.06	.33	.31	.68	.39	.99	.24
Hardware & plumbing & heating equip. & supplies (6,770)	80.92	19.08	2.42	.63	.11	.35	.40	1.02	.50	.38	.25
Beer, wine, distilled alcoholic beverages (2,973)	84.61	15.39	.98	.25	.05	.05	.28	3.34	.30	1.23	.21
Dry goods & apparel (8,035)	83.84	16.16	2.26	.73	.04	.21	.52	.62	.26	.52	.16
Drugs, chemicals & allied products (5,211)	79.19	20.81	1.31	.41	.08	.16	.19	.66	.41	2.06	.31
Lumber & construction materials (5,996)	86.39	13.61	1.81	.53	.13	.41	.47	.67	.63	.31	.17

†Source Book of Statistics of Income, U. S. Treasury Dept. Internal Revenue Service, Statistics Division   *Statistics of Income, 1961-62, Preliminary   §Excludes Federal Income Taxes

SOURCE: Dun & Bradstreet, Inc.

Other significant indicators in the form of financial ratios drawn from the balance sheet and income account are effective in detecting business weaknesses before they become fatal. Dun & Bradstreet uses 14 ratios to analyze 75 lines of business—manufacturing, wholesaling, and retail. The retail section of this annual compilation is shown in Table 16–10. Careful study of the table will indicate the significance of many

TABLE 16–10

Upper Quartile
MEDIAN
Lower Quartile

14 important ratios in 13 RETAIL lines

Line of Business (and number of concerns reporting)	Current assets to current debt	Net profits on net sales	Net profits on tangible net worth	Net profits on net working capital	Net sales to tangible net worth	Net sales to net working capital	Collection period	Net sales to inventory	Fixed assets to tangible net worth	Current debt to tangible net worth	Total debt to tangible net worth	Inventory to net working capital	Current debt to inventory	Funded debts to net working capital
	Times	Per cent	Per cent	Per cent	Times	Times	Days	Times	Per cent	Per cent	Per cent	Per cent	Per cent	Per cent
Clothing, men's and boys' (151)	5.08 / 2.74 / 1.84	6.38 / 2.78 / 0.52	11.79 / 5.74 / 0.78	18.79 / 8.91 / 0.81	4.36 / 2.37 / 1.56	4.87 / 2.99 / 2.05	** / ** / **	5.1 / 3.7 / 2.8	6.7 / 15.0 / 29.0	19.9 / 41.9 / 87.3	38.2 / 73.1 / 142.8	59.1 / 85.9 / 125.5	32.2 / 66.8 / 97.8	9.5 / 30.9 / 50.2
Clothing, men's and women's (76)	4.09 / 3.02 / 1.91	3.64 / 1.28 / 0.43	8.89 / 3.66 / 1.02	18.57 / 4.21 / 1.90	5.15 / 2.70 / 1.63	6.32 / 3.67 / 2.76	** / ** / **	5.1 / 4.1 / 3.5	7.5 / 21.8 / 38.7	18.1 / 36.7 / 73.9	58.4 / 90.6 / 152.5	60.0 / 79.2 / 116.8	36.9 / 66.7 / 98.0	18.9 / 33.5 / 47.0
Department stores (278)	5.60 / 3.53 / 2.25	2.52 / 1.30 / 0.65	9.01 / 4.65 / 1.71	11.43 / 6.34 / 2.04	4.47 / 3.08 / 2.33	6.07 / 4.30 / 3.04	** / ** / **	6.4 / 5.2 / 3.7	13.0 / 25.9 / 47.1	17.1 / 29.4 / 62.1	36.1 / 69.7 / 101.8	50.8 / 69.7 / 102.8	38.6 / 59.6 / 91.8	12.0 / 27.8 / 57.6
Discount stores (236)	2.10 / 1.59 / 1.34	2.20 / 1.05 / 0.54	20.04 / 11.52 / 3.97	29.60 / 15.32 / 5.47	12.98 / 8.48 / 5.93	19.93 / 11.93 / 8.07	** / ** / **	7.9 / 5.8 / 4.4	15.5 / 28.9 / 53.9	68.9 / 120.6 / 206.2	109.6 / 169.4 / 262.5	128.5 / 183.7 / 278.1	64.5 / 84.2 / 109.0	23.1 / 48.0 / 85.8
Dry goods (82)	5.30 / 3.14 / 2.00	4.73 / 2.87 / 1.41	15.80 / 9.64 / 3.23	25.82 / 12.32 / 5.30	6.00 / 3.15 / 1.90	9.74 / 3.90 / 2.15	** / ** / **	6.1 / 4.5 / 3.0	7.6 / 16.9 / 28.6	13.9 / 34.5 / 67.3	36.7 / 82.7 / 138.4	63.6 / 96.5 / 144.9	25.5 / 51.3 / 77.1	15.9 / 32.0 / 47.4
Furnishings, men's (36)	4.86 / 3.49 / 2.05	3.95 / 1.98 / 0.40	8.28 / 4.99 / 1.35	12.01 / 7.43 / 1.71	4.10 / 2.48 / 1.88	5.31 / 3.77 / 2.40	** / ** / **	7.5 / 3.9 / 3.2	6.5 / 14.9 / 21.8	20.7 / 36.6 / 80.8	55.6 / 78.1 / 147.8	70.1 / 100.9 / 137.3	33.5 / 54.2 / 83.7	8.2 / 18.6 / 32.6
Furniture, 50 per cent or more instalment (168)	7.01 / 3.99 / 2.35	6.44 / 3.10 / 1.00	8.79 / 4.91 / 1.71	10.59 / 5.75 / 2.01	2.42 / 1.59 / 1.19	2.82 / 1.70 / 1.30	124 / 164 / 231	6.9 / 4.5 / 3.3	3.7 / 9.4 / 24.8	14.8 / 35.5 / 74.5	37.5 / 61.9 / 124.0	22.7 / 39.2 / 59.0	52.9 / 93.2 / 173.5	6.8 / 16.6 / 30.3
Groceries and meats, chain (66)	2.85 / 1.94 / 1.48	1.35 / 1.02 / 0.67	12.68 / 10.32 / 6.80	29.06 / 18.99 / 11.46	12.09 / 8.73 / 6.84	26.15 / 17.71 / 13.45	** / ** / **	19.1 / 14.7 / 12.3	39.2 / 54.0 / 70.8	31.7 / 44.0 / 74.6	56.3 / 62.2 / 100.6	92.1 / 117.7 / 159.6	60.0 / 71.9 / 103.7	32.3 / 49.0 / 91.9
Groceries and meats, independent (66)	2.18 / 1.52 / 1.13	1.87 / 1.09 / 0.35	15.10 / 8.62 / 3.14	50.37 / 22.60 / 8.54	13.81 / 9.17 / 5.92	83.35 / 31.02 / 16.77	** / ** / **	26.4 / 20.9 / 12.1	25.9 / 59.7 / 103.8	32.0 / 49.0 / 90.5	59.2 / 90.3 / 128.8	93.0 / 144.6 / 284.9	82.7 / 118.5 / 169.6	19.2 / 68.3 / 257.4
Hardware (67)	14.82 / 5.97 / 2.49	4.33 / 1.87 / 0.93	6.80 / 2.89 / 1.41	8.96 / 4.82 / 1.86	3.78 / 1.57 / 1.07	3.82 / 2.29 / 1.65	** / ** / **	4.0 / 3.4 / 2.8	7.1 / 14.9 / 31.5	5.1 / 16.5 / 40.7	24.8 / 46.1 / 83.9	52.3 / 74.3 / 109.3	15.2 / 38.7 / 68.1	11.9 / 22.5 / 34.1
Lumber and building materials (185)	9.59 / 4.76 / 2.47	3.16 / 1.70 / 0.68	6.43 / 3.17 / 1.25	9.09 / 4.51 / 1.69	2.55 / 1.88 / 1.33	3.61 / 2.68 / 1.73	58 / 79 / 109	5.8 / 4.9 / 3.5	9.2 / 17.3 / 28.8	9.0 / 20.1 / 44.0	32.5 / 51.6 / 111.8	40.4 / 56.9 / 79.7	25.8 / 50.5 / 92.7	10.1 / 24.7 / 49.3
Shoes (75)	4.30 / 2.70 / 1.88	4.15 / 1.97 / 0.47	10.35 / 4.60 / 1.50	16.34 / 8.57 / 1.92	4.85 / 3.05 / 1.30	9.04 / 4.38 / 2.65	** / ** / **	4.9 / 3.6 / 2.9	8.6 / 20.9 / 35.2	20.0 / 40.9 / 74.4	47.8 / 90.3 / 131.7	89.6 / 125.0 / 173.2	21.7 / 49.4 / 76.9	11.3 / 24.2 / 65.0
Women's specialty shops (196)	3.57 / 2.13 / 1.62	3.93 / 1.83 / 0.32	12.49 / 5.05 / 0.93	21.52 / 6.90 / 1.46	6.01 / 3.61 / 2.24	8.54 / 4.93 / 3.11	** / ** / **	8.8 / 6.2 / 4.4	11.7 / 20.9 / 45.3	25.4 / 60.9 / 103.5	64.1 / 102.6 / 163.5	53.2 / 92.6 / 126.1	64.3 / 97.8 / 139.3	16.9 / 35.2 / 72.4

**Not computed; necessary information as to the division between cash sales and credit sales was available in too few cases to obtain an average collection period usable as a broad guide.

Note: In the tables, three figures appear under each ratio heading, to reflect the inter-quartile ranges. The first figure is the **Upper Quartile**, the second, in bolder type is the **Median**, and the third figure is the **Lower Quartile**. An example of how these ranges are tabulated is given on this page under "Clothing, Men's and Boy's." This procedure has been followed throughout the entire series of ratios.

SOURCE: Dun & Bradstreet, Inc.

of the ratios. In the case of current assets to current debt (the current ratio), this is generally regarded as a test of solvency, and a ratio of less than one and a half to one is regarded as a danger signal.

Dun & Bradstreet computes these ratios each year, and the most effective way to use these data is to compare figures for your company with the D&B standard (median) figures. In this way, you can tell whether your company is doing better, worse, or average when compared with the composite ratios for a large number of companies in your line. For example, a basic test of a company is its ability to make money. The three net-profit ratios measure this capacity. The differentiation between the good, average, and poorer firms is quite clear and needs no elaboration. The next two ratios—net sales to tangible net worth and net sales to net working capital—are capital-turnover ratios. These measure the efficiency in the use of capital. As the turnover rate increases, efficiency increases. Too high a ratio would indicate an insufficiency of either working capital or equity capital to do the volume of business. Too low a rate means that capital is not active enough, i.e., is not being used sufficiently.

The net-sales-to-inventory ratio shows whether the inventories are out of proportion to the demand being made upon the firm for its products. The ratio indicates how many times the finished goods on hand are turned over during the course of the year. The normal period in which stocks should be converted into cash or receivables through sales varies with the particular line and must be known before the significance of merchandise turnover in a particular case becomes clear. In comparison with the normal figure, the higher the turnover, the better the inventory control and the more favorable generally the condition of the firm. The lower the turnover, the poorer the control of inventory.

The next three ratios—fixed assets to tangible net worth, current debt to tangible net worth, and total debt to tangible net worth—tend to show whether the firm is financing its operations more on other people's funds than on its own. They indicate the measure of protection which owners are providing to creditors. The lower the ratio, the greater the protection; the higher the ratio, the more it indicates that the firm is depending too heavily on financing by its creditors.

The ratio of inventory to net working capital is an additional measure of inventory balance. If an excessive percentage of net working capital is reflected by unsold inventory, there may be difficulty in meeting currently maturing obligations. Ordinarily the relationship of inventory to net working capital should not exceed 80 percent.

Dividing the current debt by inventory yields yet another indication of the extent to which business relies on funds from disposal of unsold inventories to meet its debts.

The ratio of funded debts to net working capital is used to determine whether or not long-term debts are in proper proportion. Ordinarily this relationship should not exceed 100 percent. Dun & Bradstreet has prepared a Worksheet to enable anyone to compare ratios in a given industry with figures for a company in that industry. This is shown in Figure 16–8.[7]

Which Form of Business Organization Is Best?

It is not easy to say whether the single proprietorship, the partnership, or the corporation is best for the type of business you have in mind. Each form has its advantages and disadvantages. There are literally hundreds of thousands of small businesses in the form of family-held corporations, so the widely held notion that the corporate form is only for big business just is not so. Probably, from the viewpoint of initial organization and red tape, the easiest way of getting into business is via the single proprietorship. This is simple and inexpensive. As the owner, you have a free hand, and you are least affected by government regulation. The income of the business is taxed as your personal income, and you are personally responsible for all its debts. Upon your death, the business may have to be liquidated, unless your wife or son can take over. The firm's ability to borrow and its credit are your ability and your credit.

If your need for resources is greater than your own personal savings and credit, then a partnership may be logical. This enables two or more people to pool their money, talent, time, and credit for a bigger enterprise, which may be either a bigger success or a bigger bust. If it is the latter, each partner is liable to the full extent of his own personal resources for all obligations of the partnership. Any partner can act as agent for the business and can by his unilateral act commit and obligate all other partners. A substantial error of judgment by one partner can throw the others into bankruptcy. It is advisable, therefore, to "know your partners." Tax-wise, the partnership is no different than the single proprietorship. Each partner's income from the business is taxed at regular personal income tax rates, although the partnership as such must file a tax return. This, however, is largely for informational purposes.

If you are the worrying type and do not quite trust your partners or prospective partners, then the corporate form of organization with its essential feature—limited liability—may be just the thing for you. The owners' personal assets are beyond the reach of creditors, and the act of one officer cannot obligate another as an individual or jeopardize his personal property. There is more red tape, restriction, and regulation to the corporate form; but, as your business grows larger, there are two

---

[7] A free copy of "14 Important Ratios in 75 Lines of Business" and of "Cost of Doing Business in 185 Lines" may be obtained by writing to Dun & Bradstreet at 99 Church Street, New York, N.Y., 10007.

FIGURE 16–8

worksheet

—for comparing financial and operating ratios as well as cost of doing business ratios of your business with those of your industry. If your line of business is not included in these studies, use the ratios of the industry most closely related or most nearly comparable to your own.

		RATIOS FOR YOUR INDUSTRY	RATIOS FOR YOUR COMPANY		COST OF DOING BUSINESS FOR YOUR INDUSTRY	COST OF DOING BUSINESS FOR YOUR COMPANY
Current Assets to Current Debt	Upper Quartile MEDIAN Lower Quartile	_____ _____ _____	_____	Cost of Goods Sold	_____	_____
Net Profits on Net Sales	Upper Quartile MEDIAN Lower Quartile	_____ _____ _____	_____	Gross Margin	_____	_____
Net Profits on Tangible Net Worth	Upper Quartile MEDIAN Lower Quartile	_____ _____ _____	_____			
Funded Debts to Net Working Capital	Upper Quartile MEDIAN Lower Quartile	_____ _____ _____	_____	Compensation of officers	_____	_____
Net Sales to Tangible Net Worth	Upper Quartile MEDIAN Lower Quartile	_____ _____ _____	_____	Rent paid on Business Property	_____	_____
Net Sales to Net Working Capital	Upper Quartile MEDIAN Lower Quartile	_____ _____ _____	_____	Repairs	_____	_____
Collection Period	Upper Quartile MEDIAN Lower Quartile	_____ _____ _____	_____	Bad Debts	_____	_____
Net Sales to Inventory	Upper Quartile MEDIAN Lower Quartile	_____ _____ _____	_____			
Fixed Assets to Tangible Net Worth	Upper Quartile MEDIAN Lower Quartile	_____ _____ _____	_____	Interest Paid	_____	_____
Current Debt to Tangible Net Worth	Upper Quartile MEDIAN Lower Quartile	_____ _____ _____	_____	Taxes Paid	_____	_____
Total Debt to Tangible Net Worth	Upper Quartile MEDIAN Lower Quartile	_____ _____ _____	_____	Amortization Depreciation Depletion	_____	_____
Inventory to Net Working Capital	Upper Quartile MEDIAN Lower Quartile	_____ _____ _____	_____	Advertising	_____	_____
Current Debt to Inventory	Upper Quartile MEDIAN Lower Quartile	_____ _____ _____	_____			
Funded Debts to Net Working Capital	Upper Quartile MEDIAN Lower Quartile	_____ _____ _____	_____	Pension & Other Employee Benefit Plans	_____	_____

SOURCE: Dun & Bradstreet, Inc.

reasons why, if you started with the proprietor or partnership form, you may be tempted to switch to the corporate form. First, you can raise additional capital for expansion more easily by selling stock; and second, you will probably be able to save on taxes, for, as your personal income grows, you are taxed at higher and higher brackets, and a point is reached where the flat corporate rate is exceeded by the personal rate.

Your Credit Status and Credit Information

When you are in business for yourself, you have to worry about your own credit and about the other fellow's, too. This makes life even more complicated as a small businessman than it has seemed up to this point. You may recall reading in Chapter 3 that the credit of individuals was recorded in the files of credit bureaus all over the country. In the same way, the small businessman's credit is a subject of concern not only to his suppliers and creditors but also to the national credit agencies, such as Dun & Bradstreet and the National Credit Office, which may be asked for written credit reports on him. Not only do these agencies use trade sources, such as banks, suppliers, creditors, salesmen, and trade associations, but they also send out reporters to interview the head of a firm and obtain necessary information and impressions upon which to prepare a written report. Thus a small firm will be investigated by, as well as use the resources of, an agency like Dun & Bradstreet in the course of ordinary business life. An example of a Dun & Bradstreet report on a small business may be seen in Figure 16–9. It will be noticed that this report involves a rating—in fact, a change of rating, from E 2½ to E 2. The E 2½ rating means that the Simpson Hardware Co. estimated financial strength was about $20,000–$35,000, with a "good" composite credit appraisal. Now it has been advanced to E 2, which raises its composite credit appraisal to "high."

Dun & Bradstreet provides two important services for businessmen: subscribers on request obtain special reports on individual firms and, secondly, regularly receive reference or rating books. These books are lent, not sold. The old volumes must be returned when a new edition is issued or when the subscription contract expires. Rating books are issued every two months in the United States and Canada. They contain nearly 3,000,000 United States and 250,000 Canadian names. Data are arranged alphabetically, by states, cities, towns, and villages within each state and by names in each community. The rating books contain maps of states, lists of banks, and a compilation of state collection and bankruptcy laws. Population and banking facilities of each community are given. The line of business is indicated by a symbol and an abbreviation. A rating covers two points: capital and credit. The "key" to the ratings is shown in Figure 16–10. The "key" indicates that capital and credit ratings are correlated. In particular, in the lower brackets (below $10,000), the very fact that capital is limited prevents a high

FIGURE 16–9

Dun & Bradstreet Report

RATING
CHANGE

SIC	NAME & ADDRESS					STARTED	RATING

| 52 51 | SIMPSON HARDWARE CO | CD 26 FEB 2 19-- N | | | | 1948 | E 2 |
| | SIMPSON, WILLIAM J., OWNER | HARDWARE & PAINTS | | | | | Formerly E 2½ |

495 N MAIN ST.
SPRINGFIELD OHIO

TRADE DISC-PPT
SALES $89,446
WORTH $27,908
EMPLS I + I P.T.

SUMMARY

AN ESTABLISHED BUSINESS CONDUCTING A STEADY AND PROFITABLE VOLUME.
FINANCIAL CONDITION IS WELL BALANCED.

TRADE

HC	OWE	P DUE	TERMS			
1551	356		2-10-30	Jan 19 19-- Disc	SOLD	1948 to date
900	600		2-10	Disc	yrs	
400			2-10-30	Disc	1950 to 11-1-6-	
1600	300		30	Ppt	Active acct	
733	112			Ppt	yrs	

FINANCE

Statement Dec 31 19--

Cash on hand & bank	$ 4,604	Accts Pay	$ 3,064
Accts Rec	1,315	Accruals	621
Mdse	19,158		
Total Current	25,077	Total Current	3,685
Fixt & Equip	4,008		
Auto	2,113		
Ppd & Def	395	NET WORTH	27,908
Total Assets	31,593	Total	31,593

Net Sales January I, 19-- to December 31, 19--, $89,446; gross profit
$19,551; monthly rent $175; lease expires 19--. Fire insurance on fixtures
$4,000; on merchandise $20,000.
Signed Jan 30, 19-- SIMPSON HARDWARE CO. by W.J. Simpson, Owner
-----0-----

When Simpson took over the business in 1948, sales were about $45,000
a year. By working long hours and advertising in the Suburban News he
built up volume a little every year. Also there has been an increase in
residential building on his side of town. Profits have increased as sales
have expanded. Cash withdrawals from the business have been conservative.
Merchandise turns satisfactorily and Simpson has been able to improve his
financial condition a little each year. Carries good balances at his bank
and has not borrowed since 195-.

OPERATION

Retails shelf hardware and tools (65%), S & W Paints (20%) and housewares, cutlery, garden implements, glass, lawn mowers, seeds and sporting
equipment (15%). About 90% of sales is for cash; 30 day credit is extended to contractors and householders. Two clerks, one part-time, are employed. LOCATION: Rents a store 25 x 60 in a residential shopping area
on the outskirts of town. Premises are well maintained.

HISTORY

Style was registered by Simpson July 17, 1948. Used for buying and
advertising. Owner purchased this established business July 1, 1948 from
Ralph T. Meyers. Capital was $18,000 of which $10,000 was a loan since
repaid.
William J. Simpson, born 190-, is married, a native of Ohio. After
graduating from Miami University in 1930, taught school until 1936. 1937-
1945 employed by the Wilson Wholesale Hardware Co., Columbus, Ohio, latterly
In the accounting department. 1946-48 was a salesman for Davis & Crocker,
wholesale builders supplies, Springfield.
2-2 (201 49)

Source: Dun & Bradstreet, Inc.

FIGURE 16–10

KEY TO RATINGS

ESTIMATED FINANCIAL STRENGTH				COMPOSITE CREDIT APPRAISAL			
				HIGH	GOOD	FAIR	LIMITED
Aа	Over		$1,000,000	A1	1	1½	2
A+	Over		750,000	A1	1	1½	2
A	500,000	to	750,000	A1	1	1½	2
B+	300,000	to	500,000	1	1½	2	2½
B	200,000	to	300,000	1	1½	2	2½
C+	125,000	to	200,000	1	1½	2	2½
C	75,000	to	125,000	1½	2	2½	3
D+	50,000	to	75,000	1½	2	2½	3
D	35,000	to	50,000	1½	2	2½	3
E	20,000	to	35.000	2	2½	3	3½
F	10,000	to	20,000	2½	3	3½	4
G	5,000	to	10,000	3	3½	4	4½
H	3,000	to	5,000	3	3½	4	4½
J	2,000	to	3,000	3	3½	4	4½
K	1,000	to	2,000	3	3½	4	4½
L	Up	to	1,000	3½	4	4½	5

CLASSIFICATION AS TO BOTH
ESTIMATED FINANCIAL STRENGTH AND CREDIT APPRAISAL

FINANCIAL STRENGTH BRACKET			EXPLANATION
1	$125,000 to	$1,000,000 and Over	When only the numeral (1, 2, 3, or 4) appears, it is an indication that the esti-
2	20,000	to 125,000	mated financial strength, while not definitely classified, is presumed to be within the range of the ($) figures in the corre-
3	2,000	to 20,000	sponding bracket and that a condition is
4	Up	to 2,000	believed to exist which warrants credit in keeping with that assumption.

NOT CLASSIFIED OR ABSENCE OF RATING

The absence of a rating, expressed by the dash (—), or by two hyphens (--), is not to be construed as unfavorable but signifies circumstances difficult to classify within condensed rating symbols and should suggest to the subscriber the advisability of obtaining additional information.

SEE REFERENCE BOOK FOR EXPLANATION OF ABSENCE OF A LISTING AND ADDITIONAL SYMBOLS USED IN REFERENCE BOOK

Dun & Bradstreet, Inc.

Offices in Principal Cities of the United States

Source: Dun & Bradstreet, Inc.

credit rating. In considering ratings, "G 3" may be regarded as comparatively better than "Aa1." The former is the best credit rating that can be obtained with the capital involved, while the latter may imply some adverse opinion of the firm. The third and fourth grades of credit generally indicate slowness of payment.

The subscriber who desires more exhaustive and possibly more recent information than that contained in the rating book asks for a credit report on the concern in which he is interested. His contract with the agency calls for a specified number of credit reports per year, excess reports being subject to an additional charge. There are three types of credit reports sold by Dun & Bradstreet. The "Synopsis" report is written on the majority of names in the Reference Book, mostly on the smaller enterprises. The "Analytical" report is written by a staff of analysts on larger concerns with complicated capital structures. The "Specialized" report is written on manufacturers, wholesalers, and larger retailers who have a less complicated structure than "Analytical" names but are important from a credit viewpoint. "Specialized" reports generally deal with medium-sized firms emphasizing individual trade features.

There are a variety of other Dun & Bradstreet services, including a Mercantile Claims Division for the handling and collection of past-due accounts. When you are considering buying a business, it is useful to obtain a D&B report on the concern and get an idea of how it is rated (assuming it is) and what D&B thinks of it. Once you take over, if you do, you will be subject to the same type of credit scrutiny.

If you sell for cash only, then your only credit problem is your own vis-à-vis your suppliers. But if you sell on credit, either charge or installment, then you have another major business area and problem on your hands. If you are operating a single proprietorship with little help, then you should make every effort to stick to cash sales only, because you have enough to do as it is without trying to be a credit man as well. It is a highly specialized function that is not done easily or well along with eight other business functions the same day. Of course, you may not have a choice; the nature of your business may require the extension of credit. A drugstore, for example, may be able to operate successfully on a strictly cash basis, but an electrical appliance store, on the other hand, will have to sell on credit. The nature of your competitor's operations may, of course, force you into credit accommodations. If this is the case, then you had better start reading up on and studying credit and collections.[8]

Insurance for the Business

In starting a new business or buying an existing one, after you have talked to your business broker, accountant, lawyer, etc., be sure to

---

[8] Clyde W. Phelps, *Retail Credit Fundamentals* (4th ed.), International Consumer Credit Association, St. Louis, Mo., 1963.

schedule a long conference with your insurance agent. You will need his help. If your life savings go into the purchase of a store and its fixtures and equipment, what if there is a fire—and you have forgotten about fire insurance? If your delivery truck hits and kills someone, and you face a $25,000 damage suit—because you had neglected to take out the right kind of insurance—could your business settle this out of its cash reserves? You could lie awake at night having nightmares thinking of the countless other types of hazards or misfortunes which might befall your business. But since many of them can be covered by insurance, it is more restful and logical to consult your insurance agent.

While there are more than 300 varieties of business insurance available, they may be classified into seven categories. *Business life insurance* is merely life insurance used to meet the hazards of loss to a business from the death of someone importantly associated with it. This type of life insurance involves nothing new or different from the basic life insurance policies and provisions, but it does require a special application of these provisions to meet the problems peculiar to the business. There are numerous specific purposes for which business life insurance is written.

Chief among these are: (*a*) Key-man protection, to reimburse for the loss of a key employee or to provide replacement in the event of his death. This insurance provides the funds with which to hire the needed successor and to help meet the financial burden that the employee's death might cause. To illustrate: a soap-manufacturing firm had its buying of essential oils and other raw materials centered in one veteran employee whose knowledge and contacts resulted in very economical buying; at his death, there was a costly interlude before a successor had the buying of these specialized materials in hand. (*b*) Partnership insurance, to retire a partner's interest at death. As a partnership automatically dissolves at or shortly after the death of any one of the partners, there is an especially vital need for life insurance protection to safeguard the business against forced liquidation. Partnership insurance enables the surviving partner to reorganize at once and continue in business; it liquidates the interest of the deceased partner without loss; it enables the beneficiaries of the deceased partner to secure full, fair value for his interest in the firm, at once and with a minimum of trouble; and it lends support to the credit standing of the firm. (*c*) Corporation insurance, to retire at death a major shareholder's interest in a small, closely held corporation. This type of insurance is of special concern to the small corporation where the shareholders are few and their interests keep them close to the management of the firm, possibly being one and the same. The great bulk of the country's corporations are in this category. Large numbers of them are small, closely held businesses which adopted the corporate form merely for its legal, tax, and continuity advantages. Such insurance gives the deceased shareholder's heirs full value for his holdings at once and reduces the shock of changes in ownership. (*d*) Proprietorship insurance, to provide for maintenance of a business upon the death of a sole proprietor. There is no set pattern; each case has to be determined on its own merits. One plan may call for the sale of the business to stated employees, with the purchase money provided by the insurance; another may provide that the business be run by the executor or the heirs, etc. The specific plan is important, however. Many small businesses flounder upon the death of the sole owner merely because he did not provide the business insurance with which to maintain it. Numerically, businesses of the individual-proprietor type are by far the most numerous, comprising approximately 70 percent of all business units.

The second type of business insurance is *property insurance.* Most important in this category is fire insurance, with its various auxiliaries which insure against sprinkler leakage, boiler explosions, smoke damage, and other losses not covered under the basic policy. Not only the fixtures and equipment but the inventory as well should be insured, and the building too, of course, if the firm owns it. The third type of business insurance is *liability insurance.* The most common form is the "comprehensive liability insurance" policy, which covers claims against you for damages or injuries to property or persons that occur during the normal operation of your business or that are due to the products sold or to the acts of employees during working hours. Special liability policies have been devised for individual kinds of businesses. For example, there is a druggists' liability policy that covers claims arising from mistakes in filling prescriptions. Accountants can buy a liability policy that insures them against damage claims arising out of their mistakes. Restaurant owners can protect themselves against damage suits that may arise if some of the food served has been contaminated.

Workmen's compensation and disability insurance is essential in order to pay claims arising out of injuries employees may sustain while working for the firm. Most states require this type of insurance; but, even if they do not, it is worthwhile, because the courts have consistently held that the employer is responsible for the health and safety of his employees while they are on the job.

Burglary, theft, and dishonesty insurance is a fourth type. Businessmen buy what is known as the "three D" policy. This covers loss due to dishonesty, disappearance, and destruction. You can, of course, buy straight burglary or theft policies, but the "three D" policy is better. Also you can buy a fidelity bond to protect yourself against losses due to the dishonesty of your own employees. Then there is *business-interruption insurance.* Commonly called "use and occupancy," this type covers loss of income resulting from temporary interruption of the business following fire, explosion, or some other disaster. Another form of use and occupancy insurance pays the extra expense you incur when your business is forced to move to another location after a fire or because a lease is canceled. *In-transit insurance* provides coverage against losses while goods are in transit and should be used when expensive merchandise is shipped. *Auto and truck insurance* is essential, of course, but since coverage for commercial firms is roughly the same as, but more expensive than, that for private individuals, no further explanation is needed.

Clearly, you cannot afford, in your new business, to overlook the insurance angle. You may very likely not be able to afford all the coverages described above, but your agent can suggest priorities to enable you to buy the most essential policies first and other coverages later, as you can afford them.

The Business Information Service of the U.S. Department of Commerce worked out a business insurance program for a small retail grocery store doing $72,000 of gross annual sales. A two-phase insurance program was developed, with the first, most essential, phase designed to cover early operations and the second, an expansion of the original plan, to provide for future insurance needs as the enterprise grew. As shown in the accompanying tabulation, the types of insurance policies carried by the company and planned for the future represent a logical coverage for a business with a sales volume large enough to support a full program without penalizing some other phase of the business. All policies are carried on an annual basis; each is renewed annually. Costs are figured on gross annual sales of $72,000. The four types of insurance shown are now carried and represent 0.19 percent of gross sales. Other types on insurance, to be obtained later, are shown in the second tabulation. To obtain these additional types of coverage would cost an additional 0.31 percent of gross sales. This should give you a working idea of what an insurance program for a small business includes and costs. The insurance agent can tell you a good deal more with respect to any specific situation.

Type of Insurance	Coverage	Actual Value	Annual Cost
1. Fire insurance and extended coverage......................	$3,000*	$5,000	$ 35.00
2. Public or premise liability........	$5,000 and $10,000	....	19.55
3. Delivery truck:			
a) Collision....................	$50.00 deductible	$1,200	
b) Broad-form theft.............	Full value	New	(a.b.c.)
c) Fire and lightning............	Full value	....	60.00
4. Burglary.......................	$1,000 in store; $1,333 away from store	....	25.00
Total......................	....	....	$139.55

* Carried on stock only—$3,000 or less for damage from fire, windstorm, hail, hurricane, explosion, riot, civil commotion, smoke, aircraft, or land vehicle.

Type of Insurance	Coverage	Annual Cost
5. Workmen's compensation....	$1.07 per $100 of payroll plus $20.00	$ 31.00 min.
6. Public liability.............	$5,000 and $10,000, and $5,000	40.00
7. Product liability............	$5,000	20.00
8. Use and occupancy or Business interruption...........	$5,000	25.00
9. Life insurance (each partner)	$5,000*	100.00
10. Fidelity insurance...........	$1,800†	10.00
Total.................	....	$226.00

* Ten-year term insurance carried by each partner at the firm's expense and payable to the partnership to liquidate any obligation at the death of partner.
† This covers loss only from proven employee dishonesty.

Self-Employment and Social Security

Persons self-employed in trade or business or the professions are covered under social security. This is a good thing because, contrary to a widespread view of the economic status of the self-employed, satistics show that over one third of the families dependent on self-employment earnings have incomes too small to permit significant systematic savings. Moreover, the majority of the self-employed are in the upper age brackets. Fifty-five percent are over 45, as contrasted with 32 percent of the employees who are over that age. The self-employed also continue in self-employment longer. The proportion over age 65 still engaged in earning a living is four times that of employees who continue working after that age. It is estimated that more than 5,000,000 persons who work for themselves are now covered under the self-employment provisions of the social security law, as amended.

Here are some questions and answers on social security for the self-employed:

1. *What kinds of self-employment income are covered by the social security law?* In general, the net earnings from most kinds of busi-

nesses, trades, or crafts in which the owner or partner "works for himself." The sole owner or partner operating a store, shop, garage, lunchroom, etc.; the independent contractor; self-employed engineers, architects, accountants, lawyers, dentists, optometrists, clergymen, and the artist and the writer may build up old-age and survivors insurance protection under this part of the law. Only doctors are not covered.

2. *What about farm operators?* They too are now covered under the self-employment provisions of the Social Security Act. For social security purposes, the term "farm operator" includes people who operate farms or ranches as sole owners, partners, renters, or lessees.

3. *What amount of earnings must a self-employed person have to be covered by social security?* If net earnings from self-employment are $400 or more in any one year, the person is covered by the law even though he may not be active in the business. His self-employment income will count toward social security payments.

4. *Does a self-employed person report income from investments?* No. Your income from stocks or bonds will not be credited for social security purposes, unless you are a dealer in securities; and your rentals from real estate held for investment purposes will not count toward social security benefits unless you are a real estate dealer.

5. *Are reporting self-employment income and paying the self-employment tax optional?* No. Any person whose self-employment is covered by the law must report his earnings and pay the self-employment tax.

6. *What is the contribution rate for self-employed persons?* The following tabulation shows the tax rates and the scheduled increases:

Calendar Year	Percent
1963–65	5.4
1966–67	6.2
1968 and later	6.9

Only the first $4,800 of total wage and self-employment income is taxable.

7. *How will the self-employed person pay his self-employment tax?* His contribution toward old-age and survivors insurance protection for himself and his family will be payable at the time he files his federal income tax return every year. At that time, he will enter the amount of his self-employment earnings and tax on separate Schedule C, which is a part of his income tax return, Form 1040. The schedule will be detached from his income tax report form by the Director of Internal Revenue, who will forward it to the Social Security Administration. Self-employment income will then be credited to his social security account.

8. *How will prior "covered" employment affect the self-employed?* Any wages a self-employed person previously earned in a job covered by social security will still be listed on his social security account. These earlier earnings will help to establish his insured status and will be considered in determining his average earnings for retirement or survivors insurance payments.

9. *What if husband and wife are business partners?* If they operate a business as a true partnership or a joint venture, each should report his respective share of the business profits as net earnings from self-employment on separate schedules even though they file a joint return. Each will receive social security credit if each has net earnings of $400 or more.

10. *What about father and son partnerships?* A father and his son may work together to conduct a business as partners or joint venturers. In either case both are self-employed and are covered under the law, if each has net earnings of $400 or more per annum.

Remember, as a small businessman, that if your self-employment income is $400 or more a year, you must report your self-employment income on Schedule C and pay the social security tax. You have no choice. Coverage under the Social Security Act is mandatory. For each full year in which his self-employment income is $400 or more, the self-employed person will receive credit for four quarters of coverage. Eligibility for benefits, as was indicated in Chapter 8, is based on quarters of coverage and is the same for the self-employed as for the employed. Furthermore, the self-employed have exactly the same rights and benefits—old-age insurance and survivors benefits—under the Act as have the employed. If you forget what these are, turn back to Chapter 8 to refresh your memory.[9]

Your Chances of Success

How long may you expect to stay in business? What are your chances of survival? The answers to these questions depend less on general economic conditions than upon your own business qualities and personal good fortune. The first five years are the hardest. Dun & Bradstreet declares that "if a concern is destined to be a failure, it usually does not take much time in becoming one." Table 16–11 reveals that about 55 percent of the concerns that fail have been in business for five years or less. Failure liabilities and trends are shown in Tables 16–12 and 16–13.

During a given year, about one seventh of all business enterprises in

---

[9] For greater detail see *Social Security Information for Self-Employed People*, OASI Bulletin No. 22, U.S. Department of Health, Education and Welfare, Washington, D.C.

TABLE 16–11

Trend in Age of Business Failures, 1945–1963

Year	% in Business 5 Years or Less	% in Business 6 to 10 Years	% in Business over 10 Years
1945	59.1	19.8	21.1
1946	71.8	13.9	14.3
1947	77.6	13.3	9.1
1948	76.5	12.5	11.0
1949	74.6	14.5	10.9
1950	68.2	19.0	12.8
1951	63.2	23.5	13.3
1952	59.9	25.8	14.3
1953	58.5	26.7	14.8
1954	57.2	27.3	15.5
1955	56.6	26.0	17.4
1956	58.6	23.1	18.3
1957	58.9	21.8	19.3
1958	57.2	21.4	21.4
1959	57.1	22.3	20.6
1960	58.6	20.8	20.6
1961	56.2	22.4	21.4
1962	55.4	22.2	22.4
1963	55.4	21.7	22.9

Source: Dun & Bradstreet, Inc.

TABLE 16–12

Business Failures by Size of Liability, 1950–1963

Year	Under $5,000		$5,000 to $25,000		$25,000 to $100,000		$100,000 to $1 Million		Over $1 Million	
	No.	%	No.	%	No.	%	No.	%	No.	%
1950	2,065	22.5	4,706	51.4	1,975	21.6	407	4.4	9	0.1
1951	1,832	22.7	4,160	51.6	1,634	20.3	412	5.1	20	0.3
1952	1,428	18.8	3,884	51.0	1,769	23.3	512	6.6	18	0.2
1953	1,383	15.6	4,317	48.7	2,375	26.8	748	8.5	39	0.4
1954	1,640	14.8	5,640	50.9	2,946	26.5	829	7.5	31	0.3
1955	1,785	16.3	5,412	49.3	2,916	26.6	820	7.5	36	0.3
1956	2,032	16.0	6,152	48.4	3,431	27.1	1,022	8.1	49	0.4
1957	2,001	14.6	6,699	48.8	3,847	28.0	1,147	8.3	45	0.3
1958	2,028	13.5	7,015	46.9	4,456	29.8	1,408	9.4	57	0.4
1959	1,841	13.1	6,664	47.4	4,202	29.9	1,284	9.1	62	0.5
1960	1,688	10.9	6,884	44.6	5,078	32.9	1,703	11.0	92	0.6
1961	1,903	11.1	7,378	43.2	5,725	33.5	1,973	11.6	96	0.6
1962	1,647	10.4	6,700	42.5	5,425	34.4	1,876	11.9	134	0.8
1963	1,296	9.0	5,781	40.2	5,115	35.6	2,031	14.1	151	1.1

Source: Dun & Bradstreet, Inc.

TABLE 16–13

Failure Trends, 1929–1963

Year	Number of Failures	Total Failure Liabilities	Failure Rate per 10,000 Listed Concerns	Average Liability per Failure
1929	22,909	483,252,000	104	21,094
1930	26,355	668,282,000	122	25,357
1931	28,285	736,310,000	133	26,032
1932	31,822	928,313,000	154	29,172
1933	19,859	457,520,000	100	23,038
1934	12,091	333,959,000	61	27,621
1935	12,244	310,580,000	62	25,366
1936	9,607	203,173,000	48	21,148
1937	9,490	183,253,000	46	19,310
1938	12,836	246,505,000	61	19,204
1939	14,768	182,520,000	70	12,359
1940	13,619	166,684,000	63	12,239
1941	11,848	136,104,000	55	11,488
1942	9,405	100,763,000	45	10,713
1943	3,221	45,339,000	16	14,076
1944	1,222	31,660,000	7	25,908
1945	809	30,225,000	4	37,361
1946	1,129	67,349,000	5	59,654
1947	3,474	204,612,000	14	58,898
1948	5,250	234,620,000	20	44,690
1949	9,246	308,109,000	34	33,323
1950	9,162	248,283,000	34	27,099
1951	8,058	259,547,000	31	32,210
1952	7,611	283,314,000	29	37,224
1953	8,862	394,153,000	33	44,477
1954	11,086	462,628,000	42	41,731
1955	10,969	449,380,000	42	40,968
1956	12,686	562,697,000	48	44,356
1957	13,739	615,293,000	52	44,784
1958	14,964	728,258,000	56	48,667
1959	14,053	692,808,000	52	49,300
1960	15,445	938,630,000	57	60,772
1961	17,075	1,090,123,000	64	63,843
1962	15,782	1,213,601,000	61	76,898
1963	14,374	1,352,593,000	56	94,100

Source: Dun & Bradstreet, Inc.

the United States normally close and an equal number open for business. This is an impressive figure and might discourage you, but you should also know that, contrary to popular notions, retail trade has the lowest birth and death rates of all fields. Failures are of two types. There are the formal ones that get into court, where creditors lose. But a much larger number of failures occur each year which do not occasion legal action. They are the ones in which owners lose their capital, find that it has been eaten away, that they cannot make ends meet. The high hopes and enthusiasm with which they started are gone and, as they sadly lock the door for the last time, they say "never again."

What Causes Failures?

Here, two popular notions are wrong. Business recessions are not the chief cause of business failures, although they have often furnished plausible alibis. A study by the National Cash Register Company indicates that in 82 percent of the cases surveyed, failures were due to the faults of those failing. A Dun & Bradstreet study set the figure higher. As Figure 16–11 reveals, lack of experience and incompetence are responsible for the great bulk of all failures. Breaking failure causes down more precisely, the leading ones are as follows:

1. *Picking the Wrong Business.* After the war, a great many exservicemen who had been trained by the armed forces as radar and radio men opened their own radio and TV repair shops. The resulting overcrowding drove most of them out in a short time. The same was true of exporting-importing. Many GI's who came back from overseas, having established a few contacts abroad, went into the export-import business on their own. After a good year or two, most of them were forced out.

2. *Lack of Managerial Experience.* Many a good mechanic or wonderful salesman makes an unholy mess of his own business the first time he sets out on his own. He may be expert in his own line, but he just lacks managerial experience or ability. Having to handle so many aspects of a business that he had never handled or thought about before frustrates, tires, and bewilders him, leading to neglect and, finally, failure.

3. *Incompetence.* Some people just have bad dispositions, cannot get along with anyone, or are lazy and shiftless. They cannot hold a job, or they drift from one job to another. Finally they persuade some foolish relative to finance a business venture for them. They fail, of course, because, if you cannot keep a job, it is not likely that you can run a business successfully.

4. *Lack of Working Capital.* An underfinanced business is doomed almost from the start unless it is in the hands of an ingenious and specially talented manager. It just does not pay to try to start a business with less than the average amount of capital shown by surveys to be necessary for the particular line or field chosen.

Classification of Causes of Business Failures in United States in 1963 Based on Opinions of
Informed Creditors and Information in Dun & Bradstreet's Credit Reports

LINE OF BUSINESS		UNDERLYING CAUSES		METHOD OF OPERATION	ALL	
NUMBER	PERCENT		ALL	APPARENT CAUSES	NUMBER	PERCENT
390	2.7	NEGLECT:	Due to	Bad Habits	88	0.6
				Poor Health	192	1.3
				Marital Difficulties	52	0.4
				Other	58	0.4
260	1.8	FRAUD:	On the part of the principals, reflected by	Misleading Name	9	0.1
				False Financial Statement	51	0.3
				Premeditated Overbuy	19	0.1
				Irregular Disposal of Assets	139	1.0
				Other	42	0.3
1345	9.4	LACK OF EXPERIENCE IN THE LINE	Evidenced by inability to avoid conditions which resulted in:	Inadequate Sales	6440	44.8
2891	20.1	LACK OF MANAGERIAL EXPERIENCE		Heavy Operating Expenses	1264	8.8
2779	19.3	UNBALANCED EXPERIENCE*		Receivables Difficulties	1600	11.1
6096	42.4	INCOMPETENCE		Inventory Difficulties	1057	7.4
				Excessive Fixed Assets	742	5.2
				Poor Location	601	4.2
				Competitive Weakness	3140	21.8
				Other	415	2.9
111	0.8	DISASTER:	Some of these occurrences could have been provided against through insurance.	Fire	54	0.4
				Flood	2	—
				Burglary	8	0.1
				Employees' Fraud	9	0.1
				Strike	4	—
				Other	34	0.2
502	3.5	REASON UNKNOWN				
14,374	100.0	TOTAL		Because some failures are attributed to a combination of apparent causes, the totals of these columns exceed the totals of the corresponding columns on the left.		

* Experience not well rounded in sales, finance, purchasing, and production on the part of an individual in case of a proprietorship, or of two or more partners or officers constituting a management unit.
Source: Dun & Bradstreet, Inc.

5. *Excessive Debt.* This is not necessarily the same as, or a different way of putting, cause No. 4. You may have the required initial capital, but you may overbuy, be too optimistic and hire too large a staff, or sign a lease at too high a rental. All these things spell failure.

6. *Poor Salesmanship.* You may be an excellent manager, but if you cannot sell and do not hire someone who can, you will have a well-run storage warehouse on your hands, because your inventory will not move. In very few businesses does the stock sell itself. Chances are that it will not in your business.

7. *Bad Location.* If you are on the wrong side of the street—and in most cases there is a good side and a poor side—you will not get the customers; and without customers you are licked before you start. Most chains spend a good deal of money in the effort to choose good locations; they do it scientifically, employing a variety of techniques, such as clocking passers-by at varying times, in varying weather, before they locate.

8. *Failure to Keep Records.* To operate your business effectively, you must know at all times what your cash position is; how much your inventory amounts to and at what rate it is turning over; which items are selling and which are slow; what your costs are, fixed as well as variable; which sales yield the best profit and which yield none at all. These and a hundred other facts are needed to enable you to control and judge your business trends competently. You cannot know or find out any of these facts unless your records are kept carefully and up to date.

9. *Loose Credit Policies.* You can expand sales by not asking people to pay you for what they buy, but you will not be in business very long if you do. Granting credit too freely and loosely amounts to the same thing and has the same consequences. You might just as well give away the goods. The results in the end will be just the same as an unsound credit-sales program.

10. *Lack of Insurance.* Fire, theft, embezzlement, or a large damage suit by a customer who injures himself in your store can all spell a quick end to your small business if you do not have the necessary insurance protection to cover such hazards.

11. *Poor Judgment of People.* In buying goods, in hiring an employee, in choosing an accountant or a lawyer, in advertising, in choice of styling or display, in selecting a partner, inability to judge wisely and select well can be costly, if not disastrous.

12. *Neglect.* If you prefer your stockbroker's office, or the race track, or your leisure to your business, you cannot expect it to make its own decisions, to buy and sell its own goods, and generally to run itself. The man who devotes his full time and attention to his business may

possibly not succeed, but he stands a much better chance of doing so than one who likes leisure.

Conclusion

A small business of your own may be a wonderful way to invest your savings. It may free you from the monotony of a job you do not like and also yield a fine return. But it will do so only if you devote time, care, and your best judgment both to selecting it and running it. The first five years are the hardest. If you survive these, you have done well. In the course of them you will find that running a business is not a game, as you may have imagined, but hard work—probably much harder then the job you left.

SUGGESTED READINGS

1. *Starting and Managing a Small Business of Your Own* (rev. ed.), Small Business Administration, Washington, D.C., 1962.
2. White House Committee on Small Business, *Small Business in the American Economy,* Washington, D.C., May, 1962.
3. Olin S. Pugh, "Small Business Investment Companies," *Business Topics,* Michigan State University, Autumn, 1963.
4. J. K. Lasser, *How to Run a Small Business* (3d ed.; New York: McGraw-Hill Book Co., Inc., 1963).
5. P. C. Kelley and K. Lawyer, *How to Organize and Operate a Small Business* (3d ed.; Englewood Cliffs, N.J.: Prentice-Hall, Inc., 1961).
6. *14 Important Ratios in 75 Lines of Business,* Dun & Bradstreet, Inc. Issued annually. A free copy may be obtained by writing to the firm at 99 Church St., New York, N.Y., 10007.
7. *10 Keys to Basic Credits and Collections* and *Terms of Sale Generally Used in 90 Lines of Business Activity,* both Dun & Bradstreet, Inc. Issued annually. Free copies may be obtained by writing to the firm at 99 Church St., New York, N.Y., 10007.
8. *A Handbook of Small Business Finance,* Small Business Administration, Washington, D.C. Latest edition.
9. Martin B. Solomon, Jr., *Investment Decisions in Small Business* (Lexington, Ky.: University of Kentucky Press, 1963).
10. John H. Bunzel, *The American Small Businessman* (New York: Alfred A. Knopf, Inc., 1962).
11. *Managing the Independent Business,* Lee E. Preston (ed.) (Englewood Cliffs, N.J.: Prentice-Hall, Inc., 1962).
12. *Expenses in Retail Businesses,* Merchants Service, National Cash Register Co., Dayton 9, Ohio. A free copy may be obtained upon request.
13. Small Business Administration publications of interest include:
    a) Management Aids
    How Trade Associations Help Small Business

How the Public Employment Service Helps Small Business
How to Analyze Your Own Business
Loan Sources in the Federal Government
Choosing the Legal Structure for Your Firm
Analyzing Your Cost of Marketing
Checking Your Marketing Channels
Cash Management in Small Plants
Key Marketing Words—What They Mean
Getting Results from Your Budget
Payroll Savings Helps Small Business
Business Life Insurance
Sole Proprietorship Life Insurance
Corporation Life Insurance
Partnership Life Insurance
Pointers on Meeting Competition
Retirement Plans for Small Business
Getting Money for Long-Term Growth
Reducing Transportation Costs
New Depreciation Guidelines—Realistic and Flexible
Tax Dates for Small Plants
What Kind of Money Do You Need?
Checking Your Management Methods
Financial Planning in Closely Held Businesses
b) Small Marketers Aids
Trade Regulations and Small Business
Depreciation Costs—Don't Overlook Them
Checklist for Going into Business
Direct Mail Advertising for Small Retailers
Understanding Why They Buy
Specialized Help for Small Business
Can You Afford Installment Selling?
Tax Dates for Small Marketers
Pricing Your Services for Profit
c) Small Business Bibliographies
Operating Costs and Ratios—Retail
Operating Costs and Ratios—Wholesale
Distribution Cost Analysis
Buying for Retail Stores
Motels
Discount Retailing
d) Management Research Summaries
Facts about Small Business Financing
Organization Patterns in Small Business
Forecasting in Small Business Planning
Financial Analysis and Small Business
Pricing Decisions in Small Business
Investment Decision Making in Small Businesses
Small Business Success and Failure Cases

A Study of Industry Financial and Operating Ratios
Accounting in Small Business Decisions
Equity Financing of Small Manufacturing Firms
Sources of Equity and Long-Term Financing for Small Manufacturing Firms
Insurance Management in Small Retail Firms
Accounting Practices in Small Firms
Site Evaluation for Small Retailers
Small Business Use of Trade Association Programs
Attitudes of Bankers toward Small Business Financing
Small Business Experiences in Seeking Credit
Choosing a Form of Business Organization
A Study of Business Terminations
Small Business Instability and Failure
Small Manufacturers and the Financial Gap
Management Planning in Small Firms
Ten Small Retailers and Their Problems
Measurement of the Risk Attitudes of Banks
Solving Small Retailers' Problems
Characteristics in Small Business Success
Buying and Selling a Small Business
Success Patterns in the Real Estate Business
Management Counseling of Small Business
The Estate-Tax Valuation Problem in Family-Owned Firms
Federal Taxes and the Legal Form of Small Firms
Profitability and Size of Firm
Factors in Small Business Success or Failure
How Small Firms Handle Their Legal Problems
A Study of Retailer Survival
The Franchise System of Distribution
Tax Compliance Costs in Small Firms
Financing Problems of Small Manufacturers
e) Small Business Management Series
   One Hundred and Fifty Questions for a Prospective Manufacturer
   A Handbook of Small Business Finance
   Ratio Analysis for Small Business
   Equity Capital and Small Business
   Guides for Profit Planning
f) Starting and Managing Series
   Starting and Managing a Small Business of Your Own
g) Small Business Research Series
   Cash Planning in Small Manufacturing Companies
   The First Two Years: Problems of Small Firm Growth and Survival

CASE PROBLEMS

1. Visit one of the types of stores listed in Table 16–10. Prior to this visit, list on the Worksheet Form (Figure 16–8) the average ratios and aver-

age costs for the line of business you have selected. Ask the owner of the store to cooperate by providing his figures to enable you to compare them with the averages. Prepare a brief written report for him developing your findings as to the effectiveness of his operation.

2. Donald Browter is graduating from an eastern college of business administration this June. He is now in the process of deciding between two business ventures.

Donald has always been interested in cameras and photography. During college he was photography editor of the university daily and in the summers he worked in a large photography store in Minneapolis, Minnesota. While in the U.S. Army he did a good deal of official photographing.

Donald has approximately $15,000, which was left to him upon the death of his father. Mr. Lampson, owner of the Minneapolis Camera Shop, has urged Donald to come back to his shop as a junior partner. Mr. Lampson plans to retire in five years and would allow Donald to buy the business for $10,000 down now and $7,000 to be paid in the next ten years. For the coming five years, while working under Mr. Lampson, Donald would receive a straight salary of $100 a week. The Minneapolis Camera Shop is in an excellent location and enjoys a fine reputation.

One of Donald's classmates, Jim Peterson, is also interested in photography. Jim wants to settle in Long Island, where both he and his wife have their families and a large circle of friends. He has approached Donald about the possibility of establishing a partnership and jointly operating a camera store. Jim has done some investigation and thinks that it would be feasible to start such a business venture if he and Donald were each to invest $13,500.

Would you advise Donald to join Mr. Lampson or to form a partnership with Jim Peterson? Why?

3. Charlie, 30, has recently been promoted to assistant buyer in the housewares department of a small but good department store in his home town, population 90,000.

Charlie has always been handy with tools and has built his own home almost completely by himself. When he was in the Army he had some accounting experience. At present he is making $6,000 a year.

He is interested in going into business for himself, even though it appears that he has a good future in the department store. There is a hardware store in the town that has not been doing very well. The store opened four years ago and has been losing money ever since. The owner is lazy and careless and has not used sound business judgment. There is another hardware store in town that has prospered. Charlie thinks there is room for two stores, especially because a new real estate development promises to bring an additional 500 families into the town in the next few years.

Although the proprietor allowed the first store to run down, it is in a good location and the proprietor has recently renewed his five-year lease. This store is offered at $10,000, $7,000 being the cost of inventory. Charlie thinks he can buy the proprietor out for $8,000. Charlie has $5,000 to invest and the other $3,000 he must raise through financing.

In your opinion, what should Charlie do? Why?

4. When Mr. and Mrs. James Littleton were about to open their new bar and grill, they sat down with their lawyer and accountant to list the various licenses, reports, tax returns, etc., to which they would be subject in their new business (which they intended to operate as a partnership). What would the requirements be in your locality?

5. Peter Antonelli had worked for a manufacturer as a mechanical engineer for over ten years. He and his wife had managed to save (all told) about $22,-000. Now Peter's physician advises him to go to the Southwest (far from his former home) for health reasons; it will probably be necessary for him to remain there indefinitely. Peter and his wife realize that they must have some means of support at their new place of residence. A business broker whom they consult offers, for $10,000, a combination greeting card and toy business which, he says, has been doing about $38,000 of business a year. This business is located in a store whose rent is $150 a month, subject to a lease which still has eight years before expiration. What are some of the things that Peter and his wife should consider before they buy such a business?

6. Jerome Greenway is 27 years old. He has been married three years and has a baby daughter. After graduating from Dartmouth College, he served as an officer in the Army for two years. Recently he has had several years of varied business experience. When the local Plymouth automobile agency (in a middle-western city of 100,000 people) is offered for sale for $50,000, Jerome's father-in-law offers to let him have the money to buy it. Discuss some of the factors Jerome should consider before buying this business.

7. Peter Arnstein is negotiating to purchase a restaurant in a large city. This restaurant occupies leased premises. The terms of the lease (which has nine years to run) require a fixed monthly rent of $150 plus 5 percent of gross monthly receipts in excess of $7,500. How do you react to this provision? In connection with it, what other things might you want to consider?

8. Jeremiah Rich is branch sales manager for a firm which manufactures and sells equipment for dry-cleaning shops. He earns an annual average income from his commissions of about $8,000. Knowing the business as well as he does, he feels that if he (being worth about $15,000) invested about $7,000 in a dry-cleaning store of his own, he could earn about $12,000 a year. Would you advise him to open his own dry-cleaning establishment? Why?

9. Book & Card Mart, Inc. (family owned), is for sale. You are told that it does an annual volume of $150,000 of sales and that, if you buy it, you should make $15,000 a year for yourself. The purchase price is $50,000. How good does this proposition look to you? What factors would you need to examine?

10. After working as buyer and merchandise manager in a department store in a large city, Eldon formed a department-store corporation to operate a new department store in a city of 75,000 people. Consider the various types of insurance that might be appropriate for a business of this type.

11. Visit your local department store and discuss Appendix Tables 16-A and 16-B with the owner. Volunteer to help him check his sales people's activ-

APPENDIX TABLE 16–A

HOW MUCH A SALESPERSON SHOULD SELL

WEEKLY SALARIES ▶	$15.00	$17.50	$18.00	$19.00	$20.00	$21.00	$22.00	$23.00	$24.00	$25.00	$27.50	$29.00	$30.00	$32.50	$35.00	$37.50	$40.00	$42.50	$45.00	$47.50	$50.00
											SALARY	COST									
$ 150	10.0	11.7	12.0	12.7	13.3	14.0	14.7	15.3	16.0	16.7	18.3	19.3	20.0	21.7	23.3	25.0	26.7	28.3	30.0	31.7	33.3
160	9.4	10.9	11.3	11.9	12.5	13.1	13.8	14.4	15.0	15.6	17.2	18.1	18.8	20.3	21.9	23.4	25.0	26.6	28.1	29.7	31.3
170	8.8	10.3	10.6	11.2	11.8	12.4	12.9	13.5	14.1	14.7	16.2	17.1	17.6	19.1	20.6	22.1	23.5	25.0	26.5	27.9	29.4
180	8.3	9.7	10.0	10.6	11.1	11.7	12.2	12.8	13.3	13.9	15.3	16.1	16.7	18.1	19.4	20.8	22.2	23.6	25.0	26.4	27.8
190	7.9	9.2	9.5	10.0	10.5	11.1	11.6	12.1	12.6	13.2	14.5	15.3	15.8	17.1	18.4	19.7	21.1	22.4	23.7	25.0	26.3
200	7.5	8.8	9.0	9.5	10.0	10.5	11.0	11.5	12.0	12.5	13.8	14.5	15.0	16.3	17.5	18.8	20.0	21.3	22.5	23.8	25.0
210	7.1	8.3	8.6	9.0	9.5	10.0	10.5	11.0	11.4	11.9	13.1	13.8	14.3	15.5	16.7	17.9	19.0	20.2	21.4	22.6	23.8
220	6.8	8.0	8.2	8.6	9.1	9.5	10.0	10.5	10.9	11.4	12.5	13.2	13.6	14.8	15.9	17.0	18.2	19.3	20.5	21.6	22.7
230	6.5	7.6	7.8	8.3	8.7	9.1	9.6	10.0	10.4	10.9	12.0	12.6	13.0	14.1	15.2	16.3	17.4	18.5	19.6	20.7	21.7
240	6.3	7.3	7.5	7.9	8.3	8.8	9.2	9.6	10.0	10.4	11.5	12.1	12.5	13.5	14.6	15.6	16.7	17.7	18.7	19.8	20.8
250	6.0	7.0	7.2	7.6	8.0	8.4	8.8	9.2	9.6	10.0	11.0	11.6	12.0	13.0	14.0	15.0	16.0	17.0	18.0	19.0	20.0
260	5.8	6.7	6.9	7.3	7.7	8.1	8.5	8.8	9.2	9.6	10.6	11.2	11.5	12.5	13.5	14.4	15.4	16.3	17.3	18.3	19.2
270	5.6	6.5	6.7	7.0	7.4	7.8	8.1	8.5	8.9	9.3	10.2	10.7	11.1	12.0	13.0	13.9	14.8	15.7	16.7	17.6	18.5
280	5.4	6.2	6.4	6.8	7.1	7.5	7.9	8.2	8.6	8.9	9.8	10.4	10.7	11.6	12.5	13.4	14.3	15.2	16.1	17.0	17.9
290	5.2	6.0	6.2	6.6	6.9	7.2	7.6	7.9	8.3	8.6	9.5	10.0	10.3	11.2	12.1	12.9	13.8	14.7	15.5	16.4	17.2
300	5.0	5.8	6.0	6.3	6.7	7.0	7.3	7.7	8.0	8.3	9.2	9.7	10.0	10.8	11.7	12.5	13.3	14.2	15.0	15.8	16.7
325	4.6	5.4	5.5	5.8	6.2	6.5	6.8	7.1	7.4	7.7	8.5	8.9	9.2	10.0	10.8	11.5	12.3	13.1	13.8	14.6	15.4
350	4.3	5.0	5.1	5.4	5.7	6.0	6.3	6.6	6.9	7.1	7.9	8.3	8.6	9.3	10.0	10.7	11.4	12.1	12.9	13.6	14.3
375	4.0	4.7	4.8	5.1	5.3	5.6	5.9	6.1	6.4	6.7	7.3	7.7	8.0	8.7	9.3	10.0	10.7	11.3	12.0	12.7	13.3
400	3.8	4.4	4.5	4.8	5.0	5.3	5.5	5.8	6.0	6.3	6.9	7.3	7.5	8.1	8.8	9.4	10.0	10.6	11.3	11.9	12.5
425	3.5	4.1	4.2	4.5	4.7	4.9	5.2	5.4	5.6	5.9	6.5	6.8	7.1	7.6	8.2	8.8	9.4	10.0	10.6	11.2	11.8
450	3.3	3.9	4.0	4.2	4.4	4.7	4.9	5.1	5.3	5.6	6.1	6.4	6.7	7.2	7.8	8.3	8.9	9.4	10.0	10.6	11.1
475	3.2	3.7	3.8	4.0	4.2	4.4	4.6	4.8	5.1	5.3	5.8	6.1	6.3	6.8	7.4	7.9	8.4	8.9	9.5	10.0	10.5
500	3.0	3.5	3.6	3.8	4.0	4.2	4.4	4.6	4.8	5.0	5.5	5.8	6.0	6.5	7.0	7.5	8.0	8.5	9.0	9.5	10.0
525	2.9	3.3	3.4	3.6	3.8	4.0	4.2	4.4	4.6	4.8	5.2	5.5	5.7	6.2	6.7	7.1	7.6	8.1	8.6	9.0	9.5
550	2.7	3.2	3.3	3.5	3.6	3.8	4.0	4.2	4.4	4.5	5.0	5.3	5.5	5.9	6.4	6.8	7.3	7.7	8.2	8.6	9.1
575	2.6	3.0	3.1	3.3	3.5	3.7	3.8	4.0	4.2	4.3	4.8	5.0	5.2	5.7	6.1	6.5	7.0	7.4	7.8	8.3	8.7
600	2.5	2.9	3.0	3.2	3.3	3.5	3.7	3.8	4.0	4.2	4.6	4.8	5.0	5.4	5.8	6.2	6.7	7.1	7.5	7.9	8.3
625	2.4	2.8	2.9	3.0	3.2	3.4	3.5	3.7	3.8	4.0	4.4	4.6	4.8	5.2	5.6	6.0	6.4	6.8	7.2	7.6	8.0
650	2.3	2.7	2.8	2.9	3.1	3.2	3.4	3.5	3.7	3.8	4.2	4.5	4.6	5.0	5.4	5.8	6.2	6.5	6.9	7.3	7.7
675	2.2	2.6	2.7	2.8	3.0	3.1	3.2	3.4	3.5	3.7	4.1	4.3	4.4	4.8	5.2	5.6	5.9	6.3	6.7	7.0	7.4
700	2.1	2.5	2.6	2.7	2.9	3.0	3.1	3.3	3.4	3.6	3.9	4.1	4.3	4.6	5.0	5.3	5.7	6.1	6.4	6.8	7.1
725	2.1	2.4	2.5	2.6	2.7	2.9	3.0	3.2	3.3	3.4	3.8	4.0	4.1	4.5	4.8	5.2	5.5	5.9	6.2	6.5	6.9
750	2.0	2.3	2.4	2.5	2.7	2.8	2.9	3.1	3.2	3.3	3.7	3.9	4.0	4.3	4.7	5.0	5.3	5.7	6.0	6.3	6.7
775	1.9	2.2	2.3	2.4	2.6	2.7	2.8	3.0	3.1	3.2	3.5	3.7	3.9	4.2	4.5	4.8	5.2	5.5	5.8	6.1	6.4
800	1.9	2.2	2.2	2.4	2.5	2.6	2.7	2.9	3.0	3.1	3.4	3.6	3.7	4.1	4.4	4.7	5.0	5.3	5.6	5.9	6.2
825	1.8	2.1	2.2	2.3	2.4	2.5	2.7	2.8	2.9	3.0	3.3	3.5	3.6	3.9	4.2	4.5	4.8	5.1	5.4	5.7	6.1
850	1.8	2.1	2.1	2.2	2.3	2.5	2.6	2.7	2.8	2.9	3.2	3.4	3.5	3.8	4.1	4.4	4.7	5.0	5.3	5.6	5.9
875	1.7	2.0	2.0	2.2	2.3	2.4	2.5	2.6	2.7	2.8	3.1	3.3	3.4	3.7	4.0	4.3	4.6	4.8	5.1	5.4	5.7
900	1.7	1.9	2.0	2.1	2.2	2.3	2.4	2.5	2.7	2.8	3.1	3.2	3.3	3.6	3.9	4.2	4.4	4.7	5.0	5.3	5.5
925	1.6	1.9	1.9	2.0	2.2	2.3	2.4	2.5	2.6	2.7	3.0	3.1	3.2	3.5	3.8	4.0	4.3	4.6	4.9	5.1	5.4
950	1.6	1.8	1.9	2.0	2.1	2.2	2.3	2.4	2.5	2.6	2.9	3.0	3.1	3.4	3.7	3.9	4.2	4.5	4.7	5.0	5.3
975	1.5	1.8	1.8	1.9	2.0	2.1	2.2	2.3	2.5	2.6	2.8	3.0	3.1	3.3	3.6	3.8	4.1	4.3	4.6	4.9	5.1
1000	1.5	1.7	1.8	1.9	2.0	2.1	2.2	2.3	2.4	2.5	2.7	2.9	3.0	3.2	3.5	3.7	4.0	4.2	4.5	4.7	5.0

(Left margin, reading vertically: A M O U N T O F W E E K L Y S A L E S)

The figures in the top line of the table represent weekly salaries. Those in the extreme left and right columns are the weekly sales required to justify the salaries according to salary cost percentages.

To determine how much a salesperson should sell, select the column headed with the weekly salary of the salesperson. Follow this column down to the salary cost percentage nearest that of your store. The dollar figures on the same line in the AMOUNT OF WEEKLY SALES column (extreme left or right) show what the salesperson should sell each week to earn his salary.

Example: A salesperson receives $75.00 per week in a hardware store having annual sales of $300,000 in a county with a population of over 2,000,000. The salary cost percentage for stores in this classification is 14.9%, as shown on page 15. Under the column marked $75.00, locate this salary percentage or the one closest to it. In this case the

ity against the norms set forth in these appendix tables. Prepare a brief written report for him setting forth your findings.

APPENDIX TABLE 16–A (Continued)

$52.50	$55.00	$57.50	$60.00	$62.50	$65.00	$67.50	$70.00	$72.50	$75.00	$77.50	$80.00	$82.50	$85.00	$87.50	$90.00	$92.50	$95.00	$97.50	$100.00	WEEKLY SALARIES
									PERCENTAGES											
35.0	36.7	38.3	40.0	41.7	43.3	45.0	46.7	48.3	50.0	51.7	53.3	55.0	56.7	58.3	60.0	61.7	63.3	65.0	66.7	$ 150
32.8	34.4	35.9	37.5	39.1	40.6	42.2	43.8	45.3	46.9	48.4	50.0	51.6	53.1	54.7	56.3	57.8	59.4	60.9	62.5	160
30.9	32.4	33.8	35.3	36.8	38.2	39.7	41.2	42.6	44.1	45.6	47.1	48.5	50.0	51.5	52.9	54.4	55.9	57.4	58.8	170
29.2	30.6	31.9	33.3	34.7	36.1	37.5	38.9	40.3	41.7	43.0	44.4	45.8	47.2	48.6	50.0	51.4	52.8	54.2	55.6	180
27.6	28.9	30.3	31.6	32.9	34.2	35.5	36.8	38.1	39.5	40.8	42.1	43.4	44.7	46.1	47.4	48.7	50.0	51.3	52.6	190
26.2	27.5	28.7	30.0	31.2	32.5	33.7	35.0	36.2	37.5	38.7	40.0	41.3	42.5	43.8	45.0	46.3	47.5	48.8	50.0	200
25.0	26.2	27.4	28.6	29.8	31.0	32.1	33.3	34.5	35.7	36.9	38.1	39.3	40.5	41.7	42.9	44.0	45.2	46.4	47.6	210
23.9	25.0	26.1	27.3	28.4	29.5	30.7	31.8	32.9	34.1	35.2	36.4	37.5	38.6	39.8	40.9	42.0	43.2	44.3	45.5	220
22.8	23.9	25.0	26.1	27.2	28.3	29.3	30.4	31.5	32.6	33.7	34.8	35.9	37.0	38.0	39.1	40.2	41.3	42.4	43.5	230
21.9	22.9	23.9	25.0	26.0	27.1	28.1	29.2	30.2	31.2	32.3	33.3	34.4	35.4	36.5	37.5	38.5	39.6	40.6	41.7	240
21.0	22.0	23.0	24.0	25.0	26.0	27.0	28.0	29.0	30.0	31.0	32.0	33.0	34.0	35.0	36.0	37.0	38.0	39.0	40.0	250
20.2	21.2	22.1	23.1	24.0	25.0	26.0	26.9	27.9	28.8	29.8	30.8	31.7	32.7	33.7	34.6	35.6	36.5	37.5	38.5	260
19.4	20.4	21.3	22.2	23.1	24.1	25.0	25.9	26.8	27.8	28.7	29.6	30.6	31.5	32.4	33.3	34.3	35.2	36.1	37.0	270
18.7	19.6	20.5	21.4	22.3	23.2	24.1	25.0	25.9	26.8	27.7	28.6	29.5	30.4	31.3	32.1	33.0	33.9	34.8	35.7	280
18.1	19.0	19.8	20.7	21.5	22.4	23.3	24.1	25.0	25.9	26.7	27.6	28.4	29.3	30.2	31.0	31.9	32.8	33.6	34.5	290
17.5	18.3	19.2	20.0	20.8	21.7	22.5	23.3	24.2	25.0	25.8	26.7	27.5	28.3	29.2	30.0	30.8	31.7	32.5	33.4	300
16.1	16.9	17.7	18.5	19.2	20.0	20.8	21.5	22.3	23.1	23.8	24.6	25.4	26.2	26.9	27.7	28.5	29.2	30.0	30.8	325
15.0	15.7	16.4	17.1	17.8	18.6	19.3	20.0	20.7	21.4	22.1	22.9	23.6	24.3	25.0	25.7	26.4	27.1	27.9	28.6	350
14.0	14.7	15.3	16.0	16.7	17.3	18.0	18.7	19.3	20.0	20.7	21.3	22.0	22.7	23.3	24.0	24.7	25.3	26.0	26.7	375
13.1	13.8	14.4	15.0	15.6	16.3	16.9	17.5	18.1	18.8	19.4	20.0	20.6	21.3	21.9	22.5	23.1	23.8	24.4	25.0	400
12.3	12.9	13.5	14.1	14.7	15.3	15.9	16.5	17.0	17.6	18.2	18.8	19.4	20.0	20.6	21.2	21.8	22.4	22.9	23.5	425
11.7	12.2	12.8	13.3	13.9	14.4	15.0	15.6	16.1	16.7	17.2	17.8	18.3	18.9	19.4	20.0	20.6	21.1	21.7	22.2	450
11.0	11.6	12.1	12.6	13.1	13.7	14.2	14.7	15.3	15.8	16.3	16.8	17.4	17.9	18.4	18.9	19.5	20.0	20.5	21.1	475
10.5	11.0	11.5	12.0	12.5	13.0	13.5	14.0	14.5	15.0	15.5	16.0	16.5	17.0	17.5	18.0	18.5	19.0	19.5	20.0	500
10.0	10.5	10.9	11.4	11.9	12.4	12.8	13.3	13.8	14.3	14.8	15.2	15.7	16.2	16.7	17.1	17.6	18.1	18.6	19.0	525
9.5	10.0	10.4	10.9	11.4	11.8	12.3	12.7	13.2	13.6	14.1	14.5	15.0	15.5	15.9	16.4	16.8	17.3	17.7	18.2	550
9.1	9.6	10.0	10.4	10.9	11.3	11.7	12.2	12.6	13.0	13.5	13.9	14.3	14.8	15.2	15.7	16.1	16.5	17.0	17.4	575
8.7	9.2	9.6	10.0	10.4	10.8	11.2	11.7	12.1	12.5	12.9	13.3	13.8	14.2	14.6	15.0	15.4	15.8	16.3	16.7	600
8.4	8.8	9.2	9.6	10.0	10.4	10.8	11.2	11.6	12.0	12.4	12.8	13.2	13.6	14.0	14.4	14.8	15.2	15.6	16.0	625
8.1	8.5	8.8	9.2	9.6	10.0	10.4	10.8	11.1	11.5	11.9	12.3	13.1	13.5	13.8	14.2	14.6	15.0	15.4		650
7.8	8.1	8.5	8.9	9.2	9.6	10.0	10.4	10.7	11.1	11.5	11.8	12.2	12.6	13.0	13.3	13.7	14.1	14.4	14.8	675
7.5	7.9	8.2	8.6	8.9	9.3	9.6	10.0	10.4	10.7	11.1	11.4	11.8	12.1	12.5	12.9	13.2	13.6	13.9	14.3	700
7.2	7.6	7.9	8.3	8.6	9.0	9.3	9.6	10.0	10.3	10.7	11.0	11.4	11.7	12.1	12.4	12.8	13.1	13.4	13.8	725
7.0	7.3	7.7	8.0	8.3	8.7	9.0	9.3	9.7	10.0	10.3	10.7	11.0	11.3	11.7	12.0	12.3	12.7	13.0	13.3	750
6.8	7.1	7.4	7.7	8.1	8.4	8.7	9.0	9.3	9.7	10.0	10.3	10.6	11.0	11.3	11.6	11.9	12.3	12.6	12.9	775
6.6	6.9	7.2	7.5	7.8	8.1	8.4	8.7	9.1	9.4	9.7	10.0	10.3	10.6	10.9	11.3	11.6	11.9	12.2	12.5	800
6.4	6.7	7.0	7.3	7.6	7.9	8.2	8.5	8.8	9.1	9.4	9.7	10.0	10.3	10.6	10.9	11.2	11.5	11.8	12.1	825
6.2	6.5	6.8	7.1	7.3	7.6	7.9	8.2	8.5	8.8	9.1	9.4	9.7	10.0	10.3	10.6	10.9	11.2	11.5	11.8	850
6.0	6.3	6.6	6.8	7.1	7.4	7.7	8.0	8.3	8.6	8.8	9.1	9.4	9.7	10.0	10.3	10.6	10.9	11.1	11.4	875
5.8	6.1	6.4	6.7	6.9	7.2	7.5	7.8	8.0	8.3	8.6	8.9	9.2	9.4	9.7	10.0	10.3	10.6	10.8	11.1	900
5.7	5.9	6.2	6.5	6.7	7.0	7.3	7.6	7.8	8.1	8.4	8.6	8.9	9.2	9.5	9.7	10.0	10.3	10.5	10.8	925
5.5	5.8	6.0	6.3	6.6	6.8	7.1	7.4	7.6	7.9	8.1	8.4	8.7	8.9	9.2	9.5	9.7	10.0	10.3	10.5	950
5.4	5.6	5.9	6.1	6.4	6.7	6.9	7.2	7.4	7.7	7.9	8.2	8.5	8.7	9.0	9.2	9.5	9.7	10.0	10.3	975
5.2	5.5	5.7	6.0	6.2	6.5	6.7	7.0	7.2	7.5	7.7	8.0	8.3	8.5	8.8	9.0	9.3	9.5	9.8	10.0	1000

(Right margin, read vertically: AMOUNT OF WEEKLY SALES)

nearest figure is 15.0%. The amount in the AMOUNT OF WEEKLY SALES column opposite 15.0% is $500. This is the average amount of merchandise the salesperson should sell each week to earn his salary of $75.00.

If you know the average weekly sales of your salespeople, you can determine which ones deserve salary increases with this table. Find the salesperson's amount of weekly sales and follow that row across to your salary cost percentage. The weekly salary at the top of that column is what your salesperson is actually earning. If you're paying him less than the table indicates he should be paid, he may be entitled to a raise. But if you're paying him more, the difference is coming directly out of your profit.

MERCHANTS SERVICE, THE NATIONAL CASH REGISTER COMPANY
Dayton 9, Ohio

APPENDIX TABLE 16–B

HOW MUCH A SALESPERSON SHOULD SELL

SALARY COST PERCENTAGES

$55.00	$57.50	$60.00 (6)	$62.50	$65.00	$67.50	$70.00	$72.50	$75.00 (1)	$77.50	$80.00	$82.50	$85.00	$87.50	$90.00	$92.50	$95.00	$97.50	$100.00	WEEKLY SALARIES
	38.3	40.0	41.7	43.3	45.0	46.7	48.3	50.0	51.7	53.3	55.0	56.7	58.3	60.0	61.7	63.3	65.0	66.7	$ 150
	35.9	37.5	39.1	40.6	42.2	43.8	45.3	46.9	48.4	50.0	51.6	53.1	54.7	56.3	57.8	59.4	60.9	62.5	160
	33.8	35.3	36.8	38.2	39.7	41.2	42.6	44.1	45.6	47.1	48.5	50.0	51.5	52.9	54.4	55.9	57.4	58.8	170
	31.9	33.3	34.7	36.1	37.5	38.9	40.3	41.7	43.0	44.4	45.8	47.2	48.6	50.0	51.4	52.8	54.2	55.6	180
	30.3	31.6	32.9	34.2	35.5	36.8	38.1	39.5	40.8	42.1	43.4	44.7	46.1	47.4	48.7	50.0	51.3	52.6	190
	28.7	30.0	31.2	32.5	33.7	35.0	36.2	37.5	38.7	40.0	41.3	42.5	43.8	45.0	46.3	47.5	48.8	50.0	200
	27.4	28.6	29.8	31.0	32.1	33.3	34.5	35.7	36.9	38.1	39.3	40.5	41.7	42.9	44.0	45.2	46.4	47.6	210
	26.1	27.3	28.4	29.5	30.7	31.8	32.9	34.1	35.2	36.4	37.5	38.6	39.8	40.9	42.0	43.2	44.3	45.5	220
	25.0	26.1	27.2	28.3	29.3	30.4	31.5	32.6	33.7	34.8	35.9	37.0	38.0	39.1	40.2	41.3	42.4	43.5	230
	23.9	25.0	26.0	27.1	28.1	29.2	30.2	31.2	32.3	33.3	34.4	35.4	36.5	37.5	38.5	39.6	40.6	41.7	240
	23.0	24.0	25.0	26.0	27.0	28.0	29.0	30.0	31.0	32.0	33.0	34.0	35.0	36.0	37.0	38.0	39.0	40.0	250
	22.1	23.1	24.0	25.0	26.0	26.9	27.9	28.8	29.8	30.8	31.7	32.7	33.7	34.6	35.6	36.5	37.5	38.5	260
20.4	21.3	22.2	23.1	24.1	25.0	25.9	26.8	27.8	28.7	29.6	30.6	31.5	32.4	33.3	34.3	35.2	36.1	37.0	270
19.6	20.5	21.4	22.3	23.2	24.1	25.0	25.9	26.8	27.7	28.6	29.5	30.4	31.3	32.1	33.0	33.9	34.8	35.7	280
19.0	19.8	20.7	21.5	22.4	23.3	24.1	25.0	25.9	26.7	27.6	28.4	29.3	30.2	31.0	31.9	32.8	33.6	34.5	290
18.3	19.2	20.0	20.8	21.7	22.5	23.3	24.2	25.0	25.8	26.7	27.5	28.3	29.2	30.0	30.8	31.7	32.5	33.4	300
16.9	17.7	18.5	19.2	20.0	20.8	21.5	22.3	23.1	23.8	24.6	25.4	26.2	26.9	27.7	28.5	29.2	30.0	30.8	325
15.7	16.4	17.1	17.8	18.6	19.3	20.0	20.7	21.4	22.1	22.9	23.6	24.3	25.0	25.7	26.4	27.1	27.9	28.6	350
14.7	15.3	16.0	16.7	17.3	18.0	18.7	19.3	20.0	20.7	21.3	22.0	22.7	23.3	24.0	24.7	25.3	26.0	26.7	375
13.8	14.4	15.0	15.6	16.3	16.9	17.5	18.1	18.8	19.4	20.0	20.6	21.3	21.9	22.5	23.1	23.8	24.4	25.0	400
12.9	13.5	14.1	14.7	15.3	15.9	16.5	17.0	17.6	18.2	18.8	19.4	20.0	20.6	21.2	21.8	22.4	22.9	23.5	425
12.2	12.8	13.3	13.9	14.4	15.0	15.6	16.1	16.7	17.2	17.8	18.3	18.9	19.4	20.0	20.6	21.1	21.7	22.2	450
11.6	12.1	12.6	13.1	13.7	14.2	14.7	15.3	15.8	16.3	16.8	17.4	17.9	18.4	18.9	19.5	20.0	20.5	21.1	475
11.0	11.5	12.0	12.5	13.0	13.5	14.0	14.5	15.0	15.5	16.0	16.5	17.0	17.5	18.0	18.5	19.0	19.5	20.0	500
10.5	10.9	11.4	11.9	12.4	12.8	13.3	13.8	14.3	14.8	15.2	15.7	16.2	16.7	17.1	17.6	18.1	18.6	19.0	525
10.0	10.4	10.9	11.4	11.8	12.3	12.7	13.2	13.6	14.1	14.5	15.0	15.5	15.9	16.4	16.8	17.3	17.7	18.2	550
9.6	10.0	10.4	10.9	11.3	11.7	12.2	12.6	13.0	13.5	13.9	14.3	14.8	15.2	15.7	16.1	16.5	17.0	17.4	575
9.2	9.6	10.0	10.4	10.8	11.2	11.7	12.1	12.5	12.9	13.3	13.8	14.2	14.6	15.0	15.4	15.8	16.3	16.7	600
8.8	9.2	9.6	10.0	10.4	10.8	11.2	11.6	12.0	12.4	12.8	13.2	13.6	14.0	14.4	14.8	15.2	15.6	16.0	625
8.5	8.8	9.2	9.6	10.0	10.4	10.8	11.1	11.5	11.9	12.3	12.7	13.1	13.5	13.8	14.2	14.6	15.0	15.4	650
	8.9			10.0	10.4	10.7		11.1		11.8	12.2		13.0			14.1	14.4		675

(Right-hand vertical label: AMOUNT OF WEEKLY SALES)

As mentioned on the chart, HOW MUCH A SALESPERSON SHOULD SELL, can be used to determine industry of salespeople. To explain further, let us take the case of the salesperson receiving a salary of $75 per week in a store having a salary cost percentage of 15.0%.

Under the column headed $75 (1), find the figure 15.0 (2). To the side in the "Amount of Weekly Sales" column, you will find that he should sell $500 (3) worth of merchandise to justify his salary.

But suppose at the end of the week he has sold but $400 worth of merchandise. Obviously, he is below quota. Now locate this figure (4) in the weekly sales column and then follow along the line to the left until you reach 15.0 (5). At the top of this column you will see that a weekly salary of $60 (6) is indicated. This means that the salesperson's efforts for the week have earned only $60 in salary — *$15 less than he is being paid!* This difference must be advanced to the employee from your own earnings or from the earnings of other profitable employees.

And suppose your other salespeople are not up to par. You again must make up the loss from your earnings.

In thinking over the situation, this question logically comes up: *Am I working for my salespeople, or are they working for me?* Does each one bring in his share of business . . . or must a few work harder to make up for the lack of industry of one or two? This chart points out one way to find the answer as to whether or not salespeople are profitable.

Source: Merchants Service: National Cash Register Company.

17

ESTATE PLANNING: WILLS, TRUSTS, ESTATES; DEATH AND GIFT TAXES

If your riches are yours, why don't you take them with you to the other world?

—*Benjamin Franklin*

RESIDING in a small village was a lawyer who was famous throughout the state for drawing up wills. When a wealthy man died, there was much speculation as to the value of his estate, and the town gossip set about to find out. He went to see the lawyer, and after a few preliminary remarks about the deceased, said rather bluntly:

"I understand you made his will. Would you mind telling me how much he left?"

"Not at all," answered the attorney, resuming his writing, "he left everything he had."

Estate Planning

"Amid the gin mills and night spots of New York's Fifty-second Street stands a dignified town house called 'The Home of Estatology.' It is there, in its worldly neighborhood, to help prepare men of means for an orderly (and moderately taxed) departure from this world. Its function is 'estate planning.' " Thus begins a *Fortune* article on "Estate Planning: New Growth Industry." Estate planning has been called an "old trade with a new name." At one time it appeared to involve merely will making, but today it is recognized that making a will is just one part of a more elaborate process that should run for most of a person's adult lifetime.

"Estate Planning is a process of arranging a person's affairs so as to produce the most effective disposition of his capital and income. It is an attempt to work out an arrangement which best suits the financial requirements, personalities and welfare of those concerned, and at the same time produces the most economical method of disposition." The tools of estate planning include:

1. *Outright Gifts during Life.* Too often this aspect is ignored. Gifts may include cash, securities, real estate, life insurance, annuities, etc.

2. *Gifts in Trust Created during Owner's Lifetime.* This is particularly useful as a device for endowing minor children.

3. *Annuities.* These can be used in many ways to assist in estate planning.

4. *Life Insurance.* Contrary to popular belief, life insurance proceeds, except under certain circumstances are part of one's *taxable* estate.

5. *Passing Property by Will.* When personal property is passed, it is called a "bequest"; when real property is involved, it is called a "devise."

6. *Trusts Created at Death.* Just as you can create a trust or trusts during your lifetime, you can also create one by will at death.

7. *Special Devices and Mechanisms.* There are a variety of devices, such as use of a business, which attorneys, experienced in estate planning, have developed.

All these tools, or several of them combined, are involved in estate planning. You can either use them wisely or you can do nothing. Not making an estate plan *is* making an estate plan, in a way, but one you may not really want to make. If you do nothing, the state takes over. Your property passes to those people and in such proportions as the state legislature has decreed.

What Happens if You Do Not Leave a Will

If you die and leave no will, you are said to have died "intestate." In effect, the state makes your will for you, and your property passes in accordance with the fixed provisions of the law of the state in which you are domiciled. No matter how small or large your estate, not leaving a will causes much trouble and inconvenience for your survivors. A woman who died in Pennsylvania in 1936 left lawyers there a lot of work and a legacy of disappointment to a lot of other people. She left more than $17 million, but no will. Because some 26,000 persons claimed kinship, there were over 2,000 hearings in the probate court. The testimony of 1,100 witnesses filled 390 volumes and 115,000 pages. The estate was not settled until 1952—sixteen years after the owner's death.

But, you may say, no one would be interested in a small estate, and why does one have to make a will if one has very little to leave? Assume that you are married, have one small child, and leave $18,000—but no will. Your wife, under the laws of many states, will receive only one third of your estate. The child will inherit two thirds, but since it is a minor, a guardian will have to be appointed by the probate (or surrogate's) court. It may very well be that your wife will be that guardian; yet she will be anything but a free agent in the handling of your child's money. She will have to provide a bond; she will be under constant supervision of the court; she will have to file annual accountings. All told, guardianship is an expensive and cumbersome procedure. It can be avoided by a properly drawn will.

How Property Passes if There Is No Will

While the statutes of descent and distribution which govern the disposition of one's estate if there is no will vary from state to state, it is possible to give a general impression of what is usually found in them, as follows:

1. On death of unmarried man or woman (including widow or widower)
    a) In the absence of children or their descendants, property goes one half to each parent or entirely to the surviving parent.
    b) In the absence of children or their descendants, and parents, property goes equally to brothers and sisters. Children of a deceased brother or sister divide equally their parent's share (*per stirpes*).
    c) In the absence of children or their descendants, parents, brothers, sisters, or their descendants, property is divided among next of kin.
    d) In the absence of all relatives, property escheats to the state of the domicile of the deceased.
2. On death of married man or woman
    a) In the absence of children or their descendants, a stipulated amount (perhaps $5,000 or $10,000) and half of the remaining balance go to the surviving spouse, with the remainder going to the parents of the deceased; in the absence of parents, the surviving spouse is apt to take the entire estate.
    b) In the presence of children or their descendants, either one third or one half goes to the surviving spouse, and the balance is divided equally among the children, descendants of a child dividing their parent's share equally. The amount herein stipulated for the surviving spouse is in addition to the life-interest in real estate granted by the homestead statutes. An option may be given the surviving spouse of taking an amount mentioned in a will or provided by rights of dower and curtesy, if it is larger than would be secured under the statutes

of descent and distribution. The right of dower is the wife's right to one third of the income for life from her husband's real estate after his death; curtesy is a like right giving a husband one third of the income for life from his wife's real estate after her death. In some states these rights no longer exist; in others they have been written into law in the form of a wife's (or husband's) right to elect to take the intestate share against the will rather than accept the share provided in the will.

3. On death of widow or widower with children or their descendants

   a) Children take the property equally, descendants of deceased children dividing equally their parents' share.

The estate law of each state may have a table showing the way in which property passes in intestacy under differing and varying relationships. Figure 17–1 shows the pattern for New York, New Jersey, and Connecticut.

The Inadequacies of Intestacy

The will written for every man and woman *by law* is rarely an acceptable substitute for the will that the law permits every legally competent person to write for himself. The state, whose laws of intestacy are inflexible and cannot be adapted to the needs of your dependents, will distribute your property in a manner which you might not think desirable.

For example, assume that you are married and have one child, age four. The real asset of your estate is your retail business, which you own individually and which pays a good living. You die without leaving a will, and, upon her petition to the probate or surrogate's court, your wife is appointed guardian for the child. A special guardian will also be appointed by the court to check on your wife's disposition of the estate—on her accounting to the court. She may wish to continue the business; but the special guardian will insist that the business be sold in order to liquidate and settle the estate. If retained, it would provide a good living; when sold, it brings only a moderate sum, which, when invested, will not provide a good living. Yet the special guardian and the court will require that the business be sold, since you left no will granting the power to continue the business. By a simple will with such power, you could have left your wife a going business and a good income.

To take a second example: Assume that you are age 60 and that your wife is age 54. You have one son, age 30, who is employed, earning a good income but who likes a good time and is a spendthrift. You die without leaving a will. Your wife, who has no other means of support

FIGURE 17–1

How An Estate Is Distributed If There Is No Will

Surviving Heirs	New York	New Jersey	Connecticut
Wife and one child	½ to wife ½ to child	To wife—life use of ½ the realty plus ⅓ of personal property outright. Child or children take rest	⅓ to wife ⅔ to child
Wife and two or more children	⅓ to wife ⅔ to children	Same as above	Same as above
Child or children, but no wife	All to children	All to children	All to children
Wife and parent(s), but no children	$5,000 plus ½ the balance to wife. Rest to parent or parents	All to wife	$5,000 plus ½ of balance to wife. Rest to parent or parents
Grandchildren	Grandchildren and more remote descendants do not share unless their parent is dead. Then each set of grandchildren divides the share their parent would have taken if alive		
Wife, and brothers and sisters or their descendants	$10,000 plus ½ the balance to wife. Rest to brothers and sisters or their descendants	All to wife	All to wife
Wife, and uncles, cousins, etc. (no descendant, parent, brother, sister, nephew, niece)	All to wife	All to wife	All to wife
No wife and no children	All to parent or parents or, if none, to brothers and sisters or their descendants	Equally to parent or parents and brothers and sisters or their descendants	All to parent or parents or, if none, to brothers and their descendants

NOTES: A surviving husband takes the same share of his wife's estate as she would of his.

Descendants of a brother and sister (for example nieces or nephews) take their parent's share only if the parent is not alive to take his or her share.

If there are no relatives closer than cousins, the property normally goes to the "distributees" or "next of kin," usually the closest surviving relatives, for example, surviving first cousins (but if there are surviving first cousins, descendants of deceased first cousins will not share).

SOURCE: Irving Trust Company.

and who may be too old to go to work after being a housewife for so many years, gets only one third of your $90,000 estate; the son, who does not need it and who will probably squander it, gets two thirds, or $60,000. Obviously, you would not have intended this decision; but, in the absence of a will, that is how your estate is divided.

A third example may interest you. Tom and Ethel Young have no children; Tom's father is living and is quite wealthy. Ethel has no resources of her own. Yet, on Tom's death, since there was no will, Ethel received $5,000 plus half of the remainder of Tom's estate, while Tom's father received the other half. The father had no need of the funds; the wife did, but the law is inflexible.

If you die intestate (without a will), an administrator for your estate must be appointed by the court, and a bond equal to the size of the estate must be posted. The wrong person may be selected to administer the estate. The court may pick your widow, who knows little about money matters, whereas you would have made your brother, who has been your business partner for years, your executor had you bothered to make a will. No tax-savings devices will be available to your estate if you do not leave a will. There is no room for charitable dispositions. Your estate will not be distributed among your heirs in accordance with either sentiment or need. Your parents, or other persons you may have in mind, however much they may need or deserve your help, may not receive anything from your estate.

For example, assume that your wife is quite wealthy in her own right and that her parents are very well off too. Your parents, on the other hand, are poor, retired, not well, and wholly dependent upon you for support. Moreover, they do not, unfortunately, get along with your wife, nor she with them. You have two small children. You die and leave no will. All your property goes to your wife and children; nothing goes to your parents. Your wife could easily take care of herself and the children from her own resources, but, because you left no will, your death leaves your parents destitute.

The Young Family and "Guardianship"

You are young, gay, carefree, and nothing could be further from your mind than death, wills, estates, etc. Who cares—why bother? But consider one young, gay, carefree family.

Jim and Mary Fantini had been married for three years. They had a son, aged one. On a family summer vacation, they were in an automobile accident. Jim was killed. Mary was in the hospital for a month. Miraculously, the little boy was unhurt. Jim had no will. With the house they owned, the estate amounted to about $70,000. They lived in a state where the law said that in the case of death of a husband and no will, one third must go to the widow, two thirds to the child.

When Mary recovered she was shocked to learn that she could not administer her child's money, or even act as guardian without consent of the court. She had to apply to the court to administer the estate and post a bond, the premium cost of which was $210. Then she had to apply for legal guardianship of her son and post another bond, at an additional cost of $380. Because she had to sell the house, she had to secure court approval to do so. There were additional fees, including payments to lawyers, totaling $750 more. The first year, then, her expenses came to almost $1,400.

That isn't the end, however, for her lengthy legal involvement with the court will continue until the boy reaches 21. Each year she will have to post bonds and the fees will be about $500 per annum. Altogether, the cost of Jim's not having drawn a will cost Mary and her son about $10,000 of a modest estate. It could have financed the boy's college education. And it was all so unnecessary. A simple will drawn by Jim, leaving everything to Mary and naming her executrix to serve without bond, would have avoided most of the involvement with the court and eliminated almost all the cost.

Modern Estate Planning

The limitations and inadequacies of intestacy are so apparent, and inequities which frequently arise as a result are so glaring, that the informed person today plans the disposal of his lifetime accumulation and the protection and welfare of his family in the light of their special circumstances. Just as modern insurance programing, when coupled with social security and annuities, provides for planned security in old age and retirement, so modern estate planning permits you to use your resources to protect your wife, your children, and your parents in the best possible way in the light of your circumstances. Your business and investments can be left in the most competent hands, estate expenses and death taxes can be minimized, and family protection can be maximized through a carefully planned, flexible, and liquid estate program. Trusts may be established for those not competent to handle funds themselves, double estate taxes can be avoided, and your life insurance and real property can be tied in with other assets, such as stocks and bonds, so that forced sales, with costly shrinkage of values shortly after death, can be eliminated.

A man of means does a grave injustice to his family if he does not sit down with a competent lawyer specializing in estate planning and with an official of the trust department of his commercial bank to discuss a co-ordinated plan for the disposal of his assets upon death.

Just how the trust company goes about analyzing an estate situation is shown in Figure 17–2. The information needed to plan intelligently for estate purposes is shown in Figure 17–3. Before you discuss your problem with your lawyer, you should set down all the facts required in

FIGURE 17–2

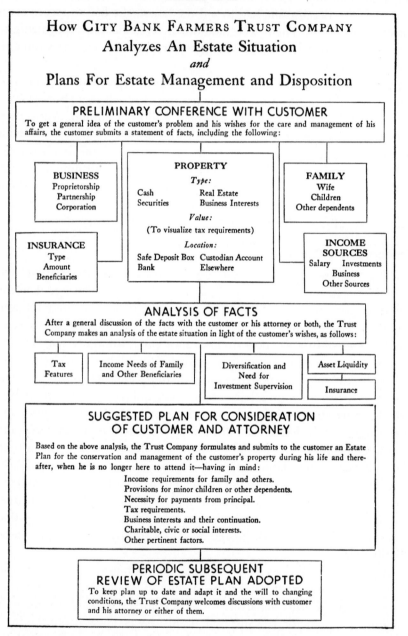

How City Bank Farmers Trust Company
Analyzes An Estate Situation
and
Plans For Estate Management and Disposition

PRELIMINARY CONFERENCE WITH CUSTOMER

To get a general idea of the customer's problem and his wishes for the care and management of his affairs, the customer submits a statement of facts, including the following:

BUSINESS
Proprietorship
Partnership
Corporation

PROPERTY
Type:
Cash   Real Estate
Securities   Business Interests

Value:
(To visualize tax requirements)

FAMILY
Wife
Children
Other dependents

INSURANCE
Type
Amount
Beneficiaries

Location:
Safe Deposit Box Custodian Account
Bank   Elsewhere

INCOME SOURCES
Salary   Investments
Business
Other Sources

ANALYSIS OF FACTS

After a general discussion of the facts with the customer or his attorney or both, the Trust Company makes an analysis of the estate situation in light of the customer's wishes, as follows:

Tax
Features

Income Needs of Family
and Other Beneficiaries

Diversification and
Need for
Investment Supervision

Asset Liquidity

Insurance

SUGGESTED PLAN FOR CONSIDERATION OF CUSTOMER AND ATTORNEY

Based on the above analysis, the Trust Company formulates and submits to the customer an Estate Plan for the conservation and management of the customer's property during his life and thereafter, when he is no longer here to attend it—having in mind:

Income requirements for family and others.
Provisions for minor children or other dependents.
Necessity for payments from principal.
Tax requirements.
Business interests and their continuation.
Charitable, civic or social interests.
Other pertinent factors.

PERIODIC SUBSEQUENT REVIEW OF ESTATE PLAN ADOPTED

To keep plan up to date and adapt it and the will to changing conditions, the Trust Company welcomes discussions with customer and his attorney or either of them.

Source: *Planning Your Estate*, City Bank Farmers Trust Co., New York.

FIGURE 17–3

Getting the Facts for Estate Planning

Statement of Facts

The following suggests some of the facts concerning yourself and your dependents which you ought to take into consideration to formulate a sound plan. It is not necessary to prepare the statement before discussing the subject with us but having it available would be helpful. All information which we may receive is held in confidence.

(Approximate amounts are sufficient)

NAME..

PRESENT ADDRESS... LEGAL RESIDENCE...........................

YOUR BUSINESS INTERESTS

(a) ....Corporation ....Partnership ....Proprietorship

(b) Kind of business...

(c) Who owns control?..

(d) Do you desire to have your business continued after your death?.........................

(e) What plans have you made to have it continued?..

....

(f) Describe any written contracts, business insurance agreements or other arrangements you have made for the disposition of your business interests:...

....

(g) Give any other important details with respect to your business:.............................

....

YOUR APPROXIMATE WORTH

	Net Value	Annual Income
(a) Value of business interest	$...................	
(b) Salary, commissions, fees, income from business, etc.		$...................
(c) Stocks	$...................	$...................
(d) Bonds	$...................	$...................
(e) Mortgages	$...................	$...................
(f) Real Estate	$...................	$...................
(g) Other property and income	$...................	$...................
TOTAL NET WORTH AND INCOME	$...................	$...................

Describe any trust interests you may have: (including powers of appointment)..........................

....

How much of your net annual income is available for investment each year?...........................

SOURCE: *Planning Your Estate*, City Bank Farmers Trust Co., New York.

this form so that both of you will have all the essential information available. Figure 17–4 is a graphic illustration of what a completed estate plan will look like. In an actual case, of course, exact facts and figures will be described precisely. You cannot leave a planned estate, however, without a will. The central feature of estate planning is the will.

FIGURE 17–3 (Continued)

YOUR LIFE INSURANCE

How PAYABLE:

	Lump Sum Payment	Insurance Company Plan	Trust Company Plan	Other Plan
(a) To named beneficiary	$................................	$................................	$................................	$................................
(b) To estate	$................................			

Approximate annual net premiums $................................

Have you made a will?................................ Has your wife made a will?................................

YOUR WIFE'S NET ESTATE

Wife's total separate net worth $................................

Approximate annual income of wife $................................

YOUR HEIRS AND DEPENDENTS

NAME	RELATIONSHIP	AGES, if children
....	....	....
....	....	....
....	....	....
....	....	....

What approximate minimum annual income will be required to maintain your family in its present standard of living after your death? $................................

Please state to whom you wish the income of your estate to be paid after your death.

NAME	Amount or Percentage of Annual Income
....	....
....	....
....	....
....	....

Within legal limits, any desired disposition of an estate can be made. On the following pages there are two charts indicating two different plans for the distribution of an estate.

Your "Last Will and Testament"

The expression "last will and testament" is historical and comes from the time when a distinction was drawn between a "testament"—a term derived from the Latin—which disposed of personal property, and a "will"—a term derived from the Anglo-Saxon—which disposed of real

FIGURE 17–4

A Completed Estate Plan

The following chart illustrates one plan for the disposition of the estate of Mr. John Doe after his death. It shows how his general estate and the proceeds of his insurance can be held in trust. Under this plan, the proceeds of his insurance can be made payable to his estate or can be made available to his executor to pay inheritance taxes and other cash demands by providing in the insurance trust that the trustee may lend money to or purchase securities from the executor. This plan is one which is not designed to effect any estate tax saving through use of the marital deduction which is available under the Federal Revenue Act of 1948 with respect to devises and bequests from one spouse to the other subject to the limitations and conditions contained in the law. This plan is recommended in some cases *after an analysis of the estates of both husband and wife indicates its desirability.*

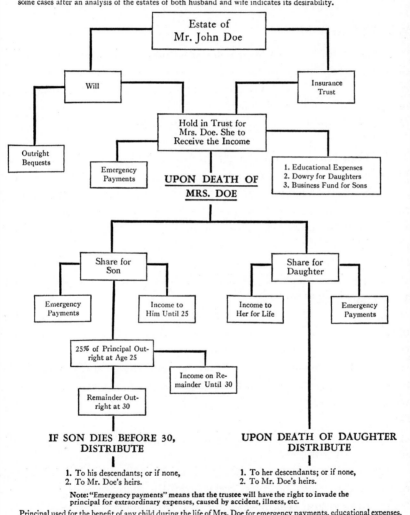

IF SON DIES BEFORE 30, DISTRIBUTE

1. To his descendants; or if none,
2. To Mr. Doe's heirs.

UPON DEATH OF DAUGHTER DISTRIBUTE

1. To her descendants; or if none,
2. To Mr. Doe's heirs.

Note: "Emergency payments" means that the trustee will have the right to invade the principal for extraordinary expenses, caused by accident, illness, etc.

Principal used for the benefit of any child during the life of Mrs. Doe for emergency payments, educational expenses, dowry or a business fund, may be charged against such child's share.

Upon Mrs. Doe's death, a share may also be set apart for the descendants of any deceased child. Descendants who have attained majority will receive their pro-rata parts of such share outright. Minors will receive their pro-rata parts of such share upon attaining majority.

SOURCE: *Planning Your Estate*, City Bank Farmers Trust Co., New York.

property. The word "will" is the current modern equivalent of both, although the heading of a will customarily employs the longer form. Some states make a distinction as to the descent of real property, on the one hand, and personal property, on the other. In New York, for example, a person 18 years old, whether male or female, may make a will disposing of personal property but must be age 21 to make a will disposing of real property.

Why Make a Will?

Aside from the fact that if you die without a will your estate will be distributed according to the intestate laws, the provisions of which are necessarily general and inflexible, there are a number of other valid reasons why a will is decidedly advisable—in fact, almost necessary. *It is well to remember that if you die intestate—*

1. Your family will find itself unnecessarily involved in certain court procedures, of which, the chances are, it has little or no knowledge.
2. Your knowledge of the property that you own and your advice as to its disposition cannot be passed on. It dies with you.
3. Indifference on your part is indicated. It is, therefore, not unlikely that this indifference will be transferred to those who administer your estate.
4. You lose the privilege of naming your executor—and this may be a very costly loss indeed.
5. You lose the privilege, afforded by the laws of most states, of naming a guardian for your minor children. This is vital, particularly if your wife should not survive you.
6. In some instances, if you leave no immediate family, your failure to leave a will may result in the passage of your property to persons in whom you have no particular interest, or even in its escheat to the state.
7. The procedure involved in intestacy is likely to increase the shrinkage of your estate.
8. You lose the opportunity of minimizing estate and inheritance taxes, as can often be done by a carefully planned will.

In *contrast,* a will gives you the advantage of specifying—

1. To whom your property should go.
2. When it should go.
3. In what amounts it should go.

4. How it should be safeguarded.

5. By whom it should be handled.

Disposition of Property by Will

Usually a person may dispose of his property by will as he wishes. We have already seen one possible exception to this rule, in that, if a husband (or wife) leaves his spouse less in his will than she would have under the statutes of descent and distribution or under the laws of dower and curtesy, the surviving spouse may elect to take the larger amount granted by the statutes or laws. That is, one spouse may not usually, in most states, disinherit the other, although it is possible to disinherit children. Another exception is provided by the homestead laws, which are found in nearly every state. The purpose of such laws is to provide a roof over her head for a wife in spite of her husband's possible desire to deprive her of it.

Certain provisions or bequests in wills may be against "public policy" and hence will be invalidated. For example, a man who had lived in a certain house during all of his adult life provided that his home be boarded up for 20 years after his death and then be given free of charge for two years to any deserving young married couple. The probate court held that, while it recognized the sentimental purpose, the closing of a needed dwelling for 20 years was against public policy. Also, a condition in a will to the effect that a person who has never married shall only receive a bequest providing he or she remain unmarried for life is usually against public policy, since it is thought that marriage and the founding of families is to the best interest of society. While it is impossible to prevent a person who has never married from getting married, you are usually permitted to restrict a person from remarrying a second or third time on pain of losing the gift set forth in your will. It is also possible in some states to insert provisions that your beneficiaries marry only persons of certain religions. A mother bequeathed her wealth to her daughter only on condition the daughter divorce her husband or was widowed at the time the will was probated. The court held that the will was valid.

There are certain bequests which, as a group, are invalid; these are usually political in nature. For example, a gift to the Communist party or to any other organization dedicated to the overthrow of the United States government is obviously against public policy and void.

Certain property will pass automatically on death and is not subject to disposition by will. This may be because of the nature of the property or the technical legal title by which it is held; because the testator is married; or for a combination of reasons. For example, if property is held by two persons as joint tenants with right of survivorship, or by husband and wife as tenants by the entirety, and one of them dies, the survivor becomes sole owner of the property, regardless of the will of the decedent.

Although insurance may be payable to the executors or administrators of the insured, so that the proceeds will become part of his estate and be subject to his will, insurance is generally payable to named beneficiaries, with the proceeds payable to them regardless of the terms of the insured's will. United States savings bonds, held in the name of one person and payable on death to another, are a further example of property which passes outside of the will. In the so-called "community-property" states a substantial portion of the property of a decedent may not be subject to disposal by will at all.

Who May Make a Will

In general, anyone of full age and sound mind is capable of making a will. In some states, males and females must be 21 years of age, but other states sometimes use 18 years as the minimum for both sexes or require females to be 18 and males to be 21. The person making a will ("testator" if male; "testatrix" if female) must possess sufficient soundness of mind to make the instrument a valid expression of his testamentary wishes.

Validity of Wills

It is the generally accepted rule that the validity of a will which bequeathes personal property depends upon the law of the state or country where the deceased had his domicile (home) when he died; whereas the validity of a will which devises real estate depends on the law of the state or country where the real estate is located (its "situs"). Most states have loosened the principles of local sovereignty in order to give validity to wills made in other states and countries. Many have adopted the Uniform Wills Act or similar statutes. The power to dispose of property by will is neither a natural nor a constitutional right. It depends wholly upon statute, i.e., it may be given, revoked, or circumscribed by act of the legislature.

"Domicile" is a very important concept in wills, especially from a tax standpoint. A person may have a number of residences; he usually has but one domicile. This is based on his intent and is judged by such things as where he voted, where he paid taxes, etc. In the famous Dorrance case, both New Jersey and Pennsylvania claimed that John T. Dorrance (sole stockholder in the Campbell Soup Company) had been domiciled in their respective states. The U.S. Supreme Court refused to take jurisdiction, and both states assessed and collected death taxes on his estate, New Jersey $12 million, Pennsylvania $14 million.

Formalities in Wills

There are several steps in the ritual that is required to make a valid will. While these may seem excessively precise to you, remember that the law insists on these steps to prevent fraud, as safeguards for the protection of all concerned. A will must be in writing, and the more important aspects of the ritual with which the maker must comply are outlined in the following paragraphs.

Signature of Testator. A valid will must be signed by the maker. Although the signature may be made satisfactorily by pen, pencil, or typewriter, it is only common sense to write it in ink, by hand. The signature should be placed right after the last sentence of the will itself. The will must be signed *at the end* to prevent fraud—to eliminate the possibility that someone might add a typed paragraph either before or after the signature and thus change the terms and intent of the will. A surprisingly large number of cases are brought to court to determine whether the signature was at the end of a will, particularly where a rather confusing printed form was used by a testator (maker of a will) who tried to write his own will. Where the signature of the decedent was not at the end, the will was denied "probate." That is, it was held no valid will, and the testator's property was divided up, when he died, as if he had died "intestate," i.e., without a will. It is a further legal requirement that the signature be written in the presence of the subscribing witnesses. Confusion is avoided if the testator's signature agrees in all respects with his name as given elsewhere in the will. To avoid question as to other pages of the will, the testator's signature, or at least his initials, should be written on each of the other pages, customarily in the margin. This is also to prevent fraud—to prevent the substitution of a new typed page for one of the originals.

Witnesses. State statutes generally require at least two or three witnesses to a will. The witnesses should also be of full age and of sound mind. It is also good if they are healthy, and younger than the testator. Often a will is not offered for probate for some years after it is made. In case of dispute, it is helpful if the witnesses are then living and still mentally able, so that they can give any necessary testimony. No beneficiary under a will or spouse of a beneficiary should sign as a witness, since anything left to him may be lost by his doing so.

Witnesses should see the testator write his signature or be told by him that the signature is his. They should see each other sign, and the will itself should state that all witnesses signed in the presence of each other. If the addresses of witnesses are added, it may help later in locating them. Although the witnesses need not read the will, and the testator may not want them to read it, the testator should tell them that he wants them to witness his signature to his last will and testament.

Absence of Alterations. Alterations should not be made in a will after it has been signed and witnessed. Any alterations made prior to signatures should be incorporated in a fair copy, free of erasures or any other changes which later might be the cause of misunderstanding. Once a will has been completed, changes can be effected through a codicil or addition, executed with all the formalities of the will itself.

A few examples of errors will serve to show the importance of the ritual. An intelligent, literate woman bought a will form at a stationery store, on which she wrote her wishes for the disposal of her property. There was not enough room for her to write all she wanted above the dotted lines for signatures of maker and witnesses, so she continued her writing below. She and the witnesses signed on the dotted lines. Everything seemed in order. There was no question but that she was of sound mind at the time; no doubt as to how she wished to dispose of her property; no dispute that the witnesses saw her sign, knew she meant the document to be her will, and signed as witnesses. Nor is there anything necessarily wrong with a will made out on a printed form. But she hadn't signed it at the end; and, in the state where she lived, the law required that a will be signed at the end. The court would not permit the document to be given effect as her will—could not consider the writing above the signature as a will and ignore what followed—inasmuch as she had written it all as a single, consecutive expression of her wishes.

Mr. Thomas asked two friends if they would come over to the home of his sister, Mrs. Conway, to witness the signing of her will. Two or three days later he drove them to her house. They waited in the living room while Mr. Thomas went into the dining room. In a few minutes the two witnesses were called into the dining room; then Mrs. Conway was wheeled in. Mr. Thomas told her to "sign this paper here," and she did. Then the witnesses signed. Later, after Mrs. Conway's death, this paper was offered for probate; but the court would not accept is as her will. The witnesses testified that, at the time of signing, Mrs. Conway had not shown, either by word or deed, that she knew it was her will. Neither she nor anyone else in her presence had asked the witnesses to sign as witnesses to her will.

Thus a will is not valid unless, at the time the witnesses sign, the maker of the will, in the presence of the witnesses, "declares" or gives a definite indication that it is his will. The example given illustrates the reason for this requirement: Mrs. Conway was age 85 and infirm at the time of signing. The requirement—like the others for a valid will—is intended to protect anyone from being imposed upon in making what may be a last, and hence irrevocable, will.

Terminology

Occasionally a student will complain, "I do not understand why such unintelligible terms as 'intestate,' 'testamentary,' 'corpus,' 'issue,' 'per stirpes,' 'power of appointment,' and the like have to be used in talking—or writing—about wills and trusts. Why don't you use language I can understand?"

When it comes to using legal words in legal situations like wills and trusts, there is a good reason why lawyers use them. Over the years, through definition by statute and interpretation by the courts, these terms have acquired precise meanings—meanings that might take pages of words to explain fully. Technical words and terms are a means of exact and comprehensive expression; and when properly used in wills and trust agreements, they are a protection to the people whose interests are served and can be an economy, too, in the avoiding of litigation. You should, therefore, understand a few of these terms:

Administrator. This is the term applied to the person appointed by the court to administer an estate of a person who died intestate. Applied to a woman, the term is "administratrix."

Administration Expenses. The cost of settling an estate—court costs; the fees of executors, attorneys, and appraisers; and other expenses.

Ancillary. An ancillary executor is subordinate to the one named in your will and is appointed to dispose of property in another state or country which does not permit your chosen executor to represent you.

Beneficiary. A beneficiary is one who is named in the will as a recipient of property under it.

Bequeath. In connection with wills, this is a word with a technical legal meaning, the giving of a bequest of personal property (as contrasted with real property), the recipient being a "legatee."

Codicil. An addition to a will or a change executed with the same formalities as required in the will itself.

Decedent. The deceased, or deceased person.

Devise. This is the gift of real property (not personal property) to a person known as the "devisee."

Estate. Your estate is all you own—real estate, cash, stocks, bonds, and other property. You can pass these on by will, subject to the deduction of debts, estate and inheritance taxes, and administration expenses.

Exculpatory Clause. "None of my Executors or Trustees shall be liable for any act or omission in connection with the administration of my estate or any of the trusts or powers hereunder nor for any loss or injury to any property held in or under my estate or any of said trusts or powers, except only for his or her actual fraud; and none of my Executors or Trustees shall be responsible for any act or omission of any other Executor or Trustee."

Executor. The person named in a will and appointed to administer an estate according to the provisions of a will. Applied to a woman, the form is "executrix."

Holographic Will. Such a will is written entirely in the handwriting of the person making the will.

Intestate. This term refers to one who dies without leaving a valid will.

Legatee. This is a person who receives personal property under a will, as contrasted with a "devisee," one who receives real property.

Letters Testamentary. The court's certificate of the probate of a will and of the executor's authority to act under it.

Nuncupative Will. Such a will is an oral disposition of personal property made by a person during his last illness or by a soldier or sailor during battle. It should be put in writing by witnesses as soon as possible and offered promptly for probate. This is the only sort of oral will commonly held to be valid.

Personal Property. This is all property which is not real estate.

Probate. This is the name of courts having jurisdiction of wills and of the court's procedure in proving the validity of wills. "Probating a will" means presentation of proof to the court after your death of the legality of your last will and testament, whereupon the court grants authority to the executor to carry out your intentions as expressed in the will.

Real Estate. Land and the buildings thereon.

Surrogate. This term (used in New York) means the same as "probate judge."

Testate. A person leaving a valid will is said to have died "testate."

Testator. A person who makes and leaves a will. The feminine form is "testatrix."

Trust. A trust puts your money or other property into the hands of a trustee (either financial institution or individual, or both) for management and disposition of income and of principal as you direct in your will or trust agreement. There are "living trusts," "insurance trusts," and "testamentary trusts," to be described later. A person who receives the income from a trust during his or her lifetime is known as a "life-tenant" or "life-beneficiary," while the person who receives the principal of the trust after the death of the life-tenant is a "remainderman."

Common Provisions

Since the purpose of a will is to direct the distribution of an estate to the person or persons whom the testator wishes to have it, the following comments may prevent omission of important provisions which might otherwise be overlooked. It is common to mention the testator's just debts and funeral expenses, which must be paid before anything can be left for anyone else. Customarily, notice is given to creditors; they have a reasonable time in which to submit their claims for payment. The testator may find it desirable to state in his will the type of funeral and burial services he wishes in order that a great deal more or a great deal less than he thinks appropriate will not be paid for them.

Distribution of real and personal property to family, relatives, friends, and charities should be set out in clear and concise terms; in connection therewith, disposition of personal effects should be dealt with in such a way as to avoid dispute. It is usually advisable for the testator to nominate the person of his choice as executor; and if there are minor children, it may be expedient to nominate a guardian for them. The will

> ### Names Clipped From Will Restored by Surrogate
>
> BUFFALO, N. Y. (UPI) — Surrogate Thomas J. O'Donnell recently told nine persons they could not be cut out of the will of a relative even though they literally were.
>
> One paragraph of the will of Mrs. Lillian G. Briggs of suburban Kenmore, who died Feb. 21, 1962 was scissored out. It provided for bequests to nine relatives. The will was contested.
>
> In what Surrogate O'Donnell called "a rare move," he accepted a carbon copy of the will and awarded $6,000 to the relatives. It was not determined who did the cutting.

can set up any trusts thought advantageous for wife, children, or others and can make special provision for anything else the testator desires.

Too much care cannot be devoted to the drawing of a will; in spite of care, ambiguities are frequently found in them, and dissatisfaction and unfairness often result. When distributing property by will, attention should be directed toward other property already owned by the beneficiaries and any money coming to them as beneficiaries of life insurance policies in order to achieve an equitable over-all result.

If individual pieces of property are left to each of several children, there is always the question as to whether some of them may increase in value by the time of the testator's death, whereas others may decline in value, thus effecting an unequal distribution. It might be better to give each child an equal interest in all properties or the proceeds from the sale of them all. Some years ago, a certain wealthy individual left stipulated amounts to serveral charities, thinking that he was leaving such a substantial estate that there would be plenty left over for his family. The depression of the 1930's, however, so depleted his assets that, after the designated amounts were distributed to the charities, little remained for the family.

What Is in a Will?

There are five principal sections to a will: the opening recitation, the dispositive clauses, the administrative clauses, a testimonium clause, and an attestation clause. Each has a special and important function.

The opening recitation tells who you are, where you live, may say that you are of sound mind and competent to make a will (though saying it does not prove it is so), may revoke all previous wills, direct that all just debts and funeral expenses be paid, and give instructions as to burial (though this latter feature is better done in a separate letter of instruction rather than in a will, since the will may not be opened until after the funeral). A typical introductory clause is as follows:

IN THE NAME OF GOD, AMEN. I, Joseph Taffet, of the Borough of Manhattan, City, County and State of New York, being of sound mind and memory, but also aware of the uncertainties of this life, do hereby make, publish and declare this to be my Last Will and Testament. I hereby revoke all wills and codicils made by me at any time heretofor.

The dispositive clauses are the heart of the will. They indicate who is to get what. There are four types of legacies—specific, general, demonstrative, and residuary. There are also lapsed and preferred legacies. A *specific* legacy occurs when a particular piece of property in an estate is set aside and given to a named individual: you bequeath your gold watch to your son, Thomas. A *general* legacy exists when you leave a given sum of money, such as $5,000, to an individual. A cash bequest is payable out of the general assets of the estate. When the testator does not leave sufficient property to pay all the general legacies, the specific legatees would nevertheless receive the particular items bequeathed to them, whereas general legacies would be proportionately diminished and abated. In fact, where it is necessary to raise money to pay debts, the general legacies will first completely abate before recourse is had to the sale of items specifically bequeathed. In other words, a specific bequest has priority over a general or cash bequest.

A *demonstrative* legacy is usually one of a stated amount of money coupled with a specification in the will of a source of funds for its payment. In the case of a true demonstrative legacy, if the indicated source of funds is nonexistent—or to the extent that it is insufficient—

the legacy is payable out of general assets, like a general legacy. This has, however, occasioned considerable litigation, so that many draftsmen prefer to avoid demonstrative legacies completely.

A *residuary* legacy, as the term implies, is payable from the remainder of the estate after administration expenses, debts, and specific, general, and demonstrative legacies have been paid. The danger, as pointed out previously, is that you may make a will with a number of specific and general legacies and then leave the remainder—the bulk of your estate—as a residuary legacy to your wife or child. A shrinkage of the assets of the estate may sharply reduce the residuary legacies without impairing or touching the specific and general bequests. Since this, of course, was not your intent, you can guard against such an eventuality by inserting an abatement clause, which provides that if the entire net estate, or residuary estate, is less than a certain amount, or shrinks a certain percentage from value at the time the will was drawn, then the general legacies shall be reduced proportionately or eliminated altogether. When you leave your residuary estate to your nearest and dearest, such an abatement clause should always be used.

A *lapsed* legacy occurs when the legatee predeceases the testator. To provide for such contingencies, the will should make provision for alternate disposition. A *preferred* legacy is, of course, one where the testator in his will indicates that preference shall be given in the event that the estate is insufficient to satisfy all legacies in full.

The third major part of the will is the section which contains the administrative clauses. These set up the machinery for carrying out all your instructions. Here you name your post-mortem agents, your executors, and your guardians (if you have any minor children). The executor is the person (or persons, since there can be more than one; or institution, since it can be a trust company) responsible for having the will approved by the court, locating heirs and property, paying bills, distributing bequests, and so on. You may select anyone—your wife, a business partner, your brother, your lawyer, your banker, etc.—as your executor; but you will want to ask them if they will accept, and you will want to be reasonably sure that they are able to handle the complicated business of settling an estate and are young enough so that they are not likely to predecease you. You may also wish to name an alternate or substitute executor in case your first choices decline to serve or die. The guardian you appoint for your minor child may, of course, be your wife, in which case you will want to provide that she may serve without bond and have absolute discretion in the handling of any funds you may leave to the child. If you own and operate a business, you will want to give your executor very broad powers if you want the business continued, because otherwise he will either be forced to liquidate it or may not have sufficient authority to operate it efficiently. These are all highly technical matters, the settlement of which should never be attempted without the advice of a lawyer.

The fourth part of a will is the testamonium clause. Actually this is very simple. It ends the will and says that, in approval of the foregoing, you are signing your name. Do not sign your name, however, until the witnesses are present. The testamonium clause is likely to read: "IN WITNESS WHEREOF, I have hereunto set my hand (and seal, in some states) this 5th day of May, 1966."

Mr. Kelly's "Humorous" Will

"FOR YEARS I have been reading Last Wills and Testaments, and I have never been able to clearly understand any of them at one reading. Therefore, I will attempt to write my own Will with the hope that it will be understandable and legal. Kids will be called 'kids' and not 'issue' and it will not be cluttered up with 'parties of the first part,' 'per stirpes,' 'perpetuities,' 'quasi judicial,' 'to wit' and a lot of other terms that I am sure are only used to confuse those for whose benefit it is written."

So begins the Last Will of John B. Kelly of Philadelphia, one-time bricklayer, founder of two of the country's largest brick contracting firms, former Olympic rowing champion, and father of H. S. H. Princess Grace of Monaco.

It was typed on twelve full-size legal sheets, prompting his parting observation: "If I don't stop soon, this will be as long as Gone With the Wind."

Finally, there is what the lawyers call the "attestation clause." This is the clause for witnesses, so that a record will exist reciting the circumstances under which the signing of the will was witnessed and by whom. Remember that they must hear you announce that this is your will, see you sign it, and then sign in the presence of each other as well as in your presence. Remember, too, that a beneficiary under a will should not witness it. The will remains valid, but the witness is likely to lose his or her legacy.

Duties of an Executor

One institution entitled a section such as this, describing the functions of an executor, as "How (Not) to Give a White Elephant." There was once, it declared, a wily rajah, who punished all those who earned his disfavor by giving them a "sacred" white elephant. Refusal was out of the question; working the dedicated beast was taboo. The eating habits of elephants being what they are, these ponderous, idle pachyderms eventually ate the recipients out of house and home, which was the potentate's plan. And so it is that Webster's dictionary describes a white elephant as "Something requiring much care and expense and yielding little profit; any burdensome possession." High on the list of modern-day white elephants is the job of executor when it is bestowed on an inexperienced individual. The path that today's executor must follow winds through a veritable jungle of laws and regulations.

The duties of an executor have been described in detail as follows:[1]

Locates and Reads Will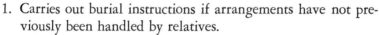

1. Carries out burial instructions if arrangements have not previously been handled by relatives.
2. Arranges for living expenses of family, where necessary.

Takes Preliminary Steps to Safeguard Assets

1. Retains counsel to probate will.
2. Confers with persons familiar with decedent's affairs.
3. Examines checkbooks, books of account, and other records pertaining to assets, where such records are available.
4. Obtains immediate information as to decedent's business interests.
5. Notifies postmaster, banks, safe-deposit companies, and other depositaries, of death.
6. Makes preliminary inventory.

Probates the Will

This proceeding is judicial. It consists of petitioning the court through your attorney to admit the will to probate and to issue letters testamentary to the executor named in the will, as authority to carry out the testator's wishes.

The proper parties must be notified, and the required proof must be submitted by witnesses to satisfy the court that the will is valid and that any attempts to contest the probate should be resisted.

Appointment of a temporary administrator is possible if delay of probate occurs because of a contest or for other reasons.

---

[1] Adapted from *Executor and Testamentary Trustee*, City Bank Farmers Trust Co., New York, no date.

Assembles the Estate Property

1. Life insurance
   a) Obtains proofs and collects.
2. Household and personal effects
   a) Makes proper provision for their care.
3. Securities and mortgages
   a) Locates safe-deposit box.
   b) Removes contents in presence of representative of state tax commission.
   c) Obtains tax waivers and collects securities in custody of others.
   d) Liquidates indebtedness if any securities have been used as collateral.
4. Real estate
   a) Inspects and reports on condition of property.
   b) Ascertains status of taxes, mortgages against property, and leases.
   c) Arranges for management and collection of rents.
   d) Files exemplified copy of will in counties where real estate is situated.
5. Cash
   a) Obtains tax waivers and collects.
6. Miscellaneous assets
   a) Collects money due decedent, bank accounts, and interests in other estates or trusts, present or future.
   b) Adjusts conflicting claims and liquidates them.
7. Inventory
   a) Makes complete list of property.
8. Ancillary administration
   a) Takes necessary steps to obtain property located outside the state.

Has Appraisals Made

Has appraisals made to establish values as of date of death, when necessary.

Manages Assets

Sets up a separate set of accounts for estate. Segregates assets specifically bequeathed and arranges for any income thereon to be held separately, pending distribution. Sets up accounts as follows:

1. Household and personal effects
   a) Determines best time and method for disposal of personal property, with special consideration to valuable collections.
2. Business interests
   a) Investigates and determines policy as to continuance, liquidation, or sales of business after securing information about the particular lines of business affected, always having due regard to the testator's wishes.
3. Securities and mortgages
   a) Examines desirability of investments.
   b) Determines propriety of retention or sale. Varying factors should be considered, sometimes one and sometimes others, e.g.:
      (1) Funds for taxes.
      (2) Other cash requirements.
      (3) Investment powers in will.
      (4) Market conditions.
      (5) Results of statistical research.
      (6) Taxable gains or losses.
      (7) Ultimate disposition of estate.
4. Real estate
   a) Investigates leases, encumbrances, condition of buildings, and determines rental revenue.
   b) Considers anticipated conditions of locality and neighborhood and, where desirable, consults with real estate specialists.
   c) If circumstances require a sale, lists property with leading brokers.

Settles Claims and Debts

1. Claims
   a) Advertises for claims when required by law.
   b) Considers propriety of claims and rejects those deemed improper.
2. Nature of claims and expenses encountered
   a) Bills for current expenses.
   b) Funeral expenses.
   c) Taxes or adjustment of taxes.
   d) Unmatured charitable subscriptions and pledges.
   e) Liability as endorser or maker of promissory notes.

f) Liability on leases; special partnership or business contracts.

g) Administration expenses and legal fees.

Settles Taxes

The procedure for proper assessment and payment of modern taxes is highly technical. Special forms of information and tax returns must be prepared and filed with the respective taxing authorities.

1. Income taxes
    a) Federal, state, and local. Considers propriety of all claims for taxes and, where practicable, resists those deemed improper.
    b) On income before death: files necessary returns and pays taxes due; makes final settlement with tax authorities.
    c) On income after death: files necessary returns and pays taxes, if any.
2. Estate and gift and inheritance taxes
    a) Federal
        (1) Files preliminary notice.
        (2) Makes return and pays taxes.
        (3) Makes final adjustment after review and audit.
    b) State of domicile
        (1) Obtains waivers for transfer of securities.
        (2) Considers payment in time to obtain discount.
        (3) Institutes proceedings for fixing tax.
        (4) Final adjustment of tax payment.
    c) Foreign states and countries
        (1) Takes necessary steps to file returns and pay taxes so that property affected can be released for transfer.
3. Real estate and other miscellaneous taxes
    a) Attends to adjustment of all outstanding taxes, including state, city, and local property and other miscellaneous taxes.

Accounts to Court and Distributes Net Estate

1. Payment of legacies
    a) Pays legacies.
    b) Delivers specific bequests.
    c) Obtains final receipts and releases from legatees.

2. Audit of administration of estate and accounting
   a) Causes a detailed statement of account of its acts as executor to be prepared and submitted either to the interested parties or for judicial settlement by the appropriate court.
   b) Upon the settlement of the account to the satisfaction of the interested parties and such court, distributes the balance of the estate remaining in the hands of the executor as required by the terms of the will.
3. Establishment of trust funds
   a) Turns over securities or cash or other property to trustee to constitute corpus of any trust provided for in will.
   b) Adjusts income due trust fund from date of decedent's death.

the important role of executor

Executors are, of course, compensated for such services, but an inexperienced person would either spend an excessive amount of time at the task or perform it inadequately. For this reason, if you appoint your wife as executor, you may wish to name your lawyer as coexecutor in order to take adequate care of such involved matters as probating the will, settling the estate, meeting claims, providing for estate taxes, and filing an accounting with the court. Choose your executors carefully— not on the basis of friendship alone, but on the basis of competence and ability to handle money matters. When you have chosen them, tell them where you keep your will and give them each an unsigned copy of it.

Fees for independent executors, such as those appointed by courts, are fixed by state law. A typical example of the sliding scale usually used would be the following:

4 percent on the first $10,000 of the estate,
2½ percent on the next $290,000, and
2 percent on any amount in excess of $300,000.

Thus, for a $50,000 estate, an executor could charge $1,400; for a $100,000 estate, $2,650; and for a $200,000 estate, $5,150. Only in the very large estates does the fee really pay for the time and problems involved. On a $1 million estate, for example, the fee would be $21,650. While executors' commissions vary from state to state, the fee is generally 2 to 2½ percent of estates over $50,000.

Simultaneous Deaths (Common Disasters)

You often read about a husband and wife who die in the same accident. In the absence of a will, all the property would probably pass to their children. If there were no children, there would probably be an argument as to which person died first. The same sort of difficulty could arise if each had left a will. If it was established that the husband died first, the wife would take whatever her husband willed her; and this property, together with any other she owned, would pass as stipulated in her will, except that her husband would not be living and could not receive anything left to him in that will. In the absence of a will, any property she left would go to her relatives, to the exclusion of his.

Gross inequities often result. For example, Johnson and his wife are traveling, and there is an accident. Johnson is killed instantly. Mrs. Johnson dies a few hours later. Neither had wills. What happens to Johnson's quite substantial estate? All of it would go to his wife's relatives. Johnson's father, mother, brother, sister—even his own children by a former wife—would receive nothing. If there is no will and it cannot be determined who died first, there may be endless and very costly litigation between the two sides of the family to determine which inherits.

To prevent unwanted results as far as possible, it may be helpful for a will to state how the property is to be disposed of if both husband and wife die at the same time. A well-drawn will usually contains a *common-disaster clause.* Such a clause may read: "Any person who shall have died at the same time as I, or in a common disaster with me, or under such circumstances that it is difficult or impossible to determine which died first, shall be deemed to have predeceased me."

If the will contains only one bequest—for example, a gift of all property to the testator's wife and, if she does not survive the testator, then to the testator's daughter—a useful wording of a common-disaster clause would be as follows: "All of my property, I give, devise, and bequeath to my wife, Mina, and if she does not survive me or if she and I die at the same time or in a common disaster or under such circumstances that it is difficult or impossible to determine which died first, then to my daughter Carla, if she survives me."

A Child Is Born—a Will Is Broken

It is sometimes possible for children not mentioned in a will to argue successfully that they were inadvertently forgotten when the will was made and that they should receive part of the estate. If the testator wishes to leave practically nothing to one or more of his children, he can do so by naming them and leaving each $1.00; this will show definitely that they were not forgotten. It would also be well if the testator explained why he was, in effect, cutting them off.

Often a husband wishes to give the wife control of the entire estate and therefore disinherits a child or children on the assumption that his wife will care for the child. Such a clause might read: "As it is my wish that my wife shall have the entire control of my estate, I have deliberately omitted any provision for bequests to my children, Dorothy and Anne, since I am confident that my wife will make all necessary provisions for them." If your wife, however, is a financially irresponsible type or is very likely to remarry upon your death and possibly neglect the children or not provide adequately for them, then such a clause is inappropriate, and the children should be separately and carefully protected by preferred legacies.

You may have drawn a will leaving all to your wife, explaining that you are leaving nothing to your little daughter because you are confident that your wife will provide for her. Several years later a son is born. Then the husband dies. The son may be entitled to one third of his father's estate. The widow receives two thirds. The daughter gets nothing. Why? Because the law in most states provides that when a child is born after a will is made, that child is entitled to take his "intestate share" as if no will existed—unless some provision has been made in advance for afterborn children, or unless it is clear from the language of the will that no provision for them is intended. A useful rule for every family is: Whenever a child is born, have both parents' wills checked by the family lawyer.

Review of Wills

Here is a streamlined statement of facts in a court case:

Mrs. J owned 75 shares of General Electric stock when she executed her will. The will gave a niece "Seventy-five shares (75 sh.) of common stock of General Electric Company." Between the time the will was signed and Mrs. J died, General Electric effected a three-for-one stock split. As a result, there were 225 shares of General Electric in Mrs. J's estate at the time of her death.

In the same will Mrs. J bequeathed "ninety (90) shares of International Paper Company stock" to a nephew. After the will was signed, the company paid dividends in its own stock. As a consequence, there were 104 shares in Mrs. J's estate at her death.

Was the niece entitled to 75 shares of General Electric or 225?

Was the nephew entitled to 90 shares of International Paper or 104?

A court proceeding was necessary to decide what Mrs. J intended. It was finally held that the niece was entitled to all 225 shares of General Electric. But it was also held that the nephew was entitled to only 90 shares of the Paper Company; the balance went to the person to whom Mrs. J willed her residuary estate.

Here trouble and expense could have been avoided by wording the will in a way that would have anticipated the possibility of stock splits and dividends. But a review of the will after the extra stock had been received would have revealed its weakness.

We live in a dynamic, not a static, world. A will which makes a sensible distribution of property at one time may result in a foolish distribution at another, later time. When a will has been made, therefore, it should not be put aside and overlooked for many years. It is good practice to review its stipulations at regular intervals to ascertain whether any of the provisions should be changed.

The safest way to make changes is to have a new will drawn, although a codicil to the old will may be effective.

A *codicil* is an instrument which amends or changes a will. An example will indicate how it is drawn. Assume that you want to change your executor:

I, Joseph F. Taffet, of the County of Confusion, City of Confusion, State of Confusion, do hereby make, publish and declare this Codicil to my Last Will and Testament:

I hereby ratify each and every provision of my will executed the 24th day of September, 1958, except insofar as such will is inconsistent with the terms of this instrument.

I hereby direct that Henry Takelittle be substituted as my executor, in place of Thomas Graball.

In witness whereof I have hereunto set my hand (and seal) this 20th day of January, 1959.

The same formality must be employed in executing and witnessing a codicil as was done with the will. You need not have the same witnesses, but you must have the same number. You must announce to the witnesses that the instrument is the codicil to your will. Then you must sign, and they must sign, all in the presence of one another. You should then fasten the codicil securely to the will itself.

Revocation of Wills

The safest way to revoke a will is to tear it up and burn the pieces in the presence of informed witnesses. If it is burned, canceled, torn, or otherwise destroyed by the testator or by another person in the testator's presence and at his order, the law will consider it revoked. A new will under a later date and stating the testator's intention to revoke prior wills will revoke them. A later will which is inconsistent with the provisions of previous wills serves as a revocation of the earlier wills to the extent that it is inconsistent with them.

Where to Keep a Will

Being valuable documents, wills should be kept with other important papers. Above all, they should be left where they will come into the hands of persons who will see that they are presented to the court for probate. Frequently they are left for safekeeping with one's attorney; logically, they should be left with one's executor-to-be.

A safe-deposit box is not recommended as a place to keep a will because when the person dies his safe-deposit box is sealed by the safe-deposit company. It may be opened only upon application to the probate court, and then only in the presence of a representative of the Estate Tax Division of the state's Tax Department. It must then be resealed, and the contents may not again be touched until the will is probated and the executor is given authority and access to the box. It is better, therefore, to keep your will either in a strongbox at home or with your lawyer or executor. Of course, if your wife has a safe-deposit box in her own name, you can keep your will in her box, and hers in yours.

Letter of Last Instructions

You should give your executor or your lawyer a letter of last instructions, which is separate and apart from your will. This letter, to be opened upon your death, should contain the following:

1. A statement as to where your will may be found.
2. Instructions as to funeral and burial. You may wish to specify for example, that, as a veteran, you be buried in a certain national cemetery rather than in the family burial plot.
3. Where your birth or baptismal certificate, social security card, marriage or divorce certificate, naturalization and citizenship papers, and discharge papers from the armed forces may be found. The latter is important if you wish to be buried in a national cemetery, which is the privilege of any veteran.
4. Where your membership certificates in any lodges or fraternal organizations which provide death or cemetery benefits may be found.
5. A list of the locations of any safe-deposit boxes you may have, and where the keys may be found.
6. A list of your insurance policies, and where they may be found.
7. A statement concerning any pension systems to which you belonged and from which your estate may be entitled to receive a death benefit.
8. A list of all bank accounts, checking and savings, and their locations.
9. A list of all stocks and bonds you own, and where they may be found.
10. A statement of all real property owned by you.
11. A list of all other property—personal, business, etc.
12. Instructions or directions concerning your business in the event your will suggests or provides that it be continued.
13. A statement of reasons for actions taken in your will, such as disinheritances. It is sometimes better to place the explanation in a separate letter available to the court, rather than in your will, to avoid a complicated will and expensive litigation in connection therewith.

TRUSTS

"The Federal Tax Court ruled today that trust funds amounting to $64,000 set up for the two children of Joe Louis must be used to pay part of the $1,199,437 he owed the government in back taxes.

"The judge estimated that during his long reign as heavyweight champion from 1937 to 1948, Mr. Louis made about $4,600,000. But when he retired, the judge said, he was $500,000 in debt". . . thus ran a newspaper account. Fortunately most trusts have happier outcomes than those Joe Louis established. In some circles they are used very extensively. *Fortune* remarked, "If you don't have a trust fund in Boston, it's as if you didn't have clothes on."

A trust is an agreement whereby the person who establishes the trust—the settlor or grantor—gives his property to a trustee or trustees for the benefit of the beneficiary or beneficiaries of the trust. Individuals, and institutions such as trust companies and banks, act as trustees. According to the desire of the grantor, a trust may be revocable or irrevocable. Formerly it was the practice to choose an individual or individuals as trustees. Then it was necessary to choose honest, able, responsible men for this important undertaking. The advent of the trust company brought a continued life not enjoyed by individuals. Sooner or later an individual is sure to die; a trust company usually enjoys a perpetual charter. Furthermore, the large volume of trust business handled by such institutions gives them an experience and organization beyond the scope of the individual. By teaming an institution and an individual as cotrustees, many of the advantages of each may be secured for a trust.

Life-Tenants and Remaindermen

Those who receive incomes from trusts during their lifetimes only are known as "life-tenants"; those beneficiaries who get the corpus or principal of the trust upon the death of the life-tenants are called "remaindermen."

Living Trusts

A living trust, or trust *inter vivos,* or voluntary trust is in effect while the grantor is still living; in fact, he may be a beneficiary. Any person having enough property to warrant it can set up such a trust for his own protection. Unless he has a minimum of $10,000 or $20,000, he will probably not be able to find competent trustees who are willing to undertake the responsibility. The trustee takes the legal title to the property and administers it to preserve the principal and earn a relatively safe income with it, although both principal and income may be distributed currently under the agreement, in which case the beneficiary would be very much like an annuitant.

In addition to the advantage of putting the property into skillful hands, there are some tax advantages in setting up living trusts. If the settlor really parts definitely with the property put into the trust by (1) making the trust irrevocable, (2) receiving no income, and (3) not retaining the power to change the beneficiary, although he will be answerable for gift taxes when the trust is established, no estate or inheritance taxes will be levied on this property when he dies. The living trust is one alternative manner of parting with one's property. Should the settlor retain the power to revoke the trust, receive the income, or change the beneficiary, he has in important respects not really parted with his property at all. He still has it under his control and could not reasonably expect to obtain an extate tax advantage. Important income tax advantages may still result, however.

A valid trust may be established orally as to personal property if the words used indicate clearly that the legal title is to be held by one person for the benefit of another; but a writing is required for real property, and a writing is always preferable for the purpose of eliminating dispute as to the agreement. It shoud go without saying that the drawing of a trust instrument is a technical undertaking which should be left to an experienced lawyer; an ordinary individual drawing such an instrument could raise difficulties involving far more money than a lawyer would have charged to create an effective instrument.

Testamentary Trusts

A testamentary trust is a trust under the will of a deceased person and becomes effective as of his death. Trustee and executor may or may not be the same person. The purpose of such a trust is to lodge the property in skillful hands so that it may be advantageously administered for the beneficiaries. If the same money were handled by an inexperienced person, the chances of doing as well with it, either from the viewpoint of income or of safety of principal, would probably not be bright.

This type of trust is often set up so that the widow (a life-tenant) may receive the income for life and the children (the remaindermen) may have the principal upon her death. In the absence of a widow, the income may be left to the children for a number of years, usually during their minority, at the end of which time the corpus (principal) of the trust is to be paid to them. It is possible to incorporate a provision in the trust agreement whereby the trustee may use part of the principal to supplement the income should income alone be inadequate. Testamentary trusts are often useful as a means of reducing taxes, as will be shown later.

The Trust Term-Rule against Perpetuities

In nearly all, if not all, states there is a public policy against the continuance of trusts or suspension of powers of alienation beyond periods defined by certain rules. The common-law rule fixed the period at lives-in-being plus twenty-one years, but this has been modified in some states. For example, in several states a trust under a will can be created for a term measured by the lives of not more than two persons who are named in the will and who are living at the testator's death; these are the so-called "measuring lives."[2]

The persons whose lives are specified in the will as the measuring lives need not necessarily be, although they most frequently are, the same persons as those who are to receive the income from the trust. Furthermore, the rule against perpetuities does not limit the number of beneficiaries but only the duration of the trust. Thus, a trust can be created to continue during the life of A and thereafter during the life of B, with a direction that the income during the continuance of the trust be paid to X, Y, and Z and as many other persons as the testator desires to receive the income during the continuance of the trust.

In the above example, although A and B must be persons in being at the date of death, X, Y, and Z need not be, since they are not measuring lives. In other words, there is no objection to creating a trust for the payment of income to a person born after the date of the testator's death, provided that such person's life is not a measuring life. In such a case, the measuring life must be that of a person specified in the will who is living at the testator's death. Therefore, a testator can establish a trust in which he directs that the income shall be paid to his widow during her life and that, after her death, the trust shall continue during the life of their son (who was living at the time of the father's death), during which time the income from the trust shall be divided among such of the testator's grandchildren as are living at the date of the widow's death. Even though some of the grandchildren may not have been born at the date of the testator's death, they will nevertheless be entitled to share in the income of the trust so long as B, the son—the second measuring life—lives. Upon the son's death, the trust terminates, and the grandchildren—the remaindermen—receive specified shares of the corpus or principal of the trust.

---

[2] In New York the law now provides that a testamentary trust may run for the duration of any number of lives as long as the individuals are all alive when the testator dies. The only restriction is that a trust cannot be measured by such a large number of lives that it would be "unreasonably difficult" to establish when it came to an end.

Powers of Appointment

A frequent and valid criticism of the conventional type of trust created in a will is that the beneficiary of the income is given no control over the disposition of the trust property and that, in many cases, it would be better to allow the beneficiary to exercise such control in order to provide for conditions which the testator cannot foresee when he draws his will.

For example, consider the conventional type of trust created for a son or daughter, with directions for the payment of the income to him (or her) during his or her lifetime, the principal to be distributed to his children living at his death in equal shares, per stirpes.[3] This trust leaves no room for any provision for the son's widow. The principal of the trust bypasses her completely. If the son has little property of his own to dispose of at his death, his widow must be content to see the principal of the trust pass to her chidren or more remote descendants. Perhaps the testator considers this appropriate, but he might recognize that it would

---

[3] There is a significant difference between per stirpes and per capita. An example will make the very real difference clear.

Let us say that the will of John Adams created three trusts for his three children, Arthur, Barry, and Catherine. The sons marry and, in the course of time, have children. Arthur has one son, Albert. Barry is blessed with three daughters, Barbara, Betty, and Brenda. But Catherine, who outlives both her brothers, dies without ever having children. According to Mr. Adams' will, the principal of the trust for Catherine, if she leaves no descendants, is to be paid to the "issue, *per stirpes*" of Mr. Adams who survive Catherine.

The word "issue" has the same general meaning as "descendants." In this case, the "issue" are the grandchildren (and their descendants, if any). *Per stirpes* means that the issue take through their ancestors—that is, in the proportion their parents would have taken. Under this scheme the principal of Catherine's trust is split into two equal shares for the two ancestors—Arthur and Barry. Arthur's only son stands in Arthur's place and will take one share. Barry's three girls stand in his place and divide the other share. Thus, under the *per stirpes* division, the grandson gets one half the trust principal, but each granddaughter gets only one sixth.

The *per stirpes* provision is traditional. But many men, having been told how it works have this reaction: "I don't like that kind of distribution—I am equally fond of all my grandchildren. I would like them to share equally."

Is the answer, then, a direction that the trust principal be paid to "issue, *per capita* and not *per stirpes*"? Perhaps, but maybe not. The possibility of the birth of great-grandchildren would have to be considered. They would usually be deemed "issue" and would be entitled to a share if the division were on a *per capita* basis. Thus, in Mr. Adams' case, if there had been three great-grandchildren, in addition to the four grandchildren, each of the seven would have taken the same amount under a *per capita* division.

The "issue, *per capita*" division is not as often used. It seems inappropriate to give a grand-grandchild (who may have been born long after the will-maker dies) the same share his parent gets. An alternative that combines both the *per stirpes* and *per capita* methods of division may be better. It would take the form of a direction to pay the trust principal "in equal shares to my grandchildren surviving the termination of the trust, the share of any grandchild who dies before such event, to be divided among his issue, *per stirpes*." That direction has the advantage of equalizing the shares of the grandchildren while at the same time making provision for the offspring of a grandchild who might die before the trust ends.

be desirable to allow his son to make the decision as to whether it would be appropriate to provide for his widow out of the principal of the trust, the income of which was enjoyed by the son during his married life.

Furthermore, the trust vests the principal in the son's children in equal shares, *per stirpes*. It is reasonable to suppose, however, that when the son dies, the economic status of his children will vary. Some may have married wealthy spouses. Some may have been disabled by chronic illness. Some may have predeceased the son, leaving children of their own, with little property for their support and education. Nevertheless, under the rigid plan provided in the will, the principal of the trust must be distributed without regard to the differing needs of the remaindermen.

If the testator is disposed to allow the son to determine how to meet these problems, the creation of a power of appointment offers an excellent solution. In general, a *power of appointment* is a provision in a will granting another the power to decide, after the will-maker's death, how property left in trust shall eventually be distributed. For example, in the case above, the father (the testator) would give the son a power of appointment, which would allow the son to specify, in his will, how and to whom the principal of the trust should be distributed upon his death. The son does not own the principal of the trust, but he is permitted on his death to decide how it should be distributed. A typical power-of-appointment clause in a will would read: "Upon the death of my said son, my Trustees shall pay over the then principal of the trust in such shares, and in such manner, outright or in lesser estates, in trust or otherwise, as my said son may by his last will and testament appoint. . . ."

Power of Invasion *Of Principal*

The income return on invested funds decreased with the generally lower level of interest rates in the quarter century prior to 1958. Future developments cannot be foreseen, especially during a trust term which may run for many years. Furthermore, no one can predict whether the investments of a trust will retain their value or will depreciate. Hence, inadequacy of income is a contingency which must be faced and covered in the drafting of the trust, particularly where the initial corpus of the trust is not large and where the purpose of the trust is to support the testator's immediate family.

For example, assume that a testator has accumulated $100,000, and, up to the time of his death, is earning $10,000 a year. When he dies, he leaves a widow and young children. In his will he has directed that his entire estate be held in trust, with income to be paid to his wife during her life and the principal to be divided among his children on her death. Assume that his net estate is $90,000, which forms the principal of the trust. On the basis of the present yield of so-called "trust investments," this might produce no more than $3,000 per year. From this there must be deducted trustee's commissions and any income tax payable by the widow, which means that the amount available for the support of her family will be only a small proportion of her husband's income at the time of his death.

In this hypothetical example the principal, although much needed for the support and education of the young children, cannot be used by the trustee because the will contains no permissive language to that effect. The hardship which will arise in such a situation is obvious and might have been avoided by appropriate language allowing an invasion of the principal.

There are many ways of taking care of such a situation. The testator can provide that if, in any year, the income from the trust fund is less than a stated amount, the deficiency is to be made up out of the principal. Or the testator may prefer to leave it to the discretion of the trustee to determine how much of the principal shall be paid over to the wife from time to time, in order to enable her to support her family. Or, alternatively, the testator may wish to vest this discretion in his wife, giving her the right to require the trustee to pay over whatever amounts of principal she may request. Various combinations are possible.

Life Insurance Trusts

Live insurance is being used increasingly in estate planning and in a variety of ways. For example, it is used:

1. To increase the estate. You can increase the size of your estate by adding to your insurance protection.

2. To solve the problem of liquidity. On your death a variety of charges must be paid, debts settled, taxes paid, etc. Life insurance will provide your estate with immediate liquid funds to meet these liabilities.

3. To keep your business going. You can have a trust created with the proceeds of your insurance, and it can buy assets from the estate or lend money to the estate, and by this means provide the liquid cash to keep your business going.

4. To provide staggered or long-term income. Rather than have your beneficiaries paid a lump sum you may wish the funds paid out over a period of time either as interest from a trust, or as interest and principal under the annuity method.

5. To provide management. A great many people accumulate more money through life insurance these days than in any other way. It would be a disaster if, upon their deaths, their beneficiaries were forced to administer the proceeds of these policies, because in many cases they have not the experience and training to do so effectively. Fortunately, several options are open. The insured can, before his death, stipulate that the proceeds be payable to a trustee for the benefit of his loved ones. If this is not done, the beneficiaries may find that they can leave the funds with the insurance company and receive an annuity for a period of years. Or they can accept the proceeds of the policies and turn them over to a trustee of their own choosing under a trust agreement acceptable to them.

Choosing a Trustee

Care must be taken when choosing a trustee. Only a good one, whether an individual or an institution, should be appointed. There are some arguments for the choice of an individual. The main one is that the settlor knows just who is going to handle his money in behalf of his beneficiaries. The weakness in this argument lies in the fact that the man appointed may die, thereby necessitating a successor. It may be difficult for ordinary persons to locate a qualified individual and to induce him to bother with the administration of limited funds.

For reasons such as these, more and more persons in ordinary circumstances are turning toward corporate trustees—trust companies and the trust departments of commercial banks. Permanency of corporate trustees, their experience and familiarity with legal details, the fact that they are unlikely to abscond, and the possibility that they can often be more easily found than experienced individuals—all of these considerations have led to a great growth of trust business in institutions.

Duties of Trustees

When a trustee has been chosen, what may be expected of him? It is his duty to strive diligently to preserve the principal of the trust estate, to keep it invested to the best of his ability, and to secure as good a return on the investment as is reasonably possible. He is engaged in a fiduciary undertaking and must observe the stipulations of the trust agreement to the utmost. Where the trust agreement allows him a choice, he must exercise the choice within the requirements of law. In some states, trustees may invest only in securities named on an approved list issued by the state. In the absence of statutory restrictions, the trustee must abide by the common law, which differs among the states. However, it is universally required that the trustee act in good faith and prudently.

The usual trust estate earns only a conservative, moderate income. In recent years there has been a growing movement to permit trustees to combat inflation by investing in common stocks, which, before this century at least, were considered too speculative for trust estates. Compensation of trustees depends upon the size of the trust estate and the income; it differs in the various states. If beneficiaries are dissatisfied with the actions of trustees, they may petition a court to (1) remove the trustee and appoint another, (2) cause the trustee to do certain things or refrain from doing others, (3) nullify any wrongful doings of the trustee, (4) assess money damages against the trustee, or (5) punish the trustee for criminal acts.

The Advantages of Trusts

It is obviously undesirable to bequeath or devise property directly to a minor, because a minor cannot receive or manage his or her property. Such a gift would require the appointment of a guardian, who is usually required to file a bond; an annual accounting by the guardian to the court; the necessity of obtaining a court order before any property can be used for the minor's maintenance; and the limitation of the guardian to so-called "legal investments" in investing any of the minor's funds. Then, too, the sale of a minor's real estate requires approval of the court, and it is an expensive and lengthy proceeding to obtain the necessary permission. All these difficulties can be avoided by creating a trust for the infant's benefit.

In the case of a widow, a trust may be advantageous to free her from the responsibility and worry involved in the investment and administration of funds, which can better be entrusted to other, more experienced hands. Also, she is shielded from the consequences of dissipating, by improvident investments or gifts, any money left to her outright.

A trust is likewise advantageous where a testator feels that other beneficiaries, in addition to his widow, ought to be protected from financial worry in general and from their own financial irresponsibility in particular. In many states the income from such a trust may be protected against garnishment or attachment by creditors of the beneficiary and even against voluntary assignments by the beneficiary. These are the so-called "spendthrift trusts." A typical clause would read:

The income reserved to the beneficiaries of the trusts created by this will shall not be subject to anticipation, commutation, hypothecation, pledge, assignment, sale, transfer, or alienation in any manner, nor shall any beneficiary have power to charge or encumber any such interest, nor shall any such interest be in any manner liable for or subject to the debts, contracts, liabilities, engagements, torts, or obligations of any beneficiary or claims against any beneficiary.

Tax Advantages of the Trust

One of the main reasons, today, for creating trusts is the tax advantage. If a testator leaves his estate to his widow outright, an estate tax will be payable on his death. When the widow dies, there is a further estate tax on what she leaves, including the property received from her husband. Assuming that she leaves her property to her children and that this property continues to be owned by the children until their deaths, their estates, in turn, will pay estate taxes thereon (subject to a tax credit with respect to the property inherited from her if their deaths occur within five years after her death).

Thus, three sets of estate taxes will have been paid in the course of the transmission of the original property left by the testator. If, on the other hand, the property is left in trust, with the income payable to the widow for her life and thereafter in further trusts, with the income payable to the children for their respective lives, and the principal of the trust for each child to be paid outright to that child's issue on the death of such child, only one estate tax will be payable; namely, on the death of the testator.

The Estate Tax

The federal estate tax is a tax on the right to transfer property, including not only transfers taking effect at death but also certain *inter vivos* transfers, such as one made in contemplation of death. The federal estate tax, like all death duties, is not a tax on property. Nor is it an inheritance tax, which is imposed on the right to receive property. Instead, it is a tax on the right to transmit property at death, and it is measured by the value of the property. To prevent avoidance of the tax, a transfer which is deemed to be in lieu of a testamentary disposition— as, for example, a gift made in contemplation of death—is also subject to the estate tax.

The starting point in computing federal estate tax liability is the gross estate. The gross estate of a decedent is the total vaue of his property, whether real or personal, tangible or intangible, except real property situated outside the United States. Once the property that makes up gross estate has been determined, the next step is the valuation of such property. The executor or administrator has the option of valuing the estate either at the date of the decedent's death or as of the date one year from date of death. Estate taxes due the federal government, which are much heavier than those due the state where you live, are payable 15 months after death. State estate and inheritance tax laws vary as to the time of payment, usually from one year to 18 months.

Your Gross Estate—What Is Included?

Estate tax laws refer to the "gross estate." This means the fair market value of all the real and personal property which you own at your death. In addition to your house and its contents, cash, stocks, bonds, mortgages (owned by you), notes (held by you), jewelry, automobile, and all other such property, the following are also included:

1. Life insurance on your life is taxable (no matter how payable) if you pay the premiums on the policy directly or indirectly, or if you possess "incidents of ownership in the policies," such as the right to change the beneficiaries, to borrow on the policies, or to collect cash surrender values. If your wife pays the premiums out of money you give her for household expenses, you are considered to have paid indirectly. Most people labor under the illusion that because life insurance proceeds are not taxable under the personal income tax, they are also exempt from the federal estate tax. This is not the case.

However, the 1954 tax revision made an important change. Formerly, even if you retained no "incidents of ownership," that is, for example, the right to borrow on the policy, or receive dividends, or elect settlement options, or name the beneficiary, etc., the insurance principal was taxed to your estate to the extent that you paid the premiums yourself, directly or indirectly. Now, if you do not retain any "incidents of ownership," you can have someone else take out a policy on your life, or you can assign your policy to someone else and the principal at your death may not be taxed to your estate, even if you continued to pay all the premiums on the policy directly.

2. Another illusion is that if all your property is in joint ownership with rights of survivorship, your estate will not have to pay taxes on it. The property passes outside your will, just as does insurance to a named beneficiary, but both are subject to the federal estate tax. Property of any kind which you own jointly with someone else, with right of survivorship, is taxable to the extent of your contribution to its purchase price or other interest therein. Under the federal law, and generally under state laws, when the first joint owner dies, it is presumed that he (or

she) supplied all of the purchase price of the jointly owned property, so that all is considered taxable in the deceased joint owner's estate, except to the extent that it can be proved that the survivor contributed to the purchase.

3. Gifts made within three years of your death, unless your executor can prove they were not made in contemplation of death, are taxable.

4. Trusts you have created in your lifetime wherein you have reserved certain rights or powers or wherein the enjoyment of the trust property by the beneficiaries depends on their surviving you are taxable. For example, bank accounts which you establish in trust for your children are taxable, since you can add to them or withdraw at will. For tax purposes, it is the same as if the bank accounts were solely in your name.

5. All other forms of property, or rights in property, are taxable, such as powers of appointment (which powers require special scrutiny to determine whether the value of the trust property they control is taxable or not. For the most part, general powers of appointment are taxable, limited powers are not).

The Limitations of Joint Ownership

Owning property jointly with a wife may be a convenient way of handling a family checking account, but if you carry the idea much further, say the estate planning experts, you are inviting trouble. Why?

Your property may wind up wholly or partly in the wrong hands. A middle-aged man puts his property into joint ownership with his wife. They have no children, but the husband has an aged parent still living, and the wife has two brothers. The husband dies unexpectedly. A short time later the wife dies without having made a will. Since the joint property was entirely the wife's at her death, it all goes to her brothers (under state law). Probably, both husband and wife would have wanted to care for the husband's parent as well.

Will joint tenancy avoid taxes at death? No! On the contrary it often attracts higher tax or expensive tax complications—particularly in the usual case where the money or property all came from the husband originally. Suppose, for instance, that the wife dies first. If everything is in joint names, and the amount is substantial, the husband will have to report the property in the estate tax return on her estate. Then he will have the job of proving that it was all his money or property in the first place. If he cannot, he will be in the unhappy position of paying a tax to get his own money back. On the other hand, if both contributed to the joint estate, he has the job of tracing the contributions of each.

Your Net Estate—What Is Included?

The federal estate tax law allows certain exemptions and deductions in determining the "net estate," which is the base on which the tax is computed. An overall, basic exemption of $60,000 is allowed by the federal law. Most state estate or inheritance tax laws allow similar deductions and also exemptions of varying amounts, usually depending on the relationship of your beneficiaries.

Among the permissible deductions are funeral expenses and claims, loans, and mortgages against your property. Expenses for the administration of your estate, including fees for legal services and commissions of your executor, are deductible, and this reduces the net cost of these services to your estate. Bequests to qualified charities and other tax-exempt institutions are deductible. There may be circumstances under which property which you recently inherited—property previously taxed to another estate *within five years of your death*—may also be deducted. The most important deduction, if your wife (or husband) survives you, is the "marital deduction."

The Marital Deduction—What It Means

Under the marital-deduction feature of the tax laws, a specified portion of a married person's estate may pass to the surviving spouse free of federal (since 1948) and state (New York, for example, since 1950) death taxes when particular requirements of the law are met. A husband or wife may leave up to one half of his or her adjusted gross estate (gross estate less debts, claims, and administration expenses but before exemptions or charitable bequests) to a surviving spouse as an outright legacy or in trust, providing the survivor receives all the income at least annually and has the unrestricted power to dispose of the property during his or her lifetime or upon death, by will or otherwise.

The marital deduction makes a very real difference in your estate-tax liability, as may be seen in Figure 17–5. It may be much more than all other deductions put together. In some cases it may wipe out your tax entirely. For example, you leave an estate of $100,000. Your marital deduction is $50,000, thereby bringing your net estate down to $50,000, or $10,000 less than the $60,000 exemption; there is, therefore, no tax liability. Assume that your estate is $300,000 and that you leave your property in such a way that the marital deduction amounts to the maximum allowed—$150,000. With the $60,000 exemption subtracted, only $90,000 remains to be taxed; and on this the tax is $17,500. On the $300,000 estate without the marital deduction, it would be $59,100.

If you cut the estate in half, you always reduce the tax by more than

FIGURE 17–5

A Sample Computation of Estate Taxes with and without Using the Marital Deduction

Gross Estate:

Real estate...	$ 50,000	
Jewelry, automobile, etc.............................	15,000	
Cash and securities.................................	370,000	
Savings account.....................................	5,000	
Life insurance......................................	100,000	$540,000

Deductions:

Debts and funeral expenses..........................	$ 10,000	
Administration expenses*............................	30,000	40,000
Adjusted Gross Estate.........................		$500,000

Using Marital Deduction

Adjusted Gross Estate...............................		$500,000
Less:		
Maximum marital deduction (one half Adjusted Gross Estate)...	$250,000	
Charitable bequests................................	50,000	300,000
Net Estate (before exemptions).................		$200,000

Estate Taxes:

Federal...		31,500
New York State...................................		2,500
Total..		$ 34,000

Without Using Marital Deduction

Adjusted Gross Estate...............................		$500,000
Less:		
Charitable bequests................................		50,000
Net Estate (before exemptions).................		$450,000

Estate Taxes:

Federal...		$102,100
New York State...................................		11,500
Total..		$113,600

* NOTE: Administration expenses include the executor's commissions and attorney's fees, both of which are deductible for estate tax purposes. The amount in any particular case depends on the number of executors and your attorney's charges. In making estimates, an arbitrary figure of 5–6 percent may be used to illustrate the aggregate of such expenses.

SOURCE: Morgan Guaranty Trust Company of New York.

half. The marital deduction, or any other deduction, comes "off the top" of the estate, where the rates are highest. Thus, if there is a surviving spouse, the specific exemption plus the marital deduction totals $120,-000, and a 10 percent estimate for other deductions and credits would make the estate tax inapplicable to estates of less than $132,00. The savings which result from the marital deduction at different estate levels may be seen in Table 17–1.

The Credit for State Death Taxes

The federal estate tax is really a little more complicated than it has been made to appear in the presentation above, since in reality two federal estate taxes are actually imposed, namely, the basic estate and the additional estate tax. The federal estate tax payable is the sum of the net basic estate tax and the net additional estate tax. The function of the basic estate tax is the computation of the amount of credit allowable for

TABLE 17–1

Estate Tax Savings Due to Marital Deduction

Net Estate before $60,000 Exemption	Tax without Marital Deduction*	Tax with Marital Deduction*	Tax Saving
$ 100,000	$ 4,800	....	$ 4,800
150,000	17,500	$ 1,050	16,450
200,000	31,500	4,800	26,700
250,000	45,300	10,700	34,600
500,000	116,500	45,300	71,200
750,000	191,800	80,500	111,300
1,000,000	270,300	116,500	153,800
2,500,000	830,000	351,400	478,600
5,000,000	2,038,800	830,000	1,208,800
10,000,000	4,975,000	2,038,800	2,936,200

*After maximum credit for state inheritance taxes.

estate, inheritance, or death taxes paid to the states and to foreign countries. A credit of up to 80 percent of the basic estate tax is allowed for death taxes paid to a state. The basic tax remaining after the credit for state taxes, plus the additional estate tax, add up to the total estate tax. The effective rates of the total tax, allowing maximum credit for state taxes, may be seen in Table 17–2 (also see Figure 17–6).

State Inheritance and Estate Taxes

An inheritance tax differs from an estate tax in that the former is levied on the right of the beneficiary to receive a bequest and is based on his or her share, while the estate tax is levied on all the property of the person dying and must be paid out of the estate by the executor.

All states, except Nevada, levy either inheritance or estate taxes. In some states they are known as succession taxes. Don't hurry to Nevada. It won't help. The federal estate tax is constructed to equalize state

TABLE 17-2

Federal Estate Tax Burden on Representative Net Estates

Amount of Net Estate*	Maximum Gross Tax†	Maximum Credit for State Taxes	Net Total Tax	Effective Rate‡
$ 5,000	$ 150	$ 40	$ 110	2.2%
20,000	1,600	160	1,440	7.2
50,000	7,000	400	6,600	13.2
100,000	20,700	1,200	19,500	19.5
200,000	50,700	3,600	47,100	23.5
600,000	180,700	18,000	162,700	27.1
1,000,000	325,700	38,800	286,900	28.7
5,000,000	2,468,200	402,800	2,065,400	41.3
10,000,000	6,088,200	1,082,800	5,005,400	50.0
50,000,000	36,888,200	7,482,800	29,405,400	58.8

*Includes amount of net estate after all deductions and exemptions.
†Totals are for both the basic and additional tax.
‡Based on net tax.

practices by allowing a credit against the federal tax for the amount paid to the state. Thus, if you pay nothing to the state, you receive no credit and your federal tax is just that much higher.

Most states—Colorado, Illinois, Indiana, Kansas, Maine, Pennsylvania, Texas, Virginia, West Virginia, and Wisconsin, for example—have inheritance taxes. Only a few, New York, for example, have estate taxes. Some states, such as Ohio, have both.

The state inheritance tax is usually levied at a much lower rate than the federal estate tax—1 to 20 percent in most cases. The rate varies with (a) the degree of relationship between the decedent and the beneficiary, and (b) the size of the bequest. In Kansas, for example, a widow is given a $75,000 personal exemption, a child only a $15,000 exemption. In Ohio a widow, or a child under 21, have only a $5,000 exemption, and a son or daughter over 21 receives only a $3,500 exemption. Practices vary so widely that it is useless to attempt to generalize. This is especially true of rates, kinds of property taxed, and types exempt. Usually the states are not only lower in rates but also more generous in their exemptions on types of property taxed than is the federal government. The chief tax officer of your state can provide you with a copy of your state inheritance or estate tax law.

The Federal Gift Tax

The federal gift tax is commonly regarded as a supplement to estate taxes to prevent avoidance of the latter by transfers of property during

FIGURE 17-6

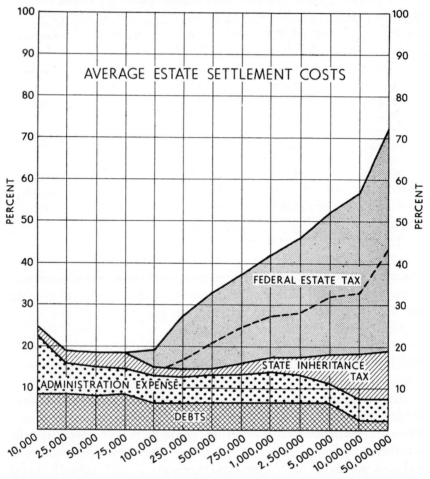

AVERAGE ESTATE SETTLEMENT COSTS

SIZE OF ESTATES (DOLLARS)

This graph was prepared by the Estate Recording Company, an independent statistical organization, from a survey of the court records of over 10,000 estates probated in all parts of the United States. "Debts" comprise mortgages payable, income and real estate taxes, and everything else the decedent owed; "Administration Expense" includes funeral costs, fees, court costs, and miscellaneous charges; "State Inheritance Tax" is the average found as a result of this study.

The broken line indicates the extent of the Federal Estate Tax in those estates where the full marital deduction was taken but in those estates where no marital deduction was taken the complete Federal Estate Tax applied.

Source: Reproduced by courtesy of Estate Recording Company, San Diego, Calif., 92105.

the owner's lifetime. A gift, however, must be in the nature of a windfall. It must be unearned; otherwise, it is taxable as income. "Gifts" are broadly defined under the federal law as all gratuitous transfers of property, direct or indirect, real or personal. Four types of gifts must be distinguished to determine whether they are taxable under the gift or estate levies: (1) a gift to take effect at death; (2) a gift *causa mortis* (in anticipation of death); (3) a gift *inter vivos* (during life); and (4) a fictitious sale or exchange in which the property is transferred for a consideration less than its true value. The first two cases are taxed under the estate tax, the latter two under the gift tax. The rates of the federal gift tax are fixed at three fourths of those of the additional estate tax, so that it is less expensive to give property away during your lifetime than it is to part with it on death.

What Gifts Are Taxed?

All gifts and transfers of property, real and personal, including life insurance policies and certain transfers of property to joint ownership, are subject to the tax. Where, however, a person creates a joint bank account, having the right to regain the entire fund without the consent of the other joint owner, the gift does not occur until the latter withdraws for his or her own benefit from the fund; and the gift is the amount so withdrawn. Gifts to qualified charitable, religious, educational, and other tax-exempt institutions are deductible for gift tax purposes as well as for income tax purposes. The tax is computed on the total gifts made during the calendar year.

What May Be Excluded

The first $3,000 given to any one person during any calendar year is excluded from the amount of gifts for the year. Thus, $3,000 a year may be given to each of one or more persons without incurring a gift tax for that year. In addition to this annual exclusion there is an overall specific exemption of $30,000 against all taxable gifts which a person may make during his lifetime. This exemption may be used entirely in one year or be spread over a period of years until it is exhausted.

For example, if a person makes a gift of $10,000 to another in one year, $3,000 of the gift will be free from the tax under the annual exclusion, and the balance of $7,000 may be applied against the $30,000 exemption, leaving $23,000 of the exemption to be used in subsequent years. No gift tax will be due as the result of such a gift, but it must be reported on a gift tax return.

To take another example, if a person makes gifts of $5,000 to each of two others in one year, $3,000 of each gift will be free from tax under the annual exclusion, and the balance of $2,000 of each gift (or a total of $4,000) may be applied against the $30,000 exemption, leaving $26,000 of the exemption to be used in subsequent years. No gift tax would be due as the result of such gifts, but they, too, must be reported. Not only the donor but also the recipient of a gift (except qualified public and charitable organizations) must report it.

The Marital Deduction

As in the case of the federal estate tax, the federal gift tax also provides for a marital deduction. This was introduced by the Revenue Act of 1948 and applies to gifts made after April 2, 1948, by citizens or residents only. If you make a gift to your wife or she makes a gift to you, there may be deducted one half of the value of the gift before applying the annual exclusion and the specific exemption. The marital deduction is available only if the gift meets tests similar to those necessary to obtain the marital deduction for federal estate tax purposes, as previously described.

Joint Gifts by Husband and Wife

Gifts made after April 2, 1948, to third persons by you or your wife may be treated for gift tax purposes as made one half by you and one half by your wife if each of you consents to this procedure, in writing, on the gift tax returns. Thus, you and your wife report only one half of the gift in your respective gift tax returns, and the annual exclusion and the specific exemption are then used by each of you separately. However, if you and your wife elect to treat any one gift to another person as made jointly, then all gifts made to other persons by either of you during that calendar year must be treated the same way.

It is thus possible for a husband and wife to make a joint outright gift of $66,000 to one person without incurring gift tax liability if no previous gifts of more than the allowable annual exclusions have been made by either in the past. However, one result of such a gift would be that the present specific exemption of both husband and wife would no longer be available against any subsequent gifts to the same person or to others. You save taxes by splitting gifts, of course. For example, assume that a man puts $200,000 into a trust for the benefit of his daughter. If he were taxed on the whole gift, his tax would be $30,600. By splitting the gift, however, so that he gives $100,000 and his wife gives the same amount, the aggregate tax is only $17,190.

Why Gifts Save Tax

There are several reasons why gifts during a lifetime save taxes. In the first place, the federal gift tax rates are lower than the federal

TABLE 17–3

FEDERAL GIFT TAX

Amount of Gift	A Federal Gift Tax (unmarried donor)	B Federal Gift Tax (married donors to third parties)	C Federal Gift Tax (married donor to spouse)
$ 30,000	$ 0	$ 0	$ 0
60,000	2,250	0	0
100,000	9,225	2,400	1,200
150,000	20,025	8,850	4,425
200,000	31,275	18,450	9,225
250,000	42,525	28,950	14,475
300,000	54,075	40,050	20,025
350,000	66,075	51,300	25,650
400,000	78,075	62,550	31,275
450,000	90,075	73,800	36,900
500,000	102,075	85,050	42,525
600,000	127,650	108,150	54,075
700,000	153,900	132,150	66,075
800,000	180,450	156,150	78,075
900,000	208,200	180,150	90,075
1,000,000	235,950	204,150	102,075
1,500,000	386,700	334,050	167,025
2,000,000	554,775	471,900	235,950
2,500,000	737,625	617,250	308,625
3,000,000	935,475	773,400	386,700
5,000,000	1,836,975	1,475,250	737,625
10,000,000	4,549,050	3,673,950	1,836,975

Amount of Gift: This column represents the amount of gift *after* deducting the annual exclusion or exclusions but *before* deducting the lifetime exemption or exemptions.

Column **A** Gift tax payable on gifts to third parties where donor is unmarried or prescribed consent of spouse has not been given.

Column **B** Combined gift tax payable on gifts by married donors to third parties where prescribed consents have been given.

Column **C** Gift tax payable on gifts by one spouse to the other.

APPLICABLE TO GIFTS MADE AFTER APRIL 2, 1948

SOURCE: Manufacturers Hanover Trust Company, New York, N.Y.

estate-tax rates. Federal gift tax rates may be seen in Table 17–3. Secondly, by making gifts, you divide the taxation of your property between estate tax and gift tax. This is a saving, because each tax—the gift tax and the estate tax—has its own exemption and its own rising scale of rates. It keeps the property out of the high brackets. This is somewhat similar to the way in which savings can be made in income taxes if a given amount of income is divided between two taxpayers instead of all being taxed to one of them.

Finally, a gift may save on income taxes. Assume that you want to help your married son. You give him stocks and bonds (which you formerly owned) which will now yield him a monthly income of $100. By making the gift, your annual income subject to taxes is $1,200 less than it would have been had you held the securities in your own name and paid out the $100 a month to your son.

Relationship of Gift Tax to Estate Tax

If the maker of a gift lives three years after making it, his estate is not required to pay an estate tax on the property which was the subject of the gift. On the other hand, a gift made within three years of death is, for estate tax purposes, presumed to have been made in contemplation of death, unless it can be proved that the gift was in fact not so made. Even though a gift tax has been paid on a transfer of property, such property may also be subject to the estate tax, as, for instance, in the case of a gift in contemplation of death. To help the taxpayer in such situations, the federal estate tax law allows a "gift tax credit" to be taken off the estate tax. The credit is the amount of the gift tax that was paid, with one very complicated and rare exception.

Since gifts made during a lifetime may be considered as coming from the top estate tax bracket of an individual, sizable tax savings may result from a program of lifetime gifts. For example, if Thomas Farmer has a net estate of $200,000, which he wishes to transfer to his son (since his wife is independently wealthy), the estate tax (if it passed at his death) would be:

Net estate	$200,000
Minus $60,000 exemption	140,000
Federal estate tax on $140,000	32,700

If, however, he decided to transfer the major portion of the estate by gifts, say over a ten-year period, taking advantage of marital option to split the gift, the tax results would be as follows:

GIFT TAX COMPUTATION

Outright gifts of $60,000 against lifetime exemption ($30,000 each parent)	$ 60,000
Ten years annual exclusion of $6,000 ($3,000 each parent)	60,000
Total gifts	$120,000
Gift tax	0
Final estate at father's death	$ 80,000
Net estate after exemption	20,000
Federal estate tax on $20,000	1,600

Conclusion

What are the highlights of this complicated business of estate planning?

1. Everyone should make a will regardless of the size of his or her estate.

2. Everyone should leave a letter of last instructions.

3. Every individual has an exemption of $60,000 before federal estate taxes accrue.

4. Because of the marital deduction one half of a husband's or wife's estate already belongs to the survivor and is therefore not subject to the estate tax.

5. A person may give up to $3,000 a year to as many individuals as he desires without its being subject to gift or estate taxes.

6. A husband and wife can together give up to $6,000 under the above conditions.

7. An individual may give away as much as $30,000 without its being subject to gift or estate taxes. This is a lifetime exemption. It is in addition to the annual $3,000 exclusion.

8. A husband and wife together have a $60,000 lifetime exclusion.

9. For a person of means, estate taxes are minimized by making gifts during one's lifetime to the full extent of the gift tax exemptions.

10. Gift taxes rates, even when they apply, are three quarters of estate tax rates.

11. Insurance, handled in certain ways, aids in estate planning and may, under special circumstances, not be subject to the estate tax.

12. The trust is a very effective way of passing an estate on to children, or even grandchildren, and minimizing estate taxes.

Of the many complex and involved financial problems one inevitably faces through life: insurance, debts, mortgage financing, taxes, investments—all of which we have now surveyed—none is more difficult or technical than wills, trusts, estates, and death and gift taxes. Nowhere is it more saving of time and trouble to pay the fee of a lawyer or other expert for careful, competent, precise, and correct advice. Invariably, a shortsighted attempt to save a fee will result in a much more serious loss.

All that this book has attempted is to provide the framework and background to enable you to talk more intelligently about your personal financial problems with the various experts—lawyers, accountants, insurance agents, bank mortgage officers, internal revenue agents, trust officers, etc.—whom you will encounter in due course in your "four score and ten." It would be a real disservice to you to leave you with the impression that you are now competent to deal with all these complicated matters on your own. Remember: "Many persons might have attained to wisdom had they not assumed that they already possessed it."—SENECA

SUGGESTED READINGS

1. *Wills and Trust Agreements: Suggestions for Their Preparation,* Morgan Guaranty Trust Company of New York, 1963.

2. *How to Safeguard Your Estate,* Connecticut Mutual Life Insurance Company, Hartford, Conn., 1963.

3. *How to Choose Your Executor,* First National City Bank of New York, 1963.

4. *Personal Trusts for Practical People,* First National City Bank of New York, 1963.

5. W. J. Bowe, *Tax Savings through Estate Planning* (Nashville, Tenn.: Vanderbilt University Press, 1963).

6. J. K. Lasser Institute, *Estate and Gift Tax Planning,* American Research Council, Larchmont, N.Y., 1962.

7. *Changing Times, The Kiplinger Magazine:*
    a) "Your Will: Why, What and How," April, 1963.
    b) "Joint Ownership—Right for You?" June, 1962.
    c) "How to Help Your Widow," November, 1961.
    d) "Estate Planning," September, 1960.

8. William R. Spinney, *Estate Planning* (10th ed.), Commerce Clearing House, Chicago, 1963.

9. *Federal Estate and Gift Taxes Explained,* Commerce Clearing House, Chicago, 1963.

10. *Gifts of Securities or Money to Minors; A Guide to Laws in 50 States,* Association of Stock Exchange Firms, 120 Broadway, New York, N.Y., 10005, Latest annual edition.

11. Rene A. Wormser, *Personal Estate Planning in a Changing World* (New York: Simon and Schuster, Inc., latest edition).

12. Earl S. MacNeill, *What Women Want to Know about Wills* (New York: Harper & Row, latest edition).

13. A. J. Casner, *Estate Planning* (Boston: Little, Brown & Co., 1963).

14. L. Cusack and T. Snee, *Documents and Data for Your Estate Planning* (Englewood Cliffs, N.J.: Prentice-Hall, Inc., 1963).

15. W. K. Stevens, "Estate Planning: Basic Principles and Special Techniques," *Journal of Taxation* (May and June, 1962).

CASE PROBLEMS

1. Norman Roberts is 28 years old and an employee of a large advertising concern. He is married and the father of a year-old son. He has life insurance payable to his wife, owns a car, and recently was given by his parents a small ranch house worth about $20,000. He has stock in his name totaling about $10,000, and has a joint savings account with his wife in which they have deposited about $4,000. It has not occurred to him to make a will, but his wife suggests that he should do so. Norman is not impressed, saying that what he has would automatically go to her. How would you advise them?

2. Jack Lobart was a successful young engineer who, as an employee of a large electronics corporation, drew a salary of about $20,000 yearly. He died when he was in his late thirties, leaving an estate totaling about $150,000, primarily the result of several successful investments. In his will, he directed that a trust be created, with the income to be paid to his wife during her lifetime and the principal to be divided equally among their children after her demise. His wife was left with three children, whose ages ranged from 9 to 17. The net estate, on which she was totally dependent for support, amounted to about $130,000. This estate yielded an income of about $6,000. From this sum, far beneath her accustomed income, income taxes and trustee commissions had to be deducted. Although she needs and will continue to need a larger sum for the support and education of the children, Mrs. Lobart has no way of obtaining any of the principal, because her husband's will contained no provision to that effect. The trustee, her late husband's brother, sympathizes with her predicament, but is unable to help her obtain more money under the will. How could Jack Lobart have avoided such a situation?

3. John Smith, aged 26, was killed in an accident, leaving a blind wife and two children (ages 1 and 3). Having just commenced his career, John left very little money. His father, Fred Smith, a widower, has cancer and the doctors give him only a year to live. His will, as it stood at the time of the accident, named his son as sole heir. Fred now wishes to rewrite the will so as to aid his daughter-in-law and his grandchildren. What are your suggestions?

4. Mr. Jones is extremely wealthy. He is married, but has no children. He has, however, a permanently crippled unmarried younger sister, whose support he has assumed. For the last few years Miss Jones has been living with her brother and his wife. For business reasons, Mr. Jones is to move to another part of the country. His sister would prefer to remain in their home town. She has friends with whom she can live, but Mr. Jones would like to make her

financially secure for the years to come. What might be sensible financial arrangements?

5. Martin Morse, a 60-year-old businessman, has a net estate of $75,000. His son is earning a good income, but his daughter is a widow with two small children. She is living on a barely adequate pension. Mr. Morse would like to help her now and also to finance her children's education. What would be a good way of accomplishing this?

6. John Randall, age 64, has never made a will and does not see any reason for making one. His wife, age 58, and his five children, four of whom have large incomes, are still living. Randall's net estate is worth about $60,000. His only son is concerned that, upon Randall's death intestate, his entire estate would not go to Mrs. Randall, who would have no other income. Mr. Randall refuses to speak to a lawyer about the matter, but his son thinks that his father may listen to him. What points should the son bring to the attention of the father?

7. Branch Burlingame (age 59) is a successful account executive in an advertising agency. He makes $40,000 a year and has a wife (age 50) and three children: a son, age 27, and two daughters, ages 16 and 17. In addition to a mortgage-free home worth $50,000, which will go to his wife upon his death, and substantial annuities and insurance coverage to send his daughters to college and provide himself and his family with a comfortable income after his retirement, he has assets of $300,000. Burlingame would like to have this money go to his wife and daughters; he does not get along well with his son and does not want him to receive any of this money. What are your suggestions?

8. Allen Rubens has a huge income and pays heavy income taxes. Besides his wife, he supports his daughter-in-law and her three children by sending them $800 monthly, since his son was shot down in Viet Nam. Can you help him reduce his tax liability?

9. Peter Tompkins inserted in his will a specific legacy of old gold coins, worth $3,000, to a local museum; a demonstrative legacy of $8,000 to his grandson, to be taken from $10,000 deposited in a savings bank; and residuary legacies of $57,000, all to be taken from his estate, which he believed was worth $68,000. After his death it was found that burial expenses, debts, and taxes absorbed $10,000. At his death he still owned the gold coins, and his savings account amounted to $14,000. The balance of his estate consisted of stocks and bonds, which brought $32,000 upon their sale. The residuary legacies were for $20,000 to his grown, successful son and $37,000 to his elderly, crippled wife. Tompkins and his wife had been living for years on his $8,000 annual salary. Comment.

10. Frank Corbett made his wife beneficiary of $100,000 of straight life insurance on his life. She died when their three children were 3, 6, and 7 years of age. He has built up a successful grocery business (netting $8,000 a year), owns his own home free and clear (worth $15,000), has $9,000 in various banks, and owns $35,000 of securities, yielding 5 percent. This morning he was almost run down by an automobile as he went to work. Accordingly, he begins thinking of the future and his three children. He wonders whether he should go to the local lawyer and have a will drawn. Meantime, he ponders the disposition of his property. Can you help him with his estate planning?

11. Gerald Craig lived and died in your state. Although he made and signed a will, he had no witnesses to it. His estate amounted to $90,000. He left a wife (age 61), who was accustomed to living on a scale befitting an annual income of $10,000, and a ne'er-do-well son 33 years of age, who has a wife and three young children. Comment.

12. Lucretia Smith, a widow, inherited $300,000. She wanted to retain $100,-000 and give $100,000 each to her son and her daughter, but they were only 8 and 10 years of age. How would you advise her to handle this money?

13. When widower Peter Turgeon died, he left a residence worth $15,000; a summer home worth $5,000, which all his children liked very much; and $25,000 invested in stocks and bonds. He was survived by two sons and two daughters, all of whom he loved equally well. What would have been a suitable disposition of his property in his will?

The New Medicare and Social Security Provisions

by JEROME B. COHEN

Supplement to

PERSONAL FINANCE
Principles and Case Problems, Third Edition

by Jerome B. Cohen and Arthur W. Hanson

 1965

RICHARD D. IRWIN, INC.

HOMEWOOD, ILLINOIS